SOCIOLOGY / a text with adapted readings

HARPER & ROW, Publishers / New York

SOCIOLOGY

a text with adapted readings

LEONARD BROOM The University of Texas

PHILIP SELZNICK University of California, Berkeley

THIRD
EDITION

SOCIOLOGY, THIRD EDITION

COPYRIGHT © 1955, 1958, 1963 BY

HARPER & ROW, PUBLISHERS, INCORPORATED

Printed in the United States of America

All rights in this book are reserved. No part of the book may
be used or reproduced in any manner whatsoever without written
permission except in the case of brief quotations embodied in
critical articles and reviews. For information address Harper
& Row, Publishers, Incorporated, 49 East 33rd Street, New York
16, N. Y.

Library of Congress catalog card number: 63-10974

Acknowledgments

We are grateful for the professional contribution of the following colleagues who prepared the indicated chapters in close collaboration with us and in accordance with the basic plan of the book:

BURTON R. CLARK, University of California, Berkeley:
EDUCATION

DONALD R. CRESSEY, University of California, Santa Barbara:
CRIME AND DELINQUENCY

RICHARD T. MORRIS, University of California, Los Angeles:
SOCIAL STRATIFICATION

GERTRUDE JAEGER SELZNICK, University of California, Berkeley:
SOCIALIZATION

RALPH H. TURNER, University of California, Los Angeles:
THE FAMILY

We are greatly indebted to Gretchan N. Broom for her creative and unstinting collaboration in editing and writing, and for carrying the burden of administrative tasks.

For generous collaboration in this and earlier editions we extend thanks to Helen Beem Gouldner on INDUSTRIAL MAN, William A. Kornhauser on POLITICAL MAN, and Gertrude J. Selznick on RELIGION.

In addition to those whose help we acknowledged in previous editions, we express our appreciation for the assistance and guidance of Robert Blauner, Benjamin S. Bradshaw, Robert E. L. Faris, Father Joseph Fitzpatrick, S. J., Jack P. Gibbs, Norval Glenn, Charles Y. Glock, Paul Jacobs, John I. Kitsuse, John Larkins, Leo Lowenthal, Sheldon L. Messinger, William Petersen, Donald A. Petesch, Tamotsu Shibutani, Fred E. Templeton and Charles R. Wright. Other of our debts are recorded in footnotes and credit lines, but we wish to thank especially the authors of the original works from which our Adaptations were drawn.

LEONARD BROOM

PHILIP SELZNICK

Chapters

Table of Contents

Text and Adaptations

* Items marked with an asterisk are brief illustrative materials.

Chapter **14** **Crime and Delinquency**—*Continued*

PART **THREE** Master Trends

Chapter **15** **Urban Man**

Chapter **16** **Industrial Man**

PART ONE

Elements of Sociological Analysis

Chapter I

Introduction

Section 1   The discipline of sociology

Sociology is one of the social sciences. Its long-run aim is to discover the basic structure of human society, to identify the main forces that hold groups together or weaken them, and to learn the conditions that transform social life. In this, sociology, like any pure or basic science, is a disciplined, intellectual quest for fundamental knowledge of the nature of things. Most sociologists believe that they stand only at the outermost rim of this understanding.

Although some sociologists devote themselves to the development of first principles and fundamental concepts, others pursue relatively restricted inquiries, including careful reporting of significant events, the compilation and interpretation of sociological statistics, and the testing of hypotheses about limited topics. Some of this work has a practical orientation, such as the desire to control juvenile delinquency or to reduce absenteeism of factory workers; much of it is stimulated by intellectual curiosity, the desire to understand a puzzling fact or to comprehend an important event. In this book we shall draw on the sociological enterprise as a whole, both on attempts to formulate basic principles and on

more modest efforts to contribute to the fund of verifiable knowledge.

When one seeks to draw general conclusions, he must be *selective*. The scientist is interested in *kinds* of things, in placing phenomena into categories, and this means looking at special aspects of the concrete world. The same "thing" can be understood in a number of different ways. Consider your instructor's chair. If a specialist in the branch of physics called mechanics were to study it, he would see it as a combination of weights and balances; a biologist specializing in anatomy would see it as a receptacle for the human form and might assess its effect on the spinal column; an economist might see it as a product of mass production, a unit of cost and price; the psychologist might see it as part of the perceptual frame of the student; and the sociologist might see the chair as a symbol of status.

Like any other field of inquiry, sociology is selective in its approach. It highlights and illuminates aspects of social life that otherwise might be only obscurely recognized and understood. Its specialized knowledge about basic elements and processes in the social

August Comte (1798–1857), French social philosopher, gave sociology its name. As a "positivist" Comte stressed the need to base scientific theories on observation, but his own writings were highly speculative. He saw in human history three stages of "universal progress"—theological, metaphysical, scientific. He also offered elaborate proposals for a new Positivist State in which there would be a supreme priesthood of sociologists to direct society. Few of Comte's specific ideas are now accepted, but he gave impetus to the discussion out of which present-day sociology emerged. His major work was The Positive Philosophy, *first published in French, in six volumes, 1830–1842.*

world can enrich understanding and may have practical uses as well. The sociologist may be called upon for help with a special problem, such as the effectiveness of propaganda or the recurrence of "crime waves." However, sociology's present capacity to give "answers" to social problems should not be exaggerated. At this time the sociologist's practical contribution lies in the ability to clarify the underlying nature of social problems, to estimate more exactly their dimensions, and to identify aspects that seem most amenable to remedy with the knowledge and skills at hand.

Adaptation 1, pages 11–14, discusses some of the objectives, methods, and problems of sociological inquiry.

SOCIOLOGY AND THE SOCIAL SCIENCES

There has been diminishing controversy about whether sociology should be called a science or a more neutral name such as "discipline." Some believe that sociology is not a science at all and that because of the nature of its subject matter it cannot be one. Some, for example, point to the difficulty of applying the experimental method to social phenomena as a major obstacle. Such scholars do not usually hold, however, that the field does not merit study or that its findings are not worthwhile.

By a variety of research methods, the social scientist attempts to go as far as he can toward uncovering what is persistent and repeatable in the social world. He recognizes, however, that for him "nature" is more elusive and inconstant than it is for the physical scientist. This problem is raised in "The Variability of Social Facts," page 5.

Science is not to be defined by a single method or routine, such as the classic before-after experiment or the use of special implements such as glass tubing or lenses or precise measuring instruments. Each of the old and established sciences has developed more or less distinctive techniques, instruments, and routines. The specialized routines and equipment of the scientific enterprise, which vary from discipline to discipline and from time to time, should not be confused with science itself. All science is characterized more nearly by an attitude, an approach, a point of view, than by any special technique. One is entitled to call sociology a science if theories are progressively refined and tested

The Variability of Social Facts

Abridged from Morris R. Cohen, "The Social Sciences and the Natural Sciences," in William Fielding Ogburn and Alexander Goldenweiser (eds.), *The Social Sciences and Their Interrelations* (Boston: Houghton Mifflin, 1927), pp. 455–57. Used with permission of the publisher.

In the following comments, the American philosopher Morris R. Cohen (1880–1947) points up some of the difficulties of reaching firm generalizations about social phenomena. He did not doubt the value of social inquiry but asked that due regard be paid to the complexity and variability of social facts.

Cohen is best known for *Reason and Nature* (1931) and for *Introduction to Logic and Scientific Method* (with Ernest Nagel, 1943).

Any cubic centimeter of hydrogen will for most purposes of physics or biology be as good as another. But observation on one community will not generally be so applicable to another. Even purely biologic facts, for example, the effects of diet, seem to be more variable in the human than in other species. In the social realm reasoning from examples is intellectually a most hazardous venture. We seldom escape the fallacy of selection, of attributing to the whole class what is true only of our selected instances.

It is, of course, true that for certain social questions we can treat all individuals as alike. Thus, for vital statistics, every birth or death counts the same, no matter who is involved. Likewise, in certain economic or juristic questions we ignore all individual differences. Yet there can be no doubt that the applicability of such rules in the social sciences is more limited and surrounded with greater difficulty than the application of the laws of the natural sciences to their wider material.

In any fairly uniform realm like that of physics, where we can vary one factor at a time, it is possible to have a crucial experiment; that is, it is possible to reduce an issue to a question of yes or no, so that the result refutes and eliminates one hypothesis and leaves the other in possession of the field. But where the number of possible causes is indefinitely large, and where we cannot always isolate a given factor, it is obviously difficult to eliminate an hypothesis; and the elimination of one hypothesis from a very large number does not produce the impression of progress in the establishment of a definite cause.

The last observation suggests that the greater complexity and variability of social fact also make its purely theoretical development more difficult. In general, social situations are networks in which one cannot change one factor without affecting a great many others. It is, therefore, difficult to determine the specific effects of any one factor. Moreover, social elements seldom admit of simple addition. The behavior of the same individuals in a large group will not in general be the same as their behavior in a smaller group.

Agreement based on demonstration is less easy in the social than in the natural sciences because the greater complexity of social facts makes it less easy to sharpen an issue to an isolable point and to settle it by direct observation of an indefinitely repeatable fact.

by observation, and if the ideals of objectivity and exactness guide inquiry.

Sociology shares with other social sciences —notably anthropology, economics, political science, and social psychology—the task of scientific exploration of social behavior and its products. There is no hard and fast division between one social science and another, nor should there be. There is hope in social science that problems arising where these fields meet and requiring interdisciplinary cooperation will lead to fruitful perspectives and research. There are, however, important differences of emphasis that mark off one social science discipline from another.

Social psychology is largely concerned with connections between group experience and the psychology of the individual. This is an area of knowledge to which both sociologists and psychologists have contributed. In their attempts to understand individual behavior and personality, social psychologists have recognized the need to see the influence of interpersonal relations and group membership. This has led to studies of social roles, of the emergence of personality in social interaction, of the analysis of attitudes, and the investigation of small groups. In social psychology the emphasis is placed on the effect of group influences directly on the person. Aspects of social psychology are treated in the study of SOCIALIZATION,[1] PRIMARY GROUPS, and COLLECTIVE BEHAVIOR. In this book psychological mechanisms are treated only lightly, and physiological psychology is omitted.

Anthropology is partly a biological and partly a social science. Physical anthropology deals especially with the biological origins of man and with variations in the human species, including the study of race. Because of the social importance of race differences, sociology texts have traditionally given much attention to this problem. We have not done this because the study of races (though *not*

of race-conscious groups) is now recognized as a technical problem in genetics and human biology, and it could not be adequately introduced here. We have also excluded discussion of such topics as fossil men and the characteristics of the lower animals. These interesting subjects do not directly illuminate sociological inquiry, and we thought it better to leave them for courses in physical anthropology, biology, or comparative psychology, where they can be properly developed.

Social and cultural anthropology have contributed greatly to the comparative analysis of societies by exploring the ways of life among preliterate communities throughout the world. We have drawn upon these materials and the ideas developed from them largely in CULTURE, SOCIALIZATION, and Part Three. In many ways, anthropology and sociology have drawn closer together in recent years, particularly as anthropologists have turned to the study of literate societies. A central emphasis on the analysis of culture, however, continues to characterize anthropological inquiry. In sociology this is a significant but not a predominant preoccupation.

Economics deals with the phenomena of cost and price, of savings and investment, of supply and demand. The economist necessarily makes assumptions about the goals men seek in economic life, and sometimes he questions those assumptions. When he does, psychological and sociological analyses are indicated. Furthermore, the economic order is related to and dependent upon many noneconomic forces, including government, public opinion, family life, and migration. Sociologists help to explore these relations and to see their significance for industrial stability and change. The chapter on INDUSTRIAL MAN is in part an introduction to the sociological analysis of economic institutions.

Political science is mostly concerned with the study of government, and traditionally it has had a strong legal and administrative orientation. In recent years, however, there has been a growing interest among political sci-

---

[1] To facilitate cross reference, the titles of chapters appear in small capital letters throughout the book.

entists in exploring all of the factors that influence political and administrative decisions, not merely the legal and official relationships. The political order does not stand alone but is rooted in culture and social organization. These considerations, added to the rapidly increasing importance of political decisions for many areas of social life, have stimulated a renewed interest in political sociology. This subject is treated in POLITICAL MAN.

Some historians classify their discipline as a social science; others, as one of the humanities. In either case historical documentation is invaluable for sociological research, and sociological analyses are of interest to historians of the contemporary scene.

Sociology is complementary to the other social sciences. It explores the varieties of group structure and the ways they affect political, psychological, and economic relationships. Sociologists are not interested in business decisions *as such,* but they are interested in the social conditions that make certain types of business relations possible. For example, they study the effect of kinship on economic participation in newly industrialized countries or the effect of internal and external group relations on factory output and morale. Sociologists are not specialists in military science, but they can and do study leadership and morale in air force squadrons and army units.

Section 2 Plan and content of the book

THE OLD AND THE NEW

Most of the material covered in this book has been part of sociology for a long time, and we have not tried to impose a fundamentally new perspective. We have presented the funded knowledge of the discipline, including new research, according to categories and principles on which there is a high degree of consensus.

There is a basic continuity in the subject matter of sociology, even though it is a rapidly growing discipline. New research findings and new ideas are being actively sought in many centers of the Western world, although many of these ideas are not yet ready for presentation in an introductory text. However, much is included here that has not previously appeared at this level:

1. There is a growing emphasis on sociology as an intellectual perspective, a set of tools for analyzing special areas of experience. The systematic application of ideas developed in Part One to the subjects treated in Part Two reflects this approach; and Part Three presents modern man's patterns of life in three major areas.

2. We have adopted a recent trend toward putting older sociological concepts to work in new contexts. This may be seen in the expanding study of primary groups, where a classic idea has been applied with outstanding results to new areas, notably factory organization and military life.

3. Studies of simple research techniques have been introduced, and we have drawn upon a number of historical studies and case reports, which play a major role in sociological research and theory.

4. We have also developed a number of topics not ordinarily covered in introductory texts. For example, the sociology of political and economic development is treated in some detail.

PLAN

In order to present a systematic introduction to sociology, this book was written according to a carefully designed but simple and direct plan. An understanding of the plan is essential to the most efficient use of the book. Reference to the detailed Table of Contents (pp. vii–xviii) will be helpful in reading the following discussion.

Part One: Elements of Sociological Analysis

Part One might be called the "elements of sociological analysis," and it covers the main aspects of the subject matter of sociology. The distinction between Part One and Part Two reflects two kinds of specialization in sociology. First, a sociologist may be interested in certain phenomena found in all societies or in most areas of society. For example, he may be a specialist in the study of social stratification, in the analysis of population data, or in the study of how personality is influenced by group experience. These specialties are discussed in Part One, which sets out the main skills and interests comprising the sociologist's tools of analysis. Secondly, a sociologist may specialize in applying the tools of sociological analysis to a particular area of society, such as religion or education. These specialized applications are carried out in Part Two.

The division between Part One and Part Two is *not* a strict division of theory and application. Each Part One chapter includes factual material as well as concepts, application as well as theory. However, Part One draws on many different areas to illustrate points, while each Part Two chapter concentrates on a special area. For example, the chapter on ASSOCIATIONS in Part One includes material on political parties and factories, drawn upon to illustrate general principles regarding the sociology of large-scale organizations.

Taken together, the Part One chapters present the main tools with which the sociologist approaches any special area. However, we have not meant to do more than organize the subject matter according to established categories. The number of chapters, and the way they are divided, is largely a matter of con-

venience and emphasis. For instance, Chapter IX combines two closely related fields, POPULATION AND ECOLOGY, while separate chapters are given to ASSOCIATIONS and PRIMARY GROUPS. Nor have we sought to make the chapters neat and watertight compartments. The subject of SOCIAL ORGANIZATION, for example, includes the study of primary groups, associations, and social stratification. But these important and specialized elements of social organization are also given detailed treatment in separate chapters.

Part Two: Analysis of Special Areas

In Part Two we bring sociological analysis to bear on specialized areas of interest. Each Part Two chapter is divided into *sections* corresponding to the Part One chapters. The elements of sociology are re-examined in several specialized areas of social life. For example, the study of SOCIAL STRATIFICATION or COLLECTIVE BEHAVIOR is not limited to its treatment in Part One; it is pursued in Part Two in chapters on THE FAMILY, RELIGION, EDUCATION, MINORITIES, and CRIME AND DELINQUENCY.

The list of topics in Part Two could have been extended to include the sociology of rural or military life. It would be a challenging project for the student or class to apply the pattern of Part Two chapters to a field not included in this book, that is, to develop one's own Part Two chapter. One of the topics just mentioned might be used, or the approach might be applied in the study of a geographical area, such as the Near East. Our experience has taught us that this is a good way to sharpen one's understanding of sociological concepts and at the same time to achieve a broad introduction to a special area. We do not intend to imply that all of the elements of sociology are equally relevant to all areas of social life. For narrow subjects, only some of the sociological elements are relevant, and even broad areas do not call for equal emphasis of the several elements.

Part Two chapters provide background

materials for problems of public policy. Indeed, the interest in these areas has largely derived from the practical problems that arise in a changing society and that seem to require and are amenable to sociological analysis. Three of the five chapters in Part Two—THE FAMILY, MINORITIES, and CRIME AND DELINQUENCY—deal with fields in which theoretical sociology has long converged with the more immediate concerns of applied sociology. In these chapters we have presented material that is relevant to decisions regarding social policy. But we offer the caution that sociological analysis as such can tell only what must be taken into account in policy-making. It cannot make policy.

Part Three: Master Trends

Three major themes characterize modern society: (1) the development of the city as the predominant site of human residence, association, and work, (2) the ascendance of an industrial order with new problems of organization and control, and (3) the transformation of the political order. These themes are the subjects of three related chapters that form a distinct unit of the book. The chapters are presented within a framework emphasizing social change; at the same time they introduce the student to the main ideas and findings of urban, industrial, and political sociology. Illustrations are drawn from emergent as well as advanced societies, from nations still at the threshold of modernity as well as from the more fully developed industrial societies. The chapters are entitled URBAN MAN, INDUSTRIAL MAN, and POLITICAL MAN. Modern man is all these things.

FORMS OF PRESENTATION

The subject matter is handled in two main ways, in *text* and in *Adaptations*. The text gives a coherent exposition and analysis. Set off from the text and separately identified are the adapted readings. These present aspects of important studies published in books, monographs, and learned journals. Because much of the material was prepared originally for a professional public, we have often simplified, condensed, and reorganized it to make it as useful as possible to beginning students of sociology. That is, we have "adapted" to the introductory level studies that illustrate or further develop discussions in the text. In a number of cases we have adapted only a portion of a major work or we have presented in Adaptation format our own summaries and interpretations of important books. In every case, Adaptations further develop points covered in the text discussion or are complementary to it.

Some Adaptations are primarily reports of research and are included for their factual and interpretive detail: for example, "The Web of Friendship," "The Church and the Sect," and "Fertility in Ceylon." Others are more theoretical: "The Primary Group: Essence and Accident" and "Mind, Self and Society." Still other Adaptations are given as examples of research technique or methodological problems: "Public Opinion Polls" and "The Technique of the Sociogram."

Brief illustrative materials highlighting particular items are presented against a shaded background.

The book makes extensive use of charts and tables and some pictorial illustrations. Although most of the charts and tables are rather simple, they are essential parts of the text and should be studied with at least as much care as a page of exposition.

Research Exercises

Summaries of research procedures, such as "Methods of Stratification Research," are organized to encourage the student to try his hand at original research. Such work should be undertaken, however, only after careful review and planning with the instructor. Furthermore, studies that depend on observation or interviewing are, in a sense, an invasion of privacy. There should be a clear understanding that the privacy of informants and subjects will be protected. Real people and real social relations are the subject matter of the sociologist. He shares with other scientists the obligation of objectivity and rigor. To these, whether he be a mature scholar or a new student, he must add a respect for the privacy of his subjects.

TO THE STUDENT

It is unwise to read a textbook as one reads a novel. Depending on the difficulty of the material and the objectives, different reading techniques are useful. The plan we suggest for studying this book is not meant to be a hard and fast set of rules but an approach that should help in your study. You will need to adapt the procedure to your own study habits and abilities, but we have recommended it to our own students with some success.

1. To get a general idea of the material covered in a chapter, read through the whole chapter or the part assigned *rapidly* at one sitting, if possible. Make a *brief* topical outline as you read to gain an overview of the chapter plan. Headings and subheadings in the text will help you do this, but we suggest you do not make detailed notes or underscore during the first reading which is intended to *familiarize* you with the subject matter.

2. After you have a perspective of the chapter, you are ready to *study* it in detail, section by section, while the first reading is still fresh in your mind. Each major section of a chapter, and each Adaptation your instructor assigns, is a unit that should be studied without interruption. If you plan your work so that you have enough unbroken time to cover thoroughly each section you begin, it will take less time than several short periods of study, and you will learn the subject matter more efficiently.

During this second *close* reading, make marginal notes, underscore important points, and transfer summary notes and questions to your notebook. We advise that you underscore only the most important phrases. A

book in which almost every sentence is underlined is much like a book that has not been underlined at all, except that it is a bit more difficult to read. Your notes and marks should *assist,* not hinder, you when you review.

The objective of the second reading is to get the material *under control.* At this time you might add details to your original topical outline.

3. After each section has been studied, another rapid reading of the entire chapter will reinforce your mastery of the material. Be sure that you are clear about items on which your notes show problems or which your instructor has emphasized or qualified. If you follow this scheme, review for examinations should be relatively brief and painless.

TO THE INSTRUCTOR

In this new edition we have been able to benefit more fully from the advice and teaching experience of colleagues in many types of institutions. This advice and the real, if uneven, development of sociology in the past few years have led us to make extensive changes. Sociologists familiar with an early edition will notice that both text and adaptations have been substantially modified. We have substituted fresh material when there was an opportunity to make a more effective presentation. However, we have deliberately avoided presenting new material just because it is new. Significant older studies are retained, and we have again reached into the storehouse of sociological writings for the old as well as the new.

We are convinced that the perspectives of sociology are invaluable tools for understanding the modern scene, but we do not think of sociology as the study of the latest news. A degree of topicality is useful for imparting a sense of relevance, but the studies cited ought to be the best available regardless of age, and ought to strike as closely as possible to the fundamentals of the discipline. For example, in our opinion no study of a race riot equals the report of the Chicago Commission on

Race Relations, and we have, therefore, retained from the first edition Adaptation 22, the report of the 1919 riot. We think Mead's *Mind, Self and Society* is a classic with which all students of sociology should be acquainted, and we have retained Adaptation 7 from the second edition. Adaptation 46, new in this edition, is from another classic, Tocqueville's *Democracy in America*. We hope not only that the Adaptations of these meritorious works communicate sociological understandings, but that they also communicate to the student a sense of sociology as a sustained effort over many years and by many minds.

No one can know the needs of his students better than the instructor, and we have tried to furnish him with some of the tools to do his job. From our own experience and from that of other teachers, we feel that the combined format of original text and Adaptations provides both coherence of exposition and flexibility of instruction.

The Part Two chapters, each of which recapitulates the chapter topics in Part One, were, as we intended, often used as a basis for review. We had not anticipated that preparation of (and for) examinations would thereby be greatly simplified. A number of instructors have found that the thematic repetition in the Part Two chapters makes it possible for the student to review the key elements of the course without doing a large amount of re-reading of the early chapters. The students have, therefore, been able to continue their study of leading ideas, but with fresh materials.

In one-semester courses chapters or Adaptations are sometimes omitted or are used to enrich the course for part of the class. Some instructors concentrate on Part One, assigning only selected Part Two chapters as required reading or permitting students to choose from the Part Two chapters according to individual interests. Part Two has been reorganized and reduced to five chapters, including new chapters on RELIGION and EDUCATION. We think that reinforcement of the student's understanding of the Part One principles is effectively accomplished by the Part Two chapters.

The Part Three chapters add another perspective, introduce further teaching flexibility, and allow for the development of problem-oriented instruction.

Notes on Sociological Research

Adapted from an unpublished paper by Martin A. Trow.

Growing up in a society teaches its members much about how it works, but there are kinds of knowledge one is not likely to gain in the ordinary pursuits of life. For example, most adult Americans are aware of the existence of prejudice and discrimination against Negroes. But in the ordinary course of life the individual may not learn much about what lies behind these feelings. Nor is he likely to know very accurately how widespread anti-Negro sentiments are, what forms they take, how they differ in different parts of the country and among different groups in the population, and whether such sentiments are on the rise or are declining in extent and intensity. Similarly, many people are aware that college enrollments are growing rapidly, but few people know how fast, what kinds of institutions are absorbing the bulk of the growth, and how this growth is affecting the character of higher education.

Sociological research is the purposeful effort to learn more about society than we are likely to learn in the ordinary course of living. In carrying on this work, the sociologist uses a variety of methods. How he goes about his work depends on (1) what his objectives are, and (2) what materials or data he can procure.

Sociological Description

For many purposes, what is needed is a factual account of an event, such as a political rally, or a summary of the characteristics of a population, such as the proportion of aged or the number of divorced persons. In this sense, sociology is a kind of reporting. However, sociological reporting has two special characteristics:

1. *Precision.* The sociologist tries to be as precise as possible in his descriptions. If he can do so, he finds ways of counting and measuring, but much valuable sociological research does not involve the use of statistics. It may consist of the careful study of historical records or the close observation of some single event, situation, or group. The evidence may be assembled and analyzed with care even though numbers are not used.

Accurate reporting and analysis has two basic requirements: *objectivity* in observation and *skepticism* toward other people's reports of what is going on. Objectivity does not require that the observer approach the world with a blank mind; rather, he should be equally prepared to find that the facts do or do not support his prior beliefs. Skepticism does not require that the scholar doubt everything he hears or reads, only that he try to distinguish reliable from unreliable reports, "official" pronouncements from genuine opinions, knowledge from prejudice.

In numerical descriptions of populations a number of questions must be considered. For example, were the data collected or reported according to uniform criteria? The importance of uniform criteria is illustrated in the following hypothetical case. Suppose a sociologist compared juvenile delinquency rates

for a number of small and large cities and found higher rates in the larger cities. He might then go on, very sensibly, to investigate what it is about large cities that makes for greater delinquency. His efforts might be pointless, however, if it happened that the smaller cities were in states that defined a juvenile as any person under eighteen, while the larger cities were in states that defined a juvenile as anyone under twenty-one. Thus the higher delinquency rates of the larger cities might reflect merely a more inclusive legal definition of who is a juvenile.

Many similar problems arise in the use of official statistics. Record-keeping is often more complete and detailed in cities than in rural areas. This may distort comparisons between areas. There are similar problems in making comparisons over periods of time. Part of the reported increase in juvenile delinquency in recent years is due to changes in official reporting rather than changes in juvenile behavior.

Besides using public records, sociologists gather data on their own, often by interviews and questionnaires. A sociologist interested in a community's attitudes toward an increase in school taxes would have to gather his own data. Since he could not interview everyone, he would select a sample. If his findings are to describe with accuracy the distribution of attitudes in the population, his sample must be "representative," that is, must be a reflection in miniature of the whole community. There are scientific ways of constructing such samples and of estimating the probability that they are representative. When the characteristics of a whole group or population are to be described by means of a sample, the precision with which the sample is chosen is of fundamental importance.

On the other hand, much can be learned from studies that do not have representative samples. Detailed interviews with ten members of one college fraternity can tell many things about fraternity life. Unless the men interviewed (the "respondents") are selected according to principles of scientific sampling, it cannot be concluded that the findings apply to the fraternity as a whole.

2. *Guidance by sociological ideas.* Precision alone does not make a description distinctively sociological. The sociologist has a fund of ideas that help him to form hypotheses about the particular situation or problem he is studying. These ideas or "concepts" comprise a large part of what he learns as a student of sociology. They are his armory of analysis, his guides to inquiry.

From Description to Explanation

Sociologists are rarely content with simply counting things or with straight reporting. They want to understand and explain, to go beyond descriptive fact-gathering to comparison, interpretation, and the assessment of how different aspects of the social world are related.

The reported facts often raise questions that call for additional information. For example, it has long been known that high school boys from working-class backgrounds are less likely than middle-class boys to go to college. Why? Some of the difference, but not all, can probably be accounted for by the expense of a college education. But this is not the whole story. In pressing for a fuller explanation, sociologists have applied another idea—the notion of a group atmosphere or "climate." Recently researchers have investigated the influence on college-going of different high school climates, determined largely by attitudes toward academic achievement in the student body.

One study demonstrated the effects of this climate: middle-class boys in predominantly working-class high schools were less likely to go on to college than boys from the same backgrounds who had attended high schools with predominantly middle-class students. Conversely, working-class boys in predominantly middle-class high schools were more likely to aspire to college than boys from similar backgrounds in high schools whose stu-

dents were mostly working-class in origin. By thus looking more closely at the students, studying their school environments as well as their origins, a more accurate and a more sophisticated understanding of the conditions affecting college attendance can be achieved. Description quickly becomes a search for explanations.

Empirical Indicators

Many things sociologists want to study cannot be seen or measured directly. An example is the "morale" of a team of workingmen or a company of soldiers. Morale is said to be high when there is cheerful obedience to orders, confidence in supervisors or officers, willing participation in the life of the organization. But to refine this idea, and to study the factors that affect morale, one needs some way of measuring the level of morale in one group as compared with others.

Morale cannot be measured directly, but its presence and strength can be *indicated* by directly observable events that usually accompany high or low levels of morale. Thus morale can be measured by such indicators as rates of absenteeism, rates of infraction of rules, number of men who report themselves sick, willingness to put in extra work, and other acts or attitudes. An empirical indicator is an *observable* sign that some *un*observable characteristic of an individual or a group exists. To rely on empirical indicators in sociology is like relying on the observation of smoke as an indicator or natural sign of the probable existence of a fire.

One of the continuing tasks of social research is to test the *validity* of empirical indicators. For example, using the number of men who report themselves sick as an indicator of low morale may not always give valid results. Unhealthful living or working conditions might also produce higher sick-call rates in one group than in another with which it is compared. For this reason sociologists often try to find more than one indicator for the same phenomenon. In the case of army units it would be expected that low morale would be shown by high rates of absence without leave (AWOL), high rates of sick call, high rates of disobedience, and perhaps other evidences of discontent.

The search for valid indicators also helps to clarify ideas. For example, the meaning of morale, as given above, includes *both* willing participation in group life *and* confidence in leaders. But when morale is measured, it may be found that participation and confidence do not necessarily go together. The members of a group may work well together, with considerable satisfaction, but in opposition to their leaders. Conversely, men may have confidence in their leaders but show little interest in active participation, as is often the case in trade-unions and political organizations. Such findings invite a clarification of the working definition of morale.

Critical analysis of indicators may also lead to the discovery that the same behavior may have different meanings for different people. For example, is cutting classes a good indicator of "commitment to education"? Some students cut classes because they are indifferent to studies; for them high rates of cutting indicate low levels of commitment to education. For other students, however, cutting classes may point to a serious but independent pursuit of learning.

Sociological research is a union of observation and analysis, of gathering data and reflecting on it. Doing research on social life and theorizing about it can scarcely be distinguished. At every step the design of research is guided by and contributes to the body of sociological ideas. Theories and hypotheses about social life are at once the fruit of past and the seed of future research.

SOURCES AND READINGS

Periodicals

The following journals in English contain articles on topics pertinent to each of the chapters in this book. They contain basic readings for all fields of interest and will not be separately listed in succeeding chapters.

American Journal of Sociology, established in 1895. Until 1935 it was the official journal of the American Sociological Society (as it was then called). See the Index to Volumes I-LII, 1895–1947.

American Sociological Review, established in 1936. Official journal of the American Sociological Association. See the Index to Volumes I–XXV, 1936–1960.

American Catholic Sociological Review

Annals of the American Academy of Political and Social Science

Behavioral Science

British Journal of Sociology

Current Sociology

Journal of Abnormal and Social Psychology

Rural Sociology

Social Forces

Social Problems

Sociological Abstracts

Sociological Inquiry

Sociology and Social Research

Sociometry

A number of regional societies in the United States issue periodicals or proceedings which are becoming increasingly important. See especially:

Pacific Sociological Review

Sociological Quarterly (formerly *Midwest Sociologist*)

Southwest Social Science Quarterly

The *Transactions* of the World Congresses of Sociology now appear every three years. Published by the International Sociological Association.

Encyclopedia of the Social Sciences, published in 1930–1935.

Chapter II

Social organization

Section 1   The individual and social organization

A major objective of this book is to explore the following general principle: *the way men behave is largely determined by their relations to each other and by their membership in groups*. The more fully these relations are understood, the better will be the comprehension of why and how people act as they do. Social relations are at the foundation of both motivation and control. The goals and aspirations that set people into motion are greatly influenced by their social relations. Social relations are also instruments of control, for they limit action and restrain impulses that might threaten the orderly arrangement of independent lives.

In observing and analyzing the influence of social relations on behavior, the sociologist also studies the structure of society. This means that he is interested in the *elements* that, taken together, give form to the dynamic social world and permit the work of that world to go on despite tremendous complexity and potential confusion.

In this chapter the basic elements of social organization are examined. Section 1 deals with the way individuals are influenced by social relations and integrated into society.

Section 2 analyzes the formation of new groups, the changing relations among major groups, and the significance of these relations for the development of society as a whole. Section 3 reviews some basic trends in the history of Western society. The concluding section outlines the scope of social organization as a field of study.

INTERACTION AND RELATEDNESS

In his daily life an individual continually meets people, co-operates with them, obeys them, irritates them, ignores them. Even to begin a list of such actions shows how diverse are the ways human beings deal with each other. The process of acting in awareness of others, and adjusting responses to the way others respond, is called *social interaction*. Much interaction follows an established pattern; as soon as an individual identifies another person as his teacher or employer, for example, he knows how he is expected to respond.

Other interactions, however, are less closely governed by established patterns. In Western society the individual is faced with many alternatives—whom to have as friends, whom to marry, where to work, what political party to join, and many others. In the course of making these choices, he establishes ties with other individuals, accepts membership in many groups (for instance, when he becomes a student or employee) and gradually comes to have a settled place in the world. The individual's interactions, and group memberships, are determined more nearly by the ways he solves the problems of everyday life than by a fixed set of rules. As an outgrowth of the individual's daily choices and decisions, enduring relations are established, and he thus makes a contribution to social organization. These topics are illustrated in Adaptation 2 which describes interaction and social organization in a suburban housing development.

The sociologist is mainly concerned with interactions that attain stability, that is, those that are recurrent and patterned. This central concern for stable, recurrent interactions does not mean that the less stable ones are uninteresting or unimportant. Sociologists also study spontaneous, relatively uncontrolled forms of human behavior, such as fads and fashions, panics and riots, but in doing so particular attention is given to the emergence of shared patterns of behavior, even though they are transitory. Sociologists also recognize that in the more stable relations, such as marriage, there is room for a variety of responses and adjustments. While searching for what is orderly, it must be remembered that change and instability are characteristic of social life. Much interaction is casual, tentative, or unstable, and does not lead to enduring social bonds.

The variety of social relations is enormous. Friendship, fatherhood, employment, leadership, neighborliness, partnership, citizenship, marriage, and a host of other terms signify important and differing relations. The sociologist tries to understand the nature of these relations by examining their elements, classifying them, and studying what happens to them under changing conditions.

Some social bonds are strong and others weak. A shipboard romance is a notoriously weak social relation; marriage, even in present-day society, remains a relatively strong and stable relation. Some social relations, such as family relations, have lasting significance for the entire life of the individual while others, even if they endure, are far less meaningful. Some relations are of great importance to the community because they involve tasks that must be performed, such as the care of children. Other relations, for example a friendship, may be of little concern to anyone except those who are immediately involved.

The strength of a social relation depends in part upon its scope and whether it fits into a larger pattern. For example, if a marriage involves the husband in economic ties to his wife's family, this broadens and often strengthens the foundation upon which the marriage rests, despite the fact that it also introduces unusual strains. In addition, the strength of a relation depends on whether it serves or frustrates the needs of the individual. Both aspects of any social relation—its place in a larger social setting and its significance for personal satisfaction—affect whether the relation is strong and enduring or weak and transitory.

ROLES AND ROLE STRAIN

The concept of "role" can help in viewing social relations as part of the orderly structure of society.[1] The basic idea is quite simple: a "role" (sometimes called "social role") is a *pattern of behavior associated with a distinctive social position,* e.g., that of father, teacher, employer, or patient. Most roles specify the rights and duties belonging to a social position; they tell the individual what he ought to do in his role as father, or teacher, to whom he has obligations, and upon whom he has a rightful claim.

[1] See Theodore R. Sarbin, "Role Theory," in Gardner Lindzey (ed.), *Handbook of Social Psychology* (Cambridge, Mass.: Addison-Wesley, 1954), Vol. I, pp. 223–58.

Complementary Roles

Roles are usually *complementary,* or reciprocal. The role of superior is complemented by the role of subordinate, the role of teacher by that of student, the role of employer by that of employee. The behavior specified for each role helps to make social interaction an orderly and reliable process. Students know how to behave toward teachers, housewives how to behave toward grocers. The fixing of roles also helps to insure the co-ordination of individual behavior into a meaningful whole. The roles of worker, foreman, salesman, and manager are related to each other so as to constitute a functioning, co-operative business enterprise.

The elaboration of roles is closely related to the division of labor. Roles include ways of fixing responsibility for all the jobs that have to be done, from feeding babies to deciding for war or peace. The greater the complexity of society or of a particular group, the more different roles there will be. Some roles are so common that all members of society are familiar with them, but others are so highly specialized that only a few people know about them or are called upon to fill them or respond to them.

Most roles are more complex than they appear to be at first glance. A mother is a mother in relation to a child; yet being a mother is more than just one social relation. It is a bundle of relations to other members of the family and to the community, as well as to the child. Part of the role of mother may involve membership in the P.T.A. just as part of the role of employer may involve membership in a Chamber of Commerce. Although many roles are rather definitely specified, in practice they are often too complex to be learned except through experience. The mother, the employer, the student, the foreman only gradually learn through their interactions with others what is expected of individuals in their social position.

To analyze a role completely it is necessary to specify in detail the social position with which it is associated. In some respects, all students occupy similar social positions. Insofar as this is true, it is possible to describe general features of the student's role. But there are many ways of being a student, even within a particular college. The married student, the disciple, the "big man on campus" are all significantly different in the positions they occupy within the social structure of the college. Close analysis usually reveals specific roles, reflecting the particular way a given family, school, or other group is organized.

Role Conflict

In the course of his role behavior the individual is subject to conflicting pressures and strains.[2] Some of these strains arise because different and inconsistent kinds of behavior are required. For example, a role may call for friendship or intimacy but also may require impersonal judgment or command. To the extent that a professor's role leads him to attempt to influence some students deeply, he needs to be on friendly terms with them, to treat them as unique persons, and to develop a sense of mutual loyalty. But the role of professor also requires that the man be a judge, evaluate the work of the student, and make decisions that may affect the latter's entire career. These conflicting aspects of the role may require painful adjustments by both professor and student.

Some roles are designed to meet this type of problem. To preserve authority, close personal relations between those in command and their subordinates may be carefully avoided. For example, the impersonality and severity of military discipline are supported by creating a strong sense of social distance between officers and enlisted men. This is not always a satisfactory solution, however. A more personal leadership is necessary to win deep loyalty or to summon extraordinary energies in battle; and distance between ranks is a handicap to effective communication even

2 William J. Goode, "A Theory of Role Strain," *American Sociological Review,* **25** (August, 1960), 483–96.

in everyday activities. Hence, the wise leader seeks various ways of overcoming the distance between himself and his command. For example, he may show by public acts that he understands the problems of his subordinates and is proud of them.

Many role conflicts in industry and military life arise when the attempt is made to create a bridge from the commanding group to those who must obey. Many noncommissioned officers in the army, and foremen in industry, play this bridging role. They are men "in the middle." They must communicate orders from above, but they must be close enough to the working group to understand how these orders will be received; they must have the confidence of the working group lest fear and hostility undermine effective communication and the will to co-operate. At the same time, these lower-level leaders must be able to take the point of view of their superiors whose orders are to be communicated and enforced. The result is a continuing necessity to take account of two approaches to daily experience and of two sets of interests that are often in conflict.

Thus strains and inconsistencies are *built into the role*. When these built-in conflicts are known, the problems set for the individual by his role are also known. His role involves him in relations that make demands upon him, limit the alternatives he can choose, and create the problems he must try to solve. Much behavior can, therefore, be understood by determining the individual's place in the social structure.

SOCIAL ORGANIZATION AND SOCIAL CONTROL

The individual gains much from his involvement in social organization, but he always pays a price. That price is the acceptance of restraints, of limitations on the freedom to do as he pleases.

The achievement of orderly social life depends on law-enforcement agencies only to a limited degree. Social order depends also on two basic sources. One of these is the fund of shared understandings or agreed-upon rules governing how men ought to behave. This may be called the *normative order,* and is analyzed in the next chapter, CULTURE. The other source of order is social organization, the patterned relations of individuals and groups.

Social organization produces social control mainly because people are *dependent* on each other. One of the chief ways of mapping the social structure of a group or community is to explore the mutual dependencies that have been created. The more people an individual is dependent upon for his satisfactions, the more claims will there be upon him to exercise self-restraint lest he offend those he needs and risk the loss of their co-operation.

Dependency is not just a matter of narrow self-interest. Dependency of others upon the individual invokes ideals that might otherwise be inoperative. The social ideals of parenthood, even if he fully approves of them, are not instruments of social control for the bachelor. His behavior cannot be restrained by responsibility to children he does not have. It is only through relations to others and by participating in social institutions that responsibilities arise; only in this way do ideals become effective instruments of social control.

Isolation and Control

Social isolation weakens social control. If a person is uninvolved with others, there are fewer occasions to assess the consequences of his actions either for himself or for others dependent upon him. Durkheim's explanation of the different rates of suicide (see Adaptation 3) is grounded in a theory of social organization. He pointed out, for example, that unmarried people are "freer" to choose suicide as a response to despair than are married people because the unmarried are relatively isolated from controlling social bonds.

Of course, an individual may seek isolation in his search for personal independence, but almost no one avoids *all* entangling relations. Rather he seeks the development of skills and resources to make himself less dependent on the good will of others or on their constant companionship. Isolation is indeed one way of minimizing social control, but from the standpoint of personal well-being the loss of positive values must also be considered. Too much freedom (freedom of this sort should not be confused with *political* freedom) can disorient the individual, and may rob his life of direction and meaning.

The Web of Friendship

Abridged and adapted from *The Organization Man* by William H. Whyte, Jr. (New York: Simon and Schuster, 1956), pp. 330–61. Published in this form by permission of William H. Whyte, Jr.

Students of social organization are interested in both the *sources* and the *consequences* of patterned interaction. In the new suburb, one may observe the spontaneous growth of social organization among people previously unrelated to each other. The effects of this patterning on the personal lives of the residents can then be analyzed.

This procedure is followed in Whyte's description and interpretation of life in Park Forest, Illinois. He traces the emergence of different micro-communities that develop their own social characteristics. These characteristics are based on the physical placement of homes by the designers of the housing development and on the patterns of relations established by the first residents.

Also considered are the effects of the highly patterned and intense social life of these small subcommunities on (1) civic participation and (2) the individual's dilemma of personal autonomy and group loyalty.

In suburbia, friendship has become almost predictable. Given a few physical clues about the area, you can come close to determining its flow of "social traffic," and to a diagnosis of who is in the gang and who is not.

Park Forest has the principal design features found in other suburbs: its 60 x 125 plots are laid out in the curved superblocks typical of most new developments, and the garden duplexes of its rental area are perhaps the most intense development of court living to be found anywhere. Park Forest is like other suburbs, only more so.

The architects wanted a good basic design that would please people and make money for the developers—but not since the medieval town have there been neighborhood units so well adapted to the predilections and social needs of its people. In many ways, the courts are remarkably similar to the workers' housing of the fifteenth century. Like the Fugger houses in Augsburg, the courts are essentially groups of houses two rooms deep, bound together by lines of communication, and the parking bay unifies the whole very much as did the water fountain of the Fugger houses.

When the architects designed the 105 courts and the homes area, they tried hard to introduce some variety, and no two courts or superblocks are physically alike. But neither are they alike socially; some neighborhood units have been a conspicuous social success from the beginning, others have not. Each court produces a different pattern of behavior, and whether newcomers become civic leaders or bridge fans or churchgoers is determined to a large extent by the gang to which chance assigns them.

Court residents talk about these differences a great deal. In some areas, they will tell you, feuding and cussedness are chronic. "I can't put my finger on it," says one resident, "but as long as I've been here this court has had an inferiority complex. We never seem to get together and have the weenie roasts and parties they have in B 18 across the street." In other courts they will talk of their *ésprit de corps*. "At the beginning we were maybe too neighborly," says one housewife, "your friends knew more about your private life than you did yourself! But it's still real friendly. The street behind us is nowhere near as friendly. They knock on doors over there."

A routine plotting of the rate of turnover in each area, the location of parties, and similar data revealed geographical concentrations that could not be attributed to chance. For example, when the location of leaders of church and other civic organizations was plotted, certain courts displayed a heavy concentration while others showed none at all. The pattern, furthermore, was a persistent one. When leaders for the same organizations as of two years earlier were studied, the same basic pattern emerged. Several leaders were still hanging on, but there had been enough turnover

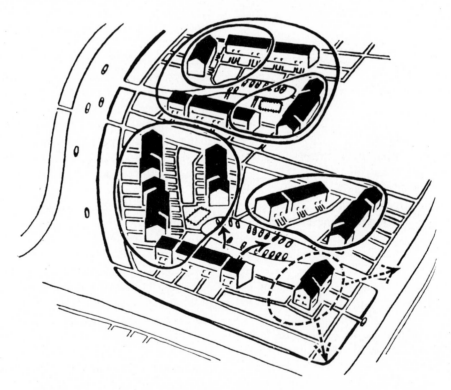

What Makes a Court Clique: In the rental courts formed around parking bays social life is oriented inward. In the large court at the bottom, for example, wings whose back doors face each other form natural social units. Buildings sited somewhat ambiguously tend to split the allegiance of their inhabitants, or else, like the lonely apartment unit at lower right, isolate them. Smaller courts like the one at the top are usually more cohesive; and though there may be subgroupings, court people often get together as a unit.

to show that the clustering was closely related to the influence of the court.

Other indexes show the same kind of contagion. The map of active members of the United Protestant Church indicates that some areas habitually send a good quota of people to church while other areas send few. Voting records show heavy voter turnouts in some areas, apathy in others, and this pattern tends to be constant—the area that had the poorest showing in the early days is still the poorest (six people voting out of thirty-eight eligibles). The same courts may also make more complaints to the police about parking-space encroachments, litter left on the lawns, and similar evidences of bad feeling. Courts that keep on producing an above-average number of complaints prove to be the ones with relatively poor records of churchgoing and voting. Another key index is the number of parties and such communal activities as joint playpens. Some courts have many parties, and though the moving van is constantly bringing in new people, the partying and the group activities keep up undiminished. On closer investigation, areas with high partying records usually prove to be the ones with the physical layout best adapted to providing the close-knit neighborly group that many planners and observers feel needs to be re-created.

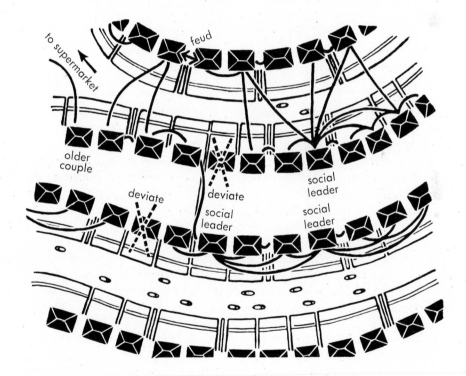

How Homeowners Get Together: (*1*) *Individuals tend to become most friendly with neighbors whose driveways adjoin theirs.* (*2*) *Deviates or feuding neighbors tend to become boundaries of the gang.* (*3*) *People in the most central positions make the greatest number of social contacts.* (*4*) *Street width and traffic determine whether or not people make friends across the street.* (*5*) *People make friends with those in back of them only where some physical feature creates traffic—such as the short-cut pavement one woman on the lower street uses on her way to the supermarket.*

Court Traditions

Of all the factors making for differences among the courts, the character of the original settlers seems the most important. In the early phase, the court's inhabitants must function as a unit to conquer such now-legendary problems as the mud of Park Forest, or the "rocks and rats" of Drexelbrook. During this period, though the level of communal sharing and brotherhood is high in all courts, the impact of the strong personality, good or otherwise, is magnified. Two or three natural leaders concentrated in one court may so stimulate the other people that civic work becomes something of a tradition in the court; or, if the dominant people are of a highly gregarious temper, the court may develop more inwardly, along the one-big-family line. Conversely, one or two troublemakers may fragment a court into a series of cliques, and the lines of dissension often live long after the troublemakers have gone.

In time, the intensity of activity weakens. As the volunteer policemen are replaced by a regular force, as the mud turns to grass, the old *esprit de corps* subsides into relative normalcy. First settlers will tell you that the place is in a dead calm. But what seems like dead calm to them will not seem so to anybody from the outside world, and for all the settling down the court continues to be a hothouse of participation. Occasionally, there are sharp breaks in the continuity of tradition; in one court, several forceful women ran for the same post in a community organization, and the effect of their rivalry on the court spirit was disastrous. Most courts, however, tend to keep their essential characters. Newcomers are assimilated, one by one, and by the time the old leaders are ready to depart, they have usually trained someone to whom they can pass on the baton.

Space and Sociability

The social patterns show rather clearly that a couple's behavior is influenced not only by which court they join but by the particular part of the court in which they are placed.

It begins with the children. There are so many of them and they are so dictatorial in effect that a term like *filiarchy* would not be entirely facetious. It is the children who set the basic design; their friendships are translated into the mothers' friendships, and these, in turn into the family's. "The kids are the only ones who are really organized here," says the resident of a patio court at Park Merced in San Francisco. "We older people sort of tag along after them." Suburbanites elsewhere agree. "We are not really 'kid-centered' here like some people say," one Park Forester protests, "but when your kids are playing with the other kids, they force you to keep on good terms with everybody."

That they do. With their remarkable sensitivity to social nuance, the children are a highly effective communication net, and parents sometimes use them to transmit what custom dictates elders cannot say face to face. "One newcomer gave us quite a problem in our court," says a resident in an eastern development. "He was a Ph.D., and he started to pull rank on some of the rest of us. I told my kid he could tell his kid that the other fathers around here had plenty on the ball. I guess all we fathers did the same thing; pretty soon the news trickled upward to this guy. He isn't a bad sort; he got the hint—and there was no open break of any kind."

Placement of driveways and stoops: If you are passing by a row of houses equally spaced and want a clue as to how the different couples pair off, look at the driveways. At every second house there are usually two adjacent driveways; where they join makes a natural sitting, baby-watching, and gossip center, and friendship is more apt to flower there than across the unbroken stretch of lawn on the other sides of the houses. For the same basic reasons the couples who share adjoining back stoops in the courts are drawn together, even though equidistant neighbors on the other side may have much more in common with them.

Lawns: The front lawn is the thing on which homeowners expend most time, and the sharing of tools, energies, and advice tends to make family friendships go along and across the street rather than over the back yards. The persistence of this pattern furnishes another demonstration of the remarkable longevity of social patterns. At first, some people thought that lack of over-the-back-fence fraternization was strictly temporary. It has not proved to be so. As the areas have matured, some of the reasons for the concentration of activity in the front area have disappeared; but despite this fact and despite the turnover, over-the-back-fence socializing is still the exception.

Centrality: The location of your home in relation to the others not only determines your closest friends; it also virtually determines how popular you will be. The more central one's location, the more social contacts one has. In the streets containing rental apartments there is a constant turnover; yet no matter who moves in or out, the center of activity remains in mid-block, with the people at the ends generally included only in the larger gatherings.

Some Park Forest veterans joke that a guide should be furnished newcomers so that if they had a choice of sites they would be able to tell which would best suit their personality. Introverts who wished to come out of their shell could pick a house in the middle of a block; while introverts who wished to stay just as they are would be well advised to pick a unit more isolated.

Barriers: The rules of the game about who is to be included, who left out, are not simple. Suppose you want to give a party? Do you mix friends out of the area with the neighbors? How many neighbors should you invite? Where, as social leaders chronically complain, do you draw the line? Physical barriers can provide the limiting point. Streets, for example, are functional for more than traffic; if it is a large street with heavy traffic, mothers will forbid their children to cross it,

and by common consent the street becomes a boundary for the adult group.

Because of the need for a social line, the effect of even the smallest barrier is multiplied. In courts where the parking bays have two exits, fences have been placed across the middle to block through traffic; only a few feet high, they are as socially impervious as a giant brick wall. Similarly, the grouping of apartment buildings into wings of a court provides a natural unit whose limits everyone understands.

Ambiguity is the one thing the group can not abide. If there is no line, the group will invent one. They may settle on an imaginary line along the long axis of the court, or, in the homes area, one particular house as the watershed. There is common sense behind it. If it is about time you threw a party for your neighbors, the line solves many of your problems for you. Friends of yours who live on the other side understand why they were not invited, and there is no hard feeling.

In this need, incidentally, the deviant can be of great benefit. The family that doesn't mix with the others or is disliked by them frequently furnishes a line of social demarcation that the layout and geography do not supply. So functional is the barrier family in this respect that even if they move out, their successors are likely to inherit the function. The new people may be normal enough themselves, but unless they are unusually extroverted the line is apt to remain in the same place.

The Outgoing Life

The effect this web of friendship has on the individual is a problem suburbanites think about a great deal. One of the first points they make is how it has altered their personality—or how they and the rest of the group altered someone else's. For the good. "I've changed tremendously," says one typical transient. "My husband was always the friend-maker in the family—everybody always loves Joe; he's so likable. But here I began to make some friends on my own; I was so tickled when I realized it. One night when the gang came to our house I suddenly realized I made these friends."

The cumulative effect can be summed up in a word. People are made *outgoing*. If the person is too shy to make the first move, others will take the initiative. In almost every court, patio, or superblock there is usually someone who enjoys doing the job, and the stiffer the challenge, the more the enjoyment. "When Mr. and Mrs. Berry came, they wouldn't give you the time of day," one leader recalls. "But I knew they were real shy and unhappy beneath it all. I said to myself, 'I'm going to conquer them if it kills me.' I have, too. She was one of the organizers for the Mothers' March and he's gotten tremendously interested in the school. They're part of the gang now—you wouldn't know they were the same people."

The Sin of Privacy

On the matter of privacy, suburbanites have mixed feelings. Fact one, of course, is that there isn't much privacy; people don't bother to knock and they come and go furiously. The lack of privacy, furthermore, is retroactive. "They ask you all sorts of questions about what you *were* doing," one resident puts it. "Who was it that stopped in last night? Who were those people from Chicago last week? You're never alone, even when you think you are."

Less is sacred. "It's wonderful," says one young wife. "You find yourself discussing all your personal problems with your neighbors—things that back in South Dakota we would have kept to ourselves." As time goes on, this capacity for self-revelation grows; and on the most intimate details of family life, court people become amazingly frank with one another. No one, they point out, ever need face a problem alone.

In the battle against loneliness even the architecture becomes functional. Just as doors inside houses are disappearing, so are the bar-

riers against neighbors. The picture in the picture window, for example, is what is going on *inside*—or, what is going on inside other people's picture windows. Walls in the new apartments are thin, but there is more good than bad, many transients say, to the thinness. "I never feel lonely, even when Jim's away," goes a typical comment. "You know friends are near by, because at night you hear the neighbors through the walls."

Even the most outgoing, of course, confess that the pace of court life occasionally wears them down, and once in a while they reach such a point of rebellion they don't answer the phone. One court resident moves his chair to the front rather than the court side of his apartment to show he doesn't want to be disturbed. Often a whole court or a wing of it will develop such a signal; a group in one Drexelbrook court has decided that whenever one of them feels he or she has finally had it, she should draw the venetian blinds all the way down to the bottom of the picture window. The rest spot it as a plea to be left alone —for a little while, anyway.

But there is an important corollary of such efforts at privacy—people feel a little guilty about making them. Except very occasionally, to shut oneself off from others like this is regarded as either a childish prank or, more likely, an indication of some inner neurosis. The individual, not the group, has erred. So, at any rate, many errants seem to feel, and they are often penitent. "I've promised myself to make it up to them," one court resident recently told a confidant. "I was feeling bad that day and just plain didn't make the effort to ask them in for coffee. I don't blame them, really, for reacting the way they did."

Privacy has become clandestine. Not in solitary and selfish contemplation but in doing things with other people does one fulfill oneself. Nor is it a matter of overriding importance what one does with other people; even watching television together—for which purpose several groups have been organized— helps make one a more real person.

The Moral Basis of Conformity

However one may view this responsiveness to the group, it is important to acknowledge its moral basis. That friendship in the new suburbia transcends personal characteristics so much is due in part to the increasing homogeneity of American middle-class values. But it is also due to a very active kind of tolerance, and unless this is recognized one cannot appreciate the true difficulty of the suburbanites' dilemmas.

Very consciously, they try to understand one another's backgrounds and prejudices, and make a great effort to meet one another half way. Farm-bred Republicans learn to appreciate that not all urban Democrats are Communists. "The people who lived in the other half of our duplex," recalls one Republican, "were as different as could be from us. They were the kind who worshipped F.D.R.'s name. But we got to like them just the same. We just didn't talk politics. We used to go bowling together and that sort of thing. I didn't make him a Republican, but I think he appreciates my views a lot more than he did before, and I understand him better."

This seeking of common values applies markedly to religion. The neighborhood friendship patterns would be impossible unless religious beliefs had lost much of their segregating effect. And it is more than a passive, live-and-let-live attitude.

Even where there is conflict, suburbanites lean over backward to see the other point of view. "When Will and Ada had to dash East last month—they're devout Catholics—I took care of little Johnny for them," recalls one non-Catholic. "It really tickled me. Here I was picking Johnny up at St. Irenaeus School every afternoon and seeing to it that he said his Rosary every night before he went to bed." Park Forest abounds with such stories, and the good will implicit in them is real.

The suburban group also has a strong effect on relations between husband and wife, in many ways a beneficient one. The group is a foster family. In the transient organization life the young family has to take a good part of its environment with it; no longer is there the close complex of aunts and uncles and grandparents to support the couple, and when they come to their first crisis this absence can have a devastating effect. All the other young couples are in the same boat, and in a sort of unspoken mutual assistance pact they provide for one another a substitute for the big family of former years.

What unites them most are the concerns of parenthood, and this preoccupation with children is a potent factor in keeping marriages on keel. "The kind of social situation you find here discourages divorce," says United Protestant Church minister, Dr. Gerson Engelmann. "Few people, as a rule, get divorces until they break with their groups. I think the fact that it is so hard to break with a group here has had a lot to do with keeping some marriages from going on the rocks."

The Group as Friend and Tyrant

But the group is a jealous master. It encourages participation, indeed it demands it, but it demands one kind of participation—its own kind—and the better integrated with it a member becomes the less free he is to express himself in other ways.

When we first went to Park Forest we thought that the courts and blocks most notable for their friendliness and social activity would contribute the greatest number of civic leaders. As a check we plotted the location of all the leaders in the principal community organizations. To our surprise, the two did not correlate; if anything, there was a reverse relationship. By and large, the people who were active in the over-all community did not tend to come from the courts that were especially "happy."

The cause-and-effect relationship is not too difficult to determine. For some people, of course, it does not make much difference whether the neighborly gang is a happy one or not; they would be leaders in any event.

But such people are a minority. The majority are more influenced by the good opinion of the group, and its cohesiveness has a considerable bearing on whether they will become active in community-wide problems. Where the group has never jelled enough to stimulate a sense of obligation, the person with any predilection for civic activity feels no constraints. The others would not be annoyed if he went in for outside activity; they don't care enough. If the group is strong, however, the same kind of person is less likely to express such yearnings. It would be divisive. There are only so many enthusiasms a person can sustain, only so many hours in the day, and the amount of leisure one expends outside the group must be deducted from that spent inside.

It is not merely that the group will resent the absenteeism. The individual himself feels a moral obligation to the group. A young housewife had been toying with the idea of getting involved in the little theater, for she felt she and her husband were culturally very lacking. But she decided against it. "If we do it'll mean we'll have to spend more of our free evenings away from the gang. I'd hate to be the first to break things up. The two play areas for the kids—my, how we all pitched in on that! I know we spend too much time just talking and playing bridge and all. Frankly Chuck and I are the only ones around here who read much more than the *Reader's Digest*. But have we the right to feel superior?

I mean, should we break things up just because we're different that way?"

Is this simple conformity? Consider the man who is wondering about something he knows would upset the group—like not painting his garage white, like the rest. He may have been one of the first settlers of a block where the people have suppressed potential dislikes in a very successful effort to solve their common problems. Quite probably, a piece of bad luck for one of the group might have further unified them. If one of the wives had come down with polio, the rest might have chipped in not only with their money but with their time to help out the family through the crisis.

In other words, there had been a great deal of real brotherhood, and the man who is now figuring about his garage faces a decision that is not entirely ludicrous. He knows instinctively that his choice will be construed by the others as an outward manifestation of his regard for them, and he does feel a real obligation to help sustain the good feeling.

If he goes along with them he is conforming, yes, but he is conforming not simply out of cowardice but out of a sense of brotherhood too. You may think him mistaken, but grant at least his problem. The group is a tyrant; so also is it a friend, and *it is both at once*. The two qualities cannot easily be separated, for what gives the group its power over the man is the same cohesion that gives it warmth. This is the duality that confuses.

Suicide and Social Integration

A summary and interprétation of Emile Durkheim, *Le Suicide* (Paris: Alcan, 1897). English translation and Introduction by George Simpson (Glencoe: The Free Press, 1951).

The French sociologist, Emile Durkheim, was interested in the various types of social integration and in social disorganization, the weakening of social bonds. He studied the differing rates of suicide and used them as an index of social integration among various European groups. At the time Durkheim wrote, it was known that the suicide rate varied for different groups and for different periods. It was higher for Protestants than for Catholics, higher for the unmarried than for the married, higher for soldiers than for civilians, higher for noncommissioned officers than for enlisted men, higher in times of peace than in times of war and revolution, and higher in times of both prosperity and recession than in times of economic stability.

Durkheim reasoned that since different groups have different suicide rates, there must be something about the social organization of the groups that prevents or fails to deter people from committing suicide, and which may even prompt them to it. He acknowledged that individual reasons for committing suicide were many and varied: financial distress, disappointment in love, failing to pass an examination, ill health, and so on. But these reasons did not explain why some groups are more inclined to suicide than others.

Durkheim suggested that the degree to which the individual was integrated into group life determined whether he could be motivated to commit suicide. However, he recognized that no one simple set of circumstances explains suicide. The individual can be motivated to commit suicide at either of two extremes: if he is highly integrated or if he is only superficially integrated into society.

Altruistic Suicide

When the individual is tightly bound into a highly integrated group with a strong sense of solidarity, he accepts the values and norms of the group as his own. He does not distinguish between his interests and those of the group, nor is he likely to think of himself as a unique individual with a life separate and apart from the group. Under these circumstances what would prompt him to commit suicide?

He will be willing to sacrifice his life for group goals. The Japanese *Kamikaze* of World War II is an example of military self-sacrifice. Japanese airmen dove their planes

Emile Durkheim (1858–1917), a profound student of social organization. His lifelong interest was in the forces that hold a society together or tend to disorganize it. In The Elementary Forms of the Religious Life, *he studied the contribution of religion to social cohesion; his* Division of Labor in Society *analyzed two basic types of social solidarity and introduced the concept of* anomie. *Another of his studies of social integration was* Suicide, *one of the first modern examples of the use of statistical method in social research.*

onto enemy ships in order to disable them, despite the fact that it meant certain death. In highly integrated societies, where there is a strong sense of social solidarity, self-destruction may be looked upon as self-affirmation and fulfillment; death, as well as life, has meaning and value. Closely related to this kind of suicide is ritualistic self-sacrifice. In India a practice called *suttee,* now outlawed, was sometimes performed by a woman upon the death of her husband.

The ultimate personal act may reflect the strength or weakness of group ties.

If the individual fails to meet group standards, death may appear preferable to life. Identification with the group can be so intense that group condemnation is tantamount to self-condemnation. Failure in such a case is total and absolute. The individual puts all his eggs in one basket. He stakes his entire self-respect on approval of one particular group; when that is withdrawn, he has no other basis for self-esteem.

Suicide that results from an excessive degree of group integration Durkheim called *altruistic,* and it is committed for the sake of the group or according to group norms of right conduct. Altruistic suicide may be found where the individual is overcommitted to one group and is socially isolated from other groups.

Durkheim used his theory of altruistic suicide to explain why the suicide rate was higher for soldiers than for civilians, higher for noncommissioned officers than for enlisted men, and higher for volunteers and those who re-enlisted than for conscripts. He suggested that suicide increases as the soldier identifies himself more completely with the values and norms of military life. The officer is better integrated into the military organization than the ordinary soldier, the volunteer more committed to military life than the conscript. The more the soldier is integrated into military life, the greater is his isolation from other groups in society; the more committed he is to military values, the more he stakes his self-respect on success in the army. No other paths are open to him.

Egoistic Suicide

What happens to the individual when he is only weakly attached to the social order?

1. He lacks the restraints that intense participation in group life imposes on him. If he has an inclination to commit suicide, he is not deterred because of deeply felt commitments to others. Nor does he consider the consequences of his suicide for the group. An individual not bound to others is free of any

claims that they may have on his survival.

2. The individual lacks the emotional attachments that make life worth while and less self-centered—attachments to others as persons.

3. The individual lacks the emotional supports which deep immersion in group life can provide. He is thrown back upon his own resources. He gains no satisfaction from the achievements of the group; success or failure are his alone. Wrongdoing is not defined solely by group standards, but is a matter of personal judgment and responsibility. Under the burden of individual responsibility, the individual is susceptible to the emotional disturbances which may lead to suicide, and he cannot fall back upon relations with others to help him over a personal crisis.

This kind of suicide Durkheim called *egoistic*. It is self-centered rather than group-centered. Altruistic suicide occurs because the individual is deeply involved in group life; egoistic suicide occurs because the individual is uninvolved and detached.

According to Durkheim, the relatively higher rate of Protestant suicide could be explained as egoistic. Both Catholicism and Protestantism condemn suicide, but Catholicism makes its injunction effective by attaching the individual to the church as a social institution. Protestantism, on the other hand, makes salvation an item of individual faith and religious belief, a matter of personal responsibility. It tends to detach the individual from all religious constraint except his own conscience. In doing so, however, it removes those social restraints that would be most effective in deterring him from suicide.

The relatively higher suicide rate among the unmarried is also an instance of egoistic suicide. The unmarried are both socially and emotionally isolated from others. They have fewer responsibilities as well as fewer attachments. The married are restrained by both formal obligations and emotional ties. They are also apt to be less self-centered. Their lives are perforce taken up with the care

of others, and they develop shared interests and values and find emotional support in their personal relations with others.

During wars and revolutions people are led to forget themselves and their troubles in uniting for a common effort. At least temporarily, social crises result in a stronger integration of society. For this reason, Durkheim claimed, the suicide rate tends to fall during social disturbances and wars.

Anomic Suicide

When a group is highly integrated and unified, it develops a set of norms to regulate behavior and interpersonal relations. The norms include a clearly defined code of what is proper and improper for people of various ranks and classes. When it is felt that the individual should not presume beyond his station in life, the norms set strict limits on individual aspiration and achievement, but they provide people with a sense of security. Success may be limited, but it is genuine. Not only in matters of achievement but in matters of moral behavior, the individual knows what is expected of him. If he conforms to the standards set by the group, he is assured of its approval. The group provides the individual with a sense of security by establishing clear rules of right and wrong and by limiting his aspirations to what he can achieve.

When group norms are weakened, there is less restraint set upon the individual's aspirations and behavior. At the same time, however, he loses the security that group control and regulation can provide. His aspirations soar beyond possible fulfillment; he is uncertain of what is right and wrong.

According to Durkheim, a society that lacks clear-cut norms to govern men's aspirations and moral conduct is characterized by *anomie,* a French word meaning "lack of rules." Suicide resulting from anomie Durkheim called *anomic.*

Anomic and egoistic suicide both spring from low social integration, but they are nevertheless independent. Although the individual who commits egoistic suicide does not have the personal bonds that would deter him from suicide, he has not necessarily rejected the norms of the group. On the contrary, the egoistic suicide may be a highly moralistic person who feels a deep sense of personal responsibility for his behavior. His morality, however, usually stems from "principle" rather than from emotionally felt commitments or loyalties to other persons. Indeed one of the sources of his emotional disturbance may be that he is overdisciplined; he conforms in an overly rigid way. According to Durkheim, egoistic suicide is apt to occur among intellectuals and professionals, people whose primary commitment is to ideas rather than to persons.

In anomic suicide, on the other hand, the individual may be deeply involved in society, but group life fails to provide him with controlling standards of behavior. The egoistic suicide may find life unbearable because of *excessive* self-discipline; the anomic suicide may find life unbearable because of *inadequate* self-discipline.

Durkheim found two kinds of evidence to support his theory that the lack of limiting norms might increase the suicide rate. He noted that the rate was higher in countries that permitted divorce than in countries that did not permit it, and the rate was still higher where divorce was frequent. He suggested that where divorce was allowed, one of the most important regulative principles in society was weakened and that the weakening of marriage norms was associated with a less firm application of other group norms.

Durkheim found evidence that suicide is related to economic crisis. This is most clear in periods of recession but also occurs during periods of sharp business expansion. Durkheim interpreted this as a result of *anomie*. Although recessions bring hardship, poverty by itself does not inspire suicide. Spain was poorer than France but had only a tenth as many suicides. In France the suicide rate was higher in areas with a relatively large number of persons of independent means. Economic shifts unsettle people's lives and make for greater uncertainty. Consequently, people do not act on the basis of limited traditional aspirations and may find it difficult to accept frustrations.

Conclusion

The main significance of Durkheim's study is the analysis of the kinds of relations that people can have to groups and to group norms. His study was published in 1897 and was based on statistical data that now seem somewhat crude. On the other hand, most of his observations have been generally supported by later studies,[3] and the ingenuity and aptness of his analysis and interpretation are a challenge to contemporary scientists.

[3] For more recent studies of suicide see:

Ruth S. Cavan, *Suicide* (Chicago: University of Chicago Press, 1928).

Louis I. Dublin and Bessie Bunzel, *To Be or Not To Be* (New York: Harrison Smith and Robert Haas, 1933).

Andrew F. Henry and James F. Short, Jr., *Suicide and Homicide* (Glencoe: The Free Press, 1954).

Austin L. Porterfield and Robert H. Talbert, *Crime, Suicide and Social Well-Being in Your State and City* (Fort Worth: L. Potishman Foundation, 1948).

Calvin F. Schmid and Maurice D. Van Arsdol, Jr., "Completed and Attempted Suicides: A Comparative Analysis," *American Sociological Review*, **20** (June, 1955), pp. 273–83.

Section 2 **The group structure of society**

TYPES OF GROUPS

The word "group" is used in a very general sense. It refers to any collection of persons who are *bound together by a distinctive set of social relations*. This includes everything from members of a family, adherents to Catholicism, participants in a mob, to citizens of a national state. Two persons form a group if they are friends or partners or otherwise *held together and set apart from others* by their relationship. Groups can be highly organized and stable or very fluid and temporary.

Groups and Social Categories

People who have similar incomes or who are alike in other ways, such as age, occupation, or reading habits, do not necessarily form social groups. Such classifications may be called statistical aggregates or social categories. They are important in sociological analysis because people who are similar in these ways often enter into social relationships and form groups. People who have similar incomes often have much else in common. They may share a style of life, be aware of their position in a society, and form groups on the basis of this consciousness. A persistent interest of sociology is the study of the conditions under which various social categories become or produce social groups.

The aged are a significant social category, and there is considerable interest today in the kinds of groups older people are likely to form or accept. Is there an old-age style of life that can be the natural basis for separate housing? Or do older people feel little sense of identity with each other despite their similar age and dependency? There have been some old-age political pressure groups, such as the Townsend movement of the 1930's. Should more

and increasingly powerful groups of this sort be expected as the proportion of older people in the population rises? What effect would this have on the political order? These questions indicate the problems raised when the group potential of a social category is explored.

Although consciousness of kind—the awareness that one belongs to a certain category—is an important element in the formation of groups, it is not indispensable. Many workers belong to lodges, bowling clubs, and other groups that are distinctively working-class in character; yet if asked, they would not necessarily identify themselves as belonging to any particular social category. Nevertheless they unconsciously enter and create ways of group life based on similarities of occupation and income. Similar life experiences lead to social interaction and the formation of groups, even though people are not aware of why and how this takes place.

Communities

A community is an inclusive group with two chief characteristics: (1) within it the individual can have most of the experiences and conduct most of the activities that are important to him; (2) it is bound together by a shared sense of belonging and by the feeling among its members that the group defines for them their distinctive identity. Theoretically, the member of a community lives his whole life within it; he feels a sense of kinship with others who belong to it; and he accepts the community much as he accepts his own name and family membership.

Communities are usually based on locality —a village, city, or nation. The geographical area and a sense of place set the boundaries of common living and provide a basis for solidarity. However, without respect to geography, one may speak of the "Catholic community," in the sense that there is a unique set of Catholic activities and institutions which, taken together, permit many Catholics to live out much of their lives within boundaries set by religious affiliation. They can be educated as Catholics, live in a Catholic neighborhood, work for a Catholic organization, belong to a Catholic professional society, and read a Catholic newspaper. Similarly, one may speak of a Japanese-American community, a Jewish community, and even an academic community. However, most fully developed communities do share a common locality.

In American society the development of a national community has been limited by strong sectional feeling, particularly in the South, by segregation of Negroes and whites, by the problems of assimilating millions of immigrants with diverse origins, and by a system of government that allows a large degree of local autonomy. On the other hand, rapid changes in the technology of communication, increasing centralization of industry and government, a mobile population, and the emergence of the United States as a world power have greatly increased the significance of the national community for the lives of its members.

Associations

Special-purpose organizations, such as trade-unions, corporations, and political parties, are called associations. In this category are factories, where the main incentive to participation is money income, as well as "voluntary associations," such as clubs or veterans' groups. There are many thousands of such organizations in the United States.

Associations are usually based on limited, utilitarian interests. However, there are variations in the range of interests served and in the resulting meaning of membership. In general the more specific and practical an association's objectives, the more impersonal

and narrow will be the individual's relation to the group.

Recent discussions of the "organization man" have centered about this problem, emphasizing the personal dilemmas that arise when a large, basically impersonal business enterprise seeks to win a broader loyalty from the employee, as well as a high degree of conformity to an approved pattern of life.[4]

Institutions

When an association serves public rather than merely private interests, and does so in an accepted, orderly, and enduring way, it may be called an "institution." The word "institution" also refers to practices, to *established ways of doing things*. Constitutional government, marriage, private enterprise, and Thanksgiving dinner are called institutions, although they are practices rather than groups. This book follows common usage and refers to both of these related phenomena as institutions. An institution, therefore, may be a type of group or it may be a formalized practice or procedure. In this sense, the Methodist church is an institution, and it conducts itself in institutionalized ways.

The most important public interests are *cultural values* and *social order*. Groups that promote and defend these interests are, correspondingly, the most important institutions. Cultural values are ways of action and belief that make up a society's sense of identity, its "way of life." For example, Americans value churchgoing, public education, and equal justice under law. Churches, schools, and courts are institutions based on and serving these cultural values.

The public interest in social order concerns the regulation of internal conflict and the safety of the community against external threats. These are the main functions of government institutions. Other public interests include the promotion of economic welfare, science, public health, and peace. Public

---

[4] See William H. Whyte, Jr., *The Organization Man* (New York: Simon and Schuster, 1956).

interests are sensed as urgent when a key value is affected or social order is believed to be at stake.

GROUP RELATIONS

The major groups just reviewed receive extended discussion in later chapters. The present discussion is intended to underscore the fact that society is not merely an aggregate of interacting individuals. It has a group structure, and each type of group makes a distinctive contribution to maintaining society as a "going concern."

At any given time, there are dominant groups and subordinate ones, allies and enemies. Some are dependent, others relatively independent. Some are strategically located and can communicate with or influence many parts of the community; others are on the fringes with limited access to other groups. Knowing the pattern of group relations is essential to understanding a community or society and the processes of social control.

Group structure is not static; it is the product of continuous interaction in which the relations among groups are tested and transformed. A few of the basic forms of group interaction, and the stable relations that they produce are considered here.

Competition, Rivalry, and Conflict

The interests of one group are often inconsistent with those of others. For example, several organizations may seek to recruit the same people: colleges may compete for the better students or staff; several nations may want the same economic resources; many retail stores want to sell to the same customers. *Competition* is this mutually opposed effort to secure the same scarce objectives.

Competition is a relationship that does not necessarily involve direct interaction; it may be impersonal and unconscious. Cotton farmers in Mississippi compete with cotton farmers in Egypt, but they may be unaware of each other. When groups become aware that they are in competition they are called

rivals. *Rivalry* is a form of conscious competition between specific groups: for example, the Democrats and Republicans, the Ford Motor Co. and General Motors, the Army and the Air Force, the U.S.A. and the U.S.S.R. This kind of competition is more direct, with mutual awareness and often self-conscious strategy and tactics.

When the clash of interests is so keen that groups do not merely compete for the same scarce goals but seek to injure or even destroy each other, there is *conflict,* and the group itself is endangered in a direct way. Intense feelings may be aroused and, as a result, the rules governing competitive and rivalrous activity may be abandoned.

Rivalry and conflict are *dissociative* forms of interaction. They pull groups apart rather than bind them together. However, these processes are not *purely* dissociative. Rivalry is usually based upon commonly accepted rules, as in athletics. Conflict tends to increase the *internal* solidarity of the contending groups.

Communication between the conflicting groups tends to be suspended. The sense of threat and an increased concern for internal solidarity leads to a blocking of communication channels. For example, when labor-management conflict is intense, union leaders avoid all except the most official and circumscribed contact with the employers, partly because they would be exposed to criticism from their own members. A rapid decline in communication between the United States and the Soviet Union after 1946 accompanied the onset of the "cold war." Exchange of news and of scientific information, as well as travel, was sharply restricted.

It is sometimes believed that conflict is a result of poor communication, that conflict arises because people do not understand each other. If communication means the ability to see another's point of view, then some conflicts truly rooted in false perceptions may be eased by increasing communication. However, many conflicts are grounded in the mutually inconsistent needs and aspirations of groups. Moreover, increased contact and improved communication may intensify conflict by making groups aware of their differences, increasing their fears, and revealing opposing interests of which they were unaware.

Accommodation and Assimilation

After a long and bitter strike, union and management may come to agreement and the men go back to work. Feelings of hostility and antagonism may persist. Each side may prepare to renew open conflict at another time. Under such circumstances, the agreement represents an unstable accommodation. *Accommodation* is the mutual adjustment of groups that retain their own identity and interests. In an unstable accommodation a temporary adjustment is made and the conflicting groups adapt themselves to immediate realities, despite the existence of unresolved issues.

In settling conflicts, accommodation must first be achieved. The problem is not so much one of communication, of mutual understanding, as it is of discovering what is essential to each group if it is to cease hostilities and offer the minimum co-operation that is needed. This was the problem of the American states after the Revolution. The Constitution they created in 1787 was an accommodative document. It adjusted the interests of large and small states, of Southerners and Northerners, and thereby won support for the foundation of the United States. It was not essential that the states see all things alike or that the citizens cease to view themselves as Virginians and New Yorkers.

A stable accommodation resolves the major differences of interest, particularly those deemed vital to continued group existence. When a stable accommodation is reached, there is a basis for deeper harmony involving more extensive mutual understanding. Groups can then enlarge their contacts and even come to think of themselves as sharing a single identity.

The process by which the identity of groups is fused is called *assimilation*. In this process the breakdown of communication barriers is essential. In the assimilation of immigrants to the United States the schools have carried a heavy burden. Many classes were conducted in large cities to teach adult immigrants the English language and some essentials of American history and government. Despite these efforts, few first-generation immigrants are really assimilated. Differences in social background persist as barriers to effective communication.

Co-operation

Group co-operation is agreed-upon joint action. Such agreement may be based on similar group aspirations, e.g., organizations interested in preventing delinquency; groups may have a common enemy and thus have temporarily convergent interests; or they may agree upon a set of common rules to regulate their competition. The amount of communication depends on the basis of co-operation; when people act together out of loyalty to family or community, there is much more communication than when there is a limited alliance in defense against a temporary threat.

In co-operation each group gains, either in an immediate advantage or indirectly in seeing its ultimate goals advanced. However, they need not gain *equally*. Weak groups usually gain more from co-operation than do strong groups, and the latter are therefore often reluctant to enter agreements with weaker groups. They may feel impelled to do so, however, when they share or must conform to a social ideal holding that co-operation as such is a good thing.

Co-operation as well as conflict can threaten group independence. When two groups co-operate, communication between them is greatly increased. The boundaries of group membership may become obscure, and leaders may be called upon to justify the independent existence of their organizations. If pressure is generated for the amalgamation of groups, it may threaten the vested interests of the leaders as well as the long-run aims each group represents. This is a serious problem among churches, government agencies, and political groups. Leaders of government agencies—for example, of the different military services—carefully examine proposals for administrative co-operation with other agencies to see what the consequences will be for the sharing of public credit, for the justification of independent budgets, and for maintaining the distinctive loyalties and outlooks of their staffs. Co-operation among community welfare agencies raises similar problems. They need to be reassured that their independent existence is not threatened by a proposed joint venture, such as fundraising through a Community Chest.

Because co-operation is highly valued, the word easily becomes a symbol to which people must pay their respects. In fact, however, responsible group leaders always try to answer the question, "Co-operation for what and with whom and at what price?"

Isolation and Integration

In mapping the social structure, one of the most important things to consider is the *degree of integration* of social groups, that is, the extent to which they share a common outlook, communicate with each other, depend on each other, and share responsibility for maintaining the social order.

Complete isolation of groups within the same society is excluded by definition because membership in a society presumes some social ties. Even remote mountain communities or frontier settlements are subject to outside legal control, however weakly enforced. Nevertheless, some groups are more isolated than others.

The existence of relatively isolated groups is particularly important to *social control*. The connection between individual isolation and social control was discussed in Section 1, pages 18–19. By the same logic, the isolation of groups reduces the chances that they will

act responsibly, that is, in accordance with the needs and ideals of the larger society of which they are a part.

The history of trade-unionism shows a development from a high degree of isolation and low social control to increasing integration and greater social responsibility. This transition is still incomplete and unstable: a number of unions continue to display characteristic signs of isolation.

For many years, the organization of workers into trade-unions was treated as a criminal conspiracy. After that legal interpretation was abandoned, the right to organize was still denied in many quarters and when such organizations did appear, they encountered hostility. It was not respectable to belong to trade-unions nor was union leadership a respectable occupation.

Since trade-unions were not accepted as legitimate institutions, few established avenues of communication between them and other groups in the society developed. Employers often refused even to talk to union leaders, particularly if they were not their own employees. No government agencies existed to adjust trade-union affairs and the public interest. Thus trade-unions were isolated from the "respectable" community in two senses: *attitudes of mutual rejection* and *an absence of ties to other groups* set them apart.

The early stages of unionism were also characterized by reliance on the strike and on aggressive tactics, including violence. This, too, can be traced in large part to the social isolation of the unions, and especially to the absence of effective channels for peaceful negotiation. The rejection of the unions' right to exist put them in the position of fighting for their lives, and this same rejection meant that a peaceable accommodation was not acceptable until an effective show of strength had been made. For this reason both labor and management often resorted to violence, one to show its strength, the other to forestall the creation of a strong union. Both sides used intimidation because no arrangements for negotiation and compromise were acceptable to the employers. The most bitter conflicts took place over the issue of union recognition, not over differences about wages or working conditions.

At the present time in the United States, a number of fundamental changes have taken place in the relations among unions, employers, government, and the general community. Most large industrial employers have accepted the unions as rightful participants in industrial life. Conflict now tends to be over narrower, practical issues, rather than a life-and-death struggle over principle.

Adaptation 4 offers a different, but related, perspective on how groups interact and how they are bound together. Two communities living side by side are described, the Negroes and forest pygmies of Ituri in the Congo. The account shows (1) how the mutual dependence of two groups gives the subordinate group a certain amount of leverage; (2) that group interaction cannot be fully understood without knowing the feelings that are brought into play—for example, the grudging way a sensed duty is fulfilled; (3) that living together in mutual dependence may lead to enlarged and perhaps unplanned co-operation —for example, the participation of pygmies in the Negro "circumcision school."

ADAPTATION 4

Negro-Pygmy Relations

An American sociologist among the African pygmies. Ellsworth Faris (1874–1953) revisited the Belgian Congo in 1949. His book, The Nature of Human Nature, *includes a study of the Forest Bantu. See also Adaptation 10, pp. 141–43.*

From "The Pygmies of the Ituri Forest" in Carleton S. Coon, *A Reader in General Anthropology* (New York: Holt, 1948), pp. 323–25. The account, which was condensed by Coon, was narrated by Patrick Putnam, who had been living with the people of whom he spoke for nearly two decades. Reprinted by permission of Henry Holt & Co. For a somewhat different perspective, see Colin M. Turnbull, "The Lesson of the Pygmies," *Scientific American,* **208** (January, 1963), 28–37, and *The Forest People* (New York: Simon & Schuster, 1961).

The Ituri forest is inhabited by two kinds of people, Negroes and pygmies, who maintain an almost symbiotic relationship, based on trade. A Negro village may own approximately 100 square miles of forest territory. In this territory are the Negro village and the pygmy village. The former is permanent, in a clearing; the latter is temporary, under the forest trees. In maintaining their relationship, it is the pygmies' job to take in honey and meat, while the Negroes' obligation is to give them plantains. In addition, the pygmies may bring in a certain amount of wild baselli fruit in season, or roofing leaves, or rattan and fibers for net making; in return they may acquire ax blades, knives, and arrowheads from the Negroes.

There is no strict process of barter involved, and no accounting kept, other than through general observation. If the pygmies are stingy, the Negroes will hold back their bananas. If the Negroes are stingy, the pygmies will leave the territory and go to live with other pygmies serving other Negro hosts.

This relationship is interfamilial, between a pygmy family and a Negro family. It is a matter of close personal relations, inherited, on both sides, from father to son. These alliances may change from time to time, but when they do there are usually hard feelings; if a man's pygmy leaves him to serve another host, it is a kind of divorce. In the old days, a frequent cause of intervillage warfare among the Negroes was the luring away of each other's pygmies.

Before the Belgians stopped intervillage and intertribal warfare, the most important single duty of the pygmy was to act as scout and intelligence agent in the forest. As soon as he became aware of a raiding party crossing the boundary of his host's territory, he would hotfoot it to the village to give warning. This eternal vigilance on the part of the pygmy was probably of more value to his hosts than the meat that he brought in. Now that the need of this has ceased he is fulfilling only half of his contract; the Negro, who still provides plantains and manufactured objects, is still fulfilling all of his. Yet both are satisfied.

Ordinarily, the pygmy keeps inside the territory of his Negro hosts. Individuals and small family groups may go outside to visit relatives in other bands, but this causes no disturbance because the visitors turn in their game to the hosts of the kinsmen whom they are visiting. This constant milling about evens up on the whole, and the number of pygmies in any band at any one time is about the same. There are occasions, however, when the hunters of a band may have a strong reason to pass beyond the landmarks which designate their hosts' territorial boundaries. If there is a lot of game just over the border and no

pygmies there to catch it, the pygmies will tell their Negroes, who in turn tell the Negroes owning that part of the forest. An agreement will be made between the two groups of Negroes, and the pygmies will be allowed to take the game, provided that they pay a part of it to the owners of the forest, and another part to their own hosts. This kind of economic treaty, therefore, brings the pygmies of a given band into contact with two groups of Negroes, and may initiate new relationships.

Pygmy Attitudes toward Their Negroes

The pygmies consider themselves inseparably attached to their hosts and think it their duty to provide them with meat. Although they feel that they are supposed to turn over all honey and elephant meat, in each case they eat all they can before taking it into the village. They never preserve or store any food. Their duty of feeding the Negroes meat is therefore regarded as somewhat of a nuisance. On the other hand, when the pygmy wants something from a Negro, he wheedles and "begs" for it. He may thus "borrow" a mortar, a skin-headed drum for dancing, etc., and will not return it until the Negro comes after it or sends for it. He will not put any of these things under cover, or care for them; he leaves them out in the rain to mildew and rot. The owner has to see that his property is cared for, and this forms a subject on which the Negro can make fun of the pygmy.

The form of this relationship is therefore a grudging duty in the case of giving, and a wheedling begging in the case of receiving. These outer forms fail to reveal the inner feeling of loyalty and affection between the parties concerned, but rather symbolize the existing situation in which the Negro is at the top of the scale and the pygmy at the bottom.

Negro Attitudes toward Their Pygmies

The Negroes distinguish four ranks or orders of living beings: people, pygmies, chimpanzees, and other animals. The pygmies are thus considered a species apart, neither human nor animal, but in between. The main point of distinction lies not in their size or physique, but in the fact that the pygmies do no cultivation.

The Negroes think of their pygmies as barbaric and uncultured, but at the same time they are often fond of them. A Negro may occasionally marry a pygmy woman, and the children are considered real children, complete human beings; they are brought up with the Negro's other children. The Negroes say that pygmy women are good in bed, cheap, and prolific, but that they are useless for women's work—cultivation and cooking. For a pygmy woman it is a great rise in the scale of living to marry a Negro as his second or third wife, despite the fact that pygmy wives are usually the butt of humor from the Negro wives. This is, however, a one-way process; no Negro woman could endure the pygmy way of living, and none of them ever marries a pygmy.

The interplay between Negroes and pygmies may be illustrated by a number of examples in which they disagree on historical facts. The Negroes say that the pygmies once went naked, like animals. The pygmies hotly deny this and assert that they always wore loin cloths. The Negroes admit that they themselves were once cannibals, but say that the pygmies ate more human flesh than they did. This, too, the pygmies deny; they claim that they never ate human flesh except when the Negroes gave it to them.

In addition to the exchange of food and, formerly, protection, which form the basis for Negro-pygmy interaction, another activity helps to cement their relationship. The Negroes hold a "circumcision school" for the indoctrination of young men about once in four or five years. There is no specific interval; probably they wait until there are enough boys ready to form a class of the right size. These boys are anywhere from nine to fourteen years of age. Now the pygmies associated with these Negroes may send their boys through this same school with the sons of their hosts. Thus, the pygmy boys are away from home for several months, are in close association with the Negro boys, and are taught the same secrets that the Negro boys learn. At the end they are all circumcised together, and their parents come to the Negro village to dance and get drunk with the parents of the Negro boys.

The pygmies are thus age-graded like the Negroes. Each class has its own cheer, or song, as in American colleges. Each class also has its own name, such as "Hurricane" or "Great Army Worm," depending on some event which occurred during its period of isolation. This not only forms a strong bond between the pygmies and their hosts but it gives them a formal sequence of age-grades in their own society. There are no special scarifications or other insignia for each class. It is a common experience to hear one person asking another, when strangers meet, "What class were you in? I am a Hurricane."

Section 3 Basic patterns of social organization

Individual and group relations are more meaningful when viewed in the historical and sociological *context* within which those relations have developed. For this reason, students of social organization attempt to describe the general features of whole societies or social orders. For any period of history, they try to locate the most important institutions, the most pervasive social relations, the basic social trends.

When the broad patterns of organization and change are known, individuals and groups are seen as part of larger settings. The roles of factory worker, professor, minister, and middle-class mother are all placed within the context, for example, of industrial society. The implications of industrial society for work, education, religion, and family life are thus brought into focus. No study of an important group or role is complete without some consideration of how it reflects a pattern of change, such as increasing specialization, or how it fits into the dominant features of the society or the epoch.

Because human societies are so complex, it is difficult and risky to formulate generalizations regarding broad patterns or trends in social organization. Nevertheless, much scholarship has been devoted to this task, and it is possible to state some conclusions with confidence.

This section discusses five *key forms* of social organization: (1) kinship, (2) fealty, (3) status, (4) contract, and (5) rational coordination. In various societies or historical periods one or the other of these modes of organization has been especially important. In some cases it is considered the chief foundation of social order in that society or age and thereby gives the society its distinctive character. But no matter how dominant a principle of order may be, *all* of the key forms will be found *in some degree*.

KINSHIP

The oldest and most enduring social bond is kinship or family membership. Common biological ancestry is universally the foundation of kinship. In addition, married persons may be recognized as kin, but this is not always so; in some societies, husband and wife remain separately attached to the kin groups of their birth.

Kinship is important in all societies, both past and present. But in some societies kinship is the most important social bond and families are the key units of social organization. The "family firm" and the "family farm" are current reminders of the way economic activities are based upon the family. Only a few centuries ago, in England, families vied for pre-eminence in politics, for the right to rule as the Royal House, or to be counted among the more favored nobility. Nor is this unknown in contemporary United States, as the activities of the Kennedy family make plain.

Societies may be called *familistic* when the family is the dominant type of social group and carries the main burden of maintaining order, producing goods, and propitiating the gods. In such a society the individual is dependent on his relatives. They are his chief sources of practical aid, and they hold the keys to social esteem. The interests of the family tend to be placed above the interests of the individual.

In Western society, kinship has declined in importance in the total fabric of social organization. Although the family is still strong, it has lost many of its old functions, especially in economic life, and fewer obligations and relationships are determined by family membership. Other groups carry the main burden of social organization.

FEALTY

Another fundamental social bond is the *personal relation of follower and leader*. Fealty is the recognized obligation of one person to be faithful to another, to be "his" man. More than a contract of service is involved. Fealty presumes a personal commitment to do whatever may be needed to serve the interests of the leader, to take the bad with the good. In a limited sense, it is a kind of marriage. And indeed, oaths of fealty have sometimes matched the sacredness and binding character of marriage vows.

In Europe and England, for about four hundred years, fealty was a principal social bond. This was the epoch of *feudalism,* which may be roughly dated from about the tenth century, when its outlines were already clear, to the thirteenth century, when it began a gradual decline.

A chief characteristic of feudal life was lordship. This is a system of political obligation in which a powerful individual is owed the personal loyalty and service of a group of followers, allies, and more servile dependents. An especially powerful lord might be called a duke or a king. In the heyday of feudalism, a great hierarchy of lords and their respective dependents, all knit together by bonds of loyalty and protection, gave the social order a remarkable symmetry and a precarious cohesion.

The development of lordship presumed that no effective central authority existed, and this was so in western Europe and England after the decline of Roman power. Moreover, lordship was an alternative to the bond of kinship. Some men sought the protection of lords, who were not their relatives, because there was no kin group capable of establishing order at the local level.

The following account applies to seventh-century England:

A man without kindred, or a man cast out by his kin, was without rights, an outlaw, unless he was adopted by another kindred, or found a lord to vouch for him. Social discipline was still maintained largely by the kin, so that a man or woman might be involved in the misdeeds of their kin group. For example, if a man of another kindred was killed the whole kindred of the killer was responsible either for paying *wergild* or blood money to the kin of the murdered man, or, if this compensation were refused, for sustaining the blood feud. When a tribesman was accused of an offence, he could clear himself by the oath of a given number of his kindred swearing to his innocence. (A man's circle of kindred included both maternal and paternal relatives.) But homicides within a kindred group occurred frequently, a sign of its disintegration and growing ineffectiveness. The practice of a man *seeking lordship* increasingly provided an alternative social discipline. For a

good lord gave his man the material support which a father gave his sons, and the social protection which the kindred gave its members.[5]

Functions of Fealty

As feudalism developed, increasing emphasis was placed on the fidelity of a man to his lord. The most important crime was treason against a lord. The bond of fealty had a dual importance. First, fealty helped create a small but decisive band of personal followers for the king or local lord. In the formative period of feudalism, power was in the hands of small bodies of armed men. The lord was in effect the leader of such a band and his influence depended on his capacity to maintain continuing loyalty. The development of a code of honor, emphasizing loyalty to the lord as a supreme virtue, was helpful in sustaining this relationship.

Second, fealty was a device for maintaining the cohesion of a society made up of local domains, each ruled by a supreme personal leader. As feudalism matured, the local barons became entrenched in their power. They were vassals of the king and took an oath of fealty to him, but they had independent power, with troops and resources of their own. Fealty and vassalage were in effect ways of recognizing an alliance or creating a federation. It was as if the governors of the fifty United States were considered personal rulers and recognized the central government by taking an oath of personal loyalty and submission to the President.

As a social bond, fealty does not belong only to a remote and exotic age. It is an important part of the working of contemporary society. Many executives of large enterprises would be far more frustrated and less competent if they were unable to rely on the personal loyalty of a few staff members. When an executive is promoted or moves to another organization, he often takes with him a small

5 Marion Gibbs, *Feudal Order* (New York: Henry Schuman, 1953), p. 21.

Feudal society is symbolized and remembered in d'Entrevaux in the French Alps. The walled town sits at the base of a cliff dominated by the lord's castle.

group of key assistants on whose personal loyalty he can rely and who are of inestimable value to him in establishing effective control over the organization he is supposed to manage.

Ties of fealty are of continuing significance in modern political life. Because elections are often popularity contests, and center on the man rather than on the party, politics tends to be based on personal leadership. In many areas, candidates create their own political organizations to supplement the work of the regular political party. To build campaign organizations often requires ties of personal loyalty. In practical politics, the capacity to win loyalty is of great value to the leader; and the capacity to give it is highly prized in the follower.

Despite the continuing importance of fealty, it cannot be said to be a major principle of social organization in modern society. The trend is toward more impersonal modes of organization. The areas within which ties of fealty count are being narrowed.

STATUS

The term "status," as used by students of society, has two different but related meanings that must be distinguished according to the context in which they are used.

1. Status may refer simply to a person's social position. Each role in society is associated with a social position or status. (See above, p. 16.) In this meaning, status does not necessarily have any connotation of "higher" or "lower."

2. Status is also used to designate an individual's place within a system of social ranking. Thus in the army, sergeants have a higher rank than privates, and the whole set of ranks may be referred to as a "status system." This second meaning is narrower than the first, and is focused on the idea of rank.

There are status distinctions in every society, but where status is a dominant principle of social organization, the society depends for its stability on the widespread belief in the rightness and permanence of "one's station in life." Social discipline is maintained by inculcating and reinforcing the view that every man has a *proper* place within the social scheme of things. That place tells him how to conduct himself in relation to others; it defines the limits of his aspirations.

A society based on status emphasizes rank and has many devices by which distinctions of place and privilege are maintained. On the other hand, in such a society even a man's occupational status, without direct concern for rank, is stable and is usually transmitted from generation to generation. The cobbler sticks to his last and teaches his trade to his son.

Ninth-century Japan in many ways resembled the status-based society of European feudalism:

At all levels the lamentable principle prevailed that a man's status was irrevocably fixed at birth; and to the present day Japanese life is governed by the subtle ubiquity of the concept of *mibun* (personal position); a person's *mibun*, which depends on his sex, age, birth, education, rank, and occupation, governs his behavior at all stages. This means that the same conduct can be praiseworthy, indifferent, or actually reprehensible, depending on a person's *mibun*. The merchant's duty is to enrich himself, but a samurai who concerns himself with money is unworthy of the name; a second son is permitted amorous adventures; indeed they earn him applause and respect; his elder brother, however, is expected to behave irreproachably. . . .[6]

As European and English feudalism matured, status was increasingly emphasized as the foundation of social order. In the earlier period, kingship was highly personal. The hereditary principle was not well established. A king was a king because he won and maintained the personal loyalty of a group of followers. Later, however, a subtle and decisive transformation took place. The king received loyalty as a right *because he was king*. At

[6] Fosco Maraini, *Meeting with Japan* (New York: Viking, 1959), p. 240.

the same time, hereditary monarchy, based on status fixed by birth, was strengthened. Thus status joined fealty as a cardinal principle of feudal order.

In the contemporary world *fixed* statuses are less important to the social order. But the quest for status, and the effects of status, are continuing features of everyday life, for the assignment of status remains a powerful device for allocating *respect* and defining an individual's social worth. Man's desire for the respect of his fellows is a large part of the "human condition."

The allocation of status in modern society is treated in SOCIAL STRATIFICATION.

CONTRACT

One of the great books of the nineteenth century is Sir Henry Maine's *Ancient Law,* first published in 1861. This was a study of legal institutions and the changing conditions of society. Part of the work traces the growing autonomy of the individual in society and the declining importance of family and group ties. He summarized the legal implications of his findings in a famous generalization: ". . . the movement of the progressive societies has hitherto been a movement *from Status to Contract.*" [7]

This generalization is in some respects too sweeping, as Maine himself would have readily admitted. The development of feudalism, for example, was in part a movement the other way, from contract to status:

In the really feudal centuries men could do by a contract . . . many things that cannot be done now-a-days. They could contract to stand by each other in warfare "against all men who can live and die"; they could (as Domesday Book says) "go with their land" to any lord whom they pleased; they could make the relation between king and subject look like the outcome of agreement; the law of contract threatened to

swallow up all public law. Those were the golden days of "free," if "formal," contract. The idea that men can fix their rights and duties by agreement is in its early days an unruly, anarchical idea. If there is to be any law at all, contract must be taught to know its place. [8]

Under feudalism men could determine their obligations by entering into free agreements, mainly to exchange services for the lord's protection. This was a supplement to fealty, and was especially important for the lower classes, to whom the idea of fealty, with its connotation of personal honor, was not relevant. Later, rights originally established on the basis of contract and fealty became entrenched, made hereditary, and conceived of as attributes of status.

Despite these qualifications, Maine was largely correct in observing a basic trend, in the post-feudal era, toward contract as a principle of social organization. By the sixteenth century, society was beginning to be seen in a new light. The Renaissance, the Protestant Reformation, and the growth of business enterprise all helped give the individual a new hold on the political, economic, and philosophical imagination. More and more, the basis of obligation was sought in the agreements made by freely acting, personally responsible individuals. This perspective advanced steadily and reached its greatest influence in the nineteenth century.

In contract a bond is created based upon an exchange of one promise for another; or a promise may be made in consideration of some act already done. The relation is a *specific* one, in that it covers only those matters with respect to which the promise is made. No commitment beyond the terms of the contract is intended or required. In contrast, marriage and fealty are more than contracts, since they entail a broad responsibility of one person for another. "Marriage contracts" are typically either promises to marry or agreements

---

[7] Sir Henry Sumner Maine, *Ancient Law* (London: Oxford University Press, The World's Classics, 1931), p. 141. Emphasis in original.

[8] Sir Frederick Pollock and Frederic M. Maitland, *The History of English Law Before the Time of Edward I* (Cambridge: Cambridge University Press, 1898), p. 233.

to define some special aspects of the relationship, such as the disposition of property. For the most part, marital responsibilities are *diffuse* rather than specifiable; they cannot be completely foretold nor restricted to a particular exchange of services.

When the principle of contract is a dominant feature of social organization, individuals independently take on the job of establishing groups and arranging for the conduct of much of the work of society. The legal enforcement of contracts encourages private initiative and autonomy. Especially during the nineteenth century, contract became almost a sacred principle to those who believed most strongly in individualism and in private rather than government initiative.

The Social Contract

Although contract has mainly to do with economic affairs, including the relations of employers and employees, the force of the idea has had a great impact on legal and political philosophy. In the seventeenth and eighteenth centuries, especially in France and England, the contract model was relied on to explain and justify the obedience of citizens and the powers of rulers. This was the doctrine of "social contract," perhaps the most explicit formulation ever offered of contract as the foundation of social order. The most influential proponents of this theory were Thomas Hobbes (1588–1679), John Locke (1632–1704), and Jean Jacques Rousseau (1712–1778).

The various theories of social contract differed on a number of vital points, but they had this much in common. They purported to describe the *origins* of political society. Rational men, it was held, agreed to surrender some or all of their individual freedom to a sovereign, who might be a king, a republican government, or any other ruler. In exchange, the sovereign would maintain order and provide the essential security without which, in the famous words of Hobbes, life would be "solitary, poor, nasty, brutish and short."

The Declaration of Independence of 1776, adopted by men who had been greatly influenced by John Locke, reflected these views when it held that men, created equal and endowed with "unalienable rights," instituted governments to secure those rights.

Although phrased as a theory of origins, the idea of social contract was mainly a way of asserting that governments *ought* to rest on the consent of the governed. At least, it was held, a government might be rightfully overthrown if it did not fulfill its part of the contract. Thus neither tradition nor theology nor force alone could explain or justify the continuing authority of government. As a theory of the origins of political community, the contract model has limited value, in view of the evidence that basic human institutions emerge gradually and without so rational a foundation. Nevertheless, in limited circumstances, when a community is "founded" in a deliberate manner, such as might occur in international relations, the social contract theory does have explanatory merit. But that is not the main point of the doctrine. It is primarily a justification, only secondarily an explanation.

In today's commercial civilization, contract is perforce a significant part of social organization. It is the institutional mainstay of the market economy. Nevertheless, there are signs that unregulated, voluntary agreement is losing ground within the social order. Government is assuming an increasingly active role in limiting freedom of contract by setting standards, especially where the parties to the bargain are unequal in power. The most striking examples have occurred in the field of labor relations, but the trend is considerably broader.[9]

BUREAUCRACY

The principle of social organization most characteristic of twentieth-century industrial

[9] See W. Friedmann, *Law in a Changing Society* (Berkeley and Los Angeles: University of California Press, 1959), Chap. 4.

society may be called *rational co-ordination.* In this pattern men are brought together in complex organizations run by professional managers. These managers are often called "bureaucrats" and the organizations they run are known as "bureaucracies."

During the past two generations, many writers have called attention to the increasing bureaucratization of human activity. By this they mean that more and more spheres of life are dominated by large organizations and increasing numbers of people are becoming employees of the big corporation or government enterprise. The "organization society" produces the "organization man."

Few aspects of modern society can be studied without reference to the bureaucratic trend. This is most obvious in the business world and in modern military establishments, where the co-ordination of specialists in accordance with an impersonal logic of efficiency is highly developed. The same trend may be observed in educational institutions and even in church organization.

Wherever bureaucracy develops, there is increased specialization, impersonality, reliance on general rules, and distance between top management and the ordinary worker, citizen, or soldier. Up to a point, this is usually associated with increased efficiency, but there is growing evidence that new techniques are needed to offset some of the characteristics of bureaucracy[10] that tend to limit initiative and personal satisfaction.

THE MASTER TREND

The key patterns, discussed above, indicate a master trend. Over many centuries, Western society has shifted from an emphasis on kinship and status to a reliance upon more impersonal and instrumental modes of organization.

This broad historical development is characterized by two attributes: (1) special-

Herbert Spencer (1820–1903), was one of the most influential English writers of the late nineteenth century. He developed a theory of evolution which he summarized in the following famous "formula": "Evolution is an integration of matter and concomitant dissipation of motion; during which the matter passes from an indefinite, incoherent homogeneity to a definite, coherent heterogeneity; and during which the retained motion undergoes a parallel transformation."

On the basis of this resonant principle Spencer worked out a sociological system emphasizing an evolution toward greater social complexity and increased individualism. Society, he said, is like a complex organism in delicate balance and only natural processes of evolution should be allowed to affect its development. This emphasis on individualism and on natural adaptation led him to oppose reform through governmental action.

[10] For the characteristics of bureaucracy see ASSOCIATIONS, p. 224; INDUSTRIAL MAN, pp. 640 ff; POLITICAL MAN, p. 682.

ization, and (2) secularism and rationality.

Specialization

The historical trend toward *social differentiation* (specialization and heterogeneity) may be seen in the separation of major institutions from one another, in the development of the division of labor, and in the growth of many social groups with varying perspectives and interests.

1. *Differentiation of institutions.* The major economic, political, and religious institutions have become increasingly distinct and specialized. In earlier times, for example, church and state were usually fused or, at least, their responsibilities overlapped. Citizenship made one subject to the jurisdiction of the church, which could use force to command obedience. The head of the state was also the "defender of the faith." Secular and religious education were not distinct. The separation of these institutions was marked by centuries of conflict, sometimes violent, sometimes carried on in the obscurity of legal argument over the jurisdiction of ecclesiastical and secular courts.

This disentanglement of institutional spheres is the basis of political freedom as we know it. At the same time, many urgent problems of co-ordination and control have been created.

2. *Division of labor.* Even primitive society has a division of labor, based largely on age and sex. Modern industry and commerce have pushed specialization to great extremes. Consequently, many new interests and groups are created, because those engaged in the same specialized activities tend to see the world alike and have a common stake in it. In addition, the individual's life is less unified and more compartmentalized.

Durkheim[11] raised the question whether the specialized division of labor necessarily undermines the integration of society. He pointed out that specialized activities are interdependent, that a highly differentiated society has an "organic solidarity" similar to the functional interdependence of parts of the body.

He contrasted "organic" with the "mechanical solidarity" of folk societies, based upon likeness rather than difference. The individual follows all of the group's movements automatically or mechanically because he is an undifferentiated part, and his reactions are like those of everyone else.

Durkheim realized that economic and technical interdependence had to be supplemented by a set of commonly agreed-upon rules and aims. Otherwise there would be an "anomic" division of labor, with the parts fighting against each other and with individuals so compartmentalized that they would be unable to see beyond their immediate tasks. Durkheim concluded that there must be a mixture of the two types of solidarity if social cohesion is to be maintained.

Secularism and Rationality

Western society has moved away from reverence for and uncritical acceptance of established institutions. Few things are "holy," and therefore removed from worldly, secular judgment. Modern man feels freer to ask, "what good is it?" The world has become "disenchanted," more "sensate," more "materialistic," less "spiritual," to use some of the terms that have been applied to this trend toward *secularism.*

Secularism encourages *rationality* in social organization. Group ways of acting are consciously designed and measured by effectiveness and efficiency. Weber[12] studied the increasing emphasis on rationality in modern industry, military organization, and other spheres of life. He saw that the business world, in its drive for efficiency, was becoming increasingly impersonal and machinelike.

---

[11] George Simpson (tr.), *Emile Durkheim on the Division of Labor in Society* (New York: Macmillan, 1933).

[12] See the picture and biographical note, p. 630. In his *The Protestant Ethic and the Spirit of Capitalism,* Weber studied the contribution of religious austerity and self-discipline to the development of rationality in early capitalism. (See INDUSTRIAL MAN, pp. 630 ff.)

Weber traced the development of what has already been mentioned as one of the characteristic social forms of our time, the bureaucratic administrative hierarchy, in which the principle of rationality in social organization has had perhaps its fullest development.

Secularism and rationality are associated with *impersonality* in human relations. With a weakened sense of kinship and with a utilitarian orientation, it is easy to treat people as means rather than as ends. Georg Simmel showed how the growth of a money economy contributes to impersonality in social relations. When compensation is worked out in strictly monetary terms, people tend to restrict their relations with one another and to ignore personal considerations. The use of money brings into association many persons who are otherwise unrelated. Their relations may be limited to the exchange of goods or services for money without more extensive involvement.[13]

From Gemeinschaft to Gesellschaft

In 1887 Tönnies contrasted two types of society, which he called *Gemeinschaft* and *Gesellschaft*.[14] A *Gemeinschaft* ("communal society") is a society in which people feel they belong together because they are of the same kind. Broadly speaking, they are kin, and cannot freely renounce their membership, for it involves great emotional meaning for the group as well as for the individual. People do not decide to join a *Gemeinschaft*. They are born into it or "grow" into it in the way the bonds of friendship grow. In a true *Gemeinschaft* people have definite functions to perform. These roles are "natural" by-products of being a woman or having a certain father or being born in a certain place. This model of a communal society closely fits the

Georg Simmel (1858–1918) was a German philosopher who influenced the pioneers of sociology in the United States, particularly through the translations of Albion W. Small. A generation ago Simmel was best known for his effort to identify the distinctive subject matter of sociology, which he saw as the study of "forms of social interaction," such as subordination, competition, and division of labor. Today there is greater interest in his perceptive analyses of sociability, city life, the money economy, and the consequences of group size.

"folk" or primitive society and the ideal conception of the feudal social order. The decline of *Gemeinschaft* is a decline of the sense of kinship with other members of a community.

To this type of society Tönnies contrasted the *Gesellschaft* ("associational society"), in which the major social bonds are voluntary and based upon the rational pursuit of self-interest. People enter relations with one another, not because they "must" or because it is "natural," but as a practical way of achiev-

---

[13] See *The Sociology of Georg Simmel*, translated and edited by Kurt H. Wolff (Glencoe: The Free Press, 1950); also N. J. Spykman, *The Social Theory of Georg Simmel* (Chicago: University of Chicago Press, 1925), pp. 219 ff.

[14] Ferdinand Tönnies, *Gemeinschaft und Gesellschaft* (1st ed., 1887), tr. and ed. by C. P. Loomis as *Fundamental Concepts of Sociology* (New York: American Book Co., 1940). (See PRIMARY GROUPS, p. 139.)

ing an objective. The typical relation is the contract, and the typical group is the voluntary special-purpose association. The long historical trend has moved toward the *Gesellschaft,* with more and more activities governed by the voluntary action of freely contracting individuals.

Gesellschaft produces the "mass society." [15] The weakening of traditional bonds, the growth of rationality, and the division of labor, have created societies made up of individuals who are only loosely bound together. In this sense the word "mass" suggests something closer to an aggregate than to a tightly knit social group.

Mass society means mass participation. It is the "participant society." [16] In earlier periods, small well-insulated minorities controlled decision-making in the major institutions. The rest of the people lived out their lives within the confines of work, household, and parish. Mass society is the spread of democracy, not only in the making of political decisions, but in the enlargement of participation and influence in many areas of life, for example, education and participation in politics. Mass democracy is discussed in POLITICAL MAN, pages 708 ff.

Counter-trends

The trends culminating in mass society represent a movement away from a highly integrated social order to a more loosely knit one based on individualism and group autonomy. In the twentieth century these trends have come to their fullest development, but this century has also seen the rapid development of counter-trends leading to closer social integration. Two of these counter-trends are centralization and the "quest for community."

1. *Centralization* is a dominant theme in modern society, especially in political and economic life. The centers of decision have moved away from local areas and small units to the capital cities of government and industry. Although there is a proliferation of associations, some are far more important than others. Centralization is greatest in the totalitarian nations, but the trend is world-wide.

2. The *quest for community* is another trend running counter to the emphasis on rationality and individualism. Millions feel the need to find or reaffirm a common identity, and this has sometimes led to a denial of individualism and a revived but distorted sense of kinship. The most striking example is Hitler's Germany, which purported to offer a rebirth of *Volksgemeinschaft,* a communality of "blood and soil."

In every age there are certain key words which by their repetitive use and re-definition mark the distinctive channels of faith and thought. . . . In the nineteenth century, the age of individualism and rationalism, such words as *individual, change, progress, reason,* and *freedom* were notable. . . .

Today a different set of words and symbols dominates the intellectual and moral scene. It is impossible to overlook, in modern lexicons, the importance of such words as *disorganization, disintegration, decline, insecurity, breakdown, instability,* and the like. What the nineteenth-century rationalist took for granted about society and the nature of man's existence, as the result of an encompassing faith in the creative and organizational powers of history, the contemporary student of society makes the object of increasing apprehension and uncertainty. [17]

The fate of rationality and of individual freedom depends upon man's ability to solve the problems which these ideals, together with industrialism and urbanization, have set for the modern world.

---

[15] See especially Karl Mannheim, *Man and Society in an Age of Reconstruction* (New York: Harcourt, Brace, 1949); also Jose Ortega y Gasset, *The Revolt of the Masses* (New York: Norton, 1932).

[16] See Daniel Lerner, *The Passing of Traditional Society* (Glencoe: The Free Press, 1958), p. 60 *et passim.*

[17] Robert A. Nisbet, *The Quest for Community* (New York: Oxford, 1953), pp. 3–4, 7. Reprinted by permission of Oxford University Press.

Section 4 **Social organization as a field of study**

This chapter has introduced some of the elements of social organization: interpersonal relations, roles, groups, and the relations among groups. The levels of social organization are enumerated below and are discussed in this section.

It is evident that social organization is a quite general phenomenon, and in a broad sense this topic comprises most of sociology. Many aspects of social organization have become subjects of specialized study, and whole chapters are devoted to them in this book.

However, there is an important sense in which sociologists have a *general* interest in social organization. The student of social organization, as such, is primarily interested in the *relatedness* of persons and groups. Usually, relatedness is not studied abstractly, by

itself, but in a particular context, such as the family, industry, politics, or community life. However, as a scientist the sociologist seeks to discover generalizations that apply to many different situations and groups. He studies criminals, church congregations, bomber crews, rural villages, cities, and whole societies. At the very least, in order to make these studies, he needs *guiding ideas,* concepts and theories that will tell him what to look for and how to develop his findings in an orderly way. Theories of social organization are designed to help fill this need. They necessarily deal with a wide range of phenomena, from relatively simple to very complex forms of group life. This range may be classified as follows:

1. *Interpersonal relations.* In Section 1 of

Levels of Social Organization

The INTERPERSONAL Level	Ordered interactions Role behavior
The GROUP Level	Initiates, builds upon and sustains interpersonal relations Distinctive characteristics of various types of groups Relations among groups
The SOCIAL ORDER Level	Broad patterns of group life that characterize an entire community or society

this chapter (pp. 15–30) the involvement of the individual in relations with others was discussed. An interpersonal relation is the simplest social bond, occurring when two persons stand in some relation to each other, such as leader to follower or neighbor to neighbor. The term *interpersonal* means "between persons" and does not imply that the relation must be a "personal" one; it may be either impersonal or intimate.

Although groups are different, most of them depend upon interpersonal relations that are similar in kind to those that appear in other groups. In a criminal gang, some men are in authority over others, some are friends, some may be teachers. The more that is understood about authority and friendship, as general phenomena, the more readily will the criminal gang or any group be understood. Therefore the student of social organization may be found devoting himself to a detailed investigation of the dynamics of leadership, as such, or some other important interpersonal relation. He will study the conditions that sustain the relation and the strains to which it is subject. In doing so, he contributes to knowledge of the basic elements of all groups.

Although the study of interpersonal relations seems to focus attention on very limited elements of social life, sometimes quite the contrary is true. Particular interpersonal relations, such as those involved in kinship, slavery, or the relations to a feudal lord, may be of crucial importance to the functioning of an entire society. In that case, intensive analysis of the interpersonal bond is vital to understanding whole communities and broad social changes. Therefore, studies of the social organization of industry, politics, or rural society may properly emphasize some key interpersonal relation.

2. *Group relations.* Section 2 (pp. 31–38) treated the interaction of groups and the stable arrangements that result. Group relations, too, such as accommodation or interdependence, are general and occur in many diverse settings. The theory of group relations can utilize studies of labor and management in the United States and of the pygmies of the Congo.

In the Part Two chapters, the *pattern of group relations* is sometimes the main theme of a section on social organization. For example, that section of MINORITIES deals with the patterns of segregation and integration of Negroes and whites in the United States and South Africa.

3. *Social orders or systems.* The student of social organization is interested in groups and activities that are interdependent, that form unified "social systems." He attempts to discover what pattern of relatedness among people and groups *holds the system together* and gives it *a distinctive character.* For example, feudal social organization had a number of key characteristics: a personal tie of loyalty between lord and vassal, the binding of serfs and villeins to the soil, a manorial system of agriculture, and decentralized military control by barons who dominated the countryside from fortified castles. These and other features help to define the essential ingredients of a feudal order, including its weakness and strength.

Sociologists are also interested in the distinctive features of nomadic societies, the modern American community, totalitarian social organization, and other large social systems. Not all of these are readily reducible to a few simple ingredients, but the primary objective is to find out what the social order is as a functioning system, what it depends upon, and what the main points of inner strain and conflict are.

In this sense, the field of social organization has been largely the province of historical sociologists interested in social orders that embrace and give form to large communities and long epochs. However, the study of social systems can also be applied to limited areas of life. The medical world, for example, is heavily influenced by professional organization, by its specialized technology requiring centralization of many activities in large hospitals, by the doctor-patient relationship, and by the way the private physician is related to the hospital personnel. Anyone interested in the social aspects of medical care would need to understand this network of relations in modern medicine.

Ordinarily, the term "educational system" refers to public schools and the way they are run. But the student of social organization sees the schools as part of a larger setting, including the pattern of local politics, the influence of university schools of education, and the role of the schools as vehicles of social mobility. These and other interdependent characteristics give American public education its distinctive capabilities, limitations, and internal stresses. The term "social system" is used to designate these interconnected groups and activities.

No sharp separation can be made between studying large institutional settings and small-scale situations. The social organization of the medical world reaches into the hospital ward and affects the human relations within it, just as the social organization of feudalism left its mark on personal interaction in the baronial hall and in the fields.

SOURCES AND READINGS

H. H. Gerth and C. W. Mills, *Character and Social Structure* (New York: Harcourt, Brace, 1953), Part Three.

Scott A. Greer, *Social Organization* (New York: Doubleday, 1955).

George C. Homans, *The Human Group* (New York: Harcourt, Brace, 1950).

George C. Homans, *Social Behavior: Its Elementary Forms* (New York: Harcourt Brace & World, 1961).

Robert K. Merton, *Social Theory and Social Structure* (revised and enlarged ed.; Glencoe: The Free Press, 1957).

Robert E. Park and Ernest W. Burgess, *Introduction to the Science of Sociology* (Chicago: University of Chicago Press, 1924).

Robin M. Williams, Jr., *American Society: A Sociological Interpretation* (2nd ed.; New York: Knopf, 1960), Chaps. 12–14.

Chapter III

Culture

Section 1 Introduction

As used in the social sciences, the term "culture" refers to man's entire *social heritage,* all the knowledge, beliefs, customs, and skills he acquires as a member of society. A man who grew up apart from human association would lack culture because he had not communicated with other men and would, therefore, not share the knowledge of earlier generations. He would, however, solve problems and learn from experience, as do other animals. By the acquisition of culture, by tapping the heritage of his past, man becomes distinctively human. Man has, therefore, been called the culture-bearing animal. The problem of whether or not animals other than man possess culture need not concern us here. The other animals, of course, are capable of learning and problem-solving, and the vertebrates at least learn from each other by example. But the amount of their communicative learning is relatively small and rudimentary.

The culture or social heritage of any society is always specific; it is the "distinctive way of life of a group of people, their complete design for living." [1] Culture presumes the ex-

istence of human society and provides the necessary skills for making society work. Viewed another way, culture is a large part of what is transmitted in the process of socialization, discussed in Chapter IV.

THE STUDY OF CULTURE

Man's distinctive humanity may be achieved through any culture. A forest pygmy, an Eskimo, an ancient Roman, or an advertising account executive are equally human. In contemporary scientific usage cultures, whether primitive or civilized, are viewed as equal in the sense that each one is a self-contained design for living. This usage is largely the outgrowth of research of cultural anthropologists. Their firsthand studies of numerous preliterate peoples led them to reject the earlier idea that all cultural evolution followed a single path, culminating in the high civilizations of the Western world. Furthermore, they observed that all aspects of a particular culture are not evenly developed. For example, the Australian aborigines, whose technology is rudimentary, have a highly developed kinship system; but Americans, whose technology is most advanced, have a much simpler kinship system, one that

---

[1] Clyde Kluckhohn, "The Study of Culture," in Daniel Lerner and Harold D. Lasswell (eds.), *The Policy Sciences* (Stanford: Stanford University Press, 1951), p. 86.

Participant Observation

No one has experienced a culture precisely as it is described in studies of primitive or contemporary peoples. These studies attempt to describe the *regularities* in behavior, and they are based on a *series of observations*. Behavior peculiar to a specific incident is identified, but the regular, repeated, "patterned" behavior is emphasized. For example, a social scientist from a remote culture might study American college classes. After attending a number of sessions, he would see regularities: the meetings have a ritual starting and ending marked by the sounding of a bell; one person faces all the others; this individual differs from those he faces in a number of ways, such as age, frequency of speech, style of dress, and freedom of movement. The observer might see that he is addressed with more deference than the other members accord each other.

After a while, he would learn that the older man is a "teacher" and that he is transmitting information to the others, called "students." However, even if he achieves a full description of the regularities of classroom behavior, his task has only begun. He would need to learn why the society encourages its youth to spend their time and energy in this way, how individuals are selected to attend the classes, what the standards of performance are, and why the youth accept this interference with their leisure. He would then begin to understand the norms governing educational behavior. As he mastered the rudiments of the culture, he might begin to act as a member of the class, at which point he is no longer a scholarly outsider but a participant observer.

An actual experience* of a participant-observer team that studied medical students is paraphrased as follows: "We went to lectures with students taking their first two years and to the laboratories in which they spend most of their time, watching them and engaging in casual conversation as they dissected cadavers or examined pathology specimens. We sat around their fraternity houses while they discussed their school experiences. We accompanied students in the clinical years on rounds, watched them examine patients in wards and in clinics, sat in on discussion groups and oral exams. We ate with the students and took night call with them. We pursued internes and residents through their crowded schedules of teaching and medical work."

The participant-observer method yields a wealth of detailed description and rich and varied insights. Because it is time consuming and costly, it is perhaps best used in the exploratory phases of research preliminary to the development of more precise research instruments and to the exact statement of hypotheses.

Caution: Overidentification. There is always a risk that the participant observer will become too successful, that having crossed the line between pure observer and participant-observer, he will cross the next line into full participant. When this occurs, research objectives are sacrificed to human involvement and full identification with the subjects.

* Howard S. Becker, "Problems of Inference and Proof in Participant Observation," *American Sociological Review*, **23** (December, 1958), 652–60.

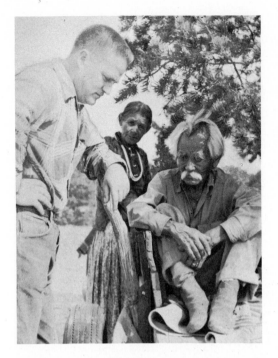

Anthropologist at Work: Harvard anthropologist, E. Z. Vogt, author of Navaho Veterans: A Study of Changing Values, *interviews Navaho informant.*

would be regarded as "primitive" by Australian standards.

There is perhaps another reason for the anthropological attitude toward culture. One of the basic features of contemporary field research is the prolonged face-to-face encounter of the anthropologist and his subjects. Under ideal conditions research goes on for many months, even years, during which time the fieldworker becomes a close observer of and actual participant in many aspects of their daily life. He often becomes a partisan and defender of "his" people. To have lived entirely detached from one's own culture is a unique intellectual experience that permits one to look at his own society from a fresh perspective. It is not surprising that under these circumstances Western culture does not always come out first in the comparison.

The anthropologist accepts a broad, impar-

tial orientation toward culture that is well represented in the following:

Culture is not restricted to certain special fields of knowledge; it includes ways of behaving derived from the whole range of human activity. The designs for living evident in the behavior of the Eskimos, the natives of Australia, or the Navahos are as much a part of culture as those of cultivated Europeans and Americans. Culture includes, not only the techniques and methods of art, music, and literature, but also those used to make pottery, sew clothing, or build houses. Among the products of culture we find comic books and popular street songs along with the art of a Leonardo da Vinci and the music of a Johann Bach. The anthropologist does not employ the contrast "cultured versus uncultured," for this distinction of popular usage represents only a difference in culture, not its absence or presence.[2]

The viewpoint outlined in this quotation is a rejection of narrow provincialism and underscores the positive, accepting approach that the social scientist uses in studying other cultures or the cultures of subgroups within Western society. There is a keen awareness of the risk that the standards of a particular culture will be used to judge men of another culture, to whom these standards are alien. To fail to understand cultures by their own standards is to deny respect to people who have solved the problems of group life in their own way.

Cultural Values

Nevertheless, some comparisons are legitimate, particularly *within* a given society. Because culture includes a set of "designs" for carrying on the life of society, there must be cultural *ideals*. Ideals involve standards of perfection, whether in the skills of the fisherman, the behavior of parents, or the performance of the artist. This is true of all societies—preliterate as well as Western. The medicine

[2] Ralph L. Beals and Harry Hoijer, *An Introduction to Anthropology* (New York: Macmillan, 1953), p. 207.

man, the expert storyteller, the skilled craftsman, stands in a different position relative to his culture than does the average participant. Similarly, the culture of Western society can be known in different ways and to different degrees. The knowledge of a passenger in a plane is not equal to that of the designer, even though they are both participants in what might be called the aeronautical culture complex.

Moreover, certain aspects of a culture are more important than others in defining the society's distinctive way of life, its culture as a whole. In various societies and at different times religious, legal, intellectual, and aesthetic ideals have had this central role. In any society a limited number of people stand out from the general population in being sensitive to these key ideals, in having a sense of responsibility for them, and in possessing a basic understanding of their origins and functions.

Sociologists are primarily interested in the part of culture that defines the norms and standards for human behavior. This selective approach is used in this book. The *cultural aspects* of special spheres of life are treated in the culture sections of the Part Two chapters. These sections deal primarily with the way cultural values and norms affect and are affected by the family, minorities, crime, and the educational and religious institutions. For example, sociologists are interested in discovering how the standards of criminals conflict with those of the large society (culture conflict) and how the norms defining crime and punishment have changed over the years (culture change).

CULTURE AND SOCIAL ORGANIZATION

Social organization is made up of interpersonal and group relations. The family is a unit of social organization, and the form of the family and much familial behavior are prescribed by the culture. One culture may value a kind of family in which the father is dominant; another may relegate him to a lesser role. Culture is the design and the prescription, the composite of guiding values and ideals. Hence, culture and social organization are interdependent. The separate treatment of the subjects is a matter of selective interest and emphasis.

On the other hand, much of social organization is not culturally prescribed but arises out of the give and take of personal and group interaction that is not entirely governed by definite rules. For example, a hierarchy of social classes may be culturally defined as it was in medieval Europe or Classical China. In American society stratification exists, but it has much less support in the "design for living."

The interrelations between culture and social organization may be illustrated by the Tanala,[3] a hill tribe of Madagascar. Originally they subsisted by the cultivation of *dry rice*. They cut down and burned jungle growth, thus clearing the land for planting. After one or two crops the land had to be abandoned until the jungle overran it again. The jungle about a village was thus exploited until it was exhausted, and then the village was moved. There was no individual ownership of land; the village as a whole held the territory. Within the village *joint families*—groups of households connected through a common head—were the chief units of organization. Joint family members worked as a group and owned the crops from the land they cleared. The head of the joint family divided the crops among the households, and there was little variation in wealth between families. Forest products, such as game, belonged to whoever took them.

The adoption of *wet rice* cultivation from a neighboring people disrupted Tanala culture and social organization. Because at the outset wet rice planting was done on relatively small plots, it was cultivated by single

[3] Ralph Linton, *The Study of Man* (New York: Appleton-Century, 1936), pp. 348–55; and Ralph Linton, *The Tanala: A Hill Tribe of Madagascar*, Anthropological Series Vol. XXII (Chicago: Field Museum of Natural History, 1933).

At two points in Western history distinctive forms of architecture symbolize the institutional aspirations of the people. The Secretariat of the United Nations (twentieth century) and the Chartres Cathedral (thirteenth century).

households, and unlike the dry rice system, the land was in continuous cultivation. The idea of exclusive ownership of real estate developed, and because there was only a limited amount of suitable land, two classes —landholders and landless—became distinguished. Those who held wet rice land no longer needed to be involved in the large joint family effort in jungle clearing, and they did not want the villages to be moved. The landless, who continued dry rice cultivation, had to move into the jungle too far to return to the village at night. As a result they too began to develop separate household organization. There were numerous other effects: changes in the kinship and marriage system, in the practice of warfare, in the design of villages and village defense, in slavery, and in the growth of a centralized authority with autocratic control.

The Tanala case shows how changes in social relations are affected by changes in the key activities of a group and how the particular forms of adaptation and interaction are embedded in custom. When the food gathering technology was changed, the social system changed along with it. The sequence of changes was initiated by a modification in the technology—the shift from dry rice to wet rice cultivation. This was accompanied by changes in social organization: greater emphasis on the individual household, declining emphasis on the large joint family, and the stabilization of the site of the village. Accompanying these changes were shifts in cultural values: the joint family was displaced by the household as the chief object of loyalty, and land became valued not as something to be used temporarily but to be permanently possessed. Thus culture and social organization interact in the working out of man's relations to his environment and his fellow men.

ETHNOCENTRISM

Each group considers its way of life the natural and the best way. Strange groups, beliefs, or practices are treated with suspicion and hostility simply because they are strange. Intense identification with the familiar and the devaluation of the foreign is called *ethnocentrism*. It is the feeling that one's own culture is the best in all respects and that others are in varying degrees inferior—barbaric, heathen, or outlandish. Extreme ethnocentrism leads to a needless rejection of the richness and knowledge of other cultures. It impedes the sharing of ideas and skills that might bring a society closer to its own goals. Historically, man has improved his ability to cope with his environment through the exchange of techniques and knowledge among cultures. Ethnocentrism tends to inhibit this proved method of culture growth. Finally, ethnocentrism, whether practiced by primitive or modern man, denies the basic unity and humanity of mankind. In the modern world with ease of communication and travel it becomes progressively difficult for sophisticated people to sustain ethnocentrism in its more flagrant forms.

In less virulent form ethnocentrism appears as a cultural nearsightedness that takes one's own culture for granted and that passively rather than actively rejects others. Even a book like this, which tries to be sensitive to such problems, falls into ethnocentric terminology. The authors freely, if reluctantly, use "America" and "Americans" in the American (sic) way. By "Americans," people in the U.S.A. mean nationals of the U.S.A. But it is a correct designation of all the people in North and South America. Latin Americans resent the proprietary way we use a word that belongs to them as much as to us. In polite parlance they use the term "Norte Americano," in colloquial speech the term Yankee, which can carry connotations ranging from friendly to bitter depending on intonation, and a repetoire of terms beginning with Gringo and ending with unprintable. From the standpoint of the "American" there is no convenient, neutral, all-purpose word that is the natural and readily-understood private property of citizens of the United States of America. The reader is invited to think of one—and to think of another country in the same predicament.

If a social event is to be fully understood, it must be interpreted against the social setting in which it occurs. The context provides the meaning of the event, connects it with other events, with the values of the society, and makes sense out of what otherwise seems unreasonable. An ethnocentric orientation precludes the possibility of a rounded interpretation of behavior because all behavior is viewed from a single point of view, that of the individual's own culture.

Selective Learning

Although a culture is a "complete design for living," no one fully masters all of the knowledge and skills nor is motivated by all of the values of any culture, however simple. The learning of culture is always selective. The individual learns some aspects of his culture because of his sex, his age, the group into which he is born, and the locality in which he lives. However, he shares many other ways of doing things with all members of his society because of their common culture. The individual must learn what of the "blueprint of behavior" applies to him and what he can avoid with impunity. He will become a *human* being as a member of so-

ciety, and the *kind* of human being he becomes depends in large part on the culture of which he partakes.

SOURCES AND READINGS

Ralph L. Beals and Harry Hoijer, *An Introduction to Anthropology* (2nd ed.; New York: Macmillan, 1959).

Carleton S. Coon, *A Reader in General Anthropology* (New York: Holt, 1948).

C. Daryll Forde, *Habitat, Economy and Society* (London: Methuen, 1934).

Walter Goldschmidt (ed.), *Ways of Mankind* (Boston: Beacon, 1954).

Edward Adamson Hoebel, *Man in the Primitive World* (2nd ed.; New York: McGraw-Hill, 1958).

John J. Honigman, *The World of Man* (New York: Harper, 1959).

A. L. Kroeber, *Anthropology* (New York: Harcourt, Brace, 1948).

Ralph Linton, *The Study of Man* (New York: Appleton-Century, 1936).

George P. Murdock, *Our Primitive Contemporaries* (New York: Macmillan, 1935).

Robin M. Williams, Jr., *American Society* (2nd ed.; New York: Knopf, 1960), Chaps. 10, 11.

PERIODICALS

American Anthropologist
Comparative Studies in Society and History
Human Organization
Journal of the Royal Anthropological Institute
Southwestern Journal of Anthropology

Section 2 **Cultural variation**

No aspect of man's life is untouched by culture. Even his biological needs, such as eating, elimination, sleeping, and sex behavior, bear the mark of his culture. These underlying impulses are hedged, controlled, and defined by ethical and aesthetic norms.

Nevertheless, man's basic character, which includes his social nature, generates fundamental problems that must be dealt with by

all societies. For example, all societies regulate the division of labor, procreation, and the rearing of children. The alternative ways these problems are solved accounts for the almost infinite variety of human culture. Not all culture, however, is rooted in necessity. Man can survive in society without joking, artistic expression, games, or religion, but no culture is completely lacking in these elements. One can not fail to be impressed by the wide variety in the solutions of different cultures to the small and large tasks of dealing with the environment and with human association. Such differences among cultures are much more than amusing variations on a theme.

PERVASIVENESS OF CULTURE

The rules and values of a culture influence and redirect the expression of deeply motivated behaviors and even the forms of individual maladjustment. Table III:1 compares the use of alcoholic beverages and associated effects in three elements in the U.S. population.[4] In one, drinking is common, ritualized and regularly practiced, but alcoholism is

[4] Selden D. Bacon, "Social Settings Conducive to Alcoholism: A Sociological Approach to a Medical Problem," *The Journal of the American Medical Association*, **164** (May 11, 1957), 177–81.

virtually unknown; in another, drinking is rather common but has little group support, and there is a high incidence of alcoholism; in the third, drinking is rare, but among the few who drink, the alcoholism rate is high.

For Orthodox Jews (the most religiously conservative of Jews) drinking is a normal part of everyday life. The practice is learned from early childhood in the family circle and by all members of the group. It is highly regulated, and deviations are severely sanctioned. The function of drinking is to draw the group together in intimate association of family and friends, and there are strong religious overtones. Almost everyone drinks, but alcoholism is practically nonexistent.

Among "old" Americans (persons at least three generations in the U.S.) of British Isles backgrounds, drinking alcoholic beverages is less clearly defined. It is learned in late adoles-

Table **III:1**   Use of Alcohol in Three American Subcultures

	ORTHODOX JEWS	ANGLO-AMERICANS	MORMONS
Social Functions	Closer adherence to moral norms Cements bonds of family and of larger group	Relaxation from moral norms Creates transitory solidarity	Individual, not social Drinkers identified as deviants
Rules and Procedures	Ritualized	Varying rules, depending on group or situation	Always taboo
Sanction for Violations of Rules	Quick, severe, uniform by prestigeful group members	Source and nature of sanctions irregular and uncertain	Taboo Sanctions by whole group
When Learned	Early childhood	Adolescence, sometimes secretly	Post adolescence, secretly
From Whom	Adults	Other adolescents	Deviants or Gentiles
Emotional Feeling	Neutral to mild Little or no excitement	Strong Marked variation	Very strong
Incidence of Alcoholism	Practically unknown	High	Generally low Among drinkers, very high

Source: Chiefly from Bacon, *op. cit.*

cence, often within the peer group and sometimes secretly. It is accompanied by guilt, hostility, and exhibitionism. Instead of being supported by and in turn supporting group norms, as among Orthodox Jews, drinking represents a relaxation of moral norms. The act is vaguely defined. Instead of being part of family life and other intimate associations, it is often done away from home and frequently in public places. Although drinking is far less common than among Orthodox Jews, there is a far higher incidence of alcoholism.

Mormons strictly forbid drinking. The very act is a defiance of group norms. Drinking is rare, but those who do drink show an exceedingly high rate of alcoholism.

The variations in the rates of alcoholism among these groups can not be explained by varying incidence of personal maladjustment. The kinds of things people do, either when they are normal or when they are psychologically disturbed, depend upon the alternatives open to them by their culture. If alcoholism is low in one group, it does not follow that the amount of psychological maladjustment is correspondingly low. There is no evidence that Orthodox Jews are less maladjusted than Anglo-Americans. Because the form that maladjustment takes is governed by culturally ingrained customs and values, the individual maladjustment of these Jews is expressed in other ways than through alcoholism. The same is also true for almost all Mormons, but in this case, because their culture *forbids* the use of alcohol. Anglo-American culture leaves much to individual choice and judgment, and alcohol is neither consistently forbidden nor regulated and ritualized in its use. The lack of consistent norms and practices in the use of alcohol probably increases the likelihood that it will be used in uncontrolled ways.

Subcultures

The groups mentioned are only three of a large number of identifiable populations of a heterogeneous society. Complex societies like the United States contain not one homogeneous culture but a multitude of ethnic, regional, and occupational subcultures with which people identify and from which they derive many distinctive values and norms. Some writers have suggested that there is no such thing as American culture, but instead, that there is a conglomeration of subcultures. "American culture" can be thought of in several ways: as including all the subcultures, as consisting of only those norms that all subcultures share, or as restricted to those norms subscribed to by a dominant group or majority of the population.

Subcultures are distinguishable from one another and from the dominant culture forms by such manifest characteristics as language, clothing, gesture, and etiquette. There are also less public but equally important differences in norms and values.

Ethnic subcultures. Ethnic subcultures played an important part in American society during the nineteenth and early twentieth centuries. Although ethnic groups have intermingled, combining their beliefs and practices with those of other ethnic groups and with the dominant culture, some of these remain as subcultures. Some immigrant areas are still easily discernible, but the life-styles of others have practically disappeared. Visible distinctions of dress, food habits, child-rearing techniques, and language steadily diminish as the ethnic subcultures have become "Americanized" and as the dominant culture has adopted some of the ethnic practices.

Regional subcultures. The regions of the United States still retain some of the character and flavor of their diverse histories and settlement. Some of the differences derive from the cultures of their settlers. Other distinctive characteristics originated in the economic activities that varied from region to region. The industry and commerce of New England created different problems, adjustments, and culture patterns from the plantation economy of the South. The leveling effect of the expansion of industry, commerce, and mass communications has reduced regional variation to minor matters of dialect, mannerisms, diet, knowledge about and loyalty to the locality. Local distinctions, however, are still important to the old residents of stable regions.[5]

Occupational subcultures.[6] What people do for a living has always effected many other phases of their lives. Occupations create friendship patterns, determine class position, and affect life-styles. The degree to which subcultures are associated with occupations is illustrated by the specialized languages of occupations, which sometimes mean nothing to outsiders.

Despite the wide cultural variation in the United States, as exemplified by subcultural differences in class, sex, and age as well as the regional, ethnic, and occupational subcultures just mentioned, there is an underlying conformity: common knowledge, beliefs, and norms which can be recognized as American.

LANGUAGE AND CULTURE

Each language is a product of the culture with which it develops and the environments in which it works. It, therefore, has special capabilities and vocabulary suited to a particular technology and social organization. A language, like its culture, is ever adaptive, ever changing. It is shaped and reshaped as it performs communicative tasks for young and old, male and female, scholar, scientist, technician, thief, and illiterate.

The uniqueness of a language is most fully appreciated when one tries to study another, and this is part of what is meant in the frequently reinvented adage that no one understands his own language who has not learned another. All but a handful of people are completely bound to one language, and even

<hr>

[5] See Howard W. Odum, *Southern Regions of the United States* (Chapel Hill: University of North Carolina Press, 1936), especially Chap. 16.

[6] See Everett C. Hughes (ed.), "The Sociology of Work," special issue of the *American Journal of Sociology,* **57** (March, 1952).

those who are successful students of foreign languages are unlikely to free themselves completely from their mother tongue.

The educational system of the United States has long been deficient in language study. Unlike Europeans, and especially nationals of the smaller countries, most Americans have little exposure to foreign languages except in the artificial environment of the classroom. The powerful assimilative quality of the United States has tended to downgrade and wipe out the subcultures of immigrant communities. Immigrants were regarded not as bridges to the old world but as ethnic minorities to be Americanized as soon as possible. The value of assimilation was largely accepted by the immigrants and to a greater degree by their children, who in the course of rejecting the old-world language and culture sometimes rejected the carriers of the language and culture—their parents.

Learning Languages

Recently there has been a shift in the national attitude to language study (and study in general) and to language communities, although, except for a few regional cases such as Spanish speakers, the pools of linguistic diversity are drying up. As language study comes to be understood as something more demanding than the literal translations of elementary exercises, more Americans are having the intellectual excitement and pain of finding themselves isolated from the sound of English. In connection with a teaching experiment a group of 20 college students who had studied Russian were sent to the U.S.S.R. aboard a Russian ship pledged that they would not use English until their return. The pedagogical and linguistic results of the experiment need not concern this discussion. The cultural and social experiences are pertinent.

The students are candid in saying the "pledge" imposed immense emotional burdens on them, yet most of them maintain that it should be required in future programs. Pressures mounted as days in the Soviet Union went by. It was not that the students could not express themselves well in talking with Russians. It was that in undergoing what was a most exciting, confusing, and emotionally charged experience, they were unable to share their impressions with each other in their own language, to reveal the depths and nuances of new experiences and feelings. This is painful.

On the other hand, there is no doubt that maintenance of the pledge forced the students to try to express ideas instead of making mere comments on the state of weather or food. Although they were undergoing a very stimulating experience, the students felt that in some ways they had grown intellectually stale. One young man wrote: "For three months we have been living on thought capital previously acquired. We have not had the time to read seriously, and to renew these resources." He went on to point out a paradoxical morale problem: that the students were subjected to group living and never had time for prolonged solitude; yet, he said, "Each of us was ever alone; communication, on levels deeper than those of everyday conversation, was rendered impossible by our limited ability in Russian. Meeting other people in a real sense is difficult even in English. The problems of resources and morale are not independent: they combine to form a strange, dream-like background for intensive language study, where a man is never alone yet always alone—unable to exercise many dimensions of his mental capacity, and unable to refresh them."[7]

A World Language

It is often suggested that a world language would bring peace closer by increasing understanding between peoples. At the same time growing national self-consciousness and the establishment of new nations has increased the number of languages with a solid national identity and perhaps has reduced the chances of any one language becoming a general world tongue. Efforts to develop

and promulgate artificial languages such as Esperanto seem doomed to failure.

Once scholars in Europe all read Latin, which was perhaps a "neutral" language. Today there is no neutral scholarly language, and it appears that no one of the present "world languages" is, in fact, gaining ground. The problem goes beyond science and scholarship. The medieval European separation between scholar and citizen is not possible with modern technology. But if a common language of the future is necessarily "vertical," it must also serve all parts of a world tied by social and economic bonds. One answer might be selection of an existing "natural" language that happens to be (1) unusually easy to learn for speakers of most other languages and (2) proven capable of easily incorporating concepts of science. Malay and Turkish have been suggested as fulfilling these criteria; but dozens of other languages may be equally well suited. A natural language has the advantage (as Margaret Mead wrote) of having been "shaped and tested by time and speakers of many degrees of intelligence and types of imagery, both sexes, all ages, etc." If it also has the two characteristics mentioned, and has no great "political" disadvantages, it might succeed where artificial languages have failed.[8]

Space and Time

Some subtle and profound differences among cultures are reported in Adaptation 5, which describes how communication is affected by attitudes so ingrained by culture that they are usually below the level of consciousness.

1. Units of time gain their meaning in social situations that are culturally defined. Being an hour late in one culture is the equivalent of being five minutes late in another.

2. Comfortable interpersonal distance for a Latin American connotes undue inti-

[7] Abridged from "Americans Learn Russian in the Soviet Union," Carnegie Corporation of New York, *Quarterly,* **7** (October, 1959), pp. 5–6.

[8] Abridged from Sol Tax, Letter No. 13 to Associates, *Current Anthropology,* **3** (April, 1962), 168-B.

macy or aggression to a North American.

3. Non-verbal communication (the "silent language") may be as decisive as words in determining the effectiveness of the interactive process. Time and distance elements of a culture should, therefore, be studied with the same seriousness as the overt symbolic behavior of gesture and verbal and written language.

4. Failure to be aware of such variations will increase "culture shock," the strangeness and insecurity of being in a foreign culture.

The Silent Language

Abridged and adapted from Edward T. Hall, *The Silent Language*, Chapters 1, 9, and 10. Copyright © 1959 by Edward T. Hall. Used in this form by permission of the author and Doubleday & Company, Inc.

THE VOICES OF TIME

Time talks. It speaks more plainly than words. The message it conveys comes through loud and clear. Not long ago the superintendent of the Sioux came to my office. I learned that he had been born on the reservation and was a product of both Indian and white cultures, having earned his A.B. at one of the Ivy League colleges.

During a long and fascinating account of the many problems his tribe was having in adjusting to our way of life, he asked: "What would you think of a people who had no word for time? My people have no word for 'late' or for 'waiting,' for that matter. They don't know what it is to wait or to be late." He then continued: "I decided that until they could tell time and knew what time was they could never adjust themselves to white culture. So I set about to teach them time. There wasn't a clock that was running in any of the reservation classrooms. So I first bought some decent clocks. Then I made the school buses start on time, and if an Indian was two minutes late that was just too bad. The bus started at eight forty-two and he had to be there."

He was right, of course. The Sioux could not adjust to European ways until they had learned the meaning of time. The superintendent's methods may have sounded a bit extreme, but they were about the only ones that would work. The idea of starting the buses off and making the drivers hold to a rigid schedule was a stroke of genius; much kinder to the Indian, who could better afford to miss a bus on the reservation than lose a job in town because he was a day late. There is, in fact, no other way to teach time to people who handle it as differently from us as the Sioux. The quickest way is to get very technical about it and to make it mean something.

A well-known authority on children in the United States once stated that it took the average child a little more than twelve years to master time. This estimate is probably somewhat conservative. Why does it take a child so long to learn time? The answer is not simple. In fact when one begins to discover how many complications are involved he may wonder whether the full subtleties of time can be mastered at all.

In the social world a girl feels insulted when she is asked for a date at the last minute by someone whom she doesn't know very well, and the person who extends an invitation to a dinner party with only three or four days' notice has to apologize. How different from the people of the Middle East with whom it is pointless to make an appointment too far in advance, because their informal time system places everything beyond a week into a single category of "future," in which plans tend to "slip off their minds."

Even physiological urgency is handled quite differently by people around the world. In many countries people need less of what Americans would call urgency in order to discharge a tension. In the United States the need must be highly critical before people act. The distribution of public toilets in America reflects our tendency to deny the existence of urgency even with normal physiological needs. I know of no other place in the world where anyone leaving home or office is put to periodic torture because great pains have been taken to hide the location of rest rooms. Yet Americans are the people who judge the advancement of others by their plumbing.

Punctuality

Informally, for important daytime business appointments in the eastern United States between equals, there are eight time sets in regard to punctuality: on time, five, ten, fifteen, twenty, thirty, forty-five minutes, and one hour early or late. In regard to being late there are "mumble something" periods, slight apology periods, mildly insulting periods requiring full apology, rude periods, and downright insulting periods. No right-minded American would think of keeping a business associate waiting for an hour; it would be too insulting. No matter what is said in apology, there is little that can remove the impact of an hour's heel-cooling in an outer office.

Even the five-minute period has its significant subdivisions. When equals meet, one will generally be aware of being two minutes early or late but will say nothing, since the time in this case is not significant. At three minutes a person will still not apologize or feel that it is necessary to say anything (three is the first significant number in the one-to-five series); at five minutes there is usually a short apology; and at four minutes before

or after the hour the person will mutter something although he will seldom complete the muttered sentence. The importance of making detailed observations on these aspects of informal culture is driven home if one pictures an actual situation.

An American ambassador in an unnamed country interpreted incorrectly the significance of time as it was used in visits by local diplomats. An hour's tardiness in their system is equivalent to five minutes by ours, fifty or fifty-five minutes to four minutes, forty-five minutes to three minutes, and so on for daytime official visits. By their standards the local diplomats felt they couldn't arrive exactly on time; this punctuality might be interpreted locally as an act relinquishing their freedom of action to the United States. But they didn't want to be insulting—an hour late would be too late—so they arrived fifty minutes late. As a consequence the ambassador said, "How can you depend on these people when they arrive an hour late for an appointment and then just mutter something? They don't even give you a full sentence of apology!" He couldn't help feeling this way, because in American time fifty or fifty-five minutes late is the insult period, at the extreme end of the duration scale; yet in the country we are speaking of it's just right. If he had been taught the details of the local time system just as he should have been taught the spoken language, it would have been possible for him to adjust himself accordingly.

Coming to the Point

Our pattern allows very little switching of the position of "intervals" once they are set in a schedule, nor does it allow for much tampering with either the content or the position of the points on the time scale. How much this is a factor in other cultures has not been determined precisely. There are cases, however, where the content or "agenda" of a given period of time is handled quite differently. In the Middle East refusal to come to the point and discuss the topic of a meeting often means that the party cannot agree to your terms but doesn't want to turn you down, or simply that he cannot discuss the matters under consideration because the time is not yet ripe. He will not, moreover, feel it is improper to meet without ever touching on the topic of the meeting.

Our pattern calls for the fixing of the agenda informally beforehand. We do not, as a whole, feel too comfortable trying to operate in a semi-public situation, hammering out an agenda, the way the Russians do. We prefer to assume that both parties want to talk about the subject, otherwise they wouldn't be there; and that they are sufficiently involved in the topic to make it worth their while. With the Russians there is some indication that, while this is true, negotiation over the separate points of the agenda signals to the other side how the opponent is going to react during the actual conference. Softness on our part in early negotiation, because we do not technically fix the agenda but agree informally about what should be taken up, is often interpreted as weakness. Or it may give the impression that we are going to give in on certain points when we aren't at all.

By and large, the overriding pattern with us is that once you have scheduled the time, you have to use it as designated, even when it turns out that this is not necessary or advantageous. All of which seems very strange to the Arab. He starts at one point and goes until he is finished or until something intervenes.

It is not necessary to leave the country to encounter significantly different time patterns. There are differences between families and differences between men and women; occupational differences, status differences, and regional differences. In addition there are two basic American patterns that often conflict. I have termed these the "diffused point pattern" and the "displaced point pattern."

Contrasting the behavior of two groups of people participating in the two patterns, one observes the following: Taking 8:30 A.M. as the point, participants in the "displaced point" pattern will arrive ahead of time anywhere from 8 A.M. to 8:27 A.M. (cutting it fine), with the majority arriving around 8:25 A.M. Diffused point people will arrive anywhere from 8:25 A.M. to 8:45 A.M. As can be seen, there is practically no overlap between these two groups.

A person asked to spend the evening and arrive about "nineish," wouldn't think of using the daytime "diffused point" pattern. The "displaced point" pattern is mandatory, usually at least ten or fifteen minutes after the hour but not more than thirty-five or forty minutes. If asked for dinner, with cocktails before, the leeway is much less. It is permissible to arrive for a seven o'clock engagement at 7:05 but not much later than 7:15. The "mutter something" period starts at 7:20, and by 7:30 people are looking around and saying "I wonder what's happened to the Smiths!" The hostess may have a roast in the oven. In New York City there is a big difference between a "5 to 8" cocktail party, when people arrive between 6 and 7:30, and dinner-party time when ten minutes late is the most allowed.

In practice the attitude toward punctuality depends on three things: (*a*) the type of social occasion and what is being served; (*b*) the status of the individual who is being met or visited; (*c*) the individual's own way of handling time.

SPACE SPEAKS

As one travels abroad and examines how space is handled, startling variations are discovered—differences we react to vigorously. Literally thousands of experiences teach us unconsciously that space communicates. Yet this fact would probably never have been brought to the level of consciousness if it had not been realized that space is organized differently in each culture. The associations and feelings that are released in a member of one culture almost invariably mean something else in the next. When we say that some foreigners are "pushy," all this means is that their handling of space releases this association in our minds.

"It's as much as your life is worth to ride the streetcars. They're worse than our subways. What's more, these people don't seem to mind it at all." As Americans, we have a pattern which discourages touching, except in moments of intimacy. When we ride on a streetcar or crowded elevator we "hold ourselves in," having been taught from early childhood to avoid bodily contact with strangers. Abroad, it's confusing when conflicting feelings are being released at the same time. Our senses are bombarded by a strange language, different smells, and gestures, as well as a host of signs and symbols.

Whenever people travel abroad they suffer from a condition known as *culture shock*. Culture shock is simply a removal or distortion of many of the familiar cues one encounters at home and the substitution for them of other cues which are strange. A good deal of what occurs in the organization and use of space provides important leads as to the specific cues responsible for culture shock.

The Latin house is often built around a patio that is next to the sidewalk but hidden from outsiders behind a wall. It is not easy to describe the degree to which small architectural differences such as this affect outsiders. American foreign aid technicians living in Latin America used to complain that they felt "left out" of things, that they were "shut off." Others kept wondering what was going on "behind those walls." In the United States, on the other hand, propinquity is the basis of a good many relationships. To us the neighbor is actually quite close. You can borrow things, including food and drink, but you also have to take your neighbor to the hospital in an emergency. In this regard he has almost as much claim on you as a cousin.

Another example has to do with the arrangement of offices. In this case one notices great contrast between ourselves and the French. Part of our over-all pattern in the United States is to take a given amount of space and divide it up equally. When a new person is added in an office, almost everyone will move his desk so that the newcomer will have his share of the space. This may mean moving from positions that have been occupied for a long time and away from favorite views. The point is that the office force will make its own adjustments voluntarily. In fact, it is a signal that they have acknowledged the presence of the new person when they start rearranging the furniture. Until this happens, the boss can be sure that the new person has not been integrated into the group.

Given a large enough room, Americans will distribute themselves around the walls, leaving the center open for group activities such as conferences. That is, the center belongs to the group and is often marked off by a table or some object placed there both to use and save the space. Lacking a conference table, members will move their chairs away from their desks to form a "huddle" in the middle.

The French, by contrast, do not make way for each other in the unspoken, taken-for-granted way that we do. They do not divide up the space with a new colleague. Instead they may grudgingly give him a small desk in a dark corner looking toward the wall. This action speaks eloquently to Americans who have found themselves working for the French. We feel that not to "make a place" accents status differences. If the rearrangement which says, "Now we admit you to the group, and you are going to stay," fails to take place, Americans are likely to feel perilously insecure. In French offices the key figure is the man in the middle, who has his fingers on everything so that all runs smoothly. There is a centralized control. The French educational system runs from the middle, so that all students all over France take the same class at the same time.

Conversational Distance

Spatial changes give a tone to a communication, accent it, and at times even override the spoken word. The normal conversational distance between strangers illustrates how important are the dynamics of space interaction. If a person gets too close, the reaction is instantaneous and automatic—the other person backs up. And if he gets too close again, back we go again. I have observed an American backing up the entire length of a long corridor while a foreigner whom he considers pushy tries to catch up with him. This scene has been enacted thousands of times— one person trying to increase the distance in order to be at ease, while the other tries to decrease it for the same reason, neither one being aware of what was going on. We have here an example of the tremendous depth to which culture can condition behavior.

This was suddenly brought into focus one time when I had the good fortune to be visited by a very distinguished and learned man who had been for many years a top-ranking diplomat representing a foreign country. After meeting him a number of times, I had become impressed with his extraordinary sensitivity to the small details of behavior that are so significant in the interaction process. Dr. X was interested in some of the work several of us were doing at the time and asked permission to attend one of my lectures. He came to the front of the class at the end of the lecture to talk over a number of points made in the preceding hour. While talking he became quite involved in the implications of the lecture as well as what he was saying. We started out facing each other and as he talked I became dimly aware that he was standing a little too close and that I was beginning to back up. Fortunately I was able to suppress my first impulse and remain stationary because there was nothing to communicate aggression in his behavior except the conversational distance. His voice was eager, his manner intent, the set of his body communicated only interest and eagerness to talk. It also came to me in

a flash that someone who had been so successful in the old school of diplomacy could not possibly let himself communicate something offensive to the other person except outside of his highly trained awareness.

By experimenting I was able to observe that as I moved away slightly, there was an associated shift in the pattern of interaction. He had more trouble expressing himself. If I shifted to where I felt comfortable (about twenty-one inches), he looked somewhat puzzled and hurt, almost as though he were saying, "Why is he acting that way? Here I am doing everything I can to talk to him in a friendly manner and he suddenly withdraws. Have I done anything wrong? Said something that I shouldn't?" Having ascertained that distance had a direct effect on his conversation, I stood my ground, letting him set the distance.

Not only is a vocal message qualified by the handling of distance, but the substance of a conversation can often demand special handling of space. There are certain things which are difficult to talk about unless one is within the proper conversational zone.

The Army, in its need to get technical about matters that are usually handled informally, made a mistake in the regulations on distance required for reporting to a superior officer. Everyone knows that the relationship between officers and men has certain elements which require distance and impersonality. This applied to officers of different ranks when they were in command relationship to each other. Instructions for reporting to a superior officer were that the junior officer was to proceed up to a point three paces in front of the officer's desk, stop, salute, and state his rank, his name, and his business: "Lieutenant X, reporting as ordered, sir." Now, what cultural norms does this procedure violate, and what does it communicate? It violates the conventions for the use of space. The distance is too great, by at least two feet, and does not fit the situation. The normal speaking distance for business matters, where impersonality is involved at the beginning of the conversation, is five and a half to eight feet. The distance required by the Army regulations borders on the edge of what we would call "far." It evokes an automatic response to shout. There are, of course, many subjects which it is almost impossible to talk about at this distance, and individual Army officers recognize this by putting soldiers and junior officers at ease, asking them to sit down or permitting them to come closer. However, the first impression was that the Army was doing things the hard way.

In Latin America the interaction distance is much less than it is in the United States. Indeed, people cannot talk comfortably with one another unless they are very close to the distance that evokes either sexual or hostile feelings in the North American. The result is that when they move close, we withdraw and back away. As a consequence, they think we are distant or cold, withdrawn and unfriendly. We, on the other hand, are constantly accusing them of breathing down our necks, crowding us, and spraying our faces.

Getting over a spatial accent is just as important, sometimes more so, than eliminating a spoken one. Advice to the foreign traveler might be: Watch where people stand, and don't back up. You will feel funny doing it, but it's amazing how much difference it makes in people's attitudes toward you.

Section 3 Norms

TYPES OF NORMS

All societies have rules or *norms* specifying appropriate and inappropriate behavior, and individuals are rewarded or punished as they conform to or deviate from the rules. The norms are blueprints for behavior, setting limits within which individuals may seek alternate ways to achieve their goals. Norms are based on cultural *values,* which are justified by moral standards, reasoning, or aesthetic judgment. For example, in the United States sophisticated behavior is admired and rewarded in the middle and upper classes. The value says "sophistication is a good thing," and the·norms associated with it specify what a sophisticated person is. He knows how to handle money and can meet anyone on an equal footing; he knows how to be polite and when and how to be impolite or insolent. He is competent and confident in any social situation.

Punishment of deviation and rewards for conformity may be subtle and, therefore, difficult to observe. Only in extreme cases would an unsophisticated individual be openly taunted or ridiculed. Usually he experiences nothing more than a vague sense of being ignored. If he is unperceptive as well as unsophisticated (and a sensitive awareness is a large part of sophistication), he may not even be aware that he has deviated from a norm.

Punishments and rewards are most direct in the socialization of children, who are rewarded for *efforts* at conformity, for success in *learning* norms, and for successful *performance.* Although children are rewarded for an approximation to norms, or even for unsuccessful effort, adults are rated more strictly on performance. The adult is assumed to have adequate knowledge of the norm appropriate in the situation and the behavior appropriate to the norm.

Most people are so unconsciously governed by norms that they do not see clearly the functions norms perform. It is impossible to imagine a normless society, because without norms behavior would be unpredictable. The standards of conduct contained in the norms give order to social relations. Individuals who conform are able to communicate easily with each other, and conforming behavior is predictable. Interactions go forward smoothly if participants follow the rules appropriate to the situation.

Mores and Folkways

Norms, classified as mores and folkways, vary in importance according to the extent to which they are invested with the social good. As Sumner put it, "When the elements of truth and right are developed into doctrines of welfare . . . we call them mores." In choosing the Latin word *mores* Sumner observed that "The Romans used *mores* for customs in the broadest and richest sense of the word, including the notion that customs served welfare and had traditional and mystic sanction so that they were properly authoritative and sacred." He indicated that modern nations (his examples are all Western) have no word equivalent to mores or the Greek *ethos*. He was, however, not interested in the ethical and philosophical problems of right and wrong but in the mores as limitations on both the ends and means of human action.[9]

In Figure III: 1 norms are classified according to the strength of sanctions associated with them (top to bottom) and the degree to which they are institutionalized or crystallized into law (left to right). The more powerful the norms governing a social behavior, the more likely it is that the controls will have been formally recognized by legislation. Mores stand at the upper range of the scale and folkways at the lower range of noninstitutionalized norms. Laws are also distributed on a scale from high to low intensity of feeling. The figure is shown to grow narrower at the top, an indication of the fact that norms

[9] This distinction was first made in William G. Sumner *Folkways* (Boston: Ginn, 1906), especially Chap. I, Secs. 34, 42, and 43. See also Richard T. Morris, "A Typology of Norms," *American Sociological Review,* **21** (October, 1956), 610–13.

William Graham Sumner (1840–1910), influential sociologist and author of Folkways *and* The Science of Society (*with A. G. Keller*). *Sumner's work emphasized the conservative influence of custom. He was also a staunch conservative on both political and economic issues. Perhaps the best-known chapter title in social science is from* Folkways: *"The Mores Can Make Anything Right and Prevent Condemnation of Anything."*

warranting the strongest sanction are almost certain to be institutionalized into laws.

The incest taboo, the prohibition of cannibalism or murder, and the protection of private property are salient norms in Western society. Their violation strikes at the roots of social order, and this disruptive potential calls forth a strong emotional response. If murder is committed, the emotional reaction may be fear, anger, or hatred, and the full resources of the society are mobilized.

Mores are often salient norms in that they

are important to the cohesion and functioning of society; their violation threatens crucial values. Monogamy is an example of such a value. A bigamist is regarded as an adulterer who is immoral, dishonest, or mentally unbalanced. There are legal punishments for bigamy, but in addition there are the extra-legal punishments of ostracism or unwillingness to hire such a man, even if he can fulfill the technical requirements of a job. However, in societies where polygamy is practiced, monogamy may be disdained: Tibetan women " . . . sneer at the dullness and monotony of monogamic life. Thus, the ethics follow the customs." [10]

Norms are classified as folkways when the intensity of feeling associated with them is low and the modes of enforcing them, either by rewards or punishments,[11] are not clearly defined or rigidly applied. Norms specifying

[10] Sumner, *op. cit.*, p. 353.
[11] The term *sanctions* is used by some authors to refer to punishment and reward. Reward is positive sanction, and punishment is negative sanction.

appropriate dress, for instance, evoke little emotion. At worst, a guest incorrectly attired for a formal occasion may be asked to leave. But the clothes of the clergy and military are, from the viewpoint of the norms, not merely clothes, but badges of membership and rank, which are not susceptible to the flexibility of lay civilian etiquette. A multitude of folkways govern fashion, table manners, the language used in addressing old people, tone of voice, grooming, posture, and many other kinds of behavior. These folkways seem right, proper, and rational, although objectively they may not be rational, that is, the most efficient ways of achieving desired ends. For example, although it is generally recognized by nutritionists that the varietal meats (entrails, etc.) have high food value, there is little or no market demand for many of them.

Laws

Laws are also norms. The intensity of feeling associated with them varies from the low emotional reaction elicited by the folkways to

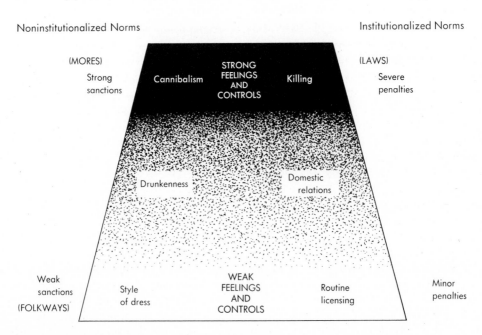

Fig. III:1   Types of Norms

the intense reaction following a violation of the mores. Laws that prohibit holding parades without obtaining licenses have little feeling associated with them. A law that requires a man to support his wife has intermediate intensity, and a law that punishes killing has the highest intensity. (See Fig. III: 1.)

If we are to study crime in its widest social setting, we will find a variety of conduct which, although criminal in the legal sense, is not offensive to the moral conscience of a considerable number of persons. Traffic violations do not often brand the offender as guilty of moral turpitude. In fact, the recipient of a traffic ticket is usually simply the butt of some good-natured joking by his friends. Certain church groups and service clubs regularly conduct gambling games and lotteries for the purpose of raising funds. Professional gamblers rationalize that there cannot be anything very unethical about their games when "legitimate" groups are in the same business.[13]

There are laws covering behavior about which few of us are concerned and laws directed at controlling violations of our most crucial norms. Laws are distinguished from folkways and mores in that laws are *institutionalized*. They are designed, maintained, and enforced by the political authority of the society, the state. Folkways and mores are designed, maintained, and enforced by public sentiment.

Most laws originate in public opinion and consensus, but they may survive long after the public has lost interest. Some "blue laws," such as the prohibition of dancing on Sunday, remain in the statutes as forgotten relics of an earlier period when they were topics of public concern. Sometimes legislation anticipates public opinion. Fair employment practices laws, prohibiting discrimination against Negroes and other minorities, have been enacted in some states. These laws have usually been

championed by groups attempting to improve their position in the job market and are often supported by political idealists. Although such laws may lack general support, or even popular awareness, they have the creative effect of developing public knowledge of a problem, of mobilizing opinion, and of giving expression to standards that may in time become popularly accepted norms. When and if this occurs, fair employment practices laws would gain strength and be invested with enforcement provisions now largely lacking or unused.

CONFORMITY AND DEVIATION

Most norms are regarded as binding rules by most people, but they may change in importance over a period of time. In the early part of the twentieth century, women who smoked were looked upon as immoral. The norm was strongly felt and would have been classified among the mores. Today there is little feeling about women's smoking. Because of growing concern over the effects on health, smoking may once again become a deviation, and habitual smokers may some day be regarded in the same way as alcoholics. There have been legislative proposals to discourage the use of cigarettes by requiring labels that would describe them as dangerous.

A way of behaving may violate the norms in one situation and not in another. Getting drunk may be tolerated on New Year's Eve, at a stag party, after an emotionally painful experience, or as celebration of good news. Getting drunk frequently without ceremonial reasons violates the norms. The same expansive behavior may prevail in both situations, but one is permitted and the other is wrong.

Conflict in Norms

The working of the normative order may be illustrated by exploring extreme cases in which fundamental and strongly held norms come into conflict. Nothing is more repugnant to Western man than murder and cannibalism; no assertion is less debatable than

[13] Richard C. Fuller, "Morals and the Criminal Law." Reprinted, by special permission, from the *Journal of Criminal Law and Criminology* (Northwestern University School of Law), **32** (March-April, 1942), 624–30.

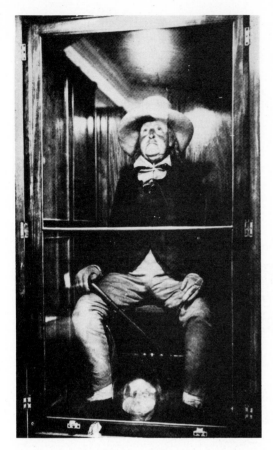

Eccentricity with a purpose: Jeremy Bentham (1748–1832) was a persistent critic of tradition and urged that all social practices be assessed according to their utility and the criterion of maximizing pleasure and minimizing pain. In his gift to the University of London, he required that his remains be preserved in University College, where his clothed skeleton is kept in a case with his skull between his feet.

"Self-preservation is the first law of nature." What happens when these two norms directly conflict?

During the seventeenth century a small fishing party was driven far out to sea by a storm in the Caribbean.[13] Their few provi-

sions were soon exhausted, and it became evident that it would take many days to reach land. One of the men proposed that lots be cast and that the loser sacrifice himself to be eaten, so that the others might live. Lots were cast, and it so happened that the original proposer lost. However, no one would act as executioner and butcher, and it was necessary to cast lots again. A butcher was thus chosen, the man was killed and eaten. After 17 days the small boat reached port in a French island where the Magistrate did not hold the survivors. Because they were English, their case was again examined by an English judge on the island of St. Kitts. He released the prisoners outright saying " . . . the inevitable necessity had washed away the crime."

Can it be taken as a general principle that under the compulsion of *necessity* the strongest of laws and mores may be overridden? Examine this case from an incident in 1884.

At the trial of an indictment for murder it appeared, upon a special verdict, that the prisoners D. and S., seamen, and the deceased, a boy between seventeen and eighteen, were cast away in a storm on the high seas, and compelled to put into an open boat; that the boat was drifting on the ocean, and was probably more than 1000 miles from land; that on the eighteenth day, when they had been seven days without food and five without water, D. proposed to S. that lots should be cast who should be put to death to save the rest, and that they afterwards thought it would be better to kill the boy that their lives should be saved; that on the twentieth day D., with the assent of S., killed the boy, and both D. and S. fed on his flesh for four days; that at the time of the act there was no sail in sight nor any reasonable prospect of relief; that under these circumstances there appeared to the prisoners every probability that unless they then or very soon fed upon the boy, or one of themselves, they would die of starvation.[14]

[13] See *Cox's Criminal Law Cases* (London, 1886), Vol. XV, p. 629.

[14] Regina *v.* Dudley and Stephens (1884), *Ibid.,* pp. 624–38. For another case bearing on the problem of necessity and a thoughtful assessment of norms and the law, see Edmond Cahn, *The Moral Decision* (Bloomington: Indiana University Press, 1955), pp. 61–71.

The court held the prisoners guilty of murder and sentenced them to death. On the argument that the killing was an act of necessity, the court had this to say:

Who is to be the judge of this sort of necessity? By what measure is the comparative value of lives to be measured? Is it to be strength, or intellect, or what? It is plain that the principle leaves to him who is to profit by it to determine the necessity which will justify him in deliberately taking another's life to save his own. In this case the weakest, the youngest, the most unresisting, was chosen. Was it more necessary to kill him than one of the grown men? The answer must be "No." [15]

It is probable that this court would have found that murder had been committed even if lots had been cast and one of the mature men had been the victim, for the verdict emphasized the importance of the normative principle:

We are often compelled to set up standards we cannot reach ourselves, and to lay down rules which we could not ourselves satisfy. But a man has no right to declare temptation to be an excuse, though he might himself have yielded to it, nor allow compassion for the criminal to change or weaken in any manner the legal definition of the crime. [16]

Although sentence of death was passed, it was afterwards commuted by the Crown to six months' imprisonment. The original sentence defended a principle regarded as essential to the moral order; the commutation of the sentence acknowledged the exceptional circumstances of the crime.

Some norms are more specifically stated than others; some have wider ranges of application than others; some permit individual interpretation to a greater extent than others. Limits are indeed set by the norms, but variation in conformity is often permitted, and

exceptions are also provided for. There are a number of reasons why norms are not followed without deviation:

1. Some norms are perceived as less important than others. A driver who hits another automobile to avoid hitting a child has violated one norm so as to conform to another. The fact that he does this "automatically" shows how deeply ingrained are the underlying values. In this case the relative importance of the norms is clear and there is no conflict.

2. Norms may conflict with each other so that an individual must disobey one if he is to conform to the other. The cannibalism cases exemplify this type of normative conflict. Less dramatically, a student who sees a friend cheating on an examination must choose between conflicting norms. One norm instructs him to see that honesty is upheld, and another tells him to be loyal to his friend.

3. An individual may evade a norm because he knows it is weakly enforced. Using company stationery for personal letter-writing and taking home company supplies are rarely punished.

4. Some norms are not learned by all people even in the same society. For example, there are class differences in etiquette and life styles.

Individual evasion of the norms does not necessarily threaten them, but when large numbers of people evade the norms over long periods of time, they are weakened. On the other hand, some norms are so important that they persist in spite of deviations. The widespread evasion of norms regulating sex behavior might seem to constitute a threat to the continuation of the norms themselves. [17] However, it is unlikely that these deviations will change the sex norms, either as laws or as mores. Although behavior may only approximate the sex norms, they stand as explicit

---

[15] *Cox's Criminal Law Cases, op. cit.,* p. 637.
[16] *Ibid.*

[17] For a discussion of the social and legal limitations on sexual behavior and the violations of those norms, see A. C. Kinsey, W. B. Pomeroy, and C. E. Martin, *Sexual Behavior in the Human Male* (Philadelphia: Saunders, 1948), pp. 263–96.

ideals for the members of the society, i.e., they remain as standards to guide and evaluate conduct.

Patterning

Many early studies tried to delineate cultures by describing the concentration of traits in geographic localities. For example, aboriginal North America was divided into a number of regions, called *culture areas,* each containing several tribes that shared common cultural elements. Because these studies emphasized the smallest units of cultural analysis (traits, or even items), they conceived cultures as collections of elements. Even this atomistic approach, however, contained the germ of the idea of patterning. The observers recognized that traits did not exist and work as isolated units but hung together in clusters that have been called trait complexes. The bow is an example of a culture *trait,* which is made up of a number of *items:* a special kind of wood, a specified length, sinew string, etc. Any item alone would be meaningless, but combined they make up the trait, a bow. The bow grouped with the arrow, quiver, and the technique of shooting, is a *trait complex.*[18]

In more recent years, anthropological research has given increasing attention to the patterning of *norms* rather than the patterned distribution of culture objects. A norm does not operate as a separate trait any more than does a single trait in the bow complex. Norms are interrelated in *culture patterns* that give a unified focus to the culture or to parts of it.

Military status etiquette illustrates the interrelatedness of norms. All soldiers and officers are required to have respect for and behave respectfully toward those in positions of authority. The relations between soldiers and officers are reinforced in many kinds of activity by this underlying authority norm. Men in subordinate positions show deference

to those in superordinate positions. Standing at attention and speaking only when officially recognized help to reinforce this norm, deemed essential to the survival of the system. A break in the disciplined reaction to persons of higher or lower status threatens authority. The rules enumerated in army manuals suggest the variety of situations in which the authority norm and the etiquette of status are expected to function, and the selections from the *Basic Field Manual* (see "Military Courtesy and Discipline," p. 76) show a sophisticated awareness of the functional significance of military etiquette.

Normative patterning can also be seen in the American culture taken as a whole. For example, the achievement of success is a salient norm that directs behavior in business, in schools, in child rearing, and in many other aspects of life. The norm that "people ought to try to be successful" is so strong that other goals may be ignored or rejected in the pursuit of success. The high value placed on succeeding, as measured by getting good grades in school, may result in cheating or other forms of dishonesty. A student may be so set on being "successful" that he uses ulterior means to achieve this goal, and impairs the high value placed on education and the accompanying norm that people go to school to learn.

A suggestive effort to summarize the major value orientations in the United States has been made by Williams. One merit of this statement is its propositional form, which invites the reader to test the validity of each theme against his own knowledge. The list of themes follows a cautionary note:

(In the nature of the case, anyone—including the author—can think of numerous exceptions to each of these generalized formulations, as well as widespread alternative themes.)

1. American culture is organized around the attempt at *active mastery* rather than *passive acceptance.* Into this dimension falls the low tolerance of frustration; the refusal to accept ascetic renunciation; the positive encouragement

---

[18] See Ralph Linton, *The Study of Man* (New York: Appleton-Century, 1936), pp. 397 ff.

of desire; the stress on power; the approval of ego-assertion, and so on.

2. It tends to be interested in the *external world* of things and events, of the palpable and immediate, rather than in the inner experience of meaning and affect. Its genius is manipulative rather than contemplative.

3. Its world-view tends to be *open* rather than closed: it emphasizes change, flux, movement; its central personality types are adaptive, accessible, outgoing and assimilative.

4. In wide historical and comparative perspective, the culture places its primary faith in *rationalism* as opposed to *traditionalism;* it deemphasizes the past, orients strongly to the future, does not accept things just because they have been done before.

5. Closely related to the above, is the dimension of *orderliness* rather than unsystematic *ad hoc* acceptance of transitory experience. (This emphasis is most marked in the urban middle classes.)

6. With conspicuous deviations, a main theme is a *universalistic* rather than a *particularistic* ethic.[19]

7. In interpersonal relations, the weight of the value system is on the side of *"horizontal"* rather than *"vertical"* emphases: peer-relations, not superordinate-subordinate relations; equality rather than hierarchy.

[19] A "universalistic" ethic emphasizes the application of uniform rules or principles, e.g., that all men are equal before the law or should have equal opportunities. A "particularistic" ethic emphasizes claims to special treatment on the basis of friendship, kinship, social status, or other specific criteria.

8. Subject to increased strains and modifications, the received culture emphasizes *individual personality* rather than group identity and responsibility.

In broadest outline, then, American society is characterized by a basic moral orientation, involving emphases on active, instrumental mastery of the world in accordance with universalistic standards of performance. It is a pluralistic system in which it is not easy to secure unitary commitment to collective goals. It permits a wide range of goals for achievement.[20]

Thus whole cultures are sometimes characterized by values that reinforce each other and affect the most varied and important kinds of behavior. For example, "the pattern of Tlingit culture was exuberant, with property as the goad to action, with the display of wealth as the symbol of virtue, with pride and arrogance as the dominant personality motifs. These reappear in every facet of Tlingit social life." [21] Benedict [22] called the dominant life patterns of the Northwest Indians (including the Tlingit) "Dionysian." She dis-

[20] Robin M. Williams, Jr., *American Society: A Sociological Interpretation* (2nd ed., rev.; New York: Knopf, 1960), pp. 469–70.
[21] Walter Goldschmidt (ed.), *Ways of Mankind* (Boston: Beacon Press, copyright, 1954, by the National Association of Educational Broadcasters), p. 10.
[22] Ruth Benedict, "Psychological Types in the Cultures of the Southwest," *Proceedings of the Twenty-third International Congress of Americanists*, September, 1928, pp. 572–81.

Table **III:2** Dionysian and Apollonian Cultures *

Dionysian: Northwest Indians	Apollonian: Southwest Pueblo Indians
Wide range of emotionality	Restrained expression of emotion
Ceremonial drunkenness	Sobriety
Torture used to heighten sensory experiences	No torture
Frenzy and visions part of religious experience	Disapproval of frenzy, visions, and trances
Use of intoxicants and drugs	No use of drugs or alcohol
Fasting a religious practice	Fasting not understood
Ritualistic eating of filth	No ritualistic eating of filth
Ceremonial and nonceremonial suicide	No suicide

* Constructed from Ruth Benedict, "Psychological Types in the Cultures of the Southwest," *Proceedings of the Twenty-third International Congress of Americanists*, September, 1928, pp. 572–81; and Ruth Benedict, *Patterns of Culture* (Baltimore, Md.: Penguin Books, 1934).

Military Courtesy and Discipline

Selected from *Basic Field Manual: Military Courtesy and Discipline,* FM 21–50, War Department (Washington, D.C.: Government Printing Office, 1942), pp. 4–5, 16, 22, 36–37.

CUSTOMS OF THE SERVICE

Validity. Over the long period of our Army's existence, certain customs and practices have grown up through force of necessity. They have stood the test of time and are effective and binding today as regulations. These unwritten laws of the Army derive their force from the necessity and consent of those who comprise the service. Usually, the breach of one of these customs merely brands the offender as ignorant or thoughtless; but there are some, the violation of which will bring official corrective measures.

GUIDES TO LEADERSHIP

Setting a good example. Absolute loyalty is fundamental, and that loyalty should extend downward as well as upward. If by actions or words you are disloyal to your superiors, your men will doubt your loyalty to them, and their loyalty to you will suffer correspondingly.

The leader should set his subordinates an example of courtesy. A courteous manner in dealing with your men will increase their self-respect and increase their respect for you.

You must demonstrate that the authority of your grade is deserved through moral worth. Moderation in the use of intoxicants naturally follows as an important precept. Excesses on the part of an officer in matters of sex, gambling, and incurring debts indicate poor judgment and instability, and forfeit the respect of superiors and subordinates alike.

MILITARY COURTESY

Article 6. Salutes. The most important of all military courtesies is the salute. This is because it is at once the most obvious and the most used. The proper execution of the salute distinguishes the military man. The salute serves two purposes: as the act of recognition between members of the military profession, and as an indication of respect for authority. The salute is not a mark of subservience, it is an indication of the possession of military courtesy and discipline by those who render it. Its omission indicates a lack of courtesy which is a mark of poor discipline.

Article 12. Personal courtesies. Military persons enter automobiles and small boats in inverse order of rank and leave in order of rank. Juniors, although entering an automobile first, take appropriate seats in the car. The senior is always on the right.

---

tinguished an "Apollonian"[23] culture among the Pueblo Indians of the Southwest. Table III: 2 summarizes the elements she assigned to each culture type. These point to profound differences in underlying values of two distinct cultures. However, it has not been demonstrated that other cultures fit into the Apollonian and Dionysian categories or that the terms may be confidently assigned to other cultures. This kind of analysis emphasizes, perhaps overemphasizes, a few key elements. In striving to isolate the essence of a culture, it may minimize variability within a culture or between two similar cultures.

[23] Such names have been applied to historical epochs by Friedrich W. Nietzsche and his followers. For example, see Oswald Spengler, *The Decline of the West* (New York: Knopf, 1926), first published in German in 1922.

Courtesy and Military Discipline

Section 4   **Cultural adaptation and change**

No culture, however isolated from outside influences, adjusted to its environment, and conservative in its outlook, is truly stable and unchanging. This section examines several aspects of culture dynamics: (1) the interaction of culture and environment, (2) cultural growth and technology, and (3) acculturation.

CULTURE AND ENVIRONMENT[24]

The first task for every culture is to cope with its physical environment. Each environment affords different kinds of opportunities

[24] For resource material and extensive bibliography on the topics in this section, see William L. Thomas, Jr., *Man's Role in Changing the Face of the Earth* (Chicago: University of Chicago Press, 1956).

and imposes distinctive restrictions and limitations on cultural development. Cultural growth is, therefore, in part a process of trial and error, of working out against the environment solutions to the problems of daily life. The culture selects from the range of environmental opportunities, but obviously trials are limited to the materials at hand. In this sense culture begins to take shape at the very moment that man copes with his environment in an active way.

In the polar environment, for example, agriculture is impossible (a negative limitation). Hunting and fishing offer manifest opportunities, but the efficiency with which opportunities are exploited depends upon the culture.

There is nothing in the polar environment that determined the ingenious adaptations of the Polar Eskimo.[25] It *allowed* the development of the igloo and the dog sledge, but it did not *require* those particular solutions to the problems of housing and transport. Other peoples living in similar environments did not develop these possibilities. Although the Eskimo was remarkably successful in coping with his environment, Indian tribes in similar environments used different and by-and-large less impressive solutions.

It may be thought that the mandatory rule of Eskimo hospitality and the communal attitude toward food are direct adjustments to a rigorous climate. However, the communal attitude does not extend to other areas of Eskimo life, and dogs and manufactured possessions are private property, even though they, too, are essential to survival.

Having made a successful adaptation to one of the harshest environments in the world, the Eskimo appears to have an active approach to the material world that stands him in good stead when he is obliged to deal with the weapons, tools, and machines of Western civilization. He has highly developed his mechanical abilities and his understanding of the

qualities of physical materials. He shows the same mastery over instruments and machines of steel and glass that he does over tools of bone and wood.

In summary, the environment provides the framework within which cultural specialization and selective exploitation go on. Opportunities may be rich or meager, but the environment does not tell what will be done with them. Environmental limitations contribute to cultural variability throughout the world. Figure III : 2 illustrates the use of land in the temperate zone and indicates which type of crops will grow best under given conditions of rainfall and temperature. Although it would be inaccurate to say that the environment *determines* the type of agriculture, it would be equally inaccurate to reject the *limiting* nature of environment.

The interaction between culture and environment may be further illustrated by the types of adaptations found in three major regions of South America.[26] The ability to deal with the environment ranges from a bare survival technology in the Marginal zone to a surplus economy providing the basis for a high civilization in the Andes.

The Marginal people lived mainly on the coasts of southernmost South America in a cold and wet climate. They relied on hunting, fishing, and gathering for sustenance. In order to maintain a minimum subsistence, small bands had to travel almost continuously, chasing herds of guanaco (wild mammals related to the llama) or digging rodents out of burrows. When the food in an area was exhausted, the bands moved on. Some used canoes for fishing, but their material possessions were meager, and population density was low.

The Tropical Forest people of northeastern and north-central South America

[25] See George Peter Murdock, *Our Primitive Contemporaries* (New York: Macmillan, 1936), Chap. VIII.

[26] See Julian H. Steward (ed.), *Handbook of South American Indians,* Bureau of American Ethnology Bulletin 143 (Washington, D.C.: Government Printing Office, 1949), 6 Vols., especially Vol. 5, Steward's "South American Cultures: An Interpretive Summary," pp. 669–772. He distinguishes four culture types: the Marginal, the Tropical Forest, the Andean, and the Circum-Caribbean peoples. The first three are considered here.

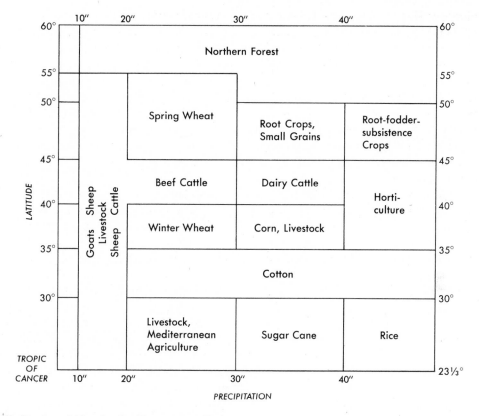

Fig. III:2 Land Use in the Temperate Zone

developed a remarkably uniform culture throughout a wide area of the rain forest. They engaged in slash-and-burn agriculture, fishing, hunting, and the gathering of forest products. Their settlements were stable and densely populated, as many as a thousand inhabitants living in a single community. Abundant crops of manioc, yams, maize, and fruit provided surplus products and leisure—conditions that further cultural growth. Their dugout canoes, thatched houses, hammocks, ornaments, and looms contrast with the few possessions of the Marginal people.

The Andean people lived in Peru, most of Bolivia, southern Ecuador, and northern Chile, where there are a variety of climates. The coasts are desertlike, but the high plateau region, the home of the Inca, is friendly to the domestication of plants. The

Andeans practiced crop rotation, irrigation, and fertilizing, and the yield of half an acre could support one person. Domesticated animals were used for transportation and wool, and every technique of textile making was known to the Incas. Their metallurgy included the use of alloys and bronze. The Inca achieved the highest population density in the New World, their material culture was richer than any of the other cultures of the continent, and their civilization is regarded as one of the most advanced in the history of man.

Although domesticable plants and animals gave a surplus that contributed to the achievements of the Inca civilization, no purely environmental factors determine the total nature of a culture. Where there is no need to struggle with the environment for essential needs, the probabilities of developing a high culture are greatly increased. Surpluses of time and man power are probably essential to the elaboration of culture, the division of labor, and the growth of complex social organization.

Changing the Environment

Primitive cultures, even those characterized by great practical ingenuity, such as the Eskimo, are able to control only small parts of their environment. Eskimo housing and clothing effectively control climate in a very small area. More advanced cultures for good or ill manipulate major aspects of their environments, for example, through deforestation, irrigation, the diversion of streams, and changes in the contours of land. Modern civilization with its control of great sources of power can create numerous specialized environments and can exploit the same regions in many different ways. The limiting forces in environment, therefore, diminish in importance as the range of possibilities is more completely exploited.

CULTURE AND TECHNOLOGY

From the perspective of recent history, rapid change in technology and a questioning of standards and values seem a normal state of affairs. By contrast, other periods in history seem stagnant, and, relatively speaking, most of them were. Few other cultures valued change as does the American version of Western civilization, and few have been so inclined to equate change in general with progress in particular. Discussion of change should, therefore, proceed upon the understanding that no member of Western civilization can be immune to a strong bias toward change, either favorable or unfavorable.

For most of mankind's history, the growth of culture was slow. (See Table III:3.) The Old Stone Age (the Paleolithic Period), which lasted perhaps one million years, saw the mastery of fire, of tools made of wood, stone, and bone, of some artistic skills, and undoubtedly of language and social understandings. The few thousand years of the New Stone Age witnessed far more rapid accumulations of knowledge and skills: the practice of pastoral and agricultural arts, the domestication of animals, the making of pottery and textiles, and the growth of carpentry. These advances supplied the necessary conditions for population expansion and for the rise of cities. In the urban civilizations, culture cumulation was still more rapid.[27]

Innovation

The roots of invention reach back into the cultural resources of a society. Each invention depends on the previous body of knowledge. If the gaps in the supporting knowledge are too numerous or large, there will be no effective invention, although a man of great talent may have ideas that anticipate the necessary supporting knowledge. Leonardo da Vinci, for example, invented many machines that became practical in succeeding centuries, but in his day (fifteenth century) the base of technological skills and knowledge was not ready to translate most of his ideas into practical reality.

His sketchbooks are full of technical studies. The models shown in [the International Business Machines] exhibition are constructed after his original sketches and demonstrate how completely practicable Leonardo's designs are . . . . Almost all these projects could be carried out without alteration, for not only is the drawing itself perfectly clear in all of them but the mechanism itself is so correct in principle that the models made from his plans function without a hitch.[28]

A partial list of his innovations and inventions follows. The starred items were actually built in his lifetime.

[27] Ralph Turner, *The Great Cultural Traditions* (New York: McGraw-Hill, 1941), Vol. 1, Part One.

[28] Ludwig Heinrich Heydenreich, "Leonardo da Vinci, The Scientist" (catalogue prepared for an exhibition of working models based on Leonardo's drawings, Collections of the Fine Arts Department, International Business Machines Corporation, copyright, 1951), pp. 7–8. The list of inventions is indebted to the catalogue.

Table III:3   The Growth of Culture in the Western World*

Approximate Earliest Dates	Centers of Culture Growth	Chief Developments
Iron Age Beginning 1,400 B.C.	The Mediterranean, Southern and Eastern Europe	First mechanical power from water wheels Alphabetic writing Iron (made possible extensive stone sculpture) Wide dispersion of knowledge of the Bronze Age Coins and money economy
Bronze Age Beginning 3,000 B.C.	The river valleys of the Nile, Tigris-Euphrates, and Indus	Earliest cities with populations of several thousands in river valleys Public edifices: temples, city walls, administration buildings Seals as symbols of property Wheeled vehicles; wheel-made pottery Sun dials; astronomy Writing Metallurgy; glass Sail boats Canal irrigation, plow
Neolithic Beginning 7,000 B.C.	Hilly regions east of the Mediterranean	Permanent village settlements with populations of several hundred Animal and plant domestication Handmade pottery and weaving
Upper Paleolithic Beginning approximately 50,000 B.C.	Western Europe [Homo sapiens exclusive human form]	Skin clothing, needles Missile weapons: bow and arrow, harpoon, throwing stick Artificial dwellings Graphic art
Lower Paleolithic Beginning approximately 1,000,000 B.C.		Hunting traps Formal burial Fire Stone, bone and wood implements

*This compilation is indebted to George W. Brainerd. For additional background see Grahame Clark, *From Savagery to Civilization* (New York: Henry Schuman, 1953). Clark uses E. B. Tylor's terminology, which may be roughly equated as follows:
Savagery   =Paleolithic (Old Stone Age)
Barbarism   =Neolithic (New Stone Age)
Civilization =Age of Metals
See also Gordon Childe, *What Happened in History* (Baltimore: Penguin Books, 1942).

Aerial bomb

*Air conditioning unit

*Clock with double escapement (first to indicate minutes as well as hours)

Diver's apparatus

Helicopter (credited by many authorities as the forerunner of the propeller)

*Hydraulic pump

Hydraulic screw (forerunner of the turbine)

Jack (for lifting weights, foreshadowed the automobile jack)

Machine gun

Military tank

*Parachute

Projector (for throwing an enlarged image of an object on a screen)

*Revolving stage

Streamlined and double hull for ship

Variable speed driver (meshing cogged wheels of different diameters with the same lantern wheel to obtain different speeds of rotation—an idea found in the automobile)

When the cultural base is ready for an invention, however, the possibility of a development may be so apparent that essentially the same invention is made independently by a number of men at the same time.

Culture Lag

Sociologists have long observed that changes do not occur in a co-ordinated way even in closely related parts of the culture. Although the different parts of culture—for example, industry and education—are interdependent, changes go on at different rates. Industry may develop a need for skilled personnel that the educational system is unable to supply without retraining of teachers. Such a change brings pressure on the school system to make adaptive changes in its training methods, but while this adaptation is going on, a period of maladjustment occurs. This period of delay has been called *culture lag.*[29]

Ogburn emphasized that changes in material conditions (especially in the physical environment) and in things[30] (including houses, factories, raw materials, and other objects) often outdistance the ways of using these things and of adapting to these conditions. The ways of adjustment may be called the *adaptive* culture, which includes wholly adaptive elements, such as technical rules, and partly adaptive elements, such as the folkways and mores.

The efficient use of the newly invented automobile required drastic improvements in the road systems, but the development and building of highways suitable for motor vehicles were long delayed. Traffic codes and techniques of traffic control have been worked out even more slowly, and an etiquette of automobile driving is yet to develop. The consequences are inefficiency, wasteful delay in utilizing new techniques, stress, and maladjustment.

The general use of the typewriter was delayed in part because—

Many questioned the value of paying approximately $125 for a machine that would do the same work as a 1-cent pen . . . . [In addition] questions of the status of women in society . . . became involved in the controversies over its utilization. The girl typist became a symbol of women's emancipation and aroused responses accordingly. In 1881 when the New York YWCA announced typing lessons for women, vigorous protests were made on the grounds that the female constitution would break down completely under the strenuous 6 months' course offered. . . .[31]

Lag in the adoption of the typewriter for

---

[29] W. F. Ogburn, *Social Change* (New York: Viking, 1950), Part IV, especially pp. 200–213; first published in 1922. Ogburn illustrated the central idea of lag in the conservation policy in forests (pp. 200–212), in workmen's compensations laws (pp. 213–36), and suggested its application to a number of other cases (pp. 237–56).

[30] The common distinction between material and nonmaterial culture raises some difficult problems, especially in a discussion of change. The physical objects of the "material culture," strictly speaking, do not change; the technology, including knowledge, skills, and language that govern the fabrication of material things, does change.

[31] Bernhard J. Stern, "Resistances to the Adoption of Technological Innovations," in *Technological Trends and National Policy*, National Resources Committee (Washington, D.C.: Government Printing Office, 1937), p. 49.

office use is schematically shown in Figure III:3. The dates indicated in the figure are arbitrary, but if the dates can be determined and if the rates of change can be plotted as shown in the figure, a more accurate representation of lag will be gained. The change is thus seen not as an all-or-none matter but as a progressive adjustment over a period of years.

Caution: Two common assumptions should be qualified:

1. That material conditions will be the first to change. This need not be the case. For example, adaptive changes associated with a war effort may stimulate drastic changes in the technology.

2. That the fastest possible adjustment involves the least maladjustment. This is not necessarily so. A delayed adaptation may be based on fuller experience and a better assessment of what is required for effective adjustment.

Mass Culture

When the technology of mass communication makes literature, music, drama and other activities available to very large numbers, as it does in contemporary America, intellectual and aesthetic standards are likely to be lowered. Under such circumstances, concern arises over maintaining creative ideals. This problem is not peculiar to the twentieth century. In eighteenth-century England, for instance, there was a mass market for literary goods, such as popular novels and magazines, and much discussion of the threat to standards of taste and morality.[32] Today there is similar concern among intellectuals that standards are being debased, that "mass culture" is pushing "high culture" into a precarious position.

Mass culture is oriented toward entertainment of large numbers of people, and of

[32] Leo Lowenthal and Marjorie Fiske, "The Debate over Art and Popular Culture in Eighteenth Century England," in Mirra Komarovsky (ed.), *Common Frontiers of the Social Sciences* (Glencoe: The Free Press, 1957).

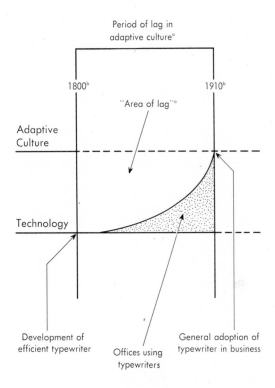

Fig. III:3 Use of the Typewriter

This illustration adapts Ogburn's diagram to the case of the typewriter. Cf. Ogburn, *Social Change* (New York: Viking Press, 1950), p. 206.

[a] Lag may be used as a measure of waste by indicating the rate of change between the two dates. The hypothetical curve shows the increasing use of the typewriter and the decline of the "area of lag."

[b] The dates are hypothetical.

course has become a major industry. It offers easy access to a part of the world of art and letters, and this is a key to its success. In order to win and hold their audiences, the producers of mass culture are ready to "give the people what they want" even if this means radically lowering standards.[33]

There is no doubt that some lowering of

[33] See Bernard Rosenberg and David M. White (eds.), *Mass Culture* (Glencoe: The Free Press, 1957); Max Lerner, *America as a Civilization: Life and Thought in the United States Today* (New York: Simon and Schuster, 1957). For an early but still valuable treatment of this subject, see Alexis de Tocqueville, *Democracy in America* (New York: Knopf, 1945), Vol. II, pp. 48, 51–52.

'N Mennischte Maedel (*a Mennonite girl*) *and two Amish girls.*

standards has occurred, but it is quite possible that improvement in popular taste has also taken place. This is not known to be so, nor is it known what effect mass culture has on the production of truly creative works of high standard. Perhaps the main question is whether relatively low-grade forms of art necessarily drive out the good, or whether they can exist side by side in successful but uneasy accommodation. As yet these matters have not been carefully studied.

Folk cultures, too, are threatened when technology breaks down their isolation. The Amish [34] folk society has survived for many decades as an integrated conservative community. The old world Amish culture took root in the new world, and a strong religious sectarianism and patriarchal authority defended the group against culture change. In recent years the pressure of a dynamic secular society shows signs of breaking down the folk culture. It is not that the representatives of the mass culture are determined to destroy the folk culture. On the contrary, if they had any choice in the matter, they would probably prefer the Amish to continue in their old ways. However, it becomes progressively harder for folk culture to survive in the face of pressure from a mass culture.

ACCULTURATION

Acculturation refers to a group's taking on elements from the culture of another group. The term has also been used as a synonym for *socialization,* the acquisition of ways of behaving and valuing by individuals. All cultural acquisitions are learned, and some writers use acculturation and socialization interchangeably. In doing so, they signify that they are chiefly interested in the molding of individual personality and behavior. (See SOCIALIZATION.) In this book we reserve the word *acculturation* for the process of cultural change induced by contact with foreign cultures. Usually both cultures in a contact situation are changed, although one may be more profoundly influenced than the other. In the modern world no culture is completely isolated and unaffected by others, but the intensity and duration of contact vary from place to place and from time to time. Many primitive peoples as well as modern men travel great distances, and in doing so, they carry with them cultural forms that are adopted by others and from whom in turn they acquire new practices. The Indians of North America traded their wares over a wide area. In the Southeast the population of whole villages visited neighboring tribes for a season of contests and recreation, and in the course of these social relations, acculturation took place.

[34] The Amish, Mennonite, and Dunkard sects are cultural enclaves, together referred to as "Pennsylvania Dutch."

Selectivity of Acculturation

Except at the very end of the process, acculturation goes on selectively. This was the case, for example, at the time of the Norman Conquest (1066), which established a new upper class in English society as well as a new political control. The Norman French influence was reinforced by continuous contact with France. Changes induced in the English language testify both to the depth of French influence in English society and the high status occupied by the French in other than political facets of English life.

It is a remark that was first made by John Wallis and that has been very often repeated, especially since Sir Walter Scott made it popular in *Ivanhoe,* that while the names of several animals in their lifetime are English (*ox, cow, calf, sheep, swine, boar, deer*), they appear on the table with French names (*beef, veal, mutton, pork, bacon, brawn, venison*). This is generally explained from the masters leaving the care of the living animals to the lower classes, while they did not leave much of the meat to be eaten by them. But it may with just as much right be contended that the use of the French words here is due to the superiority of the French *cuisine,* which is shown by a great many other words as well, such as *sauce, boil, fry, roast, toast, pasty, pastry, soup, sausage, jelly, dainty;* while the humbler *breakfast* is English, the more sumptuous meals, *dinner* and *supper,* as well as *feasts* generally, are French.[35]

Foreign influences are received differently by different parts of a population. Some occupational or status groups, such as entrepreneurs or land holders or legal experts, may be in a strategic position to benefit from the introduced technology and knowledge—or, at least, they may so conceive the situation. Others, such as technicians in aboriginal crafts or ceremonial experts, may perceive the foreign culture as threatening and destructive to vested interests and to be resisted at all costs.

French culture and language did not innundate England, but many elements were absorbed, forming a new cultural amalgam with the French influence stronger at the top of the status hierarchy than at the bottom. The processes of cultural exchange usually flow in both directions, but when not marked by some abrupt event the changes may be so gradual as to be hardly noticed except by scholars. Such are the changes in American English induced by the presence of European immigrants.

Culture Contacts of Migrants

Even the tourist in his native land encounters a sense of strangeness and unsureness in a different community. The customs of the new place must be learned if he is to be comfortable in it. But because the language difficulties are small, a minor matter of accent or dialect, and because customs are similar, he soon feels at home. The tourist in a foreign land has greater practical difficulties. Language and customs are strange, and he may be unsure of himself. Nevertheless, his tourist status lends him a degree of invulnerability, and he is not obliged to adjust fully to the land he is visiting. He is expected not to know; he can err without reprisal; he may even break some laws with impunity. His relations tend to be of a surface character, and if there is strain or conflict, it, too, is superficial. His ties to his homeland are unimpaired, and his native culture remains a steady reference for his judgments and actions.

The immigrant, however, by the very act of his movement alienates himself from his native culture. For an English immigrant to the United States or Australia or for a Portuguese immigrant to Brazil, the adjustment is relatively easy because cultural differences are not very great, but even in cases like these, there is strangeness, dislocation, and perhaps rejection of the new land and of its different ways.

---

[35] Otto Jespersen, *Growth and Structure of the English Language* (New York: D. Appleton & Co., 1923), p. 89. Reprinted by permission of Appleton-Century-Crofts, Inc.

For millions of immigrants, however, the cultural gaps are very great, and some people remain for the rest of their lives strangers in a strange land. The extent of dislocation of eighteenth- and nineteenth-century immigrants and their feelings of extreme insecurity are hard to appreciate in a time when cultural barriers have been reduced by easy travel and mass communication and when people of most nations are aware of other nations and, in a sense, prepared for differences. Although immigrants to the United States have come from diverse origins and statuses, many were peasants displaced from their land by economic and population pressures and the changing character of European society.[36] Some had little conception of what awaited them in the New World, or indeed, of what their own land was like beyond their provincial confines. They knew intimately only their own locality, their neighbors, and the town to which they went to trade and for the Fairs. They were illiterate and uninformed or misinformed about the city and transportation, and the trip from farm to town to port city to the New World was a series of arduous experiences in which luck and native wit had to substitute for sure knowledge.

The qualities that were desirable in the good peasant were not those conducive to success in transition. Neighborliness, obedience, respect, and status were valueless among the masses that struggled for space on the way. They succeeded who put aside the old preconceptions, pushed in, and took care of themselves. This experience . . . [brought] into question the validity of the old standards of conduct. . . .[37]

The first culture conflict of the migrant was expressed as a conflict between the folk culture of the peasant and the cosmopolitan forms of an emerging commercial society. The conflict began in the migrant's homeland in his dealings with government officials and shipping agents who operated on the basis of rules strange to the migrant and mistrusted by him. It increased in the new land, where much more was strange and therefore suspect. In the New World the sense of rootlessness, of *anomie,* was compounded by more profound differences of language and custom. Only the expanding economy of America permitted so many with the skills of a folk culture to make their way in the culture of the New World. However well the immigrant learned the ways of his new country, there remained throughout his life important areas of knowledge and experience in which he was insecure and to which his adjustments were faulty. He was, in a sense, "marginal" between the Old World and the New. (See MINORITIES, pp. 504 f.)

Stimulated Invention

Acculturative influences may stimulate inventions as well as modify or replace existing forms. One of the most remarkable cases of this kind was the invention early in the nineteenth century of a system of writing by Sequoyah, a Cherokee Indian. The stimulus for Sequoyah was an understanding of the function of writing as performed by the white man, and he wished to bring this art to his own people. Over a period of years he tried out a number of techniques, including picture writing, until he hit upon devising a separate symbol for each of the eighty-odd syllable sounds in Cherokee. The full execution of the idea required years of disciplined endeavor as well as the initial stroke of genius. The quality of Sequoyah's singlehanded invention of writing and the extent of its immediate application are probably unique in recorded history.

The syllabary proved highly practical. Cherokee speakers needed only to memorize the symbols with their associated sounds in order to become literate in their language. In this respect the Cherokee system of writing is superior to English. A Cherokee can master

[36] Oscar Handlin, *The Uprooted* (Boston: Little, Brown, 1951), *passim.*

[37] *Ibid.,* p. 61. Quoted by permission of Little, Brown & Co.

Break with tradition: After World War II, young Japanese rapidly adopted "progressive" Western styles.

reading and writing in a matter of a few months compared with the three or four years of schooling required for basic knowledge of written English. On the other hand, compared with classical Chinese, for example, English has a writing system of only moderate difficulty. Chinese takes several times as much schooling as does English for comparable levels of literacy.

In a very short time after Sequoyah's invention was accepted, the Cherokee nation became literate, and this stimulated further developments. Type was cast in the syllabary, the Bible and other religious works were translated into Cherokee, and a newspaper was established. An unanticipated consequence of the invention was to give the medicine men a means for perpetuating their tribal learning. Traditions that had been handed down by word of mouth for many generations were preserved for posterity in the notebooks of the medicine men. A folklore became a literature.

Acculturation of Preliterate Peoples

The most studied form of acculturation is that resulting from the impact of Western civilization on the simpler cultures of the Americas, Africa, and Oceania. From the standpoint of Western observers the most obvious consequence of these contacts has been the adoption of elements from Western culture: weapons, tools, clothing, and the like. Very often the impact on preliterate peoples was so heavy that the native cultures were submerged, or at least seemed to be. More sensitive studies, focused on the non-material culture, have un-

covered a greater amount of cultural persistence than had been assumed. There is also evidence that the primitive peoples did not blindly accept the "superior" culture of the Europeans even when defeated in combat. In art and drama the primitive peoples lampooned the white man and represented him as ignorant and destructive. Neither the manners nor the morals of the conquerors are objects for admiration as seen through the eyes of the primitive artist. Clearly the "small" cultures of preliterate peoples are not so vulnerable as was thought a few years ago. Undoubtedly most of them are living on borrowed time, but while they still survive, they represent a great intellectual resource and a unique opportunity for modern man to understand the varied capacities of mankind.

Adaptation 6 is a case study describing the contact between two American Indian peoples. This situation is notable for the lack of acculturation between the two groups despite a prolonged period of intimate contact.

The Hopi and the Tewa

ADAPTATION 6

Abridged and adapted from Edward P. Dozier,[18] "The Hopi and the Tewa," *Scientific American*, **196** (June, 1957), 127–36. Used in this form with permission of author and publisher.

The problem of the relations between a dominant population and a minority—Negroes, Jews, or an immigrant group—is one of the most interesting, as well as one of the most important, in the realm of social science. Sociologists and anthropologists have carried out many and varied studies in efforts to understand the factors that make for assimilation, on the one hand, or separation, on the

other. This adaptation reports a case study of a unique situation. It concerns the Hopi and a small colony of Tewa Indians, two groups of Pueblo Indians living side by side in the mesa country of Arizona. Ethnically and in many other ways they are very much alike. Yet for more than 200 years they remained aliens in practically the same village. Then, through what might be considered a historical accident, the two groups were rapidly brought together, barriers fell and they began to live in harmony.

[18] For the full report see Edward P. Dozier, *The Hopi-Tewa of Arizona* (Berkeley and Los Angeles: University of California Press, 1954), University of California Publications in American Archaeology and Ethnology, Vol. 44, No. 3, pp. 259–376.

The Spanish occupation of the Southwest in the sixteenth century fell as a catastrophe on the peaceful Pueblo Indians. The white man's diseases and fanatical attempts to Christianize and "civilize" the Indians took a great toll, and finally in 1680 the Indians rebelled and drove the Spaniards from Santa Fe.

Among the leaders of the rebellion were a Tewa group, whose numbers had been reduced from 4,000 to less than 1,000. When the Spaniards were driven out, these people moved into Santa Fe. But thirteen years later a well-armed Spanish force returned and quickly subdued them. Most of the Tewa were taken as slaves. A few hundred escaped, remained rebellious, and three years later made a final raid on the city, after which they fled 400 miles to Hopi country.

A Tale of Betrayal

The Tewa took up residence literally next door to the Hopi. Their houses are indistinguishable; the Tewa village has all the appearances of a typical Hopi town. But for more than two centuries both groups have been keenly aware of a sharp boundary separating the two villages.

The 200 men, women, and children who made the journey did not find the bounteous welcome they had expected. According to the Tewa legend, Hopi chiefs had repeatedly promised the Tewa land, food, sexual privileges with Hopi women, and assistance in settling in a permanent home. These inducements were offered because the Hopi needed the brave Tewa as warriors to drive off their enemies. But after the Tewa had performed this service, says the legend, the Hopi failed to make good their promises, and the Tewa received only a meager village site at the end of a mesa (a "table" of land with steeply sloping sides). The Tewa responded by putting a "curse" upon the Hopi. They dug a pit between their village and the neighboring Hopi one, made the Hopi spit into the pit, then spat upon the spittle of the Hopi, and filled the pit with earth. This action was intended to seal the Tewa culture forever from appropriation by the Hopi.

Whether or not this legend is literally true, it has kept the two peoples separate for hundreds of years, although in fact they live in the same settlement. The legend has reinforced basic psychological and social factors that operated against assimilation.

Why the Cleavage Persisted

First, and perhaps most important, the Tewa were a small but proud minority—only about 200 against several thousand Hopi. They refused to be assimilated: the passive Hopi, on the other hand, made no effort to impose their language or customs on the handful of militarily useful newcomers.

Secondly, while the two peoples were alike in many respects—both are Pueblo Indians with much the same ceremonial forms, and farmers at about the same technological level —they were temperamentally very different. The Tewa had come from a border region where they constantly had to defend themselves against the Plains Indians and later against the Spaniards. They had lived in a country of rivers—the Rio Grande and its tributaries—in which it was possible to work with nature to irrigate their crops. They had been exposed to a century of Spanish example in asserting control over the environment. As a result the Tewa had developed a high measure of active self-reliance.

The Hopi, in contrast, lived in a region where men easily persuaded themselves that there was little they could do about the environment. In the mesa country there were no streams, and agriculture was at the mercy of the weather. They planted maize, beans and melons in the flat washes below their mesas. When too little rain fell, their plants withered and died in the hot sun; when it poured, raging floods uprooted the plants and washed them away. Thus weather was the most important concern of the Hopi, and it shaped their attitude toward nature and human existence.

The contrasting attitudes of the Tewa and the Hopi are expressed in their religious beliefs and practices. The Tewa religion has its share of magical concepts, but the Tewa fortify their appeals to magic with practical steps. Their medicine men not only perform magical rites but also administer medicinal herbs, massage, and treatments for the injured: they are expert in setting broken bones. Their songs and dances exalt warrior prowess. When enemies threatened in the past, they formed war parties to meet them. In any crisis the Tewa offer prayers and then take action.

In the Hopi religion the dominant theme is reliance on the mystical forces believed to control the weather and natural environment. Elaborate ceremonies have been developed to coax these powers to favor the petitioners with bountiful harvests. The Hopi believe that if their rites and ceremonies are properly and regularly performed with a "good heart," there will always be enough to eat and everyone will be healthy. They depend upon the magical powers not only to provide rain for their crops but also to thwart sickness and ward off their enemies; rather than take up arms against attackers, they appeal to the deities to deflect or immobilize the enemy. The deities believed to control the destinies of men are a group of vaguely conceived ancestral gods called the *katcina*.

The religious differences between the Tewa and the Hopi clearly illustrate the nature of the two peoples—the one aggressive and self-reliant, the other passive and mystical. From the start their incompatibility of outlook, together with the Tewa's resentment as an unhonored minority, made them hostile neighbors. The Hopi feared and disliked their protectors; the Tewa responded with aloofness and contempt.

The sharpest division is in language. With constant invocation of the curse against transmission of their culture and secrets to the Hopi, the Tewa have restricted their language to their own group. Even when a Hopi marries a Tewa, the Hopi does not learn the Tewa language. The Tewa, on the other hand, do speak Hopi: to maintain necessary communication they have become bilingual. Yet they have succeeded in defending their own language so well that only a single Hopi term ("thank you") has crept into the Tewa language, and this word has gained only a partial entry—the Tewa men use the Hopi term, but the Tewa women still use the Tewa term.

Differences in Social Organization

The Tewa have borrowed the Hopi system of maternal descent, but it serves to preserve their exclusiveness. In the Tewa village, as among the Hopi, women are the important members of the family. They own the land and houses, dispense the food and make the important decisions. The men perform religious rites, exercise disciplinary powers, support the family and teach the children how to "make a living," but they have little authority in the home. Residence and family allegiance belong strictly to the mother. When a man marries, he goes to live in his wife's house, but he frequently visits his mother's house and considers that his home.

It is clear that this system supports the Tewa determination to maintain their own culture. A Tewa household is impervious to Hopi influence, even in the rare cases of intermarriage. The Hopi husband would find it extremely difficult to impose Hopi values and customs on his children, even if he were disposed to do so. Any attempt at such subversion would be countered by the mother's authority and by reminders of the curse.

The Tewa have maintained an important difference in social organization from their neighbors. A Hopi village is a loose aggregation of clans, and the maternal clans are virtually independent units. Once a year the clan heads meet to discuss the welfare of the village, but by and large ceremonial and political activities are controlled by the individual clans. The Tewa village, on the other hand, has a centralized organization. It is divided into two groups—the "winter people," and the "summer people." Every child is initiated into one of the two groups between the ages of six and ten. Each group has its own *kiva* (ceremonial house) and its own chief. The two chiefs co-operate in conducting the village's ceremonial and governmental activities, and each has special responsibilities for one half of the year.

The Hopi tolerated the independent Tewa as mercenaries who performed useful functions as protectors and go-betweens in their relations with outsiders. They turned over to the Tewa the handling of all their relations with other Indian tribes and with the white authorities, but the Hopi looked down upon these functions as work suitable only for inferiors.

This state of arm's length separation might have continued indefinitely if whites had not begun to move into the mesa country of the Hopi toward the end of the last century. The new white settlers had no intention of introducing social changes among the Indians; indeed, they were probably unaware of the differences between the Hopi and Tewa. But their coming brought an important change.

The Tewa suddenly found themselves in a situation in which their qualities were highly valued. The white scheme of values favored the practical and aggressive spirit over the mystical. The practical Tewa readily and enthusiastically took to stock-raising, wagework and the white man's schools. Their children, already trained in two languages, learned English more quickly than the Hopi's. Moreover, their higher ardor as a minority spurred them to excel in the classroom. They became models for the Hopi children.

The Hopi began to develop a new respect for the Tewa. The Tewa's role as emissaries and interpreters to the white people grew in importance and prestige. Their value orientation, remarkably like that of the new white residents, no longer had to take a back seat. The Hopi saw that "it paid to be like the whites." They were greatly impressed by the achievements of some of the Tewa in the

new climate. One of these was an interpreter who spoke five languages (Tewa, Hopi, Navaho, Spanish, and English) and had been a leader in contacts with the U.S. Indian Service and other outsiders. He became a prosperous livestock raiser, built a large house below the mesa and started a new community, now named for him. Equally impressive were the accomplishments of a Tewa woman who revived the art of pottery-making, copying old designs excavated from Indian ruins. This quickly became an important industry among both peoples.

With remarkable speed the antagonism and distinctions between the Hopi and Tewa began to disappear. The Tewa were accepted as "equals" and shed their onus as a minority. Their population has doubled in the past half century. Intermarriage has become common. The Hopi and Tewa work together in pottery manufacture, in cattle co-operatives and even in religious rituals and ceremonies. The ancient legend that had divided the groups faded in influence, and social differences began to disappear. Curiously the Tewa have remained clannish about their language, but since they are fluent in Hopi, there are no barriers to communication.

Today hostility between the two groups has virtually disappeared. Only the old men try to keep alive the ancient Hopi "injustices," but the young people tend to laugh off their admonitions and bury the memory of the "curse."

_____

The Hopi-Tewa account is a case study, and for scientific purposes has all the limitations of the case study method. A case study cannot tell what must happen or what cannot happen. It can tell only what happened and what is possible within a specific set of circumstances. If the peculiar combination of historical, environmental, and cultural factors could be very closely reproduced, similar results might be predicted, but the chances are very slight that a complex combination of factors would appear again in similar form. However, a number of important observations can be made, although they are not in any strict sense scientific generalizations:

1. The capacity of a culture to retain its integrity even while it is in intimate and prolonged contact with another culture is clearly demonstrated. On the basis of all the external circumstances, a trained observer might have expected acculturation, but it did not occur.

2. Because the Tewa were heavily outnumbered by the Hopi, their absorption might have been predicted, but this did not take place. The rugged independence of the Tewa minority and the passivity of the Hopi majority combined to permit the persistence of the Tewa as an independent population.

3. The drastic change in the orientations of the two groups toward each other was due to a change introduced from the outside. This change caused the Hopi to re-evaluate the Tewa, and a new basis for association was established.

4. Intergroup problems are not likely to be "solved" in the short run if one waits for minorities to disappear. On the other hand, this study suggests that once a pattern of change is initiated, it may go on very rapidly. That is, the relations between two peoples may proceed for a long time with little alteration. Then introduction of some new factor or event may cause a "break-through," completely restructuring relations.

Chapter IV

Socialization

By **GERTRUDE JAEGER SELZNICK**

in collaboration with L. B. and P. S.

Section 1 Introduction

The human infant comes into the world as a biological organism with animal needs and impulses. From the beginning, however, the organism is conditioned to respond in socially determined ways. The individual learns group-defined ways of acting and feeling, and he learns many of them so fundamentally that they become part of his personality. The process of building group values into the individual is called *socialization*.

From the point of view of society, socialization is the way culture is transmitted and the individual is fitted into an organized way of life. Socialization begins very early, and in due course the child learns to take part in group life and to embody in some degree the values of his society and of groups within it. Socialization also continues into adult life. As the individual participates in new social forms and institutions, he learns new disciplines and develops new values. For example, learning to be a parent and assuming family responsibilities are for most people important parts of their adult socialization. While parents are usually the chief agents for socializing the child, they are themselves socialized in taking on the parental role and the values of parenthood.

From the point of view of the individual, socialization is the fulfillment of his potentialities for personal growth and development. Socialization humanizes the biological organism and transforms it into a *self* having a sense of identity, capable of disciplining and ordering behavior, and endowed with ideals, values, and ambitions. Socialization regulates behavior, but it is also the indispensable condition for individuality and self-awareness.

BIOLOGICAL BASIS OF SOCIALIZATION

Man's biological nature makes socialization both possible and necessary. For example, socialization could not occur if man did not have the inborn capacity to learn and use language. Yet, apart from socialization, this potentiality cannot be realized. The following are some of the biological characteristics of the human animal upon which socialization is based:

Absence of Instincts

An instinct is a relatively complex behavior pattern that is biologically fixed for the species. The nest-building instinct of birds is a familiar example. If man possessed such biologically fixed behaviors, they would place limits upon his learning and his socialization, and variation or change in important areas of his life would then be impossible. However, man has no true instincts. He does have a number of built-in reflexes; for example, the human infant spontaneously sucks when his lips are stimulated, and the pupil of the eye contracts in the presence of light. But except for reactions of this kind, man's behavior is not rigidly determined by his biological make-up.

Instead of by instincts, human behavior is impelled by less specific biological drives. A drive, such as hunger or sex, is an organic tension that is felt as discomfort or impulse but does not direct behavior to specific goals. It impels activity but does not determine it. The fact that man is activated by drives rather than by biologically fixed behavior patterns makes his needs amenable to social direction.

The observations of Maslow indicate that biological drives can be redirected, even among infrahuman primates.[1] He observed that much sexual behavior in monkeys had a more *social* than biological significance. Monkeys used sexual forms of behavior to establish dominance and express submission.

Childhood Dependence

Man has a long period of physical dependence upon others, further prolonged by his need to learn the social and technological skills of social living. Because of the biological helplessness of the infant and the social ineptness of the young, it is necessary to fix responsibility for child care and training. Social control over biological mating transforms it into the social institution of the family, the helplessness of the child thus contributing to the socialization of adults.

The long period of physical dependence

encourages emotional dependence, and ties of feeling develop between the child and those who care for him, whether they are his biological parents or others.

Capacity to Learn

The long period of childhood dependence would be relatively fruitless if the child were not highly educable throughout. Although abilities vary from one individual to another, the high level of man's intelligence is one of his innate biological potentialities. The human being can learn more than other animals and can continue to learn more over a longer period of time. The young chimpanzee learns as well as, and in some respects better than, a human infant of the same age, but his rate of learning soon declines.

Language

Man's ability to learn is directly related to his capacity for language. Other animals have intelligence, but because he has language man alone has reason. When a chimpanzee fits some poles together to secure an otherwise unobtainable banana, he might be said to have insight into the principle of addition. But without language he can neither reflect upon the principle nor elaborate it, nor can he convey it *as a principle* to his offspring. Only through language can insight be formulated as knowledge and transmitted to and shared with others, thus becoming a social rather than merely an individual possession.

Language can also express and arouse emotion, conveying values and attitudes as well as knowledge. Whether as a vehicle for knowledge or for attitudes, language is the key factor in the creation of human society. By making possible the communication of ideas, it frees response and interaction from the limited confines of the purely biological. It makes possible *symbolic* interaction, upon which human society depends. For example, through the symbolic forms of debate and discussion, opposing interests may be ex-

---

[1] A. H. Maslow, "The role of dominance in the social and sexual behavior of infrahuman primates: III. A theory of sexual behavior of infrahuman primates," *Journal of Genetic Psychology*, **48** (1936), 310–38.

pressed and settled without a show of force. Some other animals follow leaders, but language makes possible the conception of leadership and its eventual elaboration into the institution of government.

AIMS OF SOCIALIZATION

Through socialization society teaches the child what he needs to know if he is to be integrated into the community and what he needs to learn if he is to develop his potentialities and find stable and meaningful satisfactions. The individual is not born with the ability to participate in group activity but must learn to take account of others, to co-ordinate his behavior with that of others, to share, and to co-operate. Socialization is a kind of social control exercised both to strengthen group life and to foster the development of the individual.

1. Socialization inculcates basic *disciplines,* ranging from toilet habits to the method of science. Undisciplined behavior is prompted by impulse—fleeting needs and impressions. It ignores future consequences and stable satisfactions. Disciplined behavior restricts immediate gratifications by postponing, foregoing, or modifying them, sometimes for the sake of social approval, sometimes to insure a future goal.

Disciplines vary in the extent to which they are internalized, that is, built into the individual. In American culture much behavior is regulated by time schedules: employees and students are expected to be on time. The alarm clock testifies to the inadequate internalization of this particular discipline, but the fact that late risers are usually apologetic is evidence that some internalization has taken place.

Disciplines can reach so deep that they modify physiological responses; many people waken early whether they want to or not. Sometimes individuals become incapable of performing socially prohibited acts. A person may become physically ill after eating tabooed food. The sexual impulse may be so hemmed in by social prohibitions that impotence results.

2. Socialization instills *aspirations,* such as the desire to be a good mother. Disciplines and aspirations are closely related. For the individual, disciplines are often arduous and unrewarding in themselves, but aspirations help to sustain disciplines by making it easier and more meaningful to give up immediate satisfactions.

Society transmits not only general cultural values that define its way of life but also more specific aspirations. A religion organized around a priesthood must be able to motivate some of its adherents to become priests. An economy built upon an advanced technology must be able to motivate some of its members to become scientists and engineers. Such aspirations often entail considerable self-denial, and socialization must succeed in inculcating these aspirations as ideals to be pursued for their own sake rather than merely for material reward.

3. Socialization teaches *social roles* and their supporting attitudes. Group membership requires more than a general ability to take account of others in a social relation; it requires the more specific ability to play specialized roles. Leaders and followers, pupils and teachers, play different and complementary parts. The individual learns how to co-ordinate his behavior with that of others and to adjust to particular circumstances by means of roles.

A role also specifies the virtues, feelings, attitudes, and personality traits proper to it. Pupils are supposed to be eager and alert, teachers patient and wise, the army officer aloof, the enlisted man obedient.

4. Socialization teaches *skills,* providing the individual with a basic preparation for participation in adult activities. Many skills are specifically social, such as writing letters, dealing with neighbors, using the telephone, and ordering dinner. Social skills can be important preconditions of effective participation in political or other associations.

DELIBERATE AND UNCONSCIOUS SOCIALIZATION

Much of the socialization of the child, especially within the family, the school, and the church is deliberate. Adults hold certain values explicitly, convey them verbally to the child, and support them with rewards and punishments. Cleanliness, promptness, obedience, and manliness are familiar examples.

Socialization is also a product of spontaneous human interaction and occurs without deliberate intent to train. Because the individual is part of the environment of others, people may try to control and direct his behavior, not in order to educate him but to insure their own comfort and well-being. The child who spoils a game of baseball because he has not learned the rules may be socialized by the scorn of his playmates, although their interest is in protecting their own enjoyment, not in socializing him. Parents are under many different kinds of pressure to socialize the child, but not the least of these is the fact that the undisciplined child is disruptive of the adult environment.

The child responds at least as much to postural cues and expressions of feeling as to statements of approval and disapproval. Implicit values and unverbalized attitudes can be the most important elements in socialization when they are embodied in behavior toward the child. Verbal injunctions that are not reinforced in the lives and attitudes of parents are relatively ineffective.

SOCIALIZATION AND CONFORMITY

Socialization inevitably produces a degree of conformity. People brought up under similar circumstances tend to resemble each other in habits, values, and personality. However, socialization need not result in complete conformity. Many factors are present that encourage individuality and uniqueness. Only three are mentioned here:

1. Socialization is not smooth and uniform. The individual is socialized by many agencies—the family, the school, his play-mates, his occupation, and in a literate society by the written word. If they emphasize different values, the agencies may compete for the loyalty of the individual and, therefore, reduce his conformity to any one group's values. Bright children of lower-class families may be encouraged in school to pursue advanced study, but family values may discourage intellectual aspirations.

2. Nonconformity may be a value in itself and be transmitted, like any other value, through the socialization process, e.g., individuals learn to think well of someone who has a mind of his own.

3. The kind of socialization to which the individual is exposed is to some extent modified by his unique capacities. Very little is known about the relation between the biological potentialities of the newborn infant and the abilities of the mature adult. Although all capacities depend on training for their full realization, some seem to be inborn —for example, intelligence and mathematical and musical talent. It may be that irritable or placid, responsive or passive temperaments are also biologically innate tendencies. To some extent, how a person is socialized depends upon these potentialities and tendencies. The child learns only what he is taught, but what he is taught depends to some degree upon what he can learn. This is evident in the case of extraordinary talent or lack of it, but the same principle is involved when parents adjust their discipline to the responses of the average child.

Section 2 treats the socialization of the child and the emergence of the self with special attention to personal interaction and the interplay of response between parent and child. In Section 3 the agencies of socialization are considered, especially their unique functions and their distinctive capacities to reach the individual. Section 4 discusses adult socialization, including the importance of social roles in the development of individual personality. Section 5 deals with culture, personality, and human nature.

SOURCES AND READINGS

James H. S. Bossard and Eleanor S. Boll, *The Sociology of Child Development* (3rd ed.; New York: Harper, 1960).

Robert E. L. Faris, *Social Psychology* (New York: Ronald, 1952).

Hans Gerth and C. Wright Mills, *Character and Social Structure* (New York: Harcourt, Brace, 1953).

John J. Honigmann, *Culture and Personality* (New York: Harper, 1952).

Edwin M. Lemert, *Social Pathology* (New York: McGraw-Hill, 1951).

Alfred R. Lindesmith and Anselm L. Strauss, *Social Psychology* (New York: Dryden, 1949).

Gardner Lindzey (ed.), *Handbook of Social Psychology*, 2 vols. (Cambridge: Addison-Wesley, 1954).

William E. Martin and Celia Burns Stendler, *Child Development* (New York: Harcourt, Brace, 1953).

Daniel R. Miller and Guy E. Swanson, *The Changing American Parent* (New York: Wiley, 1958).

Theodore M. Newcomb, *Social Psychology* (New York: Dryden, 1950).

Jean Piaget, *Language and Thought of the Child* (New York: Harcourt, Brace, 1926).

David Riesman, in collaboration with Reuel Denney and Nathan Glazer, *The Lonely Crowd* (New Haven: Yale University Press, 1950).

Muzafer Sherif and Carolyn W. Sherif, *An Outline of Social Psychology* (rev. ed.; New York: Harper, 1956).

Tamotsu Shibutani, *Society and Personality* (Englewood Cliffs: Prentice-Hall, 1961).

Anselm L. Strauss (ed.), *The Social Psychology of George Herbert Mead* (Chicago: Phoenix Books, University of Chicago Press, 1956).

Journal of Abnormal and Social Psychology.

Sociometry.

Section 2 **Socializing the child**

The molding of the child, whether deliberate or unintentional, is accomplished through person-to-person interaction. The social response of the parent, though geared to an immediate life situation, is based upon needs and values already formed in a particular culture and society. The child responds in turn, and in this mutuality of interaction the drama of socialization is acted out.

RESPONSES TO THE CHILD

The newborn infant is responded to as a biological organism; he is taken care of and given physical attention. His primary need is food, and his most important early experiences center around the act of feeding and being fed. Between maximum satisfaction and starvation lies a wide range of variation. Feeding habits differ from culture to culture and from family to family. In some groups the infant may be fed whenever he cries, in others, only at rigidly prescribed intervals. He may be nursed until well into childhood, or may be weaned early. Some infants experience alternate periods of satiation and neglect. The way the infant's biological needs are met and the degree of satisfaction and deprivation he experiences convey an image of the world as either niggardly or indulgent, capricious or reliable. This image may remain as a permanent part of adult character, especially if it is reinforced by later experience.

The infant is also responded to in an emotional way. Attitudes of rejection or acceptance, approval or disapproval, tension or relaxation color the physical care he receives. The act of feeding, for example, is accompanied by the mother's attitudes and physical postures, which are prompted by cultural values or psychological traits. In the 1920's the middle-class culture of the United States dictated a degree of aloofness and rigidity toward the child, but in the 1940's permissiveness was encouraged in child rearing. The mother may regard the infant as a fulfill-

The child has more than one kind of guardian, and the ways of being cared for are many and diverse. While one is entertained to forestall restless boredom, another is held for comforting and nearness.

ment or a nuisance, a natural product of marriage or a disruption of her life and interests.

Importance of Emotional Responses

As the infant grows to childhood, emotional responses to his behavior take on increased importance. The adult's responses change from efforts to satisfy his bodily needs into attitudes of approval and disapproval designed to encourage him to exercise self-control. Thus the child is encouraged to feed himself and to renounce the satisfactions of being fed. He must learn to control his elimination and to stop depending upon his mother for cleanliness.

There are also emotion-laden responses to the child as a person, toward his appearance, his intelligence, and his temperament. The parents have cultural and personal images of what they are and what they expect the child to be. They respond to the child in terms of their own psychological needs, their position in the class, status, and role structure of society, and their ambitions for the child.

RESPONSES OF THE CHILD

The earliest reactions of the human infant are biological responses to his own inner states of comfort and discomfort. When he cries, he neither knows that he cries nor does he purposefully cry to gain attention. Gradually the infant associates his crying with the attention and satisfaction he receives. He learns to employ the cry as a purposive act to call forth a ministering response. By employing the cry to stimulate response in another, the infant enters in a primitive way into interpersonal communication. Later the child is able to forego crying and say instead, "I am hungry."

The physical dependence of the child upon the parents and in particular upon the mother soon develops into emotional involvement. This emotional involvement arises largely because the parents are a source of *both* frustration and satisfaction.

1. *Rage and hostility*. The human organism does not suffer deprivation and frustration passively. It reacts by manifesting rage, anger, hostility, and aggression. As the child matures and is expected to control his impulses, part of his frustration and deprivation may be expressed as hostility and resentment against those adults who are the source of his frustration. One of the important problems the child faces in the course of socialization is the management of his aggressive impulses and his frustration.

2. *Anxiety*. Rage and hostility are immediate, sharply defined emotional responses, capable of being "discharged" by some act of aggression against the offending object. Anxiety, in contrast, is a diffuse emotional state that arises from threatening uncertainty, doubt, and inner conflict. Anxiety is a kind of fear, but whereas fear is a response to a definite danger, anxiety is a vague, uneasy apprehensiveness. It is experienced when the outcome of a situation is in doubt or when one feels threatened by an unknown danger.

Man has been called the rational animal and the social animal. He has also been called the anxious animal. It may be that the prolonged dependence of the human child upon the care of others makes man peculiarly prone to anxiety. In Western society, where the natural parents are usually the primary source of attention and care, the child's anxiety is probably greater than in societies where more people care for him.

As the child matures, other sources of anxiety are introduced. In Western society, a premium is placed upon independence and self-sufficiency. Before he enters school, the child is expected to be independent of his mother to the extent of feeding himself, managing his bodily functions, and controlling his aggressions and expressions of rage and hostility. He is then introduced to a formal and competitive system of education, where further demands are made upon his self-control. He is supposed to set goals for himself and to achieve them. Later, he is expected to choose a career, trade, or profession, to leave the parental home, and to make his own way. At every hand is the possibility of failure, and the fear of failure carries its burden of anxiety.

3. *Love and affection.* Little is known about the origins of human love, but the love of the child for the parents probably begins as an extension of the aura of satisfaction resulting from care and attention. Momentary and transitory feelings, at first tied to immediate satisfactions, are reinforced and strengthened and come to have an autonomy and independence of their own.

The child needs to be able to evoke positive feelings from the parents. Clinical studies of delinquent and maladjusted children show the destructive effects of parental rejection and lack of love. The failure to evoke love in the parents may result in the atrophy of the ability to love and in what has been called a "fear" of loving. In extreme cases, even when they were removed to environments of love and satisfaction, some delinquent children were unable to return the positive feelings extended toward them with anything but further hatred and hostility.[2] In less extreme cases, the failure to evoke love results in anxiety, in a sense of uncertainty, threat, and personal inadequacy.

THE EMERGENCE OF A SELF

Whenever the individual takes on group values, some change in him and in his selfhood occurs. Furthermore, the initial creation of the self takes place in the process of socialization.

Two important contributors to the understanding of the emergence of the self within the socialization process are the pragmatist philosopher, George Herbert Mead, and Sigmund Freud, the founder of psychoanalysis. Their views are by no means incompat-

ible, but each stressed different aspects of the relation between the self and the social group. Mead, whose views are summarized in Adaptation 7 (pp. 105 ff.), emphasized the emergence of human rationality and creativity within the socialization process. Freud,[3] on the other hand, emphasized the repressive and frustrating aspects of group life. Where Mead was interested in the potentialities of society for freeing the individual, Freud was interested in the ways group life constrains and distorts the self.

Both Mead and Freud divided the self into "parts." Mead saw the self as partly conventional, that is, part of the self takes the attitudes and opinions of others into account; but he saw another part of the self as spontaneous and creative. Mead called this part the active "I," and the conventional and passive part of the self, the "me." If group life is rigid and restrictive, the "me" dominates the "I" and individuality is minimal. But, under appropriate social conditions, the "I" can actively and creatively influence and restructure the social process.

Freud divided the self into "id," "ego," and "superego." The superego is roughly equivalent to Mead's "me." The id is essentially the biological core of the self that society tries to but can never thoroughly domesticate. The ego is a kind of mediator trying to effect a compromise between the individual's biological needs and the demands of society. Where Mead saw the possibility of harmony between the "I" and the "me," Freud saw the potentialities for conflict among the various parts of the self.

From these views can be derived at least three important ways in which socialization creates a self.

1. *Socialization creates a self-image.* Through interaction with others and through language, the individual comes to think of himself as an "I." As he perceives the attitudes of others toward this "I," he de-

[2] Fritz Redl and David Wineman, *Children Who Hate: The Disorganization and Breakdown of Behavior Controls* (Glencoe: The Free Press, 1951).

[3] Sigmund Freud, *An Outline of Psychoanalysis* (New York: Norton, 1949), pp. 19, 121.

Margaret ignores the camera . . .   *Karl and his playmate confront it tentatively . . .*

. . . while Dotty's class poses proudly.

GROWING SELF-AWARENESS

velops a self-image. He takes on a view of himself from observing the way others respond to him. For this reason Cooley spoke of a "looking-glass self." [4] The behavior of others toward him is the mirror in which the individual sees himself.

The attitudes that enter into the individual's self-image are, for the most part, emotive; they are attitudes of approval and disapproval, acceptance or rejection, interest or indifference. They are judgments upon the child, sometimes based on his genuine potentialities, sometimes reflecting the meaning of his potentialities for the life of the significant adults around him. In either case, the judgments that others direct toward the child, expressed in their attitudes toward him, are judgments the child is likely to make of himself.

The importance of self-images is most easily observed in pathological behavior, where socialization has created a self-image harmful to the person. In situations of neglect, deprivation, and rejection, the child may come to think of himself as inadequate; because he is unloved, he may think of himself as inherently unlovable. In extreme situations he may develop self-hatred. The child who steals may be socially defined by others as delinquent, and may come to identify himself as delinquent, and may seek out other delinquents to gain approval for his self-image.

2. *Socialization creates the ideal self.* From the attitudes of others toward himself, the individual also creates an image of what he ought to be in order to secure love and approval. The tendency of socialization to arouse in the child a need for love and approval and to construct an ideal version of himself is a double-edged sword. The identification of the self with ideal values, goals, and roles is an important aspect of socialization because it helps to sustain disciplines. On the other hand, if there is too great a discrepancy between the potentialities of the person and his ideal self, or if the ideal self makes extreme and unrealistic demands, the result will be a sense of inadequacy and failure.

3. *Socialization creates an ego.* Much of the behavior of parents toward their children after infancy is directed toward insuring the child's self-control and independence. As he matures, he is expected to develop *inner* controls, to establish his own relations to the world, and to set his own goals. Socialization is directed, therefore, toward creating a self capable of controlling and directing its own behavior.

The ego is what it does. It is a name for the integrative, controlling functions of the self, some of which are listed in Table IV: 1. In recent years the importance of these functions for the well-being of personality and its integration into society has been increasingly recognized.

STATIC AND DYNAMIC ADAPTATION

Part of socialization is more or less routine learning and adjustment, in which habits are formed and perceptions of the self and the world are acquired. Some adjustments, however, have deeper impact upon the personality and generate inner tensions, needs, and strivings. Fromm has distinguished static and dynamic adaptation:

By static adaptation we mean such an adaptation to patterns as leaves the whole character structure unchanged and implies only the adoption of a new habit. An example of this kind of adaptation is the change from the Chinese habit of eating to the Western habit of using fork and knife. A Chinese coming to America will adapt himself to this new pattern, but this adaptation in itself has little effect on his personality; it does not arouse new drives or character traits.

By dynamic adaptation we refer to the kind of adaptation that occurs, for example, when a boy submits to the commands of his strict and threatening father—being too much afraid of him to do otherwise—and becomes a "good" boy. While he adapts himself to the necessities of the situation, something happens in him. He may de-

[4] Charles Horton Cooley, *Human Nature and the Social Order* (rev. ed.; New York; Scribner's, 1922), p. 184.

Table **IV:1** Functions of the Ego*

Ego Function	Adequate Ego	Inadequate Ego
Tolerating frustration	Can substitute another goal for one that is blocked	Has a temper tantrum
Coping with insecurity, anxiety, and fear	Is able to develop psychological "defense mechanisms"	Can only flee or attack
Resisting temptation	Can resist immediate gratifications for the sake of long-range goals	Has impulses stirred by whatever promises immediate gratification
Assessing reality	Adjusts behavior to particular circumstances and people	May see all authority figures as replicas of parents
Facing guilt	Has guilt feelings and can right a wrong	Has few guilt feelings and tries to evade them
Establishing inner controls	Can substitute inner control when external supervision is withdrawn	Quickly falls into disorganized behavior when outside controls are removed
Resisting group intoxication	Is slow to respond to group excitement	Easily loses control under impact of group excitement
Being realistic about rules and routines	Does not feel persecuted by rules and routines	Interprets rules and routines as directed against self
Dealing with failure, success, and mistakes	Can correct a mistake and is proud of success	Takes mistake as sign of absolute worthlessness, success as a sign of absolute worth
Maintaining ego integrity	Expresses, but does not lose, own values in group activity	Gives in easily to the authority of the group

*Adapted from Fritz Redl and David Wineman, *Children Who Hate: The Disorganization and Breakdown of Behavior Controls* (Glencoe: The Free Press, 1951), Chapter III, "The Ego That Cannot Perform," pp. 74–140. This is a study of delinquent children with severe psychological and social difficulties.

velop an intense hostility against his father, which he represses, since it would be too dangerous to express it or even to be aware of it. This repressed hostility, however, though not manifest, is a dynamic factor in his character structure. It may create new anxiety and thus lead to still deeper submission; it may set up a vague defiance, directed against no one in particular but rather toward life in general. . . . This kind of adaptation creates something new in him, arouses new drives and new anxieties.[5]

In part because of dynamic adaptation, there is often a considerable discrepancy be-

tween what parents want their children to be and the way they actually turn out.

IDENTIFICATION

One of the important mechanisms by which the individual takes on the values of others is *identification*. The term is loosely used to sum up a number of different ways in which one person puts himself in the place of another. People are said to identify with others when they are able to feel sympathy for another's plight, to understand and perhaps even experience the emotions someone else is experiencing, and to treat others as they themselves would like to be treated.

[5] Erich Fromm, *Escape From Freedom* (New York: Rinehart, 1941), pp. 15–16. Reprinted by permission.

The normal tendency of the child to take the same attitudes toward himself that others take toward him is also a form of identification. If the average child does not steal, it is not because he has reached the rational conclusion that it is unwise or inexpedient to do so. Rather he takes the same morally disapproving attitude toward such behavior that others take toward it. He identifies with the adult point of view, and the thought of stealing prompts feelings of guilt.

It is also normal for the child to take the same attitudes toward his environment that his "significant others" take toward him. The little girl who is spanked by her mother may in turn spank her dolls, acting toward her dolls as her mother acts toward her. She identifies with her mother according to her limited experience of what a mother does and feels.

There is a stronger and more specific sense in which children identify with others. Some adults in the child's experience appear to him as ideal figures; the child wants to be like them and *models* himself upon them. In early childhood, he identifies with one or both of his parents. Later, he may develop "crushes" on teachers and peers and take them as ideal images to be emulated. Identification of this sort is often temporary, but it can permanently shape character and personality.

This type of identification is not well understood. Some believe that identification with a parent or other authority figure, such as a teacher, is an effort to take over adult mastery and power, which appear overwhelming and desirable in the child's eyes. Some believe that it is an effort to gain approval, while others relate identification more closely to the child's efforts to establish self-esteem. To be like those one admires is a way of admiring oneself. In this way the ego finds internal gratification in self-approval and becomes less dependent upon the approval of others. Still others interpret identification as an effort to guarantee self-control and self-discipline. Among the greatest threats to the child's sense of security are his own aggressive impulses and his tendency to revert to uncontrolled behavior, e.g., a temper tantrum. This kind of behavior meets with rejection and counteraggression. One way to insure mastery over his impulses and to establish an inner control is to take over the values of an admired figure as a guide.

Identification is part of the normal process of growing up and becoming a mature adult. Through it, ideals are taken on by the growing child, and models of behavior are transmitted from one generation to the next. Identification continues throughout life, although the mature adult is likely to identify himself less with persons than with principles, roles, jobs, organizations, and causes. There are degrees of identification. A person identifies with his job to the extent that his self-esteem depends upon continuing in it and doing it successfully. A person identifies with an organization to the extent that he takes on its values.

Conclusions

1. *The child is active in socialization.* (*a*) Parents respond and adjust to the characteristics of the child. (*b*) The child does not absorb values as a sponge absorbs water; values may be smoothly accepted, or rejected, or modified in the course of dynamic adaptation.

2. *The self is social.* There is no self prior to interaction; the self develops only out of communication with others.

3. *The most significant interactions are emotional.* Not all communicative interaction has equal weight in the formation of personality. When interaction has emotional import, it reaches most deeply and has a more lasting effect on the core of personality.

4. *The management of impulse and tension is a strategic goal of socialization.* As a necessary condition for social participation and learning, this management is a critical point at which the normal and pathological begin to divide.

Caution: To say that the self is social does not mean that it transcends its biological origins. The social self transforms but does not eradicate the biological. Nor is the self necessarily socialized in all its aspects. Some biolog-ical impulses may not be adequately integrated with social goals. Furthermore, the idea of a social self does not imply that the individual lacks a unique identity or is not a whole and independent person.

Mind, Self and Society

A summary and interpretation of George H. Mead, *Mind, Self and Society* (Chicago: University of Chicago Press, 1934). Quotations by permission of The University of Chicago Press.

Though George Herbert Mead was a fundamental and highly influential thinker, he never presented his ideas in book-length form, and the four volumes published under his name are for the most part stenographic reports of lectures. *Mind, Self and Society* represents notes taken during 1927 and 1930 in Mead's Social Psychology, a course he had given since 1900.

Both as philosopher and social psychologist Mead was concerned with socialization. As a philosopher he was interested in the question: Which came first, the individual or society? Many philosophers, in trying to account for the existence of society, assumed that individuals endowed with mind and self-consciousness could exist prior to or outside society. According to one version of the contract theory of society, man first lived in a state of nature in which each individual pursued his desires as best he could. This wholly individual pursuit of satisfaction resulted, however, in "the war of all against all." Therefore, in the interests of self-preservation and to render their satisfactions more secure, men "contracted" with each other to accept authority and live according to some "rules of the game," that is, they agreed to create society. Sophisticated contract theorists probably did not believe that a pure state of nature ever actually existed, and in any case were more concerned to *justify* social norms than to trace their historical origins. Nevertheless, their argument did assume that it made sense to talk of a "natural man," who was possessed of mind and selfhood.

Together with such other pragmatists as John Dewey, Mead insisted that the human individual endowed with mind and self is the *product,* not the creator, of society. "The self . . . is essentially a social structure, and it arises in social experience. After a self has arisen, it in a certain sense provides for itself its social experiences, and so we can conceive of an absolutely solitary self. But it is impossible to conceive of a self arising outside of social experience." (*Mind, Self and Society,* p. 140)

Minds and selves, Mead argued, arise only in the process of social interaction and communication; they cannot antedate society. But how can social interaction and communication occur before there are minds and selves? Mead reasoned that the capacity to interact and communicate is a biological endowment of the higher orders of animal life. Indeed communication by non-verbal means within the context of some shared activity is a precondition for the emergence of language. Why then does only man have society? The answer lies in language, which man alone possesses. Language adds a new dimension to primitive, subhuman interaction and communication by making socialization possible. Through lan-

George Herbert Mead (1863–1931) was for many years a member of the faculty of philosophy at the University of Chicago. More than anyone else he can be said to have clarified and illuminated the nature of social psychology. A thoroughgoing empiricist, Mead nevertheless disagreed sharply with the atomistic conception of man characteristic of seventeenth- and eighteenth-century "scientific" philosophy. This philosophy placed man firmly in the natural order of things; yet it made the error of assuming that man was "naturally" endowed with both reason and self-consciousness. Mead contended that reason and self-awareness, though natural potentialities of man, could not be realized except in society. Early empiricism was atomistic because it conceived of individuals "forming" society the way atoms form matter. Mead recognized the atomistic analogy as a false one and showed that the individual is dependent upon society for his distinctive attributes as a human being, that is, for mind and self.

guage man internalizes the attitudes of other individuals and of the social groups in which he participates. In this way social control arises. Finally, mind and self-consciousness emerge when social interaction is accompanied by, and accomplished through, language.

Mead argued that the distinctive task of social psychology is to explain how society "gets into" the individual, determines his behavior, and thus becomes part of his psychology, or of his "selfhood." He also advanced specific hypotheses concerning stages in the development of the self from the narrow capacity to take on the attitudes of other individuals to the more generalized capacity to relate to the community.

The essentials of Mead's point of view may be stated in a few key propositions. These are briefly presented and explained in the following discussion.

PRE-VERBAL INTERACTION

Social interaction precedes language, mind, and self-consciousness. Among many animal species sexual union and care of the young make necessary at least some continuing interaction with another individual; thus, rudimentary family life exists among species lower than man. In most cases common co-operative acts are necessitated by biological differences in capacity or function, of which sexual differentiation is the most striking example.

Sometimes physical differentiation is so pervasive as to make almost the entire life process a common act. In the case of ants and bees, some individuals are biologically equipped to perform only one function, such as reproduction or food-getting. The survival of both individual and species depends upon the interaction of highly specific biological roles in a complex pattern of co-operative acts. In this way ant and bee "societies" arise.

But their organization is, strictly speaking, a biological one, and interaction is based on physical and chemical cues.

Non-verbal communication must precede language. Interaction, even on the biological level, is a kind of communication; otherwise, common acts could not occur. A dancing male bird does not deliberately intend to communicate a readiness to mate; yet communication occurs because it is more or less guaranteed by the nervous system of his species. As a rule, the dance does arouse an appropriate response in a female, much as if she "understood" the meaning of the male's behavior.

The dance communicates because it stands for something else. It is not an isolated, meaningless bit of behavior. It is a *natural sign,* a product and manifestation of a state of organic tension, of a physiological readiness to mate. The impulses behind the mating dance, moreover, require for their relief appropriate behavior on the part of another. Thus, because the dance is a natural sign directed toward another, it can be viewed as a *gesture,* that is, as non-verbal communicative behavior.

If man could not first participate in a non-verbal "conversation" of gestures, he could never communicate by means of language. Before language can convey meaning *to* the child, the behavior of his mother must have meaning *for* him. He could never understand the meaning of "angry" or "hungry" unless he could comprehend an angry or a nurturing gesture. Nor would his mother's gesture have meaning for the child unless both were participants in an ongoing mutual activity. The emergence of language depends upon the existence of already established, albeit primitive, social interaction.

THE IMPORTANCE OF LANGUAGE

Language creates minds and selves. Despite interaction and communication, neither mind nor self-consciousness need be present in these primitive social acts; indeed without language they cannot be. Language alone makes possible ideas and communication by means of ideas.

The male bird's mating dance has meaning for the female when it prompts an answering response from her, but it cannot be said to have meaning for the dancing male. He is simply behaving. *He* is not telling the other he is ready to mate; if anything "tells" the other, it is the dance and not the dancing bird. The bird's behavior communicates, but not the bird.

Language makes it possible to replace behavior with ideas. Though the mother can teach her child the meaning of "I am angry" only by behaving in appropriate ways, once the child learns the words, the mother need not behave in an angry fashion in order to communicate displeasure. Having learned what the words mean, the child now has the *idea* of anger. Because mother and child now share an idea, the child can respond to what the mother says as well as to what she does. It is the mother (not merely her behavior) that now communicates.

Furthermore, having the idea of anger, the child can *think* about his mother's anger; it can have meaning for him even when she is absent or not angry. Thus as the child acquires language he acquires mind. He also becomes self-conscious as he reflects not only about his mother's anger but about himself and his own behavior. Thus he acquires a self. The attitudes of others, such as his mother's anger, lead him to modify his inner self as well as his external actions. As he matures, the child no longer adjusts merely to the immediate expression of approval and disapproval; he changes himself and his ways in order to achieve a stable adjustment to other people and his environment. He *takes the attitudes of others* into himself as enduring guides and standards, as part of his own personality.

THE SOCIAL SELF

Mind and self are social. Much of language is factual, simply identifying objects about which people communicate. Though factual, these meanings are nevertheless social; they are shared and common meanings. In time "dog" and "cat" and "cow" come to have the same factual meaning for the child that they do for others.

Through language the child also learns the attitudes and emotions with which objects are viewed by his parents and others. The factual and emotive meanings of words are separable in analysis, but in practice they are learned together, and language transmits not only names of objects but appropriate or pre-scribed attitudes toward the objects named. Some of these are designed to enable the child better to deal with his physical environment; for example, attitudes of wariness and cau-tion go along with "dog" and "fire." Others are, however, social in a more distinctive sense. Factually "cow" means the same to a Hindu as to an American, but to the Hindu child the meaning of "cow" also includes at-titudes of religious reverence and respect. Thus as he learns language the child is initi-ated into a world of shared and social mean-ings; he shares the meanings that objects have for his social group.

Just as the child learns to take the same attitudes toward objects in his environment that others take toward them, so he learns to take the same attitudes toward himself that others take toward him. When the mother tells the child that he has done something good or bad, right or wrong, she is not trying to teach him merely what the words mean. She treats the child as an object toward which she takes a certain attitude, and tries to in-duce the child to do the same. He is encour-aged to take himself as an object to be evalu-ated and controlled in the same way that he evaluates and controls other objects, and to do so from the standpoint of someone else. He is taught, in short, to make appropriate or prescribed responses to his own behavior just as he has been taught to make appropri-ate or prescribed responses to other objects in his environment.

Because this control occurs through taking the attitudes of others toward oneself, because it is control from the standpoint of someone else, it is distinctively social in nature. In this way society "gets into" the individual. Of all the animals, man alone is able to excercise self-criticism; but all self-criticism is social criticism insofar as the principles that guide it are the result of internalizing the attitudes of others toward oneself.

Prior to using the attitudes of others to think about himself, the young child is not *self*-conscious. As an animal, the human child is conscious. He has sensations, feelings, and perceptions of which he is aware. It is by thinking about himself in the light of the at-titudes of others toward him that the individ-ual becomes self-conscious and begins to acquire a social self.

As the individual matures he develops the capacity to respond to a "generalized other." All higher forms of communication depend upon the capacity of each to put himself in the place of the other, that is, to control his own responses in terms of an understanding of what the other's responses are likely to be. As he learns to control his behavior in the light of another individual's attitudes either toward that behavior or toward the environ-ment, the individual can be said to be learn-ing to take the role of the other. He responds to himself and to the world as he anticipates the other would respond. The capacity to put oneself in the place of the other emerges only with maturity and in the process of social in-teraction and communication.

The child first internalizes the attitudes of particular individuals, primarily his parents, toward himself. At this stage he does not have the capacity to participate in organized group life or to engage in complex, co-operative games governed by impersonal rules. Social interaction is limited to interaction with spe-cific individuals, and behavior is largely de-termined by the child's experience with those who are not merely others but *significant* others for him. At this stage of development, his play consists largely of simple role-taking. He plays at being a mother, father, doctor, or postman. He re-enacts the behavior and attitudes of others as individuals.

The child gradually learns, however, a less personalized, more complex form of role-taking as expressed in his developing ability to participate in organized games. In baseball, for example, it is not the acting out of a highly specific individual role that is required. The player adjusts his behavior from moment to moment, and does so in the light of what a number of others are doing and of the rules and purposes of the game. In performing his role, he responds to a *generalized other.*

Mead used this term to designate "The organized community or social group which gives to the individual his unity of self. . . ." (*Op. cit.,* p. 154) One who takes the standpoint of the generalized other knows what is required to keep the group to its distinctive aims and rules. He sees not only his own role, not only the roles of particular others, but the ways roles are related in determining the outcome of group activity. Gradually the individual takes on the point of view of the community as a whole.

THE "I" AND THE "ME"

The social self has a creative, spontaneous aspect. To stress the essentially social nature of the self may seem to imply that the self is completely determined by the internalized attitudes of others. This is not so. To be sure, the internalized attitudes of others represent what the individual takes into account when he acts; they are the demands that group life actually or supposedly makes upon him. Nevertheless, his behavior has a large element of freedom and spontaneity. The demands of the social situation pose a problem to the acting individual, but there is considerable leeway in how he meets the problem. Furthermore, the individual can never predict precisely what his response in a given situation will be. The baseball player wants to play good ball; in this sense his behavior is deter-

mined by accepting the demands and standards of the group. But whether he will make a brilliant play or an error neither he nor anyone else knows beforehand.

Mead called the acting self the "I." The "me," on the other hand, is that part of the self that is an organization of the internalized attitudes of others. The "I" represents the self insofar as it is free, has initiative, novelty, and uniqueness. The "me" represents the conventional part of the self. The "I" responds to the "me" and takes it into account, but it is not identical with it.

There may be varying amounts of "I" and "me" in behavior. In impulsive behavior the "me" is absent; in Freudian language, the "I" is not being censored by the "me." Social control is present to the extent that the "I" is controlled by the "me." The over-institutionalized individual is over-determined by his "me." In more normal circumstances the individual responds to a situation in its social aspects but does so with some regard for his own unique capacities and needs. The most gratifying experiences are those in which the demands of the "me"—or of the social situation—permit the expression, and realize the potentialities, of the "I."

In primitive society the individual self is more completely determined than in civilized societies by the "me," that is, by the particular social group to which the individual belongs. Primitive society offers much less scope for the "I." Indeed, the development of civilization is largely dependent upon the progressive social liberation of the individual self. The "I" is the innovator, the source of new ideas and energy to initiate social change.

The enlargement of the self is dependent upon and in turn supports the breadth of community values. What the self is and how it develops depends upon the nature of the community whose attitudes the individual has internalized. Membership in a community is more than physical presence in it; the small boy belongs to his gang, not to the city in which he lives: ". . . until one can respond to himself as a community responds to him, he does not genuinely belong to the community." (*Op. cit.,* p. 265)

The self will be isolated and alienated from other selves if it is a member of a socially isolated group or one with narrow or provincial values. The self becomes enlarged to the extent that it belongs to a group engaged in activities that bring it into contact with other groups. The rise of national states, which seems to be and often is a constraining and limiting influence, nevertheless encourages the development of internationalism and the extension of man's effective community. It does so because it fosters communication among nations rather than limiting it to communication among intra-national groups. Similarly the self becomes enlarged to the extent that it belongs to a community whose values are universal, for example, science, or religions that emphasize brotherhood.

Summary

1. Language is a biologically given potentiality of man. But man could not develop this potentiality without first being able to interact socially and communicate with others in a non-verbal, gestural way within shared, ongoing activities. Without social interaction language would not be possible. Out of social interaction accompanied by language human reason and self-consciousness emerge.

2. Social interaction, when accompanied and facilitated by language, leads "naturally" to social control and the development of human society.

3. Through language the individual takes on or internalizes the attitudes of others toward both the environment and himself. In this way the human being acquires a social self. The young child internalizes the attitudes of those who are significant others to him. With maturity the individual learns to relate to a generalized other, that is, to organized group activity and the community as a whole.

4. The individual need not and indeed cannot be totally controlled by the internalized attitudes of others, that is, by the "me" part of the self. The individual is also an "I," that is, someone who takes account of the "me" but is not necessarily dominated by it. The "I" may indeed act upon, influence, and modify the social process.

Section 3 Agencies of socialization

Many groups and institutions play a part in socializing the person. These agencies of socialization teach different things at different times. The delegation of specialized responsibilities to particular groups is partly a reflection of what the groups are competent to do. For example, although the family does much to educate the child, it cannot be relied upon to supply the degree of literacy that business and industry require of even "unskilled" employees. Consequently in Western society public education has become a basic social institution.

Socializing agencies may complement and support each other, but sometimes they inculcate independent and even conflicting values. This can lead to psychological conflict for the individual, but it is the necessary condition for freedom of choice among values and ways of life. During early childhood, his experience in the family is the only source of satisfactions and frustrations he knows, and the young child characteristically regards parental values as universal. As he grows older, particularly in a complex and varied society, he learns that there are alternative sources of satisfaction and approval and that a choice among values exists. However, conflict for the individual is minimized when the values he encounters are mutually supportive.

REACHING THE PERSON

In primitive and folk societies a great part of the culture has access to the child. The life of the society is lived out before his eyes; very little is not open to his direct observation; and most of the agencies support each other in socializing him. There is little competition for access to him. On the other hand, in a large and heterogeneous society, the agencies of socialization are faced with the problem of *gaining access* to the individual and of establishing the conditions which make for deep rather than superficial influence. A number of factors determine a group's ability to reach the individual and exert a significant socializing influence.

Conditions of Effective Access

Communication is necessary in order to influence the person. In early life communication requires actual physical access to the child. Whoever wishes to influence the child from a distance can do so only through those who come into direct contact with him—his parents, his peers, or his school. In a literate society, the person is soon reachable from a distance through books, newspapers, movies, radio, and television. However, not all communication is equally effective in influencing the person.

Early access is likely to be most influential because the personality is still unformed. Groups that reach the individual in his formative years have this advantage, and this largely explains the special importance of the family as an agency of socialization.

When *person-to-person interaction* permits the free play of emotion, it encourages intensive socialization. Such groups as the family, in which emotional relations are prominent, are called primary groups partly because they are "primary" agencies of sociali-

zation. The greater the need for influencing the person deeply, the more important it is for socialization to take place in and through primary group experience.

The individual must be *psychologically accessible*. The person is "ready" for different influences at different times in his life. What appeals to him is related to his psychological needs and capacities. His present availability is also affected by the values he has acquired in the past. Some agencies of socialization, especially the early ones, tend to limit the areas in which the individual is open to influence by other agencies.

The more *exclusive* the access of a group to the individual, the more effective its influence is likely to be. For example, the initiation of the "swab" into the life of the Coast Guard Academy includes a two-month period of isolation from the outside world. Cut off from his former ties, he is more accessible to the Academy's influence. (See Adaptation 8, pp. 123 ff.)

Competition of Socializing Agencies

If the groups that reach the individual have similar values and goals, they are mutually supportive, and socialization is reinforced. If, however, they compete for the opportunity to impress the individual with their values, he must choose between them, and he may be less effectively socialized by either group. For example, children of immigrants are exposed to two sets of values, often sharply divergent, one held by their parents, the other by the host society. Because the parents' values are unsupported outside the home, their influence is weakened. Because the values of the host society are unsupported in the home, the child may accept them in an incomplete and superficial way. He may obey the letter of the norms without understanding their spirit.

The family, the first and most basic socializing agency, is treated in a separate chapter. (See especially pp. 373–75.) The agencies of socialization change as the individual matures. Through childhood and adolescence the school and peer group increasingly compete with the family for access to the individual. With adulthood the occupational group and the newly established family achieve ascendant importance.

PEER GROUP

The individual is socialized both by his elders and by his equals. In the peer group the individual associates with others who are approximately his own age and social status. The childhood peer group is typically a *play group*. In adolescence it takes on the character of a *clique* or "social set" which introduces the child to status and class values. In adult life peer groups continue to provide a setting for social intercourse among equals.

Childhood Peer Groups and Social Control

1. The peer group helps to introduce the child to *impersonal authority*. In the family, authority is vested in the parents as *persons,* and they determine what is right and wrong. In the play group, the child learns to obey the impersonal "rules of the game," to take "objective" roles such as pitcher or catcher in a game of baseball, and to develop a concept of justice which is applicable to all.[6] In time he himself becomes a representative of "law and order"; he conceives himself as a protector of the rules, and exercises social control over playmates who break them.

2. Within the peer group the child *tests the limits of adult tolerance* with reduced fear of parental reprisal. Children in groups often behave more provocatively toward adults than the individual child feels free to do. At the same time, the child tests the extent to which his peers will go in defying the adult world and the degree to which he can rely on peer support.

3. The peer group may or may not support adult values. If it does, it is one of the most effective agencies for the *transmission of adult values*. The following example il-

lustrates the power of the peer group and its role as the representative of adult class and status values:

Bill was a late adolescent who began to run around with a girl who not only lived on the other side of the railroad tracks, but who had most of the traits associated with that oft-used phrase. Bill's family was upper class, Bill was personally most attractive, and his mother knew the power of a peer group. Calling Bill to her, she explained with disarming friendliness that she had heard of his new girl and wanted to meet her. Wouldn't he bring her to the house, and to make it less formal, she would invite a few of his favorite friends. Upon securing Bill's wondering and semi-reluctant consent, the mother proceeded to promote, secretly, a gala event, to which she invited all of Bill's extended clique. Bill's relations with the new girl just barely survived until the end of the party.[7]

Peer Group Values

The peer group exists for the sake of "sociability." But behind this innocuous interest is a powerful force for conformity. Like any other socializing agency, the peer group represents a system of rewards and punishments, of approval and disapproval. It rewards the skills of sociability. It rejects the personality that disrupts the flow of good feeling and hinders smooth personal relations.

Because the peer group has no other basis for existence than sociability, and because differences disrupt sociability, there are strong pressures for *uniformity* within the peer group. Actual differences in achievement and status tend to be minimized, and strong differences in belief and conviction suppressed.

Peer groups transmit the skills and values of sociability. Such ideals as co-operation and tolerance, sharing and participation become important to the person. He is taught not to be eccentric or to "show off." Although peer groups provide an opportunity for the development of friendships and genuinely intimate and spontaneous relations, they do not

---

[6] See Jean Piaget, *The Moral Judgment of the Child* (London: Kegan Paul, 1932).

[7] James H. S. Bossard, *The Sociology of Child Development* (New York: Harper & Bros., 1948), p. 507.

necessarily take account of or value the "whole person." The conventional responses required within the peer group often inhibit the development of deep personal attachments.

Other-directedness [8]

Riesman suggests that the peer group is becoming the most important socializing agency. In present-day society people look primarily to their contemporaries for guidance and direction; modern man values most the judgment and approval of others in his environment. The most important values to modern man are also the values typical of the peer group, for example: sociability, which minimizes differences and emphasizes similarities, co-operation, and getting along with others.

Riesman calls modern man "other-directed," and contrasts him with the "tradition-directed" and the "inner-directed" man. The tradition-directed type, e.g., in primitive

[8] David Riesman, in collaboration with Reuel Denney and Nathan Glazer, *The Lonely Crowd* (New Haven: Yale University Press, 1950).

and folk societies, looks to tradition and the past for guidance and models of behavior. The inner-directed type, exemplified by nineteenth-century man, guides his behavior by abstract ideals implanted in him as a child by family authority—ideals such as wealth, knowledge, and the moral life. The other-directed man is equipped instead with an internal "radar" device; he makes his way through the complexities and intricacies of modern life by picking up cues from his environment. Like the inner-directed man, modern man has a strong drive for success. But where the inner-directed man has internalized criteria of success, the other-directed man depends upon the approval of his peers to tell him what success is. (See Table IV: 2.)

The importance of the peer group and of peer group values is a product of the structure of modern society and the emerging nature of the family:

1. The urban family is small, and the areas in which it participates as a unit are limited. The peer group fills a larger part of the child's life.

2. The high degree of social and techno-

Table IV:2 Socialization and Modes of Conformity*

Social Character	Who Socializes?	What Guides Behavior?	Psychological Mechanism of Conformity	Life-Style
Tradition-directed	The clan, the tribe, the village	Adherence to detailed norms of village life learned by direct observation	Shame: wrongdoing is a transgression against the group	Politically indifferent; subsistence oriented
Inner-directed	The parents	Adherence to general principles laid down early in life; freedom for nonconformity within these limits; built-in gyroscope steers individual	Guilt: wrongdoing is a violation of personal ideals	Politically moralistic; production oriented
Other-directed	The peer group	Cue-taking in particular situations; being "in the know"; built-in radar steers individual	Anxiety: the ultimate evil is being unloved and unapproved	Politically manipulative; consumption oriented

*Adapted from David Riesman, in collaboration with Reuel Denney and Nathan Glazer, *The Lonely Crowd* (New Haven: Yale University Press, 1950).

logical change characteristic of modern society widens the gap between generations. Parental knowledge is rapidly outdated, and the peer group becomes more important as the avenue to contemporary values and "know-how."

3. In modern society there is a relatively high degree of mobility. Children tend to move upward on the social ladder, especially through a college education. The family no longer feels competent to instruct the child in his newly acquired class and status values and, therefore, leaves these matters to the peer group.

4. The economy is changing from one based upon the expansion of production to one organized around consumption. In a period of expansion, innovation, and pioneering, there is need for people with extraordinary courage, adventuresomeness, drive, ruthlessness, imagination, talent, and even moral insensitivity. At present the main task is to run the mass-production economy with its standardized methods; this often requires a high degree of skill, but it depends less upon the extraordinary and unique character traits of individuals. The less important the unique contribution of the individual, the more important in the competitive struggle is "selling" his personality.

Section 4 **Adult socialization**

Adult experiences continue to shape and develop personality. Adult socialization is most intensive during critical periods when adjustment to new situations must be made. If these adjustments are difficult to make and far-reaching in their effects, the individual may undergo great changes in his self conception, habits, and values. Marriage, parenthood, divorce or death of a spouse, unemployment or financial success may serve to break up old behavior patterns and transform orientations. The person who moves from an urban center to the suburbs or from a Southern city to a Northern one has new experiences that may produce significant revisions of old attitudes and habits.

Specialized adult roles that depend on deeply internalized social control require intensive socialization. Adaptation 8 describes how a civilian youth is transformed into a military officer. (See pp. 123 ff.)

Two problems in continuing socialization are considered here: parent-youth conflict, which may undermine earlier socializing influences, and the interplay of roles and personality as an aspect of adult socialization.

PARENT-YOUTH CONFLICT IN AMERICAN SOCIETY[9]

In contemporary society adolescence is marked by conflict between the generations, and earlier close relations between parent and child may disappear. The adolescent looks to other authorities for guidance and support and often rejects parental values and ways. Some disparities between youth and age occur in all societies, but there are special conditions that aggravate adolescent-parent antagonism in the United States.

Differing Rates of Socialization. Socialization continues throughout life, but it does so at a decreasing rate. The adolescent is at a stage of development where learning is rapid and basic, but by the time the adult is a parent, he is no longer so able to acquire

[9] This discussion is based on Kingsley Davis, "The Sociology of Parent-Youth Conflict," *American Sociological Review,* **5,** No. 4 (August, 1940), 523–35.

new ways or to undergo fundamental personality changes. If there is rapid social change, the habits and outlooks of the older generation will become "obsolete."

Differences in Opportunity and Participation. Youth is a period of opportunity and choice among alternatives. The adult has already made his choices. He has a settled way of life, an occupation, a defined position and role. He consolidates gains instead of exploiting opportunities. The choices open to youth may result in anxieties about the future.

Conflict between young and old may be less in societies that clearly specify appropriate behavior at all age levels. The young know that as they grow older they will automatically rise in the social hierarchy, and they do not experience anxieties about the future. The adult, backed by his superior ascribed status, is not so readily judged a failure by his children.

"The much publicized critical attitude of youth toward established ways is partly a matter of being on the outside looking in." [10] The young soldier who is "old enough to die for his country but not old enough to vote" may resent being excluded from political responsibility. The adolescent who knows how to drive an automobile may resent restrictions on his holding a license.

During an earlier period in the history of the United States children were employed in industry, and their assumption of the adult role of worker led to their being treated as adults in other areas as well. Laws prohibiting child labor and increasing educational requirements have combined to postpone the transformation of child to adult, and there is a longer period of "being on the outside looking in."

Adult Realism, Youthful Idealism. By its very nature, socialization encourages youthful idealism. As part of their education, children are taught the "official" ideals of the culture, and these are often at variance with its

"operating" standards. Youth becomes exasperated with adult "hypocrisy," or may become cynical, dismissing all ideals as worthless and irrelevant.

Where the education of the child is informal and carried on as part of everyday life, he learns the official ideals and the working pattern simultaneously. He learns to "make allowances"; he sees very early that society provides for deviations and departures from the norm. In the United States education is more formal, and children participate in the life of the community in a more peripheral and minor way. This is inevitable because economic and political activities are carried on by distant and impersonal agencies, which cannot be known through direct participation. The child takes on many of his ideals outside everyday social experience, and he is often deliberately shielded from "the facts of life." When this occurs, events are judged in the light of formal education, and disillusionment may result.

Parental Authority. Authority exercised by impersonal agencies is not interpreted as a judgment of the total person, but when it is combined with personal and intimate relations, it tends to be onerous. Within the personal relations of parent and child, the parent's authority tends to invade every area of life and to frustrate the youth's expectations of unlimited love and approval. The conflict that stems from resentment of parental authority may be expressed openly when the adolescent's behavior has the approval of competing authorities, such as his peer group.

SOCIAL ROLES AND PERSONALITY

Part of the socialization process is learning the specified and expected behaviors appropriate to social positions. A doctor's formal role specifies that he try to cure the ill, relieve suffering, help people, and be loyal to his profession. Additional behaviors are informally expected of a role, but these are not essential to it. A doctor is expected to be kind,

[10] *Ibid.,* p. 529.

Socialization and courage: The matador puts his long training and discipline to the test.

well groomed, poised, and hard-working. These attributes are a kind of "halo effect" around the formal role, and a doctor can discharge his formal role without conforming to them.

Anticipatory Socialization

By specifying the terms of relationships, roles articulate the interactions of one person with another. The individual learns how to be a patient in relation to a doctor, a student in relation to a teacher, a husband in relation to a wife. Roles and their complementary roles, taken together, organize and integrate shared experience.

Insofar as roles consist of definite and known patterns of behavior, they provide blueprints for anticipatory socialization. The individual can prepare himself beforehand for an expected or hoped-for future role. Learning professional skills is one example of anticipatory socialization.

More significant than the learning of technical and social skills for the formation of personality is the acquisition of values, self-conceptions, and perspectives appropriate to an expected or admired role. The aspiring employee may view his fellow workers from the perspectives of the employer he would like to be. The prospective priest or nun may very

Socialization and courage: A member of the French Resistance smiles defiantly at his German executioners.

early begin to acquire habits of self-discipline in preparation for the religious life. The medical student may take the role of doctor in his relations with nurses though he continues to see himself primarily as a student in his relations with faculty.[11]

Few roles are taught or learned in a wholly conscious and deliberate way. They emerge from personal interaction, and people learn what is expected of them by taking cues from others. The socialization of the person occurs in the role as he adapts himself to its requirements and to the expectations that others have of him in that role. The medical student, for example, comes to realize that patients expect him to be wise and reassuring by observing their reactions to him when he is not.

To say that the patient "searches your face for clues" is no overstatement. . .when trying to palpate a baby once, I got a little confused and frowned in puzzlement. [I] sensed at once that the mother saw the frown and was alarmed. So, I re-assured her that everything was all right.

[11] Mary Jean Huntington, "The Development of a Professional Self-Image," in Robert K. Merton, George G. Reader, M.D., and Patricia L. Kendall (eds.), *The Student-Physician* (Cambridge: Harvard University Press, 1957), pp. 179–87; and Howard S. Becker, Blanche Geer, Everett C. Hughes, and Anselm L. Strauss, *Boys in White* (Chicago: University of Chicago Press, 1961).

I have always tried to remember not to do it again.[12]

Informal Roles

Although many roles are associated with clearly defined positions in the social structure, other roles are informal and unofficial. Much organizational activity is based, not merely on formal procedures and positions, but on the interplay of informal roles. In discussions among directors of a company, highly differentiated roles may show up despite the fact that each, except for the chairman, may occupy the same formal position. The compromiser, the "spark plug," the "idea man," the debunker may each make his unique contribution to the decision-making process. To some extent informal roles affect behavior in formal roles. The perennial compromiser may make a poor leader but a good administrator, the "idea man" a poor administrator but a good administrative assistant.

Roles and Personality Integration

All roles organize behavior, but some roles are so important that they serve to integrate the personality. They become part of the individual's self-conception, which is built around the behavior and the attitudes that go with a role. The individual sees the world from the point of view of a particular role and may find it difficult to take on other roles or to behave in ways alien to his critical role. Such roles are usually sex roles, family roles, and occupational roles, but an individual may also see himself as the "life of the party." He will be unhappy when this role is taken over by someone else, and he may try to act out this role even when it is inappropriate.

When identification is intense and a role is critical in personality integration, the individual may stake his self-respect on it. When deprived of his role, he loses self-esteem. People for whom a job has been the integrating element in life are disturbed by retirement unless they are able to find self-esteem and meaningfulness in some other way.

Capacities and Limits

Roles determine which potentialities are to be realized and which suppressed. Each person is potentially many things; what he actually becomes depends largely upon the role he chooses or has assigned to him. The skills and personality traits of leadership, for example, are fully realized only when they are exercised. This full realization of potentialities requires, however, that the role be socially supported. The individual then can behave in the role without anxiety and cautious self-doubt.

Roles are also limiting and restrictive, particularly in the case of caste roles. Some parts of the white community expect the Southern Negro to be improvident, carefree, and musical in a folksy and primitive way. To the extent that he acts out the role defined by this image, he is granted a measure of security and approval. Such a role may become part of the person's self-image. Caste divisions are difficult to overcome, not only because of opposition from above, but because the role of subordinate may be internalized and become a part of personality structure.

Even where roles are satisfying to the individual and provide him with the opportunity to exercise his capacities, they may have a negative side. Attached to the role are characteristic risks, anxieties, and limitations. For example, successful business executives show common personality characteristics.[13] On the "positive" side are high achievement desires, strong mobility drives, an attitude toward authority as helpful rather than inhibiting, high ability to organize unstructured situations, decisiveness, a strong sense of self-identity, and aggressiveness. These personality traits are "positive" in the sense that they support the social role and find expres-

---

[12] Merton *et al.*, *op. cit.*, p. 227.

[13] William E. Henry, "The Business Executive: The Psychodynamics of a Social Role," *American Journal of Sociology*, **54** (January, 1949), 286–91.

sion within it. The "negative" traits are uncertainty, constant activity, continued fear of losing ground, inability to be leisurely introspective, ever-present fear of failure, and limitations on the play of emotion in interpersonal relations.

Conflicts of Role and Personality

Although roles express and form personality, role and personality may conflict. A woman with an aggressive and dominating personality finds it difficult to take the submissive role expected of her, while a man with an anxious and mild temperament will experience strain in fulfilling the role of decision-maker within a patriarchal family.

Some roles make conflicting demands upon the person. A leader, for example, is supposed to be accessible to his followers so that he can respond to their desires and interests. Yet the leader is also often required to make decisions based on special foresight and understanding, and this requires a certain degree of isolation from membership influence and pressure. Although there is nothing inherently contradictory in accessibility at one time and isolation at another, it is rare for the same individual to be equally skillful at achieving both.

The conflict may result in the choice of different kinds of leaders in different periods. In times of stability, when the organization "runs itself," the accessibility of leadership is important; in times of danger and stress, when decision can be crucial, there is more need for maintaining the independence of the leadership role. Two distinct personality types may successfully fill leadership roles during different periods of an organization's history.

RESOCIALIZATION

Over the total life span, individuals change their attitudes, values, behavior, and self-conceptions as they assume new roles and undergo new experiences. This occurs as they pass from one job to another, from the single to the married and from the married to the widowed state, from youth to old age. Though the long-run change may be profound, single steps along the way are often gradual and partial: a little of the person is changed a little at a time.

New roles and experiences vary, however, in the extent to which they require or induce drastic changes in the individual:

1. A new role may affect only one aspect of a person's identity or it may encompass virtually the entire self.

2. It may require only superficial or minor changes in behavior or it may necessitate acquiring a whole new set of habits.

3. It may be consonant with the individual's past roles or it may be radically dissonant with them.

4. It may be a projection of past values or it may require a moral break with the individual's past and a repudiation of his old self, past loyalties, and former social commitments.

Adult change that is gradual and partial is called *continuing socialization. Resocialization* denotes change that is more basic and more rapid, especially the abandonment of one way of life for another that is not only different from the former but incompatible with it. Important examples of attempts at resocialization are "brainwashing," the rehabilitation of criminals, and the conversion of "sinners" to a religious way of life. In these cases, the aim is to make the person over in fundamental ways and to effect a break with the past.

Certain occupational and life roles demand extensive and intensive socialization, and training for them approaches resocialization. The role of priest or nun requires that the new religious life be all-encompassing and that a thorough break be made with the ways of the secular order. Adaptation 8 (pp. 123 ff.) describes some resocializing aspects of cadet life at the Coast Guard Academy.

Resocialization of the mature individual is difficult to accomplish. Generally speaking, it requires that the conditions of childhood socialization be reproduced in heightened, intense, and extreme form. Attempts at resocialization—whether forced upon the individual or assented to voluntarily—include some if not all of the following elements:

1. *Total control over the individual.*[14] The individual is isolated from society, from the countervailing influences of competing institutions and groups, and from his own past life. The resocializing institution has not only sole access but total access to the individual; every aspect of his life is under surveillance. The person is totally dependent upon the institution even for satisfaction of his physical needs. More significantly, he is dependent upon the institution for cues and "information" as to what is right and wrong, true and false, in his new environment.

2. *Suppression of past statuses.* Former statuses for which the person had approval or in which he took pride or pleasure are ignored. Within the resocializing institution the individual is initially devoid of status and is given approval only for the achievement of a new status defined by the resocializing agency.

3. *Denial of the moral worth of the old self.* Not only are past statuses ignored, the individual's past perspectives are seen as rad-

[14] See "On the Characteristics of Total Institutions" in Erving Goffman, *Asylums* (Garden City: Anchor Books, Doubleday, 1961), pp. 1–124.

Resocialization is becoming recognized as important in the rehabilitation of the mentally ill.

ically faulty, morally inferior, and blame-worthy.

4. *Participation of the individual in his own resocialization.* The individual is encouraged to participate actively in the resocialization process by engaging in self-analysis, self-criticism, and "confession" of past and present failings.

5. *Extreme sanctions.* Resocialization agencies often employ extreme sanctions ranging from the negative sanctions of physical cruelty and social isolation to the positive sanction of the promise of eternal salvation.

6. *Intensification of peer group pressures and support.* Resocializing institutions rarely rely on "reforming" the individual by invoking a punishment and reward system administered from on high. Instead, efforts are made to increase the informal influence of the peer group, which is able to give and to withhold from the individual the often subtle but crucial satisfactions of group life and personal interaction.

Brainwashing

The term "brainwashing" is a translation from the Chinese and was first used in Communist China to refer to the re-education of the Chinese people whereby all vestiges of the old, pre-Communist system would be "washed away." In the present context, the term refers to efforts at conversion of Westerners to the ideology of the Chinese Communist Party while they are being held prisoner.

Under the impact of brainwashing, many prisoners confessed to crimes of espionage that they could not possibly have committed and that they immediately repudiated upon liberation and arrival in Hong Kong. A few, however, appear upon release to have been "converted." Despite the brutality of their imprisonment, and their innocence of any crime, they made statements like the following: [15]

In China today a person who is not guilty of a crime could never be arrested or convicted. Before I was arrested in my heart I knew that I was guilty of being a spy. The People's Government took care of us so well! We had no pressure put on us. In order to gain self-respect one has to confess. We are grateful for such light sentences.

Such apparent conversions led to the widespread belief that the Communists had discovered "a new and powerful weapon to use against the mind of man." [16] However, reports by repatriated Westerners indicate that, although actual physical torture plays a part, brainwashing consists of an extreme, intensive, and in itself brutal application of the entire range of resocialization measures.

The process of "thought reform" or the "ideological remolding" of the individual begins with "total" imprisonment; the individual is entirely cut off from all contact with the outside world. Although he is charged with being a spy or an enemy of the Chinese people, no specific and refutable accusations are made. Instead he is made to review his past life in order to discover for himself what he did that was, from the point of view of his captors, morally wrong. In order to be able to make a "sincere" confession that will satisfy his captors and secure his release, the prisoner must abandon his own concept of guilt and innocence learned in his past life, discover the concept of guilt and innocence held by his captors, and then use the latter to inspect and judge his past life. His confession must in effect consist of a moral condemnation of his entire previous self as the product of a capitalist, imperialist society. Although his confession must be buttressed by specific details —real or fabricated—the individual is required to repudiate, not only this or that specific act, but his entire past self as criminal.

Prisoners are commonly placed in a cell with other prisoners—usually all Chinese— who are well on the way to being reformed

[15] Quoted by Edgar H. Schein with Inge Schneier and Curtis H. Barker, *Coercive Persuasion* (New York: Norton, 1961), p. 15.

[16] *Ibid.*

and who subject him to a process known as the "struggle" to help him recognize and admit his criminality. Hour after hour, from morning to night, they repeat the accusations against him and urge him to confess. They respond to him in no other way than as a criminal and as an object of a "struggle." The prisoner's past status as priest, doctor, or missionary is treated only as a "cover up" for his "spy personality."

. . . Each attempt on the part of the prisoner to reassert his adult human identity. . .("I am not a spy. I am a doctor"; or "This must be a mistake. I am a priest; I am telling the truth.") was considered a show of resistance and of "insincerity" and called forth new assaults.[17]

The prisoner is never left alone, not even to perform the most intimate body functions. Until he is able to embark on the long road to a full and satisfactory confession, the prisoner is often put into chains. Besides being subjected to pain, he is rendered as helpless as an infant, and made totally dependent upon others for the satisfaction of every physical need.

When you get back [to your cell] you are obliged to stand with chains on your ankles and holding your hands behind your back. They don't assist you because you are too reactionary. . . . You eat as a dog does, with your mouth and teeth. You arrange the cup and bowl with your nose to try to absorb broth twice a day. If you have to make water they open your trousers. . . .[18] [Subjected to such treatment, the person feels himself] deprived of the power, mastery, and selfhood of adult existence . . . men began to exist on a level which was neither sleep nor wakefulness, but rather an in-between hypnogogic state. In this state they were . . . more readily influenced.[19]

But the prisoner sometimes begins to internalize the attitudes of others toward himself and to view himself in the mirror of the de-

grading and humiliating treatment he is given. He begins to believe in his own guilt, to acknowledge his utter dependence upon his captors, and to earnestly desire to be once again restored to human society on any terms.

Sudden leniency on the part of prison officials is often decisive at this point.

. . . An official came to see me and he spoke to me in a very friendly voice. "The government doesn't want to kill you. It wants to reform you. We don't want to punish you at all, we just want to re-educate you." . . . It was my first glimmer of hope. I felt finally there might be a way out. I wasn't feeling so hopelessly alone any more. The official had actually shown some human quality.[20]

Once the prisoner begins to confess, he is subjected to intensive "re-education." Group study programs, lasting as long as ten to sixteen hours, focus not only on academic discussions of Marxist theory and practice but on self-criticism and analysis to insure total intellectual and emotional agreement with official doctrine. Confession and self-condemnation are continuously refined and elaborated during the period of imprisonment.

The evidence now available suggests that brainwashing is rarely successful in achieving a permanent transformation in the ideas and values of individuals subjected to it. This evidence is based almost entirely on the experience of repatriated prisoners who returned to a Western setting. It is not known how successful brainwashing might be among prisoners who continue to live in China where their "thought reform" would be supported and reinforced daily or among Chinese themselves.

Several conclusions can be tentatively stated concerning both the success and the failure of resocialization by brainwashing techniques.

1. Resocialization is apt to be unsuccessful when, as in brainwashing, it is submitted

[17] Robert Jay Lifton, M.D., *Thought Reform and the Psychology of Totalism* (New York: Norton, 1961), p. 67.
[18] *Ibid.*, p. 22.
[19] *Ibid.*, p. 67.
[20] *Ibid.*, p. 73.

to under duress, against the individual's will, and without "anticipatory socialization" on his part.

2. Attempts at "reform" can achieve some success if they are related to values already held by the individual. Accounts of brainwashing often include reports of efforts to arouse a sense of personal guilt by invoking the failure of the individual to have lived up to his own values in the past. This is illustrated in the following exchange between a priest and his prison "instructor":

Instructor: Do you believe man should serve others?

Priest: Yes, of course I do.

Instructor: Are you familiar with the Biblical saying, "I come on earth to serve, not to be served"?

Priest: Yes, as a priest it is my creed.

Instructor: Did you have a servant in your mission [in China]?

Priest: Yes, I did.

Instructor: Who made your bed in the morning and swept the floor?

Priest: My servant did this.

Instructor: You did not live up to your doctrine very well, did you, Father? [21]

3. Resocialization seems to succeed insofar as it induces "spiritual humility" as in the above example. But it is not likely to be successful if it degrades and humiliates the person in his own eyes and those of others.

4. Resocialization is unsuccessful in working a genuine transformation if it gains compliance merely by disorienting the person and then offering him a way out of his plight. When the individual is deprived of all social supports and psychological satisfactions, he is likely to suffer a mental breakdown or, at best, become confused, apathetic, and compliant in an external, mechanical way.

[21] *Ibid.*, p. 77.

Socializing the Cadet

Abridged from Sanford M. Dornbusch, "The Military Academy as an Assimilating Institution" in *Social Forces*, Vol. 33, No. 4, May, 1955, pages 316–21. Published in this form by permission of the author and *Social Forces*.

The function of a military academy is to make officers out of civilians or enlisted men. The objective is accomplished by a twofold process of transmitting technical knowledge and of instilling in the candidates an outlook considered appropriate for members of the profession.[22]

The Coast Guard Academy, like West Point and Annapolis, provides four years of training for a career as a regular officer. Unlike the other service academies, however, its cadet corps is small, seldom exceeding 350 cadets. This disparity in size probably produces differences in the methods of informal social control. Although all the findings reported here may not be applicable to the other academies, many of the mechanisms by which this academy socializes the cadet will probably be found in a wide variety of social institutions.

[22] In the original paper the process of instilling an appropriate outlook is referred to as the "assimilating function" of the military academy. Cf. Robert E. Park and Ernest W. Burgess, *Introduction to the Science of Sociology* (Chicago: University of Chicago Press, 1921), pp. 735, 737.

The Suppression of Prior Statuses

The new cadet, or "swab," is the lowest of the low. The assignment of low status encourages the cadet to place a high value on successfully completing the steps in an Academy career, and requires that there be a loss of identity based on pre-existing statuses. This clean break with the past must be achieved in a relatively short period. For two months, therefore, the swab is not allowed to leave the base or to engage in social intercourse with non-cadets. This complete isolation helps to produce a unified group of swabs, rather than a heterogeneous collection of persons of high and low status. Uniforms are issued on the first day, and discussions of wealth and family background are taboo. Although the pay of the cadet is very low, he is not permitted to receive money from home. The role of the cadet must supersede other roles the individual has been accustomed to play. There are few clues left which will reveal social status in the outside world.

Learning New Rules and Adjustment to Conflicts Between Rules

There are two sets of rules which regulate the cadet's behavior. The first of these is the body of regulations of the Academy, considered by the public to be the primary source of control. These regulations are similar to the code of ethics of any profession. They serve in part as propaganda to influence outsiders. In addition, official regulations help support the second set of expectations, the informal rules. Offenses against the informal rules are merely labeled as breaches of the formal code, and the appropriate punishment according to the regulations is then imposed. This punitive system conceals the existence of the informal set of controls.

In case of conflict between the regulations and tradition, the regulations are superseded. For example, it is against the regulations to have candy in one's room. A first classman orders a swab to bring him candy. Caught en route by an officer, the swab offers no excuse and is given fifteen demerits. First classmen are then informally told by the classmate involved that they are to withhold demerits for this swab until he has been excused for offenses totaling fifteen demerits. Experience at an Academy teaches future officers that regulations are not considered of paramount importance when they conflict with informal codes.

The Development of Solidarity

The control system operates through the class hierarchy. The first class, consisting of cadets in their third or fourth year at the Academy, are only nominally under the control of the officers of the Academy. Only one or two officers attempt to check on the activities of the first classmen, so that they are able to break most of the minor regulations with impunity. The first class is given almost complete control over the rest of the cadet corps. Informally, certain leading cadets are even called in to advise the officers on important disciplinary matters. There are one or two classes between the first classmen and the swabs, depending on the existence of a three- or four-year course. These middle classes haze the swabs. Hazing is forbidden by the regulations, but the practice is a hallowed tradition of the Academy. The first class demands that this hazing take place, and, since they have the power to give demerits, all members of the middle classes are compelled to haze the new cadets.

As a consequence of undergoing this very unpleasant experience together, the swab class develops remarkable unity. For example, if a cadet cannot answer an oral question addressed to him by his teacher, no other member of his class will answer. All reply, "I can't say, sir," leaving the teacher without a clue to the state of knowledge of this student compared to the rest of the class. This group cohesion persists throughout the Academy period, with first classmen refusing to give demerits to their classmates unless an officer directly orders them to do so.

The basis for interclass solidarity, the development of group feeling on the part of the entire cadet corps, is not so obvious. It

New Cadets:
Swabs brace under the doubtful gaze of an upper classman.

occurs through informal contacts between the upper classmen and swabs, a type of fraternization which occurs despite the fact it traditionally is discouraged. The men who haze the swab and order him hazed live in the same wing of the dormitory that he does. Coming from an outside world which disapproves of authoritarian punishment and aggressiveness, they are ashamed of their behavior. They are eager to convince the swab that they are good fellows. They visit his room to explain why they are being so harsh this week or to tell of a mistake he is making. Close friendships sometimes arise through such behavior. These friendships must be concealed. One first classman often ordered his room cleaned by the writer as a "punishment," then settled down for an uninterrupted chat. Such informal contacts serve to unite the classes and spread a "we-feeling" through the Academy.

In addition, the knowledge of common interests and a common destiny serves as a unifying force that binds together all Academy graduates. This is expressed in the identification of the interest of the individual with the interest of the Coast Guard. A large appropriation or an increase in the size of the Coast Guard will speed the rate of promotion for all, whether ensign or captain. A winning football team at the Academy may familiarize more civilians with the name of their common alma mater. Good publicity for the Coast Guard raises the status of the Coast Guard officer.

The Coast Guard regulars are united in their disdain for the reserves. There are few reserve officers during peacetime, but in wartime reserve officers soon outnumber the regulars. The reserves do not achieve the higher ranks, but they are a threat to the cadets and recent graduates of the Academy. The reserves receive in a few months the rank that the regulars reach only after four grueling years. The Academy men therefore protectively stigmatize the reserves as incompetents. If a cadet falters on the parade ground, he is told, "You're marching like a reserve." Swabs are told to square their shoulders while on liberty, "or else how will people know you are not a reserve?" Myths spring up—stories of reserve commanders who must call on regular ensigns for advice. The net effect is reassurance that although the interlopers may have the same rank, they do not have equal status.

An increase in the cadet's self-esteem develops in conjunction with identification in his new role. Told that they are members of an elite group, respected by the community, most cadets begin to feel at ease in a superordinate role. One may be a low-ranking cadet, but cadets as a group have high status. When cadets visit home for the first time, there is a conflict between the lofty role that they wish to play and the role to which their parents are accustomed. Upon return to the Academy, much conversation is concerned with the way things at home have changed.

This feeling of superiority helps to develop self-confidence in those cadets who previously had a low evaluation of themselves. It directly enters into relationships with girls, with whom many boys lack self-confidence. It soon becomes apparent that any cadet can get a date whenever he wishes, and he even begins to feel that he is a good "catch." The cadet's conception of himself is directly influenced by this new way of view-

ing the behavior of himself and others. As one cadet put it, "I used to be shy. Now I'm reserved."

Social Mobility

The cadets are told that they will be members of the social elite during the later stages of their career. The obstacles that they meet at the Academy are then viewed as the usual barriers to social mobility in the United States, a challenge to be surmounted.

Various practices at the Academy reinforce the cadets' feeling that they are learning how to enter the upper classes. There is a strong emphasis on etiquette, from calling cards to table manners. The Tactics Officer has been known to give long lectures on such topics as the manner of drinking soup from an almost empty bowl. The cadet must submit for approval the name of the girl he intends to take to the monthly formal dance. Girls attending the upper-class college in the vicinity are automatically acceptable, but some cadets claim that their dates have been rejected because they are in a low-status occupation, such as waitress.

Another Academy tradition actively, though informally, encourages contact with higher status girls. After the swabs have been completely isolated for two months, they are invited to a dance at which all the girls are relatives or friends of Coast Guard officers. A week later the girls at the nearby college have a dance for the swabs. The next week end finds the swab compelled to invite an acceptable girl to a formal reception. He must necessarily choose from the only girls in the area whom he knows.

Justification of Institutional Practices

In addition to the social mobility theme which views the rigors of Academy life as obstacles to upward mobility, there is a more open method of justifying traditionally legitimated ways of doing things. The phrase "separating the men from the boys" is used to meet objections to practices which seem inefficient or foolish. Traditional standards are thus redefined as further tests of ability to take punishment. Harsh practices are defended as methods by which the insincere, incompetent, or undisciplined cadets are weeded out. Cadets who rebel and resign are merely showing lack of character.[23]

Almost all cadets accept, to some extent, this traditional view of resignations as admissions of defeat. Of the 162 entering cadets in 1944, only 52 graduated in 1948. Most of the 110 resignations were entirely voluntary, without pressure from the Academy authorities. Most of these resignations came at a time when the hazing was comparatively moderate. Cadets who wish to resign do not leave at a time when the hazing might be considered the cause of their departure. One cadet's history illustrates this desire to have the resignation appear completely voluntary. Asked to resign because of his lack of physical co-ordination, he spent an entire year

[23] "At each step of the ceremonies he feels that he is brought a little closer, until at last he can feel himself a man among men." A. R. Radcliffe-Brown, *The Andaman Islanders* (Glencoe, Ill.: The Free Press, 1948), p. 279.

building up his physique, returned to the Academy, finished his swab year, and then joyously quit. "It took me three years, but I showed them."

Every cadet who voluntarily resigns is a threat to the morale of the cadet corps, since he has rejected the values of the Academy. Although cadets have enlisted for seven years and could theoretically be forced to remain at the Academy, the usual procedure is to isolate them from the swabs and rush acceptance of their resignation. During the period before the acceptance is final, cadets who have resigned are freed from the usual duties of their classmates. This action isolates them from cadets who might be affected by their disenchantment.

Conclusion

Socializing the cadet goes beyond combat training or seamanship. Cadets are systematically isolated from the outside world, given a new personal and social identity, and instilled with a sense of solidarity. The new role is a new social world.

Section 5 Culture, personality, and human nature

Through socialization each culture places its distinctive mark on human personality. The more homogeneous the culture, the more likely it is to produce a characteristic type of person who reflects the dominant ethos or culture theme. In one society the representative personality may be relaxed and easygoing, careless of time, and tolerant of uncleanliness. In another society, quite opposite characteristics occur.

This sort of observation has been the commonplace of travelers for many centuries; but it is recognized that untrained observers

leap easily to generalized images or stereotypes. Americans are apt to think of the English as "stuffy" and "unemotional," the English to think of Americans as "brash" and "crude," and both to think of Latins as "undependable" and "volatile."

BASIC PERSONALITY[24]

Anthropologists and sociologists approach the subject of representative personalities

[24] For a discussion of "basic personality," see A. Kardiner, *The Psychological Frontiers of Society* (New York: Columbia University Press, 1945).

with caution because of the wide variation in personality observed within cultures and the difficulty of defining what is "representative." The concept of representative personality (sometimes called "basic personality," "modal personality," or "social character") points toward a *common core* of traits shared by members of a society, but there is some disagreement about the meaning of this.

1. "Representative" may mean simply the statistically frequent. Any item of behavior exhibited by a large number of people in a society would then be part of its "representative personality."

2. "Representative" may mean those common characteristics of personality which exist despite differences in overt behavior. Attention is then directed not toward the minutiae of observable behavior and response, but toward basic underlying orientations and outlooks. Riesman's "tradition-directed," "inner-directed," and "other-directed" types distinguish basic personalities according to different psychological mechanisms of conformity. The tradition-directed type conforms because wrongdoing makes him ashamed, the inner-directed because it makes him feel guilty, the other-directed because it makes him anxious lest he lose the approval of his peers. (See Table IV:2, p. 113.)

3. "Representative" personality sometimes means the personality which most fully expresses the spirit or ethos of a culture. In this sense the representative personality may be shared by only a minority. It is the kind of personality most easily integrated into dominant social institutions. The cultivated Englishman, product of a distinctive system of education, is representative in this sense.

Basic personality is culture as it is reflected in the individual's organized way of responding. If we assume that a culture tends to make the same kind of impress on the personalities it touches, the culture itself may be studied through the regularities in personality among the members of one society compared with another. This perspective reminds us that norms and patterns have reality only as they occur in someone's behavior or personality.

National Character

The emphasis on propaganda in contemporary international relations and the importance of national morale have led to efforts to assess national character, which is another term for basic personality when the subject of study is a whole nation. It is assumed that knowledge of basic personality will give evidence of the dispositions of a people to respond to certain types of propaganda, to go to war, to accept defeat, or to withstand great stress. Studies of national character have usually been carried on from a distance because they have been stimulated by interest in understanding an actual or potential enemy. Notable examples are the studies of Japanese character during World War II and more recent studies of Russian character.[25] These efforts involve considerable speculation, but they suggest the potential importance of studying basic personality.

Three limitations to this approach should be mentioned:

1. Modern societies are complex and heterogeneous. There are class differences, urban and rural differences, and ethnic differences, all of which may influence basic personality and lead to not one but a number of core types.

2. Even if there is a basic personality, it does not follow that decisions by political leaders are directly affected. Political decision is the outcome of many factors, and attitudes built up because of basic personality dispositions may be offset by other forces.

3. Even sound knowledge of basic personality is not necessarily specific enough to permit us to predict how people will behave

[25] See Ruth Benedict, *The Chrysanthemum and the Sword* (Boston: Houghton, 1946); Margaret Mead, *Soviet Attitudes Toward Authority* (New York: McGraw-Hill, 1951); and Alexander H. Leighton, *Human Relations in a Changing World* (New York: Dutton, 1949).

in particular situations. If the representative personality of a culture is aggressive, for example, this does not tell what the object of aggression will be.

Despite these problems, it is clear that similar social experiences can create a considerable degree of uniformity in personality, especially in homogeneous societies, where the agencies of socialization support and reinforce each other.

SEX AND TEMPERAMENT

All societies distinguish between the roles of men and women, assigning to each sex special tasks, duties, and prerogatives. In Western society, differences in the roles of men and women are associated with sharp and contrasting differences in temperament. The female is regarded as naturally nonaggressive and passive, the male as naturally aggressive and active. The contrasting temperaments of men and women have been associated with the dominance of one and the submission of the other. Thus, the more dominating a man, the more masculine he is thought to be; the more passive and pliant a woman, the more feminine.

Mead analyzed three primitive societies (Arapesh, Mundugumor, and Tchambuli), on the island of New Guinea, to test the hypothesis that temperamental differences between males and females are universal.[26]

The ideal *Arapesh,* man *or* woman, is gentle, responsive, unaggressive, and "maternal." A child is not regarded as the result of a single act of impregnation, but must be fed and shaped in the mother's womb by repeated unions of mother and father. The verb "to bear a child" may refer either to a man or a woman. After an infant is born, the husband lies down at his wife's side and is said to be "in bed having a baby." Husband and wife together observe the taboos and perform the ceremonies that accompany the

birth of a child. Later, the husband shares in child-care.

The minute day-by-day care of little children, with its routine, its exasperations, its wails of misery that cannot be correctly interpreted, these are as congenial to the Arapesh men as they are to the Arapesh women. And in recognition of this care, as well as in recognition of the father's initial contribution, if one comments upon a middle-aged man as good-looking, the people answer: "Good-looking? Ye-e-s? But you should have seen him before he bore all those children." [27]

Sexual aggressiveness is attributed to neither sex. Rape is unknown among the Arapesh; their image of male sexuality makes it psychologically alien to them. The Arapesh permit polygyny (one husband, multiple wives), but it is not regarded as an ideal state.

Among the *Mundugumor,* both men and women are aggressive, harsh, and violent. In the structure of Mundugumor society the father and his daughters form one group, the mother and her sons another. Pregnancy is welcomed by neither parent, for the father fears a son and the mother a daughter. The crying infant is suckled only as a last resort, and then with the mother in a strained, standing position. The infant is removed as soon as he stops suckling. Weaning consists of slapping the child and thrusting him away.

Both sexes are regarded as sexually aggressive, and sex play, especially in premarital encounters in the bush, take the form of mutual scratching and biting. Polygyny is an ideal. Wives bring wealth and power by growing and curing tobacco, but new marriages are a further stimulus to hostility. Throughout life there is antagonism between the sexes. In this battle women ". . . are believed to be just as violent, just as aggressive, just as jealous [as men]. They simply are not quite as strong physically, although often a woman can put up a very good fight, and a

---

[26] This discussion is indebted to Margaret Mead, *Sex and Temperament in Three Primitive Societies* (New York: Morrow, 1935).

[27] *Ibid.,* p. 39. Reprinted by permission of William Morrow & Co., Inc.

husband who wishes to beat his wife takes care to arm himself with a crocodile-jaw and to be sure that she is not armed." [28]

Among the *Tchambuli,* sharply divergent roles are prescribed for the sexes and are accompanied by marked temperamental differences. The roles reverse Western notions about what is naturally male and female temperament. Tchambuli economic life is supervised by the women, and the men devote themselves in separate establishments to art and ceremony. The women work together in easy and bantering camaraderie, and the men are anxious, distrustful of each other, and given to "catty" remarks. The women are efficient and unadorned, the men self-conscious and arrayed in bird-of-paradise feathers. The women work and support the community; the men arrange ceremonies and dances to entertain and amuse the women.

Women are regarded as more actively and urgently sexed than men. The men's emotional life centers around the women. One source of this emotional dependence is the experience of the young male child. In infancy and early childhood he lives as an integral part of the women's community, where his experiences are pleasant and intimate. For a number of years, when he is considered too old to spend all his time with the women but is still too young to be accepted into the adult male community, he lives in a kind of emotional limbo. His earliest and deepest ties are to women, and these ties are never counterbalanced by his experiences in the male community.

Caution: Although men and women do take on distinctive personality traits in different cultures, in no society is there a dead level of temperament. Among the Arapesh, for example, there were noticeable differences in the degree to which individuals were unaggressive and nonviolent. Never-

theless, even the most active Arapesh child is less aggressive than a normally active American child.

HUMAN NATURE

Because the individual's own responses seem spontaneous and natural to him, he often regards them as part of his essential humanity rather than as the result of a particular training and experience. On the other hand, once the efficacy of socialization is understood, it is easy to fall into the opposite fallacy and to deny that there are limitations to human malleability.

When we speak of the "nature" of wood and water, we mean that it responds in ascertainable ways to known conditions. If we drive too large a nail into hard wood, it may crack; if we heat water to 212° F. at sea level, it will boil. To know the nature of anything is to know also its potentialities and limits. The problem of human nature should be understood in the same matter-of-fact way.

The idea of human nature is clear enough when it refers to the study of man as a physical organism. The more we learn about body chemistry and physiology, the more we can say about the organism's responses to the invasion of bacteria and to changes in temperature, pressure, and nutrition. Similarly, various psychological phenomena, such as learning and perceiving, seem to follow laws that are characteristic of the whole species. But there is more to man than his biological and neurological equipment. He also has personality, characterized by dispositions to respond in emotional ways, by the development of a self, and by psychological defenses. Special problems in the study of human nature arise when we turn to the socially relevant aspects of man's psychic structure.

Such challenging questions as the following are raised: Are there universal psychological characteristics which affect the way men relate themselves to each other? Do these characteristics, if they exist, set limits on the kinds of social arrangements that are

[28] *Ibid.,* p. 210.

psychologically acceptable? Or are psychic tolerances so broad that *any* kind of social organization is possible? Are some aspirations, such as the quest for power, part of essential human nature, or are they products of socialization in a given culture?

Some of these questions have been explored in the comparative study of personality and society. These kinds of study can test whether or not asserted uniformities in human nature really exist. Mead's study of sex and temperament and Malinowski's investigation of the Oedipus complex (see Adaptation 9, pp. 132 ff.) are of this kind.

Communication and Basic Humanity: A New Guinea native, knowing no English, binds an Australian soldier's wounds and guides him for two days and nights through the jungle to his camp.

A recent approach to the study of human nature is the attempt to identify emotional needs which demand satisfaction in social arrangements. (See Adaptation 44, pp. 692–95.) Fromm asserts that man has a fundamental need for belonging, for being securely part of a community which can give him emotional support. The growth of economic and political freedom in Western society has tended to isolate the individual and to bring about the withdrawal of older social supports. Fromm's analysis is based on "neo-Freudian" psychology. This point of view recognizes the importance of social influences but maintains that the human psychic structure is naturally fragile, because it grows out of and depends upon social interaction. The continued support of others through love, affection, and social approval is needed. The neo-Freudians hold that man is *anxiety-prone* and that social groups must provide conditions that alleviate anxiety. If these supports are lacking, the individual will seek a way out of anxiety, sometimes with severe consequences for political order. Anxiety may manifest itself in several ways; in overaggressiveness, submission to authority, or in apathetic withdrawal.

A common human nature does not necessarily lead directly to uniformities in behavior. What is observed depends on the conditions within which response takes place, and what is learned is *the disposition of the person to respond*. If the need for personal security is a fundamental part of human nature, the need will be revealed in a wide variety of ways. An understanding of the underlying psychic condition can reveal much about potential responses of children and adults to anxiety-provoking situations.

Authority and Socialization in a Primitive Society

A partial summary of Bronislaw Malinowski, *Sex and Repression in Savage Society* (New York: Harcourt, Brace, 1927).

Freud's Theory

According to Freudian psychoanalytic theory, the family universally gives rise to a typical constellation of feelings called the "Oedipus complex," in which the male child feels hostility toward his father because the child desires exclusive access to his mother. This hostility must be suppressed, but it manifests itself in later life as antagonism toward male authority figures. Freud held that the source of hostility to the father was sexual feeling on the part of the child for the mother. He believed that the Oedipus complex appears in disguised form in fairy tales, legends, and myths. For example, in the Greek mythical drama for which Freud named the complex, Oedipus unknowingly but inevitably killed his father and married his mother. Freud regarded the myth as evidence for the existence of the complex. The myth was a symbolic and socially acceptable form for expressing the repressed desire to return to a warm and intimate relation with the mother.

Malinowski's Theory

Malinowski approached the study of the Oedipus complex from the standpoint of anthropological studies, which show wide variation in family structure. He held that the pattern of "conflicts, passions, and attachments" within the family varied according to the structure. Malinowski's hypothesis was that the hostility of the male child was directed against the father not in his role as husband of the mother, but in his role as authority over the child, and that the source of the Oedipus complex was not sexual jeal-

ADAPTATION 9

ousy but resentment of the father's power to dominate. He reasoned that if his hypothesis were correct, the Oedipus complex was not universal but a product of the middle-class family in Western society. This family is patriarchal, and the father has the dominant power within it. Other societies, however, distribute power differently, and the father has power in varying degrees. There are some societies in which he has very little power. Malinowski tested his hypothesis in the light of his extensive knowledge of the Trobriand Islanders of Northeastern New Guinea, who vest authority over the child in the mother's brother rather than in the father.

The Father

The Trobriand Islanders are matrilineal, that is, kinship is reckoned through the mother only, succession and inheritance descend in the female line, and children belong to the mother's family, clan, and community. A boy inherits the social position and the possessions, not of his father but of his maternal uncle.

Matrimony is monogamous except for chiefs. The Trobrianders are ignorant of conception and do not regard the husband as the father of the children. He gives the children loving care and tender companionship in early childhood, but his authority over them is only by virtue of his personal relations with them. The mother's brother is the socially recognized source of authority.

Marriage in the Trobriand Islands is patrilocal: the wife goes to live with her husband in a house in his community. The children *live* with the father in childhood, but they *belong* to the mother's community. Their real home is where their maternal uncle lives.

The Maternal Uncle

The child is integrated into the life of the community and learns his role and obligations in society from his mother's brother.

This maternal uncle, not the father, directs the boy's occupations, teaches him tribal laws and prohibitions, and requires certain of his services. The work that he does with his uncle contributes to his own community in which he will eventually take his place. However, he continues to work with his father, too, but he does so out of good will and friendship, as this work contributes to his father's community of people who are legally strangers to him. The uncle holds the key to the boy's social status, wealth, power, and family pride. Therefore, to the Trobriand boy, the uncle is idealized as the model of right behavior and is the person to please and imitate.

During adolescence the young boy learns his duties, is instructed in traditions and magic, in arts and crafts. At this time relations between the boy and his uncle are most intimate and satisfactory, and the father suffers a temporary eclipse in the child's life.

The authority and discipline exercised by the uncle inevitably prove irksome to the child, and the ideal of behavior provided by him, a burden. Although the education received from his uncle is the road to mature status in the community, it requires from him the renunciation of childhood pleasures and the repression of childhood impulses. The child's attitudes toward the uncle include not only reverence but also dislike and hostility, which must be repressed and denied.

Unlike the father in our society, the Trobriand father is immune to these feelings of hostility. Without authority and the power to discipline, he invokes no dislike on the part of the child. As a matter of fact, he provides a haven and a refuge when friction between the child and his uncle develops.

Myth and Reality

In accordance with Freud's suggestion that repressed feelings find outlet in myth and legend, Malinowski examined Trobriand stories. He found that the father is not mentioned in their mythology. Myths are based upon the matrilineal family pattern, and the central male role is usually taken by the maternal uncle, who is typically the villain. He abandons the nephew or withholds the art of magic from him and is murdered by the nephew. These myths are double-edged. They can be interpreted to mean either that in practice the uncle finds his duties to his nephew irksome or that the nephew would be glad to be rid of his debt of gratitude to his uncle.

The mutual hostility and suspicion between uncle and nephew in myths have their parallel in reality. While it is the duty of the uncle to pass on to his nephew the family possessions, the nephew is in fact bound to make a substantial payment for inheritance. When a father gives gifts to his son, he always does so out of sheer affection, and magic is as often received from the father as a gift as it is inherited from the uncle. However, when magic is inherited from the uncle, there may be a suspicion in the nephew's mind that he has been cheated of his full share. Suspicion does not arise when the magic is a gift from the father.

Conclusion

Malinowski disagreed with Freud on two counts. He concluded (1) that the Oedipus complex, as Freud described it, is not universal but a product of the patriarchal family in Western society, and (2) that the hostility found in the Oedipus complex is directed against the father, not because of his sexual relation to the mother, but because of his social relation to the child. This social relation is an authority relation, and hostility will center around whoever has dominant authority within the family.

The authority problem of the maternal uncle in Trobriand society lies in the divided loyalties of the uncle-father and the dilemma of authority and intimacy.

1. The family system of the Trobriand Islanders is subject to *divided loyalties.* The uncle is father to his own children and bound to them by ties of affection, and he may resent his obligations to his nephew—obligations which must have preference over his personal relations with his children and his wife. The nephew's fear of abandonment, hostility, and suspicion may, therefore, be not so much the result of rebellion against the uncle's authority as a recognition of the uncle's divided loyalties. By the standards of Trobriand culture, the uncle ought to be wholly committed to the nephew, but the nephew knows he is not.

2. The uncle is not only an authority figure for the nephew but his educator as well. Education must involve him in intimate relations with his nephew. When authority is combined with intimacy, it is likely to generate hostility. The intimacy leads to expectations that the person will be treated with affection and leniency, while the authority relation leads to a measure of impersonal judgment. In other words, it is not authority alone that engenders hostility, but authority combined with a personal or primary relationship.

Caution: While Malinowski's study is an interesting attempt to test psychological hypotheses by anthropological investigation, it should not be concluded that the issue raised here is settled.[29]

---

[29] For some of the debate on this topic see Ernest Jones, "Mother-Right and the Sexual Ignorance of Savages," *International Journal of Psychoanalysis,* VI, Part 2 (April, 1925), pages 109–30. See also Harold D. Lasswell, "A Hypothesis Rooted in the Preconceptions of a Single Civilization Tested by Bronislaw Malinowski," in Stuart A. Rice (ed.), *Methods in Social Science* (Chicago: University of Chicago Press, 1931), pages 480–88.

Chapter V

Primary groups

Introduction

In exploring the forms of human association, students of society have given much attention to a type of relation called the primary relation and a type of group called the primary group. This chapter identifies these phenomena and shows their significance for the individual and society.

THE PRIMARY RELATION

We must first distinguish between the primary *relation* and the primary *group*. A primary relation has the following chief characteristics:

1. *Response is to whole persons rather than to segments*. In the primary relation the participants interact as unique and total individuals. Uniqueness means that response is to a particular person and is not transferable to other persons. "Wholeness" should not be taken literally. It means (*a*) that one responds to many aspects of another's character and background, and (*b*) that one responds spontaneously and freely, as a unified, naturally organized self, permitting true feelings to enter the relationship. The less transferable the response and the more complete the interaction, the more primary is the relation.

Many human relations are not primary because they are highly transferable and very narrowly confined. For example, the relation between clerk and customer is a transferable one; each acts in standardized ways that are applicable to other clerks and other customers. In addition, the relation involves only parts of each person, those parts relevant to the conduct of business. If, however, this relation were to ripen into friendship, the transferability of response would decrease and more aspects of the person would be taken into account in their interaction. To "take account" of another as a person, instead of as a clerk or a customer, for example, is to become aware of and to adapt one's own responses to the many facets of the other's personality.

Entering a primary relation presumes acceptance of a whole person. This is recognized in the relation between husband and wife, which is understood to be not a contract but an unlimited commitment one to the other, where each assumes full responsibility for the other's well-being. In contrast nonprimary relations (often called "secondary") usually entail only limited responsibility of one individual to another, for ex-

FACE TO FACE

Each of these pictures is a study in
personal relations, a blend of behavior
defined by social roles and spontaneous person-to-person interaction.
Spontaneity and intimacy afford opportunity for personal response and
self-expression, but interaction is also
governed and constrained by the situation, by the role, and by the past history of interpersonal experience.

Upper left: A survey engineer talks
with the captain of a labor gang in
New Guinea.

Upper right: A circus bicycle per-
former holds his sleeping baby just
before his act goes on.

Lower left: The proprietor and
friends are gathered around the stove
in his Vermont general store.

Lower right: Rafer Johnson, Olympic
decathlon champion, and C. K. Yang
of Nationalist China. College friends,
international competitors.

ample, the relation between many employers and employees.

2. *Communication is deep and extensive.* In the primary relation fewer limits are placed on both the range and the mode of communication. In nonprimary relations communication is limited to a few areas. In the primary relation, communication tends to occur as readily by means of non-verbal and private behavior as by words, and feelings and needs are revealed that are hidden in public situations. Nonprimary relations are not meant to reveal the deeper layers of personality and tend to be restricted to formal and public modes of interaction.

The differences in communication between primary and nonprimary relations are important because the expression of feelings and beliefs tends to influence the feelings and beliefs of others. Although communication does not guarantee agreement, it does facilitate and encourage it, and where communication is deep and extensive, similarities in attitudes and feelings naturally tend to develop. In nonprimary relations, though there may be agreement or understanding on some matters, it may not be carried over to others. In the primary relation, however, increased communication brings with it an increased opportunity for individuals to influence each other deeply. Cooley emphasized the contribution of the primary group to the formation of character, for example, in the influence of parents upon children.

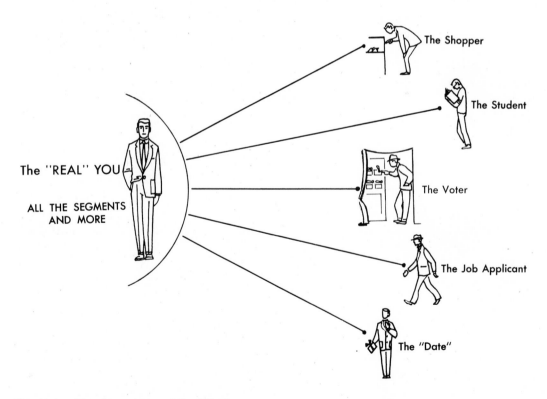

Fig. **V:1**   The Segment and the Whole

The more segmental the relation, the more people see and respond to each other according to the roles they play. However, roles differ in the extent to which they allow the spontaneous expression of personality. In the ideal primary relation, the mutually free response of integrated persons is at a maximum.

Although primary relations do not preclude hostility, they cannot subsist on antagonism. The primary relation entails a positive valuing of the other, a sense of "we-ness," of belonging together and sharing a common identity. When a personal relation is characterized by antagonism, communication is restricted and response is usually limited to a part of the other's personality. It is not, then, a primary relation. Strong antagonisms amounting to hatred may develop when an individual is frustrated in his expectations of a primary relation. The hate may be a distortion of a primary relation.

3. *Personal satisfactions are paramount.* Individuals enter into primary relations because such relations contribute directly to personal security and well-being. Because direct personal satisfactions are gained, the primary relation is not a utilitarian means to further ends but is valued for itself. In the primary relation the individual is accepted for himself and not merely as a means for some impersonal objective. Although a man's job may support his family, it may not be in itself a source of psychological satisfaction. To the extent that a job gives direct satisfaction, one may expect to find that primary relations have developed in the work situation.

These chief characteristics of the primary relation—response to whole persons, deep and extensive communication, and personal satisfactions—may be expected when the quality of "primaryness" is most fully developed. In experience, of course, primary groups do vary from the "ideal," and most primary relations are incomplete, even those among friends and lovers. Nevertheless, knowing what the fully developed primary relation is can help to diagnose situations in which the incompleteness of the relation is a source of tension and frustration.

THE PRIMARY GROUP

A group is primary insofar as it is based upon and sustains primary relations. Some groups, like the family, arise from primary relations and are especially capable of sustaining them. Where people live or work together closely for some time, groups based on primary relations usually emerge. However, barriers to communication, such as the enforcement of sharp differences in status, can block the development of primary relations.

It follows from this that families, play groups, and neighborhood circles, which offer congenial conditions for primary group development, should be examined to determine the degree to which they approximate the model. On this point note the discussion in Adaptation 10, which follows. Communication is lower and contact more fragmentary in some cases than in others.

Moreover, not all small groups are primary. For example, a committee working together over a considerable time, but composed of men of varying backgrounds, ages, and ranks, may offer little opportunity for primary group formation. Smallness is one condition facilitating primary group formation but in itself is not sufficient.

On the other hand, largeness, although not a congenial condition, does not necessarily prevent formation of primary groups. Sociologists sometimes speak of whole communities as based on primary relations. The German word *Gemeinschaft* or "primary community" is used to designate a type of society characterized by (1) an assignment of status to the whole person, so that his job and the rest of his life form a unity; (2) a high degree of cohesion based on the widespread sharing of common attitudes and aims; and (3) a sense of unlimited commitment to the community, which is conceived as an enlarged kinship group, the source of one's personal identity. (See SOCIAL ORGANIZATION, p. 47.)

Various primary groups, such as families, soldier groups, boys' gangs, and factory cliques, can be classified together only because they are based to a significant extent on primary relations. In addition, they perform functions normally expected of primary groups, such as giving the individual emotional support. Clearly, however, these groups are very different. They do not all protect or gratify the individual in the same way or to the same degree. A primary group within a factory can do some important things for the individual and can affect the factory organization; but it cannot do the family's job, just as the family cannot perform the factory group's peculiar functions. To know what a primary group can do, one must know the social context within which it has developed.

Caution: Because of this topic's connection with such experiences as love, friendship, and family life, the student may mistakenly draw the conclusion that primary relations are necessarily good and nonprimary relations are somehow inherently bad. It is true that primary relations are closely related to personal satisfaction. This does not mean, however, that just because a relation is primary, it is desirable, nor that direct personal satisfaction is the only criterion of social worth.

In many situations, it is advantageous to maintain relatively impersonal relations. Much business, military, educational, and legal experience suggests the wisdom of formalizing relations in order, for example, to establish equality of treatment. Formalization permits decisions to be made with reference to the task at hand. Professional standards can be upheld or individuals assigned to hazardous duties free from the pressures that arise when personal claims can be made on those in authority.

The relationship between faculty and students is an instance of the problem of formal *vs.* primary relations. Quite properly both professors and students value informal and easy contacts; yet such contacts are engaged in with real risks. The professor who is too easily accessible may find it more difficult to make objective judgments about grades, or he may be suspected of being influenced by his personal attachments. Because of this, many professors sacrifice part of their friendly relations with students rather than jeopardize impartiality and objectivity. The problem arises even more seriously for judges and other government officials. The long historic effort to achieve "a government of laws and not of men" reflects the social value of nonprimary relations in situations where objectivity is of paramount importance.

SOURCES AND READINGS

Dorwin Cartwright and Alvin Zander (eds.), *Group Dynamics* (Evanston: Row, Peterson, 1953).

Paul A. Hare, Robert F. Bales, Edgar F. Borgatta (eds.), *Small Groups* (New York: Knopf, 1955).

George C. Homans, *The Human Group* (New York: Harcourt, Brace, 1950).

Helen H. Jennings, *Leadership and Isolation* (2nd ed.; New York: Longmans, Green, 1950).

Josephine Klein, *The Study of Groups* (London: Routledge and Kegan Paul, 1956).

Paul F. Lazarsfeld and Robert K. Merton, "Friendship as Social Process" in Morroe Berger, Theodore Abel, and Charles H. Page, *Freedom and Control in Modern Society* (New York: Van Nostrand, 1954), pp. 18–66.

J. L. Moreno, *Who Shall Survive?* Nervous and Mental Disease Monograph, Series No. 58, 1934.

Michael S. Olmsted, *The Small Group* (New York: Random House, 1959).

Edward A. Shils, "The Study of the Primary Group" in Daniel Lerner and Harold D. Lasswell (eds.), *The Policy Sciences* (Stanford: Stanford University Press, 1951), pp. 44–69.

John W. Thibaut and Harold H. Kelley, *The Social Psychology of Groups* (New York: Wiley, 1959).

American Sociological Review, "Special Issue on Small Group Research," Vol. 19, No. 6, December, 1954.

Periodicals: *Human Relations;* and *Sociometry.*

The Primary Group: Essence and Accident

Abridged and adapted from "The Primary Group: Essence and Accident" by Ellsworth Faris, *American Journal of Sociology*, **38** (July, 1932), 41–50. Published in this form by permission of The University of Chicago Press.

The term "primary group" was first used by Cooley: [1]

By primary groups I mean those characterized by intimate face-to-face association and co-operation. They are primary in several senses, but chiefly in that they are fundamental in forming the social nature and ideas of the individual. The result of intimate association, psychologically, is a certain fusion of individualities in a common whole, so that one's very self, for many purposes at least, is the common life and purpose of the group. Perhaps the simplest way of describing this wholeness is by saying that it is a "we"; it involves the sort of sympathy and mutual identification for which "we" is the natural expression. One lives in the feeling of the whole and finds the chief aims of his will in that feeling.

It is perhaps a moot point whether Cooley saw face-to-face contact as necessary to the primary group. However, social scientists have often equated primary groups with face-to-face groups. In the following adaptation we present the gist of an attempt by Ellsworth Faris to arrive at a more adequate and a more generalized understanding of the essence of the primary group.

The medieval schoolmen made a distinction between the essence and the accident. Your table may be square and oaken, but being square and oaken is not essential to its being a table. It would still be a table if it

[1] Charles Horton Cooley, *Social Organization* (New York: Scribner's, 1909), p. 23.

were round or oval, or if it were made of maple or of steel. Such characteristics of particular tables are called accidents. If we want to arrive at a definition of a table, we must be careful not to confuse such accidental characteristics of particular tables with the essence of all tables, the essence of all tables being those properties which all tables share, and without which they would no longer be tables.

The primary group is often defined as a face-to-face group. But how essential to the definition of a primary group is the property face-to-face? Are all face-to-face groups primary groups? Are any groups primary groups whose relations are not face-to-face? Or is the face-to-face relation merely an accident?

In an American criminal court, the judge, jury, defendant, and counsel are in a face-to-face nearness. Yet the court has none of the essential properties of the primary group set forth by Cooley. It is externally controlled and governed by rules made by absent and ancient authorities. A legislative body, even a small one, or a board of directors with formal procedures, are additional examples of face-to-face groups which cannot be called primary groups. A primary group may be as small as two, but you and an unwelcome salesman at your door do not form a primary group. Nor would a delinquent student and the dean into whose office he has been summoned constitute a primary group. Not all face-to-face groups are in essence primary groups.

Do any groups not face-to-face have the properties of the primary group? There is reason to think so. A kinship group widely scattered in space and communicating by letter may be characterized by a common feeling of unity, exhibit "a certain fusion of individualities in a common whole," and be accurately classed as a primary group. "The sort of mutual identification and sympathy for which 'we' is the natural expression," suggests that Cooley did not mean to make the face-to-face relation the essence of the primary group.

If our reasoning be sound, it follows that not every family is a primary group and that a school group may or may not be so defined. A domestic tyrant may, with commands, threats, and punishments, assemble his subjects around a table thrice daily as a group; but such a group would lack the essential qualities of a primary group. The father who has alienated his children may be viewed with hatred or treated as an outsider in a company where there is no feeling of "we."

The primary group is to be contrasted, therefore, not with the group whose members are separated in space, but with the group whose members are related to each other only in formal, impersonal, and institutionalized ways.

The importance of primary relations lies in the fact that they give rise to the essentially human experiences, so that human nature may be said to be created in primary group relations. To the degree that relations are impersonal and fractional, they are ineffective in generating the sentiments which are distinctly human. If children in home and school are to participate in the culture of their people, it is necessary that the home and school be primary groups. But the mere fact that children meet face-to-face with the members of their families and their schools does not guarantee the emergence of primary group relations.

This is not to say that the primary group is superior to other types of groups. Some kinds of human needs may be better satisfied by institutions than by primary group relations. Indeed, primary group relations may intrude in a disorganizing manner, for example, when a police officer refuses to arrest a man because he is a friend. Here is the root of much of the corruption, bribery, nepotism, and "graft" of our modern life. Formal and institutional groups cannot perform their functions unless the distinction between them and the primary group is kept with scrupulous clarity.

As we have shown, it is in the institution that we find the essential opposite of the primary group. In institutions forms are fixed, rules are prescribed, offices are laid down, and duties are set forth with definite clarity and relative inflexibility. Under typically institutional circumstances the person does not act freely but instead performs a definite institutional function, and personal relations are at a minimum. An institution might almost be defined as a social device to make emotion unnecessary. But the primary group has as an essential element the emotional character which binds its members into a relation.

Conclusion

Not all face-to-face groups are primary groups. It is essential to the primary group that a certain kind of relation exist among its members, a relation that is personal, spontaneous, emotional. Such primary relations may exist without face-to-face contact, and they may be absent even where there is face-to-face contact. The opposite of the primary group is the group in which relations are formal and impersonal. A family is, therefore, not necessarily a primary group, although it is true that the family is, among all social groups, the one most likely to develop and sustain primary relations.

This essay by the late Ellsworth Faris is representative of an important trend in recent sociology. This trend has shifted emphasis away from the external and static traits of groups (like face-to-face nearness) to the internal dynamics of relations within groups.

Caution: Faris contrasts the primary group with the institution. Here he uses "institution" to mean a group or activity characterized by formal, impersonal rules. Many sociologists, however, would not restrict the term "institution" in this way, but would use it to refer to any well-established group or activity, including those that are based upon and sustain primary relations. (See SOCIAL ORGANIZATION, pp. 32–33.) The family, according to this usage, would be termed an institution quite independently of whether or not it also fulfilled the requirements of being a primary group. Impersonal relations and groups

are called "secondary" by some sociologists.

Note also that "primary" is used both to designate a type of relation and to indicate the significance of that relation for socialization. Primary groups play a primary role, that is, a fundamental role, in the socialization of the individual. This point is recognized by Faris when he notes that the family *ought to be* a primary group. When the family does not develop primary relations, its fundamental role is not fulfilled, and inadequate socialization of the child may be expected.

Section 2 The primary group and the individual

When Cooley first identified primary groups, he called them the "nurseries of human nature" [2] because of their importance in giving social direction to the individual's developing personality. The socializing function of primary groups has been considered in the preceding chapter, and it is further treated in THE FAMILY, pages 373–75. This section discusses the *individual-sustaining function* of the primary group, the kinds of support it can give to the person.

The primary group is the main link between the individual and society. It can do the work society requires, largely that of getting the individual to want to work or fight or exercise self-restraint, because it serves his personal needs. Membership in a primary group gives him emotional support which binds him to the group and, through it, to the aims of the larger society.

The need of the individual for group support has long been recognized and is often used as a powerful instrument of social control. The extreme form of control based on

this need is banishment, a technique regarded in some societies as equivalent to capital punishment. However, the severity of this punishment will vary with the completeness of the personal isolation forced upon the individual. The more isolated an individual is from his immediate primary group and from the opportunity to create new primary relations, the greater is his distress. A political exile isolated from home ties may experience severe distress, but if he goes abroad with his family and a retinue of followers, he continues to be supported by primary group ties.

The problems of aging are undoubtedly aggravated by the weakening of primary group ties. The decay has two sources. First, the old person is deprived of companionship as his friends die; second, the limited number of home-centered activities in urban America provides slender basis for sustained mutual interests among the generations. Perhaps the rural home is a better environment for the aged because its larger group and multiplicity of activities afford varied opportunities for primary group interaction. This suggests that it is not merely the fact of group

[2] *Op. cit.,* see especially Chap. 3.

Charles Horton Cooley (1864–1929) is rightly regarded as one of the founders of sociology. He is best known for his work on socialization and the primary group. Like the American pragmatists, George H. Mead and John Dewey, Cooley emphasized the social nature of the self. It had been customary in Western thought to treat the relation between the individual and society as a philosophical problem and to ask: Why should the individual take on social values? Cooley and others held that the relation between the individual and society is an empirical one, and that the proper question is: How does the individual take on social values? They viewed socialization as a natural process.

membership that counts but the repeated opportunity to validate that membership by participation in activities meaningful to the group. Even activities of a routine and unemotional character can perform this function, as long as they draw the individual into the group.

The experience of the citizen soldier newly inducted into the army is another case in point. The organization, as he first encoun-

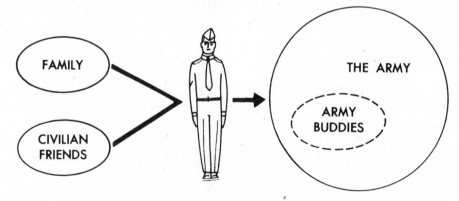

Fig. **V:2**   The new soldier depends greatly on continuing support from primary relations outside the army; but this dependence decreases as he finds new friends who will take account of him and protect him as a unique individual.

ters it, is impersonal, almost inhuman. All of the people in it are unknown quantities, and especially the recruit himself, for he finds that what he means, what he is, depends on the knowledge and judgment of people with whom he is intimate. Separated from them, he is unsure of himself. In his early career in the army he depends heavily on his old ties to his family and friends. He tries to interpret his new training activities in terms of the old relationships. Letters from home, visits from friends and relatives, and daydreams about civilian life fill a large part of his unoccupied hours.

As new friendships are made with his barracks mates, he comes to think of himself as a member of his army unit, and his dependence on civilian primary groups is lessened. In time of war the civilian primary group continues as a source of moral support. In peacetime the regular army soldier's primary group may monopolize his relations. If he is married, his family often becomes a part of the community of the army post. His wife is an army wife; his children are "army brats." In extreme instances, associations with civilian groups may be reduced to the vanishing point.

HOW THE PRIMARY GROUP HELPS

What does the individual get out of the primary group? Just how does it sustain him?

This soldier receives as he gives, acting out and reliving his own primary group experience.

This is not yet fully understood, but the following elements are undoubtedly present:

1. In the primary relation uniqueness counts. The individual recognizes that he is accepted and wanted for himself. He does not need continuously to be on guard, to put forth his best effort, to *prove* himself. He can *be* himself.

2. From his primary group membership the individual derives an image of himself; his continued membership in the group sustains that identity. When the "sharp dresser" or the "big wheel" or "Joe's pal" moves to a new environment, he must re-establish his identity, or find a new one, sometimes under great difficulties.

In Adaptation 12 Long John was identified in the Norton Street gang as "Doc's pal." When Doc left the Norton Street group for Spongi's gang, John lost his old identity with the Nortons and could not establish it with Spongi. No longer thought of as "Doc's pal," Long John lost his self-confidence and his bowling deteriorated. Unprotected by his old identity, he became an object of attack by the Nortons. He was unable to establish a new image of himself either in his own or the group's eyes, and his psychological difficulties were not removed until Doc saw to it that Long John was once more identified as "Doc's pal" both by Spongi's gang and the Nortons.

3. Because the primary group takes account of the whole person, knowing him and adapting to his many individual characteristics, it can soften the impact of externally imposed rules and regulations. *The primary group protects the individual by reinterpreting and modifying goals and rules, and by adapting them to the capacities of the individual and to his special personal circumstances.* In Adaptation 11 the distant authority (management) of a large factory set standards that failed to take account of the working primary group. Although the primary group could not directly "get at" the distant authority, it did very effectively modify the expression of that authority, because the supervisor was to some extent integrated into the workers' primary group. His difficult role was to compromise and interpret the formal standards of the factory in a way acceptable to management and workers. Clearly neither worker nor management interests could operate exclusively very long. Reasonable production levels had to be maintained, but they did not have to be achieved in the precise way set down in the formal rules. Had the supervisor tried to make the formal system work in a literal way, he would have been rejected by the primary group, and his usefulness to the company would have ended. On the other hand, he could protect the members of the group in their minor violations of the rules only while the main objective of production was being satisfied. The workers were not interested in undermining production, but they wanted some control over their situation to reduce their dependence upon an impersonal industrial machine.

The large society often must develop rules based on experience with average individuals. Groups which know the individual best, especially the family, intercede in his behalf and regulate his participation in the community. For example, parents may blunt the impact of the school by requiring a minimum of the child. Or they may support the standards of the school while assisting the child to compensate for his learning difficulties or to exploit fully his special talents.

The Bank Wiring Room

Abridged and adapted from F. J. Roethlisberger and W. J. Dickson, *Management and the Worker* (Cambridge: Harvard University Press, 1939), Part IV. Published in this form by permission of the authors and Harvard University Press.

Between 1927 and 1932 an important program of studies on employee satisfaction and dissatisfaction at work was carried out at the Western Electric Hawthorne Works in Chicago by the company's research organization and the Harvard Department of Industrial Research.[3] The data for these studies include management records of production, absenteeism and labor turnover, on-the-spot observation and record-taking, and an extensive and long-range interview program with management and workers.

The investigation reported here, one part of the Hawthorne studies, deals with the interpersonal relations and social organization of a small group of factory workers in the bank wiring room.

The detailed study and observation of the bank wiring room was undertaken late in the research program. There was already evidence that social groups in shop departments were capable of exercising strong control over the work behavior of individuals. In some groups the wage incentive systems were rendered ineffectual by group pressure for controlled output. Informal practices which put certain workers under pressure and kept them in line were brought to light. There was evidence of informal leadership by persons who assumed the responsibility of seeing that the members of a group clung together

[3] Henry A. Landsberger, *Hawthorne Revisited* (Ithaca, N.Y.: Cornell University, 1958) is an analysis of the bank wiring room research and a commentary on published critiques of the study.

and protected themselves from interference by company representatives.

These reports of social organization among employees, and its effects, were derived almost entirely from interviews. The investigators had little opportunity to observe the groups at work, they knew little about their output except what could be learned from departmental records, which were kept for practical rather than research purposes, and they knew almost nothing about the behavior of the employees toward one another and their supervisors. In order to get a more systematic and exact understanding of behavior in the shops, it was decided to study one group intensively.

THE SETTING

For six months detailed observation was made of a group of fourteen men in the "bank wiring" room. The work group consisted of nine wiremen, three soldermen, and two inspectors, who turned out parts for telephone switchboards. A completed job involved three main types of work: (1) a wireman connected the projecting points of "banks," (2) a solderman fixed the connections in place, and (3) an inspector tested the work of both men. The wired banks were assembled into a final product called an "equipment," which was ten or eleven banks long and two or three banks high.

Management's Incentive System

The men worked under a system of group piecework. Part of their weekly earnings was based upon the number of equipments turned out by the group as a whole during the week. The wage incentive plan had the following three principal elements:

1. Every man was assigned an hourly wage

rate based largely upon his own average individual output established by past performance. His basic hourly rate multiplied by the number of hours he worked constituted a worker's basic individual weekly wage. His basic wage was guaranteed by the company irrespective of group output.

2. The basic wage was supplemented by a "bonus" which depended upon the number of equipments the group as a whole had completed during the week. If group output went above a certain level, each man received his share of the increased earnings.

3. Since individual hourly wage rates were based upon a man's average output per hour, allowance was made for time lost by stoppages beyond his control. Otherwise the efficiency ratings of men who had been delayed would suffer when compared with those of men who had lost little time.

This wage incentive plan was instituted by management to promote efficiency and to provide a fair means of apportioning earnings among the employees. The plan assumed that the men wanted above all to maximize their earnings.

1. Since each individual's total wage was determined to some degree by group output, each worker would try to increase output.

2. If the workers exerted pressure at all, it would be to increase the output of the slower workers.

3. To increase his hourly wage rate, each worker would strive to increase his individual average output.

The plan also assumed a high degree of cooperation between employees and management. Efficiency ratings, for example, were meant to assure a fair distribution of wages. In order to establish efficiency ratings, however, it was necessary to keep detailed records, both of individual output and of time lost. The plan could be fair, therefore, only if the employees did not thwart management's efforts at objective record-keeping and if management could establish adequate supervision of the records.

Management's wage incentive plan was a workable one, promoting both efficiency and a fair distribution of earnings, only if the men acted in accordance with management's assumptions.

THE ACTUAL SITUATION: RESTRICTION OF OUTPUT

Actually, the men behaved quite differently. They had their own idea of a proper day's work—about two completed equipments per man—and they felt that no more should be turned out. So far as the company was concerned, total output was satisfactory, and the foreman felt that his "boys" worked hard. Nevertheless, the men had adopted an informal norm setting output below the level it might have reached had each man worked as hard as he could.

If a man worked too fast or produced more than the group thought right, he would be ridiculed as a "rate-buster" or "speed king." On the other hand, if he produced too little, he would be called a "chiseler." Another penalty for nonconformity was a practice the men called "binging." This was a sort of game in which one man might walk up to another and hit him as hard as he could on the upper arm. His victim was then entitled to retaliate with a similar blow. One of the objects of the game was to see who could hit the hardest. But this practice was also used as a penalty and played a role in regulating the output of some of the faster workers. Thus:

First wireman: "Why don't you quit work? Let's see, this is your thirty-fifth row today. What are you going to do with them all?"

Second wireman: "What do you care? It's to your advantage if I work, isn't it?"

First wireman: "Yeah, but the way you're working you'll get stuck with them."

Second wireman: "Don't worry about that. I'll take care of it. You're getting paid by the sets I turn out. That's all you should worry about."

First wireman: "If you don't quit work I'll bing you." (He strikes him and finally chases him around the room.)

Observer, a few minutes later to the man who

was "binged": "What's the matter, won't he let you work?"

Second wireman: "No, I'm all through though. I've got enough done." (He then went over and helped another wireman.)

The employees also believed that their weekly average hourly output should show little change from week to week. They felt that if their output showed much change either from day to day or from week to week "something might happen." An unusually high output might thereafter become the standard their supervisors would expect them to maintain. The men felt it would be a way of confessing that they were capable of doing better. On the other hand, they felt that a low output would afford their supervisors a chance to "bawl them out." If output were kept fairly constant, they thought, neither possibility could happen.

In attempting to keep his production record constant, the worker was repudiating management's assumption that he would try to increase his production and with it his hourly rate. Since average hourly output was calculated by dividing total output by hours of work, the men could keep their output records constant by claiming either more or less than their actual output or more or less than the time actually spent. In practice both methods were used. Most men reported more connections than they completed, but two men who worked quite fast usually reported a little less than their actual count. The men who reported less than their actual output also claimed the least time out.

Attitudes Toward Supervision

The group felt that no worker should give the supervisor information which could be used to the detriment of his fellow workers. Anyone who did so was branded a "squealer" and made to feel unwelcome. One inspector was driven from the group with this treatment.

The group also felt that those in authority should not attempt to maintain social dis-

tance or act officious. The wage incentive plan provided one of the means by which the group was able in an informal way to decrease the social distance between themselves and their supervisor. To measure individual output the supervisor was supposed to make a daily count of the number of connections made by each wireman. But he did not have time for the job and left it to the wiremen to do themselves. Much the same thing occurred with regard to claims for time lost. The supervisor was responsible for deciding which stoppages were allowable and which were not, but because a clear distinction was often impossible, he approved most of the claims made. In effect, therefore, the workers supervised their own records, and by doing so were able to hold the supervisor to their own informal work norms.

Conclusion

The work norms of the bank wiremen may be summarized as follows:

1. You should not turn out too much work. If you do, you are a "rate-buster."

2. You should not turn out too little work. If you do, you are a "chiseler."

3. You should not tell a supervisor anything that will be detrimental to an associate. If you do, you are a "squealer."

4. You should not attempt to maintain social distance or act officious. For example, if you are an inspector, you should not act like one.

These norms, and the behavior supporting them, were spontaneously elaborated and enforced by the workers themselves, and were contrary to management's assumptions.

The Function of the Norms

When the men were asked why they tried to limit output and to keep their output records "steady," their replies were varied. Someone might be laid off, hours might be reduced, the slower workers would be reprimanded, the rate would be cut. Although

ADAPTATION 12°

workers elsewhere have had experiences of this kind, the men at Hawthorne had not encountered any of the things they said they were guarding against.

Their behavior seemed to be guided by the desire to protect themselves from interference of any sort on the part of management. Fearing changes which might be detrimental to their interests, the workers guarded against all change. Despite the wage incentive system, the workers maintained by their own informal controls constant group and individual output.

The work norms also controlled and regulated behavior within the group. The activities ordinarily labeled "restriction of output" represented attempts at social control and discipline and were able to transform a collection of individual workers into a social group.

The Primary Group and Individual Security

Abridged and adapted from William Foote Whyte, *Street Corner Society* (Chicago: University of Chicago Press, 1943), especially pp. 3–25 and 255–68. Published in this form by permission of William Foote Whyte and The University of Chicago Press. The second edition issued in 1955 contains an extended appendix describing the field research methods used in the study.

A stable and satisfying pattern of primary relations is of critical importance to self-security. In the following account of street corner groups, psychological difficulties and a breakdown in performance are traced to the disturbance of interpersonal relations.

The account is presented in the first person by the author. It concerns two street corner groups—the Norton Street gang and Spongi's gang—and the difficulties of two street corner members, Long John and Doc.

LONG JOHN'S NIGHTMARES

Long John's position among the Norton gang was ambiguous. Although he was close friends with the Norton leaders, Doc, Danny, and Mike, and shared some of their prestige, he was not a leader himself and had little influence over the rank and file of the gang.

When Doc and Danny left the Norton Street gang to join Spongi's gang and Mike drifted away, the Nortons regrouped under the leadership of Angelo, a previous follower. Long John divided his time between Spongi's and the Norton Street corner, but the realignment of the two groups placed him in a new and vulnerable position.

Those who hung around Spongi's "joint" (a local gambling house) were divided into an inner circle and the hangers-on. Danny, Doc, and three others were in the inner circle. When Spongi went for "coffee-ands," for a drive, or to the movies, he would invite them, but not Long John. Long John was excluded from the inner circle.

Without the support of Doc, Danny, and Mike, Long John lost his old standing among the boys who remained on Norton Street. Long John's bowling soon deteriorated, and he finished next to last in the individual competition that season. The first part of the next season brought no improvement. Doc and Danny, who still occasionally bowled, would say to him, "Well, it looks like you're not the man you used to be. This year maybe you won't be good enough to make the first team."

These remarks were made in a joking manner, but they were symptomatic of the changes in personal relations that had taken place. As if they sensed Long John's defenseless position, the Nortons redoubled their verbal attacks on him. The former followers had always attacked him more than they attacked Doc, Danny, or Mike, but now they subjected him to an unrelenting barrage that was calculated to destroy his self-confidence. When he was bowling poorly, there was little Long John could say to defend himself.

One afternoon Doc came to consult me about Long John. He had confided to Doc that he had not slept well for several weeks. As Doc said, "I talked it over with him. . . . Whenever he gets half-asleep and the sheet comes up over his face, he wakes up thinking he's dead. . . ." I suggested to Doc that he might be able to dispel Long John's anxieties if he took him into Spongi's inner circle and if he and Danny began to defend Long John's bowling and encourage him when the others attacked him. Doc was doubtful but agreed to try. Within a short time he had fitted Long John into Spongi's inner circle. As he explained:

I didn't say anything to Spongi, but I already fitted with him. I just made a lot of noise about Long John. If he wasn't around, I would ask the boys where he was. When he came in, I would say to him, "Here's Long John, the dirty bum," and I would ask him where he had been. I gave him so much attention that he moved in there right away. Spongi began asking him to go places with us. Now even when I'm not around John is right in there.

At the same time Doc and Danny began to support him at the bowling alleys. Long John's bowling began to improve. In a short time he was bowling as well as he had in the season of 1937/38. In the individual competition that climaxed the 1939/40 season, he won the first prize. He never again consulted Doc about his nightmares.

DOC'S DIZZY SPELLS

Doc's dizzy spells came upon him when he was unemployed and had no spending money. He considered this the cause of his difficulties, and, in a sense, it was. But many Cornerville men adjust themselves to being unemployed without serious difficulties. Why was Doc so different? To say that he was particularly sensitive is to name the phenomenon without explaining it. The observation of Doc's changing patterns of primary group relations provides the explanation.

Doc was accustomed to a high frequency of interaction with the members of his group and to frequent contacts with members of other groups. While he sometimes directly originated action for his group, usually someone would suggest a course of action, and then Doc would get the boys together and organize group activity. In 1938 Doc decided to run for the state legislature (he later withdrew from the campaign). The events of Doc's political campaign indicate that his usual pattern of interactions had broken down. Mike appointed himself Doc's campaign manager and was continually telling Doc what to do about the campaign. At the same time I was telling him what to do about getting a job. However, while we were suggesting action for him with increasing frequency, he himself was unable to originate action in group events. Lacking money, he could not participate in group activities without accepting the support of others and letting them determine his course of action. Since such a pattern conflicted with Doc's image of himself as a leader, he avoided associating with his friends on many occasions—that is, his frequency of interaction was drastically reduced. When he was alone, he did not get dizzy, but, when he was with a group of people and unable to act in his customary manner, he fell prey to the dizzy spells.

When Doc finally got a job as the director of a recreation center, the spells disappeared. He was once again able to organize action, first for the boys in his center, but also for his own corner boys. Since he had money, he could again associate with his friends and could also broaden his contacts. When the job and money ran out, in the winter of 1939/40, the manner of interaction to which Doc was adjusted was once more upset. The dizzy spells came back, and shortly before Doc got a WPA job in the spring of 1941, he had what his friends called a nervous breakdown. When I visited Cornerville in May, 1941, he was once again beginning to overcome the dizzy spells. He discussed his difficulties with me:

When I'm batted out, I'm not on the corner so much. And when I am on the corner, I just stay there. I can't do what I want to do. If the boys want to go to a show or to Jennings or bowling, I have to count my pennies to see if I have enough. If I'm batted out, I have to make some excuse.... I don't want to ask anybody for anything. Sometimes I say to Danny or Spongi, "Do you want a cigarette?" They say, "No, we've got some," and then I say, "All right, I'll have one of yours." I make a joke out of it, but still it is humiliating. I never do that except when I'm desperate for a cigarette. Danny is the only one that ever gives me money.

I have thought it all over, and I know I only have these spells when I'm batted out. I'm sorry you didn't know me when I was really active around here. I was a different man then. I was always taking the girls out. I lent plenty of money. I spent my money. I was always thinking of things to do and places to go.

Conclusion

Whyte's examples illuminate the importance of primary group support for individual security. They suggest that individual security is not merely a matter of belonging. Long John and Doc always belonged; neither was ever ostracized, but their old ways of belonging were upset.

Whyte's study suggests that even though primary relations approximate the free, personal, and spontaneous conditions set forth by Faris (see Adaptation 10, pp. 141 ff.), they are nevertheless patterned and structured in definite social ways. In the study at hand patterning was in terms of social rank. Long John and Doc were accustomed to interactions based upon their social rank within the group. Deprived of their social rank, they were also deprived of those particular interpersonal relations that had been satisfying and supporting.

The study also suggests that personal maladjustment occurs within a social context and can be aggravated or ameliorated by changes within the individual's social situation. Doc helped to cure Long John's nightmares by changing his social situation. By bringing him into Spongi's inner circle, Doc re-established the close relationship between Long John, Danny, and himself. In so doing, he protected Long John from the aggressions of the former followers. Then Long John's mental difficulties disappeared, and he began acting with the same assurance that had previously characterized his behavior.

Doc showed that he was well aware of the nature of his own difficulties, but understanding was not enough to cure him. He needed an opportunity to act in the manner to which he had grown accustomed. When that was lacking, he was socially maladjusted. If he had been a man with low standing in the group and had customarily been dependent upon others to initiate action for him in group activities, the dependence which resulted from having no money would have fitted in with the pattern of his behavior in the group. Since he had held the leading position among his corner boys, there was an unavoidable conflict between the behavior required by that position and the behavior necessitated by his penniless condition. Not until this conflict was resolved could Doc master his dizzy spells.

Section **3** **Primary groups in large-scale organizations**

Thus far, the work done by the primary group has been discussed. It has been treated as a value-transmitting agency, molding the personalities of new members in socially approved ways, and in Section 2 its contribution to the psychological well-being of the individual was noted. We now consider the function of the primary group in *sustaining the cohesion of large organizations*.

PRIMARY RELATIONS IN FORMAL STRUCTURES

Every organization of some size and duration (such as a church, university, business, army, trade-union) has both "formal" and "informal" relations and both a "formal structure" and an "informal structure."

The formal structure is the official pattern which determines the lines of authority and communication within the organization. Definite offices are provided for, like president or treasurer; officials are assigned their powers and duties; the limits of their authority are set; and rules are prescribed for the conduct of the organization. The members of these organizations are thus related to each other in certain formal ways. They have official roles to play and official tasks to perform. Where such official patterns prevail, the organization is sometimes called a "formal" organization.

In the study of associations, the phrase "informal structure" is used to denote those patterns that arise from the spontaneous interaction of personalities and groups within the organization. This distinction is discussed further in ASSOCIATIONS pp. 227 ff., but here we shall deal with only one aspect of informal structure, the effect of primary relations upon the capacity of the organization to do its job effectively.

In general, whenever individuals relate themselves to each other as persons rather than according to their assigned roles, they initiate primary relations. The universal tendency to initiate primary relations in formal organizations leads to the formation of friendships and cliques. The significance of this process is that *new lines of communication and influence* develop which are not accounted for in the officially approved patterns. For example important information may be passed among friends even though they are not entitled to it according to the rules. Or a subordinate may have personal and informal access to a high official and be able to "go over the head" of his immediate superior. As individuals "get involved," mixing their personalities with the job, official acts and relations become shaped by psychological and other personal needs.

SUSTAINING THE INDIVIDUAL

Why do these primary relations arise? The answer can be inferred by combining general knowledge about the individual-sustaining function of the primary group with knowledge about formal organizations. Such organizations use individuals as *tools*. Since the goals of organizations are impersonal, individual needs tend to be subordinated. Because the members of formal organizations are not merely "members" but persons as well, they feel the need to be treated as unique individuals and not as impersonal "cogs in a machine." If the impersonality of command cannot be influenced, they work to establish personal relations with other participants. If they fail they feel helpless and exposed to arbitrary treatment.

The most obvious way of escaping impersonality is to "make friends with the boss."

A Note on Manipulation

Any treatment of the social functions of the primary group, particularly its contribution to the cohesion of large organizations, is likely to carry overtones of manipulation, suggesting a calculated subordination of the individual to group goals. This is sometimes called the "managerial" approach, and many persons object to what they think of as a cold-blooded and even cynical effort to use the primary group as a means of wringing more work or morale from the individual. This is an important problem and deserves careful thought. The following points should be considered:

a) One may deliberately assume the perspective of promoting organizational cohesion in order to learn something about the nature and potentialities of primary groups. This does not mean that the social scientist himself is committed to promoting any organization's objectives.

b) If the sources of a group's strength are known, we often know how to weaken or destroy it. Adaptation 13 emphasizes the cohesion of the German army, but that study was carried on by the Allies to discover how best to use propaganda against it.

c) The fostering of primary groups can be simply a method of developing smoother and more satisfying human relations. On the other hand, if people are tied by primary group attachments into organizations with which they really disagree or which are not in their best interests, serious moral problems may arise. Probably this is the most justifiable basis for distrust of the "managerial" approach.

d) Those who wish to build on primary relations for improving organizational effectiveness must adapt their plans to the personal needs of the individual. Then, however, the individual, through his participation in primary groups, will have increased opportunity to influence the organization's goals or at least those methods of operation that affect him immediately.

e) While the problem is not fully understood, there are probably definite limits to the possibility of manipulating individuals through managerial control of primary groups if the manipulation violates personal integrity. Indeed, effectiveness of manipulation depends on the capacity of the organization to provide some protection and positive gratification to the individual.

But co-operation with others of the same rank is also helpful. The Hawthorne wiremen banded together informally as a defense against feared arbitrary action by management. Many groupings of this kind occur in formal organizations. They act as havens where the individual may find treatment that takes account of his personal needs. For example, if he is occasionally unable to do his work effectively, the group will protect him. On the other hand, he pays a price for his protection, for he must abide by the informal norms set up by the group.

DOUBLE-EDGED SIGNIFICANCE OF THE PRIMARY GROUP

Primary groups may either support or undermine the officially approved pattern of communication and command. They may help to mobilize the participants for the achievement of prescribed goals or, on the other hand, they may have a subversive effect. Adaptation 14 pp. 163 ff. illustrates one of the ways a primary group may *support* the objectives of a formal organization. The "leadman" created conditions that helped to protect the individual worker, to make him feel less isolated, and to reduce his fears. An illustration of the *subversive* effect a primary group may have within a formal structure is the case of the Hawthorne wiremen who developed an organization of their own and whose activities resulted in a self-determined limitation of output (Adaptation 11). In general, all primary relations and groupings are *potentially* subversive to large-scale organizations because the special goals or interests of the self-protective group may be given priority over the official goals of the organization.

THE "MEDIATING" PRIMARY GROUP

A generalization from Adaptation 14 may be restated as follows: *where members are attached to a large organization through a primary group, the capacity of the organization to mobilize and control them is increased.* We may think of such primary groups as having a "mediating" function,

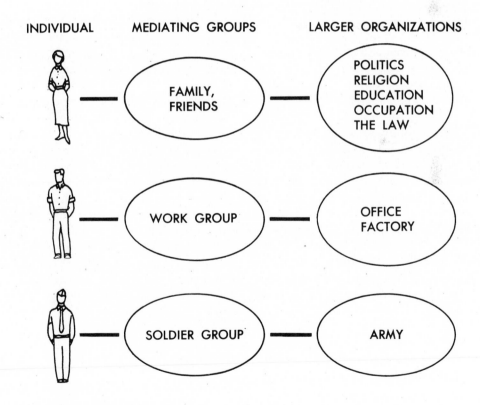

INDIVIDUAL   **MEDIATING GROUPS**   **LARGER ORGANIZATIONS**

FAMILY, FRIENDS — POLITICS RELIGION EDUCATION OCCUPATION THE LAW

WORK GROUP — OFFICE FACTORY

SOLDIER GROUP — ARMY

Fig. **V:3**   Mediating Primary Groups

Primary groups offer the individual personal affection and response as well as protection from arbitrary rules. If the primary group is effectively linked to a larger organization, it can heighten participation, but if the link is broken, morale and discipline may suffer.

binding the individual firmly into a larger social structure much as the family mediates between the individual and the larger society. The stronger the mediating primary group, the firmer this integration will be. This assumes that the primary group is itself geared into the organization. It does not follow, however, that strong mediating primary groups are indispensable to the functioning of organizations. Many enterprises do not fully mobilize the energies and loyalties of their employees or members, and yet accomplish their purposes reasonably well. However, when ordinary incentives are inadequate, the individual's attachment to a mediating primary group may encourage him to greater or more disciplined participation and even personal sacrifice.

The role of mediating primary groups received special attention in the study of cohesion and disintegration in the Nazi army. Although primary groups were important, they were not the only source of integration. The "hard core" of indoctrinated Nazis was a strong cohesive force which held the primary group to the organization's goals. The leadman described in the Mayo study performed a similar function. For a primary group to perform a mediating function, supporting rather than undermining an enterprise, something must bind it to official aims and policy.

PRIMARY GROUPS AND SOCIETY

If the primary group contributes to cohesion of large organizations, it may be expected to have an important role in knitting together whole societies. Many have speculated about the deterioration of primary relations and groups in modern industrial society, and it is sometimes suggested that this is the root cause of many symptoms of social and personal disorganization. Perhaps increasing mobility and urbanization have weakened individual ties to the extended family, the local community, and to small circles of lifelong friends. When such ties are weakened, social disciplines and aspirations are less effectively transmitted, and there may be new and sometimes pathological efforts to regain the benefits of primary group experience. Adaptation 44, pp. 692 ff., traces the rise of facism to weakening primary group ties.

But it is not certain how much ties have been weakened, how far social disciplines and aspirations have deteriorated, nor the extent to which the new forms are pathological. The sociologist studies the weakening of primary relations and its consequences, as one possible factor in any specific instance of social disorganization, just as he analyzes the influence of primary group ties on absenteeism in a factory. If there is evidence of high rates of mental illness, suicide, delinquency, or other manifestations of social disorganization, the sociologist will want to determine if the participants are deprived of normal primary group experience. The possible significance of the primary group in these cases offers a diagnostic hypothesis to be tested in the light of empirical research findings.

Primary Groups in the German Army

Abridged and adapted from Edward A. Shils and Morris Janowitz, "Cohesion and Disintegration in the Wehrmacht in World War II," *The Public Opinion Quarterly*, Summer, 1948; pp. 280–315. Published in this form by permission of the authors and *The Public Opinion Quarterly*.

This study was carried out by the intelligence unit of a Psychological Warfare Division. It analyzes the relative influence of primary and secondary group situations on the high degree of stability of the German

Army in World War II. It also evaluates the impact of the Western Allies' propaganda on the German Army's fighting effectiveness.

Methods of collecting data included front-line interrogation of prisoners of war, intensive psychological interviews in rear areas, and a monthly opinion poll of random samples of prisoners of war. Captured enemy documents, statements of recaptured Allied personnel, and the reports of combat observers were also analyzed.

Although outnumbered and inferior in equipment, the German Army maintained its integrity and fighting effectiveness through a series of almost unbroken retreats over a period of several years. Disintegration through desertion was insignificant, and the active surrender of individuals or groups remained extremely limited throughout the Western campaign.

This extraordinary tenacity of the German Army has frequently been attributed to the strong National Socialist political convictions of German soldiers. It is the main hypothesis of this paper, however, that the unity of the German Army was sustained only slightly by the National Socialist political convictions of its members, and that the determined resistance of the German soldier was due to the steady satisfaction of his *primary* personality needs.

THE FUNCTION OF THE PRIMARY GROUP

Modern social research has shown that the primary group, the chief source of affection and accordingly the major factor in personality formation in infancy and childhood, continues to be a major social and psychological support through adulthood. In the army, when isolated from civilian primary groups, the soldier depends more and more on his military primary group. His spontaneous loyalties are to the members of his immediate unit whom he sees daily and with whom he develops a high degree of intimacy.

A German sergeant, captured toward the end of World War II, was asked by his interrogators about the political opinions of his men. In reply, he laughed and said, "When you ask such a question, I realize well that you have no idea of what makes a soldier fight. The soldiers live in their holes and are happy if they live through the next day. If we think at all, it's about the end of the war and then home."

The combat effectiveness of the majority of soldiers depends only to a small extent on their preoccupation with the major political issues which might be affected by the outcome of the war and which are of concern to statesmen and publicists. There are, of course, soldiers to whom such motivations are important. Volunteer armies recruited on the basis of ethical or political loyalties, such as the International Brigade in the Spanish Civil War, are affected by orientation toward major political goals. In the German Army, the "hard core" of National Socialists was similarly motivated.

In a conscript army, on the other hand, the criteria of recruitment are much less specialized, and the army is more nearly representative of the total population. Political or social values and ethical schemes do not have much impact on the determination of such soldiers to fight to the best of their ability and to hold out as long as possible. For the ordinary German soldier the decisive fact was that he was a member of a squad or section that maintained its structural integrity and coincided roughly with the *social* unit which satisfied some of his major primary needs. If he had the necessary weapons, he was likely to go on fighting as long as the group had a leadership with which he could identify and as long as he gave affection to and received affection from the other members of his squad and platoon. In other words, as long as he felt himself to be a member of his primary group and therefore bound by the expectations and demands of its other members, he was likely to be a good soldier.

PERSONNEL

OVERSEA FOUR-MAN TEAM REPLACEMENTS

SECTION I

GENERAL

1. General.—*a.* It is the intent of the Department of the Army to provide the means and methods by which the morale, effectiveness and administrative control of oversea replacements can be improved. Experience has indicated that individuals who remain throughout the replacement stream with other individuals with whom they have received their basic training, maintain a higher esprit de corps and become more readily adjusted to their duties in their initial unit of assignment.

SECTION II

ADMINISTRATION AND ORGANIZATION AT TRAINING INSTALLATIONS

6. Formation of four-man teams.—*a.* Personnel completing the 12th week of basic training, except those ineligible under *b* below, will be formed into four-man teams. All team personnel will possess the same MOS. The method of forming four-man teams will be as prescribed by the training installation commander. The choice of the individual will be considered whenever possible. Care must be exercised that these combinations are such that maximum morale effects can be gained. The purpose of the team will be explained. Individuals will be informed that such teams will move intact to the unit of assignment overseas. Assignment as a team in an oversea unit will be considered an initial assignment only and will not preclude opportunities for individual advancement.

SECTION III

RESPONSIBILITIES

17. Army personnel center.—*a.* *Housing.*—Housing at the Army personnel center will be provided for carrier companies on a unit basis. Accommodations will be provided so that four-man team integrity can be maintained as well as unit integrity.

b. *Administration.*—The movement of the carrier company to the oversea command will be accomplished by an appropriate indorsement to the movement order. This indorsement will be accomplished by the Army personnel center.

c. *Processing.*—The Army personnel center will limit processing to the minimum necessary. It will be assumed by the Army personnel center that record maintenance is correctly conducted by the company personnel and that each individual is POR qualified.

18. Port of embarkation.—*a.* *Movement.*—Movement of the carrier company to the port of embarkation from the Army personnel center will be on call of the port commander only. Movement to oversea destination will be by military water transportation to the maximum extent practicable.

b. *Quartering aboard ship.*—The port of embarkation will be responsible to insure that so far as possible the company and all four-man teams are physically located aboard ship in a manner sufficient to maintain easy communication within the company and the integrity of each four-man team.

The relation between primary groups and morale is recognized in this Army regulation. Note the provision for maintaining the integrity of the four-man teams in the period between completion of training and attachment to a regular infantry unit.

Table **V:1**   Allied Leaflet Propaganda Themes Remembered
by German Prisoners of War

	Dec. 15–31 1944	Jan. 1–15 1945	Jan. 15–31 1945	Feb. 1–15 1945
Number of Ps/W	60	83	99	135
Themes and appeals remembered:				
a. Promise of good treatment as Ps/W and self-preservation through surrender	63%	65%	59%	76%
b. Military news	15	17	19	30
c. Strategical hopelessness of Germany's position	13	12	25	26
d. Hopelessness of a local tactical position	3	1	7	7
e. Political attacks on German leaders	7	5	4	8
f. Bombing of German cities	2	8	6	—
g. Allied Military Government	7	3	—	—
h. Appeals to civilians	5	4	2	—
	**	**	**	**

** The percentages add up to more than 100 per cent since some Ps/W remembered more than one topic. Only Ps/W remembering at least one theme were included in this tabulation.

WEAKNESS OF SECONDARY SYMBOLS

Problems and symbols remote from immediate personal experience had relatively little influence on the behavior and attention of the German soldier. Interrogation of prisoners showed that they had little interest in the strategic aspects of the war. There was widespread ignorance and apathy about the course of the fighting. Three weeks after the fall of the city of Aachen, many prisoners who were taken in the adjoining area did not know that the city had fallen. For at least a week after the beginning of the Battle of the Bulge—an important German counteroffensive toward the end of the war—most of the troops on the northern hinge of the bulge did not know that the offensive was taking place and were not much interested when they were told of it after their capture.

Neither did expectations about the outcome of the war play a great role in the integration or disintegration of the German Army. The statistics of German soldier opinion show that pessimism about the outcome of the war was compatible with excellent fighting behavior. The relatively greater importance of considerations of self-preservation is shown by German prisoner recall of the contents of Allied propaganda leaflets (Table V:1). During December, 1944, and January, 1945, more than 60 per cent of the sample of prisoners taken recalled references to the preservation of the individual, and the figure rose to 76 per cent in February of 1945. On the other hand, the proportion of prisoners recalling references to the total strategic situation of the war and the prospect of the outcome of the war seldom amounted to more than 20 per cent, while references to political subjects seldom amounted to more than 10 per cent. The general tendency was not to think about the outcome of the war unless forced to do so by direct interrogation. Pessimism was counterbalanced by reassuring identification with a strong and benevolent Führer, by identification with good officers, and by the psychological support of a closely integrated primary group.

Ethical aspects of the war did not trouble the German soldier much. When pressed by Allied interrogators, the prisoners said that Germany had been forced to fight for its life. There were very few German soldiers who said that Germany had been morally wrong to attack Poland or Russia. Most of them thought that if anything had been wrong about the war, it was in the realm of technical decisions. The decision to exterminate the Jews had been too drastic, not because of its immorality, but because it united the world against Germany. The declaration of war against the Soviet Union was wrong only because it created a two-front war. But these were all arguments which had to be forced from the prisoners of war; left to themselves, they seldom mentioned them.

On the other hand the significance of political ideals was pronounced in the case of the "hard core" minority of fervent Nazis in the German Army. But National Socialism was of little interest to most of the German soldiers. "Nazism," said a soldier, "begins ten miles behind the front lines."

The soldiers did not react noticeably to the various attempts to Nazify the army. When the Nazi party salute was introduced in 1944, it was accepted as just one more army order, about equal in significance to an order requiring the carrying of gas masks. The *National Sozialistische Führungsoffiziere* (Nazi indoctrination officer), known as the NSFO, was regarded apathetically or as a joke. The NSFO was rejected not for his Nazi connection but because he was an "outsider" who was not a real soldier. The highly Nazified Waffen SS divisions were never the object of ordinary soldiers' hostility, even when they were charged with atrocities. On the contrary, the Waffen SS was esteemed, not as a Nazi formation, but for its excellent fighting capacity. Wehrmacht soldiers felt safer when there was a Waffen SS unit on their flank.

In contrast to the apolitical attitude of the German infantry soldier towards most secondary symbols, an intense and personal devotion to Adolph Hitler was maintained throughout the war. There is little doubt that a high degree of identification with the Führer was an important factor in prolonging German resistance. Despite fluctuations in expectations regarding the outcome of the war, the trust in Hitler remained strong even after the beginning of the serious reverses in France and Germany. The attachment grew in large part from the feeling of strength and protection which the German soldier gained from his conception of the Führer personality.

However, as defeat became imminent, and the danger to physical survival increased, devotion to Hitler deteriorated. The tendency to attribute virtue to the strong and immorality to the weak boomeranged, and devotion to Hitler declined. Moreover, for the vast horde of dishevelled, dirty, bewildered prisoners, Hitler was of slight importance compared with their own survival problems and the welfare of their families.

IMPACT OF ALLIED PROPAGANDA

A monthly opinion poll of German prisoners found there was no significant decline in attachment to Nazi ideology until February and March, 1945. In other words, the propaganda attacks on Nazi ideology seem to have been of little avail until the smaller military units began to break up under heavy pressure. Much effort was devoted to ideological attacks on German leaders but only about five per cent of the prisoners mentioned this topic, confirming the general failure of ideological appeals. Allied propaganda presentations of the justness of our war aims, postwar peace intentions, and United Nations unity were all ineffective.

Promises of good treatment as prisoners of war gained most attention and were best remembered. In other words, the best propaganda referred to immediate situations and concrete problems. The most effective single leaflet in communicating the promise of good treatment was the "safe conduct pass." It was usually printed on the back of leaflets which stressed self-preservation. The rank and file were attracted by its official language and legal, document-like character. Where General Eisenhower's signature did not appear on the leaflet, doubt was cast on its authenticity.

As a result of psychological-warfare research, a series of leaflets was prepared which was aimed at primary group organization in the German Army and omitted reference to ideological symbols. Group organization depended on the acceptance of the immediate leadership and mutual trust. Therefore, this series of leaflets tried to stimulate group discussion and to bring attention to concerns which would loosen solidarity. One leaflet declared, "Do not take our [the Allies] word for it; ask your comrade; find out how he feels." There followed a series of questions on personal concerns, family problems, the immediate tactical situation, and supply problems. Discussion of these problems was expected to increase anxiety.

FACTORS AFFECTING PRIMARY GROUP COHESION

If the primary group was a crucial element in the German Army, it is important to know what factors strengthened or weakened primary group cohesion.

1. *The "hard core."* The stability and effectiveness of the military primary group depended in large measure on the Nazi "hard core," who approximated 10 to 15 per cent of the total of enlisted men; the percentage was higher for noncommissioned officers and was very much higher among the junior officers. Most of these were young men between twenty-four and twenty-eight years of age who as adolescents were imbued with the Nazi ideology during its zenith. They were enthusiasts for the military life. The presence in the group of a few such men, zealous, energetic, and unsparing of themselves, provided models for the weaker men, and their threats served to check divisive tendencies. Although, as we have seen, political ideology was not important to most soldiers, the "hard

core" provided the link between the ordinary soldier in his primary group and the political leadership of the German Army and state.

2. *Community of experience.* German officers saw that solidarity is fostered by the recollection of jointly experienced gratifications and, therefore, the groups who had gone through a victory together should be maintained as units. This principle also guided replacement policy. The entire personnel of a division would be withdrawn from the front simultaneously and refitted as a unit with replacements. New members added to the division while it was in the rear had the opportunity to assimilate themselves into the group; then the group as a whole was sent forward. This system continued until close to the end of the war and helped to explain the durability of the German Army in the face of the overwhelming numerical and material superiority of the Allied forces.

Poor morale toward the end of the war was found most frequently in hastily assembled units. These were made up of new recruits, dragooned stragglers, air force men who had been forced into the infantry (and who felt a loss of status in the change), men transferred from the navy into the infantry, older factory workers, concentration camp inmates, and older married men who had been kept in reserve throughout the war and who had remained with their families until the last moment. It was clear that these reluctant infantrymen, so diverse in age composition and background, could not become effective fighting units very quickly. They had no time to become used to one another and to develop the type of friendliness which is possible only when loyalties to outside groups have been renounced—or at least put into the background.

3. *Family ties.* Correspondence between soldiers and their families was generally encouraged, but the families of German soldiers were given strict instructions not to mention family hardships in their letters to the front. Even so, preoccupation with family affairs

GERMAN PRISONERS OF WAR

Note the varied ages of these German prisoners, captured near the end of World War II. This is the kind of mixed unit referred to in Adaptation 13.

often conflicted with loyalty to the military primary group.

The strong pull of the civilian primary group became stronger as the coherence of the army group weakened under the pressure of Allied victories. Sometimes the strength of family ties was used to keep the men fighting in their units. For example, soldiers were warned that desertion would result in severe punishment of the deserter's family. Some men reasoned that the shortest way home was to keep the group intact and to avoid capture and a long period in an enemy prisoner of war camp. They thought those remaining in the defeated but intact army units would have only a short wait before demobilization.

4. *Proximity.* Spatial proximity is important in maintaining the solidarity of military groups. In February and March of 1945, isolated remnants of platoons and companies surrendered in groups with increasing fre-

quency. The tactical situation forced soldiers to take refuge in cellars, trenches, and other underground shelters in small groups of three and four. The isolation from the nucleus (officers and "hard core" elements) of the primary group reinforced fears of destruction and helped to break down primary group relations.

Conclusion

At the beginning of World War II, many publicists and specialists in propaganda attributed much importance to psychological warfare operations. The legendary successes of Allied propaganda against the German Army at the end of World War I and the expansion of the advertising and mass communications industries in the ensuing two decades had convinced many people that human behavior could be extensively manipulated by mass communications. They emphasized that military morale was to a great extent a function of the belief in the rightness of the "larger" cause which was at issue in the war; good soldiers were, therefore, those who clearly understood the political and moral implications of what was at stake.

Studies of the German Army's morale and fighting effectiveness during the last three years of the war throw considerable doubt on these hypotheses. It was found that solidarity in the German Army was based only very indirectly and partially on political convictions or broader ethical beliefs. Where conditions allowed primary group life to function smoothly, and where the primary group developed a high degree of cohesion, morale was high regardless of the political attitudes of the soldiers. Certain types of propaganda did become effective when conditions fostered disintegration of the military primary group. The effective propaganda, however, ignored political issues and exploited the desire to survive.

Primary Groups and Industrial Efficiency

Abridged and adapted from Elton Mayo and George F. F. Lombard, *Teamwork and Labor Turnover in the Aircraft Industry of Southern California*, Harvard Business School, Business Research Studies No. 32 (October, 1944). Published in this form by permission of George F. F. Lombard and Harvard University.

The late Elton Mayo and his associates studied primary groups at work in large-scale, industrial organizations. They investigated the causes of high rates of absenteeism and labor turnover in the southern California aircraft industry during World War II. The study concludes that the chaotic demands of the war had broken up the old spontaneous worker teams, and that absenteeism and labor turnover were directly related to the absence of primary group relations among new workers.

THE PROBLEM AND ITS SETTING

Under the pressure of production needs of World War II, southern California became an industrial community in a few short years. The small airplane plants of southern California "exploded" into large industries. While the plants were expanding, however, their trained workers were being drained off by the draft. Attracted by the drastic need for workers in the rising industries, thousands of persons migrated to the area.

It is not surprising that labor turnover and absenteeism were high in the aircraft industry. Each month of 1943, 14,000 to 15,000 new workers entered the factories, but approximately the same number terminated work. Faced with huge defense orders and drained of its old trained workers, the industry recognized a growing threat to aircraft production and the war effort. Social research was undertaken to discover the sources of absenteeism and labor turnover.

THE PRIMARY GROUP AND WORKER CO-OPERATION

Attention was concentrated on absenteeism, since the absentee would return to the job, and could be observed in his work situation. A preliminary study of individual absentee records disclosed that not all workers contributed equally to the high absentee rate. On the contrary, some attendance records were consistently poor, others consistently good. What made some workers come faithfully while others had many absences? In order to find an answer, a comparison was sought between work units that showed high absenteeism rates and units that had low rates. By comparing the two situations, the factors that made for the difference could be discovered. This was not easy, however. When the records of the various departments (each numbering as many as several hundred workers) were examined, they showed that significant differences in absenteeism did not occur at that level. High absenteeism was not concentrated in some departments and low absenteeism in others. Since a comparison of high and low groups was needed, it was evident that study of the large work unit could not help to explain the differences among individual workers.

Within the large work units, however, were small work groups, and these were analyzed in the hope that some would show high and others low absenteeism. If this were found to be the case, further observation might reveal what made for good attendance in one work group and poor attendance in another.

Seventy-one work centers in two aircraft plants were chosen for study on the basis of certain criteria: they had to be composed of workers who were together day by day, who had come to know one another, and who understood the interrelation of their various jobs. It turned out that significant differences did exist among these work groups. Some had excellent attendance records, others a high absentee rate. One group with an excellent attendance record was singled out for special observation and study.

This group of 19 workers had an output per man-hour considerably above the plant average and a reputation for "working like beavers." They thought of themselves as a team, different from the other workers in the plant who in turn regarded them as somewhat clannish.

The team relations in this group did not occur by chance. The persons responsible were the leadman, Z, and the senior assistant foreman, who gave Z his support. Although Z was in many respects "just another worker" —officially his job as leadman did not require him to do more than take care of minor interruptions in the work of his group—he actually did several things to strengthen job relations:

1. *The individual worker.* Z's chief attention was given to the personal needs of his workers. He introduced a new employee to his companions and tried to get him congenial work associates. After an employee had worked a few days, Z took him to the assembly line to see the part he made installed in the complete machine. In addition, Z listened to the personal problems of his workers.

2. *"Trouble shooting."* Z tried to anticipate material shortages and worked to eliminate them when they occurred.

3. *The outside world.* Requests for raises went through Z to the foreman. Z also dealt with inspectors, efficiency men, and the like. He acted for his group both as buffer against the rest of the plant and as an effective link with it.

In conversation both Z and the senior assistant foreman expressed a strong conviction that the achievement of group solidarity is necessary for sustained production. This leadman made it his self-imposed task to secure happy and effective relations among his workers. The result was a well-knit primary group, superior to other work groups in morale and efficiency.

Furthermore, in the process of primary group interaction, Z created a condition in which the objectives of the industrial organization had become linked to the needs of the workers. If a group member failed to meet work requirements, such as regular attendance, he thereby failed to meet the demands and expectations of his fellow group members and brought their displeasure. Since the gratification of the individual's needs depended on his having the approval of his fellow workers, the primary group constituted a powerful mechanism of social control, operating to further the aims of the industrial organization.

Conclusion

Under disorganized conditions primary group relations are not easily established. When co-operative social organization emerges, however, it is not a matter of chance, but a response to definite conditions in a concrete situation. In this study the leadership of Z determined that the primary group relations among his fellow workers would be positive rather than negative in securing the group's purposes.

Caution: The existence of primary group relations in a plant need not result in low absenteeism. It is conceivable that high absenteeism might for some reason be a primary group norm and enforceable through primary group pressures. Adaptation 11 suggests that a factory work group can undermine the ends of management as readily as it can implement them. Both studies, however, support the basic conclusion that primary and informal relations can influence decisively employee attitudes and actions. The direction of this influence depends on the specific content of the group norms as they emerge in the work situation.

Section 4 Variations in internal structure

Primary groups are characteristically more spontaneous than secondary, formal associations but, like all groups of significant duration, primary groups develop an internal structure. Structure is the pattern of relatively stable relations or ways of behaving among the members, including the expectations they have of each other's conduct. One way of describing group patterning is outlined in Adaptation 16, pages 170 ff.

Primary groups usually develop within socially prescribed forms and are often given socially prescribed tasks. The family is a good example of this. It is in effect a socially defined pattern for the expression of primary relations. Who is to be included within the family, how feelings are to be expressed, how roles and status are to be assigned, what duties are to be fulfilled and how, are all matters that depend upon the social image of the family group.

Where prescribed forms emphasize differences in the roles and status of the participants, primary relations may be impaired. However, not all prescribed forms limit primary relations. The American family has been moving from a patriarchal form to a more equalitarian one. The father is no longer assigned a rigidly differentiated role and a high authority status. The result has been an increase in his participation in primary relations, especially with his children. However, this development has been accompanied by a narrowing definition of the extent of the family, so that primary relations with relatives other than the immediate family are more limited now than they once were. (See THE FAMILY, pp. 357–58.)

TASK GROUPS AND SOCIAL CONTROL

Many stable primary groups have goals to fulfill and tasks to perform. They are more than products of primary relations; they are also co-operative enterprises with common goals. This kind of group has work to do, and the fulfillment of its tasks encourages structuring of the group and the exercise by its members of some control over each other's behavior. Activity must be initiated and directed, instructions carried out, and in general some division of labor takes place. The more tasks a primary group performs, the greater are the satisfactions it must supply. The task-oriented primary group through positive forms of social control attempts to satisfy the needs of its members for affection, respect, and a sense of meaningful participation. As Jennings has pointed out, in the process of relating individual needs to group performance, those who are able to make personal relations easier and more gratifying will become leaders. (See Adaptation 15.) Similarly, the leadman in the Mayo study tried to fulfill the group's task by taking account of the individual needs of his co-workers.

In other groups social control is exercised in a negative way by aggressive and hostile behavior. This is illustrated in the behavior of the bank wiremen, who employed ridicule and even a form of physical violence.

When a group's members are concerned mainly with self-protection and defense against real or imagined attack rather than the positive fulfillment of a task, hostile and aggressive behavior frequently emerges as a pattern of social control. If a "united front" is thought necessary for the protection of the group, there is more interest in winning conformity than in satisfying individual needs. Deviation from group norms is apt to be treated harshly, so that social control in this case tends to be repressive and constraining. Since such a group's aim is to win a passive unity rather than to mobilize energies in a positive direction, it need not provide as many personal satisfactions to its members.

Both positive and negative forms of social control are often found in the same group, particularly if it mobilizes as well as disciplines its members. The study of primary groups in the German Army describes how both types of influence were exercised (Adaptation 13, pp. 156 ff.).

One should not infer that all cohesion and incentive stem from primary relations. Individuals may be united by fear of a common danger, and they may be coerced or persuaded to work or fight, quite apart from membership in primary groups. If, however, control is exercised through primary groups, then the conditions that make such groups effective must obtain. Among these conditions, in the case of task-oriented primary groups, is the creation of satisfying interpersonal relations.

PATTERNS OF COMMUNICATION

An experimental study [4] of supervised play groups investigated the effects of different kinds of supervision on two groups of children, ten to twelve years of age. One type of supervision was *authoritarian:* the children were allowed little voice in determining their own activities; direction was almost completely in the hands of the adult leader. The other type was *democratic:* the adult leader encouraged the children to make their own decisions and to plan group activities themselves.

Detailed observations were made of the children's conversation, behavior, and attitudes, both toward each other and toward the adult supervisor, in order to discover what differences existed under the two kinds of direction. The investigator found sharp differences in the patterns and quality of communication in the two groups. These differences were due to the kind of supervision over the children. The children under "democratic" supervision, where communication was relatively free, were able to form a more stable and complex group than the "authoritarian" supervised group. When communication is thwarted, as it was in the "authoritarian" group, individual needs are unexpressed and therefore may be unfulfilled.

If patterns limiting the free flow of communication develop within a primary group, the group is threatened by instability and divisiveness. A free flow of communication is

[4] Ronald Lippitt, "An Experimental Study of the Effect of Democratic and Authoritarian Group Atmospheres," University of Iowa *Studies in Child Welfare*, **16**, No. 3 (February, 1940), 43–195.

necessary so that individual interests, especially of more passive members, can be known and taken into account. Another experimental study of communication within a small group (not, however, a primary group) showed that those who were not deeply involved in the communication process set up by the experimenter were deficient in morale. (See ASSOCIATIONS, pp. 225–27.)

Where self-protection and defense become the principal goal of a group, communication tends to be more limited and more repressive, designed not so much to evoke creative energies as to constrain and channel them.

Individual Choice and Group Leadership

Abridged and adapted from Helen Hall Jennings, *Leadership and Isolation, A Study of Personality in Inter-Personal Relations* (2nd ed.; New York: Longmans, Green, 1950). Published in this form by permission of Helen Hall Jennings and Longmans, Green & Co., Inc.

Every group is structured or organized in some way. What is this structure, and how does it come about? To some extent the structure of a group is a reflection of the feelings its members have toward one another as persons. One can imagine that there are lines of attraction and repulsion between various members, holding the group together in some ways and pulling it apart in others. The sociometric test was devised to uncover these attractions and repulsions. It does this by asking the members of a group whom they want to be with. The test usually asks that choices be made in terms of some particular activity. The persons one might choose to work with, for example, are not necessarily those with whom he would like to spend his leisure.

The population studied consisted of over 400 subjects in the New York State Training School for Girls, twelve to sixteen years of age and of normal intelligence. Though choices ranged over all 400 subjects, the statistical data apply only to a selected group of 133 subjects who were at the institution long enough to be retested.

The present study asked the subjects to choose and reject companions on the basis of four different activities: living together, working together, leisure, and studying. No limit was put upon the number of choices and rejections that could be made. The instructions were worded as follows:

You will notice that your paper is divided into eight squares or boxes. In the first "Yes" box, marked "live with," write the names of whatever girls there are anywhere on the campus or in your own house whom you would prefer to live with. In the "No" box of "live with," write the names of whatever girls there are anywhere on the campus or in your own house whom you would prefer not to live with. Do the same for the "work with" boxes. Then, those you would prefer not to work with, place in the "No" box for work. Next, do your "recreation or leisure" and then, your "study or school" boxes, having in mind the same instructions. . . .

The group was retested after an interval of eight months in order to see what had happened to the choice scores. Each girl tended to choose the same *number* of individuals on both tests, whether or not she was chosen by others. That is, each girl seemed to have a relatively fixed need for others, a need which was independent of the extent to which she was chosen. At the same time the extent to which an individual was chosen remained fairly constant.

LEADERSHIP AND SOCIOMETRIC CHOICE

The following observations are based on the patterns displayed with reference to but two of the four kinds of association: living together and working together. Data on studying-together choices were not analyzed because academic divisions necessarily restricted the range of choice. The leisure time choices will be discussed separately.

The positive choices made on the basis of living and working together tended to cluster around a few individuals. Subjects in the top layer of choice received from 15 to 44 positive responses; compared to the average, they were "over-chosen." Subjects in the bottom layer of choice received two or less positive responses and some none at all; they were the "under-chosen."

Those who were highly chosen on the sociometric test were leaders in the school community. An analysis of the Community Council, which was elected by the school community, showed that of 20 of its members receiving the most votes in the election, 18 were subjects who ranked as "over-chosen" on the sociometric test.

WHAT MAKES A LEADER?

What accounts for the large discrepancy between the over-chosen and the under-chosen? Sociometric ranking depended on what a person did—how she behaved toward others in group activity situations—rather than on what she was as a unique individual. Traits like moodiness, generosity, and personal cleanliness seemed not to influence sociometric choice. What did matter was a person's capacity for interplay with other personalities within a group activity.

Leaders are able to recognize and to respond to the needs of others and to support these needs in ways that further group activity and expand group life. Leaders widen the area of social participation for others and foster tolerance among group members.

This point about what a leader does is reflected in what the subjects said. In talking about their reasons for choosing those in leader positions, they made such observations as the following:

> She makes you feel a part of things.
>
> She tries to make you better than yourself.
>
> She can lead and not make the girls feel they are being overpowered but rather that they are doing things of their own accord.
>
> She gives you advice in a way that makes you think for yourself.
>
> When you have a grudge against a girl, she can reason it out for you.
>
> She is good even to the people she doesn't respect and will lend them things.

The under-chosen, on the other hand, tend toward behavior that divides individuals and blocks or disrupts group activity. They are self-centered, having little ability to identify with others or come to terms with a wide range of personalities.

The under-chosen were spoken of as follows:

> She's always out for credit and not for the thing itself.
>
> She plays people off against each other.
>
> She likes to do things the opposite of what others like to do whether it's right or wrong.
>
> She goes around with a look on and makes you feel that you have done something.
>
> She doesn't keep anything to herself.
>
> She works hard but if she has a disagreeable job to do, sometimes she thinks she is being imposed upon.
>
> She always seems afraid she'll do more than another person does, more than her share I mean.

The housemothers were asked to evaluate the behavior of the subjects. A catalog of their estimates showed that the under-chosen exhibited, for example, five times as much quarrelsome and irritable behavior and twice as much aggressively dominating behavior as the average subject; the over-chosen only one-third as much in both cases.

What especially marks the capacity of those in leader positions to take account of others is their attitude toward the under-chosen. Leaders protect the under-chosen both from their own destructive impulses and from the aggressive impulses of the other members of the community. In talking about one of her rejections an average member made the following observation: "Personally I never bother to speak to her. Jean [a leader] does though, but then she's fortunate, she's got a large heart, room for everybody no matter how nasty they are. Jean tells me I am narrow-minded. For a time I act different but soon Vera [the rejected girl] gets on my nerves again and I just stay away or walk off from her."

ORGANIZED GROUPS AND SPONTANEOUS GROUPS

It will be noted that the leaders helped to make things easier and pleasanter for the members of work groups and groups of girls who lived together in the same housing unit. In these groups, interaction was not completely spontaneous but involved a certain degree of control and the ability to co-operate in a common effort. Leaders able to facilitate interpersonal relations were needed in such groups, and they tended to be heavily over-chosen on the sociometric test when the choice was based on living together or working together.

A different pattern was found when the choices were based simply on the desire to be with a schoolmate in her free time, because the problems of co-operation were then less important. Leisure choices could more closely reflect feelings toward others as unique individuals rather than as persons skilled in group co-operation. The leisure choices showed much higher reciprocity than the living-working choices. Subjects tended to want to be with the same people who

wanted to be with them. In addition, more girls were unchosen for leisure time relations. Only 5 out of the 133 girls were unchosen on the combined living-working criteria (on the second test), whereas 15 were unchosen on the leisure time criterion.

This suggests that in the informal situation of leisure, compared with more formal settings of housing or work units, the individual cannot as readily "promote" relationships in the sense of winning others to choose him. In working or living together, the individual's behavior as a group member may count and advance his position. He may find numerous opportunities within the range of the activities to make himself useful to group endeavors.

In the leisure setting, it may be that an individual simply "cares about" another as a person in a more total sense, and there may be little he can do about either gaining or losing the relationship. Similarly, there may be little the second individual can do about his response to the first. The basis of feeling in many instances may be less within the realm of control and less within the possibility of "change," regardless of either individual's conscious or overt effort.

As choice becomes more freely based on personality, the "model" primary relation is approached. But the groups usually called primary groups are likely to combine both goal-orientation and personality-orientation, even if the goal is no more specific than the maintenance of a family unit or of long-standing friendship. Therefore, in studying the inner dynamics of the primary group, we need to consider how the interpersonal relations are affected by this mixture of social control and spontaneity. As we have seen, this often means that the individual seeks, within a task group, leaders and associates who permit him the most satisfying person-to-person relations and the fullest protection and expression of his own personality, consistent with the goals of the group. In the goal-oriented primary group, people must make compromises. As their choices become freer, unrestrained by the necessities of group co-operation, they can more readily afford to act spontaneously.

Conclusion

1. Sociometric choice is related to leadership. (*a*) The kind of choice expressed on the sociometric test is the kind of choice which selects leaders. (*b*) The sociometric test can be used to discern leadership patterns within a group.

2. Leadership is not a personality trait; it is a way of relating oneself to others. Leadership accrues to those who take account of others in ways that facilitate group life and group cohesion. We can express this in another way by saying that leadership is functional in two senses: it is a function of (it is dependent upon) interpersonal relations; it has a function (it performs a task) in group life.

3. Leadership is situational: who the leaders are depends upon the concrete circumstances. A leader in one group is not necessarily a leader in another, nor is a leader related to every member of a group in the same way.

Caution: The degree to which sociometric choice is related to leadership, and leadership in turn is dependent upon interpersonal processes within a group situation, probably depends on the character of the group. The community studied by Jennings was marked by relatively personal, informal, direct, and spontaneous relations. We should not expect the same results in associations of a more formal, indirect, and "secondary" character, where leaders and members have little intimate relation to each other.

Since the sociometric test asks subjects to choose on the basis of group activities, it is not surprising that those chosen should be the individuals best able to further group activities. What a test shows depends on how it is constructed. Just as an intelligence test gives little information regarding musical talent, so a sociometric test cannot uncover leadership of a different sort from that described in the Jennings study. The kind of "leadership" enjoyed by Albert Einstein in physics or by T. S. Eliot in literature emerges not from interpersonal relations but by virtue of special achievement. If, however, Einstein or Eliot attempted to exercise influence in primary group situations, they would require the kinds of skills investigated by Jennings.

The Technique of the Sociogram

Groups develop distinctive *patterns of interaction.* They contain subgroupings, which differ from group to group and within a particular group over time. Some individuals are admired and sought out by many; some are isolated.

A casual participant or observer may notice some of the relationships and may sense the "tone" of relations within a group. If, however, the group exceeds a few members,

it is unlikely that even an astute and experienced observer will have a thorough grasp of the basic relationships without prolonged observation or the aid of objective measures. One of the sociometric techniques which has been devised for the objective presentation and interpretation of relations within groups is called the *sociogram.* It is a diagram of the *informal* relations within a group. (Charts of the *formal* relations are discussed in ASSOCIA-

ADAPTATION 16

TIONS, pp. 220–21.) A sociogram shows the informal group structure, such as subgroup and friendship patterns, and the position of each individual among his fellows. A sociogram is a preliminary step in understanding group action or individual action in a group setting. It may be used to summarize verbal choices, the written choices of a sociometric test, or the direct observation of a competent observer.

The student should gather data from a small group, preferably 12 or less in number, and follow through the basic steps outlined below. He may wish to ask questions getting at leadership or some other characteristic rather than friendship. The questions depend entirely upon the problem being investigated, but they must be phrased clearly and unambiguously. It is usually advisable to pretest the questions to insure that they ask what is intended. One may measure the degree of his insight into group relations by predicting the choice that the members of the group will make and comparing them with the actual choices.

As an illustrative exercise a third-grade teacher of fifteen boys and fifteen girls asked her class to "Write the name of the child you like best in this class," and then "the name of the child you like second best." For simplicity we shall explain the processing of the boys' choices only. It is not necessary to show the whole sociogram because only three boys chose or were chosen by girls. The procedure is described below.

INTERPRETATION

1. The outstanding finding of the first choices is William M's position as the *star*. He received 5 first choices from the other 14 boys and 2 of the possible 14 second choices. Clinton received 2 first choices and 5 second choices, making him a strong runner-up to William M. Between them they received 14 of the possible 30 choices, and their choices of Alfred create a *triangle*, which dominates the sociogram. The three boys combined received 19 of the possible 30 choices.

2. In the first choice sociogram, there is one *mutual choice,* or *pair*, between boys— William M and Alfred—and one between a boy and a girl—Robert and Sally. Additional pairs show when the second choices are counted.

3. There is an *island* consisting of Melvin, Charles, Herbert, Robert (and Sally) on the first choices. In the second choices a bridge is thrown from the island to the main group of boys by Melvin's choice of Clinton, and there are additional ties between this group and the girls. The island has other girls who do not appear in the figure, and it is interesting that the girls in this group are only weakly integrated with the main group of girls.

4. There are seven *isolates:* Skipper, Michael, Herbert, Donald, Morgan, Richard L, and William R. These boys received no choices.

5. One *error* appears in Richard L's failure to make a second choice.

Note that such errors reduce the *total* number of choices made by the group.

VARIATIONS IN THE USE OF SOCIOGRAMS

This example of friendship choices is only one of many possible uses of the sociogram. By comparing the patterning of choices on different criteria (athletic partner, study companion, etc.) the consistency and diversity of ratings in a group can be observed. Sometimes investigators wish to study a particular factor or process in relation to group structure. Whyte (Adaptation 12, pp. 150–52) wanted to know how individual security was related to patterns of primary group relations. Although he did not ask the Nortons direct questions, such as "Who are your three best friends in this group?" his observations of group interaction provided him with data on their relations. He closely observed group activities until he was able to plot the informal relations of the group members. He was than able to relate behavior (for instance, Long John's nightmares) to breaks in the individual's usual pattern of primary group relations.

Roethlisberger and Dickson (Adaptation 11, pp. 147–50) studied group norms and informal controls in relation to group structure. Sociometric techniques were used to determine the informal structure of the bank wiring room group. The authors observed who talked most frequently to whom, which cliques played what sorts of games, between whom arguments took place, etc., and they were then able to plot the informal structure of the group. This led to a more detailed understanding of how group norms emerge and how they are enforced.

Cautions: Like any other research technique, the sociogram has its limitations.

1. Validity. Responses are influenced by the subjects' willingness to record their true feelings. If the respondents lack confidence in the investigator or if he is known to have strong preferences for certain individuals in the group, the results will probably be influenced. If there is resistance to making responses or to signing names to responses, it is unlikely that the results will be valid.

2. Reliability. It should not be assumed that a chart made at any given time is a reliable indicator of relations at some other time. Especially in groups of young children, there is evidence that relations are unstable. A series of sociograms would be needed to trace changes over a period of time.

3. Cues. We have already mentioned the possibility of cues from the investigator's preferences. Other cues should be avoided, too. For example, there should be no lists enumerating the group in an arbitrary order. It is common knowledge that the order in which names appear on a ballot affects the number of votes candidates receive.

4. Privacy. The group should be confident that their choices will not be made known to others. If respondents are not assured of privacy, their choices may reflect fear or some factor other than the criterion asked for.

5. Applicability. The sociogram is especially useful in well-defined and limited groups. A small dormitory or fraternity house would provide a good experimental setting.

6. The sociogram is a beginning and not an end. It is usually a first step in the analysis of leadership, morale, or some other aspect of informal structure.

PROCEDURE

1 We wrote each chooser's name on the left-hand side of a slip of paper with an arrow pointing to the name of his first choice, which was written on the right-hand side.

2 After a slip had been made for each choice, we sorted the slips of those who had named the same person as best friend. We found four subgroups, called *sets*, in which the same person had been named as best friend by several persons:

William M, chosen by Donald, Skipper, Michael, Clinton, and Alfred.
Alfred, chosen by William M and Morgan.
Clinton, chosen by William R and Curtis.
Robert, chosen by Charles and Herbert (and Sally).

3 The set with the most slips (William M's) was arranged to converge on his name.

4 William M chose Alfred, who was a member of another set. Because William M's and Alfred's choices were *mutual*, their slips were placed parallel to each other. The other choice in the 2nd set (in this case Morgan's choice of Alfred) was placed in position with the 1st set.

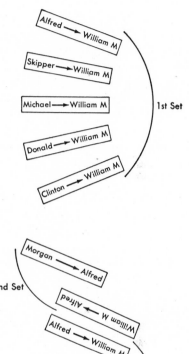

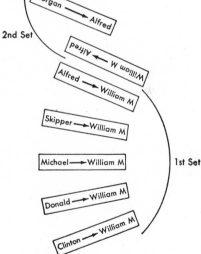

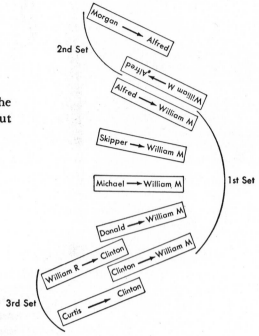

5 Another set which could be attached to the arrangement was Clinton's, and it was put in position.

6 The 4th set (Robert's) did not attach to the other sets, and it was arranged by itself. Robert's choice was then placed in position.

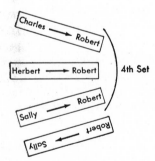

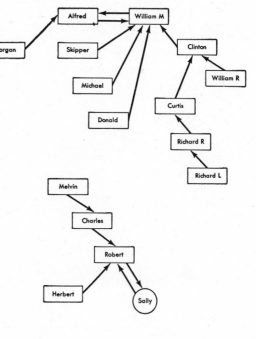

SOCIOGRAM OF FIRST CHOICES

7 The remaining individual slips were fitted into the arrangement, and the sociogram of 1st choices was completed by sketching the arrangement as a diagram.

SOCIOGRAM OF FIRST AND SECOND CHOICES

8 The second choices were processed in the same way, but a rearrangement of the diagram was necessary to prevent an undue amount of crossing of choice lines. The completed sociogram of first and second choices is shown here.

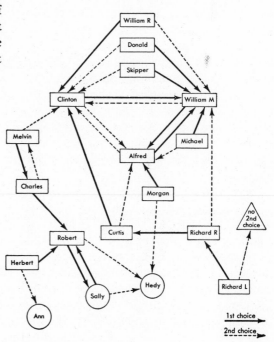

Social stratification

Chapter VI

By RICHARD T. MORRIS

in collaboration with L.B. and P.S.

Section 1 Introduction

Most people are born in societies in which the members classify each other into categories and place these categories above or below one another on a scale of superiority and inferiority.

It is possible for individuals to see each other as separate, unique human beings who do not fall into any categories. It is also possible to have categories that are equally evaluated. In either case, there is no stratification. Small groups, such as boys' gangs, bridge clubs, or fraternities often have little or no internal stratification because each member is seen as a separate individual. Stratification is possible, however, even in a small group: pledges and actives, duds and experts, new members and old-timers are all strata.

Once a stratification system is well established and recognized, members of the various strata tend to develop feelings of solidarity and to present a common front in their relations to other strata. Often the members of a stratum tend to restrict association to members of their own stratum. They may develop distinctive organizations, friendship groups, and occupational cliques, and may marry only within their own category. Special experiences tend to produce unique patterns of behavior and beliefs about etiquette, dress, entertainment, preferences in music and art, in politics and religion. These differences in interests, motivations, skills, and styles of living are important clues to the understanding and prediction of human behavior. (See Sec. 4, pp. 202–3.)

Since stratification is a matter of classification and evaluation, there is an almost unlimited variety of ways in which societies have been structured. Some have two strata, others have twenty-two; some are based on personal qualities, e.g., bravery, beauty, intelligence, others are based on possessions alone; some are built like a triangle with a very large base made up of the lowest stratum and a tiny group at the top, others take on a diamond shape, with a large middle stratum and small upper and lower strata; some are clear and agreed upon by everyone in the society, others are vague and indefinite and not seen in exactly the same way by any two people in the society; some allow easy access to different strata, others have categories that are tight and rigid, which an individual can neither move out of nor into from the moment of his birth; some stratification systems remain the same for centuries, others shift from year to year. Two contrasting types of stratification systems are briefly described below. Not only are they interesting in themselves; they afford a perspective from which American society may be viewed.

STRATIFICATION IN IMPERIAL CHINA[1]

For over 2,000 years, stratification in China retained basically the same form. Even though different groups occupied the top positions and the structure periodically became dislocated by war, revolt, and social upheaval, it returned to the same shape, made up of the same strata, with the same basic characteristics. From the second century B.C. until the early 1900's, the Confucian principles of leadership were maintained without a break. These principles were simple: there are three important social bonds—father-son, husband-wife, and sovereign-minister. In each the relation is the same, absolute submission and obedience of the latter to the former in the pair. Government was a direct projection of the patriarchal family. At the top was the Emperor, the Son of Heaven, who received his power to rule from Heaven and retained his mandate as long as he was able to keep things running smoothly in accordance with the order of nature. Natural disasters—famines, floods, earthquakes—were seen as his personal responsibility and served as either warnings from Heaven or proof that his prerogatives were at an end.

Beneath the Emperor and responsible to

him was an enormous bureaucracy made up of Confucian scholars. Once every three years civil examinations were held throughout the country for appointments to the various offices. The examinations were largely in the areas of literature, history and Confucian classics. The Emperor showed his righteousness by giving honors and advancement to worthy men in the society. They showed their worthiness by literary knowledge in the examinations rather than by political talent. Once in office, the intellectual had a great deal of prestige and power and could, if he wished, amass a fortune. Above all, he had leisure to continue his studies in the art of being proper and to train his children in the same tradition. The bureaucratic elite was recruited largely from the gentry, i.e., the large landholders. Though technically possible for a peasant to pass the examinations and achieve office, in practice it was rare, since the difficulty of the language and the complexity of the subject matter were so great that extensive leisure time and tutoring were essential. The examinations were so exacting that even among the gentry only one person in a hundred was ordinarily able to pass.

Beneath the gentry was the great peasant base of the society. A few of the more successful farmers could accumulate enough land to move up into the gentry and consolidate their positions with the aid of scholarly sons. The great bulk of peasantry, however, were apt to remain small landowners, or even more likely, because of population pressure, heavy taxation, and the limited availability of arable land, to slip down to the level of tenants and farm laborers. On the other hand, there was no downward movement of the gentry to the peasant level. With the gentleman's abhorrence of manual labor, the poorest of the gentry, helped by his kinsmen, managed to hang on to his position regardless of reverses.

The peasantry was subdivided into several strata along occupational lines: the farmer at

[1] See John K. Fairbank, *Chinese Thought and Institutions* (Chicago: University of Chicago Press, 1957), pp. 235–50; Hsiao-Tung Fei, ''Peasantry and Gentry: An Interpretation of Chinese Social Structure and Its Changes,'' *American Journal of Sociology,* **52** (1946), 1–17; Shu-Ching Lee, ''Administration and Bureaucracy: The Power Structure in Chinese Society,'' *Transactions* of the Second World Congress of Sociology (Vol. II), London: International Sociological Association, 1954, pp. 3–15; and Robert M. Marsh, *The Mandarins: Circulation of Elites in China, 1600–1900* (Glencoe: The Free Press, 1960).

元指揮千戶金公宏業

團兵衛鄉
一以當百
太湖一區
崔苻屏迹

1. *Chin Hung-Yeh, a military commander during the Mongol period, thirteenth century* A.D., *cleared* Tai Hu (*Grand Lake*) *area of bandit gangs.*

2. *Ku Yung, prime minister of the Kingdom of Wu during the Three-Kingdoms period, third century* A.D.

3. *Miao T'ung, receiving the highest score in the triennial examinations, was automatically appointed Imperial tutor. (Late seventeenth century, Manchu Period)*

the top, and in descending order, the gardener, woodsman, herdsman, artisan, merchant, weaver, servant, and unskilled laborer. At the very bottom were outcasts: the jobless, bandits, smugglers, convicts, slaves, actors, rag-pickers, barbers, and prostitutes. This stratum made up the bulk of the army, particularly as the peasantry increasingly resisted conscription. Outcasts were not permitted to take the civil examinations, even if they had wished to. Their main path of upward mobility was through the army or organized banditry on a large scale; and this was often successful, particularly in the wake of the periodic famines or revolts when dynasties were overthrown and replaced. In war and peace, the whole military structure, including the powerful war lords, was parallel to but never quite accepted by the peasant-gentry with their ideals of scholarly gentility and decorous behavior.

Figure VI: 1 shows the main features of this amazingly stable stratification system, which began to break down about the beginning of the twentieth century. The causes of its failure were many and complex: the inefficiency of the bureaucracy, the overthrow of the last dynasty and the establishment of the Republic, industrialization from the West, religious missions, the growth of the treaty ports, the Japanese invasion, the coming of the Communists—all played a part. But survivals of the old order may still be detected in the communist system.

STRATIFICATION IN SOVIET RUSSIA[2]

In contrast to the ancient, stable system of dynastic China, the newly established stratification system of Soviet Russia has, in its forty years of existence, been in a constant state of readjustment and realignment. Based upon a clear-cut economic and political doctrine, the original design for stratification in Russia was very simple: there were to be no class distinctions. The aristocracy and *bourgeoisie,* i.e., the owners of the means of production, were to be overthrown and to disappear or be absorbed. The peasantry were indistinguishable from their urban working cousins, and very little was said about the political hierarchy as a basis for stratification in a classless society. Marx saw government as a tool used by the ruling class (the owners) to maintain itself, and it followed that with no ruling class, there would be no need for government, except as a minor bookkeeping operation.

It became evident soon after the Russian Revolution of 1917 that theory and practice were often far apart. The new government took over the task of establishing its position and converting a semifeudal society into an efficient industrial nation. Complex and pow-

[2] See Alex Inkeles and Raymond A. Bauer, *The Soviet Citizen* (Cambridge: Harvard University Press, 1960), pp. 67–100; Alex Inkeles and Kent Geiger (eds.), *Soviet Society: A Book of Readings* (Boston: Houghton Mifflin, 1961); and S. V. Utechin, "Social Stratification and Social Mobility in the U.S.S.R.," *Transactions* of the Second World Congress of Sociology (Vol. II), London: International Sociological Association, 1954, pp. 55–63.

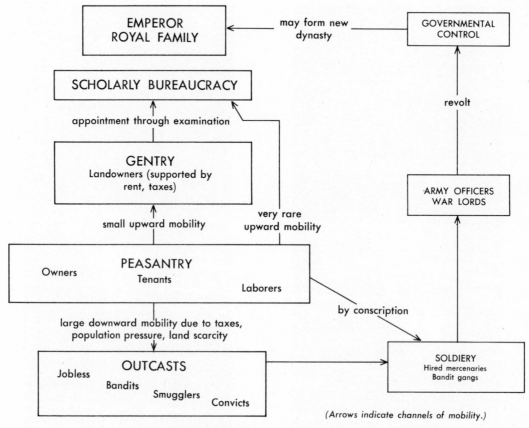

Fig. **VI:1**   Stratification and Mobility in Imperial China, 200 B.C.–1900 A.D.

erful organizational machinery was essential in the planning and carrying out of the conversion. A new governing group emerged based upon the political dominance of the Communist Party.

In addition the traditional occupational differences in prestige reasserted themselves: professionals (especially scientific and military) at the top, managers, skilled technicians, clerical workers, skilled laborers, unskilled laborers, and peasants, in descending order. The ranking appears to be based on job characteristics such as amount of training and the nature of the work (dirty *vs.* clean, manual *vs.* nonmanual), and resembles very closely the occupational prestige structure in the United States and other industrialized countries. (See p. 200.) These two princi-

ples of stratification—the political and the occupational—combined to create the system outlined diagrammatically in Figure VI:2. It is a shifting, changing system as relations between the two principles are worked out, and as a third principle of stratification common in Western Europe and America begins to operate—income differentials and the amassing and inheritance of property.

There was no upward mobility from the forced labor camps. The average peasant child as well as the children of disadvantaged or average workers have little chance of high school careers because of tuition fees and the absence of scholarships at this level. Without such education, the path up is through increased worker skill or movement to larger, more productive collective farms.

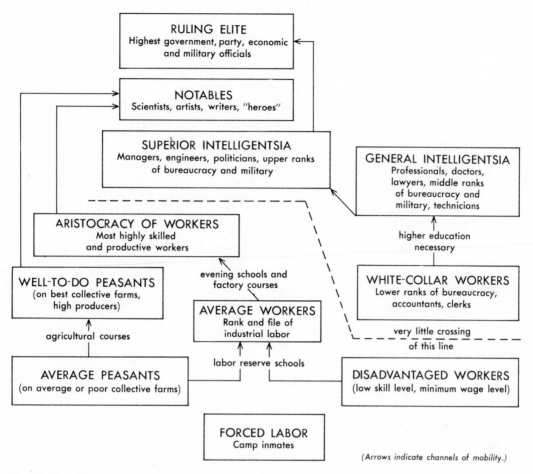

Fig. VI:2 Stratification and Mobility in the U.S.S.R., 1940—1955

It is virtually impossible for these children to move into the ruling elite by becoming intelligentsia.

A few of the most productive or talented workers may become notables, but they are more or less decorations and are not apt to be given real power. There is an increasing tendency for positions in the ruling elite and the superior intelligentsia to be filled from the ranks of those who have had higher education, but higher education is difficult to attain for the children of uneducated parents. The positions of those at the top are consolidated by abolishing inheritance taxes and by an income tax that levels off at about $6,000, instead of steeply increasing at the higher income brackets. Some notables earn over $150,000 per year and keep most of it. It is now possible for the wealthy to maintain savings with interest and to accumulate houses and personal property. The vision of a classless society seems to be dim indeed with mobility channels slowly closing and "proletarians" taking positions ever more clearly at the bottom of a rigid stratification system. There still exists, however, the official ideology, which is important as a propaganda device especially in Asia and Africa, that Communism means a classless society, or at least, a society in which "the ruling class" is made up of peasants and workers rather than the old elites.

SOURCES AND READINGS

H. Dewey Anderson and Percy E. Davidson, *Occupational Trends in the United States* (Stanford: Stanford University Press, 1940).

Bernard Barber, *Social Stratification* (New York: Harcourt, Brace, 1957). This book contains an extensive bibliography.

R. Bendix and S. M. Lipset (eds.), *Class, Status and Power: A Reader in Social Stratification* (Glencoe: The Free Press, 1953).

Ralf Dahrendorf, *Class and Class Conflict in Industrial Society* (Stanford: Stanford University Press, 1959).

Alba M. Edwards, *Comparative Occupation Statistics for the United States, 1870–1940* (Washington, D. C.: Government Printing Office, 1943).

Milton M. Gordon, *Social Class in American Sociology* (Durham: Duke University Press, 1958).

A. J. Jaffe and Charles D. Stewart, *Manpower Resources and Utilization: Principles of Working Force Analysis* (New York: Wiley, 1951).

Joseph A. Kahl, *The American Class Structure* (New York: Rinehart, 1957).

S. M. Lipset and R. Bendix, *Social Mobility in an Industrial Society* (Berkeley and Los Angeles: University of California Press, 1958).

David C. McClelland, *The Achieving Society* (Princeton: Van Nostrand, 1961).

T. H. Marshall, *Citizenship and Social Class* (Cambridge: Cambridge University Press, 1950).

Kurt B. Mayer, *Class and Society* (Garden City, N. Y.: Doubleday, 1955).

Herman P. Miller, *Income of the American People* (New York: Wiley, 1955).

C. W. Mills, *White Collar: The American Middle Classes* (New York: Oxford University Press, 1951).

Albert J. Reiss, Jr., *Occupations and Social Status* (Glencoe: The Free Press, 1962).

Leonard Reissman, *Class in American Society* (Glencoe: The Free Press, 1959).

Pitirim A. Sorokin, *Social and Cultural Mobility* (Glencoe: The Free Press, 1959).

T. Veblen, *The Theory of the Leisure Class* (New York: Macmillan, 1912).

BIBLIOGRAPHIES

Current Sociology, "Social Stratification and Social Mobility," Vol. II, No. 1; Vol. II, No. 4, 1953–1954.

S. M. Miller, "Comparative Social Mobility," *Current Sociology*, **9** (1960), 81–89.

Harold W. Pfautz, "The Current Literature on Social Stratification: Critique and Bibliography," *American Journal of Sociology*, **58** (1953), 391–418.

The extensive literature from the Warner studies is referred to on page 190. Further references are given on pages 202–3.

Section 2 The study of social stratification

Social scientists have used three methods in studying social stratification: (1) the reputational approach, (2) the subjective approach, and (3) the objective approach.

The Reputational Approach

One way to study stratification is to ask people how they classify one another, how many and what kinds of categories they use, how they evaluate those categories, and how they rank them in a hierarchy. The sociologist usually selects a small community and asks a number of long-term residents to serve as judges or raters and to indicate how they stratify the other members of that community. Some investigators have asked informants to place personal acquaintances and other individuals whom they know about (by reputation) into categories, to give their general impressions about the stratification system of the town, and to mention terms that are commonly used to refer to the various social categories—such terms as "upper crust," "wrong side of the tracks," and "hoi polloi." The judges' evaluations and observations are combined by averaging or some other technique to determine the stratification system of that community. Other investigators have asked resident judges to sort cards, on which are written the names of a large number of families in the community, into piles containing families of the same social rank or position. They then ask the judges to rank their categories and to say why they placed the families where they did, in order to discover what criteria the judges used.

A number of other techniques have been used in studies of this kind, but the logic of all of them is essentially the same: the members of a community or organization constantly stratify one another, and the way to find out how they do it is to ask them. The strata discovered by this method, regardless of refinements of technique, are commonly called *reputational strata*. The method is called the *reputational approach,* because the categories are based upon the reputations that various members of the community have in the eyes of other members. (See Adaptation 17, pp. 186 ff.)

The Subjective Approach

The logic of the *subjective approach is* straightforward: to discover the effective stratification system, ask the members where they place *themselves,* not others. The sociologist merely asks, "In what class (or stratum, or category) do you belong?" On the basis of the answers, the investigator can construct a picture of the number, size, and arrangement of *subjective strata* in that particular society, community, or organization. This method has an obvious advantage: it can be applied to much larger units than the reputational approach, which is limited by the extent of the acquaintance of the judges. Sociologists who use the subjective approach further argue that to determine the effectiveness of stratification, i.e., its effects on behavior, it is more important to know where a person *thinks* he is than it is to know where others place him. (See pp. 185 ff.)

The Objective Approach

A third method used to study the stratification system of a society or organization is called the *objective approach.* It is based upon detailed observation to determine the strata that exist, whether or not the members are aware of the strata. To determine *objective strata,* the scientist "stands outside" the society and tries to discover the criteria that accurately divide the population into strata most significantly affecting the social behavior he is trying to understand and predict.

Marx [3] (see p. 648) thought that in any society an individual's position and function in the production process, e.g., whether he owns the means of production or works for someone else, largely determines the beliefs and actions of that individual and of all others in that particular category. Marx felt that members of a category would develop common interests out of their common position and under specified conditions would enter into an organized effort to reach common goals. On the other hand, Max Weber [4] (see p. 630) saw *three* basic criteria which stratified the society simultaneously: the possession of economic goods and opportunities, the possession of political power, and the possession of social honor or prestige. Although the distributions of these three criteria are often highly interrelated, he maintained that they can be and often are separate and that each in its own way is important in determining the behavior of individuals, their style of life, and their life chances. Other social scientists have come to the conclusion that occupation, power, income, education, or combinations of these criteria are crucial and permit the most accurate prediction of social behavior.

The sociologist using the objective approach may decide to make income his cri-

---

[3] Cf. Reinhard Bendix and S. M. Lipset, "Karl Marx' Theory of Social Classes" in Bendix and Lipset (eds.), *Class, Status and Power* (Glencoe: The Free Press, 1953), pp. 26–35; and Ralf Dahrendorf, *Class and Class Conflict in Industrial Society* (Stanford: Stanford University Press, 1959), "Karl Marx's Model of the Class Society," pp. 3–35.

[4] Max Weber, *From Max Weber: Essays in Sociology,* translated and edited by H. H. Gerth and C. W. Mills (New York: Oxford University Press, 1946), Chap. VII.

terion and divide an income range into three categories: less than $3,000, $3,000–$4,999, and $5,000 or over. He may call these three categories "socio-economic levels" or "strata" and give them names, such as "lower," "middle," and "upper." He then may investigate the characteristics (correlates) of each stratum, such as differences in sexual behavior, drinking patterns, political attitudes, or buying habits, as they vary by income categories. (See Sec. 4, pp. 202–3.) Most of the class or stratification studies reported in the public press are of this kind. The investigator selects a criterion, usually income, occupation, or education (or some combination of these characteristics), sets up his categories with arbitrary boundaries, and then proceeds with the investigation of correlates.

In both the reputational and the subjective approaches the investigator gathers his data from statements made by members of the society about the way *they* see stratification taking place, whereas the *investigator* does the stratifying in the objective approach, regardless of how the individuals feel about the structure or see it. This logic is basically the same in all of the *objective approaches*. (See pp. 188 f.)

Caution: The reputational and subjective approaches are "objective" in the sense that they are scientific efforts to gain unbiased knowledge.

COMPARISON OF THE THREE METHODS

The differences in method have led to increasingly widespread and important differences in the terminology used in stratification theory and research. The term *stratum* or *level* is often used to refer only to those categories determined by the objective method, whereas the term *class* or *social class* is reserved for those categories determined by the subjective or reputational method. In other words, if the members of a society provide the information on how they stratify

one another or themselves, if they are aware of the strata, there are social *classes* in that society. If, on the other hand, the members of the society are not aware of their position in categories but the investigator finds significant categories, his classifications are called *strata*. However, these strata are significant for behavior and for the development of possible future class consciousness, even though at the time the population is unaware of such a classification.

Discussion of the three approaches to stratification study raises many questions. If there is a difference between the structure as seen by the scientist and as seen by members of the community, which one is correct? If the community members differ from one another in the way they see the structure, who is right? If some judges in a reputational study see three classes, others see seven, others four, five, or nine, is the sociologist justified in picking the majority view and dispensing with the others? Research[5] shows that individuals at lower levels consistently see a different structure and use different criteria from those who are in the middle or in the higher positions. Who *really* sees the structure? Or can it be said that there are as many structures as there are people looking at them? It is quite possible for an individual or group to be assigned to one stratum by a scientist, to several others by several sets of community members, and to still another by himself. The various stratifiers may use different criteria; they may use the same criteria and estimate the cues, the symbols, the possession of them by the individual differently. On the other hand, they may agree upon these points and simply categorize differently. For example, they may all use income as a criterion and estimate its possession in the same fashion but disagree over the number of income categories.

The schoolteacher is a case in point. *Ob-*

[5] E.g., Allison Davis, B. B. Gardner, and M. R. Gardner, *Deep South* (Chicago: University of Chicago Press, 1941), p. 65.

jectively, using income as a criterion, she may be in a lower stratum. She probably makes less than the zoo cook. *Reputationally,* using the criteria of service to children or place of residence, she may be placed in the middle class by members of her community. *Subjectively,* because of her association with intellectuals and her advanced training and degrees, she may place herself at a higher level. Which is her *real* class position?

The answer may be disappointing, since it cannot be a flat statement, and since it is perhaps not really the crucial question. If an important purpose of stratification studies is to classify individuals in a society or to discover how they classify one another, so that their behavior may be predicted and understood with greater precision and insight, then a number of classifications may be made, and one may excel another depending upon *what prediction* the scientist wishes to make. This argument holds that there is no "real" stratification or class structure and, therefore, that there is no "real" position of an individ-

ual, but that there are a variety of structures seen from a variety of points of view. The question must always be asked: "Class from whose point of view?" The point of view that is "best" depends entirely upon what is to be predicted with it.

For example, the subjective method may be most useful for predicting political attitudes. Where a person *thinks* he is may determine how he will vote. On the other hand, if differences in sexual behavior are to be investigated the objective method using education as a criterion may afford the best results. However, if associational membership is to be predicted and understood, the reputational method may be best.

It is possible, in an especially rigid and clearly stratified society, that the different methods would arrive at approximately the same description of the structure, i.e., all members would agree upon the placement of an individual, he would see himself in the same position, and any social scientist would stratify the society similarly.

Methods of Stratification Research

THE SUBJECTIVE METHOD

The Sample

Use a large class in your school, or a number of small classes, or an organizational meeting. Try to get at least 100 people to participate. If you can get them all at once, so much the better.

The Data

Ask your subjects to write the answers to the following questions:

1. To what class *in America* would you say you belong? (Write just the name of the class.)

2. To what class in America would you

say your father belongs (or did belong if he is now deceased)?

3. To what class *in your own community or home town* would you say you belong?

4. To what class in his community does your father belong (or did he belong)?

5. Now, please write the following words, one under the other: "Upper, Lower upper, Upper middle, Middle, Lower middle, White collar, Working, Upper lower, Lower." Please mark with an "O" your own class, the class in America to which you think you belong. Please mark with an "F" your father's class, the class in America to which you think your father belongs (or belonged).

6. Now please write the following words, one under another: "Upper, Middle, Working, Lower." Mark one of these with an "O" to indicate your own class and an "F" to indicate your father's class in America.

7. What is it about your father which made you place him in the class you did? What characteristic did you use to place him?

8. What made you place yourself where you did?

9. What is (or was) your father's main occupation. Be specific: do not just say "businessman"; say what kind of business and his position in that business.

10. What occupation do you plan to enter?

11. (Optional) If you were to vote in the next presidential election, would you be apt to vote Democrat or Republican?

12. (Optional) How do you think your father will vote?

The Findings

To analyze the results, list separately all of the class names used in questions 1 through 4 and enter the number of people who used each of these names. Enter separately the number of people who placed themselves and their fathers in the various classes provided in questions 5 and 6. For each class in question 6 list separately the fathers' occupations from question 9 and the intended occupations from question 10. This might be compared with the occupational distribution in the classes derived from questions 1 through 5. For each class in question 6 list the criteria used for placement of self, question 8, and for father, question 7. For each class enter the number of political affiliations, questions 11 and 12.

The Interpretation

A study such as this will help you to answer the following kinds of questions, tentatively at least, as they apply to your particular sample:

1. Where do people place themselves when class names are not provided?

2. How does this differ from their self-placement when names are provided?

3. What does the "middle" or "working" class consist of?

4. How do occupations spread themselves over the classes?

5. Does voting intention differ by class?

THE REPUTATIONAL METHOD

The Judges

Use a small community (up to 5,000) for your study. Ask approximately five people who know a large number of individuals in the town to serve as judges. Bankers, clergymen, doctors, established businessmen, town officials, or a newspaper editor might be good possibilities. If you choose judges in the upper income and occupational brackets, however, bear in mind that you will get a picture of the class structure of that community as seen *from the top*. To make a comparison of this view with the views from other levels, several investigators might choose judges from different strata in the same community. These judges should also know a large number of families. They might be milkmen, bill collectors, handymen, mail carriers, or policemen. (See the comment on privacy in INTRODUCTION, pp. 9 f.)

The Sample

Take a sample of the town's adults. If possible, get a city directory or other list which includes *all* of the people in the community. Take each *n*th name. (For example, if there are 5,000, take each fiftieth name for an easily manageable sample of 100.) Write the name and address of each of the selected people on a separate card. If they are not included, add the judges' names to the set of cards. Number each card. You might use a telephone directory, but if you do you will automatically bias your sample by excluding those who do not have telephones. A city directory is a less biased listing.

Judge A (5 Classes)	Judge B (5 Classes)	Judge C (3 Classes)	Judge D (4 Classes)	Judge E, F, G...
Upper. 6, 50	Upper 6, 36	Upper 6, 50	Upper 6, 7, 36	
Upper-Middle 7, 12, 36, 41, etc.	Upper-Middle 50, 7, 12, 34, 22, etc.	Middle 7, 12, 36, 41, 22, etc.	Upper-Middle 12, 50, 34, etc.	
Middle 22, 9, 34, 52, etc.	Middle 9, 41, 52, 8, etc.		Middle 41, 22, 52, etc.	
Lower-Middle 8, 10, 26, 46, etc.	Lower-Middle 10, 26, 17, etc.			
Lower 47, 17, 18, etc.	Lower 46, 18, 47, etc.	Lower 18, 47, etc.	Lower 17, 47, 65, etc.	

Fig. VI:3 Example of Plotting Arrangement for Reputational Study

The numbers in the cells are the card numbers of the individuals ranked. *Etc.* indicates that additional rankings were made in the cell. Most judges will not rank all individuals in the sample.

The Data

Ask the judges to do each of the following operations in turn:

1. Go through the cards and discard the ones listing people whom they do not know.

2. Sort the remaining cards into piles which represent groups of people who seem to belong together in terms of the general standing they have in the community. (They may make any number of groupings they wish.)

3. Arrange the piles in order of evaluation, with those who are most highly regarded in the community at the top, those least valued at the bottom. (They may rate two or more groupings as having about equal value.)

After they have done this, ask the following information of the judges:

1. What do people generally call these groupings (if they have names for them)?

2. Do the groupings have any particular characteristics: in personality, character, or behavior?

3. What would you estimate is the percentage of the community in each grouping?

4. Are any important groupings omitted from this arrangement? (The judge may not personally know any people in them, or representatives of these groupings may not have been included in the original set of cards.)

5. Why did you group the individuals as you did? (What were the characteristics or

criteria the judge used in his groupings?)

As the information is collected the investigator must:

1. Make a record of the cards discarded and of the groupings and ratings made by each judge.

2. During each interview record the characteristics, estimated size, criteria, and names used for each of the groupings by each of the judges.

The Findings

After the data have been collected from all of the judges, make a summary of your findings. List the name or number of each judge, his position as estimated by the other judges and himself, the number of people he placed, the number of groupings he made, and their relative size.

Next, plot the rated individuals according to the positions assigned to them by the various judges. Use a large sheet of graph paper and enter the number of each individual's card in the class groupings made by each judge. This arrangement will provide a quick visual image of agreement between the judges in their perceptions of the social structure of the community. (See Fig. VI: 3.)

Make a summary statement of the characteristics, criteria, sizes, and names of the classes as perceived by the several judges.

The Interpretation

From such a study you may get a fairly clear picture of the class structure as seen by certain community members, the degree of agreement among them, and differences in the way the structure is seen from different vantage points.

THE OBJECTIVE METHOD

The Sample

Try to get about 100 people as subjects from a large college class or several small ones. Ask them the questions while they are in class.

The Data

Ask the students to write answers to the following questions, or give them mimeographed forms.

1. What is (or was) your father's main occupation? Be specific. Do not just say "businessman," but state what kind of business and your father's position in that business.

2. (Optional) What is your intended occupation? Be as specific as possible.

3. What was your father's approximate annual average income during his best five years?

4. (Optional) What income do you realistically expect to be making ten years after you graduate?

5. What educational level did your father attain? Use one of the following terms: grade school, some high school, high school graduate, some college, college graduate, some postgraduate, postgraduate degree.

6. What educational level did your mother attain? (Use the same terms as above.)

7. Now we would like to get some information about the personal tastes and preferences of your parents.[6] What sort of pictures are (or were) displayed in your living room at home? Use one of the following terms to indicate the kind of picture. If there is more than one kind displayed, indicate the most frequent kind by "1" for most frequent, "2" for second most frequent, etc.

   a. photographs of family members or friends

   b. photographs of scenery or animals

   c. reproductions of traditional or representational paintings

   d. reproductions of abstract or modern painting

   e. original traditional or representational paintings, including family portraits

   f. original abstract or modern paintings

   g. if others, describe

   h. no pictures

[6] Cf. Russell Lynes, *The Taste Makers* (New York: Harper, 1954), pp. 310–33.

8. What kinds of entertainment do your parents prefer? If they had equal choice and opportunity to attend one of the following events, which would they choose? If more than one, number in order of preference. If mother and father differ, indicate separately by "F" and "M."

    a. ballet
    b. stage play
    c. night baseball, football, or basketball
    d. automobile races
    e. lecture or discussion
    f. symphony concert
    g. night club entertainment
    h. movie
    i. if others, describe

9. What magazines do your parents regularly read? Number in order of frequency if more than one. If mother and father differ, indicate separately.

10. (Optional) Ask questions 7, 8, and 9 of the students themselves.

The Findings

When the data have been collected, separate the occupations of the fathers as follows:[7]

1. Professionals, proprietors and high officials of large businesses, including gentlemen farmers

2. Semiprofessionals and lower officials of large businesses, clerical, sales, and kindred workers, skilled workers, proprietors of small businesses

[7] For a finer breakdown see Warner, *Social Class in America*, pp. 140–41.

3. Semiskilled workers and unskilled workers

Separate the educational levels into:
1. College education
2. High school education
3. Grade school education only

Separate the income levels into:
1. Over $10,000
2. $3,000 to $10,000
3. Under $3,000

Now distribute the answers to questions 7 through 9 according to the three kinds of strata. If you separate the strata differently, or make finer groupings, e.g., into seven categories instead of three, the differences in distribution may show up more clearly.

The Interpretation

A number of questions can be answered by the analysis of your data. Does income, occupation, or education make the most difference in the preferences and tastes of your sample? Which area of preference is most clearly differentiated by which criterion, i.e., does artistic preference vary most by education while entertainment preference varies most by occupation? What is the relation between occupation, education, and income in your sample? If the optional questions are asked about students' own positions and preferences, how do they differ from their parents? Which students differ most? Many other comparisons can be made. (See Sec. 4, pp. 202–3.)

Section 3 **Studies of stratification in the United States**

REPUTATIONAL STUDIES

Perhaps the most influential series of studies using the reputational approach is that of W. Lloyd Warner and associates.[8] They interviewed people in three communities: a New England town of about 17,000 population called "Yankee City," a Southern town of about 10,000 called "Old City," and a Midwestern town of about 6,000 variously called "Jonesville," "Prairie City," "Elmtown," and "Hometown." In these communities six (sometimes five) social classes were distinguished and named by the investigators as follows:

1. The *upper-upper* class is an aristocracy of birth and inherited wealth. The "old families" have a way of life characterized by ritual behavior and intricate codes of etiquette. Community members refer to this class as "the 400," "the aristocrats," and "the people with family and money."

2. Members of the *lower-upper* class, like

the upper-uppers, live in costly houses in exclusive districts, and have similar patterns of participation, income, and occupation. They engage in such occupations as finance, industry, and the professions. But they lack the distinguished ancestry of the upper-uppers and the tradition of the upper-class behavior. Their money is too new and their achievement too recent to warrant the same prestige as the upper-uppers. In Jonesville, however, these two upper classes are combined, making only five classes in all.

3. The *upper-middle* class is composed of professionals and substantial businessmen. These respected members of the community often act as civic leaders, but they are not "society." They live in comfortable houses in the "better" residential sections. They are referred to by community members as "above average but not tops."

Warner calls these three higher classes the "level above the common man." The "level of the common man" is composed of the lower-middle and upper-lower classes and contains the largest number of people.

4. The *lower-middle* class is composed of small-business men, white-collar workers, and a few skilled workmen. Their small neat houses are in the "side streets." They are proper and conservative, careful with their money, concerned about respectability, and labeled as "good common people."

5. Members of the *upper-lower* class are the "honest workmen" and the "clean poor." They are semiskilled workers in factories, service workers, and a few small tradesmen. They live in the less desirable sections and have lower incomes, but they are "respectable." They are often referred to as "the poor but hard-working people."

6. The *lower-lower* class is not "respecta-

[8] The "Yankee City" Series (New Haven: Yale University Press): W. L. Warner and P. S. Lunt, *The Social Life of a Modern Community* (1941); W. L. Warner and P. S. Lunt, *The Status System of a Modern Community* (1942); W. L. Warner and Leo Srole, *The Social Systems of American Ethnic Groups* (1945); W. L. Warner and J. O. Low, *The Social System of the Modern Factory* (1947); W. Lloyd Warner, *The Living and the Dead* (1959).

The "Old City" study: Allison Davis, B. B. Gardner, and M. R. Gardner, *Deep South* (Chicago: University of Chicago Press, 1941).

The "Bronzeville" study: St. Clair Drake and Horace R. Cayton, *Black Metropolis* (New York: Harcourt, Brace, 1945).

The "Jonesville" studies: W. Lloyd Warner, Robert J. Havighurst, Martin B. Loeb, *Who Shall Be Educated?* (New York: Harper, 1944); W. L. Warner and Associates, *Democracy in Jonesville* (New York: Harper, 1949); W. L. Warner, Marchia Meeker, and Kenneth Eels, *Social Class in America* (Chicago: Science Research Associates, 1949); R. J. Havighurst and Hilda Taba, *Adolescent Character and Personality* (New York: Wiley, 1948); and A. B. Hollingshead, *Elmtown's Youth* (New York: Wiley, 1949).

For a summary statement see W. Lloyd Warner, *American Life, Dream and Reality* (Chicago: University of Chicago Press, 1962).

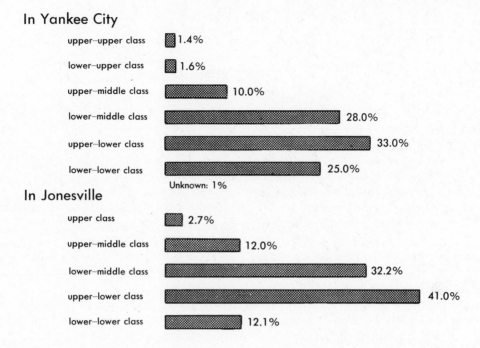

In Yankee City

upper–upper class	1.4%
lower–upper class	1.6%
upper–middle class	10.0%
lower–middle class	28.0%
upper–lower class	33.0%
lower–lower class	25.0%

Unknown: 1%

In Jonesville

upper class	2.7%
upper–middle class	12.0%
lower–middle class	32.2%
upper–lower class	41.0%
lower–lower class	12.1%

Fig. **VI:4** Size of Classes

Source: For Yankee City data, Warner and Lunt, *The Social Life of a Modern Community* (New Haven: Yale University Press, 1941), p. 88. For Jonesville data, Warner and Associates, *Democracy in Jonesville* (New York: Harper, 1949), pp. 50–51.

ble." They are the "level below the common man," live in the worst sections and are semi-skilled and unskilled workers. In Yankee City they comprised the largest proportion of individuals on relief. They are regarded as immoral by the other classes and are referred to as "poor but not respectable," "the river rats," etc.[9]

According to Warner, the same class levels, showing similar characteristics, are to be found with minor variations throughout the country. He holds that the social classes he has identified are real entities: "The designations of social levels are distinctions made by the people themselves in referring to each other. . . ."[10]

The number of classes identified by the members of a community varies, however, according to the social class of the informant. Furthermore, the more remote the classes are from the position of the informant, the less clearly are distinctions made. The criteria for judging class membership also vary. The lower classes use money as the main criterion; the middle classes, money and morality; and the upper classes, style of life and ancestry.

These differences in perspective make it difficult to picture a single class structure in a community. Furthermore, not all of the members of the community, especially if it

[9] For detailed discussion see Ruth R. Kornhauser, "The Warner Approach to Social Stratification," in Reinhard Bendix and S. M. Lipset (eds.), *Class, Status and Power* (Glencoe: The Free Press, 1953), especially pp. 230–31. See also Milton M. Gordon, *Social Class in American Sociology* (Durham: Duke University Press, 1958.)

[10] Warner and Associates, *Democracy in Jonesville*, p. xiv.

Social Rank and Disaster at Sea

Britain of the Edwardian period was characterized by well-defined social strata and a strong sense of class identity. The great trans-Atlantic liners of the time with their sharp demarcations between classes of passengers were an expression of the status system in extreme form. The *Titanic,* a ship of the British White Star Line, was commissioned in 1912. The largest and most luxurious liner of her day, she was reputed to be the safest. She carried lifeboats for about 1,200 passengers, or only 30 per cent of her total capacity, but safety regulations of the time required even fewer lifeboats. On her maiden voyage she collided with an iceberg in the North Atlantic and sank with the loss of more than 1,500 of her 2,200 passengers and crew.

A few years earlier when another White Star Liner, the *Republic,* sank, Captain Sealby told passengers entering the lifeboats, "Remember! Women and children go first, then the First Cabin, then the others." * There was no such rule aboard the *Titanic,* but the survivors were not a random sample of the passengers. Historical research and cold statistics suggest that a convergence of indifference, carelessness, luck, and location worked in favor of the first-class and against the third-class passengers. Of 143 women in first class only 4 were casualties (2.8 per cent), and 3 of these were casualties "by choice." Of 93 women in second class there were 15 casualties (16.1 per cent). Of 179 women in third class, 81 were casualties (45.3 per cent). Only one of the 29 children in first and second class was lost, but only 23 out of 76 children in steerage were saved.

Investigations were held in both Britain and the United States, but in neither country was the moral drawn nor the statistical inference made. After the disaster new rules were passed governing lifeboats and safety measures. As Lord put it, "The night was a magnificent confirmation of 'women and children first,' yet somehow the loss rate was higher for Third Class children than First Class men. It was a contrast which would never get by the social consciousness (or news sense) of today's press." †

* Walter Lord, *A Night to Remember* (New York: Holt, 1955), pp. 107–9 *et passim.* Quotation at p. 109.

† *Ibid.,* p. 108.

is very large, *can* be placed by an individual or set of individuals. We can place only those of whom we are aware, and we are particularly aware of those with whom we have social contact. In a small, folk society everyone may be placed by everyone else. The same is probably not true in our society, even in small communities. In one reputational study of a community of only 3,300 population, the judges had lived in the community for a long time, but the most active rater (a person from the upper-upper class) still could place only 148 of the 190 families selected as the sample.[11] In other words, individuals in our society do not know, are not aware of, do not place everyone in the society, or even in their own communities.

This creates difficulties when attempts are made to generalize from community placements to the class structure of the whole society. Political and economic strata which exercise very important controls in the country at large are not represented in the small com-

munity. A picture of the nationwide class structure which does not systematically include the stratum of national industrial and political leaders in Washington and New York gives a distorted view. It is impossible to predict certain kinds of national political or economic changes by looking at Jonesville alone. Most reputational studies are limited to placements *within* the small community and do not inquire into views about the class structure of the metropolis, the state, or the country.

It should not be inferred, however, that people can place others only if they know them personally. In an occupational prestige study, for example, persons could rate or rank the occupation of airline pilot even though they have never known one personally.

The vague image of national stratification seen by most Americans is partly due to the leveling of life-styles brought about by mass production and the extensive distribution of uniform consumer goods. For example, it has become increasingly difficult to estimate the occupation or income of a person by the way he dresses, the kind of car he drives, or the place in which he spends his vacation.

[11] Wayne Wheeler, *Social Stratification in a Plains Community* (Minneapolis: 1949), pp. 30–36. See also Otis Dudley Duncan and Jay W. Artis, *Social Stratification in a Pennsylvania Rural Community* (State College: Pennsylvania State College School of Agriculture, 1951).

Table **VI:1** Subjective Perceptions of Class Position*

Upper	1.6%	2.9% Upper
Best, highest, etc.	1.3	
Upper middle	1.7	
Above average, etc.	.8	
Middle	38.6	47.0% Middle
In between, moderate, etc.	5.5	
Lower middle	.4	
Working, laboring	10.6	10.6% Working
Lower	1.2	
Poor, poorest, etc.	2.8	4.3% Lower
Unemployed, etc.	.3	
Miscellaneous	7.7	
Don't know	27.5	
Total	100.0%	
Number of cases: 5,217		

* Reprinted by Special Permission of the Editors from the February, 1940, FORTUNE Survey of Public Opinion; Copyright 1940 Time Inc.

SUBJECTIVE STUDIES

In 1940 the *Fortune* Survey asked, "What word would you use to name the class in America you belong to?" The responses were as shown in Table VI:1.

When those who had *not* used the actual words "upper," "middle," or "lower" were asked to pick one of these three words to describe the class to which they belonged, the total distribution among the three classes appeared as follows:

Upper class	7.6%
Middle class	79.2%
Lower class	7.9%
Don't know	5.3%

In the same year, the Institute of Public Opinion[12] asked, "To what social class in this country do you think you belong—the middle class, the upper, or the lower?" It found almost the same results:

Upper class	6%
Middle class	88%
Lower class	6%

When Americans are asked to name the class they belong to, three-quarters of them answer, and they assign themselves a variety of terms and positions, although nearly 40 per cent say "middle." If, on the other hand, only three alternatives—upper, middle and lower—are presented to them 80 to 90 per cent place themselves in the middle class. Because of the widespread ideology of equalitarianism, there is undoubtedly hesitancy to say that one is upper class. There is also reluctance to say that one is lower class, possibly because it implies that he is not only poor but also immoral or inferior.

In 1945 Centers[13] used the term "working class," which allowed a somewhat different meaning and position from "middle" but

without the opprobrium attached to the word "lower." A national sample of 1,097 white, male adults was asked to use one of *four* names for their social class: middle class, lower class, working class, or upper class. Their answers were as follows:

Upper class	3%
Middle class	43
Working class	51
Lower class	1
Don't know	1
Don't believe in classes	1
Total	100%

If the aim of the investigation is to discover whether the members of a society are actually aware of class membership, that is, feel that they belong to a class, the validity of supplying respondents with particular class names may well be questioned. It is not safe to assume the existence of a working class whose members so identify themselves in their day-to-day behavior and who act politically or economically in behalf of that class, simply because there are a number of people who choose that name among others when a list is presented to them. If a list of class names which included "upper-upper middle," "upper middle," "middle middle," "lower middle," and "lower-lower middle" were presented to a nationwide sample, no doubt sizable proportions of the population would distribute themselves into these categories.

Subjective findings compared with reputational findings suggest that there are large variations in the way Americans stratify their society depending upon (*a*) whether they are stratifying their own community or the country, and (*b*) whether they are placing themselves or placing others. People make rather fine distinctions in the class structure of their own community, if it is a small one, and particularly if they are in the upper strata looking down. Those at the top have better knowledge of the community than those in the lower strata. This is due to greater activity in community affairs, better education, more

[12] George Gallup and S. F. Rae, *The Pulse of Democracy* (New York: Simon and Schuster, 1940), p. 169.

[13] Richard Centers, *The Psychology of Social Classes* (Princeton: Princeton University Press, 1949), p. 77. See also Joseph A. Kahl and James A. Davis, "A Comparison of Indexes of Socio-Economic Status," *American Sociological Review*, **20** (1955), 317–25.

Communist Russia presents itself as a friend of the working class: Flanked by sculptures of Nehru and Hemingway, a painting of Khrushchev purports to show the admiration and affection of American working men for the Soviet leader. In the United States, however, even the terms "worker" or "working class" are not generally accepted by blue-collar employees. The painting says more about Communist ideology than about social class in the United States.

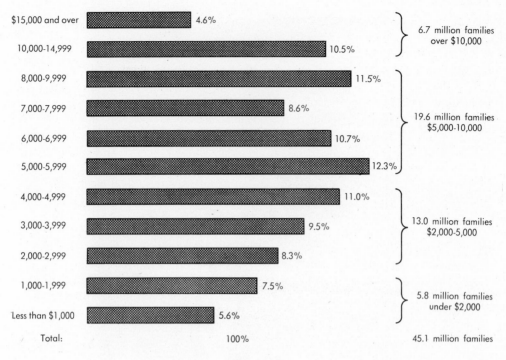

Fig. **VI:5**

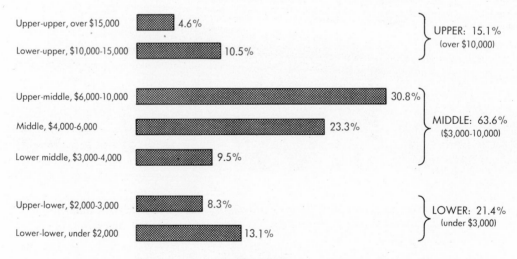

Fig. **VI:6**

Figs. **VI:5** and **VI:6**   Stratification of U.S. Families by Income, 1959

Source: U.S. Bureau of the Census, *U.S. Census of Population: 1960. General Social and Economic Characteristics, United States Summary.* Final Report PC(1)-1C. (Washington, D.C.: U.S. Government Printing Office, 1962), pp. 225–26.

concern about community structure because of the desire to maintain their own positions, a greater interest in civic affairs and organizational activities, and a greater sense of responsibility for the community.

On the other hand, people placing themselves in the national class structure make very few distinctions among classes. Nearly all of them place themselves somewhere in the middle. This is confirmed by at least one study showing that the number of classes perceived and the subjective placement of respondents is in large part a function of the variation in class names provided.[14]

There are probably two kinds of class order in the United States: (1) a number of separate class structures in small communities all over the country—structures seen and agreed upon only by certain members of those communities, and (2) nationwide classes, perceived vaguely by about three-quarters of the population.

OBJECTIVE STUDIES

Most objective studies made for the purpose of discovering correlates use the criteria of income, education, or occupation. In part these particular criteria are used because the data may be compiled, measured, and compared with relative ease. There are also sound theoretical reasons for using income and occupation as the chief objective criteria. The "best" objective criteria are those which most accurately predict the greatest number of important correlates. Income and occupation in an industrial society are very good criteria because they determine so many other characteristics. It may be noted, too, that Warner found occupation to be the best single predictor of reputational class position.

One picture of economic stratification in the United States is shown in Figure VI : 5, which is based on the findings of the 1960 census. Because the census was conducted in April, 1960, the incomes reported are for the calendar year 1959.

Increase in Family Income[15]

For the country as a whole, the average money income of families and persons rose substantially between 1949 and 1959. The average (median) income of families was $5,700 in 1959, a gain of $2,600, or 84 per cent, over 1949. However, only part of the increase in income represented a gain in real purchasing power since prices also rose during this period. In terms of actual buying power the median family income increased by about 50 per cent.

Underlying the rise in median family income has been a major shift of families upward along the entire income scale. The proportion of families with incomes of less than $5,000 declined from 80 per cent in 1949 to 42 per cent in 1959. In contrast, the proportion receiving incomes between $5,000 and $10,000 increased from 17 per cent in 1949 to 43 per cent in 1959, and the proportion of families with incomes of $10,000 and over rose from 3 per cent to 15 per cent. Despite the marked rise in incomes that has taken place, somewhat more than one in every five families reported less than $3,000 in money income in 1959.

The income data discussed here cover money income only. Many farm families receive an important part of their income in the form of housing and of goods produced and consumed on the farm rather than in money. In evaluating the economic condition of farm families and others who receive income in kind rather than money, this fact should be taken into consideration.

Arbitrary Categories

When income categories are regrouped into broader strata, they appear to be class group-

[14] See Neal Gross, "Social Class Identification in the Urban Community," *American Sociological Review* **18** (1953), 398–404.

[15] U.S. Bureau of the Census, *U.S. Census of Population: 1960. General Social and Economic Characteristics, United States Summary.* Final Report PC (1)–1C. (Washington, D.C.: U.S. Government Printing Office, 1962), pp. xxxviii–xxxix.

College education	16.5%	4 or more years 7.7%
		1-3 years 8.8%
High school education	43.8%	4 years 24.6%
		1-3 years 19.2%
Less than high school education	39.8%	8 years 17.5%
		5-7 years 13.9%
		1-4 years 6.1%
		none 2.3%

N = 99.4 million

Fig. VI:7   Stratification of U.S. Population (Twenty-Five
Years Old and Over) by Education, 1960

Source: U.S. Bureau of the Census, *U.S. Census of Population: 1960. General Social
and Economic Characteristics, United States Summary.* Final Report PC(1)-1C. (Washington, D.C.: U.S. Government Printing Office, 1962), p. 207.

ings rather than income strata. (See Fig. VI: 6.) They are, however, arbitrarily lumped income strata based on a single objective criterion. Figures VI: 5 and VI: 6 show that the "class" structure that emerges from the objective approach depends upon the cutting points and categories used by the analyst. The same data can show stratification pictures having completely different shapes, meanings, and political implications. Depending upon how the categories are grouped, America can be shown to have an enormous lower class, an overpoweringly large middle class, or to have classes of roughly equal size. Stratification data based upon education or occupation can be manipulated in the same way. (See Figs. VI : 7 and VI : 8.)

Although it is easy to rank incomes and education—the more of either, the higher the stratum—it is not so simple to rank occupations. Occupations must be ranked *before* they can be used as criteria for stratification.

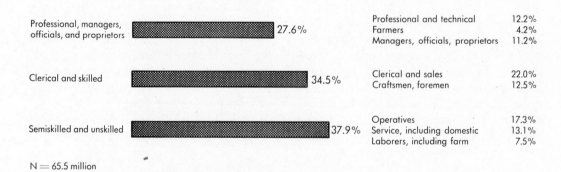

Professional, managers, officials, and proprietors	27.6%	Professional and technical 12.2%
		Farmers 4.2%
		Managers, officials, proprietors 11.2%
Clerical and skilled	34.5%	Clerical and sales 22.0%
		Craftsmen, foremen 12.5%
Semiskilled and unskilled	37.9%	Operatives 17.3%
		Service, including domestic 13.1%
		Laborers, including farm 7.5%

N = 65.5 million

Fig. VI:8   Stratification of Employed Population of U.S.
by Occupational Groupings, 1961

Source: U.S. Bureau of the Census, *Statistical Abstract of the United States: 1961*
(82nd ed.) (Washington, D.C.: U.S. Government Printing Office, 1961). Derived
from Table No. 287, p. 215.

More than thirty studies made in the United States since 1925 have asked judges to rank occupations. The investigations show a remarkable consistency in the way occupations were ranked over a thirty-year period.[16] A nationwide sample (2,920 people) was asked to rate some 90 occupations in 1947. The findings of this study are presented in Table VI : 2.

The rankings do not strictly follow an ordering by income. The prestige ranking of minister, priest, and college professor are far above what would be indicated by income alone. On the other hand, undertaker, singer in a night club, and bartender are ranked below the position that would be determined by income. Occupation serves as a clue to a number of important characteristics used in social ranking. It is normally used as a fairly good indicator of income, education, association with others, authority over others, contribution to the community or society, morality and responsibility, intelligence and ability. The occupation of physician, for example, is characterized by a very high degree of *all* of these features, and it has a consistently high rating. Because occupation is readily available information, and because it indicates other important characteristics by which individuals may be placed, it is widely used as a criterion for stratification.[17]

It should be remembered, however, that an occupational prestige ranking is not in itself a stratification system any more than is a continuous range of income from $0—$10,000.

The prestige scale must be broken down into categories in order that strata may appear. As with education and income, the cutting points are arbitrary when the study is made by the objective method. When the reputational or subjective methods are used, there is a good deal of overlap and disagreement among the members of American society as to which occupations belong in what class. (See if you can get any one of your classmates to agree with you how to stratify the occupations listed in Table VI: 2 on page 200.)

SUMMARY[18]

The American system of stratification is vague and loose with much blurring and overlapping of the strata. There are no sharp lines which separate classes but rather a merging of each class with those adjacent.

The broad, shifting, diffuse top level is composed of the highest business managerial groups and the professional elite, especially the scientific and military. The "upper-uppers," or family elite groups, are probably in a secondary position in the whole country, although they may be at the top in smaller communities. Compared with Japan or France, there are no hereditary ruling families on a national scale. There is no clear break between the elite groups and the upper-middle class, which also contains business and professional people and an increasing number of civil servants and military men as governmental functions expand.

Traditionally, the line between the middle and lower classes is between white-collar occupations and labor. Even this distinction is blurred in America because the high income of the laboring man often exceeds that of a white-collar worker, and because they have common life-styles.

[16] Maethel E. Deeg and Donald G. Paterson, "Changes in Social Status of Occupations," *Occupations*, **25**, No. 4 (1947). There is also consistency in occupational prestige rankings among different nations that are at the same level of industrialization. See Alex Inkeles and P. H. Rossi, "National Comparisons of Occupational Prestige," *American Journal of Sociology*, **61** (January, 1956), 329–39.

[17] A more sophisticated socio-economic index for ranking occupations has been devised by Duncan. The index incorporates values for education and income and permits the assignment of ratings to 400 occupations instead of 90 as given in the North-Hatt scale (Table VI:2). See Otis Dudley Duncan, "A Socio-economic Index for All Occupations" in Albert J. Reiss, Jr., *Occupations and Social Status* (Glencoe: The Free Press, 1961), pp. 109–38.

[18] This summary is indebted to Talcott Parsons, "A Revised Analytical Approach to the Theory of Social Stratification" in Bendix and Lipset, *op. cit.*, especially pp. 122–25. Also see a five class system based upon life-styles and values in Joseph A. Kahl, *The American Class Structure* (New York: Rinehart, 1957), pp. 120–21, 184–217.

Table **VI:2**   The Ratings of Occupations *

Occupation	Score	Occupation	Score
U. S. Supreme Court Justice	96	Reporter on a daily newspaper	71
Physician	93	[AVERAGE	69.8]
State governor	93	Manager of a small store in a city	69
Cabinet member in the federal government	92	Bookkeeper	68
Diplomat in the U. S. Foreign Service	92	Insurance agent	68
Mayor of a large city	90	Tenant farmer—one who owns livestock and	
College professor	89	machinery and manages the farm	68
Scientist	89	Traveling salesman for a wholesale concern	68
United States representative in Congress	89	Playground director	67
Banker	88	Policeman	67
Government scientist	88	Railroad conductor	67
County judge	87	Mail carrier	66
Head of a department in a state government	87	Carpenter	65
Minister	87	Plumber	63
Architect	86	Garage mechanic	62
Chemist	86	Local official of a labor union	62
Dentist	86	Owner-operator of lunch stand	62
Lawyer	86	Corporal in the regular army	60
Member of the board of directors of a large		Machine operator in a factory	60
corporation	86	Barber	59
Nuclear physicist	86	Clerk in a store	58
Priest	86	Fisherman who owns his own boat	58
Psychologist	85	Streetcar motorman	58
Civil engineer	84	Milk route man	54
Airline pilot	83	Restaurant cook	54
Artist who paints pictures that are exhibited		Truck driver	54
in galleries	83	Lumberjack	53
Owner of factory that employs about 100		Filling station attendant	52
people	82	Singer in a night club	52
Sociologist	82	Farm hand	50
Accountant for a large business	81	Coal miner	49
Biologist	81	Taxi driver	49
Musician in a symphony orchestra	81	Railroad section hand	48
Author of novels	80	Restaurant worker	48
Captain in the regular army	80	Dock worker	47
Building contractor	79	Night watchman	47
Economist	79	Clothes presser in a laundry	46
Public schoolteacher	78	Soda fountain clerk	45
County agricultural agent	77	Bartender	44
Railroad engineer	77	Janitor	44
Farm owner and operator	76	Sharecropper—one who owns no livestock or	
Official of an international labor union	75	equipment and does not manage farm	40
Radio announcer	75	Garbage collector	35
Newspaper columnist	74	Street sweeper	34
Owner-operator of a printing shop	74	Shoe shiner	33
Electrician	73		
Trained machinist	73		
Welfare worker for a city government	73		
Undertaker	72		

(continued)

* Source: *Opinion News*, Vol. IX (September 1, 1947), by permission of the National Opinion Research Center. The survey on which the findings are based was done for the President's Scientific Research Board on the basis of plans developed originally by Paul K. Hatt and C. C. North.

The indefinite class lines separating the large middle class from the top and the bottom become even more vague as the effective compression of income range takes place. The tax structure reduces the top of the scale, while the shrinkage of the lower prestige occupations due to mechanization sends streams of workers into the white-collar jobs.

The most important pressure groups, e.g., business, labor, agriculture, and veterans, represent interests and members spread widely through the status range. The classes do not feel a common interest and, therefore, do not operate clearly as political entities.

Section 4 Correlates of social stratification

Positions in the social strata are associated with characteristic attitudes, behavior, and life chances. The associations (correlates) discovered in a variety of studies conducted in the United States are summarized in compact tabular form in this section. Table VI: 3 presents findings which show that life chances and privileges are not randomly distributed but vary in an orderly way from lower to higher strata. This table also gives findings on behavioral correlates and attitudes. The lower, middle, and upper strata of the tables are rough categories which vary from study to study, e.g., a low income stratum in one study may be below $2,000; in another, below $3,500. Similar variations occur in the boundaries of occupational and educational strata. Although the location of the boundaries between the strata cannot be precisely fixed, they may serve as general guides, and the main findings from a number of independent studies may be summarized.

Interpreting the Table of Correlates

Some of the relationships shown in Table VI : 3 may not seem surprising, e.g., the fact that broken homes, restricted travel, and fewer organizational memberships are associated with the lower strata. Low income and education, in themselves related, can probably account directly for many of the findings presented above. Self-evident or not, it is important to appreciate the far-reaching influence of socio-economic status. It may also be tempting—but erroneous—to apply an economic interpretation to other findings: high psychoses rates in lower-income groups, fewer close friends in the lower occupational categories; more severe discipline of children in the lower-income brackets. The fact is, however, that the correlations reported in the table are, for the most part, *simply correlations.* No causal relationships are claimed or demonstrated by most of the authors. It is one thing to show a connection between two phenomena; it is quite another to explain and to prove the nature of the relationship. Therefore the following cautions are listed.

Cautions in Interpreting the Correlates

1. The correlations are by no means perfect. The behavior of people of any one stratum is not uniform: not all lower-income people have fewer friends, vote less, or read fewer magazines than those in higher-income strata.

2. Correlation is not a statement of causation. Low income, little education, or low-prestige occupation do not necessarily cause a person to think, feel, or act in a given way, nor do they necessarily determine his life chances directly. For every correlation cited in the tables, there is an extensive literature which tries to interpret, understand, and explain the relationships. Most of these expla-

Table VI:3   Correlates of Social Stratification, United States

RELATED FACTORS	(*)	LOWER STRATA	MIDDLE STRATA	HIGHER STRATA
		Life Chances and Privileges		
Standardized mortality ratios	1930[a](O) 1950[b](O)	Unskilled workers: 151 Unskilled workers: 120	Skilled workers: 93 Skilled workers: 96	Professionals: 81 Professionals: 82
Education[c] (applicants for college)	(O)	21% of factory workers' children	45% of white-collar workers' children	73% of professionals' and executives' children
Lifetime income[d]	(E)	1–4 years of elementary education: $143,808	High school graduates: $241,844	College graduates: $419,871
Annual mean income[e]	(E)	8 years elementary: $3,769	4 years high school: $5,567	4 years or more college: $9,206
Admission rates for psychoses[f]	(I) (O)	Significantly higher than average		Significantly lower than average
Psychoanalysis and psychotherapy for neuroses[g]	(E) (O) (D)	4.9%	20.9%	46.9%
Custodial care for neuroses[g]	(E) (O) (D)	23.0%	4.3%	0.0%
Parental consent for trial polio shots[h]	(O) (E)	57% of lowest SES did not give consent	16% of middle SES did not give consent	14% of highest SES did not give consent
Broken families[i] (after 15 or more years of marriage)	(R)	50–60% of lower-class families	15% of upper-middle-class families	
		Attitudes		
Political attitudes[j]	(O) (I)	Favor social security measures, labor unions, government regulation of business		Disapprove strong labor unions and large government role in economy

* Parenthetical letters indicate the following bases for stratification used in the studies cited: (I) income, (O) occupation, (E) education, (R) reputational method, (D) dwelling area.

[a] J. S. Whitney, "Death Rates by Occupation Based on Data of the U.S. Census Bureau, 1930" (New York: National Tuberculosis Association, 1934). (Ratio between the number of deaths and the number of deaths expected, adult white males)

[b] L. Guralnick, "The Study of Mortality by Occupation in the United States" (Washington, D.C.: National Office of Vital Statistics, September, 1959). (Ratio between the number of deaths and the number of deaths expected, adult white males)

[c] Elmo Roper, Factors Affecting the Admission of High School Seniors to College (Washington, D.C.: American Council on Education, 1949). (National sample, white high school seniors, 1947)

[d] Statistical Abstract of the United States: 1961, Table No. 142, p. 110. (National sample, 1958)

[e] Statistical Abstract of the United States: 1961, Table No. 143, p. 111. (Males 25 years and over, 1958)

[f] Robert E. Clark, "Psychoses, Income, and Occupational Prestige," American Journal of Sociology, 54 (1949), 433–40. (Sample, male first-admission cases, Chicago, 1922–1934)   Also see A. B. Hollingshead and F. C. Redlich, Social Class and Mental Illness (New York: Wiley, 1958), and J. K. Myers and B. H. Roberts, Family and Class Dynamics in Mental Illness (New York: Wiley, 1959). (Sample, total population and psychiatrically ill, New Haven, Conn., 1950)

[g] Based on Table 26, p. 267 in Hollingshead and Redlich, Social Class and Mental Illness.

[h] Leila C. Deasy, "Socio-economic Status and Participation in the Poliomyelitis Vaccine Trial," American Sociological Review, 21 (1956), 185–91. (Sample, mothers of second grade children, Virginia, 1954)

[i] (Through separation, desertion, divorce, or death.) A. B. Hollingshead, "Class Differences in Family Stability," Annals of the American Academy of Political and Social Science (November, 1950), pp. 39–46. (Sample, Midwestern community, 1949)

[j] Angus Campbell et al., The American Voter (New York: Wiley, 1960).

Table VI:3   Correlates of Social Stratification, United States (page 2)

RELATED FACTORS	(*)	LOWER STRATA	MIDDLE STRATA	HIGHER STRATA
Tolerant attitudes on civil liberties[k]	(O)	Manual workers: 30%	Clerical and sales workers: 49%	Professionals and semiprofessionals: 66%
			Behavioral Correlates	
Organizational membership[l] (belong to one or more associations)	(O)	Unskilled laborers: 21%	Clerical and sales: 41%	Professional and managerial: 53%
Report no close friends[m]	(O)	30% of unskilled workers	13% of skilled, small business, and white-collar workers	10% of professionals, top business and officials
Average life-time travel[n]	(R)	Radius of 145 miles		Radius of 1,100 miles
Reading[o]	(I)	35% do not read magazines; 82% read less than one book per month		7% do not read magazines; 59% read less than one book per month
Reading the **New York Times**[p]	(E) (O) (D)	4% read the **Times**	24% read the **Times**	51% read the **Times**
Voting in presidential elections[q]	(E)	Grade school education: 62% said they voted	High school education: 80% said they voted	College education: 90% said they voted
Child-rearing practices[r]	(I) (O)	More severe, more physical punishment, less demonstrative	More permissive and warm, use praise and reasoning, allow aggression toward parents	

[k] From S. M. Lipset, "Democracy and Working-Class Authoritarianism," *American Sociological Review*, **24** (1959), Table 2 p. 486. Data from a national survey conducted by Samuel A. Stouffer. See Samuel A. Stouffer, *Communism, Conformity and Civil Liberties* (New York: Doubleday, 1955). (Male workers)

[l] Data from a national survey conducted by N.O.R.C. in 1955, reported in Charles R. Wright and H. H. Hyman, "Voluntary Association Memberships of American Adults: Evidence from National Sample Surveys," *American Sociological Review*, **23** (1958), Table 3, p. 289.

[m] Joseph A. Kahl, *The American Class Structure* (New York: Rinehart, 1957), pp. 137–38. (Sample, Cambridge, Massachusetts, 1953) Also see Robert S. and Helen Lynd, *Middletown* (New York: Harcourt, Brace, 1929), p. 272; and Peter H. Rossi, *Why Families Move* (Glencoe: The Free Press, 1955), pp. 34–40. (Sample, Philadelphia, 1953)

[n] John Useem, Pierre Tangent, and Ruth Useem, "Stratification in a Prairie Town," *American Sociological Review*, **7** (1942), 331–42. (Sample, South Dakota town, 1941)

[o] Genevieve Knupfer, "Portrait of the Underdog," *Public Opinion Quarterly*, **11** (Spring, 1947), 103–14. (Sample, Ohio town, 1944)

[p] Hollingshead and Redlich, *Social Class and Mental Illness*, p. 403. Data for first column are for Class V, second column for Class III, third column for Class I. (Sample, New Haven, Conn., 1950)

[q] Robert E. Lane, *Political Life* (Glencoe: The Free Press, 1959), pp. 48–49. Lane also cites data on nonvoting by occupation and income. See also Angus Campbell *et al.*, *The Voter Decides* (Evanston: Row, Peterson, 1954). (Nationwide survey, 1948, 1952)

[r] Eleanor E. Maccoby and Patricia K. Gibbs, "Methods of Child Rearing in Two Social Classes," in W. E. Martin and C. B. Stendler (eds.), *Readings in Child Development* (New York: Harcourt, Brace, 1954). (Sample, Boston, 1952) Cf. Robert J. Havighurst and Allison Davis, "A Comparison of the Chicago and Harvard Studies of Social Class Differences in Child Rearing," *American Sociological Review*, **20** (1955), 438–42; and Robert R. Sears *et al.*, *Patterns of Child Rearing* (Evanston: Row, Peterson, 1957). A study of 206 families in Eugene, Oregon, found no general class differences in socialization practices; see Richard A. Littman *et al.*, "Social Class Differences in Child Rearing: A Third Community for Comparison with Chicago and Newton," *American Sociological Review*, **22** (December, 1957), 694–704. Daniel R. Miller and Guy E. Swanson, *The Changing American Parent* (New York: Wiley, 1958), found differences within the middle class in child rearing according to father's occupation.

nations are stated tentatively as hypotheses suggested for further testing.

3. A stratum is not automatically an acting group, nor are the members necessarily aware of their likeness. People with low or high incomes may or may not be aware of each

other's common problems, beliefs, and desires.[19]

[19] An interesting interpretation of a number of stratification correlates may be found in Genevieve Knupfer, "Portrait of the Underdog," *Public Opinion Quarterly*, XI (Spring, 1947), 114. This article is reprinted in Bendix and Lipset, *op cit.*, pp. 255–63.

Section 5   **Social mobility**

Thus far this chapter has emphasized the more stable aspects of social stratification, although reference has been made to mobility and change. This section specifically deals with mobility within and between classes. It covers the kinds and conditions of movement, mobility aspirations, and mobility trends in the United States.

KINDS OF MOBILITY

Stratification is only one kind of differentiation. A large industrial organization may have the familiar levels of top management, second level management, foremen, and workers. It may also have divisions, such as sales, manufacturing, and engineering, each with its own hierarchy. The differences between divisions may be clear to everyone in the plant, but the divisions may be equally evaluated.

In distinction to strata, *equally* valued categories may be identified by the term *functional category* or *situs*. The divisions of the industrial organization are such functional categories, because although they are differentiated, they are given equal evaluation. Such functional categories may also be found in military, religious, political, and other organizations.

The occupational structure of a whole society may be analyzed in terms of situses as well as strata. For example, the Finance and Records situs would include all occupations

primarily concerned with the handling of monetary affairs or the processing of records, accounts, or correspondence, and could range through all the strata from bank president to mail clerk or pawnbroker's assistant. The Manufacturing situs might include all occupations primarily concerned with the fabrication of articles or the processing of raw materials on a production-line basis, ranging from a top-stratum official to an unskilled production worker [20] (see Fig. VI:9). Other situses not listed in Figure VI:9 include Commerce, Education, Law Enforcement, and others.

Functional categories may change into strata if they become *differentially* evaluated and placed one above the other, or, vice versa, strata may change into functional categories if they become equally valued. Mobility may take place in movement from stratum to stratum, *vertical mobility,* or from situs to situs, *horizontal mobility.* As a student moves from freshman to senior in his college career, he is vertically mobile. If he changes majors, he is horizontally mobile, moving from one functional category (situs) to another.

There have been few systematic studies of

[20] See Richard T. Morris and Raymond J. Murphy, "The Situs Dimension in Occupational Structure," *American Sociological Review*, **24** (1959), 231–39. For some of the correlates of situs, see Raymond J. Murphy and Richard T. Morris, "Occupational Situs, Subjective Class Identification, and Political Affiliation," *American Sociological Review*, **26** (1961), 383–92.

mobility based upon the subjective or reputational approaches, i.e., studies which investigate mobility as seen and evaluated by members of the community or by the mobile individuals themselves. Most mobility studies have used the objective approach, and they frequently rely on occupation as the sole criterion of vertical mobility. They may attempt to measure change in occupational status between fathers and sons, and in some cases grandsons. This is called *generational mobility*. Or, they may investigate the changes in occupational status during one individual's work life, called *career mobility*.

Distinguishing between *changes in* the occupational structure and *movement within* it is one of the chief problems of mobility studies. If an individual during his lifetime (or compared with his father) remains a bookkeeper, there appears to be no mobility. But, if during this period the prestige of bookkeeper drops and the salary falls below that of a skilled workman, is the bookkeeper to be considered downwardly mobile even though he has not changed his occupation? Obviously it is necessary to keep the different

aspects of mobility sharply separated. Statements of mobility must clearly identify both the type of mobility and the framework in which it takes place. Unless otherwise specified, the term *mobility* as used in this book refers to vertical mobility of individuals in the nation at large from the objective point of view.

ASCRIBED AND ACHIEVED STATUS

In medieval Europe, in British India, and in ancient Rome and China, there was relatively little vertical mobility. A man was born to his station in life and usually stayed there, as did his children and grandchildren. However, in each society, no matter how rigid, there were a few narrow avenues through which members of the lower strata might pass upward. Through strength of arms, successful banditry, religious training, exceptional intelligence and devotion to studies, or financial luck, individuals did on occasion manage to fight or buy or write themselves out of their inherited positions. Nevertheless, the strata lines were clearly drawn and extremely difficult to cross. (See pp. 177–78.) These so-

FUNCTIONAL CATEGORIES (Situses)

STRATA[a]	FINANCE AND RECORDS	MANUFACTURING	TRANSPORTATION
High (Score 60 and over)	Accountant (H) Bank Manager	Industrial Engineer Lithographer	Airline Pilot Railroad President
Middle (Score 30-59)	Bookkeeper Bank Teller	Bookbinder Tool and Die Maker	Railroad Conductor (V) Mail Carrier
Low (Score 0-29)	Office Boy Shipping Clerk	Forgeman Laborer, Steel Mill	Bus Driver Telegraph Messenger

V = vertical mobility, from stratum to stratum
H = horizontal mobility, from situs to situs

Fig. **VI:9**   Types of Mobility

[a] Strata scores derived from Otis Dudley Duncan, "A Socio-economic Index for All Occupations" in Reiss, *Occupations and Social Status*, pp. 109–38, and Appendix B, pp. 263–75.

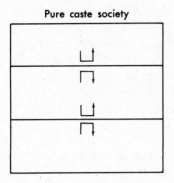

Pure caste society

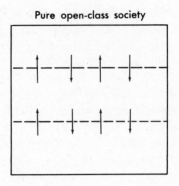

Pure open-class society

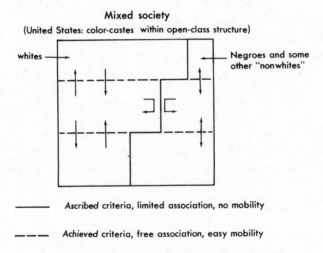

Mixed society
(United States: color-castes within open-class structure)

whites →

← Negroes and some other "nonwhites"

———— *Ascribed* criteria, limited association, no mobility

– – – – *Achieved* criteria, free association, easy mobility

Fig. **VI:10** Caste, Open-Class, and Mixed Societies

cieties were stratified by *ascribed* [21] criteria, characteristics with which one is born and over which one has no control, e.g., sex, family lineage, skin color, and the like. Where ascribed statuses are predominant, the future existence of an individual is largely determined at birth: his occupation, income, religion, associates, wife, education, and probably even the length of his life are predetermined within set limits.

At the other extreme are societies that are stratified largely by means of *achieved* criteria, characteristics which the individual is

able to control and change, e.g., income, occupation; religion, residence, education, political affiliation, and the like. Individuals may move where they wish in the structure, limited only by their own efforts, ability, and luck.

CASTE AND OPEN-CLASS SOCIETIES

Depending upon the kinds of criteria used, the amount and kind of association between the strata, and the possibility of vertical mobility between strata, two types of social structures have been distinguished:

The *caste* society in its pure form is composed of strata based entirely upon ascribed criteria. There is very little association be-

[21] Cf. Ralph Linton, *The Study of Man* (New York: Appleton-Century-Crofts, 1936), pp. 115 ff.

tween members of the different strata, and the few relations permitted are severely limited and formally prescribed, e.g., master-servant, professional-client relations. Marriage between castes is prohibited, and there is neither career nor generational mobility in the pure caste society. Each person is born into a caste, marries within his caste, and has children who stay in the caste. Although there has probably never been a society which met all the criteria of caste organization, traditional India and the ancient Incas had caste-like structures.

The *open-class* structure is based upon achieved criteria. There is complete freedom of association between the members of all strata, including intermarriage and equalitarian social relations. Vertical mobility is possible and probable from the bottom to the top. However, just as there has never been a pure caste society, there has never been a completely open-class structure. The United States, for example, tends toward an open-class system, but ascribed criteria, such as race, sex, and family position, are applied in many areas. The United States has historically approved of achievement. Although it has not frowned too severely on the ascription and continuity of high status, it has favored the log-cabin-to-White-House ideal.

Because of the use of ascribed criteria in the United States, a great deal of discussion has arisen whether or not this country contains castes within its predominantly open-class structure. There are some characteristics of a caste society in Negro-white relations: skin color is an ascribed criterion; association is formally prescribed and limited; intermarriage is prohibited; mobility between the two color groups is almost impossible except in rare cases. However, *within* the Negro community, as well as within the white community, there is mobility, the predominant use of achieved criteria, and relatively free association patterns—all characteristics of an open-class society. (See Fig. VI : 10. See also MINORITIES, pp. 515–16.)

FACTORS AFFECTING MOBILITY

A number of other factors help determine the nature of mobility patterns in the United States: (1) changes in the occupational and economic structure, i.e., the opening of new positions and the disappearance of old positions; (2) differences in reproduction rates, i.e., the inability of certain strata to reproduce themselves without recruitment from other levels (see POPULATION AND ECOLOGY, pp. 328–29); (3) the concentration of immigrants at certain levels; (4) the opening of new channels of vertical mobility through increased education; and (5) the mobility aspirations of individuals, i.e., whether people *want* to move or not.[22]

Mobility Aspirations

Upward mobility depends not only on aspiration but also on opportunity. And a realistic aspiration requires that opportunity be recognized. An unrecognized opportunity is not a "real" one, because people cannot strive toward an unrecognized goal. An understanding of the differences between positions and knowledge of what it takes to achieve them are essential conditions of vertical mobility. Even in a mobile society, groups for whom mobility is highly probable see the chances for and the desirability of social movement differently from those groups whose movement is hindered. People do not necessarily correctly perceive the chances for mobility, but their perceptions influence their striving toward or rejection of goals and, therefore, affect mobility rates.[23]

[22] For a discussion of the relative contributions of some of these factors to occupational mobility in the United States see Joseph A. Kahl, *The American Class Structure* (New York: Rinehart, 1957), pp. 252–62.

[23] For a review of the relevant research on mobility aspiration see Seymour M. Lipset and Reinhard Bendix, *Social Mobility in Industrial Society* (Berkeley and Los Angeles: University of California Press, 1959), pp. 227–59. For recent empirical studies see Harry J. Crochett, Jr., "The Achievement Motive and Differential Occupational Mobility in the United States," *American Sociological Review*, **27** (1962), 191–204; and Fred B. Silberstein and Melvin Seeman, "Social Mobility and Prejudice," *The American Journal of Sociology*, **65** (1959), 258–64.

Professionals and executives have very different ideas about economic opportunity from factory workers.[24] Workers do not think they can get ahead as easily as do professionals and executives. Factory workers feel that personal connections and "pull" are responsible for advance, but professionals and executives feel that their own abilities and efforts are more important. A study of the status orientations of shipyard workers found many attitudes similar to those of the factory workers.[25] Most of the shipyard workers did not see clear channels for getting ahead. They felt that luck was the decisive factor, and most of the men had no aspirations beyond the position of foreman. This may have been a realistic estimate of their chances. They

[24] Reported by Herbert Hyman, "The Value Systems of Different Classes," in Bendix and Lipset, eds., *Class, Status and Power.* pp. 426–42.

[25] Katherine Archibald, "Status Orientations Among Shipyard Workers," *ibid.,* pp. 395–403.

sneered at the men in the top positions who had formal and specialized education. They did not want education for themselves or their children, and they did not see it as a way to the top.

Differences in the ways the channels of mobility are perceived are shown in a study of attitudes toward college education.[26] (See Table VI : 4.) The higher groups, as measured by occupation, education, or rent, recommend college education as essential to advancement more often than the lower groups. Whether the advice is based on the respondents' rationalizations about the positions they already hold, or whether they objectively see education as a good or poor mobility channel, the fact remains that the views are different.

The extent and distribution of educational opportunities is an important condition of

[26] Reported by Herbert Hyman, *op. cit.,* p. 430.

Table **VI:4**   Differences in Emphasis upon College Education as Essential to Advancement*

	Per Cent Recommending College Education
Occupation	
Professional	74
Businessmen and proprietors	62
White-collar workers	65
Skilled labor	53
Semiskilled	49
Domestic and personal service workers	42
Farmers	47
Nonfarm laborers	35
Highest Education Achieved	
Attended college	72
Attended high school	55
Attended grammar school	36
Among Renters, Monthly Rental	
Above $60	70
$40-60	64
$20-40	54
Below $20	37

*Adapted from Herbert Hyman, *ibid.,* p. 430.

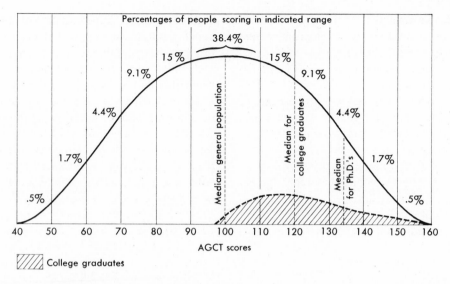

Fig. **VI:11**   Intelligence and College Education

Figure VI:11 indicates that only a small fraction of the talent in this country is fully utilized. The large curve represents the distribution of the general population on the Army General Classification Test —roughly equivalent to IQ scores. The small, shaded curve shows the distribution of college graduates, who fall mainly in the upper AGCT scores. It is possible to estimate the amount of wastage of talent by comparing the two curves. For example, about 16 per cent of the population scores 120 (the median of college graduates) or better, but only 5 per cent of the population graduate from college—a wastage of two-thirds. If these figures are compared with the evidence on the relation between income of parents and college attendance, we may hypothesize that differences in occupation and income limit educational mobility and the full use of talent in the United States. (Combination of figures redrawn and adapted from Dael Wolfle, "Intellectual Resources," *Scientific American*, September, 1951, p. 45.)

mobility. (See Fig. VI : 11.) Where education is reserved for a limited number of strata, it is more difficult for a "circulation" of the elites to take place. Persons from other than the select groups cannot achieve positions which require formal and specialized training. The increasingly widespread educational facilities in the United States make for higher vertical mobility rates, even though there are still differences in opportunity among the income strata.

Low mobility rates may be due to poor opportunities for motivated individuals, faulty perceptions of the opportunities, or lack of motivation. It should not be assumed, however, that an individual in a lower stratum

who does not *want* to move up the occupational or income ladder, or who does not wish advancement for his children, is in some sense deficient in will power, moral character, energy, or intelligence, or that he is frustrated and unhappy where he is. He may like it where he is and prefer to remain there. His position may give him rewards that he feels he could not get at other levels. For example, during World War II many enlisted men refused commissions. They had friends and knew the situation where they were. They did not want to accept the risks of a new situation, new friends, and the responsibilities of a higher position even for an increase in money and prestige.

Generational Mobility

Although the data on mobility are scanty, there is fair consensus that generational mobility, as measured between father's occupation and son's occupation, is limited, i.e., sons tend to follow their fathers' occupations or occupations of similar prestige and income.[27] However, Table VI : 5 suggests that this gen-

[27] Section IV, "Social Mobility in the United States," in Bendix and Lipset, op. cit., pp. 371–500. See also Reinhard Bendix and Frank W. Howton, "Social Mobility and the American Business Elite—II," British Journal of Sociology, 9 (1958), 1–14, for a comparative evaluation of research findings on the movement of individuals into the business elite.

eralization varies by occupation level. Most stability is found in the middle of the occupational structure. More white-collar workers and skilled workers have fathers at their own level than do the higher occupations or the lower ones. There is evidence of a good deal of upward mobility: over half of the professionals and businessmen had fathers who were in lower occupational categories than they were; about a fifth of them had fathers who were in the lowest occupational category of semiskilled, service workers, or laborers.

There is also evidence of a large amount of downward mobility: white-collar and

Table VI:5 Generational Mobility *

Father's Occupation	Son's Occupation,[a] 1950						
	Professional	Business	Clerical and Sales	Skilled Labor	Semiskilled	Service Workers	Laborers (including farm)
Professional	19	9	7	4	3	4	3
Business	25	34	22	10	10	15	8
	44%	**43%**	**29%**	**14%**	**13%**	**19%**	**11%**
Clerical and sales	12	7	15	4	4	5	3
Skilled labor	19	22	24	35	24	18	17
Farmers and farm mgrs.	5	13	8	15	20	26	39
	36%	**42%**	**47%**	**54%**	**48%**	**49%**	**59%**
Semiskilled	13	8	15	19	23	11	11
Service workers	5	4	5	4	5	12	3
Laborers (including farm)	3	3	5	8	12	8	15
	21%	**15%**	**25%**	**31%**	**40%**	**31%**	**29%**
Total percentage (deviations from 100% due to rounding)	101%	100%	101%	99%	101%	99%	99%
Number of sons (in thousands) projected from sample of 11,400 families	218	356	324	509	483	202	150

*Source: Herman P. Miller, Income of the American People (New York: Wiley, 1955), pp. 31–33. Miller derived the figures from unpublished data from the Occupational Mobility Survey conducted in 1951 in six cities: Philadelphia, New Haven, San Francisco, Chicago, Los Angeles, and St. Paul. For details of the survey see Gladys L. Palmer, Labor Mobility in Six Cities (New York: Social Science Research Council, 1954).

Note—Within each cell of the table is entered the percentage of sons whose fathers were in each occupational category. Bold-face type indicates the subtotal of each cell. Thus, in the upper lefthand cell 19% of the professional sons had fathers who were also professionals; 25% of the professional sons had fathers who were in business; 44% (the subtotal) of the professional sons had fathers who were either professionals or in business.

[a] The number of sons in farming was too small to be analyzed separately.

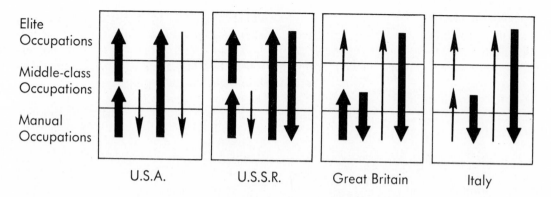

<table>
<tr><td>Elite
Occupations</td></tr>
<tr><td>Middle-class
Occupations</td></tr>
<tr><td>Manual
Occupations</td></tr>
</table>

U.S.A.   U.S.S.R.   Great Britain   Italy

Heavy arrows indicate high mobility
Light arrows indicate low mobility

Fig. **VI:12**   Comparative Generational Mobility:
                 National Profiles

Diagrams derived from S. M. Miller, "Comparative Social Mobility," *Current Sociology*, **9** (1960), Table XX, p. 56. Elite occupations are the higher business and independent professional occupations. Middle-class occupations are white-collar, professional and business occupations, except those in the elite. Manual occupations are skilled and unskilled workers. The rates of mobility are based on the distribution of the occupations of sons of fathers in given occupational positions, e.g., of 100 white-collar fathers 20 of their sons are in manual occupations, 15 are high professionals, etc. The diagrams, reading from left to right, show on a comparative basis the extreme of upward mobility, with limited downward mobility in the U.S., to the extreme downward mobility with limited upward movement in Italy. The high-low distinctions are made on the basis of comparing 18 countries.

skilled workers are almost as apt to be recruited from above as from below. Surprisingly, those in the lowest occupational level are *least* likely to be recruited from their own ranks. About two-thirds of the semiskilled, service workers, and laborers had fathers who were in higher occupational categories. Professionals are most frequently recruited from business, businessmen from their own ranks, white-collar workers from skilled labor, skilled laborers from their own ranks, semi-skilled laborers about equally from skilled labor and their own ranks, and both service workers and laborers from farmers. Farmers' sons who enter urban occupations seem for the most part to fall in the lower occupations.

When changes in the occupational structure are taken into account, it appears that there was not much change in generational mobility rates during the first half of this century.[28]

Cautions in Interpreting Generational Mobility Data

It is difficult to estimate the meaning of mobility rates without some basis for comparison, either over time within the United States, or by comparing across societies. When it is said of sons in the professions that 44 per cent of their fathers were also professionals, is this unusually high or unusually low or just about what we might expect in any society at any time?[29] Depending on what point the

[28] Natalie Rogoff, "Recent Trends in Urban Mobility," in P. K. Hatt and Albert Reiss (eds.), *Reader in Urban Sociology* (Glencoe: The Free Press, 1951), pp. 406–20.
[29] Cf. Herbert Hyman, *Survey Design and Analysis: Principles, Cases and Procedures* (Glencoe: The Free Press, 1955), pp. 126 ff. See "Evaluating Percentages" on page 212.

Evaluating Percentages

Abridged and adapted from Herbert Hyman, *Survey Design and Analysis* (Glencoe: The Free Press, 1955), pp. 126–28. Used by permission.

How shall an analyst appraise the implication of a finding that 82 per cent of a national sample believe that radio stations are doing an "excellent" or "good" job? Does this represent *overwhelming* public satisfaction? Shall the analyst note that *as many* as 18 per cent were not satisfied, or shall he stress that *only* 18 per cent did not show satisfaction? The extremes of zero *vs.* universal satisfaction are perhaps easy to evaluate, but here the analyst faces an intermediate figure that could be appraised in a variety of ways.

On attitudes towards advertising on the radio, about one-third of the public was found to be opposed to radio commercials. Does this represent serious criticism of the current pattern of American radio, or is this to be expected and regarded as innocuous from the point of view of change in the institution? The public was also queried on radio's degree of impartiality in handling controversial issues. Eighty-one per cent regarded radio stations as being fair to both sides in general. Is this high praise of the radio industry, or should the fact be stressed that *as many as* 19 per cent did not explicitly express the view that radio was fair?

In all these instances, the analyst can report the bare facts. Or he can use such neutral terms as "a majority," "a minority," and the like. But this is after all not the point of a descriptive survey. Such facts must be evaluated to be of some use, and they are bound to be capricious in the absence of norms for deciding whether such findings are large or small, frequent or rare.

Findings, apparently clear in their implications, can be misinterpreted in the absence of a standard of comparison. In a survey by the National Opinion Research Center, 37 per cent of a national sample indicated that they had a favorable feeling towards the English government. Should the analyst regard this finding as indicative of serious hostility to England? While 37 per cent is not a very high figure in absolute magnitude, when attitudes toward England were compared with attitudes toward other countries, 37 per cent represented an unusually favorable attitude on the part of the American publicity. Only toward Canada did a larger proportion of the public indicate a favorable feeling.

To safeguard interpretations, the analyst usually sets norms by collecting data on parallel phenomena from the same individuals. A similar juxtaposition of parallel phenomena provided norms for the previously mentioned 82 per cent of the sample who were well satisfied with radio. Parallel questions on satisfaction with the churches, newspapers, schools, and local government did not yield a figure as high as the 82 per cent for radio. Radio is therefore seen to stand in *unusual* public favor.

These examples illustrate one problem in the use of norms and a method for treating it. It is obvious that there can be considerable arbitrariness in choosing the parallel phenomena to be compared. For example, one might pick only institutions towards which there is great public dissatisfaction and thereby present a misleading picture of relative satisfaction with radio. The analyst must therefore pick a series of parallel phenomena ranging over the whole probable spectrum.

analyst is trying to make, he can say, "*Fully* 44 per cent of their fathers were professionals," or he can say, with very different implications, "*Only* 44 per cent of their fathers were professionals." A study of time trends in the United States does not help much with this problem, because as noted above, the rates have been fairly stable. A comparative analysis of mobility rates among different societies shows the United States as having a very similar mobility pattern to the U.S.S.R. and a very different one from Italy [30] (see Fig. VI : 12).

Career Mobility

Although the movement of individuals during their work life is relatively high, a large part of the movement is between occupations on the same level or into adjacent occupational categories. People tend to advance occupationally during their careers *but not very far*. The formal educational requirements for some of the higher-level jobs act as effective barriers.[31]

There is less career mobility among those in the top and the bottom strata than there is in the middle. In the career of any individual it is most difficult to move from manual to nonmanual occupations.

Mobility and the Changing Social Order

Extensive changes in American society during the last two centuries have been brought about by the industrial revolution, the increase in population, the expanding frontier, and the general rise of the standard of living. Built largely upon an agrarian but non-feudal base, the stratification system in America since Colonial times has been characterized by high vertical mobility rates, vague and shifting class lines, and the use of many different criteria in different parts of the structure. The equalitarian spirit of early America encouraged the development of an open-class society with a strong tradition of equal opportunity for advancement.

Until World War I immigrants filled the lower occupational and income positions, displacing native Americans and contributing to an upward mobility of the native born. Geographic expansion and the pushing back of the frontier, with shifts in land use and the development of new resources, have kept the structure fluid. Technological and occupational change, the lower reproduction rates of the higher strata, the increasing opportunities for higher education, and the possibilities for geographic mobility have maintained a high rate of vertical and horizontal mobility.

Figure VI : 13 is an attempt to summarize the major outlines of the stratification system and the chief paths of mobility in the United States. It may be compared with the diagrams for classical China (Fig. VI : 1, p. 180) and the U.S.S.R. (Fig. VI : 2, p. 181). Obviously they are partly arbitrary and cannot reflect the details discussed in the text. If these cautions are kept in mind, the diagrams can be studied for a broad overview of stratification and mobility in the three countries.

The general upward flow, the overlapping of "Society" and the stratum of persons of highest responsibility, and the importance of eduation for mobility are indicated in Figure VI : 13. The figure suggests that the national elite, defined by tasks performed, is not identical with the elite based on lineage and wealth and that higher education has become almost an essential to high positions. Although the figure shows generational mobility, it depicts less fully the mobility of individuals in their lifetime and the low-volume downward movement.

Since the 1870's there has been an enormous shift in the occupational structure: farming and the extractive industries have shrunk; manufacturing and mechanical industries are beginning to contract with the

[30] S. M. Miller, "Comparative Social Mobility," *Current Sociology*, **9** (1960), 1–89.

[31] S. M. Lipset and Reinhard Bendix, "Social Mobility and Occupational Career Patterns," *American Journal of Sociology*, **57** (1952), 494–504. See also A. J. Jaffe and R. O. Carleton, *Occupational Mobility in the United States, 1930–1960* [projection to 1960] (New York: King's Crown Press, 1954).

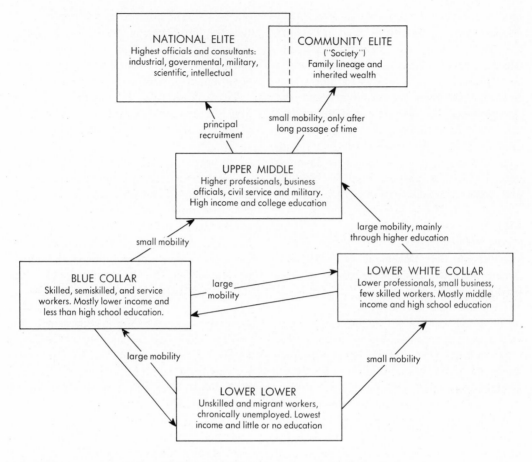

Fig. **VI:13**   Stratification and Generational Mobility in the United States

use of automatic machinery; the public service, business, clerical, and professional occupations are expanding. The lower status occupations have diminished, and the higher status occupations have increased both relatively and in absolute numbers.

The transition from blue-collar to white-collar work can be taken as a rough index of upward occupational movement. Considering only transfers between these two very broad categories and disregarding vertical mobility within each one, changes in the national economy between 1870 and 1930 produced a very marked upward shift in the center of occupational gravity. . . . Some 9,000,000 persons who were white-collar workers in 1930 would have been engaged in manual labor if the occupational distribution of 1870

had persisted. On the average, about 150,000 workers per year ascended from blue-collar to white-collar jobs.[32]

Although the effects of mass immigration upon upward mobility have diminished (and have even been reversed at times with the immigration of professionals), differential birth rates have contributed to upward mobility. Lower fertility in the higher occupational and income brackets creates a

[32] Elbridge Sibley, ''Some Demographic Clues to Stratification,'' *American Sociological Review,* **7** (1942), 322–30. For recent summary and interpretation of mobility in the U.S., see Seymour M. Lipset and Reinhard Bendix, ''Ideological Equalitarianism and Social Mobility in the United States,'' *Transactions* of the Second World Congress of Sociology, pp. 34–54.

vacuum in the upper strata, and this is filled by individuals from the lower strata.

The Persistence of Poverty

High mobility rates, however, have not eradicated differences in life chances and life-styles. The gap between a member of the Ford family and an unskilled worker in the Ford plant, between a sharecropper and an oil millionaire, cannot be ignored. Discussion of the "affluent society," the rise in average income, and the substantial rate of upward mobility tend to obscure the reality of hard-core poverty and deprivation in the United States.[33] In 1959 nearly 6 million

[33] See Fig. VI:5, p. 196. Cf. Gabriel Kolko, *Wealth and Power in America* (New York: Praeger, 1962); Robert J. Lampman, *The Share of Top Wealth-Holders in National Wealth, 1922–1956* (Princeton: Princeton University Press, 1962); and Conference on Economic Progress, *Poverty and Deprivation in the United States, The Plight of Two-Fifths of a Nation* (Washington, D.C.: Conference on Economic Progress, 1962).

family units had total money income of less than $2,000, an amount below the level of subsistence. More than 8 million adults had a fourth-grade education or less, so little that their chances of significantly improving their lot were slight. (See Fig. VI : 7, p. 198.) No less than 5 million employed workers were at the absolute bottom of the occupational ladder and nearly 25 million were in the lower occupational brackets. (See Fig. VI:8.) About 3.5 million people, amounting to 5 per cent of the labor force, were unemployed in 1960. These facts must be borne in mind in order to maintain a perspective on the workings of the American economy and the system of stratification.

Strains and Compensations

How can such differences exist without serious conflicts? To discover the answer, it is necessary to analyze both the strains and the alleviating factors in the present social order in the United States.[34]

The strains may be outlined as follows:

1. Inequalities in wealth, opportunity, and privilege are emphasized by advertisements of costly goods and the publicity given to wealthy individuals.

2. Even achieved position is not believed to be a sure mark of honest effort and ability. Many working men are convinced that success is due to luck or "pull." The wealthy may be envied, but they are not regarded as moral paragons.

3. Restrictions on occupational and educational opportunities for minority groups are widespread and publicized.

4. Strong pressures and motivations for upward mobility exist in almost all strata of the society, but there are only a limited number of positions open at the higher levels. The limited number of opportunities in the medical profession is a case in point.

5. Economic fluctuations, periods of mass unemployment, and fear of their recurrence have raised doubts about the effectiveness of the present economic system and its control. In view of this insecurity, there are increased pressures on government and corporations for health, employment, welfare, and retirement programs. The programs complicate federal tax policies and become issues in union-management controversies.

The tensions between strata suggest a highly volatile society on the verge of far-reaching and disruptive changes. The surprising fact from this viewpoint is that there is so little class conflict or awareness of class divisions, so few political organizations along lines of class interest, and such a dearth of class concepts or action programs. There are powerful factors that alleviate or cushion strains and tensions.

The compensating factors include the following:

1. The majority of the population has a "comfortable" level of living. The similarity of many mass-produced items, regardless of price, tends to minimize differences in wealth and possessions. The automobile, the television set, and the meal of the rich man may be more elaborate and may cost more, but many men in the lower strata own and consume items which are not so very different.

2. Even though there is display of high income consuming behavior in the mass media, men from the lower strata rarely observe upper-class behavior directly. The phantasies seen in the movies or read in the magazines are quite different from real experience. The tendency for association—friendship, visiting, cliques, dating, marriage—to be restricted to a given stratum limits contact with those of widely dissimilar positions and prevents resentment or conflict which might otherwise develop.

3. The ease with which a person may move into situations where his social position is either unrecognized or where it does not matter diminishes the effect of low position. The wide latitude in clothing and appearance allowed in eating places and at entertainment events is a source of surprise to foreign visitors. Free public services and facilities—parks, libraries, camp grounds—reduce the number of situations where class differences matter.

4. Although restrictions upon minority groups make for tension and conflict, in another sense the very presence of minorities diminishes the likelihood of organized conflict along income or occupational strata lines. Unionization, for example, often has been retarded by antagonisms and cleavages between religious, racial, and ethnic groups.

5. Although many individuals have their mobility aspirations frustrated, enough people move to the top to keep alive the belief in the possibility of achievement.

6. The large middle class mediates and cushions the strains within the structure.

[34] This discussion is indebted to Robin M. Williams, Jr., *American Society* (Rev. ed.; New York: Knopf, 1960), pp. 138–49.

People in the middle strata may have sympathetic feelings for the strata on either side of them—they may aspire to the higher ones and come from the lower ones—and thus may tend to advocate middle-of-the-road solutions. Because of its diversity in occupation, income, and origin, the middle class probably tends toward an attitude of compromise and a resistance to abrupt or drastic change.

This discussion suggests that apart from unforeseen technological or political events, new trends in the stratification system of the United States may appear only gradually. The composition of social strata is complicated and confused. The occupants of most social ranks do not have well-developed class consciousness, and strains and tensions appear at the individual rather than at the class level.

Chapter VII

Associations

Section 1   **Introduction**

In order to earn a living, get an education, or exert influence in politics, we usually find it necessary to become members or employees of specialized organizations. Corporations, trade-unions, churches, colleges, clubs, political parties, and a host of other associations make up an important part of society, particularly of contemporary *associational* society.

There are, of course, great differences among organizations, depending on the ends they are meant to serve. Schools, prisons, factories, and lodges all have distinctive characteristics, as do organizations of rural dwellers or of minorities. Different environments and different functions produce widely varying patterns of participation. The Associations sections of the Part Two chapters of this book treat the sociological features of organizations as they are shaped by special social environments. Although organizations differ in many ways, they have much in common. Whatever its special purpose, every organization attempts to co-ordinate the activities of human beings. This leads to a number of common characteristics, which will claim most of the attention of this chapter.

The sociologist views an organization figuratively as a "little society." He sees in specialized associations many of the features of societies, including the processes that bind them together or disrupt them. For example, stratification, socialization, and primary group formation are important phases of organizational experience, affecting the capacity of the organization to do its job.

This chapter considers how the essential elements of organization are influenced by social processes. (See Fig. VII:1.) Every association must:

1. Provide *incentives* to its members so as to win and sustain their participation;

2. Set up an effective system of internal *communication;*

3. Exercise *control* so that activities will be directed toward achieving the aims of the organization;

4. Adapt itself to external conditions that may threaten the existence of the organization or its policies, that is, maintain *security*.

If these requirements of effective organization are to be fulfilled, the social relations among the persons involved must be consistent with them. A major task of the soci-

INCENTIVE is increased when	COMMUNICATION is facilitated when	CONTROL is strengthened when	SECURITY is fostered when
SOCIALIZATION builds organization's goals into personality by identification.	**SOCIALIZATION** transmits the organization's point of view —"decisional premises."	**SOCIALIZATION** creates homogeneous organization—permits authority to be delegated without loss of control.	**SOCIALIZATION** strengthens group loyalty —members protect the organization, e.g., its reputation.
PRIMARY RELATIONS provide personal satisfactions which reinforce monetary or other rewards.	**PRIMARY RELATIONS** break down formal barriers to communication.	**PRIMARY RELATIONS** provide a source of informal discipline.	**PRIMARY RELATIONS** create personal attachments that bind the individual to the organization.
STRATIFICATION affords added rewards of prestige and privilege.	**STRATIFICATION** tells if the message comes from an authoritative source.	**STRATIFICATION** locates and stabilizes authority.	**INSTITUTIONAL- IZATION** adapts the organization to its social environment.

Fig. **VII:1**   Social Relations and Effective Organization

ologist is to explore the ways incentive, communication, control, and security depend on the underlying relations among persons and groups.

SOURCES AND READINGS

Peter M. Blau and W. Richard Scott, *Formal Organizations: A Comparative Approach* (San Francisco: Chandler, 1962).

Amitai Etzioni, *A Comparative Analysis of Complex Organizations* (New York: The Free Press of Glencoe, 1961).

Erving Goffman, *Asylums* (New York: Anchor Books, 1961).

Rensis Likert, *New Patterns of Management* (New York: McGraw-Hill, 1961).

James G. March and Herbert A. Simon, *Organizations* (New York: Wiley, 1958).

Robert Presthus, *The Organizational Society* (New York: Knopf, 1962).

Section 2 Formal structure

The distinction between "formal" and "informal" relations is important in understanding the sociological aspects of organizations. See PRIMARY GROUPS, pages 153–54. While sociologists have given most attention to the informal patterns, it is necessary to have a clear understanding of the meaning and significance of formal structure. Indeed, the formal system provides the environment within which informal relations arise; the working organization is a product of the interaction of both formal and informal patterns of behavior.

FOUR ELEMENTS OF FORMAL STRUCTURE

Figure VII : 2 is a simplified chart showing the formal structure of a large oil company. It introduces the following elements of company organization:

1. *Division of labor.* The chart shows that the company's operations have four main divisions: one produces the oil, another refines it, still another handles transportation, and a fourth is responsible for marketing. Moreover, we see that problems of personnel, purchasing, and finance are also divided. This division of labor according to some definite plan is the most obvious element of any formal organization. It occurs primarily for reasons of economic efficiency. *Specialization* is the guiding principle. Note that in the division of labor certain responsibilities are *delegated* to particular individuals and groups. Note also that this delegation of responsibilities creates new groups within the larger association, which becomes an organization of organizations.

2. *Delegation of authority.* The boxes and

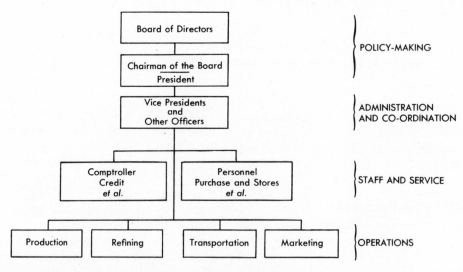

Fig. **VII:2**   Abbreviated Organization Chart (Standard Oil
Company of California)

From Planning and Developing the Company Organization by Ernest Dale
(New York: American Management Association, 1952), p. 28.

lines of the organization chart show the "chain of command." Typically, there is a *hierarchy,* in which certain individuals and groups are assigned the right to issue orders to others. The chart shows that the four main operating divisions are on the same level in the hierarchy. Also, the personnel department does not have the formal right to give direct orders to the operating divisions.

Ordinarily, a personnel department is a "staff" or "auxiliary" group. It receives instructions (as in Fig. VII:2) from the higher administrative and policy levels, and makes recommendations to those levels without directly supervising the operating divisions. However, actual practice may differ considerably from the official or formal pattern.

3. *Channeled communication.* The organization chart also shows the officially approved paths for information, requests, and commands. Some complex organizations, notably the military services, go to some pains to insure that individuals transmit information or requests "through channels." According to the chart (Fig. VII : 2), if a Vice President wants to communicate with a member of the Board of Directors, he will not by-pass the President of the company. Similarly, if the manager of an oil field, who is subordinate to the chief of the Production Division, wishes to communicate with the manager of an oil refinery on a matter of policy, he will be expected to do so through his chief. The latter will in turn communicate with subordinates in the Refinery Division only through the chief of that division. Rules of this sort are not rigidly held to because they tend to interfere with the ability of subordinates to solve their problems quickly and easily. But even in the most relaxed organization, the wise subordinate remembers his "channels" whenever anything important comes up. Otherwise, his chief will not have the information he needs to make intelligent decisions or to defend the actions of his division when called upon to do so by higher authority.

4. *Co-ordination.* In order to attain the advantages of specialization, labor is divided, but it is also necessary to maintain a united and consistent effort by the organization as a whole. This is the job of the administrative and policy levels (Fig. VII:2) which review the activities and recommendations of the various divisions, consider the conflicts that must be resolved, and develop the new policies that may need to be established. Such co-ordinating officials often act as judges, weighing the arguments presented by divisions which may differ on company policy or which may have complaints against each other. Organizations differ in the extent to which top management initiates activity or simply reviews actions initiated at the working level.

The organization chart does not show all of the elements of formal organization. There are many *procedural rules and sanctions* that do not appear on the chart, such as the rules governing hours of work. In addition, we may include the *official goals* of the organization as part of the formal system.

These elements of formal structure are governed by two related ideals: *rationality* and *discipline*.

Under a system of *rationality,* the goals of the organization are to be attained as completely as possible and at the lowest cost. This assumes that the goals are attainable and can be formulated in a clear-cut way. Within many associations, including churches, universities, political groups, and even business enterprises, the formulation of specific, attainable aims is exceedingly difficult and, consequently, administrative rationality is only partly achieved.

The ideal of *discipline* is necessary because the organization is basically a system of roles. When a man is given a job, he is expected to play out the role assigned to him. This always requires self-discipline. Since it is *activities* that are divided and co-ordinated, not persons, a single individual may be assigned more than one role within the organization. He "wears two hats," it is said. But he is expected to keep his two roles separate, and this calls for a special degree of self-discipline. Disciplined role behavior is a necessary foundation of rationality in formal systems. But, like rationality, it is an ideal that is never completely fulfilled.

FORMAL STRUCTURE DEFINED

The formal structure of an organization is a system of rules and objectives defining the tasks, powers, and procedures of participants according to some officially approved pattern. This pattern specifies how the work of the organization is to be carried on, whether it be producing steel, winning votes, teaching children, or saving souls.

The "officially approved pattern" is not necessarily codified or even written down, nor is it always fully comprehended by the participants. There may or may not be an organization chart. Sometimes the official, formal relations are so simple and well understood that there is no need to write them down. On the other hand, the relations may be so complex that a chart of the whole system would be too complicated to be helpful. In a complex organization, to find out what patterns will be *openly recognized and enforced* as part of official policy is itself no simple task. Many patterns receive official approval (or are denied it) only when they are challenged and must be submitted to the controlling officials for review.

The formal organization may be thought of as a *legal* system. As in the case of law set forth by courts and legislatures, it is a recognized authority that tells what patterns of behavior will be officially defended or punished within the organization. Moreover, like the formal organization, the legal order does not deal with all behavior, but only with that which is thought necessary to control in order to maintain public order or to meet other community needs. For example, the law of contracts deals with promises, but

not with all promises. Only those promises which meet the conditions of a legal contract are enforceable under the law. Similarly, formal relations in an organization are designed to control only those aspects of behavior which affect the achievement of the organization's aims. The law, also, is often discovered only as ways of acting are challenged and submitted to the courts for review.

DEMOCRATIC AND AUTHORITARIAN FORMS

Some organizations allow their members to participate in decision-making, while others restrict this privilege. For example, the Parent-Teachers Association, the League of Women Voters, the Republican party, and the United Automobile Workers Union are so organized as to permit, at least formally, a wide degree of membership control. On the other hand, bank tellers, soldiers, students, and boy scouts are not expected to participate significantly in the control of their organizations. We may refer to those associations that permit major decisions to be made by majority vote or through elected representatives as "democratic." Those that restrict their members or employees to the disciplined acceptance of orders transmitted from above may be called "authoritarian."

These differences in organizational form have practical roots. In general, authoritarian controls develop where sustained and co-ordinated activity is undertaken. If a group does no more than meet occasionally for discussions, democratic forms of decision may be adequate. As a group seeks to carry on more extensive and continuous activities, authoritarian forms are usually added. It is convenient and effective to charge a single individual or small group of executives with the responsibility for getting the job done. They, in turn, select others who accept direction and thus permit a unified effort according to some definite plan. All large organizations follow this procedure, though

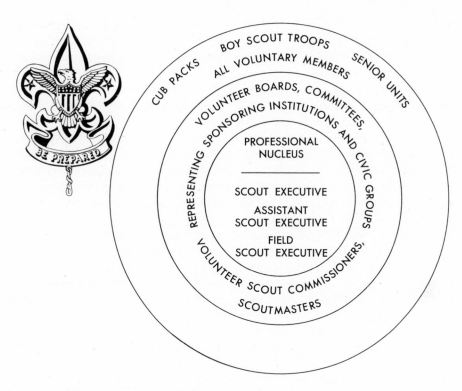

Fig. **VII:3** Local Boy Scout Organization

A Boy Scout local organization is a complex mixture of volunteer and professional membership. There is a clear administrative hierarchy among the professional Scout executives. Their job is to hold together and guide a large number of voluntary groups of adults and youths.

they vary widely in the rigidity of discipline, extent of supervision, and the autonomy of component units.

On the other hand, democratic forms arise not only because they are valued but also because they induce participation where other incentives are not available or are insufficient. Usually where participation is not voluntary, or where it is fully compensated in money or services, democratic forms are only weakly developed. They are not needed to induce or sustain participation. But if high levels of loyalty and zeal are required, or if the individual is asked to take large risks voluntarily, democratic forms are appropriate. Even in a factory, where authoritarian controls predominate, the effort to maintain high morale may lead the com-

pany to introduce limited forms of democratic participation in decision-making.

The universe of formal organizations is not neatly divided into democratic and authoritarian types. In fact, both forms are found in many large organizations. The United Steelworkers of America, the American Farm Bureau Federation, the National Association of Manufacturers, and the Standard Oil Company are alike in their formal provisions for meetings and elections to be held by members or stockholders; and they all have large staffs of employees whose activities are controlled from the top in accordance with the ideals of rationality and discipline. The ultimate source of legal authority lies in the members. Democratic forms control the relation between the members and the top officials. But those officials have an authoritarian relation to the employees of the organization. On the other hand, many organizations give substantial autonomy to constituent groups of employees. For example, academic departments in some universities have a large voice in determining their own programs and personnel. Furthermore, as members of academic senates, departments may influence general policies of the university.

Not all organizations ultimately controlled from the top are equally authoritarian, in the sense noted above of "restricting their members or employees to the disciplined acceptance of order transmitted from above." In some corporations and agencies there is considerable decision-making by committees, wide autonomy for subordinate officials, and much action initiated from below. Organizations that encourage these patterns may be thought of as democratic in spirit, and to some extent in form, even though final responsibility and authority necessarily remain at the top.[1]

Sometimes an executive is criticized as "authoritarian" because in his relations with his employees he issues orders in a way that shows a lack of regard for their opinions or feelings. This kind of authoritarian behavior may be found in authoritarian organizations but should not be confused with them. Some army commanders or corporation officials are authoritarian in their dealings with subordinates; others show tolerance and respect. Some may pride themselves on "lone wolf" decisions; others frequently consult with subordinates. But in all armies and in most businesses, authoritarian *procedures* predominate.

The word "authoritarian" has a sinister ring, because of the heavy cultural support for democratic forms. Indeed, if the kind of discipline and decision-making that prevails

in an army or even a corporation or government agency were extended to the whole society, we would have lost our system of representative government. But these authoritarian forms, when limited to specific activities and controlled by the laws and customs of a democratic society, do not necessarily challenge our cultural ideals. So long as the men at the top, who stand in an authoritarian relation to their subordinates, are themselves responsible to some membership or electorate, and are controlled by legal or other norms that restrain arbitrary action, we can readily accept and even require authoritarian forms. For example, there is authoritarian administration within the U.S. Department of Defense, but the Secretary of Defense is responsible to a President who must stand for election.

BUREAUCRACY

Much of what we have called "formal" structure is often referred to as "bureaucratic" structure. That term is widely used but occasions some misunderstandings. The following points should be kept in mind:

1. "Bureaucracy" as used in social science refers to the formal organization of *administrative officials*. It does not include the nonsupervisory work force in a factory or the members of a trade-union. Nor does it usually include the top policy-making leaders or directors. "Formal structure" is a more general term, designating the prescribed roles and procedures of *all* participants.

2. In Webster's *New International Dictionary* we find the following definition of *bureaucracy:* "A system of carrying on the business of government by means of departments or bureaus, each controlled by a chief, who is apt to place special emphasis upon routine and conservative action . . . . Hence, in general, such a system which has become narrow, rigid, and formal, depends on precedent, and lacks initiative and resourcefulness." This definition, reflecting our ordinary usage, associates bureaucracy with something undesirable,

---

[1] On the balance between compliance and initiative in bureaucratic structures see Reinhard Bendix "Bureaucracy: The Problem and Its Setting," *American Sociological Review,* October, 1947, pp. 493–507.

even pathological. It is important to be clear that most social scientists do not *define* the term in this way, though they may agree that under certain conditions officials are indeed "apt to" over-emphasize routine and otherwise take on the traits suggested in the dictionary definition. Rather, the social scientist defines a bureaucrat simply as an official within a formal system. He may then go on to study the likelihood that bureaucrats will exhibit certain pathological tendencies, such as narrowed perception and lack of initiative. But ordinarily he does not limit the idea of bureaucracy to these tendencies.

Communication Patterns in Task-Oriented Groups

Abridged and adapted from "Communication Patterns in Task-Oriented Groups" by Alex Bavelas, *Journal of the Acoustical Society of America, **22*** (1950), 725–30. Published in this form by permission of Alex Bavelas and the Acoustical Society of America. The experiment was conducted by Sidney Smith. The full article may also be found in Dorwin Cartwright and Alvin Zander (eds.), *Group Dynamics: Research and Theory* (Evanston: Row, Peterson, 1953), pp. 493–500, from which Figs. VII:4 and VII:5 are taken.

Formal structure is a way of fixing communication patterns. How do these fixed patterns affect the work and life of a group? Bavelas and his associates undertook some experiments to find out whether different *imposed* patterns of communication make for differences in group performance, leadership, and morale. This work is in an early stage, but it already (1) provides a fresh way of looking at formal structure and (2) shows how certain features of formal organization may be studied on an experimental basis.

COMMUNICATION LINKS

Let us vary the ways in which five individuals are linked to one another, it being understood that every individual in the group will be linked to at least one other individual in the same group. To be "linked" means that individual p can communicate to q and q to p. What different kinds of communication patterns may we produce that might affect human beings in some way? First impressions of the patterns may prove misleading. (See Fig. VII: 4.) Students commonly remark, upon seeing patterns C and D for the first time, that pattern C is "autocratic," while pattern D is a typical "business setup." Actually, of course, insofar as linkage goes, they are identical. The only difference is the arrangement of the dots on the paper. Among patterns A, B, and C, however, we may point to some real differences. For instance, in pattern A each individual can communicate with two others in the group directly—that is, without relaying a message through some other person. In patterns C and D there is only one individual in the group who can communicate directly with all the others.

To make another comparison, any individual in pattern A can communicate with any one of the others with no more than a single "relay." In pattern B two individuals must relay messages through three others in order to communicate with each other.

AN EXPERIMENT

Do the patterns make a difference? One experiment will be described. Eight groups of college students were studied, using patterns A and B shown in Figure VII : 5. Each subject was given a card upon which had been printed five symbols from among these

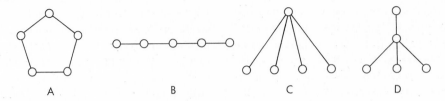

Fig. VII:4 Some Different Communication Patterns

Each line represents a communication linkage.

six: $\bigcirc \triangle * \square + \diamondsuit$. While each symbol appeared on four of the five cards, only one symbol appeared on all five cards. Each group's task was to find the common symbol in the shortest time possible. The subjects sat in separate cubicles. In each subject's cubicle was a box of six switches, each switch labeled with one of the six symbols. The task was considered finished when each member of the group indicated that he knew the common symbol by throwing the appropriate switch. The switches operated a board of lights visible to a laboratory assistant who recorded individual and group times and errors, an error being the throwing of an incorrect switch. The subjects communicated by writing messages which could be passed through slots in the cubicle walls. The slots were so arranged that any desired linkage pattern could be imposed by the experimenter. No restriction whatever was placed upon the content of the messages. A subject who had the "answer" was at liberty to send it along. The cards upon which the messages were written were coded so that a continuous record of the communication activities could be maintained.

Each experimental group worked on 15 successive problems. The same six symbols were used throughout, but the common symbol varied from trial to trial. Four groups worked in pattern *A,* and four other groups worked in pattern *B*. No group worked in more than one pattern.

Each of the subjects answered a questionnaire immediately after the end of the fifteenth trial. One of the questions read: "Did your group have a leader? If so, who?" The answers are shown in Figure VII: 5. The findings suggest that the individual occupying the most central position in a pattern is most likely to be recognized as the leader.

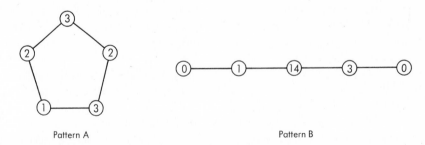

Pattern A   Pattern B

Fig. VII:5 Emergence of Recognized Leaders in Different Communication Patterns

The number at each position shows the total number of group members who recognized the individual in that position as the leader.

From direct observation of the subjects while they worked, it appears that the morale of the individuals in the most peripheral (least central) positions of pattern *B* is the poorest.

Further experiments strengthened the hypothesis that leadership is related to "centrality" of position in the communication pattern. This principle is recognized in the design of administrative organizations, where there is usually some attempt—not always successful—to give persons in high authority the readiest access to communication channels.

In another experiment using the same patterns the subjects were asked "How did you like your job?" and "How satisfied are you with the job done?" The answers to both questions show again that those who occupy the more peripheral positions have the poorest morale. This conclusion supports the general view that participation and group morale are closely related.

Caution: Conclusions from laboratory experiments using small groups are not directly applicable to large, complex organizations. However, such experiments can suggest new ways of looking at organizations and help formulate hypotheses to be tested in studies of "the real thing."

Section 3   Informal structure

The rules of the formal system account for much but by no means all of the patterned behavior in associations. The phrase "informal structure" is used to denote those patterns that emerge from the spontaneous interaction of personalities and groups within the organization. This key idea may be developed more logically if we put the matter as follows: An organization's informal structure is made up of the patterns that develop when the participants face persistent problems that are not provided for by the formal system. These problems arise in a variety of ways:

1. *Impersonality of the formal system.* The definite rules and prescribed roles of the formal structure are necessarily impersonal. The individual is treated as a unit in a technical, task-oriented system. This has many advantages, but it also has limits. In practice, it is often necessary to reach individuals as *persons,* if their best efforts and their highest loyalty are to be mustered. Some leeway must be allowed for interpersonal and group relations to supplement the formal patterns of communication and control. (See Adaptation 14, pp. 163–65.) The importance of "personal contact" in all organizations, not only for private advantage but to get the job done, is well known to all experienced participants. Even in armies, where formal relations are most fully expressed, friendship and pride in one's "outfit" are important ingredients of effective organization. The impersonal system is modified to permit greater access to the individual's personal motivations. Socialization and the development of primary relations are particularly important in this connection.

2. *Lag of the formal system.* Like any other code of rules or laws, the formal system of an organization tends to lag behind changes in its operations, for example in a work situation. (See the discussion of cultural lag, CULTURE, pp. 82–83.) Despite the lag, those who do the work must solve new problems, even if these problems have not yet been recognized officially and there are no rules to meet them. For example, the official pattern controlling the behavior of a foreman may have

been developed prior to the organization of the factory's workers by a union. The union's elected shop stewards seek to act as spokesmen for the workers on day-to-day grievance problems. The foreman will be under great pressure to find a way of dealing with these men, even though the company has not recognized the union and has developed no formal procedures for co-operating with it. The temporary solution may be an informal pattern of consultation between the foremen and the shop stewards. After a period of time this informal procedure, usually modified and made consistent throughout the factory, may become formalized.

3. *Generality of the formal system.* The rules that make up the formal system are general. Each rule deals with a class of cases or a type of problem. No set of rules can anticipate all the problems the man on the job will face, although organizations vary in their attempts to devise formal systems that will do so. In every organization there are some informal patterns that provide more detailed control than the formal system. In time some of these patterns may become formalized; others will remain outside official recognition. The test of formalization, it may be well to repeat, is not whether a rule has been written down, or neatly formulated, or universally accepted, but whether the official authority in the organization will approve it and, if necessary, enforce conformance to it. The same holds true in the law. The courts and legislatures decide what customs ought to become part of the enforceable rights and duties of individuals and groups.

The fact that rules remain general is not a matter of whim or ineptitude on the part of the rule-makers. Inefficiency often results from the effort to provide detailed guidance when circumstances are not completely predictable. The man who has to do the job may be greatly hampered if he is not given some freedom to work out special ways of handling new situations. By keeping rules general, ways of acting may be tested informally be-

fore they are given official approval. This is often important, because when a procedure is officially approved (for example, a way to communicate with outside groups), the leaders of the organization will have to defend the practice. It is often convenient to let a practice remain unofficial so that it can be more easily changed or repudiated.

4. *Personal problems and interests.* The foregoing comments on impersonality, lag, and generality indicate some of the aspects of organizational experience that cannot be adequately handled by the formal system *even when we assume that the participants are solely interested in attaining the organization's aims.* When this is so, the participants simply do their best to supplement the formal rules in informal ways. In fact, we cannot assume that individuals are solely interested in helping the organization to reach its goals. We know that the emotional needs of individuals affect the way they act in organizations. As a result of their interaction with others, patterns outside of the formal system are likely to emerge. For example, a new supervisor may allay his anxieties by cultivating the friendship of an experienced worker. He thereby gains access to valuable information about the work and the employees. Perhaps his friend will defend him when things go wrong. This relation, if stabilized, becomes part of the informal structure of the plant. It cannot be officially enforced, yet it is a significant fact that must not be overlooked by anyone who seeks to understand or influence that segment of the organization.

Upon entering an organization, one does not eliminate all past ideas and attitudes or one's attachment to other groups and values. (There are rare exceptions, in the case of some religious and political groups.) These attachments, especially to old ways of thinking, may significantly shape behavior inside the organization. Where there is leeway on policies to be pursued, one's prior attitudes may come into play. For example, one who hires new employees may allow his personal

Informal structure: patterns that develop during spontaneous interaction of persons and groups within the organization.

VALUES and NORMS

INFORMAL GROUP NORMS within the organization, e.g., "Don't be a rate buster."

BASIC ATTITUDES about work, co-operation, loyalty, etc. brought into the organization as a result of prior socialization.

SOCIAL CONTROL DEVICES, e.g., expressing approval or ridicule.

GROUPS

FRIENDSHIPS exert prior claims on the individual. (May be within group or from outside.)

CLIQUES show personal loyalty. (May be friendship groups or merely alliances.)

INTEREST GROUPS share a stake in existing social arrangements. (May be any groups, including formal units.)

STATUS

INFORMAL PRIVILEGES attached to positions in the formal hierarchy.

POWER RELATIONS, e.g., balance of power between local and headquarters units, depending on source of funds, locus of membership, etc.

DEPENDENCY PATTERNS, e.g., dependence of "staff" on "line."

Informal structure critically affects COMMUNICATION and POWER. It is indispensable to effective functioning but may also undermine it.

Fig. **VII:6** Elements of Informal Structure

likes and dislikes for various classes of people to influence his decisions. Loyalty to an outside interest group may be very specific, not simply a matter of general beliefs and attitudes. If a person joins an organization while retaining loyalties to outside groups that want to influence it, he may act inside the organization as the agent of the outside group, sometimes consciously, sometimes unconsciously.

Informal structure arises as the individual brings into play problems and interests other than those defined by his role in the organization. Formal relations co-ordinate roles or specialized activities, not persons. Formal rules apply to foremen and machinists, to clerks, sergeants, and vice-presidents, but no durable organization is able to restrict inter-action to these formally defined roles. In actual practice, men tend to interact as many-faceted persons, adjusting to diverse daily experiences in ways that spill over the neat boundaries set by their formal roles. Much of this adjustment is idiosyncratic, reflecting the unique responses of unique persons to unique situations. The sociologist is not concerned with these idiosyncracies but with the way such behavior produces a social structure composed of informal codes, groups, hierarchies, and aims.

Sociologists who have studied associations have given special attention to informal structure. Much contemporary research in this area has amounted to demonstrations that group processes do go on inside industrial, military, and other formal organizations. However, the associations individuals participate in are made up of *both* formal and informal relations. In experience they are interrelated, jointly affecting the ability of the association to solve the major problems that arise in any attempt to co-ordinate the activities of human beings. Therefore, the sociology of special-purpose associations stresses the *interdependence* of these aspects. In the following sections, while emphasizing informal processes, we shall show their relation to the formal devices for attaining organized, concerted effort.

Section 4 **Cohesion and morale**

Associations are devices for mobilizing human effort. The most effective organizations are able to win from their members a sense of *personal* commitment. The work they do, the initiative they display, and the loyalty they give go beyond the minimum requirements of keeping a job. When this occurs, we say that morale is high. The organization becomes more than a technical arrangement of co-ordinated parts. It becomes a cohesive social group.

SOCIALIZING THE ORGANIZATION MEMBER

It is common to refer to someone as a "Harvard man," a "Forest Service man," or a "military man." These labels suggest that the individual has been influenced by his associational experience, that he has been effectively socialized by an organization. We feel that certain key attitudes have been transmitted which give him a special stamp and allow us to make some reliable predictions about his behavior. Not all organizations, however, are capable of such effective socialization.

The examples we have given may suggest that the products of socialization in organizations are highly visible, but this is not always so. Sometimes organizations leave no particular mark on the individual, or the organization's influence is recognized by only those who are "in the know." Socialization tends to be important in organizations that require a high degree of personal dedication and loyalty. Some organizations call for distinctive ways of thinking and responding; still others must offset influences that work against the organization's aims or policies, e.g., the civilian outlook and habits of the draftee.

The reshaping of the person in organizational settings is done through habituation and the learning of social roles. The individual becomes adapted to certain ways of thinking and working. He learns how to be a foreman or a team member, just as he learns how to be a father or a neighbor.

This influence on the individual has been called the *"internalization of influence,* because it injects into the very nervous systems of the organization members the criteria of decision that the organization wishes to employ. The organization member acquires knowledge, skill, and identifications or loyalties that enable him to make decisions, by himself, as the organization would like him to decide." [2]

The effects of organizational socialization are:

1. *To link personal satisfactions and organizational aims.* If the individual feels personally attacked when the organization is attacked and personal failure when it fails, he will work harder, be readier to pitch in in crises, and require less discipline than if iden-

[2] H. A. Simon, *Administrative Behavior* (2nd ed.; New York: Macmillan, 1958), p. 103. Italics supplied. See SOCIALIZATION, pp. 123-27.

tification had not taken place. Hence socialization helps provide incentives to high levels of participation and responsibility.

2. *To make official communication easier.* If the individual has absorbed the general outlook of the organization and its distinctive "approach" to its task and to its relation to other organizations, it will be easier to communicate instructions. They will not have to be spelled out laboriously, because their background and intent will be understood. As Simon puts it, the socialized organization member has absorbed the "decisional premises" of the enterprise, that is, the bases on which decisions are made. One advantage of this deeper understanding is that the member will know, without being explicitly told, when he may modify or even disregard instructions. Because he understands the basis of an order, he need not follow it mechanically or literally.

3. *To permit greater delegation of authority without loss of control.* When decisional premises are adequately communicated, the person who gives an order shares the same understanding of what is to be accomplished as the person who executes it. The latter may then be permitted a great deal of freedom. In this way, organizational socialization substitutes informal social controls for formal administrative controls. Personnel come to have similar ways of thinking and responding. The fact that they share values and aspirations permits the college president to delegate decision-making to a dean with confidence that the decisions will conform to the college's basic policies and interests. No such assurance would be possible if the dean were not instilled with the values and point of view of the college.

4. *To strengthen group loyalty and thereby organizational security.* Socialization increases the likelihood that the members will stand united against threats from the outside. This is obviously important in voluntary associations. But it is also significant where employees have dealings with other organizations and the public, especially at the administrative level. For example, loyal employees are expected to defend the reputation of their organization and to pass on useful information, even if it is acquired off the job. It is probable that assessments of organizational loyalty play a very important part in determining the careers of professional or executive personnel.

These effects of socialization in organizations parallel the effects of socialization in society itself. When aspirations and disciplines are built into the individual, a linkage is established between personal satisfactions and such social aims as hard work and patriotic sacrifice; specific rules are more thoroughly understood and more flexibly applied; and the individual can be expected to act in accordance with social values even when the official agencies of the society are not present or effective. The weaker the socialization, the more society must depend upon formal controls.

Organizations need to emphasize socialization whenever impersonal incentives, such as wages, are not adequate to sustain participation at required levels; whenever instructions are so complex that the persons who are to carry them out require extensive indoctrination in decisional premises; and whenever circumstances require extensive delegation of authority, for example, if subordinate offices are geographically distant or isolated.

Caution: Important as socialization is for winning increased involvement and conformity from organization members, the significance and persistence of formal devices should not be overlooked. Socialization usually *supplements and supports* the formal structure. Moreover, there are some circumstances, an army in wartime is the best example, when primary emphasis is necessarily placed on *both* socialization and the maintenance of extensive formal controls. Neither alone is adequate to meet the stresses that are encountered in combat.

Finally, a word should be said about the *price* paid for socialization. When an organization attempts to influence its members, it facilitates its work in the ways we have mentioned. This takes much of the burden off the formal system of communication and control. But this advantage has two attendant risks:

1. *Rigidity.* The process that makes a man uniquely adapted to a particular way of thinking and working may make him ill adapted to other ways of behaving. He may become so set in his habits and outlook that he cannot readily accept new ideas or new tasks. This may be of no great consequence, if the organization does not need to make any important changes in its orientation. However, if significant change is required, the organization will face difficulties. (See Sec. 7, pp. 250–54.)

2. *Loss of unity.* Identification takes place at many levels in a large organization, but very often the individual's primary loyalty is to his working group. This is valuable to the organization as a whole, for it means that the individual's energies are being harnessed at the proper place, that is, where he works. But this attachment may prove to be disruptive if the member of a subordinate unit places the interests of that unit above those of the total enterprise. A major task of top leadership is to overcome this potential disunity while retaining the advantages of identification with the working unit.

IDENTIFICATION

Through the process of identification, a man may come to think of an organization as an extension of himself. He may respond to the organization as a whole person, give more of himself than the job requires, and make the organization's problems his own. He gains direct personal satisfaction from the relation, and he permits himself to be shaped by it. The characteristic signs of a primary relation emerge: wholeness of response, depth of communication, and orientation to personal satisfaction. However, this organizational loyalty and identification is often mediated by attachment to particular persons: the relation is to some other person and through him to the organization.

On the other hand, person-to-person interaction may be lacking. The individual may attempt to act toward an impersonal organization as if it could sustain a primary relation. This may work out reasonably well if the organization is flexible and if it takes account of the individual as a person and does not treat him as a mere tool. If identification occurs when these conditions are absent, the individual may be faced with continuous frustration, constantly attempting to bend the "ungrateful" organization to his will.

ORGANIZATION UNITS AS SOCIAL GROUPS

The effect of personal interaction is to create social groups within the formal organization. In many cases, the social group and the organization unit have the same membership, name, and history. When a particular division or the organization as a whole becomes the object of personal identification, develops a homogeneous personnel, and shares a common fund of tradition, it becomes more than a narrowly utilitarian organization. It takes on the character of a community. Colleges often show this kind of integration, West Point and Annapolis being perhaps extreme instances.

The social groups arising out of immediate work situations, however, do not necessarily follow the boundaries of formal organization units. Clerical and professional personnel, though in the same formal unit, may belong to distinct working groups with different identifications, perceptions, and interests. Differences in status and social background, combined with differences in the nature of the work done, often create social groups that do not reflect the formal division of labor.

Sometimes, when social groupings cut across formal organization lines, problems of divided loyalty arise, especially for individuals whose daily work takes them outside the formal unit and brings them into co-operative contact with members of other units or even with members of other organizations. The problem has practical implications in the relation of staff units to the operating or line organization. (See Sec. 2, p. 221.) Suppose a Personnel Department has the job of maintaining standards of recruitment, promotion, training, and employee morale in a large firm. A member of the Personnel Department may be permanently assigned to work with one of the operating divisions; for example, the Refining Division in Figure VII : 2. If he has daily contact with members of that division over a period of time, he may share its special perspectives and be accepted by its members. To the extent that he identifies with the Refining Division, he will tend to act as its representative, presenting its arguments and points of view to his superiors in the Personnel Department. On the other hand, if this member of the Personnel Department is given a variety of assignments, which place him in contact with many operating units, his main identification will probably stay with the Personnel Department or, more accurately, with the particular section of that department to which he belongs.[3]

The way the lines of identification develop in the case just cited will be important to the Personnel Department. If its technicians are absorbed into working groups of the program or operating divisions, its staff acquires other points of view, and this may weaken the policies of the Personnel Department. It might even endanger the continued existence of some sections of the department. Weakened identification of its members would make it vulnerable if the operating divisions demanded that they be allowed to work out their own personnel procedures. To forestall this, the Personnel Department might decide to limit any given staff member's contact

with a particular operating division, in order to avoid the possible integration of that staff member into a working group of the division.

SUMMARY

We have discussed here and in PRIMARY GROUPS, pages 153–65, a number of ways primary relations contribute to the cohesion and effective functioning of organizations. These influences may be summarized as follows:

1. *Primary relations help morale,* that is, the maintenance of participation at desired levels. This is accomplished by modifying the impersonality of the formal system. The individual's fear of arbitrary treatment is reduced, and he is given direct personal satisfaction in companionship and identification with his work and with the enterprise.

2. *Primary relations aid communication.* By adapting formal rules to the individual's immediate situation, primary relations not only protect the individual but also break down communication barriers. Instructions thus adapted will be better understood and more readily accepted.

3. *Primary relations aid control of organization members.* When a man is absorbed into a primary group, he accepts its discipline. If that group is part of a larger association, it can hold its members to the aims and methods of the whole. For example, the pressures exerted within the primary group may help reduce absenteeism. In this way, primary relations supplement the more formal controls.

Cautions: (1) There is a disruptive potential in primary groups. The discussion of "the double-edged significance of the primary group" (pp. 154–55) should be recalled. (2) The constructive contributions of primary relations are not equally available or necessary in all associations. The more dependence there is on high morale, the greater will be the significance of primary relations. Some organizations, however, can get along well enough to serve their purposes without high levels of personal commitment.

[3] Based on the discussion in H. A. Simon, D. W. Smithburg, and V. A. Thompson, *Public Administration* (New York: Knopf, 1950), p. 101.

Section 5 **Communication and social status**

Most discussions of stratification deal with whole societies or communities, and this is the emphasis in SOCIAL STRATIFICATION. But the basic processes of stratification also occur in special-purpose associations, where they affect communication, incentive, and control. In this section we emphasize the importance of stratification for communication within large organizations.

FORMAL RANKS AND SOCIAL STRATA

The study of social stratification in organizations includes both the *formal ranking system* and the *informally patterned experiences* of the persons who occupy the positions. The formal ranking system is readily observed. It is easy to make lists of the official ranks that intervene between a five-star general and a private, between a corporation president and an unskilled worker, between the president of the American Federation of Labor and a member of a trade-union local, or between a university president and a teaching assistant.

These formal ranks tend to be associated with distinctive attitudes and interests. The diverse experiences and problems of men at different levels condition (1) how individuals in like social positions view the world and themselves, and (2) the stake they have in the organization. A man's position in the hierarchy tends to influence his general social behavior—his manners, outlook, opportunities, and power—and in this way social stratification develops.

Status is symbolized in many ways. The American office "is a veritable temple of status." [4] The carpeted office, the memo pad, the privilege of smoking or of first-naming one's colleagues—all are cues to differential status. The way names are used is important, but

the significance attached to names depends on whether one is looking up or down the hierarchy. The rank order of address by executives is definitely outlined by that student of human relations, Potter, in the case of a Lumer Farr, a company director, who liked to be called "The Guv'nor":

In the science of Christian-naming, Lumer is associated with Farr's Law of Mean Familiarity. This can be expressed by a curve, but is much clearer set down as follows:

The Guv'nor addresses:
Co-director Michael Yates as MIKE
Assistant director
    Michael Yates as   MICHAEL
Sectional manager
    Michael Yates as   MR. YATES
Sectional assistant
    Michael Yates as   YATES
Apprentice Michael Yates as MICHAEL
Night-watchman
    Michael Yates as   MIKE [5]

Organizations are both aided and hindered by the transformation of formal, technical rankings into social strata. On the one hand, the development of appropriate attitudes helps to sustain the system of authority. Men who have feelings of deference toward their superiors more readily accept commands. On the other hand, the development of special interests and attitudes may introduce rigidities into the organization.

The Economy of Incentives

Incentives leading to wholehearted participation are scarce, and remuneration is no guarantee that individuals will give freely of their energy and zeal. A system of status, in addition to fixing the lines of authority and

[4] W. H. Whyte, Jr., "Status in the American Office," *Fortune* (May, 1951).

[5] Stephen Potter, *One-upmanship* (New York: Holt, 1952), p. 44.

communication, helps to provide additional incentives.[6] High status conveys social prestige, inside and outside the organization, accompanied by deference and respect from others. Many persons work hard and sacrifice to attain even relatively small advances of status. Sometimes merely the proper choice of job titles, with no change in actual authority or salary, is an effective incentive.

In addition to prestige, higher status offers special privileges of many kinds, including the opportunity to execute one's own ideas. These and other social concomitants of the formal ranking system help to win fuller cooperation. The design of status systems from the standpoint of the economy of incentives has not been closely studied, but its general importance is widely recognized.

Communication and the Chain of Command

The significance of social stratification in the operation of an organization is illustrated

[6] This point has been emphasized by Chester I. Barnard, who did much to lay the groundwork for the sociology of large-scale organizations. See *The Functions of the Executive* (Cambridge: Harvard University Press, 1938) and "Functions and Pathology of Status Systems in Formal Organizations" in William Foote Whyte (ed.), *Industry and Society* (New York: McGraw-Hill, 1946).

by its effect on internal communication. Gardner and Moore (Adaptation 19, pp. 235–40) show how information is filtered as it moves up and down the chain of command. The employees' efforts to protect their security result in distortions in communication. A job is not merely a technical arrangement for getting something produced; it is also a life situation for the person, with distinctive stresses, limitations, and opportunities.

Although stratification may *distort* communication, the formal status system is actually designed to *facilitate* it. For example, when a man receives an order or request, he wants to know if it comes from someone who is in position to know the facts and who will back up the action taken. Usually knowledge of the sender's place in the formal status system answers his questions quickly and easily. As formal ranking is reshaped by social relations, more detailed knowledge is necessary to interpret orders. One man at a given formal rank may not need to be taken seriously, but another at the same level might command prompt action. For example, communications from a "lame duck," a high official known soon to be leaving office, are treated more casually than if his tenure were continuing.

The Line of Authority and Communication

Abridged and adapted from *Human Relations in Industry* by B. B. Gardner and D. G. Moore (Rev. ed.; Chicago: Irwin, 1950), pp. 33–65. Published in this form by permission of the authors and Richard D. Irwin, Inc.

The formal line of authority or chain of command provides a *channel of communication* extending from top to bottom. But it is not the simple, direct channel it is often thought to be. By its very nature as a linkage of man-boss relationships, it has a number of peculiarities which affect the quality, accuracy, and speed of communication. In fact, much of the transmission is so difficult that

it is rare for a superior who is several steps removed from the work level to have comprehensive knowledge of what goes on in the shop. This adaptation reviews some of the sources of communication difficulties up and down the line organization.

Communication "Down"

Because each person is so dependent on his boss for recognition and communication up the line, and because each person is so sensitive to his boss's moods, opinions, likes, and

ADAPTATION 19

dislikes, there is often much confusion and misunderstanding in communication down the line. For example, we see the superintendent passing through the shop convoyed by the foreman. Being in a jovial mood, he comments that "the girls seem happy this morning, the way they are talking and laughing." The foreman thinks, "Is he hinting that I shouldn't allow them to talk? Does he think I don't keep proper discipline? Those girls ought to have sense enough to stop talking and act busy when he's around. Maybe I better move Mary off by herself because she always gets the others started talking." The boss leaves, quite unaware that his comments have been interpreted as criticism. As soon as he is gone, the foreman bawls out the girls for talking and not paying attention to their work; he moves the Marys around, and it is weeks or even months before the final ripples of disturbance have died down.

Distortion "Up" the Line

Because of sensitivity to the boss and dependence on him, there is much distortion in communicating up the line. Along with concern for "giving the boss what he wants," there is a tendency to "cover up," to keep the boss from knowing about the things that go wrong or the things that do not get done. No one wants to pass bad news up the line, because he feels that it reflects on him and that he should handle his job so there is no bad news. Consequently, he does not tell the boss what a poor job he did or how stupid he was. That is, he does not unless he thinks someone else will get to the boss first. (See "A Case of Jitters," p. 238.) When he does have to break some bad news to the boss, he will probably have everything fixed up or have developed a good excuse. People at each level develop defenses, often complicated and ingenious, to protect themselves from criticism from those above them in the chain of command.

The subordinate selects what to tell the superior, trying to anticipate what the boss wants to know or what he may want to know later, trying to present things in such a way that his boss will feel that things are not too bad, or, if they were, that they are now under control, and trying to give him good news to take the sting out of the bad. The boss goes away feeling that he knows what is going on, that he has his finger firmly on the pulse of the shop.

Filtered Information

Each individual in the line acts as a filter who sorts the information coming to him and selects what he will pass on to his boss. Because the boss responds most favorably to good news, good news goes up the line quite easily and rapidly. Information about improvements in output, quality, costs, and so on are transmitted readily from level to level. On the other hand, bad news moves more slowly; everyone is reluctant to communicate his mistakes or failures. The what-will-the-boss-think-of-me feeling encourages delays, excuses, and the development of tact in presenting bad news. The filtering of information operates at all levels in the hierarchy.

The Foreman's Orientation

The foreman, who is usually considered the first level of management, has the most direct and detailed knowledge of the job and the workers. He plans and supervises their work; he checks and judges it; he maintains discipline and enforces the rules. To the workers he is the one who gives orders, who rewards and punishes. It is through him that the downward pressures, the demands and orders, are transmitted to the work group.

The foreman develops an orientation toward the work which is different from that of the rest of the hierarchy. In the first place, his attention is focused on the everyday details. He sees the immediate difficulties and complexities of getting the work out, and he usually knows the workers and their attitudes. As a result, he tends to be impatient with higher levels or with staff people who try to generalize on the basis of partial knowledge and make decisions which affect his job. He frequently feels that his superiors impose tasks on him and on his group without understanding the difficulties of the job.

1. *Worker-oriented foremen.* Foremen have a variety of attitudes about their superiors and their subordinates. In some cases they have strong feelings of sympathy with the work group. The foreman identifies with the workers, acts as though he were one of them, and constantly defends them from his superiors and from outside organizations. In this situation, the foreman generally maintains little social distance between himself and his work group.

There is often a much greater distinction between the foreman and his department chief. In some cases the foreman may actually avoid contacts and force the department chief to come to him. The foreman tries to keep the department chief away from his group, to be present when he is around the job, to cover up mistakes, protect individual workers from his criticism, and otherwise to build strong barriers between them. He resists demands from above for changes, finding reasons for not accepting them or for their failure if they are forced upon him.

2. *Management-oriented foremen.* The opposite type is the foreman who has a strong identification with management and his superiors, and he holds his subordinates at a distance. He tends to be critical of the workers and feels that they are not dependable or are not trying to do a good job. They correctly feel that he is aloof, and they hesitate to talk freely to him or to discuss problems with him. He is likely to seek out his superiors, both on the job or outside. He is concerned about his relationship with his department chief and tries to make a good impression. There is a close relationship between foreman and department chief and considerable distance between foreman and worker.

In this type of situation the workers feel forced to be on their guard against their fore-

man and think of him as someone who is against them rather than for them. They develop various defenses: they watch their behavior whenever he is in sight; they may restrict output without his knowledge; and they may complain about him to the union. Sometimes the tension makes contacts so uncomfortable that even he is aware of it and may withdraw to some extent from the work situation. In extreme cases, he spends most of his time at his desk, talking to his superiors, or entirely out of the department.

3. *Isolated foremen.* Sometimes a foreman is isolated from both his department chief and the work group. In these cases, there is avoidance on the part of all concerned. If the job will run with a minimum of direct supervision, the foreman may stay out of the group most of the time and stay away from his department chief, too. As long as the work goes on, the department chief also avoids the foreman and the group, and all contacts are very formal and uncomfortable. If the job does not go well, the foreman is in difficulties because his boss will be critical of him and may make arbitrary demands. At the same time, the group is defensive and does not respond to the foreman's demands. The foreman is generally critical of them, just as his boss is critical of him. Under these conditions, both the foreman and the workers are uncomfortable, and whenever there is pressure on the foreman from above, he feels isolated and defenseless and takes it out on his subordinates. In other words, such situations may be fairly stable as long as the work is running well, but under pressure a great deal of friction between foreman and workers develops.

4. *Integrated foremen.* Sometimes, on the other hand, we find a situation in which there is strong identification and integration between all three—the workers, the foreman, and the department chief. In such cases we see very easy interaction between workers and department chief, and the department chief is usually in close touch with the details of the job and with the individuals. The fore-

A Case of Jitters

From *Human Relations in Industry* by B. B. Gardner and D. G. Moore (Rev. ed.; Chicago: Irwin, 1950), pp. 37–38. Reprinted by permission.

Take the case of Bob, foreman in the machine department, when he suddenly discovers that he does not have enough bronze rod on hand to complete the order of part number X37A22 for the end of the week and that it will keep two hand screw machines going steadily to make delivery on time. So he talks to Charley, the machine operator who came to him asking for the rod:

Bob: "Are you sure there isn't any of that rod over in the rack? When we started on this job, I checked the storeroom records and there was plenty on hand."

Charley: "There sure isn't now. You remember when we first started on this order somebody gave us the wrong specifications and we turned out a lot that had to be junked."

Bob: "That's right. Well, I'll call the stockroom and get some more over right away." (*Thinking,* I sure did slip up on that. I completely forgot to order more rod.)

(*He calls the stockroom.*) "I'll need two hundred pounds of that ⅜th bronze rod for part number X37A22. We're in a rush for it, got to get the order out right away and a couple of machines are waiting. Can you get it right over?"

Stockman: "Sorry, we are out of that rod. Won't be able to get it in before Friday. Why didn't you call last week?"

Bob: "Can't you get hold of any before that? If I don't deliver those parts before Monday, the gadget assembly department will be tied up."

Stockman: "We'll do the best we can, but don't expect it before Friday. Why don't you guys give us a little more notice instead of waiting until your machines shut down and then expecting us to do miracles?"

Bob: (*Thinking:* This is a terrible note! I slip up on ordering that rod the one time the stockroom is out of it. Why can't they keep some stock on hand instead of trying to work from hand to mouth. Just trying to make a good showing by keeping down inventory and they tie up production. They ought to realize that they are there to help the shop, not to give us all this trouble. Wonder what I can do now. The boss sure will give me hell when he hears this. Maybe I ought to check with Joe in gadget assembly to see how many parts they have on hand and how long before he will need more. Maybe I better let him know what's happened so he will know what to expect. Maybe he can plan his work so the people on that assembly job can do something else for a few days.

But if I tell him what's happened, he will tell his boss, and his boss will jump on my boss, and my boss will jump on me for letting this happen and not letting him know. So before I tell Joe anything I better tell my boss. Maybe if I tell him, he can tell Joe's boss, and I won't have to say anything to Joe. Joe's going to be plenty sore anyway. He got kind of hot the other day when I tried to get him to let me make some changes in the base plate for that Model N job. Seemed like he was just being stubborn. Wonder if he might have enough parts on hand so he could just go along and say nothing about this affair. If I knew he had enough, I just wouldn't say anything and take a chance on getting some to him before he runs out. I'm afraid to risk it, though, without being pretty sure, because if he did have to shut down, my boss sure would raise cain. Yeah, and Joe called the other day to know how we were coming on that lot we delivered yesterday, said he didn't want to get caught short. But Joe always does that. He starts crowding you for things long before he actually needs them. He seems to think no one will keep their promises unless he rides them. If I ask Joe how much he has on hand, he will suspect something and I will have to tell him.

Guess I better not take a chance on Joe. I will have to tell my boss first. But gee, how I hate to tell him! I know just what he will think. I know I should have remembered to order more when we spoiled that first run, but I was so busy getting caught up that I forgot. Anyway, you never would expect the stockroom to be out of a standard item like that. And if they ran this place right, they never would be. But my boss won't care about that. All he'll think is that I must be asleep on the job. He expects me to keep track of everything; and if I have to do the stock-room's job for them to keep my job going, he expects me to do that. What will I tell him, anyway, that won't make me look like a fool who doesn't know his job? Maybe I better not tell him now. It won't hurt to wait till tomorrow, and maybe then the stockroom will know when I can expect the rod. Maybe they will do better than Friday, and I might squeeze by. When I do tell the boss, I want to be able to tell him just when we will be able to start on the job again, and maybe I can plan it so we won't hold up the assembly. Guess I will wait till tomorrow and see what I can figure out.)

And Bob spends the rest of the day in a state of jitters trying to figure a way out of the predicament, or at least a partial solution which he can present to his boss when he finally is forced to tell him. He goes home that night with a terrible grouch, is cross to the children because they are so noisy, gets annoyed with his wife because she seems so cheerful, can hardly eat his supper, sleeps poorly, and hates to go to work the next morning. Such is the human element of communication up the line.

man is comfortable under these conditions, does not worry about the presence of the department chief, and need not cover up mistakes or try to protect the group. In many instances of this kind, the whole department stands as a unit against outside pressures or against demands from above. These are the most comfortable and satisfactory work situations for the foreman and for the workers.

THE FOREMAN, COMMUNICATION, AND MORALE

As we have seen, a foreman is in constant contact with the workers and has the respon-sibility of putting into action many of management's policies and decisions. He is the one who interprets management to the workers; he is, to a large degree, the only representative of management with whom the workers have much contact; he is the one who imposes management's controls upon them. For these reasons he influences the workers' attitudes toward the job, management, and the company generally. He is the one who can most directly affect their morale and loyalty. While his importance to employee morale has long been recognized, recent studies have shown that in many respects he is also the most important factor in the work situation.

Caution: The above description of the complications and limitations of communication, especially through the line of authority, might give the impression that communication between levels in the industrial status system is completely ineffectual. Actually, of course, this is not true. People at the bottom of the structure do produce the goods, and those at the top do control production and maintain their authority over those below. But because of the nature of man-boss relations and because it and other status relations in the system are neither clearly recognized nor understood, communication sometimes actually interferes with satisfactory work relations and effective production.

Section 6 Interest groups and leadership

Those who do the same work or occupy similar positions within an organization have similar experiences and problems; their attitudes and evaluations distinguish them from other participants; they share a stake in existing social arrangements. This social differentiation significantly affects (1) the division of labor out of which, indeed, it largely arises, and (2) the distribution of power.

Some attention has already been given to the emergence of groups based on shared life situations, for example, soldier groups in a modern army. These primary groups are also products of social differentiation and can act as interest groups. But interest groups are not necessarily primary groups. They may take many forms within large organizations, from small informal groups of workers seeking protection from potentially arbitrary supervision to the large department that can win the loyalty of its members and therefore act as a social unit. Some internal interest groups are weak; others are strong. Some muster support only from within the enterprise or association; others find external allies. For example, the Army Corps of Engineers acts as an interest group within the U.S. Government, but it is also supported by private associations outside the government, such as the National Rivers and Harbors Congress. Some interest groups coincide with the formal structure and transform technical units into unities of persons. Other interest groups cut across the officially approved lines of communication and weaken the formal structure.

INTEREST GROUPS AND THE DIVISION OF LABOR

In many large organizations, the formation of interest groups is an expected and desired outcome of the division of labor. At least some of the units of a complex administrative structure foster particular standards or aims. The personnel department upholds standards of employee selection and training; accounting is supposed to maintain standards of reporting and fiscal control; the sales department protects lines of communication to buyers; production is committed to a schedule of output. All of these units are expected to defend the values as well as to execute the functions entrusted to them. They become interest groups, often vigorously promoting their special aims and methods. Within limits, and depending on the type of organization, some competition and even conflict among units may be tolerated, because the directors are then confident that each unit is making the most of its potentialities. It is presumed, of course, that top officials are able to settle the resulting conflicts and hold the competing groups to the aims of the organization as a whole. The amount of leeway permitted internal interest groups depends largely on the extent to which the organization wishes to encourage initiative developed from below. A university, for example, must depend on the initiative of its academic departments to develop their respective fields of knowledge. These departments often act as interest groups, pressing for recognition and increased budgets and protecting standards of education and research.

A good example of the social differentiation that produces interest groups is the staff-line conflict reported in Adaptation 20, pages 244–47. Dalton shows that the difference between staff officials and line supervisors is not merely one of job assignment. It extends to their images of themselves and of each other, and it reflects the insecurities they feel on the job. This differentiation is strongly influenced by the social backgrounds of the staff personnel, including both attributes that are developed within the factory and characteristics they bring with them from their earlier social experience. In this case, as in the case of the Hawthorne bank wiremen (Adaptation 11, pp. 147–50), the formal division of labor leads to a cleavage of interests and attitudes.

Just as in the society as a whole, some groups are stronger than others because of their greater ability to influence opinion or to control essential activities and resources. The struggle for power is usually less obvious in special-purpose organizations than in society at large. Partly because of this covert quality, an important phase of the sociological study of organizations is the discovery of the relative strength and weakness of the constituent groups, not as defined by formal position alone but as conditioned by their place within the social structure of the enterprise.

The Dalton study reflects this interest. One of its main themes is the relative weakness of the staff compared with the line, but this is only partly due to the formal authority of the top line officials. The staff personnel are also dependent on line officers who are *not* formally their superiors. The staff men (who often seek promotion through transfer to the line organization) are dependent because of their problems of advancement and because the line supervisors can interfere with the work of the staff. Similar cases of conflict among officials in government, business, and other organizations have been reported, though few have been so carefully documented and analyzed. For example, a perennial strain is expected between the sales and production divisions in businesses, and there is often a marked difference in perspective, influence, and career line between the teaching and administrative groups in schools and colleges.

SELF-PERPETUATING LEADERSHIP

The leaders and executives of large organizations tend to develop special interests that set them apart from the rank and file. A classic analysis of this development and its consequences is summarized in Adaptation 21. Michels describes (1) the divergence of interest between rank-and-file members of political parties and their leaders who have a stake or interest in the positions to which they have been elected, and (2) the ability of men who control the organizational machinery to protect their vested interests and perpetuate their tenure in office.

There has been much controversy about the interpretation of Michels' thesis. Some claim it means that democracy is impossible. Actually, however, he meant that democracy is limited by its need for leadership, a need it shares with all other forms of organization. More important, Michels indicated certain inherent dangers in the democratic process that must be taken account of and guarded against. He suggested that when a voluntary political association becomes a militant, disciplined "action" organization, in distinction to a loose grouping of like-minded individuals, tendencies toward oligarchy are likely to appear. There is, of course, no implication that every organization is or must become controlled by a tight oligarchy.

A similar pattern in the modern corporation was identified by Berle and Means.[7] In the very large corporation there is a wide *dispersion of stock ownership:* no individual or group owns more than a small fraction of the total shares. For example, in 1929 no one owned more than 1 per cent of the outstanding stock of the Pennsylvania Railroad, American Telephone and Telegraph, or United States Steel. Breaking ownership into tiny fragments permits the massing of large quantities of capital for industrial development but the individual stockholder can then have only a small voice in the company's affairs.

With dispersion of stock ownership, there arises a *separation of ownership and control* which is most marked in cases of "management control."

When the largest single interest amounts to but a fraction of one per cent—the case in several of the largest American corporations—no stockholder is in the position through his holdings alone to place important pressure upon management or to use his holdings as a considerable nucleus for the accumulation of the majority votes necessary to control. . . . In such companies where does control lie? To answer that question, it is necessary to examine in greater detail the conditions surrounding the electing of the board of directors. In the election of the board the stockholder ordinarily has three alternatives. He can refrain from voting, he can attend the annual meeting and personally vote his stock, or he can sign a proxy transferring his voting power to certain individuals selected by the management of the corporation, the proxy committee. As his personal vote will count for little or nothing at the meeting unless he has a very large block of stock, the stockholder is practically reduced to the alternative of not voting at all or else of *handing over his vote to individuals over whom he has no control and in whose selection he did not participate.* In neither case will he be able to exercise any measure of control. Rather, control will tend to be in the hands of those who select the proxy committee by whom, in turn, the election of directors for the ensuing period may be made. Since the proxy committee is appointed by the existing management, the latter can virtually dictate their own successors. Where ownership is sufficiently subdivided, the management can thus become a self-perpetuating body even though its share in the ownership is negligible.[8]

Insofar as the managers are no longer the simple agents of the owners, subject to easy removal, there is always the possibility that they will act in their own interests, which are not always identical with those of the ordinary stockholder. Sometimes the controlling group can profit more at the expense of the company than by making profits for it. Even though most corporate managers may be responsible and devoted to their companies' interests, this *danger* in self-perpetuating leadership is widely recognized.

The foregoing conclusions must be qualified by two points:

1. A member of a special-purpose organization, such as a union, corporation, or political party, usually gives only a small portion of his total life to the organization. The leaders, however, give much greater attention and energy. This difference in degree of involvement influences the relative ability of members and leaders to control decision-making, including the choice of new leaders. In many organizations, the members abdicate their theoretical right to make decisions, even important ones. They are quite happy to have someone else take over the task as long as *their own special interests* (for example, the continued flow of reasonable dividends) are not severely damaged. In trade-unions, con-

---

[7] A. A. Berle and G. C. Means, *The Modern Corporation and Private Property* (New York: Macmillan, 1933).

[8] *Ibid.,* pp. 84, 86–88. Reprinted by permission of The Macmillan Company.

MANAGEMENT PROXY   THE NEW YORK CENTRAL RAILROAD COMPANY

403747

The undersigned Stockholder(s) of said Company hereby appoint(s) WM. WHITE, HAROLD S. VANDERBILT, JAMES A. FARLEY, WILLIAM E. LEVIS and SIDNEY C. MURRAY, or any one of them, to vote as the attorney and proxy of the undersigned at the Annual Meeting of the Stockholders of said Company, appointed to be held in the Armory, 195 Washington Avenue, in the City of Albany, New York, on Wednesday, May 26, 1954, at 12 o'clock Noon, E. D. S. T., and at any adjournment thereof, in respect of the following matters set forth in said Company's Proxy Statement, receipt of which is hereby acknowledged: (1) for the election of Directors of said Company and of Inspectors of Election; (2) Against ( ) or For ( ) proposed Resolution No. 1, relating to cumulative voting; (3) Against ( ) or For ( ) proposed Resolution No. 2, relating to change of date of Annual Meeting (management favors a vote against each of these Resolutions); and (4) in their discretion in the transaction of each other business as may be lawfully brought before the meeting; and in the name of the undersigned to act and vote at such meeting, and at any adjournment thereof, according to the number of shares of stock which the undersigned would be entitled to vote, and as fully as the undersigned could do, if personally present, with full power of substitution to them or any one of them; hereby ratifying all action of said proxies or any of them or their or his substitutes or substitute by virtue hereof; and hereby revoking any authorization to vote such shares heretofore given by the undersigned to anyone. A majority of such of my attorneys and proxies, their substitutes or substitute, as shall be present and shall act at said meeting (or if only one be present and act, then that one) shall have and may exercise all of the powers of all of said attorneys and proxies hereunder. It is understood that the shares represented hereby will be voted against adoption of said Resolutions Nos. 1 and 2, unless a contrary direction is indicated by the

Dated and signed, _____ 1954.

THIS IS YOUR PROXY

Proxy for the
Alleghany-Young-Kirby Ownership Board
The New York Central Railroad Company

The undersigned, a holder of stock in THE NEW YORK CENTRAL RAILROAD COMPANY, hereby appoints ROBERT R. YOUNG, ALLAN P. KIRBY, THOMAS J. DEEGAN, Jr. and CHARLES T. IRELAND, Jr., the proxies, and each of them (with full power to act without the other), the proxy of the undersigned (with full power of substitution in each), for and in the name of the undersigned to attend the Annual Meeting of the stockholders of said Company to be held at the Armory, 195 Washington Ave., in the City of Albany, New York (or at such other place as the Company in any notice of said meeting shall legally appoint), on May 26, 1954, at 12:00 o'clock noon, and there, or at any adjournment thereof, to vote the number of votes or shares of stock which the undersigned would be entitled to vote if then personally present, with respect to (1) the election of fifteen Directors of said Company and of three Inspectors of Election at the meeting, (2) for ☐ against ☐ the proposal for cumulative voting; (3) for ☐ against ☐ the proposal to change the date of the annual meeting and (4) in the transaction of such other business as may properly be brought before such meeting or any adjournment or adjournments thereof; hereby ratifying and confirming all that said proxies, or any of them, or their substitute or substitutes, may lawfully do or cause to be done by virtue hereof; and hereby revoking any authorization to vote such shares heretofore given by the undersigned to anyone.

Dated and signed, _____, 1954.

(Signature of Stockholder)

Please execute exactly as your name appears to the left. A corporate proxy should be signed by its president or vice-president and its seal should be affixed. When signing as attorney, executor, administrator, trustee or guardian, please give your full title as such. For joint accounts, each joint owner should sign personally.

PLEASE SIGN AND RETURN PROXY IN ACCOMPANYING PREPAID ENVELOPE
PLEASE DO IT NOW!

Proxies Mailed To Central Stockholders

NEW YORK, April 8 (P)—
The fight for control of the New York Central Railroad was tossed into the homes of 40,000 shareholders today.

The starting gun for this new phase of the battle went off when the railroad announced that April 19 was the record date for stock eligible to vote at the annual stockholders' meeting May 26.

Within a few hours, both the management group headed by William White, Central's president, and the opposition forces, led by financier Robert R. Young, were dispatching bales of proxy material.

It was placed in the mail hastily with the aim of getting to the stockholder first and with the heaviest punch.

The management's proxy statement showed that the present 15 directors who seek re-election own 106,622 shares, or 1.6 per cent of the 6,447,410 shares of outstanding common.

VOTING STRENGTH

White stated, however, that this total by no means represents the management's aggregate voting strength.

The opposition proxy statement showed that its nominees own 1,089,880 shares and that an additional 30,000 shares is held by companies controlled by one nominee, Daniel E. Taylor of Norfolk, Va.

This brings the opposition total to 1,118,880 shares, or 17.4 per cent. It includes the 800,000 shares bought from the Chesapeake & Ohio Railway by Young's Texas friends, Clinton W. Murchison and Sidney Richardson.

CHASE BANK

The Central, however, has attacked the validity of the transfer of this stock to the two Texans and challenged the right of the stock to be voted unless proper papers are filed before the record date.

Management's proxy material stated that the Chase National Bank of New York is still the record holder of the 800,000 shares and "as of the date of this proxy statement such shares have not been transferred on the books of the company."

Sparks Fly at N. Y. Central Meeting

Proxy Count Expected Next Week

ALBANY, N. Y., May 26 (P)—
The bitter war for control of the vast New York Central Railroad was climaxed today as 2000 stockholders assembled in a meeting marred by disorder and confusion—but the result of the fight may not be known for days.

The meeting in an armory recessed, after a noisy four hours and forty minutes, until noon Tuesday, when election inspectors will report on the tabulation of stock voted.

Until then no one will have official word on whether the management headed by William White, Central president, will remain in the saddle or whether it has been unseated by the opposition forces of Texas-born financier Robert R. Young.

OFFICIAL REPORT

White said tabulation of the vote for the new board of directors would take at least until Tuesday when the election inspectors are due to make their first official report.

But Young claimed an overwhelming victory.

"We have deposited proxies for more than a majority of the outstanding stock, so that if every share is voted we will still be elected," Young asserted.

Young, however, has been making claims for victory for weeks, as has management.

SINCE FEBRUARY

The fight for the $2,600,000,000 railroad, the world's second biggest, has raged since February. The Central board then rejected Young's demand for the board chairmanship and a directorship for his associate, Allan P. Kirby, president of Alleghany Corp.,

which Young heads as board chairman.

Three inspectors of election—each a law professor—are scheduled to go into session from 9 a. m. to 8 p. m., daily, without holidays, until the vote count is complete.

One informed source predicted the count could take weeks.

White gaveled the meeting to order promptly at noon and promised that it would be conducted "in a fair and orderly manner."

But the proceedings were thrown into confusion an hour later, after White had disposed of preliminaries, and the polls were opened, as

Mrs. Vilma Soss, president of the Women Shareholders of American Business Inc., challenged the agenda of the meeting.

"There should be discussion before the voting," she shouted. "I protest the legality of this meeting."

She mounted the steps to the platform and began to argue with White.

The meeting went out of control as hundreds of stockholders milled toward the platform amid noise and confusion.

Proceedings came to a dead halt as a uniformed railroad patrolman took Mrs. Soss firmly by the arm and led her back to the floor.

White ordered the polls open at 12:51 p. m. (EDT) and stockholders formed three long lines before a large steel-meshed teller's area in a corner of the huge Armory.

Young entered the meeting with a known total of 1,118,880

shares or 17.4 per cent of Central's 6,447,410 shares of outstanding common. Management's estimated strength ahead of the meeting was 256,122 shares or almost 4 per cent.

The largest single block of stock outstanding, 800,000 shares owned by Young's Texas friends, Clint W. Murchison and Sid W. Richardson, were voted on a single ballot each—400,000 shares apiece. Shortly after they were voted, a State Court ruled that the action, contested by management, was legal.

Both Young and White came to Albany on a special stockholders' train from New York city. Each greeted as many of the approximately 1000 stockholders, riding the two sections, as he could.

Fig. **VII:7**   New York Central Railroad Proxy Fight

sumer co-operatives, political parties, and corporations, it is usually difficult to get more than a handful of members to attend the meetings where organizational decisions are made.

If members could always intervene when their welfare is threatened, there would be less reason for concern. But when members abdicate their power in normal periods, the incumbent leaders are able to consolidate their positions. Leaders can usually meet all but the most determined and well-organized assaults of an aroused membership. In practice only severe crises bring out the members, and even then the outcome may be in doubt.

2. The relatively weak status of members can be improved if they band together in organized factions. Then they are no longer lone individuals against powerful leaders. New power centers within the organization are created, and if these are strong enough, they can call the leaders to account. This is of course what happens in the organization of pressure groups and parties in a political democracy. But the social conditions in spe-

cial-purpose organizations, particularly the narrowness of member interests, do not easily sustain permanent opposition groups which can mobilize opinion and supply alternative leadership.

The analyses of Michels and of Berle and Means, discussed above, call attention to a basic trend in large-scale organizations toward the creation of self-perpetuating oligarchies. It should not be concluded, however, that leaders of corporations or trade-unions are never challenged or ousted. In fact, this does occur, and in 1954 the business pages of American newspapers carried a number of stories of internal contests for control of large corporations, the most notable of which was the successful effort of a financier to oust the incumbent management of the New York Central Railroad. (See Fig. VII:7.) Internal conflicts are exceptional, however. Although an appeal to the stockholder is necessary, controversies presume a rather high degree of organization on the part of an opposition that is prepared to take over control.

Staff-Line Conflict in Industry

Abridged and adapted from "Conflicts Between Staff and Line Managerial Officers," by Melville Dalton, *American Sociological Review,* June, 1950, pp. 342–51. Published in this form by permission of Melville Dalton and the *American Sociological Review.*

This is a study of social differentiation and its consequences in two major groups of management: the line organization and the staff organization. *The line* consists of the foremen and their superiors who direct the actual work done and who are responsible for production. *The staff organization* consists of specialists who have a research and advisory function in the plant. Staff groups are relatively new in industry. They provide specialized knowledge and technical advice in such

diverse fields as chemistry, statistics, public and industrial relations, personnel, accounting, and engineering.

Data on staff-line relations in this study were drawn from three industrial plants in related industries. They range in size from 4,500 to 20,000 employees and from 200 to nearly 1,000 management officials.

THE PROBLEM

The staff has specialized knowledge gained from training and research. In theory it applies this knowledge to problem areas and advises the busy line officers how they can increase production and efficiency. The ideal situation involves two assumptions: (1) that the staff specialists are reasonably content to function without a measure of formal authority and are content with their advisory role; and (2) that their suggestions for improvements are welcomed by the line officers and carried out. This study examines how these assumptions and the theoretical ideal are affected by the actual relations of the two groups as they work out their distinctive problems.

It must be emphasized that the staff-line conflict discussed here is only one of many frictions in the plants. For instance, there is competition and tension among departments, among individuals, and between union and management.

SOURCES OF FRICTION

There are two major sources of friction between the staff and line in the plants considered. One is the *social background* or composition of the two groups, that is, the personal characteristics they bring to the plant. The other source of friction is the differentiation that takes place within the plant, the differences in *social position* they assume once there.

Social Composition

The two groups differ in age, formal education, and social behavior (appearance, manners, etc.).

1. *Age*. The staff members on the average are significantly younger than the line officers. This is a source of friction revealed in the ill-concealed attitude of the older line officers. They resent receiving what they regard as instructions from younger men. The staff officers often attribute their lack of success in "selling ideas" to the line to this attitude. As one assistant staff chief remarked: "We're always in hot water with these old guys on the line. You can't tell them a damn thing. They're bull-headed as hell! Most of the time we offer a suggestion it's either laughed at or

not considered at all. The same idea in the mouth of some old codger on the line'd get a round of applause. They treat us like kids."

2. *Education*. The staff members necessarily have more education than the line officers. Education is part of the qualifications for staff jobs; experience is emphasized in the choice of line officers. The staff is in a position to exploit this difference in education, and it probably contributes to a feeling of superiority among them. The line, however, resents the proposals of the staff because of the educational difference involved as well as the age differential. The line often refers to the staff as "college punks," "slide-rules," "crackpots," and "chair-warmers."

3. *Social behavior*. Attention to personal appearance, cosmopolitan recreational tastes, facility in speaking and writing, poise and polish in social intercourse—these also distinguish the staff from the line. The line receives occasional snubs from the staff and feels that their emphasis on social prestige is a threat to the line man's own position and not in the best interests of the plant. To quote a line officer on the matter of social intercourse during the working day: "They don't go into the cafeteria to eat and relax while they talk over their problems. They go in there to look around and see how somebody is dressed or to talk over the hot party they had last night. Well, that kind of damn stuff don't go with me. I haven't any time to put on airs and make out I'm something I'm not."

Social Position Within the Plant

The different functions the two groups perform in the plant and the different opportunities they have for advancement, salary, power, prestige, and responsibility are major sources of friction.

1. *Chances for advancement*. Line officers have better chances for advancement than staff personnel for at least three reasons: (*a*) there are approximately twice as many positions of authority in the line; (*b*) the line or-

ganization reaches higher, for it has six status levels whereas the staff has only three; (*c*) line salaries for comparable positions are usually higher.

2. *The staff is on trial.* Continuous dispute over the relative worth of the two groups is another source of friction. The line regards the staff as on trial rather than as a managerial division of equal importance. To the line officer, his authority over production is something sacred, and he resents the implication that after many years in the line he needs the guidance of an inexperienced newcomer. He is ready with charges of "crack-pot experimentation" and "costly blunders" by the staff. The lower foremen are inclined to suspect that the staff is less an engineering and technical assistance division than a weapon of top management to control the lower line officers.

The staff member is painfully aware of these feelings and of the need of his group to prove its worth. He feels bound to contribute something significant in the form of ideas helpful to management. By virtue of his greater education and knowledge of the latest theories of production, the staff man regards himself as a management consultant, an expert. He feels that he must be, or appear to be, almost infallible once he has committed himself to top management on some point. Whereas in practice adoption of their suggestions depends upon the amount of co-operation that can be won from line officers, the staff prefer to see themselves as agents of top management, independent of the lower line, and superior to it.

3. *The line resists innovation.* The different pressures upon the staff and upon the line in day-to-day operations create additional tension. As we have seen, the staff must make contributions in the form of suggested changes in order to prove its worth. But it is the line that is called on to change its work habits. The experienced line officer fears being "shown up" before his superiors for not having thought of improvements himself. Moreover, changes in methods may bring

personnel changes which threaten to break up cliques and other informal arrangements and to reduce the line officer's area of authority. Or such changes may expose forbidden practices and departmental inefficiency and waste. In some cases these fears have led line officers to strike informal bargains with the staff to postpone the initiation of new practices for a period of time in exchange for some other co-operation from the line.

The pressure on staff personnel is to develop new techniques, but they also have to consider how their plans will be received by the line. They know from experience that lower line officers can give a "black eye" to staff contributions by deliberate malpractices. Line officers may verbally accept a change, but they are in a position to sabotage it in practice. For this reason, there is a tendency for staff members to withhold improved production schemes when they know an attempt to introduce them might fail or bring personal disrepute.

The study found evidence that the accommodation of staff to line demands included the manipulation (but not embezzlement) of company funds. Pressures from the lower line organization forced some staff groups to "kick over" some of the funds appropriated for staff use. The line was then able to hide inefficiencies and meet the constant pressure from the top to show low operating costs. In return the staff received more co-operation from the line in accepting innovations, and some staff personnel who wished transfer to the line were recommended.

WEAKNESS OF THE STAFF

It is clear in the plants studied that the line is the more powerful branch of management. The position of the staff is weak and defensive. This is due to its lack of authority over production and its dependence upon top management for approval and for advancement.

The ultimate authority in the plant rests with top *line* officials. Usually, they have risen to the top by way of the line organization. They understand and sympathize with the daily problems of the line in getting the main work done, and their functions as top officials bring them close to the day-to-day pressures and responsibilities of the line. Top officials also have influence over promotions in the higher staff positions. A staff member knows that if he aspires to one of the higher staff jobs, or wishes to transfer to the line, he must satisfy the top line officer. The staff member must show his ability to work with the line and to understand its problems. He must make contributions the line will accept, and be able to minimize the conflicts occasioned by the social differences in background and role we have described.

Conclusion

The ideal conception of staff-line relations assumes that the staff is willing to function in an advisory capacity and that the line is willing to accept staff suggestions for improvement. The sources of tension inherent in this situation have been described. One result is a morale problem among new staff members, reflected in disillusionment and high turnover.

The new staff member, often selected because of his academic record, enters industry prepared to engage in logical, well-formulated relations with other members of management, and to carry out the precise, methodical functions for which he has been trained. He believes he has much to contrib-

ute and that his efforts will win early recognition and rapid advancement. He soon discovers that his freedom to function is snared in a web of informal commitments, that his academic specialty may not be relevant to his actual assignments, and that he must learn who the informally powerful line officers are and what ideas they welcome. The result is a disillusionment that contributes to a relatively high turnover of younger staff personnel.

In the plants studied, ambitious staff men, frustrated by the relatively low hierarchy through which they could move, appeared eager to increase the number of personnel under their authority. And in fact the personnel of staff groups did increase disproportionately to those of the line. There was also a trend of personnel movement from staff to line, presumably reflecting the drive, ambition, and qualifications of staff members who were striving for positions of authority, prestige, and higher income.

In general, staff-line friction reduces the distinctive contribution of staff personnel. Their relatively weak position, requiring accommodation to the line, tends to restrict their ability to engage in free, experimental innovation. On the other hand, the natural resistance of the line to staff innovations probably usefully restrains over-eager efforts to apply untested procedures on a large scale. The conflicts, however, introduce an uncontrolled element into the managerial system. Under such conditions, it is difficult to know when valuable ideas are being sacrificed.

The "Iron Law" of Oligarchy

A summary and interpretation of *Political Parties: A Sociological Study of the Oligarchical Tendencies of Modern Democracy* by Robert Michels (Glencoe: The Free Press, 1949). First published in English in 1915. Quoted material used by permission of The Free Press.

"Who says organization says oligarchy." With these words the German political sociologist, Robert Michels (1876–1936), summed up his famous "iron law of oligarchy."

ADAPTATION 21

Although his "law" is stated in unqualified form, Michels' analysis showed *not* that organization alone leads to oligarchy (the control by a few), but rather that certain kinds of organization have that tendency, and then only when certain additional processes are at work. The study was based mainly on the history of socialist and trade-union organizations in Europe before the first World War.

His influential book attempts to trace a connection between the basic necessities of organization and the evolution of self-perpetuating oligarchies. Following Michels' argument, we shall first consider the general need for organization and then the special circumstances that make for the drift to oligarchy.

THE NEED FOR ORGANIZATION

1. *Democratic action, like any action that strives for definite ends, requires organization.* In any group, especially in one where disciplined action is required, there is a division of labor. This simple, fairly obvious statement is the starting point of the argument.

2. *Organized, concerted action requires the delegation of special tasks, responsibilities, and powers to a few leaders.* This is a special phase of the division of labor. No organization of any size or duration can exist without leaders. Someone has to organize meetings or determine the consensus of opinion, represent the group and its decisions to other organizations or the public, and make the countless small and large decisions that are necessary to carry out its aims.

The degree of organization and the importance of leadership vary with the size of the group, the permanence of its aims, and the complexity of the organization. In a small undifferentiated group leadership may be but weakly developed; leaders arise spontaneously and serve temporarily, unofficially, and without many rewards. The leaders remain members of the group, sharing its interests and influenced by the same social conditions as the members. Since the group is small, all

or most members may participate in decisions and actions. The delegated authority is limited and temporary and may be exercised by any member.

The mere fact of organization, that is, the division of labor generally and delegation of tasks and powers to leaders, *is not in itself undemocratic.* The conditions that give rise to oligarchy have not yet been stated. Michels develops his thesis in the *additional* processes that can be expected once this division of labor has been established.

CONDITIONS MAKING FOR OLIGARCHY

1. *The delegation of tasks and powers to leaders results in a concentration of skills and informal prerogatives in their hands.* Not all members can perform the tasks of leadership in complex organizations. The jobs become specialized and require experience, knowledge, and individual aptitude.

a. Administrative skills are required to keep the organization functioning and to get things done. Relations with the outside world, such as diplomacy, collective bargaining, or public relations, require technical skills that the leaders alone possess. Their skills set them apart from the rank and file, and social differentiation begins. This specialization makes the members dependent on the leaders in office, because they are the ones who can keep things going and get things done that further the aims of the group. The dependence of the rank and file—a central theme in Michels' work—makes the leaders indispensable and hence gives them increased power.

b. Leadership carries prerogatives. When he chooses the organization's staff, the leader can select men whose first loyalty is to him. Thus personal machines are built. Leaders also control the channels of information within an organization, and their control gives them special access to and influence over the opinions of the members. These prerogatives and similar opportunities that characterize the social position of leadership tend to make leaders independent of the rank and file, and the power inherent in the concentration of skills is consolidated.

2. *The position of leaders is strengthened by the members' political indifference and by their sense of obligation to those who guide them and do the main work.* The ordinary member does not have the inclination or time to participate in the demanding, complex tasks of an organization, and he is glad to have the work done by someone else. Moreover, he recognizes his own incompetence compared with the skills of his leaders. The rank and file then submit willingly rather than reluctantly to the widening power of the officials.

3. *The concentration of skills and prerogatives in the leaders' hands and the willing submission of the rank and file create opportunities for the self-perpetuation of the leaders.* It is not surprising that they take advantage of this and try to stay in office. Michels holds that leaders try to keep their power because it is inherent in human nature to seek power and retain it. "The desire to dominate, for good or for evil, is universal." (Michels, p. 206) This is a dubious and unnecessary assumption, and perhaps Michels' weakest point.

He gives other more acceptable reasons for the self-perpetuation of leaders. Certainly leaders have a desire for personal security, and the prerogatives of leadership give them social status distinct from the ordinary members. They wish to retain their status and prerogatives, including the accustomed way of living and type of employment. The union official resists returning to the shop. Leaders may also believe sincerely that they are serving the best interests of the organization and that a threat to them is a threat to the group as a whole.

4. *Self-perpetuation of leaders tends toward subversion of the aims of the organization.* If leaders are independent of rank and file control, there is a temptation to use the organizational machinery and power to fur-

ther personal aims, a condition which results from the absence of effective democratic control. There is a divergence of interest between the leaders and the led, and leaders follow policies that may not serve the aims for which the group was organized.

Because he was studying social reform movements, Michels was especially interested in the subversion that comes from the conservatism of oligarchic leadership; the objective of stability and security for the organization (and for the leaders) is put above all other action aims. Action is slow and cautious, risks are minimized, powerful enemies are placated, and aims are modified to assure stability. There was a strong tendency among the trade-unions of Europe to move from revolutionary to more conservative aims once they had achieved extensive membership, financial security, and discipline. Organization was necessary for the achievement of the original goals, and it introduced new interests that modified group aims.

5. *Oligarchy is inherent in democracy and cannot be eliminated.* Michels holds that the social differentiation between leaders and led is universal. This does not mean that tyranny abounds everywhere but that there is a predisposition to oligarchy which requires definite social checks. "Nothing but a serene and frank examination of the oligarchical dangers of democracy will enable us to minimize these dangers, even though they can never be entirely avoided." (Michels, p. 408)

To minimize the dangers, it is necessary to capitalize on a counter-tendency of democracy to stimulate and strengthen the individual's aptitude for criticism and control. "This predisposition towards free inquiry, in which we cannot fail to recognize one of the most precious factors of civilization, will gradually increase in proportion as the economic status of the masses undergoes improvement and becomes more stable, and in proportion as they are admitted more effectively to the advantages of civilization. A wider education involves an increasing capacity for exercising control. Can we not observe every day that among the well-to-do the authority of the leaders over the led, extensive though it be, is never so unrestricted as in the case of the leaders of the poor? . . . It is, consequently, the great task of social education to raise the intellectual level of the masses, so that they may be enabled, within the limits of what is possible,

to counteract the oligarchical tendencies of the working-class movement." (Michels, pp. 406 f.)

An equally important regulative principle blocking the oligarchic drift is found in social and political pluralism, that is, the existence of effective opposition groups that challenge the indispensability and self-perpetuation of leaders. Michels does not develop this principle. (See POLITICAL MAN, pp. 707–8.)

Section 7   Institutionalization

In the course of time, the net impact of the processes thus far discussed is to build into the organization many habits, values, vested interests, and other rigidities. The organization reflects its own peculiar history, the people who have been in it, the groups formed, and the way it has adapted to its environment. It becomes more or less institutionalized depending on how much leeway there is for personal and group interaction. The narrower an organization's goals, the more specialized and technical its operations, the less opportunity will there be for social forces to affect its development. A university has more leeway than most businesses, because its goals are less clearly defined and it can give freer play to internal forces and historical adaptation. But no organization of any duration is completely free of institutionalization.

By institutionalization we mean the development of *orderly, stable, socially integrating* forms and structures out of unstable, loosely patterned, or merely technical types of action.[9] Such important institutions as representative democracy and public education contribute

to the integration of the total society, while churches and clubs are only effective within a particular community or group. Stable, highly formalized technical procedures in science and industry, such as those which govern the shipment of freight or the assembly of a complicated machine, do not necessarily contribute to the formation or maintenance of a social group and are, therefore, not institutional. On the other hand, some technical procedures, such as piloting a ship, may symbolize an occupation or profession and take on, for its members, an institutional meaning.

We may distinguish four institutionalizing processes, which perform important functions in the life-history of associations; (1) Formalization, (2) Self-maintenance and conservatism, (3) Infusion with value, and (4) Development of a distinctive social composition and social base.

Formalization

The most obvious type of institutionalization in associations is the development of formal organization. This often emerges out of trial-and-error informal practices, as discussed on page 228. Social integration is directly and explicitly promoted by formal devices of co-ordination and communication

---

[9] Discussions of institutions by Robert C. Angell, Talcott Parsons, and others have emphasized this integrating aspect. See "Institutions and Social Integration" by Werner S. Landecker, *Papers of the Michigan Academy of Science, Arts, and Letters,* **39** (1954).

rather than by spontaneous social bonds. This transformation of informal groups and practices into legally recognized and formally established institutions occurs continuously, not only within associations but in the larger society as well. For example, in the law of domestic relations many pre-existing practices and duties regarding marriage and family life are formalized. Similarly, zoning ordinances in a city often formalize patterns of land use that have already developed in an unplanned way.

Formalization is a way of increasing control. Practices hitherto spontaneous, controlled only by tradition or the give-and-take of personal and group interaction, become subject to explicit rules and limitations. For example, labor-management legislation formalized practices that were already worked out, but at the same time it made collective bargaining subject to greater public scrutiny and control. Nonconformists were brought into line, and links were established between particular practices and the interests or values of the larger community. To take a simpler case, when the informal "coffee break" in an office is formalized, the practice is made legal, but it is also more readily controlled.

Self-maintenance and Conservatism

A living association is a complex social group made up of both formal and informal relations, blending technical aims with personal desires and group interests. The various elements of the association have a stake in its continued existence. Moreover, the aims of the organization usually require a certain permanence and stability. There is a need to accommodate internal interests and adapt to outside forces: (1) to maintain the organization as a "going concern," (2) to minimize risks, and (3) to achieve long-run rather than short-run objectives. The leaders become security-conscious and are often willing to sacrifice quick returns for the sake of stability.

The institutional analysis of trade-unions is concerned, among other things, with the effort of union leaders to win survival and security for their organizations. The history of the labor movement is largely dominated by efforts to win "union security" through provisions for compulsory membership (the closed shop and its variants), for automatic deduction of dues payments from wages (the "check-off"), and for joint consultation with management. These objectives look to the long-run maintenance of the union rather than to immediate gains for the members.

Large corporations are also concerned with institutional security and in recent years have been particularly sensitive to the need for a favorable climate of public opinion. So-called "institutional advertising" reflects this trend. Expensive newspaper and magazine space is bought not to promote sales, at least in the short run, but to build up favorable attitudes toward the corporation and toward business in general.

Infusion with Value

When an individual identifies with an organization or becomes habituated to its methods, or otherwise mixes his personality with it, the organization becomes for him a valued source of personal satisfaction. (See Sec. 4, p. 232.) Administrative changes are difficult when individuals are habituated to and identified with long-established procedures. For example, the shifting of personnel is inhibited when individuals resist changes that threaten personalities. This infusion with value helps to institutionalize the organization, giving it a greater stability and social integration, transforming it from a mere tool into something that is valued for itself.

If an organization is merely an instrument, it will be readily altered or cast aside when a more efficient tool becomes available. Most organizations are thus *expendable*. When value-infusion takes place, however, there is a resistance to change. People feel a sense of personal loss; the "identity" of the group or community seems somehow to be violated;

they bow to economic or technical considerations only reluctantly, with regret. The Marine Corps has this institutional halo, and it resists any administrative measures that would submerge its identity. In 1950, President Truman became irritated with political pressure favoring Marine Corps membership on the Joint Chiefs of Staff. He wrote a letter calling the Marines the Navy's "police force" and likening their "propaganda machine" to Stalin's. This raised a storm of protest which ended with a presidential apology.

From the standpoint of the national community, most of the many thousands of organizations in the country are not highly valued for themselves, although certain principles on which they are based, such as free speech or competition, may have deep cultural roots. With some very important exceptions, such as the Supreme Court, when any particular organization is threatened or dies, no national outcry is heard. On the other hand, special groups or localities are often urged to keep some organization from dying for lack of support. For example, appeals were made to keep various major league baseball teams in their "home" cities. For those who participate directly in an organization, it may acquire much institutional value, yet it may be readily expendable in the eyes of the community.

Development of a Distinctive Social Composition and Social Base

In its day-to-day activities, an organization makes many kinds of decisions. Most are easily revised and have no permanent effect on structure or method. Other decisions, however, are more binding and give an organization a particular "character," especially when the *social composition* of the organization is affected. For example, selective recruiting may bring persons with distinctive backgrounds or orientations into an organization. Sometimes this is done deliberately, e.g., a private school or college attempts to preserve its traditions by admitting students with ap-

propriate family backgrounds. More often the development of a distinctive social composition is gradual and inadvertent, resulting, for example, from the unplanned selectivity that takes place because of the tendency to bring in people who share the backgrounds and perspectives of incumbent personnel. Whether deliberate or not, the result is a membership or personnel characterized by distinctive attitudes and habits of work.

The *social base* of an organization is closely related to its social composition. Many organizations, such as political pressure groups, are connected to a particular clientele or constituency upon whose support they are dependent. Because of this dependency the personnel and methods of the organization tend to reflect the social characteristics of the constituency. Even in business, adaptation to a particular market (by locality or quality of goods) may strongly affect the habits and outlook of the sales and production departments. For example:

The first boats made by Gar Wood were high quality craft, made of the finest materials by master boat builders. Later the company decided to mass-produce a comparatively low cost speed boat for wide distribution. It developed that the entire organization found itself unable to cope with the effort to shift commitments. Workmen and shop supervisors alike continued to be preoccupied with high cost quality craftsmanship. Members of the selling staff, too, could not shift emphasis from "snob appeal" to price appeal. The quality commitment was so strong that an entirely new division—operating in a separate plant hundreds of miles away and therefore recruiting from a different labor market—had to be created to do the job successfully.[10]

Analysis of an organization's social base can reveal the pressures that play upon it and can help one understand its historical evolution and the role it plays in the community. The social base of the American Federation

[10] From notes by the late Edward Boehm, formerly a Vice-President of Gar Wood Industries.

Institutions are known by their meetings. Characteristic campus gatherings are shown here: a dormitory bull session; a students' sing; a seminar, conducted by Robert Frost.

of Labor lay in the craft-organized skilled workers; and the split that led to the formation of the Committee for Industrial Organization (later the Congress of Industrial Organizations) in 1935 reflected the effort to shift that base so as to include the semiskilled workers in the mass production industries. The emergence of new social forces in the American electorate, particularly the labor and minority-group vote, has changed the social base of the Democratic party, with significant consequences for its program and its chances of victory. The Anti-Saloon League was based on the rural Protestant churches from which it drew heavy support but whose influence in American life was waning. (See Adaptation 23, pp. 289 ff.) The structure and policies of the National Association for the Advancement of Colored People were affected by the paucity of leadership in the Negro population and an orientation toward the Negro middle class. (See Adaptation 36, pp. 522 ff.)

The social base of an organization is usually broader than its membership. It is the group toward which the organization is oriented and from which it draws its support. Hence, the social base influences social composition, because it supplies members and leaders. The interdependent relations of so-cial base, membership, and leadership are often quite complex and depend on a number of variables. For example, some minority and immigrant groups, the aged, and the labor movement at certain periods, have been relatively dependent on outsiders for leadership, because skills were lacking within the group, the risks were great, and it was necessary to have people able to communicate effectively with government and with other groups in society. In such cases, the social base may accept leaders, such as demagogues or racketeers, who are not representative or who may not be subject to effective control.

These institutionalizing processes lend stability and integration to an organization but give it a particular stamp and often effectively determine its capabilities and limitations. During the New Deal the older agricultural agencies in government were bypassed, and new agencies were created to administer new programs. It was felt that the older organizations had become institutionalized; they had assumed ways of working and attitudes toward government operations and made allies in the farm community. Consequently, it was difficult for them to undertake programs requiring a fresh approach. The assessment of organizations from this standpoint is a major problem of policy and administration.

Chapter VIII

Collective behavior

Introduction

By common agreement the term "collective behavior" designates the study of relatively *unstructured* social situations and their products such as crowds, riots, revivals, rumor, public opinion, fads and social movements. These phenomena are characterized by behavior that is not fully controlled by cultural norms and ordered social relations. In such situations there is room for free play of emotions, for a high degree of personal interaction and influence, for the give and take of political competition, and for the emergence of transitory opinions and allegiances.

Collective behavior is important, not only because riots make headlines and sometimes affect great events, but also because spontaneous activities may give rise to new norms and values. The early phases of social change are usually marked by unstructured forms of action. The organization of workers often began in spontaneous protests against some immediate threat to jobs or wages. Many of the more respectable religious denominations of today originated in religious movements that excited crowd behavior. (See Adaptation 31, p. 431.) Once-popular fads, such as wearing wrist-watches, collars attached to shirts, and low-cut shoes, have become customary. The study of collective behavior illuminates the dynamics of social change and the ways new customs and institutions become established.

Through collective behavior new forms of action and new groups are created in response to felt needs, pressures, and excitements, rather than as a result of consciously coordinated activity. The development of informal structure in associations is a product of collective behavior. (See ASSOCIATIONS, p. 227.) On the other hand, collective behavior is usually combined with less spontaneous forms of social control. This combination has marked some of the most important events in history, particularly mass protests and insurrections. (See Adaptation 45, pp. 698 ff.)

It should be emphasized that collective behavior is part of the everyday life of society, though it does not always take dramatic form. In studying collective behavior the social world is viewed from the standpoint of action, of constant regrouping and continuously changing perspectives. There is always some degree of unstructuredness in human situations, if only because situations are never exactly alike and the rules cannot fully take account of uniqueness. However, some circumstances are more likely than others to elicit spontaneous activity.

GENERAL CONDITIONS OF COLLECTIVE BEHAVIOR

Three general conditions characterize relatively unstructured and unstable situations:

1. *Absence or weakness of social forms.* Where existing social arrangements do not prescribe what is proper and acceptable behavior, people are obliged to improvise. A crisis or disaster, such as a flood or famine, a revolution or an invasion, is something for which people are usually unprepared. Action is called for, yet routines to cope with the emergency are lacking or inadequate. The ordinary and orderly processes of communication break down, and rumors, often exaggerated and fear-provoking, take their place. Panic may result. In a pioneer country where law-enforcement agencies are weak or nonexistent, vigilante groups often go beyond their legitimate limits.

In crowds, for example, people come into contact with each other outside the restraining influence of a social structure. Race riots, for example, happen where individuals of different races encounter each other but have no pattern of social relations to guide and direct their behavior. Religious expressions of the Holy Roller variety occur in churches with little social organization.

2. *Ambiguous and open decisions.* Especially in a democratic society, much government policy is deliberately left undetermined, waiting upon the expression of public opinion. While a broad framework of orderly rules is maintained, decisions are not reached by agreement on a traditional and commonly accepted authority but are worked out in the interplay of competing interest groups. It is assumed that public opinion is not predetermined and fixed but may be influenced. As political contests progress, appeals may take on the emotional character associated with collective behavior.

3. *Changed perspectives and values.* Innovations, such as the growth of factory technology, bring about changes in goals and outlooks. Old ways are questioned, and pressure is exerted on custom and tradition. A period of fluidity ensues. When the prevailing patterns cannot be readily changed in prescribed ways, individuals often band together outside the official framework. Such conditions make for social movements, often with radical ideologies and a high degree of emotional involvement. If the movement is successful and its new perspectives are accepted, institutionalization occurs and the collective behavior aspects diminish in importance.

These conditions, widespread in modern society, lend importance to the study of spontaneous and temporary social relations and groups. Section 2 discusses group behavior based on emotional contagion. Section 3 deals with publics, public opinion, and propaganda. Section 4 reviews collective behavior and social change.

Collective behavior, socialization, and the study of primary groups are the fields in sociology most closely related to psychology. Indeed, they are often studied and taught under the title "social psychology." An understanding of these topics depends in part on the development of knowledge about human motivation, emotion, perception, and communication. In sociology the chief concern is with the social conditions that produce collective behavior and the effect it has on group conflict, morale, consensus, and changing patterns of social organization.

SOURCES AND READINGS

GENERAL WORKS:

Herbert Blumer, "Collective Behavior," in A.M. Lee (ed.), *New Outline of the Principles of Sociology* (New York: Barnes & Noble, 1951).

Joseph Klapper, *Effects of Mass Communication* (Glencoe: The Free Press, 1960).

R. T. LaPiere, *Collective Behavior* (New York: McGraw-Hill, 1938).

Wilbur Schramm, *Process and Effects of Mass Communication* (Urbana: University of Illinois, 1954).

Neil J. Smelser, *Theory of Collective Behavior* (New York: The Free Press of Glencoe, 1963).

R. H. Turner and L. M. Killian, *Collective Behavior* (New York: Prentice-Hall, 1957).

Charles R. Wright, *Mass Communication* (New York: Random House, 1959).

ON PUBLIC OPINION AND PROPAGANDA:

Gordon W. Allport and L. Postman, *The Psychology of Rumor* (New York: Holt, 1947).

Bernard Berelson and Morris Janowitz (eds.), *Reader in Public Opinion and Communication* (Rev. ed.; Glencoe: The Free Press, 1953).

Daniel Katz (ed.), *Public Opinion and Propaganda: A Book of Readings* (New York: Dryden 1954).

Elihu Katz and Paul F. Lazarsfeld, *Personal Influence* (Glencoe: The Free Press, 1955).

Walter Lippmann, *Public Opinion* (New York: Harcourt, Brace, 1922).

ON SURVEYS AND POLLING:

Hadley Cantril, *Gauging Public Opinion* (Princeton: Princeton University Press, 1947).

Herbert Hyman, *Survey Design and Analysis: Principles, Cases and Procedures* (Glencoe: The Free Press, 1955).

Mildred Parten, *Surveys, Polls, and Samples: Practical Procedures* (New York: Harper, 1950).

Social Science Research Council, *Pre-election Polls of 1948* (New York: Social Science Research Council, 1949).

Public Opinion Quarterly publishes articles in this field and also reports the findings of current polls.

Section 2 Emotional contagion

Emotional contagion is found in a wide range of related phenomena, including crowd behavior, panics, bank runs, collective hallucinations, crazes, and *esprit de corps*. These phenomena, and others that are less dramatic, show a *common mood,* a state of mind affected by emotion. The mood shared in a group colors the thought and action of the participants by facilitating some acts and inhibiting others. This is most apparent in the protest of an angry mob, but is also true of more conventional situations. A solemn religious ceremony has no place for levity, and even disbelievers share the common mood. At a congenial party formality and personal reserve break down, resulting in flirtations and other acts ordinarily inhibited.

A common mood is experienced by a group of interacting persons as something "in the air," an impression created when people perceive one another's expressive movements, which communicate feelings and develop emotional atmospheres. Feelings are revealed in part through speech, but even more in accompanying expressive movements—the pitch of a man's voice, the rapidity of speech, the look in his eyes, the speed and rhythm of breathing, muscular movement, changes in facial expression, and the color and moisture of his skin. Each individual contributes to an emotional atmosphere to the extent that he reveals his feelings. Each person is affected to the extent that he perceives how others feel and modifies his conduct accordingly. The contributions of each are reciprocal and mutually sustaining. Being enveloped in an emotional atmosphere, the participants are constrained to act along certain limited lines, some impulses being reinforced while others are restrained.

When interaction has developed strong dispositions to behave in a given way, the mere perception of someone else engaging in the activity releases already organized sets. A man who is frightened and disposed to flee breaks upon seeing others run. There is an unconscious imitation of models of action by those who share a common mood. In contagious behavior people generally act similarly, rather than according to some intricate division of labor.

ELEMENTS OF EMOTIONAL CONTAGION

The psychological processes that induce or sustain emotional contagion are not fully understood, but they include the following:

1. *Heightened suggestibility.* In unstructured situations people tend to look to others for cues. The readiness to take cues can be heightened by the presence of emotional tension, because *emotional tension narrows the field of consciousness.* A fearful person is alert to signs of danger and responds to cues that promise relief from anxiety. At the same time, he is apt to ignore other stimuli in his environment. An important consequence of heightened suggestibility is the *loss of critical ability.* When tension dominates consciousness, the weighing of alternative courses of action and the costs of action recede into the background.

2. *Heightened stimulation.* Different personalities show different degrees of suggestibility. However, suggestibility can be induced and the field of consciousness narrowed when there is an increase in the volume and intensity of stimuli from other persons who are excited. In large crowds where there is close physical proximity, stimulation takes the form of *circular response. A* stimulates *B* to fear. *B's* fear not only stimulates *C* in turn but is reflected back to *A* and stimulates him further. Propinquity also calls to attention such physical manifestations of emotion as heavy breathing, perspiration, and muscular tension. If emotion is present in one participant, others are likely to be aware of it.

3. *Homogeneity of experience.* To sustain emotional contagion, there must be shared dispositions and background. Crowd stimuli are not strong enough to make a guard join a prison riot. Fads and crazes are often limited to a particular age, class, or ethnic group whose members share emotional needs and attitudes. A mixed group, composed of people from different social, ethnic, age, and educational categories is less likely to develop emotional contagion.

SIGNIFICANCE OF EMOTIONAL CONTAGION

The social significance of emotional contagion may be summarized as follows:

1. *Emotional contagion provides a psychological unity when other sources of social integration are lacking.* Psychological unity is based on common emotional responses to similarly perceived situations, rather than on definite rules and group structure, but a group based on psychological unity is usually temporary. For example, people searching for a lost child disperse after the emergency is over. However, the social integration of established groups also may be reinforced by emotional contagion, which promotes solidarity and *esprit de corps.*

2. *In groups based on emotional contagion, discipline tends to be low, the release of inner impulses is encouraged, and unconventional behavior is permitted.* Revival meetings, mobs, and similar groupings usually attempt to evoke and canalize the emotions of individuals, who are thus freed from normal restraints. Emotional unity is developed and allowed to run its course. Sometimes this results in behavior excesses, such as acts of violence, either heroic or cowardly. Because emotional contagion is so often accompanied by the weakening of individual responsibility and social control, collective excitement in panics, crowds, revivals, and other emotion-laden activities leads to destructive behavior.

3. *The boundaries of emotional contagion are not set by physical proximity or even group membership, but by the limits of effective communication.* To the extent that feelings are transmitted through the media of mass communication—press, radio, and television—an entire nation may be caught up

The Casting-Out: Group identity is reaffirmed in a storm of emotions as this collaborationist is jeered and reviled in Chartres after the liberation of France from the Nazis. The shaved head stigmatizes the traitor.

in collective excitement, leading to politically irresistible decisions on war or the treatment of nonconformists. Leaders may feel they must bow to the popular mood. Or they may excuse their own lack of moderation by reference to presumed public excitement. Popular "hysteria," however, is often exaggerated by the tendency for news to be reported in dramatic fashion.

The remainder of this section considers some of the more important manifestations of emotional contagion, particularly crowds, mobs, panics, rumor, and popular extravagances known as crazes and fads.

CROWDS

In common usage any large number of people gathered in one place is called a crowd, but crowds differ in the extent to which interaction occurs or leads to unity of feeling and behavior. The "sidewalk superintendents" gathered around a building under construction form a *casual* crowd in which interpersonal relations are at a minimum. What captures attention is of no great emotional import. Nevertheless, a crowd is a potential medium for arousing emotion and for encouraging its expression. Large gatherings provide congenial conditions for emotional contagion. Stimulation and suggestibility are heightened; the presence of others gives the individual a sense of security and approval; and crowds convey a feeling of anonymity. In times of social unrest or of racial tension, street crowds have often been transformed into *acting crowds* or *mobs,* when the event that attracts attention is exciting and stimulates existing hostilities.

The House of Commons and Parliamentary Psychology

Abridged from *Closing the Ring* by Winston S. Churchill (Boston: Houghton Mifflin, 1951), pp. 168–69. Reprinted by permission of Houghton Mifflin Company.

On October 28 [1943], there was the rebuilding of the House of Commons to consider. One unlucky bomb had blown to fragments the Chamber in which I had passed so much of my life. I was determined to have it rebuilt at the earliest moment that our struggle would allow. I had the power at this moment to shape things in a way that would last. Supported by my colleagues, mostly old Parliamentarians, and with Mr. Attlee's cordial aid, I sought to re-establish for what may well be a long period the two great principles on which the British House of Commons stands in its physical aspect. . . . The first is that its shape should be oblong and not semicircular. Here is a very potent factor in our political life. The semicircular assembly, which appeals to political theorists, enables every individual or every group to move round the centre, adopting various shades of pink according as the weather changes. I am a convinced supporter of the party system in preference to the group system. The party system is much favoured by the oblong form of chamber. It is easy for an individual to move through these insensible gradations from Left to Right, but the act of crossing the Floor is one which requires serious consideration. I am well in-

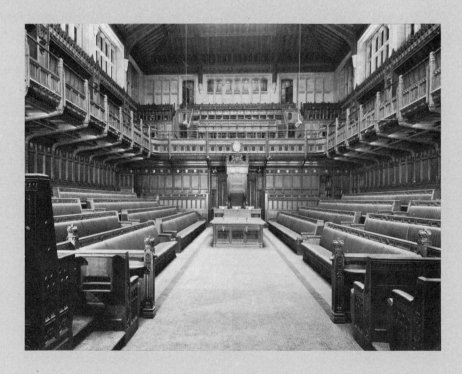

formed on this matter, for I have accomplished that difficult process, not only once, but twice. Logic is a poor guide compared with custom. Logic, which has created in so many countries semicircular assemblies with buildings that give to every member not only a seat to sit in, but often a desk to write at, with a lid to bang, has proved fatal to Parliamentary government as we know it here in its home and in the land of its birth.

The second characteristic of a chamber formed on the lines of the House of Commons is that it should *not* be big enough to contain all its Members at once without overcrowding, and there should be no question of every Member having a separate seat reserved for him. The reason for this has long been a puzzle to uninstructed outsiders, and has frequently excited the curiosity and even the criticism of new Members. Yet it is not so difficult to understand if you look at it from a practical point of view. If the House is big enough to contain all its Members, ninetenths of its debates will be conducted in the depressing atmosphere of an almost empty or half-empty chamber. The essence of good House of Commons speaking is the conversational style, the facility for quick, informal interruptions and interchanges. Harangues from a rostrum would be a bad substitute for the conversational style in which so much of our business is done. But the conversational style requires a fairly small space, and there should be on great occasions a sense of crowd and urgency. There should be a sense of the importance of much that is said, and a sense that great matters are being decided, there and then, by the House.

By their very nature casual crowds and mobs are not part of an organized and controlled system of social relations. They arise spontaneously without orderly preparation. There is no etiquette of crowd behavior. If feelings of hostility, anger, or resentment are aroused, the socially uncontrolled interaction of the crowd may have serious consequences. (See Adaptation 22, pp. 267–74.) In recent history the calling of general strikes has often been a prelude to revolutionary attacks upon governments. (See Adaptation 45, pp. 698–703.) The effect of a general strike, in addition to raising the level of tension and excitement, is to draw people away from stable institutionalized activities at work and home, and to encourage the formation of street crowds. One of the first moves of a fearful government is to attempt to break up gatherings of more than two or three people, because even small knots of excited people might expand into uncontrollable street crowds.

Integrative Crowd Behavior

Not all crowd behavior is spontaneous and unguided. Controlled emotional contagion is often encouraged and can serve a useful social function. It may offer release for emotions and tensions that ordinarily find no expression, and may stimulate feelings that enhance group solidarity. Organized gatherings of many kinds provide settings that articulate crowd behavior with the social structure.

1. *Expressive crowds.* Parties, dances, and some spectator sports are gatherings in which certain emotions and tensions can find an ordered release. In parties and dances emotional contagion makes for freer interpersonal relations. Football games permit and encourage shouting, singing, and a degree of aggressiveness. Without the unity of the crowd, people would not feel so free to engage in emotional or boisterous behavior.

2. *Audiences.* Many audiences are similar

to casual crowds in their passivity and low degree of emotional unity. Nevertheless they may be susceptible to emotional contagion. In some audience situations, like lectures or concerts, the presence of others encourages expressions of enthusiasm. Performers have been known to employ claques, people hired to cheer and stimulate the spread of approval.

3. *Religious services*. Services that arouse contagious emotions of humility and piety may support deep religious feelings. In some religious sects, emotional contagion is encouraged and results in relatively uncontrolled and predominantly expressive behavior. As institutionalization develops, more restrained services appear. (See RELIGION, pp. 437–39.)

4. *Mass meetings and deliberative assemblies*. Meetings of voluntary associations usually have two functions. As deliberating bodies they hear and pass upon reports from leaders and choose new leaders. They are also designed to stimulate feelings of solidarity. Meetings in a political campaign are largely of the latter kind, and people go as they do to a football game, expecting to cheer and otherwise express their feelings. When large numbers are involved, it is common for deliberative meetings to become subject to emotional contagion. Although conventions of unions, veterans, and political parties are usually highly organized, the leaders are aware of the danger that the meeting may get out of hand. An unimportant individual may gain the attention of the meeting and develop influence he might not otherwise have.

Assemblies are called "mass meetings" when the solidarity aspect is predominant and emotional demonstrations are expected and encouraged. The emotions displayed are often stereotyped, however, and need not reflect real feelings. The "demonstrations" at national political conventions are often calculated efforts to put on a show of enthusiasm for a candidate.

In "The House of Commons and Parliamentary Psychology," page 260, Churchill takes account of the crowd potential even in the highly institutionalized British Parliament. The small rectangular chamber has two effects. At ordinary meetings, it encourages a conversational style. On the other hand, at historically significant sessions when all members are present and the chamber is packed, there results a "sense of crowd and urgency."

MOBS AND RIOTS

A mob is a crowd bent upon some aggressive act such as lynching, looting, or the destruction of property. As a rule the term "mob" refers to one crowd that is fairly unified and single-minded in its aggressive intent. The word "riot" connotes more randomly destructive behavior, occurring in several places and possibly involving many crowds. Rioting tends to express generalized resentment and rebellion rather than definite purpose. Prison riots, though usually undertaken to force prisoners' demands, often entail random destructiveness. (See pp. 569–70.)

Mob aggression is socially oriented. Its targets are socially defined, usually some ethnic or racial group, social class, or public institution that is perceived as the source of frustration. The socially defined nature of the target is evident in "scapegoating," in which aggression is *displaced* from objective sources of frustration, such as economic distress, to some group or individual defined as a legitimate object of hostility.

Of all the forms of emotional contagion, mob activity is the most goal-oriented and the most dependent upon leadership for its direction. Mobs divide into a nucleus of active and militant leaders and an acquiescing mass of spectators. The spectators provide the leaders with a sense of support and approval. The leaders in turn provide the mass with cues for aggressive behavior. Mob leaders are often those least likely to achieve leadership under ordinary circumstances.

Because of the role of leadership and rumor-mongering in mob activity, situations of group conflict and social unrest are fertile soil for fanatical and irresponsible persons. In the 1919 Chicago race riot [1] gangs of hoodlums and "athletic clubs" formed the nuclei of mobs. (See Adaptation 22, pp. 270 ff.) Although the initial clash between Negroes and whites occurred at a relatively isolated bathing beach, rumors and gang activity carried the conflict beyond its original locale. Spontaneous outbreaks between Negroes and whites were soon followed by organized raiding by neighborhood gangs in search of victims.

The release of tension and the expression of aggression in mobs signify not an individual but a group phenomenon. Even in a riot situation, where tension is high and personal danger seems to threaten, violence is not usually committed by isolated individuals but by organized gangs or crowds transformed into mobs. The average individual is not able to engage in socially destructive or violent behavior except as a member of a group or an emotionally unified mob. Riot violence is, therefore, intermittent and concentrated, sparked by the transformation of crowds into mobs or the organization of raids. In order to suppress riots, the law enforcement agencies must be able to control known gangs and prevent the formation of crowds.

PANIC

Panic occurs in the face of danger, usually to physical survival—as in a fire or on a sinking ship. The threat may also be to economic or social status, as in financial panic. Panic is not dependent upon emotional contagion, for people panic when they are alone. They may become disorganized, compulsive, or paralyzed; they may engage in irrelevant or ineffective behavior or may be unable to do anything at all.

Panic is related to emotional contagion in two ways: (1) The presence of others can,

[1] Cf. A. M. Lee and N. D. Humphrey, *Race Riot* (New York: Dryden, 1943) for a study of the Detroit race riot.

through heightened stimulation and the circulation of rumors, enormously increase the sense of overwhelming danger; and (2) a disastrous unity of action may result from emotional contagion. On a sinking ship or in a burning theater, it is essential that individual action be differentiated and co-ordinated, that everyone not rush to the same lifeboat or exit. Yet in the face of danger a mechanical, emotion-based unity may replace coordinated action. Sometimes the sight of a man irrationally jumping overboard stimulates others to do so. Unlike the irrational impulse to follow a man jumping overboard, the impulse to run to the nearest exit in a burning theater may be a rational response by those individuals near the exit. But other frightened people, stimulated by their behavior, also rush to the same exit and thereby make escape impossible.

Knowledge is a preventive of panic, especially if there is no real danger. An eclipse can lead to panic if people do not understand that it is a natural phenomenon. Prior knowledge of what to do and the habit of using knowledge can help prevent panic. In this sense, civilian defense is an anti-panic device if it is realistic in its preparations and is able to engender confidence in the public.

FADS AND CRAZES

The term "fad" usually refers to the spread of some relatively superficial and external pattern of behavior, such as a game or a way of dressing. "Craze" has more emotional connotations. While a fad involves neither great emotional investment nor the revision of ordinary routine, a craze seizes the whole person, often occupying all his time and energy. The line between the two is not always clear: if a fad becomes a great preoccupation, it is apt to be called a "craze." Crazes range all the way from religious manias to solving jigsaw puzzles. What characterizes this wide range of phenomena, extending from the sublime to the trivial, is that the activity seems all-

Wall Street in the Panic of 1929: A common mood of anxiety spread out of the offices into the streets.

important, at least for the time being. In the craze the field of consciousness may be narrowed to the point where critical ability is virtually extinguished and future consequences are ignored.

Very little is securely known about fads and crazes. Fads seem to spread primarily among individuals in similar social circumstances; they represent heightened cue-taking from other members of one's own social group or from members of some group to which one would like to belong. One of the underlying emotions seems to be *anxiety concerning social status,* which readily encourages taking cues from those "in the know." Literary and fashion fads often have snob-value: a leading figure sets the trend, and others who wish to be identified as "intellectuals" or "modish" follow suit. With the development of mass communication and advertising techniques, some fads spread through the whole society. The content of advertisements indicates at a glance that they both assume and further stimulate in their readers anxiety concerning social status.

Status anxiety has a special bearing on the psychology of youth and group discrimination. Adolescents of subordinate minorities seem especially prone to fads. They take their behavior-cues from each other, both in protest against more conventional models of behavior and in an effort to gain security from their special group membership. In recent years there has been a tendency for lower-class and minority-group adolescents to adopt unconventional and socially disapproved manners, clothes, and haircuts. To be sure, not all fads are based on anxiety, nor do they have equal emotional significance.

A craze involves irrationality. When people are caught up in a craze they tend to act in foolish or even disastrous ways. The irrationality is the continuous and single-minded pursuit of the craze, so that other interests and obligations are neglected and the consequences are ignored. In financial crazes people behave in self-defeating ways

much as in some types of panic. What is rational action for one individual may be disastrous when many undertake it. In the seventeenth century the people of Holland were seized by the Tulip Mania. In the preceding century the possession of tulips had come to signify wealth and good taste. As the middle classes began to acquire tulips, perhaps from a desire to achieve social status, the price of the bulbs rose to great heights. Speculation was widespread, and many speculators became wealthy. This encouraged a general stampede toward investment in the bulbs. When the prices reached fantastic heights, the rich ceased to acquire tulips for their pleasure and sold them to realize a profit. The price of tulips fell, and many people were ruined.

During the depression of the 1930's a "send-a-dime" chain letter craze developed in the United States. The letters promised that the investment of a dime would eventually bring a return of $1,562.50. The chain letter craze, occurring during a severe economic depression, expressed the economic anxiety of the period.

RUMOR

A rumor is an unconfirmed communication usually transmitted by word of mouth in a situation of anxiety or stress. Rumors spring up in unstructured situations when information is needed but reliable channels do not exist. The role of rumor in a race riot is discussed in Adaptation 22, pages 271–72. Note that newspapers also were "full of rumors" because normal controls over reporting and editing were weakened.

Because they are so readily influenced by emotions, rumors tend to be *rapidly disseminated* and to *distort or falsify* the facts. A rumor may begin as an inaccurate or distorted report because of the narrowing of perception in emotionally charged situations. It may also become progressively more distorted, because all oral communication is subject to distortion. Even when emotional elements are lacking, factual reports tend to become shorter and simpler as they are passed on, with distortion of details in accordance with personal and cultural predispositions or "sets."

Truth or falsity of rumor is irrelevant: a story is told and believed not because it is demonstrably true but because it serves a need for the teller and for the listener who becomes a teller. Sometimes the need is to achieve status in the eyes of the listener, and the story will be distorted in ways that will please him. The story may represent mere wishful thinking, as in the "send-a-dime" chain letter craze, or be an outlet for hostility, as in a race riot. The aim is not to convey information but to induce in the listener the same emotional attitude toward the alleged information that the teller has.

Rumor both contributes to and is a product of emotional contagion.

1. Rumors make for an atmosphere of tension and crisis. By means of rumors, feelings are conveyed from one person to another and from one locale to another. The study of the 1919 Chicago race riot (p. 273) points out the role of rumor in spreading the riot beyond its originally isolated area and in creating a general air of tension and excitement. Anger- and fear-provoking rumors exaggerate the hostile intent of the other side and tend to justify emotional and behavioral excesses.

2. Emotional contagion narrows the field of consciousness and diminishes critical ability. In times of distress, perception, which is always selective, is rendered even more so. People are apt to accept anything they hear and to revise it in accordance with their momentarily overpowering needs. Moreover they tend to misinterpret what they themselves observe. During the 1919 Chicago race riot the newspapers were unreliable partly because their informants became untrustworthy under the riot conditions.

In times of crisis and emergency, though information is of supreme importance, it is often unavailable. In a disaster like a flood or an invasion, official sources of information often disintegrate; in periods of social tension, they are often distrusted and lose their aura of authority. In such situations rumor rushes in to take the place of more secure knowledge.

MORALE AND EMOTIONAL CONTAGION

Morale is a quality of group experience and is measured by the degree to which the members believe in a group's goals, have confidence in its leaders, and engage in concerted effort. Most groups persist even if they have low morale. They are held together by the interdependence of their members and by social codes.

Emotional contagion can contribute to morale by creating a common mood of self-sacrifice, of shared danger, or of devotion to a cause. Consciousness of belonging together and being of the same kind pervades the group, breaking down personal reserve and releasing feelings of affection and sympathy. Under such conditions mutual inspiration is possible and individuals may rise to great heights of courage and effort. As we have seen in PRIMARY GROUPS, page 153, and ASSOCIATIONS, page 233, morale in organizations is also closely related to participation in primary groups.

Unifying symbols and ceremonies are evident when morale is supported by a common mood. In wartime, symbols of national unity are widely displayed and their very quantity helps to create an atmosphere in which consciousness of group goals is increased. Social movements and military organizations also make wide use of uniforms, badges, rallies, funerals, and many other symbolic forms and activities. Even the way men walk and look can have a symbolic meaning and contribute to the emotional atmosphere, a fact which some religious sects and military organizations have long understood.

Emotional solidarity is closely related to

feelings of *antagonism toward out-groups.* People drawn together by a shared hatred temporarily and often gladly forget their own differences. Self-glorification and hatred of enemies are themes repeatedly used in bolstering morale through emotional contagion. On the other hand, when an external but impersonal threat, such as a flood, requires intense participation, the fact of shared experience may produce a common mood of well-being and togetherness.

For many groups the ultimate test of morale is tenacity in the face of danger. Other groups, such as workers in a factory, are never called upon in this way. Their morale is largely expressed in interpersonal co-operation and in a willingness to accept orders, carry on day-to-day tasks, and contribute to production.

Emotional contagion alone cannot long sustain high levels of morale. A group of soldiers may be stirred by a prevailing mood to an act of heroism, but in the long run it is the stable group life of the army that determines morale. The emotional cohesion of a crowd is fleeting and may sometimes be dissipated by a pistol shot, a fire hose, or a rain shower. However, in a time of crisis, temporary periods of cohesion may tip the scales and decide the course of events.

Race Riot: Chicago, 1919

Abridged and adapted from *The Negro in Chicago,* by the Chicago Commission on Race Relations (Chicago: University of Chicago Press, 1922). Copyright 1922 by the University of Chicago. The staff of the Commission was headed by Graham R. Taylor and Charles S. Johnson. Published in this form by permission of The University of Chicago Press.

This is a case study of one of the worst race riots in American history. Although the event occurred more than a generation ago, the study remains a classic in sociological writing. It has not been excelled as an interpretive account of the development of contagious behavior, marked by collective excitement, mob leadership, rumor, and the breakdown of institutional controls. It shows that in a sustained riot situation unorganized spontaneous behavior is combined with more organized and deliberate action.

In the United States most race riots have occurred between Negroes and whites. Though a race riot usually flares up spontaneously over an incident, in retrospect often trivial, it has a history of accumulated tension and mutual hostility. A riot may be unpredictable, sparked by a real or imagined provocation, but some conditions are conducive to riots. In the United States, race riots have occurred mostly in Northern cities into which Negroes have migrated at a pace too rapid for gradual adjustment and accommodation, and where conscious efforts are not being made for their integration and acceptance. Under such conditions Negroes and whites have not yet had time to participate together in joint enterprises or to share common endeavors, and thus to work out even a formal and impersonal pattern of social relations. Their relations are marked by prejudice and competition, especially for jobs and housing. Under such circumstances the only contact Negroes and whites have is in public facilities, in streetcars, in theaters, in playgrounds, and at the beach. Contact in these areas, though highly impersonal, is nevertheless of a direct nature. Negroes and whites meet under conditions in which (1) personal feelings, especially of a hostile nature, are most apt to be stimulated and (2) personal feelings are least subject to social control. Where personal relations occur within and are controlled by a social context, prejudice may not be eliminated but intense feelings both of hostility and resentment are less likely to arise.

Soon after the episode the Governor of Illinois appointed a biracial Commission on Race Relations to study the causes of the riot and to make recommendations for the prevention of further disturbances. The Commission's investigative staff which included trained sociologists prepared a voluminous report not only on the riot but on the general situation of the Negro in Chicago. In their description and analysis of the riot three facts stand out: (1) Race riots have a background of old unresolved hostilities, prejudices, and grievances. (2) A race riot of the sort described is a spontaneous, unplanned flare-up. (3) If a race riot continues, it may develop a nucleus of leaders who conduct organized raids.

BACKGROUND OF THE RIOT

Between 1910 and 1920 the Negro population of Chicago increased 148.5 per cent, from 2 per cent of the city's total population to 4.1 per cent. In 1918, because of the war, an acute housing shortage developed, which did much to aggravate whatever tensions already existed. Whites became hostile toward further expansion of the "Black Belt," and Negroes resented their forced crowding, high rents, and inferior housing. Prior to 1919 twelve bombings had occurred of homes not only of Negroes but of real estate men, white and Negro, who had sold or rented property to Negroes in white neighborhoods. (The bombings increased after the 1919 riot.) Propaganda on the part of white property owners was at times reckless and inflammatory.

The 1919 Chicago riot began on Sunday, July 27, with a clash of whites and Negroes at a bathing beach in Chicago, and resulted in the drowning of a Negro boy. Violence and rioting continued for days afterward until the state militia was called out to assist the police. The danger of further clashes was not considered over until August 6. Twenty-three Negroes and 15 whites were killed; at least 342 Negroes and 178 whites were injured.

BEGINNING OF THE RIOT

Sunday, July 27, was hot, one of a series of days with temperatures in the 90's. At four o'clock in the afternoon Eugene Williams, a seventeen-year-old Negro boy, was swimming offshore in Lake Michigan at the foot of Twenty-ninth Street. Although the beach flanks an area thickly inhabited by Negroes, it was used by both races. The part near Twenty-seventh Street had by tacit understanding come to be considered as reserved for Negroes, while the whites used the part near Twenty-ninth Street. Williams, who had entered the water at a point used by Negroes, drifted south into the part used by the whites. White men, women, and children were in the vicinity and on the beach in considerable numbers. Four Negroes walked through the group of whites and into the water. White men summarily ordered them off. The Negroes left, but soon returned with others of their race. Then began a series of attacks, retreats, counterattacks, and stone-throwing. Williams, who had remained in the water during the fracas, found a railroad tie and clung to it, stones meanwhile frequently striking the water near him. A white boy of about the same age swam toward him. As the white boy neared, Williams let go of the tie, took a few strokes, and went down. When examined later, his body showed no stone bruises, but rumor had it that he had actually been hit by one of the stones and drowned as a result.

Guilt was immediately placed upon a certain white man by several Negro witnesses who demanded that he be arrested by a white policeman who was on the spot. No arrest was made.

For an hour both whites and Negroes dived for the boy without results. Awe in the face of the tragedy gave way to excited whispers. "They" said he was stoned to death. The report circulated through the crowd that the police officer had refused to arrest the murderer. The Negroes in the crowd began to mass dangerously. At this crucial point the accused policeman arrested a Negro on a white man's complaint. Negroes mobbed the white officer, and the riot was under way.

The two facts, the drowning and the refusal to arrest, or widely circulated reports of such a refusal, must be considered together as marking the inception of the riot. A police captain later testified that the first reports after the drowning were that the situation was calming down. White men had co-operated with Negroes in diving for the body of the boy. Furthermore, since the scene of the clash was isolated, no outsiders had gathered to augment the disturbance. Without the stimulus of reports concerning the policeman's conduct, the clash might well have ended.

SPREAD OF THE RIOT

Reports of the drowning and of the alleged conduct of the policeman spread out into the neighborhood, and two hours after the drowning of Williams, another fatality occurred. The Negro crowd from the beach had gathered at the foot of Twenty-ninth Street. As it became more and more excited, a group of officers was summoned by the policeman who had been at the beach. James Crawford, a Negro, fired into the group of officers and was himself shot and killed by a Negro policeman who had been sent to help restore order.

During the remainder of that Sunday afternoon many distorted rumors circulated swiftly through the neighborhood. The Negro crowd from Twenty-ninth Street went into action, and white men coming into contact with it were beaten. In all, four white men

were beaten, five were stabbed, and one was shot. As the rumors spread, new crowds gathered, mobs sprang into activity spontaneously, and gangs began to take part in the lawlessness.

As darkness approached, white gangs farther to the west in the Stock Yard district went into action. Negroes in white districts suffered severely at their hands. From 9:00 P.M. until 3:00 A.M. twenty-seven Negroes were beaten, seven stabbed, and four shot.

Few clashes occurred on Monday morning. People of both races went to work as usual and even continued to work side by side without signs of violence. But as the afternoon wore on, white men and boys living between the Stock Yards and the "Black Belt" sought malicious amusement in directing mob violence against Negro workers returning home. The main thoroughfares along streetcar routes were thronged, especially at transfer points, with white people of all ages. Trolleys were pulled from wires and the cars brought under the control of mob leaders. Negro passengers were dragged to the street, beaten, and kicked. The police were apparently powerless to cope with these numerous assaults. Four Negro men and one white assailant were killed, and thirty Negro men severely beaten in the streetcar clashes.

By Monday night, both whites and Negroes showed signs of panic. Each race grouped by itself. Small mobs began systematically in various neighborhoods to terrorize and kill. Gangs in the white districts grew bolder and made raids through neighborhoods into which Negroes had recently moved. Many Negro homes in mixed districts were attacked and several of them burned. Furniture was stolen or destroyed.

At midnight, Monday, streetcar clashes ended because of a general strike on the surface and elevated lines. The tie-up was complete for the remainder of the week. On Tuesday morning there was a new source of terror for those who tried to walk to their places of employment. Men were killed en route to their work through hostile territory. Idle men congregated on the streets, and gang rioting increased. A gang of white soldiers and sailors in uniform, augmented by civilians, raided the "Loop," the downtown section of Chicago, early Tuesday, killing two Negroes and beating and robbing several others, and incidentally destroying property of white business men.

Wednesday saw a material lessening of crime and violence. Though the "Black Belt" and the district immediately west of it were still storm centers, other more peripheral areas had quieted down. On Wednesday evening at 10:30 the mayor yielded to pressure and asked for the militia, which had been mobilized in nearby armories as early as Monday night. Rain on Wednesday and Thursday drove idle people of both races into their homes and broke the heat wave. Friday witnessed only a single reported injury.

The riot virtually ceased on Saturday, though for the next few days injuries were occasionally reported. By the following Thursday, August 8, the riot zone had settled down to normal and the militia was withdrawn.

SUMMARY OF THE RIOT PATTERN

The total riot period was 13 days in length, from Sunday, July 27, through Thursday, August 8, the day on which the troops were withdrawn. Of this time only the first seven days witnessed active rioting.

In the seven active days, rioting was not continuous but intermittent, being furious for hours, then fairly quiescent for hours. The change in the nature of the clashes day by day showed (1) an increase in intensity of feeling, (2) greater boldness of action, and (3) greater organization. This development reached its peak on Tuesday.

For the most part the riot was confined to the "Black Belt" and the Stock Yards district, the home of many all-white organized gangs and "athletic clubs." Violence centered on streetcar routes, partly because of the known heavy concentration of Negroes on certain transportation lines.

Streetcar Contacts

In 1919 the Negroes constituted only 4 per cent of the city's population. Negro traffic, however, was concentrated upon 12 streetcar lines which connected Negro residence areas with the manufacturing districts where Negroes were largely employed. The proportion of Negroes to whites on these 12 lines was much higher than 4 per cent, and on some lines the majority of the passengers were often Negroes.

These transportation contacts were significant. Many whites had no other contact with Negroes. Unlike contacts in school or at work, transportation contacts are unsupervised and uncontrolled. If there is a dispute between passengers over a seat, it usually rests with the passengers themselves to come to an understanding. Any feeling of suspicion or prejudice on either side because of the difference in race accentuates misunderstanding. Finally, transportation contacts, at least on crowded cars, involve a degree of physical contact between Negroes and whites which rarely occurs under other circumstances, and which sometimes leads to a display of racial feeling.

Gangs and "Athletic Clubs"

Gangs were responsible for extending the riot beyond the first clash. Both organized gangs and those which sprang into existence spontaneously seized upon the excuse of the first conflict to engage in lawless acts.

The gangs which figured so prominently in the riot were all-white gangs, or "athletic clubs." Judges of the municipal court said that there were no gang organizations among Negroes to compare with those found among young whites.

However, there was evidence that Negro gambling clubs, or their leaders, were also active in the rioting. Police raids were made on some of the "Black Belt" clubs on August 23, some weeks after the riot. At the Pioneer Club, eight guns, four packages of cartridges, and twenty-four knives were taken.

Crowds and Mobs

During the riot many crowds of curiosity seekers were transformed into vicious mobs when exciting rumors circulated and suggestions of vengeance were made by leaders. Such suggestions were frequently accompanied by some daring act, stimulated by the excitement.

The mob in its entirety usually did not participate actively. It was one in spirit, but it divided in performance between a small active nucleus and a large proportion of spectators. The nucleus was composed of young men from sixteen to twenty-one or twenty-two years of age. Sometimes only four would be active while 50 or 150 looked on, but at times the proportion would be as great as 25 in 200 or 50 in 300. Fifty is the largest number reported for a mob nucleus. This occurred when six Negroes were beaten, dragged off a streetcar and chased, one of them being killed. Here there were three stages of crowd formation. First came the nucleus of 50 active men who did the beating, chasing, and killing. Closely aiding and abetting them were 300 or 400 others. After the Negroes had been forced off the car and were being hunted through the neighborhood, a crowd of about 2,000 gathered and followed the vanguard of attackers and spectators. These were present out of morbid curiosity, but sufficiently imbued with the spirit of the mob not to interfere with its outrages.

Without the spectators mob violence would probably have stopped short of murder in many cases. An example of the behavior of the active nucleus when out of sight of the spectators bears this out. A Negro was chased from a streetcar. He outstripped all but the vanguard of the mob by climbing fences and hiding in a back yard, thus concealing himself from the rest of the crowd. The young man who had followed him left without striking a blow, upon his mere plea for mercy. In regard to the large nonactive elements in the crowds, the coroner said during the inquest, "It is just the swelling of crowds of that kind that urges them on, because they naturally feel that they are backed up by the balance of the crowd, which may not be true, but they feel that way."

Mobs committed atrocities at the direct suggestions of the leaders. Prepared by rumors mobs were easily aroused to action. A streetcar approaching and the cry, "Get the _____!" was enough. Prompt action clinched the idea, and the emotion of the attack narrowed the field of consciousness. Countersuggestion was not tolerated when the mob was rampant. A suggestion of mercy was shouted down with the derisive epithet, "nigger lover!" Silenced objectors made no further effort to thwart mob action. There are no records of such persons notifying the police or persisting in their remonstrances.

Not only did action once under way make interference hazardous, but it brought into the mob a greater number of participants and increased its energy. If five men jerked a trolley from the wires, ten men gathered to board the car, and twenty-five chased and beat the routed Negroes.

A sharp diversion of attention sometimes caused the dispersal of mobs. An unexpected revolver shot was the most effective means of such diversion. For example: A mob chased a Negro off a streetcar into an alley. A policeman with presence of mind followed the group into the alley, fired a few shots in the air, and the crowd ran. However, shooting which was part of the mob's own action did not have the same effect.

Rumor

Newspapers printed more rumors than facts, often because their sources of news,

Table **VIII:1**

Date	Injured Reported by the "Tribune" and "Herald-Examiner" in First Four Days			Facts from Police, State's Attorney, Hospitals, and Olivet Baptist Church			
	White	Negro	Total	White	Negro	Unknown	Total
July 27	29	19	48	10	31	5	46
July 28	64	60	124	71	152	6	229
July 29	62	72	134	55	80	4	139
July 30	40	21	61	20	20	2	42
Total	195	172	367	156	283	17	456
Percentage of total	53	47	100	34	62	4	100

though trustworthy in ordinary times, were highly unreliable under the riot conditions. In general the tendency of newspaper reports was toward exaggeration and the exacerbation of the riot. An illustration of the unreliability of news reports is provided by Table VIII:1.

The table shows that while total injuries and injuries to Negroes were understated, the number of whites injured was exaggerated and the proportion of whites injured greatly exaggerated. Reports of numbers of dead and injured were apt to feed the riot, because they tended to produce the feeling that the score must be evened up on the basis of "an eye for an eye," a Negro for a white, or vice versa.

Police and Militia

The police were handicapped in dealing with the riot because of their inadequate numbers, their lack of training in riot control, and their anti-Negro prejudices. Furthermore, the white police were distrusted by the Negro population. This distrust had grown seriously during the six months preceding the riot because no arrests had been made in cases where the homes of Negroes had been bombed.

The evidence points to a greater readiness of policemen to arrest Negroes than whites. Of 229 persons accused of various criminal activities during the riot, 154 were Negroes and 75 were whites. Of this number, 81 Negroes and 47 whites were indicted. At first glance these figures indicate greater riot activity on the part of Negroes. Yet out of a total of 520 injured, where race was reported, 342 were Negroes and 178 whites. The fact that twice as many Negroes were injured, yet twice as many appeared as defendants, indicates that whites were not apprehended as readily as Negroes.

The militia, which had been given special drills in the suppression of riots and insurrections for a year and a half previous to this occasion, was called in only after the worst of the riot was over. In general, though they were all white, they appeared to be welcomed not only by the police and white citizens, but by Negro citizens as well. The only show of hostility to the troops came from white gangs who fired on some detachments when they first came in. Later militia activities were directed principally against gangs of hoodlums, most of which were white.

Conclusion

1. Most riot *violence occurred after working hours.* Work acted as a restraining influence in two ways: (*a*) People continued to go to work; (*b*) there was no violence in places of employment. In spite of the riot atmosphere, work habits were sufficiently in-

Detroit Race Riot, 1943: Not all are caught up in the mob; two youths show their humanity.

stitutionalized so that business and industry were not interrupted.

2. *Rumor* kept the crowds in an excited, potential mob state. The press, though stressing tolerance and order in its editorials, was responsible for wide dissemination of much of the inflammatory material. Given a riot at-mosphere, in which fear- and anger-provoking rumors freely circulate, a crowd was easily transformed into a mob. It is important, therefore, in a riot situation to establish some agency to provide reliable information and counteract the exaggeration and emotionalism of rumors.

3. *The riot violence was intermittent.* So long as the riot atmosphere continued, violence was always potential, capable of being sparked by almost any kind of incident. But violence was usually the result of organized raiding or of the development of a mob spirit in a crowd.

4. *Release of tension was usually a group phenomenon.* Only under special conditions did people feel "free" to engage in violence. These conditions were present when mob leaders felt they had the support of others and when the critical faculties of the more passive were overwhelmed by being caught up in a mob situation. Much violence can be controlled in a riot situation if crowds and mobs can be kept from forming.

5. The greatest number of *injuries* occurred on main thoroughfares and at transfer points along streetcar lines. Some of this violence was no doubt due to the fact that main thoroughfares were crowded. Riot violence seems to take place in areas where contacts between the races though direct are superficial and impersonal. Where contact is institutionalized and occurs in a social context, at work or at school for example, there is less likelihood of violence.

6. *Crowds and mobs* engaged in rioting were usually composed of a small nucleus of leaders and an acquiescing mass of spectators. Most leaders were young men, between sixteen and twenty-one. Gangs of young whites formed the nucleus of much crowd and mob leadership.

7. Sporadic clashes and *spontaneous mob outbreaks* were characteristic of the earlier phases of the riot. These were followed by organized raids, usually of gangs, which did much to extend the riot beyond its "normal" limits.

8. The police lacked sufficient forces to control the riot, but they were also hampered by the Negroes' distrust of them and by their own prejudice. The machinery of justice was also affected by prejudice, and by political rivalries. The all-white militia was welcomed by both Negroes and whites. A militia can be effective in controlling a riot because (*a*) it can be isolated from the riot atmosphere and (*b*) if its personnel is drawn from other areas, it does not have the community ties that hamper the objectivity of the police. The sheer fact of prejudice in law enforcement officers seems not to hinder their ability to control riots. There is no evidence that as individuals the militia were any less prejudiced than police.

Section 3 **Public opinion and propaganda**

In emotional contagion, individuals are united by psychological bonds. The links are temporary, the groups are shifting, and the influence of the immediate situation is strong. However, emotional contagion is not the only source of temporary and shifting unities. Some groupings of this kind arise out of common interest rather than shared emotional experience.

PUBLICS

A public consists of people who (1) regard themselves as affected by an event or activity, (2) can in some way register that concern, and (3) are taken into account. This is a very general term that may apply to magazine subscribers, stockholders, voters, and many other groups or categories. Our chief interest is in *political publics*. These arise when there is an issue, that is, a disagreement within the population concerning what ought to be done, such as whether or not the federal government should support a program of medical care. Politics occurs when the public is split into factions and rival groups pursue their respective interests.

A public may be a dispersed group. It need not have a definite membership nor a formal organization of roles. Since a public consists of those concerned with the consequences of an event, the composition of the public changes as the situation changes and the same event comes to be seen in a different light. New people become interested; others lose interest and turn elsewhere; there may be a realignment within the public. When government support of medical care is labeled "socialized medicine," some shy away from discussions; others may join a health plan at their place of work and lose interest in the general issue. Publics are temporary collectivities that can be identified only by common concern with an event, and their size and composition vary with each issue.

When issues are recurrent, some political publics tend to become more stable. Within each area of interest there arises a core of people who follow developments more closely and whose support can be expected. On an issue like medical care, business groups can be counted upon to take one side, labor unions the other side, and veterans' groups split. The existence of relatively stable publics implies a continuity of interest in a succession of related issues. Such publics can sometimes be identified by the books, newspapers, and magazines they read. By participating in common communication channels, they tend to define situations alike. Consequently, they consistently take the same sides on a variety of issues. Such publics, however, are only partially organized, and their composition continually changes. They may provide the *social base* out of which organized groups emerge and on which such groups are dependent. (See ASSOCIATIONS, p. 252.)

Like crowds, publics arise in unstructured situations. But in the public free play of interest rather than emotion is released. Within the broad framework set by law and custom, competition can take place. In its "pure" form, political competition occurs without the heightened stimulation and emotional rapport found in crowd behavior. Whereas crowd behavior leads to a loss of self-consciousness, in political publics there may be progressively more explicit recognition of one's own interests and an intensification of both personal and group self-consciousness. The member of a public ideally shows more self-control and more ability to assess tactical and strategic lines of action than the member of a crowd. The farmer responding to an act of government according to his interests has a point of mooring for his thought and is largely free of the pressures that make for emotional contagion.

Caution: The differences between crowds and publics, although significant, are not absolute. In actual experience members of publics show some crowdlike behavior: (1) Calculated self-interest does not completely govern action even when direct practical interests are at stake. (2) When acting groups are formed out of publics, the emotional ties that enhance solidarity come into play. (3) Propaganda tends to play upon and arouse emotions.

VALUES, ATTITUDES, AND OPINIONS

Personal integrity is highly prized in American culture. A man should be secure in what is most intimately his, such as his body, his ideas, and his family. This *value* affects a wide range of thought and behavior, in part by generating *attitudes*. For example, valuing personal integrity may dispose one to react negatively to the use of informers (who violate personal confidences), wire tapping, and the forcible pumping of a man's stomach to secure evidence against him. "An individual's attitude toward something is his predisposition to perform, perceive, think, and feel in relation to it."[2] Attitudes are in turn reflected in *opinions,* which are specific judgments on particular issues. The sequence from value to attitude to opinion moves from the general to the specific, from a broad mental set or disposition to a narrower one and finally to a specific and concrete expression of it.

Opinions are *situational,* and therefore do not reflect values directly. An opinion may run counter to a mental set because of pressures in the immediate situation. An opinion is often the complex resultant of many attitudes. For example, attitudes derived from the value of personal integrity may call for rejection of wire tapping. But a belief that the community is in danger may bring other attitudes into play. The resultant opinion may accept wire tapping, perhaps with some reservations. When opinions reflect situational pressures, they may be held weakly, as in the case of legislators who respond to group threats or to shifting climates of opinion. (See Adaptation 23, p. 289.)

CONSENSUS

Where an opinion is current and widely shared, there is *consensus.* For example, there has been a developing consensus in the

[2] Theodore Newcomb, *Social Psychology* (New York: Dryden, 1950), p. 118.

United States on the desirability of a federal social security program. Although there is still disagreement on the extent of social security, the principle itself is no longer a matter of significant controversy. This development is probably a specific expression of an underlying shift in values and attitudes affecting individualism and social responsibility.

As a consensus develops, the subject is removed from political competition, and old alignments based upon it may be changed. For example, the fact that many New Deal measures were widely accepted by both Democrats and Republicans in 1952 probably hurt the Democratic cause in that year. (See Table VIII:2.) The Republican candidate, Dwight Eisenhower, disarmed his opponents by explaining that he did not intend to repeal the New Deal.

What the New Deal stood for had reached such a degree of acceptability, had become so noncontroversial by 1952, that even had Stevenson tried to draw the fire of Eisenhower on the issue, he would have met with little luck. . . . The memory of the depression of the 1930's had faded sufficiently so that less than a majority of the voters were willing to vote on this basis alone, and the actual New Deal remedial measures of fifteen and twenty years ago now seemed like a good thing. The only rub as far as the Democrats were concerned was that the New Deal had become ancient history. In the absence of any

Table **VIII:2**   Regular Republicans View the New Deal *

	Good Thing (Per Cent)	Mistake (Per Cent)	Neither Good nor Bad (Per Cent)	No Opinion (Per Cent)
Social Security laws	84	6	7	3
Farm price supports	39	34	13	14
Tennessee Valley Authority (TVA)	58	15	10	17
Recognition of labor unions	42	24	11	23
Marshall Plan	47	18	19	16

* From Louis Harris, *Is There a Republican Majority?* (New York: Harper, 1954), p. 41. Data are from the 1952 election studies of the Elmo Roper research organization. National cross sections of from 2500–4000 people were polled at intervals from January to October.

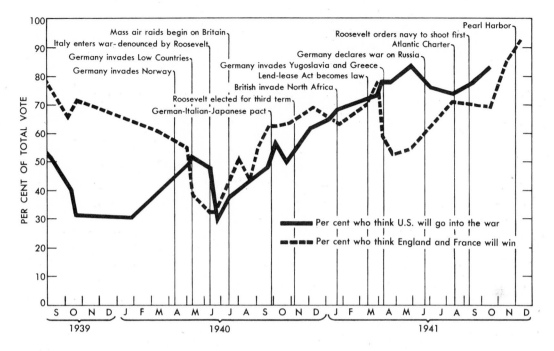

Fig. **VIII:1** Events and Opinions Prior to Pearl Harbor

Replies to two questions are plotted: (1) Do you think the United States will go into the war in Europe or do you think we will stay out of the war? (2) Which side do you think will win—Germany and Italy or England (and France)? [Data from Office of Public Opinion Research, Princeton University. Modified from Bruner, 1944, pp. 21 and 23, and Cantril, 1944, p. 221. Reproduced by permission of Harcourt, Brace & Co. from Ernest R. Hilgard, *Introduction to Psychology* (New York: Harcourt, Brace, 1953), p. 506]

Eisenhower opposition over it, the New Deal had ceased to be a potent vote-getter.[3]

Amendments to the U.S. Constitution usually reflect near-consensus, because the amending process is deliberately cumbersome and can be blocked by a strong minority. There are many occasions when the political community foregoes rule by simple majority, permitting a minority veto. Examples are the requirement that three-fourths of the states ratify an amendment, that a two-thirds majority is necessary for certain congressional acts, and the tolerance of filibusters in the Senate. On key issues a wide degree of consensus is sought in order to avoid serious disunity. If an amendment is passed hastily and in response to high-pressure political tactics, it may not reflect a true consensus, particularly if the long-run balance of forces in the community is changing. The victory of the Anti-Saloon League reflected very wide popular support for prohibition but not all who agreed did so with equal conviction. (See Adaptation 23.) The consequences of the proposed legislation were not fully understood, with the result that many people were willing to abandon prohibition after the enforcement problems were recognized. In addition, prohibition sentiment was weaker in the cities than in the rural areas, yet the cities were growing in political importance. The discovery and creation of consensus on the aims and key policies of government are two

[3] Louis Harris, *Is There a Republican Majority?* (New York: Harper, 1954), p. 42.

of the most important and difficult tasks of statesmanship. For an understanding of these problems, scientific studies of values and attitudes, based in part on public opinion surveys, will probably become progressively more useful.

GROUP BASIS OF PUBLIC OPINION

Public opinion is relatively unstable and tends to fluctuate with changes in the immediate situation even in matters of the gravest consequence. For example, opinions regarding U.S. entry into World War II were heavily influenced by events in Europe. (See Fig. VIII:1.) As this country becomes more exposed to rapid technological change and to pressures from the rest of the world, it is increasingly difficult to make statements beginning, "The American people will never stand for. . . ." Even matters on which near-consensus has been reached may become issues again in the swift movement of events. There is a large degree of unpredictability in the ebb and flow of public opinion, because the judgments are specific and the influence of the immediate situation is great. The more general a judgment—for example, "The English people are our natural allies"—the more likely it is to endure. But opinions on specific policies and events—such as, "The British are right in recognizing Communist China" —tend to reflect immediate pressures.

Despite this instability, public opinion develops within a *social setting*. The more we understand about that setting, the less arbitrary and unpredictable do the shifts in opinion appear. Though opinion emerges from day-to-day interaction, people have definite social backgrounds and group affiliations: they are not separate atoms moving about randomly.[4]

1. *Social background*. An individual's social background affects the way he responds to events and consequently the opinions he

forms. For example, when opinions on foreign policy were analyzed according to the social backgrounds of the respondents, the following conclusions were reached: (*a*) Younger people are more apt to be optimistic than their elders about the prospects of international organization. (*b*) Lower-income groups are more pessimistic about the future of international relations, in contrast to the moderate optimism of the middle and wealthy groups. There is more nationalism and isolationism among the lower-income classes. (*c*) Rural people are more pessimistic than city people and have less of a sense of power to influence events. These attitudes were *inferred* from the expression of specific opinions on foreign policy matters.[5] Table VIII:3 shows how three income groups differ in their opinions.

2. *Reference groups*. Differences in social background affect perspectives, and therefore opinions, because they make people sensitive to different things, provide experiences that give them feelings of weakness or strength, make them more or less verbal, more or less tradition-centered, and more or less prone to join organized groups. In addition, people tend to see themselves and the world through the framework provided by the groups in which they participate. However, we cannot automatically conclude that a person's "reference group" (that group whose perspectives he assumes) is derived from his occupational role or economic position. For example, many low-income people identify with and accept the standards of middle-class life. In modern society, with wide-open communication channels, people may assume the perspectives of groups they *aspire* to be in as well as (or in place of) those to which they actually belong. Furthermore, an individual may have many reference groups, affecting his opinions on specific subjects. He may be an alumnus, an auto dealer, a brother, a baseball fan, and a

[4] See "Public Opinion and Public Opinion Polling," by Herbert Blumer, *American Sociological Review*, October. 1948. pp. 542–49.

[5] Gabriel Almond, *The American People and Foreign Policy* (New York: Harcourt, Brace, 1950). Chap. VI.

Table **VIII:3**   Income Groups and Foreign Policy*

	Upper	Middle	Lower
Per cent who say the United States must buy abroad in order to sell abroad (August, 1946)	83	79	67
Per cent who belong to groups or organizations which discuss national and international problems (May, 1947)	28	16	8
Per cent who think there is something the United States could do to prevent a war (May, 1947)	62	59	46
Per cent who approve of this country's joining a "majority rule" type of world organization (February, 1947)	49	43	26
Per cent who advocate a high tariff policy for United States (August, 1946)	53	53	42
Per cent who gave "No opinion" or "Don't know" answers	10	13	22

* From *The American People and Foreign Policy* by Gabriel Almond (New York: Harcourt, Brace, 1950), p. 125. The table is adapted from public opinion polls of the American Institute of Public Opinion (Gallup), the *Fortune* Survey, and the National Opinion Research Center.

Southerner. Any or all may serve as reference groups for him. Reference groups should be distinguished from social categories, e.g., people in the same income level, and membership groups, such as trade-unions. Social categories and membership groups often *become* reference groups. In studying opinion it is important to know to what extent social categories and membership groups have been transformed into reference groups. It is also necessary to know which of the many reference groups actually influence the individual on a given issue.[6]

3. *Strong and weak groups.* Although many groups influence public sentiment, they are not equally effective. There are wide variations in group prestige, size, resources, and in the significance they have for the individual. To the extent that people think of themselves as "middle class," regardless of income, this reference group plays a significant role in the formation of opinion. A man's middle-class manners, speech, and physical appearance may make him an acceptable political candidate, and if his personality approaches the middle-class ideal, he may become influential. Although middle-class values and attitudes are widely held, organization among white-collar workers and consumers is relatively weak. On many specific issues, therefore, well-organized labor and business groups have greater weight. Special legislation, on tariffs and labor, for example, reflects the views of these organized groups. Even strongly held opinions may not influence decisions unless they are expressed through organizations. On most subjects, no popular vote is taken and differences in organization and resources determine the final outcome. (See Adaptation 23, p. 292, on the reluctance of the prohibition forces to accept a direct popular vote.)

A very large group may seem influential, but its real influence depends on how significant the group is for the member. A college alumnus may be a member of many groups, some of which play a far greater role in his life than the alumni association. This overlapping or *multiple membership* tends to limit the influence of particular groups. The demands upon the members, to support a policy or to give funds, compete with similar demands by other groups.

Multiple membership accounts in part for the relatively unstable and shifting character

[6] See *Fundamentals of Social Psychology* by Eugene L. Hartley and Ruth E. Hartley (New York: Knopf, 1952), pp. 465–81.

of public opinion. The individual is constantly pulled in different directions by his various memberships and roles. Consequently, group strength is not to be judged by mere size. One interest group may have 50,000 members yet have little influence upon them. Another of the same size may include a core of devoted workers who effectively mobilize the opinions of less committed members. A group may be strengthened by withdrawing its members from other attachments, but few organizations are able to do so. Communist parties and some religious sects, however, have gained strength in this way.

4. *Active and passive groups.* Those most concerned with controversial issues join or form interest groups. Others make up a large spectator-like body, interested enough to follow developments but not sufficiently concerned to participate directly. The passive groups are not necessarily without importance. As an audience whose reactions must be taken into account, they are arbiters in the struggle among interest groups. The naked pursuit of interests is limited not only by law and custom but also by the other members of the public whose approval is required. Interest groups try to show that their interests are tied to the general welfare. In this way, active groups bid for the support of the spectators, who judge whether private and public interests are truly related. That is why trade-unions, business associations, and professional groups like the American Medical Association, spend so much time and effort on public relations.

In summary, knowledge of the group structure of society is indispensable to a proper understanding of public opinion. Opinions are affected by social experience; and the interaction of groups, varying in strength and activity, determines the weight and direction of public sentiment.

ASCERTAINING OPINION

In a free society people "vote" in many ways. They speak out at home and among their friends and associates, write letters to newspapers and legislators, join or quit organizations, and go to the polls. Because opinion is registered in many ways, it must be studied in many ways. One way is to study the rise and decline of organizations, for example, to determine the fate of socialist ideology or prohibition sentiment in the United States. Another way is to find out what the most active people (the "opinion leaders") in a community think. Another approach is to assess opinion in influential business, professional, and government circles. Finally, there is the problem of determining how people vote and what their votes mean.

The prediction of election returns has been justly considered an important achievement of modern social science. The polls have helped to demonstrate that the behavior of large populations can be studied through the sophisticated use of sampling techniques. In Adaptation 24, page 297, Likert shows how accurately a small nationwide sample can reflect certain characteristics of the population as a whole.

Election polls are designed to predict a single, highly complex event. This is an exacting task, for it requires not merely one prediction but a whole chain of subordinate ones. The polls must be able to analyze the "don't know" or undecided responses and predict how they will divide on election day. The pollsters must predict how many people will vote and from what groups in society they will come because many who state their preferences when asked do not take the trouble to vote. Analyses of the 1948 election polls showed that inadequate handling of these problems probably led to the failure to predict President Truman's election.

The prediction of elections is only part of the broad study of public opinion. As we have seen, the weight and effectiveness of public opinion depends on the group structure of society; it is not a mere summation of the views held by separate and equal individuals. The polls have devised techniques well suited to the study of consumer preferences and elections. Standardized products like soap are purchased by almost everyone—and in roughly equal quantities. Many elections are in essence popularity contests, and some election campaigns have employed the same advertising techniques used for the sale of soap. Just as one man's purchase roughly equals another's, so one man's vote counts as much as another's, irrespective of differences in status or power.

The election poll, however accurate, has all the limitations of the election itself as a way of ascertaining public opinion:

1. *Intensity.* A person who expresses his preference to an interviewer may or may not take his vote seriously; he may be very unhappy or quite undisturbed if his candidate loses. The strength of his opinion, of course, affects the chances that he will actually cast his ballot.

2. *Meaning.* A vote may mean quite different things to different people. Was the election merely a popularity contest? Did the voters mean to give the new administration a mandate on specific issues? Which issues were central and which peripheral? These questions remain unanswered, and there is room for interpretation after the election is over, especially when the results are very close, as they were in the Nixon-Kennedy contest of 1960.

3. *Action.* As a result of variation in intensity and meaning, it is difficult to say whether an expressed preference will lead to any action. This applies most immediately

to whether a man votes at all, but beyond that it is important to know whether voting a certain way leads to other forms of political action. The bare expression of preference does not tell.

Modern and sophisticated public opinion surveys that go beyond the simple expressions of preference attempt to overcome these limitations. Intensity can be gauged by avoiding simple yes-no answers and providing graded alternatives from which to choose. People may be asked directly whether they "strongly approve," "approve," "don't care," etc., or a more elaborate and carefully worked out series of alternatives may be presented. The problem of meaning can be handled by offering a series of increasingly specific questions on the same topic. Each succeeding question requires a more precise answer about what the words mean and what the implications of the point of view are. Superficial responses can be filtered out in this way, as shown in Table VIII:4.

In the future public opinion analysis will probably place less emphasis on specific predictions and more on general understanding of underlying trends. It is more important to know whether the coalition of social groups that contributed to the Democratic majorities from 1932–1948 is basically intact or split than to predict a specific election. An election may result in part from accidental circumstances, whereas a trend may be related to more enduring changes in population composition, such as the assimilation of ethnic minorities, the improvement of the

Table **VIII:4**   Filtering Conventional Responses *

Do you believe in freedom of speech?	Yes	97%
	No	1
	Don't know	2
If "yes": Do you believe in it to the extent of allowing Fascists and Communists to hold meetings and express their views in this community?	Yes	23%
	No	72
	No opinion	5

*From *Gauging Public Opinion* by Hadley Cantril (Princeton: Princeton University Press, 1944), p. 22. The questions were asked by the American Institute of Public Opinion in November, 1940.

economic condition of some groups, or the development of new values. (See POLITICAL MAN, pp. 709 f.)

INFLUENCING OPINION

Propaganda may be defined as the calculated dissemination of partisan ideas with the intent of influencing group attitudes and opinions. It is a form of special pleading in which truth may be, and often is, subordinated to effectiveness. Some regard propaganda as morally neutral, justified or not according to the ends it serves. Others feel it is inherently manipulative and tends to corrupt the free formation of considered judgments, whether in choosing a toothpaste or a foreign policy. This debate turns largely on a matter of degree. Most propaganda operates within limits, foregoing the bare-faced lie and the more strident emotional appeals.

In an older and more restricted usage, "propaganda" is the dissemination of a systematic doctrine, such as Catholicism. The Communists hold to this usage, distinguishing "propaganda" from "agitation." The former refers to intensive work among small groups, with emphasis on communicating fundamental ideas, e.g., Marxist economic and political theories. Agitation is the spreading of a few ideas, usually with a heavy emotional content, to a great many people. In its restricted sense "propaganda" is closer to "indoctrination" and does not have many of the characteristics associated with the use of mass communications. We shall use "propaganda" in the more general sense, without distinguishing it from agitation.

Propaganda usually refers to writings, speeches, pictures, gestures, and other symbols. In addition the term "propaganda of the deed" has been used in connection with the dramatic actions of nineteenth-century anarchists who attempted to win attention to purported evils by assassinations or other acts of violence. However, recent history has seen many examples of government action taken with a view to influencing attitudes. Even so

vast an action as the Korean war had its propaganda significance. It showed the determination of the free world to resist Communist aggression. Military defeats, too, such as the abortive invasion of Cuba in 1961, are weighed for their propaganda effects. Any event can have a symbolic meaning, communicating the intentions as well as the strength or weakness of the actor.

The nature and effectiveness of propaganda depend on objectives and on the characteristics of the target population. If the aim is to sell a particular brand of cigarettes, certain techniques of attention-getting may suffice. But if the aim is to win support for a political belief or economic doctrine, different methods may be needed. If ideas of this sort are to "get across," they must be adapted to the experiences of the listener, and this usually requires a highly selective approach to various types of audiences. The "cold war" has taught United States propagandists the necessity for more intensive knowledge of the group basis of opinion in Europe and Asia. This discussion considers some characteristics of propaganda aims, methods, and targets.

Aims

As a mass-communications activity, propaganda tends to have short-run, situationally-defined aims. The appeal is to a diverse population on the basis of immediate interests, fears, or desires. The propaganda of advertisers, interest groups, and political parties is largely of this kind. The objective is not so much to influence the individual deeply as to win his support for some immediate issue, candidate, or product. The more short-run and superficial the aims, the easier it is to use propaganda tricks and gadgets. Long-run aims, which attempt to change basic attitudes, are more difficult to achieve.

Although it seems obvious that the objective of propaganda is to win active approval, in fact it may seek only passive acquiescence. A revolutionary group preparing a *coup d'état* does not necessarily require mass support so long as the population passively accepts the insurrection. Similarly, much Communist propaganda since World War II has not been aimed at winning allegiance to Communism but is content to induce passivity and confusion. The objective is to isolate the U.S. from popular support abroad.

Some propaganda, though ostensibly directed outward, is really a way of bolstering group morale. Political meetings usually bring together people already committed to the organization or candidate. They are "pep rallies" designed to stimulate confidence and increase involvement, though they may also be effective propaganda as demonstrations of strength. Propaganda activity gives a group something to do and therefore strengthens its cohesion. During a long period of its history, Communist propaganda seemed especially inept, using esoteric language and slogans that had little relevance to the experience of those to whom the propaganda was directed. Yet it helped to build the "hard core" of the Communist movement.

Methods

In the study of propaganda most attention has been given to techniques and relatively little to aims or targets. A number of characteristic propaganda methods have been identified:

1. *Gaining attention.* Many varied techniques have been used, from luminous paint to the "big lie." The effectiveness of attention-getting techniques depends on the nature of the medium used as well as the disposition of the audience. Charges against an individual often receive wide publicity in the press, whereas answers to these charges seem inherently less interesting and are given less prominent display. An emphasis on negative attitudes, as in the anti-saloon propaganda (see Adaptation 23, p. 292), is often successful in winning attention and support because it is easier to get agreement on the existence of an evil than on some particular solution.

2. *Associating a partisan cause with existing values, attitudes, and symbols.* The propagandist, pleading for a special interest, tries to identify himself with a wider community. He uses symbols that are known to elicit favorable responses, such as highly sentimentalized propaganda playing upon warm feelings toward children, mother, and the home town. *Glittering generalities* are emotionally loaded symbols that associate a cause directly to a general value. It is also very common to employ prestigeful figures, sometimes merely to grace a letterhead, as a way of legitimizing propaganda. (This is not necessarily to be deplored, because if the members of a public know the views of prestige figures, and prestige figures are involved, the device can help to identify the appeal and its source.)

In modern history the struggle for valued symbols has been a common feature of propaganda contests. Adolf Hitler took advantage of the fact that "socialist" was a high prestige word for many Europeans when he called his party the National Socialist German Labor Party. The Russian Communists continue to call themselves "democratic" and their satellites "people's governments," despite their dictatorial regime.

3. *Concealing identity and aims.* The attempt to associate a cause with existing community sentiment is often jeopardized when the true aims and special interests of the sponsors are known. An evasive technique is the use of "front" organizations that have innocuous names and objectives but are controlled and manipulated by covert interests. The use of front organizations by extremists of various kinds has greatly increased the sophistication needed for effective political participation.

4. *Raising anxieties.* The critical ability of an audience may be impaired by techniques that induce anxiety and fear. This is widely practiced in advertising that makes people anxious about health, love, and status. In political propaganda *hidden* enemies are commonly emphasized.

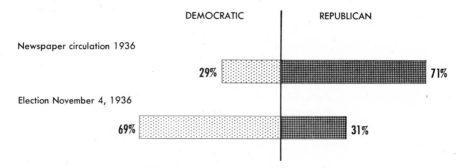

Fig. **VIII:2**   Public Opinion Often Differs from Newspaper Opinions

The popular vote for Franklin D. Roosevelt did not coincide with the editorial opinions of newspapers in the fifteen largest cities. Editorial opinion may neither express nor profoundly affect public opinion. See "The Press and the Public," *The New Republic*, **90** (March 17, 1937), 178–91.

5. *Showing strength.* Propagandists are sensitive to the reluctance of people to support a weak cause, and much effort is expended in putting on displays of strength. Sometimes this consists in propagating an ideology that history is necessarily moving in a particular direction and that "the cause" represents this "wave of the future." Parades, meetings, strikes, and similar demonstrations are also effective, but the turnout must in fact be impressive, lest the effort boomerang. Effective organizational work is necessary to supplement the propaganda and to sustain its effects.

6. *Excluding competition.* The exercise of critical ability depends in part on the competition of ideas. If only one side is presented, the tools of criticism are lacking. However, it appears that a mere preponderance of propaganda does not necessarily determine opinion. Large city newspapers with editorial policies opposed to Franklin D. Roosevelt greatly outnumbered those that supported him, but this had little relation to the vote. (See Fig. VIII:2.)

Targets

An understanding of the target group is a vital condition for effective propaganda. The social composition and organization of the population must be understood as well as psychological factors that influence susceptibility.

1. *Social composition and organization.* Propaganda must be adapted to the backgrounds and experiences of the target group. An advertisement that assumes the "typical American" lives on Main Street in a small town and has a grandfather who used "spunk water" to cure warts is not likely to mean much to the urban son of an Italian immigrant.[7] A knowledge of the social composition of a population reveals a great deal about its *prior dispositions* to accept or reject certain propaganda emphases. For example, immigrant groups often retain some loyalty to their country of origin, and suburban populations are especially conscious of social status. Knowledge of such interests and aspirations affects the choice of propaganda themes and methods.

It is also important to know how the population is *organized,* for this determines the acceptable channels of communication. Where local leaders or special organizations are powerful, propaganda that by-passes these channels may be suspect and go unheeded. Some groups are more accessible to

[7] See William H. Whyte, Jr., *Is Anybody Listening?* (New York: Simon and Schuster, 1952), pp. 30–33.

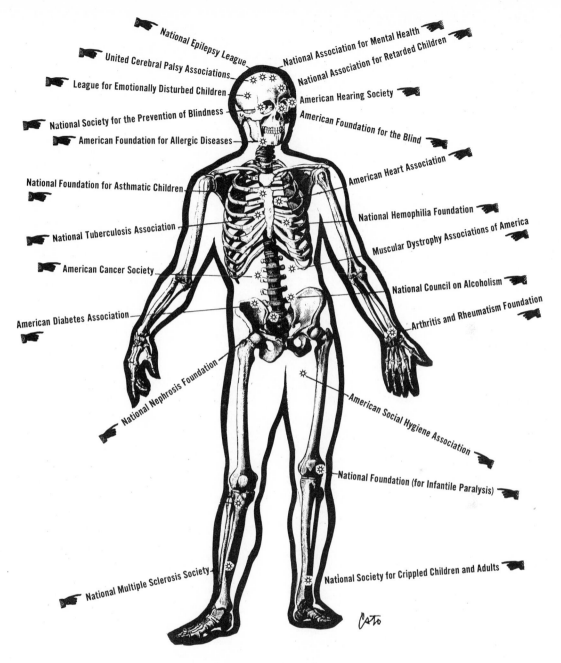

Competing Sovereignties

National Epilepsy League

National Association for Mental Health

United Cerebral Palsy Associations

National Association for Retarded Children

League for Emotionally Disturbed Children

American Hearing Society

National Society for the Prevention of Blindness

American Foundation for the Blind

American Foundation for Allergic Diseases

American Heart Association

National Foundation for Asthmatic Children

National Hemophilia Foundation

National Tuberculosis Association

Muscular Dystrophy Associations of America

American Cancer Society

National Council on Alcoholism

American Diabetes Association

Arthritis and Rheumatism Foundation

National Nephrosis Foundation

American Social Hygiene Association

National Foundation (for Infantile Paralysis)

National Multiple Sclerosis Society

National Society for Crippled Children and Adults

CATO

appeals based on self-interest; others respond to ideological propaganda. This is not a matter of accident but a product of the special backgrounds and experiences of various elements in the population.

A community is made up of many different audiences, and each must be approached in a special way. For example, propaganda directed at the *elites* (the most influential or self-conscious groups in a community), requires a more sophisticated and more pointed approach than propaganda aimed at a wider audience. An example of elite-oriented propaganda is the attempt to reach potentially disaffected Communists behind the "iron curtain," a project that must be based on a high degree of knowledge of the history and problems of Communism and Socialism.

2. *Susceptibility.* Some general psychological mechanisms are known to affect vulnerability or resistance to propaganda. In ambiguous situations, people look for cues. They are more suggestible to ideas and rumors than they would be if the situation were clearly defined. Hence, propagandists play an important role during times of unrest. In general, whenever propaganda meets some *felt need* in the population, if only the relief of anxiety, it is likely to get a hearing. On the other hand, people *evade* propaganda by filtering out what they want to hear and rejecting the rest.

Although propaganda is significant in unstructured situations, it is not the only way opinion is influenced. In transmitting ways of looking at the world and one's self, socialization makes some ideas congenial and others alien. Furthermore, most opinions are acquired in the course of group participation rather than in response to mass communications.

FEARS AND PROSPECTS

When several publics exist, and each has the opportunity to weigh conflicting views according to the criterion of self-interest, the multigroup character of society is preserved. Because of heterogeneity and self-interest, the conditions that make for emotional contagion are lacking. (See above, p. 278.) However, modern mass communications tend to make many millions available to similar and simultaneous influences. There is a danger that emotional contagion, based upon common fears of war or subversion, will sweep society and lead to excessive and irresponsible reactions. This has been referred to as the degeneration of publics into crowds. Lederer [8]

said that the "mass-state," built upon the eradication of groups, replaces reason by propaganda, and enslaves man by delivering him to his emotions. In such a society, public opinion is not the result of the slowly working interplay of interests and ideas, but is the crowdlike response of an amorphous population.

A similar view has been expressed by Neumann:

Mob psychology, when it seizes a whole nation, destroys the web of its complex structure. Like the individual differentiation of its members, so the innumerable associations of the living community are melted into one gray mass. This process of "massification"—the dissolution of free organizations, the flattening of the social pyramid—in a way preceded the rise of modern dictators. They were the product of this disintegration of society which in turn became the basis of their established rule. [9]

Views of this kind, which emphasize the extension of crowd behavior to many aspects of social life, have been common during the past century. [10] They are usually stated in exaggerated terms, but they probably point to an underlying trend and danger.

A graphic depiction of an imaginary society dominated by the calculated manipulation of symbols is found in George Orwell's novel *Nineteen Eighty-Four.* Orwell describes a society ruled by Big Brother and his Ministry of Truth. The Ministry systematically rewrites history and has for its slogans WAR IS PEACE, FREEDOM IS SLAVERY, IGNORANCE IS STRENGTH. The machinery of propaganda and intimidation is highly developed, including an official language, Newspeak, much of whose vocabulary is deliberately constructed for political purposes. (See "Language and Politics *in Extremis,*" p. 288.) Orwell's account is a projec-

[8] Emil Lederer, *The State of the Masses* (New York: Norton, 1940).

[9] Sigmund Neumann, *Permanent Revolution* (New York: Harper & Bros., 1942), p. 115.

[10] See especially Gustave Le Bon, *The Crowd* (London: Unwin, 1917); and E. A. Ross, *Social Psychology* (New York: Macmillan, 1908).

The Tricks of the Trade

Abridged from Institute for Propaganda Analysis, *The Fine Art of Propaganda* by Alfred McClung Lee and Elizabeth Briant Lee (New York: Harcourt, Brace & Co., 1939). Reprinted by permission.

Some of the devices now so subtly and effectively used by good and bad propagandists are as old as language. All have been used in one form or another by all of us in our daily dealings with each other. Propagandists have seized upon these methods we ordinarily use to convince each other, have analyzed and refined them, and have experimented with them until these homely devices of folk origin have been developed into tremendously powerful weapons for the swaying of popular opinions and actions.

The chief devices used in popular argument and by professional propagandists—together with our symbols for them—are:

Name calling—giving an idea a bad label—is used to make us reject and condemn the idea without examining the evidence.

Glittering generality—associating something with a "virtue word"—is used to make us accept and approve the thing without examining the evidence.

Card stacking involves the selection and use of facts or falsehoods, illustrations or distractions, and logical or illogical statements in order to give the best or the worst possible case for an idea, program, person, or product.

Transfer carries the authority, sanction, and prestige of something respected and revered over to something else in order to make the latter acceptable; or it carries authority, sanction, and disapproval to cause us to reject and disapprove something the propagandist would have us reject and disapprove.

Testimonial consists in having some respected or hated person say that a given idea or program or person is good or bad.

Plain folks is the method by which a speaker attempts to convince his audience that he and his ideas are good because they are "of the people," the "plain folks."

Band wagon has as its theme "Everybody—at least all of *us*—is doing it"; with it, the propagandist attempts to convince us that all members of a group to which we belong are accepting his program and that we *must therefore* follow our crowd and "jump on the band wagon."

Once we know that a speaker or writer is using one of these propaganda devices in an attempt to convince us of an idea, we can separate the device from the idea and see what the idea amounts to on its own merits.

Language and Politics in Extremis

From "The Principles of Newspeak," Appendix to *Nineteen Eighty-Four* by George Orwell; copyright, 1949 (New York: Harcourt, Brace & Company, Inc.), pp. 309–11. Used with permission.

The name of every organization, or body of people, or doctrine, or country, or institution, or public building, was invariably cut down into the familiar shape: that is, a single easily pronounced word with the smallest number of syllables that would preserve the original derivation. In the Ministry of Truth, for example, the Records Department was called *Recdep,* the Fiction Department was called *Ficdep,* the Teleprograms Department was called *Teledep,* and so on. Even in the early decades of the twentieth century, telescoped words and phrases had been one of the characteristic features of political language; and it had been noticed that the tendency to use abbreviations of this kind was most marked in totalitarian countries and totalitarian organizations.* It was perceived that in thus abbreviating a name one *narrowed and subtly altered its meaning,* by cutting out most of the associations that would otherwise cling to it. The words *Communist International,* for instance, call up a composite picture of universal human brotherhood, red flags, barricades, Karl Marx, and the Paris Commune. The word *Comintern,* on the other hand, suggests merely a tightly knit organization and a well-defined body of doctrine. *Comintern* is a word that can be uttered almost without taking thought, whereas *Communist International* is a phrase over which one is obliged to linger at least momentarily. In the same way, the associations called up by a word like *Minitrue* are fewer and more controllable than those called up by *Ministry of Truth.*

What was required, above all for political purposes, were short clipped words of unmistakable meaning which could be uttered rapidly and which roused the minimum of echoes in the speaker's mind. For the purposes of everyday life it was no doubt necessary, or sometimes necessary, to reflect before speaking, but a Party member called upon to make a political or ethical judgment should be able to spray forth the correct opinions as automatically as a machine gun spraying forth bullets. His training fitted him to do this, the language gave him an almost foolproof instrument, and the texture of the words, with their harsh sound and a certain willful ugliness, assisted the process still further.

The Newspeak vocabulary was tiny, and differed from almost all other languages in that its vocabulary grew smaller instead of larger each year. Each reduction was a gain, since the smaller the area of choice, the smaller the temptation to take thought. Ultimately it was hoped to make articulate speech issue from the larynx without involving the higher brain centers at all. This aim was frankly admitted in the Newspeak word *duckspeak,* meaning "to quack like a duck." Provided that the opinions which were quacked out were orthodox ones, it implied nothing but praise, and when the *Times* referred to one of the orators of the Party as a *doubleplusgood duckspeaker* it was paying a warm and valued compliment.

* For example, "Gestapo" from Geheime *Staatspolizei,* "Comintern" from *Communist International,* "Inprecorr" from *International Press Correspondence* (official organ of the Communist International), "Agitprop" from *Agitation* and *Propaganda* department.

tion of some of the features of the totalitarian societies of Nazi Germany and Soviet Russia.

Some of the anxiety about the future of public opinion is based on the *strong pressures toward conformity* in the mass communications industries. Since profit-making is the criterion of successful operation, there is a tendency to try to please as many people as possible and to avoid antagonizing highly vocal groups. The industries are fearful of minority views and tastes. Sensitive or controversial issues are likely to be avoided. The forums that should be available to divergent opinion if the general public is to be well informed may be closed. It is also feared that a dead level of uniformity in taste, stirring no antagonisms yet rising to no new heights, may stultify the arts. No doubt these fears have some justification. On the other hand, new technological developments may change the situation drastically, making many more channels of communication available to experimental and educational activities.

The Anti-Saloon League

Abridged and adapted from Peter H. Odegard, *Pressure Politics: The Story of the Anti-Saloon League* (New York: Columbia University Press, 1928). Published in this form by permission of Peter H. Odegard and Columbia University Press.

In 1920 the Eighteenth Amendment to the U.S. Constitution was ratified, prohibiting "the manufacture, sale, or transportation of intoxicating liquors." The "noble experiment" ended thirteen years later, so far as national legislation was concerned. Enforcement had proved difficult and, in many urban areas, virtually impossible, bringing the bootlegger into American life and with him the high point of gangsterism. In addition, prohibition sentiment, old in American history, was mainly rural and Protestant. Repeal in part reflected the waning of rural dominance in national politics. We shall not deal here with the shift in sentiment that led from prohibition to repeal but only with the coming of national prohibition itself.

Passage of the Eighteenth Amendment can largely be attributed to the national Anti-Saloon League, formed in 1895. This organization transformed the existing temperance movement from a moral appeal to the individual into a political power. The following account describes the nature and strategy of the Anti-Saloon League. Some implications for understanding public opinion and propaganda are noted in the concluding summary and interpretation.

THE SOCIAL BASE OF PROHIBITIONIST OPINION

Although in theory the Anti-Saloon League was a nonsectarian organization, in fact it was almost entirely an instrument of the Protestant churches, principally the Methodist, Baptist, Presbyterian, and Congregational denominations. Prohibitionist sentiment was strong among these groups, and the Anti-Saloon League was organized to give them effective political organization. The League was what would today be called a "front" organization. In theory it was open to anyone; in practice it was controlled by the Protestant churches from whom it drew both its leadership and its principal membership support. The churches opened their pulpits to Anti-Saloon League speakers and provided the League with an extraordinary access to church membership. According to one account, pastors in more than two thousand churches in Illinois discussed a pending temperance measure on a single Sunday.

During the prohibitionist heyday, the Protestant church in America was predominantly rural and native. Even in the cities, Protestant churches were composed largely of people born in rural areas. Where Protestants were in the majority, as in the South, prohibitionist sentiment was strong: nine of the Southern states adopted prohibition prior to 1916. Connecticut and Rhode Island never ratified the Eighteenth Amendment; Catholics made up 67 per cent and 76 per cent, respectively, of the total church population in these states.

The Anti-Saloon League did not have to create prohibitionist sentiment; it already existed in the rural, native, Protestant areas. Nor did it have to organize prohibitionist sentiment; it was already organized in the Protestant churches. But with singular success, it *mobilized* the existent and organized sentiment and directed it toward a political purpose, the passage of prohibitionist legislation.

MORAL SENTIMENT INTO POLITICAL ACTION

The Anti-Saloon League, formed as a national organization in 1895, was, as its name suggests, a league of already existing temperance organizations. Behind it lay almost a century of temperance agitation, some of which had tried with only indifferent success to achieve prohibition legislation. One local organization, however, the Oberlin Temperance Alliance, had secured the passage of such legislation in Ohio. In 1887 the Oberlin Temperance Alliance circulated petitions demanding the passage of a state-wide Township Option Bill, by which individual municipalities might vote to outlaw the sale of liquor. The bill was put through the House and went to the Senate where, according to a preliminary poll, it had a majority of one. Two days before the vote was to be

taken, Senator Crook of Dayton, one of the bill's supporters, announced that after having been visited by three committees of Dayton brewers, distillers, and saloonkeepers, he had been persuaded to vote against the measure.

Senator Crook's frankness was his own undoing. The prohibitionists reasoned that if he could be influenced by pressure from the liquor interests, he could be encouraged to return to the straight and narrow by greater pressure from the other side. That afternoon, the Rev. H. H. Russell, employed by the Alliance to push the bill, went to Dayton. Soon letters, telegrams, and petitions from citizens of that city poured in upon the recalcitrant Crook demanding that he support local option. The Senator did vote for it, and the measure was passed by a majority of one.

Senator Crook and his three committees of brewers, distillers, and saloonkeepers provided the Anti-Saloon League with a lesson in politics. Thereafter the temperance movement diverted its efforts from appealing to the conscience of the individual voter to exerting direct influence on legislators themselves.

PRESSURE POLITICS

With the Ohio experience as a model, the national Anti-Saloon League organized itself into a legislative pressure group. It set itself up as a single-purpose organization, concentrating solely on the passage of prohibition legislation. Some prohibitionists had earlier formed themselves into a Prohibition party, arguing that the existing parties would not and could not institute prohibition. But it had never won significant electoral support, and in 1896 it split on the silver and gold issue, each side putting its own presidential candidate into the field. The Anti-Saloon League avoided all side issues upon which disagreement and factional splits could occur, and which might alienate potential supporters. Advocates of silver or of gold, of free trade or of a high tariff could all join in the Anti-Saloon League's drive for prohibition legislation without endangering their other loyalties.

Instead of entering politics as another party, the League worked through the Republican and Democratic parties, supporting whatever dry candidates were nominated. It did not care what else a candidate stood for, so long as he stood for prohibition. It frequently supported both Republicans and Democrats in the same election, provided both candidates were dry. Nor did the Anti-Saloon League insist that a candidate be a personal abstainer. The League's theory was that it is better to have a drunkard who will "vote right, than to have a saint who will vote wrong."

The League's objective was to hold the balance of power. With virtual control of a large block of voters, the League frequently forced the major parties to nominate candidates friendly to its interests, since the dry vote often spelled the difference between victory and defeat.

Having decided on a satisfactory candidate, the League did all it could to see that he was elected. Women and children were urged to gather near the polls to act as reminders of the evil of the saloon. They often paraded before polling places wearing badges: "Vote Against Whiskey and For Me," or "Vote Against the Saloon—I Can't Vote." The following report in the *New York World* of May 13, 1919, describes a North Carolina election scene:

When a voter came within range he was immediately surrounded by . . . ministers . . . women and children. The clergymen employed words of advice and confined their activities to the proprieties. But the women and children were less tactful. They clutched at the coats of the voter. They importuned him to vote the dry ticket. A phrase constantly employed was "Mister, for God's sake don't vote for whiskey," repeated with parrot-like accuracy that results from thorough coaching. . . . A few of the wets

ran the gauntlet of the women and children . . . but the greater majority of the voters viewed the conflict from afar and returned to their offices and homes. The drys won the day.

The League provided funds and personnel for more routine campaign activities, often employing organizers to canvass voters in their homes. In 1906 in New York it promised aid in his current campaign to any state assembly member who had voted dry and was being opposed on that account. Thirty-six dry members requested such assistance, and all were re-elected.

When prohibition legislation was pending, the Anti-Saloon League employed many kinds of direct action techniques designed to impress recalcitrant legislators with the size and strength of dry opinion. As in the campaign of the Oberlin Temperance Alliance, local League organizations saw to it that legislators received letters and telegrams from dry voters. Petitions were also effective. When national prohibition was up for debate in the House of Representatives in 1913, long slips of paper listing the names of over six million petitioners hung from the balconies filled with prohibition supporters. One Congressman suggested that the House move out of Washington to avoid pressure from the drys. That same year Congress had been petitioned to submit prohibition to the states by a parade of four thousand men and women, many of them grown gray and infirm in the long campaign, wearing the white ribbon of temperance and marching to the strains of "Onward, Christian Soldiers."

The threat of defeat for wets and the promise of victory for drys was, however, the principal political weapon of the Anti-Saloon League. In 1917, just before the House passed the resolution to submit prohibition to the states, the *Washington Times* asserted, "If the ballot on the constitutional amendment were a secret ballot, making it impossible for the Anti-Saloon League bosses to punish disobedience, the Amendment would not pass." The newspaper implied that national prohibition was about to be passed not out of conviction but out of fear of political reprisal. The League's electoral effectiveness depended on two things: (1) its control of the rural vote and (2) the dependence at that time of both the state and national legislatures on rural areas. If the rural vote had not been very nearly a block firmly committed on the dry issue, the League's promise to deliver votes would have been far less effective than it actually was. If the legislatures had been as dependent on the cities as they were on the rural areas, the League's hold over the rural voters would have been a less potent political weapon.

INFLUENCING THE LEGISLATORS

When the Anti-Saloon League turned its energies from reforming the individual to pressing for the passage of prohibition, it sought to exert its influence where the rural population had its political power. This was in the state legislatures, which tend to over-represent rural and small town areas wherever representation is based on geographical area rather than population. In the United States Senate a sparsely settled rural state like North Dakota has as many senators as a densely populated state like New York. In addition, the movement toward the cities tends to weight legislative bodies toward rural overrepresentation, since reapportionment lags behind actual population changes. In 1917, when the League put on its strongest drive for national prohibition, one of its leaders pointed out, "We have got to win it now because when 1920 comes and reapportionment is here, forty new Congressmen will come from the great wet centers with their rapidly increasing population."

In most cases the Anti-Saloon League opposed submitting the prohibition issue to direct popular vote, trusting rather to its influence in the state legislatures. In the debate on national prohibition it was pro-

posed that ratification be by state conventions elected by popular vote for that purpose. To this the League spokesmen objected and insisted that the more usual procedure of ratification by state legislatures be followed. They argued that since state conventions would be chosen by the same electorate that had chosen the state legislatures, the proposal to submit ratification to a more direct vote was merely a delaying tactic. Although the League had itself pressed for a seven-year ratification period in case ratification in some states would prove difficult, three-fourths of the states ratified within fourteen months. The speed with which the amendment was ratified surprised the wets as well as the drys. "The grip held by the Anti-Saloon League over the state legislatures was never better illustrated than in the manner in which these bodies obeyed the command to ratify. In vain were suggestions made that the lawmaking bodies were without instructions from the people on this most important question. In vain were efforts made to have the sentiment of the electorate tested by referendum voting." [11]

PROPAGANDA STRATEGY

The League directed its propaganda not so much *for* prohibition as *against* the saloon and its evils. This was an effective device because even drinkers who balked at the idea of absolute prohibition were willing to admit that the American saloon had become a noisome thing. The United States Brewers' Association itself had recognized the need for reform. Reform, however, would not satisfy the League, and it pictured the saloon as hopeless beyond redemption.

"The saloon is the storm center of crime; the devil's headquarters on earth; the schoolmaster of a broken decalogue; the defiler of youth; the enemy of the home; the foe of peace; the deceiver of nations; the beast of sensuality; the past master of intrigue; the

[11] *Year Book of the United States Brewers' Association,* 1919, p. 18.

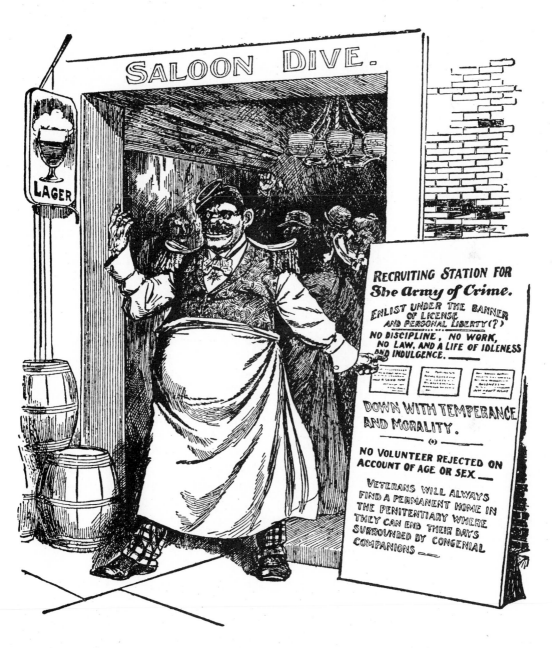

The Recruiting Sergeant for the Army of Crime: This cartoon, depicting the saloon as a natural center for vice and crime, was widely used in Anti-Saloon League publications.

vagabond of poverty; the social vulture; the rendezvous of demagogues; the enlisting office of sin; the serpent of Eden; a ponderous second edition of hell, revised, enlarged and illuminated." [12]

The anti-saloon propaganda of the League tried to induce a favorable attitude toward prohibition by attaching it to an already existing attitude, a negative attitude toward the saloon. It used the same strategy when it attached its fight for local option to democratic values. Local option, by which any political unit—county, city, town, or even ward—could vote to ban the saloon, was presented as an extension of self-government and home rule. Many people who personally disliked prohibition felt obliged to support the drive for local option as consonant with democracy. Woodrow Wilson, then Governor of New Jersey and no partisan of prohibition, wrote, "I am in favor of local option. I am a thorough believer in local self-government and believe that every self-governing community which constitutes a social unit should have the right to control the matter of the regulation or the withholding of licenses." [13]

National prohibition was first written into the law as an aspect of food conservation during the first World War. A bill was passed under the pressure of the drys prohibiting the manufacture of foodstuffs into distilled spirits, and giving the President authority to extend the restriction to beer and wine. The war gave considerable impetus to dry propaganda, prohibition being presented as part of the war effort. Nor did the League hesitate to play upon anti-German attitudes prevalent at the time. "German brewers in this country have rendered thousands of men inefficient and are thus crippling the Republic in its war on Prussian militarism. . . ." [14]

[12] Quoted from the Kentucky Edition of *American Issue*, April, 1912, the national organ of the Anti-Saloon League, also published in state editions.

[13] *American Issue*, Vermont Edition, March, 1912.

[14] *American Issue*, Ohio Edition, August 3, 1917.

Conclusion

1. Public opinion is usually ineffective unless it is transformed into political power. The Anti-Saloon League was distinguished from its predecessors by its use of prohibitionist opinion as an electoral weapon. It developed the political skill to defeat wets and elect drys. It concentrated its efforts on state legislatures, where prohibitionist votes were influential because of overrepresentation of the rural population.

2. Public opinion has a social base. Prohibitionist sentiment was not a matter of random individual opinion but was concentrated in native, rural, Protestant areas. It never gained significant following in large cities nor among immigrants and non-Protestants. The effectiveness of public opinion in determining governmental policy depends in large measure upon the social and political resources of its social base. The passage of prohibition legislation reflected the political and social importance of the rural population in American life, especially in the state legislatures. Its repeal can be attributed in part to the growing dominance both of the political power of the city dweller and of the values and attitudes of urban life. (See URBAN MAN, pp. 596–97.)

3. Since usually only a relatively small minority feels strongly about any issue, propaganda to influence others and gain allies is important in making public opinion effective. Such propaganda does not usually set out to create entirely new sentiments but to focus, strengthen, and extend old opinions. If the saloon had not become a reprehensible institution and if temperance sentiments had not already been present in large sections of the American people, the Anti-Saloon League would probably not have succeeded in its drive for legislation. But given temperance attitudes and the repugnance which many people felt toward the saloon, it was easy to transform these feelings into attitudes favorable to prohibition legislation.

4. A consensus may be temporary and unstable.

a. The social base which supports a given opinion may melt away. The conditions under which the rural population lives are quite different from what they were in the nineteenth century and early twentieth century, and the changes in these conditions have brought with them changes in attitudes and values.

b. The social base which supports a given opinion may lose its political dominance. The success of the prohibition movement came at the end of the period of rural political power. With a decline in political power, the rural population was less able to give to legislation the stamp of its own special attitudes and values.

c. Propaganda may gain allies and win a consensus on superficial or on unrealistic grounds. The adherence of many legislators to prohibitionist sentiments was not a matter of principle but of political expediency. Many people supported prohibition as a moral ideal but revoked their support when enforcement proved difficult.

Public Opinion Polls

Abridged and adapted from "Public Opinion Polls" by Rensis Likert, *Scientific American*, **179**, No. 6 (December, 1948). Published in this form by permission of Rensis Likert and the *Scientific American*.

The following adaptation presents an assessment of public opinion polls. Likert concludes that their failure in 1948 to predict the Democratic presidential victory by no means discredits public opinion polling but does dramatize the need for improvements in their techniques.

In 1948 Gallup forecast a 44.5 per cent vote for President Truman, who actually received 50 per cent of the vote and won the election. The failure of Gallup and other pollsters in predicting the outcome of the 1948 election has reinforced the skeptics of public opinion polling, who argue that the samples are too small or otherwise inadequate, that the problems are too complex to be dealt with in a few simple questions, and that the investigators are biased. How valid are these criticisms? How sound are the present polling techniques, and how reliable are their results? Is it possible to improve public opinion polling?

POLLING METHODS

The polling process divides conveniently into two major parts: (1) the population sample used; (2) the questionnaire, the method of interviewing, and the analysis of the replies. The accuracy of any poll obviously depends upon the accuracy of each of these parts.

Let us consider first the sample. In 1936 the now defunct *Literary Digest* magazine conducted a poll which forecast a Republican victory. Its conspicuous failure dramatized the fact that the design of a sample is as important as its size. Although the sample totaled more than two million persons, it erred by 20 percentage points because it was not representative of the total population. First, the poll was restricted to *Literary Digest* and telephone subscribers, that is, to those of a relatively high economic status. Second, it required that a mailed questionnaire be returned. This resulted in a further selection from an already highly-selected group; it selected out those who answer mailed questionnaires or who felt strong enough in this case to go to the trouble to do so.

The present public opinion polls use samples based on the so-called "quota-controlled" method. This method depends for its accuracy on finding those variables that have a high correlation with the behavior being studied. Thus to design a sample for predicting an election, the pollsters use their knowledge of how voting correlates with party affiliation, age, economic status, and so on. They then attempt to find out how these variables are distributed in the whole population. For example, census data will tell them how many people in the total population are Negro, how many are women, how many live in cities, and how many earn above and below certain amounts. These characteristics may be related to how people vote, and the sample must contain its proportionate quota of Negroes, women, etc. When the social composition of the sample is determined, quotas are then assigned to interviewers, that is, the interviewer must poll a certain number of persons in each age group, socio-economic group, etc.

For maximum accuracy, however, a pollster would need to know all of the variables correlated with voting behavior, such as previous voting behavior, education, income, occupation, religion, party affiliation of the voter's father, mother, and close friends, and so forth. He would also need precise information on the distribution of all these variables in the population. Unfortunately for public opinion polling, these two conditions almost never exist. In the first place, many of the variables that affect voting or other behavior are unknown. In the second place, no data are available on the distribution in the population of most of the variables that are known.

In spite of these difficulties, pollsters using the quota method have usually been able to make surprisingly accurate predictions. The methods generally employed are, briefly, as follows. Quotas are set, usually on the basis of geographical region, size of community, age, sex and socio-economic level. In some parts of the country, race also is included. In making election predictions, the results that these quota samples yield are generally tested by asking respondents how they voted in the previous presidential election and checking the percentages obtained with the actual election figures. Any discrepancy that exists is eliminated by weighting the results. For example, in a poll taken in Maine in 1944, 38 per cent of the persons interviewed said they planned to vote for Franklin D. Roosevelt. An analysis of the replies showed that the sample contained an underrepresentation of persons who had voted for Roosevelt in 1940. When a ratio correction was applied, a weighted estimate of 48 per cent for Roosevelt in 1944 was obtained.

ERRORS IN THE SAMPLES

A major source of bias in quota samples is the fact that interviewers, in a perfectly human fashion, endeavor to fill their quotas in the easiest manner possible. They go to places where people are readily available and seek any who will fill the age, sex, and socio-economic specifications of their quotas. They tend, therefore, to secure a sample which is biased in that it includes more people who are easily contacted than a truly representative sample should include.

An analysis of samples obtained with the quota-controlled method shows that this method tends to obtain data with biases which at times may be serious. For example, quota samples tend to include too few respondents from high income families, too few from the lowest income groups, too many with at least high school education, and too few with only a grade school education or less.

The basic weakness of the quota-controlled method is that it does not employ a random sample. A general human failing among interviewers, or errors in the fixing of quotas, may produce a sample which is systematically biased in the same direction. In other words, when deliberate human choice enters into the final selection of respondents, the usual laws of probability governing the sampling phenomenon do not apply; the errors or deviations may not balance one another as they tend to do in a purely random sample, but at times may become cumulative and produce a bias of large and unpredictable dimensions.

A MORE ACCURATE METHOD

All this indicates that a method which rigorously follows random procedures will produce more accurate samples than the quota method can. Acting on this basis, a few government and university groups have developed new methods of sampling which do indeed produce much more reliable results. These methods are called *probability sampling*. The fundamental requirement of probability sampling is that the final determination of just which persons are to be polled must be left to chance. Because this procedure is in conformity with statistical laws, it is possible to calculate precisely the probability that the margin of error in any sample will not exceed a given amount.

A method based on these principles, now being used, is known as the "area" sample. The basic principle of this method is that each person in the population is given an equal, or known, chance to come into the sample. This is done by associating each person with one, and only one, very small geographic area and then selecting a random sample of the small geographic areas into which the country is thus divided.

The first step is to make a purely random selection of counties and metropolitan areas. Then within each of these areas a sub-sample of small geographic segments is selected, again by random methods. The final sample may include all the dwellings in each selected segment, or every *k*th dwelling, depending on the size of sample desired. The selection of persons actually interviewed in each dwelling will then depend on the purpose of the survey; if its purpose is to predict an election, the sample will consist of all the eligible voters in the designated dwellings or certain voters selected at random.

When this method is used, the interviewer has no choice whatever. He goes to the specified dwelling and interviews the specified person or persons. If a respondent is not at home he calls again and again until he gets the interview; if he finds it impossible to do so, he reports that fact to headquarters.

RESULTS

The representative character of the samples obtained by the area sampling method has been amply proved in practice. The Survey Research Center at Michigan has compared the composition of small nationwide samples (of only 500 to 3,500 persons) with the U. S. Census figures for the nation as a whole, and has found that samples obtained by the area sampling method reflect rather accurately the composition of the national population. In an analysis based upon an area sample of only 1,151 persons, the following results were obtained:

In the Survey Research Center sample, 91 per cent of the persons interviewed were white; the census figure for the percentage of white persons in the whole population was 90.6.

In the sample 23 per cent turned out to be in the age group 21 to 29; the census figure for the same group was 22.8 per cent. In other age groups the correspondence was equally or almost equally close.

In the results on schooling, the proportion who had gone no farther than grade school was 44 per cent in this survey and 46.1 per cent in the census; those who had finished high school were 23 per cent of the sample, 22.9 per cent in the census; those who had finished college, 5 per cent of the sample, 5 per cent in the census.

The chief disadvantage of the area sample method is that it is more expensive. It costs more to design the sample and it costs much more for interviewers to take time to locate each designated respondent. But the increased accuracy of this method outweighs its additional cost. Because of the greater cost, most pollsters have resisted using probability samples and have adhered to the quota-sample method. Until the best available methods of sampling are used by those making election predictions and publishing polling results, it will be well to keep in mind that the sampling methods now employed may have a substantially larger error than is claimed. The formula now used by pollsters to compute the probable error in their polls is not applicable to quota samples; because the formula used is actually based on the assumption that the sample is a truly random one.

INTERVIEWING

Now let us consider the other part of the polling process—the questions that are asked, the quality of the interviewing, and the competence shown in the analysis and interpretation. In ordinary election polling there are two main problems: first, how to get frank and accurate replies, and second, how to estimate which of the people interviewed will actually go to the polls.

Several different procedures have been used to encourage respondents to answer accurately. One of these is publicity, intended to inform people about the poll so they will be prepared to be interviewed. Pollsters also try to win the co-operation of respondents by assuring them that their answers will be treated as confidential. One of the most useful devices for getting accurate answers is the indirect approach. Instead of asking the voter bluntly whether he is going to vote and, if so, for whom, the interviewer first asks a series of questions on the major issues in the campaign. People who are reluctant to say whom they expect to vote for will almost always tell how they feel about the issues, how strongly they feel, and which candidate

they believe will handle each of the different problems best. The answers to all these questions can then be analyzed to predict the probable proportion of each group who will vote and how they will vote.

The prediction of elections involves a particularly knotty problem which often is neglected. This is the "turnout problem"—predicting who will vote. To predict an election it is not sufficient to know what candidates are favored; it is necessary to know what candidates are favored by those persons who will actually go to the polls. This means that the pollster must know which voters are most likely to vote and which are most likely to stay home. Unfortunately, the pollsters have made few attempts to develop questions to measure the intensity of the determination to vote, and the results consequently have a large possible error.

After the 1948 election, Gallup is reported to have stated that his polls indicated a relatively small turnout, but that he did not mention this factor of uncertainty because his newspaper clients would have accused him of "hedging." As a rule, the larger the turnout, the greater the Democratic vote, but this rule may not have applied. In any case, it appears likely that the "undecided" vote and the size and character of the turnout played a large part in the miscalculations of the pollsters. Had they obtained more data on these factors and analyzed them adequately, their predictions might have been less positive and less wrong.

THE QUESTIONS

The measurement of opinion on social, economic, and international issues, and of public knowledge about these issues is more difficult, as a rule, than the prediction of elections. The problems in this field of polling are still so serious that opinion-poll results should be taken with even greater caution than predictions about elections.

Perhaps the greatest of these problems is that of meaning. Most of the issues of the day involve words and concepts that have different meanings for different people. On some issues large sections of the population may have no understanding of the major dimensions of the issue or the terms used. To understand the meaning of the percentages obtained in a poll, it is essential to know what respondents meant when they answered each question. Unfortunately, such data are not available. Yet polling results are often presented and discussed with the implicit assumption that each respondent understood the question and answered it from precisely the same point of view as that of the person conducting the poll.

An indication of the inadequacy of the usual polling questions can be obtained by asking a very small sample of respondents a question taken from any poll on a complex current problem and permitting these respondents to answer in their own words and to elaborate their answers. Several tests of polling questions have been made in this fashion. Quite consistently evidence has been obtained that questions on complex issues have different meanings for different people who are called upon to answer them.

Richard L. Crutchfield and Donald A. Gordon while at Swarthmore College ran a test on the following Gallup Poll question which appeared in news releases of August 22, 1943:

"After the war, would you like to see many changes or reforms made in the United States, or would you rather have the country remain pretty much the way it was before the war?"

To test interpretations of this question, the investigators interviewed a cross-section sample of 114 New York City residents. After recording the respondent's initial reaction to the question, "the interviewer then encouraged the respondent to enlarge upon his answer in an informal conversational manner." The interviewers found that the initial response of their New York respondents gave substantially the same results as

those obtained by Gallup for the country as a whole. But they also found that their respondents had seven different frames of reference in mind when answering the question. Some persons thought the question referred to "domestic changes or reforms"; others "technological changes"; others changes in the "basic political-economic structure of the U.S."; and still others thought it referred to changes in "foreign affairs of the U.S."

Respondents also had quite different meanings in mind when they answered "change" or "remain the same." For example, among those who answered in terms of "domestic changes and reforms" the word "change" for some persons meant shifts in a more liberal direction, such as "increases in social security," "higher pay levels," and "greater social equality for members of minority groups." Other persons meant a shift in the conservative direction, such as "change to a Republican administration," "less government control of business," and "more control of labor unions." Similarly, some of those who answered "remain the same" had in mind conservative aspects of our economy; others giving the same answer referred to liberal aspects, such as "maintaining high wages." It is obviously impossible to interpret percentages which combine into single totals answers which have such widely different meanings.

This study of what the respondents really meant by their answers substantially altered the interpretation of the poll. Thus, in their first answers, 49 per cent of the New York City respondents said they wanted the country to "remain the same," and 46 per cent voted for "changes or reforms." But further questioning of those who were thinking in terms of domestic changes showed that 60 per cent wanted "changes or reforms," and 40 per cent favored "remain the same"—a direct reversal of the results with respect to this phase of the question. Most of those who thought the question meant technological change favored such change, while those who thought it referred to the basic political-economic structure of the U.S. did not want change.

Many of the polls dealing with complex current issues use questions which are very likely to be as misunderstood as was the question tested by Crutchfield and Gordon. The importance of knowing what questions mean to respondents and what the latter mean by their answers is illustrated by the following two questions, which seemed similar in wording but produced substantially different results. The Gallup Poll asked: "Do you think the U.S. and all the Western European countries participating in the Marshall Plan should join together in a permanent alliance—that is, agree to come to each other's defense immediately if any one of them is attacked?" The answers: *Yes,* 65 per cent; *No,* 21 per cent; *No opinion,* 14 per cent. At about the same time (the results of both polls were published in the same week —May 31 and June 2, 1948), the National Opinion Research Center asked: "As you may know, England, France, and other countries of Western Europe recently signed an agreement to defend each other against attack. Do you think the U.S. should promise to back up these countries with our armed forces if they are attacked by some other country?" The answers: *Yes,* 51 per cent; *No,* 39 per cent; *No opinion,* 10 per cent. Thus on what was essentially the same question—the formation of a military alliance— there was a difference of 14 percentage points in the *Yes* answers and 18 points in the *No* answers. Unless data are obtained showing what respondents in a poll actually mean by their replies, the percentages obtained are of limited significance and sometimes may be seriously misleading.

The problem becomes even more difficult when attempts are made to take polls on complex issues in several different countries at the same time. The language and cultural differences, added to all the other difficulties, are likely to make the results seriously inaccurate. In an international poll it is virtually impossible to have a complex question mean the same thing to all respondents.

THE FUTURE OF THE POLLS

The public opinion poll is only one area of application of a far more important instrument: the sample interview survey. The sample interview survey is one of the research tools of the social sciences. It is being used increasingly to study such widely different problems as the behavior of consumers, the distribution of income, principles of organization and management, religious behavior, the factors affecting political behavior, the production plans of farmers, and the processes of propaganda. Either alone or in combination with experimental methods, this tool enables the social sciences to deal with their problems quantitatively and on a large scale.

A great deal of research on improvements in the technique is now going on. Some of this research is being done by the public opinion polling agencies. More, however, is being done by the federal government and educational and research organizations. Important methodological advances are flowing and will continue to flow from this research on all phases of polling, such as sampling, interviewing and research design.

Section 4   **Collective behavior and social change**

In a rapidly changing society, the fluid conditions congenial to collective behavior are prevalent. Race riots take place when migrations lead to unordered contact between hostile social groups. Religious sects arise when established churches are unable to meet the needs of new life situations. Swift alternations of war and peace bring widespread shifts in public opinion. Collective behavior *reflects* these underlying changes, but in responding to them it *creates* new perspectives, new lines of action, and new institutions.

PERSPECTIVES AND DOCTRINES

A "perspective" is a complex pattern of attitudes, values, and perceptions which together give an ordered view of the world. It includes what one sees as foreground and as background, one's hierarchy of values, one's specific judgments concerning persons and groups, and one's conception of himself in relation to others (e.g., whether he feels weak or strong). People in similar situations tend to have *shared perspectives:* they see the world alike, evaluate it similarly, and have the same assessments of what is plausible and possible. When circumstances change, a period of uncertainty and division occurs until a new perspective or "definition of the situation" is adopted that seems to fit the world as it is subjectively experienced by people in like circumstances.

In the study of social change, nothing is more fundamental than an understanding of altered perspectives. Every new epoch has been marked by its distinctive evaluations of the role of the individual and the meaning of history. The nineteenth century was a period of great industrial expansion and self-confidence. Ideas that stressed the power of the individual and hailed change as progress

were widely held. The twentieth century is typically an age of wars and revolutions, of pessimism and anxiety, and the idea of progress is questioned. These changes in perspective have, for better or worse, made possible and perhaps inevitable many of the movements and institutions that characterize our time, such as collectivism and increased state control.

Two types of perspectives are very often associated with fundamental historical changes:

1. *Perspectives affecting group identity.* Perhaps the most potent force in history is the sense of common belonging felt by many people. When changes occur, it is always important to know whether new perspectives will alter established groupings. Hence we ask: Will Asians think of themselves in racial terms, marking themselves off in hostility and suspicion from the Caucasian world? Will workers think of themselves as a distinct class having special aspirations and interests? Will internationalism break down older national loyalties? Did the war weaken or strengthen perspectives that make second-class citizens of ethnic and racial minorities?

2. *Perspectives that set people into motion.* In the perspectives of rulers and merchants, the geographical position of England in the fifteenth and sixteenth centuries shifted from the perimeter to the center of the maritime world. The result was an epoch of trade and conquest that has only recently run its course. Religious and political ideas have also broadened perspectives and sent men out as missionaries, colonists, and warriors. Before the Pilgrims could come to New England, ordinary men had to transform their conceptions of what the world was like and what kinds of action made sense.

Ideologies

When self-conceptions and world views change, people grope uncertainly for some way of expressing their new understandings and hopes. The time is ripe for *ideologies,* doctrines that purport to formulate the distinctive perspectives of social groups.[15] These ideologies profess to be "true" not only in upholding certain values but in giving a correct picture of what the world is really like. Some go far in attempting to provide detailed formulations of group perspectives. In an epoch of change, ideologues are active, proposing many different systems of belief for groups to adopt. Only a few ever gain wide acceptance because to be effective the beliefs must fit the shared perspectives of many people and be related to historical experience.

The twentieth century has seen a waning of individualism and a development of collectivist ideologies, doctrines that stress the importance of social cohesion and planning. There are many variations and vital differences among these doctrines. Socialist and "welfare" states retain political freedom while Communism and Fascism have instituted unparalleled tyrannies. Despite these differences, collectivist ideologies are alike in calling for increased social control, a strong and active government, and more social responsibility, solidarity, and community. These ideologies have gained wide acceptance because they are in some way consistent with the understandings and aspirations of millions. It is probable that proposed alternatives to Communism and Fascism must likewise be consistent with underlying perspectives if they are not to fall on deaf ears.

SOCIAL MOVEMENTS

For the most part, social change occurs gradually and without design. However, new perspectives and aspirations often generate collective action to combat presumed evils and to institute new ways of life. Sometimes the action is sporadic and temporary, as in the case of isolated uprisings against oppressive conditions. When collective action is more unified and lasting and has certain characteristic features, we call it a "social movement." The main features of a social movement are:

1. *A distinctive perspective and ideology.* The women's suffrage movement arose out of redefined perspectives regarding the place of women, and these were formulated in a doctrine that was widely accepted. The ideology of a movement provides direction and self-justification; it offers weapons of attack and defense; and it holds out inspiration and hope.[16] Social movements place great emphasis on ideology, particularly when other sources of orientation and cohesion are lacking.

2. *A strong sense of solidarity and idealism.* Membership in a "movement" typically means more to the individual than other affiliations. He is a "dedicated" man and feels part of an idealistic and active enterprise. (See Adaptation 31, p. 431.) Idealism plays a role in all movements, political or religious, "progressive" or "reactionary," and it is especially important in the early stages.

3. *An orientation toward action.* The very word "movement" suggests unconventional methods of appeal, such as street meetings and the sale of propaganda tracts. Small movements can sometimes gain wide attention by dramatic actions, particularly if they involve violence. The stress on action in part

---

[15] "Ideology" is sometimes defined as a pattern of ideas that justifies and helps preserve a particular social system. This defensive and justifying function usually follows if a doctrine successfully formulates a group perspective. Even if an ideology includes reformist or revolutionary ideas, it is usually self-justifying from the standpoint of the group that accepts it. On the other hand, an ideology will have other characteristics and consequences as well. For the more restricted view, see Karl Mannheim, *Ideology and Utopia* (New York: Harcourt, Brace, 1936), and on the general topic of the "sociology of knowledge" see R. K. Merton, *Social Theory and Social Structure* (Glencoe: The Free Press, 1957), Chap. XII.

[16] See Herbert Blumer, "Social Movements," in A. M. Lee (ed.), *New Outline of the Principles of Sociology* (New York: Barnes & Noble, 1951), pp. 210–11.

Mass Media in Emergent Nations

It is estimated that there are 2 billion people who do not now have access to the news.* UNESCO hopes that cheap radio (a $5 transistorized set), a sharp increase in literacy, the training of personnel in news media techniques, and better use of films are feasible steps toward universal access to the news. The target date for this achievement is 1975 and the estimated cost of the program is $3.4 billion. The UNESCO "vital minimum" standard for information facilities is the following for every hundred persons:

Ten copies of daily newspapers
Five radio receivers
Two cinema seats
Two television receivers

Of the news media radio has grown most rapidly in underdeveloped countries because neither distance nor literacy is a barrier to its use.

The United States has approximately the following facilities per hundred persons:†

33 copies of daily newspapers
More than 100 radios
31 TV sets

These facilities, far in excess of the UNESCO "vital minimum," pose the question whether there can be too much access to the news, too many opportunities to read, view, and listen.

* Mary Burnet, "2,000 Million People Without Access to News," UNESCO Courier, June, 1962, pp. 4–13.
† Harry Hansen (ed.), The World Almanac (New York: World-Telegram, 1962).

reflects the problem of maintaining interest and solidarity. There is a constant need to "give the members something to do" to keep them from slipping away to other interests and involvements.

A movement is usually made up of *a variety of forms and groupings*. For example, the prohibition movement included the Anti-Saloon League, the Prohibition party, the Women's Christian Temperance Union, and many church groups. The socialist movement in England has included a number of different political parties, trade-unions, newspapers, and groups of intellectuals such as the Fabian Society. This tends to give a movement a somewhat amorphous character, because there is usually no official leadership for the movement as a whole, and there is often much discussion about what constitutes the boundaries of the movement. Socialists and Communists began as part of the same social movement but have long since come to view each other as foes.

A social movement tends to follow a roughly discernible "career," from its origins in unrest to its end in institutionalization.

Chapter IX

Population and ecology

Introduction

Sociology necessarily uses a wide range of research methods. For example, the study of socialization employs the intensive examination of individual life histories to determine how a person acquires the basic skills of behaving in his society and how he takes on the basic values of his culture. The study of the primary group uses case analyses of groups as well as of individuals and certain special techniques, such as sociometry. The techniques of population analysis and ecology offer very different approaches to the study of society and are particularly useful in organizing information on large numbers of people.

Even if the topic for investigation is the behavior of individuals in small groups, an understanding of population is essential for the selection of the individuals to be studied, that is, the construction of a sample. Through determining how representative subjects are of the universe from which they were selected, one can tell whether conclusions about the sample can be applied to a large part of the society or only to a small part of it, or, perhaps, only to the cases being studied.

An understanding of population phenomena offers clues to underlying forces in the society which it would be difficult or impossible to acquire by compiling the opinions of people or studying their life histories. For example, one of the great problems in the modern world is the population change which has taken place in Western Europe and North America but which is only beginning in the countries of Asia. Western Europe and North America are in the late stages of a population growth cycle. The countries of Asia, on the other hand, are in the early stages of a growth cycle. Their massive populations are increasing with great rapidity and will continue to do so for the foreseeable future. The population pressures being generated in the countries of the East will have profound effects on the organization of their societies and probably on the relations among nations.

Some characteristics and changes of population deserve to be understood for their own sake. Even if they were not important to our daily lives or those of our descendants, the great population movements deserve study just as the movements of the stars or planets deserve study by intellectually curious people.

Social or human ecology is closely related to population analysis. A good part of the data of ecology, as we shall see in Section 5 of

Thomas Malthus (1766–1834)

Modern work in population began with Thomas Malthus,[1] whose "Essay on the Principle of Population, etc." was first published in 1798. Malthus posed the problem of the unchecked growth of human population versus the slower growth of the means of subsistence. He held that population tends to increase up to the limit of the food supply, thus preventing any considerable rise in the standard of living.

In later editions of his work, he brought together empirical data and developed the idea of the positive checks *which keep population growth from approaching a geometric ratio. These positive checks are: (1) hunger, (2) disease, (3) war, and (4) vice. He also recognized* preventive checks *which might depress the birth rate. These are: (1) deferred marriage, and (2) celibacy. He regarded the use of contraception as a "vice," which permitted men to escape the consequences of intercourse.*

[1] See D. V. Glass (ed.), *Introduction to Malthus* (London: Watts and Company, 1953).

this chapter, is similar to population data, and the skills required for research in this field are essentially the skills of the population expert. The problem of population increase in Asia can be viewed as a problem in ecology in that it involves a drastic change in the relation between mankind and natural resources and an increasing competition for limited land.

Because population analysis and ecology provide objective indices to social relations, they are valuable to the sociologist, but they cannot give definitive answers to sociological questions. They do indicate, however, where to look for definitive answers, and they help to formulate testable hypotheses. A drastic decline in the birth rate, for example, may call attention to other changes. The decline might be due to the postponement of marriage, and this fact would show up in the study of population data. This, in turn, could be traced to social and cultural factors: for example, to an attempt to reduce the birth rate by postponing marriage, or to establishing a dowry system requiring young people to accumulate substantial wealth before they were eligible for marriage. Knowledge about the birth rate and the changing age at marriage would then lead to a more intensive study of social and institutional relations or of the changing valuations of a social order. The usefulness of population analysis and of ecology can be seen in their interplay with more conventional sociological inquiry as well as in the providing of a rich body of knowledge and a set of research techniques.

The major source of information on population is the census, conducted in many countries every ten years. The numerous blanks and question marks about the populations of many underdeveloped countries impede their progress and planning. No modern state can develop wise, long-term plans for the training and effective use of its human resources without the sort of knowledge compiled by sophisticated census taking. Adaptation 25, page 308, briefly reviews the history and operations of the United States Census, which has become a continuing, year-round activity rather than a population count conducted each decade.

The addition of the new states of Alaska and Hawaii creates some minor reporting problems to which the reader should be alert. Many earlier U.S. statistical series are for continental United States. Although in percentage terms the populations of the new states do not loom large in the national total, precision dictates that the distinction be made between the 50 states taken as a whole and the continental states, excluding Alaska. When the latter is intended, the term *conterminous* is used in the Census reports and in this book. Otherwise, the designation "United States" refers to the country as composed at the period indicated in context. The same caution applies in comparing long time series during which the geographic areas varied.

Section 2 of this chapter discusses some of the main characteristics of population and some of the elementary techniques used to summarize population data, such as the sex ratio and the population pyramid. A brief summary of the population of India is presented to afford a perspective on population problems and characteristics of the United States.

Section 3 discusses the measures of fertility and mortality, trends in the birth and death rates, a comparison of differences in these rates in various parts of the world, and the prospects for longevity. Attention is given to the problems of interpreting this knowledge.

Section 4 reviews in broad perspective the sweeping changes in the rates of population growth in the Western world as well as in less developed areas, and summarizes information about migration.

Section 5 introduces the study of ecology, the spatial distribution of populations, and some of the conceptions used to order ecological information. Although ecology in this text is grouped with population analysis, it is a distinct specialization for sociologists.

SOURCES AND READINGS

See p. 344 for readings in ecology.

See p. 312 for the chief guides for using United States Census information and other official sources.

TEXTS

Paul H. Landis and Paul K. Hatt, *Population Problems* (2nd ed.; New York: American Book Co., 1954).

William Petersen, *Population* (New York: Macmillan, 1961).

T. Lynn Smith, *Population Analysis* (New York: McGraw-Hill, 1948).

Warren S. Thompson, *Population Problems* (4th ed.; New York: McGraw-Hill, 1953).

Dennis H. Wrong, *Population* (Rev. ed.; New York: Random House, 1962).

SYMPOSIA AND REFERENCE WORKS

Donald J. Bogue, *The Population of the United States* (Glencoe: The Free Press, 1959).

Kingsley Davis (ed.), "A Crowding Hemisphere: Population Change in the Americas," *Annals of the American Academy of Political and Social Science*, Vol. 316 (March, 1958).

Paul K. Hatt (ed.), *World Population and Future Resources* (New York: American Book Co., 1952).

Joseph J. Spengler and Otis Dudley Duncan (eds.), *Demographic Analysis* (Glencoe: Free Press, 1956).

Joseph J. Spengler and Otis Dudley Duncan (eds.), *Population Theory and Policy* (Glencoe: Free Press, 1956).

Conrad Taeuber and Irene B. Taeuber, *The Changing Population of the United States* (New York: Wiley, 1958).

PERIODICALS

Population Index (formerly *Population Literature*) is a periodical chiefly devoted to an annotated bibliography. Hundreds of items are cited each year. There is excellent coverage of governmental publications of foreign countries.

The Milbank Memorial Fund Quarterly, New York.

Population, the quarterly review of the National Institute of Demographic Studies, France. (In French.)

Population Studies, a quarterly of the Population Investigating Committee, England.

Statistical Bulletin, issued monthly by the Metropolitan Life Insurance Co.

Demographic Yearbook of the United Nations continues the *International Statistical Yearbook* published under the auspices of the League of Nations from 1927–1945. The U.N. has also assumed publication of the *Monthly Bulletin of Statistics*, formerly put out by the League.

The United States Census

Based in part on *Bureau of the Census, Factfinder for the Nation, 1948; The Story of the Census, 1790-1916;* U.S. Census of Population and Housing, 1960, *Principal Data-Collection Forms and Procedures* (1961); and other publications of the Bureau, Washington, D.C.

BACKGROUND

The United States was the first modern nation to make a legal provision for regular census taking. This is required in the apportionment clause, Article I, Section 2 of the *Constitution,* which reads in part as follows:

Representatives and direct Taxes shall be apportioned among the several States . . . according to their respective Numbers, which shall be determined by adding to the whole Number of free Persons, including those bound to Service for a Term of Years, and excluding Indians not taxed, three-fifths of all other Persons. The actual Enumeration shall be made within three Years after the first Meeting of the Congress of the United States, and within every subsequent Term of ten Years. . . .

The First Census in 1790 related solely to population, and its scope, although very limited, was somewhat greater than that required by the *Constitution*. The name of the head of each family was recorded and the total number of persons in the family, classified as free or slave. The free persons were further classified as white or other, the free whites as male or female, and the free white males as over or under sixteen years of age. (See Table IX:1 Growth of the Decennial Census.)

The First Census was taken under the supervision of the 17 United States marshals, and the actual work of enumeration was performed by about 650 marshals' assistants. The enumeration began in August, 1790, and according to law should have been completed in nine months, but double this time elapsed before the returns were all in. The returns were made by the marshals direct to the President, and he turned them over to the Secretary of State, who transmitted them to the printer. No clerical force was employed for compilation, verification, or correction, and the results were printed without explanatory text, percentages, and detailed analyses which now accompany census statistics. The report of the First Census is contained in a pamphlet of 56 pages.

Not until the 5th Census (1830) were printed schedules used. Before that the marshals' assistants had used such paper as they happened to have, ruling it, writing in the headings, and binding the sheets together themselves. Before 1850 the family was the unit of enumeration, but beginning with the 7th Census a number of important improvements were made. The individual became the unit of enumeration, and additional data, such as age, sex, race, and occupation were reported. The change of unit greatly increased the analytic usefulness of the census by improving the accuracy of enumeration, by permitting detailed tabulations of the additional data, and by facilitating cross-tabulations. The 9th Census (1870) made the first use of machine tabulation. Another innovation was the employment of maps, charts, and diagrams to present graphically the more significant facts. These were published in a separate volume called *The Statistical Atlas of the United States.*

In 1880 field operations were reorganized. Specially qualified supervisors were appointed, and they were able to give closer supervision to the work of enumeration.

The number and types of inquiries were greatly increased in the censuses of 1880 and 1890 and resulted in reports on a wide variety of subjects, but in spite of new tech-

Table 9.—POPULATION OF THE UNITED STATES, BY REGIONS, DIVISIONS, AND STATES, AND OF THE COMMONWEALTH OF PUERTO RICO: 1790 TO 1960

[Insofar as possible, population shown in that of present area of State]

Region, division, and State	1960	1950	1940	1930	1920	1910	1900	1890	1880
United States	179,323,175	151,325,798	132,164,569	123,202,624	106,021,537	92,228,496	76,212,168	¹62,979,766	50,189,209
Regions:									
Northeast	44,677,819	39,477,986	35,976,777	34,427,091	29,662,053	25,868,573	21,046,695	17,406,969	14,507,407
North Central	51,619,139	44,460,762	40,143,332	38,594,100	34,019,792	29,888,542	26,333,004	22,410,417	17,364,111
South	54,973,113	47,197,088	41,665,901	37,857,633	33,125,803	29,389,330	24,523,527	20,028,099	16,516,568
West	28,053,104	20,189,962	14,378,559	12,323,800	9,213,889	7,082,051	4,308,942	3,134,321	1,801,123
Northeast:									
New England	10,509,367	9,314,453	8,437,290	8,166,341	7,400,909	6,552,681	5,592,017	4,700,749	4,010,529
Middle Atlantic	34,168,452	30,163,533	27,539,487	26,260,750	22,261,144	19,315,892	15,454,678	12,706,220	10,496,878
North Central:									
East North Central	36,225,024	30,399,368	26,626,342	25,297,185	21,475,543	18,250,621	15,985,581	13,478,305	11,206,668
West North Central	15,394,115	14,061,394	13,516,990	13,296,915	12,544,249	11,637,921	10,347,423	8,932,112	6,157,443
South:									
South Atlantic	25,971,732	21,182,335	17,823,151	15,793,589	13,990,272	12,194,895	10,443,480	8,857,922	7,597,197
East South Central	12,050,126	11,477,181	10,778,225	9,887,214	8,893,307	8,409,901	7,547,757	6,429,154	5,585,151
West South Central	16,951,255	14,537,572	13,064,525	12,176,830	10,242,224	8,784,534	6,532,290	4,740,983	3,334,220
West:									
Mountain	6,855,060	5,074,998	4,150,003	3,701,789	3,336,101	2,633,517	1,674,657	1,213,935	653,119
Pacific	21,198,044	15,114,964	10,228,556	8,622,011	5,877,788	4,448,534	2,634,285	1,920,386	1,148,004
New England:									
Maine	969,265	913,774	847,...					661,086	648,936
New Hampshire	606,921	533,242	491,...						346,991
Vermont	389,881	377,747	359,...						
Massachusetts	5,148,578	4,690,514	4,316,...						
Rhode Island	859,488	791,896	713,...						
Connecticut	2,535,234	2,007,280	1,709,...						
Middle Atlantic:									
New York	16,782,304	14,830,192	13,47...						
New Jersey	6,066,782	4,835,329	4,16...						
Pennsylvania	11,319,366	10,498,012	9,90...						
East North Central:									
Ohio	9,706,397	7,946,627	6,9...						
Indiana	4,662,498	3,934,224	7,2...						
Illinois	10,081,158	8,712,176	5,2...						
Michigan	7,823,194	6,371,766	3,1...						
Wisconsin	3,951,777	3,434,575							
West North Central:									
Minnesota	3,413,864	2,982,483	2,...						
Iowa	2,757,537	2,621,073	2,...						
Missouri	4,319,813	3,954,653	3,...						
North Dakota	632,446	619,636							
South Dakota	680,514	652,740							
Nebraska	1,411,330	1,325,510							
Kansas	2,178,611	1,905,299							
South Atlantic:									
Delaware	446,292	318,085							
Maryland	3,100,689	2,343,001							
District of Columbia	763,956	802,178							
Virginia	3,966,949	3,318,680							
West Virginia	1,860,421	2,005,552							
North Carolina	4,556,155	4,061,929							
South Carolina	2,382,594	2,117,027							
Georgia	3,943,116	3,444,578							
Florida	4,951,560	2,771,305							
East South Central:									
Kentucky	3,038,156	2,944,806							
Tennessee	3,567,089	3,291,718							
Alabama	3,266,740	3,061,743							
Mississippi	2,178,141	2,178,914							
West South Central:									
Arkansas	1,786,272	1,909,511							
Louisiana	3,257,022	2,683,516							
Oklahoma	2,328,284	2,233,351							
Texas	9,579,677	7,711,194							
Mountain:									
Montana	674,767	591,024							
Idaho	667,191	588,637							
Wyoming	330,066	290,529							
Colorado	1,753,947	1,325,089							
New Mexico	951,023	681,187							
Arizona	1,302,161	749,587							
Utah	890,627	688,862							
Nevada	285,278	160,083							
Pacific:									
Washington	2,853,214	2,378,963							
Oregon	1,768,687	1,521,341							
California	15,717,204	10,586,223							
Alaska	226,167	128,643							
Hawaii	632,772	499,794							
Puerto Rico	2,349,544	2,210,703							

¹ Includes population (325,464) of Indian Territory and India... cially enumerated in 1890 but not included in general report 1890.
² Includes persons (6,100 in 1840 and 5,318 in 1830) on public... of the United States, not credited to any region, division, or Sta...
³ OHIO.--Population of Territory Northwest of the River Ohio.
⁴ INDIANA.--1810 figure includes population of Indiana Territory... includes population (3,124) of those portions of Indiana Territory... form Michigan and Illinois Territories in 1805 and 1809, respect... tion which was separated in 1816.

SCHEDULE of the whole Number of PERSONS within the several Districts of the UNITED STATES, taken according to "An Act providing for the Enumeration of the Inhabitants of the United States;" passed March the 1st, 1790.

DISTRICTS.	Free white Males of sixteen years and upwards, including heads of families.	Free white Males under sixteen years.	Free white Females including heads of families.	All other free persons.	Slaves.	Total.
*Vermont	22,135	22,328	40,505	255	16	85,539
New-Hampshire	36,086	34,851	70,160	630	158	141,885
Maine	24,384	24,748	46,870	538	NONE	96,540
Massachusetts	95,453	87,289	190,582	5,463	NONE	378,787
Rhode-Island	16,019	15,799	32,652	3,407	948	68,825
Connecticut	60,523	54,403	117,448	2,808	2,764	237,946
New-York	83,700	78,122	152,320	4,654	21,324	340,120
New-Jersey	45,251	41,416	83,287	2,762	11,423	184,139
Pennsylvania	110,788	106,948	206,363	6,537	3,787	434,373
Delaware	11,783	12,143	22,384	3,899	8,887	59,094
Maryland	55,915	51,339	101,395	8,043	103,036	319,728
Virginia	110,936	116,135	215,046	12,866	292,627	747,610
Kentucky	15,154	17,057	28,922	114	12,430	73,677
North-Carolina	69,988	77,506	140,710	4,975	100,572	393,751
South-Carolina	-					
Georgia	13,103	14,044	25,739	398	29,264	82,548

	Free white Males of twenty one years and upwards, including heads of families.	Free Males under twenty-one years of age.	Free white Females, including heads of families.	All other Persons.	Slaves.	Total.
S. Western Territory	6,271	10,277	15,365	361	3,417	35,691
N. Do.						

Truly stated from the original Returns deposited in the Office of the Secretary of State.

TH: JEFFERSON.

October 24. 1791.

* This return was not signed by the marshal, but was enclosed and referred to in a letter written and signed by him.

Table **IX:1**   Growth of the Decennial Census: 1790–1960 *

Census Year	Number of Enumerators	Length of Enumeration (Months)	Cost Per Capita	Population Enumerated Conterminous U. S. (in Thousands)
1790	650	18.0	$0.011	3,929
1810	1,100	10.0	0.024	7,239
1830	1,519	14.0	0.029	12,866
1850	3,231	20.5	0.061	23,191
1870	6,530	15.0	0.087	38,558
1890	46,804	1.0	0.183	62,947
1910	70,286	1.0 ª	0.173	91,972
1930	87,756	1.0	0.321	122,775
1950	151,814	1.0	0.601	150,697
1960	159,321	3.8 ᵇ	0.60 (est)	178,464

* The Story of the Census, 1790–1916, p. 22. Data for 1930–1960 supplied by courtesy of the Bureau.
ª Not including time spent in making investigations and recounts in places where fraudulent enumeration had been detected.
ᵇ Enumeration was 99 per cent complete in six weeks.

niques which made possible more rapid enumeration and tabulation, publication was delayed. Two things became apparent. First, the decennial census had become burdened with fields of investigation that might better be subjects of continuous inquiry throughout the decade. Second, the process of building a completely new temporary organization for each census was no longer economical of time or money and a permanent organization was needed.

In recognition of the first problem, the 1900 decennial census was limited to four subjects: population, manufactures, agriculture, and mortality. Shortly thereafter, in 1902, the second problem was solved when the Bureau of the Census was established as a permanent agency, known as the Census Office.

The 1960 Census introduced a number of innovations: it gathered a larger amount of information on a sample basis than in previous years; for the first time it asked householders to fill out questionnaires instead of only responding to enumerators' questions; and it made extensive use of high-speed, electronic data-processing equipment. The census has long been a leader in experimentation with statistical processing machines. Because

of the electronic equipment used in 1960, the information was entered on a schedule designed for FOSDIC (Film Optical Sensing Device for Input to Computers). FOSDIC scanned microfilm of the completed schedules and from the position of the marks on the schedules converted the information into magnetic impressions on tape. The tape was then processed by electronic computers. The use of FOSDIC eliminated the card-punching operation, and thus, one important source of clerical error. The enormous capacity of the electronic computer made it possible to do much more uniform editing and coding than in earlier censuses and to ensure consistency among a large number of interrelated items.

ACCURACY

The census, which is essentially a vast reporting procedure, can be only as accurate as its reporters and respondents. Many countries have great difficulty in conducting their censuses because the people mistrust the intentions of the government and elude the enumerator or give him incomplete and faulty information. Although some people in the United States mistrust the census and regard it as an invasion of privacy, it has been remarkably free of this kind of impediment. This fact probably reflects a general feature of American culture.

On the other hand, the competitive spirit, another aspect of American culture, has occasionally affected not only the interpretation of census statistics but also their actual gathering. *The Story of the Census* reports:

Dishonest enumerators may sometimes yield to the temptation to increase their pay (which in most cases is based on the number of names turned in by them) by returning fictitious names. But the "padding" of returns from motives of personal gain has been a less serious obstacle to accurate census taking than . . . organized attempts on the part of certain cities and towns to inflate their population figures. The voice of local business interests—disguised as that of local patriotism—has sometimes called more loudly to the supervisor or the enumerator than has the voice of honor, duty, or fidelity to oath of office. After the census of 1910, 69 indictments were brought against enumerators and others believed to be responsible for the falsity of the returns in 14 cities and towns. In 13 cases the defendants were imprisoned and fined, and in 40 cases fines alone were imposed. The jail sentences ranged from one day to six months, and the fines from $50 to $1,500.

In 1960 some cities with aspirations to be as large as possible questioned the accuracy of census figures. For example, the census reported in many areas that a central city had not grown very much or had even declined in population, an expected fact in view of the movement of population to the suburbs. This news was received with angry protests from some municipal officials and local patriots and in some cases the cities incurred considerable expenses to check on the accuracy of published figures. Sociologists had predicted the census finding of slow growth or decline in many central cities as well as the civic indignation at the findings.

The management of the census must consider basic social attitudes as well as the improvement of such techniques as enumeration, computing, and tabulating. Sociologists are alert to the cultural and social influences that may distort statistics. They also look upon these distorting influences as clues to underlying social attitudes.

Checking Census Accuracy

To check on the accuracy of the census a number of techniques are used.[2] For instance, birth and death statistics for the period between censuses are examined, and an estimate of "expected" population is made. This is done for the country as a whole and for regions and cities. Then the actual count is compared with the "expected" population. Where a significant difference exists, close analysis is made for possible error.

Toward the end of the enumeration period in 1960 many newspapers published "Were You Counted?" forms, which contained the questions asked of 100 per cent of the population. The reader was urged to fill in the form and send it to the Census District Office if he believed that he or members of his household had been missed in the enumeration.

In 1950 a direct sample check was undertaken in a Post-Enumeration Survey. The Census had actually counted 150,697,000 people in 1950. The Post-Enumeration Survey, which was performed by specially trained and supervised enumerators, found in its sample recount that many people had been erroneously omitted or had been erroneously enumerated. The techniques of the Survey were far too costly to be used for the whole Census, but they did provide a valuable check on its accuracy. We may compare the findings of this survey with the regular enumeration for continental United States:

Census population	150,697,000
Post-Enumeration survey estimated population	152,788,000
Persons erroneously omitted	3,400,000

[2] This discussion is based on U.S. Bureau of the Census, *U.S. Census of Population 1950*, Vol. II, *Characteristics of the Population*, Part 1, U.S. Summary, Chapter C. (Washington, D.C.: Government Printing Office, 1953), pp. xxviii-xxxi.

Persons erroneously included   1,309,000
Net error   2,091,000

A similar evaluation program was conducted for the 1960 Census.

SAMPLING IN THE CENSUS

There are additional ways in which sampling is used in the U.S. Census. It would be impossible for the Bureau to gather the amount of data that it does during the regular decennial census or to conduct current surveys (see p. 313), were it not for the development of sampling techniques. Much population information for 1950 and 1960 is based on samples—20 per cent for 1950 and 25 per cent for 1960—and is so identified in the census reports.

Estimates of the total number of persons with specified characteristics are obtained by multiplying by five the number of persons with these characteristics in the 20 per cent sample; by four the number in the 25 per cent sample. This procedure of deriving overall figures from sample figures is, of course, a matter of probability. For example, the 1950 Census shows that 17.6 per cent of the males twenty-five years and over *in a 20 per cent sample* had completed four years of high school. On the basis of this sample, the Census reports that 7,500,000 or 17.6 per cent of all males *in the total population* twenty-five years and over have completed high school, but it does not mean that the national figure is exactly 7,500,000. On the contrary, it presents the figure with the following understanding: The chances are approximately two out of three that the figure for the total population lies between 7,500,000 plus 5,440 and 7,500,000 minus 5,440. (The degree of probability and the range of accuracy claimed are derived from the mathematics of statistics.) The figure 7,500,000 falls at the midpoint of a fairly narrow range within which the actual figure probably lies.

You might argue that two out of three chances are not very good odds. One chance out of three remains that the actual figure lies outside the 7,500,000± 5,440 range. It is easy to increase the chances of accuracy. If you are willing to take as a reasonably accurate figure a total of 7,500,000± 13,600, then the chances increase to *one hundred to one* that the actual figure for the total population lies between 7,500,000 plus 13,600 and 7,500,000 minus 13,600.

In one sense total census figures based on sampling, like all such figures, are never precise. They are presented and must be used with the understanding that the actual figures are probably close to the computed figures. In another sense, however, they are precise, because once the acceptable range of accuracy is specified, the degree of probability that it has been attained (e.g., odds of 2-1 or 100-1) can also be specified. Suppose a publisher is interested in estimating the potential market for a book on carpentry designed to be read by men of at least high school education. He would doubtless be pleased to know that the chances are as high as one hundred to one that his potential market lies between 7,500,000± 13,600. In fact, he should be satisfied to know that the chances are two out of three that his potential market lies between 7,500,000± 5,440.

Although sample statistics for the U.S. as a whole may be accepted as approximating very closely the results that would have been obtained from a complete enumeration of the population, this is not true of smaller populations. In general the smaller the sample and/or the smaller the total population, the less reliable are the results of the sample.

CENSUS SOURCES

Guides for using the United States Census cover both decennial census publications and the results of other census surveys:

1. *Catalog and Subject Guide*, issued quarterly, cumulative since January, 1946.

2. *Catalog* of U.S. Census Publications, 1790–1945, U.S. Bureau of the Census, Washington, 1950.

The divisions of the *Catalogs* follow the organization of the Bureau of the Census:

1) *Agriculture,* first taken in 1840, quinquennial since 1920.

2) *Business,* first complete census taken in 1929, subsequently in 1933, 1935, 1939, 1948, and became quinquennial in 1954.

3) *Foreign trade.*

4) *Governments,* reports on finance and employment on state and local levels.

5) *Industrial,* prepares "Facts for Industry" series, annual surveys of manufactures since 1949; Census of Manufacturing first taken in 1810, subsequently at varying intervals, now quinquennial.

6) *Population and Housing,* the categories most frequently used by sociologists. See also U.S. Census of Population: 1960, *Availability of Published and Unpublished Data.*

SUMMARY SOURCES

Statistical Abstract of the United States, an annual summary of statistics on population, industry, and social, political, and economic characteristics. Convenient source book available from the U.S. Government Printing Office.

Historical Statistics of the United States (Colonial Times to 1957) should be used in conjunction with the *Statistical Abstract.* Contains a compilation of about 3,000 statistical time series. An excellent reference guide as well as a direct source of data.

CURRENT POPULATION REPORTS

In addition to the decennial census, the Bureau conducts periodically the Current Population Survey, covering a sample of about 35,000 households throughout the country.

OTHER UNITED STATES GOVERNMENT SOURCES

Department of Labor, Bureau of Labor Statistics: *Monthly Labor Review* gives characteristics of the labor force. Covers some subjects formerly published by the Bureau of the Census.

Department of Health, Education, and Welfare, Office of the Secretary: *Indicators* (monthly) summarizes vital statistics, morbidity and accident rates, and various data concerning health, education, and welfare. A good multi-purpose first reference.

Trends, annual supplement to *Indicators.*

National Health Survey, Series A (Program descriptions, survey designs, concepts and definitions), Series B (Health Interview Survey results by topics), Series C (Health Interview Survey results for population groups), and Series D (Developmental and Evaluation Reports).

National Office of Vital Statistics: *Monthly Vital Statistics Report* reports deaths, births, and marriages.

Weekly Morbidity and Mortality Report.

Vital Statistics of the United States, Annual Report gives detailed breakdown of vital statistics for the year by states and smaller areas and by such characteristics as sex, age, race, etc.

Vital Statistics—Special Reports. Topic and frequency of issue vary.

In 1963 publications of Health Survey Statistics and Special Vital Statistics were revised. A new set of series, *Vital and Health Statistics,* was initiated encompassing program reports, research methods, health survey statistics, and vital statistics (supplementary to annual and monthly *Vital Statistics* reports).

Section 2 Composition

Composition refers to the distribution of a population by significant biological or social categories, such as race, nativity, religion, sex, age, occupation, education, and urbanization. Population figures may be gathered and presented in a great number of ways to answer the needs of government, science, and industry. For example, the number unemployed, the number with specified income levels, and the number with specialized higher education provide indices of important social phenomena. The proportion of unemployed is often used as an index of the health of the economy; changes in income levels may be a

Table **IX:2**   Population Composition, U.S., 1960*

Age Group	Population (in Thousands)	Component
14 years and over	69,877	In labor force (Males: 67.9%, Females: 32.1%)
	56,399	Not in labor force
	10,327	Enrolled in school
	1,760	Inmates in institutions
	12,443	Retired and over 64 years old
	28,918	Women, 14–64, chiefly homemakers
	2,951	Males, 14–64
5–13 years	29,296	Enrolled in school
	3,431	Not in school
Under 5 years	20,322	Preschool

* Source: U.S. Bureau of the Census. *U.S. Census of Population: 1960. General Social and Economic Characteristics, United States Summary.* Final Report PC(1)-1C. (Washington, D.C.: U.S. Government Printing Office, 1962), Tables 65, 73, 82.

sign of new stratification patterns; the rate of growth of the population trained in engineering may indicate whether or not educational institutions are keeping pace with the needs of an expanding technology.

A crude summary of the population composition of the United States by age, sex, and major activity is given in Table IX:2. A finer breakdown would give a more comprehensive picture but would be correspondingly more complicated. However, even this short statistical summary reveals the way the population may be differentiated into meaningful clusters.

A description of composition gives a static, cross-sectional view of population, but, in fact, no population is ever truly stable. To make effective use of composition data one must: (1) compare different populations, or (2) study a series of cross sections, that is, study the trends and changes in the same population. There are basic categories, particularly age and sex, which may now be found in any census.

Smith has summarized the importance of understanding the age and sex compositions of populations:

Variations in the age and sex make-up of populations have a direct effect upon almost every significant item of demographic accounting. The distribution of ages and the proportions of the sexes influence the marriage rate, the birth rate, the death rate, the ratio of producers to consumers, the percentages in the school or military ages, the numbers eligible for old-age assistance, and almost every other significant item of national bookkeeping and planning. In social and economic spheres, valid comparisons are possible only if precautions are taken to ensure that comparable age and sex groups are being used.[8]

THE SEX RATIO

The proportion of males to females within a population is called its *sex ratio* and is stated as the number of males per 100 females. A sex ratio of 100 means that the population is evenly divided between males and females; a figure greater than 100, that there are more males than females; a figure less than 100, that there are fewer males than females. For example, Alaska's sex ratio (132) is higher than that of Washington, D.C. (SR=88); that is, the proportion of males to

[8] T. Lynn Smith, *Population Analysis* (New York: McGraw-Hill, 1948), p. 112.

females is higher in Alaska than in Washington.

A sex ratio that deviates markedly in either direction is thought to be biased or "out of balance."[4] This attitude is traceable to the values of a monogamous marital system. A polygynous family system (one with plural wives) would not be concerned about an excess of females, and a polyandrous system (one with plural husbands) would welcome an excess of males.

At birth the sex ratio for whites in the United States approximates 106, but at successively older ages the proportion of males diminishes; that is, the sex ratio declines with increasing age. The American female seems to be a more durable organism than the American male; the life expectancy for females is higher than for males. In some other countries this is not the case, and at earlier periods in American experience, this may not have been so.

In 1960 the sex ratio in the United States had declined from 106 in 1910 to an all-time low of 97. In the preceding century it had fluctuated between about 102 and 105, but never in the country as a whole did the number of females exceed the number of males until the 1940's. This was due, at least in part, to the heavier immigration of males than females.

The over-all sex ratio for Negroes in the U.S. has been consistently lower than for whites, but the reasons for this are obscure. Whatever the cause, this low ratio contributes to the adjustment problems of the Negro family. (See Adaptation 35, pp. 509–12.) For immigrants the sex ratio historically has been higher than for the native born, because males are usually more heavily represented in international migrations. (This was not true, however, of the light immigration of the 1930's and 1940's.) The high proportion of males of marriageable age among immigrants complicates the problems of adjustment and impedes family building, especially in the early stages of the growth of an immigrant community.

Viewed regionally, New England had the lowest sex ratio (95) in 1960, and the Mountain States the highest (101). Massachusetts had the lowest sex ratio of any state (93) and Alaska the highest (132).

The American city has a strong attractive power to women. In 1960 the urban sex ratio was about 94, the rural 104. The urban sex ratio was even lower between the ages of 20 and 29 (SR=92) and consequently reduced or eliminated the chances for marriage for many women. The rural sex ratio in the same age group was about 106 and consequently there was a surplus of rural males of marriageable age. These biased sex ratios reduce the rate of marriage and tend to lower the crude birth rate. Cities vary in their sex ratios, depending on the character of industry in the area. Heavy industry, such as steel, is associated with a relatively high sex ratio. On the other hand, commercial activities and light industry, such as the assembly of small equipment requiring manual dexterity, are associated with a low sex ratio.

The social significance of the low sex ratio has not been closely studied. Changes in sexual morality have been attributed to the biased sex ratio, but it is probably only a partial explanation. The accompanying decay of the large family system with the loss of old familial roles and ties may be at least as important as the statistical fact of the sex ratio in leading to the change in sex mores. The urban concentration of women probably contributed to the development of women's political activities, which resulted in the suffrage movement and ultimately in the Nineteenth Amendment (1920) extending the franchise to women. In contrast to the association between a low sex ratio and urbanization in the U.S. and other Western countries, the relationship is reversed in India, where urbanization is associated with a high sex ratio. (See page 321.)

---

[4] Cf. Hans von Hentig, "The Sex Ratio," *Social Forces*, **30**, No. 4 (May, 1952), 443.

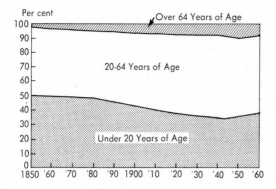

Fig. **IX:1**   Population of the U.S. by
Age Groups: 1850–1960

The frontier towns of the last century exemplify a very high sex ratio, associated with little stability and much violence. It would be too simple to say that these facts are *attributable* to the lack of women. More accurately, the instability and violence can be ascribed to the high mobility of the men and their general *anomie* (state of detachment), in this case, no doubt, engendered and encouraged by the absence of the conservative and restraining influences of family responsibilities. In addition, the frontier movement probably selected and appealed to the kind of men already disposed to choose male communities, men who prized their mobility and detachment.[5]

AGE COMPOSITION

In large part the industrial and military potentials of a nation depend on its age composition. A population with heavy concentrations in the productive years has a larger labor force and a larger potential force for mobilization in time of emergency. A population with smaller proportions in the productive years is less able to respond to threats against its security and is probably less adaptable to technological change. A population

concentrated at either extreme of the age distribution has a heavy dependency ratio, that is, the number of nonproductive individuals is relatively great and burdens the productive population.

Throughout most of its history, the United States has had a young population. Large numbers were concentrated at the early ages, the birth rate was rather high, and the death rate was fairly high. In the long-term trends both birth and death rates have declined with a consequent reduction in the proportion of the population in the lower ages. Figure IX:1 depicts the change in the proportion of the major age groups over more than a century. Although for much of that period the population in the most productive years increased faster than the old and the young, this is not now the case.

Population Pyramid

The study of the population pyramids affords a more intensive analysis of changes in the age (and sex) composition of a population. Figure IX:2 shows the age-sex distribution of the population of the United States for 1900, 1940, and 1960. The population pyramid, sometimes called "the tree of ages," summarizes the age and sex characteristics of a population at a given time. A vertical line divides the percentages of males on the left from the percentages of females on the right. The percentages, indicated on the scale at the bottom, are calculated from population figures compiled by age groups, that is, males under 5 years of age, between 5 and 9 years old, and so on. The age groups are shown on the pyramid steps. The figure for 1900 has the shape of a true pyramid, typical of a population increasing because of a high birth rate but also showing a high death rate. ". . . each year's crop of babies was larger than that of the year before, and the older birth classes, besides being smaller to begin with, had tended to die at a relatively early age." [6]

[5] See Paul H. Landis, *Three Iron Mining Towns, A Study in Cultural Change* (Ann Arbor: Edwards Brothers, 1938), Chaps. 3 and 7, for a study of male-dominated frontier towns.

[6] Frank W. Notestein, "Population," *Scientific American*, **185**, No. 3 (September, 1951), 30.

The 1940 figure describes a much different population. The birth rate had declined, and the death rate had declined. The proportion of population in the most productive years (between 20 and 50) had increased. The proportion in the older dependent ages had also increased, but the proportion of children had declined. The very sharp reduction in the percentages of children under 10 years of age is undoubtedly related to the depression of the 1930's.

The pyramid for 1960 shows an increase in the population under 20 years of age—the result of the high birth rate in the 1940's and 1950's. The increase reversed the trend of the 1930's toward lower birth rates. (See Sec. 3, p. 328.) The short age bars, which were at the base of the pyramid in 1940, moved up in 1960 to become a notch at ages 20–24 and 25–29. This shows how the population pyra-

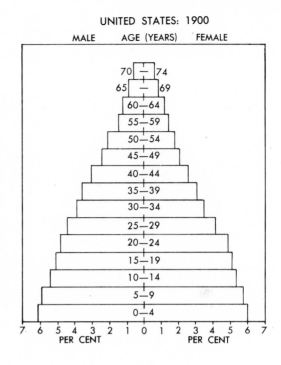

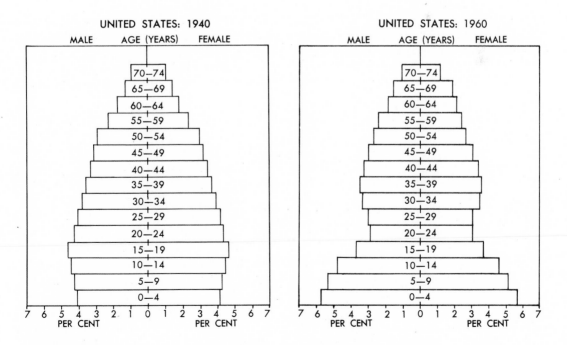

Fig. **IX:2** Population Pyramids, United States: 1900, 1940, and 1960

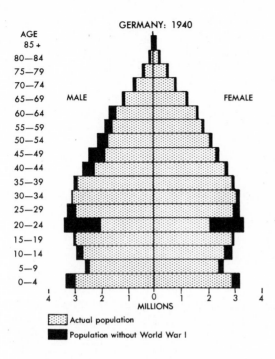

Fig. **IX:3**   Population Pyramid for
Germany—Actual and
without World War I

After Frank W. Notestein, *The Future Population
of Europe and the Soviet Union* (Geneva: League
of Nations, 1944), Fig. 27, p. 101.

mid graphically reveals the earlier history of a population. Of course, it does not tell the reasons for irregularities and changes, but it does direct attention to important questions. The notch in the U.S. 1960 figure is attributed to a depression.

Wars and epidemics leave their scars on the population pyramid, not merely for the lifetime of the directly affected age group but for generations. Figure IX:3 indicates the effects of World War I on the German population of 1940. First, note the war casualties, males aged 40–64 who were of military age in 1914–18. Next, observe the notch in the age group 20–24, a consequence of the depletion of these potential fathers. Finally, the effects of this notch reappear at the bottom of the pyramid in the reduced size of the youngest age groups.

The Populations of India and the United States [7]

Suggested by *The Population of India and Pakistan* by
Kingsley Davis (Princeton: Princeton University Press,
1951), from which the early data are drawn. Supplementary data are from United Nations *Demographic
Yearbook* (various dates) and publications of the U.S.
Bureau of the Census and the National Office of Vital
Statistics.

[7] The India referred to in this adaptation is post-partition India, which includes Kashmir and Jammu but excludes Pakistan. The United States refers to conterminous U.S. only to preserve the principle of comparison between continental nations. In all cases the latest available data, even though estimates, are presented for India, but U.S. data are given for the most closely comparable year. The Indian census is con-

The population problems illustrated by India loom ever larger in international affairs. They may be best understood if India's characteristics are compared with those of a technologically advanced country like the United States. At the same time such comparison

ducted the year following that for the U.S. Where not specifically noted in the text, comparisons are for the nearest census years, e.g., India, 1951, U.S., 1950.

ADAPTATION 26

may contribute to an understanding of the United States.

SIZE AND DENSITY

Figure IX:4 shows the relative sizes of India and the United States. India, somewhat less than half the size of conterminous U.S., sustained a population of about 438 million in 1961 compared with a U.S. population of about 178 million in 1960. The approximate corresponding densities:

India (1961), 347 per square mile

United States (1960), 60 per square mile

Although other countries have higher densities (Japan, 625 in 1955, England and Wales, 750 in 1950), India's density is by far the greatest of the large countries and is much higher than that of China. By world standards the United States is thinly settled.

Average density figures for countries as large as India and the United States, however, are hardly more than suggestive. Both countries have great regional concentrations and larger areas of relatively sparse settlement. But even an "area of relatively sparse settlement," the mountainous Indian frontier state of Kashmir, had a density of 51 in 1951, the same as the U.S. average for that year. India, which is a predominantly agricultural country, has very high *rural* densities, whereas the heavily populated areas in the United States are predominantly *urban*. This is suggested in Figure IX:5. In 1951 only about 16.7 per cent of the population of India was in cities of more than 5,000 compared with more than 50 per cent in the United States. By this criterion, India was about as urban as the United States a century earlier. Some purely agricultural districts in India have densities exceeding 1,000 per square mile, and densities over 500 are common. In the United States densities as high as 1,000 are found in towns or suburbs. In the nature of its heavy rural concentration, India resembles Java, Egypt, Japan, and China.

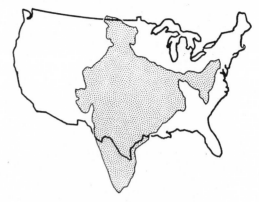

India, 1961—1,263,000 sq. miles
United States, 1960—2,971,000 sq. miles

Fig. **IX:4**   Comparison of Areas

A more sophisticated statement of agricultural density is as follows: nearly 70 per cent of the population of India was directly supported by agriculture in 1951, but less than 20 per cent of the population of the United States was dependent on agriculture in 1950.

GROWTH

The size and density of India leads to the assumption that it has been historically an area of rapid population growth. As compared with the United States, a relatively industrialized country, or as compared with Europe, this has not been so. Figure IX:6 shows the population growth of the United States compared with India in two ways. The upper

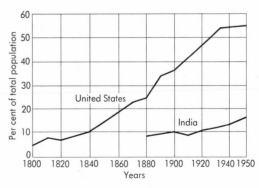

Fig. **IX:5**   Population in Cities of
5,000+

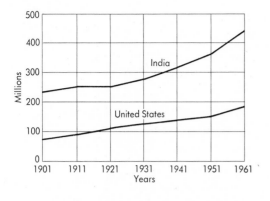

Fig. **IX:6**   Population Growth

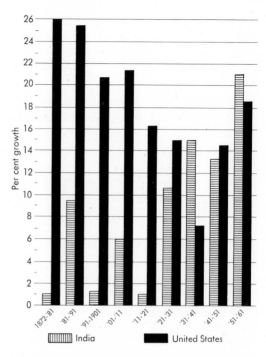

Fig. **IX:7**   Per Cent Population Growth
by Decades

part of the figure expresses growth in millions, and the lower graph is stated as percentages of the 1900–1901 populations. Before 1950 the Indian rate of increase exceeded that of the U.S. only in the depression decade of the 1930's.

On the other hand, because of its age characteristics, India is now entering upon a period of exceedingly rapid growth both in numbers and percentage. (See Fig. IX:7.) In the decade of the 1950's India increased at a rate faster than the U.S., despite the rapid growth of the U.S. at that time. The periods of small Indian increase were marked by famine or epidemic, and as India reduces these catastrophes, she will grow at an explosive rate. In contrast to India, note the rather steady decline in the rate of growth in the United States through the 1930's, a decade of

abnormally small immigration and natural increase. The following two decades show a recovery to high levels of growth.

IMMIGRATION

Indian growth is little influenced by either immigration or emigration, whereas in the United States immigration has added very heavily to the gains of natural increase. This is indicated in the figures for the foreign-born populations of the countries at 1950–1951. India's 8,667,000 foreign born made up 2.4 per cent of the total population of the country. The 10,147,000 foreign born in the U.S. amounted to 6.7 per cent of the total population.

AGE PYRAMIDS

Figure IX:8 shows the population pyramids for India and the United States in two forms: as percentages and as millions of persons. On page 316 the population pyramid is introduced but only in terms of percentages of the population. The lower part of Figure IX:8 shows the distribution by age and sex for the two countries, expressed in absolute numbers, that is, in millions of persons. As a result of high mortality and high fertility, India has a very young population. Its pyramid has a broad base and a quickly attenuated top. It is sharply contrasted with the pyramid of the United States, a country of low mortality and relatively low fertility. India in 1951 had more than twice as many people as the United States. It had roughly the same number of people aged 65 and over, but about three times as many children under 5 years of age. Consequently in India most of the dependents are children, but in the United States an increasing proportion of the dependents are oldsters.

If mortality in India continues to decline, the very large numbers in the lower years will produce an enormous growth of the population. By contrast the narrower base of the United States in 1950 will not sustain such a heavy growth as India's broad base.

SEX RATIO

Although the rural sex ratios for India and the United States are quite similar, the urban ratio for India reverses the relationship observed throughout the Western world:

	Urban	*Rural*
India, 1951	116	104
United States, 1950	95	106

India's cities in the last half century have become highly masculine, counter to trends in Western Europe and the U.S. This may be related to the seclusion of women in Hindu-Muslim society and to the characteristics of the Indian urban economy. The general masculinity of India, both urban and rural, indicates mortality differentials unfavorable to females.

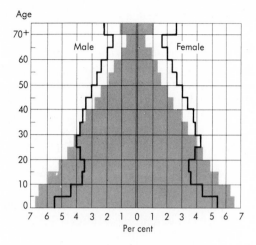

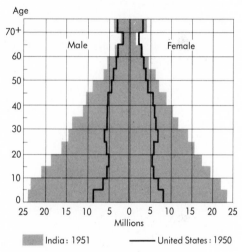

Fig. **IX:8** Population Pyramids

Source: United Nations, *Demographic Yearbook, 1960*, Table 5.

MORTALITY AND FERTILITY

Published birth and death rates for India have serious limitations because of extreme under-registration. However, estimates based upon sophisticated reinterpretation of vital statistics records and census reports are closer to the facts than the reported rates on births and deaths. Therefore, estimates for India based on a demographic analysis of 1941 and

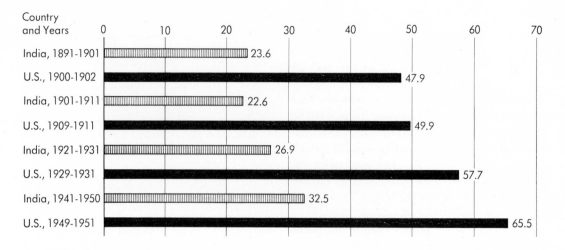

Fig. **IX:9**   Average Life Expectancy in Years at Birth for Males

Source: United Nations, *Demographic Yearbook, 1957*, Table 24.

1951 census reports are presented for comparison with the U.S. as follows:

Crude birth rate, 1950:
India, 39.9
United States, 23.5

Crude death rate, 1950:
India, 27.4
United States, 9.6

The death rates for India are not only much higher than for the United States, they are also erratic. This is because the major causes of death in India, apart from famine, are epidemic and infectious diseases, such as cholera, smallpox, plague, respiratory diseases, and the like. These diseases are subject to control by medical and public health techniques, which are now well understood, and for this reason alone a sharp decline in India's death rate is taking place, and a great increase in population will result. In the United States, on the other hand, the major causes of death are nonepidemic and degenerative disorders such as diseases of the heart and circulatory

system, and cancer. It is less likely that they will be effectively controlled, and the death rate for the United States is therefore not so likely to decline.

Just as the death rates for India are higher than for the United States, the birth rates for India are higher. One of the urgent questions of our time is whether or not Asian countries will be able to check their fertility by means other than catastrophe. Some of the considerations that must be taken into account in assessing this problem are reviewed in Adaptation 27, pages 340 ff.

Finally, Figure IX:9 reports another consequence of the high death rate of India compared with the low death rate for the United States. Note the great wastage in the population of India. The low average life expectancy in India means that the society is burdened by large numbers of people who never reach their productive years or who have a short working life. In the United States on the other hand, people tend to live through their economically useful years. (Cf. Fig. IX:12, p. 330.)

Section 3 **Fertility and mortality**

The future of a population is determined by the interplay of its birth and death rates and by immigration and emigration. If migration is held constant, the analysis of detailed birth and death rates can be used to predict the size of a population, its potential growth or decline, and its age structure.

In population literature *fertility* refers to *actual* reproduction; *fecundity,* on the other hand, refers to *potential* reproduction, that is, the population that would result from the biologically maximum number of births. The fertility of populations in modern urbanized and industrialized nations is only a small part of their fecundity, and even in the agrarian countries of Asia where fertility is very high, it does not reach the biological maximum.

THE MEASURES OF FERTILITY

A simple way to measure fertility is to calculate the percentage of new births in a population. The percentage states the number of births for each 100 persons in the population. For example, in 1960 [8] there were 4,247,000 births recorded in the U.S. On the basis of a total population of 179,323,000 new births constituted 2.37 per cent of the total, or 2.37 births for every 100 persons in the population. Conventionally, the calculation is made for each 1,000 population and is called the *crude birth rate*. The formula is:

$$\frac{\text{registered births in year}}{\text{midyear population}} \times 1,000 = \text{crude birth rate}$$

Substituting the 1960 figures [9] in the for-

mula, we obtain the U.S. crude birth rate:

$$\frac{4{,}247{,}000}{179{,}323{,}000} \times 1{,}000 = 23.7$$

There are difficulties in the interpretation of crude birth rates and other measures based on birth registration figures for the United States. Early in this century the "registration area," the area legally requiring birth registration, covered only ten states, chiefly in the northeast. In 1933 the registration area finally included the whole country, but until that time there was a shifting geographic base as more and more states were added. The setting up of standard birth registration procedures marks a great improvement in American vital statistics, but progress is yet to be made before the U.S. records are as good as those of some other countries, such as Sweden.

The completeness of the registration area does not, however, assure completeness in birth reporting. The National Office of Vital Statistics estimated birth registration in the U.S. in 1960 as only 98.9 per cent complete.[10] Therefore, for the United States and other areas where the records are not complete, a *corrected birth rate* (that is, crude birth rate adjusted for under-registration of births) may be computed. Recorded births are increased by an estimate of the percentage of all births that are not reported. The 1960 U.S. corrected rate was 23.9.

A crude birth rate of 23.9, corrected or not, may be either comparatively high or comparatively low, depending on the number of women of childbearing age in the population.

---

[8] Census figures are given to the nearest thousand.
[9] The figure for the population of the United States is for the census date of April 1, 1960. To be more nearly exact, the mid-year population should be taken, but the difference In the calculated rate would be very small.
[10] "Monthly Vital Statistics Report, Provisional Statistics," NOVS, Vol. 39, No. 13 (May 31, 1961), p. 2.

Table **IX:3** Estimated Birth and Death Rates and Age
Composition in Various World Regions*

Region	Rates Per Thousand of Population		Estimated Percentage of Population		
	Births (Col. 1)	Deaths (Col. 2)	Under 15 Years (Col. 3)	15–59 Years (Col. 4)	60 Years and Over (Col. 5)
World	36	19	34	58	8
Africa:					
Northern Africa	45	26	39	55	6
Tropical and Southern	47	28	43	49	6
America:					
North America	25	9	27	61	12
Middle America	45	18	42	53	6
South America	42	19	39	56	5
Asia:					
South West Asia	46	21	38	56	6
South Central Asia	44	26	37	57	6
South East Asia	44	23	43	53	4
Eastern Asia	39	21	37	56	7
Europe:					
Northern and Western Europe	18	11	24	61	15
Central Europe	19	10	24	62	14
Southern Europe	21	10	28	61	9
Oceania	25	9	30	61	12
U.S.S.R.	25	8	—	—	—

*Source: United Nations *Demographic Yearbook 1956*, Tables A and B, pp. 2, 8; and *Demographic Yearbook 1960*, Table 2

If one country has 250 females of childbearing age per 1,000 population and a second country has only 200, and if both have the same crude birth rate, the fertility of the second is obviously greater.

The need for a finer measure of fertility is shown in Table IX:3, which gives the crude birth rates for the regions of the world in column 1. These rough figures indicate that there are important differences between regions in the degree of fertility, for example, between Africa (crude birth rate = approximately 46) and the U.S. and Canada (crude birth rate = 25). To interpret these birth rates, we may refer to column 4. This reports the percentage of the population between ages 15 and 59 and contains the women of childbearing age. Because the percentage is larger in the U.S. and Canada than it is in Africa, there is good reason to suppose that the difference in fertility between the two regions is even greater than is indicated by their crude birth rates. To be more confident of this generalization, it would be necessary to eliminate males and females past the menopause from the percentages in column 4. Because much data, especially from underdeveloped areas, are of doubtful accuracy, the preceding comments are meant to point to problems of analysis rather than fact.

Measures of fertility calculated in terms of the reproduction of women of childbearing age have real advantages if the data are good. One such measure is the *age specific birth* rate,[11] obtained by dividing the number of births to mothers of each age group by the number of women of that group and multiplying by 1,000. For example, in 1959 there were 571,000 births to mothers 15 to 19 years of age, and the age specific birth rate for that group was 90.9. Figure IX:10, using age specific birth rates, shows why it is necessary to take into account not only the number of females capable of bearing children, but also their age distribution. In the United States at least, births are heavily concentrated in the age range 20–29, and relatively few births occur to women under 20 or over 34. "The Case of the G. E. Babies," pages 326–27, shows the necessity of applying appropriate measures of fertility to the correct segment of the population.

The detailed knowledge required to calculate the age specific birth rate (and more advanced measure based upon it) is a serious impediment to its use. This knowledge is lacking or imperfect in all but a few countries where human bookkeeping is most highly developed. The *fertility ratio,* on the other hand, may be computed directly from census data without recourse to vital statistics. To calculate the fertility ratio, it is necessary to know only the age and sex distribu-

tion of the population. The ratio is a statement of the number of small children to the number of women of childbearing age defined arbitrarily, for example, 15–44 years of age. A typical calculation is as follows:

$$\frac{\text{Number of children under 5 years}}{\text{Number of women aged 15—44 inclusive}} \times 1{,}000 = \text{fertility ratio (FR)}$$

Substituting U.S. Census figures for 1960:

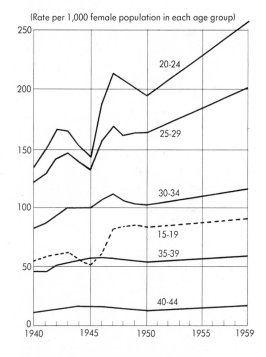

(Rate per 1,000 female population in each age group)

Fig. **IX:10**   Birth Rates by Age of Mother: United States, 1940–1959

Source: Vital Statistics—Special Reports, National Summaries. "Births by Age of Mother, Race and Birth Order," Vol. 37, No. 13 (November 27, 1953); U.S. Department of Health, Education, and Welfare—Public Health Service, NOVS. 1959 data from *Vital Statistics of the United States, 1959,* Vol. I, Table 39A.

[11] Demographers use the age specific birth rate to construct a more refined measure of fertility, called the *standardized birth rate.* For a discussion of this measure, see the references on p. 307.

Two other measures based on the age specific birth rate are the gross reproduction rate and the net reproduction rate. They are attempts to determine whether or not populations in the long run are maintaining their numbers. The *gross reproduction rate* tells us to what extent a given group of women are replacing themselves with daughters, assuming (1) that they live through their childbearing period and (2) that the age specific birth rates are maintained. To be practically useful, corrections need to be made to the gross reproduction rate. The *net reproduction rate* makes one of these corrections. It applies the age specific death rates prevalent at a given time. It assumes certain age specific birth rates, as does the gross reproduction rate. The net reproduction rate is usually expressed as follows: A net reproduction rate of 1.00 means that if the age specific birth and death rates existing in a given year continue, the population of women would just replace themselves in one generation; 1.50 means that in one generation they would increase by 50 per cent; 0.50 means that in one generation they would decrease by 50 per cent.

The Case of the G. E. Babies

Reprinted from the January, 1954, issue of *Fortune* by Special Permission of the Editors; Copyright, Time Inc.

The perils and complexities of birth forecasting were encountered . . . in rather extraordinary circumstances, by General Electric. January 14, [1953] G.E. announced that it would award five shares of its common stock to any employee who had a baby on October 15—the company's seventy-fifth anniversary. Originally the company said it expected about thirteen winners. It arrived at this figure by applying a daily U.S. birth rate to its own 226,000 employees. This computation actually yielded a prediction of fifteen births; but a G.E. public-relations man thought it might be nice to trim the figure to thirteen, the number of original G.E. investors. The mathematics suffered from more than public relations, however. G.E. employees, since they include no children and no one over sixty-five, are obviously a much more fertile group than the population as a whole. When this fact sank in, a company statistician made a new assault on the problem. He estimated that the size of an average G.E. family was 4.2. This meant that the total number of people in the G.E. families was close to a million. Applying the crude annual birth rate to *this* group, and dividing by 365, he came up with a new prediction of seventy-two births on the big day.

As it turned out, there were not thirteen, fifteen, or seventy-two babies born to G.E. employees on October 15. There were 189.

Subtracting the company's highest expectation of seventy-two from 189 gives 117, "extra" babies. Where did G.E. go wrong? Well, among other things, the company made no allowance for the incentive provided by its own stock. This oversight, remarkable in a company that has had a lot to say about capitalist incentives, was apparently rectified by the employees. The latter not only enjoy having children, but, it appears, they rather enjoy the idea of becoming capitalists. And they seem to have known a good thing. In a generally declining stock market, G.E. common stock rose during the pregnant months from $69\frac{1}{8}$ to $78\frac{7}{8}$.

Where Did G. E. Go Wrong?

They applied the wrong rate to the wrong group. They applied the crude birth rate to G.E. employees, assuming that only the *employees* would have the babies. If the crude birth rate were to be used at all, it should have been applied to the whole population of G.E. *families,* not just the workers but their wives, children (and other relatives). This they finally did when they included families in their calculations of the crude birth rate. But the crude birth rate requires a cross section of the total population, and they did not have one. Even the whole population of G.E. families is not representative of the whole population of the U.S. For instance, G.E. families contain an abnormally large proportion of individuals in the productive (and reproductive) years and few aged persons. The G.E. statistician also failed to consider these characteristics which affect the birth rate: (1) the section of the country, (2) the size of the communities where the employees lived, (3) their income, (4) their education, and (5) their race.

Could G. E. Have Done Better?

They could have made a closer approximation by applying age specific birth rates to the women of childbearing ages in G.E. employee families. This could have been further refined by correcting for seasonal fluctuations in births. Corrections for the characteristics G.E. failed to consider would be far more difficult to make and, under the conditions noted below, pointless.

Because figures for the characteristics of the G.E. population are not available, a more refined estimate cannot be calculated. It is probable but not certain (as *Fortune* assumes) that the announcement of the award was an incentive. The influence of incentive

could have been estimated and the quality of the prediction further improved by interviewing a sample of G.E. wives. Of course, if G.E. had wished to, it could have eliminated the incentive factor entirely by announcing the award eight instead of ten months before October 15. As it was, the announcement was probably timed to create maximum motivation. And a number of births may have been induced (hastened) by physicians.

There is at least one additional complication. Any estimate of a daily birth rate, even for a rather large population like the G.E. families, is subject to an additional source of error. Daily birth rates vary even more widely than seasonal or monthly birth rates. In 1950 U.S. registered crude birth rates ranged from 20.9 for the month of April to 25.5 for September. The shorter the time period, the greater the range of variation in birth rates (and the smaller the population, the greater the range of variation in birth rates). The chances of getting close to the mark on any particular day for any particular group are, therefore, not very good.

$$\frac{20,320,901}{36,078,973} \times 1,000 = 563$$

Assuming equally good enumeration of the young and the mature, and also assuming equally good over-all enumeration, the fertility ratio can be readily used for comparing the fertility of different countries or trends within the same country. However, if comparisons are made between interdependent areas, it is important to know if children are domiciled with their mothers. For example, rural mothers may migrate to the city, leaving their children to be cared for in the

rural areas. The comparison of fertility ratios for country and city would then be misleading. The rural fertility ratio would be too high because of the "extra" children, and the urban fertility ratio would be too low because of the presence of mothers separated from their children.

FERTILITY TRENDS

Figure IX:11 shows the fertility ratio for the United States since 1800. Two facts should be observed:

1. The steady decline in the fertility ratio from about 1,000 in 1800 to 342 in 1940.

2. The recovery in the ratio following World War II to over 472 in 1950 and to 563 in 1960. The reasons for the decline in fertility through 1940 and for the differential rates noted above are topics for conjecture. The dissemination of efficient methods of birth control is a precondition to the decline in fertility and to the "controlled" fertility that has been characteristic of Western and Central Europe as well as the United States and Canada. Why people use the techniques, the immediate "cause" of the changes, is far more obscure. Probably it is related to changes in the desire for children, or at least for large families, and increased emphasis on individualism, and aspirations for a higher standard of living and a higher educational standard both for oneself and one's children.

As is pointed out in the discussion of trends in Section 4, the increase in fertility since World War II was contrary to most population predictions, which assumed an extension of the prolonged decline in the birth rate. It is too soon to tell if the change is a temporary or relatively permanent one, but as Dorn has observed, it is reasonable to expect a *controlled* fertility to increase as well as decrease in response to historical events and economic changes.[12]

FERTILITY DIFFERENTIALS

Groups within a population reproduce at different rates. For example, some of the fertility differentials that have been fairly well established for the U.S. are as follows:

1. Rural farm areas have higher fertility than rural nonfarm areas.

2. Rural areas have higher fertility than urban areas.

3. The larger the city, the lower is the fertility; that is, size of city is inversely related to fertility.

4. In general, manual workers' wives have more children than do the wives of white-collar workers.

5. Catholic fertility tends to be higher than Protestant fertility.

In the Western world, in recent decades lower income groups and those with relatively low education have shown higher birth rates than the middle and upper classes and the relatively well educated. However, in the recent baby boom there is evidence that well-educated elements shared more than proportionately in the increase. Furthermore, where large samples have permitted fine analyses of income categories, it becomes clear that the very highest income groups have greater fertility than the middle and medium high groups in such places as England, the United States, and the Scandinavian countries.

These differences in fertility have important social consequences. For example:

1. The burden of dependency is not evenly distributed through the population. Rural areas have a relatively greater burden of supporting young children.

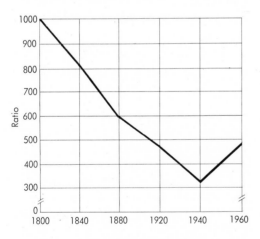

Fig. **IX:11**   Fertility Ratio for the
United States: 1800–1960

Children under 5 years of age per 1,000 women 16–44, United States. Adapted from *Population Problems* by Warren S. Thompson (New York: McGraw-Hill), p. 175. Data for 1960 from U.S. Bureau of the Census, *Census of Population: 1960*, PC(1)-1B, p. xiii.

[12] Harold F. Dorn, "Pitfalls in Population Forecasts and Projections," *Journal of the American Statistical Association*, **45**, (September, 1950), 332.

2. More fertile groups may become increasingly preponderant in the population, where fertility is not offset by migration or other factors. Thus, high Catholic fertility is the subject of anxious comment by some individuals from religious groups of lower fertility.

3. Some areas or groups cannot maintain themselves and must draw members from outside their number in order to persist. In the past this has been the relation between urban and rural areas, the city drawing upon the fertile countryside.

MORTALITY

The calculation of death rates and the registration of deaths encounter the same problems discussed under fertility. The best-known death rate, the crude death rate, is calculated as follows:

$$\frac{\text{registered deaths in year}}{\text{midyear population}} \times 1,000 = \text{crude death rate}$$

In 1960 the U.S. crude death rate was

$$\frac{1,702,000}{179,323,000} \times 1,000 = 9.5 \quad \begin{array}{l}\text{per thousand} \\ \text{of enumerated} \\ \text{population}\end{array}$$

This was a bit more than half of the 17.2 recorded in 1900 in the death registration states.

Table IX:3 compares in column 2 the North American death rate with estimates for Asia and Africa. As in the discussion of fertility, it is necessary to relate crude rates to age structure in order to make useful interpretations. If this is done, the advantage of North America (and also of Northwest and Central Europe) as expressed by the crude death rate is an understatement of their relative superiority, because the populations of these countries are older. The high African and Asian death rates occur in populations with heavy concentrations under 15

years of age: about 40 per cent in Africa and Asia, compared with 27 per cent in North America. (See page 324.)

Age specific death rates are calculated on the number of deaths per thousand persons of specified ages. In 1959 the U.S. age specific death rates ranged from 0.5 in ages 5–14 to 202.8 per thousand for persons 85 years and over.[13] The preoccupation of health officers with the mortality of certain groups has led to the development of special measures for these particular groups. Three of these follow:

1. The *infant mortality rate* reports for 1,000 live births how many infants die in the first year. The United States infant death rate was 25.7 in 1960, compared with rates for Sweden of 17, New Zealand of 24, and for Romania of 77.

2. *Neonatal mortality rate.* As the infant mortality rate has been brought under control, more attention has been given to the large proportion of infant deaths occurring during the first month. One-third of all infant mortality is concentrated in the first day of life; three-fifths of infant deaths occur in the first week; and more than two-thirds are in the first month.[14] A *neonatal mortality rate* is nothing more than an age specific death rate for the age group, birth to one month. The very existence of this measure suggests how developments of medical technology and awareness of problems lead to changes in record-keeping. Viewed another way, vital statistics point out to the medical scientist and practitioner where serious problems lie and where his efforts might be expected to produce most immediate benefits.

3. The *maternal mortality rate* states the number of mothers dying per 10,000 live births. The current American rate is under 5 maternal deaths per 10,000 live births, a

[13] *Vital Statistics of the United States,* 1959, Vol. I, Table 6-C.
[14] *Statistical Bulletin,* Metropolitan Life Insurance Co., February, 1952, p. 1.

Number of Survivors

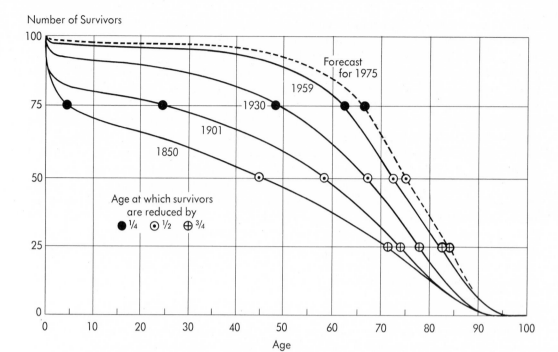

Fig. IX:12 Survivors from Birth to Successive Ages: United States, 1850–1959

Forecast for 1975 on the basis of low mortality forecast by Bureau of the Census, 1947. Source: *Statistical Bulletin*, Metropolitan Life Insurance Company (March, 1952, and March, 1960).

decline from 58 in 1935. Sometimes it is useful to study the rates at different ages, so that *age specific maternal mortality rates* are calculated. Interest is also directed toward the relationship between maternal deaths and the order of birth. In general the risk of childbirth is greatest at the highest ages, and the most favorable period for childbearing is the early twenties. Maternal mortality statistics bear out the popular belief that the first birth is relatively the most hazardous for the mother.

THE CHANCES OF SURVIVAL

Figure IX:12 shows how dramatically the chances of survival have improved in a century and forecasts a slight continued improvement. In 1850 only three-fourths of the newborn in the United States reached age 5; in 1901 the same proportion reached age 24; and in 1959, the same proportion survived more than 60 years. The age to which one-half of the newborn survive increased from 45 in 1850 to more than 73 years. Great advances in medical science and technology, in public health practice, and improvement in nutrition and the standard of living are responsible for the great gains. These changes have had and will continue to have profound effects on the society. A few of these consequences are:

1. An increasing number of persons will live and are living through their working years with a consequent improvement in the productive efficiency of the nation.

2. A larger number of persons will reach

and are reaching old age, thereby creating a dependency problem. Old age is attracting increased scientific attention, age is being redefined in popular thought, and a change is taking place in what is believed to be the proper functions of the aged.

3. With the marked reduction in deaths of the young, the population will be able to sustain or increase its numbers with relatively fewer births.

4. "Premature" deaths have been reduced and may be reduced somewhat further, but at this time it seems unlikely that the upper limits of human existence will be significantly increased. To assume so is to misread the statistics and to interpret improved average longevity as an extension in the limits of the human life span. Figure IX: 13 shows how the age at death has changed since 1900. Note in Figure IX: 12 that the gain in survivors at the three-fourths point and above is not nearly so impressive as at one-half and one-fourth. Indeed, the 1959 curve presses closely against the 1975 forecast, suggesting relatively little anticipated improvement. It would take a major break-through in control of the disorders of age to extend significantly the human life span.

MORBIDITY

Morbidity refers to the occurrence of disease, and the morbidity rate is usually expressed as the incidence of a disease per 100,000 of population. The gathering and interpretation of medical statistics is an exceedingly complex operation. For example, changing classifications of diseases impose difficulties in the interpretation of morbidity rates over a period of time, and diseases that are socially stigmatized are often not correctly reported. The lists of disease are being reviewed and revised constantly, and the continuing National Health Survey has greatly improved morbidity records in the United States.

Full and reliable morbidity statistics have a significant influence on medical research and

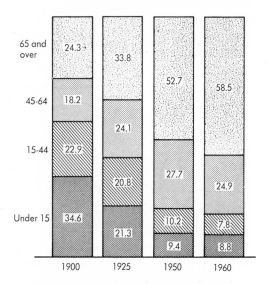

Fig. IX:13 Per Cent Distribution of Deaths by Age for the United States, 1900–1960

From *Statistical Bulletin*, Metropolitan Life Insurance Company, **34**, No. 9 (September, 1953), 4. Data for 1960 added.

practice. They can indicate where research is most needed and perhaps where and when protective measures should be applied. For example, in countries where some diseases, such as malaria, are widespread (pandemic), individual diagnosis and treatment are impossibly expensive, and techniques of mass prevention or treatment are the only feasible approaches. In such countries substantial gains in reducing illness and mortality may be achieved with relatively few trained personnel and at relatively little cost per person. For much of the world pandemic diseases affecting whole populations are mass public health problems rather than problems of individual medical care.

On the other hand, in the modern Western world much less can be expected of mass treatment. In countries such as the United States, with the postponement of death and the accompanying increase in the diseases of old age, emphasis must be given to far more costly individual diagnoses and treatment. For this kind of care more doctors and medical facilities are needed per thousand of population. Wise public health administration and medical practice need to take into account not merely the statistical summaries of morbidity and mortality rates but also detailed death and illness rates in the light of the characteristics of the population.

Section 4 **Population change**

WORLD POPULATION GROWTH

The population of the world has increased nearly sixfold in the past three centuries. Improvements in the means of production and transportation, advances in agricultural technology, and the manifold effects of the industrial revolution have combined in a large part of the world to reduce death rates, to prolong life, and at least in the West to raise the standard of living. Carr-Saunders [15] estimates that there were about 545 million inhabitants of the world in 1650. In two centuries the population more than doubled, and in 1850 the total was 1,171 million. In the last century it has again more than doubled, and the U.N. *Demographic Yearbook* [16] sets its estimate for 1959 at 2,907 million. The increase, of course, has not been uniform. People of European ancestry made up about one-sixth of the population of the world in 1650; by 1959 they constituted almost one-third of the world's people. Asia still accounts for more than half of mankind, although her share of the world's population has decreased.

The rate of increase in Western Europe and North America has been slowing up. The sharp decline in death rates was followed by a decline in birth rates. By the beginning of World War II the trend had proceeded to a point where the countries of Western Europe had reached or were approaching stable populations, and the rate of increase in the U.S. had declined so far that a stable population was predicted for the near future. Western and Central Europe were described as areas of stationary population and subject to incipient decline. Postwar trends suggest that a stable population is less certain or at least less imminent for Western Europe and North America.

DEMOGRAPHIC TRANSITION

Students of population have tried to identify basic stages of growth and decline in the populations of various parts of the world. When a population seems to be passing from one stage to another, it is called *demographic transition*. Beginning about the middle of the seventeenth century Europe's population passed through these stages:

1. A period of explosive growth as the death rate declined

2. A leveling off of growth as the birth rate declined

3. A change in the age structure and a trend toward population stability or decline The prewar condition of Western Europe with its stable or incipiently declining population appeared to be the natural end product of a cycle, and the series of stages was thought to be a *necessary* sequence. The U.S. also seemed far advanced in the cycle. Following these assumptions, population forecasts for the U.S. predicted a stable or declining population to be reached in the

[15] A. M. Carr-Saunders, *World Population* (Oxford: Clarendon Press, 1936), p. 42.
[16] United Nations, *Demographic Yearbook*, 1960.

approximate future at numbers which now appear to be very conservative. The "baby boom" following World War II arrested the trend toward stability and made obsolete estimates that were only a few years old. Indeed the population of the U.S. has already exceeded some of the prewar predictions of its ultimate maximum.

Are we to conclude that such predictions based on the analyses of long-term trends are pointless and irresponsible? The predictions were certainly erroneous in detail, and some undoubtedly were deficient in method. Each one, however, is subject to re-examination, and painstaking assessment of error is one of the ways that science advances. Although this highly technical problem cannot be reviewed here, it seems likely that many of the estimates were incorrect in assuming that the underlying values and beliefs that motivated the declining birth rate were permanent features of American culture and society.[17] We have already referred to Dorn's opinion that a controlled birth rate can readily move up as well as down. This seems to be verified by the persistence of the "baby boom," and it may be concluded that the predictions erred in paying too little attention to social and cultural factors. The baby boom may be either a transitional phenomenon or the signal of a long trend. World War II undoubtedly had the effect of postponing some births to the immediate postwar period, at which time they contributed to the baby boom. Even if the boom in births abruptly terminates, it has made an important impact on the age structure of the country and the reproductive po-

tential of coming generations. It has also warned population specialists to apply with caution generalizations about demographic transitions. Even though some detailed predictions have proved faulty, the main ideas of the demographic transition are provocative. Thompson [18] groups the countries of the world in three broad categories according to the extent of their control over birth and death rates:

Group 1 countries have achieved significant control over death rates and have also gained increasing control over birth rates. Despite postwar changes, Western peoples now have relatively low death rates and birth rates. Thompson predicts that they will do no more than maintain relatively low rates of natural increase. This group contains the United States, Canada (except Quebec), the United Kingdom, Australia, New Zealand, and most of the countries of northern, western, and central Europe. In all they represent about one-fifth of the world's population.

Group 2 countries show a declining death rate, but their birth rates have only begun to decline. They lag behind Group 1 in their population trends. Their exceedingly high rates of natural increase may continue for some time. In this group are the countries of southern and eastern Europe, the Soviet Union, Japan, Quebec, and possibly north Africa, Brazil, Argentina, and Uruguay. These regions also contain about one-fifth of the world's population. It is uncertain how long it will take Group 2 countries to complete the sequence of changes to a stable or declining population—or indeed if they will complete the cycle.

Group 3 countries, such as most of Asia and Negro Africa, have high but variable death rates and high and steady birth rates. Population trends depend largely upon what Malthus called positive checks (famine, war, disease, etc.), but the checks have been altered by the introduction of modern health

---

[17] For a bibliography on population forecasts and an incisive critique, see Dorn, *op. cit.* A manual for making population forecasts for sections of the U.S. is: Van Beuren Stanbery, "Better Population Forecasting for Areas and Communities" (Washington, D.C.: U.S. Department of Commerce, Government Printing Office, 1952). For recent examples of population projections see Bureau of the Census, *Current Population Reports* (November 10, 1958), Series P–25, No. 187: "Illustrative Projections of the Population of the United States, by Age and Sex, 1960 to 1980," prepared by Meyer Zitter and Jacob S. Siegel; and (June 22, 1961) Series P–25, No. 232: "Illustrative Projections to 1980 of School and College Enrollment in the United States."

[18] A summary may be found in *op. cit.*, pp. 267–72.

measures in some areas. These countries contain about three-fifths of the world's population and most of the undeveloped areas.

Population Change in Undeveloped Areas

The rates of growth in Group 3 countries are so great that any program for improvement of health and standards of living in undeveloped areas ought to take into account its effects on population increase. An improvement in production without an increase in the standard of living and without social changes affecting fertility "may result . . . in ever larger masses of humanity living close to the margins of existence and vulnerable to every shock in the world economic and political structure. Such 'progress' may amount to setting the stage for calamity. Much of Asia seems to be perilously close to this situation. . . ."[19] Moreover, the mothers of the next generation are already born, and a further enormous population increase seems inevitable. Formosa, the Philippines, Java, and Korea have had considerable development, primarily in agriculture, but little change in the social structure and the birth rate. Stable governments and slight improvements in agricultural techniques and sanitation reduced death rates, so that before World War II the populations were growing at a rate which would permit them to double in one generation.

"No more striking illustration of the limitations, from the demographic point of view, of 'good government and economic development' can be given than the case of Java."[20] Between 1860 and 1930 marked advances were made in sanitation and agricultural production, and in that time the population tripled. In 1930 Java had a density of 800 per square mile. The customary way of life had changed little; there was no evidence of sig-

nificant improvement in the standard of living of the masses; the limits of agricultural production were being approached; and there were few signs of a decline in fertility. If the rates of increase are maintained, by 2000 Java will have a density of 1500 per square mile. The problems of undeveloped areas do not stop with improvements in agricultural or industrial productivity and sanitation. The population problem affects all aspects of planning and development.

In the Western world the decline in birth rates accompanied industrialization and urbanization. Perhaps Western-style urbanization would have the same effects in the East. The experience of Japan suggests that this is so, but similar evidence from India or China would be more compelling. Even if urbanization reduces the birth rate, the population pressures of the East are too great to wait upon urbanization. The problem, therefore, may be posed this way: Can agrarian countries with large family systems and high fertility modify the values, beliefs, and practices responsible for high fertility *without* undergoing urbanization? If this is not done, or can not be done, the efforts to improve the undeveloped areas may prove self-defeating.

Adaptation 27 reports the findings of research in a high-fertility area, Ceylon. The study suggests what must be considered before answers may be formulated to the momentous problems of population growth. The factors include the nature of the family pattern, the value placed upon relations between the sexes, the value placed upon women and children, the location of authority in the family and community, and the relationship between the family and larger kin and locality groups. The analysis shows the necessity of taking such social and cultural factors into account and indicates the futility of using purely biological criteria in studying vital human trends. Even if Ryan's study gave a definitive answer for Ceylon, which it does not presume to do, a series of comparative studies over a fairly long period are

[19] This discussion is largely based on Frank W. Notestein, "Summary of the Demographic Background of Problems of Undeveloped Areas," *The Milbank Memorial Fund Quarterly*, **26**, No. 3 (July, 1948), 249–55. Quotation at p. 252.
[20] Notestein, *loc. cit.*

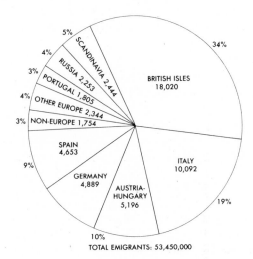

Fig. **IX:14** Intercontinental Migration,
Country of Origin:
1846–1932

For countries specified the period covered is
1846–1932. Various dates apply for unspecified
countries. Numbers inside the circle are emigrants
in thousands. Numbers outside the circle are percentages of the total. [Computed from A. M. Carr-
Saunders, *World Population* (Oxford: 1936), p. 49.]

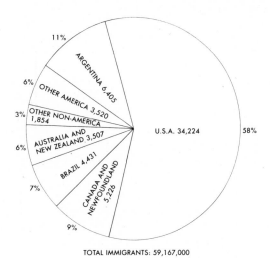

Fig. **IX:15** Intercontinental Migration,
Country of Destination:
1821–1932

For U.S.A., Canada, and Brazil the period covered
is 1821–1932. Various dates apply for all other
countries. [Computed from A. M. Carr-Saunders,
World Population (Oxford: 1936), p. 49.]

needed before even tentative predictions may
be made for the Asian world. At very least,
however, the Ryan study points to the kind
of knowledge essential to predict the course
of fertility in undeveloped areas.

INTERCONTINENTAL MIGRATION

The largest migration prior to 1800 was
the movement of slaves from Africa mainly
to the New World. Estimates of the number
of Negroes transported are unreliable and
variable, but the actual number may fall between 10 and 20 millions. Most of the slave
traffic was during the eighteenth century. By
comparison, the number of migrants from
Europe to the New World prior to 1800 may
not have exceeded 4 to 5 million. However,
by the nineteenth century a massive movement from Europe had developed, and perhaps as many as 70 million people have

entered the Western Hemisphere since the
beginning of the nineteenth century. This
spread of European peoples is the largest intercontinental population movement in recorded history.

The opening of the New World came at
an opportune time in the demographic history of Europe. Migration to the Western
Hemisphere relieved population pressure
during a period of explosive increase. It must
not be assumed, however, that emigration is
always generated by population pressure.
Small Portugal, for example, experienced a
drain of man power during the period of
exploration and weakened her demographic
structure in attempting to man her far-flung
colonies from Asia to Brazil.

Although the early data are hardly more
than educated guesses, it is possible to find
estimates for the nineteenth and twentieth

centuries that deserve interpretation. These are summarized in Figures IX:14 and IX:15 which present the sources and destinations during the period of maximum intercontinental migration. All but 2 million of the 53 million people involved in intercontinental migration between 1846 and 1932 were from Europe, and more than three-quarters of the total movement were from five countries: the British Isles, Italy, Austria-Hungary, Germany, and Spain.

The figures for the countries of destination (Fig. IX:15) exceed the reported emigration (Fig IX:14) by some 6 million. This discrepancy is due to the difference in time span, 111 years compared with 86 years for the emigration data, and to the fact that there are somewhat better records on immigration than on emigration. Both statistical summaries are undoubtedly incomplete, but the broad outlines are clear and would not be altered significantly by addition of more recent data. The chief donor countries were European; the chief receiving countries were in the Americas, and the United States alone received three-fifths of the total immigration.

Not all of this intercontinental movement was of permanent settlers, and it is impossible to tell how many of the migrants were temporary residents. Carr-Saunders estimates that about 30 per cent of those entering the United States (1821–1924) returned to their homes and that 47 per cent of Argentine immigrants returned.[21] It is often implied that those who returned did so because they were failures in the new countries. Insofar as they adjusted poorly and did not find useful employment, this is so. However, many immigrants had intended when they left their homelands to return, and others who planned to be sojourners turned out to be permanent settlers. Whatever their initial plans, temporary migrants may play a significant part in the development of new lands, and this was certainly true of many

who eventually repatriated. For example, between 1901 and 1930 Australia had an immigration of 2,773,000 but a net gain (immigration minus emigration) of only 536,000. Yet the transient labor supply was invaluable in the building of the nation.

The United States has been a chief beneficiary from intercontinental migration. As a receiving country, it gained great human resources at relatively small cost. The expansion of the American frontier, the maintenance of an adequate labor force, the broadening of the consumer market, and the introduction of knowledge and skills were all accelerated by the uniquely sustained and diverse migration. Until recently the immigration was disproportionately composed of males in their productive years, and although this fact was an economic gain, the biased sex ratio impaired the integration of the new groups into American society. Even without the complicating factor of the high sex ratio, the task of resocializing a large number of immigrants generated stresses in the society.

Table IX:4 reports the immigration to the United States by decades and the chief contributing countries for each period. The cumulative impact of this immigration is shown in Table IX:5. The peak number of foreign born in the United States, more than 14 million, was reported for 1930. Since then, both the number and the percentage of the population foreign born have declined. The 1960 Census reported less than 10 million for the fifty states, below the number in 1900. The 10.4 million in 1900 were nearly 14 per cent of the total population; the 9.7 million in 1960 were only 5.4 per cent of the total. The decline in the importance of immigration is a consequence of many influences including a restrictive immigration policy.[22] During the 1950's the reported rate of immi-

[21] Carr-Saunders, op. cit., p. 49.

[22] See William S. Bernard (ed.), American Immigration Policy (New York: Harper, 1950); Whom We Shall Welcome, Report of the President's Commission on Immigration and Naturalization (Washington, D.C.: Government Printing Office, 1953); B. M. Ziegler (ed.), Immigration (Boston: Heath, 1953).

Table **IX:4** Immigration to the United States *

Decade	Immigration (in Thousands)	Chief Contributing Countries
1820–1830	152	Ireland, Great Britain, France
1831–1840	599	Ireland, Germany, Great Britain
1841–1850	1,713	Ireland, Germany, Great Britain
1851–1860	2,598	Germany, Ireland, Great Britain
1861–1870	2,315	Germany, Great Britain, Ireland
1871–1880	2,812	Germany, Great Britain, Ireland
1881–1890	5,247	Germany, Great Britain, Ireland
1891–1900	3,688	Italy, Austria-Hungary, Russia, Germany
1901–1910 ᵃ	8,795	Austria-Hungary, Italy, Russia
1911–1920	5,736	Italy, Russia, Austria-Hungary
1921–1930	4,107	Italy, Germany, Great Britain
1931–1940	528	Germany, Italy, Great Britain
1941–1950	1,035	Germany, Great Britain, Italy
1951–1960	2,515	Germany, Canada, Mexico, Italy

* Sources: U.S. Bureau of the Census, *Statistical Abstract of the United States: 1961* (Washington, D.C., 1961), p. 93. Annual Report of the Immigration and Naturalization Service, United States Department of Justice, Washington, D.C., for the fiscal year ended June 30, 1950, Table 4.

ᵃ Heaviest single year 1907: 1,285,000 immigrants.

gration recovered from the low levels of the 1930's and 1940's, but at least part of the increase was "statistical" rather than real, that is, immigration from Mexico and Canada was more accurately reported than in earlier periods. There is also evidence of a slight relaxation of the stringent immigration policy that has prevailed in recent decades and a sign of willingness to adapt immigration practice to the cold war. It appears that in percentage terms the foreign born will continue to diminish in importance. The origins of the

Table **IX:5** Foreign-born Population of the United States, 1850–1960 *

Year	Foreign Born Number (in Thousands)	Per Cent of Total Population Foreign Born
1850	2,244 ᵃ	11.2
1860	4,136 ᵃ	15.0
1870	5,567	14.4
1880	6,679	13.3
1890	9,249	14.8
1900	10,445	13.7
1910	13,630	14.8
1920	14,020	13.2
1930	14,283	11.6
1940	11,657	8.8
1950	10,431	6.9
1960	9,738	5.4

* Sources: for the period 1850–1890, U.S. Bureau of the Census: *Historical Statistics of the United States, 1789–1945* (Washington, D.C., 1949), p. 30. Data for 1900 to 1960 from U.S. Bureau of the Census, *Census of Population: 1960*, PC (1) 1C, *United States Summary, General Social and Economic Characteristics*, Table 66.

ᵃ White and free colored population only.

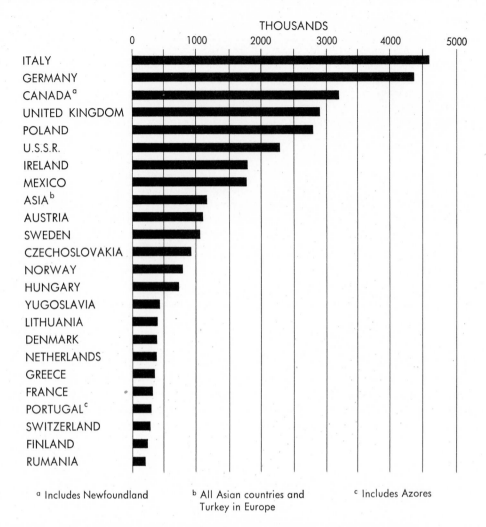

THOUSANDS

Fig. **IX:16** Foreign Stock of the United States, by Country of Origin, 1960

Source: U.S. Bureau of the Census. *U.S. Census of Population: 1960. General Social and Economic Characteristics, United States Summary.* Final Report PC(1)-1C. (Washington, D.C.: U.S. Government Printing Office, 1962), Table 69. Not separately listed: Other America, 581,000; Other Europe, 492,000; Not reported, 251,000; All other, 140,000.

foreign stock of the United States are given in Figure IX:16. Compare this with Table IX:4, which reports the chief contributing countries at various periods. "Foreign stock" includes the foreign-born and the native-born population of foreign or mixed parentage. The category thus comprises all first- and second-generation Americans. The third and subsequent generations in the U.S. are called "native of native parents." In 1960 there were 34,050,000 persons of foreign stock in the U.S., or about 19 per cent of the total population.

The American quota system of immigration control and the exceptions to it are extremely complicated both as products of legislation and in the problems they create for the immigration machinery. It is not pos-

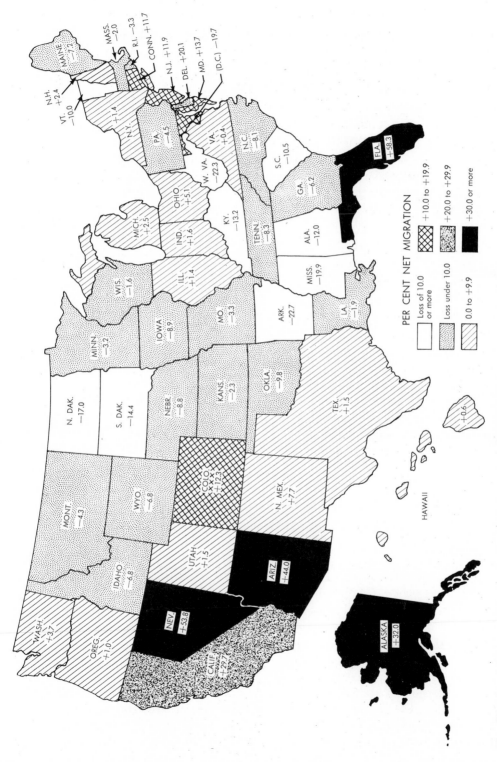

Fig. IX:17   Net Migration, 1950 to 1960, as Per Cent of 1950 Population, by States

Source: Bureau of the Census, *Current Population Reports*, Series P-25, No. 227 (April 26, 1961).

PER CENT NET MIGRATION

Loss of 10.0 or more	+10.0 to +19.9
Loss under 10.0	+20.0 to +29.9
0.0 to +9.9	+30.0 or more

MASS. —2.0
R.I. —3.3
CONN. +11.7
N.J. +11.9
DEL. +20.1
MD. +13.7
(D.C.) —19.7
N.H. +2.4
MAINE —7.2
VT. —10.0
N.Y. +1.4
PA. —4.5
W. VA. —22.3
VA. +0.4
N.C. —8.1
S.C. —10.5
OHIO +5.1
GA. —6.2
MICH. +2.5
IND. +1.6
KY. —13.2
TENN. —8.3
ALA. —12.0
WIS. —1.6
ILL. +1.4
MISS. —19.9
IOWA —8.9
MO. —3.3
ARK. —22.7
LA. —1.9
MINN. —3.2
N. DAK. —17.0
S. DAK. —14.4
NEBR. —8.8
KANS. —2.3
OKLA. —9.8
TEX. +1.5
FLA. +58.3
MONT. —4.3
WYO. —6.8
COLO. +12.3
N. MEX. +7.7
IDAHO —6.8
UTAH +1.5
ARIZ. +44.0
WASH. +3.7
OREG. +1.0
NEV. +53.8
CALIF. +25.7
HAWAII +0.6
ALASKA +32.0

sible to discuss here the manifold pressures and considerations that lie behind the restrictive American immigration policy. One demographic observation can be made, however. It is often suggested that the purpose of relieving population pressures in other parts of the world should enter into the formulation of immigration policy. However, emigration cannot play a significant part in relieving the problems of such countries as India and China. The populations of these countries are so large and their reproductivity is so high that emigration of a great many people would give only fleeting relief and at the same time would transfer the problem elsewhere.

INTERNAL MIGRATION

Just as the United States has been the most important single goal in international population movements, it has also been the scene of impressive internal migrations. The westward migration, the settlement of the hinterland, the urban movement, and high contemporary mobility are all elements in the development of American society. The westward movement, which populated the area west of the Appalachians and consolidated the American hold on the continent, has overshadowed all other interregional migrations

in the United States and has persisted into the twentieth century. It may be worth mentioning in passing that Russia's movement toward her thinly settled areas in the east resembles in some respects the westward movement of the United States.

Figure IX:17 shows net interstate migration (immigration minus emigration) for the 1950 decade. The indicated high rate of mobility is a continuation of a long historical trend and a national attitude toward free and opportunistic movement. This geographic mobility suggests a great flexibility in the American labor force, a flexibility that reduces the immigration needs of the nation and probably affects its immigration policy. If the population tended to remain geographically fixed, the development of man power demands in a given locality would encourage a policy of open migration. But because man power is relatively fluid in its adaptability to job opportunities, the labor force approaches the condition of a national pool and is used relatively more efficiently. Labor shortages tend to be filled from within the nation, and because of this there is less need to recruit workers from foreign countries. At least temporarily, however, such mobility impedes the establishing of community solidarity.

Fertility in Ceylon

Abridged and adapted from "Institutional Factors in Sinhalese Fertility" by Bryce Ryan, *The Milbank Memorial Fund Quarterly*, XXX, No. 4 (October, 1952), 359–81. Published in this form by permission of Bryce Ryan and the Milbank Memorial Fund.

Many Asian areas are now experiencing rapid increase, but there is no assurance that birth limitation will be practiced there. In this adaptation Bryce Ryan examines the social and cultural factors in Ceylon which may maintain high birth rates contrary to the experience of Western Europe.

It should not be assumed that what happens in Ceylon must happen elsewhere in Asia any more than it can be assumed that what happened in the United States must necessarily happen in Ceylon.

In Ceylon one decade has witnessed a phenomenal decline in death rates but no significant change in birth rates. Although it is possible that fertility is declining, the rate of natural increase is nearly 3 per cent per annum. Even if urban fertility is changing, a matter undemonstrated, it cannot be assumed that Ceylon will follow the Western pattern of persistent diffusion of the small family system. Ceylon is overwhelmingly a rural country, and the difference between city and village is much greater than in most Western nations. It is unrealistic to expect the rapid diffusion of new values and new techniques from an urban population which itself is probably largely unresponsive to them. A revolutionary development is even less likely to appear spontaneously in the countryside. Controlled fertility is typically associated with the individualistic and romantic marital union. No such social climate exists in Ceylon, nor is it likely soon to exist. If the small family pattern and birth limitation are to be introduced, they must be imposed upon a society now tied to large-family values.

THE MARRIAGE PATTERN

In Ceylon marriage is a calculated and rational extension of kinship; as a relation between two persons dominated by thoughts of each other, it is immoral and atypical. The individual is subordinated to the family. Evidence of social change may be found in the frequency of romantic suicides, which are protests against the control of the kin group, but these also show the continuous power of community and kin. As the society is organized, the individual has a lifelong dependence upon kin, even among urban sophisticates.

Not only is the old system sacred, the accepted scope of individualism simply does not provide for personal preferences in marriage. Previous acquaintance is usually a matter of unconcern to all parties involved, and there is virtually no comprehension of the concept of romance and seldom even a hint of rebellion. There is a potent and intricate *interdependency* between individual and kin, within which the arranged match is crucial and romantic marriage abhorrent and socially disorganizing. The demonstration of

this lies in the rigid criteria in spouse selection: (1) membership in the same ethnic community, i.e., Sinhalese; (2) identity of caste; (3) bride younger than groom; (4) bride a virgin; (5) horoscopes of each closely matched. In addition, the dowry power of the girl's people, security and occupational prestige of the boy, and the status of family lines are considered in matchmaking.

A number of factors support the familial concept and are inconsistent with the romantic complex. The greatest moral duty of a father is a "good" marriage for his daughter, and this duty falls on a son at the father's death. These are responsibilities to blood kin, fully as much as to the child. Desire for family prestige may press the father or brother toward almost impossible financial sacrifices.

In marriage the individual is both caught and sheltered within his kinship group. The son helps with his sister's dowry and in so doing protects his own status which in turn is rewarded in dowry. Challenge to the arranged match as such is a challenge to the prerogatives of kin. The lineal family as a status-bearing entity in the community has its most critical times in the period of approaching marriage. Every relative has his funds or status at stake. Romantic marriage is not consistent with the rigid dictates of caste, prestige, and house honor. It threatens not merely the father's rightful authority but the honor of the generations, past and future, of which the father is the legitimate guardian. Marriage by choice has no claim upon kin for dowry, no claim for help in harvest and no claim for co-operation in marrying some ultimate daughter of the union. Although the infrequent romantic marriages in villages do not necessarily meet with ostracism if caste propriety and other rigid matters have been observed, there is partial or complete estrangement from kinfolk. In the closely knit affairs of the village, life for such a couple may be far from pleasant.

The requirement of astrological suitability deserves special mention. Almost universally the Sinhalese, young and old, educated and uneducated, believe that suitably matched mates are perfectly revealed in the horoscopes.

DOMINANCE OF THE MALE

The Sinhalese family is usually patrilineal (see definition in THE FAMILY, p. 356) and patrilocal in the limited sense that the couple settles in the husband's village. A new marital unit is dominated by the husband's kin through their very proximity. The father-husband is the social authority, and his relation to all except small children is devoid of overt expressions of affection but replete with evidence of his dignity and prerogatives. It is not implied that this patriarchalism is harsh; few relationships between Sinhalese are that.

From early childhood the male is schooled in his superiority. A family of many males is a "fortunate one"; one of many daughters is "burdened." To the father's position services are due and deference is paid. There is a deeply seated belief that in marriage the loyalty and subservience of the wife to husband must be complete. He stands in the place of her father as well as in the role of her husband. On the other hand, it is generally agreed that the husband owes his first allegiance to his own parents rather than to his wife. Rarely a rigid disciplinarian, the father is still *master* in a society where that concept has a living feudal history.

FERTILITY IN A PEASANT VILLAGE

The village utilized for intensive investigation is in the Ceylon "Low Country," six miles from a market town. The mean age at marriage for village women (based on a one-fourth sample of existing marital units) was 21.9 years, and for men, 28.4 years.[23] There is some reason to believe that the age of women at marriage is rising, but there is no evidence of such a change among men. It is probable

that the high ages at marriage are influenced by the difficulties of dowry. About one-fourth of the marriages had no dowry, due to poverty, impositions upon the kin for providing a daughter, and a few romantic marriages. The proportion of dowryless matches has not changed with passing years. Marriages by personal choice but with parental approval account for 13 per cent of marriages and show no increase. Only 4 per cent claim to have married in spite of their parents' wishes. More than 80 per cent of all marriages and more than two-thirds of recent marriages were arranged by the parents. Most marriages conform closely to traditional patterns.

Children are viewed by all as products of destiny. When women say "all children are a blessing," they are expressing the mores of the community; but for a substantial proportion of mothers, it might be said that *many* children are *imposed* as a blessing. Many mothers accept only reluctantly a pattern of childbearing that approaches fecundity (the biological limit). Women do not face continuous pregnancies without misgivings, although most accept them with fatalistic composure.

Birth Control

To wish that destiny might be kind is one matter; to seek actively the prevention of birth is another. In response to this suggestion a woman said: "If a dead 'soul' wishes to be born into your family, it would be a terrible sin to prevent its birth. We will pay for such acts in our next life. Children that are to be born to you must be allowed to be born. That is how life goes on. We cannot and should not prevent this." Here speaks the voice of the community, echoed by men and women alike. A rebirth in the great cycle must not be denied to any being.[24] A former Prime Minister of Ceylon supported this village interpretation, a position not held, however, by several other prominent Buddhist

[23] The mean age at marriage for women in the United States is about the same and for men somewhat younger.

[24] The belief in reincarnation is a basic tenet of Sinhalese culture.

political leaders. In spite of verbal conformity by the villagers, the interviewers agree that a majority of the mothers would welcome some morally suitable relief from the imminent arrival of the next baby. They also agree that the fathers see no cause for worry and have nothing ill to say of the most fertile marriage.

The attitudes of men toward family size and birth control are not modified by the burden of childbearing and child care. Men sincerely want large families, and especially many sons: "children are prosperity." Not once in the extensive discussions with village men was there a mention of the difficulties of child care. The personal trials and burdens of parenthood are almost wholly the mother's. Father is proud parent toward his neighbors, a caresser of infants in the home, and contributor to his kin status through well-calculated marriages. He is served by his household, and the larger his small kingdom, the greater his dignity and glory. Through children, especially sons, he gains status as a man, is assured that his responsibilities will be inherited by others and that he himself will have security in his old age. The wife has no avenue of escape from the increasing demands upon her made by the growing family. The father works no harder to provide for a large family. He merely lives less well until the youth begin earning.

The husband's sexual authority is the most important single element for an understanding of fertility. Time and again the word "property" appears, describing the wife, and frequent allusions are made to the transfer of paternal authority from the wife's father to the husband. The woman's lot is cast with an unknown male bred to the role of patriarch. Economic dependence supports this pattern. Once a woman is given in marriage, she is expected to stick to her husband regardless of how trying married life with him may be. Her parents cannot afford to maintain his and her children or meet the expense of a second marriage.

In respect only to age at marriage is the Sinhalese pattern inconsistent with high reproductivity. (In the more remote districts, however, girls are frequently married soon after puberty.) In other spheres family structure and mores are consistent with high reproduction, and the economic cost of children is slight. The village girl fears the fate of spinsterhood or of being a childless wife; infertility is treated with contempt. However, the threat of infertility is relieved with the birth of even a single child, and the difficulties of childbearing and child care increase in at least arithmetical ratio to numbers. With these difficulties the husband has no part and rarely much concern, for they are the natural functions of his wife and her god-given means of pleasing him. The husband is also motivated by something the wife can never fully share. Children are contributions to *his* family, not to hers; the wife is an agent for the husband's kin; he is of its very substance. To her, children may be assets of the conjugal union, but to him they are also assets in the society to which his first loyalties belong.

Doubtless a substantial minority of village women are today trying to reduce the frequency of pregnancies. Lack of technical knowledge is perhaps no greater a handicap than the unsympathetic attitudes of dominant males. It seems fair to conclude that *if* women were provided with simple contraceptive techniques which were made consistent with moral precepts, and *if* the techniques were used without their husbands' knowledge, the more youthful mothers of several children would use them. The "moral rationalization" of contraception should present no great difficulties, for the Buddhist position is not doctrinaire, and the people are skilled in compromise with even rigid precepts. However, the secret use of contraceptive devices is improbable. The combined effects of male sex dominance and the distinctive male rewards for numerous progeny may retard a small-family movement more than might be expected from Western experience.

Section 5 Ecology

INTRODUCTION

Ecology is the study of the way living things relate and adjust themselves to their environment. The environment includes both other organisms and the inanimate physical setting, and the basic data for ecology are spatial distributions. Ecology as an orderly discipline within biological science developed during the nineteenth and twentieth centuries. It was greatly influenced by Charles Darwin.

An important theme of ecology is *co-operation–competition*. Organisms and species compete with each other for limited space and resources. Some organisms help each other to achieve a stable adjustment and a control of the environment (man and certain bacteria which help in the digestion of food). Others compete directly and tend to displace each other (man and predatory animals or pathogenic organisms). In the course of this competition, certain organisms or species tend to become dominant in a given natural area and achieve a relatively stable adjustment to the physical environment and network of relations with other organisms. The basic ideas of ecology (e.g., co-operation–competition) are strongly sociological, as Darwin was aware and intended. It is not surprising, therefore, that efforts were soon made to study the location of human groups and their institutions in the same context. The fact that the discipline cuts across biological and social sciences has encouraged some to suggest that ecology may contain the seeds of a unifying science.

Social or *human ecology* is closely related to population analysis. Many of its data are population data, and the skills required for research in this field are essentially those of the population expert. However, ecology is not concerned with all population data but only with those which can be expressed as spatial distributions. Furthermore, as we have indicated, it has a distinctive theoretical focus, competition for physical space and resources. Some ecological studies have been made of areas as large as regions (and studies of regionalism [25] have some of the same basic ideas as ecological research), but the American metropolis has been the chief topic for the social ecologist.

SOURCES AND READINGS

A. W. Hawley, *Human Ecology* (New York: Ronald Press, 1950).

R. E. Park, *Human Communities* (Glencoe: The Free Press, 1952).

J. A. Quinn, *Human Ecology* (New York: Prentice-Hall, 1950).

George A. Theodorson (ed.), *Studies in Human Ecology* (Evanston: Row, Peterson, 1961).

William L. Thomas, Jr., *Man's Role in Changing the Face of the Earth* (Chicago: University of Chicago Press, 1956).

ECOLOGICAL SUCCESSION: THE HAWAIIAN CASE

The principle of *succession* may be conveniently illustrated by referring to Lind's [26] analysis of changes in land use and the changing occupational distribution of the various racial groups in Hawaii.

Prior to extensive contacts with Western civilization, Hawaiians lived under conditions of *closed* resources; that is, at their level of technological development the land and

[25] See, for example, H. W. Odum, *Southern Regions of the United States* (Chapel Hill: University of North Carolina Press, 1936); and H. W. Odum and H. E. Moore, *American Regionalism* (New York: Holt, 1938).

[26] Andrew W. Lind, *An Island Community* (Chicago: University of Chicago Press, 1938).

other resources were supporting the largest feasible population. It was a balanced relationship between man and the natural environment. The advent of settlers from outside the Islands disturbed this relationship, and over the years new opportunities were created. Western technology opened up new uses for the land and changed the condition of closed resources to one of *open* resources. The subsequent history of land use in the Islands has been the progressive utilization of the land by advanced agricultural technology, and progressive steps toward another state of closed resources based on new uses of the land. This took the form of a plantation economy with large production of money crops, sugar and later pineapple, for the world market.

If the land were to be fully exploited by the new methods, additional manpower was required, for the Hawaiians could not long supply the demand for workers. The plantations, therefore, imported contract labor largely from Asia. "But under the conditions of open resources [then] prevalent . . . in Hawaii the population recruited for the plantation has been unwilling to accept plantation labor as a permanent occupational and social adjustment, and a series of movements away from the plantation and into vocations believed to be more remunerative and socially desirable has occurred." [27]

The movement away from the plantation caused a constantly recurring problem of

[27] Lind, *op. cit.*, p. vi.

labor replacement, which the plantations solved by successive importations. [28] The problems of the internal adjustment of the Island community were complicated by the fact that the several corps of workers were drawn from different nations (see Table IX:6).

"Each of the major immigrant groups . . . may be conceived as invaders whose position in the new land is determined by the intensity of the existing occupation and their ability to compete. The latest arrivals occupy the places of lowest esteem in the region, and their subsequent locations measure their rise in status." [29] The earlier immigrants had advantages over those who came later, so that at any time the hierarchy of status found more of the early groups toward the upper levels. Over a period of years, the several "races" entered positions recently vacated by their predecessors as they moved up the status ladder. The Hawaiian case is almost a model illustration of the operation of the process of *invasion* and *succession* as the racial groups entered the labor market and then succeeded each other up the occupational hierarchy. This is suggested in the following table, which reports the sequence in which three major immigrant groups left agricultural la-

[28] Although plantation systems based on slavery also had serious man power problems, they were designed to hold their labor on the estates whether or not there were good work opportunities elsewhere. Nieboer's thesis is that slavery arises as an attempt to hold the labor on the land when there are ample unsettled areas, a condition of open resources. See H. Nieboer, *Slavery as an Industrial System* (The Hague: Martinus Nijoff, 1900).
[29] Lind, *op. cit.*, p. v.

Table **IX:6** Principal Immigrant Groups to Hawaii

Group (In Order of Immigration)	Chief Period	Total Immigrants * (Estimate)
Chinese	1876–1900	45,000
Japanese	1890–1919	140,000
Filipinos	1909–1934	125,000

* Estimates courtesy of Norman Meller.

Table **IX:7**   Per Cent of Male Labor Force in Agricultural Labor
for Three Racial Groups, Hawaii, 1910–1940 *

Racial Group	1910	1920	1930	1940
Chinese	38.4	32.7	18.4	5.1
Japanese	55.3	47.5	26.5	19.7
Filipinos	——	82.2	83.0	69.9

* Data from U.S. Bureau of the Census.

bor for other employment. Compare Table IX:7 with the sequence of immigration summarized in Table IX:6. Note that by 1910 the process of leaving plantation labor was already far advanced for the Chinese, the first immigrant group, and well under way for the Japanese.

Although the sequences of succession are clearest in the occupational realm, a similar series of changes occurred in the demographic characteristics of the racial groups, their degrees of residential segregation in the metropolitan area of Honolulu, and the part they played in racial mixture.

ECOLOGICAL PATTERNS IN CITIES

The ideas of ecology were adapted to the study of the city by Park, Burgess, and McKenzie and provided the framework for an important series of books, chiefly on Chicago.[30]

A number of different schemes have been devised to describe the spatial patterns of cities. Each is an attempt to give order to a multitude of facts about areas containing large populations. There is no definitive method that tells how all cities are or must be organized. Figure IX:18 diagrams three of the schemes for describing the internal structure of cities: (1) the concentric zone theory, (2) the sector theory, and (3) the multiple nuclei theory.

1. *The concentric zone theory.* The best known approach to the ecological analysis of

cities is the Burgess concentric zone theory.[31] The elementary features of the approach may be outlined as follows (see Fig. IX:18).

Zone *1* is situated in the center of the city, the area of the main business district and of the most intensive land use. In Chicago, where the Burgess scheme was worked out, Zone *1* is known as "The Loop." The administrative functions for the commerce, finance, and management of the city are located here. The populations of the area are transient residents in hotels and the daytime population [32] of commuting workers in offices and stores.

Zone *2,* labeled in the figure "Wholesale Light Manufacturing," is also called "the zone in transition." It lies just outside Zone *1,* and land is often held by real estate speculators in anticipation of Zone *1* expansion and consequent higher land values in Zone *2.* In many cities land speculation in Zone *2* proved to be a good risk. A part of the zone in transition lived up to its name and became merged with the central business district. In other cities the central business district did

[30] For bibliography and discussion of the Chicago studies see Adaptation 40, p. 607–12.

[31] Robert E. Park, Ernest W. Burgess, and Roderick D. McKenzie, *The City* (Chicago: University of Chicago Press, 1925), Chap. 2; Ernest W. Burgess, "The Determination of Gradients in the Growth of the City," *Publications of the American Sociological Society,* **21** (1927), 178–84. See also Figure X:7, p. 394, which uses this technique to summarize the distribution of family types. Figure IX:18, which is used here for purposes of comparison with other theories, differs slightly from the conventional labels given the Burgess Zones. Note that each theory emphasizes different aspects of the city.

[32] Its daytime population has been a topic for special study. See Gerald Breese, *The Daytime Population of the Central Business District* (Chicago: University of Chicago Press, 1949).

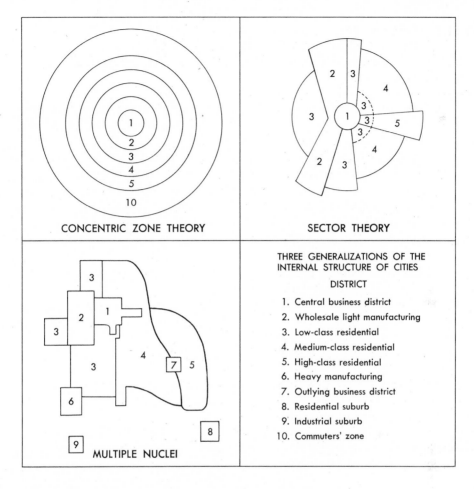

CONCENTRIC ZONE THEORY

SECTOR THEORY

THREE GENERALIZATIONS OF THE
INTERNAL STRUCTURE OF CITIES

DISTRICT

1. Central business district
2. Wholesale light manufacturing
3. Low-class residential
4. Medium-class residential
5. High-class residential
6. Heavy manufacturing
7. Outlying business district
8. Residential suburb
9. Industrial suburb
10. Commuters' zone

MULTIPLE NUCLEI

Fig. **IX:18**   Generalizations of Internal Structure of Cities

From Chauncy D. Harris and Edward L. Ullman, "The Nature of Cities," *Annals* of
the American Academy of Political and Social Science, **242** (November, 1945), 12.
Reproduced by permission of the American Academy of Political and Social Science.

not greatly expand, and the zone in transition became a blighted area because speculators were unwilling to risk improving property. Whether it is an area of transition or blight, it tends to be associated with delinquency and crime and to provide residences for groups, which because of financial or other reasons are unable to find more desirable places to live.

Zone *3,* "the zone of workingmen's homes," is a lower-class residential district, and includes immigrant groups who have improved their status and have been able to move out of Zone *2.*

Zones *4* and *5* comprise "the residential zone," where apartments and private dwellings have higher rentals than Zone *3,* and there is a higher rate of home ownership.

Zone *10,* "the commuters zone" of residential communities, lies on the outer periphery of the city. It includes suburbs beyond the city limits. This outlying area has been the location of a large part in recent population growth.

Burgess and his associates found in Chicago that a number of social characteristics [33] which could be expressed as rates were distributed in an orderly way from the center of the city to the periphery. For example, home ownership was lowest in the center of the city and progressively higher in the outlying zones, i.e., home ownership increased with distance from the center of the city. The percentage of the population foreign born, the rate of male juvenile delinquency, and the sex ratio were all highest in the center of the city and declined toward the periphery.

Studies in St. Louis and Rochester, New York, verified the zonal theory for those cities.[34] On the other hand, the analyses of Davie and Firey show that the concentric zone theory is not directly applicable to New Haven and Boston.[35] Firey found that "sentiment and symbolism," the valuation of particular neighborhoods, such as the traditionally upper-class area of Beacon Hill in Boston, prevented "rational" forces from operating. The area retained an upper-class character long after it would have changed if the forces of zonal development had determined land use.

The concentric zone theory appears most applicable to cities of rather rapid growth that (1) were not impeded unduly in their orderly expansion by hills or other peculiarities of the topography, (2) were not greatly influenced by the automobile, and (3) developed during the period of mass European immigration. Although the theory has not been found to be a universal generalization,

the negative cases do not reject its usefulness. They do direct attention to the reasons for inapplicability and to consideration of alternative theories.

2. *Sector hypothesis.* A second theory is the Hoyt *sector hypothesis,*[36] which views the large city as a number of sectors rather than concentric zones (see Fig. IX:18). These sectors are products of the growth patterns of cities, just as the zones are. Hoyt's analysis is largely based on a study of rental values and residential characteristics. He found that populations tended to move along well-defined axes of transportation as the city grew, with higher income groups showing a greater rapidity of movement than lower income groups.

According to this view, fashionable areas, for example, do not occupy a whole concentric zone, but rather occupy segments of zones just outside the fashionable areas of earlier periods. A fashionable area located in the eastern quadrant of the city would move outward as the city grew, but would remain in the eastern quadrant. This is suggested in Figure IX:19. Other kinds of housing located in other sectors would also move toward the edge of the city but would tend to remain in their original *sectors.*

3. *Multiple nuclei.* (See Fig. IX:18.) Still another approach to the problem of describing the internal structure of cities was made by Harris and Ullman.[37] They suggest that the land-use patterns of many cities are organized around several distinct nuclei rather than a single center. The nuclei are distinguished by their functions and the relation of the functions to certain kinds of terrain or communication. Four main factors are sug-

---

[33] See Ernest W. Burgess, "Urban Areas," *Chicago: An Experiment in Social Science Research,* ed. by T. V. Smith and L. D. White (Chicago: University of Chicago Press, 1929), pp. 113–38, and Burgess, *op. cit.*

[34] Stuart A. Queen and David B. Carpenter, *The American City* (New York: McGraw-Hill, 1953), p. 101; and Raymond Bowers, "Ecological Patterning of Rochester, New York," *American Sociological Review,* 4 (April, 1939), 180–89.

[35] Maurice R. Davie, "The Pattern of Urban Growth," in *Studies in the Science of Society,* ed. by G. P. Murdock (New Haven: Yale University Press, 1937), pp. 133–62; and Walter Firey, *Land Use in Central Boston* (Cambridge: Harvard University Press, 1947), *passim.*

[36] Homer Hoyt, *The Structure and Growth of Residential Neighborhoods in American Cities* (Washington, D.C.: Federal Housing Administration, 1939), especially Chap. IV; and Homer Hoyt, "The Structure of American Cities in the Post-War Era," *American Journal of Sociology,* 48 (January, 1943), 475–92.

[37] Chauncy D. Harris and Edward L. Ullman, "The Nature of Cities," *Annals of the American Academy of Political and Social Science,* 242 (November, 1945), 7–17.

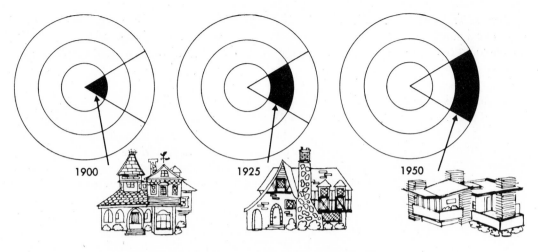

Fig. **IX:19**   Shifts in Location of Fashionable Residential Districts
According to the Sector Theory (An Idealized Example) [36]

gested as determining the development of nuclei:

1. Certain activities require specialized facilities. The retail district, for example, is attached to the point of greatest intracity accessibility, the port district to suitable water front, manufacturing districts to large blocks of land and water or rail connections, and so on.

2. Certain like activities group together because they profit from cohesion. . . . Retail districts benefit from grouping which increases the concentration of potential customers and makes possible comparison shopping. Financial and office-building districts depend upon facility of communication among offices within the district. The Merchandise Mart of Chicago is an example of wholesale clustering.

3. Certain unlike activities are detrimental to each other. The antagonism between factory development and high-class residential development is well known.

4. Certain activities are unable to afford the high rents of the most desirable sites. . . . Examples are bulk wholesaling and storage activities requiring much room, or low-class housing unable to afford the luxury of high land with a view.

The number of nuclei which result from historical development and the forces of localization varies from city to city. The larger the city, the more numerous and specialized are the nuclei. [38]

The Effects of Terrain

The characteristics of the terrain condition the internal structure of all cities, modify the location of functions, break up areas and impose difficulties in the application of generalizing theories, such as the concentric zone theory and the sector theory. Chicago's water front location, for example, is more nearly a segment of a circle than circular, with Zone *1* fronting on Lake Michigan. Hills, the underlying geological structure, and other features of the natural environment may divert land use, interrupting the sequences of growth and the functional relations between areas that would have occurred if the surface had been uniformly flat. [39]

ECOLOGICAL SEGREGATION

The pattern of original settlement of New Orleans was also influenced by the nature of the terrain, which afforded only a limited

---

[38] *Ibid.,* pp. 14–15. Reprinted by permission of the authors and the American Academy of Political and Social Science.

[39] Queen and Carpenter, *op. cit.,* pp. 95–99.

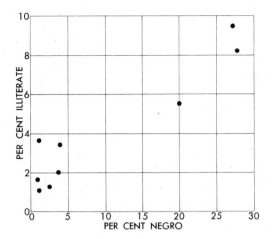

Fig. **IX:20**   From W. S. Robinson, "Ecological Correlations and the Behavior of Individuals," *American Sociological Review*, **15** (June, 1950), 352.

amount of land well suited to residence. With the *invasion* of the Americans, sharp *competition* developed between them and the Creole French for the use of the land. Certain localities became segregated Creole or American areas, and the values attached to ethnic segregation circumscribed subsequent land use. Adaptation to the terrain and its efficient use were, therefore, limited by sentiments and loyalties to segregated ethnic areas. Even after technological advances in transportation and drainage opened up additional areas for residential settlement, ethnic segregation continued important in determining land use.[40]

Segregation is more obvious in the enforced isolation of racial groups in separate enclaves, such as "black belts" (see MINORITIES, p. 496), but ecology is interested in the *fact* of segregation, irrespective of whether it is forced or voluntary.

Cautions: 1. *Ecological determinism.* There is a risk that ecology as a topic for inquiry and research will lead to a kind of determin-

ism: that is, it may be thought that space and its characteristics *determine* the social forms that lie within it. Clearly space *influences* and *limits* the condition of social life and relations, but space does not determine what the relations must be.[41]

2. *Analogies.* The ideas of human ecology have been drawn from observations of the adaptation of the lower animals and plants to their environments. These generalizations when applied to man are, at least in part, analogies and should be used with caution. Man's behavior is not merely an immediate adaptation to an immediate environment. It is adaptive in a much broader sense. Man is capable of modifying his environment in many ways, and he may attach sentiments and values to his environment. He may then adjust according to the dictates of sentiments rather than directly to the natural environment.[42]

ECOLOGICAL CORRELATIONS

A substantial amount of work in the field of ecology has attempted to relate characteristics of areas as measured by rates, averages, and the like to the characteristics of individuals within those areas. It has been shown that correlations between rates or averages for areas need not and often do not accurately represent the characteristics of the individuals within the areas.[43]

To illustrate the risks of inferring individual characteristics from ecological correlations, Robinson first plotted for each of the Census Bureau's nine geographic divisions (groups of states) the percentage of the population ten years old and over which was Negro in 1930 and the percentage of the population in each division which was illiterate. This is shown in the scattergram (Fig.

[40] H. W. Gilmore, "The Old New Orleans and the New: A Case for Ecology," *American Sociological Review*, **9** (1944), 385–94.

[41] Cf. Walter Firey, *Land Use in Central Boston* (Cambridge: Harvard University Press, 1947), *passim;* and Warner E. Gettys, "Human Ecology and Social Theory," *Social Forces*, **18** (May, 1940), 469–76.

[42] See Firey, *op. cit.*

[43] W. S. Robinson, "Ecological Correlations and the Behavior of Individuals," *American Sociological Review*, **15** (June, 1950), 351–57.

IX:20) in which the per cent Negro for each division is plotted on the x (horizontal) axis and the per cent illiterate on the y (vertical) axis. He then calculated the Pearsonian correlation for the figure and found it to be .946. It is at this point that the dangers of reasoning from ecological correlations become apparent. The scattergram shows only that the divisions with relatively large proportions of Negroes are also the divisions with relatively large proportions of illiterates. One may erroneously assume that the Negroes contribute to illiteracy to the extent suggested by the correlation. In this case, because the correlation approaches 1.00 (unity), this faulty reasoning would lead to the conclusion that the Negroes were responsible for practically all of the illiteracy. In fact this is not so. Table IX:8 shows how many thousands of Negroes and whites in the United States were literate and illiterate in 1930.

Negroes did include among their number a larger percentage of illiterates, but the correlation between race and illiteracy for individuals is only .203, about one-fifth of the ecological correlation. Whites as well as Negroes in the divisions of high illiteracy were illiterates. One cannot tell from an ecological correlation *which* individuals in an area are responsible for the correlations.[44]

In political ecology the problem may present itself in the following way. Suppose that a dominantly Catholic district moves from its traditional place in the Democratic column into the Republican column by a modest margin. If individual voting was not studied, three hypotheses are plausible: (1) the Catholic-Democratic bloc may be breaking down, and enough Catholics may have voted Republican to swing the district. (2) On the other hand, a minority of Protestants who had previously voted Democratic may have turned Republican, and the change in a "Catholic-Democratic" district may actually be caused by Protestants. (3) The change may be due to a difference in turnout. Individuals who did not participate in earlier elections may have decided to vote, and they may have been the decisive factor; or persons who had voted Democratic in earlier elections may not have voted at all.

[44] To complete this analysis it is necessary to study separate tables like IX:8 below for each geographic region of the United States. See Robinson, *op. cit.*

Table **IX:8**   The Individual Correlation Between Color and Illiteracy, United States, 1930*

	Negro	White	Total
Illiterate	1,512 (16.1%)	2,406 (2.7%)	3,918 (4.0%)
Literate	7,780 (83.9%)	85,574 (97.3%)	93,354 (96.0%)
Total	9,292 (100%)	87,980 (100%)	97,272 (100%)

* Robinson, *op. cit.* (For population ten years old and over. Figures are in thousands.)

Units of Ecological Analysis: Census Tracts

The cost and difficulty of making individual case studies of many urban phenomena stimulated the ecological approach to urban analysis. By studying areas instead of individuals, research on great population centers became feasible. According to the concepts of ecology, the units of analysis should be *natural areas,* that is, areas of land inhabited by a single dominant species. In the case of human ecology the areas should be dominated by one type of population or land use. This, however, was one of the problems the social ecologists were trying to solve: what and where were the natural areas of the city?

When quantitative urban studies were first made in the United States, political and administrative divisions, such as precincts and wards, were the units used for the compilation of statistical data. Although the divisions vary in size in different municipalities, most such units are too large for convenient statistical analysis. Their boundaries are not permanent, and the populations they contain are often quite heterogeneous.

THE CENSUS TRACT

In 1906 the late Dr. Walter Laidlaw, director of population studies for the Federation of Churches in New York, divided the city into relatively small and homogeneous tracts,* which he persuaded the Bureau of the Census to adopt for enumeration and tabulation of the 1910 Census. The seven other cities, which at that time had populations of 500,000 or more (Baltimore, Boston, Chicago, Cleveland, Philadelphia, Pittsburgh, and St. Louis), were also tracted. In 1920 census

tract data were again tabulated for the list of cities. In New York a Census Committee put out the first major publication based on tract data, and soon afterward tract data were used for ecological research in Chicago.

The number of tracted cities, in some cases including their adjacent areas, has been increased, and in 1960 there were 180 tracted areas. A list of tracted areas may be found in any *Census Tract,* PHC (1) bulletin.

Census tracts usually contain from 3,000 to 6,000 persons. Where feasible, natural boundaries (rivers, etc.) are used, and each tract is drawn so as to include as nearly as possible a homogeneous population. The same tract boundaries are retained for each Census, so that studies of changes in an area are facilitated. If an area increases greatly in population, the tract may be subdivided, but it is possible to recombine the statistics of the subdivided tract. Only in exceptional cases are the external boundaries of tracts changed; for instance, tracts for Providence were completely revised in 1950.

Tract bulletins report such information as the following:† race, national origin of foreign stock, family composition, marital status, education, residence in 1955, income, age by sex and race, and labor force and housing characteristics. For tracts with 400 or more nonwhites, there are details on the nonwhite population.

---

* Census Tract Manual. Fourth Edition, Bureau of the Census, 1958.

† Some of the data reported by census tracts are based on a 25 per cent sample. In using such information, care must be taken to refer to the instructions on sampling contained in the tract bulletins.

Block Statistics Bulletins, HC (3) supply limited data on the characteristics of dwelling units for many cities that are not tracted. Reports are available for 467 places with population exceeding 50,000.

PART TWO

Analysis of Special Areas

Chapter **X**

The family

By RALPH H. TURNER

in collaboration with L.B. and P.S.

Section 1 **Introduction**

The study of the family shows how elemental biological facts, such as mating and the helplessness of the human infant, are translated into a set of socially defined relationships. For example, in every society a woman who has borne a child is expected to develop certain feelings toward the child and to accept an elaborate set of obligations. Similarly, some man, not necessarily the biological father, is always designated to assume a special set of responsibilities and attitudes known as fatherhood.

The family everywhere constitutes a unit with certain specified functions and general consequences for the operation of the society. After the Russian Revolution of 1917, for example, the Soviet Government tried to weaken the family lest it perpetuate attitudes and relationships which would reinforce the prerevolutionary way of life. On the other hand, after the new system was established, the government returned to a policy of supporting the family.

The family is itself a social group of a special sort within which theories concerning the nature and processes of groups may be tested. Conflict, accommodation, and un-

equal dominance of members are observed within the family and are probably governed by the same principles which apply to other small groups. The family is also the fundamental unit in the socialization of the child and continues to serve as a socializing agency for the adult. If we want to explain juvenile delinquency or exceptional eminence or profound humanitarianism or deep-seated prejudice, we always investigate the kind of family in which the individual was reared.

FAMILY TYPES

The family is a variable conception. In one sense the family is the *nuclear* (or conjugal) unit, consisting of husband and wife and those children toward whom they assume the role of parents. In another sense the family is the larger *extended* (or consanguine) unit, consisting of "blood" relatives and their several nuclear family units. Some recognition of both types of units is found in every society, but there is great difference in the degree to which each constitutes a significant functioning group. In American society, particularly among the urban middle classes, the family for practical purposes is the nuclear unit. In many societies the nuclear unit is merely a part of an extended family, which has a single head, contiguous residence, and shared economic and living arrangements.

Among the many other bases for classifying types, the most frequent is the placement of formal authority and dominance in the family, as follows:

patriarchal—father dominant

matriarchal—mother dominant

equalitarian—equal dominance of father and mother

Marriage, the recognized union of husband and wife, is the basis of the conjugal family. Among the ways of classifying marriage are the following:

1. According to the number of persons united in any marriage:

monogamy—marriage of one man to one woman

polygamy—marriage involving either more than one man or more than one woman, of which there are two subtypes:

polygyny—one man to two or more women

polyandry—one woman to two or more men

2. According to the manner in which descent of the married pair is recorded:

patrilineal—the privileges and duties of descent follow the male line (e.g., child to father to father's father, etc.)

matrilineal—the privileges and duties of descent follow the female line

bilineal—the privileges and duties of descent follow both lines

3. According to the place of residence of the married pair:

patrilocal—husband and wife take up residence with the parents of the husband

matrilocal—husband and wife reside with the parents of the wife

neolocal—husband and wife reside by themselves

SOURCES AND READINGS

Of the many textbooks on the family, six may be singled out as representing major approaches:

Ernest W. Burgess and Harvey J. Locke, *The Family: From Institution to Companionship* (2nd ed.; New York: American Book Co., 1953) emphasizes characteristics of the family passing through a period of historical transition.

William M. Kephart, *The Family, Society, and the Individual* (Boston: Houghton Mifflin, 1961) follows the institutional approach to family study.

Clifford Kirkpatrick, *The Family as Process and Institution* (New York: Ronald, 1955) emphasizes the variety of conceptions of family roles that each generation inherits and must adjust to under new circumstances of life.

Stuart A. Queen, Robert W. Habenstein, and John B. Adams, *The Family in Various Cultures* (Philadelphia: Lippincott, 1961) reports on family life in thirteen different societies, past and present.

George Simpson, *People in Families: Sociology, Psychoanalysis and the American Family* (New York: Crowell, 1960) applies psychoanalytic theory to the sociology of family life.

Willard Waller and Reuben Hill, *The Family: A Dynamic Interpretation* (New York: Dryden, 1951) emphasizes family interaction from a social-psychological standpoint.

Two collections of previously published papers are:

Norman W. Bell and Ezra F. Vogel, *A Modern Introduction to the Family* (Glencoe: The Free Press, 1960), functionalist in point of view and rather technical.

Robert F. Winch and Robert McGinnis, *Selected Studies in Marriage and the Family* (New York: Holt, 1953).

The following symposium includes a number of specially written papers exploring the sociological, anthropological, and psychological frontiers of family theory:

Ruth N. Anshen (ed.), *The Family: Its Function and Destiny* (Rev. ed.; New York: Harper, 1959).

Three comprehensive analyses of national statistics about the family are available:

Eleanor H. Bernert, *America's Children* (New York: Wiley, 1958).

Paul C. Glick, *American Families* (New York: Wiley, 1957).

Paul H. Jacobson, *American Marriage and Divorce* (New York: Rinehart, 1959).

A journal devoted to inquiry about the family and application of knowledge to counseling and education is *Marriage and Family Living*.

Section 2 **Social organization**

The family is both a group with its own internal organization and a unit in the organization of the society. Though we may begin by examining some aspects of internal family organization, the characteristic relations and processes within the family can be understood only as reflecting the place of the family as an operating part of a particular kind of society.

INTERNAL ORGANIZATION OF THE FAMILY

The relative predominance of the nuclear and extended units in the family system is an important aspect of the internal dynamics of the family. The relatively self-sufficient American nuclear family severely limits both the rights of relatives to invade the privacy of the small family circle and their obligations toward it. In sharp contrast is the Hopi pattern in which the married couple lives with the wife's parents and her sisters and their husbands, sharing in many communal activities.[1]

The contrasting significance of divorce in these two systems illustrates a difference in the problem of stability. Under the American system divorce, or even disharmony between the married pair, requires extensive readjustments in economic arrangements, care of children, social participation, and emotional involvements. Loss of an adult from the Hopi extended family on the other hand requires only minor internal economic and social readjustments. Children's readjustments are simplified, since all the adults have served to some degree as parents. With the husband-wife intimacy only slightly greater than that among all the adults in the extended unit, the suffering attendant upon

shifting the object of one's affection and identification is superficial and transitory.

The preceding section shows that family systems vary in the placement of formal authority. Unequal formal authority, however, tends to be offset by informal controls of subordinates. For example, in colonial America almost unlimited formal power was given to the husband, but he seldom exercised all the power at his disposal. Because of the importance to him of services performed by his wife, the husband in a patriarchal system benefits from treating her with some consideration. When the wife cannot otherwise ameliorate her status, she may make herself unavailable or unresponsive in sex relations, either in an open bargaining relation of the sort frequently found among American lower-class families, or in the more subtle manner of the middle class.

Conditions of suburban life in the United States have given rise to a *matricentric*[2] family pattern within a formal patriarchalism. Because commuting keeps the husband out of touch with the family during daylight hours, because the wife controls day-to-day expenditures, and because she is the family "social secretary," she makes most decisions about the domestic and social life of the family, and the children look to her as the seat of effective authority. The tension created by this imbalance between formal authority and working control is a recurring theme in popular comic strips. The husband may resort to arbitrary acts to validate his formal authority, and the wife may fret alternately over the authority the husband does exercise and over his failure to be a sufficiently strong and masculine figure.

[1] Stuart A. Queen and John B. Adams, *The Family in Various Cultures* (Philadelphia: Lippincott, 1952), pp. 23–43.

[2] Ernest W. Burgess and Harvey J. Locke, *The Family* (New York: American Book Co., 1953), pp. 111–13.

The preceding discussion suggests that the internal organization of the family is affected by the environing society. We may examine these influences either in terms of the more or less stable *functions* that the family performs or in terms of the short-range *crises* with which the family must cope.

FAMILY FUNCTIONS: INDIVIDUAL GRATIFICATIONS

During the last century or two social change has stripped the family of many functions which have traditionally made it indispensable to the individual. Industrialization, by opening up opportunities for women's employment and making available for sale the essential goods and services which were formerly the work of the housewife, has eliminated the economic compulsion to marriage. As achieved status has become more important and ascribed status less important in society, family membership has become merely one among many avenues to recognized social standing. Increased dependence upon wages and salaries combined with the substitution of city living for the family homestead have meant that the family no longer provides insurance against destitution and loneliness in old age. With the loss of these and other formerly indispensable functions, marriage has become increasingly a matter of choice rather than necessity. This change, shown graphically in Figure X:1, undoubtedly accounts for the increase in the divorce rate, since the decision to divorce is a product of weighing the discomfort of the marriage relationship against the sensed alternatives to the existing marriage. Figure X:1 also shows the divorce peak during World War II.

While family stability has declined, there is no apparent decline in the acceptance of family living (see Fig. X:2). Most of the increase in per cent of the population married during the last two decades can be attributed to reduction in the average age at first marriage, especially for men. But when allowance is made for this factor and certain others, marriage still shows no decline and a possible increase between 1890 and 1956.

To explain the continuing popularity of family life in the face of its declining indispensability, we observe that the family is still the preferred avenue for securing many of the traditional gratifications and that other functions may be increasing in importance. In particular the family tends to be identified with the gratifications of an *intimate* and *durable* type of interpersonal relation. In an earlier era of predominantly rural and folk living, this function of the family was relatively less important because of the many opportunities for intimate and lasting relations within the stable neighborhood. Especially in urban middle-class settings we are likely to find relatively few individuals among our business associates, neighbors, or even members of recreational groups to whom we feel it would be safe or proper to express our deepest hopes and fears. In the face of only partially satisfying interpersonal relations outside the family, people increasingly seek through the family a distinctive, intimate, intense, and exclusive type of relationship.

While social changes have probably intensified the *need* for the family to perform this type of function, changes in the internal structure of the family have both increased and decreased the *capability* of the family in this respect. Increasing equality, elimination of formal modes of address, relaxation of inhibitions against the expression of both anger and affection, and the acceptance of sexual partnership as a relation of mutual response—all signify adaptation of the family to this newer functional emphasis. On the other hand, widespread doubts concerning the permanence of any marital union and the tendency to carry over impersonal instrumental attitudes from the outside world into the family threaten its ability to provide an intimate and durable relation. Whether or not the family in a few

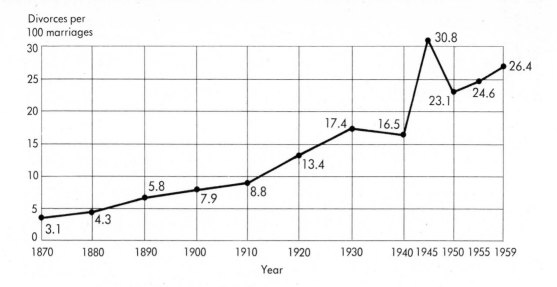

Fig. X:1 Divorces per 100 Marriages Occurring
in the Same Year: United States

For simplicity of presentation, decade figures are used, except for the 1945 peak and
data since 1950. [From Ruth S. Cavan, *The American Family* (New York: Crowell, 1953,
pp. 645–47, and *Statistical Abstract of the United States*, 1957, p. 73; 1961, p. 65.]

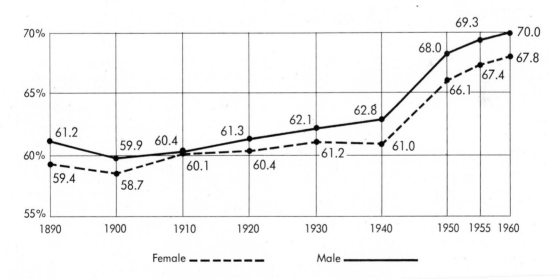

Fig. X:2 Per Cent of the Population Fourteen Years Old and
Over Who Are Married, Standardized for Age

Because the age distribution of the United States population has changed since
1890, figures reporting only per cent married would be misleading. Above percentages
are, therefore, standardized to the 1950 age distribution, i.e., each per cent married has been recomputed as if the age distribution were the same as that in 1950
(From data in the *Statistical Abstract of the United States*, 1961, p. 35.)

generations will stabilize around its new function is a question which the sociologist cannot confidently answer.

FAMILY FUNCTIONS:
SOCIETAL MAINTENANCE

The family is inevitably concerned with every aspect of society's operation. For example, the family is always in some way a unit through which the economic system, the political system, and the religious system operate. The particular place of the family will vary, as is shown by the recent change in the American family from the main *producing* unit in the nation's economy to the central unit of economic *consumption*. Some important aspects of society's functioning which are channelled through the family may be noted here.

1. The family is crucial in keeping society's members in "working condition." The family is a small enough unit to achieve an effective mutual responsibility for each individual's physical and mental welfare. The assurance of a sense of belonging and provision of a needed response relationship helps *sustain the individual* in his social participation.

2. Another function served is *population maintenance,* since it is through the family that every society motivates people to bear and rear children. Some examples of this motivation are to perpetuate the family line, to provide security in old age, to secure the gratifications of being looked up to by one's children, or to attain credit from the achievements of children.

3. Society delegates to the family the responsibility for protecting infants and children and caring for their physical needs. The family also keeps these incompletely socialized individuals from being a disruptive influence in society. In contemporary America the emphasis on speed, orderliness, and the acquisition of tangible but fragile property accentuates the disruptive potential of the child and accordingly brings this function, the *custody of the immature,* into unusual prominence, making it a source of friction within the family.

4. The family performs the *socialization* function in two ways. It develops in the young and maintains in the adult the social sentiments which are indispensable to societal functioning. It also acts as a culture transmitting agency. From the family the individual gains his first experience in social participation and his first attitudes toward attainment and acceptance of social status.

5. The family's status in the community is automatically assigned to its individual members, and this determines the individual's initial orienting status. "Farmer Jones's boy" and Doctor Brown's son" are assigned statuses according to their families' reputations, and they are treated and expected to behave in ways appropriate with their family status. This status determines how others are expected to act toward the individual until he changes or consolidates his status by his own actions. The family performs the function of *induction into the society* and helps to insure that no individuals are without assigned positions governing their interaction with others.

6. Finally, the family is an important *social control* agency, pressing toward conformity. In developing his self-conception the individual cannot escape the revealing judgments of himself that are made in the intimate family situation, even when he is relatively isolated from such criticism outside the family. The consequences of any individual's nonconforming behavior fall upon all members of his family. A man may be restrained from extramarital sexual behavior or from becoming identified with an unpopular political viewpoint primarily for fear of bringing scandal to his family or of threatening their economic well-being.

FAMILY CRISES

The intimate interdependence of family and social structure insures that family equilibrium will suffer when the normal operation of society is disturbed. Economic difficulties, for example, often lessen family stability and cohesion. A study of the effects of a severe drop in income during the depression showed that the ability of the family to make necessary adjustments without serious disruption of personal relations depended on the degree to which family members were committed to a given standard of living. To the extent that certain material levels of living were a crucial value in family life, the worth of the family relationship and of the members to one another was damaged by a reduction of income.[3]

Komarovsky found (see Adaptation 28) that the ability and right of a man to perform the husband role may be dependent upon his success in performing the breadwinner portion of that role. Failure damages his own self-respect and the respect of family members toward him. However, as the study reveals, some types of family or-

ganization shield the husband from the impact of external crises while other types make him vulnerable.

Dependence of family stability upon economic conditions is highly complex, however, as indicated by historical studies which show that both marriage and divorce rates decline during periods of business recession. While a definitive explanation of such a correlation between economic conditions and divorce cannot be given, two points should be mentioned. First, a business recession severely limits the sensed alternatives to the existing marriage arrangements, so that people probably remain longer in inharmonious marriage and are less likely to take uncompromising positions of the sort which alienate them from the marriage partner. Second, the impact of poverty on interpersonal relations is probably less when it is widely shared, as in the case of a general business depression. The breadwinner's failure can then more easily be attributed to conditions beyond his control, and the family is less likely to be socially isolated.

[3] Robert C. Angell, *The Family Encounters the Depression* (New York: Scribner's, 1936).

Authority of the Unemployed Husband

Abridged and adapted from *The Unemployed Man and His Family* by Mirra Komarovsky (New York: Dryden Press, 1940). Published in this form by permission of the author and The Dryden Press, Inc.

Among studies of the depression's effect on family life, *The Unemployed Man and His Family* is distinctive in two respects. First, it makes important refinements in the methods for gathering and analyzing individual case data. In particular, it advances a method called *discerning,* which makes explicit and subject to careful check the various logical steps an investigator must

follow in concluding that any specific cause-effect relation actually applies to a particular family history. It also refines procedures for interviewing and for classifying cases into types. Second, the study is distinctive in focusing upon the father's authority as the variable which might be affected by the depression. The father's authority was examined in relation to each member of the family. However, only findings regarding the husband's authority over his wife are presented here. Discussions of the husband's relations with other members of the family and

ADAPTATION 28

methodological details have been omitted.

The purpose of this investigation is to study the relation between the man's role as economic provider and his authority in the family. Depression and unemployment provided a tragic opportunity to study this relationship. What happens to the authority of the man of the family when he fails as a provider? It is reasonable to expect that unemployment will tend to undermine the authority of the husband and father, because economic success is one of the chief bases of prestige in our society. To the extent that a family shares this attitude, the economic failure of the man might tend to lower family esteem for him and, therefore, his authority. Furthermore, if the family is not dependent upon him, he cannot exercise any indirect coercion by granting or withholding economic benefits.

The unemployed husband's status may also suffer for another reason. In the traditional patriarchal view of the family, the husband is expected to support and protect his wife, and she, in turn, is expected to take care of his household, to honor and obey him. A degree of subordination to the authority of the husband is part of the woman's share in their reciprocal relations. In so far as the husband's claim to authority is based upon his supporting his wife, unemployment may tend to undermine it.

In order to determine whether a deterioration of the husband's authority resulted from unemployment, 59 native-born, white, urban Protestant families were interviewed during the winter of 1935/36. In all families the husband was a skilled laborer or a white-collar worker who had been unemployed for at least one year. He had been the sole provider of the family prior to his unemployment. Three private interviews were conducted with individual members of the family: one each with the husband, the wife, and a child, usually the oldest.

The *deterioration of the man's authority* was defined as a *decline in the willingness* of the family to accept his control whether or not he succeeded in maintaining it through added coercion. In the light of this definition, the criteria of deterioration of authority are twofold: (1) loss of a man's control over one or more spheres of family relations, or (2) changes in grounds of acceptance. In some cases, the decline in status was inferred from some defeat of the man; in others, there were changes in attitudes of members of the family; still other cases contained evidence of both.

PATTERNS OF DETERIORATION

Omitting one case in which the evidence was incomplete, only 13 out of 58 cases showed a deterioration of the man's authority. Three patterns stood out among these 13 cases. In the first pattern, *crystallization of an inferior status,* unemployment merely made more explicit a previously existing inferior status of a despised husband. It caused a concealed lack of respect for the husband to come into the open, or, if antagonistic sentiments had been openly expressed prior to the depression, it increased the aggression toward the husband. These changes were expressed by increased conflicts, blaming the husband for unemployment, constant nagging, withdrawal of customary services, sharp criticism in the presence of the children, irritability at previously tolerated behavior, and indifference to his wishes.

In the second pattern, the *breakdown of coercive control,* unemployment undermined the authority of a more or less dominant husband over a subordinate and resentful wife. These wives had lacked love or respect for their husbands, but the husbands were stronger than their wives. Unemployment resulted in partial or complete emancipation of the wife from the husband's coercive authority. In some cases, the relations were completely reversed; the dominance of the husband changed to his complete subordination. In other cases, the husband suffered defeat in particular spheres. For example, a Protestant man, in spite of his wife's persistent efforts, refused to send the children to a Catholic school. However, after he was unemployed for two years, the children were transferred to a parochial school.

In the third pattern, unemployment *weakened the authority of the husband over a loving wife.* These marriages were characterized by some love and admiration for the husband, or, at very least, by the absence of serious dissatisfaction in the wife. Subtle changes in the wife's attitude led to more equalitarian relations, or the husband's status declined through defeat in some spheres of the marriage relation.

The breakdown of the husband's authority, described above, took place in only one-fifth of the families. In the majority of cases, whatever other consequences unemployment of the husband may have had for family life, it did not change his relative status in husband-wife relations. What determines the husband's authority during his unemployment?

TYPES OF AUTHORITY

The way in which the husband's authority had been accepted by the wife before the depression of the 1930's was important to the adjustment of the family to the man's unemployment. Three types of authority were distinguished, namely, primary, instrumental, and mixed. (See Table X: 1.)

1. Primary authority stems from either of two sources: from love and admiration of the husband by the wife or from acceptance by the wife of the husband's traditional authority. In both cases, authority is vested in what the husband *is,* either as a person or as the bearer of certain traditional and institutional prerogatives.

2. Authority is instrumental, on the other hand, when the wife submits to it either out of fear or as the price for the satisfaction of such needs as physical comfort and economic security. Where authority is instrumental, it tends to be divorced from leadership of either a personal or a traditional sort.

3. Mixed authority has both instrumental and primary aspects. When the husband's authority was primary, the family showed a remarkable stability in the face of unemployment. Unemployment did not change the sentiments of the wife towards the husband but it made explicit unsatisfactory sentiments that already existed. Out of 35 cases of primary attitudes, only 2 showed deterioration of the husband's authority. Out of 12 cases of instrumental attitudes, 8 showed loss. Mixed attitudes were intermediate between the two extremes: out of 11 cases, 3 showed loss.

The fate of the husband's authority is to some extent in his own hands. His behavior during unemployment is a factor in the loss or preservation of his authority. A considerable portion of the men exhibited a certain deterioration of personality: loss of emotional stability, breakdown of morale, irritability, new faults such as drinking, unfaithfulness, and so on.

Apparently, the fate of the unemployed husband's authority depends largely upon two factors—the predepression attitude of the wife and his own behavior during unemployment. In the bulk of the cases the loss or preservation of the husband's authority may be explained in terms of these two factors.

Primary authority is the surest safeguard a husband has against loss of status. Whatever the pattern of dominance prior to unemployment, whatever his behavior during unemployment, his status is secure. Only 2 out of 35 cases with primary authority showed loss.

If the grounds of authority are mixed, he is also secure, provided his behavior does not deteriorate. Even if his personality does change for the worse, he still has a reason-

Table **X:1**   Basis of Authority, Husband's Behavior
and the Effect of Unemployment

| Basis of Authority | Husband's Behavior | Effect on Authority | |
		Loss	No Loss
Primary	No deterioration	1	22
Primary	Deterioration	1	11
Mixed	No deterioration	0	5
Mixed	Deterioration	3	3
Instrumental	No deterioration	3	3
Instrumental	Deterioration	5	0
Total		13	44

able chance of maintaining his authority.

When the basis of authority is instrumental, the husband wages a losing battle. If his behavior deteriorates, there is no chance of preserving his status, but even if there are no changes in his personality, he still runs the risk that his authority will be lost.

Conclusion

This study has attempted to determine the circumstances under which the balance of authority in the family is disturbed by an external economic crises. Some family relationships are more vulnerable to external economic conditions than others. Crises alter family relations when they touch already weak points in family organization.

Section 3   Culture

The family takes many forms in different societies and even in different classes and ethnic groups. But to the people of any particular culture or subculture only one or two types of family organization are likely to seem "natural" or "right." From constant exposure to the culture—through the approved verbal admonishments, through the constant pressure of exemplary models, and through rewards to the conformist—each individual acquires his culture as a set of expectations which guide his conduct and serve as the criteria for judging the conduct of others.

Three aspects of culture influence family patterns: *norms, values,* and *sentiments.* Norms are the fairly obvious and specific directives or rules governing family life. Values are the more subtle and vague notions of what is worth while, the only partially conceptualized criteria from which people get a sense that one particular family arrangement is a good and satisfying one, while another is empty, uninteresting, or downright unpleasant. Sentiments are the deep feelings which people attach to particular experiences or persons in family life, such as mother love, romantic love, and family loyalty.

SOCIAL NORMS

Social norms define the expected size, composition, and living arrangements of the family, and lay down the qualifications and rituals involved in entering or leaving the family. They define the roles, or sets of responsibilities and privileges, that go with each position in the family. Norms also include mores which are intimately connected with family functioning, such as the mores governing sex behavior in the society.

Double and Single Standards

While the middle-class American is likely to regard groups with different moral standards from his own as nonconformists, examination of the pattern in any culture or subculture will usually reveal a well-defined code which "makes sense" in the light of the conception and functions of marriage within that group. William F. Whyte has shown that the apparent promiscuity of Italian boys in an Eastern slum conceals a well-adhered-to code containing several elements. Heterosexual relations at regular intervals are thought to be necessary to health and constitute a major avenue to the attainment of prestige among the boys. Sex relations are strictly limited to girls who are not acceptable as marriage partners, which means a well-guarded taboo against sex relations with virgins and with relatives of close friends. Nonvirgins are arranged in a hierarchy of desirability as sex partners. Intercourse with prostitutes brings least prestige, "conquest" of a promiscuous but noncommercial girl carries intermediate prestige, and relations with a girl who will be exclusive for a period of time brings the most prestige.[4]

The preceding illustration points to a distinction in sex codes between a *double standard* and a *single standard*. Double standard refers to the general acceptance of two different codes, one for men and one for women. Where the true double standard prevails (which is rare), a man who prides himself on his premarital sex exploits will still demand virginity in his wife, and the girl

[4] William Foote Whyte, "A Slum Sex Code," *American Journal of Sociology*, **49** (July, 1943), 24–31.

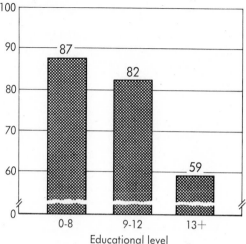

Per cent with experience

Fig. **X:3**   Incidence of Premarital Intercourse for Men by Age Twenty-four

Based on data from Alfred C. Kinsey, Wardell B. Pomeroy, and Clyde E. Martin, *Sexual Behavior in the Human Male* (Philadelphia: Saunders, 1948), p. 550.

who prides herself on her virginity would be ashamed to marry a man so lacking in masculinity as to be celibate at marriage.

Absolute Standard

Under many of the traditional American sex mores no allowance is made for varying degrees of seriousness of an offense. When mores have this *absolute* character, a single act brands the offender for life and classes him indiscriminately with the habitual violator. Such a code also recognizes no circumstances which would make some violations more or less serious than others. The absolute principle has been applied particularly to women, who could be regarded only as either virgins or "fallen women." No *degrees* of chastity were recognized, and a single offense made a woman "no better than a prostitute." In this respect the sex codes have differed from many norms, such as those

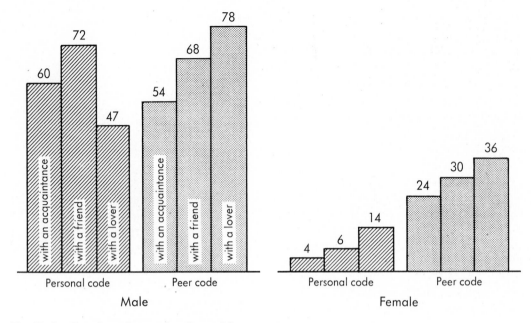

Fig. **X:4**   Per Cent Approving Sexual Intercourse
According to Type of Partner

Based on data from Winston Ehrmann, *Premarital Dating Behavior* (New York: Holt, 1959), p. 179.

prohibiting theft. In the appraisal of theft we take into account the temptation and need and the value of the object stolen in judging a person. The habitual thief is sharply differentiated from the great majority of people who have stolen once or twice in their lifetime. The result is that people are arrayed along a continuum from the most honest to the least honest, rather than placed in the "either-or" categories of the absolute scale.

There are many indications that the American sex code is coming to be less absolute than heretofore. However, popular discussions of sex behavior and some scientific studies are still phrased in terms of the absolute standard. For example, Figure X: 3 shows the per cent of men who will have had premarital sex relations by age twenty-four, which was the approximate median age at first marriage for American men in 1940. The graph shows that the majority of men are not virgins at marriage and that there are fewer male virgins in the

lower classes than in the higher classes. These figures also show that the behavior of most American men is not controlled by an absolute code prohibiting premarital relations. But to the degree to which there is a code that is not absolute, the percentages in Figure X: 3 are not particularly informative. We do not know how many of the men have had only one or two experiences, while adhering to the code most of the time. Nor do we know how discriminating these men have been regarding the types of relations into which they have entered.

Personal and Peer Codes

A study of college students enrolled in "Marriage and Family" courses shows that codes people accept for themselves do not always correspond to the codes imposed by the group.[5] Information on dating, sexual

[5] Winston Ehrmann, *Premarital Dating Behavior* (New York: Holt, 1959), esp. Chap. V.

In this Sumatran party, wives and children stand and wait until the men are finished.

behavior, and codes was secured by questionnaire from 990 students, and supplementary interviews were held with 100 from the same sample. In the interview each student told what he regarded as an acceptable degree of intimacy for himself (personal code) in relation to an acquaintance, a friend, and a person with whom he was in love. The same questions were asked regarding acceptable behavior for his associates (peer code). The percentages of students who thought it acceptable to go as far as sexual intercourse are reported in Figure X: 4. Women appear to employ a personal code that is stricter than the code they would expect of their peers, although the relative acceptability of sexual partners is the same. For men two things should be noted. First, they are far more permissive than are the women in both their personal and peer codes. Second, their pattern of acceptability is different from the women's pattern. Perhaps personal codes reflect a more traditional norm than peer codes, the women's preserving traditional strictness and the men's the traditional double standard. Of course, the study does not address itself to actual sexual conduct.

SOCIAL VALUES

By imparting values, the society prepares the individual to expect certain gratifications in the family and provides the criteria by which he will judge the adequacy of the family. The nature of the values emphasized and the definiteness with which they are comprehended vary from society to society. The relative prominence of economic considerations, to some degree a value in all family systems, will serve as illustration. Under one system, matchmaking may be openly dominated by efforts to improve one's economic position, and failure to maintain expected levels may be reason for divorce. In much of contemporary America economic advancement is regarded as a worthy secondary value in marriage only if it can be secured in accompaniment with the primary value of personal response and love. The culturally defined values are so pervasive that even individuals who deliberately choose to marry only for money, social standing, or security often find themselves dissatisfied in the absence of affection.

While the examples of love, money, and social standing all refer to individual satisfactions, in many societies the prime value lies in advantage to the family, and individual satisfactions are subordinated. Under such circumstances, marriages are likely to be arranged by the elders with a view to perpetuating family lines and making advantageous linkages between families. Zimmerman[6] has called the extreme in this direction the *trustee* family.

SENTIMENTS

A sentiment involves subjective feelings, compelling tendencies to act, and characteristic reshaping of perception, conceived by the individual in culturally defined catego-

[6] Carle C. Zimmerman, *Family and Civilization* (New York: Harper, 1947).

ries as a meaningful whole. It is exemplified in romantic love which is so fully internalized by middle-class Americans that it is difficult for them to understand that only a few generations ago within Western European culture the nearest thing to youthful love was a pattern unrelated to marriage. Similarly, the belief in mother love, another culturally shaped sentiment, is so intense that many mothers who find themselves annoyed with their children interpret this as a deficiency in mother love.

A love sentiment is a culturally learned way of interpreting and responding to an infinite variety of types of spontaneous attractions. Unsocialized attractions, like those of the small child, are ephemeral and do not incorporate altruistic and self-sacrificing behavior patterns, as we expect adult love to do. As the individual develops within American society, the culture pattern of romantic love is held constantly before him as a natural and inevitable development, so that by the time he reaches the appropriate age, and often well before, he expects to fall in love and to behave as lovers do. When he finds himself attracted to a member of the opposite sex who conforms to the cultural criteria of a suitable love object, he seeks the signs that will show he is in love. As he discovers these signs and decides he may be in love, he will unwittingly—or if internalization of the culture pattern is incomplete, even deliberately—act as a person in love is supposed to act.

The culture surrounds a sentiment with devices which ward off disbelief. Thus the conviction that true love once kindled can never die is preserved by the culturally defined notion of "infatuation." An individual who "falls out of love" concludes he was never really in love, but merely infatuated. The individual who never finds within himself an experience which he can define as love may preserve for years his belief that everyone naturally falls in love by borrowing from the culture the notion that he has just not met the right person.

CULTURAL CHANGE

Some of the marked changes that are taking place in the Western family system have already been noted. One consequence of extensive and fairly rapid cultural change is usually instability and disorganization, as reflected in heightened conflict and misunderstanding between husband and wife, parent and child, and within the larger extended family.

Inconsistent Change

The effective control of culture over the members of a society is largely dependent on the fact that its various aspects, such as norms, values, and sentiments, ordinarily are mutually supporting in their effect on the individual. During periods of transition this supporting relation is weakened, so that cultural sentiments may not suit the approved family roles, or social norms may change while the deep convictions of value are altered more slowly. For example, men may accept as *norms* the newer views of equality between the sexes and may assist their wives in domestic tasks without any supporting feeling that they gain anything by this arrangement. The absence of a culturally imbued sense of *value* reduces the new norms to unpleasant duties, so that each man looks with envy on the occasional husband who gets away with following the older patterns and regards his own wife as insufficiently grateful to him for his broad-mindedness in assisting with what are essentially her tasks.

Conflicting Norms

Cultural change also threatens family stability through the co-existence of mutually incompatible social norms. Difficulty arises when husband and wife are not equally "modern" or equally traditional in their role conceptions. Difficulty also develops when an individual accepts for himself incompatible elements from both the old and the new. A consistent finding from several studies is the correlation between diversity of cultural background of husband and wife and marital maladjustment. Not all combinations from different backgrounds have the same effect, however.

The problem of partial acceptance by an individual of both the old and new patterns is more subtle. Kirkpatrick (Adaptation 29) has analyzed a phase of this confusion and described the elements of three roles from which the woman must choose today.

Ethical Inconsistency in Marriage

Abridged and adapted from "The Measurement of Ethical Inconsistency in Marriage" by Clifford Kirkpatrick, *International Journal of Ethics*, **46** (July, 1936), 444–60. Published in this form by permission of Clifford Kirkpatrick and the *International Journal of Ethics*.

There are many informal observations about the conflicting conceptions of the husband and wife role in modern society. If we are to proceed beyond common-sense discussions, however, several steps are required. First, some effort must be made to describe the alternative role conceptions with precision. Second, some effort must be made to designate the specific ways in which the conceptions can come into conflict. And third, there must be empirical tests which will enable us to demonstrate and measure such conflicts of role conception. Clifford Kirkpatrick takes these three steps in this study.

ADAPTATION 29

Modern family life has developed from a rich and varied cultural heritage. From this heritage has come confusion over the place of women in the modern world. At the present time we may distinguish between three roles that may be played by the married woman, each implying certain privileges and certain obligations. Few women may be classified unambiguously with reference to any one of these roles, but these "ideal types" are useful tools of analysis.

1. The *wife-and-mother* role is the traditional role of the married woman. It implies these privileges: security, the right to support, alimony in the case of divorce, respect as a wife and mother, a certain amount of domestic authority, loyalty of husband to one who has borne him children, and a more or less sentimental gratitude from husband and children. The corresponding obligations include: bearing and rearing children, making a home, rendering domestic service, loyal subordination of self to the economic interests of the husband, acceptance of a dependent social and economic status, and the acceptance of a limited range of interests and activity.

2. The *companion* role is essentially a leisure-class phenomenon. The privileges pertaining to this role include: sharing pleasures with the husband, receiving a more romantic emotional response, being the object of admiration, receiving funds adequate for dress and recreation, having leisure for social and educational activity, and the receiving of a certain amount of chivalrous attention. On the other hand it implies as obligations: the preservation of beauty under the penalty of marital insecurity, the rendering of ego and libido satisfaction to the husband, the cultivation of social contacts advantageous to him, the maintenance of intellectual alertness, and the responsibility for exorcising the demon of boredom.

3. Finally, there is the *partner* role, corresponding to a new definition of the cultural situation which is gradually emerging.

This entails: the privileges of economic independence, equal authority in regard to family finances, acceptance as an equal, exemption from one-sided personal or domestic service to the husband, equal voice in determining locality of residence, and equality in regard to social and moral liberty. The obligation side of the balance sheet includes: renouncing of alimony save in the case of dependent children, a contribution to the common fund in proportion to earning ability, acceptance of equal responsibility for the support of children, complete sharing of the legal responsibilities of the family, willingness to dispense with any appeal to chivalry, abrogation of special privileges in regard to children, and equal responsibility to maintain the family status by success in a career.

This multiplicity of roles contributes to personality conflict in at least four ways. Personality tensions may develop out of women's difficulty in choosing among the roles. Or a woman may be frustrated by performing one role through duty or habit while longing for a different role. Again, there may be personality conflict by virtue of misunderstanding between husband and wife in regard to the role each expects the married woman to play. Finally there is *ethical inconsistency* in attitudes toward distribution of obligations and privileges.

This study is concerned with the last of the types of role confusion. To permit testing by quantitative empirical evidence, a specific hypothesis may be stated as follows: *There is a tendency on the part of women to approve more strongly than men of privileges of more than one feminine marriage role. There is a corresponding tendency on the part of men as compared with women to endorse the obligations of more than one marriage role.* Putting the matter more briefly: Women want a double dose of privilege, and men want them to have a double dose of obligation. If this hypothesis is confirmed, much marital discord stands explained.

The data for this study consisted of questionnaires filled out by 161 male and 241 female University of Minnesota students in 1934, and by 152 fathers and 165 mothers of the same students. The questionnaire consisted of a number of statements of attitudes concerning the status of women, to be endorsed or rejected. A number of the statements could be classified as specifying either an obligation or a privilege which belonged to one of the three types of marital roles. In order to test the hypothesis, the statements were grouped for analysis into pairs. The pairs consisted of statements, each of which endorsed an obligation of a different role, or each of which endorsed a privilege of a different role. To be confirmed, the hypothesis requires that relatively more men will endorse both statements in the first type of pair and relatively more women will endorse both statements in the second type of pair. A sample of each type of pair is presented:

Privileges of both Partner and Wife-and-Mother roles
"Women have the right to compete with men in every sphere of economic activity." "Alimony is an appropriate protection for women as members of the weaker sex."
Obligations of both Partner and Wife-and-Mother roles

"There is no particular reason why a girl standing in a crowded street car should expect a man to offer her his seat." "It is only fair that male workers should receive more pay than women, even for identical work."
Privileges of both Companion and Partner roles
"A woman to be truly womanly should gracefully accept chivalrous attentions from men." "It is desirable that women be appointed to police forces and empowered to protect the rights of women offenders."
Obligations of both Companion and Partner roles
"A husband has the right to expect that his wife be obliging and dutiful at all time." "As newcomers into industry women should accept the arrangements of men in regard to hours and conditions of work."
Privileges of both Companion and Wife-and-Mother roles
"The 'clinging-vine' wife is justified provided she clings sweetly enough to please her husband." "Women should demand money for household and personal expenses as a right rather than as a gift."
Obligations of both Companion and Wife-and-Mother roles
"Women should be guided by men's view of decency in dress." "Retention by a wife of her maiden name is selfish and fanatical."

Table X:2 summarizes the findings. In the first column the average percentage of all

Table **X:2**　Endorsement of Privileges or Obligations of Two Roles

Role Combinations	Average Per Cent Endorsing Both			
	Male Students	Female Students	Fathers	Mothers
Partner and Wife-and-Mother				
(a) Privileges (5 pairs)	15.2	20.4	19.9	25.7
(b) Obligations (10 pairs)	23.6	10.6	27.0	16.1
Companion and Partner				
(c) Privileges (5 pairs)	23.1	29.6	18.8	26.7
(d) Obligations (8 pairs)	20.0	9.0	23.0	13.2
Companion and Wife-and-Mother				
(e) Privileges (2 pairs)	42.5	44.9	32.6	45.5
(f) Obligations (3 pairs)	12.0	8.0	12.9	9.7

male students who endorsed both statements is given for each of the six kinds of pairs. Similar average percentages for female students, for fathers, and for mothers are given in succeeding columns.

Row (a) summarizes the endorsement of privileges from both the Partner and the Wife-and-Mother roles, based on five pairs of statements. On the average about 15 per cent of the men students endorsed privileges from both roles. However, a larger percentage of women students (about 20 per cent) endorsed privileges from both roles. Row (b), which deals with obligations from the same two roles, shows a difference in just the opposite direction. Nearly 24 per cent of men students compared with about 11 per cent of women students endorsed obligations from both roles. The evidence so far supports the hypothesis, namely, that women want a double dose of privilege and men want them to have a double dose of obligation. Ethical inconsistency seems to follow self-interest.

The evidence for students is similar regarding the other two pairs of roles. More women students than men students endorse double privilege, as reported in rows (c) and (e), while more men than women students endorse double obligation, as shown in rows (d) and (f).

To the extent that confusion of roles is a product of cultural change, it should affect successive generations to different degrees. During the period when new roles are just developing, the greatest confusion might be expected. As the new roles become more established and the alternatives facing a wife are more clearly recognized, inconsistency should decline. Thus as women tend more and more to make deliberate selection of their roles by weighing just what they will gain and what they will give up in following

each alternative, the confusion we are describing should decrease.

By examining the percentages of endorsements by the parents of the students (third and fourth columns), it is possible to test the hypotheses on an earlier generation. In each case the trend of differences is the same for the older generation as it was for the students. The older generation shows a similar tendency for women to claim double privilege and men to expect double obligation of their wives. In rows (a) and (b) all the percentages for the fathers and mothers are higher than the corresponding percentages for the students. This finding could be regarded as some slight evidence for the hypothesis that the younger generation is less inclined to ethical inconsistency than the older generation. Note, however, that the same difference is not found in the remaining rows of the table. Therefore it cannot be concluded that the hypothesis of generational differences is supported by these data.

Conclusion

In sum, Kirkpatrick has taken a common-sense notion, refined it, operationalized it, and tested it. Out of the confusion over the contemporary wife role he has abstracted three logically coherent types. His hypothesis is that when alternative roles are available, each sex will tend to select a combination of elements from two or more roles which is to its own advantage. Through a careful classification of questionnaire responses he is able to confirm that this is the case. In this tendency for women to claim more privileges than men grant them and for men to pose more obligations for women than they are willing to accept, we have pinpointed what may be an important source of much contemporary marital disharmony.

Section 4 **Socialization**

The family is the major agency through which socialization takes place. Within the family the parents and others try deliberately to mold children into conformity with acceptable cultural models. In addition there are effects, often unintended and unrealized, from the pattern of interpersonal relations within the family and from the type and intensity of the sentiments expressed in family interaction. Finally, socialization continues throughout life and hence operates through the family on its adult members.

DELIBERATE SOCIALIZATION OF THE CHILD

Deliberate attempts to train the child are governed by parents' images of what a child ought to be, and these in turn are often influenced by the social settings within which parents live. Miller and Swanson suggest that a general shift away from the traditional entrepreneurial pattern in American society has brought with it a widespread change in child-rearing practices. The classic *entrepreneurial* setting involves small-scale organizations with modest capitalization and limited division of labor, with risk-taking and competition as essential conditions for financial success. Middle-class parents living in such a setting encourage their children to be "highly rational, to exercise great self-control, to be self-reliant, and to assume an active, manipulative stance toward their environment." [7] The newer *bureaucratic* setting involves large-scale organizations that reward workers with wages and protect them from much insecurity by company insurance and welfare programs. Success depends more upon developing specialized skills and participating well in the organization than

on risk-taking. Middle-class parents from such settings encourage their children to be "accommodative, to allow their impulses some spontaneous expression, and to seek direction from the organizational programs in which they participate." [8] Miller and Swanson interviewed parents who were representative of each of the two settings, which coexist in American society today. On the basis of a number of specific questions about child rearing they found modest support for the hypothesis that entrepreneurial middle-class parents more than bureaucratic parents stress self-control and an active approach to the environment. Thus child-rearing practices are affected by changing forms of economic organization.

Direct and Indirect Methods

Societies also differ in the degree to which children are thought to be more effectively handled by direct dealing through command and obvious punishment and reward or by indirect dealings. In the latter case parents are supposed to control the child by providing pleasant alternatives to disapproved behavior and by depending principally on "reasoning with the child" rather than on punishment and threat. [9] The dominance relationship will not greatly differ in the two situations, since a child begins quite early to identify the effective meaning of many of the indirect techniques being used on him. But the second method trains for a manipulative approach to people and strengthens the "salesman" personality fostered by conditions of modern urban life.

[7] Daniel R. Miller and Guy E. Swanson, *The Changing American Parent* (New York: Wiley, 1958), p. 57.

[8] *Ibid.,* p. 58.

[9] This pattern of socialization is discussed by David Riesman in *The Lonely Crowd* (New Haven: Yale University Press, 1950), pp. 45–54, *et passim.* See also SOCIALIZATION, p. 97.

Value of Children

The pattern of deliberate socialization is also shaped by the ways children acquire special value to their parents. In contemporary urban society, children are important in determining the family reputation among neighbors and associates. Within the suburban neighborhood and among apartment dwellers, children usually have a much wider range of nearby contacts than their parents, so that many adults are known to each other only by whose parents they are. And with the reserve characterizing urban relations, even among friends, children's spontaneous and uninhibited behavior is extensively used as a clue to concealed characteristics of their parents. One study of a group of Midwestern mothers reports that those with older children tended to place greater emphasis on the traditional virtues of children, such as cleanliness, obedience, respect for adults, than did mothers with children under five years of age. Interviews with the mothers suggested that they retreat to traditional values in child raising as the awareness is forced on them that teachers and other parents judge them according to the propriety of their child's conduct.[10]

Mediating Function

An important aspect of deliberate socialization is the parents' function in *mediating* the child's relations with other agents of socialization. Parents mediate or "stand between" the child and other groups by attempting to control the child's spontaneous associations, by placing the child in formal groups, by motivating his participation in various associations, and by helping to interpret to him his learning from groups outside the family. The broken home is often unable to perform this function, so that the child is unduly socialized by groups into which he happens by chance.

Whether parents encourage extensive socializing experiences with the child's peers or isolate him from such experiences will be important in his development. Piaget, through an ingenious set of studies of children in Switzerland, showed that characteristic types of moral attitudes develop in each case.[11] Relations between adult and child tend to be unequal, with final authority wielded by the adult. When the child's conception of morality is patterned in this kind of relationship, rules tend to be regarded as ends in themselves. Strict conformity to the letter of the law is demanded, with little attention paid to the spirit of the law or the motives of people. Piaget calls this the "morality of constraint." In contrast, relations among peers are characterized by give and take, and decisions are reached by discussion and compromise. According to the "morality of co-operation" which develops in this type of environment, rules exist for the benefit of the group and by mutual consent of its members. Consequently, the purpose of the rule is understood, and a moral judgment always takes into account the motives behind any action.

INTERPERSONAL RELATIONS IN THE FAMILY

Parents probably socialize the child more by the pattern of interpersonal relations which they establish unwittingly than by their deliberate efforts. Through parental example and through the role which the child finds for himself within the family, the basic skills of *gesture interpretation* and of *interpersonal technique* are learned. Through repeated experience in the home, the child learns to interpret an angry word either as something passing or as a sign of deep-seated hatred, to interpret criticism either as an impersonal or as a highly personal matter, and either to accept a compliment at its face value or to look for a hidden insult behind

[10] Evelyn M. Duvall, "Conceptions of Parenthood," *American Journal of Sociology,* **52** (November, 1946), 193–203.

[11] Jean Piaget, *The Moral Judgment of the Child* (New York: Harcourt, Brace, 1932).

it. The child may learn that problem situations are to be dealt with by adjusting himself to them, or he may learn that they are best handled by taking active steps to modify the situation. In the latter instance he learns either that direct threat and force are the effective means for modifying the behavior of another, or that persuasion, negotiation, assumed martyrdom, or some other technique is the way. The grown individual from an inharmonious family background may unwittingly precipitate crises in his own marriage by making the gesture interpretations and using the interpersonal techniques he learned in childhood. Defective patterns of interaction may thus persist.

The child learns these basic skills by a combination of *adopting* them from family models and *adapting* to the roles of others in the family. The child learns his own role by trying out various roles he sees about him for their effectiveness in his own situation. He settles upon a single role for himself, or he learns several alternate roles from which he selects according to his estimate of what the roles of others in any given situation will be. For example, the child who tries out his father's domineering role and meets sudden punishment may then try out the "helpless" role he sees his mother use and find that it works better. If his mother is also domineering toward him, and his siblings and playmates are all able to dominate him, he may learn to use only this single role in all types of situations. However, if he has several weaker siblings and playmates, he may successfully ape the parents' domineering role with his playmates, reserving the submissive role for situations in which he is the weaker person.

Section 5 **Primary relations**[12]

The assertion sometimes made that the family is the prototype of the primary group is a half-truth which requires careful qualification. Relationships within the family are on a highly personal basis, they are face-to-face and lasting, and there is a strong "we-group" feeling. But besides these standard characteristics of the primary group, we must note some features which differentiate it from other primary groups: (1) Membership in the family is not voluntary, or at least not completely so. (2) Authority patterns which are determined by the culture and re-inforced in the society impede the development of spontaneous leadership patterns which characterize the ideal primary group. (3) Inequality is intrinsic and marked in the family because of the age differential, unlike the ideal primary group, which is a body of peers. (4) The intimacy of family relations varies, as we have indicated, from society to society and from family to family. In American society the adolescent-parent relationship is quite likely to be less intimate than the relationship among fellow adolescents. The semblance of intimacy which is sometimes maintained merely out of duty and propriety in both parent-child and mate relationships is very different from the spontaneous intimacy of the gang. In our discussion, there-

[12] Several of the ideas presented in this section have been most fully developed in Willard Waller and Reuben Hill, *The Family: A Dynamic Interpretation* (New York: Dryden, 1951.)

fore, it will be necessary to think of the family as a *special kind* of primary group.

IDENTIFICATION

Family relations are characterized by *identification,* which is a process of experiencing the actions of another person as if one had performed them himself. Some identification is a part of any group membership, but it is especially important to the primary group. The pride which a family member feels because of the accomplishments of any other member is an important source of solidarity in the family relationship. On the other hand, identification is also a source of disharmony, since it leads the individual to feel the same discomfort when another member of the family commits a social error or violates a social norm that he would if he had committed it himself, except that he may perceive its inappropriateness even more clearly. For this reason, many persons who seem broadly tolerant and at ease with all kinds of people outside of their families display an intense intolerance over minor actions of their mates or children. Tolerance in the former situation is based on the absence of identification.

Limitations on Intimacy

The idealization of marriage as total intimacy with each party having no secrets from the other and finding his greatest pleasure in activities with the other, is likewise a source of both solidarity and dissension. While fairly intense intimacy characterizes other primary relations, the individual's reaction to family intimacy may reflect the nonvoluntary character of family relations and the attitudes of sex competition which are promoted in many societies. These considerations may cause a person to define great intimacy as an encroachment upon his own individuality and to resist too great involvement. Boys' gangs and fraternities and girls' groups are particularly likely to stress competition between the sexes, to define a ro-

mance as a "conquest," and treat any member who admits he has fallen in love as one who has been bested by a member of the opposite sex. The individual may thus find himself caught in the ambivalent position of both demanding and resisting extreme intimacy.

Involvement of members in any group is likely to be unequal, and in an intense relationship such as the family, one member is likely to exercise considerable dominance by virtue of his being less intensely involved than others.[13] In courtship, for example, a boy dating an extremely popular girl may find himself making numerous concessions to maintain the relationship, while the girl, who senses the abundant alternatives available to her, experiences little incentive to compromise. However, the restricted sphere of life permitted to most married women in America makes them more dependent upon the family for a larger portion of their satisfactions in life than their husbands. Therefore, in spite of equalitarian ideology and the matricentric pattern (see Sec. 2, pp. 357–58), on the major issues the wife may be the more motivated to make whatever adjustments are required to keep the relationship satisfactory. Inadvertently by so doing she reinforces her traditional subordinate status. The parents of adolescent children in contemporary society find it difficult to implement their formally dominant position. Their need to feel that their children are dependent upon them is countered by the adolescents' feeling that parents are relatively superfluous.

PATTERNED RELATIONSHIPS

People as close to one another as are family members tend to acquire stable ways of dealing with each other. These may be called patterned relationships. Such patterns develop when interpretations placed

---

[13] This idea has been called the "principle of least interest" by Willard Waller and Reuben Hill, *op. cit.,* pp. 190–92.

on an individual's gestures in specific situations become generalized expectations for future situations. For example, a wife places an interpretation on her husband's explanation of his late arrival home—he is over-conscientious on the job, he doesn't love her enough to want to get home early, he is hopelessly inefficient and slow-moving, he is working hard to get ahead for the benefit of the whole family, etc. After several such incidents, she settles on one interpretation which is thereafter evoked *before* the husband offers his explanation and which determines the wife's response to her husband more than does his own explanation. If the same expectation seems to fit other situations, it will be generalized. Meantime, the husband has gone through a similar process of interpreting his wife's response to his late arrivals and may have established his own generalized expectation.

The ability of a married couple or parents and children to make novel adjustments or to solve recurrent problems is sharply limited by patternings of this sort. It is characteristic of family relations that to an outsider arguments appear trivial and easily resolved through common-sense compromises. But when a couple cannot agree on a specific issue, such as how to reduce family expenditures, the issue at hand may be serving merely as a vehicle for a more general conflict pattern. The wife's interpretation of everything her husband says as a reflection on her competence makes her resist his suggestions regardless of their merit. Meanwhile, the husband's feeling that the wife is trying to dominate every decision makes it impossible for him to accept any suggestion she makes.

Actual roles in the family tend in time to grow into increasing consonance with the prevailing expectations. The wife who believes that her husband thinks her irresponsible in financial matters may find little reward in efforts at financial planning. Irresponsibility does not entail great penalties

when the husband is already prepared for it.

Patterned Conflict

Much of the material already discussed bears on the nature and causes of family conflict and instability. Some additional generalizations can be made, however, concerning the *pattern* of conflict, particularly as it is shaped by the predominance of primary relations within the family.

Conflict may be *chronic* or *progressive*. The former is intermittent, sometimes more and sometimes less intense, but showing no long-term trends. Chronic conflict may become so stable a part of family life that the same arguments recur periodically for several decades and may even be sentimentalized to the participants. Progressive conflict, on the other hand, is cumulative, each incident adding to the stored up antagonism from the preceding incidents and moving a step nearer to separation, or in the case of children, to open rebellion.

The factors which make conflict become progressive or remain chronic are not well understood, but certain hypotheses can be suggested: (1) The greater the value placed upon the issues of recurring conflict, the more likely is conflict to become progressive. The very determination to settle the issue "once-and-for-all," which is common when the issues are important to the participants, breeds intolerance and extreme behavior. (2) Serious personality disorganization of one of the partners tends to make conflict progressive. (3) Strong negative feelings about overt conflict tend to make conflict progressive. Some people expect open and recurrent conflict as an accompaniment to normal living and adjust readily to frequent argument. To others harmony is a prime value in the family and if it cannot be achieved, there is no alternative but progressive deterioration of the relationship.

In one characteristic pattern, progressive conflict proceeds between husband and wife or parent and child until the participants are confronted with a dramatic climax which makes them suddenly aware that the entire relationship itself is threatened. There ensues a panicked retreat into reconciliation and a period of intense and reassuring— perhaps anxious—intimacy, out of which another cycle of progressive conflict may emerge.

Because of its primary group quality, the marriage relationship cannot be terminated with the ease of a secondary association. The intense involvements and identifications must be broken by a process known as *alienation*. The involvement of a married couple is an elaborate intertwining of many phases of their lives, so that a break in one area still leaves many involvements and identifications in other areas. Even in a predominantly antagonistic relationship, the members may be quite dependent upon one another emotionally, and full alienation will require that each assume a new personal independence. Incomplete alienation is exemplified in cases of a divorced husband or wife spying on his ex-spouse or seeking out ways to discredit him.

PREDICTION OF MARITAL SUCCESS

One of the most important research areas in the sociological study of the family has been the attempt to ascertain what characteristics of individuals and couples before marriage are related to the kind of adjustment they will make in marriage. Some studies have dealt with a single factor, such as religious background, conceptions of the husband and wife roles, and elopement versus sanctioned marriages. Others have attempted not so much to explore fully the relation of any single factor to marital success as to identify a wide range of possible factors which are related to success. In several of these studies, as in Adaptation 30, the findings have been presented in the form of a device for predicting success in marriage. The score any couple receives places them in an actuarial risk category and tells them the proportion of successes within that group. For example, from filling out such a schedule, a couple may ascertain that 90 per cent of persons with their score have successful marriages. Although the "odds" strongly favor their marital success, the couple have no way to tell whether they will be among the 90 per cent or among the 10 per cent who are unsuccessful.

At the present stage of development of tests designed to predict marital success the tools should be regarded as exploratory research instruments. These studies can not provide exact guides for choosing a marital partner or for governing the lives of people. They are meant to add to an understanding of the dynamics of adjustment and to the building of a body of verifiable knowledge about the family.

The Prediction of Marital Success

Abridged and adapted from *Engagement and Marriage* by Ernest W. Burgess and Paul Wallin (Philadelphia: Lippincott, 1953). Published in this form by permission of the authors and the J. B. Lippincott Co.

Efforts to devise a questionnaire which can be used by an unmarried pair to estimate their chances of a successful marriage have a few basic steps in common. First, the investigator decides on some way of telling a successful marriage from one that is unsuccessful. The device he uses to sort the marriages is called the criterion of success. One criterion might be objective evidence such as whether or not the couples are divorced. Many studies, however, depend on questionnaires containing items which are thought to be self-evident measures of success. After the criterion of success is established, the investigator makes out a questionnaire consisting of items which he thinks might turn out to be good predictors of marital success. For example, if he thinks long engagements lead to successful marriages and that neurotics are unlikely to have successful marriages, he will include a question on length of engagement and questions from a standard personality inventory of neurotic tendencies. Then, he administers the questionnaire to a group of people whom he can sort into successful or unsuccessful marriages according to his predetermined criterion. Finally, the items from the questionnaire on which the successful and unsuccessful differ are weighted and combined into a prediction schedule. The nondifferentiating items are eliminated.

In reviewing the main steps in developing a prediction questionnaire we shall refer to the Burgess-Wallin study which follows this general pattern but with significant innovations. In their study, couples first filled out questionnaires *before* marriage and then were followed up for a rating of their marital success (the criterion) after a few years of marriage. Furthermore, a more elaborate criterion of marital success was employed than in earlier studies.

SUBJECTS AND METHOD

A sample of engaged couples was first secured to serve as an experimental group. A battery of items derived from earlier predictive studies and from various theoretical considerations was administered to this experimental group. All questions were worded so that their answers could be objectively scored and so that they could be answered before marriage.

Of 6,000 sets of schedules distributed through college classes and by students to engaged friends and acquaintances, 1,200 were returned by mail, and of these the first 1,000 complete sets were used. After from three to five years of marriage, 666 of these married couples could be given the marital adjustment inventory. The subjects were all residents of metropolitan Chicago, and in the great majority of couples one member at least had attended college for a year or more.

Students who assisted in distributing schedules supplied certain information about the couples to whom they gave the forms. On the basis of this information it was possible to compare those who returned the schedules with those who did not. Participant couples tended to be of higher education, non-Catholic, younger, rated radical or liberal rather than reactionary or conservative, and were assigned a higher forecast of marital success by those distributing the questionnaires. Because of the nature of the sample, the results can be applied with some confidence only to middle-class white, native-born, urban, Protestants who have completed high school or attended college.

Personal interviews were also conducted before marriage with 226 of the same couples. An additional questionnaire including more intimate matters such as sex experience was also filled out by these engaged subjects at the time of interview. Interviews were conducted with 124 of the couples after marriage.

CRITERIA OF MARITAL SUCCESS

The choice of a criterion or measure of marital success is a difficult but crucial step because there are many different and sometimes conflicting ideas concerning just what kind of marriage should be regarded as successful and what kind unsuccessful. The most objective measure, based on whether a couple is divorced, separated, or together, overlooks the many unpleasant unions which are continued because of social pressure or sense of duty. In this study not one but nine different criteria are used, each consisting of the sum of scores assigned to the answers to several questionnaire items. The criteria are as follows:

a. The respondent's evaluation of the *permanence* of the marriage and his conception of his mate's evaluation.

b. The respondent's evaluation of his own marital *happiness* and his conception of his mate's marital happiness.

c. The respondent's general *satisfaction* with his marriage and his conception of his mate's general satisfaction.

d. An inventory of *specific satisfactions* and dissatisfactions.

e. The respondent's estimate of *consensus* (agreement between husband and wife on fundamental issues).

f. The respondent's estimate of his *love* for his mate and his conception of its reciprocation by the mate.

g. The respondent's estimate of the *sexual satisfaction* of himself and his mate.

h. The respondent's estimate of the degree of *companionship* in the marriage.

i. The respondent's estimate of *compatibility* of personality and temperament between himself and his mate.

The husband and wife filled out the schedules independently, and each was assigned separate scores for the nine criteria, higher scores indicating greater success.

It was possible to have 666 of the original couples fill out the marriage success schedule at a time when about 75 per cent of them had been married between three and five years. Of the 1,000 engaged couples, 150 had not married, 33 were divorced or separated, and 10 were widowed. Thus, of the 807 eligibles, approximately 80 per cent participated in the follow-up study. It is important to remember that the findings of this study apply only to the early years of marriage. The relation to success in later years of marriage remains to be investigated.

The two most general criteria, happiness and satisfaction, correlate highly ($+.82$) with each other, on the basis of the 666 married couples studied. The others correlate moderately (from .44 to .65) with these two criteria. On the basis of this evidence *general satisfaction* and *happiness* can be used as two over-all criteria of marital success, though for certain purposes all the criteria may still be used separately or combined into a single composite index.

PREDICTIVE ITEMS

The next step is to assess the value of the various items on the original engagement schedule for predicting success in marriage. Each potential predictive item is tested by comparing the way that the more successful couples answered it with the way that the less successful replied. If there is a difference which meets certain statistical tests which show that it could not have happened by chance, the item is retained. If there is no difference or the difference is too small, the item is discarded as not being predictive. Answers to the retained items are assigned weightings ranging from $+9$ to -2. The positive weightings are assigned to answers which are predictive of success and the negative weightings to answers which are predictive of failure. Heavier weightings are assigned to those answers on which the successful and unsuccessful couples answer most differently.

When the items have been selected and the respective weightings determined, they are assembled in the form of multiple choice questions, which can be administered to other engaged couples. Each answer is assigned a numerical value, as has been described in the preceding paragraph. For example, each person will select one of the five alternative answers to the following questions and will be assigned the score which applies to the answer selected:

My childhood, on the whole, was (check):
(a) extremely happy _____; [score 4 points]

(b) more happy than average ————;
[score 3 points]

(c) about average ————; [score 2 points]

(d) rather unhappy ————; [score 1 point]

(e) extremely unhappy ————; [score 0 points]

For convenience and to clarify their theoretical relevance, the predictive items are classified into a limited number of more general factors. The items were grouped by logical analysis under (*a*) background factors, (*b*) engagement history, (*c*) personality, (*d*) engagement success, and (*e*) anticipated contingency factors. Each of these broad predictive factors was then also correlated with the marital success score.

The points assigned to the answers given by the subjects are totaled within each of these five categories, giving each couple five separate predictive totals. Each of these totals can then be converted into percentile scores which tell the couple how they compare with the group of subjects used in the original study. If the couple's score is better than that of 75 per cent of the original subjects, the evidence is judged as favorable to the success of their marriage. If their score is not better than the lowest 25 per cent of the original subjects, the evidence is unfavorable to successful marriage. Scores which place the couple in the middle 50 per cent are viewed as nonpredictive. By considering each of these five sections of the predictive schedule the couple can gain a general impression of their probable success in marriage. But, more important, they may be able to detect in advance certain areas in which they will have to make more than the usual amount of adjustment if their marriage is to be a successful one.

FINDINGS

Of the many specific findings from this research, it is possible to give only a few of the typical ones. They can be conveniently summarized under the five general factors listed above.

a. Most of the *background* items are characteristics of individuals prior to meeting their future mates and cannot be changed by interaction of the couple during engagement. A number of these items have to do with relations between the subject and his own parents. Such items as close attachment of the man to his father, very strong attachment of the couple to their mothers, and college education and income over $5,000 for their fathers were found to be predictive of success in marriage. Various items signifying that the individuals make friends easily and are active in social organizations rather than being lone-wolves are also predictive of marital success. Amount of income is not so important as personal characteristics of prudence, thrift, and stability displayed in economic activity. Wholesome sex instruction is likewise predictive. Taken together, there is a correlation of .31 for husbands and .27 for wives between background scores and multiple marital success scores.

b. The sum total of items concerning *engagement history* correlate .28 for husbands and .26 for wives with a multiple marital success score. Many of these items can be grouped together as indicating the gradual emergence of love through companionship in contrast to the more violent and hasty romantic love. Liking the future mother- and father-in-law very much, engaging in most activities together, preferring to stay at home, and confiding in the mate about everything are all predictive of success.

c. Personality items, based on self and mate ratings and on questions from standard personality inventories, correlate .25 for men and .18 for women with multiple marital success scores. The specific items from this and other studies provide a composite picture of happily married husbands and wives in contrast to the unhappily married, as being emotionally stable, considerate of

Interpreting Correlations

Correlation is a measure of how accurately the magnitude of one variable can be estimated on the basis of another. For example, the existence of correlation between a person's rating of his marital success and his earlier rating of engagement success allows the investigator to estimate one rating on the basis of the other more accurately than he could by simply random guessing. The highest possible correlation coefficient—1.00—indicates that two variables are so perfectly related that the magnitude of one can always be exactly stated on the basis of the other. A coefficient of 0.00 shows that no relationship exists between the two variables. A plus sign before the coefficient shows that the two variables change together in the same direction. A negative sign shows that as either variable increases, the other decreases. The coefficient of correlation is symbolized by the letter "r."

A low correlation (less than .50) indicates a great many individual exceptions to the relationship and must be interpreted with utmost caution. However, meaningful and high correlations (.80 and over), and even moderate ones, can be secured only when measuring instruments are precise and when the influence of interfering variables can be experimentally controlled. Sometimes deceptively high correlations are due to imperfections in the research instrument, so that the same information is included in both of the variables. A substantial correlation between ratings of marital happiness and sexual adjustment could merely mean that people take their sexual adjustment into account when they rate their marital happiness. This is called *contamination* and means that something is in fact being correlated with itself. Since ideal conditions are seldom met in practice, sociologists examine high correlations critically to be sure there is no contamination and low correlations carefully in the hope that they may supply clues to relationships. Marital happiness is so complex that we would not expect any single variable to stand out sharply; hence we cannot afford to overlook even small correlations between marital happiness and such variables as ethnic and religious similarity of mates and marriage with parental approval.

Correlation of itself never tells what is cause and what is effect. If ratings of engagement success are correlated with ratings of marital success five years later, only the time interval justifies an interpretation that the latter is not cause and the former effect. A successful engagement may help to cause a successful marriage, but it is equally possible that the same features of personal compatibility, or family background, or fortunate circumstance that cause a successful engagement also cause a successful marriage. The correlation might even result merely from a consistent tendency of respondents to rate their experience in either glowing or negative terms.

others, yielding rather than dominant, companionable, self-confident, and emotionally dependent rather than emotionally self-sufficient.

d. The highest correlations are found between a rating of *engagement success* and marital success ($r = .39$ for men and .36 for women). The engagement success inventory is a briefer set of questions covering relations that are similar to those included in some of the marital success criteria. Evaluations of their engagements by the engaged couples may sometimes be quite different, as indicated by a correlation of only .57 between the man's and the woman's engagement success scores.

e. Contingency factors are those which emerge and become observable after marriage. Length of time married, place of residence, economic success, and relations with in-laws might become factors related to success in the course of the marriage. While such information cannot be secured before marriage, it is possible to ask the respondents to anticipate some such items. Accordingly the respondents were asked where they planned to live after marriage, whether they planned to live with in-laws, whether they desired children, and questions concerning what they expected the husband and wife roles in marriage to be. Together these items correlated .21 for men and .19 for women with marital success scores.

Conclusion

Studies of the foregoing type have been used both for practical advice in marriage relations and as a fund of evidence to support or refute theories regarding family life. In addition to the practical uses already mentioned, Burgess and Wallin have suggested that the nine marital success schedules (the criteria, not the predictive schedules) may be used by married couples to identify areas of difficulty in their marriages. The authors give percentile scores for these schedules, with the suggestion that a score in the bottom 25 per cent may indicate the desirability of securing marital counseling.

There are still many limitations that are constantly pointed out both by those who have conducted such studies and their critics. The "broadside" approach of these studies often gives superficial information whose meaning can be determined only by more intensive work on particular phases of marital success. The criteria of marital success may tend to reflect the traditional conception of the family more than the less easily identified emerging forms. Most of the studies have dealt with relatively educated, urban, middle-class white samples and are not presumed to apply to the whole population. Finally, the high rate of individual exceptions to all of the findings indicates incomplete information.

However, the findings from the several major researches and many more minor studies are probably the most extensively used body of quantified data in the field of marriage relations. As studies on different populations have reported generally similar findings, a considerable body of evidence about which we can feel fairly confident is steadily accumulating.

Section 6 Stratification

It is usually through the family that individuals are located in the stratification system. Husband and wife normally share a common class position; dependent children are known by their parents' position; and in rigid class systems the children may be unable to leave the parents' stratum even on reaching maturity.

In this section the family will be examined first as an agent of the stratification system. Second, the status-seeking aspects of courtship and mate selection will be noted. Finally, the tendency for different social strata to develop distinctive forms of family organization will be explored.

FAMILY AS AN AGENT OF STRATIFICATION

The family is perhaps the principal stabilizing agent in the class system, tending to transmit the parents' station to the children in two ways. First, the higher-class families supply their children with numerous tangible advantages in their competition with lower-class children for positions of high prestige in the society. Superior financial support translated into superior education or capital to begin business ventures is only a beginning. For example, the upper-class family can assist in building a professional clientele, or in gaining suitable hospital and referral connections in medicine, or in securing high level corporation employment.

Second, the family tends to supply attitudes, interpersonal skills, and motivations which are most appropriate to membership in its own class. Even when persons of lower-class origin are able to achieve upward mobility through gaining money or other personal achievement, they are likely to be regarded as *nouveaux riches* and

placed in a class apart from and below the more genteel class because they lack the "manners" that go with high position.

The school, designed in part to facilitate upward mobility for able children from lower social strata, is often ineffectual in this respect when family values do not support it. Typically the higher-class children are taught at home to value school recognition, while lower-class children may be taught to think of a report card or scholarship certificate as a mere piece of paper. The skills taught in school, such as reading, arithmetic, and the arts, are part of the higher-class child's experience in the home and so have a meaning which motivates him to develop them, while the lower-class child, who sees no evidence of their usefulness, may lack such motivation. Consequently, a disproportion of upward mobile individuals are either from families which already possess higher level values but are in low-paying white-collar work or from families in which the mother has moved downward but has retained the attitudes of her class of origin.

Family transmission of class position prevents full correspondence between social rank and abilities, and some persons of considerable talent will be found in the lower classes. On the other hand, the family facilitates mobility. With certain exceptions, the families of the higher strata do not bear enough children to replace themselves, so that in spite of the advantages their children have, the higher classes must be constantly replenished from the lower levels.

Status Factors

The system of stratification is reinforced by a tendency for persons to select marriage partners from their own socio-economic lev-

Table **X:3**   Family Characteristics by Social Classes

Family Characteristic	Upper Classes	Middle Classes	Lower Classes
Nuclear-extended balance	Old family: extended relatively important. Other upper class: like middle class.	Isolated and small nuclear family dominant; ties to extended family tenuous.	Some isolated nuclear units; some extended family important for mutual aid and sociability.
Values in family life	Old family: family line—may approximate trustee family (see p. 368). Other upper class: may emphasize family prestige and material luxury or resemble middle class.	Individual achievement, respectability, and cleanliness, high value on close harmonious interpersonal relations in family.	More emphasis on basic material wants and pleasures; less emphasis on surface harmony in family relations; range from marked individualism to strong mutual aid.
Authority and division of labor	May be matriarchal or patriarchal depending on sex of oldest member of extended family; often tend toward equalitarian. "Companion" wife role frequent.	More equalitarian and matricentric. Woman frequently supplementary provider.	Strongest male domination. (The Negro family is an exception. See Adaptation 35, pp. 509–12.) Women most frequently share role of major economic provider.
Sex norms	Strictness or leniency, but latter concealed; double standard frequent.	Sex most strictly limited to marriage; single standard strongest.	Greater sex freedom. Frankest acceptance of double standard.
Marriage: age and rate	Late marriage. Fewest unmarried men and most unmarried women.	Intermediate.	Early marriage. Most unmarried men and fewest unmarried women.
Primary group characteristics	Ritual and formality limit intimacy. Privacy of extended unit; often difficult to maintain because of social prominence.	Strongest interpersonal identifications and intimacy. Greatest emphasis on individual privacy and privacy of the nuclear unit.	Relations more spontaneous, frequently less intimate; freer expression of antagonisms. More accustomed to dependence on outsiders; less privacy.
Parent-child roles	Close surveillance of children by governesses and tutors. Parents' socialization function frequently only mediation.	Intimate family circle. Mother major socializing agent. Emphasis on scientific technique, psychological punishment, impulse control, rivalry.	Parent-child ties more casual and custodial. Socialization less planned, more physical punishment. Father more often traditional disciplinarian.
Stability	Evidence not clear. Probably lowest rate of family dissolution in old families, others fairly high.	Moderate rate of family dissolution; divorce preferred form. Most crises over familial relations.	Highest rate of family dissolution; especially by separation. Crises mostly economic and external.

els. Although the fact of *homogamy*—the marriage of people who resemble each other —has been demonstrated with respect to socio-economic status, the reason for the practice is less clear. Do class prejudices op- erate? Do similar backgrounds lead to common interests, which serve as a basis for attraction? Or are people merely more likely to meet others from backgrounds similar to their own? Or does active intervention of parents rather than preferences of potential mates account for homogamy with respect to stratification? An exploratory study suggests that the latter pair of explanations may be closer to the truth than the former.[14] A group of 78 married student couples on the Purdue University campus were divided into 47 who had been acquainted in the environment of their parental homes before attending college and 31 who had met and married while on campus. The socio-economic backgrounds of 120 unmarried students were used as the standard in determining whether spouses were more alike in background than would be expected on the basis of a random selection of mates. The evidence showed a slight tendency toward homogamy among those who knew each other before college, but no homogamy among those who met on campus. The authors suggest that campus democratic values and freedom from parental supervision

account for the difference. The limited sample makes the conclusion highly tentative but nonetheless suggestive of the nature of the interplay between stratification and mate selection.

CLASS VARIATIONS IN FAMILY CHARACTERISTICS

Frequently in the course of this chapter, we have referred to the middle-class American family or mentioned specific class differences. These and some additional points can be brought together in a brief summary of class differences in family characteristics (see Table X:3).

Caution: A nearly full range of family characteristics is probably found at every level of stratification. The summary in Table X:3, therefore, refers merely to patterns that show a higher frequency in one class than in another.[15]

[14] Gerald R. Leslie and Arthur H. Richardson, "Family versus Campus Influences in Relation to Mate Selection," *Social Problems,* 4 (October, 1956), 117–21.

[15] For a fuller summary of variations in family characteristics by social class, see Ruth S. Cavan, *The American Family* (New York: Crowell, 1953), pp. 119–87.

Section 7 Associations

Although the family is a primary group, it is often a participation unit in associations and also has relations with associations of which it is not a part. This aspect of family study is less developed than those already discussed, but in some societies and historical periods the family has played a paramount role in economic and religious associations.

FAMILY AS A PARTICIPATION UNIT

Whether the participation unit is the entire family, the adult members of a family, or merely individuals, will have certain consequences for the functioning and organiza-

tion of any association. If an association is based on family participation, it will probably have a greater *diversity of activities* than an association whose members are individuals. The church is such an association, attracting support from many persons who first join the recreational church clubs for married couples or who send their children to Sunday school. The effectiveness of any family unit association in maintaining a large membership probably depends upon *diversity of appeal,* while the effectiveness of the contrasting type of association is more likely to depend upon the strength of a narrower appeal, such as one restricted to political or economic spheres.

Family unit membership has a *conventionalizing effect* upon any association, particularly in contrast to one-sex groups. The "toning down" of the men's service club or the women's club on "family night" is well known.

Effects of Organizational Demands

Some associations demand little more than infrequent attendance at brief meetings; others demand a great deal of time and effort as well as important commitments regarding values and behavior of members. The family tends to interfere with demands of the latter type when they do not involve the entire family. This is illustrated by the strains imposed upon the labor union leader who regards his occupation as a "calling." The demands of the job upon his time and energies conflict with the traditional ideal of the good husband who is a companion to his wife and children. The job requirement that he accept only a modest salary conflicts with the criterion of the husband as a good provider.[16]

Associations that seek to extend the demands they make upon their members tend to incorporate the family into some formal or informal type of membership. One of the traditional methods in the United States is the women's auxiliary. In some occupations, such as the Protestant ministry, it is informally but clearly understood that the wife must serve as a sort of assistant minister. Indeed, because of the very demands made upon the individual by membership in a professional or business occupation, the wife will be drawn into occupational associations through an elaborate pattern of informal activities. By the way she performs these roles she may play a crucial part in determining the success of her husband.

The Corporation Wife

William H. Whyte, Jr., concludes from 230 interviews with business executives, management consultants, and wives, that both management and the wives of business executives have formed rather clear conceptions of what a good organization wife should be.[17] The wife is supposed to make it easy for her husband to adjust to transfers, late work, and other stresses of the job. She is also supposed to be a subtle but effective operator in her husband's behalf. Among the well-understood rules are the following.

Don't talk shop gossip with the Girls, particularly those who have husbands in the same department.

Don't invite superiors in rank; let them make the first bid.

Don't turn up at the office unless you absolutely have to.

Don't get too chummy with the wives of associates your husband might soon pass on the way up.

Don't be disagreeable to any company people you meet. You never know. . . .

Be attractive. There is a strong correlation between executive success and the wife's appearance.

Be a phone pal of your husband's secretary.

Never—repeat, never—get tight at a company party (it might go down in a dossier).

Corporations are less and less willing to leave the wife's part to chance. Frequently wives are interviewed before their husbands are hired. Prizes from sales contests are often deepfreezes, mixmasters, and other objects of feminine interest, so that the wives can be counted on to join forces with the company in encouraging utmost exertion from their husbands. By getting the wife on its side the corporation minimizes the danger that loyalty to his family will interfere with the executive's whole-hearted de-

---

[16] Alvin W. Gouldner, "Attitudes of 'Progressive' Trade-Union Leaders," *American Journal of Sociology,* **52** (March, 1947), 389–92.

[17] William H. Whyte, Jr., "The Wives of Management," and "The Corporation and the Wife," *Fortune,* **44** (October, 1951), 86 ff., and **44** (November, 1951), 109 ff.

votion to the company, and hopes that the social graces of the wives will establish contacts and open the way for sales that would not otherwise be made. In large nationwide or international companies the practice of promotion through frequent transfer prevents families of executives from putting down deep roots anywhere. Consequently, they may turn to the corporation as the source of their social life and their personal as well as their economic security.

The Privacy Principle

Under conventional circumstances in middle-class American society, the relations between the family and outsiders are governed by the *privacy* principle. Family members must not share the more intimate details of family life with outsiders, and the latter must not pry unduly. Public show of dissension among family members is taboo.

The appeal to a formal association for assistance about family relations is often regarded as a violation of the privacy principle. Consequently, people are reluctant to make use of such agencies as family counseling services or even of visiting nurses. In their roles as formal representatives of secondary associations, such agents are thought to have no understanding of intimate family relations, and their use is often regarded as an admission that the family has already failed.[18] Outsiders who are called upon for advice or assistance either have been incorporated into the circle of primary relations or have special roles, such as the physician who presents a delicate balance of intimate relations and impersonality.

NEPOTISM

Nepotism is the practice of favoring relatives in filling jobs or giving other opportunities or advantages in a business or government agency. It is an expected development from the norms of kinship and family loyalty. Family members are supposed to support one another, and the father is supposed to make preparations for his children's financial future. So long as he does so by training them well and passing on property, there is no protest. But when he uses his position to secure employment or advancement for relatives in the same establishment, the charge of nepotism is likely to be heard. Favors to family members are often seen as violations of two basic norms, namely, employment and promotion according to rational criteria of efficient operation, and equality of opportunity as essential to fair treatment. Nepotism is probably most common and meets least objection in small businesses, which are ordinarily regarded as family property. However, public concern about controlling nepotism increases step by step from the family enterprise to the professionally managed business and to government operations. This suggests that inequality of opportunity is a more important source of popular indignation than fear of inefficiency.

Even in the Chinese society of several centuries ago, in which family dominance in many areas was unchallenged, several mechanisms, of which promotion by seniority was the most important, were effectively employed in the government bureaucracy to combat nepotic tendencies.[19] Periodically there is a journalistic outcry against nepotism in government, but popular indignation is muted by the positive sentiment for family integrity so that only the grossest offenses, such as a congressman's paying a salary to a relative who does no work, are affected. Discussions of large-business nepotism usually end with the conclusion that it is all right to hire a relative if he is hired on the basis of his merits. It has been suggested that the problem of nepotism disappears as large businesses develop im-

[18] Earl L. Koos, *Families in Trouble* (New York: King's Crown Press, 1946), especially Chap. 5.

[19] Robert M. Marsh, "Bureaucratic Constraints on Nepotism in the Ch'ing Period," *Journal of Asian Studies*, **19** (February, 1960), 117–32.

personal merit systems for appointment and promotion.[20] But this conclusion overlooks the fact that the problem of nepotism is one of social definition. The appointment or promotion of a family member raises the suspicion that other considerations than merit entered into the decision, because each person's own experience of the primacy of family loyalty makes him define the event in these terms. On the other hand, the adoption of an impersonal attitude by a father toward his son in the business world is a violation of the special favor to which the son feels entitled because of family bonds. The problem of nepotism is the inevitable consequence of the partial contradiction of interests between family and association. The association seeks to use family sentiments to serve association ends, and the family seeks to reap maximum benefit from the association. See the discussion in INDUSTRIAL MAN, pages 640 ff.

[20] Perrin Stryker, "Would You Hire Your Son?" *Fortune*, **55** (March, 1957), 132 ff.

Section 8 Collective behavior

While the family as a small primary group organized about roles deeply imbedded in the culture may seem a far cry from the diffuse and ephemeral products of collective behavior, there are at least two important areas where the fields relate to one another. First, collective behavior makes temporary and sometimes enduring changes in the social organization that supports the prevailing patterns of family organization and in the values which, as aspects of the general culture, carry over their influence into family life. Second, membership in the family affects a person's susceptibility to participation and the manner of his participation in many forms of collective behavior.

Family in Community Disaster

Weakening of social forms leads to a state of social unrest with a considerable amount of random exploratory behavior, some of which is collective rather than purely individual. Natural disasters such as tornadoes, earthquakes, and floods temporarily weaken social forms, and the resulting collective behavior affects the performances of family roles. A study of the destructive 1953 Vicks-burg tornado suggested several ways in which the interrelations of parent and child roles were likely to be affected.[21] Most children demanded considerably more support from their parents after the tornado, sometimes "regressing" to behavior characteristic of younger age levels. Parents who were themselves much disturbed by the disaster tended either to be unable to supply even the usual amount of support to their children or to hold their children in an overly dependent relationship. Either extreme aggravated the child's disturbance and perpetuated his demand for more than normal parental support. Even a mother who avoided these responses found herself torn between her child's demands and the community demands for voluntary service, with either neglect or guilt resulting. Adolescents, however, frequently assumed adult roles in the crises and thus augmented their already growing independence from their parents.

Family communication patterns were

[21] Stewart E. Perry, Earle Silber, and Donald A. Bloch, *The Child and His Family in Disaster* (Washington, D.C.: National Academy of Sciences—National Research Council, 1956).

among the most frequent casualties in the disaster situation. Parents either did not know how to discuss the events with their children or tried to avoid discussion entirely for fear of disturbing the children. The failure of communication or the vacillation between communicating and silence increased the child's fright and blocked normal understanding of one another's moods, which is a crucial feature of primary relations.

Fads and Fashions in Family Life

The vagaries of fashion and fad impinge on family life through patterns of recreation, styles in suburban living, conceptions of ideal family size, intellectual fads such as eugenics, and many others. Such organized movements as birth control and woman's suffrage concerned themselves directly with family roles, while progressive education had much to say about school versus family functions.

Until the late nineteenth century, patterns of child rearing were fixed in the tradition governing the roles of wife and mother. As the supports for this tradition weakened, child-rearing patterns lost their stable anchorage and became subject to determination through collective behavior. Shifts in the patterns of child rearing from 1890 to the present have been documented through analysis [22] of articles in three leading women's magazines. In many respects the patterns advocated in 1890 and 1900 are more like those of the forties and fifties than are the stern patterns of 1910 to 1930. Infant feeding practices have come full circle from allowing the infant to set his own schedule, through feeding on a strict schedule, and back to feeding when the child "demands." The strict feeding regimen of the twenties emphasized nutritional needs of the child, and the period has been described as one in which parents were afraid of spoiling their children through love. The preceding

[22] Celia B. Stendler, "Sixty Years of Child Training Practices," *The Journal of Pediatrics*, **36** (1950), 122–34.

and following periods emphasized loving the infant.

The weakening of traditional definitions appears to have given rise to the regular alterations of fashion. Having no accurate knowledge, each parental generation may have been receptive to a scheme that stressed correction of the errors of the preceding generation. The free play of fad and the regular reversals of fashion may be expected to continue until some external stabilizing force takes the place of tradition. The steady trend away from a sentimental and toward a scientific rationale of child rearing suggests that adequate scientific knowledge could well become the stabilizing force. But there are as yet no studies to show that children reared according to one formula will grow to be adults who are superior by any criterion to children reared in other ways.

Participation in Social Movements

Participation in the various forms of collective behavior is affected in numerous ways by family membership and family structure. For example, certain types of social movements appeal especially to adult couples whose lives have been made empty because their children have grown up and left home. The use of a limited range of tactics and the tendency of organizations for older people to subordinate formal aims to the sociability function weakens such movements. Other organizations appeal to nonfamily young people, who are likely to drop from the movement or become passive members upon marriage. There appears to be a conventionalization of outlook following marriage as family responsibilities multiply. Membership in vigorous unconventional movements forces the family either openly to reject the member or to incorporate itself within the movement. The family operates, then, to limit membership. To cope with this effect of family membership such movements sometimes attempt to destroy family bonds or to enlist the whole family.

When family integration weakens, the individual becomes more available for participation in some kinds of collective behavior. This availability has two aspects: (1) the individual can be more self-centered psychologically, more conscious of and concerned with his own needs and problems; and (2) his actions do not have direct, inescapable consequences for the lives of others who are dependent on him.

Socialization within the family has been examined to discover how people become susceptible to the appeal of certain types of social movements. It has been suggested that the authoritarianism of the German family conditioned people to see a strong and ruthless leadership as the way out of difficulties, while the pattern of more understanding and indulgent parenthood may create susceptibility to such leaders as Franklin Roosevelt and Dwight Eisenhower. Such hypotheses are little more than speculation.

Section 9 Population and ecology

The family is importantly related to the number, composition, and spatial distribution of the population. Variations in family pattern and individual family structure are closely related to variations in fertility and life expectancy. Family structure and the age and sex composition of the labor force are necessarily interdependent. And according to general ecological principles, various types of families tend to congregate in the specialized areas of the community.

FAMILY AND FERTILITY

Fertility is affected both by the formal value attached to children within any family system and by the way in which children fit into the family structure. The birth of children may be defined as a *sacred* matter in which humans must not interfere. (See Adaptation 27, pp. 340–43.) When this is the case, the birth rate and the infant mortality rate are usually high. Woman's status is likely to be much below that of man's because her dependency is maximized by the devotion of her life to child rearing. The large family probably necessitates the development of norms requiring children to contribute to the family's economic support and tends to make this the criterion by which the worth of children is judged.

Children in the Trustee Family

In a trustee-type family children have value as perpetuators of the all-important family line, which tends to insure a high birth rate but may be accompanied by methods for eliminating infants who will not bring credit to the family. Infant exposure to the elements as a device for disposing of a physically defective child, or of one whose birth is associated with an ill omen, is exemplified in such ancient myths as the story of Romulus and Remus. When the trustee family is strongly patriarchal and patrilineal, the birth of a son is an event of major importance, and the birth of a daughter may be regarded as a misfortune.

Children in the Urban Family

Conditions of urban life and an industrial economy alter markedly the value of children and lower the birth rate. (See POPULATION AND ECOLOGY, pp. 334–35.) Secular values replace sacred values; the living mem-

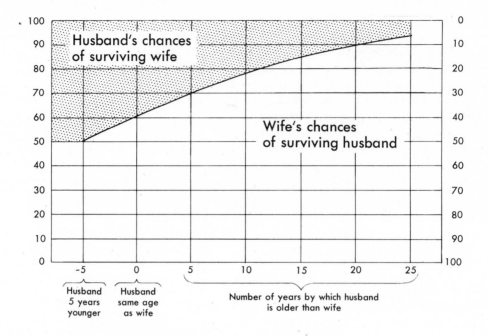

Fig. **X:5** Chances in 100 That a Married Person Will
Survive His or Her Mate

Based on mortality experience, United States, 1950. Adapted from Statistical Bulletin, Metropolitan Life Insurance Co., **34,** No. 9, (September, 1953), 2. Used by
permission.

bers rather than the family line become the
major value; children become economically
a liability rather than an asset. In the industrial economy children can contribute
economically to the family only through
wage employment. Two developments limit
their early contribution: the elaboration and
specialization of culture require a longer
period of education; children become competitors with adults for many types of employment and child labor laws are enacted.
Under these circumstances small families
become the rule, but children are valued in
new ways. In an intensely competitive atmosphere in which most persons hold unattain-
able ambitions, children may be sought in
the hope that unfulfilled ambitions may be
achieved through them. Children also acquire value as a part of the search for primary relations in the urban environment.

The trend of birth rates throughout the
world since World War II suggests that under favorable economic conditions the positive values of children are strong enough to
cause continuing population expansion.

LENGTH OF LIFE AND THE FAMILY

When the extended family is important,
widowhood is less disturbing to an individual's total life pattern than in the predominantly conjugal family system. Under the
conjugal system an individual may be deprived by widowhood of the intimate, mutual aid ties of the family for the rest of his
life. In American society, two facts combine
to make widowhood principally a problem
for the wife rather than the husband. First,
women live longer than men, on the average; second, women usually marry men
older than themselves.

The probability that a woman will outlive her husband is summarized, according to the number of years difference in their ages, in Figure X:5. Only if the husband is five years *younger* than his wife are their chances of surviving even. When husband and wife are of the same age, the chances are three to two that the wife will outlive the husband, and as the age difference increases, the wife's chances of becoming a widow rise steadily.

FAMILY AND LABOR FORCE COMPOSITION

The adult member in the labor force is usually breadwinner for a family. During the last century in America, changes in family structure and changed participation of women in the labor force have gone hand in hand. Traditionally women contributed substantially to the economic resources of the family, not through wages but by making cloth and clothing, producing and preparing food, and many other activities: As women have been stripped of their productiveness by the transfer of many activities to the factory, and as rising consumption standards demanded more money income, women have gone increasingly outside the home to seek employment. The result has been an increase in the number of married women of all ages in the labor force (See Fig. X:6.) In the last seventy years the greatest increase has taken place between the ages of thirty-five and sixty-five. The children of women in this age group are usually in school or independent, so that the mothers are free to seek work.

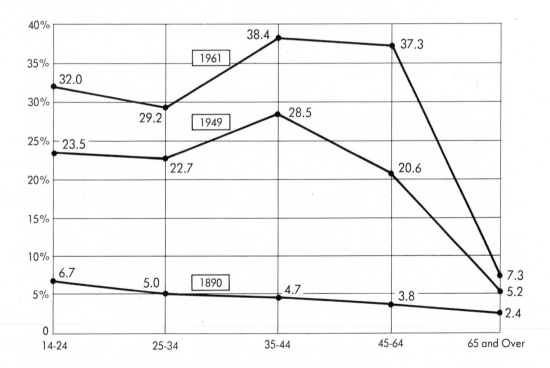

Fig. **X:6** Percentage of Married Women in the Working Force

From A. J. Jaffe and Charles D. Stewart, *Manpower Resources and Utilization* (New York: Wiley, 1951), p. 172. Data for 1961 from U.S. Bureau of Labor Statistics, "Marital and Family Characteristics of Workers, March, 1961," Special Labor Force Report No. 20 from the *Monthly Labor Review*, January, 1961, Table B.

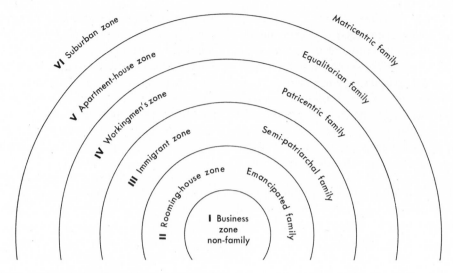

Fig. **X:7** A Theoretical Pattern of Urban Zones
and of Family Types

After Ernest W. Burgess and Harvey J. Locke, *The Family* (New York:
American Book Co., 1953), p. 101. Used by permission.

ECOLOGICAL DISTRIBUTION OF FAMILY TYPES

During the historical period when the influx of foreign migrants of peasant origin was largely shaping the growth of American cities, family patterns in common with other social phenomena were found to be distributed according to approximately concentric zones in some cities. Although the cities of today are greatly changed, abundant traces of the pattern represented in Figure X:7 in idealized form are still to be found. The central business area is the nonfamily area, where unattached men predominate. Adjacent to this area and extending out along major thoroughfares is the mobile population of childless, unstable, emancipated families who live in rooming houses. Next come the immigrant zones, typically spotted throughout the zone in transition, with a characteristic adaptation of the old-world patriarchal peasant family to conditions of urban life. The patriarchal forms are maintained, but the effective extended family cannot be re-established, and the efforts of the father to dominate his children frequently serve merely to drive the children from the family because of their knowledge of more equalitarian American practices. The zone of workingmen's homes preserves the rural patriarchal pattern as its ideal, with little alternative but disorganization for the many families who are unable to conform to the pattern under city conditions. The apartment house area brings the greatest effective equality between mates and between parent and child, but family life tends to be organized about adult interests. In the suburb is found the commuting family with its matricentric pattern.[23]

Ecological analysis is useful in suggesting possible future directions of family development. Certain types, such as the immigrant family, are bound to disappear. General trends of population movement into the city suburbs suggest that the suburbs may

[23] Ernest W. Burgess and Harvey J. Locke, *The Family* (New York: American Book Co., 1953), pp. 100–103.

set the pattern for the nation. There are a number of indications that a special family pattern is emerging in the areas on the outer fringes of the city. There families tend to be larger and to assign more positive value to children than do the central city families. Although large numbers of married and unmarried women are employed, the family still retains modified elements of traditional economic, educational, religious, and other functions. These factors contribute to its stability. In this new family form, the father probably participates more actively in the affairs of the family. He may regain some of his traditional importance within the family and again become the representative of the family in the community.[24]

[24] E. G. Jaco and Ivan Belknap, "Is a New Family Form Emerging in the Urban Fringe?" *American Sociological Review,* **18** (October, 1953), 551–57.

Chapter XI

Religion

With the collaboration of
GERTRUDE JAEGER SELZNICK

Section 1 Introduction

Religious beliefs and practices exist in every known society, from the most simple and isolated to the most complex and urbane. Not all individuals are religious, but some form of religious behavior is found wherever human communities have endured.

As important as the universality of religion is its remarkable diversity. Some religions believe in a single Supreme Being, others are polytheistic. In Buddhism the central figure is a Great Teacher and the idea of a deity is elusive and attenuated. In some preliterate societies religion centers around spirits, forces, and demons that are often capricious, willful, and malevolent.

Religious rituals, emotions, and prescriptions are no less varied than religious beliefs. A ritual may be a ceremony of adoration and supplication addressed to an all-wise and merciful God; it may be a way of propitiating a being who would otherwise bring evil upon the community; it may be solemn and dignified or include dancing, sexual rites, wild celebrations. Religious emotions run the gamut from reverence to terror, joy to self-abasement, ecstasy to peace of mind. Religious prescriptions range from the requirement of ritual murder to the commandment, "Thou shalt not kill."

Early efforts by social science to account for the universality of religion tended to see it as a socially-transmitted relic of man's pre-scientific and primitive past. Religious belief was often interpreted as a kind of error or fancy, traceable to some confusion in the mind of primitive man. For example, the anthropologist E. B. Tylor located the origin of the concept of a soul, and of spirits, in primitive man's attempt to account for his dreams and for death.[1]

Modern social science takes a different approach. The explanation of human religiosity is sought not in error and ignorance, but in certain basic functions which religion serves for the individual and for society. The universality of religion is traced not to man's propensity to make false inferences, but to persistent, recurrent traits of the human condition.

FOUNDATIONS OF RELIGION

The foundations of religion must be sought in psychology as well as in sociology, in the nature of human personality as well as in the requirements of social solidarity.

1. *Overcoming fear and anxiety.* To the

[1] Edward B. Tylor, *Primitive Culture* (London: Murray, 1873), Chap. 11.

extent that man's world is precarious, he must endure and try to overcome both specific fears and more general anxiety. Some of this unease may stem from fear of natural forces and man's sense of his own weakness compared to the overwhelming power around him. And there is always the uncertain certainty of death—when it will come and what it means. Men are made anxious by their social circumstances as well as the physical environment. There are also more general sources of anxiety: man's sense of his finiteness, his limited powers, his dependency, his unsure hold on life.

2. *Self-justification and the quest for a moral identity.* In all societies there is evidence of man's search for moral meaning. He seeks an organizing principle that will justify his most important strivings, and make sense of his sufferings. By providing for these needs, religion helps integrate the personality. The individual can relate his everyday life to larger purposes, can meet frustration with greater equanimity, and can turn potential chaos and meaninglessness into an orderly scheme.

Closely related is man's need to participate in a moral community. The members of such a group feel a deep common bond because they share a belief in what is morally "true." In the moral community the worth of the member is continuously reaffirmed: what he is and what he does is valued for itself and is not a means to some other end.

3. *Celebration of human powers and achievements.* Many religious activities and beliefs reflect self-confidence and pride rather than fear or anxiety. Human well-being seems to be enhanced when men can make the most of their strengths and successes by celebrating them and endowing them with special meaning. A victory dance, the divinity of kings, a belief in being specially chosen for a divine mission—these and many other acts and symbols celebrate man and his group.

4. *Making the world comprehensible.* In all societies, some effort is made to explain and interpret man's environment. This may take the form of a cosmology, explaining the origins of the earth and the heavens; various animals may be seen as mysterious beings whose special qualities of swiftness or cunning need special explanations; the fruitfulness or barrenness of the land, the cycles of birth and death, winter and summer, may all be represented in a more or less elaborate theology or mythology. This process of interpretation reflects an impulse to make the world more comprehensible, more familiar, and more meaningful. It is also another way of relieving anxiety.

5. *Supporting social norms and values.* Society depends on the willing co-operation of its members. For the most part, this co-operation is won through the process of socialization. But socialization is always to some degree ineffective. The socializers need all the help they can get, particularly when a large amount of self-discipline is required. By adding a divine sanction to human values, religion can effectively win compliance with the norms of society.

This classification of personal and social needs and desires does not include everything that may evoke a religious response. However, the list does cover the major sources of religious experience that have been identified and analyzed. It is obvious that not all men or groups have these requirements or motivations in the same degree. In some societies or historical periods, religion may be largely a way of handling fears; at another time or place the significant source of religion might be the quest for a moral identity, the celebration of human achievement, or the effort to make the world comprehensible.

An understanding of the variety of problems that tend to produce religious responses leads us away from any effort to locate the origin of religion in some single factor. Religion is not a unique response to a unique problem. It is a way of meeting many different problems.

It should be understood that religion is

only one of the alternative ways of overcoming anxiety, integrating personality, supporting social norms, or satisfying the other conditions mentioned above. Religion is summoned and sustained by these requirements, but other social institutions, such as politics, education, science, and the arts, serve many of the same ends. Religion supplements these other social devices, sometimes competes with them, and often fills the breach when they are absent or inadequate. Supporters of religion believe that it alone can meet the most essential personal needs and that without religion the moral foundations of society will wither.

THE BASIC RESPONSE

Thus far the characteristics of persons and groups that give rise to religion have been discussed. But what is the nature of the religious response? Many sociologists believe that the core of religion may be found in the creation of the sacred. The basic religious response consists in man's relating himself to what he recognizes as the sacred or in the transformation of what is profane and secular into what is sacred or holy.

When something is made sacred, it is invested with a special meaning or worth, treated with reverence, awe, and respect. Anything can be made sacred: a mountain, a part of the human body, a belief, a meeting place, an animal, a cup of oil or water. But if it is sacred, it must be perceived as in some way differentiated from the everyday world. What is sacred is not a mere means or instrument. Though it may be used in a ceremony, it is itself a thing apart toward which proper respect is due.

Sometimes the sacred is created by endowing parts of the world with a special and mysterious power. This does not necessarily involve a belief in particular gods or spirits. Thus the idea of *mana,* associated with the peoples of Polynesia and Melanesia, refers to an impersonal power that may be located in any object—a song, a man, a plant, a stone.

The essential point is that mana is extraordinary power and produces extraordinary results.

If a man's pigs multiply and his gardens are productive, it is not because he is industrious and looks after his property, but because of the stones full of mana for pigs and yams that he possesses. Of course a yam naturally grows when planted, that is well known, but it will not be very large unless mana comes into play: a canoe will not be swift unless mana be brought to bear upon it, a net will not catch many fish, nor an arrow inflict a mortal wound.[2]

Mana sets things apart and gives them a special significance. It transcends the ordinary. Therefore the principle of mana is a long step toward the creation of a sacred realm, even though all the attitudes usually associated with sacredness may not be present.

The recognition or creation of sacredness lays a foundation for faith and moral commitment. What is sacred has a special claim to respect and obedience. Because it is a special realm, the sacred may offer a new vision and a new truth unlimited by the criteria of the common-sense world.

To recognize, create, elaborate, and protect the sacred is the distinctive competence of religion. However, other institutions also participate in these tasks. The political community creates sacred documents and symbols, such as the Constitution, the Flag, and the Founding Fathers. Similarly, the culture can lend an air of sacredness to basic values, such as Motherhood and the Preservation of Human Life. Whatever its source, the more sacred any act or belief, the more likely it is to take on a religious quality. Thus religious institutions specialize in the sacred. And other institutions tend to become religious when they too engage in the basic religious response—the creation of the sacred.

[2] R. H. Codrington, "Mana," in W. A. Lessa and E. Z. Vogt, *Reader in Comparative Religion* (Evanston: Row, Peterson, 1958), p. 207.

Street scene in the holy Hindu city of Benares, India: A woman offers to a cow cakes prepared and sold to pilgrims for this purpose. The cow is worshiped by Hindus as a source of life, and its slaughter is forbidden.

THE ELEMENTS OF RELIGION

In the study of religion, it is necessary to distinguish the following elements or components: [3]

1. *Ritual*. All religions observe ceremonial practices or rituals. Religious rituals are prescribed acts that are sacred in themselves and also symbolize the sacred. Among Christians, the communion service is sacred and also symbolizes the sacrifice of Christ.

The ritualization of behavior is one mechanism by which sacredness is created and sustained. A way of making baskets, a family gathering, or any other socially important practice may, by being ritualized, become set apart as sacred. At the same time, whatever is sacred tends to be ritualized. In its origin the ritual practice may be simply a way of co-ordinating activity and creating respect for the group and its traditions. But as the practice takes on more symbolic meaning and is connected with other religious acts and symbols, people come to think of it, and act toward it, as a religious ceremony.

2. *Feeling*. One of the functions of ritual is to evoke appropriate feelings. The patriotic rite brings forth loyalty, pride, and a sense of closeness to one's fellow-countrymen. In this

[3] For a discussion of dimensions of "religiosity" see C. Y. Glock, "On the Study of Religious Commitment," *Religious Education*, Research Supplement, **42** (July-August, 1962), 98–110.

way the sacredness of the nation and of civic identity is affirmed. Religious emotions are not fundamentally different; they are appropriate to whatever is most sacred in the society. The religious emotion called for depends on the nature of the ceremony and of what is symbolized by it. Humility, reverence, and awe are common religious feelings, but ecstasy or terror may also be displayed. Whatever the feeling, it is prescribed as appropriate, it is expected, and it is stimulated and supported by the resources and techniques of the religion.

3. *Belief.* Conceivably, religious ritual and feeling may occur prior to, and independently of, specifically religious ideas.[4] However, in almost all societies, there is a clear emergence of beliefs that justify and support religious rituals and feelings. Moreover, beliefs have their own powerful role to play in the creation of sacredness and in meeting the human problems to which religion is a response.

In the past religious beliefs have almost always involved some notion of the supernatural. Divine beings are not of this world but "exist" outside it or above it. They are not subject to the ordinary limitations of man and beast. This strain toward the supernatural can probably be explained by reference to the functions of religion. Supernatural beings and forces can be invoked to explain natural events and thus make the world more comprehensible. They can provide a symbolic focus of unlimited power and understanding to which finite man can attach himself. Perhaps most important, a belief in supernatural power and in a supernatural realm supports the norms and values of the moral community on earth.

In theory, however, religion can exist without a belief in supernatural beings. A set of Great Truths or Principles may be given a sacred status around which a system of auxiliary beliefs and practices is organized.

The *quality* of belief may vary as well as the *content.* Some members of a religious group may be dedicated believers; others may believe in a routine way; others may "believe" in an ambiguous and detached way. Some may try to reinterpret religious doctrines so as to make them compatible with other beliefs, such as the findings of science. They may emphasize the symbolic significance of beliefs and thus avoid taking literally views about an afterlife or the origins of the universe.

4. *Organization.* Religious activities usually form the basis of a community of believers. This can take various forms, as is discussed in Section 7. Organization is needed to maintain beliefs and traditions, to conduct religious assemblies where belief and feeling are reinforced, to recruit and train specialists in religious ritual and doctrine, and to deal with the relations between the religious group and the rest of the society. In homogenous and undifferentiated societies a special religious organization may not appear. In that case other institutions of the tribe or village do the needed organizational work; the religious group is coextensive with the community.

Following Emile Durkheim, "a religion" may be defined as a *unified system of beliefs and practices relative to sacred things, uniting into a single moral community all those who adhere to those beliefs and practices.*[5] It is important to recognize, however, that any given religion is made up of a special combination of the components mentioned above—ritual, feeling, belief, and organization. Some religions may be strong on organization but make few demands on feeling; others may emphasize ritual but not belief. In comparing religions one must specify what components, or combination of them, are being considered.

The same caution applies when the follow-

See Clyde Kluckhohn, "Myths and Rituals: A General Theory," *Harvard Theological Review,* **35** (January, 1942), 45–79.

[5] Emile Durkheim, *The Elementary Forms of the Religious Life* (Glencoe: The Free Press, 1947), p. 47. (First published in 1912).

ing questions are asked: Who is more religious? Are people becoming more or less religious? Is religion declining or gaining strength? Unless the basis of comparison is specified, incorrect conclusions will be drawn. For example, an observed strengthening of religious organization, measured by increased membership, funds, or buildings, may or may not be associated with a strengthening of religious belief or feeling.

SOURCES AND READINGS

Michael Argyle, *Religious Behavior* (London: Routledge & Kegan Paul, 1958).

Emile Durkheim, *The Elementary Forms of the Religious Life* (Glencoe: The Free Press, 1947).

Sigmund Freud, *The Future of an Illusion* (London: Hogarth, 1928).

William J. Goode, *Religion Among the Primitives* (Glencoe: The Free Press, 1951).

Thomas Ford Hoult, *The Sociology of Religion* (New York: Dryden, 1958).

William A. Lessa and Evon Z. Vogt, *Reader in Comparative Religion* (Evanston: Row, Peterson, 1958).

Glenn M. Vernon, *Sociology of Religion* (New York: McGraw-Hill, 1962).

Max Weber's studies in the sociology of religion include *The Protestant Ethic and the Spirit of Capitalism* (London: George Allen & Unwin, 1930); *The Religion of China, The Religion of India, Ancient Judaism* (published by The Free Press of Glencoe, 1951, 1958, 1958, respectively).

J. Milton Yinger, *Religion, Society and the Individual* (New York: Macmillan, 1957).

Section 2 **Social organization**

During most of a man's history, religion has not been "just another institution." It has been looked to as the sanctifier of human activities, the protector of group continuity, the builder of morale and solidarity, the bridge across whatever divides man from man and group from group. However, the extent to which these functions are performed, and *how* they are performed, depends on the place of religion within the social structure.

FUSION OF RELIGION AND GROUP LIFE

In ancient Greece and Rome, religious practices and beliefs were an inseparable part of family and civic life. Religion was, at first, a religion of family and hearth. A sacred fire burned at an altar in every house, and care was taken that it should not be extinguished. Family ancestors were venerated and the head of the household was its priest. The gods of the family were their own particular gods. The family, in other words, was a religious unit.

In his classic work, *The Ancient City,* the French historian Fustel de Coulanges (1830–1889) spoke of religion as the "constituent principle" of the family in early Greece and Rome.[6] By this he meant that common worship was the foundation of family life and the criterion of membership. A son was no longer counted part of the family if he renounced the worship. An adopted son, on the other hand, "was counted a real son, because, though he had not the ties of blood, he had something better—a community of worship. . . . A family was a group of persons whom religion permitted to invoke the same sacred fire, and to offer the funeral repast to the same ancestors."[7]

The special character of this domestic religion influenced other aspects of social life. For example, it helps explain why these communities, in contrast to others, held the idea of private property in land. The hearth was

---

[6] Fustel de Coulanges, *The Ancient City: A Study on the Religion, Laws, and Institutions of Greece and Rome* (New York: Anchor, 1956), p. 40.

[7] *Ibid.*, p. 42.

perceived as permanent, remaining forever on the same site, establishing an intimate and mysterious connection with the soil. The gods thereby "owned" the soil; but the family "owned" its gods. For this reason, among others, there developed a strong identification between a particular family and its land.

The Enlargement of Religious Identity

If each family has its own god or gods, there are many gods. When common worship is the foundation of group identity, such extreme polytheism is inconsistent with the enlargement of the group beyond the boundaries of the family. In early Greece and Rome, this problem was eased in two ways. First, the family religion began to include *gods of nature*—representations of the sea, the sun, the forest, etc.—as well as deified ancestors. The gods of nature were universal and could be shared with other families. Secondly, given this possibility, the mutiplicity of gods could be modified when one family and its nature god attained a special influence:

It happened, in the course of time, the divinity of a family having acquired great prestige over the imaginations of men, and appearing powerful in proportion to the prosperity of this family, that a whole city wished to adopt him, and offer him public worship, to obtain his favors. This was the case with the Demeter of the Eumolpidae, the Athene of the Butadae, and the Hercules of the Potitii. But when a family consented thus to share a god, it retained at least the priesthood. We may remark that the dignity of priest, for each god, was during a long time hereditary, and could not go out of a certain family. This is a vestige of a time when the god himself was the property of this family; when he protected it alone, and would be served only by it.[8]

As families united into tribes and tribes into a city, religion remained both symbol and bond of the new association. The union was marked by appropriate ceremonies, such as the lighting of a sacred fire, and by adoption of a common religion. Unification was helped when the image of the divine transcended the particularity of family and place. Ultimately, universal religions were founded on principles and symbols common to all mankind.

When religious identity and social identity are fused, we speak of *communal* religion. In a communal religion a person is considered a believer, or member of the religious community, by virtue of his membership in a family, clan, city, or state. He is born into the religion, and if he renounces it, he thereby renounces his social group. It is said that in the communal religion of ancient China, "there was no choice in religious beliefs, but neither did it occur to the common man to make any other choice. Religious values were imbedded in the traditional moral order, and religion was an integral part of communal existence, inseparable from the individual's existence." [9]

One mark of communal religion is the combination of religious and secular roles. In a family-based communal religion the father is also the priest and the home is the temple. In the broader city-based communal religion political and religious authority are combined. High priest, judge, and political chief are often one.

RELIGION DIFFERENTIATED FROM OTHER INSTITUTIONS

A fundamental historical trend is the differentiation of institutions. As societies become larger and more complex, activities become more specialized. Different functions are disentangled and become lodged in distinct institutions.

The emergence of religion as a separate institutional sphere is stimulated and supported by the following mechanisms:

1. *Voluntary religious affiliation.* When religious identity is based on voluntary

---

[8] *Ibid.*, p. 125.

[9] C. K. Yang, *Religion in Chinese Society* (Berkeley and Los Angeles: University of California Press, 1961), p. 111.

choice rather than inherited status, there is a push toward differentiation. Members of the same family may adhere to different faiths. In self-defense a new faith often dissociates itself from politics. Thus early Christianity sought to distinguish what belonged to God and to Caesar; it proclaimed itself "not of this world"; it remained for many years separate from and an irritation to the political order. Thus the emergence of a new perspective—the possibility of being converted to a new faith as an individual and by free choice—helped lay the foundation for institutional differentiation.

2. *A religious officialdom.* Even when a religion is closely integrated with the political order, and membership is not voluntary, differentiation does occur. In a complex community the priesthood becomes a specialized activity. The community delegates to a high priest or archbishop the responsibility and authority for religious affairs and for ruling a church hierarchy. The mere existence of this religious officialdom creates a vested interest and a distinct occupational community. The churchmen are jealous of their privileges, and protective of the special values entrusted to them. The result is a greater religious self-consciousness and lines are drawn between religion and other institutional spheres.

3. *Independence of nonreligious activities.* When religion is fused with the social order, it not only serves other institutions—it also controls them. As society becomes more differentiated, the worlds of science, art, education, law, and economics seek freedom to develop on their own. They encourage the perception of religion as a specialized sphere and set limits to the scope of religious authority.

The differentiation of religion does not necessarily keep it from influencing the secular order. Indeed, the very autonomy of religion may give it a sense of mission and make it a source of creativity. Because they are not fused with the rest of society, religious

leaders can develop their own ideas of what the social world should be like and try to influence that world.

The social influence of religion is not always planned or self-conscious. The Protestant Reformation had a considerable but unintended impact on the development of capitalism. (See INDUSTRIAL MAN, pp. 629–32.)

RELIGION AND SOCIAL COHESION

From the standpoint of its role in society, one of the great potential capabilities of religion is the promotion of group cohesion. Emile Durkheim was so impressed by this that he built his theory of religion on it. "The idea of society," he wrote, "is the soul of religion." [10]

Durkheim sought to cut through variations in religious rites, symbols, and beliefs to find the most fundamental characteristic of all religions.

There is something eternal in religion which is destined to survive all the particular symbols in which religious thought has successively enveloped itself. There can be no society which does not feel the need of upholding and reaffirming at regular intervals the collective sentiments and the collective ideas which make its unity and its personality. Now this moral remaking cannot be achieved except by the means of reunions, assemblies and meetings where the individuals, being closely united to one another, reaffirm in common their common sentiments . . . . What essential difference is there between an assembly of Christians celebrating the principal dates of the life of Christ, or of Jews remembering the exodus from Egypt or the promulgation of the decalogue, and a reunion of citizens commemorating the promulgation of a new moral or legal system or some great event in the national life? [11]

In all of these activities Durkheim located one basic function: the celebration of the social group, be it a clan or a larger commu-

10 Durkheim, *op. cit.*, p. 419.
11 *Ibid.*, p. 427.

nity. By such celebrations the individual is bound into a group which he needs and which needs him. The symbols of religion, he thought, really represent society. "The god of the clan, the totemic principle, can therefore be nothing else than the clan itself, personified and represented to the imagination under the visible form of the animal or vegetable which serves as totem." [12] Religious worship is, in effect, worship of society.

Limitations of Durkheim's Theory

Durkheim based his analysis on anthropological reports of religion in preliterate societies, especially in Australia. However, he did not restrict his conclusions to those or similar societies. He thought he had found the fundamental significance of all religion.

As a generalization, Durkheim's view needs the following qualifications:

1. It is wrong to ignore the varied *content* of religious beliefs and symbols. Divine ancestors, or totems, may indeed be interpreted as standing for the family or clan. In such cases, it is probably correct to say that the group itself is worshiped. However, many religious ideas go beyond representation of the group. They may contain special moral principles, such as the Christian idea of self-sacrificing love. The closeness of the relation between religious symbolism and the celebration of the group should be considered a *variable*. In domestic or communal religions this relation is more marked than it is in complex and differentiated religions.

2. Not all religious experience can be understood from the standpoint of its contribution to social solidarity. The quest for salvation may be an individual act and may lead to a weakening of group ties. Religious withdrawal from society is not uncommon. The Protestant reformers emphasized man's lonely vigil: "His life is that of a soldier in a hostile territory." [13]

3. While all religion does contribute, at least to some extent, to the cohesion *of the believers,* religion does not always help integrate the entire community. Again, it is necessary to distinguish between simpler and more complex societies. Religion can be a *divisive* force when a number of different religious groups compete for communicants or when religion struggles with other institutions, such as the government, for pre-eminence. In the latter case, of course, religion is neither more nor less divisive than the other institutions.

Religious pluralism in the United States has raised many issues, especially those affecting the relation between Church and State. For example, the present public policy, as expressed by the United States Supreme Court, fosters the separation of public education and religion. It presumes that in a religiously heterogeneous society, social cohesion will be fostered if religious activity, however minor, is divorced from government sponsorship. There is question to what extent the Court's judgment on the issue of religion in the schools reflects public opinion.

[12] *Ibid.,* p. 206.

[13] R. H. Tawney, *Religion and the Rise of Capitalism* (New York: Penguin, 1947), p. 190.

Section 3   Culture

In studying culture, sociologists emphasize its significance as a normative order, a design for living. This important emphasis is the main approach to culture in this book. However, culture also includes those activities, and their products, that express the

From the symbolic to representational in religious art. Left, The Last Judgment *(1130–1140), sculptured relief above the west door of St. Lazare Cathedral, Autun, France.* Right, Christ the Teacher *(1205–1215), south portal, Notre-Dame Cathedral, Chartres.*

values and perspectives of the society. Some pursuits—notably philosophy, literature, and the arts—are important vehicles of cultural expression. They formulate, embody, and interpret the values and outlooks of a society. Religion is part of this expressive realm. It gives content and direction to the arts.

RELIGION AND ART

The connection between culture and aesthetic creativity is nowhere more evident than in religious art. Although painters, sculptors, and architects have left the most visible monuments, music, dance, poetry, and drama have also served religious ends and been sensitive to religious influences.

The intimate relation between religion and art may be accounted for, at least in part, by the importance of *symbolism* in religion. In most religions, symbols are much in evi-

dence. They dramatize belief; they inspire reverence or fear; they form the stuff of which ceremonies are made. The true significance of a symbol lies not in its literal meaning or form but in what it connotes and suggests. A king's crown is not a mere ornament but a symbol of sovereignty and authority; that the crown is placed upon his head by a high priest may symbolize the importance and autonomy of the church. Thus acts as well as artifacts have symbolic meaning.

Although the religious symbol has a use in a larger setting, it is more than a practical instrument or tool. When a book, a cup, a picture, or a way of kneeling takes on symbolic significance, it becomes an *expressive* product. By the very way it is constructed or handled, it is meant to convey sacred meanings and to evoke appropriate emotions. In the construction of such symbols, the artist has a special place. His craftsmanship can embellish acts and objects so as to enhance their function as symbolic carriers of sacred meanings.

Because a religious object is symbolic rather than utilitarian, the artist is free to exploit the expressive potentialities of his medium, whether it be clay, paint, or language. Though he may have to work within a definite, prescribed religious tradition, the artist is not expected to represent everyday reality or to evoke everyday feelings. Since distortion evokes "strange" feelings, and places the object outside everyday reality, distortion is a common feature of religious art. But distortion for the sake of expressiveness is one of the main devices of aesthetic creativity.

Religion may offer the artist a congenial framework within which to develop his talents and express his personal vision. From the standpoint of the culture, the Greek emphasis on portraying the gods was more than a celebration of religion. It was also a kind of language, a source of known and shared meanings. For the artist this solved many problems of communication with his public. At the same time, the religious context was a rich source of ideas and starting-points for creative work. The artist served religion while he drew upon it for inspiration.

Religious Orientation and Art Styles

Historians of art have examined the relation between specific religious beliefs and the art styles of particular cultures or epochs.[14] For example, Egyptian religion was a "funerary" religion, centered around the dead and the desire to assure them immortality. The Egyptian art that has come down to us is largely tomb art.

[14] See Alessandro Della Seta, *Religion and Art* (New York: Scribner's, 1914); E. H. Gombrich, *The Story of Art* (Greenwich, Conn.: Phaidon, 1961); Edith Hamilton, *The Greek Way to Western Civilization* (New York: Mentor, 1948); Arnold Hauser, *The Social History of Art* (New York: Vintage, 1957); Emile Male, *Religious Art* (New York: Noonday, 1958); Andre Malraux, *The Metamorphosis of the Gods* (New York: Doubleday, 1960).

The static quality of Egyptian painting and the fixed remoteness and weighted ponderosity of Egyptian sculpture have been attributed to the preoccupation of Egyptian religion with death and immortality. The art style seems to strive for a sense of timelessness, transcending the present, looking to the eternity of past and future.

The religions of the ancient East emphasized the unreality of this world and preached spiritual detachment from the present. This may have been a response to the brevity and misery of most human life. Salvation was to be sought in a world beyond; the religious experience was pre-eminently a quest for mystic union with the Infinite; the seen world was but illusion. This orientation had a great influence on the art of the East, producing not only the remote, abstract, and stylized Egyptian works but also the complex, mystic patterns of Hindu art. The variations are enormous, but there is a common theme: the seen world is not to be copied or glorified; it is but a starting-point for the artist's vision of a realm of spirit.

Buddhism, which conceives nature as animated by an immanent force, which force is the one order to which the whole universe conforms, must inevitably affect the whole basis of art, insofar as art is a representation of reality or of the super-reality behind natural appearances. The quality which strikes us most in Buddhism is resignation; the submission of the individual to this all-forming spirit, this destiny. The artist shares that humility, and his only desire is to enter into communion with that universal spirit. This desire has all sorts of consequences: it leads to a preference for landscape-painting above figure-painting . . . . Nature is more sublime, nearer to the universal essence, than humanity. But what the artist sees of nature he realizes is only the deceptive outward appearance of things. He will therefore not strive to imitate the exact appearance, but rather to express the spirit.[15]

In ancient Greece, on the other hand, the

[15] Herbert Read, *Art and Society* (London: Faber and Faber, 1945), p. 53.

artist's studio "was not a lonely cave of meditation but the world of moving life." [16] In its classic form the religion of the Greeks did not demand or even encourage a flight from humanity or from what was possible in this world. The Greeks sought the divine in man and in what he could do. Perfection and excellence could make the merely human into something closer to the gods. "Through perfected mortality man was immortal." [17]

Christianity followed hard upon the civilizations of Greece and Rome, but its religious art broke with the tradition that idealized man and his works. For almost a thousand years, from the fifth century to the fifteenth, Christian art turned its back on the representation of reality and sought to glorify God in abstract, stylized, and symbolic forms.[18] The apparent primitiveness and crudeness of early Christian art cannot be attributed solely to lack of skill. A religious impulse drove the artist to disregard representation and direct his attention to the world of the spirit. In depicting that world, the presentation of symbols is more important than the reproduction of exact or even idealized men, animals, or objects.

Tension between Religion and Art

The alliance between religion and art has been both uneasy and intimate. Religion can inhibit the full development of the aesthetic impulse by restricting the artist to a narrow range of forms, materials, and modes of expression. Art in its turn can corrupt religious practice by encouraging idolatry and profanation of the sacred.

Art serves religion by creating visible symbols of man's faith in the invisible. But it is easy to confuse the symbol with what is symbolized, and to worship the representation rather than what is represented. This risk is important to a religion that seeks to convey the idea of a universal and invisible

deity whose spirit is present everywhere.

The Old Testament condemns idolatry, the worship of objects as if they themselves were divine. So great was the horror of idol worship among the ancient Hebrews that the Second Commandment forbids the making of "any graven image or any likeness of anything that is in heaven above or that is in the earth beneath, or that is in the water under the earth." As a result of this orientation, the plastic arts did not develop among the Jews until recent times.

The early Christians shared this fear of idolatry. As Christianity grew in power, debates arose as to how to decorate the churches being built throughout Europe and the Near East. Lifelike sculptures were outlawed as bordering on "graven images" but there was much disagreement concerning painting. During the sixth century Pope Gregory the Great formulated the early policy of the Roman Catholic Church. He argued that many people could not read or write and that pictures in the churches would teach them the history and substance of the Christian faith. He said: "Painting can do for the illiterate what writing does for those who can read." [19]

Disagreement over religious art was a serious problem in both the Eastern Church and Western Catholicism. The Eastern Church, centered in Byzantium (Constantinople) contained a strong faction of iconoclasts, or "image smashers," who gained power in the eighth century and forbade religious art in the Eastern churches. A century later the iconoclasts lost control and the policy of the Eastern Church was revised. The new doctrine went beyond that of Pope Gregory. The Eastern churchmen argued that religious art was holy, and that Christians could worship God through visible images without committing the sin of idolatry.[20] In time the Roman Catholic Church in the West took on somewhat the same point of

[16] Edith Hamilton, *op. cit.*, p. 32.
[17] *Ibid.*, p. 37.
[18] See Hauser, *op. cit.*, Vol. I, pp. 121 ff.

[19] Gombrich, *op. cit.*, p. 95.
[20] *Ibid.*, p. 97.

view and even relaxed the ban on sculpture.

Especially during the late Middle Ages the Roman Catholic Church was plagued by the charge of idolatry. It took considerable sophistication to distinguish between worship of God, worship of Mary, and worship of a particular image of the Madonna and Child portrayed in paint or in stone. The Protestant Reformation made idolatry a major charge against the Church, and many Protestant sects took a radical stand against all religious art.

In the sixteenth century, during the Catholic Counter-Reformation, the Council of Trent reaffirmed the position of the Church favoring images and paintings as the Bible of the illiterate. The Council ordained that

. . . the images of Christ, of the Virgin Mother of God, and of the other saints are to be placed and retained especially in the churches, and that due honor and veneration is to be given them; not, however, that any divinity or virtue is believed to be in them by reason of which they are to be venerated, or that something is to be asked of them, or that trust is to be placed in images, as was done of old by the Gentiles who placed their hope in idols; but because the honor which is shown them is referred to the prototypes which they represent, so that by means of the images which we kiss and before which we uncover our heads and prostrate ourselves, we adore Christ and venerate the saints whose likeness they bear. [21]

In his classic, *The Waning of the Middle Ages,* Huizinga discusses the role of the religious image in the profanation of the sacred during the centuries immediately preceding the Renaissance and the Protestant Reformation. According to Huizinga, one consequence of the profuse use of vivid representations of Jesus, Mary, the saints, the prophets, the tortures of Hell, the Trinity, and the Crucifixion, was to make familiar and commonplace what should be mysterious, remote, revered, respected. Religion

and religious imagery began to invade all of life until there was little distinction between the sacred and the profane.

All life was saturated with religion to such an extent that the people were . . . in danger of losing sight of the distinction between things spiritual and things temporal. . . . In the Middle Ages the demarcation of the sphere of religious thought and that of worldly concerns was nearly obliterated. It occasionally happened that indulgences figured among the prizes of a lottery. When a prince was making a solemn entry, the altars at the corners of the streets, loaded with the precious reliquaries of the town and served by prelates, might be seen alternating with dumb shows of pagan goddesses or comic allegories. . . . Till late in the sixteenth century profane melodies might be used indiscriminately for sacred use, and sacred for profane. It is notorious that Guillaume Dufay and others composed masses to the themes of love-songs. . . . [22]

By the late Middle Ages artists were themselves introducing a profane or secular element into religious art, foreshadowing the eventual independence of art from religion. This secular element consisted of the freer manipulation of the artist's medium for aesthetic purposes and for the expression of human emotion and temporal reality. Religious sculpture was already becoming more supple and lifelike, less stiff and stylized, more dynamic and rounded, closer to portrait than symbol. Religious art began to point less to the realm of the divine and called more attention to itself and its own virtuosity. During the Renaissance great painters continued to work for the Church and to paint religious subjects. But they introduced the classical imagery of Greece into Christian art, and technical problems of space, color, and composition began to predominate over expressions of religious piety and the evocation of religious faith. Great religious art disappeared, to be replaced by great works of art which happened to have religious

[21] E. G. Holt (ed.), *A Documentary History of Art* (New York: Anchor, 1958), Vol. II, p. 64.

[22] J. Huizinga, *The Waning of the Middle Ages* (New York: Anchor, 1954), pp. 156 f.

figures and episodes as their subjects.

In summary, two sources of tension between religion and art are (1) the risk of idolatry, and (2) the risk of profanation, especially the weakening of religious values and their subordination to aesthetic ends.

Section 4 **Socialization**

The function of religion is not only to make people religious but to help socialize them into the secular order. While the other-worldly ideals of religion can provide the individual with a perspective from which to criticize the secular order, religion serves more often to reconcile the individual to it. Religion helps make the secular order acceptable to the individual in several basic ways. (1) By casting an aura of sanctity over such social institutions as the state and the family, religion enhances the legitimacy of their authority. (2) By reinforcing ethical norms with supernatural sanctions, religion aids in the acceptance and internalization of those norms. (3) By providing religious rewards and consolations to offset secular failure and personal tragedy, religion facilitates the continuous adaptation of the individual to the circumstances of his life.

RELIGION AND PERSONAL AUTONOMY

Christianity is sometimes said to have an overly "domesticating" influence on the individual because of its strong emphasis on the virtues of obedience, humility, submission to earthly authority, and resignation to one's fate in this world.[23] Catholicism is thought to exert an especially strong influence in this direction. (1) By emphasizing the Sacraments as the avenue to salvation,

[23] See Friedrich Nietzsche, "The Genealogy of Morals," in *The Philosophy of Nietzsche* (New York: The Modern Library, 1927), pp. 616–807. On the other hand, Christian thinkers emphasize the influence of Christianity on the development of freedom and respect for the individual in the Western world. See, for example, G. K. Chesterton, *The Everlasting Man* (Garden City: Doubleday, Image, 1955).

Table **XI:1**   Percentage Valuing Autonomy above Obedience by Class and Religion *

Class[a] and Religion	Per Cent	Number of Cases
Upper-middle-class		
Protestants	90	(48)
Catholics	70	(27)
Lower-middle-class		
Protestants	72	(65)
Catholics	63	(59)
Upper-working-class		
Protestants	66	(79)
Catholics	51	(77)
Lower-working-class		
Protestants	48	(66)
Catholics	38	(53)

* Adapted from Gerhard Lenski, *The Religious Factor* (Garden City: Doubleday, 1961), p. 201. Data for Jews and Negroes are omitted.

[a] The middle class is divided on the basis of income, with those earning $8,000 or more classified as upper-middle-class. The same is true of the working class, with $5,000 per year income for the family head providing the cutting point.

Catholicism stresses the dependence of its adherents on the Church as an institution. (2) The Catholic Church allows the layman no active direction in the affairs of his church. (3) The Catholic Church exercises authority in matters of morals—for example, divorce and birth control—that many American Protestants and Jews regard as subjects for individual decision.

A 1958 study of a sample of Detroit adults investigated whether American Catholics value "intellectual autonomy" less than do American Protestants.[24] Respondents were

[24] Gerhard Lenski, *The Religious Factor* (Garden City: Doubleday, 1961).

asked which was most important for a child to learn: to obey, to be popular, to think for himself, to work hard, or to help others. On every class level more Protestants than Catholics chose "to think for himself." However, as Table XI:1 shows, class status was far more important than religion. Upper-middle-class individuals tended predominantly to value intellectual autonomy over obedience *regardless of religion*; the figure was 90 per cent for the 48 upper-middle-class Protestants in the sample and 70 per cent for the 27 upper-class Catholics. In the lower-working-class group, regardless of religion, a majority valued obedience over intellectual autonomy. Thus, in their respect for intellectual autonomy, upper-middle-class Catholics resembled upper-middle-class Protestants more closely than they resembled their lower-working-class coreligionists. Furthermore, the proportion of Catholics valuing intellectual autonomy over obedience was higher at each higher step in socio-economic status.

A second study based on a larger sample —more than 2,000 graduate students in the arts and sciences—investigated the extent to which religious affiliation was related to the desire for personal and creative autonomy in an occupation.[25] Students were asked how important it was to them that a job pro-

vide them with an opportunity to be creative and original, to be free from supervision, and to be free from pressure to conform in their personal lives. Students who rated at least two of these job characteristics as very important were classified as "self-expressive" or autonomous in their work orientation.

At first sight, the results seem to support the view that Catholicism discourages the desire for autonomy more than does Protestantism or Judaism. (See the column at the left in Table XI:2.) However, when church attendance is taken into account, it becomes apparent that *practicing* Catholics, Protestants, and Jews resemble each other more than they resemble their less active coreligionists. Regardless of religious affiliation, the desire for autonomy in a job was uniformly less frequent among religiously observant students than among students who reported that they occasionally or never attend services. Analysis appears, then, to support the conclusion that it is observance of one's religion rather than specific religious adherence that is associated with lack of desire for personal autonomy in an occupation.

The study found, however, that virtually all Catholic students in the sample, many of whom were attending Catholic universities, attended church regularly. Of the 555 Catho-

[25] Joe L. Spaeth, "Value Orientations and Academic Career Plans: Structural Effects on the Careers of Graduate Students." (Unpublished Ph.D. dissertation, University of Chicago, 1961).

Table **XI:2**   Per Cent of Graduate Students Desiring Personal Autonomy in a Job by Current Religious Preference*

Current Religion		Attend Church			
		Frequently		Occasionally or Never	
None	56%	——[a]		56%	(676)[b]
Jewish	48%	33%	(24)[b]	50%	(216)
Protestant	37%	31%	(514)	42%	(497)
Catholic	28%	26%	(508)	53%	(47)

* Adapted from Joe L. Spaeth, "Value Orientations and Academic Career Plans: Structural Effects on the Careers of Graduate Students." (Unpublished Ph.D. dissertation, University of Chicago, 1961).
[a] There were no cases of frequent church attendance among students with no current religious preference.
[b] Numbers in parentheses show number of cases.

lic students, 92 per cent were regular attenders; of the 1,011 Protestants, 52 per cent were regular attenders; of the 240 Jewish students, 10 per cent were regular attenders.

Taken together, the above studies suggest the following tentative conclusions: (1) The desire for personal autonomy is influenced more by degree of religious involvement than by specific religious affiliation. Being religiously observant has a generally restraining influence on the desire for personal autonomy, whether the individual is Catholic, Protestant, or Jewish. (2) Though Catholics tend to desire personal autonomy less frequently than Protestants, and Protestants less frequently than Jews, the differences are not great, especially when religious observance and social class are taken into account.

Cautions: 1. While frequent church attendance and a high degree of religious commitment appear to be associated with lack of desire for personal autonomy, they may be associated with other norms of positive value to the individual and the community.

2. Religious affiliation is so closely related to cultural factors—for example ethnic origin—that it is extremely difficult to isolate the influence of religion *per se* upon attitudes and behavior. For example, one study found that Protestant and Jewish mothers expected their children to show "independence" at an earlier age than Catholics.[26] However, among the Catholic mothers, those of Irish ancestry looked for signs of independence a full year earlier than did those of Italian ancestry. In this case cultural factors appear to play at least as important a role as religious affiliation.

CONVERSION AND ASSIMILATION

Most religious bodies rely upon gradual assimilation of the individual into the church through childhood indoctrination into the tenets of the faith and early participation in church activities and ritual. No special signs of faith or belief are looked for beyond ritual observance and assent to basic doctrine. Members are rarely called on to question the depth and authenticity of their subjective faith. Regular religious observance rather than strong religious emotion is emphasized as the way to sustain a religious outlook.

While gradual assimilation into religious belief and practice is the usual process, some branches of American Protestantism stress the need for a "conversion experience," i.e., a single intensely emotional episode in which the individual "takes on" or "surrenders to" his religious faith.

Conversion is customarily associated with overt and public confessions of faith. Revival meetings are held in which individuals are urged to come forward and "make the decision for Christ." One subject described his conversion in the following way:

I had been thinking that I should have Jesus as my personal Saviour. A saintly old man, Brother Shook, preached one night. His words hammered upon me and seemed to ring in my breast. I felt I must give my life to Christ. I went to the altar where I knelt, weeping. . . . My father came and asked me if I did not love Jesus. Of course I did! And instantly my burden rolled away. I was intensely happy. All over the house I went shaking hands with everyone. My immediate aftereffect was to tell someone else about my new love. The few nights following I led three or four of my friends to the altar. I am conscious of that experience today, and it is my Bethel when I need again the joy of the Spirit.[27]

The conversion experience is encouraged by theological emphasis on man's sinfulness, a sense of the urgency of individual moral regeneration, and a belief in the capacity of religious faith to work miracles of personality transformation. Proponents of revival-

[26] Fred L. Strodtbeck, "Family Interaction, Values, and Achievement," in David C. McClelland, Alfred L. Baldwin, Urie Bronfenbrenner, and Fred L. Strodtbeck, *Talent and Society* (Princeton: Van Nostrand, 1958), p. 146.

[27] Elmer T. Clark, *The Psychology of Religious Awakening* (New York: Macmillan 1929), p. 40.

ism point out that church attendance does not necessarily signify a genuine religious commitment nor guarantee adherence to a Christian life. Nor do they trust the ordinary processes of religious education to provide the spiritual resources for leading an exemplary life.

Emphasis on the subjective experience of conversion is probably greatest among new religious movements that cannot rely upon gradual assimilation of the children of members but must win adult adherents. Leaders of new religious movements frequently report a conversion experience, which is regarded as a warrant of the authenticity of the new faith, as well as a model and inspiration for its followers.

Much of the American stress on the importance of conversion has its roots in the early nineteenth century when, it is estimated, only 10 per cent of the population were church members.[28] At this time, Protestantism resembled a "new" religious movement. Great revivals were carried on in successive waves to awaken religious feeling and build the churches.

Empirical studies of religious conversion are largely limited to Protestants.[29] The conversion experience is by no means confined to Protestantism, however, nor even to religious belief. It may occur with regard to almost any belief, though it is most likely to occur when—as in the case of religion—the "salvation" of the individual or of society is conceived to be at stake. Studies of religious conversion support several conclusions that are probably applicable to political or other types of conversion.

1. Adolescence or near-adolescence is the age during which religious conversion is most likely to occur. Adolescence is also the age, however, when church attendance falls, religious doubts appear, and rebellious attitudes are especially keen.[30] (See Fig. XI:1.)

2. Conversions are usually experienced only where the group encourages them. Of 176 college students who remembered having been subjected to a theology of sin and damnation, about two-thirds reported some form of conversion experience. Of 133 who were members of nonevangelical denominations that place little importance on sudden conversion only 8 per cent reported a conversion episode.[31]

3. Conversions are rarely a sudden change from disbelief to belief; as a rule they represent an emotional "surrender" to religious faith after a period of prior socialization in the family and the church. A study of the highly successful campaigns of the American evangelist, Billy Graham, in England during the 1950's reported that about half of the 120,000 who came forward to make a public decision were church members at the time.[32] Most of the others were probably influenced by earlier church affiliation.

THE RELIGIOUS VOCATION

The tradition in Protestantism that emphasizes the importance of conversion for the ordinary church member tends to take a similar view with respect to the requirements for the ministry. In some American Protestant congregations, it is considered not only a necessary but a sufficient qualification for the minister to have subjectively experienced a "call from God" and to demonstrate his religious inspiration through effective preaching. No formal educational requirements are laid down; the ideal is a nonprofessional ministry.

In contrast, Catholicism and Judaism, as well as the nonevangelical branches of Protestantism, regard a period of training in a

[28] Herbert W. Schneider, *Religion in 20th Century America* (Cambridge: Harvard University Press, 1952), p. 16.

[29] See Edwin D. Starbuck, *The Psychology of Religion* (London: Walter Scott, 1899), and Clark, *op. cit.*

[30] Sidney L. Pressey and Raymond G. Kuhlen, *Psychological Development Through the Life Span* (New York: Harper, 1957), pp. 481–486.

[31] Clark, *op. cit.*, p. 87.

[32] S. Herron, "What's Left of Harringway?" *British Weekly*, February 10, 1955, cited in Michael Argyle, *Religious Behavior* (London: Routledge and Kegan Paul, 1958), p. 53.

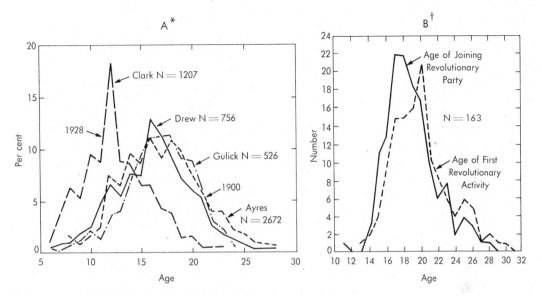

Fig. **XI:1** Adolescence and Conversion

From Sidney L. Pressey and Raymond G. Kuhlen, *Psychological Development Through the Life Span* (New York: Harper, 1957), pp. 493, 484.

* Percentage distribution of religious conversions according to age, showing age of most frequent occurrence and change of age, from 1900 to 1928. (Data of Clark, Drew, Gullick, and Ayers from E. T. Clark, *The Psychology of Religious Awakening*, New York, Macmillan, 1929, pp. 55, 63.)

†Age trends in importance of ideology and philosophy of life. Suggests ages at which ideologies are effective in producing action, as reflected in ages of joining revolutionary activity. (After J. Davis, "A study of one hundred and sixty-three outstanding communist leaders." *American Sociological Society, Papers and Proceedings*, 1929, **24:** 42–53.)

theological seminary as the only avenue to ordination, and do not insist upon extraordinary signs of "holiness" or "divine inspiration." Greater emphasis is placed upon the general suitability of the candidate for performing the duties of his religious role. The same criteria of "health, intellect, and character" are used to select candidates for the religious vocation as are used to select candidates for other professions.[33]

Recruitment

While a religious family, together with early religious training, tends to make the individual religious, recruitment to a religious

vocation appears to require a more specific socializing influence. Among seminarians and those entering religious orders, one of the most important factors determining choice of a religious vocation is contact with other religious professionals, that is, with priests, ministers, or members of religious orders. Among prospective Catholic priests, Sisters, and Brothers, approximately two-thirds have at least one close relative who is already in a religious vocation.[34] Much the same situation obtains among Protestants. A large number of ministerial candidates have fathers who are ministers.[35] Among 140 Yale

[33] Joseph H. Fichter, S.J., *Religion as an Occupation* (University of Notre Dame Press, 1961), pp. 4–5.

[34] *Ibid.*, p. 50.

[35] Ralph A. Felton, *New Ministers* (Madison, N. J.: Drew Theological Seminary, 1949), p. 24.

divinity students surveyed, three-fifths had one or more relatives in religious or social work.[36]

More than any other person, a religious professional influences the decision of the young person to enter religion. Of approximately 1500 Protestant theological students, 34 per cent named a minister as most influential in their decision as compared with 17 per cent who named their mothers and 11 per cent their fathers.[37] Among Catholics, seminarians consistently tend to name a priest as having had major influence on their decision to become a priest, Sisters a Sister, Brothers a Brother.[38] Catholic religious personnel come overwhelmingly from students who have attended parochial schools.[39]

Motivation

Studies of the motivations underlying the choice to be a priest or a minister are few in number and crude in method. In general they are limited to asking the question: Why did you enter the priesthood or the ministry? These studies do suggest, however, that—verbally at least—Catholic and Protestant motivations are different.

The expressed motivations of Catholic priests are more strictly religious than are the motivations of Protestant ministers. For Catholic priests, assurance of their own salvation is one of the most important reasons given for entering the religious life. Humanitarian service to others does not appear to be the compelling reason for entering the priesthood. In contrast, Catholic lay Brothers, who are not ordained, place the desire to "do some good in life" before all other reasons for entering the religious life.[40]

While prospective Catholic priests rarely mention "doing some good in life" as a reason for entering the priesthood, about one-fourth of 1,700 ministerial students chose "to serve mankind" as expressing their primary motivation. Another third chose "need of men and society for Christ.[41]

The different reasons given by Protestant ministers and Catholic priests cannot be interpreted as signifying that Protestant ministers are less religious than Catholic priests or that Catholic priests are less humanitarian than Protestant ministers. The expressed motives reflect long-standing institutional differences between Catholicism and Protestantism.

1. *Differences in church government.* The Protestant congregation has a voice in the affairs of its church, and the primary accountability of the Protestant minister is to his congregation. These democratic practices make for "other-directedness" and for emphasis on service to others. In the Catholic Church laymen do not have a voice in church government, and the priest is accountable only to church authorities. The priest tends, therefore, to be oriented toward the Church as an institution.

2. *Differences in Protestant and Catholic conceptions of "giving one's life to God."* For Catholics, "giving one's life to God" has traditionally been identified with withdrawing from the secular world and dedicating oneself to religious worship and devotion. For Protestants, "giving one's life to God" has more often been identified with carrying God's message into the world, partly by preaching to save souls and partly by humanitarian service.

3. *Differences in the priestly and ministerial roles.* The religious role of the priest is defined in highly specific and ritualistic terms: it is to administer the Sacraments of the Church. The religious role of the minister, on the other hand, is relatively vague and undefined, making it possible for him and others to invest it with many secular ele-

---

[36] Robert O. Smith, "Personality and Cultural Factors Affecting the Religion of One Hundred and Forty Divinity Students," *Religious Education,* **43** (March-April, 1948), 106–11.

[37] Felton, *op. cit.,* p. 7.

[38] Fichter, *op. cit.,* p. 22.

[39] *Ibid.,* pp. 41–42.

[40] *Ibid.,* p. 23.

[41] Felton, *op. cit.,* p. 15.

ments, such as "helping others" or providing community leadership.

These institutional differences probably influence the way a clergyman perceives his role and therefore the reason he will give for his decision to enter the religious vocation.

Caution: Catholic motivations have been studied by Catholic investigators, Protestant motivations by Protestant investigators. It is difficult to estimate the extent to which this has affected the findings. For example, "love of God" was fourth among the reasons given by Catholics for entering the priesthood, but this motive was not included in a checklist for entering the Protestant ministry.

Education

Three trends have characterized the education of the clergy in the United States.[42] One is the decline in the general level of education of the Protestant clergy from Colonial times until recently, when the trend was reversed. This decline was the accompaniment of American religious development in a frontier society where church organization was weak, the general level of intellectual sophistication was low, and revivalism loomed large.

A second trend, which appeared at the end of the nineteenth century, is a growing emphasis upon the "practical ministry." Seminary curricula are no longer limited to theology, church doctrine, and church history but include courses in missions, elocution, group work, social ethics, religious education, and the like. This trend began in part as a response to the early American emphasis on the practical task of inspiring conversions. It was further strengthened by the emergence during the late nineteenth century of the idea of the "Social Gospel" according to which the church was charged with the additional practical task of "doing good" in the community.

A third trend, of rather recent origin, is

the growing secularization of seminary education. The need for secular education has two related sources. One is the increasing education and sophistication of church members. The other is the increasing application of professional criteria to many of the roles historically played by the clergyman, for example, the roles of counselor, teacher, administrator.

That the clergy themselves feel the need for additional secular training is shown in a recent study of approximately 4,000 ministers from eight major American denominations. Over half agreed that they would very much like to see the clergy given more training in psychology and the social sciences. Of those who said they give psychological counseling to church members "practically daily," 75 per cent wanted very much to see more of such training.[43]

These three trends in Protestant ministerial education are surface manifestations of the influence of the secular society and the lay Protestant on the training, the character, and the personality of the clergy. In large measure, the accommodation of ministers to their congregations is inherent in the democratic structure and nonritual character of most branches of American Protestantism. It is also another aspect of the penetration of the democratic ethos into all areas of American life. The Jewish rabbi in the United States has virtually lost his former role as scholar-saint, judge, and protector of religious traditions.[44] Like many Protestant ministers he has become humanistic, social service-oriented, and respectful of science. The education of Catholic religious professionals, especially teachers, has become more secularized and scientific, while Catholic laymen have recently protested their exclusion from Church government and their

[42] See H. Richard Niebuhr and Daniel D. Williams (eds.), *The Ministry in Historical Perspectives* (New York: Harper, 1956).

[43] Robert Edward Mitchell, "Minister-Parishioner Relations," (Unpublished Ph.D. dissertation, Columbia University, 1962), Chap. III, p. 12.

[44] Jerome E. Carlin and Saul H. Mendlovitz, "The American Rabbi: A Religious Specialist Responds to Loss of Authority," in Marshall Sklare (ed.), *The Jews* (Glencoe: The Free Press, 1958), pp. 377–414.

lack of influence upon Church affairs.[45] These developments may influence the Catholic clergy as they have the Protestant minister and the Jewish rabbi.

Dilemmas of the Clergy

Many clergymen experience conflict in carrying out the ministerial role.

1. The role of clergyman has both religious and secular aspects. The Protestant minister defines his religious role as primarily that of preacher and pastor. The parishioner, too, "wants his minister to focus his energies on these tasks . . . and is prone to be critical where these expectations are not met." [46] In actuality, however, the minister finds that he spends much more time in administrative tasks than in preparing sermons or in visiting and giving spiritual aid.[47]

2. The Protestant minister faces a further dilemma stemming from the institutional character of most Protestant churches.[48] On the one hand, he would like to bring his congregation to a more religious outlook; this often entails making religious judgments on their secular conduct. On the other hand, his influence depends on maintaining good relations with his congregation; this usually entails restraining his criticism of their behavior. The socialization of the seminarian into his ministerial role often requires, therefore, that he learn how to suppress forthright expression of his religious conscience and steer a course between losing his following and abdicating his religious leadership.

---

[45] Daniel Callahan, "Problems and Possibilities," *The Commonweal*, **76** (August 10, 1962), 439–41.

[46] Charles Y. Glock and Philip Roos, "Parishioners' Views of How Ministers Spend Their Time," *Review of Religious Research*, **2** (Spring, 1961), 175.

[47] Samuel W. Blizzard, "The Minister's Dilemma," *Christian Century*, **73** (April 25, 1956), 508–10.

[48] See J. Milton Yinger, *Religion in the Struggle for Power* (Durham, N.C.: Duke University Press, 1946).

Section 5   Primary relations

Among the important functions of religion is the creation, reinforcement, and celebration of the primary group and the primary relation.

Religious stories which tell of the mythical origin of the social group link the community to a single ancestor and make all its members kin. As religion becomes more universal, that is, detached from specific groups and localities, creation myths become less important as symbols of the sense of community.

Religious rites are often centered around the dead and the relation of parents and children continues to be honored and observed even after death. Through the observance of these religious rites, living and dead continue to participate in a single and timeless community.

Many religious rites are family rites. The hearth ceremony of the ancient Greeks, mentioned earlier, is one example. The Jewish *Seder,* a ceremonial feast celebrating the Passover, is another.

Religious symbolism may be built upon primary relations, especially the family. In Christian theology God is the Father, Jesus is His Son. Men are the sons of God and by implication brothers to each other. In Catholicism the Holy Family plays a particularly important role. Mary, the Mother of God, and Joseph, her spouse, have been sanctified, and Mary is an intercessor for man to God. The celebration of the Holy Family in Catholic art, ritual, and prayer builds a bridge between religious feeling and the more familiar emotions of everyday life, and creates a locus

Mexican Americans in Los Angeles prepare for a church festival. The preparations bring religious objects into an everyday setting.

of intimacy and warmth within the austere context of religious awe.

In the Judaeo-Christian tradition, the image of God reflects the double role of the patriarchal father. God is both authority and protector, the God of judgment and punishment and the God of love and forgiveness.

RELIGION AND MARRIAGE

Most religions endure over long periods because they are passed on from generation to generation. Marriage across religious lines is thus of concern to religious groups. Partly

because it throws into question the religious adherence of the children, the major religions and denominations in the United States disapprove of interfaith marriage.

The strength of disapproval of religious exogamy (marriage outside the religious group) differs from group to group. The Old Testament forbids Jews to marry non-Jews, but religious sanctions are now rarely invoked by the American Jewish community against Jews who marry outside the faith. Conversion of the Gentile partner is generally required, however, before a rabbi will perform the religious ceremony. The Catholic Church regards the marriage of a Catholic to a non-Catholic as valid only under certain conditions; for example, the ceremony must be performed in the Catholic Church and be preceded by an antenuptial agreement that all children will be baptized and reared as Catholics. Some Protestant denominations have taken official stands against marriage to non-Protestants, especially Catholics, but the Catholic ceremony is accepted as valid.

Rates of interfaith marriage vary from religion to religion. Jews are least exogamous. Less than 10 per cent of American Jews marry outside their faith. A slightly higher per cent of Protestants are exogamous. The rate of Catholic interfaith marriage is relatively high. At the present time, among all families in which at least one spouse is Catholic, about one-fifth represent interfaith marriages. These figures include both long-standing and recent marriages, and therefore do not accurately reflect present trends.[49] Probably the figures given are lower than current rates.

The rate of interfaith marriage among Catholics appears to be increasing and may now be as high as 40 to 50 per cent in some areas.[50] Since virtually all Catholic interfaith marriages are with Protestants,[51] the Catholic rate provides a rough index to the willingness of Protestants to marry Catholics.

Interfaith marriage appears to increase with socio-economic status. In a study of over 50,000 Catholic mixed marriages in an urban area, the percentage of mixed marriages was about 9 per cent in lower rental areas but 18 per cent in upper socio-economic neighborhoods.[52]

Official religious opposition to interfaith marriage undoubtedly deters some individuals from engaging in close social relations with people of other faiths or from making marriages that might otherwise be congenial. However, the official doctrines of religious groups do not seem to account for existing rates of interfaith marriage. Three factors seem important in determining rates of interfaith marriage.

1. *The varying distribution of religious groups in the community.* In some Southern dioceses, where Catholics form no more than 2 per cent of the total population, mixed marriage rates for Catholics are as high as 60 to 70 per cent. In areas where Catholics are a majority, mixed marriage rates are often less than 10 per cent.[53] The *average* incidence of Protestant interfaith marriage—about 10 per cent—is probably as low as it is because in many areas of the United States virtually the entire population is Protestant, and there is little opportunity to marry non-Protestants.

2. *Social distance.* A particular religion may be so closely tied to ethnic background, cultural factors, residence, and socio-economic status that individuals of different faiths do not associate with each other. For example, in some areas of southwestern United States a Catholic is likely to be of Mexican origin and low socio-economic status, a Protestant of Anglo-Saxon origin and higher socio-economic status. While religious difference creates social distance, social class barriers and ethnic prejudice are important and add to the social distance that makes marriage less likely. For example, Catholics form about 30 per cent of the populations of both San Antonio, Texas, and Marquette, Michigan, but the rate of Catholic interfaith marriage is only about 5 per cent in San Antonio while in Marquette it is close to 40 per cent.[54] In San Antonio many Catholics are of Mexican origin; in Marquette the Catholics are ethnically less differentiated from the non-Catholics.

3. *Extent of primary ties to family and ethnic community.* Resistance to interfaith

[49] Bureau of the Census, *Current Population Reports,* P-20, No. 79, February 1958, Table 6.

[50] John L. Thomas, S.J., *The American Catholic Family* (Englewood Cliffs: Prentice-Hall, 1956), p. 154.

[51] *Current Population Reports, loc. cit.*

[52] Thomas, *op. cit.,* pp. 157–58.

[53] *Ibid.,* p. 155.

[54] *Ibid.,* p. 156.

marriages may reflect loyalty to family and ethnic community. Not wanting to hurt one's parents, or to be alienated from them, is apt to be more immediately important to the individual than official religious disapproval. Where the individual has close ties to an ethnic community that also shares a common religion, he may not feel at home with people of another faith—not because of religious differences but because of differences in everyday ways and attitudes.

Interfaith Marriage and Marital Success

The few empirical studies that have been made of the marital success of interfaith marriages have focused on families with children.[55] When such interfaith marriages are considered as a whole, they appear to be less successful than same-religion marriages; and no-religion marriages appear to be the least successful of all. However, when mixed marriages are classified according to various combinations of religious affiliation, the divorce (or separation) rates vary. For example, in one study Protestant father–Catholic mother marriages had a divorce rate of 7 per cent, Catholic father–Protestant mother marriages had a divorce rate of 21 per cent.[56]

One reason suggested for this variation is the inability of the Protestant mother to ad-

here to her original agreement to raise her children as Catholics. The Protestant woman who has assented to the antenuptial agreement to raise her children as Catholics may balk at actually carrying it out and training her children in a faith not her own. The Catholic father objects to the breaking of her agreement with him, and marital conflict results.

There may also be a greater willingness on the part of Protestant women to initiate a divorce when marital conflict is present. Three out of four divorces in the United States are granted to women. Though this is often a mere formality, both parties wanting a divorce, Catholic religious scruples probably deter many Catholic women from initiating a divorce.

Cautions: 1. Statistical data on interfaith marriages are crude and scattered. Until more knowledge is gained in this area generalizations should be considered highly tentative.

2. The foregoing discussion is concerned with comparisons rather than absolute quantities. Even though marriages of unaffiliated persons show a higher incidence of divorce than interfaith marriages and interfaith marriages show a higher divorce rate than in-faith marriages, the great majority of marriages in all of these categories do not end in divorce.

[55] See Howard M. Bell, *Youth Tell Their Story* (Washington, D.C.: American Council on Education, 1938); Judson T. Landis, "Marriages of Mixed and Non-Mixed Religious Faith," *American Sociological Review*, **14** (June, 1949), 401–7; and H. Ashley Weeks, "Differen-

tial Divorce Rates by Occupation," *Social Forces*, **21** (March, 1943), 334–37.

[56] Landis, *op. cit.*, p. 403.

Section **6** **Stratification**

Christianity stresses the equality of all men in the sight of God. "The Christian concept . . . is equalitarian and inclusive rather than aristocratic and exclusive." [57] Participation in the church and salvation are open to all, regardless of wealth and status.

The Christianity of the Gospels is oriented toward the poor and exalts the poor. The poor are promised a status in heaven denied to

[57] W. Lloyd Warner and Associates, *Democracy in Jonesville* (New York: Harper, 1949), p. 153.

them on earth—a status unlikely to be gained by the rich and mighty.

And, behold, one came and said unto him, Good Master, what good thing shall I do that I may have eternal life? . . . Jesus said unto him, If thou wilt be perfect, go and sell that thou hast, and give to the poor, and thou shalt have treasure in heaven: and come and follow me. But when the young man heard that saying, he went away sorrowful: for he had great possessions. Then said Jesus unto his disciples, Verily I say unto you . . . It is easier for a camel to go through the eye of a needle, than for a rich man to enter the kingdom of God. [58]

On the basis of doctrine as expressed in the Gospels, it might be expected that (1) Christianity embraces all social classes in a single religious community transcending all secular distinctions between rich and poor, the weak and the powerful; (2) church organization ignores status distinctions; and (3) the poor participate in the church more than those who have "great possessions."

SOCIAL COMPOSITION OF THE CHURCHES

A study of the religious identification and social class membership of more than 12,000 Americans was made during the 1940's by combining four public opinion polls con-

[58] Matthew 19: 16; 21–23; 24.

ducted during 1945 and 1946. The top half of Table XI:3 gives the results of this study for Protestants, Roman Catholics, and Jews. It is immediately apparent that each of the three major religious divisions in the United States has members from every social class— upper, middle, and lower. It has been suggested that there is "more heterogeneity in class status in the average church than in any other average social grouping." [59] On a national level, at least, this appears to be true. Many voluntary associations in the United States—trade-unions, business groups, professional societies—exist to further specific utilitarian interests and often have a narrow social base. The church draws its members from all social classes.

The social composition of "born" Protestants, who are in the majority in the United States, closely resembles the social composition of the population as a whole. [60] The socio-economic profiles of Catholics and Jews reflect the greater concentration of Catholics in working-class occupations and of Jews in business and the professions. As Catholics

[59] Louis Bultena, "Church Membership and Church Attendance in Madison, Wisconsin," *American Sociological Review,* **14** (June, 1949), 384–89.
[60] Herbert W. Schneider, *Religion in 20th Century America* (Cambridge, Mass.: Harvard University Press, 1952), p. 230.

Table **XI:3**   Social Class Composition of Selected Religions in Percentages, United States, 1945 *

	Upper Class	Middle Class	Lower Class	Total	Number of Cases
Protestant	14	32	54	100	(8,292)
Roman Catholic	9	25	66	100	(2,390)
Jewish	22	32	46	100	(537)
Episcopalian	24	34	42	100	(590)
Congregational	24	43	33	100	(376)
Presbyterian	22	40	38	100	(961)
Methodist	13	35	52	100	(2,100)
Lutheran	11	36	53	100	(723)
Baptist	8	24	68	100	(1,381)

*Adapted from Herbert Schneider, *Religion in 20th Century America* (Cambridge, Mass.: Harvard University Press, 1952), p. 228.   A more recent study supports these findings.   See Bernard Lazerwitz, "A Comparison of Major United States Religious Groups," *Journal* of the American Statistical Association, **56** (September, 1961), 568–79.

continue their rise on the occupational ladder, their social composition will approach that of Protestants.

Viewed as a whole, the Christian community is equalitarian and inclusive. Organizationally, however, its denominational divisions reflect some of the secular realities of status and class. The bottom half of Table XI:3 considers six major Protestant denominations separately. At the time of the study, the status profiles of Methodists and Lutherans resembled Protestants in general. Other denominations varied widely from this pattern.

Partly because of residential patterns, individual churches tend to be more homogeneous in socio-economic status than the denominations to which they belong. In one Episcopalian congregation situated in a middle-class area in a college community, 82 per cent of the adult members were college trained and more than 40 per cent had attended graduate school. Though rich and poor, educated and uneducated, are members of one religious community, they tend to worship under different roofs.

The social class differentiation of American Protestantism is partly rooted in the varying economic fortunes and different ethnic backgrounds of the groups. Among Episcopalians —who are linked in origin to the Church of England—there are large numbers of people with backgrounds in the British Isles and high status who had to overcome neither a language barrier nor ethnic prejudice. The lower proportion of American Lutherans who are upper class reflects the different history of a group that arrived in the United States at a later date and were largely of German and Scandinavian origin.

SOCIAL CLASS AND RELIGIOUS INVOLVEMENT

It is usual for Americans to identify themselves as Protestant, Catholic, or Jewish whether or not they ever attend church or synagogue and whether or not they have religious convictions. Table XI:3 is based only on such religious identification, and throws no light on the question whether the church and religion attract the poor in greater proportions than the economically privileged.

Fragmentary evidence indicates that the economically unprivileged are less involved in both the church and religion than are the more privileged. They are less likely to be members of a church congregation, to attend church regularly, and to take part in the organized activities of their church. They are also less likely to be informed about religious matters. However, when they do go to church, the less privileged tend to be both more believing and more emotionally involved in their religion than the more privileged.[61]

Social class differences in religious involvement appear even among members of the same denomination. A study of 4,000 members of 12 Congregational Christian urban churches measured the religious involvement of members along four "dimensions": (1) extent of knowledge about the Bible and religious matters in general; (2) extent of participation in the church; (3) extent of belief in church doctrine; and (4) extent of religious "feeling" as indicated by faith in prayer, daily Bible reading, and belief in the necessity of a conversion experience.[62] It was found that there was a tendency for religious knowledge and participation to be associated with higher socio-economic status, intensity of

[61] See Hadley S. Cantril, "Educational and Economic Composition of Religious Groups: An Analysis of Poll Data," *American Journal of Sociology,* **48** (March, 1943), 574–79; Bernard Lazerwitz, "Some Factors Associated with Variations in Church Attendance," *Social Forces,* **39** (May, 1961), 301–9; Lee G. Burchinall, "Some Social Status Criteria and Church Membership and Church Attendance," *The Journal of Social Psychology,* **49,** First half (February, 1959), 53–64; Harold Kaufman, *Prestige Classes in a New York Rural Community* (Ithaca, N.Y.: Cornell University Agricultural Experimental Bulletin, March, 1944); Nicholas J. Demerath, III, "Social Stratification and Church Involvement: The Church-Sect Distinction Applied to Individual Participation," *Review of Religious Research,* **2** (Spring, 1961), 146–54.

[62] Yoshio Fukuyama, "The Major Dimensions of Church Membership," *Review of Religious Research,* **2** (Spring, 1961), 154–61.

religious feeling to be associated with lower status. Differences in degree of belief were negligible for this particular denomination.

To sum up: The economically privileged tend to be religious in an intellectual, formal, and organizational way. They attend church regularly, they are active in the church, and they are informed about their religion. But, compared with less privileged churchgoers, they are apt to be less believing and less emotionally dependent on their religious faith. The economically unprivileged tend to be religious in a more emotional manner. They are less regular church attenders, their knowledge is scantier, and they participate less in church activities. But, when they are religiously involved, they are apt to be more unquestioning in their faith and more reliant on it than the more privileged. Complete indifference to religion may, however, be most widespread on the lower socio-economic levels: recent analysis of public opinion polls suggests that a larger proportion of the unprivileged than the privileged neither go to church nor evidence involvement in their nominal faith.[63]

Cautions: 1. Findings on the relation between social class and religious involvement vary from study to study. This is partly due to the different samples used. For example, some studies have investigated the relation between social class and religious involvement only among church members. Others have examined the relation in the general population, which includes both church attenders and non-attenders.

2. Measures of religious involvement are still crude and do not permit firm conclusions as to the conditions associated with "genuine" religious involvement.

RELIGION AND CLASS INTEREST

Oriented though it was to the poor, the Christianity of the Gospels did not sanction

secular rebellion against class privilege and social injustice. It projected no ideal of social reform to eliminate poverty and provided no principles to guide Christians in deciding mundane questions of social, political, and economic policy.

With its success, Christianity was transformed from a religious and moral movement of the poor into the official and powerful institution of the Catholic Church. The Church assumed social, political, and economic powers. By fusing with the secular feudal order and its ruling class, the Church inevitably became a bulwark of the status inequalities of feudal society.

During the period of its European hegemony, the Catholic Church supplemented the other-worldly ethics of the New Testament with a social philosophy and an image of society based partly on the Christianity of the Gospels, partly on classical Greek and Roman thought, and partly on the realities of the feudal social system. Though modified and often abused in practice, the social philosophy of the Church contained the following elements:

1. Poverty, as in the Gospels, continued to be exalted as a virtue. This was evident in monastic asceticism, which saw poverty as an essential aspect of the dedicated religious life.

2. There was virtually no conception of improving the material conditions of the poor. On the other hand, the poor were not condemned as failures. Poverty was regarded as a status into which one was born. In theory, if not always in practice, the poor were regarded as proper objects of Christian charity and compassion.

3. Profit-making—as opposed to merely being reimbursed for one's costs and time—was condemned. The principles of the medieval Catholic Church were explicitly anticapitalist.

4. Secular society was conceived to be a divine community at whose apex was the Church. All people were members of one

church, and all aspects of society, including the relations between the social classes, were regarded as proper subjects of religious governance.

5. Social inequalities were not only accepted but justified. Society was compared to an organism composed of different and interdependent parts, each having its own function. The ruler and the ruled, the wealthy and the poor, were likened to the mind and the hand, one fitted only to toil, the other only to govern. Social justice was conceived as giving to each one his due. But what was due to each was defined by existing differences in wealth and power rather than by a desire to achieve a more equitable distribution of the world's goods.

The Protestant Reformation

The gradual transformation of agricultural feudal society into the commercial and industrial capitalism of the modern era was accompanied in many countries by a religious revolution against the doctrines and authority of the Catholic Church. First initiated in Germany early in the sixteenth century by the clergy and the nobility, the Protestant Reformation appealed strongly to the rising middle classes desirous of ridding themselves of the religious and secular restraints of the feudal order.

Protestantism sought and received the support of the poor. It took on, however, a distinctly middle-class coloration. Not only did the middle classes support Protestantism and gain administrative control of the churches, they also suffused it with middle-class values and attitudes. Whereas Catholic social doctrine had been formed in the context of an agricultural, feudal society, Protestantism evolved a social doctrine that reflected the realities of a commercial and industrial capitalism, organized around profit-making, employers, and wage earners.

For the middle-class Protestant, it was easy to believe that to live a Christian life was to exemplify the middle-class virtues.[64] Right-

eousness became identified with industry, thrift, prudence, decorum, cleanliness, self-discipline, sobriety. Sin was almost exclusively identified with the personal vices: laziness, improvidence, frivolity, dirt, swearing, gambling, drinking. Sin acquired a distinctly lower-class look, while wealth and success, once regarded as hindrances to salvation, became its very sign and reward: "No question but riches should be the portion . . . of the godly . . .; for godliness hath the promises of this life as well as of the life to come."[65]

Poverty and Salvation

This exaltation of middle-class virtues and middle-class success led to a new approach to the problems of poverty and social responsibility. Though by no means universal among Protestants, the following attitudes characterized much Protestant activity and social policy for several centuries, and in some measure continue to do so.

1. Poverty was no longer seen as inevitable and necessary but became something to censure. The poor evoked not compassion but blame. Poverty, singled out by the Gospels as a blessed state because it was a guarantee against the sin of pride, was now associated with personal vices, with failure of character, and with spiritual unregeneracy.

2. A missionary rather than a charitable approach was taken toward the poor. Since secular society was no longer regarded as a divine community, into which all are born and all participate, Protestantism was faced with the task of gathering in the unchurched and of "converting" the nominal Christian. It would be inaccurate to say that the evangelical efforts of Protestantism were restricted to the poor. Nevertheless, the poor were regarded as most in need of salvation, since

[64] Based on R. H. Tawney, *Religion and the Rise of Capitalism* (New York: Penguin, 1947) and H. Richard Niebuhr, *The Social Sources of Denominationalism* (New York: Meridian, 1957).
[65] R. Younge, *The Poores' Advocate,* 1654, quoted by Tawney, *op. cit.,* p. 221.

they were most in need of being saved from bad habits, weakness of character, and lower-class riotousness.

3. The concept of social justice—of giving to each his due—became identified with the distribution of rewards commensurate with merit and with the withholding of charity from the "undeserving."

The law of God saith, "he that will not work, let him not eat." This would be a sore scourge and smart whip for idle persons if . . . none should be suffered to eat till they had wrought for it.[66]

The Marxist Critique

The most familiar critique of Christian attitudes toward the poor is that of Karl Marx, who formulated the famous dictum that religion is the "opium of the masses." [67] He condemned the other-worldly promises of Christianity as serving to deflect the economically oppressed from bettering their conditions in the present. Marxism sees Christianity as creating a docile laboring class, protecting the rich from threats to their wealth and power, and perpetuating secular inequalities.

In 1893, Marx's collaborator, Friedrich Engels, criticized the presence in England of several famous American revivalists, implying that this was an effort of the industrial classes to hold in check the rising protests and secular organization of the English working class.[68]

In some respects, the facts support the Marxist critique, but there are aspects of Christian doctrine and of church history that mitigate it. The church—both Protestant and Catholic—has attempted to develop concepts of social justice transcending mere expediency and setting ethical limits to the pursuit of material interests. Medieval Catholicism emphasized the social obligations of all classes in society. More recent Catholic thought has expanded the doctrine of social justice. Most notable is the encyclical, *Rerum Novarum,* of Pope Leo XIII which as early as 1891 supported the formation of trade-unions.[69] During the last century there grew up within Protestantism the concept of the Social Gospel that Christianity is required to work for social justice and the salvation of society, not merely for the salvation of individual souls.

While the Gospels hold forth no promise of material progress, their high valuation of the individual, rich or poor, and the assertion of man's spiritual brotherhood, laid an ethical foundation for secular reform and secular movements toward equality. While the church as an institution can be a powerful buttress of status and privilege, its doctrines have often inspired individuals to support social idealism and economic reform.

---

[66] Samuel Hartlib, *London's Charity Inlarged,* 1650, quoted by Tawney, *op. cit.,* p. 220.

[67] See Lewis S. Feuer (ed.), *Karl Marx and Friedrich Engels: Basic Writings on Politics and Philosophy* (New York: Doubleday, 1959), p. 263.

[68] Frederick Engels, introduction to the First English translation of *Socialism, Utopian and Scientific* (New York: International Publishers, 1935), p. 24.

[69] Anne Fremantle, *The Papal Encyclicals In Their Historical Context* (New York: Mentor, 1956), pp. 166–95.

Section 7 Associations

As religion becomes a differentiated sphere, special associations are formed to protect, nurture, and extend religious values, beliefs, and traditions. Religious associations differ on several dimensions:

1. *According to the functions they perform*

for the religion. Some religious associations embrace the entire religious community: all of the faithful are brought under a common authority and subject to a common discipline. In other religions, such as Judaism or Buddhism, there is no such unifying organization nor any clear central authority. Many religious associations are educational, e.g., parochial schools and seminaries. Other associations, such as missionary groups, are devices for extending the faith. In some religions there are monastic orders, maintained for persons dedicated to religious life and works. These are only a few of the variety of religious associations that perform distinctive functions.

2. *According to the nature of individual participation.* This dimension is significant because the extent and mode of participation strongly influence the character of the religious education, leadership, ritual, and the quality of belief. Religious participation is often restrained: what the member will do to express his feelings may be limited by his concept of respectable behavior. On the other hand, the individual may invest himself emotionally in his religion and derive deep satisfaction from it.

3. *According to the degree of integration with the rest of society.* The religious association may be isolated and self-sufficient, or it may be dependent on and allied with the economic or political order. The more isolated the group, the freer it will be to maintain and develop a distinctive identity; the more integrated, the greater will be the pressure for accommodation to the surrounding community.

On the basis of these variations, two major types of religious association have been identified, the *church* and the *sect*.

The Church

"Church" is most commonly used to designate any religious group. However, many sociologists use the term in a more restricted sense. In this meaning a church is a religious association marked by (1) a relatively high degree of institutionalization (see ASSOCIATIONS, pp. 250–54); (2) integration with the social and economic order; (3) recruitment on the basis of residence or family membership; and (4) relatively restrained and routinized participation.

Within this broad category may be distinguished the *ecclesia* and the *denomination*. The ecclesia is a church that strives for fullest integration with the rest of society and for universal membership embracing all members of the community. Unity of church and state is welcomed, and in the ideal case the ecclesia is an "established" church that counts as members all residents or citizens of a given area.

The denomination has more limited aspirations and a more restricted membership. For the most part, it is assumed that children will, in the normal course of events, be inducted into the church. Therefore family membership is the main basis of recruitment and the family is the main support of religious participation. As in the case of the ecclesia, no great demands are made upon the individual for high levels of religious commitment. Denominations are the churches of a pluralist society and are compatible with a strong belief in the separation of church and state.

The Sect

The chief features of a religious sect have been summarized as follows:

It is a voluntary association; membership is by proof to sect authorities of some claim to personal merit—such as knowledge of doctrine, affirmation of a conversion experience, or recommendation of members in good standing; exclusiveness is emphasized, and expulsion exercised against those who contravene doctrinal, moral or organizational precepts; its self-conception is of an elect, a gathered remnant, possessing special enlightenment; personal perfection is the expected standard of aspiration, in whatever terms this is judged; it accepts, at least as an ideal, the priesthood of all believers; there is a high level of lay participation; there is opportunity for the member spontaneously to express his commitment; the sect is hostile or indifferent to the secular order and to the state.[70]

Sects are concerned with purity of doctrine and with the depth and genuineness of religious feeling. As a result, demands are made upon the member to be an active participant, even a leader or missionary, as a warrant of his faith. The emphasis on purity of belief tends to create intolerance toward other groups and moves the sect toward critical assessment of the secular world in accordance with the ideals of the gospel.

Within a church, the impulse toward deeper religious commitment may be taken care of by the creation of special religious groups having selective memberships and distinctive practices. The religious orders of the Roman Catholic Church, such as the Benedictines, Dominicans, Franciscans, and Jesuits, are good examples. The partial autonomy of these groups enables them to serve a sect-like function, but they remain within the Church and contribute to its work.

Sect and Church

A number of sociologists have studied the relation between sect and church.[71] Two conclusions are important:

1. Some sects develop into denominations. If a sect is strongly interested in seeking new members, it may tend to "water down" its beliefs and take in people who are not truly committed. If in addition the sect's demands are simple, asking only that the member affirm that he feels converted, it will not be clearly insulated from the world and in time may adapt to it. Other institutionalizing processes, such as concern for a stable ministry and religious education, for respectable quarters, benefit funds, seminaries, and "good works" help this evolution along. But not all sects become denominations. One important criterion is whether the sect is *conversionist*, reaching out into the world rather than merely withdrawing from it.[72]

2. There is also a reverse movement, from church to sect. This comes about mainly by a process of schism. The watered-down belief and practice, the respectability and accommodation of the church, may become unacceptable to some of its members. Thus the poor may leave middle-class churches to form religious groups of their own, characterized by greater purity of belief, emotional fervor, a lay ministry, and an all-encompassing communal life. However, as the founders of the sect become more prosperous and respectable, they in turn become more receptive to church-like organization and behavior. They in their turn neglect the special religious needs of the poor. "This pattern recurs with remarkable regularity in the history of Christianity. Anabaptists, Quakers, Methodists, Salvation Army, and more recent sects of like type illustrate this rise and progress of the churches of the disinherited."[73]

Adaptation 31 illustrates some of these processes as it analyzes the relation of church and sect in Canada. Compare the discussion of institutionalization on pages 433–34 with ASSOCIATIONS, pages 250 ff.

---

[70] Bryan R. Wilson, "An Analysis of Sect Development," *American Sociological Review*, 24 (February, 1959), 4.

[71] See especially Ernst Troeltsch, *The Social Teachings of the Christian Churches* (Glencoe: The Free Press, 1949), Vol. I, pp. 331–41; Liston Pope, *Millhands and Preachers* (New Haven: Yale University Press, 1942), pp. 118 ff.; H. Richard Niebuhr, *The Social Sources of Denominationalism* (New York: Meridian, 1957); Bryan R. Wilson, *Sects and Society* (Berkeley and Los Angeles: University of California Press, 1961).

[72] Wilson, "An Analysis of Sect Development," *op. cit.*, p. 14.

[73] Niebuhr, *op. cit.*, p. 28.

	SECT	CHURCH
RELATION TO THE SOCIAL, ECONOMIC ORDER	Membership composed chiefly of the propertyless.	Membership composed chiefly of property owners.
	Economic poverty in church property and salaries.	Economic wealth.
	Cultural periphery of the community.	Cultural center of the community.
	Renunciation or indifference to prevailing culture and social organization, including established churches.	Acceptance of prevailing values, and political, economic order; co-operation with established churches.
	Self-centered religion based on personal experience.	Culture-centered religion based on affirmation of citizenship in an existing community.
	A moral community excluding unworthy members.	A social institution embracing all who are socially compatible.
	Many religious services regardless of interference with other aspects of life.	Regular services at stated intervals.
	Adherence to strict Biblical standards, such as tithing or pacifism.	Acceptance of general cultural standards as practical definition of religious obligation.
PARTICIPATION AND INTERNAL CONTROL	Unspecialized, unprofessionalized, part-time ministry.	Specialized, professional full-time ministry.
	Voluntary, confessional bases of membership.	Ritual or social prerequisites only.
	Principal concern with adult membership.	Equal concern for children of members.
	Emphasis on evangelism and conversion.	Emphasis on religious education.
	A high degree of congregational participation in services and adminstration.	Delegation of responsibility to a small percentage of the members.
	Fervor and positive action in worship.	Restraint and passive listening.

Fig. **XI:2**   Adapted from *Millhands and Preachers* by Liston Pope
(New Haven: Yale University Press, 1942), pp. 122–24.

ADAPTATION 31

The Church and the Sect

Abridged and adapted from *Church and Sect in Canada* by S. D. Clark (Toronto: University of Toronto Press, 1948), pages 381–429. Published in this form by permission of the University of Toronto Press and S. D. Clark.

This study is concerned with the conflict between the church and sect forms of religious organization in relation to the changing community structure of Canada. The view set forth here is that the church requires social stability, and when such a condition is not present the church gives way to the sect form of religious organization. The church seeks the accommodation of religious organization to the community. The sect emphasizes the exclusiveness of religious organization: it thinks of the worldly society as something evil and of no concern to the spiritually minded. Within the church, the spirit of accommodation tends to dominate, and within the sect, the spirit of separation.

This selection from a larger study deals with the Methodist church and the Salvation Army as they met the challenge of the Canadian city toward the end of the nineteenth century.

After about 1885, many migrants swelled the size of the Canadian city. The chief task and opportunity of religious organization became one of gaining the support of people who found themselves within a new social setting, in many cases far from their old home community and past associates. Traditional religious attachments broke down, and new ones had to be formed if religion were to maintain its hold. Established churches experienced their greatest losses to such religious movements as the Salvation Army. The Army also brought its teaching to those who had no religion. Its success came largely from its influence on the urban masses.

METHODISM'S SOCIAL BASE

The limitations of traditional religious denominationalism, which largely accounted for the rapid growth of new sectarian religious movements, can be most clearly seen in the case of the Methodist church. The failure of the Methodist church after 1885 was not a failure to grow with the growth of the city nor was it a failure to gain influence in the social life of the urban community. The building of handsome places of worship, the employment of learned and in some cases highly paid ministers, the increasing reliance upon prominent citizens in the organization of Sunday school and missionary work, and the growing participation of the pulpit in political discussion strengthened the position of the Church in the Canadian city. The Church gained support in the better residential areas of the city, and its influence declined among the poorer classes.

Methodist leaders strenuously tried to avoid placing the Church in opposition to labor. Methodist religious publications expressed their sympathy for the cause of the working man and appealed to employers to improve working conditions. But such an appeal had little relation to reality as seen by the working man concerned with strengthening his bargaining position through the organization of trade-unions. The Methodist appeal, which expressed the individualist philosophy of a natural harmony of interests of social classes, attacked the economic and social assumptions of working-class philosophy.

The predominantly rural background of the membership and the long rural history of the Church in Canada had much to do with the failure of Methodism to appeal effectively to labor. The conception of work as a virtue and of leisure as a temptation to sin persisted strongly in the thinking of Methodists. The puritan outlook of persons of rural background was little different from the individualistic outlook of capitalist employers, and, whereas Methodist membership continued to be largely of rural origin, leadership passed to the capitalist elements of the urban community. The increasing influence of employers within the councils of the Church made more difficult the development of a positive appeal to the working-class population of the cities.

Mobility of the Urban Workers

Only a small proportion of the working population of the city, however, was being drawn into trade-union organization. The bulk of urban workers, unskilled and transient, lacked a working-class philosophy or a consciousness of being a part of a distinct working class. Without permanent jobs, homes, or neighborhood attachments, they had few strong loyalties and little sense of social responsibility. These elements of the population participated little in the group life of the community. They withdrew into transitory forms of association—gangs, associations of the saloon, and ephemeral groupings based upon the casual contacts of the street, rooming house, or street-corner store.

Abandonment of the practice of street preaching, as employed by the early Primitive Methodist preachers, and reliance upon services held in imposing places of worship, cut the Church off from the floating masses of the urban community. The problem faced by the Methodist church in the latter decades of the nineteenth century was not simply one growing out of social differences between the rich and poor of the city. It was one resulting from a new kind of social mobility in the community for which the machinery of the Church was not adapted.

Limitations of Church Appeal to the Lower Classes

Mobility imposed demands upon church organization that could be met only by the development of new techniques. Methodism had abandoned the sectarian policy of recruiting members by religious conversion. It had come to rely upon the techniques of the church, seeking to perpetuate itself from generation to generation. The Sunday school developed as the chief means of keeping within the Church the new generation, but mobility rendered it increasingly less effective. Mobility was greatest among the younger people, and a growing gap developed between the membership of the Sunday school and the membership of the Church. Many who had grown up in the Sunday schools were lost to the Church through the development of new interests outside the field of religion.

The house of worship was designed to meet the needs of a settled population; it did not effectively serve a floating population which had no strong local community attachments. For the masses of the urban community the street became the center of social life. Religious organization had to adapt itself to urban ecology. In failing to do so, Methodism lost the support of the more mobile elements of the population.

The churches had to do more than reach the urban population; they had to attract support through their religious appeal. A half century of effort to build itself into a denomination had led Methodism to an emphasis upon a worldly pulpit appeal. The Church by 1885 had lost much of its evangelical drive. The polished and studied sermon took the place of the passionate exhortation calling on man to repent and seek forgiveness. The pulpit lost some of its force as a spiritually reorganizing agency among the "little people" of the city who were looking for direction and comfort and a means of securing new ties.

If churches were to be filled with people financially able to maintain them, the pulpit appeal had to be directed toward the higher social levels of the population. Revivalism and the large church edifice were incompatible. The former attracted the support of the poor, the latter required the support of the rich. In becoming a religion of the church, Methodism increasingly depended on the settled residents of the community, upon the people who enjoyed a sense of status and security.

Church-sponsored Evangelism

An effort was made by the Church to maintain a revivalist atmosphere, in part by the use of professional evangelists who appeared in the United States about the 1870's and soon became a powerful force. Though not connected with any church, and unordained, the professional evangelist worked within rather than outside the regular churches. He gained his influence not by building up a special following of his own or by developing a set of doctrinal teachings but by making a special appeal to regular church followings. In this way, the more successful of such evangelists were able to gain a hearing among hundreds of thousands of people without interfering with the work of the Church.

The value of the professional evangelist to the regular churches was limited, however, by the fact that the churches were unable to maintain the religious interest aroused by the evangelist. The non-churchgoer who took part in revivalist services in the rink or public hall did not usually attend regular religious services. Revivalism created the urge to enter into religious fellowship, but the urge was not readily satisfied within the formal organization of the Church. Revivalism was seldom successful in establishing enduring religious attachments except where it led directly to the formation of a new religious sect. Consequently, the preaching of the professional evangelists tended to strengthen new sectarian movements in the community and to weaken the regular churches. On the other hand, when the evangelists preached to people who were faithful churchgoers, they strengthened the churches, especially by getting more financial contributions.

What was needed, if the Church were to reach the highly mobile classes within the city, was a body of workers prepared to go onto the city streets, into the homes of the poor, and into the public meeting places of the common man. The need of maintaining his professional dignity made it difficult for the minister to do this. Even if the evangelists had been prepared to do such work, they were too few. It required an army of workers, and such an army could only be built by drawing upon lay volunteers. The success achieved by the Salvation Army demonstrated what could be done.

THE SALVATION ARMY

In 1883, the first Canadian branch of the Salvation Army was organized in London, Ontario—the beginnings of what was to become a dominant religious force in the Canadian urban community during the next 15 years. The Army capitalized on the great evangelical revival of 1885–1900. With its sensational methods, the Salvation Army came into sharp conflict with the traditional order of Canadian society. Deeply entrenched institutions, both secular and religious, encountered a formidable challenge in its teachings. The saloon was an obvious point of attack, but the saloon was not the only institution subjected to violent onslaught. Nothing opposed to evangelical religion escaped. Army workers made no nice distinction between what was considered the province of religious interest and what was not. There was no place—saloon, billiard parlor, or brothel—where the individual could take shelter from the scrutiny of Salvationists concerned about the state of his soul.

Challenge to the Regular Churches

The established churches relied on stated places of worship, a professional ministry, and a ritual, however simple, to maintain a sense of dignity and decorum. The professional status of the minister and the social standing of the congregation in the community depended upon ridding religion of any appearance of being "queer" or irrational.

The emphasis within Salvation Army teachings on free expression of religious feelings and the willingness of Army workers to resort to any method, however spectacular, to attract attention, threatened to destroy the "good name" of religion. The Army's teachings tended to shift the prerogative of judging spiritual worth from the institution to the convert. Religion was made popular in the sense that the understanding of its mysteries was not confined to the select few. Like all religious sects, the Army attacked directly the claims and pretensions of a professional ministry. It thus attacked the whole system of ecclesiastical control and struck at the basis of authority within the Church. The Church could not meet the Army on its own ground. The relation was not one of competition between rival religious bodies; competition gave way to a fundamental conflict between types of religious organization: the church and the sect. The loss of members by the churches to the Salvation Army represented not a shift of denominational attachments but a strengthening of a spirit of religious fellowship hostile to the whole position of denominationalism.

The Methodist church felt most strongly the effects of Salvation Army influence. The Army originated from a schism within the Methodist church in Great Britain, and its doctrines and teachings were very similar to those of Methodism. Therefore the Army tended to draw many recruits from the Methodist congregations, which were proportionately weakened.

METHODS AND ORGANIZATION

The methods employed by the Salvation Army won the support of footloose elements of the urban population. Street preaching was revived as a regular feature of religious work,

and the combination of street preaching with parades, led by brass bands, attracted attention. Crowds gathered on street corners, in public parks and other open spaces, and when a sufficient state of religious enthusiasm had been aroused, they paraded to the barracks where a revivalist meeting took place. At no point did the Army impose any serious obstacle to the participation of the individual in religious service. He could easily join the crowds on the street and as easily depart. The Army carried on religious services in barracks and public halls, where people unaccustomed to churchgoing would feel at home. The service itself was informal and encouraged the free movement of individuals. The lack of decorum in Army meetings had a quality of homeliness and ease, in contrast to the stiff formality of the church.

The centralized organization of the Army, like that of Methodism a century earlier, was highly effective for evangelical work. Military discipline became a central feature of Army organization, and while the autocratic character of the leadership led eventually to internal dispute and schism, it was an element of strength in the early years of the Army's growth.

The movement was a religious order. The property rights of the worker were surrendered to the organization: he lived in an Army residence, was clothed and fed by the Army, and earnings were turned over to Army headquarters. The recruits tended to be down-and-outs, the social outcasts of the community, who welcomed the economic as well as emotional security provided by the Army. Their enthusiasm for the Cause substituted for any individual desire for gain or self-aggrandizement. The discipline of the soldier and the devoutness of the ascetic combined to build up among workers a strong feeling of group loyalty and attachment to the leaders.

The emphasis placed by the Army upon the reclamation of the individual—the drunkard, criminal, prostitute, and wastrel—led to

practical results which could be demonstrated and dramatized. The sudden reformation of the individual assumed something of the character of the religious miracle, and colorful reports of such reformation provided effective advertising. The work of the Army among the down-and-outs of the city won for it the affection of those who did not feel welcome in the houses of worship of the more richly endowed denominations and the sympathy of those who had a philanthropic interest in the welfare of the less fortunate elements of the population. The Army worker had no hesitation in stopping to minister to the drunkard, ex-criminal, or prostitute on the street; the Army hostel was open to those who needed food and clothing. Philanthropic activities became an important part of the Army's work. Primarily, however, the force of its appeal lay in its emphasis upon the simple message of the gospel. The Army grew with all the enthusiasm of the new religious sect. It was prepared to encourage the most extravagant forms of religious expression if converts to the cause were gained.

Efforts of the older churches to adopt some of the methods of the Salvation Army were an indication of their effectiveness. But the success of the Army, in the end, was not due to any particular method. The strength of the Army lay in the fact that it was an exclusive religious sect. It expanded through its appeal to a particular class in the community. However much the older churches may have employed its methods, they were unable to make the sort of single appeal characteristic of the Army. Whatever the traditional churches did for the urban masses, the fact of social distinction was emphasized. In the Army, social differentiation disappeared in the emphasis upon spiritual worth.

INSTITUTIONALIZATION OF THE ARMY

Barracks still standing in many towns and villages provide an indication of the rapid growth of the movement. The same buildings, long since abandoned or converted to other uses, suggest an equally rapid decline. The high peak was reached about the turn of the century. Subsequent development was in the direction of limiting the field of evangelical work and strengthening the organization. Like other religious movements before it, the Army was forced away from the role of the religious sect in seeking a closer accommodation with the community.

The Salvationists' evangelism had been dominated by the consciousness of the souls still to be saved, and this restless search for the wicked and the damned gave their work its distinctive character. But the urge to spread ever further the message of religious salvation led inevitably to an impatience with the slow and laborious task of building up a permanent organization. The result was that many who were drawn into the Army were later lost through failure to follow up the early work of evangelization.

In the interests of the larger movement, Army Headquarters decided to withdraw from areas where sufficient support was not secured to maintain a strong local organization. The decision reflected the viewpoint of a leadership concerned with problems of administration and finance rather than the evangelist's main concern for saving souls. Necessarily, as the Army grew, greater attention had to be paid to building up a following loyal to the movement as a whole. Those served by the Army had to be taxed for its support. This meant an increasing emphasis on organization at the cost of reducing evangelical work.

The shift in emphasis did not come about without bitter internal conflict, which on a number of occasions led to open division and the organization of rival armies. The differences were fundamental. International Headquarters was concerned with building the movement into a permanent religious organization with its own following. The dissident evangelists were concerned with saving souls wherever they might be found, with little regard to denominational lines. The one view reflected the spirit of the church, the other the spirit of the religious sect. Although the Army suffered a serious loss of support from these defections, in the end it gained in terms of building up a strong organization. If it were to survive, it had to rid itself of some of those very attributes which had accounted for its early success.

By 1914 the Salvation Army in Canada had ceased to be a movement of the social masses. Where the typical Salvationist had been a reformed drunkard, ex-prostitute, or ex-criminal, he was now a person of some social standing with a particular competence as a religious teacher and social welfare worker. A division developed between the Salvationists, on the one hand, and those being saved on the other. Greater attention came to be paid to the educational qualifications, social position, and personality of those enlisted in officers' ranks. Establishment of a training school to equip young men and women for positions of responsibility and leadership marked the final passing of the old type of Salvationist and the emergence of the professional Salvation Army worker.

The change in the character of the Army leadership was closely related to change in the general position of the Army within the community. The movement developed into a sort of social welfare organization. Rescue work among such groups as ex-convicts, drunkards, prostitutes, and unmarried mothers led to the establishment of special homes and institutions, and the management of these came to command a greater share of attention of Army leaders. Recognition of the value of its good work won for the Army a greater measure of public good will, while the increasing financial costs of the work, in turn, forced the Army to seek greater support from the public. The World War of 1914–1918 hastened a development already under way before 1914. Its war work secured the reputation of the Army as a patriotic organization and strengthened ties with the community. Once the support of the community had been secured, it could not be easily abandoned. Vested interests operated to check any shift back to the separatist position of the religious sect.

Conclusion

1. Rapid urbanization, accompanied by increased mobility, rootlessness, and class cleavage, affected the social basis of religious participation in late nineteenth-century Canada.

2. Institutionalization of the Methodist church tied it to the more well-to-do elements of the community. This was reflected in the leadership of the Church, its social doctrine, its methods, and the nature and location of its churches. These characteristics limited the access and appeal of Methodism to the urban lower class.

3. Church-sponsored evangelism, an effort to reach a broader population, was unsuccessful because it failed to provide a new channel for religious participation and was unable to use an aggressive corps of lay workers.

4. The Salvation Army, an offshoot of Methodism, operated as a religious sect, with unconventional methods and organization. It was thus able to gain access to the mobile city poor.

5. In time the Salvation Army itself became institutionalized, with an increasingly professional ministry, limited evangelism, and an emphasis on regularized social welfare activity.

Section 8   Collective behavior

Religion is connected with collective behavior in two ways. (1) Collective rites and ceremonies are more characteristic of religion than of other social institutions. (2) Under certain circumstances, religious gatherings are more likely than other kinds of gatherings to arouse collective excitement and stimulate extreme forms of expressive behavior.

Before discussing in more detail the twofold relation of religion to collective behavior, a third, hypothetical link between the two is examined. This is the connection postulated by Emile Durkheim who saw in collective behavior of a wholly secular kind one of the sources of religious belief and feeling.[74]

COLLECTIVE BEHAVIOR AND THE ORIGIN OF RELIGION

Durkheim was concerned with the question of how primitive man came to arrive at a concept of the divine—of something possessing supernatural powers, upon which man is dependent, to which he owes absolute obedience and respect, but which is able to impart to him some of its extraordinary strength and power. Durkheim reasoned that, in order to be able to imagine divine beings, man must experience something in his everyday life that has the characteristics men attribute to their gods. According to Durkheim, society itself leads men to the idea of the divine. Like a god, society has absolute moral authority over the individual; it has

[74] Durkheim, *op. cit.*, esp. pp. 205–39.

its own ends, which often override the desires of the individual; it demands sacrifice and obedience; it seems to exist over and above the individual and to be more powerful than he. And like a god, society gives to man greater powers than he would possess without its aid. Like a god, society is, paradoxically, both master and helper to man.

But, Durkheim argues, society works in such circuitous and obscure ways that the individual does not comprehend the source of its influence on him: "Men know well that they are acted upon, but they do not know by whom." [75] Hence, man invents the concept of supernatural powers, gods, and deities to represent or symbolize his consciousness of being dependent on something greater than himself.

Durkheim saw in man's everyday social life a sufficient basis for the human concept of the divine. But he also pointed to a special relation between collective behavior and the origin of religious concepts and feelings. In collective behavior situations, the individual has the sense of being carried away by an outside force. At the same time he feels released, infused with increased energy, vitality, and intense feelings. In collective behavior situations, therefore, primitive man most easily conceives of himself as possessed by supernatural forces.

In this way, Durkheim contended, the tribal gatherings of primitive peoples are transformed into religious ceremonies. Fundamental to Durkheim's view was that "the emotional and passional faculties of the primitive are only imperfectly placed under the control of his reason and will. . . ." [76] Tribal gatherings lead, therefore, to crowd behavior and collective excitement; aided by rhythmic songs, dances, and sounds, the individual loses control of himself. He experiences exaltation; he feels transformed; he is transported to another world very different from the "uniform, languishing and dull" routine of his

everyday life. [77] In addition, the group as a whole gains a sense of emotional unity that transcends the everyday dependence of its members on each other. Such occasions become sacred to the individual and the group, and are reinforced and elaborated by means of sacred symbols, myths, and rites.

Efforts to identify the historical origin of mankind's concept of the divine are, of course, unverifiable; there is no way of going back to a prereligious period when man had no concept of the divine and to watch the transformation of secular gatherings into religious institutions. However, as a generalization about the connection between collective behavior and the creation of new faiths, Durkheim's theory has merit. New religious movements, in common with new social movements of all kinds, are apt to encourage collective excitement and emotional contagion as devices to create and spread a new faith. As new religious faiths become accepted and institutionalized, they rely less on extreme forms of collective behavior to generate commitment, and they are apt to discourage them as disruptive and as threats to existing religious forms and authority.

RELIGION AND EXPRESSIVE BEHAVIOR

In the more familiar Christian rituals, the collective nature of religious worship is highly controlled. The worshiping congregation is not a crowd, and the religious rites of most Christian churches set strict limits to individual expressiveness. Decorum, solemnity, reverence, humility are emphasized. Exuberance, noise, freedom of movement, and interaction among worshipers are virtually forbidden.

Historically, however, the religious gathering has been one of the primary settings for extreme expressive behavior. A list of expressive practices in religious gatherings would be long indeed. One of the oldest is "speaking with tongues." This phrase, used at sev-

[75] *Ibid.*, p. 209.
[76] *Ibid.*, p. 215.
[77] *Loc. cit.*

eral points in the Bible,[78] refers to the shouting of meaningless words and syllables while at the height of religious ecstasy. An individual so possessed is believed to be an instrument of the voice of God. Typically, the speaker does not understand the message, which must be interpreted by another member of the congregation who is also divinely inspired.

The extreme behavior permitted within the context of some religious rites and gatherings is usually not condoned in everyday life and may even violate the regular norms of a society. For example, American and Canadian Indians who practice the Peyote religion oppose the sale and use of peyote for nonsacramental purposes.[79]

The historical connection between religious gatherings and extreme behavior has its roots in the nature of religious belief and in the intrinsically expressive and nonutilitarian character of religious rites and practices.

1. Religious beliefs are better fitted than others to validate extreme forms of behavior. The individual who believes that he is possessed by supernatural forces feels that his extreme behavior is explainable and appropriate.

2. Many religious rites, though they arouse collective excitement, provide no outlet for it. There is some evidence that when the individual has no realistic means of dealing with excessive stimulation, he experiences physiological stress expressed as uncontrollable trembling, writhing, and similar responses.[80]

3. Finally, religious faith is difficult to experience vividly in everyday life or to demonstrate to others. Extreme manifestations of expressive behavior can demonstrate depth of faith and feeling both to others and to the active participant.

---

[78] See I Corinthians 12–14.

[79] J. S. Slotkin, "The Peyote Way," in Lessa and Vogt (eds.), *op. cit.*, pp. 482–86.

[80] See William Sargant, *Battle for the Mind* (Garden City: Doubleday, 1957).

Revivals

The most important example in recent Western history of a religious gathering generating collective excitement and extreme behavior is the English and American revival meeting of the eighteenth and nineteenth centuries.

Reports of early revivals abound in accounts of penitent sinners writhing in agony on the floor, screaming, falling into comas, and speaking with tongues. John Wesley, the founder of Methodism, described in detail the effects of his preaching at meetings during the year 1739:

Some sunk down, and there remained no strength in them; others exceedingly trembled and quaked; some were torn with a kind of convulsive motion in every part of their bodies, and that so violently that often four of five persons could not hold one of them.[81]

Early in the nineteenth century churchmen explicitly recognized that collective religious excitement, conversions, and extreme behavior, formerly thought to be divine miracles, could be induced by the use of appropriate techniques, and lay revivalism gradually emerged as an occupation distinct from the regular ministry. As the following list reveals, revivalist techniques were based on a sound grasp of the conditions that foster emotional contagion, heighten expressiveness, and break down conventional controls.

1. Preaching was intellectually simple, dramatic, and repetitive. Often it was consciously designed to arouse intense fears of Hell and Damnation. Preaching was extemporaneous; revivalists were free to gesture, move about, and adapt their exhortations to the responses of the audience.

2. Revivalists were not only lay preachers but itinerants, who would come into a town, hold meetings, and leave. In this transitory situation preacher and audience could respond to each other in terms of the immedi-

---

[81] Quoted in *ibid.*, p. 100.

ate moment and with a degree of anonymity.

3. Audience participation was actively encouraged. A hearty "Amen" from some member of the audience, besides being regarded as a visitation of the Spirit, was an encouragement to preacher and audience alike. Revivalists often explicitly exhorted audiences to be demonstrative.

> Your prayers are so very cold they do not rise more than six feet high; you must strive hard and struggle—you must groan, you must agonize, why you must pray till your nose bleeds, or it will not avail. [82]

4. Revivalists developed the "protracted meeting," which consisted of "a continuous series of meetings . . . from sunrise to midnight with time out only to eat and sleep." [83] Later the protracted meeting was abandoned and for it was substituted several weeks of nightly meetings. Since revival meetings were typically led by a single revivalist, the attention of the listener was fixed for long periods of time on one subject only—conversion—and on one person only.

5. A feature of the revival was the "anxious seat" described as "some particular seat . . . [usually the front benches or pews] where the anxious may come and be addressed particularly and be made the subject of prayers and sometimes conversed with individually." [84] Besides permitting the revivalist to concentrate upon his best prospects, the "anxious seat" placed those in it under considerable social pressure to live up to expectations.

Sustained and continual stimulation of collective excitement is not possible without social organization and institutional supports. The successful revivalist was and still is dependent upon careful organization, publicity campaigns, and—most important—the co-operation of the regular churches. Of recent revivals conducted by Billy Graham in

Great Britian it has been reported that half of the seats were reserved in advance by groups, usually from churches, and that many went intending to make a public decision. [85]

Revivals and the Church Service

Extreme emotional expressiveness is not a part of the normal Protestant church service. The staging of a revival differs radically from the traditional church ceremony, and revivalists often consciously make their meetings as unlike regular church services as possible short of outright secularization. [86]

Revivals are usually conducted in large circus tents, in barren lecture halls, sometimes under the open sky. Even when sponsored by a church, they are held, as a rule, in an auditorium, not in the church itself. Regular religious worship, on the other hand, is carried on in buildings set aside as churches and therefore to some extent sacred. Because reverence restrains the spontaneous and free expression of emotion, revivalists seek to break down reverential attitudes. The revival meeting is carried on in a setting divested of traditional religious symbolism; lively or sentimental music is played and sung; the revivalist employs broad humor, uses conversational language, translates the Bible into homey language, and sometimes attacks the regular ministry. In these and other ways the revivalist tries to break down a ritualistic and circumspect approach to the sacred.

The revival meeting is an improvisation of the revivalist, who strives for an immediate and personal relation with his audience. The order of the church service, on the other hand, is largely determined by the denomination and is far less subject to the minister's discretion. He leads a prescribed service; while a sermon may be improvised, the ideal is one carefully prepared in advance. Though the personal qualities of the minis-

---

[82] William G. McLoughlin, Jr., *Modern Revivalism* (New York: Ronald, 1959), p. 27. (Quoted)
[83] *Ibid.*, p. 93.
[84] Quoted in *ibid.*, p. 95.

[85] Argyle, *op. cit.*, p. 54.
[86] McLoughlin, *op. cit.*, p. 241.

In some New England churches the pews were enclosed. The worshipers could see the minister, but the walls reduced interaction among the congregation.

ter can add or detract from the service, members are expected, during the church service, to relate to the ministerial office rather than to the person filling that office. After a successful revival, the convert is apt to speak of the revivalist, his powers, and his saintliness, while the church member is apt to speak of a "good service" or "good sermon."

The Catholic mass has a still more restraining influence upon behavior. The order of Catholic worship is even more traditionally prescribed than the Protestant service. Much of the Catholic service is conducted in Latin, and symbolic objects are approached and handled in more formally prescribed ways.

Section 9 **Population and ecology**

The religious affiliations of mankind can be only roughly estimated. The approximate memberships of the five major religions are as follows:

Christian	900 million
Islam (Moslems)	450 million
Hindu	350 million
Confucian	300 million
Buddhist	150 million

All the variations of Christianity probably include less than one-third of the people of the world; Roman Catholics, with more than half a billion members, make up by far the largest subdivision. Indeed, there are more Roman Catholics than the total population of Islam. Catholics comprise between one-sixth and one-fifth of mankind; Protestants about one-twelfth.

It would be rash to estimate the varying rates of growth of the major religions. However, Christianity will probably not maintain its present share of the world's people because many of the adherents of Christianity live in more highly developed countries with lower birth rates. The Moslem faith may grow somewhat faster than Christianity. Unless there are large and unanticipated conversions, the religions of mankind for the foreseeable future will be predominantly other than the Christian and Moslem faiths that originated in the Middle East.

RELIGIONS OF THE UNITED STATES

Data on religious affiliation for the United States are usually compilations of reports from religious bodies rather than direct enumeration of the religion of individuals. The reliability of information based on such records is, therefore, very uneven. Some small religious organizations with few churches are not reported at all. Record-keeping is a costly enterprise that requires some education, and churches with lower-class membership and poorly educated officials are likely to have poor records. Some churches give only approximations of their memberships, and these can usually be recognized because they are reported in round numbers. (Paradoxically, reporting in round numbers can also suggest statistical sophistication.) Furthermore, religious organizations have varying definitions of membership. Most Protestant churches list only those who actually join a congregation. The Roman Catholic Church and some others include as members all who have been christened. Some churches count only family heads, others include all of the members of the ethnic-religious community. Familiarity with the basis of a denomination's report of membership is essential to a meaningful interpretation of its numerical strength. Statistics reported by religious bodies, although admittedly imperfect, are published by the National Council of the Churches of Christ in the U.S.A. in the *Yearbook of American Churches,* and are summarized in the *Statistical Abstract of the United States* and other standard reference works.

Variation in record-keeping policies suggests the difficulty of defining religious adherence with precision. Similar responses to such an ostensibly simple question as "What is your religion?" have widely varying meanings. Some people who answer "Methodist" are members of the church in all meanings of membership, were reared in the church, are active and devoted practitioners, attend services regularly, send their children to Sunday school, contribute financially to the church and its missions, tithe, participate in the non-religious activities of the church community, are visited by the minister, and are baptized, married, and buried in the church. Other respondents who answer "Methodist" merely express a preference or a sense of general identity. A full understanding of religious statistics would, therefore, depend on answers to a battery of questions on church membership, attendance, belief, and religious practice, not merely the response to one general question.

Nevertheless, even a simple question can yield valuable results when it is addressed to members of all faiths as well as nonbelievers. In 1957 for the first time the Bureau of the Census included a question on religion in one of its regular surveys. It asked a nationwide sample of persons fourteen years old and over, "What is your religion?" Of all persons in the survey 96 per cent reported a religion, 3 per cent stated they had none, and 1 per cent made no report. Answers were voluntary.

The findings of the sample survey make it possible to construct an estimate of the re-

ligious distribution of the United States. The figures given below exclude some members of the armed forces, and some children not living with their families. It is assumed that children under fourteen years, who were not in the sample, had the same religion as the head of the family. With the foregoing qualifications the 1957 religious composition may be described as follows:

Protestant	111,100,000	66.2%
Catholic	43,761,000	26.1%
Jewish	5,020,000	3.0%
Other	2,091,000	1.2%
No religion	4,717,000	2.8%
Not reported	1,189,000	0.7%
Total	167,878,000	100.0%

By restricting discussion to the actual sample, a more detailed breakdown can be made, and Table XI:4 gives the summary results of the survey by sex and color. The figures are based on sample data and are, therefore, *estimates* of the population aged *fourteen and older.* Protestants are the most numerous with about 79 million reported, Roman Catholics are the largest single denomination with about 30.7 million, and Jews number 3.9 million. Nonwhites are preponderantly Protestant, concentrated in two denominations. The majority are Baptist, and the next most numerous are Methodist. Although these two denominations are also most often reported by white Protestants, they are not nearly so preponderant. A substantially larger number of males than females say they have no religion.

By region, Roman Catholics and Jews are concentrated in the Northeast, Protestants in the South and North Central states. Jews are most urbanized, and Protestants least urbanized of the three major religions. Variation in fertility by religion is related to urbanization, socio-economic status, and other factors as well as to the influence of religious beliefs on reproduction. As shown in Table XI:5, Baptist women have the high-

Table **XI:4**   Religion Reported for Persons Fourteen Years Old and
Over, by Color and Sex, United States, 1957 *

| Religion | Number in Thousands | Per Cent Total | Per Cent Distribution | | | |
| | | | White | | Nonwhite | |
			Male	Female	Male	Female
Total, 14 years and over	(119,333)	100.0	100.0 (51,791)	100.0 (55,570)	100.0 (5,679)	100.0 (6,293)
Protestant	78,952	66.2	62.4	65.1	85.4	89.4
Baptist	23,525	19.7	15.1	15.2	59.1	62.0
Lutheran	8,417	7.1	7.9	7.7	0.3	0.2
Methodist	16,676	14.0	13.1	14.1	17.0	17.5
Presbyterian	6,656	5.6	5.8	6.4	1.0	0.8
Other Protestant	23,678	19.8	20.5	21.7	8.0	8.9
Roman Catholic	30,669	25.7	27.8	27.9	6.4	6.6
Jewish	3,868	3.2	3.6	3.6	——	0.1
Other religion	1,545	1.3	1.3	1.2	1.5	1.5
No religion	3,195	2.7	4.0	1.3	5.4	1.7
Religion not reported	1,104	0.9	0.9	0.9	1.3	0.7

* Includes about 809,000 members of the Armed Forces living off post or with their families on post. [Source: Bureau of the Census, *Current Population Reports*, Series P-20, No. 79 (February, 1958).]

Table **XI:5**   Number of Children Ever Born per 1,000 Women, Married
and Husband Present, by Religion, U.S., 1957 *

Religion	Per 1,000 Women 15 to 44 Years Old	Ratio to Nation [a] (Standardized by Age)
Total	2,218	1.00
Protestant	2,220	1.01
Baptist	2,359	1.09
Lutheran	2,013	.90
Methodist	2,155	.97
Presbyterian	2,001	.88
Other Protestant	2,237	1.02
Roman Catholic	2,282	1.01
Jewish	1,749	.79
Other, none, and not reported	2,069	.95

* Source: Bureau of the Census, *Current Population Reports*, Series P-20, as reported in Donald J. Bogue, *The Population of the United States* (Glencoe: The Free Press, 1959), p. 696.
[a] For interpreting such ratios, see MINORITIES, p. 535. Standard is the distribution by age of all women of corresponding marital status in the United States in 1950.

est fertility, Roman Catholics next, and the lowest are Jewish and Presbyterian women. The high Baptist fertility is connected to the large proportion of Negroes and the rural and Southern backgrounds of white Baptists—all factors associated with high fertility.

The decision of the Census Bureau to use such a simple and general question is indicative of the fact that religion is thought to be a sensitive topic in the U.S. A more specific question, such as "What church do you belong to?" might, it was feared, seem offensive. The question was also an experiment in anticipation of the 1960 Census—an experiment to see what results could be secured and to test public reception. Apparently the results were satisfactory: the refusal rate was small. But a question on religion was not included in the 1960 Census, and even the full findings from the 1957 sample survey have not been published. The suppression of the additional findings, publication of which had been planned, and the decision not to include a religion question in the 1960 Census are further evidence of how sensitive the topic is to some politically influential people.

INNER-CITY CHURCHES

Ecological change in the central city poses problems of religious organization as well as race relations and urban development. (See MINORITIES, pp. 534–35, and URBAN MAN, pp. 613–14.) The first residents of large cities in the United States were predominantly Protestants of British Isles or Western European background. As they moved out of the deteriorating centers of the cities, they were replaced by immigrants, many of whom were Catholics or Jews. Still later urban migrants were Protestants from the South, both Negroes and whites, and most recently, Catholic Puerto Ricans. The successive replacement of one population by another is often reflected in the occupancy of churches.

Within a fifty-year period the same houses of worship may in turn serve the three major American faiths and half a dozen denominational divisions.

A process of migration and succession is the usual adjustment to population change. The church abandons its building or sells to a successor and moves to a new location where its old members (or people like them) reside. Established inner-city churches of the major Protestant denominations are losing members at an accelerated rate, and many of them have been forced to close because they were unable to maintain a congregation large enough to support current expenses. In Boston, for example, one denomination has lost five inner-city churches in the last ten years. In New York, another denomination either abandons or merges one church every year. In Detroit, fifty-five churches were abandoned in the center of the city in a fifteen year period from 1940–1955.[87] Other churches retreat more slowly, serve their old membership as it declines, retrench on programs and operating costs, and perhaps merge with other congregations. These are "remnant" churches that leave to others the responsibility of ministering to newcomers.

Still other churches have a third policy. They try to remain in the inner city and adapt themselves to the new population base. As the neighborhood changes, so does the membership of the congregation. A church that once served a highly educated, upper-middle-class population of British Isles background may have the task of adjusting to a heterogeneous, lower-class population partly of Southern rural origins, partly of recent European immigrants. Such churches with missionary objectives must adjust to heavy demands with curtailed financial resources.

[87] "The Organization Church," *Time*, April 7, 1961, p. 53, and "Can City Churches Survive?" *Look*, April 11, 1961, p. 76.

Chapter **XII**

Education

By **BURTON R. CLARK**

in collaboration with L.B. and P.S.

Section 1 **Introduction**[1]

The sociology of education inquires into the relation of education as a specialized activity to other institutions and features of the larger society. First, it examines the social conditions that affect education. Schools and colleges are influenced by cultural values, the political system, the economic order, and social stratification. Second, sociology seeks to understand the functions performed by education for society and how it influences other institutions. The educational system transmits culture, socializes the young, and in modern society, largely determines the life chances of the next generation. It trains the brains needed by an advanced industrial society for laboratories and machine shops, and for responsible positions in industry and government.

Such questions as the following are dealt with: How does the role of the school administrator compare with that of the business leader? Can the role of college student be compared with that of factory worker,

prison inmate, or inhabitant of a mental hospital? How do the values and perceptions of the middle-class teacher interact with the characteristics of lower-class children to determine the fate of these children in the schools?

Much research in educational sociology has concentrated on social class and education, and has examined the influence of social background on educational aspiration, experience, and achievement. Other connections between society and education have been identified as fruitful lines of inquiry. For example, there is growing interest in the relation of education to the economy. Advancing technology raises educational requirements, and more occupations require longer training. This trend tends to make some schools and colleges into training centers for industry. Education is also closely connected with the development of new nations, as reflected in the training of leaders to replace colonial administrators, or the preparation of experts to man new industry and public services.

Recently sociologists have become interested in the *internal* analysis of schools and colleges. They have become interested

[1] An effort has been made in this chapter to recast for beginning students certain aspects of *Educating the Expert Society* (San Francisco: Chandler, 1962) by Burton R. Clark. A few pages of the chapter follow the book rather closely.

in student subcultures, especially the bearing of the subcultures on academic performance. Group norms among some high school students may "restrict output," a phenomenon noted among workers by industrial sociologists. They inquire into the contradictory demands of serious study and of the adolescent subworld of fun. Sociologists are also turning to the analysis of the roles of teacher, administrator, and trustee. They study the authority relation between teachers and principals, and how it affects the goals and methods of education. As schools and colleges grow more complex, new roles emerge. The *counselor* may be studied as an important part of the system, influencing the classification of students and, thereby, the role of the school in determining the fate of the young.

Education broadly defined takes place in every institution. Parents systematically instruct their children, the minister teaches his congregation, the writer influences his readers, and the artist his audience. The varieties of educational experience are almost without limit. Even the more institutionalized forms have great variety. Educational centers range from nursery schools to institutes of advanced study, poetry centers, and radiation laboratories. They include units established for adult education and part-time

study. Separately organized "schools" are also found in industry and the military, and have long been a part of many churches. This chapter concentrates on the main forms of institutionalized general education.

SOURCES AND READINGS

Orville G. Brim, Jr., *Sociology and the Field of Education* (New York: Russell Sage Foundation, 1958).

Wilbur B. Brookover, *A Sociology of Education* (New York: American Book Co., 1955).

Burton R. Clark, *Educating the Expert Society* (San Francisco: Chandler, 1962).

James S. Coleman, *The Adolescent Society* (New York: The Free Press of Glencoe, 1961).

A. H. Halsey, Jean Floud and C. Arnold Anderson, *Education, Economy, and Society* (New York: The Free Press of Glencoe, 1961).

Robert J. Havighurst and Bernice L. Neugarten, *Society and Education* (Boston: Allyn and Bacon, 1957).

A. B. Hollingshead, *Elmtown's Youth* (New York: Wiley, 1949).

Blaine E. Mercer and Edwin R. Carr, *Education and the Social Order* (New York: Rinehart, 1957).

David Riesman, *Constraint and Variety in American Education* (University of Nebraska Press, 1956).

Thorstein Veblen, *The Higher Learning in America* (B. W. Heubsch, 1918); and (Stanford, California: Academic Reprints, 1954).

Willard Waller, *The Sociology of Teaching* (New York: Wiley, 1932).

Section 2   Social organization

Like the chief economic, political, and religious institutions, education has become increasingly specialized. In earlier times, education blended with the other activities of the family, church, and community. As Western social organization developed from a homogeneous society to one characterized

by increasing division of labor, education emerged as a separate institution. The teacher became the specialized agent of instruction and the school the specialized agency for systematic transmission of culture. Responsibilities still overlap, particularly between the school on the one hand and the family and the church on the other. But differentiation of education as a separate institution is hardly in doubt, and more educational specialization and separation can be expected.

As a differentiated institution, education is dependent on other institutions and reacts to their changes. It is also an independent force that influences other institutions. This section first considers the extent to which education is independent of and integrated with the rest of society and the community. Since education is becoming increasingly important to the workings of the economy, the role of education at various stages of industrialization is also examined.

AUTONOMY AND INTEGRATION OF EDUCATION

The relation between education and other major institutions varies according to the nature of the society and its values. In totalitarian societies, education is closely integrated with the central government and the ruling party. Schools and colleges are components of the government. In practice, however, the extent of government control varies even in totalitarian societies. No large educational system is likely to remain entirely dependent on the political order. Its professional personnel develop ways of avoiding or overriding undesired directives from the state. A large institution also develops momentum of its own, and its actions may lead to consequences that are not desired or anticipated by state officials. In general, however, totalitarian societies subordinate education to political requirements as defined by the state.

In democratic societies, education is more nearly independent; but among these societies its institutional autonomy varies in both degree and in form. In some countries, control is relatively centralized in a national system of schools and colleges. In France, the Ministry of Education determines educational policy, the nature of the curricula, the qualification of teachers, and the assignment of pupils to various secondary schools by means of nationally administered examinations.[2] In centralized systems the number of students admitted to higher education may be determined by a national plan derived from a prediction of manpower needs. Local communities may exert only minor influence. Under such conditions, education is heavily involved in national politics, and interest groups attempt to influence policy in the legislative and executive branches of government.

In democratic countries with decentralized educational systems, professional personnel are largely independent of influences from the national government. The public educational system of the United States is extensively decentralized, with direct supervision of school affairs in the hands of thousands of local school boards. The schools are in politics, but in politics at the state and community levels rather than at the national level.

Democratic societies generally permit private schools. Thus a religious denomination can establish its own schools; a group of parents can initiate and support a "Three R's School"; Harvard University can exist as an independent academic municipality. The development of various private schools adds to the variety and decentralization of an educational institution.

Although many educators in the United States believe that a decentralized educational system is best, the industrializing societies of Africa, Asia, and Latin America will probably tend toward centralized systems—at least during the early stages of modernization. They will plan national systems of schools and colleges in order to train men quickly and effectively according to predicted national need. Unplanned, uncoordinated, and decentralized systems will seem expensive luxuries they cannot afford

[2] Marguerite L. Richards, "The Administration of French Education," *Current History*, **35** (August, 1958), 78–85.

Why Autonomy Is Important

The relative importance of integration and autonomy is different for every institution, but the balance between them is one of the most important problems in the study of social organization. Educators continuously strive to protect the independence of their institutions. They face encroachment from many forces in society, especially those that want to change educational policies. In resisting pressures, educational leaders feel they are protecting important public interests that have been entrusted to them. As experts and professionals, educators claim to have the training and devotion to standards that justify their autonomy.

This argument can be improperly used to avoid all criticism, but it reflects an important sociological truth. Because the values entrusted to education are general, such as "to advance learning," the work of the institution is justified on a long-run basis. Its activities cannot readily be judged by immediate results.

Most groups cannot be expected to take continuous account of the ultimate values educational institutions try to defend. This task must be left to specialists who have the necessary competence, with enough autonomy to permit them to work out and protect major policies and standards. The amount of autonomy that is needed can be determined only in the light of the specific case.

In a decentralized educational system, the optimum balance of autonomy and integration is a problem in the local community as well as in states and the society as a whole. Local interest groups try to influence school policy toward their own point of view or to serve their own needs. The school crosses the paths of the local churches in moral instruction. It interacts with local businessmen in obtaining food and other supplies and in operating its physical plant. Its teachers are vulnerable to local surveillance when laymen can bring pressure to bear through a school board. Every school district needs to decide how much it will accede to, or resist, the demands of particular local groups, and how its work should be related to other local institutions. If not decided consciously, the patterns of school-community relations are formed out of day-to-day adjustments.

The degree of autonomy helps to determine whether schools are to be passive instruments of communication or centers of initiative and change. Schools closely integrated with communities are likely to perform as they are bidden by the lay groups that comprise the local power structure. Educational personnel have little room to maneuver, little control over the extent and direction of change. Close local control produces an accommodating institution. Where schools are independent of public opinion and pressure, however, change may be initiated by the professional personnel.

Conditions of Autonomy

Whether or not a particular segment of the educational institution can maintain its autonomy depends on a number of related factors other than the general structure of the society:

1. *Firmness of the value.* If the values upheld by a school are well established and firmly accepted by the community, there is relatively little pressure upon the institution to justify itself by "results" or to adapt its policies to the immediate needs of specific groups. Medical education is a good example of a well-established and firmly accepted value, and medical programs are among the most secure educational activities. On the other hand, institutions that carry on activities weakly accepted as a public interest find it difficult to maintain their autonomy. They are insecure, and vulnerable to outside demands. Adult education, a good example, is discussed below.

2. *Professionalism.* Autonomy is dependent on the possibility of developing standards and training. Special skills and language ("jargon" to the outsider) are conducive to

social isolation, and when they are combined with professional prestige, they make it easier to resist the efforts of laymen to intrude their judgments. Physicists and mathematicians are protected by the specialized nature of their knowledge and the inability of laymen to understand their work. Elementary schoolteachers, in contrast, are vulnerable because parents live with their results and feel competent to judge their work.

3. *Source of support.* The extent of reliance on outside funds and the source from which a school or college draws its support affect its autonomy. A state college may be wholly dependent on public funds and subject to influence from the governor's office and the legislature. On the other hand, state support may free the college from the pressures of the local community, and the state constitution may protect it against gross legislative interference with educational policy. A private college may have considerable autonomy if it has large endowments and a reputation that attracts students, but it is vulnerable if it is financed on a year-to-year basis or if it cannot draw enough students to guarantee a steady income from tuition fees.

4. *Organizational scale.* Large, complex organizations are difficult to supervise from the outside. Their size obscures many activities from public view; their complexity keeps all but experienced administrators ignorant of how they actually are run—or not run. As a state college grows from 1,000 to 15,000 students, the chances of close external control decline. Authority is delegated to or assumed by the professional staff of administrators and professors. The full-time experts who are close to operations know what is going on and have the specialized competence to make informed decisions.

The presence or absence of these four conditions determines the capacity of the institution to make its own policies and protect itself from outside pressure.

Adult Education[3]

Adult education is only weakly accepted as a public interest, and the institutions that carry on this activity are insecure and dependent. The public schools are concerned primarily with the education of the young, and adult schools maintained by local school authorities compete for support and budget with the elementary and secondary schools. Supplementary funds for adult education commonly come from tuition fees or state aid, both of which are dependent on attendance. Hence, great emphasis is placed on attracting students. Classes live or die according to the enrollment of a student population that is part-time, voluntary, and casual.

The teaching staff is part-time and weakly professionalized. The program of courses must be flexible because of undependable financing and changing student interests. The career lines for teachers and principals are not well defined, and advancement often means leaving the adult school for a stable, recognized position in a high school or college.

A weakly established value, a low degree of professionalism, and heavy reliance on outside financial sources combine to place adult educators in a marginal and vulnerable position. With their low degree of independence, they often become subservient to their students.

EDUCATION AND INDUSTRIALIZATION

Education affects social organization through its intimate connection with commerce and industry. The educational institutions must produce men who are qualified to fill the jobs made possible and necessary by the society's stage of economic development.

As industrialization proceeds, the focus of the economy shifts first from agriculture to manufacturing, then to such service industries as transportation, finance, communica-

[3] Burton R. Clark, *Adult Education in Transition* (Berkeley and Los Angeles: University of California Press, 1956).

tions, wholesale and retail trade, government, professional work. In the agricultural stage, raw materials are the crucial economic resource; in the early and middle stages of industrialization, the machine and the specialized factory system are distinctive features of the economy. In advanced industrialism —the technological society of the 1960's —highly trained men are the critical resource. These stages require different kinds of education for the work force:

1. Small-scale farming requires unskilled workers who need little or no formal education, since not even minimal literacy is necessary to qualify for farm labor.

2. Manufacturing needs semiskilled and skilled as well as unskilled blue-collar labor, and some white-collar office workers. Nearly all factory workers need to be able to read signs and simple instructions. Literacy for the common man is a necessary step in the development of industrialism. Many future workers must remain in school beyond the primary grades in order to obtain a modest general education and training in specific skills.

3. Finally, when manufacturing processes are advanced and the emphasis shifts toward service industry, the economic order demands that education provide prolonged training for large numbers of future technicians, managers, and professional men. These men are trained in the schools and colleges, and increasingly in the educational systems that are springing up in industry and in military organizations.

In the United States there has been a steady rise in skill levels over the past century of industrialization, with rapid rise in the last two decades. Since some of the necessary training must be gained before employment, the educational threshold for most future workers has been steadily rising. A larger proportion of jobs falls into the upper ranges of skill and expertness. Large-scale enterprises—big business, big government, big education—demand managers, professionals,

and technicians, and increasing numbers of positions require training beyond high school.

The more highly developed the modern organization, the less it can depend on the general labor pool for its human resources. The swift rise in *levels* of skill, the proliferation of *types* of skill, and the rapid change that takes place in many enterprises have led to emphasis on training by employers. "In-service" training is widely conducted to supplement the pre-job training provided by the schools and colleges. There is a trend toward in-service training at all levels of the business corporation, and much military training is of a technical nature that has civilian applications in industry.

Of course, large organizations can and do send their employees back to schools and colleges for additional education. For example, a number of companies send their executives to the advanced programs of schools of business administration. But since colleges generally do not wish to, or cannot, gear their programs closely to the requirements of a particular organization, business firms in increasing numbers have developed their own educational systems. This trend extends the educational institution, for classrooms in the factory are also a differentiated and specialized part of the modern educational system.

Research and Development

In advanced industrial societies a small but extremely influential sector in the economy is composed of producers of ideas and technological innovations. "Research and development" (R & D) has become a large enterprise in industry, government, and higher education. Research laboratories, institutes, and bureaus produce a steady stream of new ideas that reshape technology, industry, and ultimately the other institutions of society. Industrial laboratories have proliferated; nearly all large firms and many small and moderate-sized ones maintain them, employing thousands of scientists and

An African boy examines a passage from the Koran inscribed on a wooden tablet. Islam and the Arabic language are widespread in Africa, and their influence is growing.

technicians.[4] The amount spent on research in American universities rose more than 2,700 per cent between 1939–40 and 1957–58, from $27 million to $734 million.

As higher education turns to the training of experts and as universities become centers

[4] A directory of indu___ ial research laboratories, with incomplete coverage, ___sted 290 laboratories in 1920 and over 5,400 in 1960. *Industrial Research Laboratories of the United States,* First and Eleventh Editions (Washington, D.C.: National Academy of Sciences—National Research Council, 1920 and 1960).

of research, they more actively influence industry and the economy. Among the direct effects, for example, is the location of new industry around major universities from which scientific and engineering talent can be drawn and where the advice of experts is readily available. The new industrial complex of the Los Angeles area is related to such institutions as the California Institute of Technology, the University of California, Los Angeles, and the University of Southern

California. Government money for research and engineering flows to the firms and regions with specific technical capability. As the United States Department of Defense shifted its purchases from tanks and ships to missiles and electronics equipment during the 1950's the geographic distribution of defense contracts shifted 'to the Pacific and Mountain States, where the aircraft and electronics industries developed. The East North Central States (Michigan, Indiana, Illinois, Ohio, and Wisconsin) lost industry,[5] and the shift drastically affected the economic and educational climate of both regions. Hundreds of thousands of jobs were involved, and many cities in the "loser" states have encountered recurrent unemployment. Thus major economic changes were related to the tendency for technical industry to grow in areas that have a strong and appropriate scientific base in both educational and business institutions.

Modernizing Societies

Compared to advanced technological societies, countries that are industrially underdeveloped and content to stay that way need few highly trained experts. Unskilled agricultural labor predominates, and most of the population can work effectively with little or no book learning. Such societies generally educate only a very small part of their population.

Many preindustrial nations—India, Egypt, Ghana, for instance—are attempting to accelerate their industrialization. This requires both capital investment and experts who possess modern skills. Some technicians can be borrowed from industrially advanced societies. But to foster its own development and express national independence, an industrializing country tries to get its own nationals trained for responsible positions. At least in the early stages some of the training can often be done more economically in other countries, but it is a legitimate aspiration for the state to develop its own educational facilities to train technicians, engineers, and professionals.

Nigeria, a nation of forty million, which became independent in 1960, found that it lacked the skilled personnel to carry out vast economic and educational projects.[6] "To fill the gap and train Nigerians" the government attempted through recruiting abroad to hire accountants, engineers, teachers, farm experts, fishermen, typists, scientists, technicians, surveyors, pilots, flight instructors, and a chief for a fire department. After the recruitment drive in 1961, the Nigerian government received only 30 applications from Canada and the United States for 400 vacancies. Eventually the skilled positions will probably be filled by Nigerians trained abroad, and later by graduates of Nigerian schools.

The shortage of skilled personnel is a world-wide phenomenon. A relatively few nations with educational systems capable of filling more than their own national requirements will be the source of training and trained personnel for some time. A modernized educational system is likely to go hand in hand with modernization rather than precede it.

[5] "The Changing Patterns of Defense Procurement" (Washington, D.C.: Office of the Secretary of Defense, 1962).

[6] San Francisco *Chronicle*, August 8, 1961.

Section 3 **Culture**

This section first reviews the relation of education to the general culture and then considers the subcultures of colleges.

IMPACT OF CORE VALUES

The core values of a society affect the nature of its educational system, and the American commitment to democratic values strongly influences the schools. (1) The concept of widespread political participation—every man a voter—encourages mass schooling so that the common man may become a literate, informed citizen. (2) The ideals of equalitarianism—equal opportunity regardless of social origin—encourage schooling for all, especially in childhood and early adolescence, in order that the young may begin on near-equal footing. The public school is valued for its democratic potential as a place where children of different classes and cultural origins meet and learn to understand one another. The comprehensive secondary school reflects the American interpretation of democratic values. It is different from the secondary school of most other countries in that it aims to bring together in one school students of many backgrounds.

The emphasis on literacy and equal opportunity encourages Americans to be "proeducation," to feel that education merits support. But other basic values work in the opposite direction. Many Americans hold an ethic of individualism, beliefs about achievement and success that make models of the frontiersman and the business entrepreneur. Originally rugged individualism devalued prolonged study and the contemplative life. It made schooling seem relatively unimportant, for one succeeded through personal qualities of thrift and courage and hard work in the world of action. The American value system continues to stress the importance of individual achievement, but in a less "rugged" conception than in the past. Today the ethic of individualism does not downgrade education but rather encourages an instrumental attitude toward it, stressing individual mobility and economic return.

CULTURAL TRANSMISSION

Schools and colleges transmit a common fund of culture to the young, serving to protect and perpetuate knowledge, beliefs, customs, and skills. In performing this broad task, the educational institution acts as an agent of the whole society.

The culture that the schools in most American communities transmit to the next generation is a complex of values and knowledge. It includes political ideals, such as belief in democratic government and national loyalty; economic conceptions, such as free enterprise; social practices, from telling time to monogamous marriage; and implicit religious understandings, such as the premise that there is a single God. With every general value there are related norms to be instilled. Abstract statements about democracy are short on meaning unless they are spelled out in connected assertions about how to act in conformity to the democratic ideal. The "rules" of democracy vary from constitutional clauses about freedom of speech to specific proscriptions against stuffing the ballot box or slandering political opponents.

Education's part in cultural transmission is under strain because expanding knowledge increases the magnitude of the task and leads to conflicting views of what is most important to teach. There is not enough time in the school day to do all the things asked, and difficult choices have to be made between history and science, between vocational training and general studies. Much of the conflict about education in the United States is attributable to the fact that formal education is becoming swamped by the task of cultural transmission.

Under conditions of rapid change, the schools become less sure that what was right for the last generation is right for the next. In modern society, each generation faces new technological and social tasks, and the future promises additional changes of unknown nature. Consequently educators try to train for adaptability, even at the expense of failing to impart the entire cultural heritage. But educating for adaptability is an ambiguous criterion. It may mean educating men to be compliant and to adjust easily and passively to group and institutional demands, or it may mean educating them to be perceptive and understanding of the social environment and flexible and imaginative in dealing with it.

Changing Cultural Function

In preserving and transmitting the learning of the past, education has a passive cultural role; it largely conserves society as given. But increasingly education is becoming an agent of cultural and social change. The universities especially are centers of innovation and criticism as they expand research and scholarship. The fruits of their research touch all institutions and lives. Research in physics and chemistry alters technology, which in turn affects the distribution of population, the status of occupations, and even the tenor of international relations. More scholars spend more time in research than ever before.

The educational institution also insulates and protects men who devote themselves to critical assessment and innovation. Despite its ties to economic and political institutions, education offers a relatively independent base of operations for many men. Some academic researchers and scholars remain partially detached from the mores of the general culture. Oriented to critical thought and set apart

from pressures of the marketplace, academic men can become free intellectuals, critical and innovating. With the major universities quasi-autonomous and committed to inquiry, the initiative in social change rests in the hands of men of thought as well as men of action.

The college should not be viewed as a perfect setting for free inquiry and creativity, however, since professors are subject to many constraints both from the outside and from the academic community. Junior members of a faculty may find their work disturbed by insecurity of employment, and professors, far from being fully protected, are also subject to the pressures of an academic marketplace.[7]

Colleges and universities also support groups that innovate in the arts. The artist of the medieval past was usually subsidized by a duke, a bishop, a wealthy family; later in history, writers gained a livelihood by means of sales to the small public of educated men. But in modern mass markets, there are few patron-sponsors, and livelihood by sales depends on a wide popularity. Those whose painting or writing is not in heavy demand need other work for support, and artists and writers have been attracted to employment in higher education in increasing numbers. Some intellectual magazines are located near campuses, edited by professors, and in some cases sponsored by colleges and universities. Novelists, musicians, and painters become professors or artists in residence. With the campus as shelter, artistic and literary talent is subsidized and given time to develop. Colleges and universities are now patrons of artists and writers and centers of experimentation in music and drama.

STUDENT SUBCULTURES

Another important cultural aspect of education is the system of norms and standards —the blueprint of behavior—found *within* the school or college. The student newly ar-

[7] Theodore Caplow and Reece J. McGee, *The Academic Marketplace* (New York: Basic Books, 1958).

rived on a college campus encounters a cultural environment, a composite of guiding values and ideals. In small colleges, the culture may be almost homogeneous. Usually, however, the campus culture is more diverse.

Alternative orientations are held by different groups—the faculty, the alumni, and a variety of students. Adaptation 32 reviews the major student subcultures in relation to trends in American education.

College Subcultures

Abridged and adapted from Burton R. Clark and Martin A. Trow, "Determinants of College Student Subculture." Published in this form by permission of the authors.

Collegiate

The *collegiate subculture* is a world of sports, dates, and fun. Its symbols are the star athlete, the homecoming queen, and the fraternity dance. Fraternities and sororities have set the pattern of the collegiate way of life. Fraternity participation in extracurricular activities extends the influence of this style, and many nonfraternal dormitories model themselves after it, from candlelight and song to float parades and panty raids. Important since the 1890's, the Joe College style is still the most visible model, the one from which have developed the stereotypes of college life found in movies, cartoons, and television.

The collegiate subculture usually recruits its most active supporters from the upper and upper-middle classes, for it takes money and leisure to pursue a round of social activities. It flourishes only on the residential campus.

This subsystem of values and activities is compatible with strong college loyalty. Its graduates often become devoted alumni, sentimentally tied to the college through happy memory of things past and through such events as the homecoming week and the "big" game. However, the collegiate subculture is resistant to involvement with ideas beyond what is required to pass courses and gain the diploma. This orientation is epitomized in the saw: "I have no intention of letting my studies interfere with my college education."

Vocational

A second orientation is the *vocational subculture*. In this subworld, students are narrowly and directly concerned with job preparation, and see college as courses and credits leading to a diploma and a better job than they could otherwise command. They use the college to pick up credits at a rate determined by what they can afford in time, money, and energy. Symbols of this subculture are the placement office and the slide rule hanging from the belt of the engineering student. Its patterns are most fully represented in the student who is poor, commutes to campus, works at an outside job between 20 and 40 hours a week, and has a wife and children. This subculture is not visible and coherent; it is simply the pragmatic, no-nonsense orientation promoted in many students by the expectations with which they enter a college and the conditions under which they attend.

The vocational subculture is not usually compatible with strong college loyalty since its members do not participate intensely in the extracurricular life of the college. Like the collegiate, the vocational subculture is resistant to intellectual demands beyond what is required to pass the courses. To many hard-driven students preparing for work directly after the bachelor's degree, ideas and scholarship are as much of a luxury and distraction as are sports and fraternities.

This subculture is likely to flourish at "streetcar" (or parking lot) colleges that recruit primarily the sons and daughters of lower-middle-class and working-class homes. It usually has little social unity. Its members interact with one another less than do those caught up in the collegiate subculture. The student role is narrow and, in the extreme, the student body is an atomized aggregation.

Academic

A third blueprint for behavior is the *academic subculture,* the way of life of serious students who identify with the intellectual concerns of faculty members. This subculture is carried by students who work hard, get the best grades, talk about their course work outside of class, and let the world of ideas and knowledge reach them.

Their symbols are the library, laboratory, and seminar; they are liked by the professors but are "greasy grinds" in the eyes of the collegiate crowd.

The academic subculture is generally compatible with college loyalty, through identification with the faculty. It is the dominant portion of the climate found at the academically strongest colleges. When colleges aim to upgrade themselves, they seek to recruit students already oriented in this direction. Students with serious academic orientation come from all social strata and cultural groups, but proportionately more of them are likely to come from upper-middle-class homes where parents are well educated, value books and learning, and have the financial resources to support their children through undergraduate and graduate study.

The undergraduate students most representative of this subculture look forward to graduate work or professional training. They think of graduate school as the place for pre-job training. Hence, they define their undergraduate years as a time for extending their appreciation of ideas and gaining a general education.

Nonconformist

A fourth orientation is the *nonconformist subculture.* There are many types of nonconformity among college students, but a principal type is the nonconforming intellectual. His distinctive style is a rather aggressive nonconformism. Critical of the "establishment" and seeking to be independent, the nonconforming intellectuals are usually hostile to the college administration and somewhat detached from the college as a whole. These students are often deeply "concerned" with the ideas of the classroom, but even more with issues current in art, literature, and politics of the wider adult society.

Nonconforming students often seek a personal identity, and in the process they adopt distinctive styles of dress, of speech, and of attitude. In the eyes of their more conforming classmates, they are the unwashed. The nonconformist subculture, involved with ideas but not identified with the college, apparently attracts participants from all social backgrounds. It offers the rebellious student shelter and intellectual support for his rebellious idealism.

These four types of subculture emerge from the combination of two factors: (*a*) the degree to which students are involved with ideas, and (*b*) the extent to which students identify with their college:

		Involved with Ideas	
		+	−
Identify with	+	Academic	Collegiate
the College	−	Nonconformist	Vocational

Decline of the Collegiate

The collegiate subculture flourishes when students have money, leisure, and a light heart about their college education. But proportionately fewer students are so equipped at the present time compared to the past, and there is a trend away from dominance of campuses by the Joe College life. Career orientations are changing. More students now plan to pursue postgraduate studies, and they know that deans and graduate faculties will review their undergraduate records. More students plan to pursue careers in large organizations, and are aware that job interviewers from business corporations or public agencies will examine the transcripts that record college performance. The boy going into a small family business is less typical. The closer bearing of college performance on career has a sobering effect on campus life.

Secondly, most big city campuses have a large proportion of students from working-class and lower-middle-class backgrounds, who do not have much money and feel they have no time to waste on collegiate activities. College for them is related to mobility and future security in a good job. Democratization of higher education thus tends to diminish the strength of the collegiate subculture.

Thirdly, the number of students enrolled in higher education is increasing due to the high birth rate that began after World War II and to the rising proportions of high school graduates who go on to college. The growth in numbers has created a sellers' market for colleges, and many colleges are setting higher standards of admission. In their selectivity, these colleges emphasize intelligence, good high school record, and seriousness. Selection on these grounds also weakens the collegiate subculture, and in the best colleges the collegiate is losing in competition with the academic emphasis.

These conditions of changing career patterns, democratization of college-going, and increasing selectivity in some colleges cause the collegiate subculture to decline. The fraternities and sororities on many campuses have been de-emphasizing the "rah-rah" life since the end of World War II.

Triumph of Vocationalism

The vocational orientation is increasing most rapidly, and a number of forces urge the student in this direction.

1. *Occupational change.* The professional, technical, and managerial occupations, which require advanced training, are growing rapidly. The college has more numerous and more definite training jobs to do. The growing undergraduate population is concentrated in applied fields, such as business administration, engineering, and education.

2. *Education as the means of mobility.* As an instrument for the achievement of higher status, college is defined as a way of getting the training and diplomas needed for the better paying jobs. People of lower social origins now entering college in larger numbers are likely to perceive college in these terms. For students of all socio-economic levels, however, the connection between college and work grows closer, encouraging an instrumental or vocational definition of the college years.

3. *Ascendance of public colleges.* The growth in American higher education is taking place largely in the public colleges and universities. These colleges are usually more responsive than private colleges to state and local demands, and provide training for the increasingly numerous occupations that require advanced skills. They are relatively inexpensive, often easy to enter, and conveniently located to serve large numbers of students. The rapid expansion of college attendance among job-oriented young people of lower social origins is chiefly in these service-minded institutions.

4. *Bureaucratization of academic organization.* The comprehensive colleges are people-processing institutions, whose administrative staffs must deal with and organize the scattered activities of large numbers of students enrolled in a variety of programs. Relations between teachers and students under these conditions are fleeting and impersonal. In the university, teachers involve themselves less with students because they are busy with research, professional activity, and off-campus service.

5. *Withdrawal of student involvement.* An

increasing proportion of college students enroll in nonresidential colleges. Living at home and holding part-time or full-time jobs, students visit the college campus to attend class or use the library; they drop in and out of college, some finishing in six to eight years while many do not finish at all. In brief, the student role is narrowed to course work and squeezed in among off-campus roles.

The trend toward vocational orientation indicates that a new cultural conflict is emerging in colleges. The older conflict was between the academic and the collegiate subcultures with the faculties upholding intellectual values and the majority of students opposing them with their own nonintellectual or anti-intellectual interests. With the decline of the collegiate and the growth of the vocational, the emerging conflict is between the academic and the vocational subcultures. Both of these orientations are "serious"; both are legitimate in the eyes of adults; both find proponents in the faculty as well as in the student body. The old conflict was whether students would study or play. The new conflict is whether they will study in broad fields of knowledge and concern themselves with general issues, or study in applied, narrow fields and concern themselves with acquiring the skills and certificates they need for a job.

Section 4 Socialization

A considerable part of the socializing task performed by parents in earlier times has now passed to teachers. There is less occupational succession within the modern family than in preindustrial societies, and the child is prepared for some roles different from those of his parents. With the school a center of preparation and selection, the teacher helps the child to acquire new attitudes, values, knowledge, and motivations. To help the child get on, the teacher in many cases must encourage the child to move away from the values and assumptions of his parents. In nearly all schools, and especially in the schools of the slums and the rural areas, the teacher must extend the horizons of the child, diversify his knowledge of opportunity, raise his level of aspiration, and induce him to exercise his talents so that he may find a place that is different from, and not contingent upon, the roles of his parents.

EDUCATION AS A SOCIALIZING AGENCY

Socialization in the school is based on relations of teachers and students that are part of a system of universal standards and impersonal judgment. The influence of the teacher is independent of the family and kinship group and linked to the acquisition of knowledge and skill appropriate to adult roles. The classroom is decidedly different from the family as a primary socializer in its use of objective, impersonal standards, as well as in its stress on acquisition of knowledge. It is similar to the youthful peer group in separating socialization from the family context, but it is as different from the peer group as it is from the family in its use of universal standards and its emphasis on knowledge. It also differs from the peer group in its concentration on long-term objectives rather than immediate gratification. The combination in the classroom of affective, personal relations with universal standards and serious, long-term objectives creates some distinctive problems.[8]

1. *Affection and impersonality.* Socializa-

[8] Bryan R. Wilson, "The Teacher's Role—A Sociological Analysis," *The British Journal of Sociology*, **13** (March, 1962), 15–32.

A professor emeritus maintains her place in campus life.

In the modern world school is for everybody. But it makes a difference who teaches and in what setting and with what intent. A reading lesson for second-graders in a Vermont village school.

tion in the school demands of the teacher a basic sympathy with children similar to that of parents. If the teacher is to act as a socializing agent, he must be able to foster a sustained relationship with the child. Hence the relation tends toward a primary quality. But the teacher must also engage in objective assessment and impersonal selection. The teacher, like the parent, must be judge and disciplinarian as well as supportive adult, but the teacher's role tends to become more specialized, routinized, and impersonal. The teacher-student relation is depersonalized by the increasing size of schools. Thus the larger setting of the teacher-pupil relation handicaps personal commitment to the student, a commitment that appears indispensable if the teacher is to function as an agent of broad socialization.

2. *Teacher and parent.* The roles of the teacher and parent are often divergent and competitive. The orientations of the school are alternatives to those of the home, and the teacher attempts to modify the child's perspectives. The teacher also acts as a type of parent in his personal relation with the pupil and thus may compete with the biological parent for the regard and loyalty of the child. As impersonal agent of the larger society, the teacher may also appear as a threat to parents and their hopes for their offspring.

3. *Narrow and broad socialization.* The schools have the responsibility of developing character and morality. Society asks that they produce well-rounded, sensible, good citizens, even independent men of sensitive imagination and responsible judgment in complex matters. These characteristics require a broad socialization, which in turn depends on close personal relations with frequent contacts in numerous activities. But the conditions conducive to a broad socialization must contend with the influences toward specialization that restrict the socialization work of the teacher. As teachers become more highly trained and specialized in order to handle competently a large volume of knowledge, they tend to re-

duce the area of contact with the student.

These special problems cause strain in the role of the teacher. Teachers must attempt to work out within their own settings suitable combinations of affection and impersonal judgment, narrow training and broad education, co-operation with the home and the weaning of the child from the home. These contradictory requirements of socialization are never perfectly balanced, but they are partly resolved by the school's concentration on certain approaches in the lower grades and emphasis on others at the higher levels. The lower grades are characterized by affection between teacher and pupil, familiarity of teacher and parent, and general education. Students remain in a homeroom with the same teacher for several hours a day through the school year. The higher grades are characterized by impersonality, a minimum of contact between the teacher and the parents, and specialized teaching. Students move from classroom to classroom and have many teachers and counselors during a school year. The general socialization of the early years gradually gives way to differentiated and specialized socialization.

Specialization and Socialization

As more students enter college, there is a tendency for the function of the college to change from educating the few for purely intellectual pursuits to educating the many for practical ones. This tendency has been reinforced by the growing demand of industry for skilled personnel and of the community for services, such as medicine and dentistry.

Figure XII: 1 presents part of the results of a questionnaire sent to college graduates in 1947. It lists the fields in which the respondents majored, the percentage who wished they had majored in another area, and the field most frequently mentioned as a better choice. Except for the home economics major, retrospective choice tended toward greater specialization, professionalization, and technological skill. Humanities majors expressed this trend

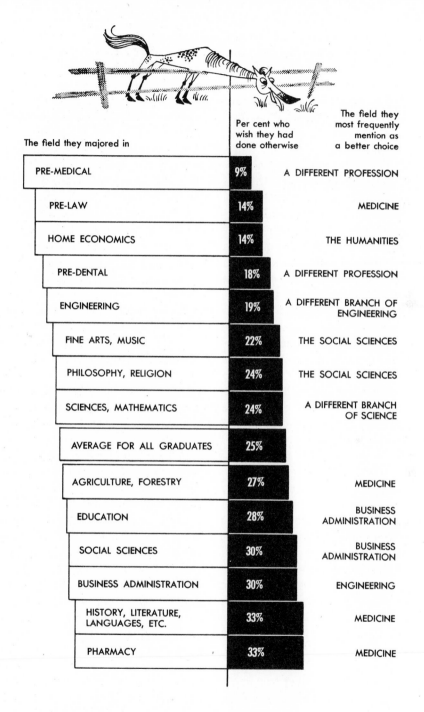

The field they majored in	Per cent who wish they had done otherwise	The field they most frequently mention as a better choice
PRE-MEDICAL	9%	A DIFFERENT PROFESSION
PRE-LAW	14%	MEDICINE
HOME ECONOMICS	14%	THE HUMANITIES
PRE-DENTAL	18%	A DIFFERENT PROFESSION
ENGINEERING	19%	A DIFFERENT BRANCH OF ENGINEERING
FINE ARTS, MUSIC	22%	THE SOCIAL SCIENCES
PHILOSOPHY, RELIGION	24%	THE SOCIAL SCIENCES
SCIENCES, MATHEMATICS	24%	A DIFFERENT BRANCH OF SCIENCE
AVERAGE FOR ALL GRADUATES	25%	
AGRICULTURE, FORESTRY	27%	MEDICINE
EDUCATION	28%	BUSINESS ADMINISTRATION
SOCIAL SCIENCES	30%	BUSINESS ADMINISTRATION
BUSINESS ADMINISTRATION	30%	ENGINEERING
HISTORY, LITERATURE, LANGUAGES, ETC.	33%	MEDICINE
PHARMACY	33%	MEDICINE

Fig. **XII:1**   On Second Thought—The Grass Is Sometimes Greener

From *They Went to College* by Ernest Havemann and Patricia Salter West
(p. 149); copyright, 1952, by TIME, Inc. Reproduced by permission of
Harcourt, Brace and Company.

by choosing the social sciences, social science majors by choosing business administration, and business administration majors by choosing engineering. The professions, particularly medicine, were the most envied and secure of occupational choices. This study has not been repeated recently on a comparable sample, and it should not be assumed that the ratings are stable.

The emphasis of college education is decreasingly on the transmission of general cultural values and increasingly on the transmission of specialized skills to prepare the individual for an occupation. This specialization tends to limit the ability of the college to reach the total personality. This does not mean that higher education leaves no mark upon personality; training for a particular occupational role transmits values and disciplines. In the case of the scientist, for example, professional attitudes of impartiality and objectivity may be deeply internalized and become a way of life. Nevertheless, the college is tending to limit its influence to the transmission of those values that are occupationally relevant or of popular interest.

Educational Isolation

When a socializing agency has special and unique values to impart, it tends to seek a degree of social isolation. It tries to minimize the access of other groups to the individual; it encourages person-to-person interaction within its own group; and it reduces its susceptibility to community pressure by relying upon private financial resources. Parochial, private, and professional schools are good examples of the effectiveness of social isolation when special values are to be transmitted.

1. *The parochial school.* The assumption behind public education is either (*a*) that a continuity exists between the values inculcated by the schools and those held by the family, or (*b*) that the family is willing to give the child over to the school, even if its influence tends to alienate the child from family ways and beliefs. For some religious groups with strong convictions, these assumptions do not hold, and the education of the child is not willingly delegated to public schools. The parochial school attempts both to strengthen traditional values by formal education and to minimize the access of other groups to the child.

2. *The professional school.* Professional schools often teach a special ethic and a sense of professional identity, as well as the requisite skills. Professional schools are usually physically separated from the rest of the university, with the result that little opportunity is provided for influence outside the specialized area.

Medical schools have been particularly successful in creating an *esprit de corps.* Of all professions, medicine is one of the best organized and most unified. Part of the success of medical education in creating a sense of professional identity and unity is probably due to the fact that instruction takes place not only in the formal setting of the classroom but in the course of intern apprenticeship, where personal interaction can come into play.

The School and the Peer Group

The school is not only a socializing agency on its own account, but it provides a setting for peer group experience.

1. Peer group interaction is assumed to be best when children are at the same level of social and psychological development, and about the same chronological age. Therefore, classes are based on rigid age ranking to facilitate peer group interaction, regardless of different intellectual capacities.

2. Classroom seating arrangements tend to reflect and support peer group interaction patterns. In many schools children are free to choose their own neighbors and to be chosen or rejected in turn.

The importance of the peer group in the school setting is not restricted to the modern school. In England during the nineteenth and early twentieth centuries the socializing power of the peer group in privately supported schools was deliberately encouraged and strengthened. Both formally and informally, upper classmen were given the right to exercise severe and often brutal social control over lower classmen.[9] This peer group experience was believed to have a salutary influence upon character and probably was effective training for the socially prized virtues of obedience and ability to "take it."

ATTITUDE AND OPINION CHANGE

It is difficult to tell precisely what changes in attitudes and values occur because of socialization in schools and colleges. The effects vary somewhat from one institution to another and often are subtle. Certain general changes are suggested by (*a*) national opinion polls that relate attitudes to level of education and (*b*) studies that compare the values of college freshmen and seniors.

The national correlation. In the general population, a variety of attitudes correlate with level of education. The strong relation of political tolerance to education is shown in Table XII: 1. The proportion of adults tolerant of political nonconformists in a 1955 nationwide poll varied considerably by educational level. At each ascending level of education, more respondents were tolerant and a smaller proportion were intolerant. A much

[9] For a vivid description of his experience between the ages of eight and twelve in such a school, see George Orwell, "Such, Such Were the Joys," in George Orwell, *A Collection of Essays* (Garden City: Doubleday, 1954), pp. 9–55.

larger share of high school graduates, compared to those with only an elementary education, were highly tolerant (42 per cent and 16 per cent, respectively); and among the college graduates more were tolerant than among the high school graduates (66 per cent and 42 per cent).

Persons with higher education are more aware of domestic and international issues and are more interested and involved in politics. (See POLITICAL MAN, p. 709.) They have greater cultural awareness. They listen more to serious radio and television programs and read more serious magazines. They read books: in a 1957 poll, 74 per cent of the college educated had read a book in the past year, compared to 43 per cent of those with a high school education, and 18 per cent of the grade school educated.[10]

In brief, education is the prime correlate of many important attitudes and habits; and the correlation usually holds up when the influence of occupation, religion, age, and other factors is controlled or ruled out. Thus, the results of national surveys suggest that mass education, whatever its limitations, significantly affects values.

The correlation within college. Studies of changes in the attitudes of students during the college years generally show a widening of perspective along with increasing liberality;

[10] Lester Asheim, "A Survey of Recent Research," in Jacob M. Price (ed.), *Reading for Life* (Ann Arbor: University of Michigan Press, 1959), pp. 3–26.

Table **XII:1**   Education and Political Tolerance*

Education of Respondent	Level of Tolerance (in per cent)				
	High	Medium	Low	Total	
College graduate	66	29	5	100	(308)
Some college	53	38	9	100	(319)
High school graduate	42	46	12	100	(768)
Some high school	29	54	17	100	(576)
Grade school	16	62	22	100	(792)

* Source: Samuel A. Stouffer, *Communism, Conformity and Civil Liberties* (New York: Doubleday, 1955), p. 90. Based on persons in a national cross section who showed some interest in the news about Communists in the United States and what is being done about them. The "more interested" people totaled somewhat more than half of the sample.

students tend to change toward the attitudes of academic men. The changes often, but not always, include a weakening of religious belief, indicating that college education is a secularizing influence.

A study of Bennington College in the late 1930's showed that the college exercised a marked influence on the political attitudes of many students.[11] The students came from politically conservative families, but the college was liberal in its political mood. One result was that the support for the conservative Republican candidate for president in 1936 (Alfred E. Landon) dropped from 62 per cent among the freshmen to 43 per cent among sophomores and to 15 per cent among juniors and seniors.

In 1952 a survey was conducted of the attitudes of 3,796 students in four Ivy League colleges (Dartmouth, Harvard, Wesleyan, Yale) and five public-supported colleges (Michigan, North Carolina, Texas, UCLA, Wayne). The students were classified in five categories, from strongly pro-civil rights to strongly anti-civil rights, and those falling in the "upper" two categories were taken as supportive of civil rights.

Table XII: 2 reports, by year in college, the percentage of students with attitudes highly supportive of civil rights (e.g., that people with dangerous social and economic viewpoints should be allowed to run for public office). The Ivy League freshmen were more supportive of civil rights than the public-supported college seniors and showed greater

change over the four years, but the change in student attitude was in the same direction in both the public and the private institutions.

A study of nearly 900 students at the University of California (Berkeley) in 1957 reported a similar trend.[12] When students were classified on the basis of their attitudes on issues such as refusing a passport to a Socialist, the proportion of "highly libertarian" almost doubled from the freshman to the senior years, from 21 to 40 per cent. The proportion only "slightly libertarian" dropped from 32 to 14 per cent.

As students progress through the educational system, they apparently become more liberal in their attitudes. The change results partly from specific knowledge and in part from being socialized to new perspectives through contact with faculties and other students and through anticipation of future careers. The higher levels of education lead to a general cultural sophistication that is characteristic of men in the professional and managerial occupations.

Cautions: 1. Most studies of students that compare one group of seniors with a second group of freshmen are not able to take into account the effect of dropouts. The apparent change in attitude may result partly from students with one attitude dropping out while students with a second attitude remain, giving the senior class a different average score from the freshman class. The best method is longi-

---

[11] Theodore Newcomb, *Personality and Social Change* (New York: Dryden, 1943).

[12] Hanan C. Selvin and Warren O. Hagstrom, "Determinants of Support for Civil Liberties," *The British Journal of Sociology*, **11** (March, 1960), 51–73.

Table **XII:2**   Year in College and Support of Civil Rights

| Type of College | Per Cent Supporting Civil Rights | | | | Freshman-Senior Change |
	Freshman	Sophomore	Junior	Senior	
Ivy League	45	57	58	68	23
Public-supported	31	40	41	44	13

From Norman Miller, "Academic Climate and Student Values," paper presented at the Fifty-fourth Annual Meeting of the American Sociological Association, September, 1959.

tudinal analysis, a *same-group comparison* that follows one group of students through the four years, noting who drops out and who remains. This method can compare the attitudes of the continuing students as seniors with their attitudes as freshmen. However, the longitudinal method is time-consuming and expensive.

2. While most studies indicate a liberalization of attitudes in the college years, there is some conflicting evidence. One study done in the early 1950's, a period characterized by an atmosphere of conservatism, suggested that students became more conservative in political philosophy.[13] A review of national surveys of attitudes toward minorities suggests that the impact of college experience varies in direction and strength. In some cases, the change may be from traditional and provincial attitudes to subtly expressed forms of prejudice rather than to a broad liberalization of attitudes.[14]

[13] Rose K. Goldsen, Morris Rosenberg, Robin M. Williams, and Edward A. Suchman, *What College Students Think* (Princeton: Van Nostrand, 1960).
[14] Charles H. Stember, *Education and Attitude Change* (New York: Institute of Human Relations Press, 1961).

Section 5 **Primary relations**

In schools, as in all kinds of institutions, individuals seek personal ties that are rewarding and sustaining. The resulting primary groups vary in strength, significance, and duration.

STUDENT PEER GROUPS[15]

Close affiliation with peers is induced and sustained by frequent and intense personal interaction and by isolation from other groups. Compared to a large campus with commuting students, a small residential college provides favorable conditions for primary groups. Students who eat, sleep, study, and play in the same dormitory are more likely to form primary attachments than are students living alone in boardinghouses or at home.

Peer relations also vary in quality and intensity because of the characteristics of the individuals who participate. Some persons need peer support more than others, and at some times more than others. Individuals under stress of a transitional phase of development are likely to seek closer association with their peers. Young children are embedded in the parental family, and most adults have their own family and other supporting ties in work and neighborhood associations. The adolescent in the process of moving out of the family of origin has not yet taken on adult responsibilities. Many teen-agers are provided with paraphernalia to act like adults —money, cars, freedom in dating, and specially-designed entertainment. But in fact these means provide the basis for a distinct adolescent social world. Adolescents are gathered together by the school, providing a base of common activities, interests, and problems on which to develop personal associations that expand into leisure-time activities.

As a result, adolescence is a period favorable to the dominance of friendship ties with peers over other social relations. Adolescent peer relations tend to be strong, intimate, encompassing, and linked to school participation. After graduation from high school, of

[15] This discussion is indebted to James S. Coleman, *The Adolescent Society* (New York: The Free Press of Glencoe, 1961). See also C. Wayne Gordon, *The Social System of the High School* (Glencoe: The Free Press, 1957), and Willard Waller, *The Sociology of Teaching* (New York: Wiley, 1932).

course, many of the ties are broken as some move away, go to work, marry, or go to different colleges.

Social relations among students reinforce some values while undercutting others; student peer groups and student subcultures are interdependent. The social patterns of the adolescent in high school support orientations toward having fun, or engaging in serious study, or turning to delinquency. In turn, the social patterns are in part determined by the subcultures:

The clusters of girls who dance together at one another's houses provide an association pattern that "resonates" to popular music and singing stars, strengthening the importance of popular music in the culture, and even providing the base for fan clubs. Yet these clusters are not only a *source* of interest in popular music: they are in part *created* by such interest.[16]

Similarly, in a dormitory or fraternity a network of close personal ties organized around dating, sports, and nonacademic campus activities upholds the collegiate subculture and in turn is sustained by it.

Student Groups and Social Status

Peer relations among students are intimately involved with the status systems of adolescents, the school, and the community. They strengthen the prestige of some persons and weaken that of others. The network of cliques in a high school *is* a status system; the student is assigned a high or low status according to his clique membership or lack of it. Some students confer status on a clique: a star athlete, a socially-prominent or wealthy boy, or a brilliant student may raise the status of his circle of friends. A student group may collectively move up or down due to its own actions; for example, it may lower its position in the school by engaging in criminal behavior. The lowered group status reflects on the individual members, and they, too, have lowered status.

The student gains membership in some groups because of his family status. Girls' cliques in high school are commonly related to social background. The status structure of the school is, in these respects, congruent with the status structure of the adult community. Boys' cliques are also based on social origins. However, athletic achievement plays an important role in membership in high-status groups in most schools, divorcing the boys' status system somewhat from the status structure of the parental community and perhaps conferring raised status on the athlete's parents. Many poor boys become successful athletes, and in winning for the school they become heroes of the system. They are rewarded with acceptance into the most popular crowd. This status is regarded by other students as more legitimate than that derived from family prestige. The athlete's status is achieved, while status that rests on family background is ascribed.

The attitudes and actions of teachers help to determine which activities become the basis for high status and who appears in the top-status groups. For example, teachers like to see the best scholars in the school serve as examples to the student body. But when teachers in three schools were asked: "If you could see any of three boys elected president of the senior class, which would you rather it would be? (Brilliant student, athletic star, or a leader in extracurricular activities)," the teachers preferred the activities leader to the brilliant student 73 per cent to 19 per cent, but only 8 per cent chose the athlete.[17] The teachers avoided naming the brilliant student for this high-status position because they thought he would not have leadership ability, be close to students, or command attention.

Lament of an Isolate

The student peer group helps the adolescent to sustain a conception of the self in a transitional period and in the face of compe-

---

[16] Coleman, *op. cit.*, p. 174.

[17] *Ibid.*, p. 193.

tition for academic and social status. Students must often weigh this support against the greater freedom they have outside the clique, for example, to study hard or to associate casually with a large number of students. Serious students frequently must choose to remain isolated, but in large schools they may band together and support one another.

Isolates are likely to have mixed feelings about their independence. Some even view their isolation as the major failure of their high school careers. One girl writes:

In school there has always been clicks [sic] and clans. I always belonged to one in grade school, one consisting of about five people, and one who wasn't the wild set. In the eighth grade, I began to separate from a single group, which I sometimes think was a mistake and started just being friendly to all the groups. This was not too good for me because it gave me a feeling of not belonging. I really didn't notice this change till I started high school but it has been that way since. Oh, to be back in a click! [18]

ADOLESCENT FREEDOM AND STUDENT CLIQUES

In childhood and especially in adolescence the child is subject to a contest of wills between parents and peers. Traditionally, middle-class parents seem to have asserted stronger control than working-class parents, supervising closer and longer through the adolescent years. This is apparently no longer so in many communities. One study asked girls if they would join a particular club in the face of their parents' disapproval.[19] In

[18] Gordon, *op. cit.*, p. 114.
[19] Coleman, *op. cit.*, pp. 287–93.

small-town schools, the daughters of the middle-class families were *less* likely to ignore or overrule their parents' judgment than were the girls from lower social origins. But in city or suburban schools, the middle-class girls were *more* likely to say they would join despite parents' disapproval. The greatest difference lay between the daughters of traditionally middle-class parents in the small towns and the daughters of modern middle-class parents in the "elite" suburbs. Lower-class girls fell between the extremes.

This distribution of girls' reactions seems associated with the concern of middle-class parents for the child's social maturity and popularity. Both at home and in the school, they attempt to give the child self-assurance and social skills, e.g., formal instruction in social dancing in the seventh grade. Early social maturity, however, produces greater liberation in adolescence. As a result, children rely more on their own judgment or on the norms of the peer group than on adult standards. They consider themselves less subject to orders from parents and teachers.

The orientation of the middle-class children of both the small town and of the city set the tone of the high school. In both kinds of communities, particularly among girls, the leading crowd is largely composed of those with higher social origins, and the top-status cliques set the norms of the informal system of the students. In the small town, the pace-setters are the girls most subject to parental constraint; in the city or suburb, they are the girls who are most liberated.

Section 6 **Stratification**

The educational system may maintain a traditional system of social status, or, conversely, it may work to alter the distribution of statuses. Whether the educational system is a servant of the status quo or a vehicle of mobility and change depends mainly on who has access to what kind of education and how much of it.

DIFFERENTIAL ACCESS

Social background, especially the social station of one's family, affects educational opportunity. This influence is strongest when social status is ascribed, assigned to persons according to the family and class into which they were born. Where status is achieved, as to a large extent it is in modern industrial nations, social background plays a lesser part. Nevertheless, social origins are influential, primarily in determining how far the young go in their schooling. This in turn limits or opens later occupational opportunity. The social level of the family affects opportunity, aspiration, and the ability to use the schools.

In general, children from the lower-classes do not have as much opportunity to obtain an education or as much interest in it as those from upper strata. Because of financial pressure and less motivation, some drop out of school as soon as they can. One study of the school attendance of sixteen- and seventeen-year-olds in New Haven, Connecticut, showed that 28 per cent were not in school. The percentage of dropouts varied across six categories of social class position, from high to low status as follows: 2 per cent, 11 per cent, 17 per cent, 26 per cent, 30 per cent, and 43 per cent.[20]

In the United States, however, compulsory attendance laws and increased interest now hold almost all students in the high school through age fifteen. Ninety-eight per cent of the fourteen- and fifteen-year-olds were enrolled in school in 1960; 83 per cent of the sixteen- and seventeen-year-olds were also in school the same year, an increase of 11 per cent in ten years (1950–1960). The proportion of boys and girls completing high school has increased considerably over recent decades. High school graduates in 1960 represented six out of ten of their fifth grade classmates, compared with less than three out of ten in 1930.[21]

Family background shows its influence on education in the decision to enter college.[22] Table XII: 3 is based on a 1955 nationwide survey of over 35,000 seniors in 500 public schools. Each student was rated on scholastic ability (as indicated by a 20-item test) and socio-educational status of family, an index based on father's occupation, father's education, and whether older brothers and sisters had gone to college. The students were classified into four categories of ability and five status groupings that ranged from well-educated professional and managerial families to poorly educated, unskilled worker and farm families. The proportion of students planning

---

[20] James S. Davie, "Social Class Factors and School Attendance," *Harvard Educational Review*, 23 (1953), 175–85.

[21] *A Fact Book on Higher Education* (Washington, D.C.: American Council on Education, n.d.), p. 65 and p. 253.

[22] Natalie Rogoff, "Local Social Structure and Educational Selection," in A. H. Halsey, Jean Floud, and C. Arnold Anderson (eds.), *Education, Economy, and Society* (New York: The Free Press of Glencoe, 1961), pp. 241–51. See also J. A. Kahl, "Educational and Occupational Aspirations of 'Common Man' Boys," *Harvard Educational Review*, 23 (1953), 186–203; W. H. Sewell, Archie O. Haller, and Murray A. Straus, "Social Status and Educational and Occupational Aspiration," *American Sociological Review*, 22 (1957), 67–73; and S. M. Lipset and Reinhard Bendix, *Social Mobility in Industrial Society* (Berkeley and Los Angeles: University of California Press, 1960), pp. 91–101 and 227–33.

to attend college varied by family status from 72 per cent in the highest category to 24 per cent in the lowest, or a difference of 48 per cent; the share of *all* students expecting to go to college was 40 per cent. Planning for college varied over the four levels of ability from 61 per cent among the top ability to 24 per cent among those of lowest ability, a range of 37 per cent.

The columns of the table show the effect of ability with family background constant. In families of top status, 83 per cent of the high-ability students and 53 per cent of the lowest in ability plan to attend college, a difference of 30 per cent. In the families of bottom status, just 43 per cent of the high-ability students plan college and 18 per cent of the low-ability students so indicate, or a difference of 25 per cent.

The rows of the table show the effect of family background on college plans, for students of similar ability. Top-ability students planning to attend college range from 83 per cent to 43 per cent according to family status, a difference of 40 per cent because of socio-educational background, or something correlated with it. The figures reflect a loss to education of talented students from lower social origins. At the next level of ability, the loss is as great, with 29 per cent in the lowest

social category compared to 70 per cent in the highest planning college, a 41 per cent difference. These two ability categories cover the upper half of high school students.

The joint effect of social background and ability on college plans can be studied by comparing any of the figures with another. The extremes are the top-status background and top ability (83 per cent) and bottom status and bottom ability (18 per cent), roughly 8 out of 10 compared with 2 out of 10. The dotted line drawn through the table separates figures greater than 50 per cent from those less than 50 per cent; it shows the decisive role played by family background. A majority of sons and daughters in families of top status expect to go to college, even when they have little ability; at no level of ability, not even the highest, do a majority of low-family-status children plan to go to college.

SELECTION AND DIFFERENTIATION IN EDUCATION

Schools and colleges affect stratification in part through their selection techniques. Selection occurs in the allocation of students to different kinds of schools and in the rating of individuals within schools. Among those who gain access to a particular level of schooling, some are identified by school personnel

Table **XII:3**   Percentage of High School Seniors Planning to Attend College*

Scholastic Ability		Family Socio-Educational Status					All Students of Given Ability Level
		(High) 5	4	3	2	(Low) 1	
(High)	4	83	66	53	44	43	61
	3	70	53	37	29	29	44
	2	65	41	31	20	21	33
(Low)	1	53	30	22	16	18	24
All students of given family status		72	47	35	26	24	40

Source: Natalie Rogoff, "Local Social Structure and Educational Selection," in A. H. Halsey, Jean Floud, and C. Arnold Anderson (eds.), *Education, Economy, and Society* (New York: The Free Press of Glencoe, 1961), p. 246.
* Based on a study of over 35,000 high school seniors who constituted the entire senior class of 500 public secondary schools. The schools were a fairly representative sample of the 20,000-odd senior public high schools in the United States, 1955.

as capable of higher education. Some are moved toward one path, some toward another, and the school's definition of the child may be decisive in determining his fate.

Classification and Social Typing

Selection and differentiation within the schools depends on the conceptions and perceptions of school personnel. Teachers, counselors, and administrators use a number of criteria in assessing the child: scores on general tests of ability, achievement, and interest; graded performance in the classroom on the basis of academic work, study habits, and social growth; personality traits; social background. Students with similar classroom performance (e.g., "B" students) may be defined quite differently from one another, depending on other characteristics. One is typed as an underachiever because his classroom performance does not measure up to the promise of high scores on ability tests; a second is seen as an overachiever because he does better than test scores predict; a third may be defined as a problem child because of unusual behavior. Such definitions affect children's progress, decisions to accelerate or retard them, and assignment to courses.

The growing complexity of occupations puts pressure on the schools to identify more closely the capability of each child and to help him make an appropriate choice of career and course of study. Schools and colleges seek ways of allocating students to educational and occupational tracks without great waste of time and effort. For this they need to measure ability and progress and to maintain a cumulative record of performance. This leads to an emphasis on testing and record-keeping. Many public school districts begin a file on the pupil in the lower elementary grades. Records accumulate and pass along through channels as the child moves up through the grades. Teachers and counselors are the custodians and interpreters of the records. The student is partially, sometimes wholly, known and judged by the file that accompanies and often precedes him. A student entering high school may be assessed before he begins his high school work by means of his achievement history, test scores, and comments of previous teachers on personality and behavior. On the basis of his record, social typing takes place, and he enters high school labeled as normal, problem, gifted, underachiever, or predelinquent. His educational and occupational possibilities are affected accordingly.

Table **XII:4**   Education and Occupational Achievement

People Who Work in These Occupations	Have This Kind of Education (in Per Cent)		
	Less Than High School Graduation	High School Graduation	Some College Education
Professional and technical workers	6	19	75
Proprietors and managers	38	33	29
Clerical or sales workers	25	53	22
Skilled workers	59	33	8
Semiskilled workers	70	26	4
Service workers	69	25	6
Unskilled workers	80	17	3
Farmers and farm workers	76	19	5

Source: *Manpower: Challenge of the 1960's* (U.S. Department of Labor, 1960), p. 17.

Table **XII:5**   Education of Business Leaders of 1928 and 1952

Highest Schooling Completed	1928 Business Leaders (in Per Cent)	1952 Business Leaders (in Per Cent)
Less than high school	27	4
High school	28	20
Some college	13	19
College graduation	32	57
Total	100	100

Source: W. Lloyd Warner and James C. Abegglen, *Occupational Mobility in American Business and Industry, 1928–1952* (Minneapolis: University of Minnesota Press, 1955), p. 108.

EDUCATION, OCCUPATION, AND INCOME

The strong relation between amount of education and occupational achievement is shown in Table XII:4. The higher occupations are composed of the better educated; for example, three-fourths of professional and technical workers have had some college education. The broad occupational categories obscure some important groups. "Proprietors and managers" includes the small shop owner as well as the corporation executive. The small-businessman need not have advanced education, but the corporation man generally does. A change has taken place in the education of businessmen holding top executive positions in the largest firms of the United States. (See Table XII:5.) The business leaders of 1952 were much better educated than the leaders of 1928. In 1952 only 4 per cent had less than a high school education, but 27 per cent did in 1928, or roughly seven times as many. About one-third were college graduates in the earlier group, compared with 57 per cent in 1952. The situation is changing rapidly; even more of today's young men who will be the business leaders of tomorrow will be even more highly educated.

Just as the relation of education to occupational attainment is strong, so is the relation of education to future income. The average annual income in 1958 of American men, ages 45–54, was directly related to the amount of education they had received: [23]

Some elementary schooling	$3,008
Completed elementary school	4,337
Some high school	4,864
Completed high school	6,295
Some college	8,682
Completed college	12,269

On the average, college graduates earned almost twice as much each year as high school graduates and almost three times as much as elementary school graduates. The difference in annual income is increasing; the largest increase between 1949 and 1958 was made by college-educated men.

The educational ladder clearly leads to higher occupations, upper social statuses, and prestigeful styles of life. Without education one has lower horizons—occupationally, socially, culturally.

What most determines life chances—social position or education, ascription or achievement? On the one hand, children from the higher social strata are likely to receive more and better education than their lower-class counterparts. Higher-level education in turn provides access to the better positions. In this

[23] Herman P. Miller, "Annual and Lifetime Income In Relation to Education: 1939–1959," *American Economic Review*, **50** (December, 1960), 962–86.

case, education stabilizes social class positions across the generations, and acts as a barrier to the social mobility of those who start from lower rungs.[24] On the other hand, some children of lower origins are upwardly mobile by virtue of the availability of schooling, persistence and success in school, and entry into some higher-status occupation to which their education admits them. In this case, education operates to change social positions rather than stabilize them. What is the balance? Until recent decades, the mobility function of education was secondary to its conservative function of maintaining family status. Father's status counted more than the classroom, and mobile individuals were often mobile without education. But the role of the school and college in social mobility grows stronger as (a) education becomes more widely available and (b) men are judged by the universal criteria of scholastic achievement and technical competence. The questions are "What do you know? What can you do?" rather than "Whom do you know?" or "What does your father do?"

From the standpoint of the society, extending and equalizing opportunity is necessary to a fuller use of talent. When high-ability children leave education early and in large numbers for various economic, racial, and motivational reasons, talent goes undeveloped. A technological society has an insatiable appetite for competence, especially in engineering and allied fields; a bureaucratic society needs trained experts for the many specialized positions of the large organization; and societies competing internationally look upon trained men as essential to national vigor. These triple pressures of technology, bureaucracy, and world tension promote the effort in the United States to open wider the doors of schools and colleges, train more persons, uncover hidden talent, and draw to higher levels those of obvious ability.

[24] Bernard Barber, *Social Stratification* (New York: Harcourt, Brace, 1957), p. 395.

EDUCATION OF MINORITIES

The schools may provide an inferior education for the members of a minority group, restricting their chances of upward social mobility. On the other hand, by offering educational opportunity to a minority, the schools may act for their social betterment. The educational system may work for the minority order as it does for the class structure, either as a servant of the status quo or as an instrument of change.

There is a sizable difference in the amount of education of whites and Negroes 25 years and older. (See MINORITIES, pp. 513–15.) Much of the difference reflects the educational histories of the older members of the population who went to school between 1900 and 1940. In the population over 65, Negroes have only half as much schooling as whites; while in the age group 25 to 29, Negroes have nine-tenths of the schooling of whites.[25] Starting out closer to zero, Negroes have made the greater gains since the Civil War. In 1860, less than 2 per cent of the nonwhites 5 to 19 years old were enrolled in school, while about 60 per cent of whites were in school, a difference of 58 per cent. By 1957 the difference between the two populations in school enrollment rate had dropped to 3 per cent.

The difference in the illiteracy rates of the two races has similarly narrowed. Eighty per cent of the nonwhites were illiterate in 1870, compared to 11 per cent of whites. In 1900, the rate was 45 per cent illiteracy for nonwhites and 6 per cent for whites; in 1959, about 7.5 per cent for nonwhites and 1.6 per cent for whites.[26]

The average (median) years of schooling of the white and nonwhite populations also indicate a closing of the gap. (See MINORITIES, p. 514.) In sheer quantity of education,

[25] Murray Gendell and Hans L. Zetterberg (eds.), *A Sociological Almanac for the United States* (New York: Bedminster, 1961), p. 21.
[26] U.S. Bureau of the Census, *Historical Statistics of the United States, Colonial Times to 1957* (1960), p. 214. *Statistical Abstract of the United States*, 1960, p. 96.

Table **XII:6**   School Enrollment Rate, 1860–1957 *
(Rate per 100 Population, 5 to 19 Years Old)

Year	Whites	Nonwhites	Difference between Rates for Whites and Nonwhites
1860	60	2	58
1890	58	33	25
1920[a]	66	54	12
1950	79	75	4
1957	88	85	3

* Source: U.S. Bureau of the Census, *Historical Statistics of the United States, Colonial Times to 1957* (1960), p. 213.
[a] Population 5 to 20 years old.

the younger generation of Negroes is not much different from white youths, but the figures do not indicate the quality of education. The kind and quality of schools in which the members of a minority are educated are determined (*a*) by patterns of segregation and integration and (*b*) by the income level of the school district.

SEGREGATION AND INTEGRATION IN THE SCHOOLS[27]

Since the Supreme Court decision in May, 1954, the integration of the public schools has been almost continuously in the courts and the press. At the time of the ruling 17 Southern and border states and the District of Columbia maintained segregation in the public schools. At the end of 1962 there were more than 6,000 school districts in the area, about half of which were biracial, that is, had both Negro and white students, and about one-third of the biracial school districts had been desegregated. By this measure an uneven but marked change had taken place.

Figure XII:2 shows the distribution of desegregated districts by state. In three states and the District of Columbia, there were no

biracial school districts still segregated; in three states, there were no integrated districts.

Analysis of desegregated districts is not an entirely satisfactory measure of the trend toward integration, because some "desegregated" districts have only a very few Negro students enrolled with whites. A count of Negroes actually attending schools with whites shows much less change. In November, 1962, about 255,000 Negroes were in schools with whites. This was one-fourth of the Negroes in desegregated districts, but only 7.8 per cent of all Negroes attending schools in the region.

Six border states and the District of Columbia had considerable integration (see Fig. XII:2) with 25 per cent or more of Negro children attending schools with whites. Eight states had a small amount of integration (less than 3 per cent of Negro children in school with whites), and three states had no Negro and white children in the same schools.

The status of school desegregation may be summarized: (1) The process of integration has been most rapid in the border states. (2) Within any state most districts integrate voluntarily, i.e., without court intervention but in response to test cases in other districts. About 85 per cent of districts integrated by 1962 had done so "voluntarily." (3) Much integration is only token integration and involves very few students. (4) Resistance to integration persists and is strongest in the Old South. This resistance is expressed in many ways: (*a*) by administrative techniques, e.g.,

[27] The context of segregation is discussed in MINORITIES, pp. 495–99.   Data in this section are derived from the *Southern School News* (Nashville: Southern Education Reporting Service), which in September, 1954, began publication of a continuing record of school segregation and desegregation, and the *Statistical Summary* (Nashville: Southern Education Reporting Service, November, 1962), *passim*. For texts of court decisions see *Race Relations Law Reporter*.

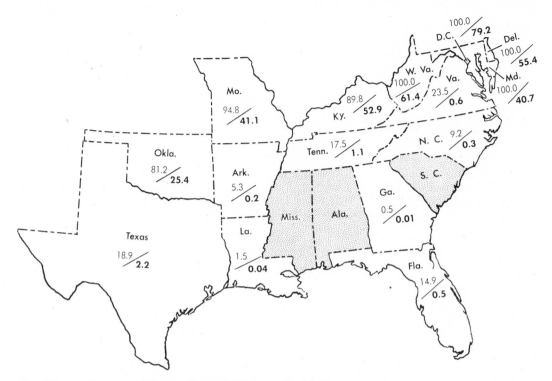

Fig. XII:2 Desegregation in the Public Schools, 1962

The numbers in this figure are percentages. Above the diagonal is the per cent of biracial districts that are desegregated in each state. Below the diagonal in dark numerals is the per cent of Negro students actually attending schools with whites. Figures are given to the nearest tenth of a per cent except for Louisiana and Georgia, which are given in hundredths. Shaded states had no desegregated districts in the Fall of 1962. Source: *Statistical Summary* (Nashville: Southern Education Reporting Service, November, 1962, p. 3).

gerrymandering the boundaries of school districts to maintain the maximum separation of the races (see also Section 9, p. 486), (*b*) by contests and delays in the courts, and (*c*) by legislation, such as encouraging private schools, amending or repealing compulsory school attendance laws, or establishing local option.

THE SLUM SCHOOL [28]

Schools located in lower-class neighborhoods are often inferior in quality, and the

[28] Based largely on Howard S. Becker, "Social-Class Variations in the Teacher-Pupil Relationship," *Journal of Educational Sociology*, **25** (April, 1952), 451–65. Teacher statements are from this study.

"slum school" has special problems and characteristics. Many children come ill-prepared and little motivated for school work. The teaching is more difficult than in middle-class and upper-class schools, and the school and teacher must make special adaptations. Most teachers try to escape by transferring to other schools.

In the slum school administrators and teachers expect less of the children. A teacher in one city says: "For instance, in the second grade we're supposed to cover nine spelling words a week. Well, I can do that up here. But the best class I ever had at [slum school] was only able to achieve six words a week and they had to work pretty hard to get that.

So I never finished the year's work in spelling. I couldn't. And I really wasn't expected to."

The gap between what the children should know and what they actually do know becomes wider in each grade: "The children come into our upper grades with very poor reading ability. That means that all the way through our school everybody is concentrating on reading. . . . At [better school] they figure that from the first to fourth you learn to read and from fifth to eighth you read to learn. . . . Well, these children don't reach that second stage while they're with us. We have to plug along getting them to learn to read. Our teachers are pretty well satisfied if the children can read and do simple number work when they leave here."

Children in lower-class schools are also considered difficult to control. They are more given to unrestrained behavior and physical violence. Many teachers adapt, if they remain long, by using sterner measures than they would in other schools, and by building a reputation that coerces the children into behaving. For all teachers, but especially for the newer, inexperienced ones, the emphasis on discipline detracts from teaching.

Teacher reaction is important in the education of minorities. Since teachers react to many characteristics of the minority child other than skin color and race, eliminating prejudice alone does not solve the problem of adequate education. The growth of Negro and other dark-skinned minority populations in Northern cities introduces into the system many children from culturally deprived and lower-class backgrounds who are —or who are seen by their teachers as—dirty, violent, and unmotivated. The teachers are likely to handle them differently, teach them less, and want to escape their teaching assignments. The consequence is a lessening of achievement, a lowering of opportunity. The problem for the school is to change the "vicious circle" of interaction between student characteristics and teacher response. This may be done by such means as increasing the pupils' motivation and strengthening the commitment of the best teachers to the worst schools.

The quality as well as the quantity of education for Negroes and others of the more deprived minorities is increasing. But the demands of society are also increasing, setting higher standards of occupational and cultural competence. The slum school may "catch up." Or with its problems of motivation, teaching technique, and teacher misunderstanding and resentment, the slum school may instead become a backwater for student and teacher.

Section 7 Associations

The large, decentralized educational system of the United States consists of hundreds of private schools, public colleges, technical institutes, nursery schools, universities, associations of teachers and administrators. These associations, established under different auspices, divide up the total educational effort. This section first examines the diversity of educational institutions and second, the nature and allocation of educational authority.

DIVERSITY OF EDUCATIONAL INSTITUTIONS

The variety of schools and colleges in the United States is the product of a number of conditions: (1) Each type of institution can perform only a few of the numerous educational tasks. (2) Private groups as well as public ones may establish schools and colleges and decide what tasks they will assume. (3) The staffs of schools and colleges influence the nature of their institutions, and attempt to give them a character distinctive from similar institutions. Some organization variety is planned: state or city educational authorities allocate tasks in a co-ordinated pattern to different institutions. But much of the variety is emergent, the unplanned result of the independent initiative of private and public groups.

Higher Education

Higher education in California illustrates organizational variety and complexity in an educational system. The public system consists of three types of colleges: the state university, composed of several campuses; the state colleges, distributed more widely throughout the state; and junior colleges, serving numerous communities. Together the colleges prepare men and women for positions that vary from the technical and semiprofessional levels (e.g., electronic technician, dental assistant) to the most advanced segments of the professions and science. Specialized tasks that relate to different sectors of the occupational structure are recognized by state officials and committees in their plans for a division of responsibility among the colleges: the university to be a center of advanced training and research as well as of undergraduate instruction; the state colleges to concentrate on four- and five-year programs, with teacher education a major task; and the two-year junior colleges to provide terminal vocational programs as well as preparation for college or university.

The three types of colleges are partially interdependent. For example, the university has fairly stringent admissions requirements for undergraduates, and approximately the top one-eighth of California high school graduates qualify. The state colleges have less stringent admissions requirements, and the junior colleges are nonselective. The selectivity of the university depends on the existence of the other two types of institutions, especially the junior college. Without the other colleges, the pressure from citizens to admit their children would probably make it impossible for the university to maintain a selective policy.

The three types of colleges have overlapping tasks in the planned division of work, and there are no clear boundaries among them. Each level is independent in its administration, and each college in part determines its own character. The needs and interests of the colleges often direct them away from their planned functions. For example, even though the state plan restricts research largely to the university, the state colleges increasingly encourage faculty research, in order to attract able scholars, raise academic quality, and achieve higher status. Generally speaking, there is a relation between self-determination and high academic quality, and many faculty and administrators aspire to improve quality in their colleges. The balance between autonomy of the college on the one hand and co-ordination of the system on the other is a serious problem in the California system.

In addition to the publicly supported institutions there are more than sixty private colleges and universities in California that are entirely independent of state co-ordination. Secular private colleges, emphasizing the liberal arts, have freedom for self-determination provided they are able to solve their financial problems. Church-related colleges pay special attention to the religious commitment of the student, and tend to be more interested than the public institutions in shaping moral values. Some private colleges have developed a distinctive character or competence. Some are nationally known institutions; others have a local following.

No single type of college could perform well all the educational and social tasks carried out by these many public and private colleges. The variety of institutions allows the individual colleges to develop particular capabilities and serve particular segments of the public while the system as a whole performs many services for a heterogeneous population.

Variety and Uniformity in the Public Schools

A primary problem in any administrative organization is whether to distribute specific functions to separate organizations or place several functions in one unit. In the United States secondary education is organized in "comprehensive schools" that combine several major tasks, e.g., the college preparatory, vocational, and general programs. In England and in European countries, the major programs appear in separate schools, and students are distributed after the elementary level to different kinds of schools that lead to different educational and occupational futures. Some large cities (e.g., New York) also follow this plan in part, and some students go to specialized academic high schools or vocational schools or schools of art and music.

These alternative forms of organization—the comprehensive versus the specialized school—are widely debated. There are several underlying issues:

1. *Democratic versus elite education.* Most educators in the United States feel that separation into different kinds of schools is undemocratic, that only the comprehensive school allows equal access to educational opportunity and encourages children of various backgrounds and abilities to mix with one another. However, educators in England and Europe for the most part maintain that specialized schools are not undemocratic as long as selection is made on the basis of ability, a position shared by some Americans.

2. *Early versus late selection.* The comprehensive secondary school smooths the way for the transferring of students from one program or "track" to another, and post-

pones the final step in educational selection until entry to college or later. The specialized school system requires that critical steps in selection be taken early, at age eleven or twelve, for example, in order to assign pupils to separate schools. Hence, sharply different philosophies of child development and educational selection are embedded in these two major forms of secondary school organization.

3. *Concentration versus diffusion of talent.* The specialized academic high school concentrates high-ability students, provides them with a challenging environment, and allows them to proceed at a rapid pace. When they are thus removed from comprehensive schools, their influence on other students is lost and most teachers are deprived of the most rewarding students. The comprehensive school, on the other hand, distributes the good students more evenly. However, it may not be able to challenge them nor protect them from nonintellectual and anti-intellectual attitudes and practices of many of the less able students.

DISTRIBUTION OF AUTHORITY

The distribution of authority in schools and colleges determines who makes educational decisions and what values or points of view influence policy. The distribution of authority also helps to set incentives; those involved in decision-making usually feel responsible for the welfare of the organization and work hard to insure its success.

Authority in education is obscure in many cases, and has features often misunderstood by the public. In the United States, authority is distributed among groups within and outside the school or college. Three governing bodies are significant: the trustees or the board of education, the administrators, and the faculty.

The Board

The control of most schools and colleges in the United States is officially vested in an

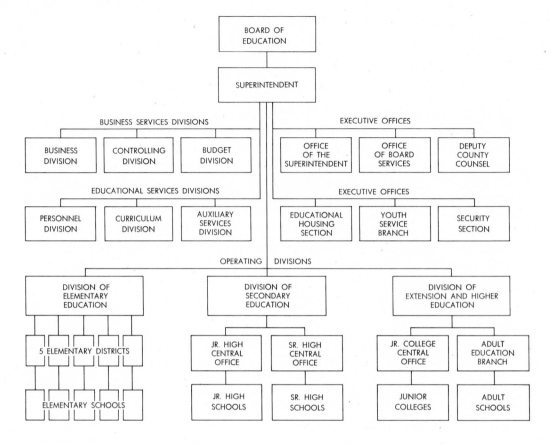

Fig. **XII:3** Formal Structure of the Los Angeles School System, 1952–1953

Source: Burton R. Clark, *Adult Education in Transition* (Berkeley and Los Angeles: University of California Press, 1956), p. 68.

elected or appointed board of laymen. The board is legally empowered to direct the organization, is held responsible for its welfare, and has final authority over the work of the employed staff. The board's position as the highest authority is reflected in organizational charts. (See Fig. XII:3.) The practice of locating authority in boards of laymen goes back to the origin of schools and colleges in the United States and grew from the belief that schools should be directed by the community rather than by the government or professional personnel. In tax-supported schools, board members are considered representatives of the whole community. In private institutions the members of the board represent the sponsoring constituency, for example, "the Quaker community." There is a tendency for the private boards to become independent of the constituency and for the institution to evolve into an autonomous organization. For example, many universities and colleges, originally established by religious bodies, now have only tenuous ties to the respective churches.

In both the public and the private sectors the board member's position is a "public trust." [29] The board is an instrument of ex-

[29] Morton A. Rank, *College and University Trusteeship* (Yellow Springs, Ohio: Antioch Press, 1959), p. 22.

ternal control and is filled by persons who are part-time and amateur rather than full-time and expert. In the case of the public schools, authority in the hands of a *local* lay board also insures that the schools will not be controlled by the state even though the local district is part of a state system.

The Administrators

The legal provision that authority rests ultimately with the lay board does not insure that laymen determine policy. Schools and colleges are staffed with full-time, paid officials. Operating authority is either delegated to senior officers by the lay board or is taken on by the school administrators in the course of routine decision-making. Board members are remote from actual operation, while the expert and informed officials are on the spot and must make the daily decisions. The board is supposed to decide policy and the hired staff to execute it, but the trained officials settle many policy questions.

Because of the strong belief in lay control of education and the legal position of the board at the top of the educational pyramid, authority in the hands of trained educators has not been fully accepted. But as educational systems grow larger and more complex their administration becomes more dependent on expert knowledge and hence on trained professionals. The organizations assume to some degree the form of a bureaucracy, with a hierarchy of officers assigned to positions with fixed responsibilities. Bureaucratic authority increases and competes with trustee authority. The larger academic systems cannot be run without layers of administrators, a network of staff units, and the advice of experts. Figure XII:3 suggests some of the administrative complexity of a large city school system (Los Angeles) where the professional staff at "headquarters" exceeds two hundred. The Los Angeles superintendent is assisted by associate and assistant superintendents, supervisors, consultants, co-ordinators, a business manager and a controller—all located in a superstructure above the administrative personnel of the individual schools and colleges of the system.

Trustee control and bureaucratic control are both hierarchical. The "higher" authorities—the school board or the superintendent, the trustees or the college president—are expected to direct the work of lower administrators, who in turn supervise the teachers and control the students. Control through hierarchy is well understood, for the idea is rooted in experience in business and government. Many board members take the business firm as a model of how to organize the school or college. The borrowed model stresses clear lines of authority and sharply demarcated jurisdictions for which officials are held responsible.

The Faculty

The chief difference in the control of colleges and universities, compared to business firms and government agencies, is the extent to which authority resides in the main professional group, the faculty. The first universities, established in Europe in the twelfth through the fourteenth centuries, were constituted of self-governing "guilds" of teachers and students.

In internal matters the universities had the prerogative of self-government. They were autonomous corporations, conceived in the spirit of the guilds; their members elected their own officials and set the rules for the teaching craft. . . . Each faculty made its own rules. Each faculty elected its own head and held its own assemblies . . . while the university as a whole had its general assembly, the congregation.[30]

From this beginning there developed a principle of the university as a self-governing community—a collegium—within which the professors control policy and practice. The

[30] Richard Hofstadter and Walter P. Metzger, *The Development of Academic Freedom in the United States* (New York: Columbia University Press, 1955), p. 6.

tradition of faculty control is strong in European universities.

This principle of collegial authority was absent in the early years of American higher education. The colonial colleges were established and supervised by religious denominations, and the teacher was hired to further the orthodoxy as defined by the board of control.[31] The president had some authority; the faculty was nearly always small and had little authority.

As American education became more secular and the colleges larger and stronger, there was less external supervision. Governing boards became more independent, and the president played a larger role. The faculties gradually increased their influence, especially after 1875 with the establishment of universities. With the university came a broadening of function. To the task of conserving and transmitting knowledge was added the creation of knowledge, a type of activity that requires greater freedom. The university also carried with it the European ideal of the faculty as a self-governing community of scholars. In recent decades faculties have continued to widen and strengthen their influence. Surveys conducted by the American Association of University Professors comparing faculty influence in 1920,

1939, and 1953 showed increases in faculty influence in seven areas of decision-making that were surveyed, e.g., faculty appointments, budgetary procedures, choosing a new president.[32]

Faculty strength in decision-making rests on a number of supports:

1. *Faculty government.* The entire faculty of a college or university is often organized in an academic council or senate that is separate from the administrative hierarchy. The faculty body has its own committees, its own administrative machinery for taking up issues and handling problems. Some powers are freely delegated to the faculty body by the trustees or the administration; other prerogatives are assumed as new matters come up; and some authority is gained by persuading the administration to relinquish control.

2. *Departmental structure.* The department is a group of faculty members who have similar interests and commitments; they usually belong to a single discipline or profession. Much day-to-day authority is delegated to the departments in the large university, making them into semi-autonomous units. In some colleges, the basic unit is the division (e.g., a social science division) embracing several related fields, and faculty

[31] *Ibid.*, p. 155.

[32] "The Place and Function of Faculties In College and University Government," *AAUP Bulletin*, **39** (Summer, 1953), 311.

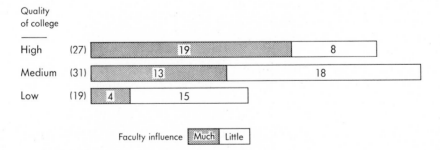

Fig. **XII:4** Quality and Faculty Influence in 77 Colleges

Source: Paul F. Lazarsfeld and Wagner Thielens, Jr., *The Academic Mind* (Glencoe: The Free Press, 1958), p. 172.

members exercise influence through divisional decision-making.

3. *Tenure.* Once the professor is granted "tenure," normally after five to seven years, his position is protected and he is freed from the fear that he will be dismissed if he is outspoken on administrative policy or controversial issues. With job security, the tenured members of the faculty can afford to insist on a voice in decision-making.

There is a positive correlation between academic quality of colleges and faculty influence. (See Fig. XII:4.) In the best colleges, the faculties usually have much authority. In relatively few colleges of low academic quality do the faculties have much influence. The medium-quality colleges are more evenly divided. On issues of academic freedom, colleges of high quality tend to allow the faculty a strong voice, while in low-quality colleges, the trustees, administrators, or outside groups are usually dominant.

Compared to higher education, elementary and secondary education have little faculty authority. Teachers in the lower grades are less inclined to insist on self-determination, and they are in a poor position to exercise strong influence. They are close to the community and vulnerable to public scrutiny. The elementary school is just around the corner physically and psychologically. Parents are concerned about the values and practices of the teachers to whom their young are exposed. However, teachers at the lower levels are likely to achieve greater autonomy and increase their authority as their work becomes recognized as expert, as their schools become larger, their salaries higher, and their sense of professional identity stronger.

Section 8   Collective behavior

The public schools of the United States are susceptible to public opinion because they are decentralized and controlled by boards of laymen. The schools are a major arena of community conflict. Some of the conflict takes the form of clashes between established groups, e.g., the American Legion versus the P.T.A., local unions against businessmen's associations, with each group attempting to influence school policy. Churches take a special interest in how schools handle moral and religious instruction. But pressure on the schools also takes less organized forms: the mood or value climate of the community; the excitation of controversy by a militant few; the occasional involvement of the apathetic majority of citizens who usually remain silent.

Community mood. The political and cultural climate of a community affects the actions of school personnel, even when the climate is not articulated by spokesmen for interest groups. An old New England town, governed by "selectmen" and an annual town meeting, is likely to have a conservative mood that encourages a traditional approach to education; a new and rapidly growing city in a metropolitan suburb usually has a climate of optimism that encourages experimentation. A community experiencing economic decline is not only short of money but is encumbered with a mood of pessimism that constrains school development.

Community moods may change rapidly under the impact of external events. After the Russians put the first Sputnik in orbit, many neighborhoods composed of well-educated business and professional families changed from support of progressive education to an interest in tougher, traditional education. These families were affected by heightened national concern over the preparation of scientists and technologists, together with a personal concern that their children qualify for college. The changed mood of the educated, upper-middle class led to a revamping of the curriculum in many communities (e.g., more language and science in the elementary school) and an upgrading of the competence of teachers in the "hard" subjects (e.g., physics, mathematics, English). Before the change in mood, the P.T.A. in the middle-class neighborhood concerned itself with the psychology of child development. After the change, the announcement for the next P.T.A. meeting was more likely to read: "Can your first-grader explain what force is? Does your sixth-grader know what influence orbit size has on centrifugal force?"

The militant minority. A few, active oppositionists, ideologically committed to a cause or motivated by the hope of power, sometimes exercise considerable influence on school policy. The oppositionists may be against all modern trends in education or convinced the schools are subversive.[33] They exert pressure on school authorities for changes in policy at meetings of the school board and elsewhere on public platforms. When every statement and action of school authorities is subject to the close scrutiny of a hostile group, they must give attention to the matters of concern to the minority, perhaps neglecting others. In order to relieve the pressure and get on with other school business, officials are tempted to appease the minority by making concessions on controversial policies.

[33] Cf. James S. Coleman, *Community Conflict* (Glencoe: The Free Press, 1957).

A few militant oppositionists can also exert pressure by threatening a general appeal to the electorate. A vocal group can stir up issues of emotional appeal and hence bring to the polls some persons who ordinarily are uninterested in the schools. School authorities must anticipate the possibility that a militant group can make good its threat and influence school programs other than the ones in immediate contention. The officials may decide it is wise to give a little rather than to risk more.

The silent vote. The various publics of the community are able periodically to express their sentiments by voting on educational issues. Such major issues as bonds for buildings and tax-limit increases for the operating expenditures of the schools are decided at the ballot box by voters who take no part in debate and express no opinions in public. The schools know what the citizens are thinking only when the votes are in.

When the voters repeatedly pass bond issues and grant tax-limit increases, the school board becomes self-confident and feels that the town supports its policies, despite the assertions of militant interests. A series of defeats at the polls constrains a system financially and leads to despair about community support. The defeats are especially vexing when they cannot be explained as the work of highly organized pressure groups. Some communities have defeated school bonds even when the bonds were supported by nearly all major associations and clubs in town.

What is the source of the "no" votes in these cases? Is there a general distrust of the school personnel? Are opposition groups working largely beneath the surface? Is there a "taxpayers revolt" based on economic self-interest? Adaptation 33 suggests what may lie behind the defeat of school proposals.

Who Votes Against School Bonds?

Abridged and adapted from John E. Horton and Wayne E. Thompson, "Powerlessness and Political Negativism: A Study of Defeated Local Referendums," *The American Journal of Sociology,* Vol. 67, No. 5 (March, 1962), pp. 485–93. Published in this form by permission of the authors and *The American Journal of Sociology.*

Studies of mass movements and political extremism indicate that the weakest support for Western political institutions is found among persons who are marginal to the centers of power in their societies. Research on local referendums also shows that among the socially and economically deprived segments of the community there is a consistent pattern of negative voting. Many persons in low-power positions apparently have negative attitudes toward community leaders and their community projects. Feeling powerless and alienated from those they identify as having power, they vote their resentment.

The data for the study consist of interviews with nearly 400 voters in two upstate New York communities, collected in March, 1957, and March, 1958, shortly after the defeat of school-bond proposals. Opinion was sampled in geographical areas roughly dividing the population according to socio-economic status. In one town, the school district was divided into tracts, and at least five interviews were gathered in each tract. In the other town, interviews were conducted proportionate to the total number of eligible voters in each election district.

Several related characteristics of the school-bond campaigns suggest that the politics of protest operated in these communities:

1. In both towns defeat of the school-bond proposal was associated with an increased turnout among persons of low income and education.

2. Each campaign was pervaded by an atmosphere of controversy generalized beyond the specific issues and directed against the experts and local leaders. This atmosphere was provoked and perpetuated by self-appointed opposition leaders—perhaps local counterparts of the demagogic leaders of mass movements—who in their opposition to the political leaders of the community professed to represent the interests of "the people."

3. During the period of community conflict there was heightened but often undirected power consciousness among persons in low positions, whose perspectives (dispositions to see the world in a certain way) colored their reactions to the issue and the direction and extent of their political action.

THE NEGATIVE ATTITUDES OF THE POWERLESS

In both communities general discontents became attached to symbols of power. In one town the symbol of power was the university, in the other, the corporation. Most persons recognized the symbols as important powers in their community; however, only persons who felt powerless were likely to see them as threatening powers. They were more likely than the politically powerful to be mistrustful of public officials and experts, to believe that the community was dominated by special interests, and to criticize and belittle education and other values central to the leaders of their community.

In the university town the persons most negatively conscious of the political structure were those who (1) felt powerless, (2) identified the university and school board as major powers, and (3) were critical of education. In the company town, the most negatively conscious were those who (1) felt powerless, (2) identified the company and the school board as central powers, and (3) identified with the union and the working class.

Each increase in awareness of power was associated with a corresponding increase in negative attitudes toward a proposal. Feeling powerless and identifying power centers had a cumulative effect. In the university town only 25 per cent were unfavorable toward the school-bond issue among those who were politically active and identified no one seat of power in the community. This compares with 68 per cent unfavorable among those who both deemed themselves powerless and identified one or more powers in the community. The corresponding figures in the company town were 31 per cent and 88 per cent, an even greater difference. The third aspect of political consciousness produced an even greater spread of positive and negative attitudes. In the university town, 74 per cent were unfavorable toward the issue among those who felt powerless, identified centers of power, *and* were critical of education. This compares with 16 per cent of those who felt politically active, identified no seats of power, *and* were not critical of education.

Although closely associated with social class position, political consciousness was an independent force in political action. At least political negativism (voting down an issue) cannot be explained only on the basis of economic self-interest. Respondents often mentioned costs as the reason for opposition to the bond issue. Yet, regardless of differences in socio-economic position, alienation still had an effect on the direction of political attitudes.

POLITICAL ACTION OF THE POWERLESS

Power consciousness was not consistently related to political participation, that is, the decision to vote. Alienation from the community powers may have produced negative attitudes, but in many cases the attitudes did

not provide sufficient incentive for voting against the plans of the powers. Feelings of alienation and hostility toward local power centers were translated into action only to the degree that the citizen was committed to living in the community. Individuals who had economic and social commitments in the community cared the most. The best indicator of involvement in the community was home ownership. The taxpayer was most likely to translate attitude into action. As seen in Table XII:7, over 80 per cent of taxpayers went to the polls, whether they felt alienated or not. (The turnout among non-taxpayers, not shown in the table, was considerably lower, except among those in the company town who were not alienated.)

But *how* did the taxpayers vote? Essentially, the non-alienated taxpayers voted "yes" for the school bonds and the alienated taxpayers "no" (Table XII:8). In the university town, only 18 per cent of the non-alienated taxpayers cast a negative vote, while 70 per cent of alienated homeowners did so, a substantial difference of 52 per cent. The same pattern appeared in the company town. (Alienation also made a difference among the non-taxpayers but to a lesser extent.) Alienation apparently determined in many cases the direction of the taxpayer's vote.

THE MASS PROTEST OF THE POWERLESS

The evidence supports the contention that among the alienated—the powerless who were power conscious—voting against the referendums may have been an expression of political protest, a vote against the local powers-that-be. But what was the nature of this protest? Was it a class-conscious protest in the Marxian sense of the term, a power consciousness based on political knowledge and identification of self-interest with class interest?

Some manifestations of class consciousness were present: the most alienated were more likely to identify a threatened "we" (the

Table **XII:7**　Voting Among Taxpayers

Attitude of Taxpayer	Percentage of Taxpayers Turning Out to Vote on School-Bond Issue
University town:	
Alienated	85% (44 of 52 persons) *
Not alienated	90% (93 of 103 persons)
Company town:	
Alienated	82% (37 of 45 persons)
Not alienated	91% (51 of 56 persons)

* Read: Of 52 taxpayers with an alienated attitude, 44, or 85 per cent, turned out to vote. Each percentage figure is calculated from a different base population (alienated taxpayers in one case and non-alienated taxpayers in the other, in each town). Therefore, the percentages shown in the table do not add to 100 per cent. (Source: Table 5 of Horton and Thompson.)

union leaders, the working class) as well as a threatening "they." Moreover, the threatened "we" had potential leaders (the taxpayers' association and the labor union). Nevertheless, other evidence suggests that the protest of the powerless resembled not so much class-conscious protest, as mass protest of persons weakly tied to any group. The following observations favor this interpretation: Although the alienated identified threatening powers in their environment, they had no precise knowledge of the bond issue, no accurate knowledge of the local power structure, nor of the specific social positions of the powers. Second, there was no convincing evidence that the alienated identified self-interest with class interest, or felt strongly attached to the leadership of the taxpayers' association or labor unions. The

alienated of the corporation-dominated community were as pessimistic about the role of the labor union in public affairs as were the less alienated and more affluent members of the community.

The alienated were undeniably suspicious of politics, even perhaps of persons who championed their economic interests, and this political suspicion was part of a broader and more pervasive cynicism. Alienation and low socio-economic positions were related both to each other and to a cluster of attitudes, a view of the world that elicits the political response of the underdog. Recurring themes in this view and consequently in the political style of the powerless were: the feeling that the world is a threatening place inhabited by the powerful and the powerless; suspicion of outsiders and of people

Table **XII:8**　Negative Voting Among Taxpayers

Attitude of Taxpayer Voter	Percentage of Taxpayer Voters Voting "No" on School-Bond Issue
University town:	
Alienated	70% (31 of 44 voters) *
Not alienated	18% (17 of 93 voters)
Company town:	
Alienated	84% (31 of 37 voters)
Not alienated	37% (19 of 51 voters)

* Read: Of 44 taxpayer voters with an alienated attitude, 31, or 70 per cent, voted "no" on a school-bond issue. As in Table XII:7, each percentage is calculated on a different base. (Source: Table 5 of Horton and Thompson.)

in general; pessimism about the future; despair; and the tendency to debunk education and other values necessary for success in a competitive society.

These findings are consistent with earlier research that suggests that persons in low socio-economic positions tend to see the world as a threatening place and that this predisposition influences specific response to reli-gious, racial, and political issues.[34] Voting down local issues may be in part a type of mass protest. It may represent a convergence of the individual assessments and actions of the powerless who have projected into available political symbols the fears and suspicions emerging from their own experience of alienation.

[34] For example, see Samuel Stouffer, *Communism, Conformity, and Civil Liberties* (Garden City: Doubleday, 1955).

Section 9 Population and ecology

The following factors largely determine the size and composition of the population in schools and colleges of a nation, although school policies and practices may have an independent effect.

1. *Birth rate.* Potential school population is determined by the national birth rate. The entering school population for the next five years can be predicted with a high degree of accuracy from current age statistics slightly adjusted for child mortality.

2. *Cultural values.* Nations vary in their traditions of how many of the young should be enrolled in elementary, secondary, and higher education. The United States encourages large proportions at each age level to enter and remain in school, interpreting democracy to mean "education for all." The English tradition, on the other hand, has emphasized selection on the basis of talent at the higher levels of schooling, and a smaller proportion attend college.

The school population is also influenced by patterns of prejudice. The enrollment of minority children is reduced when discriminatory action prevents many from entering school or shortens the time they remain.

3. *Occupational structure.* While the educational traditions of a country have some independent force, they usually reflect the changing demands of the economy. (See Section 2, pp. 447 ff.)

4. *School retention.* The student population of secondary and higher education is also determined by how well schools retain those who enroll. How long students remain in school is related to the philosophy and inclination of school personnel as well as tradition and the demands of the economy. School systems that wish to retain most students as long as possible offer alternative programs of study and extracurricular activities that increase the holding power of the high school. When attractions fail, truant officers retrieve those attempting to leave before they reach the legal age. On the other hand, teachers in the secondary schools of many countries, and in some schools in the United States, present a stern moral-academic face: "Be like us or leave." Confronted by this attitude, a large proportion of the students, especially from the lower classes, may opt out at an early age.

TRENDS IN THE SCHOOL POPULATION

The school population in the United States in 1960 was over 46 million out of a population of approximately 180 million, or over one-fourth of the total. There were 33 million in elementary schools, 10 million in high schools, and 3 1/2 million in college.

The trend is toward greatly increased numbers at every level. The number of high school graduates has risen as follows: 1870, 16,000; 1900, 95,000; 1930, 667,000; 1960, 1,803,-000.[35] A high birth rate since the end of World War II has caused rising enrollments in elementary and secondary schools and will sharply increase college enrollments, starting in the middle 1960's. College enrollments rose in the late 1950's and early 1960's because of a growing interest in attending college. This recent increase in enrollment *rate* is an extension of a long-term upswing. College enrollment compared to the population of young people eighteen to twenty-one years old was less than 2 per cent in 1870, only 4 per cent in 1900, 12 per cent in 1930, 30 per cent in 1950, and 37 per cent in 1960.[36] This rate has been increasing at an average of one per cent a year since the end of World War II and will probably continue to make its contribution to the numbers of college students in addition to the effect of population growth. In a single generation the trend toward prolonged schooling has increased by four years the median

number of years of school completed by the adult worker. The average young adult in urban areas in the early 1960's has completed high school and his rural counterpart has gone almost as far. In contrast, their parents did not go much beyond the eighth grade.

DISTRIBUTION AMONG SCHOOLS

The distribution of students between public and nonpublic (parochial and private) schools in 1960 is shown in Table XII: 9. The nonpublic enrollment for the elementary and secondary levels combined has been rising in absolute numbers and as a proportion of the total school population: 1.4 million, or 8 per cent in 1900; 2.7 million, or over 9 per cent in 1930; 3.4 million, or 12 per cent in 1950; and 6.5 million, or 15 per cent in 1960.[37] Over four-fifths of the nonpublic enrollment is in parochial schools of the Roman Catholic Church, and growth in Catholic enrollment has accounted for the increase in size of the nonpublic segment. Approximately one-half of Catholic youth attend Catholic elementary schools. Among Protestant denominations, only the Lutheran Church (the Missouri Synod in particular) has been able to maintain a sizable school system of approximately 160,000 students. Parochial schools of other churches have largely disappeared in the

[35] *A Fact Book on Higher Education* (Washington, D.C.: American Council on Education, n.d.), p. 236.
[36] Bureau of the Census, *Historical Statistics of the United States, Colonial Times to 1957* (1960), pp. 210–11; and *Higher Education* (U.S. Department of Health, Education, and Welfare), **17** (January, 1961), 18.

[37] *Health, Education, and Welfare Trends* (Washington, D.C.: U.S. Department of Health, Education, and Welfare, 1960), p. 56.

Table **XII:9** Enrollment in Public and Nonpublic Schools and Colleges, 1960

Level of Education	Public		Nonpublic		Total	
	Number (in Thousands)	Per Cent	Number (in Thousands)	Per Cent	Number (in Thousands)	Per Cent
Elementary[a]	27,900	84	5,400	16	33,300	100
Secondary[a]	8,500	89	1,100	11	9,600	100
Higher[b]	2,136	59	1,474	41	3,610	100
Total	38,536	79	7,974	21	46,510	100

[a] *Health, Education, and Welfare Trends* (Washington, D.C.: U.S. Department of Health, Education, and Welfare, 1961), p. 36. Figures for the school year ending 1960.
[b] *A Fact Book on Higher Education* (Washington, D.C.: American Council on Education, n.d.), p. 12. Figures for the opening enrollment, Fall, 1960.

long-term trend toward secularization of American education.

In higher education, the private sector is now waning in relative size. The majority of college students until the early 1950's attended private institutions. Since 1952 the majority have been enrolled in public colleges, the proportion reaching approximately 60 per cent in 1960. Between 1947 and 1960, enrollments in public colleges increased by 85 per cent, compared with an increase in private colleges of 25 per cent. This trend toward public higher education will almost certainly continue as a larger proportion of the young continue their education into the college years.

ECOLOGY OF SCHOOLS

The spatial distribution of American schools has been determined largely by the concept of the neighborhood school. Especially in elementary education, educators and parents have maintained that the school should be close to the home, serve a neighborhood, with children attending the nearest school. The neighborhood-school concept gives the elementary school a territorial base and a relatively homogeneous student body. In areas with two or more high schools, students are similarly assigned by place of residence.

Because minorities are concentrated in certain neighborhoods, the children attend segregated or largely segregated schools: the social composition of the neighborhood determines the social composition of the school. This is called *de facto* segregation in distinction from segregation by law. In a large city that has a Harlem, some schools are almost all white or all Negro, with mixed schools in the boundary neighborhoods or in areas undergoing transition.

Gerrymandering for Segregation

The idea that school population must be drawn from a geographic school district has been so fixed until recently that attempts to distribute students in preferred social patterns commonly take the form of redrawing territorial boundaries. Efforts to "purify" schools, that is, to place whites and Negroes in separate schools, or to keep middle-class children away from lower-class youth, often appear as gerrymandering. (See URBAN MAN, p. 598.) Thus in a Northern industrial city a high school district may be drawn two miles wide and ten miles long to include only white, upper-middle-class families, because a wider zone would mix races and social classes.

Gerrymandering for Integration

The neighborhood-school concept is under challenge in the United States because of efforts to integrate the schools racially. Groups opposing *de facto* segregation say that proportional racial composition should be a criterion in determining the student population of schools. They claim, for example, that if a city is 20 per cent Negro and 80 per cent white, most of its schools should have a similar ratio rather than radically unbalanced ones. This approach, too, encourages gerrymandering of school districts or, if need be, abolishing territorial zones and transporting students to schools distant from their homes. Many school boards and superintendents oppose such efforts, and those who advocate proportional integration find that the policy encounters many difficulties. New zoning plans designed to produce mixed schools are disrupted by disgruntled parents who put their children in private schools or move to new locations. Plans are soon outdated by the expansion of populations past old boundary lines, and the deliberate moving of students is costly and administratively complicated.

Effects of Migration

The flow of population into cities, and from the cities to their suburbs, complicates the problem of *de facto* school segregation. Negroes, and in some cities Puerto Ricans, have been migrating from their former rural locations into the central city, while whites have been moving from the center of the city to the suburbs in search of better homes—and to escape dark-skinned neighbors. These population movements tend to put the dark-skinned minorities in separate governmental units and school districts in the central cities of metropolitan areas, while whites concentrate in the "lily-white" suburbs. In 1960, Washington, D.C., was 55 per cent Negro; Baltimore, 35 per cent; Detroit, 29 per cent; Philadelphia, 27 per cent; Chicago, 24 per cent.[38] With over one million Negroes, New York City has the largest concentration in the country. Three-quarters of the school children of the Borough of Manhattan in New York City are Negro and Puerto Rican; two-fifths of the school children of greater New York (Manhattan, Brooklyn, Bronx, Queens) are Negro and Puerto Rican.[39] These concentrations are due to (*a*) continued in-migration, (*b*) a higher birth rate among the Negroes and Puerto Ricans, and (*c*) the flow of light-skinned people from the city to the suburbs. Between 1950 and 1957, New York City lost a white population about the size of Washington, D.C. (750,000), and gained a Negro and Puerto Rican population about the size of Pittsburgh (650,000).[40]

---

[38] *Census of Population, 1960,* PC (1)—B, Table 21.

[39] Nathan Glazer, "Is 'Integration' Possible in the New York Schools?" *Commentary,* **30** (September, 1960), 188.

[40] Dan W. Dodson, "Public Education in New York City in the Decade Ahead," *Journal of Educational Sociology,* **34** (February, 1959), 274–87.

Chapter XIII

Minorities

Section 1   **Introduction**

Nations vary widely in racial and cultural composition. The Scandinavian countries, for example, are quite homogeneous. Their internal cultural differences are slight, and few individuals are "visible," that is, racially or culturally distinguishable from the majority of their countrymen. Such homogeneous countries lack the problems of nations that have *ethnic* minorities (those set off from the main population by culture) or *racial* minorities. Presumably, homogeneous countries can achieve cohesion and consensus with relative ease because they do not experience the strain of fitting strangers into the social order. Nor do they have readily distinguishable groups whose *apparent* differences can be made the basis of differences in treatment.

On the other hand, countries like the United States, with many racial and cultural origins, necessarily encounter difficulties in building a coherent social order. This task is complicated by the fact that the diverse populations were introduced into the country rapidly, at different times, and in large numbers. Furthermore, many of the peoples are concentrated regionally or are in localities within urban areas, where they are segregated ecologically from the rest of the population and tend to develop subsocieties. Very often

isolation is imposed on the group, limiting its access to the large social order and prolonging its separate identity.

Table XIII:1 gives estimates of the minorities of conterminous United States. Racially defined populations total about 24 millions. "Negroes" include individuals ranging from persons who could easily pass as white to apparently unmixed African types. "Mexicans" include a large but unknown number of persons who are not different enough in their physical appearance to be distinguished from the white population, but this minority also includes many whose ancestry is largely or entirely American Indian. For this reason the United States census has had difficulty in enumerating Mexicans. In 1930 they were counted separately by "race," but since that time they have been included in the white population. Estimates for ethnic minorities are even less reliable than for racial groups. Many individuals in the ethnic categories are highly acculturated; others, on the other hand, are clearly set off by culture and identity from the dominant population.

Racial and cultural diversity may be obstacles to cohesion, to the building of a national community, but they are not necessarily fatal obstacles. Peoples with different

Table **XIII:1**   Minorities, Conterminous United States, 1960

Racial or Ethnic Population	In Thousands (Rounded)	
Negroes	18,860	*Racial minorities*
Mexicans	3,900	23,916,000
American Indians	590	About 13% of total
Japanese	260	(Mostly physically visible. Some,
Chinese	200	e.g., foreign-born Japanese, are cul-
Filipinos	106	turally as well as racially distinct.)
Jews	5,020	*Ethnic minorities* 9,239,000
Foreign-born whites from		About 5% of total
southern and eastern		(Mostly culturally visible, but some
Europe (excluding Jews)	4,000	have few or no culturally distinct
Foreign-born French Canadians	219	characteristics.)

Source: Racial data include native and foreign born, from *U.S. Census of Population, 1960.* Final Report PC(1)-1B, Table **44.** Foreign-born data from PC(1)-1C, Table 70. Mexicans, both native and foreign-born, estimated from preliminary reports on Spanish surname population. French Canadians estimated from unpublished foreign-born and mother tongue data. Jews, both native and foreign-born, estimated from *Current Population Reports,* P-20, No. 79, February 2, 1958. *The American Jewish Yearbook, 1962,* p. 492, estimates an additional 500,000.

cultural backgrounds can enrich the sources of national development and create a broad and cosmopolitan outlook. Modern societies have worked out very different ways of relating minority peoples and the social order. At one extreme is *assimilation* and *amalgamation,* that is, full acculturation and unrestricted intermarriage, leading to the complete absorption of the minority people and the loss of their identity. At the other extreme is rigid *segregation* of the subordinate group both geographically and functionally, so that it is nearly isolated from the large society. Distinct from either of these two policies is cultural or ethnic *pluralism,* which provides for a measure of group autonomy for minorities within a unifying social order.

No nation containing diverse groups has chosen a single solution. For example, Switzerland is a plural society in which several linguistically and culturally distinct elements have political power and cultural autonomy. But Switzerland has also experienced cultural assimilation and intermarriage among its various ethnic elements. In Soviet Russia the official policy is ethnic pluralism, which assumes cultural autonomy of the various "na-

tional" (ethnic) elements in the country, but unlike pluralistic Switzerland, these nationalities have little political independence or power. In the United States there is not one but several major policies, ranging from a variable but declining degree of segregation of Negroes to a policy permitting or even encouraging the assimilation of ethnic minorities, especially those from Western and Northern Europe.

Minorities differ in racial or cultural visibility, in the amount of discrimination they suffer, in the character of their adjustment, both as individuals and as groups, and in the length of time they survive as identifiable populations or individuals. Furthermore, in a large and diverse nation, such as the United States, wide regional differences and divergent tendencies within areas may appear. These differences are affected by regional distribution of the minorities, the economic functions they perform, and the extent to which they have developed ethnically or racially distinct systems of organization. The long-term trend in the United States as a whole, however, appears to be toward the assimilation of cultural minorities and the

Table **XIII:2**   Racial Composition, Alaska and Hawaii, 1960

	ALASKA		HAWAII	
	Number in Thousands	%	Number in Thousands	%
Total	226.2	100	632.8	100
Native whites	176.5	74.1	194.7	30.8
Foreign-born whites	7.1	3.1	7.6	1.2
Negroes	6.9	3.0	4.9	0.8
American Indians	14.4	6.4	0.5	0.1
Japanese	0.8	0.4	203.5	32.2
Chinese	0.1	0.1	38.2	6.0
Filipinos	0.8	0.4	69.1	10.9
Aleuts, Eskimos, etc.	28.6	12.7	—	—
Hawaiians, Part Hawaiians, etc.	—	—	114.4	18.1

Source: *United States Census of Population, 1960. Alaska and Hawaii*, Final Reports PC(1)-3B and PC(1)-13B, Tables 15; and *Alaska and Hawaii*, Final Reports PC(1)-3D and PC(1)-13D, Tables 96.

progressive integration of Negroes and other racial minorities.

The new states of Alaska and Hawaii are cases of regional diversity. Because they are so different in their composition, they are reported separately from the 48 states (see Table XIII:2). Hawaii is unique in the United States in its preponderance of nonwhites and its Asian background, factors that aroused opposition to Hawaiian statehood. Now that Hawaii has achieved statehood, such antagonisms are only rarely expressed. Instead, it is becoming more widely recognized that there are advantages to having a state whose origins are Asian rather than European, and Hawaii is seen as a cultural bridge with the Orient. Although this view may overstate the amount of Asian cultural survivals in Hawaii, such establishments as the East-West Center at the University of Hawaii may have a broadening influence on American education and the American outlook.

Adaptation 34 presents a perspective from which to view the minorities in American society. The racial and cultural characteristics that account for the identity, the *visibility,* of a minority, are related to two important

phenomena: (1) the degree of subordination and (2) the time estimated for its assimilation.

SOURCES AND READINGS

RECENT TEXTS AND GENERAL WORKS

Brewton Berry, *Race Relations* (Boston: Houghton Mifflin, 1958).

E. Franklin Frazier, *Race and Culture Contacts in the Modern World* (New York: Knopf, 1957).

Charles F. Marden and Gladys Meijer, *Minorities in American Society* (New York: American Book Co., 1962).

Edward C. McDonagh and Eugene S. Richards, *Ethnic Relations in the United States* (New York: Appleton-Century-Crofts, 1953).

George Eaton Simpson and J. Milton Yinger, *Racial and Cultural Minorities* (New York: Harper, 1958), contains bibliography.

COLLECTIONS

Milton L. Barron (ed.), *American Minorities* (New York: Knopf, 1957).

Andrew W. Lind (ed.), *Race Relations in World Perspective* (Honolulu: University of Hawaii Press, 1955).

Jitsuichi Masuoka and Preston Valien (eds.), *Race Relations: Problems and Theory* (Chapel Hill: University of North Carolina Press, 1961).

Race Differences*

"Scientists have reached general agreement in recognizing that mankind is one: that all men belong to the same species, Homo sapiens." † So begins the statement prepared for UNESCO by a group of experts on race problems. When biologists delimit a group of animals or plants as a species, their basic criterion is that the members of the species are interfertile when they breed with each other and that fertility is reduced when they breed with other species. All races of man have been shown to be completely interfertile. Men and women in all parts of the world with various ancestries are able to reproduce offspring whose fertility is not reduced.

According to the genetics of population, groups of animals belong to the same species if they have a similar genetic content. Many basic characteristics are apparently determined by invariable genes. Thus, every human being of whatever racial group has a four-chambered heart, the same general number and arrangement of bones in his skeleton, and so forth. There are, however, less fundamental differences within species, and man-

kind can be classified into subspecies or races on the basis of characteristics determined by variable genes. The attributes most commonly used by the man in the street to classify men into races are skin color, height, nose form, head shape, type and distribution of hair, and like characteristics. The more precise classifications made by physical anthropologists use the same attributes with more rigor and with the additional criteria of blood group genes. However, the considerable variation within each race and the overlapping between racial groups make it impossible to differentiate races according to any single criterion. Only a relatively few members of any one race combine the typical characteristics ascribed to that race. Other members approximate the "ideal" racial type in some respects but deviate from its norms in other characteristics. A race, therefore, is an arbitrary, biological grouping, and estimates of the racial composition of large populations are still based on essentially subjective opinions.

The observable differences in mankind do not connote superiority or inferiority. They are probably nothing more than adaptations to different environments. These physical adaptations are of minor consequence compared with man's efforts to achieve a mastery of his environment by cultural means.

* See L. C. Dunn and T. Dobzhansky, *Heredity, Race and Society* (New York: New American Library, 1952) and Curt Stern, *Principles of Human Genetics* (San Francisco: Freeman, 1960).

† Ashley Montagu, *Statement on Race* (New York: Henry Schuman, 1951), p. 11.

Robert E. Park, *Race and Culture* (Glencoe: The Free Press, 1950).

Marshall Sklare (ed.), *The Jews* (Glencoe: The Free Press, 1958).

Edgar T. Thompson and Everett C. Hughes (eds.), *Race: Individual and Collective Behavior* (Glencoe: The Free Press, 1958), has bibliography.

GENERAL WORKS ON THE NEGRO

Maurice R. Davie, *Negroes in American Society* (New York: McGraw-Hill, 1949).

E. Franklin Frazier, *The Negro in the United States* (New York: Macmillan, 1957).

Gunnar Myrdal, with the assistance of Richard Sterner and Arnold Rose, *An American Dilemma* (New York: Harper, 1944), has extensive bibliography.

PERIODICALS *Commentary; Journal of Negro Education; Journal of Negro History; Phylon; Southern School News.*

ADAPTATION 34

Subordinate Groups in the United States

Abridged and adapted from *The Social Systems of American Ethnic Groups* by W. Lloyd Warner and Leo Srole ["The Yankee City Series," Vol. III (New Haven: Yale University Press, 1945)], Chap. X, pp. 283–96. Published in this form by permission of the authors and the Yale University Press.

The classification of racial and cultural types in Table XIII:3 provides an overview of the factors that influence the degree of subordination of minorities and their prospects for assimilation. The analysis summarized here is part of the broad program of studies referred to as "The Yankee City Series" (see SOCIAL STRATIFICATION, p. 190). The table and this discussion have been somewhat simplified from the original.

Racial and Cultural Types

From left to right in the table are listed five *Racial Types,* ranging from Light Caucasoids to Mongoloids and Negroids (combined). Each of the Racial Types is theoretically divided into six *Cultural Types,* ranging from Cultural Type I at the top, who are most like the dominant Americans, to Cultural Type VI at the bottom, who are least like the dominant Protestant English-speaking Americans.

When these two scales, the cultural and the racial, are combined into a table, 30 possible categories logically result, since there are six cultural types for each of five racial types. For simplicity, Racial Types IV and V are combined, resulting in only 24 possible categories, but there is evidence that Mongoloids and Negroids have different degrees of subordination and will assimilate at different rates. Several of the theoretical categories do not exist in fact; they are shown by dashes in the table. For example, there are no English-speaking, Protestant, Dark Caucasoids.

Degree of Subordination

The *Degree of Subordination* indicates how each group is ranked in relation to the dominant group and to other subordinate groups. The criteria for rating a group's degree of subordination are (1) freedom of residential choice, (2) freedom to marry out of the group, (3) amount of occupational restriction, (4) strength of attitudes in the host society which prevent social participation in such institutions as associations and cliques, and (5) the amount of vertical mobility permitted in the host society for members of the ethnic or racial group.

A value from one to five is assigned to each of these criteria, the results added and the sum divided by five; the quotient gives a rough index of the degree of subordination of each group. The degrees of subordination are (1) "very slight," (2) "slight," (3) "moderate," (4) "great," and (5) "very great." Light Caucasoids who are Protestant and speak English have an index of *one* ("very slight" subordination), and most non-Protestant mixed bloods from Latin America have an index of *four* ("great" subordination).

Timetable of Assimilation

An estimate of the length of time necessary for the assimilation of each racial and ethnic group is provided in the columns *Time for Assimilation.* The criteria for determining the time period are (1) the time taken for an entire group to disappear, (2) the proportionate number of people who drop out of a group in each generation, and (3) the amount and kind of participation permitted members of the group by the host society. The same procedure as described for the degree of subordination is used to calculate a rough index number for a group's assimilation.

This scheme assumes that the relations among ethnic and racial groups in American society are largely governed by the facts of subordination and assimilation. Because the presentation is simplified and schematic, any group may be somewhat out of place, for example, Catholic French or Hungarians, but the relative positions of most of the groups are accurate.

Language and Religion

For purposes of the present analysis immigrant cultures are classified by differences of language and religion. Emphasis is placed on religious differences, because the dominant old-American religion is Protestant, and much customary behavior is closely integrated with a Protestant outlook. The customary way of life is most like the English, and the "American language" is but one of several English dialects. The ethnic people most like the dominant group are, therefore, English-speaking Protestants whose customary behavior, language, and religion deviate least from the American way. Just below this cultural type are Protestants who do not speak English and whose way of life is slightly more divergent. The third type includes English-speaking Catholics and other non-Protestants who speak English. The most divergent types are non-Christians, some of whom speak English and others who do not.

Race

The racial evaluations made by the American host society are far stronger and more lasting than the cultural evaluations. For example, English-speaking Protestant Negroes with the same culture as the rest of the American group cannot be considered a mere subvariety of other English-speaking peoples. It is obvious that their position is inferior to all Caucasoid peoples, regardless of the degree of subordination of the Caucasoids. Race, rather than culture, is the major determinant of subordination.

Interplay of Racial and Cultural Factors

Most of the peoples of the British Isles (including North Irish but not Catholic Irish) and other English-speaking peoples of the Dominions belong to Cultural Type I of Racial Type I. Their subordination is very slight, and their period of assimilation is usually less than a generation. They do not form ethnic colonies and are generally accepted as members of the dominant population.

Protestant Germans, Dutch, and Scandinavians of Cultural Type II and Racial Type I are quickly assimilated into American life. Those Scandinavians and Germans who belong to special religious sects are exceptions to the listing in the table.

Catholic Irish of Cultural Type III assimilate more slowly than Protestant Irish, despite the fact that in all other respects the two cannot be distinguished by most Americans. Whereas Catholic Irish take from one to six generations to assimilate, Protestant Irish are assimilated almost immediately.

Non-Protestant Christian groups who do not speak English are in Cultural Type IV. The strength of the Catholic Church in maintaining separate ethnic groups is illustrated here. French, German, Belgian, and Dutch Protestants assimilate rapidly and are less subordinated than those of the same nationality and language who are Catholic.

Cultural Types V and VI of Racial Type I include light Caucasoid Jews, particularly those of Western Europe. A comparison of Racial Type I with Racial Type II (dark-skinned Jews) tells much about the place and problems of Jews in American life. Jews and other non-Christians are likely to assimilate less easily than Christians, but light-skinned Jews assimilate more rapidly than their dark-skinned coreligionists.

Non-Protestants of Cultural Type IV and Racial Type II include such nationalities as Italians, Greeks, and French, who are also found in Cultural Type IV of Racial Type I. The subordination of these darker Cauca-

Table XIII:3   The Ordering of Ethnic and Racial Groups in the United States

	Racial Type I—Light Caucasoids			Racial Type II—Dark Caucasoids		
	Cultural Type	Degree of Subordination	Time for Assimilation	Cultural Type	Degree of Subordination	Time for Assimilation
I.	English-speaking Protestants (e.g., English, Scots, Canadians)	very slight	one generation or less	I. _____		
II.	Protestants not speaking English (e.g., Danes, Dutch, French)	slight	1-6 generations	II. (e.g., Protestant Armenians and other dark-skinned Protestants)	slight to moderate	6 generations or more
III.	English-speaking non-Protestants (e.g., South Irish)	slight	1-6 generations or more	III. _____		
IV.	Non-Protestants not speaking English (e.g., French, Belgians)	slight	1-6 generations or more	IV. (e.g., dark skins of Racial Type I, also Sicilians, Portuguese)	moderate	6 generations or more
V.	English-speaking non-Christians (e.g., English Jews)	moderate	1-6 generations or more	V. _____		
VI.	Non-Christians not speaking English (e.g., fair-skinned European Jews and Mohammedans)	moderate	1-6 generations or more	VI. (e.g., dark-skinned Jews and Mohammedans)	moderate to great	very long

soids is likely to be greater and their period of assimilation longer than for lighter Caucasoids, despite the fact that they are often co-religionists, speak the same language, and have the same customs. The factor of race (color), or rather the strong negative evaluation of it by American society, accounts for most of the differences in ranking of the two groups.

The future of American ethnic groups seems to be limited; it is likely that they will be absorbed. When this happens, one of the great epochs of American history will have ended.

The place of English-speaking Protestant American Negroes in American life underscores the importance of race. Negroes derive from the same cultural origins as white old-Americans. Although they are similar to the English and Scots of Cultural Type I, they occupy a very subordinate position with little likelihood of full assimilation unless great social and cultural changes occur. Racial ranking governs this degree of subordination.

Table **XIII:3** The Ordering of Ethnic and Racial Groups in the United States—Continued

Racial Type III—Caucasoid Mixtures			Racial Type IV—Mongoloids and Racial Type V—Negroids (combined)		
Cultural Type	Degree of Subordination	Time for Assimilation	Cultural Type	Degree of Subordination	Time for Assimilation
I. _____			I. (e.g., most American-born Chinese, Japanese, Negroes)	great to very great	very long to indefinitely long
II. (e.g., small groups of Spanish-Americans in the Southwest)	great	very long	II. _____		
III. _____			III. (e.g., some American Negroes)	very great	indefinitely long
IV. (e.g., most of the mixed bloods of Latin America)	great	very long	IV. (e.g., Filipinos and Negroid Puerto Ricans)	great to very great	indefinitely long
V. _____			V. (e.g., "Black Muslims" and some Orientals)	great to very great	indefinitely long
VI. _____			VI. (e.g., Orientals and Africans)	great to very great	indefinitely long

Section 2 **Social organization**

Two policies, *segregation* and *integration*,[1] define the relations of culturally or racially different peoples within a political unit and lead to very different kinds of social organization.

[1] Although many of the same ideas are applicable to ethnic minorities and to the less numerous racial minorities, this discussion emphasizes relations between Negroes and whites.

Segregation is the policy, enforced by custom or law, that excludes a group from joint participation. Characteristic forms of segregation are residence, occupation, and education. The effect of segregation is to minimize association between the races, and further, to restrict the association that does occur to clearly defined subordinate-superordinate roles. Theoretically, there could be a segregated society without subordination, but in practice this has probably never happened.

A society must be willing to pay a price for maintaining a system of subordination and segregation: it must use part of the resources of the economy in the wasteful duplication of facilities; some of its human resources (the manpower of the subordinate group) remain inadequately trained and partly wasted; and some of its dominant manpower must be used to maintain dominance. Communication between the minority and dominant populations is minimized, and cohesion and consensus of the society are impaired. Segregation also tends to retard acculturation, and to emphasize the visibility of minorities.

Integration refers to policies that permit Negroes and whites, for example, access to areas of community life on the basis of free and equal association. Integration also has its price. When integration is preceded by segregation, the integration process introduces strains and instability in the customary relations between groups. Preoccupation with the issues of housing, suffrage, and education may reduce communication between the races to "race relations." Interpersonal relations of long standing that had risen above the definitions of race may be submerged.

In nations such as South Africa and the United States the dilemma of segregation versus integration is a major issue. In both cases the dominant population is European and the chief subordinate group is African. In both cases subordination comes into conflict with the Christian ethic and liberal values. In South Africa the trend is toward increased segregation, but in the United States the tendency toward increased integration of Negroes seems clear. In both countries the direction of the trend has been set by the policies of the national government.

SEGREGATION AND INTEGRATION IN THE UNITED STATES

The areas of residence, of occupation, and of educational opportunity for Negroes are progressively expanding. By legislation, by judicial decision, and by administrative action, the arbitrary impediments to the participation of Negroes in the national life are being reduced. As these changes take place, the power of Negroes to shape their own destiny within the framework of American society and the influence they can bring to bear on the society increase.

Emphasis on economic and technological rationality is no doubt partly responsible for the trend away from segregation. Internal moral strains play their part, and probably the necessity of presenting a defensible moral order and a coherent social order in the world struggle for power is also involved.

Three changes in laws and practices in housing, education, and the armed forces suggest the entrenchment of segregation in the United States and the obstacles to achieving integration.

1. *Residential restrictive covenants.* The Supreme Court held in 1948 that restrictive covenants (agreements between property owners not to sell or rent their property to members of certain groups) were unenforceable in the courts. This means that a man may sell or rent his house to whomever he pleases without fear of punitive legal action. Yet this decision did not assure an automatic increase in the area effectively opened to settlement by Negroes or other subordinate groups. *Customary* restrictions remain, although not supported by the courts, and beliefs about the unsuitability of Negro neighbors also persist.

2. *Segregation in public schools.* In 1954 the Supreme Court held segregation in the public schools unconstitutional. This topic is dealt with in EDUCATION and is only touched upon here. It still cannot be said how rapidly educational integration will take place, but the court decision created the condition for a far-reaching change.

On the other hand, the Court's decision is probably producing increased segregation in some areas. Some school officials revised the boundaries of school districts and gerrymandered them to maintain a maximum amount of legal segregation. (See EDUCATION, pp. 486–87.) The net effect in such cases may be to increase residential segregation rather than to decrease school segregation.

Residential segregation has beome increasingly recognized as an impediment to all forms of integration, and the *de facto* segregation of schools in Northern cities has consequently become an issue. The proponents of integration assert that the schools are in fact segregated as a consequence of the high concentration of Negro residence. They claim that in a multiracial society the races need the experience of knowing each other in the schools and that only by thorough integration can schooling be made of equal quality throughout school systems. Some school boards in acceding to pressures have gerrymandered their districts so that Negroes are more *evenly* distributed. Others have permitted individual choice in the school to be attended, and this has resulted in a sharp enrollment decline in some predominantly Negro schools.

3. *Segregation in the armed forces.*[2] A third change in the position of minorities in the American social order has been in the armed forces. It had long been asserted that Negroes made inferior combat troops, that they lacked the technical ability to fly, that whites would refuse to associate with them in barracks or in combat. It was stressed that military policy could be changed only *after* civilian attitudes had changed. Nevertheless, in the decades after the close of World War II integration proceeded with great rapidity in all the armed services. The predictions of stress, disorder, desertion, and failure were not fulfilled. In mixed units Negroes are more efficient soldiers and fighting men with better morale. They apparently have been accepted by whites, and the soldierly qualities of the whites have not been impaired by the change.

[2] See Lee Nichols, *Breakthrough on the Color Front* (New York: Random House, 1954).

Integration does not proceed in a neat, orderly way in a single direction. Integration in one facet of the national life creates stress in others. For example, the integration of Negro troops in training and combat units has pointed up the inconsistency of segregating their children in the schools serving military posts or of housing their families in segregated areas. Consequently, military posts in the South have become islands of integration in a region where segregation remains the general rule. Both systems are, therefore, under pressure—the integrated system of the military camp and the segregated system of the Southern community.

APARTHEID IN SOUTH AFRICA[3]

In contrast to the United States, the Republic of South Africa through its policy of *apartheid* or "separate development" is tending toward more segregation of its non-European peoples, and now practices a more extreme subordination and control of its Negro population than has been known in the United States since the Civil War. People of European ancestry are only about one-fifth of the population of the Union, and they will probably be a decreasing proportion of the total. The native Africans are viewed by many whites as an overwhelming threat that must be rigorously controlled. In 1960 the population of South Africa was as follows:

	Thousands	*Per Cent*
Europeans	3,068	19.3
Africans	10,808	68.2
Colored	1,488	9.4
Asians	477	3.0
Total	15,841	99.9

[3] This discussion is indebted to Quintin Whyte, "Policies in South Africa," presented at the Conference on Race Relations in World Perspective, University of Hawaii, July, 1954; and John A. Barnes, "Race Relations in the Development of Southern Africa," and Absolom Vilakazi, "Race Relations in South Africa," in Andrew W. Lind (ed.), *Race Relations in World Perspective* (Honolulu: University of Hawaii Press, 1955).

People of European origin are mostly Afrikaners or British. About 60 per cent of whites are *Afrikaners,* or Boers, descendants of seventeenth- and eighteenth-century Dutch settlers. They speak *Afrikaans,* a language derived from Dutch but distinct from it. Their history is the story of a small number of people who left their homes in Europe to preserve their independence and their manner of worship. They fought the Hottentot and the Bushman; they resisted the controls of the Dutch East India Company, and rather than submit to the British, they trekked into an unknown interior. British Imperialism caught up with them again at the end of the nineteenth century. Sixty years after their defeat in the Boer War, the most uncompromising champions of Afrikanerdom, its language, culture, and tradition, hold the reins of power and have eliminated the last remnants of British power. The Afrikaners know no other home, no other allegiance.

South Africans of British stock owe allegiance to South Africa, but they would prefer to retain a wider loyalty to the Commonwealth. In 1961, however, South Africa became a fully independent Republic, and the association with the Commonwealth has ended.

To the *African* or Bantu, South African history is one of conquest and control, and of exploitation. The missionaries came with the Bible and the textbook, but education and Christianity did not prove to be the keys to power. The white man used the Bantu as a source of labor but did not permit him to be

Instrument of Apartheid: For identification and permission to travel and work in European areas, a non-European in South Africa is required to carry a pass book. Outside their own tribal areas, Bantus whose pass books are not in good order are subject to criminal penalties.

a free agent. The white man gave education and training but refused the opportunity for the exercise of ability and training.

The *Colored* amount to less than 10 per cent of the total. They are the descendants of racial crossings between early white settlers, administrators, and sailors, Bushmen and Hottentots, and slaves from the East Indies, Madagascar, and other parts of Africa. The Colored are concentrated in Cape Province, and their status has in the past been ambiguous. Apartheid tends to divest the Colored of their intermediate status and privileges and to impose controls similar to those used for the urban Bantu.

The *Asians* are mainly of Indian or Pakistani origin and are concentrated in the province of Natal, where they play a large role in trade. Although their status was an intermediate one, they have become increasingly identified with the Bantu and sometimes have co-operated with the Bantu in resisting apartheid. Relations between the governments of India and the Union have frequently been strained as a consequence of tensions in Natal.

Apartheid, as presently practiced, is an extreme form of segregation and control of the non-European peoples on rural reservations and in separate urban settlements. This policy has rapidly hardened. Constitutional changes have restricted civil liberties, and police power is applied not only to enforce segregation but to suppress debate and dissent among whites and Negroes alike.

The South African government plans to permit limited self-government in the native territories, and steps have been taken in this direction, but they are to have no direct representation in the South African Parliament. Substantial expenditures have been made to improve the economies of the Bantu territories, but the lands are not adequate for the African population and the grant of self-government is not true independent statehood. Outside the reserved areas Africans are rigorously controlled in their movements, their jobs, and their relations with whites.

The government of South Africa is in an almost hopeless dilemma. It needs African labor to operate its economy. It is determined to restrict relations between Africans and Europeans to an absolute minimum. To support their growing populations, the native areas must be developed rapidly and at high cost. Such expenditures would draw capital and trained African workers out of the white sector of the South African economy, where they are also badly needed. But the integration of Bantu into the urban and industrial economy is not to be allowed. All this is complicated by increasing political awareness and aspirations on the part of the Bantu and the growing power of the new African nations whose motto is "Africa for the Africans."

Section 3 **Culture**

The study of culture in this chapter is confined to the acculturation of ethnic minorities and the codes governing the relations between minorities and the dominant group.

The Acculturation of Ethnic Groups

Acculturation is a form of culture change in which one people takes on the cultural forms, beliefs, values and practices of another. In the course of adjusting to the new environment, each immigrant group to the United States has undergone this process to a greater or lesser degree.

Substantial populations such as Mexicans, Italians, Poles, and Russian Jews are still undergoing acculturation in the United States, and for some the process is far from complete. The American practice has been to acculturate and eventually assimilate its immigrants, and in time, these ethnic minorities will merge into the national culture.

In the early twentieth century a melting-pot policy anticipated the almost immediate absorption of immigrants. This did not take place as fast as was expected, and some disillusionment resulted. More recently a policy of ethnic pluralism has become popular, but it is unlikely that the main features of the national culture will be greatly changed by immigrant forces. The debate between the assimilationists, those who would hasten the process of acculturation and integration of ethnic groups, and the ethnic pluralists, those who would strive to maintain ethnic identities, seems to be largely academic. The United States is a plural, multigroup society in the sense that it contains many interest groups striving for diverse purposes and using political organization to attain their objectives. Ethnic minorities often behave as interest groups, but their political interests vary; there are cleavages within the ethnic minorities; and even the most segregated ethnic communities have only a limited geographic unity. Most significantly, the ethnic groups include individuals who are acculturated in varying degrees. Consequently, the United States does not have the ethnic pluralism of Czechoslovakia, for example, with linguistically and culturally distinct groups whose histories are rooted in well-defined geographic areas.

The acculturation of immigrants in a large, secular society is not very susceptible to planning. Secular universal education and the rather free movement of cultural minorities expose the minorities to the host culture and hasten their acculturation.

Two visible minorities now undergoing acculturation in the United States are the Mexicans and the Japanese. Because Mexican culture, with its Spanish language and Catholic religion, is more like American culture than is the Japanese, one might expect Mexicans to acculturate much faster than Japanese. The reverse, however, seems to be the case. The Japanese take on the new culture very rapidly while the Mexicans acculturate slowly. There are a number of reasons why this is so:

1. Japanese seem to value formal education much as Americans do. They not only want education, but they want it for what it will do for them; that is, they have an *instrumental* attitude toward it. The immigrant Mexicans, on the contrary, appear to value education much less.

2. Japanese left gang jobs rather early in their immigration history, while Mexicans have worked in ethnic gangs as agricultural laborers, railroad workers, and the like to a very great extent. This kind of employment tends to reduce the amount of contact between the ethnic group and the large society.

3. Japanese business activity has been extensive and has fostered some contact with the large society. Mexican business activity has been very limited.

4. Mexicans are more numerous than Japanese in the United States. Large numbers help to reinforce the conservative ethnic culture.

5. Japanese immigration was effectively terminated almost a generation ago. Continual Mexican immigration and contacts across the border keep immigrants in communication with Mexican culture and retard acculturation.

6. Mexicans experience more segregation in schools.

7. Light-skinned Mexicans who acculturate often cease to be Mexicans and pass into the Anglo society. Thus, the Mexican community loses the most acculturated members. Highly acculturated Japanese tend to remain within the ethnic community, serving as models for others and perhaps increasing the speed of acculturation of the less "Americanized" members of the group.

As can be seen, acculturation is not merely a matter of cultural transmission but is lim-

Race Etiquette in the Press

Reprinted from "Race in the News," a pamphlet of the Southern Regional Council, Incorporated. N.D.

Today the number of Southern dailies that persist in putting the *N* in Negro in lower case is steadily decreasing. The majority, though, still shy from the use of courtesy titles. Many papers, of course, when referring to men, reserve the courtesy title for one man —the President of the United States. Many others, however, have a style of using "Mr." before the last names of all white men except criminals, sports stars, and familiar screen and radio personalities. Less than a handful of these extend the practice to include Negro men. "Mr." conveys no information, but the custom of omitting it before the names of Negro men, when it is ordinarily used before those of whites, is but another example of the deference editors show their white readers who are accustomed to calling all Negroes by their given names.

"Miss" or "Mrs.," on the other hand, say something: they tell the reader if a woman is married or single. Clarity is often sacrificed when either is omitted, and simplicity always. Sometimes a paper's taboo against calling a Negro woman "Miss" or "Mrs." puts a great strain on the writer, with resulting violence to language. The antecedent is likely to get lost if the pronoun "she" is overworked, so to avoid that the writer painfully resorts to jargon. For example, here is an excerpt from a story appearing in a Georgia daily:

Emma Clarissa Clement, of Louisville, Ky., granddaughter of a slave, Wednesday was chosen as the American mother of 1946 by the American Mother's Committee of the Golden Rule Foundation. The first Negro elected, she is 71 years old and has seven children.
Her children include the president of Atlanta University . . . , a professor of physics, a pro-fessor of English, and an Army chaplain. *She* is former National President of the Women's Society of the African Methodist Church, and is the widow of a former bishop of the African Methodist Zion Church of Louisville.

The election was announced by Mrs. Harper Sibley, of Rochester, N. Y. . . . Telephoning Louisville to notify *the chosen* of *her* selection, Mrs. Sibley said she was told by *a* daughter that mother is speaking on a radio program right now. *Her* subject [no, not Mrs. Sibley's nor Mrs. Clement's daughter's; presumably, it's Mrs. Clement's subject] was "The Family."

More seriously, this practice can be, and often is, a cruel one. To refer to the widow of a lynched Negro as "the Mallard woman," as some newspapers did, is to deny her even the elemental dignity of grief.

Although the old rule that flatly forbade publication of Negro pictures has been relaxed during the past decade, the appearance of Negroes in photographs is still rare and decidedly special. It is no longer surprising to see pictures of Joe Louis or Jackie Robinson on the sports pages, or pictures of Duke Ellington, Lena Horne, or Rochester in the entertainment columns. But elsewhere the camera is used in much the same fashion as the reporter's typewriter. The Negro is either presented as a menace, or he is ridiculed, patronized, or applauded backhandedly.

One sees news shots of Negro criminals or Negroes in "incidents.". . . Conspicuous by their rarity are "mug shots"—portrait-like photographs kept on file for recurrent use— of local Negroes who have won honors. . . . Some papers habitually identify a pictured Negro as a Negro in the cutline—a form of redundance that, were it not for its association in the mind with the delicate matter of race, would ordinarily be caught by any half-way competent copy desk.

ited and conditioned by demographic, occupational, and organizational influences.

The "Etiquette" of Race Relations

Where relations among racial or ethnic groups are stable, behavior is guided by customs understood and adhered to by both the dominant and subordinate groups. The groups may not equally endorse the practices, but they know what to expect of each other.

The "good nigger" knows how to act and the proper Southern white "knows how to treat" Negroes. The white is addressed as "boss," "sir," "captain," "mister"; the Negro as "boy," "uncle," "george," never "mister." The Negro gives the right of way to whites; he never strikes a white; if he must contest with a white, he does it through another white. He may "have" a white man who acts as his particular sponsor. He knows where he must not be seen; he knows where he must stand. He does not "get out of line."

These examples of an etiquette of race relations are at once symbols of the subordinate status of Negroes and devices for maintaining subordination. They are closely related to the aspect of the race relations code that has been institutionalized in laws prohibiting or restricting Negro use of many facilities, such as housing, schools, libraries, parks, play-

> ⁴ For details of racial etiquette in many areas, see Bertram W. Doyle, *The Etiquette of Race Relations in the South* (Chicago: University of Chicago Press, 1937), *passim;* and Charles S. Johnson, *Patterns of Negro Segregation* (New York: Harper, 1943), Part I.

grounds, transportation, hotels, and restaurants. Although the main objective is the maintenance of segregation, there are numerous methods used to achieve this end.

Complications arise from the rules of address between Negroes and whites. Like many surface aspects of interracial custom, these are undergoing fairly rapid change. The unevenness of the changes, however, creates stress, and this is exemplified in the handling of courtesy titles in the press. (See "Race Etiquette in the Press," p. 501.)

The etiquette of control need not necessarily be consistent or rational if it is fully known, but inconsistent rules create confusion and tension for both Negroes and whites. It is virtually impossible for a Negro traveler in the South to know the multitude of rules and customs of the various localities. He is constantly in jeopardy of being "out of line." The codes, at least in urban areas, have the effect of frustrating what they are supposed to achieve—a smooth path for race relations. It would be rash to assert that the system of informal etiquette and formal codes will fall of its own weight. At least part of it is too deeply embedded to disappear very soon. On the other hand, the strains toward consistency and rationality induced by the urban environment may lead to a reduction in the number of rules. The growing sophistication and militancy of Negroes contributes to this trend, and the code is under continuous attack in the courts and legislatures as well as by informal methods.

Section 4 Socialization

The transmission of prejudice or tolerance, the development of a sense of ethnic identity, and the complications of child rearing in a biracial or bicultural environment are examples of how socialization affects minority groups.

Socialization in a Bicultural Setting

A bicultural environment poses serious problems for the effective socialization of the child. These problems may be directly attributable to culture conflict, that is, to opposing valuations and beliefs held by the host society and the ethnic group. For example, immigrant groups that place a high value on parental authority find that authority directly challenged in the United States by a family system tending toward equalitarianism. Parental authority is undermined because the immigrant's child through school and peers soon gains a better mastery of the host culture than his parents. The child, at worst, may reject his parents as greenhorns, imperfect in English and old-world in their attitudes. The parents may use repressive measures in attempting to establish control, thus further alienating their children. If the parents are victims of discrimination, they may further complicate matters by translating their anxieties and self-doubt into pressures on their children. This is part of what is known as the "second generation problem."

The problem has been relieved in two ways: (1) by accelerating the acculturation of the parents through such means as "Americanization" classes; and (2) by imparting to the children more knowledge and appreciation of their cultural backgrounds. In the case of Japanese Americans, for example, language schools were established in California and elsewhere with the co-operation of state authorities. It was hoped that parental control would be facilitated if the children had a better grasp of the Japanese language. In some cases the program was a qualified success. The adults of the minority community collaborated in supporting the program, the teaching was competent, and the children were benefited. In other cases, however, attending the language schools, which were conducted at the end of the regular school day or on Saturdays, was a burden to the children and a source of increased conflict between parents and children. Not infrequently the management of the schools created division in the community.

Because minority children undergo socialization outside the home as well as within it, they learn the prejudicial attitudes of the large society at the same time that they are objects of prejudice. In this way a conflict in values becomes a conflict within the person. If he accepts as valid the attitudes of prejudice, he must reject members of his ethnic group, his family, and in a sense, himself. If he rebels against the prejudicial attitudes, he finds himself in conflict with powerful elements in the society.

Race Awareness in Young Children

The socialization problems mentioned above are not postponed to adolescence, as has sometimes been assumed. An intensive study of a sample of 103 Negro and white children (ages 4–6) demonstrated that complex and deeply internalized racial attitudes may be effectively communicated to children at a very early age. Negro children were more aware of and more interested in color, used more racial terms, had more ideas about race, and were more concerned about it. (See Table XIII:4.)

The children's racial orientations are even more striking. Three-fourths of the Negro children preferred whites, and almost all the

Table **XIII:4** Race Awareness of Negro and White Children*

	Low Awareness	Medium Awareness	High Awareness
Negro	15%	45%	40%
White	15%	61%	24%

*Mary Ellen Goodman, *Race Awareness in Young Children* (Cambridge: Addison-Wesley, 1952), p. 57.

whites preferred whites. No Negroes felt superior to the out-group, and more than half felt inferior. Half the whites felt superior and none felt inferior to Negroes. Both Negroes and whites were more friendly to whites than to Negroes and more antagonistic to Negroes than to whites.[5]

The result of this racial awareness and prejudice among the very young is personality damage of Negro children. The preschool child apparently is neither innocent of racial matters nor fully protected from them.

Psychological Damage[6]

The fact of discrimination is the major difference in the environments of Negroes and whites. By limiting participation, discrimination prevents the Negro from achieving goals for which he is equipped and toward which he aspires. As a consequence, the individual tends to lose a sense of personal dignity and worth, and his lowered self-esteem results in increased anxiety and aggression. Since the Negro learns to fear retaliation if his aggression is expressed overtly, he must control the expression of some impulses the white man may more fully express. Therefore, the Negro compensates in one of a variety of ways, with the result that internal stress is increased and spontaneous expression is inhibited: (1) One compensatory mechanism is *underreaction,* a general apathy and depression accompanied by feelings of isolation and passivity. (2) Weak self-esteem is bolstered by *overreaction,* the attempt to raise aspirations even higher and aggressively to emulate white standards. But overreaction antagonizes others and their response brings on more self-contempt and more desperate efforts to counter it.

The dominant culture teaches that the male partner should be the "provider" and should assume a dominant role. However, a working-class Negro woman may have a more secure job than her husband. Especially in a depression, he may find it harder than she to obtain steady work. If he is unable to assume his expected role, he may lose his own self-respect and the esteem of his wife. Indirectly, economic discrimination results in a high rate of family disorganization among working-class Negroes, with high rates of desertion and of female-centered families. (See Adaptation 35, pp. 511–12.) In such homes there are further consequences for the developing personalities of children who see that their parents do not conform to the dominant cultural ideals.

The personalities of American Negroes, as of all people, are a product of adaptation to a specific social environment. The environment of an oppressed minority imposes more stress upon the individual and offers less adequate opportunities for adaptation than are afforded to "majority" peoples. Because discrimination results in psychological damage, those who are discriminated against are less effective in dealing with personal problems and less able to make a significant contribution to society as a whole.

Passing and Marginality[7]

The self develops in a multitude of associations, and the individual learns to think of himself as a particular kind of man. This is his *salient identity.* A member of an old Boston family may think of himself as first-of-all a Bostonian. A member of Jehovah's Witnesses or similar sect probably thinks of his sect membership as his salient identity. Racial or ethnic identities are also likely to be salient, but these identities usually have elements that burden and handicap the individual. Consequently, a minority individual may have ambivalent feelings about his identity, and he may wish to reject it. Perhaps such

[5] Mary Ellen Goodman, *Race Awareness in Young Children* (Cambridge: Addison-Wesley, 1952), p. 219.

[6] See Abram Kardiner and Lionel Ovesey, *The Mark of Oppression* (New York: Norton, 1951).

[7] See "Passing" by Louis Wirth and Herbert Goldhamer in Otto Klineberg (ed.), *Characteristics of the American Negro* (New York: Harper, 1944), pp. 301–19.

ideas remain in the realm of fantasy; perhaps he regards them as impractical or traitorous; or he may decide to change. Where ethnic groups have only small differences in culture, the change of membership entails little or no stress. In ethnic groups, such as Jews and Italians, which have strong in-group ties, breaking away may be quite difficult. But for racial groups, such as Negroes in the United States, the problem is further complicated. Any known Negro ancestry automatically classes the individual as a Negro. The risk of discovery is an ever-present danger, no matter how "white" the individual may be. Changing racial identity by concealing ancestry is called "passing." In the United States most Negroes who pass as white do so only temporarily, in limited areas of their lives. For example, an individual may pass in order to secure better educational opportunities, occupational advantages, or temporary convenience in traveling and leisure time activities. This may be called "segmental passing." For an individual to pass completely, he must sever connections with family and friends and re-establish himself in an entirely new life. To accomplish this successfully is literally to suffer "sociological death and rebirth": the individual must be reborn as a new social personality.[8]

Risks and consequences must be accepted by an American Negro who attempts to pass completely into the white world. First, he must dissociate himself from both Negroes and whites who knew him as a Negro. He must leave his family and attempt to compete economically and socially without the advantage of personal connections. He must move to a new place where he is unknown or attempt to lose himself in the large and anonymous metropolis. He must risk embarrassment and even reprisal if he should be discovered. If he severs himself only partially from his previous associations, he increases the risk of discovery. He must be prepared to face doubt, uncertainty, and loneliness.

Many Negroes who are able to pass never attempt to do so, and it is almost impossible to estimate with precision the number of Negroes who pass in any year. Uninformed estimates running into hundreds of thousands have appeared in popular magazines. Direct studies of genealogies of Negro families have proved difficult, since secrecy and concealment are essential attributes of passing. An estimate, based on a study of mixed-blood families, concludes that not more than 10 per cent of those who could pass permanently actually do so, and that approximately 2,500 persons change their racial classification from Negro to white in any year.[9] The current militancy of Negroes and an accompanying growth in self-respect as Negroes probably reduces the amount of passing.

"The Negro who passes as white no longer presents any contradictions to the eyes of others, but he still has the inner dilemma."[10] This "inner dilemma" is the essence of the "marginal man." The Negro who passes may have anxieties, doubts, and guilt for his act. But the Negro who can pass and chooses not to pass also has the "inner dilemma." He, too, must be considered marginal. Marginality is a more common phenomenon among ethnic than among racial groups, because the outside pressures that hold the ethnic individual to his minority status are weaker and the *marginal alternative* is more clearly perceived.

"Race" as a Social Category

Passing is a by-product of discrimination against Negroes. This discrimination occurs not because Negroes are biologically or so-

---

[8] Allison Davis, Burleigh B. Gardner, and Mary R. Gardner, *Deep South* (Chicago: University of Chicago Press, 1941), p. 42.

[9] John H. Burma, "The Measurement of Negro 'Passing,'" *American Journal of Sociology,* **52** (July, 1946), 21.
[10] Everett C. Hughes, "Social Change and Status Protest: An Essay on the Marginal Man," *Phylon,* First Quarter, 1949, p. 59. See also Everett V. Stonequist, *The Marginal Man* (New York: Scribner's, 1937); and Robert E. Park, *Race and Culture* (Glencoe: The Free Press, 1950), Part IV.

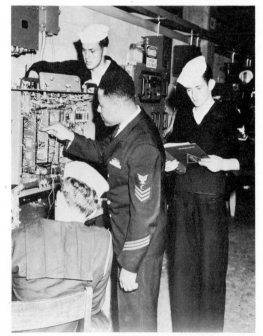

Above: Working relations become primary relations, USS Coral Sea.

Opposite: Still wearing his Steward's insignia, an electronics specialist works at his new job. His rate was later changed to Electronic Technician's Mate 1/c.

cially different from other Americans, but because they are *identified as Negroes*. The individual who passes does so because social classification as a Negro, *in itself,* is the basis of the discrimination under which he suffers.

The rigid definition of race in the United States corresponds to a social fact, not a biological fact. Obviously, in order for a Negro to pass as "white," he must look "white"; a significant proportion of his ancestry must, in fact, be Caucasian. In some other nations, notably the West Indies and Brazil, the categories of race are less arbitrary: *degrees* of racial membership are recognized and an elaborate system of terms classifying the amount of racial mixture and the social status of the individual is in popular use.

By contrast, in the United States a person with any known Negro ancestry is classified as a Negro. A person is a Negro because he is classified as a Negro and because he is treated as a Negro.

Section 5   Primary relations

PRIMARY RELATIONS WITHIN MINORITY GROUPS

Discrimination and segregation complicate socialization and throw a burden of increased responsibility on minority primary groups, particularly on the family. For example, the Negro family in the United States has been influenced by efforts of Negroes to develop relations that sustain the individual and protect him from a stigmatized racial identity. The Negro family system is tending toward a form of organization that resembles the general American norms. Adaptation 35 reviews the patterns of Negro family organization in the United States.

The pressures of prejudice do not always disrupt primary relations. Sometimes groups that suffer severe discrimination make a virtue of necessity and develop primary communities of great solidarity and richness.

The real inner solidarity of the ghetto community always lay in the strong family ties. In this inner circle deep bonds of sympathy had been woven between the members through a colorful ritual. Here each individual, who was just a mere Jew to the world outside, had a place of dignity, and was bound to the rest by profound sentiments. The adventures of each were shared by all, and enriched the store of familial lore. Through the organization in the synagogue, in turn, the family unit was given a definite status, based not so much on wealth as on learning, piety, the purity of family life, and services rendered to the community.[11]

Another consequence of segregation is the reduction of the amount of contact between groups, so that friendly relations do not have a chance to develop. Members of racial groups may travel widely through the country, but the network of in-group primary relations may completely encompass their associations. In a sense, they may never leave the segregated minority community.

PRIMARY RELATIONS BETWEEN MINORITY AND DOMINANT GROUPS

The conditions of life in the South both before and after slavery permitted primary relations to develop between Negroes and whites. Even though subordination was maintained, the friendly relations had lasting effects on the participants. Negroes had personal spokesmen in the white community; whites held warm memories of some Ne-

[11] Louis Wirth, *The Ghetto* (Chicago: University of Chicago Press, 1922), p. 37. Reprinted with permission of The University of Chicago Press.

THE FOLLOWING QUESTION WAS ASKED
OF 1,710 WHITE ENLISTED MEN

"Some Army divisions have companies which include Negro platoons and white platoons. How would you feel about it if your outfit was set up something like that?"

THE ANSWERS . . .

	Would like it	Just as soon have it as any other setup	Rather not, but it would not matter too much	Would dislike it very much
Infantrymen in a company which has a Negro platoon (80 MEN)	32%	28%	33%	7%
Infantrymen in *other companies in the same regiment* (68 MEN)	18%	33%	29%	20%
Field Artillery, Anti-Tank, and HQ units *in the same division* (112 MEN)	9%	29%	38%	24%
Cross section of other *Field Forces* units which do *not* have colored platoons in white companies (1,450 MEN)	2% 9%	27%	62%	

Fig. **XIII:1** Data based on a survey conducted in France by the Research Branch, Information and Education Division, ETO Headquarters, Report ETO-82, June, 1945: from report of President's Commission on Civil Rights, *To Secure These Rights* (Washington, D.C.: Government Printing Office, 1947), p. 86.

groes; and they assumed a paternalistic responsibility for their particular Negro friends. These relations softened discrimination. Although easily exaggerated, this background of shared experience gives some support to the claim that race relations in some Southern communities are benign. Contact between whites and Negroes has decreased with the spread of urbanization, with the tendency for controls to become formal, and the increased race-consciousness and militancy of the Negro. The Negro migrant to the North generally lives in segregated areas where the opportunities for personal association with whites are minimal.

In World War II during the Battle of the Bulge, volunteer Negro troops were hurried into combat. At that time segregation of Negro troops was the rule, and they were usually employed in noncombat duties. However, in this emergency they were sent into the line in platoons attached to white companies. Consequently, under combat conditions they worked closely with white troops. About two months later a poll was conducted of 1,710 white troops.[12] Although two-thirds of the white officers and enlisted men admitted to feeling unfavorable at first about serving in companies with colored platoons,

[12] See Samuel A. Stouffer, Edward A. Suchman, Leland C. Devinney, Shirley A. Star, and Robin M. Williams, Jr., *The American Soldier: Adjustment During Army Life,* Vol. I (Princeton: Princeton University Press, 1949), pp. 586–95.

those who had served in the same companies with the Negro troops were most favorably disposed to integration. (See Fig. XIII:1.) Those who had been most remote showed strongest negative attitudes. The white troops who had served with the Negroes were consistent in their evaluation of the Negroes as soldiers and as associates, and three-quarters of them felt that the experience had changed their attitudes in the favorable direction. This research undoubtedly played a part in the decision to integrate Negro troops fully into the armed forces.

The military experience is perhaps a special case. Military life creates fresh conditions for association in new and clearly defined situations. Such situations can readily encourage personal relations that violate customary norms. Even though the experience may have modified basic attitudes, it does not necessarily follow that these attitudes are carried over into civilian life.

Studies of housing and of admission of Negroes to schools and colleges have also found that attitudes change when formerly segregated groups are brought together. However, most people resist change, and whereas in the army much change can be managed, in schools and housing developments only the formal aspects of integration can be controlled. It would be unwise to conclude that effective integration in these situations must result in the development of firm and lasting primary associations.

The Negro Family

Abridged and adapted from E. Franklin Frazier, *The Negro Family in the United States* (Chicago: The University of Chicago Press, 1939). Published in this form by permission of E. Franklin Frazier and The University of Chicago Press.

The various types of Negro families in the United States developed in the face of unique impediments to effective family organization. African forms of family organization were largely destroyed in the course of transportation and under the forcible controls of the plantation, and slavery was not conducive to establishing new techniques of orderly integration. The Civil War and Emancipation precipitated new disorganization and a high degree of mobility. Against these obstacles the forms of Negro family organization were worked out.

Under Slavery

There were few forces at work to contribute to the establishment of stable forms of familial association among slaves. Relations between slave men and women ranged from physical contacts, sometimes enforced by the master, to stable unions characterized by deep sentiment between spouses and parental affection toward children. However, the very nature of slavery in the United States, with its separations of family groups and its emphasis on absolute control of the slave, was not conducive to stable unions. Even where they did exist, the unions might be destroyed. For example, the death of the master might occasion the breakup of his properties and the sale of his slaves.

Because of the conditions imposed by the slave system, the mother became the most dependable and important member of the Negro family. The father recognized the mother's more fundamental interest in the children and her authority in the household. A father might be sold and separated from his family, but when the mother was sold, the master had to take her children into account. Furthermore, unions between white males and slave females lacked legal and moral support, and the Negro woman was head of the household of her mulatto children.

After Emancipation

Immediately following the emancipation there was widespread disruption in all phases of Negro life. Family disorganization was noticeable in the numbers of Negroes who became wanderers "to prove they were free," cutting themselves off from family ties and forming a promiscuous and demoralized population. The destruction of the master's authority brought about the uprooting of many stable families. On the other hand, the disintegration accompanying the Civil War and Emancipation often tested and proved the strength of marital and family relations that had developed during slavery.

The reorganization of the Negro family following the initial confusion of Emancipation was assisted toward stability by five forces: Northern missionaries, missionary schools, the Negro church, the pattern established by families free before the Civil War, and developments under slavery. Where slavery was experienced in its most benign form, slave families frequently developed a degree of stability. A number of families persisted after emancipation and were able to acquire land and work it as family groups. When this happened, the family had a new cohesive element—the economic tie of working land. This corps of families early developed toward the patriarchal form, which is the American norm. But moral instruction and even force were unable to hold in check the widespread family disorganization which ensued when the Negro became a free agent in forming and breaking marital and other ties.

Present Status

Toward the end of the nineteenth century and the beginning of the twentieth century, two general tendencies were apparent in the development of the Negro family:

1. There was an extension, especially in the rural South, of the earlier mother-centered form of family.

2. In both rural and urban communities there was an increasing number of stable families modeled on the American pattern of family organization. They were not, however, characteristic of the Negro masses.

I. Rural South: *The Matriarchal Pattern*

The most striking feature of the Negro family of the rural South is the high proportion of matriarchal families, that is those with female heads.

The grandmother is often the dominant figure in this type of family, and in many cases she is the *sociological mother* of the extended family group. That is, she may be the person who directly rears the grandchildren, and perhaps also nieces, nephews, and adopted children. She exercises authority, assumes responsibility, and is called upon during the major crises of life by her own family and those outside the family. She is a repository of folk wisdom, and her superior knowledge and authority are recognized in matters concerning childbirth and child care. Midwifery is still important in the Negro South. As late as 1940, four-fifths of live births of Negroes in Mississippi and South Carolina were attended by midwives, as compared with one-fourteenth of white live births.

In isolated rural areas courtship begins at an early age and often involves sexual relations. Where sex relations result in pregnancy, the young people may or may not marry. Although the moral restraints of the larger community are absent and behavior is little influenced by white laws, the economic burden which pregnancy imposes operates as a restraint on sexual behavior. Both the girl's family and the father are obligated to help take care of the child. There is little, if any, guilt associated with illegitimacy, because the folk culture defines the bearing of children as the fulfillment of a woman's destiny. The birth of a child does, however, impose on the mother obligations which are increased if the others fail to discharge their obligations towards the child.

A large proportion of the marriages are common-law relationships; but from the standpoint of stability and community recognition, these relationships have the character of legal marriages. They conform to customs and mores which have grown up among the rural folk. As one moves from the rural South to the urban North and from

lower to upper class, one finds a steady increase in the incidence of contractual marriage and observation of the formal codes governing family behavior.

II. Urban North: *The Class Pattern*

Lower class. The lower-class Negro families, which are composed in part of recent rural immigrants who have little experience with the conventional norms of marriage and divorce, most closely resemble the rural family forms. During the mass urban migration, which began at the time of World War I, many thousands of men and women cut themselves loose from their families to seek work and adventure. Family desertion remains one of the chief forms of family disorganization among urbanized Negroes.

The lower-class families are physically segregated to a large extent in the deteriorated areas where Negroes first secure a foothold in the community. It is among this class that one finds a large proportion of families with female heads, as in the rural South. Between one-fourth and one-third of urban Negro families lack male heads. This is a result of the economic insecurity of the men and of illegitimacy. Although illegitimacy does not appear as a social problem in the rural South, sex relations and motherhood are redefined for the migrants in the city. Because of the precarious hold which women of this class have on men, their attitudes alternate between subordination to secure affection and domination because of their greater job stability and economic security.

Middle class. The effects of urban living have made possible the emergence of a substantial middle class in the Negro population. The middle class is differentiated by occupation and includes clerical and service workers and some business and professional people. Perhaps the most important accession to the middle class in the Northern cities has been the families of skilled workers. Among the middle class the male head of the family often has sufficient economic security to play the conventional role of provider for his family without the aid of the wife. The proportion of employed married women declines as the proportion of employed Negro males in industry increases.

The middle-class family is characterized by its emphasis on respectabilty in "getting up in the world," and it has a fairly democratic organization. The husband and father is recognized as the head of the family, but the wife and mother is not necessarily subordinated. She may work outside the home, temporarily or permanently, to help provide the extras for "getting up in the world." Her respected position derives from the tradition of independence among Negro women and is enhanced by her economic co-operation in buying a home or educating children.

Home ownership is an index of family stability among urban Negroes. The progressive stabilization of family life in the zones extending from the center of the community outward is indicated in some cities by a regular increase of the rate of home ownership in the successive zones. These increases are related to the tendency for the higher occupational classes to become concentrated in the peripheral areas of the Negro community.

Upper class. In upper-class urban Negro families, wives as well as husbands may be employed in professional occupations and other kinds of services. Among the upper class there are relatively few children per family and many childless couples.

Where the wife is employed, the upper-class family is usually equalitarian in its organization, and even where she is not employed, she enjoys considerable equality and freedom of activity. Respectability is taken for granted, but refinement and "culture" loom important. Individualism is a facet of upper-class behavior, and among the "emancipated" and "sophisticated" element a new type of intelligentsia has developed. The members of this group associate freely with white middle-class intellectuals and include interracial couples.

This adaptation has reviewed the evolution of the Negro family in the United States, the emergence of characteristic adjustments, and the forces making for stability and instability. The largely disorganizing heritage of slavery and the stresses of Emancipation have in part been overcome. In the rural South families based on common-law marriage and with a matriarchal organization persist, but trends toward conventional American forms are also apparent. In the urban North family types are correlated with class status. The lower-class families show the highest incidence of disorganization and the highest rate of survival of rural, matriarchal norms. The middle-class families closely approximate the characteristics of white families of similar status and are organized for upward striving. Husbands in such families are able to assume full financial responsibility, although wives may continue to work. The husband and father is the nominal family head, but the relations among the family members are democratic. The upper-class family tends to be a companionate unit. A continued trend toward the approximation of conventional American family forms may be expected.

Section 6 **Stratification**

Minorities may be studied from the stand-point of the place they occupy in the total system of stratification or from the perspective of stratification within a minority as a subsystem.

MINORITIES IN THE CLASS STRUCTURE

If the members of minorities were randomly distributed among the social strata, minority problems would be less severe. Cultural differences and group prejudice are aggravated by the fact that minorities often do not have equal life chances with the rest of the population. Discrimination and segregation result in inferior housing, jobs, and educational opportunities.

A true picture of the positions of ethnic minorities is difficult to secure. The distribution in the social strata of Jews, Italians, or other groups of European origin is not well known. Indirect evidence from the ecological study of residence gives some clues. Ethnic neighborhoods can be rated by rent, but not all members of minorities live in separate neighborhoods, and such neighborhoods contain other individuals.

Other things being equal, the longer a minority group has been in the country, the better its class position will be.[13] The groups do not, however, move up through the strata at an equal pace. The rate of vertical mobility is conditioned by the way the minority is defined or stereotyped by the dominant population, the nature of the minority's cultural background, the applicability to the new environment of the skills they bring with them, their attitude toward education, their experi-

ence in independent enterprise, and current economic conditions.

Racial minorities are much easier than ethnic groups to locate in the strata, because of the availability of census reports on education, income, and occupation. Figure XIII:2 gives the relative educational status of whites and nonwhites.[14] The advantageous position of the whites is clear. The crude figures on schooling do not completely state the real educational standing of the population, however. A disproportionate number of Negroes spend their time in schools with inferior teachers and facilities. As these conditions are corrected, nonwhites will have their share of the educational opportunities which provide the necessary conditions for occupational mobility.

Figure XIII:3 reports the occupational distribution of Negro and white male workers in 1960. The heavier concentration of whites in skilled and "clean" work is a reflection of their superior education, their access to parts of the job market in which Negroes have less opportunity, the heavier concentration of Negroes in the economically less-developed South, and the many obstacles of discrimination and segregation. If an arbitrary line is drawn between craftsmen and operatives, about one-fourth of employed Negro males fall above this line compared with more than three-fifths of the whites. The concentration of Negroes in relatively low-skilled jobs largely restricts their mobility to jobs requiring manual skills, for the

---

[13] Warner and Srole, *op. cit.,* Chap. V; and W. Lloyd Warner and Paul S. Lunt, *The Social Life of a Modern Community* (New Haven: Yale University Press, 1941), Chap. IX.

[14] Some census data are reported by "color": "white" and "nonwhite." Other data are available by "race": "white," "Negro," and "other races." Occasionally further breakdowns may be secured for "other races." The discussion here is restricted to white and nonwhite, and Negroes, of course, comprise the greater part of nonwhites.

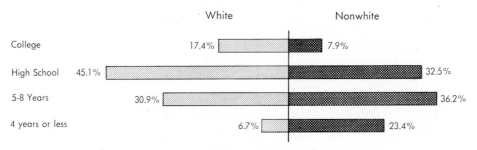

Fig. **XIII:2** Education by Color, Conterminous United States: 1960,
Persons Twenty-Five Years Old and Over

Source: *Census of Population: 1960*, PC(1)-1C, Table 76.

leap from "hand" to "head" occupations is a most difficult one to make. For more detailed discussion see pages 535 ff.

Given the foregoing data on the stratification of whites and nonwhites by education and occupation, one would expect stratification by income to show a similar bias in favor of the whites. The facts are summarized in Figure XIII:4. In 1959 the median income for white males in the United States was $4,319, for nonwhites, $2,273. Nonwhite incomes most closely approached white incomes in urban areas, but there was a substantial difference even there: the median income for urban white males was $4,792, for nonwhites, $2,794. In rural areas non-

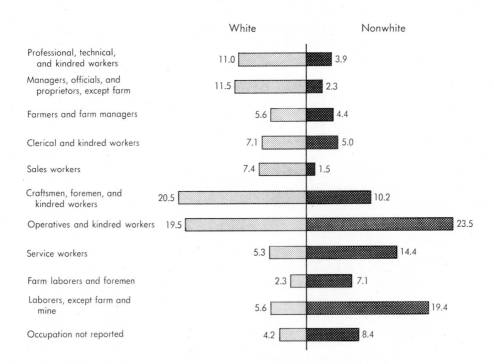

Fig. **XIII:3** Occupation by Color of Employed Males, United States: 1960

Source: *Census of Population: 1960*, PC(1)-1C, Table 88.

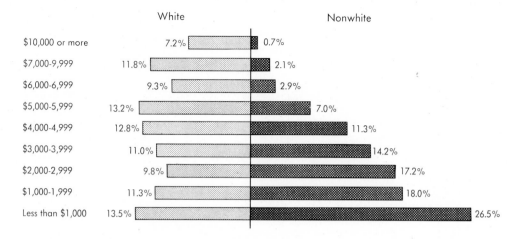

White   Nonwhite

	White	Nonwhite
$10,000 or more	7.2%	0.7%
$7,000-9,999	11.8%	2.1%
$6,000-6,999	9.3%	2.9%
$5,000-5,999	13.2%	7.0%
$4,000-4,999	12.8%	11.3%
$3,000-3,999	11.0%	14.2%
$2,000-2,999	9.8%	17.2%
$1,000-1,999	11.3%	18.0%
Less than $1,000	13.5%	26.5%

Fig. **XIII:4**   Income by Color, United States: 1959,
Males Fourteen Years and Older

Source: *Census of Population: 1960*, PC(1)-1C, Table 97.

white incomes were hardly one-third the white incomes. The relative disadvantage of nonwhite females compared with whites is even greater than for their male counterparts. Considering the large number of households dependent upon the earning power of Negro women, this factor is important in fixing the economic status of Negroes, for children must leave school at an early age to supplement the family income.

The low family income of Negroes creates a *vicious circle*: [15]

Low family income leads to early work for children.

Early school leaving restricts later job opportunities and qualifications for job advancement.

Limited job opportunities result in low family income.

Low family income leads to early work. . . .

STRATIFICATION WITHIN A MINORITY

Although Negroes are concentrated in the lower national strata, the Negro population is internally stratified not only by education,

occupation, and income, but in styles of life, in life chances (including life expectancy), aspirations, and the perceptions Negroes have of each other.

Evaluating color. Physical appearance affects the life chances of all persons, especially of the extremely attractive or ugly. Appearance enters into the placement of Negroes to a greater extent than of whites, and this is true whether the evaluations are made by Negroes or by whites. Very dark-skinned individuals are handicapped in their choice of mates, in access to congenial groups, and probably in employment. On the other hand, Negroes with "good" (not kinky) hair and light brown or "smooth" skin have an advantage. Fair skins were once featured in advertisements in the Negro press, but brown skins are now most often pictured. With the growth of race pride among Negroes, in recent years brown skins have become the idealized type of Negro beauty.[16]

Evaluating class. Negro and white class status cannot be easily equated. A semi-skilled worker with a steady income and a

[15] Cf. Gunnar Myrdal *et al., An American Dilemma* (New York: Harper, 1944), pp. 205-7.

[16] St. Clair Drake and Horace R. Cayton, *Black Metropolis* (New York: Harcourt, Brace, 1945), pp. 495-506.

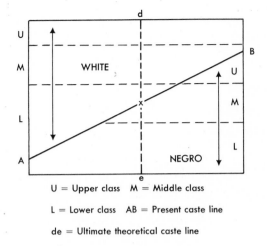

U = Upper class   M = Middle class

L = Lower class   AB = Present caste line

de = Ultimate theoretical caste line

**Fig. XIII:5   The Caste-Class System
in the Deep South**

From W. Lloyd Warner's Introduction to *Deep South*
by Allison Davis, B. B. Gardner, and M. R. Gardner
(Chicago: University of Chicago Press, 1941), p. 10.
Reproduced by permission.

stable family life would be evaluated as middle class in the Negro community, but a white with similar status characteristics would be classified upper-lower by whites. A Negro professional with a modest income but high educational qualifications would be classified in the upper strata in the Negro community, but a white with similar status would probably be rated as upper-middle by whites.

CASTE AND CLASS

The differences in the distributions of the races in the class structure are so great that they are regarded as falling in *two* class orders, one for whites and one for nonwhites. (See SOCIAL STRATIFICATION, pp. 206–7.) Each class order may be viewed as a distinct caste, separated from the other by a caste line. Individuals may change their membership from one caste to the other only by "passing" over the line. The institutional form of the caste line is segregation.

The caste cleavage originated in slavery, which held all Negroes in subordination to all whites. Even under slavery, however, there was a "class" distinction between free Negroes and slaves and between house servants and field hands. If American slavery had not been based on color, emancipation would have thrown the freedmen into free competition in the class order, and in a few decades the slaves or their descendants would have lost their distinctive identity. This happened to the white indentured servant who came to the colonies. But because American slavery was color slavery, it was easy to maintain the mechanisms of control and to institute legal controls which enforced the principle of Negro subordination.

As long as most Negroes were in fact inferior to almost all whites in education, income, and the like, discrimination and subordination were at least consistent, however unethical they may have been. But even when Negroes achieve educational and occupational advances, they remain "socially" inferior to whites.

Figure XIII:5 suggests changes which are taking place in the relative composition of the Negro and white class orders in the South. It indicates that the caste line (*AB*), the absolute barrier between the races, is rotating on the axis (*x*), permitting increased vertical mobility for Negroes and an increased approximation of Negroes to the stratified distribution of whites.

Caution: Like all schematic diagrams, the figure is only suggestive. It should not be inferred that opportunity for upward movement of Negroes presumes downward mobility of whites. In fact the upward movement of Negroes has not been accompanied by downward movement of whites.

The broad outline of Negro stratification may be viewed as follows:

1. A heavy weighting of Negroes in the lower strata, compared with whites, as shown above, pages 513–15.

2. Increased vertical mobility of Negroes and increasing opportunities for upward movement within the Negro population.

3. Pressure against the "caste barrier," separating the races, but little penetration of the barrier.

Section 7 **Associations**

The participation of minority groups in large-scale organizations reflects the broader pattern of segregation in society. This has two main aspects:

1. The exclusion of minority individuals from membership in many organizations.

2. The development of separate associations composed of members of a particular minority.

EXCLUSION

The systematic exclusion of ethnic and racial groups from fraternal organizations, labor unions, and churches enforces the more general pattern of segregation. It is characteristic of fraternal organizations in schools and colleges as well as of adult life. However, exclusion has come into conflict with the equalitarian ideal which is often strongly expressed in American educational institutions. College students and administrators alike have concerned themselves over the exclusion of minorities from fraternities. Some local chapters have challenged the provisions of their national charters or the authority of their societies' national headquarters and have insisted on admitting individuals from proscribed groups. Some colleges have barred fraternal organizations or have informally put pressure on them to change their membership rules, or have set time limits after which the rules must be changed.

In most fraternities whose exclusionist policies have been challenged, it appears that the pressure for change has come from the administration or the general student body of the colleges, or as "grass roots" movements from the active members of chapters. The "actives" find their aim of picking the "best men" obstructed when some of these best men are ineligible; but fraternity alumni who are remote from the actual choosing and do not experience this strain are often most resistant to change. To them it seems that the "actives" are lowering the standards. Their anxieties may be premature, however. The change of the formal rules will probably not markedly change the composition of organization membership for some time. It is more likely that many of the societies will remain exclusive for a time or will elect only one or two Jews or Negroes as token members. The change of formal rules does not *guarantee* more equalitarian practices; it merely *permits* ethnic or racial individuals to be elected to membership in societies from which they were formerly excluded.

MINORITY ASSOCIATIONS [17]

A large part of the associational life of members of minority groups is restricted to minority associations. This further reduces interaction between minorities and the rest of the population; acculturation is retarded; and informal as well as formal out-group relations are limited.

[17] See E. Franklin Frazier, *The Negro in the United States* (New York: Macmillan, 1957), Chaps. XV and XX; and Myrdal *op. cit.*, Chap. 39.

Segregated Parallel Associations

Many minority organizations are direct products of forced segregation. Negro schools, colleges, fraternities, and some unions and churches are perhaps the best examples. Excluded from most fraternities and sororities, minority groups have established their own. The minority organizations may make adjustment to the college environment easier, and for some of their members the feeling of discrimination may be reduced. On the other hand, ethnically exclusive organizations may seem to justify discrimination and in the long run may postpone the full acceptance of minority groups. The existence of ethnic organizations may lend support to the assertion that "they prefer to associate with their own kind." This is a dilemma of the minority association.

When the restrictions of segregation are eliminated, minority organizations may be expected either to disappear or to take in members from the dominant group, thereby changing their basic character. "Jim Crow" labor unions have tended to be absorbed by formerly exclusive unions when racial barriers have been removed. Negro colleges will be subject to great pressure now that Negroes are being admitted to a larger number of formerly "white" universities. Some of the small Negro colleges are already closing their doors or consolidating with others in a struggle to survive. The larger ones, which represent a substantial capital investment, either have begun to admit white students or are looking forward to eventual integration. A by-product of these changes in the system of higher education is the reduction in the number of job opportunities for educated Negroes as teachers, at least for the time being. Confronted by this alternative, some Negro leaders regard the prospect of integration with mixed feelings:

Unless radical changes are made in the policies at many [Negro colleges], they may find themselves in the unenviable position of obstructing the elimination of segregation in higher education.

The Negro has evinced a great courage in fighting racial segregation, but an even greater courage may be required for some to learn to live without it.[18]

Communal Associations

Many minority organizations arise as products of imposed segregation, but others are based on cultural distinctiveness. In the historical development of ethnic groups, mutual aid and fraternal associations loom large. These were often religious or national organizations with old-world ties and provided important economic aid for immigrants unfamiliar with a new country or for Negroes from the plantation. Segregated areas of residence also encourage the establishment of fraternal organizations and churches along ethnic or racial lines.

Black Nationalism

In the early 1920's Marcus Garvey, a West Indian Negro, attracted thousands of followers to his Back-to-Africa movement. Garvey believed that Negroes would never attain equality in the United States and could best improve their condition by colonizing in Africa. The movement waned when its leader was convicted of fraud in 1924. In the early 1930's the Black Muslim movement [19] was founded in Detroit by W. D. Fard, a mysterious peddler, perhaps an Arab. He told Negroes of their homeland across the sea and proclaimed himself a prophet who had come to awaken the Black Nation to its possibilities in a world temporarily dominated by whites. He exhorted Negroes to stop imitating the evil ways of whites, to abjure the white man's religion, and to worship the one true God.

[18] Ralph J. Bunche, as quoted in the Los Angeles *Tribune,* April 17, 1953.
[19] This discussion is drawn largely from C. Eric Lincoln, *The Black Muslims in America* (Boston: The Beacon Press, 1961) and E. U. Essien-Udom, *Black Nationalism* (Chicago: University of Chicago Press, 1962).

When Fard disappeared in 1934 he had attracted about 8,000 followers. Under the leadership of Fard's chief lieutenant, Elijah Muhammad (formerly Elijah Poole), Muslim membership at first declined, and the movement attracted little attention during the 1940's and early 1950's. In the late 1950's however, the movement flourished. It had at least 50 temples and missions from New England to California and Florida and an estimated membership of more than 100,-000.[20]

The Muslim ideology emphasizes the alleged evil nature of the white man and the assumed superiority of blacks. Integration of "so-called Negroes" with whites is considered degrading. Muslims oppose interracial association and intermarriage as strongly as do advocates of white supremacy. The good Muslim does not seek the friendship of whites nor of Christian Negroes. Race pride is encouraged, and the use of skin lighteners and hair straighteners is disapproved. A separate Negro economy is sought so that Negroes will not be dependent upon whites for jobs. As a step toward such a separate economy the Muslim organization has founded a number of successful business enterprises, mainly retail and service establishments. A long-range goal of the Muslims is similar to the apartheid policy of South Africa: complete segregation of Negroes and whites through the setting aside of a large area of the United States exclusively for Negroes. Although the Muslims are willing to wait for complete economic and political separation, social separation is an immediate goal.

The Black Muslim goals are vague and ill-defined. According to the Muslim myth of the origin and destiny of races, an end to white domination of the world is predestined. The "blue-eyed devils" of low physical and moral stamina were given 6,000 years to rule the world, plus a 70-year period of grace during which the Black Nation is to be awakened. The period of grace is to end in *1984*.

The early adherents to the movement were for the most part poorly educated Negroes recently from the rural South. Most Muslims still are recruited from the most underprivileged segments of the Negro population, but more of them now have urban backgrounds. A small but increasing number of college students and other middle-class Negroes have joined the movement. Muslim members are young, an estimated 80 per cent are between the ages of seventeen and thirty-five.[21] Unlike Christian organizations, the Muslims attract more men than women. Some adherents are former criminals. They reform and remain reformed as long as they remain in the movement, and apparently few have left it.

Although there are other Negro organizations emphasizing black solidarity and rejection of the white man's culture, only the Muslims have attained a sizable following. Such movements grow out of disillusionment over the prospects of Negroes soon attaining equality or near-equality with whites in an integrated biracial society. Negro aspirations for improved status have been raised by economic gains achieved during World War II, by court rulings and legislation on civil rights, and by the activities of Negro protest organizations. However, tangible improvement in treatment and relative status has been slow, especially for lower-class Negroes. In addition, the emergence of independent Negro states in Africa has fostered race pride. Impatience at the seemingly meager results of the efforts of the less militant Negro leaders and protest organizations has become widespread.[22]

The Black Muslim view that Christianity is the white man's religion and has been used to the detriment of Negroes is expressed by a prominent Muslim leader, Malcolm X:

[20] Essien-Udom, *op. cit.*, p. 5, and Lincoln, *op. cit.*, pp. 17, 22.

[21] Lincoln, *op. cit.*, p. 22.
[22] Lincoln, *op. cit.*, pp. 6–10.

Your Christian countries, if I am correct, are the countries of Europe and North and South America. Predominantly, this is where you find Christianity, or at least people who represent themselves as Christians. Whether they practice what Jesus taught is something we won't go into. The Christian world is what we usually call the Western World. . . . The colonization of the dark people . . . was done by Christian powers. The number one problem that most people face in the world today is how to get freedom from Christians. Wherever you find nonwhite people today they are trying to get back their freedom from people who represent themselves as Christians, and if you ask these [subject] people their picture of a Christian, they will tell you "a white man—a Slavemaster." [23]

Only a small minority of American Negroes belong to the Black Muslims and the other black nationalist movements. However, the influence of these movements extends beyond their adherents. As competitors to less militant organizations such as the NAACP and the National Urban League, they push the established Negro protest organizations toward stronger action. Negro churches have recently tended to change their traditional accommodative role in Negro-white relations, and the existence of the Muslims may accelerate the adoption of a militant protest policy.

Minority Action Organizations

In the United States political action and group betterment activities are important functions of minority organizations. The National Association for the Advancement of Colored People, Congress on Racial Equality (CORE), and the Urban League are among the most important groups with Negro leadership; the Anti-Defamation League, The American Jewish Congress, and the American Jewish Committee are among the best-known Jewish agencies. These organizations have different policies and tend to recruit their members from different parts of the respective minority populations. Minority associations do not always present a united front. They compete for the allegiances of the minority population and offer alternative leaders and programs. Indeed, the multiplication of "defense" organizations with different policies ranging from the militant to the accommodative poses serious problems for the effective mobilization of minority groups.

Adaptation 36 reviews the development and organizational character of the NAACP, one of the most important minority action agencies, and one that has participated extensively in joint action with other organizations. It was begun at a time when relatively few Negroes were qualified for sophisticated organizational activity. Its small corps of leaders developed alliances with white groups and guided the organization to increasing effectiveness and a substantial growth. Although the leadership was remarkably stable, its policies were flexible and responsive to crises and opportunities. The organization notably avoided involvement in mass movements which might have greatly increased its membership but at the risk of organizational instability.

[23] Quoted by Lincoln, *op. cit.*, p. 28.

Direct action: Non-violent student sit-ins have been used to combat segregation in businesses serving the public.

Above, a student is trained to withstand insult and provocation.

Below, one store is integrated.

The NAACP: A Protest Organization

Abridged and adapted from "The National Association for the Advancement of Colored People: A Study of Flexible Bureaucracy" by C. Wilson Record. Published in this form by permission of C. Wilson Record.

The National Association for the Advancement of Colored People (usually abbreviated "NAACP") is the foremost Negro action organization in the United States. Since its inception some five decades ago, the NAACP has grown from a handful of members, perhaps half of whom were white and concentrated in a few Northern urban centers, to an association of more than 300,-000 persons, predominantly Negro and distributed in hundreds of local branches over the entire nation. The history of the NAACP reflects a number of major developments in American Negro life during the past half century: the wider geographic distribution and urbanization of the Negro population, the growth of social literacy among a long-submerged racial minority, the increased use of protest and betterment activities with emphasis on the legal and political instruments, the widespread rejection of the biracial program of the postreconstruction period by Negroes, and finally, the emergence of a more mature Negro leadership. The NAACP has served both as a mirror of and instrument for the recasting of the Negro-white balance in this country. Its leading role in the Supreme Court decision which outlawed racial segregation in the public schools was a dramatic instance of the kind of activity through which it has insisted on the right of the Negro to be counted in.

The development of the NAACP may be seen as a reaction against the compromise policy of such leaders as Booker T. Washington, although the immediate spur was the Springfield race riot of 1908. Following the failure of the reconstruction, which came to its tragic demise for the Negro with the Hayes-Tilden compromise of 1876, the stage was set for the eclipse of militant Negro spokesmen, such as Frederick Douglass, and for the emergence of the "separate and subordinate" advocates of whom Washington was by far the most prominent and powerful. While Washington was ready to bargain racial peace on the Southern white man's terms, W. E. B. DuBois, his chief opponent and one of the founders of the NAACP, was not. The conflict between these two men was more than personal; it was an instance of a struggle waged on a much larger scale and for much higher stakes within the Negro community. Through the years the DuBois attitude has prevailed and with it the NAACP.

The Origins of the NAACP

As we have noted, the early NAACP was a weak and isolated grouping of Negroes and whites. For a number of years the problem of survival was ever-present. The organization's funds were limited, and only the disproportionate contributions of white liberals enabled it to make ends meet. It was necessary also to depend on the white group during this time for day-to-day leadership. In 1910 five of the six major offices in the NAACP were filled by whites; the crucial post of executive secretary was filled by Francis Blascoer, a Northern white man; the only Negro to hold a similar position was DuBois who served as editor of *The Crisis,* the official publication. It was not until a decade after the founding of the NAACP that a Negro was named executive secretary.

The Negroes who were instrumental in establishing the NAACP and carrying on its work during this period were the younger intellectuals. They were for the most part of middle-class origin, and had obtained their schooling in the North. Occupationally, they were journalists, teachers, doctors, lawyers and ministers. They regarded themselves as members of a Negro elite which had the responsibility of assuming leadership of their less fortunate brethren. Their backgrounds and self-images left their imprint on the organization which they helped to found and steer through the early difficult years.

Organizational Character and Consequences

Although its very survival was in doubt during the early 1920's and again in the early 1930's, the NAACP's basic organizational pattern had been established:

1. A small nucleus of responsible and well-informed leaders

2. A respectable, but sometimes "radical" membership, including whites

3. The absence of demagogic appeals (its aim, as Maurice Davie has put it, was to do something "for" rather than "with" the Negro masses)

4. Co-operation with other organizations —Negro and white, religious and secular, public and private—in the attainment of its goals

Certain consequences directly stemmed from these organizational conditions. The NAACP would not grow with great rapidity despite the insistence on immediate action to eliminate segregation. It would not capitalize on mass discontent or attempt to become a mass organization with roots among the black urban proletariat or the black rural workers. It would be flexible and "reasonable" in its decisions, and it would avoid identification with larger political and social ideologies. Finally, it would survive and grow if the judgment of its few top leaders was sound.

The Crisis of the 1920's

The postwar period was a difficult one, marked by unemployment of Negroes and race riots in the North as well as in the South. For the NAACP it was a time of organizational crisis. The "Back-to-Africa" Garvey Movement with its extreme Negro nationalism and race consciousness attracted the Negro masses, and by contrast the goals and methods of the NAACP seemed small and weak. The Communist party was also a threat. Although that party was unable to enlist many Negro adherents, it vigorously criticized the NAACP leaders, exploited the organizational weaknesses, and attempted to penetrate and capture local branches.

In the face of these two challenges, one expounding racial nationalism and the other revolutionary action, the NAACP was unable, without adopting some of their tactics, to develop an effective mass organization, and it decided not to try. In reaction to the challenges, however, it probably clarified and made more explicit its own major policies. It maintained its top-down organization, depending on a few able men at the national level, and it did not capitalize on spontaneous protest from the Negro population. Indeed at this stage the NAACP leadership had little communication with the mass of Negroes, and its goals were largely those of the middle class, although it was, of course, concerned with the plight of the lower strata.

During the 1920's the Association perfected certain tactics of organization and protest. The most important was the use of the courts to secure specific goals. Another significant accomplishment was the publicity and propaganda work carried on in Negro and white communities. The chief instrument was the periodical, *The Crisis,* in which stronger opinions could be presented than would have been feasible for an individual or for a local chapter. In addition pamphlets were circulated on many topics.

Attempts at direct political activity were sporadic, but the Association successfully opposed Hoover's nominee to the Supreme Court, Judge Parker, who in his early career had advocated "white supremacy." Because it lacked a mass base, the influence of white liberals and philanthropies continued to affect the organization and its policy. These allies gave the Association respectability, funds, and identification with broadly defined goals which went beyond the boundaries of the racial group and established the general strategy of *joint action*. These conditions strengthened the effectiveness of the Association, but they also imposed restraints upon it. Actions were avoided which might alienate white allies or impair respectability. During this period the membership of the NAACP actually declined from 90,000 in 1920 to 21,000 in 1929. Nevertheless, the organization remained the Negro's principal protest instrument. The aim of the NAACP continued to be the strengthening of its national office and of a few reliable branches rather than a rapid and indiscriminate numerical expansion.

The Depression Crisis

The depression, beginning in 1929, brought another crisis for the NAACP. It had developed techniques for securing justice in the courts, organizing legislative campaigns, and for publicizing the plight of American Negroes. However, the techniques of gradual change were not designed to deal with mass unemployment, poverty, housing, and welfare. The national level vigorously supported programs for the amelioration of these conditions, but the organization in the hands of conservative leaders did not mobilize the unrest among the mass of unemployed and destitute Negroes. Consequently, some lower- and middle-class Negroes turned to other organizations which represented revived nationalist movements to repatriate the Negroes to Africa or to place them on a sort of reservation in a "forty-ninth state." Radi-

cal political activities were spearheaded by the Communist Party.

Membership in NAACP declined, local branches closed down, funds for the national office were lacking, and the staff was reduced. A major decision had to be made. NAACP must expand and reach the poorer and less educated elements in the Negro population or face dissolution. Much local leadership had passed into the hands of radical political elements and labor groups. Consequently, the NAACP had to work out a closer identification with the labor movement and advance more militant political programs to recapture its previous strength and adapt to new circumstances. This alienated some of its conservatives, but its national leadership was more adventurous and accepted the risk and opportunity.

Until 1934 the NAACP had been a target of criticism for the Communist Party, but at this time the "united front" period began, and the Communist Party ceased its criticism and sought to form a working alliance with the NAACP. At the same time the Communists attempted to gain control of the organization. The centralized character of the NAACP, however, proved to be an effective defense. Its top-down leadership enabled it to ward off organizational attacks from the Communist party, for the national organization could take countermeasures through its control of the organization press and its employees whom it dispatched to chapters which were infiltrated by Communists.

The New Deal

Like the labor movement in the United States, the NAACP benefited from the New Deal program which began in 1933. In Negro communities, it revived morale and counteracted racial nationalism, but these changes alone did not assure the future of the NAACP. The New Deal employed NAACP members in administrative positions on its relief, housing, and welfare programs. This provided a channel through which the Association's opinions were effectively presented within the New Deal, and the prestige of the organization was enhanced. During this period liberal whites became increasingly sensitized to the plight of the Negro. Increased financial support for and white participation in the NAACP resulted. Organizationally, this was expressed by more direct relationships between the NAACP and liberal and labor political movements. The fact that Negro industrial employment increased made the trade-unions more cognizant of the Negro worker as a problem and as a resource. This led indirectly to added contacts between the trade-unions and the NAACP at all levels of organization. The NAACP did not officially endorse political candidates or programs, but unofficially it contributed to the large Democratic majority in Negro communities after 1936. It has played an important role in developing political consciousness among Negroes and in involving them directly in political action.

World War II

By the outbreak of World War II, the Association had recovered from the crisis of the early 1930's. Its membership had increased to more than 50,000, and new branches were established in many Southern cities. For the first time the Association had a truly nation-wide organization based on a recognition that the Negro problem was a national one and that local needs could be subsumed within a general program. The war gave the NAACP a new organizational climate:

1. *The moral factor.* America was supporting the Allied cause in the name of democracy, and the practices of segregation and discrimination were obviously inconsistent with this cause.

2. *Employment conditions.* Negro manpower was needed both in the armed forces and in industry, and the bargaining position of Negroes was, therefore, improved. The NAACP was a voice for this new strength.

3. *Political power.* The growth of the Negro electorate also strengthened the NAACP.

The organization was under attack for being too militant from two quarters—from conservative whites and from the Communist Party, following its "win-the-war" line, which had previously attacked NAACP for being too conservative. From other quarters it was criticized for being too moderate, but the leadership steered between these extremes and manifested an increasing flexibility and strength. During the war the membership grew rapidly (350,000 members by 1945), and the organization could not supply the trained personnel to serve its local branches. Furthermore, many of the new members were from the Negro working class who in education and outlook differed from the original middle-class membership. The Association's program in response both to its changing membership and to the opportunities of the times emphasized employment and similar concerns rather than political, legal, and educational rights, but NAACP did not change its leadership at either the national or local levels. Control remained in the hands of its experienced and established leaders and, if anything, the power and prestige of its executives were increased.

To perform its diverse functions expert personnel were required: lawyers, legislative experts, and research specialists. An increasing number of professionals found a place in the organization. The increasing professionalism of the top NAACP personnel reflects one aspect of organizational maturation. The need of the expert, especially the lawyer, the organizer, and the propagandist, increases as additional levels of action are embraced. Further evidences of organizational maturity are found in the relative decline of white membership in the NAACP, the ability of the Negro community to finance the activities of the organization, and finally the passing of whites from significant policy-making and executive positions. All important administrative posts in the NAACP are now filled by Negroes; this group also has an authoritative voice in making policy decisions. Although there was a decline in membership immediately after World War II, the Association was not weakened appreciably. More recently the NAACP has faced two serious challenges. The first has come from white conservatives in the South who would outlaw the organization because of its aggressive opposition to segregation. The second challenge has come from new organizations, such as CORE and the Southern Christian Leadership Conference, which believe the NAACP is too slow-moving in securing racial justice.

Conclusions

Certain critical decisions and conditions set the character of the NAACP.

1. Through its early history there was a paucity of qualified Negro leaders.

2. It did not emerge from a spontaneous mass movement, but rather out of the planning of a relatively few middle-class individuals, both white and Negro.

3. It maintained a small homogeneous organization in its early stages.

4. It maintained a top-down organization with control centered in the national office.

5. It maintained ties with white liberals and labor organizations.

6. It effectively combated, through the techniques of centralized control, efforts at Communist infiltration.

7. It became committed to action through the courts and by pressure group methods.

The foregoing conditions and decisions are related to the institutional character of the NAACP, which may be summarized:

1. A stable leadership

2. A clearly defined and centralized authority and responsibility

3. Joint action with respectable white organizations

4. Inability to organize mass protest

Its future appears to lie in a continuation of its established organizational character but with a broader based membership as the mass of the Negro population becomes better educated and able to comprehend more clearly the tactics and capabilities of the organization.

Section 8 Collective behavior

A number of conditions have stimulated the relatively unstable phenomena of "collective behavior" in race relations:

1. Population movements and industrial growth tend to break down the codes governing relations between groups and to upset stable social arrangements. Industrial development may create sudden and heavy labor demands, drawing new groups into areas, disarranging accustomed occupational roles and patterns of segregation, and creat-

ing contacts between groups for which there are no established codes.

2. Relations between groups may also be unsettled when the majority's own values are in conflict, for example, when the American creed of equality and fair play comes into conflict with prejudicial and intolerant attitudes.

3. When they become educated and acquire political skills, once submissive minorities may come openly to resent and reject

Harriet Beecher Stowe (1811–1896), daughter of a Congregational minister and wife of a theology professor. Her best-selling novel, Uncle Tom's Cabin, or Life among the Lowly, *first appeared serially in the antislavery paper,* National Era. *Published in book form in 1852, it sold over 300,000 copies in three years and was translated into twenty-three or more languages. As a play, it was widely shown and dramatically advertised, as the contemporary handbill indicates. Although both abolitionists and slaveholders criticized the work, it helped to mobilize public opinion on slavery.*

their subordinate status and may make demands on the dominant group for concessions and benefits.

Under these circumstances group contact is marked by fluidity and change, which often result in collective excitement, new interests, fresh alliances, and the creation of social movements. (See Adaptation 22, pp. 267–68.) Although much of this activity is spontaneous and unplanned, there are often conscious efforts to guide change and impose order on the loosely defined relations.

THE MODIFIABILITY OF CODES

There are two divergent views about the possibility of changing policies and practices governing race relations. One view argues that change in practices must *follow* change in public opinion. It holds that the existing practices necessarily reflect the consensus of popular belief. An opposing point of view holds that social arrangements can be changed without strong positive popular support, or even in the face of vocal opposition. Existing codes may not reflect the consensus at the time but may be survivals of outdated thinking. On such complex issues as race relations, opinion is composed of various points of view held with varying degrees of strength, and there may be no real consensus.

The analysis of opinion is most successful when it inquires into highly structured, clearly defined choices, as in elections. Public opinion on complicated problems, such as school segregation, is far more difficult to evaluate and extremely difficult to predict. Because reliable knowledge is absent, vocal and often extremist elements may be given publicity, while moderate attitudes which more nearly reflect the true consensus may not be expressed. The future may be rashly predicted by those vocal elements, even though knowledge of public opinion is lacking. Even if one knew how the majority of the public actually *felt* about race relations, it would be difficult to predict how the public

would *act* on a specific issue, such as the integration of Negroes in baseball.

An Example of Change

Until 1945 organized baseball in the United States was strictly segregated. Major leagues had teams in border or Southern cities; spring practice was held in the South; and it was commonly asserted that the intimacy of the team situation precluded the enlistment of Negro players. The fact that Negro and white players freely associated on school and college teams and in professional football did not seem to affect the argument. In 1945 Branch Rickey, the president of the Brooklyn Dodgers, initiated a chain of events which in two years completely modified the codes governing the employment of Negro players and drastically altered beliefs about the suitability of Negro players for the big leagues. Adaptation 37 tells this story.

No one knows to what extent the Jackie Robinson case actually changed public opinion or to what extent it merely expressed an underlying shift that had already taken place. It is most unlikely, however, that Rickey could have succeeded in his plan if the main body of opinion had been strongly opposed to Negroes playing in organized baseball. Probably most of the public had no clearly formed attitudes. The case itself gave shape to their opinions. *They had a real situation to evaluate instead of a hypothetical one.* Those who opposed the recruitment of Negroes were obliged to examine the strength of their opinions when they were confronted by the *fait accompli*. Much as they objected to the idea of Negroes in the leagues, they did not object strongly enough to commit unlawful acts or enough to give up baseball. One fact is clearly demonstrated in this case and in the integration of Negroes in the armed forces: the codes governing race relations are far more modifiable than has been popularly assumed.

In the case of integration of Negroes into the armed forces, officers who argued that the armed services should follow rather than lead public opinion underestimated the ability of the military to determine its own organization. The armed forces were free to act because they were supported by the sanctions of the national interest and security. The military did not have to limit its actions to the beliefs held by the general public. Furthermore, it was able to create conditions leading to the development of primary relations among members of different racial groups within the military organization. In a sense, it could change its own climate of opinion by changing its own social structure.[24] The Robinson case, however, although it has social organization aspects, clearly depended on a mobilization of public opinion and the formation, or at least the expression, of new perspectives. In this sense it is a study of collective behavior.

[24] Stouffer *et al.*, *op. cit.*, Chap. 10.

The Jackie Robinson Case

The description of the case is based principally on *The Jackie Robinson Story* by Arthur Mann (New York: Grosset & Dunlap, 1951) and also draws on the following: Bill Roeder, *Jackie Robinson* (New York: A. S. Barnes & Co., 1950); Robert Cousins' review of Roeder's book, *Jackie Robinson*, in the *Saturday Review*, July 15, 1950; articles from *Time, Life, Newsweek*, and current press reports. The quotations from Mann are published by permission of the author and from Cousins by permission of the *Saturday Review*.

This is a case study of social action designed to test and modify an accepted code. Although it would be unwise to generalize too much from this particular incident, several key points emerge:

1. The opinions and feelings about enlisting Negro players were often expressed as predictions. A prediction has much greater force than simply an expressed conviction. If Rickey had not pushed forward his plan, the judgment of those who prophesied that the plan would fail would have been confirmed.

2. Rickey was risking much and therefore carefully organized his program. In working out his tactics he deliberately saw to it that his first Negro athlete would have special personal qualities as well as outstanding baseball ability. He chose, in fact, a Negro who violated the Negro stereotype. By this choice he tacitly admitted the significance of the stereotype in popular thought.

3. The proof of Rickey's and Robinson's success was not fully established until Robinson could behave like a normally aggressive ballplayer, not like a Negro who would be permitted to play with whites only as long as he was on his best behavior.

In his review of the case, Arthur Mann wrote:

Now that Jackie Robinson is one of the established stars of baseball, and Negro players are becoming commonplace in the major leagues, it is hard to realize that there was such a storm over the entrance of this first Negro athlete into organized baseball four seasons ago (1945). In fact, the general public never did realize just how violent a storm it was. Jackie Robinson came into the Brooklyn organization over the expressed opposition of much of baseball's top brass.

Branch Rickey, president of the Brooklyn Dodgers, planned many of the events which led to this change in big-league policy. During the same period there was a movement

ADAPTATION **37**

to form a Negro league, initiated by Rickey, and in New York there was a great deal of political activity concerned with minorities. Governor Dewey sponsored the nondiscrimination Ives-Quinn Law, and Mayor La Guardia formed the Anti-Discrimination Committee, of which Rickey was a baseball subcommittee member.

Rickey saw his task as a long-term campaign:

1. To secure the backing and sympathy of the Dodgers' directors and stockholders

2. To select a Negro who would be the right man *off* the field

3. To select a Negro who would be the right man *on* the field

4. To elicit good press and public reaction

5. To secure backing and understanding from Negroes in order to avoid misinterpretation and abuse of the project

6. To gain acceptance of the player by his teammates

Rickey approached and tested the Dodgers' directors and stockholders individually, and after encountering no serious opposition, he went on to select a Negro player.

When it came to choosing a Negro player, Rickey had very encouraging reports on the playing abilities of the late Josh Bigson but rather discouraging reports on his off-the-field behavior. Rickey felt very strongly that impetuosity or aggressiveness could damage a Negro's chances, and so rejected him. As Mann put it,

Robinson had a good American-boy background —poor parents, working his way through school, tremendous athletic achievement, college experience at UCLA, Army service with an honorable discharge as a lieutenant in the cavalry, professional-football experience, track and field achievements, and a record as one of the great basketball stars on the Pacific Coast. [He was then playing for a Negro baseball team.]

On August 29, 1945, Rickey interviewed Robinson in an extraordinary three-hour scene, in which Rickey lectured, questioned, and imposed hypothetical indignities on Robinson. Rickey insisted on a "cloak of humility" as a part of his strategy to have Robinson accepted by the baseball world. Robinson asked if he wanted a ballplayer afraid to fight back, to which Rickey replied, "I want a ballplayer with guts enough not to fight back! You've got to do this job with base hits and stolen bases and fielding ground balls, Jackie. Nothing else!"

Two months later Rickey gave Robinson a Montreal contract. The publication of the signing brought forth a number of significant comments:

The commissioner of minor-league baseball, the late W. G. Bramham, is quoted as saying: "Father Divine will have to look to his laurels, for we can expect Rickey Temple to be in the course of construction in Harlem soon." Two days later he added: "It is those of the carpetbagger stripe of the white race, under the guise of helping, but in truth using the Negro for their own selfish ends, who retard the race. It is my opinion that if the Negro is left alone and aided by his own unselfish friends of the white race, he will work out his own salvation in all lines of endeavor."

Ex-star Rogers Hornsby stated flatly, ". . . Ballplayers on the road live [close] together. It won't work. . . ."

Popular Brooklyn player, Dixie Walker, commented, "As long as he isn't with the Dodgers, I'm not worried."

The National League executives issued a report which included this statement: "However well-intentioned, the use of Negro players would hazard all the physical properties of baseball." (Seven club owners tacitly accepted the statement.)

In a newspaper interview Robinson stated: "I know that I will take a tongue beating. That I can take . . . I know about the riding white players give one another and I am sure it will be much worse for me."

Rickey's plan called for a good reaction from the press and public, and, according to Mann, "Virtually all newspaper opinion and interpretation was favorable to the idea of bringing a Negro into organized ball." It was Rickey rather than Robinson who took the brunt of unfavorable publicity. "His motives, his sincerity, his integrity and even his methods were attacked. His repetitious insistence that he was after good ballplayers and believed he had them was ridiculed." Some weeks after signing Robinson, Rickey announced the signing of four more Negro baseball players: John Wright, Don Newcombe, Roy Campanella, and Roy Partlow.

The first response other than the written word came during the 1946 training season in Florida, where all municipal regulations concerning colored athletes were carefully examined to avoid violations. Jacksonville promised clearance but reversed its decision. DeLand, Florida, called off the daylight game scheduled there with the excuse that electricians had to repair the lights in the ball park that day.

Clay Hopper, a Mississippian and manager of the Montreal team, had received the news of Robinson's signing without comment or sign of antipathy, but the depth of his feelings is measured by a conversation with Rickey. During a spring training session Rickey asserted that no other human being could have made an exceptionally skillful play executed by Robinson. Hopper replied, "Mistuh Rickey, do you think he is a human bein'?" But at the end of the season his feelings and opinions had changed, for he told Rickey, "You don't have to worry none about that boy. He's the greatest competitor Ah ever saw, an' what's more, *he's a gentleman!*"

Montreal's first game of the regular season was at Jersey City, where Robinson was the hero of the game, but his wife, who was in the stands, was frightened by the tone of the crowd. In Baltimore the press predicted riots, the crowd "rode" Robinson, but his skill at running and batting soon won cheers. Syracuse fans "ragged" him even more than Baltimore, but Robinson said, "When I didn't pay any attention, they dropped it." By the end of

August ". . . Robinson was the International League's leading batsman (.378) and Montreal's standout star." [25]

During spring training (1947) when Robinson was moved up from Montreal to the Dodgers, there was an informal petition against Robinson by some of the players; Walker, a Southerner, requested a transfer, but he finished the season with the Dodgers and was then sold. Bragan, another Southerner, openly challenged Rickey but eventually made friends with Robinson.

Rickey initiated the slogan, "Don't spoil Robinson's chances," to insure etiquette of Negro fans at games. He organized the "How to Handle Robinson Committee" of leading Negro citizens. "His deportment was supervised as thoroughly as Princess Elizabeth's." [26] The committee rules included the following: he could not endorse any product; he could not sign his name to a magazine or news article; he could not object to an umpire's decision; he could not accept social invitations nor go to night spots; if insulted by another player, he must grin and bear it; and the committee felt it was as important to avoid adulation as brickbats.

During the regular season there was no hostility from his teammates, and there was indeed active support from some, notably Stanky. But it is reported that the Phillies turned the Brooklyn visiting-team dugout into a "verbal cesspool." The Phillies' president predicted serious trouble if Robinson appeared in Shibe Park. He claimed the Philadelphia players would not take the field. Rickey called the bluff, Robinson played, and there was no incident.

Robert Cousins in his review of Roeder's *Jackie Robinson* says, "Much of the bitterness . . . was undercover: an extra hard tag, deliberate spikings, crank notes, a stray pitch aimed at . . . (his) head, the rumor of a ballclub strike."

By the end of the season none of the dire

[25] *Time*, August 26, 1946.
[26] *Time*, September 22, 1947.

prophecies of rioting and bloodshed had come to pass, and Robinson was selected by the *Sporting News* (baseball's trade paper) as the "rookie of the year." Cousins writes:

Robinson wore the "armor of humility" so well that for a long while fans didn't realize that it was a disguise in his make-up. Little by little, in succeeding seasons, the armor melted away. In 1948 Robinson was thumbed out of a game for the first time. In 1949 he began to answer the needling of rival players. He kept up a rhubarb with his former manager, Leo Durocher. In a recent game these two went at it hot and heavy. The Negro whom people had assumed was tractable by nature now stands revealed as a fiery competitor—the fans' choice as the National League all-star second baseman for 1950.

He also starred in a movie about his own career. Robinson, however, had to earn the right of every white player—the right to squawk.

In the years since Robinson's success Negroes have become increasingly numerous in the big leagues and are now accepted throughout the country. In 1962 the team rosters carried more than 90 Negro players. This is not to say that all difficulties have been resolved. There are still problems of segregated housing of players, especially in some spring training camps in Florida, and interpersonal relations between teammates and between teams sometimes become race relations. There is a dearth of Negro pitchers, and as yet no Negro captains nor managers. Team management has become complicated by the recruiting of players from the Caribbean who have a different definition of race and a different style of race etiquette. The Negro's position in baseball is in a sense normalized. He is in it and successful in it, but race is in the background, an element making for instability and sometimes tension.

Section 9 Population and ecology

One cannot understand minority groups and their problems without some knowledge of their population characteristics. For instance, data on their numbers, age, and sex distributions, vital statistics, trends of increase or decrease, and occupational and educational characteristics are needed to interpret problems of assimilation and group cohesion and to predict the part these groups may play in the national life.

In this section there are three examples of population data that students of minorities have found useful:

1. A summary of the growth of the Negro population of the United States

2. A commentary on the Negro labor force
3. An exercise in the study of the population pyramid

GROWTH OF THE NEGRO POPULATION OF THE UNITED STATES

Figure XIII:6 presents the census figures on the growth of the Negro population of the United States (conterminous) compared with the rest of the population, and Figure XIII:7 gives the *rates* of increase of Negroes and whites. Throughout most of American history the white population grew faster than the Negro population. Between 1800 and 1960 the number of Negroes grew from about

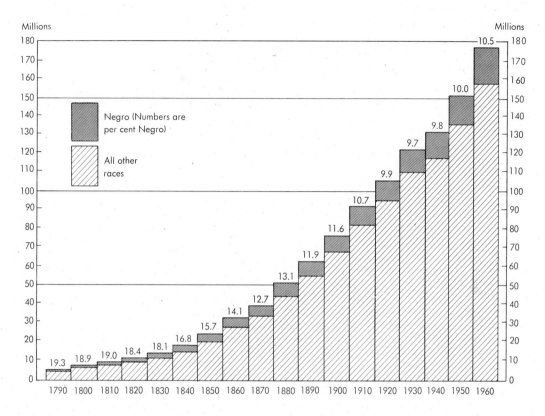

Fig. **XIII:6**   Population Growth, Conterminous U.S.: 1790–1960
(Negro and Other Races)

three-fourths of a million to nearly nineteen millions, but in that time the proportion they represent of the total population declined from about 19 per cent to about 10.5 per cent.

Since 1930 the rate of Negro increase has exceeded that of whites, and in the 1950 decade the rate of Negro growth was substantially greater. Improvements in health and living conditions are being reflected in lower death rates for Negroes than in earlier periods. The Negro population is younger and poorer than whites and its crude birth rate may be expected to remain higher for some time.

Two important generalizations may be made:

1. In the foreseeable future the Negro population is not likely to amount to much more than one-tenth of the national population.

2. The Negro problem is not self-liquidating. There will be substantial numbers classified as Negroes for the indeterminate future.

The geographical distribution of the Negro population is as important in its effect on race relations as the number of Negroes. There has been progressive dispersal of Negroes through the states, and a steady reduction of the so-called "Black Belt," the area of the South with a preponderance of Negroes. Between 1900 and 1940 the number of Southern counties with 50 per cent or more Negroes declined from 286 to 180, and from 1940 to 1960, the number declined to 134 (or 135, counting Washington, D.C.). The number of Negroes in such counties declined from about 4,000,000 in 1900 to about 2,600,000 in

1940, to under 2,000,000 in the 135 counties in 1960. Negroes have been moving from the South in large numbers, and the trend of Negro migration will probably continue. The Negro population of the South, defined in the broadest terms to include seventeen states plus the District of Columbia,[27] increased 15.3 per cent between 1940 and 1960, while the white population of the South increased 34.7 per cent. In the same period Negroes outside the South increased by more than 160 per cent, from 2,717,000 to 7,158,000. The percentage of Negroes in the South declined from about 79 per cent in 1940 to 62 per cent in 1960.

[27] For the purposes of this discussion the following are counted as Southern: Alabama, Arkansas, Delaware, District of Columbia, Florida, Georgia, Kentucky, Louisiana, Maryland, Mississippi, Missouri, North Carolina, Oklahoma, South Carolina, Tennessee, Texas, Virginia, and West Virginia.

ECOLOGICAL ISOLATION

Because of their immigration history and occupational concentration, minorities tend to be concentrated by regions within the United States and by areas within cities. (See URBAN MAN, pp. 621–22.) Most new migrants to urban areas enter the city in the transition zones and, as they secure a foothold in the economy and are able to compete for more desirable residences, they move out to preferred locations. The areas of ethnic settlement then lose their ghetto-like characteristics, and the ethnic minorities become more thinly settled, tending toward a random distribution throughout the urban population. The stages in the adaptation of immigrant groups to an urban environment can be described as a series of steps beginning with high concentration in a ghetto area—populated almost wholly by the members of the

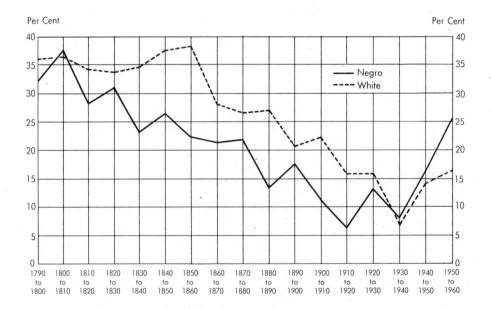

Fig. **XIII:7**   Percentage Increase in the White and Negro Population of the United States (Conterminous) by Decade: 1790–1960

Redrawn by permission. Adapted from E. Franklin Frazier, *The Negro in the United States* (New York: Macmillan, 1949), p. 174; 1950 and 1960 data added.

ethnic group with their specialized shops, restaurants, and service institutions—and ending with their dispersal throughout the metropolis and the liquidation of the enclave. The urban area of ethnic settlement is, therefore, a transitional form, but for a time it reinforces popular stereotypes about ethnic groups and, of course, maintains group cohesion and cultural continuity.

The Negro migration to the urban North is now recapitulating the history of immigrant settlement. Negro concentration in urban areas is a product of the recency of Negro entry into cities, their relatively low occupational and income status, and discrimination in housing. Rising Negro income, pressures in the field of public housing, and legal action should eventually lead to dispersion of Negro residence throughout metropolitan areas and the location of Negro homes in areas formerly closed to them. For some time, however, Negroes will remain highly concentrated in the central cities of metropolitan areas.

THE NONWHITE LABOR FORCE [28]

The nonwhite labor force in the United States differs markedly from the white labor force in its employment, occupational, sex, and educational composition as well as in other important respects.

Unemployment has been consistently higher among nonwhites, who are preponderantly Negro. At the time of the 1960 census about nine per cent of the nonwhite labor force was unemployed compared with about five per cent of the white labor force. Nonwhites are concentrated in industries and occupations in which unemployment is most common, and they tend to be the "last hired" during periods of economic expansion and the "first fired" during recessions. The differ-

[28] Based largely on Norval D. Glenn, *The Negro Population in the American System of Social Stratification: An Analysis of Recent Trends* (unpublished Ph.D. dissertation, The University of Texas, 1962), Chap. 3. Data added from U.S. Bureau of the Census, *Census of Population: 1960,* Final Report PC (1) –1C.

ence between whites and nonwhites in percentage unemployed has increased during the last two decades partly because a larger proportion of nonwhite workers held unskilled and semiskilled jobs that are eliminated by increased mechanization of industrial processes.

Nonwhites are disproportionately represented in most of the poorly rewarded occupations and are less than proportionately represented in all of the more highly rewarded ones. If Negroes were distributed in the same proportions throughout the labor force as all workers, it might be said that their proportions were "expected." Table XIII:5 shows the extent to which the representation of Negroes in each occupational group was above or below this "expected" proportion. If they were distributed among the occupational groups in the "expected" proportions, all the values would be 1.00. A ratio above 1.00 means that they are overrepresented, a ratio below 1.00, underrepresented. In addition to being concentrated in the lower occupational groups, nonwhites are concentrated in the lower paid occupations within each group. For instance, most of the nonwhites in the professional and technical category are clergymen and teachers rather than doctors, lawyers, engineers, or other highly paid professionals.

However, as can be seen from Table XIII:5, nonwhite representation is increasing in the upper and intermediate occupations. The greatest nonwhite gains are at the intermediate levels, in skilled manual and lower white-collar work. Increases at the highest levels are much smaller. The gain in the professional and technical category has been moderate, but nonwhite representation as managers, officials, and proprietors has hardly changed since 1950. Most nonwhites in the latter category are self-employed businessmen. In general, nonwhite representation has increased markedly in rapidly expanding occupational categories and has declined or increased only slightly in stable or declining

The Population Pyramid of a Minority Group

The graphic device called the population pyramid, when applied to a minority population, can yield clues to the future population or its past composition. (See POPULATION AND ECOLOGY, pp. 316–18.)

Figure *A* on the facing page really represents two populations, the American-born (Nisei), shown also in Figure *B,* and the foreign-born (Issei), shown separately in Figure *C.* The reading of these pyramids raises a number of questions:

1. Why are the foreign-born males (Fig. *C*) rather older than the females? The Japanese males who first came to the United States about the beginning of this century were young, single men who later brought younger women as their wives. We may conjecture that originally many of the men planned to return to Japan.

2. Why are there virtually no foreign-born Japanese under thirty years of age? Japanese immigration was controlled by the Gentleman's Agreement with Japan in 1907 and the Japanese Exclusion Act in 1924.

3. Why does Figure *A* deviate from the true pyramid of a "normal" population? This is explained by the immigration history of ma-ture males followed by mature females and may be understood most easily by referring to *B* and *C.* At first there were few childbearing women (arrow *1, C*), so that few persons of Japanese ancestry were born here (arrow *2, B*). A few years later more Japanese females of childbearing age (arrow *3, C*) entered as the wives of the Japanese males. These women bore the Nisei children (arrow *4, B*). But note the diminution in the number of Nisei below the age of fifteen. As the foreign-born females began to pass beyond the childbearing age, there were no foreign-born females (arrow *5, C*) to replace them, and the native-born females (arrow *6, B*) were only entering the childbearing period.

4. What can we guess about the future of this population? Barring any substantial immigration (present quotas admit only 185 Japanese per year), there should soon be an increase of native-born children as the native-born population reaches maturity. In turn, as they pass beyond childbearing age, the narrowing of the base should recur, although less clearly. The effect of the immigration pattern may be perceptible in this wavelike reproductive pattern for several generations.

ones. The increase in the proportion of the total labor force that is at high and intermediate levels has aided nonwhites by making it possible for them to move up without displacing whites. Such a situation has the hidden benefit of improving the occupational status of the minority without contributing to interracial conflict. However, in the long run, the position of minorities depends on their ability to compete freely and successfully at all occupational levels in the labor market.

The occupational distribution of nonwhites is considerably less favorable in the South than in other regions, a difference associated with the small town and rural residence of Southern nonwhites. In 1960 almost 20 per cent of Southern nonwhite workers were in agricultural occupations. Excepting the Indians and some Orientals in the West and Hawaii, almost all nonwhites in other

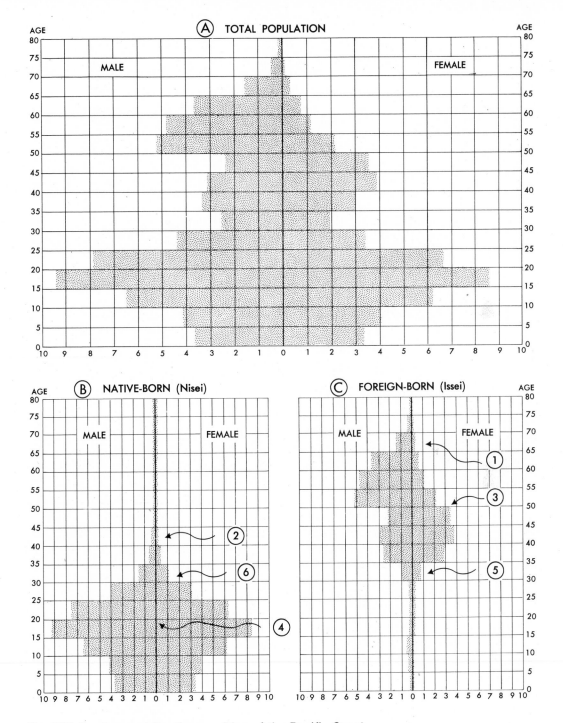

Fig. **XIII:8**   Age and Sex Composition of the Pacific Coast
Japanese Population: 1940

Source: U.S. Bureau of the Census. Figures in thousands are
given for each age group.

Table **XIII:5** Ratio of Actual to Expected Proportion of Nonwhite Workers
in Each Occupational Group, 1940–1960*

	1940	1950	1960[a]
Professional, Technical, and Kindred Workers	.36	.40	.49
Farmers and Farm Managers	1.36	1.22	.78
Managers, Officials, and Proprietors, except Farm	.17	.22	.23
Clerical and Kindred Workers	.12	.29	.46
Sales Workers		.18	.23
Craftsmen, Foremen, and Kindred Workers	.27	.38	.49
Operatives and Kindred Workers	.57	.94	1.08
Private Household Workers	4.66	5.92	5.46
Service Workers, except Private Household	1.53	2.00	2.02
Farm Laborers and Foremen	2.57	2.28	2.46
Laborers, except Farm and Mine	2.06	2.56	2.59

* Source: Adapted from Norval D. Glenn, *The Negro Population in the American System of Social Stratification: An Analysis of Recent Trends* (unpublished Ph.D. dissertation, The University of Texas, 1962), pp. 148–50. Data for 1960 are revised.
[a] Inclusion of nonwhites in Hawaii in 1960 accounts for a small part of the change between 1950 and 1960.

regions outside the South are in urban occupations. Only 16 per cent of the employed nonwhites in the South were in white-collar or skilled occupations, whereas 22 per cent of employed nonwhites in the nation as a whole were in such work. However, in metropolitan areas of 100,000 or more people, southern nonwhites do not compare so unfavorably with those in other regions. The occupational status of Negro metropolitan males is substantially the same in all regions, and that of females is only slightly lower in the South.

An appreciably higher percentage of the nonwhite labor force is female. In 1960, 39 per cent of the nonwhite and 31 per cent of the white labor force were female. The low incomes of many nonwhite males makes it necessary for their wives to seek employment to augment the family income, and women are the principal or only means of support for many matriarchal households of the Negro lower class. Of women with children under six years of age, a third of the nonwhites

but only a fifth of the whites were in the labor force in 1960. A larger proportion of both white and nonwhite females have entered the labor force during recent years. The increase has been somewhat greater for whites, and the difference in sex composition of the white and nonwhite labor forces has declined since 1940.

The low average occupational status of Negroes results both from their relatively poor qualifications and from discrimination. These two factors interact and reinforce one another. Historical discrimination of various kinds is ultimately responsible for the Negro's relative lack of education and skills. In turn, the low average level of Negro occupational qualification tends to perpetuate discrimination.

However, the educational attainments of nonwhites has risen sharply since 1940. The median years of school completed by nonwhites twenty-five years old and over rose from 5.8 in 1940 to 6.9 in 1950 to 8.2 in 1960. This improvement is more than proportional to that of whites (from 8.7 to 9.7 to 10.9), so nonwhites also experienced a relative increase in educational status. The ratio of the nonwhite to the white median was .67, .71, and .75 in the respective years. Since nonwhite education on the average is of poorer quality than white education, the ratio overstates somewhat the relative educational qualification of nonwhites. But the quality of nonwhite education may be improving faster than white education. If so, the *changes* in ratios are understated.

Because of discrimination and the poorer quality of nonwhite education, the occupational distribution of nonwhites is appreciably lower than that of whites at each educational level below college graduation. Significantly, the distributions of nonwhite and white college graduates among the occupational groups differ but little. The scarcity of Negro college graduates relative to the demand for their services in Negro institutions may account for their favorable occupational distribution.

Chapter XIV

Crime and delinquency

By **DONALD R. CRESSEY**

in collaboration with L.B. and P.S.

Section 1 ## Introduction[1]

In any society there is usually consensus about what behavior will be reacted to favorably, neutrally, or unfavorably. Some behavior is rewarded, some ignored, and some results in official punishment. However, not all disapproved behavior is made part of the criminal law. Technically, crime and delinquency refer only to behavior that violates the criminal law. Youthful offenders are called delinquents rather than criminals, but almost all acts handled officially as juvenile delinquency are acts that would be called crimes if committed by an adult. Antisocial behavior and crime are not synonymous. An act may be antisocial and not violate the criminal law, and another act may be criminal but not antisocial. A good swimmer who does not try to rescue a drowning boy has behaved immorally and antisocially, but he has committed no crime. A man who steals a loaf of bread and gives it to a starving child has behaved criminally but perhaps not antisocially.

THE SCOPE OF CRIMINOLOGY

The major objective of sociologists in the field of criminology is the development of a body of valid knowledge about the three general processes discernible in the above discussion. (1) Criminologists are interested in the process of *lawmaking,* including the conditions under which acts are defined as crimes by societies. Crime is relative; what is crime in one society may not be crime in another. In the sociology of law criminologists try to account for the origin of the criminal law as an agency of social control and, more specifically, to analyze scientifically the kinds of social organization associated with certain kinds of criminal laws. (2) Criminologists are interested in the process of *lawbreaking.* Although a society defines certain behavior as undesirable and threatens to punish it, some persons persist in the behavior and thus commit crimes. In the sociology of crime and criminality the factors associated with law violation are

[1] An effort has been made in this chapter to recast for beginning students certain aspects of the theoretical orientation of *Principles of Criminology* (6th ed.; Philadelphia: Lippincott, 1960), by Edwin H. Sutherland and Donald R. Cressey. A few pages of the chapter follow the book rather closely.

examined, and its causes are analyzed. An attempt is made to find conditions associated with high crime rates but not associated with low crime rates and to find traits or conditions that appear among criminals but not among noncriminals. (3) Criminologists are interested in *how society reacts* to lawbreaking. While a threat of punishment is contained in every criminal law, the punishment threatened for some crimes is much more severe than for other crimes. The official punishments are not imposed on all offenders, however, and the punishments threatened for some crimes are more frequently imposed than for other crimes. Some societies react to law violation primarily by annihilation of the offender; others react by corporal punishment; still others react by imprisonment or the imposition of fines. In the sociology of punishment and crime control an attempt is made to understand the differential reaction to various crimes within a society, to account for the fact that the official punishments threatened are not uniformly imposed, and to discover the conditions leading to the different reactions to crime in various societies.

Within this broad range of interests, most attention has been given to the criminal act itself and to the social conditions that produce it. This concern for crime causation, or etiology, has taken two principal forms. (1) Sociologists have studied the relation of crime rates to variations in social organization and culture. Societies and groups with different crime rates have been compared on many social characteristics, including differential mobility, culture conflict, competition, stratification, population composition and density, the distribution of wealth, income, and employment, as well as political, economic, and religious ideologies. (2) Sociologists have also investigated how people become criminals. Becoming a criminal involves the same *learning processes* as becoming a banker, a professor, or a fisherman. The content of the learning, not the

process itself, determines whether or not a person becomes a criminal. Differences in the degree of criminality have been studied in relation to the effects of the socialization process, the subcultures in which persons live, their experiences in primary groups, their associations, and their social class positions.

These two branches of criminology are necessarily interrelated. An explanation of a high crime rate must be consistent with an explanation of the criminal behavior of a person, for a crime rate is a summary of the criminal behavior of all the persons in a certain area.

INDEXES OF CRIME

The statistics of crime and criminals must be interpreted with extreme caution. They give only an approximation of the amount of crime at any given time, and they are almost useless for determining trends over a period of time. A large proportion of crimes committed go undetected; others are detected but not reported; and others are reported but not officially recorded. Since these unrecorded crimes do not appear in statistics, the statistics can only approximate the true crime rate. In order to use recorded crimes as an "index" of the crimes committed, however, it is necessary to assume that the recorded crime rate maintains a constant ratio with the true crime rate. This assumption is not warranted, for the difference between the number of crimes committed and the number of crimes recorded varies with changes in police policies, court policies, and public opinion.

Crimes reported to the police and recorded by them are called "crimes known to the police." The tabulation of crimes known to the police is the best available index of crimes committed because it is the one "closest" to the crimes. The further an index is from the crimes, the greater are the number of procedures that may affect the index. This is illustrated in Figures XIV: 1

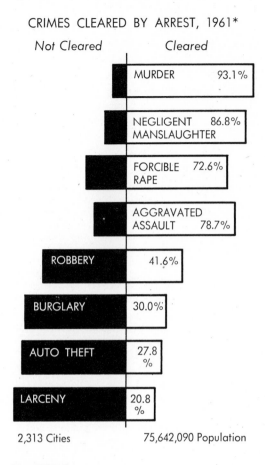

CRIMES CLEARED BY ARREST, 1961*

Not Cleared   Cleared

MURDER   93.1%

NEGLIGENT   86.8%
MANSLAUGHTER

FORCIBLE   72.6%
RAPE

AGGRAVATED
ASSAULT   78.7%

ROBBERY   41.6%

BURGLARY   30.0%

AUTO THEFT   27.8%

LARCENY   20.8%

2,313 Cities   75,642,090 Population

Fig. **XIV:1**

*Source: United States Department of Justice, Federal Bureau of Investigation, *Uniform Crime Reports—1961* (Washington, D.C.: Government Printing Office, 1962), p. 83.

and XIV: 2, which show, for example, that only 20.8 per cent of the larcenies known to the police were cleared by arrest, and that of the persons charged with larceny 45.2 per cent were found guilty. Generally, an offense is cleared by arrest when at least one of the perpetrators of the crime is identified with the crime and is arrested and charged, but there are technical exceptions. Crimes known to the police are a more reliable index than arrest statistics; arrest statistics are more reliable than court statistics; and court statistics are more reliable than prison statistics. However, even the number of crimes known to the police is not an adequate index of crime for a number of reasons:

1. The number of crimes known to the police is much smaller than the number actually committed. One study indicated that the number of cases of shoplifting known to three Philadelphia department stores was greater than the total number of thefts of all kinds in the entire city which were known to the police.[2] In 1944 and 1945 the detectives of a Chicago department store arrested two-thirds as many adult women for shoplifting as were formally charged with petty larceny of all forms (including shoplifting) by the police in the entire city of Chicago.[3] Such discrepancies are due principally to the failure of victims to complain to the police.

2. The number of crimes *recorded* as known by the police may be only a small proportion of the crimes actually known. Police departments in some cities conceal crimes known to them in order to protect the reputation of their city or department. Political administrations often try to show statistically that crime rates have declined during their terms in office. In 1928 the police reports indicated that only 879 burglaries and 1,263 robberies had been committed in Chicago; in 1931, after the system of recording crimes had been changed, the reports showed 18,689 burglaries and 14,544 robberies.[4]

3. The ratio of crimes committed to crimes recorded varies with the type of crime. Almost all murders are reported and recorded, but only an insignificant proportion of statutory rapes (sexual intercourse with a girl younger than the age of consent)

[2] Thorsten Sellin, *Crime and the Depression* (New York: Social Science Research Council, 1937), Bulletin No. 27, p. 69.

[3] Loren E. Edwards, *Shoplifting and Shrinkage Protection for Stores* (Springfield, Ill.: Charles C. Thomas, 1958), p. 130.

[4] Virgil W. Peterson, "An Examination of Chicago's Law Enforcement Agencies," *Criminal Justice*, January, 1950, 3–6.

are reported. Further, the circumstances under which crimes become known to the police affect the recording. Crimes against property usually must be reported to the police by the victim, while crimes involving drunkenness are observed by the police. It is probable that police more fully record crimes which they have observed themselves.

Since 1930 the United States Department of Justice has published in *Uniform Crime Reports* information on arrests and crimes known to the police. In 1961 the number of crimes reported to the Federal Bureau of Investigation by 7,800 law enforcement agencies, representing 96 per cent of the population of the United States, is used as an index of major crimes (homicide, forcible rape, aggravated assault, burglary, robbery, larceny, and automobile theft). "Arrests" (fingerprint records sent to the FBI) are used as an index of other crimes. The statistics on crimes known to the police cover an area that includes 82.5 per cent of the rural population, 98.3 per cent of the population in Standard Metropolitan Statistical Areas, and 90.7 per cent of the population in other cities. Table XIV: 1 shows the estimated number of serious crimes known to the police in 1961. These offenses, however, constitute only a small proportion of all offenses committed.

SOURCES

SPECIALIZED JOURNALS AND PROCEEDINGS

The sociological, psychiatric, and psychological journals carry articles on various aspects of crime and delinquency. The more important publications dealing specifically with crime and criminals are the following:

American Journal of Correction. Published by the American Correctional Association. Most articles are essays on various aspects of prison administration.

British Journal of Criminology. Most articles report on surveys of crime and delinquency in England and other European nations.

Crime and Delinquency (formerly *National Probation and Parole Association Journal*). Devoted almost

PER CENT FOUND GUILTY OF PERSONS CHARGED WITH MAJOR CRIMES, 1961*

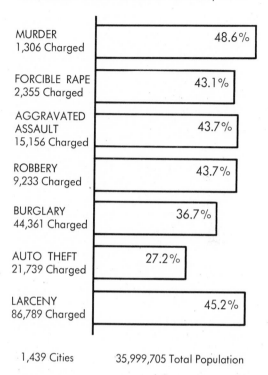

MURDER 1,306 Charged	48.6%
FORCIBLE RAPE 2,355 Charged	43.1%
AGGRAVATED ASSAULT 15,156 Charged	43.7%
ROBBERY 9,233 Charged	43.7%
BURGLARY 44,361 Charged	36.7%
AUTO THEFT 21,739 Charged	27.2%
LARCENY 86,789 Charged	45.2%

1,439 Cities   35,999,705 Total Population

Fig. **XIV:2**

*Source: United States Department of Justice, Federal Bureau of Investigation, *Uniform Crime Reports—1961* (Washington, D.C.: Government Printing Office, 1962), computed from p. 87.

exclusively to problems of rehabilitating delinquents and criminals.

Federal Probation. Published by the Administrative Office of the United States Courts in co-operation with the Federal Bureau of Prisons. Most articles deal with correctional programs—probation, prisons, and parole—but there are occasional reports of research on crime causation.

Journal of Criminal Law, Criminology and Police Science. Published by the Northwestern University School of Law. Approximately two-thirds of the articles are devoted to problems of crime causation, the remainder to techniques for detecting and apprehending criminals.

Proceedings of the American Correctional Association. Papers read at the annual prison and corrections congresses.

Table **XIV:1** Estimated Crime Rates and Major Crimes Known to
the Police: United States, 1961*

Crime	Number of Crimes	Rate per 100,000 Inhabitants
Murder and nonnegligent manslaughter	8,599	4.7
Forcible rape	16,012	8.8
Robbery	91,659	50.1
Aggravated assault	133,020	72.7
Burglary	852,506	466.0
Larceny $50 and over[a]	498,117	272.3
Auto theft	326,206	178.3
Total	1,926,119	1052.8

* Source: United States Department of Justice, Federal Bureau of Investigation, *Uniform Crime Reports—1961*, p. 33.
[a] Except auto theft.

SOURCES OF STATISTICS

Most of the statistics assembled on crime and criminals by state agencies pertain only to prisoners. There are wide variations in the kinds of data collected. The best state-collected series are the following:

California, Department of Corrections, *California Prisoners*, published annually.

Massachusetts, Department of Correction, *Annual Reports*.

New York, Commissioner of Correction, *Annual Reports on Crime Statistics*.

In addition to *Uniform Crime Reports*, mentioned above, federal agencies also collect and report criminal statistics as follows:

U. S. Department of Justice, Federal Bureau of Prisons, *National Prisoner Statistics* (Washington: Federal Bureau of Prisons). Annual statistics on commitments to federal and state penal institutions in the United States. Included are data on the number of commitments to the various institutions, the number of prisoners present at the end of each year, and the number of prisoners discharged under the various systems of release. Until 1948 this series was published by the Bureau of the Census, with the title *Prisoners in State and Federal Prisons and Reformatories*, and it included information on the type of crime, age, race, and sex of prisoners. The annual report of the Federal Bureau of Prisons, *Federal Prisons* (formerly *Federal Offenders*), gives statistical data on persons convicted of violating federal laws.

U. S. Social Security Administration, Children's Bureau, *Statistical Series*. This annual publication gives data on delinquency cases coming before approximately 400 of the 3,000 American courts that deal with children's cases.

Section 2 **Social organization**

Criminal behavior is nonconformity to the *official* values of society. This type of nonconformity increases (1) as society becomes more complex and (2) as the number of different values increases. These conditions are related, for when there are many conflicting values, mutual dependence tends to decline. As the bonds between persons become tenuous, informal ways of inspiring conformity to dominant values give way to attempts to control by force. That is, the dominant values become "official," nonconformity becomes crime, and repression of nonconformity is delegated to officials who have the power to threaten punishments and to impose them.

This section deals with some aspects of *social disorganization,* that is, the weakening of personal bonds and of institutional machinery. In the next section the emphasis is on *cultural disorganization,* that is, the breakdown and conflict of value systems.

SOCIAL DISORGANIZATION AND CRIME

People are most likely to conform when the consequences of their acts to themselves and to others are immediately apparent. The closer they are bound into a network of social relations, the greater the degree of conformity. For example, individuals in a small town are inhibited from even minor nonconformity such as not showing respect to elders. The relations between the potential nonconformist, the elders, and the rest of the community are close and intimate, and nonconformity would affect a wide range of the person's social relations. On the other hand, in metropolitan areas where people are relatively anonymous, nonconformity does not encounter concerted opposition.

As the boundaries of social interaction have extended from local areas to large cities and nations, the social consequences of various forms of personal conduct have become less discernible. The extended family and close-knit neighborhood, which were the principal agencies for inspiring conformity to a relatively consistent and unitary system of values, have declined. In their place have appeared urban communities, where consensus regarding "proper" modes of behavior has diminished, individuals have become relatively indifferent to the actions of the strangers that surround them, and a formal, official organization for discouraging and repressing crime has been created. But effective repression of crime is extremely difficult when the effects of crime are diffuse and hidden and when the society as a whole is not certain what acts should be defined as contrary to the general welfare.

POLICE, POLITICS, AND CRIME

In police departments conflicts between the efforts to control crime by force and the efforts to keep government weak become apparent. The police are expected to abide by official rules in their conduct, yet they must violate these norms and behave unofficially if they are to perform their function. Society fails to grant police departments adequate legal powers to control crime but, nevertheless, expects them to do so. Some of the weaknesses of law enforcement in the United States can be seen in (1) the *limited access* to the population for surveillance and apprehension of criminals, (2) the *political pressures* to overlook the crimes of some persons and to wring confessions from others, and (3) the *vulnerability to paid collusion* with professional and organized criminals.

1. *Limited access.* In democratic countries the police have only limited means of ferreting out criminals. The number of policemen relative to the total population is small. These men have few facilities for monitoring potential criminals, and they are restrained by the concept of "due process" from unrestricted searches, arrests, and entrapment. Under totalitarianism, however, the police have far greater access to all individuals, noncriminals as well as criminals. In Communist countries, for example, the police are supported by an extensive network of state-controlled organizations, reaching and controlling virtually every city block; the use of informers, including even family members, is widespread and normal; and the limitations of due process are not in force.[5] In the United States the status of police is ambiguous. The tendency to resort to illegal police methods reflects an underlying dilemma in our system. The suppression of crime requires a large degree of access to the population, including freedom to apprehend suspects and to go on "fishing expeditions"

[5] See Edgar H. Schein with Inge Schneier and Curtis H. Barker, *Coercive Persuasion* (New York: Norton, 1961).

for evidence in private places; on the other hand, the ideals of constitutional liberty and "due process" tie the hands of the police. This is illustrated by illegal arrests and unjustified police violence.

Generally, an officer can arrest without a warrant for a minor offense (misdemeanor) only if it is committed in his presence, and for a major offense (felony) only if he has reasonable grounds for believing a felony has been committed and reasonable grounds for believing the arrestee committed it. In many cases the law is avoided by not literally arresting the suspected person: the officer merely says something like, "We had better take a ride down to the station," and the person believes he is being arrested. Most departments have informal understandings with their police to make arrests on suspicion or in dragnet raids in opposition to the law. Under the law of arrest, if a thief were detained by a person who saw him commit a misdemeanor and a policeman subsequently arrived and arrested the offender for the misdemeanor, the arrest probably would be illegal. However, a policeman who did not arrest under such circumstances would be severely criticized, and he might even be accused of being in collusion with the offender. He must risk violating the law in order to enforce it and to maintain his position on the police force.

Violence which is not legally justified is often used at the time of arrest or between arrest and the hearing before a magistrate. Many policemen argue that it is impossible to get along without third-degree methods. Thirty-seven per cent of the police questioned in one study believed that "roughing a man up" was justified if he had shown disrespect for the police.[6] The police commissioner of a large Eastern city stated, "I've sworn to protect this community against crime. If there has to be a choice between violating my oath of office and violating the Constitution, I'll violate the Constitution every time."[7] In other words, crime will be committed in order to repress crime. Police brutality may be reconciled with a law-abiding system by attributing it to the sadistic personalities of a few policemen, not to the system. However, in other instances the public may applaud the use of violence. A bill to ban third-degree tactics was killed in the senate of an Eastern state when a senator asked, "Are we to give the criminals an even break? Does the criminal give the law-abiding citizen an even break?"[8]

2. *Political pressures.* In many cities the police are under control of politicians who do not wish and will not permit unrelenting enforcement of all criminal laws. To maintain political control, politicians must distribute special favors and privileges in return for votes, favorable newspaper publicity, and campaign funds. One such favor is immunity from arrest and prosecution for crimes such as violation of zoning ordinances, traffic laws, laws regulating weights, measures, building specifications, and labor relations. Occasionally immunity from arrest for more serious offenses, such as tax evasion, robbery, and murder, also is granted. The granting of immunity is possible because appointment and advancement of policemen from one rank to another are controlled by politicians. Policemen who are "right" will selectively enforce the law so that the political machine rather than the entire society is benefited.

3. *Vulnerability to collusion.* Law enforcement personnel are in frequent contact with criminal groups, and a major form of police lawlessness is paid collusion with professional and organized criminals. In an extreme but not rare case, a whole police department may be suffused with corruption, which then becomes self-perpetuating as an

---

[6] William A. Westley, "Violence and the Police," *American Journal of Sociology*, **56** (July, 1953), 34–41.

[7] Quoted by Frederick G. Brownell, "It Could Happen to You," *American Magazine*, May, 1949, p. 133.

[8] Quoted by J. Edgar Hoover, "Third Degree," *American Magazine*, May, 1940, p. 177.

accepted order of things. Federal and state investigating committees have uncovered graft and collusion almost every time they have looked for them. For example, the Lexow Committee in New York City in 1894–1895 found that graft was characteristic of the police system rather than of isolated patrolmen, and a generation later the Seabury Committee found the same situation.[9] The more recent studies by the United States Senate Special Committee to Investigate Organized Crime in Interstate Commerce similarly revealed collusion between criminals and law enforcement officers and evidence of extensive graft by law enforcement officers. For example, it was the committee's judgment that "outright payments for protection were most clearly established" in the case of a New Orleans sheriff whose divorced wife testified that in six years the sheriff had accumulated $150,000 which he kept in a steel box in his home.[10] She also testified that she had seen her husband receive money weekly from a slot-machine dealer and that she herself had received money every week from another slot-machine dealer. In Tampa a sheriff was the center of a criminal conspiracy to violate gambling laws, and he received direct payments of protection money. In Philadelphia there were direct payments of approximately $152,000 monthly, "not counting payments to higher ups." In New York City one bookmaking or-

ganization paid over $1,000,000 a year for police protection, and in Los Angeles an entry of $108,000 for "juice," the California term for protection money, was found in the accounts of a bookmaking organization.[11]

In many other cities evidence of a political-criminal-police triumvirate was revealed.[12] The committee, in fact, found evidence of corruption and connivance at all levels of government—federal, state, and local. Corruption in the federal government was primarily in the enforcement of income tax laws. Evidence of illegal activities on the state and local levels took four different forms: direct bribes or protection payments to the police by criminals, political influence to protect and further the interests of criminals, unusual and unexplained wealth of police officers, and direct participation by police in the business of organized crime.[13]

It may be concluded that police are often inefficient in performing their duties, as these duties are formally defined in the law, but the inefficiency is due to the fact that society fails to provide the conditions essential to efficiency in the repression and prevention of crime. The social conflicts and social disorganization that produce high crime rates produce a weak police system that cannot deal effectively with criminality. Society does not want the police to repress and prevent all crime at all costs.

[9] New York State Legislature, *Report and Proceedings of the Senate Committee Appointed to Investigate the Police Department of the City of New York* (Albany: State Printing Office, 1895), V, 5311–88; and New York State Legislature, *Report of the Joint Committee on the Government of the City of New York* (Albany: State Printing Office, 1932), five volumes.

[10] Estes Kefauver, *Crime in America* (New York: Doubleday, 1951), pp. 175–76.

[11] Special Committee to Investigate Organized Crime in Interstate Commerce, *Third Interim Report,* U. S. Senate Report No. 307, 82nd Congress (Washington, D. C.: Government Printing Office, 1951), pp. 184–85.

[12] For the Committee's finding in medium-sized cities, see its *Final Report,* U. S. Senate Report No. 725, 82nd Congress (Washington, D. C.: Government Printing Office, 1951), pp. 37–62.

[13] *Third Interim Report,* U. S. Senate Report No. 307, 82nd Congress, pp. 183–84.

Section 3 **Culture**

If there were little or no deviation from the dominant values of a society, official designation of acts as crime would be unnecessary. For example, if all members of a society were in agreement on proper respect for private property, there would be no need for laws making disrespect for property rights a crime. On the other hand, the fact that an act is formally punishable by law is evidence that some members of the society have behaved in accordance with values which contravene those of other members. Criminal behavior is one manifestation of *cultural disorganization,* the breakdown in value systems. This breakdown makes the criminal law necessary.

CULTURAL DISORGANIZATION AND CRIME RATES

The United States is perhaps the best example of a culture characterized by extensive areas of value conflict. The United States is also among the nations with the highest general crime rates. It has a complex culture in which behavior that is right according to the values of one group may be wrong according to the values of another group and crime according to political authority. Legislatures in response to the pressures of special interests pass laws defining new crimes, but this legislation need not reflect consensus in the community. If there is not a consensus, an increase in law violations will follow. For example, if a city passes a leash law, many people may choose to violate it.

The high crime rate in the United States is related to this disparity of values. Some laws are obeyed and others are not, depending on whether one believes in them.[14]

Many persons who would not think of robbing a bank or murdering will brag openly to their personal acquaintances about smuggling articles into the country, tax evasion, and various other crimes. The culture provides ready rationalizations for such acts, which may be looked upon with an attitude of amusement. Enactment of laws by interest groups is actively opposed by other interest groups, and this opposition does not necessarily cease after the laws are passed. For example, businessmen have intentionally violated laws regulating their relations with labor, and labor unions have deliberately violated the laws regulating their conduct toward management. Moreover, some persons feel relatively free to choose whether or not they shall obey even some of our ancient laws, for groups in which they have membership condone or actually encourage violation. Respect for the law decreases and crime rates increase when many of the values incorporated in the law have no society-wide basis, and this decreased respect may extend even to the most sacred values in the law.

However, in some cases the conditions under which disrespect for law develops may be entirely unintended. Some groups formally accept a basic core of the larger society's codes but develop criminal traditions in response to the society's failure to meet their needs. The needs themselves, of course, are reflections of the culture, as is the failure to meet the needs. An example is the conflict between the values stressing success in American culture and the values that make achievement of success an impossibility for some persons.[15] Merton maintains: (1) that

---

[14] For extensive illustrations of this practice, see Marshall B. Clinard, *The Black Market, a Study of White-Collar Crime* (New York: Rinehart, 1952).

[15] Robert K. Merton, *Social Theory and Social Structure* (Rev. and enlarged ed.; Glencoe: The Free Press, 1957), pp. 161–94.

values emphasizing achievement of wealth are characteristic of the culture, and the goal of success is held by persons of all social classes; (2) that values concerning the legal means of realizing this goal effectively deny success to many members of the lower classes; and (3) that this leads to efforts among the lower classes to achieve success by illegal means. In Merton's terms, "It is only when a system of cultural values extols, virtually above all else, certain *common* success-goals for the population at large while the social structure rigorously restricts or completely closes access to approved modes of reaching these goals *for a considerable part of the same population,* that deviant behavior occurs on a large scale." [16]

However, this generalization is not a sufficient explanation of criminality, for even in societies like the United States where the success goal is disproportionately stressed, most lower-class persons do not use deviant means for achieving the approved ends. Rather, in a multigroup type of society standards of conduct vary from group to group; an individual who is a member of one group uses one means for achieving the success goal, while an individual having membership in another group uses other means. Even unsanctioned means for achieving success are not available to everyone; some working-class persons may be double failures, in the sense that neither legitimate nor illegitimate means for achieving success are available to them.[17]

CULTURE CONFLICT

Disrespect for official values may be a direct product of conflicting cultural codes. Although some sociologists consider as culture conflicts the disparities of values which arise simply as by-products of increased cultural complexity, in most criminological research the term has been used to designate conflicts arising from *interpenetration of divergent cultural codes.* The concept is used here in the latter sense to refer to disparities of values arising when the official values of one culture or subculture come into conflict with those of another. Conflicts between divergent culture codes may arise in three ways: [18]

1. The codes may clash on the border of contiguous culture areas. Behavior which is not defined as crime in one culture may be crime in an adjoining culture, resulting in serious problems of identifying the "proper" ways of behaving in border areas. With the growth of communication processes, the border between such conflicting cultures has become extremely broad, for knowledge concerning divergent codes no longer arises out of limited direct personal contacts.

2. In colonization the official values of one group may be extended to the territory of another, with the result that traditional ways of behaving suddenly become illegal. When Soviet law was extended to Siberian tribes, for example, women were forbidden to wear the traditional veils. But those who obeyed the law and laid aside their veils were killed by their relatives for violating the codes of the tribe. Similarly, before French law was introduced in Algeria, the killing of an adulterous woman was the right and duty of her brother or father, but under French law such killing is crime.

3. When the members of one cultural group migrate to another culture, they may take with them values which condone ways of behaving that clash with the codes of the receiving culture and are, therefore, illegal. This process is the reverse of the one just mentioned, and it occurs when the migrant group is politically weaker than the group

[16] *Ibid.,* p. 146.

[17] Richard A. Cloward, "Illegitimate Means, Anomie, and Deviant Behavior," *American Sociological Review,* **24** (April, 1959), 164–76. See also Albert K. Cohen and James F. Short, Jr., "Research in Delinquent Subcultures," *Journal of Social Issues,* **14** (1958), 20–37; and Richard A. Cloward and Lloyd E. Ohlin, *Delinquency and Opportunity* (Glencoe: The Free Press, 1960).

[18] Thorsten Sellin, *Culture Conflict and Crime* (New York: Social Science Research Council, 1938), Bulletin No. 41, pp. 58, 63–67.

whose territory is invaded. If the Algerians in the above illustration had moved to France, they would have introduced divergent values in that nation. Similarly, migrant groups may be ignorant of many laws of the receiving culture, with the result that crimes are unintentionally committed. For example, a European peasant in America may be ignorant of many administrative laws, e.g., those regulating public health and housing. He might even unintentionally violate laws protecting private property.[19]

Culture Conflicts and Mental Conflicts

Culture conflicts sometimes appear in individuals as psychological conflicts and maladjustments. One view holds that these personality disorders lead to delinquency and crime. "Culture conflict can be said to be a factor in delinquency only if the individual feels it or acts as if it were present." [20] Juvenile delinquency is also viewed as a consequence of emotional disorders which, in turn, may be products of clashes·between the values of a mother and father from different cultures or between the values of parents and the official values of America. There is little doubt that such clashes produce mental conflicts. It is less certain that the clash of divergent values is important to delinquency *only* if it produces mental conflicts. Even when no mental conflicts are present, culture conflicts may produce delinquency and crime through any of the three processes described above. An illustration of this point is the case of a Sicilian father in New Jersey who killed the sixteen-year-old seducer of his daughter and expressed surprise at his arrest, since he had merely defended his family honor in a traditional way.[21] The killer did not know there was a conflict between his Sicilian culture code and the American code. Consequently, he could not have experienced mental conflict. Where such external conflicts occur, violations of law arise merely because the actions of persons who have absorbed the values of one culture conflict with the dominant values of another culture. This conflict and consequent law violation continue until the acculturation process is complete.

ACCULTURATION

As an immigrant group becomes acculturated, it abandons the traditional values and complementary ways of behaving that have become illegal in the new culture. However, the behavior is abandoned because it is incongruous with the new ways of behaving which the group encounters, not simply because it is illegal. Acculturated groups do not give up their conflicting customs and become law-abiding; they give up their conflicting customs and acquire in their place the ways of behaving of the new culture, including its criminal practices.

This principle was demonstrated more than seventy years ago by a French criminologist who discovered wide variations in the crime rates of the 86 *départements* (districts) of France, then made an analysis of the changes which occurred in the crime rates of groups migrating from one *département* to another.[22] He found, for example, that Corsica's crime rate ranked 65th in the 86 districts when the crime rate was computed by counting the number of crimes committed by Corsicans living anywhere in France. But Corsica's crime rate rose to second highest of the 86 districts when it was computed by counting the number of crimes by Corsicans living in Corsica. At home the Corsicans had high crime rates, but those who moved abandoned the criminal tradition. Joly showed further that "abandoning the criminal tradition" actually

[19] For illustrations of conflicts arising in this way, see E. D. Beynon, "Crime and Customs of the Hungarians of Detroit," *Journal of Criminal Law and Criminology,* **25** (January-February, 1935), 755–74.

[20] Louis Wirth, "Culture Conflict and Misconduct," *Social Forces,* **9** (June, 1931), 490.

[21] Thorsten Sellin, *Culture Conflict and Crime,* p. 68.

[22] Henri Joly, *La France criminelle* (Paris: Cerf, 1889), pp. 45–46.

meant that the Corsicans were becoming acculturated to the ways of behaving of districts that had low crime rates. The district that ranked 84th in crime rates at home rose to 36th rank when prosecutions away from home were included, indicating that persons who emigrated became acculturated to a culture containing high crime rates. Emigrants to Corsica would commit more crimes than they did at home; groups moving from Corsica to this district would commit fewer crimes than they did at home.

This same principle has also been demonstrated in the acculturation of immigrant groups in the United States. Crime rates vary widely among immigrants depending on the traditions the immigrants bring with them from the home countries and on the number and kinds of contacts they have with official values and with the values of criminal groups.[23]

[23] See, for example, Arthur Lewis Wood, "Minority Group Criminality and Cultural Integration," *Journal of Criminal Law and Criminology*, **37** (March-April, 1947), 498–510; Rose Hum Lee, "Delinquent, Neglected, and Dependent Boys and Girls of the San Francisco Bay Region," *Journal of Social Psychology*, **36** (August, 1952), 15–34; N.S. Hayner, "Delinquency Areas in the Puget Sound Area," *American Journal of Sociology*, **39** (November, 1933), 314–28; Andrew W. Lind, "Some Ecological Patterns of Community Disorganization in Honolulu," *American Journal of Sociology*, **36** (September, 1930), 206–20.

Section 4 Socialization

There are three major hypotheses about the nature of criminal socialization:

1. Many sociologists regard criminality as mainly the product of *differential association* with groups that repudiate the legal codes.[24] According to the proponents of this notion, a person may be well-socialized—in the sense that his training has not been neglected—and yet be a criminal, if the norms of his groups are at variance with the official norms codified in criminal law. Children begin life disposed neither to crime nor lawful behavior. However, they are both deliberately and unintentionally trained to conform to the behavior of the groups surrounding them, and many of the groups surrounding some children in modern society are criminalistic.

2. Criminality is regarded by some criminologists as the product of *faulty socialization* or ineffective cultural transmission. "Socialization" here is used in a limited sense and is considered the process by which the person takes on the *official* ways of behaving of the larger society in which he lives. Criminal behavior is used as evidence that a person has not been adequately indoctrinated with the official norms of that society.

3. Many psychiatrically-oriented criminologists consider criminality the product of *personality maladjustment*. The socialization process is regarded as producing either healthy or unhealthy personalities, and criminality is considered a correlate of mental disturbance.

CRIMINALITY AS A PRODUCT OF SOCIALIZATION

In a society composed of many diverse groups, it is inevitable that most families will unintentionally train their children to violate some laws. A child trained to behave according to the norms of a subgroup may deviate from the official norms of his society. That is, he may learn definitions of situations in which crime is permissible or appropriate, in which the directives for behavior implied in the general values regarding honesty and morality may be temporarily ignored. In the

[24] See Sutherland and Cressey, *op. cit.*, pp. 74–81.

socialization process persons learn that criminality is overlooked or even approved in certain circumstances. The approval of crime may be unintentionally included in the conceptions of honesty, decency, fair play, justice, and morality taught to children. An anthropologist has given us an example of how such attitudes produce nonconformity to the official norms:

The average member [of a community] neither flouts tradition at all costs nor follows its guidance through thick and thin: he compromises, rendering obeisance to fine principles in the abstract and finding excellent excuses for doing as he pleases in concrete circumstances. The Burmese are Buddhist, hence must not take the life of animals. Fishermen are threatened with dire punishment for their murderous occupation, but they find a loophole by not literally killing the fish. "They are merely put on the bank to dry, after their long soaking in the river, and if they are foolish and ill-judged enough to die while undergoing the process it is their own fault." [25]

The child of a Burmese fisherman will in all likelihood learn that it is all right to violate the general code under certain conditions. Similarly, an American child may learn that it is all right to have fun on Halloween. Of course, not all persons who learn such attitudes actually violate the law; some may never encounter the circumstance in which criminality is prescribed, and some may not go beyond the literal formula.

A person who believes that it is all right to steal a loaf of bread when starving may never get into a situation which he defines as starvation. Another may define his circumstances as starvation and steal not bread but money or jewelry. One may define as starvation a moderate reduction in his standard of living; another who experiences actual hunger may not consider himself starving.

Development of the "Criminal Personality"

Almost all members of modern societies commit some crimes, but most persons do not consider themselves criminals and are not so considered by the members of their groups. Even prisoners who do not identify themselves with the typical criminal insist that they are not really criminals. In everyday conversation we use such phrases as "criminal personality," "hardened criminal," "confirmed criminal," or "incorrigible delinquent" to refer to persons who conceive of themselves as criminals and are persistent in their criminality. Usually when we speak of a delinquent or criminal, we have in mind a person who apparently is an incorrigible outcast, but the criminality of such persons, like the criminality of persons who commit only occasional crimes, is learned.

In the efforts of families and other groups to forestall delinquency, children are often unintentionally driven into groups in which acquisition of a "criminal personality" is almost inevitable. The sequence of alienation may be outlined as follows: [26]

1. In the eyes of a child, behavior which is proper as play may include breaking windows, climbing over roofs, or greasing streetcar tracks. Such definitions of "play" are akin to "fun" on Halloween. But to many adults, including parents, policemen, and the victims of the play, the behavior is evil or delinquent and must be curtailed or suppressed. [27]

2. Demands for suppression of the evil are made on the child by community members, including his parents. The demands may lead to a shift away from the definition of the specific *acts* as evil to a definition of the *actor* as evil.

3. In the face of the demands of adults, the child feels that an injustice is being done to him and, more important, that his com-

---

[25] Robert H. Lowie, *An Introduction to Cultural Anthropology,* (enlarged edition; New York: Rinehart, 1940), p. 379. Used by permission.

[26] Cf. Frank Tannenbaum, *Crime and the Community* (Boston: Ginn, 1938), pp. 17–21.

[27] It seems probable that destructive behavior defined as "play" by middle-class children is less frequently defined as "evil" by the community than is similar "play" of lower-class children.

munity and, perhaps, his parents, consider him different from good children. This recognition on his part leads to closer integration with the group that shares his play activities, for the other members are encountering similar experiences.

4. The community then scrutinizes and looks with suspicion upon all his activities, his companions, his hangouts, his speech, and his personality, and becomes more certain of its definition of him as evil or bad.

5. The child discovers that he has been defined as bad and that even his efforts to be good are interpreted as evidence of his badness. He becomes more closely integrated with his play group, which has been redefined as a delinquent gang by both the community and the group members, and he begins to look upon himself and his companions as bad. He is defined as bad and becomes bad because he has been defined as bad.

6. Once the community has defined him as bad, it knows how to cope with him; it does not, in fact, know how to deal with him until it defines him as bad. He is threatened, punished, counseled, analyzed, supervised, and committed to an institution. He gets a "record" with the police and other agencies.

7. As the community copes with him, it crystallizes its conception of him and *his conception of himself*. He defines himself as he is defined, as an "incorrigible," a "delinquent," or a "criminal." He has adopted the community's classification system, the separation of the good and bad, the right and the wrong. He becomes loyal to groups in which the membership consists of bad persons like himself, becomes educated in crime, and learns that the community which has been defining him as bad contains many elements which support his badness. He has become socialized.

This dramatization of evil probably plays a greater role in making the confirmed criminal or criminal personality than any other experience. One process for making a crim-

inal is ". . . a process of tagging, defining, identifying, segregating, describing, emphasizing, making conscious and self-conscious; it becomes a way of stimulating, suggesting, emphasizing, and evoking the very traits that are complained of."[28]

Adult Socialization

Criminality may occur among adults who are essentially law-abiding but who almost accidentally become members of groups which engage in criminal activities. Occasionally, a law-abiding citizen, such as a cabdriver, becomes acquainted with professional criminals, learns to accept their codes and ways of behaving, and becomes a professional criminal himself. More frequently, however, an adult achieves a status which he believes is essentially noncriminal, then discovers that he must behave criminally if he is to maintain the status. If he has not learned earlier that certain kinds of crime are proper for persons of his status, he may at first experience difficulty in playing his role. But under the informal tutelage of his coworkers—including assignment of responsibilities, evaluations of his worth, ridicule of his "ideals," etc.—his conception of himself changes. He learns to commit crimes and to accept his criminal behavior as proper.

CRIMINALITY AS INCOMPLETE SOCIALIZATION

Failure of efforts to keep criminals and delinquents out of courts and prisons has led to the popular belief that those individuals are products of certain fixed biological or psychological tendencies or traits. This belief is frequently based on the assumption that there is a war between the individual and society and that all individuals possess criminal tendencies which must be suppressed if social order is to be maintained. One variety of this idea in criminology is that the criminal, because of an instinctive

[28] Tannenbaum, *op. cit.*, pp. 19–20.

something *in him,* has broken through the restrictions of society and followed delinquent patterns. "The term delinquent character disorder . . . refers to character development which leads to repeated aggressive infringements upon values of the community from which the transgressor derives gratification. In such behavior the individual is responding to the demands of his instinctual drives with little respect for reality." [29]

A variation of this viewpoint holds that the criminal's basic character make-up is egocentric rather than altruistic—he unconsciously behaves in terms of "I" rather than "we" and, consequently, follows delinquent patterns. He is unable to accept the restrictions of society because some early emotional experience has so fixed his character that he is bound by unconscious urges and desires.[30]

Regardless of whether the mainspring of action in criminality is viewed as biological or psychological, the make-up of the criminal is considered individualistic and egocentric and in opposition to the co-operative basis of social life. The criminal, then, has not been able to adjust to social living and is, hence, incompletely socialized. Both varieties of this view have been questioned by sociologists in recent years. The instinct concept has been abandoned as an explanation of behavior.[31] Moreover, the idea of a war between individual and society has given way to the view that the characteristics of the groups to which an individual belongs determine whether or not he will be in conflict with the larger society.

From another viewpoint, however, there is evidence for the hypothesis that delinquents and criminals are incompletely socialized. It is apparent that a degree of order is necessary to an on-going society, for society is basically a co-operative enterprise. Without consensus on goals and means, a society could not continue to exist. In modern societies this consensus is discernible in the official norms comprising the criminal law. A person who is not trained to behave according to these official norms and who commits crimes can, then, be considered inadequately socialized. Since the family is expected to play a major role in socializing new members of society, deviation from the official norms often reflects failure of the family to perform its socialization function.

CRIMINALITY AND PERSONALITY MALADJUSTMENT

It is widely believed that criminal behavior is due to abnormal characteristics and traits of the personality. These abnormal traits are thought to develop out of the criminal's early social life, particularly his experiences in the family, and are considered the specific causal agents of criminality. Most of the psychoses, psychoneuroses, and minor emotional disorders of criminals have their origin in the social relations of the individuals in question, but from this viewpoint the abnormalities rather than the social relations are considered the active factors that produce the criminality. For example, the practice of clinically treating personality abnormalities of criminals assumes that eradication of the personality disorder will "cure" the criminality. Thus, it is believed that criminality, like tuberculosis, can be cured in a clinic without reference to the groups from which the "disease" was acquired. Individual psychotherapy for criminals is probably the best example of a treatment program based upon this assumption.

Psychoses are characterized generally by complete breakdown or severe impairment of the ability to communicate. Psychotic persons lose contact with reality and some-

[29] Irving Schulman, "The Dynamics of Certain Reactions of Delinquents to Group Psychotherapy," *International Journal of Group Psychotherapy,* **2**, (October, 1952), p. 334.

[30] See David Abrahamsen, *Crime and the Human Mind* (New York: Columbia University Press, 1945); and Kate Friedlander, *The Psychoanalytic Approach to Juvenile Delinquency* (New York: International Universities Press, 1947).

[31] Nelson N. Foote, "Identification as the Basis for a Theory of Motivation," *American Sociological Review,* **16** (February, 1951), 14–22.

times become completely isolated from the values and norms of their social groups. In other cases the isolation is less extreme, and some semblance of group membership is maintained. Because of this isolation, many psychotics are unable to manage their lives satisfactorily, and they sometimes get into difficulty with the law. An "inner voice" that commands a psychotic to kill may be obeyed; an innocent person may be attacked as a means of defense against his imagined bad intentions; sexual inhibitions may be reduced; social conflicts and tensions of various kinds may occur. Modern societies have established hospitals where psychotics are treated and, at the same time, segregated so that they can do no harm. However, only some psychotics are dangerous, and many psychotics, dangerous or not, are not hospitalized.

Psychiatric examinations of criminals upon admission to prisons usually reveal not more than 5 per cent to be psychotic, and in many institutions less than 1 per cent of the inmates are diagnosed as psychotic. This difference may be due to variations in the personality traits of the criminals entering the different prisons, but it is greatly affected both by the preconceptions of the psychiatrists doing the examining and by variations in methods of handling defendants who plead in court that they are "insane," not "criminal." The fact that a prisoner is psychotic does not necessarily mean that his crime was due to the psychosis. The social background of 500 psychotic inmates at the Medical Center of the Federal Bureau of Prisons were markedly similar to those of nonpsychotic federal prisoners and very different from the backgrounds of psychotic persons outside prisons.[32] This suggests that the social relations which produced criminal behavior in the

nonpsychotic prisoners also produced criminal behavior in the psychotic prisoners.

"Psychopath," "psychopathic personality," and "constitutional psychopathic inferior" are used interchangeably to refer to persons who are regarded as emotionally abnormal but who do not manifest the break with reality that characterizes psychotics. The methods of diagnosing psychopathic personality are not standardized or objective, as is indicated by the fact that some prison psychiatrists diagnose over 95 per cent of the inmates as psychopaths, while in similar institutions different psychiatrists diagnose not more than 5 per cent as psychopaths. "Delinquency of one kind or another constitutes the most frequently utilized symptomatic basis for diagnosis of psychopathic personality."[33] This practice presumes exactly what needs to be investigated; namely, whether or not personality traits cause delinquency and crime. A study of the inmates of the Psychopathic Unit of the Federal Medical Center, found that the traits generally regarded as characterizing psychopaths were not useful in differentiating the "most psychopathic" group in the hospital from the "least psychopathic" group.[34]

Minor psychological disturbances, such as emotional immaturity, instability, and maladjustment have been studied independently of the concept "psychopathic personality," and delinquent and criminal behavior are frequently attributed to one or more of these traits. Some criminologists in attempting to avoid the vagueness of the psychopathic personality concept have used minor personality deviations to classify criminals. Of the 2,537 individuals coming before the psychiatric clinic of the New York City Court of General Sessions in 1948, 19.4 per cent were diagnosed as psychopathic, but 76.1 per cent were found to have minor personality

[32] Daniel Silverman, "The Psychotic Criminals: A Study of 500 Cases," *Journal of Clinical Psychopathology*, **8** (October, 1946), 301–27. See also Daniel Silverman, "Psychoses in Criminals: A Study of 500 Psychotic Prisoners," *Journal of Criminal Psychopathology*, **4** (April, 1943), 703–30.

[33] P. W. Preu, "The Concept of Psychopathic Personality," in J. McV. Hunt (ed.), *Personality and the Behavior Disorders* (New York: Ronald, 1944), II, 925.

[34] Hulsey Cason, "The Symptoms of the Psychopath," *Public Health Reports*, **61** (December 20, 1946), 1833–53.

deviations such as aggressiveness, emotional instability, and shiftlessness.[35] However, no personality tests were utilized, and the technique for locating such deviations is not precisely described. Moreover, there is no assurance that the deviations found among the criminals would not also be found in the general population.

In an analysis of 113 studies comparing the personality test scores of delinquents and criminals with the scores of control groups, not a single trait was demonstrated to be more characteristic of criminals than of noncriminals. The general observation was that "the doubtful validity of many of the obtained differences, as well as the lack of consistency in the combined results, makes it impossible to conclude from these data that criminality and personality elements are associated."[36] This, of course, is a negative conclusion; it is not a positive assertion that criminals are no different from noncriminals in personality traits. The failure to identify distinguishing personality traits suggests, however, that the explanation of criminal behavior should be sought in something other than personality traits. Most sociologists are convinced that personality traits are important to delinquency and crime only to the extent that they determine the social relations in which the person becomes involved. A child whose emotional maladjustment causes him to withdraw from or be rejected by a delinquent gang, for example, would not be so likely to become delinquent as a child whose emotional disturbance caused him to seek the companionship of the gang. In either event the social relations involved rather than the emotional disorder would determine whether or not the child became delinquent.

---

[35] Walter Bromberg, "American Achievements in Criminology," *Journal of Criminal Law and Criminology,* **44** (July-August, 1953), 166–76.

[36] Karl F. Schuessler and Donald R. Cressey, "Personality Characteristics of Criminals," *American Journal of Sociology,* **55** (March, 1950), 476.

Section 5 Primary relations

Criminal behavior is learned principally in small, intimate groups by the same processes that most noncriminal behavior is learned. There are many primary groups in modern urbanized societies, and the kinds of primary groups that encourage criminality are more numerous than in preliterate societies. Any American who has passed the age of infancy, for example, has membership in a number of primary groups, and whether he becomes criminal or not depends chiefly on the character of his primary relations. This principle can be observed in the way family and gang relations contribute to delinquency and criminality.

THE FAMILY AND CRIMINALITY

Since the family has the most intimate contact with the child during his formative years and at least some subsequent contact, it plays a uniquely important role in determining the behavior patterns a child will eventually exhibit. For this reason a large part of recent criminological research and thinking has been concerned with the relations between juvenile delinquency and home conditions and child-rearing practices.

Family life may lead to delinquency and criminality in five interrelated ways:

1. Attitudes, values, and other behavior patterns conducive to delinquency and

crime may be present in the home. A child may observe such patterns and become delinquent simply because he has learned delinquency at home.

2. The family determines the geographic and social class position of the child in the community. This, in turn, largely determines the kind of primary relations the child encounters outside the family. If the child's home is located in a high-delinquency area, the activities of play groups he encounters are more likely to be defined as delinquent than are the activities of play groups he would encounter if the home were located in a low-delinquency area. Similarly, being a member of a lower socio-economic class may bring the child into association with neighborhood primary groups that do not fully share the dominant values of the broader society.[37]

3. The family determines the prestige of various persons and consequently affects the child's preferences for certain types of social relations. He learns to appraise persons as important or not according to their language, bearing, occupation, nationality, or other traits. These preferences greatly affect his chances of becoming delinquent, for he will be prone to pay little attention to the behavior and attitudes, delinquent or nondelinquent, of persons whom he considers unimportant. If the persons to whom he assigns high prestige and with whom he seeks primary relations outside the home are delinquent in their attitudes and values, the probability is high that he will become delinquent. As a matter of fact, the *type* of delinquency like the *incidence* of delinquency, has been shown to be determined by the types of persons who are highly esteemed in a neighborhood.[38]

4. The family may fail to provide a harmonious and pleasant place for the child to live. If the primary relations in the family are obnoxious, the child may leave them, either by physically abandoning the family or by withdrawing psychologically. The family thus loses control over him and is unable to direct his membership in other primary groups. Delinquency is higher in unbroken but unhappy homes than it is in broken homes.[39] Whether a child from an unhappy or broken home becomes a delinquent, however, is determined by the kinds of outside relations he encounters when he leaves the family.

5. The family may fail to train the child to be law-abiding. It may neglect his training completely or it may overprotect him and fail to acquaint him with the rules of the outside world or with the kinds of delinquencies he will be expected to resist in the community. Whether such a "neutral" child becomes delinquent or not will, of course, depend upon the primary relations he encounters outside the home. However, the family is expected to produce not neutral children but *anti*delinquent children, whose attitudes and values will resist delinquent influences.

Most of the family conditions associated with delinquency probably become effective as indicated in paragraphs 4 and 5. Family poverty, parent alcoholism, a broken home, harsh discipline, psychological tensions or emotional disturbances in the family—all these result in failure to provide antidelinquent primary relations. Failure of the family to inculcate its children with the official values of the society is especially important, because there is no other group or agency that can so efficiently perform this function.

GANGS

The informal education a boy receives in a gang may be more influential than the education received elsewhere. From the point of view of a gang member, the gang

[37] Albert K. Cohen, *Delinquent Boys: The Culture of the Gang* (Glencoe: The Free Press, 1955); Solomon Kobrin, "The Conflict of Values in Delinquency Areas," *American Sociological Review*, **16** (October, 1951), 653–61.

[38] Richard A. Cloward and Lloyd E. Ohlin, *op. cit.*

[39] F. Ivan Nye, *Family Relationships and Delinquent Behavior* (New York: Wiley, 1958), p. 47.

Visita conyugal: *In some societies the family unit is maintained even if the father is imprisoned. Mexican prisons permit intimate association between inmates and their families.*

is the world. If this world includes delinquent and criminal activities and its leaders obtain their positions by demonstrating prowess in criminality and intimate knowledge of the underworld, the participant will almost inevitably become delinquent. "To earn the right to belong he [the youth] will adopt whatever code of behavior the gang or group prescribes, regardless of how much it conflicts with society's standards or demands." [40] If the gang's activities and codes are nondelinquent, the person obtaining membership in it will be nondelinquent. But if the gang is delinquent—if, for example, the group members make little or no distinction between going swimming and going stealing—there is a high probability that any member will be delinquent. The following quotation from a member of a delinquent gang indicates how delinquencies may be committed for fun and not for gain.

When we went shoplifting, we always made a game of it; for example, we might gamble on who could steal the most caps in a day, or who could steal caps from the largest number of stores in a day, or who could steal in the presence of a detective and get away. We were always daring each other that way and thinking up new schemes. This was the best part of the game. I would go into a store to steal a cap, by trying one on, and when the clerk was not watching walk out of the store, leaving the old cap. With the new cap on my head I would go into another store, do the same thing as in the other store, getting a new hat and leaving the one I had taken from the other place. I might do this all day and have one hat at night. It was the fun I wanted, not the hat. I kept this up for months and then began to sell the things to a man on the West Side. It was at this time that I began to steal for gain. [41]

Delinquent gangs arise chiefly from play groups that engage in delinquent or quasi-delinquent activities. The members of a play group develop a we-feeling and start referring to themselves as the "bunch" or "crowd." Group solidarity may be further promoted through rivalry with other gangs, and the delinquent character of the gang is emphasized when police and property owners try to suppress its activities. The gang then becomes a subsociety, with values and codes in conflict with those of the larger society. The conflict with other gangs, the school, the family, and the police distinguishes a gang from a play group.

Although a few delinquent gangs continue into adulthood and graduate to racketeering and professional criminal activities, the majority of them either disappear or continue as boys' gangs as their membership is replaced. A study of street corner societies, which have the characteristics of gangs, concluded that they arise spontaneously from unsupervised recreational activities, consisting largely of just "hanging around" on a particular street corner:

The corner-gang structure arises out of the habitual association of the members over a long period of time. This nuclei of most gangs can be traced back to early boyhood, when living close together provided the first opportunities for social contacts. School years modified the original pattern somewhat, but I know of no corner gangs which arose through classroom or school-playground association. The gangs grew up on the corner and remained there with remarkable persistence from early boyhood until the members reached their late twenties or early thirties. [42]

Gang formation appears to be more characteristic of urban than of rural adolescent society. Only 22 per cent of a group of the rural boys in a correctional institution were known to be members of delinquent gangs, while 87 per cent of the urban boys were members of such gangs. [43]

[40] John R. Ellingston, *Protecting Our Children from Criminal Careers* (New York: Prentice-Hall, 1948), p. 35.

[41] Clifford R. Shaw, "Juvenile Delinquency—A Group Tradition," *Bulletin of the State University of Iowa*, No. 23, N.S. No. 700, 1933, p. 5.

[42] William Foote Whyte, *Street Corner Society* (Chicago: University of Chicago Press, 1943), p. 255.

[43] William P. Lentz, "Rural-Urban Differences in Juvenile Delinquency," *Journal of Criminal Law, Criminology and Police Science*, **47** (September-October, 1956), 331–39.

The delinquent gang, like other primary groups, attempts to secure conformity by ridicule, gossip, epithets, rewards, and punishments. A boy confronted with the alternative of committing a delinquency or being called "chicken" or "square" will almost always choose the former. Loyalty to gang members and honesty within the gang are the two primary virtues. Even severe physical punishments by gang leaders are endured and kept secret from outsiders, for the alternative is ostracism by the gang. The gang influences individuals toward delinquency and crime in a number of ways: by promoting attitudes of hostility toward community agencies of social control, by teaching techniques of crime and a general pattern of destructiveness, by enforcing its system of assigning highest prestige to the most daring or skilled criminals, and by serving as a medium of contact where beginners can learn from more experienced juvenile delinquents and older professional criminals.[44]

[44] Donald R. Taft, *Criminology* (Rev. ed.; New York: Macmillan, 1950), pp. 178–79.

Section 6 **Stratification**

Studies of the socio-economic status of criminals indicate a higher official crime rate for the lower classes than for the middle and upper classes. This does not necessarily demonstrate a higher actual criminality of lower-status groups, because the administration of criminal law favors criminals of high-class position over those of lower-class position. If two persons on different class levels are equally guilty of the same offense, the one on the lower level is more likely to be arrested, convicted and committed to an institution. Furthermore, the laws are written and administered primarily with reference to the types of crime committed by people of lower-class levels.

UNOFFICIAL STATISTICS

Although most criminologists now believe that there is a higher rate of crime in the lower classes, two studies of unofficial crimes and delinquencies support the notion that crime is by no means merely a lower-class phenomenon. In the first study, 1,020 men and 678 women, largely New Yorkers, were asked to check which of 49 listed offenses they had committed. An effort was made to distribute the questionnaire to a balanced religious and racial cross section of the population, but no systematic sampling procedures were used. The group of subjects contained an excess of persons from upper social classes. Ninety-one per cent of the subjects admitted that they had committed one or more offenses, excluding juvenile delinquencies, for which they could have received a jail or prison sentence. Men had an average of 18 and women an average of 11 adult offenses. Thirteen per cent of the men admitted to grand larceny, 26 per cent to automobile theft, 17 per cent to burglary, and 11 per cent to robbery. Of the women, 11 per cent admitted having committed grand larceny, 8 per cent admitted at least one automobile theft, 11 per cent admitted to burglary, and 1 per cent admitted to robbery. Sixty-four per cent of the men and 27 per cent of the women admitted that they had committed at least one felony.[45]

[45] James S. Wallerstein and Clement J. Wyle, "Our Law-Abiding Law-Breakers," *Probation*, **25** (March-April, 1947), 107–12.

A second study found that a group of 65 college men reported having committed an average of 9.9 offenses against property, 12.3 behavior problem offenses, 9.6 offenses against persons, 16.5 sex offenses, 20.8 "casual offenses," and 12.6 miscellaneous offenses. A group of 94 training school boys reported an average of 13.4 offenses against property and 19.1 behavior problem offenses; their average number of other offenses was about the same as that of the college men. In comparison with the training school boys, the college men had only rarely been arrested for their offenses.[46] One explanation for the difference lies in the fact that many of the complaints to juvenile authorities are made by parents against their own children, and parents who send their children to college do not file complaints as frequently as do parents whose children never will attend college.[47]

WHITE-COLLAR CRIMES

White-collar crimes—crimes committed by persons of respectability and high social status in the course of their occupations—are widespread, but their frequency is not accurately reflected in police reports. Prosecution for this kind of crime frequently is avoided because of the political or financial importance of the individuals concerned, because of the apparent triviality of the crimes, or because of the difficulty of securing evidence sufficient for prosecution. Methods other than prosecution in the criminal courts are frequently used to protect society against white-collar crimes. The administration of justice under laws which apply exclusively to business and the professions, and which therefore involve only the upper classes, is quite different from the procedures

used under more general laws.[48] Persons who violate laws regulating pure foods and drugs, advertising, and restraint of trade are not arrested by uniformed policemen, are not usually tried in the criminal courts, and are seldom committed to prisons. Action usually is taken in the hearings of administrative commissions and in civil courts. However, white-collar crimes are violations of criminal laws and are punishable under those laws.

White-collar crimes most frequently take the form of misrepresentation of financial statements, bribery, misrepresentation in advertising, embezzlement and misapplication of funds, tax frauds, short weights and measures, and misgrading of commodities. Such practices are widespread:

> The manufacturers of practically every class of articles used by human beings have been involved in legal difficulties . . . with more or less frequency during the last thirty years, including the manufacturers of the surgical instruments with which an infant may be assisted into the world, the bottle and nipple from which he may secure his food, the milk in his bottle, the blanket in which he is wrapped, the flag which the father displays in celebration of the event, and so on throughout life until he is finally laid away in a casket which was manufactured and sold under conditions which violated the law.[49]

OPPORTUNITIES FOR CRIME

Types of crime are significantly related to social status. One's position in the class structure determines the opportunities, facilities, and the requisite skills for specialized crimes. Lower-class persons cannot ordinarily violate laws prohibiting embezzlement, for they are seldom in positions of financial trust. On the other hand, a person trained to carry on the routine duties of a position of trust has at the same time been trained in whatever technical skills are necessary for

[46] James F. Short, Jr., "A Report on the Incidence of Criminal Behavior, Arrests, and Convictions in Selected Groups," *Research Studies of the State College of Washington,* **22** (June, 1954), 110–18.

[47] Austin L. Porterfield, "Delinquency and Its Outcome in Court and College," *American Journal of Sociology,* **49** (November, 1943), 199–208.

[48] Edwin H. Sutherland, *White-Collar Crime* (New York: Dryden, 1949), p. 8.

[49] Edwin H. Sutherland, "Crime and Business," *Annals of the American Academy of Political and Social Science,* **217** (September, 1941), 111–18.

the violation of that position.[50] But he may have no training or skill in how to steal an automobile. Furthermore, persons of different social classes have different conceptions of the kinds of crimes which are appropriate to their statuses. An upper-class person who would not think of burglarizing his neighbor's house, because such crime is "beneath him," might file a fraudulent income tax return.

MOBILITY AND STATUS AMONG CRIMINALS

Both prisoners and criminals outside prisons rate each other according to criteria somewhat peculiar to the underworld. Perhaps the most general division is between professional thieves and other types of criminals. Professional thieves, like members of the medical and legal professions, have a number of specialized abilities and skills, and they are given high rating by other criminals. The skills include manual dexterity needed for picking a pocket, but the chief qualifications are wits, "front," and talking ability. These are the skills necessary for execution of crimes involving swindles, for selling stolen goods, and for "fixing" the case after arrest. Among criminals, thieves who lack these general abilities are regarded as amateurs, even though they may steal habitually.[51] The complex of skills developed through long informal education in association with other professional thieves distinguishes professionals from amateurs. The techniques also generally call for cooperation that can be secured only in association with professional thieves, and this allows professionals to erect and maintain barriers against invasion of the status group by amateur criminals.

Among professionals, the word "thief" is regarded as honorific, and it is used regu-

larly without qualifying adjectives to refer to the professional thief.[52] Amateur thieves are held in contempt, and many epithets are applied to them. "Snatch-and-grab thief" and "boot-and-shoe thief" refer, respectively, to a thief who steals without skill or caution and to a thief who is so incompetent that he must pick up a boot here and a shoe there. Professionals will have no dealings with persons who do not use correct methods. Many amateur criminals strive for professional status, but only a few of them reach their goal:

> Vertical social mobility functions for criminal persons as well as for noncriminal, with criminals being "on the make" in their status framework as well as others. Young thieves may begin their careers stealing automobile tires, pass from that to, say, jack-rolling drunks, and from there they may move into "heavy rackets." Professional skill, large earnings, and ability to escape imprisonment serve as the criteria for advancement and acceptability into the higher ranking criminal occupations. Many aspirants never get beyond the lower rungs of the criminal-status ladder. Others get as far as the heavy rackets but never rise to the elite status of grifters or to that of the criminal's criminal, the con man [professional thief].[53]

Professional thieves disagree about the extent of status gradations within the profession. Some class the members as either "big-time" or "small-time" on the basis of the size of their incomes and the nature of their illegal activities. Some successful confidence men, for example, feel that shoplifters are beneath them, and they try to avoid them. However, other professionals believe that there are no important gradations within the profession. One thief has written as follows:

> I have never considered anyone a small-time thief. If he is a thief, he is a thief—small-time, big-time, middle-time, eastern standard, or

[50] See Donald R. Cressey, *Other People's Money* (Glencoe: The Free Press, 1953), pp. 81–85.

[51] Edwin H. Sutherland, *The Professional Thief* (Chicago: University of Chicago Press, 1937), p. 198.

[52] *Ibid.*, p. 200.

[53] By permission, from *Social Pathology*, p. 323, by Edwin M. Lemert. Copyright, 1951, McGraw-Hill Book Company, Inc.

Rocky Mountain, it is all the same. Neither have I considered anyone big-time. It all depends on the spot and how it is handled. I recall a heel touch [sneak theft] at ten one morning which showed $21 and three hours later the same troupe took off one for $6,500 in the same place. Were they small-time in the morning and big-time in the afternoon? [54]

Within prisons, criminals make distinctions according to length of sentence, type of crime, and apparent loyalty to inmates. Generally, prisoners with long sentences are

[54] Edwin H. Sutherland, *The Professional Thief*, p. 201.

ranked higher than short-termers, but there are many exceptions to this. When prisoners are ranked according to type of crime, professional thieves, especially confidence men, are considered the "aristocrats of prisons," but notorious gangsters as well as forgers and other types of swindlers are also ranked high. Men who have engaged in the "heavy rackets"—robbery and burglary—seem to approximate a second class, and sex offenders comprise a lower class. Prisoners who have committed sexual offenses against children are at the bottom of the ladder in the social world of the prison.

Section 7 Associations

Associations among ordinary criminals not in prison develop within the broad and rather loose organization of the "underworld," held together by shared understandings about crime, law violation, and the police. Because of their hostility toward the law, the members of the underworld co-operate in protecting each other from detection and apprehension. In this setting, two principal types of association develop. First, tightly-knit groups with recognized leadership, agreements, and division of labor engage in specific crimes such as picking pockets, swindling, and blackmail. Second, "syndicates," "rings," or "combines" engage in illicit businesses, such as prostitution, and the extortion of money from legitimate enterprises. The latter activity is traditionally called "organized crime," a term which places emphasis upon the syndicate's organizational hierarchy, consisting of a top man and his lieutenants, sublieutenants and workers, and upon the alliances of such hierarchies with each other. [55]

[55] Walter C. Reckless, *The Crime Problem* (New York: Appleton-Century-Crofts, 1950), pp. 143–44.

PROFESSIONAL CRIMINALS

Small working groups of criminals often are "professionals," so-called because they engage in crime as a day-by-day enterprise, develop skilled techniques and careful planning in their occupation, have codes of behavior, *esprit de corps,* and high status among criminals. [56] The number of persons in these working groups depends upon the kind of work to be done. A group engaged in an elaborate confidence game may involve the services of four or five principals or star actors and a host of persons to play minor roles. A pickpocket troupe may consist of only two or three—a man to locate the victim, one to pick the pocket, and a third to dispose of the loot. The "hook" or "wire" (the man actually picking the pocket) ordinarily has the greatest degree of technical skill, and he usually is the recognized leader of the group. The co-operative enterprise extends beyond the actual execution of the crime. It includes preparation for "fixing" victims or the police in the event of detection

[56] See Edwin H. Sutherland, *The Professional Thief*, pp. 197-228.

and apprehension, for bail and legal services in case the "fix" fails, and for "fall dough" (unemployment insurance), for group members who are sentenced to jail or prison. Membership in the association is by invitation. A person cannot "just decide" to engage in professional crime any more than he can "just decide" to play professional baseball; existing groups must permit him to engage in the profession. Members are former hotel clerks, cabdrivers, salesmen, bellboys, etc., as well as former amateur criminals.

SYNDICATES AND RACKETS

The largest criminal associations are the vice racket hierarchies. Part of the public demands illicit gambling, narcotics, alcohol, and sexual intercourse; the "syndicates" capitalize on the demands. Usually a syndicate includes at least some persons whose legal business is law enforcement or politics. It may or may not own or run the gambling houses or places of prostitution it controls. Frequently the operators of illicit places of business are intimidated into paying a syndicate for "protection," and it is able to provide protection because it has, in turn, been granted an illegal "license" to operate in a particular locality. The syndicate type of criminal organization is feudal in character. "Serfs" work only for "lords," but several lords may be loyal to and do business with a more powerful lord, who alone or with other lords of his rank accepts the leadership of a still more powerful overlord.[57] The system assumes devotion of all members to the leaders immediately above them in the hierarchy. A serf or a lord who is able to get channels of his own to the overlord or who betrays his superiors to the honest police threatens the entire organization. Even the resignation of a member threatens the organization, for integration is based upon efficient performance of services by a variety of specialists. Consequently, great pressures, including physical violence, are exerted to keep underlings in their place.

THE PRISON COMMUNITY

American society imposes suffering on criminals by taking away their freedom and liberty. Such a system of imposing punishments was almost unheard of until less than two centuries ago. Before the time of the American Revolution, the pain and suffering imposed on criminals was physical or financial, and incarceration was most often used merely for persons awaiting trial or as a "squeezer" to get guilty persons to pay their fines. The idea of imposing pain and suffering on criminals by locking them up developed about the same time as modern ideas about democracy and freedom. The French and American Revolutions saw the beginnings of the prison system as it exists today.

Currently, society imposes punishments on criminals by forcing them into totalitarian organizations. In traditional maximum-security prisons an attempt is made to control the criminal's entire life, to see that his name is replaced by a number, that he eats when and what he is told to eat, that he works when and where he is told to work, that he sleeps when and where he is told to sleep. Theoretically, every minute of his time is watched; he is supposed to make no choices. However, there are cracks in the totalitarian monolith.[58] The complexities of prison life are such that prisoners almost inevitably are able to devise an organization giving some elements of choice and some opportunities for individual self-expression. The working of the prison is outlined in Adaptation 38, "The Prison Community," pages 565–68.

[57] Reckless, *op. cit.*

[58] See Karl W. Deutsch, "Cracks in the Monolith: Possibilities and Patterns of Disintegration in Totalitarian Systems," In Carl F. Friedrich (ed.), *Totalitarianism* (Cambridge. Harvard University Press, 1954).

Ratero en accion: *A pickpocket exploits a distracting crowd situation.*

The Prison Community

When an inmate first enters a prison, he experiences only the harsh effects of the official organization. He learns what it means to be handled impersonally. He is photographed, fingerprinted, and searched by human and electronic eyes. He is stripped, bathed, and examined. He is injected, inoculated, and immunized. He is questioned, lectured, and warned. He learns that he is anonymous and believes that the officials

have almost complete control over his actions. It takes a new inmate only a few days to learn how the official organization is set up and how to get along with the administrators. Generally, he learns to give up his individuality and learns enough rules to avoid serious trouble. In this stage he is anxious to co-operate with the prison authorities. He heeds the administrators' admonitions to "do your own time." When asked where he would like to work while in prison, he is likely to respond, "I'll do anything you want. I just want to do my time and get out of here."

Gradually, the new inmate discovers the prisoner organization. He learns that his happiness or unhappiness in prison depends to a large extent on how he gets along as a member of the inmate association, rather than how he gets along with the warden and guards. He discovers, in other words, that he has been trying to impress the wrong people. He also makes the significant discovery that he owes nothing to the officials for the food, clothing, and shelter he receives. At the same time he finds that things are not so automatic and routine as they once seemed. By observing other inmates, he discovers that his environment can be controlled to a large extent, that he does have some choices, although extralegal, that inmates do by various systems of subversion avoid the punitive conditions under which they are supposed to live, and that his task is to get along with other prisoners as well as with officials.

Types of Inmate Leaders

The informal prisoner organization is largely in the control of three types of men. There are, first, the "politicians" or "shots" or "merchants." (They have different names in different institutions.) These men have skills that enable them to hold key positions in the administrative offices of the prison, and they wield power to give inmates special privileges, good jobs, special foods, and other supplies. They get their jobs by conniving, dealing, and bribery. In some instances these politicians are racketeers, using their positions to force money and services from less powerful inmates. Only rarely do they attempt to aid inmates as a class; they are constantly "looking out for Number One." They are not trusted by the inmates, but are tolerated by the prison officials because they help maintain control of inmates.

A second group is made up of men called "outlaws," "toughs," or "gorillas." Like the politicians, they are self-centered and exploitative. They differ from the politicians principally in that they are much more prone to the use of threats and physical violence to get what they want from weaker inmates.

A third group, called "right guys" or "real men" or simply "men," has a controlling power much greater than the politicians or outlaws, for it is based on apparent loyalty and allegiance to inmates as a group. Right guys do not abuse lesser inmates, can always be trusted, and are sensible and cool headed. Unlike politicians and toughs, they are the heroes of the inmate social system, for they provide leadership for inmates rather than exploiting them. They are unmistakably against the administration, thus emphasizing the importance of solidarity in the inmate association. Ordinarily they are men serving long terms who have a stake in a quiet prison routine. They are, therefore, not troublemakers. They discourage violence, and they informally set the standards of proper behavior for convicts. Violence, foolish violations of rules that antagonize guards, and other activities that disturb the peace are disdained and controlled.

Despite the exploitative efforts of politicians and toughs, the inmate association's general orientation is toward making prison life more bearable, not toward the commission of crimes. Occasionally, to be sure, an escape or smuggling plot is dramatically assisted and kept secret by many inmates. But usually inmates are more interested in taking the edge off harsh, restrictive, prison routines than in open rebellion. The co-operative enterprise includes such activities as exchange of services, participation in the "grapevine," and sharing of personal goods with inmates who have no money.

In the system of friendships, mutual obligations, statuses, and loyalties, inmates learn that conformity to the norms of the society of prisoners (as epitomized in the right guys) is just as important to their individual welfare as is conformity to the formal controls exerted by prison officials. As a population of prisoners moves in the direction of solidarity, the pains of imprisonment become less severe, for inmate society provides the individual prisoner a meaningful social group with which he can identify and which supports him in his struggle against his condemners.[59] Thus, inmate society permits the individual prisoner at least a partial escape from the isolation and deprivations of prison life. Orthodoxy in the association is promoted by a system of rewards and such punishments as gossip, ridicule, and even corporal punishment.

The Inmate Code

This informal control may be observed in the persistence of "the code," which contains the fundamental principles of the prisoner association and has been built up through the years on the assumption that lawbreakers and law enforcers are natural enemies. The code has at least five identifiable elements.[60]

1. Don't interfere with inmate interests. An inmate must be allowed the maximum number of pleasures and privileges he can obtain. "Never rat on a con." "Don't be nosey." "Keep off a man's back." Briefly and positively: "Be loyal to your class, the cons."

2. Refrain from quarrels with other inmates and from unnecessary altercations with guards. Emphasis is put on controlling emotional outbursts. "Do your own time." "Play it cool." "Don't lose your head." "Don't bring heat" (punishment or close scrutiny of behavior).

3. Don't take advantage of other prisoners by force and fraud. "Don't exploit inmates." "Don't welsh on debts." "Be right."

4. Maintain integrity and dignity. "Don't weaken." "Don't whine." "Don't cop out (cry guilty)." Prescriptively put: "Be tough." "Be a man."

5. Don't respect prison officials or the world for which they stand. Guards are "hacks," "screws," or "hoosiers." "Don't be a sucker." "Be sharp."

This code is frequently broken, particularly by politicians and toughs. The inmate social system contains much noncohesive behavior.[61] Verbally enthusiastic supporters of the code sometimes deviate from it in practice, probably for the simple reason that it is highly profitable, if dangerous, to do so. Despite the code, inmates and prison officials are not in a constant state of conflict with each other. On the contrary, unwitting cooperation occurs at many points, for officials and elites share an interest in keeping the bulk of the inmates quiet and subdued.[62]

Strategies of Control

In a democracy, administration of a totalitarian organization is difficult. Humanitarian and treatment considerations limit the means available to prison administrators for keeping inmates quietly confined. For example, prisoners cannot all be kept in solitary confinement nor "abused" in other ways. Nevertheless, prison officials continue to be held responsible for orderly confinement of dangerous men. They must control, but the most efficient and simple means for doing so are denied them. One solution to this problem is to keep the inmates unorganized. To this end, there have been persistent efforts to substitute psychological solitary confinement for the physical solitary confinement characterizing the early Pennsylvania prisons. This practice permits in-

---

[59] Cf. Gresham M. Sykes and Sheldon L. Messinger, "The Inmate Social System," in Richard A. Cloward et al., *Theoretical Studies in Social Organization of the Prison* (New York: Social Science Research Council, 1960), p. 16.
[60] *Ibid.*, pp. 6–9.

[61] Gresham M. Sykes, "Men, Merchants, and Toughs: A Study of Reactions to Imprisonment," *Social Problems,* **4** (October, 1957), 130–38.
[62] Gresham M. Sykes, "The Corruption of Authority and Rehabilitation," *Social Forces,* **34** (March, 1956), 257–62.

mates to work together and to participate in other activities, but it minimizes the danger of escape or riot. Thus, to a large degree incentives such as parole, time off for good behavior, and privileges of various kinds are administered as rewards to inmates who heed the administrators' admonition to avoid alliances with other inmates.

A second kind of solution is to enlist unofficially the aid of some of the inmates. Because prisoners far outnumber staff members, it is nearly impossible to keep them psychologically isolated. But control is maximized if inmate elites develop and enforce norms and values that promote psychological isolation among the other inmates. Surprisingly, the inmate code and culture seem to do exactly this in spite of the code emphasis on inmate solidarity.

Inmate leaders operate so that the important administrative task of maintaining a quiet, secure institution is indirectly *supported* rather than subverted, and the code contains exact counterparts of the official admonitions. In the process of protecting their own positions of power, inmate leaders help protect the administrators' positions of power. For example, right guys, like prison officials, tell newcomers not to cause trouble by stealing from fellow-inmates, not to bring heat, and, generally, to "do your own time." Even the politicians and toughs have a vested interest in maintaining the status quo. They stress the notion that prisoners must not use official channels to gain advantage over other inmates, thus protecting their own positions of power from interference by officials, while at the same time keeping peace in the prison. Like administrators, they insist that all inmates are "equal." By equal they mean that "outside" criteria such as occupation or wealth shall not be used to determine prestige, power, or special privileges within the institution. If prestige and special privileges were awarded on the basis of extra-institutional criteria, the result would be chaotic dethroning of inmate elites. The inmate code operates to keep the bulk of the inmates unorganized and relatively powerless and, therefore, is valuable to prison officials.

To take a simple example of administrative-inmate alliances, a guard might allow an inmate to steal coffee from the kitchen in return for being co-operative, working hard, and exercising leadership that discourages violence, thus making the guard's job an easy one. The inmate then has a vested interest in his coffee-stealing privilege, and he is likely to discourage other inmates who would like to steal coffee and might cause strict control of coffee. In this way he makes the guard's job even easier, for now *he* guards the coffee, not in a literal sense, but by prohibiting other inmates from making inroads on his coffee-stealing privilege. Both the prison's coffee supply and the inmate's special coffee ration are protected by an inmate who steals while under the protection of a code that prohibits others from doing the same. As a leader, he exploits other inmates by stealing coffee allotted for their use, and he is permitted to do so by a guard who implicitly recognizes that such exploitation keeps the bulk of the inmates unorganized and under control.

SUMMARY

Parallel to the official system of the prison administration and interacting with it is an informal system of inmates. Three types of prisoners—the politicians, the toughs, and the right guys—exercise control over their fellow inmates. The first two types are motivated by overt self-interest and are manipulative or coercive in their strategies. The right guys gain the loyalty and support of other prisoners by their dedication to the welfare of inmates in general and by their opposition to the administration. The two systems of control, although nominally in conflict with each other, ordinarily operate to maintain stability and peace.

Section **8** **Collective behavior**

The characteristic phenomena of collective behavior may be observed both among criminals and among persons reacting to crime: (1) Unplanned panics and riots are relatively frequent in prisons, but some prison riots resemble organized industrial strikes. (2) Fads and fashions in crime and the spreading of strikes and riots from one prison to another have some of the characteristics of contagious behavior. (3) Public reactions to some spectacular and sensational crimes approach panic behavior. (4) The impersonal media of communication have long been considered important mechanisms in the diffusion of criminal attitudes, values, and techniques.

PRISON RIOTS

In the spring of 1952, 69 prisoners at the Trenton, New Jersey, State Prison seized four guards as hostages, barricaded themselves in the prison print shop, and said they would not surrender until a committee of citizens investigated the prison conditions. Within a week, 232 prisoners at the New Jersey Prison Farm in Rahway barricaded themselves in a dormitory with nine hostages and demanded changes in prison conditions; they smashed all the dormitory windows, tore up the plumbing and heating systems, and destroyed their own lockers. A few days later 176 inmates at the Southern Michigan Prison in Jackson seized eleven hostages, barricaded themselves in a cell block, and wrecked whatever was wreckable; prisoners in other sections of the prison armed themselves with makeshift weapons, wrecked the dining hall, set fire to the laundry, tore up the chapel, library, and gymnasium, and broke thousands of windows. Within a few months similar riots

occurred in Idaho, Illinois, Kentucky, Louisiana, Massachusetts, New Mexico, North Carolina, Ohio, and Utah. In addition, potentially serious disturbances were quelled in one prison in California, one in Oregon, and two in federal institutions.[63]

There were no attempts at mass escape, and each riot seemed to be a semiplanned strike or demonstration designed to call public attention to the conditions of prison life. The pattern was the same in all prisons: the prisoners seized hostages, barricaded themselves, destroyed property, issued demands, and engaged in bargaining with prison or political officials. The formal demands of the inmates were better food, better medical care, better recreational facilities, segregation of sex offenders, less rigid disciplinary practices, and more liberal parole practices. But some sociologists, prison officials, and even prisoners believe the demands and the bargaining process were only "second thoughts" of the prisoners. Three interpretations have been offered of the underlying causes of prison riots:

1. Riots are attributed to inmate politicians and toughs who have earlier demonstrated that they can and will keep the peace only if they are granted special favors, such as jobs that give them an opportunity to exploit fellow inmates and to obtain goods in short supply. If these men become dissatisfied with the officials' concessions, they withdraw their pretense of support and define themselves as champions of the "mistreated prisoners." This is the usual role of politicians and toughs during riots. "Most of the leaders of prison disturbances, up to the time they turned their violence against their

[63] Frank T. Flynn, "Behind the Prison Riots," *Social Service Review,* **37** (March, 1953), 73–86.

keepers, had engaged in repeated offenses against other inmates." [64]

2. The prison is seen as a "powder keg" that can be touched off by some precipitating event only when there is a shift in the semi-official government exercised by the inmates.[65] Efforts to tighten up prisons are thought to undermine control by real men or right guys, and to transfer leadership to the more aggressive toughs or gorillas, who seem intent on embarrassing the officials and, generally, giving the guards a "hard time," despite the ultimate hopelessness of their position.

3. Riots are traced to the changed social structure of prisons in the past generation.[66] Much of the power wielded informally by right guys and other inmate leaders during the 1930's was removed by prison "reform" designed to make prisons more humane and more rehabilitative. But the services that the leaders provided for the inmates and the services the administrators provided the leaders were lacking in the new organization. The riots, then, were counter-revolutions rather than revolutions, and took the form of strikes for return of inmate "rights."

FADS AND FASHIONS IN CRIME

Certain types and techniques of crime diffuse among criminals in much the same way that fashions in clothing, speech and other behavior patterns spread in the noncriminal population. A robber invents a mask or disguise which is publicized, and immediately other criminals adopt the same type of mask. A pickpocket secures three thousand dollars from a victim at a race track; other pickpockets flock to that race track. A bank robber slips a written note to a teller, rather than asking for the money, and within a short time bank robbers across the nation are using the same technique. Many criminals learn techniques from reading of the exploits of other criminals; others learn them through underworld gossip channels.

It should not be concluded, however, that the crime news presented in the newspapers has any discernible direct effect in changing noncriminals into criminals. A criminal who reads or hears of a clever technique may adopt it; on the other hand, a person whose values are essentially anticriminal will be likely to ignore the technique completely. The values themselves are not modified significantly by the news stories or gossip.

PANIC RESPONSES TO CRIME

Well-publicized sensational crimes sometimes throw the public into panics. In some instances, citizens become so frightened by a crime or a series of crimes that they will not leave their homes at night, and they take elaborate precautions to protect their homes and families from criminals. Laws may be precipitantly passed and later be found to be inconsistent, ineffective, or impossible to administer.

Enactment of sexual psychopath laws, for example, has followed panics stimulated by highly publicized sex offenses, particularly those against children. The following sequence has been observed: [67]

1. *A community is aroused* by a few serious sex crimes committed in quick succession and given nationwide publicity. Following three or four sexual attacks in Indianapolis in 1947, many householders bought guns and stood guard in their homes; the supply of locks and chains in the city's stores was exhausted. The emotional atmosphere

[64] Richard R. Korn and Lloyd W. McCorkle, *Criminology and Penology* (New York: Holt, 1959), p. 529. See also p. 480.

[65] Gresham M. Sykes, *The Society of Captives: A Study of a Maximum Security Prison* (Princeton: Princeton University Press, 1958), pp. 109–29.

[66] Maurice Floch and Frank E. Hartung, "A Social Psychological Analysis of Prison Riots: A Hypothesis," *Journal of Criminal Law and Criminology*, 47 (May-June, 1956), 51–57.

[67] Edwin H. Sutherland, "The Diffusion of Sexual Psychopath Laws," *American Journal of Sociology*, 56 (September, 1950), 142–48.

Caryl Chessman was executed in the gas chamber at San Quentin Prison, California, on May 2, 1960. A prolonged sequence of legal delays postponed the death penalty for almost twelve years. Because of the protracted legal maneuvering, world attention was drawn to the case, and he became a symbol of opposition to capital punishment. Ironically, the availability of due process made the legal system vulnerable to attack. Due process carried to an extreme was itself conceived as a punishment even though it was Chessman who pursued the series of court actions that delayed the execution.

is heightened by a protracted manhunt following the attack.

2. *The community responds in an agitated manner,* and diverse proposals are made. People in many walks of life see a need for control of the type of crime committed and a possibility that something can be done. In 1949 a radio announcer who said something should be done to stop sex crimes, such as one then being publicized in Los Angeles, received more than two hundred telegrams agreeing with him. Letters to editors demanded that sex offenders be castrated or whipped; the city council passed a resolution asking for more severe punishment of sex criminals; a woman publicly demanded that strip-tease shows be closed because they stimulated sex fiends; the state attorney general sent a bulletin to all law enforcement agencies urging enforcement of laws requiring registration of sex criminals; the superintendent of schools asked for unrelenting prosecution of sex offenders who loiter around schools; the Parent-Teacher Association held mass meetings and urged citizens to see that action was taken.

3. *A committee is appointed* to study the "facts" and make recommendations. The recommendations of the many citizens and agencies are sifted and studied, procedures in other states are reviewed, and a proposed bill for the legislature is drafted. The committee has the formal duty of following through with its proposals even after the public hysteria has subsided. The investigations are superficial, however, and the public sometimes becomes impatient if the committee works slowly and carefully. The "facts" studied consist of the information available in popular literature or discussion. The recommendations are, therefore, often based on false or questionable notions.

4. *The legislature enacts a law* based on the committee's recommendations. Very little discussion occurs in the legislatures. When the sexual psychopath law for the District of Columbia was presented in Congress, the only question asked was whether the bill would weaken or strengthen sex laws. Usually the laws are presented to the public as the most scientific and enlightened method of protecting society. However, the concept of the sexual psychopath is too vague for judicial or administrative use; therefore, the sexual psychopath laws are never used in some states and seldom used in others. Neither psychiatrists nor legal authorities have diagnostic instruments or precise criteria with which to decide if an accused person is a sexual psychopath.[68]

THE MASS MEDIA AND CRIME

Psychological, sociological, judicial, and literary authorities disagree over the effect of crime dramatization in newspapers, comic books, radio, motion pictures, and television. Generally, the mass media are charged with glorifying crime and spreading criminal techniques. Some authorities contend that the "blood and thunder" themes in comics and other mass media produce various criminal attitudes as well as emotional disturbances. These are the same charges which were directed against pulp magazines and dime novels in past years. For example, one psychiatrist has listed the following objections to comic books:

They often suggest criminal or sexually abnormal ideas; create a mental preparedness or readiness for temptation; suggest the forms a delinquent impulse may take; may act as the precipitating factor of delinquency or emotional disorder; may supply rationalizations for a contemplated act which is often more important than the impulse itself; set off chains of undesirable and harmful thinking in children; and create for young readers a mental atmosphere of deceit, trickery, and cruelty.[69]

[68] Edwin H. Sutherland, "The Sexual Psychopath Laws," *Journal of Criminal Law and Criminology*, **40** (January-February, 1950), 543–54.

[69] Marjorie Bell, "The N.P.P.A. at the Congress of Correction," *Focus*, **27** (November, 1948), p. 178, summarizing the remarks made by Fredric Wertham. See

However, objective studies do not indicate that reading comic books and viewing or hearing crime dramas *cause* delinquency and crime. Many nondelinquents read, hear, or see so-called harmful dramas and do not become delinquent. The process by which the harmful dramas may produce delinquency has not been shown. Some authorities believe that the dramatizations serve as useful outlets for children's pent-up hostilities. An aroused desire for easy money and luxury, or a spirit of bravado and adventurousness, could lead to increased activity in legitimate economic enterprise as well as to delinquency. Which course the listener, viewer, or reader takes probably depends largely upon his primary contacts and associations.[70] The mass media provide people with temporary philosophies of life, with ideas about their rights and privileges, and with fashions in dress, language, etiquette, and child rearing. Children impersonate fiction characters in play, and both children and adults imitate them in their everyday language and conduct. However, what persons perceive when they read stories, watch pictures or listen to the radio varies with socio-economic, ethnic, religious, and cultural background.[71] Many children play gangsters or robbers after seeing a gangster or crime show, but they also play gangsters or robbers after seeing a love-story or musical; and many adolescents make love after seeing gangster movies as well as after seeing pictures of romantic love-making. The techniques of crime which are presented are used by only a very few children, just as the criminal techniques known to the police are used by very few policemen. One study showed that children who reside in areas where delinquency rates are high are influenced more significantly by crime pictures and radio crime dramas than are those who reside in areas of low-delinquency rates.[72]

The mass communication media are relatively ineffective in changing attitudes and values, compared with the effectiveness of intimate, personal groups. Even when the communicator deliberately intends to modify people's attitudes, there is wide variation in responses. "Effects upon the audience do not follow directly from and in correspondence with the intent of the communicator and the content of the communication. The predispositions of the reader or listener are deeply involved in the situation, and may operate to block or modify the intended effect or even to set up a boomerang effect." [73]

Perhaps the major effect of crime dramatization and publicity is the creation and perpetuation of an attitude of indifference to ordinary criminal offenses among persons who are not the direct victims of them. Because little is said about the millions of consistently law-abiding citizens, the impression is created that crime is frequent and usual, and the reading, listening, or viewing public becomes indifferent even to the sensational, violent crimes which are dramatized, and even less concerned with ordinary offenses such as burglary and larceny. The dramatization of crime in the mass media appears to minimize public indignation when crimes are committed and perhaps to contribute

---

also Fredric Wertham, "The Comics . . . Very Funny," *Saturday Review of Literature,* May 29, 1948, pp. 6–7; Judith Crist, "Horror in the Nursery," *Collier's,* March 27, 1948, pp. 22 *ff.;* Fredric Wertham, "What Parents Don't Know About Comic Books," *Ladies Home Journal,* November, 1953, pp. 48 *ff.;* Fredric Wertham, *Seduction of the Innocent* (New York: Rinehart, 1954).

[70] Cf. Paul G. Cressey, "The Motion Picture Experience as Modified by Social Background and Personality," *American Sociological Review,* **3** (August, 1938), 516–25.

[71] Theodore M. Newcomb, *Social Psychology* (New York: Dryden, 1950), pp. 90–96. See also Eunice Cooper and Helen Dinerman, "Analysis of the Film 'Don't Be a Sucker': A Study in Communication," *Public Opinion Quarterly,* **15** (1951), 243–64.

[72] Ethel Shanas and C. E. Dunning, *Recreation and Delinquency* (Chicago: Chicago Recreation Commission, 1942). See also Howard Rowland, "Radio Crime Dramas," *Educational Research Bulletin,* **23** (November, 1944), 210–17.

[73] B. Berelson, "Communications and Public Opinion," in W. Schramm (ed.), *Communications in Modern Society* (Urbana: University of Illinois Press, 1948), pp. 168–85.

indirectly to high crime rates. A population for whom crime has become usual cannot present a consistent front against crime.

On the other hand, it has not been demonstrated that exposure through the mass media to the constant dramatization of crime is effective in changing individuals from noncriminal to criminal.

Section 9 **Population and ecology**

SEX RATIOS IN CRIME[74]

Compared with females, males have a great excess of crimes in all nations, all communities within nations, all age groups, all periods of history for which we have statistics, and all types of crime except those related to the female sex, such as abortion. In the United States, males are arrested approximately ten times as frequently as females, and they are committed to prisons and reformatories approximately twenty times as frequently as females. Of the cases coming before juvenile courts, about 85 per cent are boys. The official statistics are probably biased in favor of females, but even if correction could be made for the statistical bias, the criminal sex ratio probably would be well over 600 or 700.

The sex ratio for apprehended criminals varies with place, time, and age, however. One study indicated a sex ratio of 350 for Belgium compared with a ratio of approximately 3000 in Algiers and Tunis. It was concluded that the criminal sex ratios are highest in countries where females are rigidly supervised, and lowest in the countries in which females have the greatest freedom and the closest approximation to equality with males.[75] The sex ratio is lower in American cities than in small towns, probably reflecting the differences in the amount of freedom permitted in the two types of communities. In large cities, the sex ratio is lowest in the areas of high delinquency and crime rates and highest in the low-delinquency areas. There is some evidence that the sex ratio has been decreasing in the last few centuries and especially in the last fifty years, as women have acquired statuses more nearly equal to those of men. Finally, the sex ratios in crime vary with age. English statistics for 1940 indicated that the sex ratio was highest at age 8–10 and steadily decreased until about age 40, with little change thereafter. However, in the United States an opposite trend was apparent: at age 15–17 the sex ratio in commitments to prison is about 1500, while at age 60–64 it is about 2500.

The sex ratio indicates the difficulty of relying on "factors" which traditionally have been considered the causes of crime. For example, among boys and girls who live in the same homes, in equal poverty, in the same neighborhoods, which are equally lacking in recreational facilities, and with the same alcoholic or ignorant parents, the boys are much more frequently delinquent than are the girls. The significant difference is that girls are supervised more closely than boys and behavior consistent with legal codes is taught to girls with more consistency and care than to boys.[76]

[74] For a general discussion of sex ratios see POPULATION AND ECOLOGY, pp. 314–16.
[75] E. Hacker, *Kriminalstatistische und Kriminalaetiologische Berichte* (Miskolc: Ludwig, 1949).

[76] See Jackson Toby, "The Differential Impact of Family Disorganization," *American Sociological Review,* **22** (October, 1957), 505–12.

AGE RATIOS IN CRIME

Age appears to be closely related, directly or indirectly, to the frequency and type of crime committed. Since the statistics on the incidence of crime among various age groups are ordinarily in the form of arrests or convictions, they probably tend to exaggerate the crime rates of young adults. Children are less likely than adults to be arrested for the same offenses, and older criminals commit crimes which are less likely to be detected than those committed by young adults. Older persons have acquired prestige which can be used to avoid arrests.

After this bias is taken into account, the statistics seem to justify the following six conclusions:

1. The crime rate is highest during or shortly before adolescence. English statistics show that the age of maximum criminality is about age 12 or 13 for males and 15 or 16 for females. FBI statistics place the maximum age somewhat higher—between 18 and 24—but the English statistics probably report youthful criminality more completely than do the U.S. figures.

2. The age of maximum criminality varies with the type of crime. Among American males, the age group 15–19 has the highest official rate for automobile theft; the age group 20–24 has the highest rate for robbery, forgery, and rape; the age group 35–39 has the highest rate for gambling and violation of narcotic drug laws.

3. The age of maximum general criminality and the age of maximum criminality for most specific offenses is higher for females than for males. For example, females aged 20–24 have the highest rate for automobile theft, as well as for robbery and forgery.

4. The concentration of certain crimes, such as burglary and robbery, in the young-adult age group has been observed for several centuries. English statistics indicate that burglars and robbers of the fifteenth and sixteenth centuries were approximately the same age as the contemporary burglar and robber.

5. The crime rate, for both males and females, decreases from the age of maximum criminality to the end of life. For example, in the United States the official arrest rate of males decreases after the peak at about age 20, and the rate of females decreases after about age 23. This phenomenon has been observed in many nations.

6. The age of first delinquency and the type of crime typically committed at various ages varies from area to area. In cities, the age of first criminality is lower in areas of high delinquency than in areas with low-delinquency rates; boys aged 10–12 commit robberies in some areas of large cities while boys of the same age in less delinquent areas commit only petty thefts.

One popular notion attributes the variations in age ratios to changes in biological traits such as physical strength and vigor: crimes are committed frequently by persons who are strong and active and infrequently by persons who are weak and passive. Another biological theory attributes the variations to hereditary differences: persons strongly predisposed by heredity to crime commit crime at a very young age, while persons with a weaker tendency delay longer. However, the many variations in the age ratios are not adequately accounted for by such biological theories. Indeed, the theories do not explain even one of the facts outlined above when the full ramifications are explored. For example, the fact that age group 20–24 has the highest rate for forgery and age group 15–19 the highest rate for automobile theft in the United States cannot be attributed to differences in physical strength or heredity. On the other hand, all of the facts are consistent with the theory that crime is a product of social experiences and social organization.

REGIONAL DISTRIBUTION OF CRIMES

Crimes are not distributed evenly over a nation or city but are concentrated in cer-

Table **XIV:2**   Urban Crime Rates, 1961, by Geographic Divisions*
(Offenses known to the police per 100,000 inhabitants)

Division	Criminal Homicide	Forcible Rape	Robbery	Aggravated Assault	Burglary	Larceny $50 and Over[a]	Auto Theft
United States	4.7	8.8	50.1	72.7	466.0	272.3	178.3
New England	1.3	4.5	14.4	20.1	360.5	211.7	198.9
Middle Atlantic	3.0	6.5	38.2	63.6	361.6	282.6	163.8
East North Central	3.7	9.7	87.0	71.1	467.8	274.4	200.1
West North Central	2.5	6.4	36.6	27.9	382.2	203.5	119.2
South Atlantic	8.2	8.1	38.0	114.6	441.3	231.4	141.3
East South Central	9.4	6.3	25.9	73.1	357.9	172.8	100.0
West South Central	7.4	9.4	33.1	86.4	489.5	223.6	150.5
Mountain	4.4	10.5	56.6	46.7	546.7	365.6	250.3
Pacific[b]	3.4	15.5	74.9	94.0	784.0	443.4	283.4

* Source: United States Department of Justice, Federal Bureau of Investigation, *Uniform Crime Reports—1961*, pp. 34–37.
[a] Except auto theft.
[b] Includes Alaska and Hawaii.

tain areas. For example, the frequency of specific crimes varies in different regions of the United States, as Table XIV: 2 indicates, and in different states, as shown in Table XIV: 3. In analyzing regional crime rates, Lottier located the highest incidence of murder in the Southeastern states and found that the murder rate decreased as the distance from this center increased. Robbery was found to be concentrated on an axis running from Tennessee to Colorado, and the robbery rate decreased as the distance on either side of the axis increased. A contemporary analysis would not reveal such clear geographical trends, but interstate and interregional differences remain high.

In Lottier's statistics such crimes against property as burglary and larceny were not so definitely concentrated by regions, and Lottier attributed this to variations in the value of property in the various states. Crime rates are computed as percentages of the total population rather than as percentages of the total property values in the var-

Table **XIV:3**   High and Low Crime Rates, 1961, by States*
(Offenses known to the police per 100,000 inhabitants)

Crime	Low State	Rate	High State	Rate
Criminal homicide	South Dakota	.9	Alabama	12.9
Forcible rape	Rhode Island	1.7	California	18.5
Robbery	New Hampshire	3.4	Illinois	204.5
Aggravated assault	Vermont	5.3	North Carolina	167.4
Burglary	North Dakota	200.9	Nevada	911.0
Larceny $50 and over[a]	West Virginia	88.9	Nevada	616.1
Auto theft	Arkansas	55.3	Nevada	473.6

* Source: United States Department of Justice, Federal Bureau of Investigation, *Uniform Crime Reports—1961*, pp. 34–37.
[a] Except auto theft.

ious states.[77] Consequently, it is not certain that a high larceny or burglary rate indicates a concentration of the crime. It may indicate a concentration of property. Regional variations are attributed by Reckless to differences in traditions of orderliness and community organization.[78]

Distribution of Crime in Cities

Most crimes are concentrated in cities. The percentage of chain stores burglarized or robbed decreased regularly from the center of Chicago toward the city limits, and the decrease continued regularly for 125 miles beyond the city limits except in one zone where the rate increased slightly because of a medium-sized city.[79]

Robbery rates and the rates of crimes against property tend to increase with the size of the community. In some cases, however, the rates in cities over 250,000 are less than in cities of 100,000 to 250,000. Rape and murder are relatively more frequent in small towns of less than 10,000 than in communities from 10,000 to 25,000. Federal Bureau of Investigation data indicate that, since about 1945, the rural crime rate in the United States has been increasing more rapidly than the urban rate. As transportation and communication between urban and rural areas develop, the differences between the crime rates of the two areas may be expected to decrease.

DELINQUENCY AREAS

In a series of studies of the distribution of delinquency in large American cities, Shaw and McKay found that the rates were usually highest in the low-rent areas near the center of the city and decreased with distance from the center. Areas which had high rates in 1900 tend to maintain high rates, although the ethnic groups living in the areas

have changed. The delinquency areas are characterized by physical deterioration, proximity to commerce and industry, high proportions of populations on relief, absence of home owners, and high concentration of foreign-born and Negro populations. These findings are interpreted as follows:

From the data available it appears that local variations in the conduct of children, as revealed in differential rates of delinquents, reflect the differences in social values, norms, and attitudes to which the children are exposed. In some parts of the city, attitudes which support and sanction delinquency are, it seems, sufficiently extensive and dynamic to become the controlling forces in the development of delinquent careers among a relatively large number of boys and young men. These are the low-income areas, where delinquency has developed in the form of a social tradition, inseparable from the life of the local community.[80]

Delinquency area studies have been criticized on the ground that the official statistics of arrests and court appearances, used to measure the amount of delinquency in an area, are probably biased because of the poverty of the persons living in deteriorated areas. However, even when allowance is made for bias of this kind, there seems to be an excess of delinquency and ordinary crime. In the District of Columbia the juvenile court statistics showed *less* concentration in the deteriorated areas than did the unofficial statistics of welfare agencies.[81] The concentration, then, cannot be attributed entirely to bias against poor persons in official procedures.

Even areas of highest delinquency contain many nondelinquent persons. In one study of a high-delinquency area less than half the boys could be identified as delin-

[77] Stuart Lottier, "Distribution of Criminal Offenses in Sectional Regions," *Journal of Criminal Law and Criminology,* **29** (September, 1938), 329–44.

[78] Reckless, *op. cit.,* p. 93.

[79] Sutherland and Cressey, *op. cit.,* pp. 48, 155–56.

[80] Shaw and McKay, *Juvenile Delinquency and Urban Areas* (Chicago: University of Chicago Press, 1942), pp. 435–36. For a summary of research on delinquency areas, see Terrence Morris, *The Criminal Area* (London: Kegan Paul, 1958).

[81] Edward A. Schwartz, "A Community Experiment in the Measurement of Juvenile Delinquency," *National Probation Association Yearbook,* 1945, pp. 3–27.

quent.[82] One explanation is the limitation on contact with delinquent values, even in the most delinquent areas.[83] Delinquency may be concentrated on certain streets, and children living on other streets may associate with each other in relative isolation from the delinquent culture. Some children are kept from intimate association with delinquents because of their unaggressive dispositions and others by careful parental supervision. Generally the rate of female delinquency in such areas is much lower than the male rate, although the wealth of parents, housing conditions, and many other external conditions are the same for girls and boys.

[82] Sutherland and Cressey, *op. cit.*, p. 162.
[83] Kobrin, *op. cit.*

PART THREE

Master Trends

Chapter XV

Urban man

Section 1 The city in place and time

The concentration of population in villages began during the Neolithic Age, perhaps 8,000 years ago. These first stable communities were village-farming settlements of a few hundred people. Some of them grew substantially larger with improvements in agriculture in a friendly environment, but they cannot be called cities because they were composed largely of full-time farmers. Population size and a surplus of food are necessary, but not sufficient, conditions for urban life. Even in the modern period there are in Africa and Asia concentrations of several thousand individuals that are not true cities but rather settlements of farmers, almost all of whom regularly till their fields.

THE ORIGIN OF CITIES

Early cities were not merely great villages, dormitories for farm families, but were set off from the countryside and somewhat detached from the soil and the preoccupations of agricultural production. Somehow in several different places at different times a major break was made with the past, and the break led to changes whose details and sequence can only be guessed. The following are some of the modifications in the social

order and man's relation to the environment that were involved in the development of the first cities:

1. An increase in occupational specialization

2. The release of a few individuals from all immediately productive work and their elevation to a priesthood

3. The transformation of religious activities related to fertility, rainfall, and the streams into the administration of the water supply (the irrigation system) and the management of land and herds

4. The emergence of a political leadership and a management of the labor force

5. Differential rewards for different tasks

6. Assignment of part of the work force to ensure the continuity of the food supply and to secure the city against attack

7. A market for exchange of goods

Although it is impossible to say in what order these steps were taken, the interaction of one upon the other can be imagined. The result, although vague in knowledge of detail, is clear in principle: an ever-growing complexity and variety in human tasks, an ascendant spiral of specialization, the freeing of a few and then many men from day-to-day subsistence tasks. Some of these beginnings of urban life are outlined in an interpretation of archaeological findings in Mesopotamia in Adaptation 39, pages 591 ff.

The earliest cities in the fertile valleys of the Tigris-Euphrates, the Indus, and the Nile were followed by the growth of the Mediterranean city-states. By 600 or 500 B.C. a few Greek cities were sending colonies throughout the Mediterranean, but most of the Greek cities remained relatively small, closely integrated with the countryside, and dependent on it for food and building materials. Because the Greek terrain had a limited amount of arable land, even Athens of 400 B.C. probably did not exceed 100,000.[1]

The great Mediterranean seaports of the Ancient World were centers of government and religion as well as trade, and their growth and decline were tied to the fortunes of political and commercial empires. It is commonly agreed that Rome was the largest city of ancient times, but its exact population, like that of other early cities, is a subject of conjecture. The Roman census reported an increase from 900,000 in 69 B.C. to more than 4,000,000 in 28 B.C., but it is hardly likely that Rome increased four-and-a-half times in forty years. The statistical change may have been due to a number of causes: some increase in population, the inclusion of elements of the population not previously counted (women or children) or a rapid extension of citizenship, or counting some population that did not actually reside in the city.[2] In any case the populations of early cities probably fluctuated rather widely, and estimates of their size are based on unreliable data.

As the empires of the ancient world declined, the cities also declined. By the middle of the fourth century A.D. Rome may have had a population of less than 200,000, and by the sixteenth century only 55,000.[3] The latter figure, however, is not a low point, because Rome of Medieval times, like other Medieval cities, had begun to respond to the growth of the market and the renewal of trade and travel.[4]

The Prevalence of Cities

The development of cities in modern times is an outgrowth of an increase in agricultural productivity (which made possible surplus to support an urban population), centralization of work in machine-powered factories, and increases in population. The growth of cities has not been a smooth accumulation. Many cities have declined or disappeared, but urban life is now the characteristic form of human settlement in Europe, Australia, and North America. It is also the emergent form for most of the rest of the world.

Table XV:1 shows the distribution of large cities (over 100,000) in the major world regions. Outside of Europe and North America, the largest cities tend to be located in coastal areas.[5] The preponderantly coastal location of the major Asian and African cities is indicative of their history and function. In large part they are the outgrowth of commercial and imperial relations with the West. They are administrative centers for government and commerce, and entrepôt (transshipment) centers for handling raw materials and redistributing finished goods. Some are "preindustrial" in the sense that they are at an early stage of the industrial revolution. However, even the least industrialized have handicraft industries, organize the industry of smaller cities and villages, and are the chief locations of more advanced industrial activity in their respective countries. Through the

---

[1] Lewis Mumford, *The City in History* (New York: Harcourt, Brace, 1961), pp. 130–31 *et passim.*

[2] Cf. William Petersen, *Population* (New York: Macmillan, 1961), pp. 346–47 *et passim.*

[3] Petersen, *op. cit.*, p. 351.

[4] Henri Pirenne, *Medieval Cities: Their Origin and the Revival of Trade* (Princeton: Princeton University Press, 1925).

[5] Paul K. Hatt and Albert J. Reiss, Jr. (eds.), *Reader in Urban Sociology* (Glencoe: The Free Press, 1951), p. 147.

Table **XV:1**   Cities Over 100,000 Population in Major World Regions, 1950*

Region	1,000,000 and over	500,000 to 1,000,000	250,000 to 500,000	100,000 to 250,000	Total Cities
Africa	1	3	6	27	37
Asia[a]	20	22	43	178	263
Europe	14	28	46	187	275
U.S.S.R. (1939 figures)	2	9	20	58	89
North America	7	15	27	91	140
Oceania	2	—	3	5	10
South America	3	4	11	26	44
Total	49	81	156	572	858

* Suggested by Noel P. Gist and L. A. Halbert, *Urban Society* (3rd ed.; New York: Crowell, 1948), p. 21. Source: United Nations Demographic Yearbook, 1952, Table 8, pp. 202-14. Later data are available for some world regions, but for reasons of comparability figures for the 1950 period are used.

[a] Excludes U.S.S.R.; includes Near East.   China's list of cities was incomplete and based upon estimates.

spread of communication and trade with coastal cities and stimulated by growing nationalism, the internal regions of Asia and Africa are being drawn into the urban world. Man is becoming urban man.

THE ASIAN CITY[6]

The Asian cities in the forefront of change are the product of the interplay between East and West: political, industrial, and commercial interests from the West and manpower, raw materials, handicrafts, and trade interests of the East. Djakarta, Saigon, Manila, Hong Kong and other Asian centers are highly cosmopolitan with a background of colonial administration, organized by Europeans in the eighteenth and nineteenth centuries to tap the resources of the countryside and extend European economic and political control. Around the busy ports, systems of river, canal, and land transport developed, and these new networks of communication created national unity where none may have existed before. The commercial center was also the colonial administrative center, and the colonial capital was retained as the capital of the new coun-

try when the colonial authority withdrew.

In architecture, land use, and life-style, the cities reflect their dual origins. In the commercial quarters of Djakarta, Manila, and Hong Kong are the same kinds of streets, banks, stores, hotels, and office buildings that are found in Holland, the United States, or England. The residential suburbs of the commercial and governmental administrators are also modern and Western. But among the office buildings are small retail shops, many of them run by Chinese or Indians, and scattered through the back alleys are small factories, stalls of marginal enterprise, and itinerant peddlers who have no permanent location. A few steps from the prosperous commercial streets and the European-type residential districts is the Asian slum, a warren teeming with thousands of people, many of them homeless newcomers, who live out their lives on the streets, eating and sleeping on the sidewalks and footpaths.

The administrators of Asian countries are preoccupied with agricultural efficiency, new industry, and education, and have little energy or money left over for the underprivileged urban dwellers. Some countries hope to reverse the trend of urban migration and return some of the population to the country. But this plan runs counter to the world-wide

[6] This discussion is indebted to "The Asian City," The University of Sydney, *Current Affairs Bulletin*, Vol. 19, No. 5 (December 24, 1956). The urban centers of Japan and Communist China are not considered here.

urban trend and does not take into account the magnetic power of the city even in its least attractive form. Nor does the agricultural land shortage leave a choice for many displaced peasants.

Further migration seems inevitable, but Asian cities do not absorb newcomers as faceless, homogenous units. Hong Kong,[7] an extreme example of a commercial city, has elaborate networks of social organization, many of which have ties with mainland China through mechanisms that operated in traditional Chinese cities. Common kinship, common village or regional origin, common occupation, religion, and membership in associations (e.g., the secret societies, now outlawed in Communist China) continue to act as bonds with the homeland. Even the most unfortunate immigrant need not be cast into a situation of total anomie, for there are anti-Communist organizations, Chinese and foreign, ready to extend a welcoming hand. The typical immigrant usually finds a niche somewhere in the web of social relationships where he is protected until he can find productive employment and repay the obligation to the organization.

URBAN AND RURAL

Although almost everyone agrees that some areas and their residents are rural and that others are urban, many localities fall between the obviously urban and the obviously rural. How these localities and their populations are to be classified is important when trends in urbanization are traced or international comparisons are made.

The most commonly used distinctions are population density and size. The city is a locality in which a large number of people live and work in close proximity. The rural area, by contrast, has low population density or only a small number of people in a dense cluster. Sociologists frequently add a third criterion—heterogeneity of the population in age, sex, and occupation. This criterion excludes from the term "city" such settlements as peasant villages, mining camps, prisons, and many military installations.

The Ecological City

Having selected population density and size as criteria, one must decide at what points to draw the line between city and noncity. First, a method of delimiting the geographic area must be decided upon. Is the area to be circumscribed by administrative boundaries or by bands of countryside with lower population density? If by the latter, how wide must the separating bands be? Once this is decided, the problem remains of setting a minimum population size that is sensible even though it must be somewhat arbitrary. The following criteria are widely used by urban sociologists: (1) The *ecological* or *natural* city has a density of population great enough so that most of its land area is devoted to residential, commercial, and industrial use (including transportation). (2) It is separated from other cities by space (either land or water) devoted largely to agricultural or extractive uses or to no use at all. (3) This separating space must be broad enough to make daily commuting across it impractical for most workers. The ecological city includes the central *legal* city (which is under a municipal government), all of its contiguous suburbs, and detached satellite settlements, which are socially and economically integrated with the central city. The U.S. census unit called the "urbanized area" is roughly equal to the ecological city, which is usually larger, but sometimes smaller, than the legal city. The larger ecological cities in the United States contain several legal cities. For instance, the ecological city of Greater Chicago includes the legal cities of Evanston, Glencoe, Skokie, Cicero, Harvey, and Park Forest, to name but a few. The ecological city of New York includes Jersey City, Newark, Yonkers, and many other separately incorporated municipalities outside the limits of the legal city

[7] Based on an unpublished paper by Franz Schurmann, with permission of the author.

The great coastal cities of Asia were administrative and commercial centers of the colonial era. Above, the Raffles Hotel in Singapore, a focus of European social life in British Malaya. Below, a market in Bangkok.

and even outside the state of New York. The populations of many ecological cities now are more than double the populations of their central legal cities.

Since legal cities are often separated from one another by only an invisible boundary—the middle of a street, a river, a bay, or a short span of open countryside—the ecological city is a more meaningful sociological unit. Therefore, when available, data for the ecological city are usually employed in sociological research. The use of data for the legal city rather than for the ecological city can often be misleading. For instance, newspaper and magazine articles played up the fact that most of the largest American cities lost population between 1950 and 1960. From this one might conclude that New York, Chicago, and Philadelphia are economically decadent and that large numbers of people are moving away from them and their environs, but this is not the case. All of the largest ecological cities gained population during the decade. The population decline was in their central cities and was largely a consequence of decentralization of metropolitan areas. In part it resulted from the *expansion* of population and economic activities in the ecological cities. This expansion displaced residences from the central cities by making it necessary to use more space for transportation, parking facilities, and commercial activities.

The minimum population size for a city is placed at 2,500 by the U.S. Bureau of the Census, but a somewhat lower minimum is more meaningful in the United States, since several demographic and economic variables, such as the sex ratio, change abruptly below 1,000 population.[8] In some countries where farmers cluster in villages rather than living on isolated homesteads, a population of 10,-000 is an appropriate breaking point between rural and urban.[9] Such agricultural villages are essentially rural in their social, cultural, and economic characteristics even though their populations often considerably exceed 2,500.

International Comparisons

Since somewhat different criteria between urban and rural may be appropriate in various countries, the fact that the official definitions differ need not make comparative research impossible. However, it is unduly optimistic to assume that the most sociologically useful definition is in fact used by each country. Some countries use ecological cities as the basic urban units, others use legal cities, and, least satisfactorily, others use minor civil divisions that together comprise the entire area of the country. The latter is tantamount to considering all counties in the United States with 2,500 people or more as urban areas. Fortunately, however, few countries determine the percentage of their population urban by minor civil divisions, and most of these also use some other distinction between urban and rural. The cutting point between the city and the noncity on the scale of population size varies from 300 to 20,000. Nevertheless, Gibbs and Davis conclude that the official data on percentage urban based upon whatever criteria the particular government uses are fairly good indicators of the degree of urbanization of societies.[10] They base this conclusion on the fact that percentage urban as officially reported correlates highly with a better index of urbanization—the percentage of the population in ecological cities with 100,000 or more people. Since the latter index is not usually available in official reports and can be computed only with difficulty, Gibbs and Davis recommend that the reported urban percentages (which can generally be found in published sources) be used, although with caution, for comparative re-

[8] Otis Dudley Duncan, "Community Size and the Rural-Urban Continuum," in Paul K. Hatt and Albert J. Reiss, Jr. (eds.), *Cities and Society* (Glencoe: The Free Press, 1957), pp. 35–45.

[9] Jack P. Gibbs and Kingsley Davis, "Conventional Versus Metropolitan Data in the International Study of Urbanization," *American Sociological Review*, **23** (October, 1958), 504–14.

[10] *Ibid.*

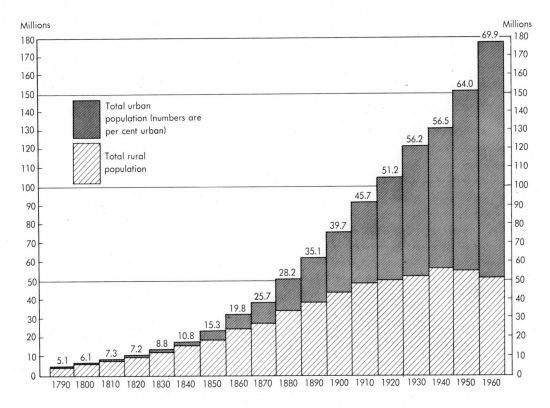

Fig. XV:1 Growth of Rural and Urban Population, United
States (Conterminous): 1790–1960

Source: *Statistical Abstract of the United States: 1960*, p. 21, and *Census of Population: 1960*, PC(1)-1A, Table 3. Figures for 1950 and 1960 are "new" definition of urban.

search. Both of these indexes of urbanization for 40 countries are given in Table XV: 2. The selected list of countries covers the full range from the United Kingdom—the most urbanized by both measures—to Thailand, Pakistan, and Haiti—the least urban. The high position of Australia on the list may be surprising because the over-all density of the country is low. In fact Australia is an extreme case of concentration, a dominant trend in the growth of urbanized societies. Argentina and Canada are other examples of high urban concentrations and low over-all densities.

By any measure the United States is one of the most highly urbanized nations in the world. Figure XV: 1 shows the growth of the population of the United States since 1790

and its change from a rural country that would have fallen near the bottom of the list in Table XV: 2. In 1960 the urban population of conterminous United States had grown to 69.9 per cent of the total.

The Rural-Urban Continuum

Many sociologists feel that a simple rural-urban dichotomy of communities and populations is inadequate. Obviously, the community of 5,000 people and the great metropolis of 5,000,000 are very different in many respects, yet their residents are indiscriminately lumped together as parts of the urban population. Perhaps communities ought to be classified not as urban *or* rural, but rather along a continuum from rural to urban.

Table **XV:2** Percentage of Population Urban and in Metropolitan Areas with 100,000 or More People, Circa 1950

Country (In Order of Per Cent Urban)	Percentage Urban	Percentage in M.A.'s with 100,000 or More *
United Kingdom	80.3	71.5
West Germany	72.4	49.3
Israel	71.3	55.8
Australia	68.9	55.4
East Germany	67.6	37.7
Denmark	67.3	37.3
United States	64.0	55.9
Belgium	62.7	41.4
Argentina	62.5	44.6
Canada	61.6	42.7
New Zealand	61.3	43.6
Cuba	57.0	26.1
France	55.9	34.7
Netherlands	54.6	45.5
Sweden	47.5	22.4
Union of South Africa	42.6	29.9
Mexico	42.6	20.6
Ireland	41.5	27.5
Italy	40.9	25.3
Japan	37.5	36.6
Spain	37.0	25.5
Switzerland	36.5	28.9
Brazil	36.2	17.5
Peru	36.1	11.0
Nicaragua	34.9	13.3
Iraq	33.8	12.2
Costa Rica	33.5	19.9
Finland	32.3	17.0
Norway	32.2	21.8
Portugal	31.2	19.6
Honduras	31.0	7.3
Egypt	30.1	19.6
Guatemala	25.0	10.5
Philippines	24.1	10.3
Turkey	21.9	9.5
India	17.3	7.8
Ceylon	15.4	9.5
Haiti	12.2	6.0
Pakistan	11.4	5.1
Thailand	9.9	6.8

Data selected from Jack P. Gibbs and Kingsley Davis, "Conventional Versus Metropolitan Data in the International Study of Urbanization," *American Sociological Review*, 23 (October, 1958) , 506–7. The original article lists 54 countries grouped according to their official definitions of urban.

* Based on revised figures kindly supplied by the authors of the original article.

It is apparent that communities form a continuum in population size, but instead of placing a cutting point on this continuum, it may be realistic to consider the largest communities more urban than the intermediate ones and the intermediate ones more urban than the smallest ones. However, students of the city sometimes judge that one community is "more urban" than another of the *same* population size. In order to take into account such differences, the proponents of the rural-urban continuum have added other defining criteria for urban and rural to the two basic ones of population density and size. These additional criteria, fertility and employment of women, for example, are social, cultural, economic, or demographic characteristics that are believed to be associated with high population density and size (in the case of the urban criteria) and with low population density and size (in the case of the rural criteria). With these criteria added, one can assert that community A with 20,000 people is more urban than community B with 20,000 people without violating the definition of urban.

The concept of the rural-urban continuum is useful to create awareness that cities possess urban characteristics in differing degrees.[11]

Metropolitan Dominance

The city does not stop at its municipal boundaries but ". . . extends as far as [it] exerts a dominant influence."[12] Ecologically the central city is the organizing core that dominates the rest of the metropolitan community and integrates it with other regions. Smaller centers within the metropolitan region are incomplete and are dependent on the main center. "The metropolitan community, therefore, comprises a cluster or constellation of centers. Smaller cities and towns tend to group themselves around larger ones somewhat as planets group themselves around a sun."[13]

The influence of a city diminishes with distance from the center, and the extent of its influence is related to its size. Cities may be conceived of as competing with each other for influence over the hinterland. In his study of metropolitan dominance, McKenzie measured metropolitan influence in several ways, for instance in the buying practices of merchants, in banking procedures, and by newspaper circulation. Comparing the circulation of papers from one city with that of other cities and with the circulation of local papers, he showed how competition between metropolitan areas is worked out and how spheres of urban influence are defined.

Unlike Great Britain, where the Manchester *Guardian* and the London *Times,* for example, have nationwide distribution, the United States has not had a national press. Because of distances, distribution costs, and time lags, competing metropolitan papers tend to be from the same or neighboring centers, the Los Angeles *Times* and the San Francisco *Chronicle,* for instance. In October, 1962, the New York *Times* began publication of a western edition, and a new phase of metropolitan competition was initiated.[14] Thus in the additional sphere of daily newspapers the metropolis of New York, nationally dominant in finance and commerce, invaded the regionally dominant centers of Los Angeles and San Francisco.

The City and the Countryside

Cities differ in the ways they are related to their countryside and the extent to which rural forms survive in the city. In climates where several crops can be produced in a year, intensive truck gardening may be carried on in the urban area. Productivity may

---

[11] For discussion and critique of the concept of the rural-urban continuum, see Duncan, *loc. cit.,* and Horace Miner, "The Folk-Urban Continuum," *American Sociological Review,* **17** (October, 1952), 529–37.

[12] R. D. McKenzie, *The Metropolitan Community* (New York: McGraw-Hill, 1933), p. 70.

[13] *Ibid.,* p. 71.

[14] The techniques of national publication and distribution were pioneered by the specialized paper, The Wall Street *Journal,* which publishes simultaneously in several metropolitan centers.

Langres (France) is close to its countryside. The city wall and a scene from the city wall.

be high enough to pay the large land rent and give the urban farmer a fair return for his work. Until recently Los Angeles was such an agricultural center, and some commercial truck gardening and fruit raising are still done.

In countries where distribution systems for foodstuffs are not highly organized, city dwellers interact closely with the countryside. Some products are sold at markets where housewives or servants bargain with farmers. Other products are sold by vendors who encompass the whole system of production and distribution from the planting of the seed to the selling of the fruit at the door of the consumer. This pattern was once common even in technologically advanced countries, but now the farmer-vendor is disappearing from the large cities, and a touch of the country has gone from the city streets. The rationalized distribution systems and the growth of cities have made this kind of vending spatially difficult and economically unsound. The change has been hastened by bureaucratization, an authentically urban influence. City and state bureaus hedge the distribution system with licenses and regulations. Small, marginal vendors find it too costly or difficult to meet these requirements and are often pushed out of business.

SOURCES AND READINGS

Nels Anderson, *The Urban Community* (New York: Holt, 1959).

Fortune (eds.), *The Exploding Metropolis* (New York: Doubleday, 1958).

Jack P. Gibbs, *Urban Research Methods* (Princeton: Van Nostrand, 1961).

Noel P. Gist and L. A. Halbert, *Urban Society* (4th ed.; New York: Crowell, 1956).

Paul K. Hatt and Albert J. Reiss, Jr. (eds.), *Cities in Society: Revised Reader in Urban Sociology* (Glencoe: The Free Press, 1957). For bibliography, see pp. 827–52.

Lewis Mumford, *The City in History* (New York: Harcourt, Brace, 1961).

Lewis Mumford, *The Culture of Cities* (New York: Harcourt, Brace, 1938).

Robert E. Park, *Human Communities* (Glencoe: The Free Press, 1952).

Stuart A. Queen and David B. Carpenter, *The American City* (New York: McGraw-Hill, 1953).

Eshref Shevky and Marilyn Williams, *The Social Areas of Los Angeles* (Berkeley and Los Angeles: University of California Press, 1949).

T. Lynn Smith and C. A. McMahan (eds.), *The Sociology of Urban Life* (New York: Dryden, 1951). For bibliography, see pp. 806–20.

See pp. 611–12 for bibliography on the Chicago studies.

The Origin of Cities

Abridged and adapted from Robert M. Adams, "The Origin of Cities," *Scientific American*, **203** (September, 1960), pp. 153–68. Used in this form with permission of author and publisher.

The rise of cities was pre-eminently a social process, an expression more of changes in man's interaction with his fellows than in his interaction with his environment. For this reason it marks not only a turning but also a branching point in the history of the human species.

Earlier achievements are closely identified with an increasing breadth or intensity in the exploitation of the environment. Their distinguishing features are new tools and techniques and the discovery of new and more dependable resources for subsistence. Even in so advanced an achievement as the invention of agriculture, much of the variation from region to region was simply a reflection of local differences in subsistence potential.

In contrast the urban revolution was a decisive cultural and social change that was less directly linked to changes in the exploitation of the environment. To be sure, it rested ultimately on food surpluses obtained by agricultural producers above their own requirements and somehow made available to city dwellers engaged in other activities. But its essential element was a whole series of new institutions and the vastly greater size and complexity of the social unit, rather than basic innovations in subsistence. In short, the different forms that early urban societies assumed are essentially the products of differently interacting political and economic—human— forces. And the interpretive skills required to understand them are correspondingly rooted more in the social sciences and humanities than in the natural sciences.

Precursors

Knowledge about the oldest civilization and the earliest cities, those of ancient Mesopotamia, rests primarily on archaeological data. By 5500 B.C., or even earlier, it appears that the village-farming community of 200–500 individuals had fully matured in southwestern Asia. As a way of life it then stabilized internally for 1,500 years or more, although it continued to spread downward from the hills and piedmont, where it had first crystallized, into the great river valleys.

Then came a sharp increase in tempo. In the next 1,000 years some of the small agricultural communities on the alluvial plain between the Tigris and Euphrates rivers not only increased greatly in size, but changed decisively in structure. They culminated in the Sumerian city-state with tens of thousands of inhabitants, elaborate religious, political, and military establishments, social strata, advanced technology, and widely extended trading contacts.

The river-valley agriculture on which the early Mesopotamian cities were established differed considerably from that of the uplands where domestication had begun. Most important, agriculture in the alluvium de-

pended on irrigation, which had not been necessary in the uplands. For a long time the farmers made do with small-scale systems, involving breaches in the natural embankments of the streams and uncontrolled local flooding. The beginnings of large-scale canal networks apparently followed the establishment of fully developed cities.

Where in this pattern were the inducements, perhaps even preconditions for urbanization? First, there was the productivity of irrigation agriculture. In spite of many natural handicaps, farming yielded a dependable surplus of food.

Second, the very practice of irrigation must have helped induce the growth of cities, but not merely to build and maintain the elaborate irrigation systems. By engendering inequalities in access to productive land, irrigation contributed to the formation of a stratified society. And by furnishing a reason for border disputes between neighboring communities, it promoted a warlike atmosphere that drew people together in offensive and defensive concentrations.

Finally, the complexity of subsistence pursuits on the flood plains may have indirectly aided the movement toward cities. Institutions were needed to mediate between herdsman and cultivator, between fisherman and sailor, between plowmaker and plowman. Whether through a system of rationing, palace largess, or a market, the city provided a logical and necessary setting for storage, exchange, and redistribution.

In any case the gathering forces for urbanization first become evident around 4000 B.C. Which of them furnished the initial impetus is impossible to say, if indeed any single factor was responsible. Growth in the size of settlements alone does not imply technological or economic advance beyond the level of the village-farming community. In our own time the Yoruba of western Nigeria maintained sizable "cities" that were in fact little more than overgrown village-farming settlements. They were largely self-sustaining because most of the productive inhabitants were full-time farmers.

Temples

The evidence suggests that at the beginning the same was true of Mesopotamian urbanization: immediate economic change was not its central characteristic. The first clear-cut trend to appear in the archaeological record is the rise of temples. Conceivably new patterns of thought and social organization crystallizing within the temples served as the primary force in bringing people together and setting the process in motion.

From the archaeological record most is known about religious institutions. Religion can be traced from small shrines in early villages to more elaborate shrines with features that later permanently characterized Mesopotamian temples. The first persons released from direct subsistence labor were probably priests, whose activities are depicted in early seals and stone carvings. Quite early, the priests also assumed the role of economic administrators, as attested by ration or wage lists found in temple premises among the earliest known examples of writing. For a long time temples seem to have been the largest and most complex institutions in the communities growing up around them.

The beginnings of dynastic political regimes are much harder to trace. Probably early political authority rested in an assembly of adult males, convoked only to select a short-term war leader to meet sporadic external threat. Later, perhaps, successful war leaders were retained even in times of peace. Herein lies the apparent origin of kingship. At times springing up outside the priestly corporations, at times coming from them, new leaders emerged who were preoccupied with warfare against neighboring city-states.

Stratification

As society shifted its central focus from temple to palace, it also separated into strata. Archaeologically the process can best be followed through the increasing differentiation in grave offerings in successively later cemeteries. Earliest graves hold only pottery vessels. Later, some royal graves were richly furnished with beautifully wrought weapons, ornaments, and utensils of gold and lapis lazuli, although many graves of the same period were less elaborate, and some resembled earlier ones. Both texts in cuneiform and archaeological evidence indicate that copper and bronze agricultural tools were beyond the reach of the ordinary peasant while graves of well-to-do have conspicuous consumption of copper in the form of superfluous stands for pottery vessels.

Temple records show substantial differences in the allotments to parishioners. Other texts describe the sale of houseplots or fields, often to form great estates held by palace officials and worked by communities of dependent clients who may originally have owned the land. Still others record the sale of slaves and the rations allotted to slaves producing textiles under the supervision of temple officials, although as a group slaves constituted only a small minority of the population.

In the temple communities on the threshold of becoming cities, full-time craft technology was directed toward supplying seals, statuary, ornate vessels of carved stone, cast copper or precious metals only for cult purposes. Production in the later city-states was stimulated by three new classes of demand. First, metal weapons, armor, and elaborate equipment such as chariots were made for the burgeoning military establishment of the palace. Second, a considerable volume of luxury goods was commissioned for the palace retinue. And third, a moderate private demand for these goods implies at least a small middle class.

By 2500 B.C. there is a fairly full picture of the general layout of a city. Radiating out from the massive public buildings toward the outer gates, were streets, unpaved and dusty, but straight and wide enough for the passage of solid-wheeled carts or chariots. Along the streets lay the residences of the more well-to-do citizenry, usually arranged around spacious courts and sometimes provided with latrines draining into sewage conduits below the streets. The houses of the city's poorer inhabitants were located behind or between the large multiroomed dwellings. They were approached by tortuous, narrow alleys, were more haphazard in plan, were less well built, and very much smaller. Mercantile activities were probably concentrated along the quays of the adjoining river or at the city gates.

Around every important urban center rose the massive fortifications that guarded the city against nomadic raids and the more formidable campaigns of neighboring rulers. Outside the walls clustered sheepfolds and irrigated tracts, interspersed with subsidiary villages and ultimately disappearing into the desert. And in the desert dwelt only the nomad, an object of mixed fear and scorn to the sophisticated court poet. By 2500 B.C. several of the important capitals of lower Mesopotamia included more than 250 acres within their fortifications. The city of Uruk extended over 1,100 acres and contained possibly 50,000 people.

From these later cities there are written records from which the make-up of the population can be estimated. The overwhelming majority (possibly as high as 80 per cent) of the able-bodied adults still were engaged in primary agricultural production, compared with perhaps 95 per cent for the temple-towns a thousand years earlier. But many who were engaged in subsistence agriculture also had other roles: herdsmen, soldier-laborers, fishermen, sailors, pilots, oarsmen, scribes, craftsmen, etc. In addition, most were expected to serve in the army in time of crisis.

Conclusion

There is, therefore, not one origin of cities, but as many as there are independent cultural traditions with an urban way of life. Whatever the initial stimulus to growth and reorganization, the process of urbanization clearly involved the interaction of many different factors. Certainly the institutions of the city evolved in different directions and at different rates rather than as a smoothly emerging totality. It is not easy to say at what stage in the whole progression the word "city" becomes applicable, but by any standard Uruk of 3000 B.C. and its contemporaries were cities. They provide the earliest examples of a process that, with refinements introduced by the industrial revolution and the rise of national states, is still going on today.

Cautions: 1. Many of the qualities we think of as civilized have been attained by societies that failed to organize cities. Some Egyptologists believe that civilization advanced for almost 2,000 years under the Pharaohs before true cities appeared in Egypt. The period was marked by the development of monumental public works, a formal state superstructure, written records, and the beginnings of exact science. In the New World scholars are still searching the jungles around Maya temple centers in Guatemala and Yucatán for urban agglomerations of dwellings. For all its temple architecture and high art, and the intellectual achievement represented by its hieroglyphic writing and accurate long-count calendar, classic Maya civilization apparently was not based on the city. These facts do not detract from the fundamental importance of the urban revolution but underline its complex character. Every high civilization other than possibly the Mayan did ultimately produce cities. And in most civilizations urbanization began early.

2. Some authorities have considered that technological advance, which they usually equate with the development of metallurgy, was a major stimulant or even a precondition of urban growth. Yet, in southern Mesopotamia at least, the major expansions of

metallurgy and of specialized crafts came only *after* dynastic city-states were well advanced. While the spread of technology probably contributed further to the development

of militarism and social stratification, it was less a cause than a consequence of city growth. The same situation is found in New World civilizations.

Section 2 **Culture of cities**

When the country and the city are contrasted, rural communities seem to be culturally homogeneous and socially unified. All groups have a division of labor, but in a non-mechanized, rural economy the division is by broad categories such as sex, age, and a few specialized skills. The common orientation to the land leads to homogeneity of outlook, which is reinforced by physical isolation and population stability.

THE SPREAD OF URBANISM

In industrial countries, the social and cultural differences between rural and urban areas are rapidly disappearing. Urban patterns of life and values now dominate much of the countryside. "The distinctive feature of the mode of living of man in the modern age is his concentration into gigantic aggregations around which cluster lesser centers and from which radiate the ideas and practices that we call civilization." [15]

The urbanization of the United States has had a profound effect on the nonurban as well as on the urban parts of the society. Urban life-styles, values, and tastes are diffused to the countryside by the mass media, the transportation network, the schools, and ties of kin and friends. The economic well-being of small-town and rural people depends to a large extent upon decisions made in Washington, D.C., in state capitals, and in the metropolises in which the giant corporations

are headquartered, and the people look more and more to the state and federal rather than to local governments for public services. The rural and small-town population can hardly escape awareness of the growing metropolitan domination of American society, but they retain an image of rural people as the source of national strength and of rural life as the good life.

Small Town in Mass Society

The relations between a small town and the mass society are analyzed in a study of social conditions in a town of 1,000 people in upper New York state.[16] "Springdale," like many other small towns, has not shared in the population growth and economic expansion that has characterized most larger American communities during the past two decades. As the countryside has been drained of its population and as automobiles and paved roads have made it possible for the remaining rural residents to speed past the once busy hamlets to larger towns for shopping and entertainment, the loci of economic and social activity in America have shifted from hundreds of "Springdales" to a smaller number of larger communities. However, unlike many communities of similar size, Springdale is not declining. The postwar prosperity of its farmers and the settlement of commuting industrial workers have pre-

---

[15] Louis Wirth, "Urbanism as a Way of Life," *American Journal of Sociology*, **44** (1938), 2.

[16] Arthur J. Vidich and Joseph Bensman, *Small Town in Mass Society* (Princeton: Princeton University Press, 1958).

vented its decline, but it probably exemplifies much that is characteristic of contemporary small-town life.

Springdalers are ambivalent toward the larger society. Technological innovations and many other cultural elements of the urban society are accepted willingly, and the professional people and other carriers of urban culture enjoy enhanced status. However, the stereotype of urban life held by Springdalers is totally negative: cities are breeders of vice, corruption, atheism, un-Americanism, and other ills. By contrast, rural America, and especially Springdale, is the stronghold of morality, honesty, Godliness, and the other traditional American virtues. The villagers believe they can enjoy the material advantages of the urban society while remaining somewhat apart from it, but they overestimate their degree of independence from the mass society. It is suggested that there is no really indigenous culture in Springdale, and that even the idealized image of rural life comes from mass media.[17]

The discrepancy between the villagers' illusions about small-town and rural life and its true dependent role in the mass society creates frustration and personality conflict, particularly among merchants who find it increasingly difficult to compete with more efficient mass merchandising in nearby cities. They react by working longer hours, extending credit more liberally, and depending on personal friendship to hold their clientele. Professionals are faced with sharp limits on their economic mobility as long as they remain in Springdale. Those who stay express their mobility strivings in patterns of consumption and leisure activities that may improve their status.

Rural-Urban Balance of Power

The decennial census was instituted to implement the apportionment clause of the Constitution. (See Adaptation 25, pp. 308 ff.)

[17] *Ibid*, pp. 102–3.

Due to changes in population distribution, there have been many reapportionments, and, as indicated in Figure XV:2, the 1960 Census called for a reallocation of seats in the House of Representatives. Twenty-five states are directly affected, nine gaining seats and sixteen losing them. Where this occurred, state legislatures are supposed to redistrict their states. If the legislatures do not redistrict, the states gaining Congressmen elect the additional ones from the whole state, that is "at large." If states lose Congressmen and do not redistrict, all candidates for the House of Representatives must run "at large."

The changes are an expression of a shift in population to the new centers of urban and industrial growth and a shift in political power from rural to the more urban states. The rural-urban shift is also occurring within states. Although 43 states have constitutional provisions requiring the reapportionment of one or both of their legislative houses at least every ten years, many states have not done so.

In 1955 some urban Tennessee voters instituted a suit in the state court, contending that although the Tennessee Constitution calls for reapportionment of the state's voting districts every ten years, the legislature had not acted since 1901. In the meantime the state had grown more than 50 per cent and the largest gains were in the big cities. By failing to act, the legislature gave disproportionate weight to rural voters. Since there was no redistricting 2,340 voters in rural Moore County elected one representative, while 312,000 voters in Shelby County, in which Memphis is located, elected only seven. In other words, a Moore County vote was worth nearly 20 Shelby County votes.

The case was eventually appealed to the U.S. Supreme Court, and in 1962 the Court held[18] that the Tennessee Constitution had

[18] See Baker *v.* Carr, 369 U.S. 186 (1962). This legal citation should be read as volume 369 *United States Reports* (Official Reports of the Supreme Court), page 186.

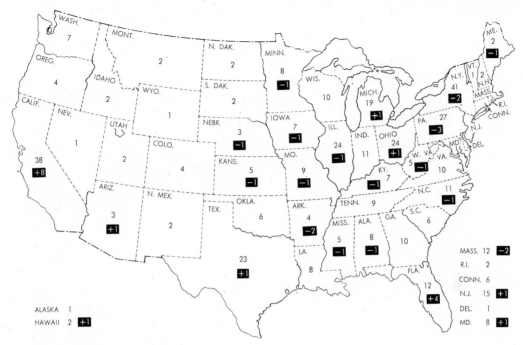

Fig. **XV:2**   Changes in Congress

Black figures indicate number of representatives after reapportionment.
White figures indicate change in congressional representation as result
of 1960 census.

been violated and that the Tennessee legis- lature must redistrict the state. The decision precipitated legislative and judicial action in other states. A major shift in political power seems to be under way, and the control of many legislatures, long in the hands of rural interests, seems to be turning to urban forces. The reapportionment process will take years to complete and of necessity will lag behind population change. The long-delayed victory for the cities will be the end of a battle, but not the end of political conflict between rural and urban interests.

CULTURAL DIVERSITY

Ancient, as well as modern, cities were places of cultural diversity. At the time of the Roman Empire, Rome's population was made up of varied social and ethnic groups from the far-flung empire, and distinctions

between victors and vanquished persisted in its social organization. Contemporary cities are heterogeneous in their segregated ethnic subcultures, extensive division of labor, and wide variations in income, power, and pres- tige.

Two factors contribute to the cultural heterogeneity of modern cities: (1) selective migration and (2) division of labor.

1. *Selective migration.* The city recruits a major portion of its population from rural areas, from other countries, and from other cities. It offers economic and social oppor- tunities to many kinds of people.

Since cities are composed of many persons whose early training and environment were rural or foreign, differences in child rearing, leisure time activities, and morals are to be expected. These differences may be rein- forced by the physical and social isolation of

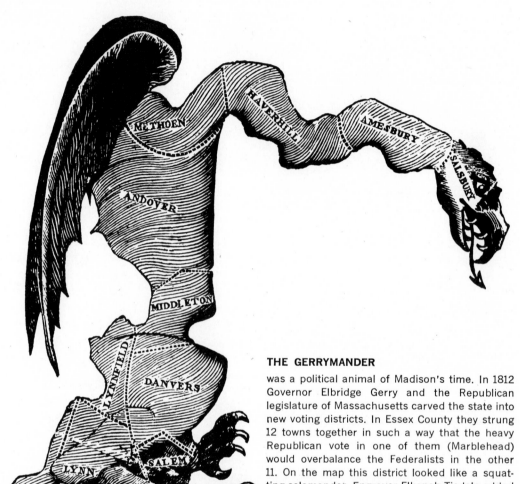

THE GERRYMANDER

was a political animal of Madison's time. In 1812 Governor Elbridge Gerry and the Republican legislature of Massachusetts carved the state into new voting districts. In Essex County they strung 12 towns together in such a way that the heavy Republican vote in one of them (Marblehead) would overbalance the Federalists in the other 11. On the map this district looked like a squatting salamander. Engraver Elkanah Tisdale added claws, wings, and fangs to the map and published it in the Boston *Weekly Messenger* as "THE GERRYMANDER!" This famous cartoon introduced a permanent word into American politics and helped defeat Governor Gerry for re-election. (He was elected Vice President on Madison's ticket later the same year.) But the gerrymander achieved its purpose. In 1812 only 11 Federalist state senators were elected in Massachusetts to 29 Republicans, although the Federalists got 51,766 popular votes and the Republicans, 50,164. This looked like cheating to most voters and caused a violent reaction against the Republicans in Massachusetts. In 1813 the original gerrymander was repealed.

ethnic and economic groups within the city. With the decrease in foreign immigration to the United States and the spread of urban ways of life to rural areas, a leveling of cultural differences is taking place. Recent studies show that migrants to the city are more and more like the city dwellers already there.[19]

2. *Division of labor.* Work in the city is compartmentalized into thousands of specialized occupations. While it would be extreme to call each occupation a subculture, broad groups of occupations do develop distinctive cultural patterns. Common interests and adaptation to similar problems tend to produce among professional groups, businessmen, or skilled workers distinctive ways of viewing the world. The artisans, the warriors, and the philosophers in ancient Greek cities perceived their environment differently, as laborers, soldiers, and teachers do today.

A contrast in and exchange of ideas and values lead to a questioning of traditional ways of thinking and generate new perspectives and new means of adaptation to the environment. The "cultural freedom" of the city is conducive to creativity, and traditionally, the city has been the birthplace of philosophy, science, and the arts. The stimulus of fresh and strange ways of interpreting events has "cross-fertilized" thought and led to bursts of creativity.

Caution: In emphasizing cultural diversity, the common values that give cohesion to the city should not be overlooked. The salient norms—the rules governing family obligations, work, and interpersonal relations—are shared by all groups in the city. Emphasis on work, achievement, and efficiency gives consistency and predictability to the behavior of

most groups. The monetary system, universal education, a common language, mass media, and mass-produced goods contribute to a standardization and leveling of culture.

Urban Diversity and City Planning

City planners are caught in a dilemma. They want to purge the city of the most deteriorated buildings, which are unsightly and sometimes dangerous. They want to reduce crowding, improve the physical environment, admit light and air, and bring trees and grass to the heart of the city. But their aspirations are more frequently than not frustrated by the scarcity and the high values of land that dictate intensive use and dense occupancy. Housing projects, therefore, tend to increase the number of persons per acre even though the amount of space between buildings is greater than before the slums were "cleared."

Second only to the density dilemma is the diversity dilemma. Many city designers try to develop areas as large and homogeneous units. They plan in "superblocks" in order to gain open space. Recently, however, city planners have become sensitive to the consequences of earlier policies that began urban renewal by knocking down everything in the neighborhood. Slum clearance without reference to prior land use destroys neighborhoods and substitutes environments without past and personality.

A recent position[20] takes as its objectives not the construction of garden cities but the rehabilitation of established neighborhoods and the preservation of the original buildings, whenever possible without displacing its residents. This viewpoint pleads for neighborhood diversity through the following means: (1) a "close-grained mix" of

[19] Ronald Freedman, *Recent Migration to Chicago* (Chicago: University of Chicago Press, 1950); Homer H. Hitt, "Peopling the City: Migration," in Rupert B. Vance and Nicholas J. Demerath (eds.), *The Urban South* (Chapel Hill: University of North Carolina Press, 1954), Chap. 4, pp. 54–77.

[20] A most vigorous (and controversial) presentation Is Jane Jacobs, *The Life and Death of American Cities* (New York: Random House, 1961). For the other side, see, for example, Lewis Mumford, *The Culture of Cities* (New York: Harcourt, Brace, 1938), and Clarence S. Stein, *Toward New Towns for America* (New York: Reinhold, 1957).

ground-floor stores and residences, (2) the preservation of short blocks, which tend to increase the possibility of neighboring, (3) the preservation of old buildings to give a sense of continuity and architectural variety, and (4) high density with much of the land covered by buildings.

In her argument for a "close-grained mix" Jacobs shows that sidewalks, for example, perform social functions beyond their manifest use: (1) The busy foot traffic of a well-used city street makes the street safe for women and children because the street is constantly under surveillance from its windows, stoops, and shops. (2) The street is a location for *un*organized play and for socialization of children by neighbors as well as peers. (3) The sidewalk and its shops are a communication network and a place where privacy is balanced against varying kinds of contact, but the emphasis on association at arm's length is an urban value.

The great uniform areas of office buildings stand in stark contrast to the round-the-clock activity of heterogeneously used blocks. In Washington, D.C., for example, massive and homogeneous offices cover acre after acre. Some of the buildings are admirable—if it is assumed that every building ought to be a monument—and the lawns lend a park-like quality to the city. But the center of a national bureaucracy, vigorously active during the working day, becomes at night a desert populated by a few janitors and police. Belatedly there has been a shift in the thinking of Washington planners. It is expected that new office needs will be met by smaller buildings located in the midst of residential areas in which at least some of the workers might live. The official buildings and their grounds would add variety to neighborhoods without overwhelming them. Washington then might become something less of a park to be looked at by tourists but something more of a city in which the nation's business is conducted and in which people live.

URBAN CULTURE AND PERSONALITY

Adaptation to city life is thought to produce distinctive attitudes and personality traits.[21] The urbanite has been characterized by his sophistication and cosmopolitanism, his rationality, matter-of-factness, and reserve in social relations. Obviously, this characterization is partly a caricature, and no true picture of *the* urban personality is possible because of the wide variation among areas and among occupations.

However, the large numbers, the density, and the diversity of people in a city necessarily affect personality and social relations. The urbanite sees many strangers every day, but he has no social relations with most of them. With many others he has only brief, impersonal contacts. While he is physically close to large numbers of people, he is socially close to few. He may think of many of them as

"numbers," "addresses," "clients," "customers," "patients," "readers," "laborers," or "employees." [The typical rural individual has fewer of these indirect communications. His] face-to-face relations (with his family, minister, teacher, neighbors, etc.) compose a much larger part of his whole system of interaction than that of a typical urbanite.[22]

Sophistication, in large part an ability to conceal feelings and to manipulate situations, is fostered by the anonymous and depersonalized urban social relations. The city dweller is highly *rational* in most of his relations. Servicemen, clerks, storekeepers, and conductors serve immediate ends and are judged by their ability to serve those ends. The urbanite expects the gas station attendant to serve him quickly and efficiently; the quality of the service will not vary a great

[21] Discussions of urban personality are found in *The Sociology of Georg Simmel,* tr. and ed. by Kurt H. Wolff (Glencoe: The Free Press, 1950), "The Metropolis and Mental Life," pp. 409–24; and Wirth, *op. cit.,* pp. 1–24.

[22] Pitirim Sorokin and Carle C. Zimmerman, *Principles of Rural-Urban Sociology* (New York: Holt, 1929), pp. 51–52. Reprinted by permission of Henry Holt & Co., Inc.

deal if the attendant likes, dislikes, or is in-different to the personality of the customer. The city dweller is dependent upon predict-able behavior; if he is to get to work on time, the bus driver must be on schedule. The per-sonal factors in the bus driver's life that cause him to be late are of no concern to the com-muter. The urbanite does not know whether someone who is in his environment today will be there tomorrow.

The *time-consciousness* of the urbanite is related to the complexity of city life and the necessity of integrating relations and ac-tivities in a workable way.

If all clocks and watches in Berlin would sud-denly go wrong in different ways, even if only by one hour, all economic life and communication of the city would be disrupted. . . . [the] tech-nique of metropolitan life is unimaginable with-out the most punctual integration of all activities and mutual relations into a stable and imper-sonal time schedule.[23]

The *blasé attitude*—a lack of reaction to new sensations—is a result of the rapidly changing stimuli presented to the city dweller.[24] He becomes indifferent to the changing panorama of faces and street scenes and to the insistent demands for his atten-tion from newspapers, advertising, radio, and television. Simmel suggests that the blasé attitude, the cool, indifferent, outer self of the city man, serves as a psychological de-fense against such pressures.

Rural and Urban Socialization

In a rural community the family is the most important source of socialization. When rural societies are isolated and have low mobility, the density of kinship ties in-creases, and, after a number of generations, "everyone is kin to everyone else." The "clans" of the Southern Appalachian moun-taineers are a case in point. This extension of the web of kin provides a way of relating

oneself to a great many people. For the child, the kin are to be treated with filial respect, and they in turn support him because of their kinship. The kin relation may even be extended to non-kin: "In the peasant or rural village neighborhood, the teacher and the neighborhood itself are often described as an extension of the family." [25]

The country household socializes the child to patterns consistent with rural life: the rural child lacks alternate models to copy, and he is constrained by the work to be done. There is, therefore, less individualiza-tion of life-styles in rural environments.

In contrast to the rural family, the city family is a small, conjugal unit. Many of its socializing functions have been taken over by other agencies, such as the playground, the day nursery, and the peer group. The ef-fects on personality of a wide variety of so-cializing agents are not well understood. Variation does, however, afford the oppor-tunity for the city child to learn alternate patterns of behavior.

Caution: Generalizations about broad dif-ferences in personality between rural and ur-ban individuals should be viewed with care:

1. Many differences in values and styles of life between urban and rural communities are rapidly disappearing.

2. Studies of rural-urban personality dif-ferences, while suggestive, are contradictory and inconclusive. They are burdened with technical difficulties, such as the lack of com-parability in personality tests. Many studies have been dominated by a bias in favor of the "folk-rural" way of life. Investigators have assumed that rural values are the criteria for "adjustment" and "integration" of personal-ity. Rural personalities are said to be more integrated and unified because of homoge-neous primary contacts, and a smaller range of personality differences has been assumed.

---

[23] Simmel, *op. cit.,* p. 413.
[24] *Ibid.,* pp. 413 ff.

[25] Charles P. Loomis and J. Allan Beegle, *Rural Social Systems* (New York: Prentice-Hall, 1950), p. 479.

The urban milieu, in contrast, is said to produce heterogeneous and unintegrated personalities. However, improved techniques of analysis and less biased investigations may uncover more heterogeneity and less personality integration in rural settings than has previously been assumed.[26]

Mental Illness and Urbanization

It is often claimed that the individuation, competitiveness, role conflict, rapid pace of activities, intense status striving, and other conditions of life in modern industrial cities result in a high incidence of mental disorders. A comparison between rates of first admissions to mental institutions in Massachusetts in the mid-nineteenth century and recent rates of admission found no increase except in the age category of fifty and older.[27] The rates for people below fifty remained about the same despite a trend toward hospitalization of patients with less extreme forms of mental illness.

Since Massachusetts became one of the most urbanized states in the intervening years, from 50 per cent urban in 1850 to 90 per cent urban in 1940, these findings suggest that city life does not produce mental disorders of the more serious types, except possibly among the elderly. It would seem that urban life is not characterized by more stress than rural life, or stress is not an important factor underlying the functional psychoses. Perhaps greater insecurity, competitiveness, and similar conditions of life in modern industrial cities produce neurotic personalities but not psychotic ones.

An increase in the number of hospitalized patients with arteriosclerotic psychoses (due to hardening of the arteries) accounts for the increase in the admission rate for older persons. The presumed greater stress or some other condition of modern urban life may have increased the incidence of arteriosclerosis, more persons with senile psychoses may now be institutionalized rather than given home care, or both of these changes may have occurred.

Although urban life as a whole may not be conducive to psychosis, the extreme forms of personality deviation are not randomly distributed through the city. There is a high concentration of mental illness in the deteriorated residential areas surrounding the main business district. In their study of mental patients in private and public hospitals in Chicago, Faris and Dunham found that the rooming-house, Negro, and foreign-born slum areas had high rates of mental illness.[28] Low rates were found along the lake-front, hotel and apartment house communities, and in outlying residential areas. The main types of mental disease were more highly concentrated in some areas than in others. For example, paranoid schizophrenia had the highest rate of incidence in the rooming-house district, and manic-depressive psychoses in areas with higher rentals.

The spatial distribution of suicide follows a similar pattern of concentration in areas of transition. In Seattle and Minneapolis, Schmid found high rates of suicide in the business districts and surrounding areas.[29]

Much further study is needed before the

[26] See Melvin Seeman, "An Evaluation of Current Approaches to Personality Differences in Folk and Urban Societies," *Social Forces*, 25 (1946), 160–65. This article presents a summary and critique of the studies of rural and urban differences in personality and character. See also T. Lynn Smith, *The Sociology of Rural Life* (New York: Harper, 1953), pp. 112–25.

[27] Herbert Goldhamer and Andrew Marshall, *Psychosis and Civilization* (Glencoe: The Free Press, 1949).

[28] Robert E. L. Faris and H. Warren Dunham, *Mental Disorders in Urban Areas* (Chicago: University of Chicago Press, 1939). Studies of other cities have shown similar patternings of mental disorders. See, for example, Clarence W. Schroeder, "Mental Disorders in Cities," *American Journal of Sociology*, **48** (1942), 40–47.

[29] Calvin F. Schmid, *Social Saga of Two Cities* (Minneapolis: The Minneapolis Council of Social Agencies, 1937); and Calvin F. Schmid, *Social Trends in Seattle* (Seattle: University of Washington Press, 1944). Similar distributions have been found in Chicago and San Francisco. See Ruth Shonle Cavan, *Suicide* (Chicago: University of Chicago Press, 1928); Ernest R. Mowrer, *Disorganization: Personal and Social* (Philadelphia: Lippincott, 1942); and Aubrey Wendling, "Suicides in the San Francisco Bay Region" (Ph.D. dissertation, University of Washington, 1954).

relations between the social and cultural milieu on the one hand and mental disease and suicide on the other are clearly understood. It is not known to what extent the various urban environments *generate* these types of behavior, that is, are underlying causes of them, and the extent to which the urban environments *precipitate* mental illness and suicidal tendencies which may have been long latent in the individual. Understanding of these problems is further complicated by the fact that there is much internal mobility in the city. Deviant personalities may tend to drift toward some areas, where their breakdowns finally occur, although the genesis of their difficulties may have been in other environments, either in the city or in rural areas. In the case of the Chicago study, many of the slum dwellers had been long-time residents, and this fact is suggestive of a direct relation between social conditions, the slum areas, and personality disturbances. If this connection is correct, the determining factors may lie in the social isolation and anomie of deteriorated areas.

Section 3 Studies of the American city

The city is investigated to guide public policy in the fields of planning, civic welfare, and urban development as well as to illuminate topics of more immediately scientific interest, such as land use, social stratification, and population redistribution. Because social differentiation is characteristic of the urban order, students of the city are interested in the phenomena of stratification, the location of social power, and the identification of distinct social areas. The work of specialists in ecology, stratification, and population distribution converge in urban research. Urban and community studies have been drawn upon earlier in this book to gain insight into broad social phenomena and specialized topics. In this section additional studies are examined and some research previously mentioned is reviewed in a different light.

STUDIES OF POWER STRUCTURE

As a social system increases in size and complexity, inequities in power probably grow. The precise location and distribution of power are hard to discover because the ability of individuals or groups to influence each other is complicated and often obscure. In the United States power and influence vary from city to city, and different interests are capable of influencing different parts of the political order. A community study, therefore, may not reveal the power of groups whose political influence operates through national rather than local channels. The major labor unions, for example, are more powerful on the national level than they are on the community level, and community studies tend to understate their importance. Nevertheless, if the studies are interpreted with care, they are valuable additions to sociological knowledge.

One of the most ambitious studies of the power structure of a city was undertaken in a Southern metropolis with a population of half a million.[30] The reputational technique was used for measuring power, a method similar to the reputational technique described in SOCIAL STRATIFICATION (pp. 182–83). First, the names of people likely to be

[30] Floyd Hunter, *Community Power Structure: A Study of Decision Makers* (Chapel Hill: University of North Carolina Press, 1953).

among the most influential in "Regional City" were obtained from several sources. The Community Council supplied names of leaders in community affairs, the Chamber of Commerce, business leaders of establishments employing more than 500 employees and of financial houses doing the largest volume of clearances. The League of Women Voters furnished lists of local political leaders, and newspaper editors and other civic leaders provided lists of society leaders and people of great wealth. The combined lists included more than 175 names.

The list of possible leaders was presented to a panel of 14 judges who selected from it those they believed to be the top leaders in the community. The judges were of all three major religions, Negro and white, male and female, young and old, and business executives and professional people. Since the judges agreed closely on the top leaders, the original list was sharply reduced, and it was finally reduced to 40 through interviews with those identified by the panel as top leaders. Hunter does not claim that these 40 were *the* top leaders of the community, but he is confident that they included at least some of the most powerful persons in the community.

The occupations of the 40 top leaders were as follows: [31]

Executives or directors in large commercial enterprises	11
Executives or directors in banking and investment	7
Professionals (five lawyers, one dentist)	6
"With major industrial responsibilities"	5
Governmental personnel	4
Labor leaders	2
Leisure personnel	5

Businessmen were more numerous in the top 40 than other occupational categories and

[31] *Ibid.*, pp. 12–13.

were also identified as more powerful. If Hunter is correct, business leadership led to general leadership. Neither wealth, prestige, nor political eminence were primary criteria for admission to the upper echelons of the decision-makers, but the top men in the economic institutions without exception had a great deal of influence in community affairs.

The noneconomic institutions were subordinate to the economic institutions in the city's power structure. The noneconomic institutions played a vital role in the execution of policy, but economic interests were dominant in policy formation. For instance, not one of the ministers in Regional City was chosen as a top leader by the panel or by the other interviewees, and the church leaders usually did not participate in the decision-making process. However, once a community project was under way, the churches had an important role in carrying it out. Neither ministers nor prominent laymen had much influence with economic leaders. Although there was no formal tie between the economic interests and government, informal relations and the composition of policy-determining committees made the local government dependent on the business leadership.

Since Regional City had a large Negro population, the same methods were used for a separate study of the power structure of the Negro subcommunity. Although there was a concentration of leadership in the Negro community, the occupational composition of the top leadership was different from that of the white community. Professionals were more numerous than businessmen, and these included six ministers and seven social workers—personnel who had little influence in the white community.

The finding of business dominance in the white community power structure agrees with several other community studies. For instance, the Lynds found business dominant in "Middletown," although this smaller community was controlled largely by one family of industrialists.[32] Mills described the concentration of power in "Central City" in the hands of large industrialists and bankers—power he believed was often wielded indirectly through manipulation of what he called the small-business "front." [33]

One should not assume from these studies that control by top businessmen of important spheres of community life is a universal phenomenon in the United States. Power systems vary from one community to another and change through time. In El Paso, Texas, for example, the influence of business interests over community issues was waning in the mid-1950's.[34] Dahl believes that access to the sources of influence over governmental action is becoming more widely distributed in America and that this general change is reflected in community power structures.[35] This opinion is a subject of controversy and of continuing research.

Furthermore, there may not be general influentials but rather people whose power is restricted to specific areas of community life.[36] Hunter suggests that there may have been several pyramids of power rather than only one in Regional City. Recent research indicates, however, that although there are many people whose influence is restricted, a handful of key influentials exercise power in several major areas.[37]

Caution: The reputational technique, which is frequently used because it is relatively economical, may not be the best way to identify the general influentials at the top of the community power structure. The validity of findings depends upon whether or not the judges know who wields power. Undoubtedly there is some discrepancy between the reputed and the real leaders, and the former may sometimes be those with the highest prestige rather than those with the greatest power.

STRATIFICATION STUDIES

Community studies of strata present some of the same problems as the power structure studies. The work of Hollingshead and of Warner and his associates (See SOCIAL STRATIFICATION, pp. 190–91) was facilitated because the size of the communities (6,000–17,000) permitted them to be examined as if they were self-contained units. Furthermore, the modest size of these cities allowed the use of reputational techniques with a reasonable hope that people knew whom they were identifying. In larger places this is impossible except in the topmost strata.

With their limited opportunities for mobility, small towns are not pictures in miniature of the stratification system of the country. Rather they are tributaries to the metropolitan centers, a special part of, and probably a relatively stable part of, a national system made up of many subcommunities and reputational systems. Within the smaller cities, each ethnic, racial, or otherwise specialized subcommunity may have its own status system and status criteria. For example, in communities with large universities, the status systems of the academic community are to a degree separate from the town.

A study of the middle classes in a Midwestern city of 60,000 population permits a somewhat broader generalization, since the subject city was selected on the basis of 36 statistical indicators as "the most typical" of all Midwestern cities of 50,000–80,000 population. A cross section of married men in "Central City" was grouped by average income of their occupations into five strata: (1) big business and executives, (2) small

[32] Robert S. and Helen Lynd, *Middletown in Transition* (New York: Harcourt, Brace, 1937).

[33] C. Wright Mills, "The Middle Classes in Middle-Sized Cities," *American Sociological Review*, **11** (October, 1946), 520–29.

[34] William D'Antonio and Eugene C. Erickson, "The Reputational Technique as a Measure of Community Power," *American Sociological Review*, **27** (June, 1962), 362–75.

[35] Robert A. Dahl, *Who Governs? Democracy and Power in an American City* (New Haven: Yale University Press, 1961).

[36] Raymond E. Wolfinger, "Reputation and Reality in the Study of Community Power," *American Sociological Review*, **25** (October, 1960), 636–44.

[37] D'Antonio and Erickson, *loc. cit.*

business and free professionals, (3) higher white-collar, (4) lower white-collar, and (5) wage workers. The first two of these include the upper class and what Mills calls "the old middle class." The white-collar workers are "the new middle class." [38]

A Metropolitan Upper Class [39]

Although one must not generalize from the characteristics of social classes in small towns to those in large cities, the upper class in at least one metropolis—Philadelphia—resembles in many respects the upper classes in Warner's Yankee City. There is a similar, although a lesser, emphasis on prominent family background and the same kind of identification with certain streets, for instance. The Philadelphia upper class, like the one in Yankee City, is an intimate association group with one major difference. Whereas small-town status elites are prominent only locally, metropolitan upper classes tend to form a national upper class. In addition to being linked by ties of marriage and friendship, by a common cultural tradition and a feeling of solidarity, the Philadelphia upper class is joined to the upper classes in New York, Boston, and other large cities.

The emergence of this national upper class may be traced to the rise of rapid communications and national corporate enterprise. Several institutions have been directly instrumental in its growth, the most important of which are the New England boarding schools and the fashionable Eastern colleges. At these, the offspring of the rich and well-born from all cities intermingle, intermarry, and form ties that endure after they return to their respective communities. The development of the Episcopal Church into a national upper-class institution has both promoted and been a result of the increased solidarity of the inter-city moneyed elite in the United States.

As the several metropolitan upper classes have become fused into a national upper class, there has been a tendency for the status-giving functions of the family to be transferred to other institutions, such as the fashionable school, college, and club. As the family firm has been replaced by the large and anonymously owned corporation, family pride in the enterprise has declined, and responsibility has been assumed by a more broadly selected group of corporate executives. These developments have made it easier for men of talent who lack prominent and wealthy ancestors to move into the metropolitan upper class. Nevertheless, the class is still composed very largely of Protestants of northern European stock.

THE CHICAGO STUDIES

In the period between World Wars I and II the University of Chicago was the dominant force in American sociology. Under the leadership of Park, Thomas, Ellsworth Faris, Burgess, Wirth (and Mead in Philosophy), it granted a large proportion of advanced degrees, published the *American Journal of Sociology,* and contributed extensively to the advancement of the discipline. A distinctive feature of this scholarly enterprise was an approach to studying the city of Chicago. The city was viewed as a "social laboratory," and it was subjected to intensive, prolonged, and systematic study. Adaptation 40 outlines some of the theoretical principles underlying the Chicago studies and some of the major lines of investigation. The monographic works growing out of the research program largely originated as doctoral dissertations and indicate the range of topics covered by the research. These monographs are listed on page 612. In the aggregate they represent an impressive body of knowledge about an American metropolis at a significant period in its growth. Adaptation 40 draws on these monographs as well as the collections of papers listed. (See also POPULATION AND ECOLOGY, pp. 346 ff.)

---

[38] Mills, *loc. cit.*
[39] See E. Digby Baltzell, *Philadelphia Gentlemen: The Making of a National Upper Class* (Glencoe: The Free Press, 1958).

SOCIAL AREA ANALYSIS

A somewhat different approach to urban research was introduced by Shevky in a study of Los Angeles.[40] In this technique the census tract is usually employed as the unit of analysis. Each tract is given a numerical score on *social rank* as measured by such factors as occupation, education, and rental value, and a score on *urbanization* as indicated by fertility, the proportion of women in the labor force, and house type. A third variable, *segregation,* is measured by the ratio of minority people in a given tract to their proportion in the city as a whole. Tracts are then grouped according to the similarity of their scores irrespective of their geographic distance from each other. Since the initial study was published in 1949, there have been a number of replications both in the United States and elsewhere and an extensive literature debating the technical merits of the method.

Because homogeneous clusters of tracts tend to be similar in other characteristics, such as life-styles, family type, and age distributions, social area analysis is of value in comparing different cities, in tracing trends in any one city, and in the general study of the spatial organization of social phenomena. This approach has the advantage of facilitating comparisons of areas with similar characteristics even when they are not contiguous.

[40] Eshref Shevky and Marilyn Williams, *The Social Areas of Los Angeles* (Berkeley and Los Angeles: University of California Press, 1949). See also Eshref Shevky and Wendell Bell, *Social Area Analysis* (Stanford: Stanford University Press, 1955).

Chicago as a Social Laboratory

The intellectual background of the Chicago studies is exemplified in the perspectives and experience of Robert E. Park. He was intimately acquainted with European sociology, and his degree from Heidelberg was earned with a theoretical treatise on collective behavior. Park had wide experience as a newspaper reporter and city editor, and this experience led him to test theories by direct observation in the field.[41] His close association with W. I. Thomas supported his own preference for viewing the surrounding city as a laboratory. He was familiar with urban studies in Europe and sensitive to the research merits of the social surveys such as the famous work of Charles Booth, *Life and Labour of the People in London* (first published in 1891–1903).

A part of the theoretical influences on the Chicago studies came from the field of plant and animal ecology. Suggestive analogies were drawn between the phenomena of plant and human communities, and the processes observed in plant ecology, such as competition, dominance, accommodation, succession and invasion, were incorporated into sociological thinking.

The development of [human ecology in the United States] was given an indigenous turn by the special conditions of American life. . . . It saw community life as a rapidly growing organism, with an expanding area, with increasing land values, and with an increasing number and complexity of institutions. Affected by the theories of *laissez faire* and free enterprise, ecologists saw an ever-competing and expanding business center as the dominant center of the community. [42]

[41] E. C. Hughes in Buford H. Junker, *Field Work* (Chicago: University of Chicago Press, 1960), pp. ix–x.

[42] Emma C. Llewellyn and Audrey Hawthorn, "Human Ecology" in Georges Gurvitch and Wilbert E. Moore (eds.), *Twentieth Century Sociology* (New York: Philosophical Library, 1945), pp. 469–70.

ADAPTATION 40

Robert E. Park (1864–1944). In association with E. W. Burgess and W. I. Thomas, he powerfully influenced the study of the urban community and race relations. See Human Communities, Race and Culture, *and* Introduction to the Science of Sociology (*with E. W. Burgess*).

In the ecological studies Park worked closely with R. D. McKenzie, whose best-known work is *The Metropolitan Community.*

Ecological Processes

Park understood the city as having ". . . a characteristic organization and a typical life history." Towns generally develop along lines of communication, at the junction of two or more land or water routes. Population and businesses concentrate about this point of maximum access, and the highest land values are found in locations where most people cross. As towns grow larger, competitively

weaker facilities, such as residences, are pushed outward. *Competition,* a key ecological concept, determines which businesses remain at the center, and thus the central business district forms. The extension of means of local transportation to the central business district increases the number of people who work and transact business there, resulting in increased land values and increased concentration of offices, banks, and stores.

In a growing city the central business district must expand, and both expansion and the anticipation of expansion affect the surrounding area, called the zone in transition. Land values in the transition zone rise, but the buildings and the neighborhood deteriorate. Old buildings are not repaired and new construction awaits the growth of the central business district. Undesirable land uses begin to encroach on the area, and the process of *invasion* is under way.

Those able to afford higher rents and the costs of commuting from outlying areas into the central business district, begin to move out. When the change in land use is complete, *succession* has taken place. In the interstices between the business and industrial developments are slums, immigrant communities, the rooming-house area, hobohemia, and bohemia. These areas tend to be separated by such barriers as transportation arteries, wedges of business and industry, park and boulevard systems, and topographical features that modify the hypothesized concentric zonal pattern. For example, lakes modify the zonal pattern of cities like Chicago and Cleveland into concentric semicircles. The areas with a predominant land use or occupancy are termed *formations* by the plant ecologist and *natural areas* by the human ecologist—natural because the areas are products of natural forces, without design. Park writes that the metropolis selects out through competition those individuals best suited to live in a particular region and milieu; every individual finds the place where he can or the place where he must live. These areas exemplify *segregation,* as understood by the plant ecologist, and in their self-sufficiency and isolation tend to resist invasion of other land uses.

Social Disorganization

The natural areas within the zone in transition, as well as the zone itself, were a major focus of interest for the Chicago studies because human ecologists hold the theory that succession, accompanied by a high rate of mobility, results in social disorganization.

The constant comings and goings of its inhabitants is the most striking and significant characteristic of this world of furnished rooms. This whole population turns over every four months. . . . And at least half of the keepers of these houses had been at their present addresses six months or less.[48]

Zorbaugh characterized the Near North Side of Chicago as one of restless succession: fashionable residential streets become rooming-house districts; rooming-houses become tenements; tenements are sometimes reclaimed for studios and shops. Frazier reporting on Negroes and Wirth on immigrants both note these populations tend to move out of the deteriorated areas as their economic condition improves.

Within the zone in transition are areas of social homogeneity such as the ghetto, which Park says "made it possible for two unassimilated peoples to live together, participating in a common economy, but preserving separate cultures," and, incidentally, representing the phenomenon termed *accommodation* by the plant ecologist. Within the zone are other areas, such as the rooming-house district, where social solidarity is completely absent.

Special institutions cater to the needs of the residents of this zone where social controls have, to a great extent, broken down. Within the rooming-house district, for example, are taxi-dance halls, established to meet the demand for companionship of homeless and lonesome men. In the zone in transition the hobo can find a cheap flop and the Skid Roader a cheap glass of wine. Many of the 1,313 boy gangs studied by Thrasher were located in this area. Here also, where social control is weak and anonymity at its highest, are the commercialized vice centers.

The slum is a bleak area of segregation of the sediment of society; an area of extreme poverty, tenements, ramshackle buildings, of evictions and evaded rents; an area of working mothers and children, of high rates of birth, infant mortality, illegitimacy, and death; an area of pawnshops and second-hand stores, of gangs, of "flops," where every bed is a vote . . . the slum . . . has reached the limit of decay and is on the verge of reorganization as missions, settlements, playparks, and business come in.[44]

The immigrant entered the slum, which served three functions for him: rents were low; it was within walking distance of work; and absentee landlords offered little resistance to people with a low standard of living and an alien culture.

The human ecologists paid less attention to the three zones beyond the zone in transition —the zones of workingmen's homes, the residential zone, and the zone of commuters, but they did study comparative indices of various social problems among zones. They found, for example, that rates of crime, delinquency, illegitimate births, family breakup, poverty, vice, mental illness, and even hotel transiency decline in relation to distance from the central business district.

When different groups move from one zone to the next, their incidence of social problems varies depending on the direction of their movement. Faris and Dunham, for instance, showed that different types of mental illness are characteristic of different areas, and Frazier showed that social problem rates vary by area for the Negro population as for the white population. The incidence of social problems of Negroes as for whites de-

[48] Harvey W. Zorbaugh, *The Gold Coast and the Slum* (Chicago: University of Chicago Press, 1929), pp. 71–72.

[44] Zorbaugh, *op. cit.* p. 9.

clines with movement toward the periphery and into the more organized social communities.

The conceptions and interpretations of the human ecologists were influenced by *laissez-faire* ideas: competition distributes and segregates residences, occupations, and businesses. For the human ecologist, each area selects those individuals who can afford it or survive in it, and each area of the city "is suited for some one function better than for any other." As Park describes it:

[The city's] growth is, fundamentally and as a whole, natural, i.e., uncontrolled and undesigned. The forms it tends to assume are those which represent and correspond to the functions that it is called upon to perform.[45]

The human ecologists held that natural growth tendencies should be taken into account in the development of city plans.

Division of Labor

A contrast between the village and the city and between communal and impersonal social controls is also a recurrent theme in the writings of the Chicago group. Except for immigrant communities, which maintain a degree of traditional solidarity, cities tend to isolate individuals and break down local attachments. The weakened restraints are related to the incidence of vice and crime.[46] Man is thrown upon himself as custom is replaced by public opinion and law. The new social order is pragmatic and experimental: education is no longer ritual, politics is empirical, religion is a quest.[47] Law, fashion, and public opinion replace traditional controls, and primary relations in general are replaced by secondary relations.

The primary force creating this new society is the division of labor, which tends to break down or to modify the older social and economic organization of society, based on family ties, local associations, custom, and status, and to substitute for it an organization based on occupational interests. Developments in urban transportation and communication, which put distance between place of residence and place of work, help to create secondary relations. There is a decline of neighborhood public dance halls and neighborhood theaters in favor of large dance gardens and movie palaces.[48] New agencies take over some of the duties that home, neighborhood, and communal organizations can no longer perform adequately.[49] But men who live in the same locality do not necessarily have the same common welfare; there is difficulty in maintaining the intimate contacts of the small town when people live in hotels or lodging houses, don't own their own homes, or are transient.[50]

With characteristic interplay between theory and documentation, Zorbaugh[51] contrasted certain areas of the Near North Side, typified by superficial and external contacts, social distance, self-absorption, and high population densities with the town or village where everyone knows everyone else "clear down to the ground." The urban diversity of cultural background increases social distance, unlike the homogeneity of cultural background in the village. Economic activities in the city take men outside their local community and give them separate interests and points of view. Urban division of labor produces an orientation of sentiment and interest along occupational rather than local lines. In the village, on the other hand, economic activities were a source of the community's com-

[45] Robert E. Park, Foreword in Louis Wirth, *The Ghetto* (Chicago: University of Chicago Press, 1928), p. x.

[46] Ernest W. Burgess, "The Growth of the City: An Introduction to a Research Project," in Robert Park, Ernest W. Burgess, and Roderick D. McKenzie (eds.), *The City* (Chicago: University of Chicago Press, 1925), p. 59.

[47] Park, "The City as a Social Laboratory," in *Human Communities* (Glencoe: The Free Press, 1952), pp. 74–75.

[48] Park, "Can Neighborhood Work Have a Scientific Basis?" in *The City, op. cit.,* p. 151.

[49] Park, "Community Organization and Juvenile Delinquency," in *Human Communities, op. cit.* p. 61.

[50] Park, "Local Communities in the Metropolis," in *Human Communities, op. cit.,* p. 90.

[51] Zorbaugh, *op. cit., passim.*

mon body of experiences. As a consequence of the separation of place of work and residence, both the range and the frequency of man's contacts are increased. This mobility results in a dissolution of public opinion and a decay of social solidarity and makes strangers out of neighbors. Recreation ceases to be spontaneous and communal. Instead it becomes commercialized and segregated in the Loop or "bright lights" area. The village fiesta is abandoned for the pool hall or the movie.

Frazier [52] wrote that the customary and sympathetic bonds that sustained the rural Negro break down when families move to the city, disorganization resulting. In the outlying areas of Chicago, where a sense of community is maintained, he found a lower incidence of various social problems among Negroes. Burgess [53] regards the taxi-dance hall as an example of the failure of the traditional devices of social control to function in a culturally heterogeneous and anonymous society. Conventional avenues for forming friendships are deficient in the city, and taxi-dance halls, lonesome clubs, and matrimonial advertising bureaus appear. Faris and Dunham [54] conclude that some types of mental disorders are more prevalent where the population is mobile and heterogeneous than where it is stable and homogeneous.

Tönnies' distinction between *Gemeinschaft* and *Gesellschaft* (see p. 47) and Durkheim's ideas about the division of labor and the interdependence of diverse social types were influential in Park's thinking. These themes are exemplified in the studies of occupations, such as *The Saleslady* and *The Professional Thief*. Like the more pointedly ecological monographs, they helped to mark off a major area of sociological research. But the occupational studies should not be thought of as entirely distinct from ecology. On the contrary, occupational types are seen in ecological terms as fitting into niches in the urban zones and in the economy. Workers find their places by natural selective processes into both work locations and residential locations.

Conclusion

Among the theoretical bases of the Chicago studies two items stand out:

1. The adaptation to human and especially urban society of ideas originally derived from plant and animal ecology
2. The theory developed by Tönnies and Durkheim that modern society is the product of evolution from a communal, relatively undifferentiated social order to a social system based on specialization, the division of labor, and the functional interdependence of diverse social types

These understandings were tested in field studies that were both descriptive and interpretive.

The growth of Chicago occurred rapidly and at a time when one after the other different populations entered the city and worked their way up the occupational and residential ladder. Furthermore, the trend of Chicago's development was well established before the automobile became the major means of urban-suburban transportation. Generalizations about the details of zonal change pertain to large, industrial, expanding cities at a particular stage in American urban history, but the Chicago studies must stand as a landmark of urban field research. (See also POPULATION AND ECOLOGY, pp. 346 ff.)

A Chronological Listing of the Chicago Studies

(Unless otherwise indicated, they are publications of the University of Chicago Press.) The numerous periodical articles are not separately referred to, but many of them appear in the listed collections. Monographs

[52] E. Franklin Frazier, *The Negro Family in Chicago* (Chicago: University of Chicago Press, 1932), pp. 249–52.

[53] Burgess, "Introduction" to Paul G. Cressey, *The Taxi-Dance Hall* (Chicago: University of Chicago Press, 1932).

[54] Robert E. L. Faris and H. Warren Dunham, *Mental Disorders in Urban Areas* (Chicago: University of Chicago Press, 1939).

about other places are excluded even though they are part of the same intellectual tradition.

Chicago Commission on Race Relations, *The Negro in Chicago* (1922).

Robert E. Park, E. W. Burgess, R. D. McKenzie, and Louis Wirth, *The City* (1925).

Ernest W. Burgess (ed.), *The Urban Community* (1927).

Frederic M. Thrasher, *The Gang* (1927).

Louis Wirth, *The Ghetto* (1928).

Clifford R. Shaw, F. M. Zorbaugh, H. D. McKay and L. S. Cottrell, *Delinquency Areas* (1929).

T. V. Smith and Leonard D. White (eds.), *Chicago: An Experiment in Social Science Research* (1929).

Harvey W. Zorbaugh, *The Gold Coast and the Slum* (1929).

Paul G. Cressey, *The Taxi-Dance Hall* (1932).

E. Franklin Frazier, *The Negro Family in Chicago* (1932).

Walter C. Reckless, *Vice in Chicago* (1933).

Norman S. Hayner, *Hotel Life* (1936).

Robert E. L. Faris and H. Warren Dunham, *Mental Disorders in Urban Areas* (1939).

Nels Anderson, *Men on the Move* (1940).

Robert E. Park, *Human Communities* (Glencoe: The Free Press, 1952), posthumous collection.

Occupational Studies

Frances R. Donovan, *The Woman Who Waits* (Boston: R. G. Badger, 1920).

Nels Anderson, *The Hobo* (1923).

Frances R. Donovan, *The Saleslady* (1930).

Clifford R. Shaw, *The Jack-Roller* (1930).

Edwin H. Sutherland and C. Conwell, *The Professional Thief* (1937).

Frances R. Donovan, *The Schoolma'am* (New York: Frederick A. Stokes, 1938).

Section 4   Changing cities

The rapid growth of cities, the accompanying redistribution of population, and the changes in social organization encompass a revolution the importance of which is only beginning to be explored. Modern man is more often than not a resident of the city and almost always oriented toward the city.

This section reviews some examples of urban change: (1) the suburban movement, (2) the emergence of the megalopolis (the super city), (3) the impact of technological change on communities, (4) the decay and reconstruction of urban neighborhoods, and (5) the effect of the concentration of economic power on civic welfare.

THE SUBURBAN MOVEMENT

Perhaps the most dramatic change in large American cities during recent years has been the movement of people from the central zones to peripheral and satellite neighborhoods. Although the suburban movement has accelerated since World War II, its beginnings were observed as early as 1899,[55] and a few commuters' settlements had grown up along railroads near large cities some fifty years earlier. This movement involved very few people, however, until the invention of the electric train and streetcar in the late nineteenth century made intermediate-range commuting both economical and convenient.[56] Metropolitan areas then expanded outward along the train and streetcar tracks and took on a star-like configuration. Most people still lived within walking distance of the public transportation routes, however, and these did not reach many of the outlying areas. The automobile provided a more flexible means of transportation and made possible an even greater dispersal of people within the metro-

[55] Adna F. Weber, *The Growth of Cities in the Nineteenth Century* (New York: Columbia University Press, 1899).

[56] William F. Ogburn, "Inventions of Local Transportation and the Patterns of Cities," *Social Forces*, **24** (May, 1946), 373–79.

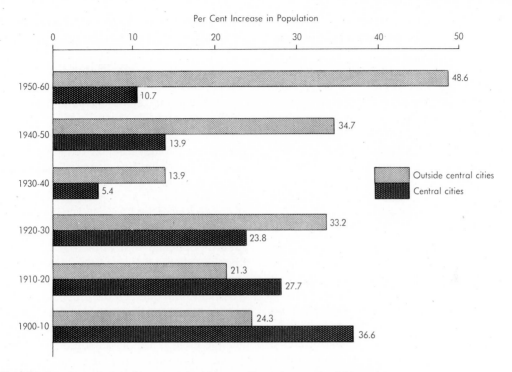

Per Cent Increase in Population

Fig. **XV:3**   Population Increase in Metropolitan Areas, Inside and
Outside of Central Cities, United States: 1900–1960

Data for 1900–1950 are for 162 territorial units that were Standard Metropolitan Areas as of 1950 [from Donald J. Bogue, *Population Growth in Standard Metropolitan Areas, 1900–1950* (Washington, D.C.: Housing and Home Finance Agency, 1953), Table 1]. Data for 1950–1960 are for 212 territorial units that were Standard Metropolitan Statistical Areas as of 1960 [*U.S. Census of Population: 1960*, PC(1)-1A, Table 33].

politan area, but the full impact of the automobile was retarded first by the Great Depression of the 1930's and then by World War II.

The size and rate of growth of the suburban population in the United States has not been precisely determined because suburban areas are not neatly separated from each other by administrative boundaries. However, it appears that roughly half of the urban population in the United States now live in suburbs and that since the end of World War II the suburban population has increased several times faster than the central portions of cities.

Figure XV:3 shows the rates of growth in Metropolitan Areas inside and outside central cities. In every decade since 1920 the per cent increase has been greater outside central cities. The growth of suburban areas has been nationwide, but most rapid in the Western states.

Suburbanization occurs in nuclei, or small communities, around the central city as well as around the satellite cities of the metropolitan area. So extensive is growth in some areas that original suburbs of the main city have merged with suburbs of satellite cities.[57]

Post-World War II suburbs have been the subjects of increasing research, and the ac-

[57] Cf. Donald J. Bogue, "Metropolitan Decentralization: A Study of Differential Growth," Scripps Foundation *Studies in Population Distribution*, No. 2, (August, 1950).

cumulating findings provide the basis for some tentative generalizations about their social, cultural, economic, and demographic characteristics.[58] The movement from the central city to the outlying areas has far-reaching social consequences. Suburbs are populated mainly by young, married adults and their children, and the family tends to be child-centered. Single and unattached adults and married couples without children are rare. There is a preponderance of people below age thirteen and between the ages of thirty-five and forty-four. Although the suburban sex ratio is well below 100, the excess of females is not as great as in the urban population as a whole. Fertility rates are higher than in the central city, but not as high as in rural areas. (See THE FAMILY, pp. 394 f.)

The socio-economic status of suburbanites averages well above that of people in the central city. Average income is higher and a larger proportion of the workers are in professional and business occupations. Many of the families are upwardly mobile and the move to the suburbs signifies their social mobility. Furthermore, high rates of geographic mobility characterize suburbia. Although most of the families are making payments on a home, the payments are regarded like rent, and equities are readily traded and sold. For those whose careers are most successful, each move may be to a more prestigeful and expensive suburb and may symbolize a step in their upward movement.

As in the rural neighborhood, primary relations in the suburbs are often based upon proximity of residence rather than upon commonality of interests. (See SOCIAL ORGANIZATION, pp. 19–23.) There is a return to "neighboring" and a trend away from the impersonality and anonymity of the central city. Participation in community organizations, including religious ones, is high. Politically, suburbanites are more conservative than people in the central city. Morally, they are more conventional and conforming.

Each suburb tends to be homogeneous in the size and appearance of homes, in the income of residents, and in the patterns of consumption. Conspicuous consumption is avoided, getting ahead of the Joneses is apparently as strongly disapproved as failure to keep up with them. Even leisure activities are highly uniform.

Caution: These generalizations undoubtedly do not apply to all suburbs. In a study of a suburb populated with workers from an automobile plant, Berger criticized many of the generalizations as "myths of suburbia." His study calls into question the propositions that organizational participation is higher in the suburbs, that residential mobility is greater, that the suburbs are characterized by political conservatism and a renewed interest in religion, and that suburban culture is essentially middle class.[59] Although the "working-class suburb" may itself be a deviant case, the generalizations based on the suburban studies thus far completed should be regarded as tentative and not without exceptions. All suburbs may tend to be alike in some respects, but most of the generalizations about them apply to neighborhoods inhabited by middle-class commuters. Industry as well as population is now being decentralized in metropolitan areas and working-class suburbs are becoming more numerous.

MEGALOPOLIS

Urban development in the industrialized world has not been merely a matter of the growth of more and larger cities. On the Northeastern seaboard of the United States, in Great Britain, in the Low Countries, and in Western Germany, a new type of urban entity has grown up—the megalopolis. The megalopolis consists of two or more cities,

[58] See especially William M. Dobriner (ed.), *The Suburban Community* (New York: Putnam, 1948), and William H. Whyte, Jr., *The Organization Man* (New York: Simon and Schuster, 1956).

[59] Bennett Berger, *The Working-Class Suburb* (Berkeley and Los Angeles: University of California Press, 1960).

once separated by broad bands of countryside, but now joined by strips of urban or semiurban settlement. Within the connecting strips there is an intermingling of urban, suburban, and rural land uses and a new relationship of the urban and the rural. The residents of the "super cities" are more widely dispersed than the residents of traditional compact cities, and their activities are not organized around any one central core. However, they have a higher degree of interdependence than the residents of any other area of comparable extent.

Although megalopolis has social and ecological unity, it lacks political unity. Unified planning and action are needed to handle effectively such problems as transportation and resource conservation, which transcend the bounds of the politically separate cities. So far, however, most planning and social action within the super cities have been piecemeal, and the adaptation of political and other institutions has lagged behind the needs of these new social entities.

Administrative Fragmentation

The numerous jurisdictions are jealous of their authorities and prerogatives, and as yet no "natural" agency has grown up to fill the gaps in management, to bridge authorities, or to devise over-all plans. The following comment, written during the *Blitzkrieg* of World War II, depicts Metropolitan London as a bombing target, and as a problem in administration.[60]

Centered on teeming Charing Cross, the London area is the most compact and circular conurbation in the world, and by the same token it is the most deadly target for aerial bombardment that man could ever have devised. . . . There are ten official Londons overlapping one another, like concentric circles around a bull's-eye, each one representing the metropolis in its various stages of governmental growth. These are the City of London, the County of London, Police London or Greater London, Port London, Drainage London, Water London, Electricity London, Transport London, Planning London, and Traffic London. Increasing in radius and in population from the London nucleus the whole southeastern corner of England is engulfed by the Metro London that began to emerge long before the present war.

Near the center of the bull's-eye is the City of London, now badly gutted by incendiary bombing, with only one square mile of territory not much larger than Chicago's Loop, and a resident population of only nine thousand souls (1937 estimate). The City plays primarily a financial and economic role, comparable to New York's Wall Street. Governmentally, too, it is still a powerful municipal corporation in spite of the fact that its Guildhall has been bombed out. It has, for example, a police force of its own that is independent of even Scotland Yard, and it exercises important extraterritorial functions including that of acting as the Port of London's Sanitary Authority.

Though its more important docks and harbors are within the City of London, Port London goes far beyond the city boundaries, for it is an elongated district extending sixty-nine miles from Teddington on the west to the Thames's mouth on the east, and is responsible for the second largest port in the world.

The analysis also enumerates the boundaries and functions of each "London," which together make up the super city.

The American megalopolis is an extreme example of political fragmentation.[61] This strip city extends from southern New Hampshire to the Virginia suburbs of Washington, D.C., a distance of some 425 miles. One can travel from one end to the other of this super city without leaving territory that is predominantly urban in its land use, its occupations, and the way of life of its people. Within the area about 20 per cent of the nation's people are concentrated on less than 2 per cent of

[60] Albert Lepawsky, "The London Region: A Metropolitan Community in Crisis," *American Journal of Sociology*, **46** (1941), 828–29.

[61] A detailed treatment of the economic and demographic characteristics of this area is given in Jean Gottman, *Megalopolis* (New York: The Twentieth Century Fund, 1961).

its land. Ten state governments, the District of Columbia, and hundreds of city, county, town, village governments—each has jurisdiction over a portion of this megalopolitan belt.

Smaller strip cities may soon develop along major transportation routes in the Midwest, in California, in Texas, and in other areas. Undoubtedly new institutional and organizational forms will develop to meet the needs of the vast urbanized regions, and sociological research must take these changes into account.

IMPACT OF TECHNOLOGICAL CHANGE

Technological change with its resulting expansion in some sectors of the economy and contraction in others is reflected in adjustments of communities, individuals, and governments. At the level of the individual the adjustment may take the form of migration to seek new opportunity, to follow a migrating industry, or to flee from an area of declining opportunity. Or if he has the financial resources and basic skills, the individual may qualify himself for new opportunities by retraining. At the level of government inducements may be made to hold industry or to attract new industry by resource development, tax concessions, or site privileges. Or government may turn its attention to retraining programs or other services for the labor force.

Vulnerable Communities

Whether change is beneficial or destructive, it is inevitably felt at the level of the community, that is the residential and local service area. The community is the crossroads of change for in it the interests of individuals and families make up a mutually reinforcing network that supports the service facilities and is supported by them. The effects of drastic change on the community may be illustrated by two accounts, one an instance of community retrenchment, the second of expansion.

Caliente [62] is a one-industry railroad town in the desert of the Southwestern U.S. It grew up as a division point to service steam locomotives. When men built their homes there they believed with some reason that their jobs on the railroad were secure. When businessmen put up their buildings, they thought the town would last, and when, collectively, the community built four churches, a 27-bed hospital, schools, and a water system, they thought they were building for the future as well as for the present.

The displacement of the steam locomotive by the diesel engine, a process greatly accelerated by World War II, spelled the death of Caliente. The relatively great efficiency of diesels (35 per cent *vs.* 4 per cent for steam locomotives) is expressed in the need for less frequent but more highly skilled service and fewer stops for fuel and water. Like many other railway division points, Caliente suddenly became technologically obsolete.

Caliente, like other towns in similar plight, was expected to accept its fate in the name of "progress." As shippers and consumers of shipped goods, the general public gains from better, faster service and eventually, perhaps, lower charges. A few of the Caliente workers who moved to other division points also gained through higher wages, but only as their seniority gave them the opportunity to work.

What are the losses, and who bears them? Before dieselization the total tax assessment on Caliente was about $9,900 of which $6,100 represented taxes assessed on the railroad. Thus the railroad valuation was about three-fifths that of the town, excluding tax-free

[62] This discussion is based on W. F. Cottrell, "Death by Dieselization: A Case Study in the Reaction to Technological Change," *American Sociological Review*, **16** (June, 1951), 358–65. The original article reports in detail the change in community sentiment, the withdrawal from *laissez-faire* principles and the attempts to use unions and political means to preserve jobs, personal income, and the financial base of the community. The field work for a follow-up study has been completed by the author, and comments about recent events are based on conversations with him. This courtesy is gratefully acknowledged.

property. The railroad can figure its losses fairly accurately. It owns 39 private dwellings, a modern clubhouse with 116 rooms, and a 12-room hotel with dining-room and lunch-counter facilities, which became useless, as did much of the fixed physical equipment for servicing trains. Some of the machinery could be used elsewhere, and some facilities, such as the roundhouse, are used for storage of standby equipment. The rest were torn down to save taxes, because the costs can be entered as capital losses on the company's books. Presumably the losses are recovered by the more efficient engines.

Probably the greatest losses were suffered by the older nonoperating employees, whose seniority extends only within the local shop and craft. A man with twenty-five years' seniority at Caliente has no priority over a similar craftsman at another point who has only twenty-five days' seniority. Moreover, some of the skills formerly valuable are no longer needed. The boilermaker's job, for example, is disappearing, and he must enter the ranks of the unskilled. The protection and status offered by the union while he was employed become meaningless now that he is no longer needed. His costs are high both in loss of income and in personal demoralization.

Operating employees also pay. Their seniority extends over a division, which in this case includes three division points. The older men can move from Caliente and claim jobs at another point, but in many cases they must leave a good portion of their life savings behind. Because of increased efficiency, however, jobs are wiped out, and three out of four operating men must seek employment outside the railroad.

The local merchants pay. The boarded windows, half-empty shelves, and abandoned store buildings bear mute evidence of their costs. The older merchants stay and pay; the younger ones, and those with no stake in the community move; but the value of property in both cases declines.

The churches pay. The smaller congregations cannot support services as in the past. As the churchmen leave, the buildings must be abandoned.

Homeowners pay. A hundred and thirty-five families owned homes in Caliente. They must accept the available means of support or rent to those who do. In either case income will be less than it was when the houses were built. The least desirable homes stand unoccupied, their value completely lost; the others are sharply devalued.

In a word, those who pay are by traditional American standards "most moral." Those who have raised children see friendships broken and neighborhoods disintegrated. The childless more freely shake the dust of Caliente from their feet. Those who built their personalities into the community watch their work destroyed, while the unentangled, the anomic, do not suffer. The chain store can move its equipment and charge the costs off against more profitable units, and against taxes. It did. The local owner had no such alternatives. In short, "good citizens," who assumed family and community responsibility, are the greatest losers. Nomads suffer least.

The first reaction to the threat against Caliente took the form of an effort at community self-preservation. Caliente became a real entity to its inhabitants, and community survival became more important than many of the individual values that had been given precedence in the past. The organized community searched for new industry, citing elements of community organization as reasons why industry should move to Caliente. But the conditions that led the railroad to abandon the town made it even less attractive to new industry than before. Although it seemed that Caliente was doomed by the forces of technological progress, by the snow-balling consequences of change that occur in all dynamic economies, some community leaders persisted in their efforts to find a new resource base. Eventually, they were successful in inducing the state to locate a Girls'

Industrial School in Caliente, and they have made strides toward developing the city as the center of a recreational area. Caliente has lost nearly half of its population, but it appears that a new basis for the economy has been established through the sustained effort and political influence of civic leaders. Although they could not cope directly with the technological problems, they appear to have surmounted some of the by-products of technological change.

Renaissance of a Community[63]

Huntsville, Alabama, began as a small town serving cotton plantations and cotton planters, some of whom moved into town and built fine homes in the early 1800's. It was a provincial place of extremes: poor Negroes, poor whites, and the gentility of the big houses. Before World War I fourteen cotton mills were built in Huntsville to be near the source of raw materials and cheap labor, and each mill had its dismal company village around it. Between World Wars I and II the mills became obsolescent, although not so suddenly and dramatically as the railway facilities in Caliente. Eventually only one mill remained in operation.

There is no readily available account of the changes that took place as the cotton mills closed down, but for Huntsville the result was retrenchment. The transient labor left, some shops cut back or closed, and the town continued but at a lower level of activity. During World War II there was a flurry of economic development with the creation of the Redstone Arsenal, but it soon closed.

Then, into the easy pace of Huntsville came the Space Age. At nearby Marshall the National Aeronautical Space Authority established the largest of its ten installations. There von Braun and his group worked on the Saturn.

If the Marshall Center had taken shape amid the aircraft and missile manufacturing complexes of southern California or amid the Northeast's vast mosaic of industry, it would doubtless remain almost invisible to the casual eye. But there is something startling and prophetic about finding it among cotton fields, loblolly pine, and people rooted in memories of the nineteenth century.[64]

In a decade Huntsville grew from 17,000 to 80,000, expanded from three square miles to fifty-six, has borrowed huge sums of money, spent $7 million for a new water system, $4 million on a new gas system, $12 million on a new electric system, and $10 million on new sewers. It built eight new firehouses, ripped out two slums and is tearing down historic Cotton Row to create a broad mall below the old town square.

It has built one new schoolroom a week for seven years, and by hiring the wives of Marshall Center scientists and technicians, has developed a teaching staff unique in small southern cities. The glare and clatter of boom is everywhere.

However . . . the boom-Huntsville is essentially a serious and quiet place. It has built sixty new churches in the last ten years but it has no bars and no night clubs. It brings the Boston Pops orchestra South for concerts, takes pride in public "clothesline" exhibits of amateur painting and in the fact that the University of Alabama is soon to build a $3-million research center in its midst. The grade schools have an international flavor; a good many Army brats now in attendance studied only last year in France or Germany. And a good deal about the town's extracurricular interests can be drawn from the fact that Clarence Ellis, a Huntsville engineer, ground a 21.5-inch mirror for the Rocket City Astronomical Association's telescope in his basement.[65]

By Caliente's standards or by the standards of most American cities, Huntsville is a success. There have been local costs in the changed pace and style of life that some conservative citizens would rather not pay. But

[63] Based on Paul O'Neil, "The Splendid Anachronism of Huntsville," *Fortune*, **65** (June, 1962), 150–55 *et seq.*

[64] *Ibid.*, p. 226.
[65] *Ibid.*, p. 226, 228.

these costs have been compensated by improved standards of living and education. Some old residents may regard this as a bad bargain, but the community has exchanged its provincialism for cosmopolitanism and its isolation for a conspicuous place in the national economy. It is now a boom town, committed to a period of vigorous expansion.

Because of their limited size, Caliente and Huntsville are excellent places in which to observe the impact of change. However, because of their limited size, they are more vulnerable to damaging trends and more profoundly affected by new opportunities. The loss of major industries or the establishment of new ones may disrupt the economy of a metropolitan center and cause the migration of many families. Prolonged, "impacted" unemployment may place overwhelming burdens on civic resources, but the change is likely to be perceived as statistical rather than communal. The sheer mass of the metropolitan area absorbs change and makes it obscure.

URBAN NEIGHBORHOODS

Metropolitan changes most nearly resembling the community examples are not the product of crises brought on by technology but of deliberately planned change. Slum clearance and urban redevelopment projects that use the formal authority of government to achieve their objectives undermine the communal structure of established neighborhoods, just as happened in Caliente. Small shops are destroyed and their customers displaced, churches lose their congregations and displaced families must live for months or years in places they did not choose. Even if the old residents eventually do return to the old localities the neighborhood is gone. A new community may grow up but this will be harder to achieve because the old shops and small service facilities have been destroyed, and with them the sense of identity that is the product of spontaneous and prolonged associations. These costs, too, are the by-product

—the unintended by-product of change. (See RELIGION, p. 442.)

Urban neighborhoods seem to have a typical life cycle—a period of rapid growth, an interim of stability, and a prolonged senescence of blight and decay. The rate at which neighborhoods go through these stages varies and depends upon a number of factors, such as the soundness of the construction of the original buildings, the encroachment of commercial and business activities, and geographical features that make the area inherently desirable for residential usage.

The typical life cycle of urban neighborhoods is due to the durability of buildings and the housing shortage, which has accompanied the rapid growth of American cities.[66] Because of these factors, old buildings remain profitable to their owners long after their condition falls below requirements of the upper and middle classes. Since to demolish these buildings would destroy property of considerable value, new residential construction is largely in previously uninhabited areas, and the old neighborhoods become slums.

The few upper- and upper-middle-class neighborhoods in large cities in which succession to lower-class residential usage has not occurred are rare enough to attract attention. Beacon Hill in Boston survives as a fashionable district, in spite of its great age and the encroachment of commercial activities, because it has become a symbol of upper-class standing and an object of strong sentiment among old Boston families.[67] An old residential area near the central business district in Chicago, the Gold Coast, has remained an upper- and upper-middle-class area, the old mansions having been gradually replaced by expensive high-rise apartments and residential hotels. A favorable location on the lake-front is a necessary although probably not a sufficient condition for this anomaly.

[66] Nelson N. Foote *et al., Housing Choices and Constraints* (New York: McGraw-Hill, 1960).

[67] Walter Firey, *Land Use in Central Boston* (Cambridge: Harvard University Press, 1947), Chap. 3.

Among the few other examples of highly desirable residential areas that have resisted decay, one warrants special attention. Its conservation as a middle-class area shows that seemingly natural and inevitable social processes can be resisted through social planning and concerted social action. At the same time it illustrates some of the difficulties involved in social planning in a democratic society.

Planned Change and Group Conflict [68]

Hyde Park–Kenwood is an area of some 70,000 people in Chicago's South Side. The community began as a railroad suburb in the 1850's and was engulfed by the growth of Chicago before the turn of the century. Residential building occurred in several waves from the era following the Civil War to 1920–1924. By the latter date, the residential plant was all but completed. By the 1950's, therefore, the newest residential buildings of any large number were more than a quarter of a century old, and a substantial proportion were at least fifty years old. The community was middle-aged and beyond.

From their beginnings, the neighborhoods in Hyde Park–Kenwood were fashionable or above average in desirability. Kenwood emerged as a cluster of large and expensive single-family dwellings on spacious lots, and most of Hyde Park was built up with commodious and substantial (although crowded) walk-up apartments and single-family dwellings. During the last major building wave in the area, a number of luxury high-rise apartments and residential hotels were built in East Hyde Park.

In 1950 the community was still far above Chicago as a whole in a number of social and economic indices, although its relative position had declined somewhat from 1940. Even though it was almost engulfed by the expansion of the "Black Belt," only 6.1 per cent of its population were nonwhite.

[68] See Peter H. Rossi and Robert A. Dentler, *The Politics of Urban Renewal* (New York: The Free Press of Glencoe, 1961).

That Hyde Park–Kenwood survived so long as an above-average residential area without concerted action to preserve its middle-class character can be attributed largely to a cluster of institutions. The most prominent of these is the University of Chicago, which has dominated the area physically and culturally almost since its founding in 1892. Other institutions in the area include The American School, George Williams College, the Chicago Osteopathic School, and the Museum of Science and Industry. The cultural attractions, the beaches, and several parks nearby have helped retain the upper-income residents of Kenwood and East Hyde Park, and the employees of the institutions comprise a large professional population.

After 1950, however, parts of the community began to deteriorate rapidly. A Negro invasion began in several localities, and the percentage of the nonwhite population increased to 36 per cent by 1956. Between 1950 and 1956, an estimated 20,000 whites left Hyde Park–Kenwood and were replaced with 23,000 nonwhites. The first of the Negro invaders were mainly business, professional, white-collar, and skilled workers, but the later arrivals were predominantly domestic servants and unskilled and semiskilled workers. Two Negro families sometimes moved into an apartment or house vacated by one white family. In the areas of Negro invasion the streets became crowded and littered. Transition to a lower-class community was well under way.

Hyde Park–Kenwood, however, was unlike most areas entering on the final stage of deterioration. (1) The large institutions in the area, particularly the University of Chicago, had heavy capital investments in the area and thus had a material interest in preserving its middle-class character. With a growing shortage of top-quality academic personnel in the nation, a slum location would be a distinct handicap to the University in its attempts to retain its position as a leading university. Furthermore, its undergraduate enrollment was dropping, in part due to a shortage of student housing in the vicinity. (2) The community in general had a liberal-intellectual orientation. Many of its residents, at least verbally, favored a biracial community, even though they wished to retain its middle-class character. Another element of the liberal-intellectual orientation was a belief in the possibility and desirability of planned social change. (3) The community was "hyperorganized" and had an above-average rate of political participation. (4) The University of Chicago, with its excellent social science departments, afforded an unusual planning resource.

Another factor which made conservation of the community possible was the timely passage of the Federal Housing Act of 1954, which authorized federal assistance for "urban renewal." Among other things, the bill provided that federal funds, supplemented by local funds, could be used to purchase blighted property to be sold below cost for private redevelopment or to be used for public housing. Launching of urban renewal projects depends entirely upon local initiative. Although the program adopted to conserve and rehabilitate Hyde Park–Kenwood came under "urban renewal," the groundwork for the program was laid before 1954.

Community Organization

The prime mover of the program to conserve and renew the community was the University of Chicago. As early as 1939 the University was active in efforts to conserve the middle-class character of its surroundings, but until 1952 its principal action had been the extension of racially restrictive covenants and the subsidizing of two community associations, which worked for enforcement of zoning and housing codes. In 1952 the University embarked upon a more positive effort at conservation. For this purpose it formed the South East Chicago Commission, which became the principal planning agency for the community. In 1954 the Commission assigned planning functions to a separate committee.

The second major participant in the efforts to conserve the community was the Hyde Park–Kenwood Community Conference, an organization with wide community support, founded in 1949 under the leadership of ministers, rabbis, and laymen from liberal religious groups. At times the Conference influenced the conservation planning process, but its chief role was to serve as a transmission belt between the Planning Unit and the citizens. The support and confidence of the citizenry was necessary for two reasons. (1) The community could not be conserved if the residents did not have enough confidence in its future to remain, and (2) popular support or at least the lack of strong popular opposition was needed if public officials were to approve the plan. The Community Conference helped provide the mass support.

Conflicting Perspectives

At first there was near consensus on the desirability of taking positive action to conserve the community. However, as details of the plan were worked out, it became evident to many that the execution of the plan would be to their detriment. Persons who at first received the plan warmly became less enthusiastic when they learned they were to be planned out of the community. Many learned that Hyde Park–Kenwood was to become so "renewed" that they could no longer afford to live there. Businessmen who at first looked with favor upon plans for a new shopping center were less favorable when they learned that the total number of business establishments would be reduced and not all of them would be able to relocate in the community. Particularly cool to the plan were the Negro residents in areas selected for clearing. For most, the movement into Hyde Park was upward mobility. Their housing was better than they had before and better than they could find elsewhere in Chicago. People who had invested money and work on their homes resented having them defined as dilapidated.

What were blighted areas to older residents were pleasant neighborhoods to the new arrivals. A vast difference in social class perspectives was evident.

Controversy arose among the leaders in the conservation movement. Racial liberals were disturbed that the renewal would greatly reduce the Negro population in the area. Racial conservatives were disturbed by the guarantees of nondiscrimination that would come with participation in the federal urban renewal program. In the end, the liberals accepted less biracialism than they desired, and the conservatives accepted more. Many middle-class Negroes were ambivalent toward the plan. As one prominent Negro put it, "every Hyde Park Negro leader is almost driven schizophrenic trying to decide whether to act as a 'Race Man' or in terms of his social class position." [69]

Opposition to the plan also arose from other sections of Chicago. The effects of the renewal would not be strictly local. If the population density in Hyde Park–Kenwood was to be reduced, the displaced population was likely to contribute to overcrowding in other parts of the city. People in other white areas bordering the "Black Belt" feared that stemming the Negro movement into Hyde Park–Kenwood would increase pressure for Negro entry into their neighborhoods. The Chicago Negro leaders generally opposed the plan because it would reduce the amount of housing available to Negroes. The NAACP, the Chicago Urban League, the Cardinal's Committee on Conservation and Urban Renewal, and the Packinghouse Workers Union were among the opponents.

Some of the opposition to the plan from within Hyde Park–Kenwood subsided as compromises were made and people became reconciled to being displaced. An association of residents in South West Hyde Park opposed through litigation the use of condemnation procedures to clear an area in that neighborhood, but the efforts were unsuccessful. The city-wide opposition to the urban renewal plan delayed approval of the plan by the City Council, but the opponents did not gain wide public support.

Final approval of the plan came late in 1958, six years after the formation of the South East Chicago Commission. In its final form the plan was a compromise that satisfied no one completely. For instance, liberals were chagrined that no guarantee for public housing was included in the plan. However, the plan was generally acceptable to the interests of the University of Chicago and those Hyde Park–Kenwood residents who wished to keep the community solidly middle class.

BUSINESS CENTRALIZATION AND CIVIC WELFARE

The growth of nationwide industrial organizations affects the fate of local communities. The resource base can be wiped out or a boom can be started by decisions made hundreds of miles away. Caliente and Huntsville are examples of vulnerable communities. Another way of viewing this problem is to study the consequences of business activities that are branches of national enterprises. (See Adaptation 41, pp. 623 ff.) The social characteristics of two very different types of cities—those dominated by one large industry and those where most of the workers are employed by a number of small firms. This study of medium-sized cities shows that the level of civic welfare is appreciably higher in the small-business cities, and that it is related to differences in the composition of the middle class, career patterns, and sources of power. The availability of leadership for community enterprises is an important factor in the level of civic welfare. In small-business cities, leadership is in the hands of a group of middle-class persons with stable incomes and positions and strong economic and social interest in their community. Their values about what constitutes a

[69] *Ibid.,* p. 181.

"good" city, a city in which they have a stake, govern in large part the direction of civic development.

Caution: Further studies are needed to determine whether the observed differences between big- and small-business cities occur generally and are due to the dominance of big business versus the prevalence of small business. It is possible that social and economic pressures and interests will lead large corporations to be more active in community enterprises. The findings of Adaptation 41 cannot be assumed to apply to the great metropolitan centers where many corporations, large and small, influence civic welfare in diverse, competitive, and perhaps complementary ways.

Small Business and Civic Welfare

Abridged and adapted from C. Wright Mills and Melville J. Ulmer, *Small Business and Civic Welfare*, Report of the Smaller War Plants Corporation to the Special Committee to Study Problems of American Small Business, United States Senate (Washington, D.C.: Government Printing Office, 1946). Published in this form by permission of C. Wright Mills and Melville J. Ulmer.

The American economy became increasingly concentrated during World War II as big business made substantial gains in an economy already characterized by extremely high concentration. A relatively few gigantic corporations are now responsible for the bulk of America's entire industrial production and employment. In 1951 firms with 1,000 or more employees accounted for about 40 per cent of all paid employees. These firms included only 0.1 per cent of all firms.

The report discusses how the concentration of economic power affects the general welfare of cities and their inhabitants. It focuses on two problems: (1) economic stability and (2) the level of civic welfare. This summary is limited to the second topic: Does the concentration of economic power raise or depress the level of civic welfare in cities?

The Plan of the Study

Three pairs of medium to small cities were chosen for study. The cities in each pair were so selected that they had several basic factors in common—geographical location, size of population, percentage of foreign born and Negroes in the population, etc. In the case of two of these pairs, however, the cities differ sharply in one important respect. One of each pair was clearly a big-business city; the other was distinctly a small-business city. A big-business city is one in which (*a*) a few large firms employ all or most of the workers; (*b*) ownership of most of the industrial facilities lies outside the city; and (*c*) business activity is concentrated in one or a very few industrial lines. Conversely, a small-business city is one in which (*a*) most of the workers are employed by a large number of small firms; (*b*) the bulk of the industrial facilities are locally owned; and (*c*) business activity is diversified. In the case of the third pair of cities the differentiation between big- and small-business was not so sharp.

The large-firm cities were chosen to represent local manifestations of a national trend —the trend toward industrial concentration, absentee ownership, and the dominance of giant corporations. Similarly, the small-firm cities were selected to represent communities which were characterized by a number of small, locally owned, and competitive enterprises.

The Measure of Civic Welfare

A "good" city may mean different things to different people. Nevertheless, there are numerous standards of welfare on which virtually everyone will agree. Clearly a city is "better" if fewer of its children die during their first year after birth, if it has more parks for children to play in and more recreational facilities for all age groups. Housing, health, utilities, cultural facilities, and per capita income, for example, are agreed upon as obvious elements in any measure of civic welfare. A composite index, which included these as well as numerous other measures, was used as a standard of evaluation of the big-business and small-business cities.[70]

The Findings

The over-all measure of civic welfare showed that in each case the small-business cities studied rated materially higher than did the comparable big-business cities. While there were discrepancies in some of the individual measures, the general pattern was clear. Infant mortality was appreciably greater in the cities where large corporations predominated. In cities dominated by small competitive firms, housing conditions were superior, church membership more frequent, and public expenditures on recreation and libraries higher. The interest of residents in literature and educational subjects was also greater. The small-business cities were more adequately provided with the common utilities—telephones and electricity.

Civic Spirit

The improvement of parks, schools, libraries, and streets is carried on extensively only if there is an active civic spirit. It was found that this value did not have firm roots in the big-business cities, and insofar as it existed, it was of a different and less active

[70] This measure was developed by E. L. Thorndike in *Your City* (New York: Harcourt, Brace, 1938). For another measure of civic welfare see Robert C. Angell, "The Moral Integration of Cities," *American Journal of Sociology*, Vol. 57, No. 1, Part 2 (July, 1951).

type than that which prevailed in the small-business cities. Big business seemed to dry up interest in community enterprises. Five reasons are given why civic spirit—and thus civic welfare—tended to be more pronounced, more widely shared, and more active in the cities with small firms:

1. *The independent middle class.* The economically independent middle class—small-businessmen, firm members, and officials of local corporations—predominate in small-business cities. The small-businessman is traditionally the chief participant in the management of community enterprises. He usually has some time and money available, and is, on the average, fairly well educated. His work in conducting a small firm trains him for initiative and responsibility. His business throws him into constant contact with the administrative and political figures of the city. Furthermore, the small-businessman often stands to benefit personally as a result of civic improvement; better highways and streets lead to greater sales for the retail merchant. By participating actively in civic affairs, he widens his circle of contacts. For retailers the good will of the community obviously has value in dollars and cents.

In the big-business cities, however, there is no particular reason for the officials of giant corporations to be personally well known. There is little economic incentive for officials of absentee-owned corporations "to be someone civically." This is one of the most important causes of the lower levels of civic welfare in the cities dominated by large firms.

A middle class consisting largely of the salaried employees of the giant corporations is characteristic of the big-business cities. There is less incentive and less chance for these salaried people to take the lead in civic enterprises. They lack the economic independence of an active small-business group. Furthermore, the mass of salaried employees, below the top executive levels, lack the necessary training in leadership.

2. *The patterns of success.* The traditional pattern of success for the independent businessman consists of: (*a*) founding a business enterprise and (*b*) conducting and expanding that enterprise. But in the big-business city, the pattern is quite different; it involves (*a*) getting a "forward looking" job in one of the existing big corporations and (*b*) working one's way up the line within this corporation. The first type of success pattern may be called that of the business enterpriser; the second, that of the business careerist.

Rising within a city's business and civic hierarchy is a far different affair from climbing within the corporate hierarchy. The business careerist looks for his advancement not to local individuals or institutions, but rather to the officials of the corporation. Corporate officials do not include active participation in civic enterprises among the standards for promoting subordinates. In addition, the truly successful business careerist moves physically because success in a great absentee-owned firm involves rising in the corporation, and eventually this means getting out of town and into the central office.

In sharp contrast, the business enterpriser founds a local business or carries on the business of his family. He remains locally rooted and locally oriented. His own business success is linked to his participation in civic affairs.

3. *The distribution of prestige.* In cities with small competitive firms, the local businessmen gain prestige by participating in civic enterprises. In big-business cities, however, prestige is gained by an entirely different route. It is achieved by "getting in with" and imitating those who hold the real power and prestige in the city, namely, the executives of the big corporations and their wives. Beside them, the standing of small-businessmen in the community is dwarfed. The tendency of the old, upper-middle class to imitate and try to "get in with" the corpora-

tion group, coupled with the tendency of the "bright young men" to leave the city or become business careerists, creates a civic vacuum in the big-business city.

Middle-class women are frequently more active than men in civic matters, especially in education, health, and charities, if for no other reason than that they have more time available. Although women participate in civic affairs for a variety of reasons, including, of course, the simple desire to be of service to the community, they will generally participate to a greater extent if (*a*) "it is the thing to do," that is, if it increases their prestige, or (*b*) it helps their husbands' business. These motivations of civic activity are much stronger in the small- than in the big-business cities. In the corporation dominated cities, a woman gains little social prestige by participating in civic affairs. Nor does the corporate official's wife help her husband's career by such activities. The power of the corporation's name will readily provide him with all of the contacts in the city that he will ever require. Executive wives need not even be concerned with civic enterprises related to education, because they send their own children to exclusive schools or to suburban schools, which are separate from the city's schools.

4. *Real and apparent power.* Although the officials of the large absentee-owned firms have little interest in civic affairs, they nonetheless actually run the big-business cities studied in this report. The answer to this apparent paradox is that corporation men, in fact, take action in civic affairs only when these civic affairs impinge upon corporation interests. In such cases, the influence of corporation men is often exerted behind the façade of local politics. It is in this sense that officials of the great absentee-owned firms possess the real power in civic affairs, although the apparent power may reside elsewhere. Their direct economic control, which may spread, for example, to the control over local banks, is taken for granted. Their in-

direct controls over virtually every facet of urban life are less obvious. By threatening to leave the town, refraining from participating in activities, or by withholding financial support, they can control, block, or encourage civic projects and improvements.

5. *Labor and civic leadership.* During recent years labor has played an increasingly active role in civic affairs. In the cities studied, labor was more likely to participate co-operatively in civic matters, along with other groups in the small-business cities.

The civic activities of business groups in a small-business city are typically of a kind more likely to elicit the co-operation of labor. There are more informal relations between owners and workers because industrial plants are smaller and because it is easier for a wage earner to visualize himself as a potential businessman. In the big-business cities, on the other hand, if labor participates in civic activities, it is more likely to do so independently and often in conflict with business groups.

It is possible that in the future labor will be more active in the big-business cities, where traditional civic leadership has practically vanished. In the big-business cities studied, labor was undertaking civic responsibilities and pushing a number of different civic projects. It was actively interested in the conduct of the city government. However, while civic vacuums may develop in big-business cities, it does not follow that labor can readily step into such vacuums. Lack of leadership training and leisure may hinder widespread participation.

Conclusion

This study of small business and civic welfare shows that communities in which small firms predominate had a higher level of civic welfare than comparable communities dominated by large corporations. In small-business cities the environment was favorable to the development and growth of civic spirit. The interests of the potential leaders of civic enterprises were generally mutual and locally rooted. In big-business cities, civic spirit was stunted or distorted. The potential leaders of civic enterprise were either powerless to act or were motivated by interests outside the city.

Caution: It is impossible to say from the available data whether such differences as infant mortality and housing are traceable to the size of business or to some other, perhaps unrelated, influence. It should also be kept in mind that the interpretations are based on only three pairs of cities.

Chapter XVI

Industrial man*

* This chapter draws on material included in earlier editions in Chapter XIII, INDUSTRIAL SOCIOLOGY, prepared by Helen Beem Gouldner in collaboration with L. B. and P. S. We wish again to acknowledge our indebtedness to her.

Section 1   Early industrialization

Among the master trends of modern history is the rise of industrialism—an economic and social order based on machine technology and on large-scale highly specialized systems of production. Industrialization began in western Europe but it has now become world-wide. Men everywhere seem destined to know and live with, to enjoy and endure, the distinctive features of an industrial society.

This chapter considers, first, some aspects of the early stages of industrialization, especially the problems of motivation and discipline that accompany the break from traditional society. The discussion draws on studies of early capitalism and on analyses of non-Western society. Section 2 traces the development of two major institutions of industrial society—the business firm and the labor union. Section 3 discusses the impact of technology on human relations with emphasis on the theory of alienation. Finally, Section 4 presents some highlights of the social composition of the labor force.

SOCIAL RELATIONS AND INDUSTRIAL CAPITALISM

Under feudalism, the matrix of social life was the economically self-sufficient manor, controlled by a lord. Economic roles were fixed by tradition and custom, and division of labor was limited to broad categories. There were farmers, supervisors, soldiers, and village artisans, such as blacksmiths, carpenters, and masons. An individual's occupational position and his status of freeman or serf were inherited and conditioned by family relations. Unfree tenants or serfs were bound to the manor by tradition and law. Everyone in the manorial group was obligated to render services to the lord and pay taxes in goods or money. The lord, in turn, resolved disputes, avenged the wrongs to his people, and protected the manorial group from foreign invasion and marauding bands.

The collapse of feudal society permitted workers to move about and seek different occupations. The new conditions, free labor

During the Middle Ages labor was divided in a few very broad categories. One worker completed a finished product. This is in marked contrast to the occupational specialization of modern economy. More than 22,000 jobs are listed in the Directory of Occupational Titles *of the United States Employment Service.*

The Butcher and His Servant

and an emphasis on achieved rather than ascribed status, made the social system more congenial to the emergence and continuation of industrial capitalism. Of course, many other changes were necessary for the growth of industrial capitalism, such as the application of science and technology to production and distribution, development of a free market and world trade, and establishment of the factory as the unit of production.

The breakdown of feudal rights and obligations between the lord and tenants freed workers to go where early capitalist enterprises were located. Large groups of propertyless workers provided the labor force necessary to industrial capitalism.

With a free labor force, the individual entrepreneur was not responsible for his workers as was the feudal lord. He could hire and fire according to the needs of his factory.[1]

[1] Max Weber, *The Theory of Social and Economic Organization* (New York: Oxford University Press, 1947), pp. 276–78; Wilbert E. Moore, *Industrial Relations and the Social Order* (2nd ed.; New York: Macmillan, 1951), pp. 420–21 and 425–27.

Under the system of free labor individuals are able to sell their labor (or their goods) wherever it is most profitable. They are not bound, traditionally or legally, to negotiations with particular persons and are not limited in their activities by rigid class distinctions. Since both laborer and enterpriser can deal with many rather than few individuals, it is possible for wide markets and competitive practices to develop.

Achieved Status

Under feudalism a person's station in life and occupational role were fixed by tradition and inheritance. The son of a serf was also a serf, and the son of a blacksmith in a feudal village was trained to become a blacksmith. With the advent of free labor, emphasis on ascribed factors in the assignment of occupational position was replaced by emphasis on individual choice and achievement. Heredity still determines, to some degree, general class status and broad occupational groups (such as manual and nonmanual

The Coppersmith

The Hatter

labor). However, the major social emphasis is on individual choice and achievement in the assignment of particular positions.

Division of labor on achieved rather than hereditary status is more congenial to the development and expansion of industrial capitalism because: (*a*) Achievement is better adapted to specialization—a characteristic feature of industrial capitalism. When occupations are inherited and training takes place within the family, the number of specializations is limited. (*b*) Technological advance has been a major feature of industrial capitalism; job requirements constantly change and new jobs are continually created. It is unlikely that the technological advances that have played a major role in the expansion of industrial capitalism could have developed to such an extent without an emphasis on achieved status and its accompanying ideals of initiative and acquisition. On the relation of achieved status and machine technology, see "Industrialism and Social Relations in Non-Western Societies," pages 636 ff.

RELIGION AND CAPITALISM

Just as an economic order requires congenial social relations, so it depends on beliefs and sentiments that make for effective participation in economic activities. Individualism, and the belief that hard work, thrift, self-discipline, accumulation of money, initiative, and rationality are virtues make up the set of values called the "spirit" or "ethos" of capitalism. These beliefs are not uniformly shared by the whole society, but are characteristic of middle-class entrepreneurs. The values are put forward as *duties* in Benjamin Franklin's "Advice to a Young Tradesman" (p. 633).

These personal aspirations and disciplines were especially important in the formative stages of capitalism. Early capitalism depended on the enterprise and work of individuals rather than on complicated and impersonal large-scale organizations. The development of capitalism required enterprisers who were motivated to work hard, to save, to compete for markets, to expand their

Max Weber (1864–1920) was one of the German economic historians and sociologists who attempted to trace the distinctive features of the capitalist social and economic order. He undertook a vast comparative study of world religions in order to see the relation between religious ideas and economic development. The best-known product of this work is The Protestant Ethic and the Spirit of Capitalism. *He also wrote extensively on bureaucracy, law, and the logical foundations of social science.*

businesses, and to accumulate capital. For both the enterpriser and his immediate subordinates, individual qualities, such as self-discipline, were important in assuring adequate attention to the requirements of the job. Insofar as the cultural supports for discipline and work extended to the working class, they helped to insure regular attendance and continuous operation of the machines in the factories. "Grass may grow and

sheep may graze if the peasant lies drunk under the hedge occasionally, but the wheels of mills cannot turn steadily if boiler stokers must have frequent debauches." [2]

The cultural source of such values as industriousness, self-discipline, initiative, and acquisitiveness has been much debated. The problem is this:

. . . how is it possible that strata of enterprisers and workers emerge that are willing to engage in methodically persistent, hard work and thereby gain a competitive advantage over less principled, more traditionalist economic agents? These men forego the traditional enjoyments of wealth—the expansion of their consumption, or the investment of wealth in ostentatious ways. How is it, then, that men arise who work hard, despite the fact that in the value terms of their economic tradition and epoch they have no understandable motives for doing so? [3]

The Protestant Ethic

One historical interpretation suggests that capitalist ideology had its main roots in the spread of Protestantism throughout Western societies. Max Weber, in his *Protestant Ethic and the Spirit of Capitalism,*[4] was one of the initiators and chief proponents of this view. The main points in his study show how Protestant doctrine shaped the personalities of the entrepreneurial middle class in which capitalism had its origins:

1. *Self-discipline and work.* The Calvinist doctrine of predestination held that men were to be either condemned to everlasting Hell or to "live in the House of the Lord forever," depending on the judgment of the Lord. Because believers in this doctrine were uncer-

[2] Charles A. Beard. "Individualism and Capitalism," In *Encyclopaedia of the Social Sciences* (London: Macmillan, Ltd.), **1**. Quotation at p. 149.

[3] Hans Gerth and C. Wright Mills, *Character and Social Structure* (New York: Harcourt, Brace, 1953), p. 215. Used by permission.

[4] Translated by Talcott Parsons (London: Allen and Unwin, 1930). See also R. H. Tawney, *Religion and the Rise of Capitalism* (New York: Harcourt, Brace, 1926). On the relation of religion and capitalism and for a general restatement of Weber's thesis, see Gerth and Mills, *op. cit.,* pp. 234–36 and pp. 360–63.

John Calvin (1509–1564), Swiss theologian, was one of the leading architects of the Protestant Reformation. At the age of twenty-six he published The Institutes of the Christian Religion, *one of the most influential religious books in history. Calvin stressed the depravity and corruption of human nature, the need for redemption through faith and repentance, and the doctrine of predestination and election. His views led to a great emphasis on such personal traits as self-denial and self-discipline, which Weber linked to the "capitalist spirit." The sponsor and leader of a theocracy in Geneva, Calvin had no idea of contributing to economic or political individualism. While he greatly influenced Protestantism as a whole, his impress was most felt in Puritan England, Scotland, and New England.*

tain whether or not they were among the elect, they had anxieties and insecurities. Strict self-discipline, the rejection of worldly pleasures, and righteous success in this world through hard work came to be regarded as signs of grace that one was in God's favor and possibly among the elect. Relief from religious anxieties was thus sought in honest, efficient toil and self-control. To work was to pray, and work was a calling. Independent, honest business was interpreted as a calling particularly acceptable to God.

2. *Initiative and acquisition.* Patterns of hard work and self-discipline won economic advantage over competitors and led to the acquisition of wealth. Avoidance of worldly pleasure, emphasis on thrift, and abhorrence of waste withheld the traditional uses of wealth from the early Puritans. They could, however, use their capital to extend production and develop additional enterprises. Individual initiative was rewarded, since success in work was interpreted as a sign of God's blessing. Furthermore, continual work in one's calling was necessary, since there was constant anxiety about salvation. No matter

what the Puritan accomplished in this world, there was no guarantee of salvation. There was no point at which he could relax. The expansion of productive enterprises also helped the Puritan establish the Kingdom of God on earth. He could give more workers the chance to prove themselves among the elect by sober, hard work.

3. *Individualism and competition.* Puritanism emphasized that man is alone before his Maker. He should not trust the friendship of men; only God should be his confidant. Even those closest to him might be among the damned. Each individual had to seek success as the sign of grace, and this striving was consistent with economic competition. While he had to deal honestly and righteously with other men, he was ready to take advantage of his opportunities even if it meant outdoing his competitors. (See RELIGION, p. 423.)

The contribution of Protestantism to the development of capitalism was not direct. Certainly the originators of Protestantism had no idea of producing or even supporting an economic order based on individualism and unlimited profit-seeking. But their religious revolution went beyond religion to influence more general cultural attitudes toward work, poverty, individual obligation, and the worth of trade and industry. The rising merchant and industrial classes of the seventeenth and eighteenth centuries linked themselves to these new values, were strengthened by them, and they in turn helped to mold religion to the requirements of a commercial age.[5]

Religion and Mature Capitalism

As capitalism became more formalized and institutionalized, and as accounting systems and other controls developed it leaned less heavily on the personal qualities of individuals. Capitalism became less dependent on religious motivations and disciplines. Utilitarian and pecuniary, rather than religious, motives predominate in the writings of Benjamin Franklin (see p. 633). As Weber suggested, once capitalism became the dominant and pervasive economic order, it no longer needed religion.

However, many of the ideas embodied in Protestantism continue to support modern industry. Self-discipline persists in the interest of attaining removed goals such as wealth and high status. Initiative, hard work, and success in one's work are still approved. These values eliminate the need for extensive socialization within industrial organizations in the Western world. Individuals come to an organization already inculcated with appropriate behavior patterns.

INDUSTRIALIZATION IN NON-WESTERN SOCIETIES

As industrialization continues to spread throughout the non-Western world, social scientists have the opportunity to observe the impact of machine technology on social organization and values and the interdependence of economic activities and social

organization. For example, preliminary studies of industrialization in underdeveloped countries suggest that the extent to which a society is integrated affects the degree of resistance to industrialization and the amount of disorganization that accompanies it.[6]

Adaptation 42 outlines the social patterns accompanying the introduction of machine technology in non-Western societies. It indicates how industrialism causes the old social order to break down by separating economic activities from the total social system, by placing new individuals in positions of power, and by changing the level of aspiration of the workers. New social relations develop in the adjustment to machines. Impersonal relations take the place of the former close personal ties between a worker and his relatives and neighbors. Achieved status, rather than family relations, becomes an important basis of division of labor and social differentiation.

The Dual Society and Labor Commitment[7]

The penetration of industrialization into nonindustrial societies has at least two possible results. (1) The old order may be completely supplanted by a homogeneous industrial society. This is likely to occur where the indigenous population is sparse and has a weakly developed technology. In Australia, for example, the small numbers of aborigines are peripheral to the industrial economy and influence it in no important way. (2) The penetration of industrialism may lead to a *dual society,* which is the coexistence of an industrial social system with a preindustrial one. This may occur when industrialism is introduced into densely populated agrarian societies. Most often the imported system is mature capitalism, but sometimes it is social-

---

[5] Cf. Tawney, *op. cit.*

[6] Wilbert E. Moore, *Industrialization and Labor* (Ithaca: Cornell University Press, 1951). See also Bert F. Hoselitz (ed.), *The Progress of Underdeveloped Areas* (Chicago: University of Chicago Press, 1952).

[7] This discussion is indebted to J. H. Boeke, *Economics and Economic Policy of Dual Societies* (New York: Institute of Pacific Relations, 1953), and Wilbert E. Moore, *op. cit.* in ftn. 6.

WORKS

of the late

Doctor Benjamin Franklin

Consisting of

HIS LIFE WRITTEN BY HIMSELF,

together with

Essays, Humorous, Moral & Literary,

Chiefly in the Manner of

THE SPECTATOR.

ADVICE TO A YOUNG TRADESMAN.

WRITTEN ANNO 1748.

REMEMBER that *time* is money. He that can earn ten shillings a day by his labour, and goes abroad, or sits idle one half of that day, though he spends but sixpence during his diversion or idleness, ought not to reckon *that* the only expence; he has really spent, or rather thrown away, five shillings besides.

Remember that money is of a prolific generating nature. Money can beget money, and its offspring can beget more, and so on. Five shillings turned is six; turned again, it is seven and three-pence; and so on till it becomes an hundred pounds. The more there is of it, the more it produces every turning, so that the profits rise quicker and quicker.

Beware of thinking all your own that you possess, and of living accordingly. It is a mistake that many people who have credit fall into. To prevent this, keep an exact account, for some time, both of your expences and your income. If you take the pains at first to mention particulars, it will have this good effect; you will discover how wonderfully small trifling expences mount up to large sums, and will discern what might have been, and may for the future be saved, without occasioning any great inconvenience.

In short, the way to wealth, if you desire it, is as plain as the way to market. It depends chiefly on two words, *industry* and *frugality*; that is, waste neither *time* nor *money*, but make the best use of both. Without industry and frugality nothing will do, and with them every thing. He that gets all he can honestly, and saves all he gets (necessary expences excepted), will certainly become *rich*—if that Being who governs the world, to whom all should look for a blessing on their honest endeavours, doth not, in his wise providence, otherwise determine.

AN OLD TRADESMAN.

ism, communism, or a blend of systems. Dual societies now exist in much of the world, including most of Eastern and Southern Asia, Africa, and Latin America.

Basic values and motivations are different in industrial and preindustrial societies, and in dual societies the divergent motives impinge upon one another in complicated and not always predictable ways. In Western society desire for more wealth is rarely satiated, and economic rewards maintain their effectiveness in influencing decisions and actions. Furthermore, monetary wealth is an acceptable reward even if it is not immediately converted into goods and services. The man whose needs are completely provided for can be induced to work for additional money— money he may not spend for years, if ever. The "economic man" of classical economics was supposed to be motivated solely by the desire to maximize wealth. Although he has never existed, his closest approximation is Western industrial man.

Preindustrial man hardly resembles economic man at all. He has no desire to accumulate wealth for its own sake. Hunger and other physical needs are the primary spurs to economic activity, and when these are satisfied, incentive disappears. Workers in nonindustrial social systems often work hard to satisfy an immediate need but cannot be spurred to further effort once that need is satisfied. In industrial societies higher pay usually holds down the rate of labor turnover. Preindustrial workers tend to leave the job when their immediate requirements are satisfied, and higher pay may, therefore, result in increased labor turnover.

Labor Commitment

Much has been written about the problems of recruiting a committed, reliable, and stable labor force in societies undergoing industrialization. The limited economic wants of workers are only one obstacle to a committed labor force. For instance, in nonindustrial societies kinship systems are also economic systems, and a marked change in the economic role of the man, such as his entering the industrial labor force, disrupts his accustomed social relations. Consequently, the social penalties of his disruption may deter him from industrial work even if he has economic incentives for working. Furthermore, peasants and artisans often dislike or think they would dislike the rigid time schedule and discipline of the factory. An anticipated loss of personal autonomy was found to be a major obstacle to industrial employment in a study of a Mexican village.[8] However, workers actually adjusted well to the schedule and discipline of industrial employment.

Although the problem of obtaining a committed industrial labor force in dual societies is formidable, it is not insurmountable. Industrialism is advancing throughout the world, perhaps impeded but never stopped by a lack of committed labor. When industrial and nonindustrial ways of life come into conflict, eventual victory of the industrial way apparently is inevitable.

Workers enter and remain in the industrial labor force despite contrary influences. The first industrial recruits are usually the landless, the hungry, the politically powerless, and the socially disaffected, who are pushed rather than pulled into industrial employment. The push is often provided by the beginning of industrialization itself. Cheap manufactured goods lessen the demand for handicraft goods and make it necessary for artisans to seek new means of livelihood. Basic needs can no longer be satisfied in traditional ways. The reduced mortality that accompanies industrialization spurs population growth, increases rural population density, and makes it difficult for peasants to subsist by tilling the land.

It has been thought that in India the conservatism of a traditional village society and a caste system would impede the develop-

[8] Moore, *op. cit.,* Chap. 12.

ment of an industrial labor force. However, the recruitment of committed workers has gone forward faster than expected.

The desperate poverty of the countryside made available a large labor supply that was eager to move into industry as opportunity appeared. Once employed in the factories, the workers on the whole rather readily adjusted to the disciplinary requirements of mechanized industry. Early in the history of the steel company at Jamshedpur an intensely committed labor force emerged. In Bombay, although the evidence is somewhat less conclusive, commitment to industrial employment was not difficult to achieve. Neither the multiplicity of language nor the institutions of caste seriously affected employers' ability to obtain a labor force committed to the factory system.[9]

The extent to which a labor force is incorporated into the industrial complex is measured by the degree to which the following conditions hold:

1. Acceptance of factory routines, time schedules, and discipline

2. Surmounting traditional obstacles to interaction on the job, e.g., caste barriers or inhibitions of race

3. Free geographic movement of labor to places of manpower shortage

4. Labor stability, i.e., little absenteeism and capricious quitting

Cautions: 1. It should not be assumed that the end product of industrialization is complete Westernization. For example, Japan has acquired an industrial technology and an efficient organization of its labor force. But the organization of the labor force is in some sectors of the economy more paternalistic and regimented than in the West. Many of the adaptations of modern Japan are evolutions of Japanese culture rather than of Western culture. The future development of Japan will be away from the traditional society but not necessarily toward Western forms.[10]

2. This discussion has focused on worker adjustment to an industrial order. Management also must assume responsibility in creating a committed labor force. Worker adjustment is retarded when management tries to maintain traditional, paternalistic authority without assuming the obligations of paternalistic responsibility, or when management treats new recruits from villages as if they were experienced and committed workers.

3. In Western societies industrialism was a gradual outcome of a combination of economic, social, and cultural conditions. This is different from imposing a highly developed industrial pattern on nonindustrialized societies that lack the social and cultural supports present in Western societies.

SOURCES AND READINGS

Reinhard Bendix, *Work and Authority in Industry* (New York: Wiley, 1956).

Peter M. Blau and W. Richard Scott, *Formal Organizations: A Comparative Approach* (San Francisco: Chandler, 1962).

Theodore Caplow, *Sociology of Work* (Minneapolis: University of Minnesota Press, 1954).

Melville Dalton, *Men Who Manage* (New York: Wiley, 1959).

Burleigh B. Gardner and David G. Moore, *Human Relations in Industry* (2nd ed.; Chicago: Irwin, 1950).

Arthur Kornhauser, Robert Dubin, and Arthur M. Ross (eds.), *Industrial Conflict* (New York: McGraw-Hill, 1954).

Rensis Likert, *New Patterns of Management* (New York: McGraw-Hill, 1961).

Delbert C. Miller and William H. Form, *Industrial Sociology* (New York: Harper, 1951).

Wilbert E. Moore, *Industrial Relations and the Social Order* (2nd ed.; New York: Macmillan, 1951).

Sigmund Nosow and William H. Form (eds.), *Man, Work, and Society* (New York: Basic Books, 1962).

[9] Morris David Morris, "The Labor Market in India," in Wilbert E. Moore and Arnold S. Feldman, *Labor Commitment and Social Change in Developing Areas* (New York: Social Science Research Council, 1960), pp. 197–98.

[10] Richard K. Beardsley, "Japan Is NOT 'Westernized,' " paper presented at the 61st Annual Meeting of the American Anthropological Association, 1962.

Eugene V. Schneider, *Industrial Sociology* (New York: McGraw-Hill, 1957).

Neil J. Smelser, *Social Change in the Industrial Revolution* (Chicago: University of Chicago Press, 1959).

Charles R. Walker, *Modern Technology and Civilization* (New York: McGraw-Hill, 1962).

William H. Whyte, Jr., *The Organization Man* (New York: Simon and Schuster, 1956).

Periodicals:

Economic Development and Cultural Change
Human Organization

Industrialism and Social Relations in Non-Western Societies

Abridged and adapted from George A. Theodorson, "Acceptance of Industrialization and Its Attendant Consequences for the Social Patterns of Non-Western Societies," *American Sociological Review*, **18** (1953), 477–84. [11] Published in this form by permission of George A. Theodorson and the *American Sociological Review*.

Some leaders of nonindustrial societies have said they want only machines from the Western world. This oversimplifies the meaning of industrialism. The extensive use of machines requires semiskilled and skilled workers, factory organization, and a money economy. The introduction of these elements in non-Western societies leads to the development of new social relations, which in time tend to resemble dominant patterns of Western industrialized society.

If it can be learned what changes must accompany industrialization in order to prevent confusion and the waste of time, money, and effort, planners may be able to anticipate and control some of the consequences of industrialization. It is also important to know what need not change, for this knowledge may

soften somewhat the impact of industrialism.

This essay suggests how industrialization causes the old social order to break down and new social relations to emerge. The social changes emphasized here are typical of many newly industrialized societies. However, there are wide variations in the social and cultural conditions of societies prior to the impact of industrialism and in the ways industrialism is introduced. Any particular society, therefore, may only approximate the changes outlined.

DISRUPTION OF THE TRADITIONAL ORDER

Before the introduction of mining and railroads, Northern Rhodesia in many respects typified nonindustrialized societies. It was inhabited by small groups living in village communities limited to a very small area and isolated from the outside world. Social relations were personal relations between kin and between lifelong intimates.

Subsistence agriculture or cattle-keeping seldom involved a man in co-operation with any save friends and relatives who lived near by. Marriage was a local affair and seldom joined families more than thirty miles apart. Religious ritual, ceremonial, warfare, hunting and fishing were only occasionally organized on any large scale; normally they were confined to the family,

[11] With illustrations on industrialization of non-Western countries from Godfrey Wilson, *Economics of Detribalization in Northern Rhodesia, Part 1* (Livingstone: The Rhodes-Livingstone Institute, 1941); Wilbert E. Moore, *Industrialization and Labor* (Ithaca: Cornell University Press, 1951); Audrey I. Richards, *Land, Labour and Diet in Northern Rhodesia* (London: Oxford University Press, 1939); and Ralph L. Beals, "The Village in an Industrial World," *Scientific Monthly*, **77** (1953), 65–75.

the village and the local district or chiefdom; and so a high degree of autonomy in each primitive community was inevitable.

The economic life of primitive Northern Rhodesia, being part of its general social life, was parochial; it consisted, above all, of the cooperation of groups of close kinsfolk and close neighbours; most things that men wanted were produced within their bounds. Hence, there was little specialization and techniques remained simple. These groups were both the main factories and the main markets of primitive life, for the circle of exchange only occasionally passed outside them.

In primitive Northern Rhodesia, then, the bonds of kinsfolk and neighbourhood were as much a matter of business—that is of reciprocal economic advantage—as of affection, duty and respect. It was upon them that a man depended for his daily bread and his whole livelihood. For a primitive African the obligations which bound him to a wife, to parents, to parents-in-law, to children, and so on, were as much determined by the fact that he could not prosper without them as by personal affection, or by the legal, moral and conventional codes of his tribe.[12]

Throughout the world, many such isolated communities have been affected by industrialism. Improved transportation facilities have brought villagers in contact with nearby cities and have made possible urban employment and trade. Modern factories or mines have been established near primitive villages, workers have been drawn from nearby communities, and the traditional social organization is disrupted. Characteristically three major changes occur:

1. *Economic relations are separated from the integrated social system.* In nonindustrialized societies, it is often difficult to separate economic activities from other areas of behavior. Trading, domestic roles, and cooperative endeavors, such as planting and harvesting, are intimately bound up with familial ties and obligations and the social life of the community. Exchange of food, for

Our man in Nigeria: a representative of the Singer Company.

example, may involve specific kinship obligations, a religious ceremony, and a display of family status.

When natives leave home to work in a distant city or a nearby factory or mine, their economic activities are separated from the system of rights and obligations in the community. As the worker gains money and skills, he is no longer economically dependent on his immediate and extended family, and his kinship ties thereby become weaker. The authority and unity of the family are undermined, and the integrity of other parts of the social organization is threatened. For example, among the Bantu of Southern and Eastern Africa,

. . . family economy is sufficiently disrupted so that the ordinary mode of supplying enough cattle for the bride price (lobola) through the obligations of the father and gifts or loans from other kinsmen no longer operates. The young man then may seek work not only to pay taxes but to *buy* cattle in order to complete the marriage agreement. This is already a radical and

[12] Abridged from Wilson, *op. cit.*, pp. 9–12. Used by permission.

disruptive step. Its logical successor is the complete commutation of the necessary cattle-price into its monetary equivalent, thereby removing the whole arrangement from its functional context in the village economy, the customs and rituals of marriage and kinship, and the symbols of familial cohesion. At this juncture the original institutions have been mortally wounded and simply collapse, leaving the individual who is money-oriented to work out new familial arrangements in the absence of precedent and tradition.[13]

2. *New individuals are placed in positions of power.* Industrialism introduces new skills, tools, and money, which bring new rewards and satisfactions, make some persons economically independent of the old order, and create new social statuses. Under industrialism there may be an emphasis on skills that were insignificant in the old system. For example, trading and mechanical abilities gain new prestige.

The creation of new economic roles, new rewards, and the increased prominence of previously unimportant resources and skills tend to place new individuals in positions of power. The new power structure challenges the old and later tends to produce a new elite. The power and influence of new merchants and manufacturers are most pronounced, and the new factory workers may improve their status. Previously higher classes who remain in agricultural pursuits may lose status. Among the Bemba of Northern Rhodesia, for example, those aspiring to leadership may gain followers through the distribution of goods. Mine workers are able to use their wages to buy goods and win positions of importance.[14]

Even if the new elite consists only of members of the old elite, the power structure is modified. The fact that they are the same individuals makes little difference, for they

must learn new attitudes, expectations, and values in order to perform their new roles.

Opposition to industrialization may be encountered from those who expect to lose most from change. While new roles are being created, old roles and skills decline in importance. The fears of the threatened members are based on sound fact and are not simply irrational reactions to change. In New Guinea, for example, workers returning to their home communities are taking over the authority of older men.

3. *Levels of aspiration are changed.* One result of industrialization, the production of large quantities of cheap goods, further disrupts the old order. It makes available to the masses material products they never expected to own. The peoples of many societies are accustomed to poverty, drought, and famine. But small improvements brought about by industrialization may suggest the possibilities of even greater betterment, and this may lead to impatience and general dissatisfaction. (See POLITICAL MAN, pp. 677 f.)

PROLONGED DISORGANIZATION

The transition from an old social order to a new one is accompanied by a conflict of social ties and values: the factory system versus the family system, orderly patterns of work versus less disciplined work habits. Obviously, not all native systems undergo equal amounts of stress in the process of change. In some cases the transition is relatively smooth; in other instances disorganization is prolonged and serious.

Industrialization introduces new economic patterns but not a total social system. When the native recruit is unhappy and discontented in the factory, it is not simply because he is nostalgic for the traditional atmosphere of his youth. It may be rather that the new environment does not afford him the satisfactions and security of a well-rounded and integrated pattern of life.

One of the most common barriers to the recruitment of a new labor force is the reluc-

[13] Moore, *Industrialization and Labor*, pp. 81–82 (used by permission of the Cornell University Press). See Monica Hunter, *Reaction to Conquest* (London: Oxford University Press, 1936).
[14] Richards, *op. cit.*, pp. 211–18.

tance of the worker to give up the secure, traditional patterns of village life. As a result, a pattern of intermittent, casual or migratory labor is often found. This allows the native laborer to enter employment at intervals while maintaining contact with his home community.[15]

NEW SOCIAL RELATIONS

Social disorganization is not likely to be permanent. New social relations develop, reflecting in part adjustment to the factory system. Because machines are expensive, they must be used economically. In the early stages of industrialization, labor is far less scarce than machinery, and there is a strong incentive to adjust labor to the machines. Teaching and enforcing of these adjustments leads to new social relations, detachment of the worker from his home community, and emphasis on achieved status in the factory. The changes are first experienced by the factory workers and through them are communicated to those who are not directly involved in industry.

1. *Impersonality.* The worker must adjust to the long hours he has to spend away from his home community. Old values, the social controls of the village, and his ties to the home community are weakened. His immediate family tends to occupy an increasing proportion of his free time and his extended family diminishes in importance.

With the introduction of mining and railroads in Northern Rhodesia, the relations of workers to kin and villagers have become more and more tenuous. In fulfillment of traditional obligations, the mine worker still occasionally visits his native village with gifts of cash and clothes. He fears to neglect his obligations both for religious reasons and because he still desires the respect and approval of his relatives. However, the bonds are weakened; the worker faces new obligations in his town and factory environment and is physically separated as well as economically independent of his kinship ties.[16]

The village of Nayon—near Quito, the capital of Ecuador—recently changed from an agricultural to a market economy. Before transportation facilities made the capital city accessible, the villagers lived primarily in association with relatives. Now villagers are often away on trading trips or in the city on business, and social relations within the village are more impersonal. There is little visiting among relatives and practically none among nonrelatives. "Characteristically, people in Nayon do not know what their neighbors are doing; moreover, they have comparatively little interest in knowing." [17]

2. *Achieved status.* In nonindustrialized communities kinship is an important basis for assigning roles. But machine operators are selected largely on the basis of technical competence. The factory system emphasizes assignment to jobs on the basis of achieved criteria rather than family relations. It is not who you are but what you can do that counts.

[15] Moore, *op. cit.*, in ftn. 13, pp. 21–35.

[16] Wilson, *op. cit.*, p. 39.
[17] Beals, *op. cit.*, p. 69.

Section 2   **Management and labor in transition**

In Section 1 it was shown that the rise of industrialism brought with it new social relations, new aspirations and disciplines. Industrial man was freed from older attachments and constraints. Especially in England and in the United States, this trend produced a great emphasis on individualism, which reached its height in the nineteenth century.

While this was going on, another and contrary trend was in the making. The logic of industrialism was creating new social institutions. These would, in time, provide industrial man with new centers of authority, new social bonds, new opportunities for collective action and group membership. Industrial man would become "organization man."

Two of the major institutions created by industrialism are the *business enterprise* and the *labor union*. This section considers the changing nature of these institutions, with emphasis on leadership and on group conflict and accommodation.

The coming of the factory system introduced a new way of organizing human effort. Workers, machines, capital, and management were brought together to create a "company," "firm," or "enterprise." Sometimes the firm was incorporated, but this legal status was not necessary. The essential characteristic of the enterprise is the creation of a new form of effective action—the business organization.

The idea of an established enterprise recognizes that organizational continuity and effectiveness are vital to productivity and profit. This was less important in the early stages of capitalism, when manufacturing was mainly handicraft and the businessman was more a trader or middleman than an organizer of production. In later stages of industrialism, the businessman becomes a builder of organizations.

The importance of organization increases as the size of the business grows. A small business, even though it is legally a corporation, may not have the internal differentiation or the continuity of an enterprise. For this reason, the latter term refers to relatively large firms that have a stable work force and a specialized managerial staff.

TYPES OF INDUSTRIAL MANAGEMENT

In the history of industrial organization the major trend has been from family-based management to professional management. These two types of management still exist, but professional or bureaucratic management is more representative of modern society. Family management (sometimes called "patrimonial") is more characteristic of an earlier era:

Patrimonial management is a common first stage in a country's march toward economic development. In countries where the family is one of the dominating social institutions in the society, the family enterprise is a simple and logical instrument of business activity. Loyalty and trust within the hierarchy are assured. The forces of tradition and religion support the essential integrity of the family dynasty. The enterprise provides the means for safeguarding the security and the reputation of the family.[18]

As the business expands family management loses ground. Even the extended family is unable to supply enough capital, ideas, or managerial personnel to meet the crises of business growth. For a time outsiders can be hired without loss of control and without changing the character of the business. But eventually the professionals outnumber the family members and take over more and more responsibility for making business decisions. At last, the family recognizes that its own interests are served best by turning over the day-to-day operation of the enterprise, and even the most important policy decisions, to professional managers.

The Ford Motor Co. postponed this development longer than many other large family enterprises, but during the past generation it has taken the same road. The fact that family members continue to be active in the business, and quickly move to executive positions, does not necessarily change the basic phenomenon. Under the new conditions, the family member in the firm becomes a part of professional management. He adapts to the

---

[18] Frederick Harbison and C. A. Myers, *Management in the Industrial World* (New York: McGraw-Hill, 1959), p. 69.

organization and does not attempt to bend it to his will. In some cases, he may be given a peripheral managerial post (a "division" of his own) instead of displacing a major professional executive at the top of the business hierarchy.

Family vs. Bureaucratic Management

The transition from family (or patrimonial) to bureaucratic organization may be more closely specified by considering (1) managerial authority, (2) rational procedure, and (3) managerial ideologies.

Managerial authority. Patrimonial management is typically one-man rule. The dominant figure resists delegation of authority and is inclined to make as many decisions as possible on his own. The relation between the "big boss" and his staff is personal and he expects unreserved loyalty and obedience.

In the bureaucratic setting authority is more impersonal, more systematic, more limited, and more effectively delegated. Respect is shown for authority based on technical competence. And all officials, including top management, accept a framework of established rules. In this sense, bureaucratic authority is "constitutional."

In many firms having professional management the principle of command is modified. Ultimate authority is still at the top, and directives are issued down the line, but there is increased emphasis on consultation. Those whose work may be affected by an impending decision are given a chance to be heard. This is not democracy, in the sense of majority rule, but the base of managerial decision is broadened to take advantage of the professional expertness and practical knowledge that exists at lower levels of the organization.

Rational procedure. The pre-bureaucratic business leader was impatient with formal rules and procedures. He liked to keep his accounts in his hat and to run the organization from day to day without clear-cut policies. Much was done in accordance with tradition—"this is the way we always do it"—

or by improvisation to fit the requirements of the moment. The intuitive understanding derived from one man's experience, often a rich experience, was the foundation of decision-making in the enterprise.

The bureaucratic way is directly contrary. Systematic procedure based on "principles of sound management" is the ideal. Rules and policies are developed to guide decision-making in all phases of activity. Men are hired in accordance with criteria worked out by a personnel department; they are trained, assigned, and supervised according to specified routines. Tradition is never its own justification but is subject to question and revision by specialists in organization planning and human engineering. A "web of rules" governs behavior at all levels of the enterprise.

The web of rules becomes more explicit and formally constituted in the course of industrialization. At the very early stages, the very notion of a rule may be alien, and individual incidents are confronted without regard to their more general implications. The continuing experience of the same work place, the growth in its size, the same workers, and the emergence of managerial staff tend to result in customs and traditions which begin to codify past practices. . . . Some rules may later emerge which anticipate problems rather than merely summarize past decisions. The statement of the rule then becomes more formal and elegant, particularly as specialists are developed in rule-making and administration.[19]

Detailed rules also existed in the early days of the factory system, but at that time the rules applied mostly to the discipline of the work force rather than to other policies and practices of management. The worker was subject to very close supervision, and was required to abide by many regulations governing his conduct both on and off the job. At a later stage rules became protective as well

[19] Clark Kerr, J. T. Dunlop, F. H. Harbison, and C. A. Myers, *Industrialism and Industrial Man* (Cambridge: Harvard University Press, 1960), pp. 198–99).

as restrictive, and applied to management as well as to the worker.

Managerial ideologies. Recent studies have shown how the perspectives and self-justifications of management have changed with the evolution of industrial organization.[20] In eighteenth- and early nineteenth-century England, the philosophy of management might be summed up as "stern and responsible tutelage." Workers were viewed as dependent rather than self-reliant; they were thought to be inherently irresponsible and unreliable, hence they needed a firm governing hand. According to this ideology, the owner-manager stood *in loco parentis* to his work force. His exercise of command was justified because it was needed, not only by society but by the workers themselves. At the same time management had a moral responsibility to the employees as well as to the enterprise. In this scheme of things, "the dependence of the poor and the responsibility of the rich are the valid moral rules of the social order." [21]

As industrial development quickened its pace, this early point of view was discarded. In the nineteenth century, and in the first decades of the twentieth, the morality of individualism, self-reliance, ambition, effort, and the "survival of the fittest" was extended from the middle-class entrepreneurs to the entire industrial community. "The militant language of an ethics of the jungle was applied to the relations between employers and workers. Riches and poverty merely reflect differences of ability and effort. The employer's success is evidence of his fitness for survival, and as such justifies his absolute authority over the enterprise." [22]

With the rise of professional management

[20] See Reinhard Bendix, *Work and Authority in Industry* (New York: Wiley, 1956); W. H. Whyte, Jr., *The Organization Man* (New York: Simon and Schuster, 1956); F. W. Howton, *The Changing Self-Image of the American Businessman,* unpublished Ph.D. thesis, University of California, Berkeley, 1959.
[21] Reinhard Bendix, "Industrialization, Ideologies, and Social Structure," *American Sociological Review,* **24** (October, 1959), 614.
[22] *Ibid.*

the influence of this ethic has waned. It has been replaced by a perspective better adapted to the needs of complex organizations run by specialized, expert, and interdependent staffs. In the ethic of "organization man" co-operation, group-mindedness, and security are the compelling themes.

UNIONS AND SOCIETY

In 1779, in Leicestershire, England, a youth named Ludd, angered by boys of the village, entered a house where stockings were manufactured and broke some of the spinning frames. The news of the act spread and became legend. In 1811–1816, English rioters who broke machinery in various textile factories were called Luddites. This was an early response by workers who thought that the industrial revolution was producing unemployment. For a modern response to a similar anxiety, see "Dead Horse and the Featherbird" (pp. 644–45), which recounts how printers and pilots cope with the impact of technological change.

Desperate outbreaks against the new technology occurred sporadically, but they had no lasting effect. The important response by workingmen to industrialization has been the creation of organizational counterparts to the business enterprise—the labor or trade-unions. Wherever there is industrialization some kind of labor organization is found. Unions have assumed diverse forms and have served both the union memberships and the larger society.

1. *Social protest and political radicalism.* Some labor unions have been primarily political and ideological, more interested in creating a mass base for political change than in establishing working arrangements with employers. Political unionism is most likely to be found when organized labor is weak. Unable to win concessions from employers, the unions turn to the political arena. The unions take the form of a general union, which is not strong at the factory level but plays a conspicuous role in politics. This pattern is found

in a number of underdeveloped countries such as Indonesia and Egypt.[23]

A similar development occurred in the United States during the latter part of the nineteenth century. The National Labor Union, organized in 1866, turned away from bargaining for better working conditions and looked to political solutions. The Knights of Labor, which had considerable influence from about 1879–1890, attempted to create a general union rather than an organization based upon the interests of particular groups of workers. "The aims of the Knights were idealistic, humanitarian, and political." [24]

A more extreme example of radical unionism in the United States was the Industrial Workers of the World—the "Wobblies"—organized in 1905. The I.W.W. program embraced ideas from a number of left-wing groups of the time, including Marxists, anarchists, syndicalists, and just militant unionists. The Wobbly program had two distinctive features. First, the organization hoped to transform society by direct economic action. The unions would take over the major industries and thus do away with capitalism. The idea was to build One Big Union that would prepare for One Big Strike. Second, the I.W.W. was more interested in agitation and strike leadership than in settlements and industrial stability:

Despite the fact that probably millions of workers came under the sway of the IWW in one conflict or another, its permanent membership never amounted to much more than 60,000. The chief reason for this was that the IWW did not concentrate on building strong permanent unions. Instead, it devoted its energies to educating the workers to its revolutionary philosophy through militant strikes. Wherever a battle was brewing, IWW leaders stepped in. Their aim was twofold: To win immediate gains for the workers involved, and to develop in them a

sense of class consciousness and a feeling of class solidarity. Though the "Wobbly" organizers often achieved these results, they rarely remained on the scene to consolidate their gains and build a strong union organization after the strike had been concluded.[25]

In the United States, radicalism played an important part in the history of trade unionism, but its influence has diminished markedly.

2. *Job control, collective bargaining, and interest-group politics.* In advanced industrial nations of the non-Communist world, the major drift has been toward non-ideological, "pragmatic" unionism. The major unions are solidly based on effective power at the factory level. They long ago rejected the Wobbly complaint:

> Why do you make agreements that
>   divide you when you fight
> And let the bosses bluff you with
>   the contract's "sacred right"?

On the contrary, the union contract is now perceived as a charter of industrial justice and a key to industrial stability.

Pragmatic unionism offers the member three main services in exchange for his loyalty and his dues: (1) protection of his job against potential competitors, (2) protection against unfair treatment by the company, and (3) continuous effort, through collective bargaining, to improve wages and working conditions. In addition, through the federation to which it usually belongs, the union may act as a political lobby and pressure-group. In this way it protects itself against restrictive legislation, and also supports more general legislation, e.g., for social insurance, that may reflect the interests of the union members. Despite its involvement in politics, the pragmatic union seeks no general reconstruction of society. It limits itself to specific objectives that may be won within the existing political and economic framework.

---

[23] See Walter Galenson (ed.), *Labor and Economic Development* (New York: Wiley, 1959), pp. 8–15.

[24] Robert F. Hoxie, *Trade Unionism in the United States* (New York: Appleton, 1926), p. 87.

[25] Aleine Austin, *The Labor Story* (New York: Coward-McCann, 1949), p. 167.

Dead Horse and the Featherbird

By Paul Jacobs. From a *Report* to the Center for the Study of Democratic Institutions, Santa Barbara, 1962, pages 3–6.

* * * * The composing room of the newspaper is comparatively quiet; no linotype machines chatter harshly, nor does the floor quiver from the running of the presses in the basement. It is the lobster shift—those off-hours when the printers set type without the pressure of a deadline. The men stand at their long composing tables adjusting metal rules, checking type against the copy for the advertisement at their elbow, and occasionally talking with each other.

The foreman walks over to a hook on the wall, a spike festooned with printed copies of advertisements that appeared in the newspaper days before. He takes one off the hook and carries it to a printer who has just finished tying up the type and metal for an ad that will run in tomorrow's paper.

"Here," the foreman tells the printer, offering him the printed ad. "We're falling behind on reset. Get this one."

The printer looks up sullenly. "What do you think I am—a lousy amateur? I don't want to set that stuff. I'm no blacksmith. Give me some live copy, not that dead horse."

The foreman does not argue. He calmly puts the advertisement down on the table and walks away, saying over his shoulder, "Get started before I call the chapel chairman over."

The printer begins to set the type for an advertisement that had already been run some months earlier. The copy announces an Easter sale in a department store, and it is now the end of summer. Mumbling to himself, the disgruntled printer starts work on the ad, knowing the foreman has authority to demand that the work be done and that the chapel chairman of the shop (the union's chief steward) would back up that authority.

The compositor slaps together whatever type he can find which fits that of the ad, encloses the type in a metal form, and walks over to a table where he slams it down beside a dozen similar forms of ads that had also appeared earlier in the paper. Soon, another printer will pick up these forms from the table and take them over to a proof press where a proof copy will be made of each one. Then, the proof copy will be checked for errors and the necessary corrections made in the type. Finally, another proof of the ad will be pulled and the printer's work will be ready for its final destiny: to be destroyed without being used—melted down in the "hell box" where used type becomes hot lead once again.

This is the process by which printers do "unwork"; work that is actually performed and paid for but goes unused. It is called "reproduction," "reset," "bogus," or "dead horse."

* * * * The jet airplane seems prepared to hang in the air forever until that moment when its wheels touch the concrete runway and it is instantly transformed from a graceful creature of the air into a screaming, speeding, metal monster, ungainly and awkward out of its natural element. With a frantic roar, the jet engines are reversed and the plane protestingly slows down. It taxies up to the landing area and in moments a horde of attendants are swarming over it, chocking its wheels, moving up the passenger ramps, unloading baggage, and readying the ship for its next voyage.

Finally, the last passenger walks down the ramp, speeded on his way by the fixed smile of the stewardess at the door, mechanically repeating the airline farewell: "Goodbye now. Come back and fly with us again." Their work finished, the crew members walk down the ramp with the captain-pilot first, followed by co-pilot and flight engineer—American culture heroes in their natty uniforms, each carrying one bag of luggage and one black valise stuffed with the maps, charts, and manuals that are the paraphernalia of their craft. They walk across the oil-stained concrete ramp to the flight operations office.

Inside the office they are met by a crew from another airline who will cajole the same jet into the skies for the next leg of the journey. They talk a bit of the new traffic pattern at the Los Angeles airport, of the near-miss one of their group had with an Air Force jet, and always of the weather. But this second group of fliers has an additional man in it, for the company that flies the next segment of the trip in the very same plane does it with four crew members instead of three.

That fourth flier is a "featherbird" airman. When he arrives back at his home base, he will walk into the flight operations office there and ask the superintendent, "Any chance of getting back to flying yet? I'm a pilot, not a damned chair-warmer." The superintendent may shake his head sympathetically. "Negative, there's nothing open for you on pistons."

* * * * Thirty thousand feet of vertical space separate the newspaper compositor setting type that will never be used from the airman squeezed into a seat with no instruments in front of him. But "unwork" is a common link between them. The industries in which they perform their "unwork" are widely separated, too—by different histories, structures, economic patterns, and by contrasting relationships to government: newspaper publishing is relatively free of state regulation while commercial aviation is subject to rigid supervision by a number of governmental bodies. There is a difference also in costs. The setting of not-to-be-used type is not a heavy economic burden upon most publishers; the presence of a fourth crew member represents an airline expenditure of millions of dollars.

But despite the differences between these two industries, setting "dead horse" and flying as a "featherbird" have much in common. They derive from the same source, could not exist without management collusion, and have the same demeaning consequences for the men who are paid to perform "unwork." Even more, the common source of "unwork" that links together pilots and printers affects millions of other workers, all of them sharing a fear of unemployment and a consequent loss of identity. Thus, they can be viewed as two examples from a catalogue of meaningless work and fruitless effort carried on in America today. Current apprehension about unemployment related to our technological advance, to automation and "cybernation," make the "unwork" of these two industries symbolic of a major issue in the 1960's—how to maintain a full and free economy without a fully employed work force.

3. *Labor discipline.* Where unions are free institutions, not controlled by the government, their main function is to represent the interests of the members. However, once firmly established at the plant level, the union assumes responsibility for fulfilling its contract. It has to maintain discipline among the members and see that they do not engage in unauthorized "wildcat" strikes and slowdowns. Without such discipline, the authority of the union leaders at the bargaining table would be undermined.

In advanced industrial countries, unions are widely accepted as integral parts of the industrial organization. Many employers, especially in large-scale manufacturing, have agreed to the "checkoff" (deducting union dues from the workers' pay), the "union shop" (requiring all employees to become members of the union), and other devices for strengthening union leadership. At first, these agreements were made with great reluctance, but after some experience, employers came to recognize the potential contribution of the union to maintaining labor discipline and reducing costly work stoppages.

In Communist countries trade-unions are controlled by the state. Strikes are not permitted. The main function of the union is to discipline the work force and raise output, but they also provide welfare services. Soviet-type unions are responsible for administering social security, allocating housing, and adjusting the grievances of workers. In effect, the union is a government agency carrying on a combination of control and service functions.

PROSPECTS

As industrialization proceeds, the business enterprise and the union become stable institutions. Conflicts become less frequent and less intense. The differences between labor and management are no longer over basic principles, such as whether unions should exist at all or what the future of society should be. Most disagreements are on matters of de-

tail and are subject to compromise. The government intervenes as mediator and stabilizer. The whole system is watched and tended to maintain production at desired levels.

The foregoing description is more nearly an image of the future than an accurate rendering of the present. However, it does fairly depict what is happening in the most advanced sectors of the economy in the most industrialized nations of the free world. The struggle for union recognition still goes on in some areas, such as in industrialized farming, even in the United States. But where stabilization has been achieved, the drift toward professional management of labor relations, involving representatives of management, labor, and government, is apparent.

Two important consequences of this trend may be identified:

1. Although many unions began as agencies of social reform, in the industrialized nations they are not proponents of major social change. Unionism as a "movement," either in itself or as part of a larger political effort, is in decline. As institutions with vested interests of their own, and with many commitments to other institutions, the unions are losing any special role they may have had as focal points of social criticism or reconstruction. Indeed, many unions in the United States have supported restrictive policies on immigration and have maintained practices of racial discrimination and segregation.

Unions do, however, make a significant contribution to building a system of industrial justice, thus enhancing the security and dignity of workers on the job.

2. When unions are militant and struggling for recognition, participation can bring psychological as well as material benefits to many members. To be a member of the union is to have a special and valued identity. Some have seen in this a basic justification for unionism:

The union returns to the worker his "society." It gives him a fellowship, a part in a drama that he can understand, and life takes on meaning once again because he shares a value system common to others. Institutionally the trade-union movement is an unconscious effort to harness the drift of our time and reorganize it around the cohesive identity that men working together always achieve.[26]

However, the limited aims of the bureauc-

ratized unions turn them into service agencies. The achievement of widespread labor recognition and labor peace makes member enthusiasm and devotion irrelevant. The significant work is done by union officials and participation of the member is not needed. The member pays his dues to support an officialdom that renders a valued service. In such an institution, psychologically meaningful participation is not likely to be achieved or sustained.

Section 3   Technology and human relations

Section 1 of this chapter analyzed some of the effects of machine technology on human relations in traditional society. It was shown that mechanization, which everywhere accompanies industrialization, disturbs and reconstructs patterns of residence, employment, status, and leadership.

In later stages of industrialism the influence of technology on society continues. Every area of modern life—from making love and rearing children to politics, war, and the arts—has been in some way affected by technological change. Some of these effects are limited, others sweeping; some have been of enormous benefit to health and welfare, while others pose grave threats for human survival.

This section considers a limited problem—the significance of technology as an *environment* within which the modern industrial worker lives and which limits or expands his chances of attaining a satisfying work experience.[27]

[27] The discussion of socio-technical systems, alienation, and automation in this section is based on materials prepared by Robert Blauner. See also Robert Blauner, *Alienation and Freedom: The Manual Worker in Industry* (in press; Chicago: University of Chicago Press, 1963).

Socio-technical Systems

It is useful to think of the setting within which a man does his assigned work as a "socio-technical system."[28] This idea emphasizes the close interdependence of technology and human relations on the job. The socio-technical system is a blending of the social and technical aspects of organization.

The technical system refers to the physical plant, the machinery, and the mechanical processes that are organized toward the goal of producing goods or services. Technical organization lays out the work and provides for the flow and allocation of materials. The technological factor—what the machines can do—and the concern for minimizing costs decisively affect the way the work is organized. Taken together, the nature of the technology and the criterion of cost limit the alternative ways of getting the job done.

It takes people to operate a technical system, and there is no technical system without a social system. The technical system fixes important aspects of the group situation. For example, the technology may dictate how

[28] F. E. Emery and E. L. Trist, "Socio-technical Systems," in Charles R. Walker, *Modern Technology and Civilization* (New York: McGraw-Hill, 1962), pp. 418–25.

Karl Marx (1818–1883). His general system, dialectical materialism, includes a sociological system called historical materialism. In this theory Marx emphasized technology as a generator of social change and a direct influence on the nature of work and human relations. Technology and the forms of economic organization constituted the "material foundations" of the social order. All else was called "superstructure," a reflection of the problems set by technology and economic class relations. Rich as it is in historical analysis, Marx's work has been marred by political dogmatism. When ideas are used as weapons, a partial truth is easily confused with the whole truth, and the self-corrective method of science is abandoned.

much detailed supervision is needed and what opportunities there are for informal contact among the workers. At the same time, the technical system depends upon the "human factor"—the skills, motivation, and discipline called for by the mechanical processes.

The socio-technical system includes (1) a specific technology, e.g., a way of recapping automobile tires; (2) the formal division of labor; and (3) the informal human relations on the job. The problem of the enterprise is to create socio-technical systems that simultaneously achieve technical goals and hold the working group together.

ALIENATION

In some of his early writings, Karl Marx advanced the theory of alienation, an influential hypothesis concerning the impact of technology on human relations in industry.[29] In Marx's view, factory technology, the in-

creasing division of labor, and capitalist property institutions brought about the estrangement of the industrial worker from his work. Highly mechanized systems replaced craft methods of production in which the artisan had been master of his tools and materials. In the new factories, the intelligence and skill previously expressed by the craftsmen were "built into" the machines. Workers were left with routine and monotonous jobs. In the pre-industrial period both skilled craftsmen and peasants had considerable control over the rhythms and movements of work. But the machine system now controlled the pace of work and restricted the employee's free movements. This loss of freedom, this subordination to the machine, threatened to turn the worker into a mere instrument or thing and to give him a sense of powerlessness.

Similarly, the increasing division of labor within the factory made jobs simpler, and each employee's area of responsibility diminished. This resulted not only from technological developments as such, but also from the managerial and engineering concepts of effi-

[29] On Marx's concept of alienation, see Erich Fromm, *Marx's Concept of Man*, with a translation from Marx's Economic and Philosophical Manuscripts by T. B. Bottomore (New York: Ungar, 1961).

ciency, of making work more rational. In rationalizing production the total work process was broken down into minutely subdivided tasks. A job made up of only one or a few operations involved no real responsibility. Nor did it require an understanding of the factory's entire activity. Responsibility, problem-solving, and decision-making, removed from the ranks of the employees by the systematic division of labor, became the work of supervisors, engineers, and others on the technical staff. The fragmented relations of the individual to his work robbed him of a sense of purpose. This loss of meaning is an aspect of alienation.

According to Marx, the property relations of capitalist society also contribute to the alienation of the employee. The factory belongs to the entrepreneur who has the legal and social power to hire labor, sell the products of the enterprise on the market, and appropriate its profits for himself. The worker does not own what he produces. He has nothing to sell but his labor. Because the factory belongs to the capitalist, the workman is not likely to identify psychologically with its fortunes or its products. Because the profits do not benefit him personally, he is not motivated to work with all his energy and intelligence. Thus the property institutions of capitalism produce a third form of alienation—the employee's sense of isolation from the system of organized production and its goals.

The socio-technical systems that grow from capitalist economic institutions and modern factory technology deprive the employee of a truly human relation to his work. Loss of control means loss of freedom, initiative, and creativity. Specialization simplifies and degrades labor; it makes the goals of the enterprise so remote that a sense of meaningful participation in a work community cannot be attained. The worker does not identify with the productive organization, but feels himself apart, or alienated, from its purposes. When work does not permit control, evoke a sense of purpose, or encourage larger identifications, the job is simply a way to make a living. Marx believed that unalienated productive work was essential to man's psychic well-being. Alienation reduced work to the merely instrumental, and this could only result in widespread suffering and degradation.

These ideas of the youthful Karl Marx of the 1840's reflected a romantic point of view widely held among intellectuals of the period. The rise of industrialism was viewed with misgivings, and intellectuals were concerned about the effects of the new order on the individual's organic relation to his community, his work, and his sense of himself as a creative and autonomous person. The concept of alienation, referring to the estrangement of man from important sources of his psychic and moral well-being, was "in the air."

As Marx sharpened his attack on capitalism, and looked to growing class conflict and political struggle, he lost interest in these more general moral issues. His emphasis shifted to the conflict of interest between workers and capitalists, and he did not pursue the theme of alienation. If he had done so, he might have come to realize that his critique was directed not toward capitalism as such. Rather, its most important elements apply to any industrial society.[30]

The theory of alienation in industry contains important insights regarding the effects of socio-technical systems on human satisfaction. It illuminates some basic trends in modern work organization and technology and accurately describes the situation of many employees. However, Marx greatly exaggerated the uniformity of modern industry. While the theory is provocative, it underestimates the diversity of socio-technical systems in a complex society.

[30] Students of Marx disagree on the extent to which he shifted his views about or his emphasis on alienation. See Fromm, *op. cit.*, pp. 69 ff.; Lewis Feuer, "What Is Alienation? The Career of a Concept," *New Politics,* **1** (Spring, 1962), 116–34; and Daniel Bell, *The End of Ideology* (New York: The Free Press of Glencoe, 1960), pp. 335–97.

INDUSTRIAL VARIATIONS

Empirical studies of modern work organization reveal that alienation is distributed unevenly in the work force. These variations become evident when three industries with different kinds of technology—craft, assembly-line, and continuous process—are compared. The printing, automobile, and industrial chemical industries are contemporary examples of each of these forms of technology. Each develops characteristic socio-technical systems.

Craft Technology

The printing industry is still largely based on craft technology. Its products are not standardized, and many traditional practices govern the way work is done. Historic craft specialities persist. The work force is predominantly skilled. There is variety and interest in the work of compositors, who set type, and pressmen, who run printed pages off the presses.

Craft workers are not dominated by the technical system. They control the pace at which they work, the quality of the product, and the quantity of output. They determine many of the techniques and methods involved in production and constantly meet to solve problems in the course of their work. Unlike other employees who often are under intense pressure, printers are able to resist external control and maintain personal independence. This reflects the opportunities presented by the technology as well as the strength of the powerful craft trade-unions in the printing industry.

The craft worker is not limited to a small, subdivided part of the product, and therefore his work has meaning as fashioning a product with which he can identify. Craft production is usually carried on in relatively small units, such as the machine shop or the construction site, rather than in very large plants. In the small shops characteristic of the printing industry, the sense of isolation and anonymity common in mass-production industry is absent. Workers in craft industry therefore suffer little alienation, since craft technology provides intrinsically challenging work, a satisfying amount of control over the process of work, and opportunity for meaningful participation in a work unit.

In a survey of factory workers in many industries, printers were the most likely to report that their jobs gave them a chance to try out their own ideas. Four out of five printers felt that they were able to express personal initiative in work, compared to one out of two in the entire sample.[31] Table XVI: 1 suggests that printers were also the least alienated from their occupational status. Only 36 per cent of the printers said they would choose a different trade or occupation if they could start over again at the age of fifteen, compared to 59 per cent of all factory workers, and 69 per cent of the automobile workers.

Assembly-Line Technology

Automobile production is based on a totally different technological principle, the assembly line. As the incomplete motor vehicle moves along a conveyor belt at a predetermined speed, workers at every point on the line assemble one of the component parts. Three features of the assembly-line work organization are (1) extreme subdivision of jobs, (2) complete predetermination of work methods, and (3) the mechanically set speed of the conveyor belt. These features color the whole atmosphere of work where this technology is used.

The average assembler's job consists of only one or two operations. Little skill or training is required. The work is extremely repetitive, and little initiative is possible because engineers and time-study personnel have figured out in advance how each job is to be done. In addition, assembly-line workers have virtually no control over their socio-technical environment. The speed of the line

[31] Blauner, *op. cit.*

Table **XVI:1**　Proportion of Factory Workers Desiring a Different Occupation, by Industry, 1947

"If you could go back to the age of 15 and start life over again, would you choose a different trade or occupation?"

Industry	Yes	No	Don't Know and Depends	Number of Respondents
Leather	71%	20%	9%	(129)
Sawmills and planing	71	24	6	(68)
Oil refining	71	27	2	(51)
Automobiles	69	23	8	(180)
Iron and steel	65	25	10	(407)
Machinery	65	29	6	(293)
Furniture	64	29	7	(259)
Apparel	63	35	2	(265)
Chemicals	58	29	13	(78)
Nonferrous metals	55	36	9	(88)
Textiles	54	37	9	(409)
Food	51	34	15	(296)
Stone, clay, glass	48	25	27	(108)
Transportation equipment	48	48	3	(93)
Paper	37	49	14	(102)
Printing	36	50	13	(107)
All factory workers	59%	32%	9%	(2,933)

Source: Robert Blauner, *Alienation and Freedom: The Manual Worker in Industry*, unpublished Ph.D. thesis, University of California, Berkeley, 1962, p. 348. Data from a Roper survey for *Fortune*, 1947. Deviations from 100 per cent are due to rounding

brings 30 to 45 cars every hour and sets the pace of work and the quantity of output. The powerlessness of the automobile worker even extends to physical movement. He cannot leave his work station on the line without being relieved by another assembler.

The assembly-line worker is more clearly alienated than the workman in any other industrial environment. Just as his job denies him control and meaning, the social atmosphere of the large assembly plant intensifies his sense of isolation. Assembly-line technology even inhibits the formation of informal work groups, which contribute to internal solidarity in most factories. The impersonality of the large plant and the meaninglessness of a repetitive job lacking responsibility are experienced by the worker as deprivations. Natural tendencies toward loyalty and identification are undermined. With little interest in the work or company, the typical job means little more than a weekly paycheck.

Caution: The assembly-line is an extreme form of technology that is highly mechanized yet relies on a large number of human operators. The assembly line has symbolized the engineering mentality associated with this sociotechnical system and has influenced other less fully mechanized work settings. However, the *numerical* importance of assembly-line workers should not be exaggerated. Perhaps less than 5 per cent of American manual workers are on the line. Even in the automobile industry, less than one-fifth of blue-collar workers were on the line in the 1950's.

Continuous-Process Technology

In a continuous-flow system, the characteristic technology of the modern oil and

Thorstein B. Veblen (1857–1929), an American economist, became a caustic critic of modern business society. His best-known book, The Theory of the Leisure Class, *analyzed the functions of "conspicuous waste" and "conspicuous consumption." Veblen believed that technology—especially the way work is organized—decisively influences institutions and habits of thought. In* The Engineers and the Price System *he stressed the conflict between "the instinct of workmanship" and the "pecuniary values" of the business world.*

chemical industries, the product flows automatically through an extensive network of pipes and reactor units. Within each of these units a particular process or reaction is carried out. Manual workers do not deal with the product directly, as they do in craft and assembly-line industries, but control the reactions of the invisible oils and chemicals by monitoring control boards, watching gauges and instruments, and adjusting valves.

Only the maintenance crew, which repairs breakdowns in the automatic equipment, uses traditional manual skill. The operator's basic job requirement is responsibility. Each team of operators is responsible for a particular

chemical process and for the expensive equipment in its unit. Yet instead of feeling dominated by the towering technology, which in physical size and capital cost is many times greater than assembly-line technology, these employees feel they control the technical apparatus. Although production is regulated automatically, the operators control the pace at which they read instruments and patrol the plant. There is freedom of movement because automated work environments are relaxed and free of pressure. When operations are running smoothly, routine readings take up only a fraction of work time, and there is considerable "free" time.

Yet unpredictable breakdowns in the operations do occur, and the energies of the workers are employed in locating the cause of the problem and restoring production to normal flow. The chemical operator's attitude toward breaks in production is in sharp contrast to that of the alienated automobile worker. The chemical worker feels in control when production is running smoothly; therefore he willingly works hard to eliminate the crisis. The assembly-line worker, on the other hand, feels powerless when the line is moving normally. He *welcomes* breakdowns and is likely to give a sigh of relief when the conveyor is stopped for repairs.

Although the generalization is not supported by responses to the question reported in Table XVI:1, evidence from interviews suggests that continuous process technology produces a socio-technical system with low alienating tendencies. The powerlessness of workers in assembly-line industry is replaced by control over automatic processes. The loss of meaning that results from an extreme division of labor is absent, because the individual's responsibility encompasses an entire productive process. The nature of the work leads to closer integration of employees with management rather than alienation from the company. Because the operator is responsible for an expensive process, and develops firsthand familiarity with its operations, he

Table **XVI:2**   Proportion of Factory Workers Whose Job Leads
to a Promotion, by Industry, 1947

Industry	Per Cent, Yes, Promotion	Per Cent, No, Promotion	Don't Know	Number of Respondents
Chemicals	79%	12%	9%	(78)
Oil refining	63	31	6	(52)
Furniture	59	32	8	(260)
Transportation equipment	57	33	10	(93)
Paper	55	30	15	(106)
Sawmills and planing	54	38	7	(68)
Nonferrous metals	52	46	2	(90)
Food	51	32	18	(297)
Machinery	49	44	7	(297)
Printing	48	32	20	(112)
Iron and steel	46	45	10	(409)
Apparel	43	50	7	(272)
Textiles	40	52	8	(410)
Automobiles	39	53	8	(180)
Stone, clay, glass	34	50	17	(109)
Leather	28	53	18	(130)
All factory workers	47%	42%	10%	(2,963)

Source: Robert Blauner, *Alienation and Freedom: The Manual Worker in Industry,* unpublished Ph.D. thesis, University of California, Berkeley, 1962, p. 357. Data from a Roper survey for *Fortune*, 1947. Deviations from 100 per cent are due to rounding.

may be consulted frequently by engineers and supervisors.

Continuous-process technology also helps reduce alienation by its effect on the occupational structure within the plant. In the oil and chemical industries there is a balanced distribution of skills. Jobs exist at all levels of skill—low, middle, and high, gradations that create opportunities for advancement. Movement from one skill and pay level to the next is a normal part of employment experience. Possibilities for advancement are reflected in the employees' optimism. Thus, in the factory survey mentioned above, chemical and oil workers were the two categories most optimistic about promotions. In contrast, as shown in Table XVI: 2, a much smaller percentage of automobile workers reported that they had jobs that would lead to a promotion. This reflects a technology associated with a rather uniform and low level of skill, in which opportunities for promotion are restricted. In printing the opportunities for promotion are also relatively low, but for a different reason. Craft technology demands a highly skilled work force, and printing craftsmen, already at the top of the skill hierarchy, have nowhere to go except into management.

There are many socio-technical systems in modern industry that cannot be classified as craft, assembly-line, or continuous process. Because of this great diversity in work environments, it is difficult to assess the general quality of human relations and the level of employee alienation. More empirical studies are needed of the technical, economic, and social factors that produce distinctive socio-technical systems. Even the development of automated production does not introduce uniformity, for not all automated work environments have the characteristics of the continuous process as it appears in the chemical industry.

AUTOMATION

For many, the word automation suggests a world of automatic factories and business concerns, run by computers without workmen. It is true that highly automated processes are being used in the manufacture of oils and chemicals, in the machining of automotive engine blocks, in the production of radio and television sets, and in the processing of insurance premiums and bank statements. Dramatic as some of these cases are, there is no inevitable progression toward a totally automated technology. Less advanced methods still predominate, and in many industries automatic techniques are not easily applicable.

The possibilities of automation depend on the nature of the end products, and on the extent to which a company is willing to commit itself to turning out a few standardized items. The production of gasoline readily lends itself to automation because gasoline is fluid and homogeneous. Automobile production is less readily automated because motor vehicles are made up of thousands of heterogeneous parts. Attempts at automation meet almost insuperable obstacles in the shoe industry because of the enormous variety of sizes, widths, styles and materials that make up a diversified product line.[32]

Automation is no single form of technology. There are many stages and types of automated production. Much controversy over the impact of automation on socio-technical systems and employee alienation is due to this diversity. Worker reaction to automation depends on the nature of the work setting *before* automation. For example, in some offices traditional clerical jobs have been displaced by the introduction of electronic data processing systems. When this takes place, the employee's job is simplified, but his control over the work and his freedom of physical movement are reduced.[33] Another study of office automation found that when a high-speed computer system was introduced into an insurance firm where clerical procedures had already been mechanized (using a keypunch card process), the result was a widening of the employee's responsibility.[34]

It is difficult to distinguish the effects of automation as such from the effects of change-over to the new system. A common finding is that installation of automation replaces physical fatigue with mental tension. However, the "jumpiness" that workers in newly automated plants report may be due to difficulties in adjusting to a radically changed way of work. In the oil and chemical industries, which have been automated for many years, operators have become habituated to the job, and complaints of mental tension are less common. But automatic technology never stands still, and the introduction of new techniques means that employees must become accustomed to frequent changes in operations. Automated processes require workers who are more adaptable and flexible than the average mass-production worker or low-skilled clerical employee. That is why automated firms seek employees with higher education and some technical knowledge.

Despite the difficulty in generalizing about automation, a number of consequences seem firmly established. Work in the factory becomes lighter and cleaner. Manual skills decline in importance. Employee responsibility is heightened. Advanced automation in both factory and office tends to enlarge jobs rather than further subdivide the work. Most important for its impact on socio-technical systems, automation enhances the interdependence of all employees and contributes to the

---

[32] James R. Bright, *Automation and Management* (Boston: Harvard Business School, 1958).

[33] Ida Russakoff Hoos, "When the Computer Takes Over the Office," in Sigmund Nosow and William H. Form (eds.), *Man, Work and Society* (New York: Basic Books, 1962), pp. 72–82.

[34] Bureau of Labor Statistics, "The Introduction of an Electronic Computer in a Large Insurance Company," (mimeographed) Number 2 of *Studies of Automatic Technology* (October, 1955).

integration of the organization. Since events in one segment of the process have immediate repercussions on the total system, communication increases both horizontally and vertically. There is more consultation between employees and supervisors, between engineers and foremen, between the office and the factory.

Dramatic long-range consequences of automation have provoked much comment, but it is too early to estimate their importance. The long-term growth in the proportion of clerical jobs in the total labor force may be reversed if computer systems continue to replace traditional office jobs. Thus the chief avenue of employment for female high school graduates may "dry up." Computer systems may also threaten the career of the typical male business college graduate who fills the middle management positions in industry, between first-line supervision and the higher executives. Many feel that the work of checking, co-ordinating, and routine decision-making can be more efficiently programmed for the electronic machine. Finally, automation may eliminate that distinction between factory and office, between hand and brain work, which has been a central element in the stratification system of every industrial society. Blue-collar operators in the new clean, office-like factories will be responsible employees, much like the white-collar employees in the new, more mechanized, factory-like offices.

STUDYING GROUP PERFORMANCE

Although most studies of work groups concentrate on "problem" behavior, such as turnover, absenteeism, morale, and low productivity, they offer insights into the basic processes underlying behavior in organizations. The findings show that the social variables of the immediate work situation, such as the attitudes of workers toward each other and toward their supervisor, the character of supervision, and group cohesiveness, are related to performance.

In investigating the interrelations between social factors and group performance, the first step, as in any systematic inquiry, is to develop a tentative theory and set of hypotheses. The actual testing of theory and hypotheses must take into account four major points: (1) *control* of factors other than the ones under investigation, (2) *reliability* of the techniques for observing and measuring the factors under study, (3) *validity* of the techniques, and (4) a *criterion* of group performance. All of these points, of course, apply to other scientific studies.

1. *Control.* Suppose the task is to determine the relation between a group's performance and the behavior of its supervisor. The hypothesis is as follows: Supervisors in high-producing groups involve their subordinates in the decision-making process more than do supervisors of low-producing groups. The study must be designed to control factors other than the supervisor's behavior. To effect controls, a number of groups similar in size and type or difficulty of work but different in productivity must be compared.

If supervisors of the high-producing groups consistently involve their subordinates in the decision-making process to a greater extent than supervisors of the low-producing groups, and if this is shown irrespective of group size, difficulty of work, and other factors, the involvement of subordinates in the decision-making process could be considered a factor in group performance. However, more rigorous and direct methods of testing the hypothesis would be required before the relationship could be firmly established. One such procedure, using experimental and control groups, is described in Adaptation 43.

2. *Reliability.* It is necessary to develop reliable techniques to observe and measure the factors under study. If an investigator administers the same questionnaire (or a similar form of the questionnaire) to the same group several times, and if the members of the group score approximately the same each time, he may assume that his questionnaire is a *reliable* measuring instrument.

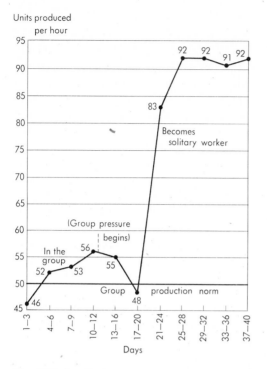

Fig. **XVI:1**   Pressure on the Presser

A presser in a pajama factory worked 20 days in a group and 20 days alone. After the presser reached the standard production rate of about 50 units per hour, he exceeded the established group level. "Scapegoating" began, and his production declined. When the group was dispersed, the presser's production increased markedly and remained high. [Data from Lester Coch and John R. P. French, Jr., "Overcoming Resistance to Change," *Human Relations*, **1** (1948), 519–20.]

3. *Validity.* The investigator strives for instruments and techniques capable of making valid observations and measurements as well as reliable ones. If the instruments measure what the investigator intends them to measure, they are *valid*. A reliable questionnaire or series of observations may not necessarily be valid. Responses to a questionnaire on the decision-making behavior of a supervisor may not describe his supervisory behavior but instead the attitudes of his subordinates toward him. If they like him, they may rate him favorably on *all* aspects of his behavior.

(This response is the so-called halo effect.)

One way to solve the problem of validity in this context is to interview subordinates—asking them to tell why they answered particular questions as they did. Another is to interview the supervisor—asking him if he involved subordinates in decision-making. Still another is to observe him on the job. If the interviews and observations agree with the results of the questionnaire, one may conclude that the questionnaire yields valid results, that it measures decision-making behavior. The final test of the validity of the questionnaire depends on the outcome of several studies. If repeated studies support the initial theory and set of hypotheses, there is good reason to believe the questionnaire is valid.

4. *Criterion.* To determine the relation between the social factors in the work situation and group performance, an adequate measure of performance is needed. Performance may mean several different things—quality of work, quantity of work, or the efficiency with which the work is produced. The particular measure of group performance used is called the *criterion*.

Few studies of work groups combine adequate controls, reliable and valid measures of relevant factors, and precise criteria of performance. The large number of variables and the difficulties of controlling and measuring them make it difficult to approach the ideal of scientific rigor. But studies with limitations *that are understood* are far better than no studies at all.

Factors Related to Work Performance

Two social factors are examined for their effect on work group performance:

1. *Group cohesiveness.* A cohesive group is characterized by "teamwork" or "group unity," and has the following features: (*a*) friendly interaction of members, (*b*) common interests and shared goals, (*c*) identification of the members with the group, and (*d*) norms that establish "proper" behavior of members.

Several indicators of these characteristics—pride in the work group, positive sociometric choices, co-operation, lack of persistent antagonisms, and acceptance of group goals—are positively associated with group performance.[35]

Adaptation 14, pages 163–65, shows the importance of group cohesion and suggests that worker "teams" reduce absenteeism and turnover and improve production. However, "teamwork" may be related positively or negatively to production. A cohesive group can control the behavior of its members toward either restricting production or raising it.

The members of a long-established cohesive group with standards of high production are likely to maintain high levels of individual and group performance. If, however, the norms of a cohesive group are oriented toward restriction of production, the performance is accordingly lower. An extreme case of the effect of group norms and pressures is illustrated in Figure XVI: 1.

2. *The behavior of the supervisor.* At least two aspects of supervisory behavior are related to high productivity of work groups:

a. An active leadership role. A supervisor who performs an active leadership role differentiates between the functions of supervisor and worker, spends more time in actual supervision than in doing the same sort of work as his subordinates, plans and oversees the work of the group, and helps his subordinates. Supervisors of high-producing groups tend to define themselves as group leaders to a greater extent than supervisors of low-producing groups.[36]

b. A "human relations" approach to supervision. A supervisor who has the "human relations" approach is not overly critical of his subordinates, shows an interest in their personal and job problems, encourages them to make suggestions for improvement of work methods and the work situation, keeps them informed about the work situation and their performance, and allows a maximum amount of freedom on the job. His supervision concentrates on people rather than on work production, and may be described as group- or person-oriented. Supervisors of high-producing groups tend to be more group- and person-oriented than supervisors of low-producing groups.[37]

Participation in Decision-Making

The apparent success of the "human relations" approach to supervision has led its advocates to urge full participation of subordinates in making decisions that directly affect them. Some feel that participation will increase production and employee morale and reduce turnover, absenteeism, and resistance to change. One study that supports this viewpoint is outlined in Adaptation 43. This experiment found that participation of workers lowered resistance to change in the production routine and increased production. Adaptation 43 also illustrates some procedures of research studies in general and of experiments with control groups in particular. Each step is illustrated by outlining what the investigators actually did.

---

[35] Rensis Likert, *New Patterns of Management* (New York: McGraw-Hill, 1961), esp. Chap. 3; and Peter M. Blau and W. Richard Scott, *Formal Organizations* (San Francisco: Chandler, 1962), esp. Chap. 4.

[36] Daniel Katz, Nathan Maccoby, and Nancy C. Morse, *Productivity, Supervision and Morale in an Office Situation* (Ann Arbor: University of Michigan, 1950); and Daniel Katz, Nathan Maccoby, Gerald Gurin, and Lucretia G. Floor, *Productivity, Supervision and Morale Among Railroad Workers* (Ann Arbor: University of Michigan, 1951).

[37] Katz *et al.*, as in ftn. 36.

An Experimental Study on Resistance to Change

Abridged and adapted from Lester Coch and John R. P. French, Jr., "Overcoming Resistance to Change," *Human Relations,* **1** (1948), 512–32. Published in this form by permission of the authors and Tavistock Publications, Ltd.

This adaptation, first, reports the findings of a study that attempted to isolate the causes of resistance to change in work groups, and to develop techniques to reduce this resistance, and, second, illustrates the use of experimental and control groups in research.

STEP 1. THE PROBLEM

The first step in any research is to delineate the problem to be studied. Unless the area of investigation is carefully defined and limited, research is apt to be unsystematic and findings inconclusive.

This experimental study was designed to discover why people resist change so strongly and what can be done to overcome the resistance. The study was made at a pajama factory, where there were frequent and necessary changes of work procedures and the shifting of personnel to different jobs. Strong resistance to these changes was expressed in grievances, high turnover, low efficiency, restriction of output, and marked aggression toward management. Special monetary allowance for transfers to different jobs did not lower the resistance.

STEP 2. COLLECTING BACKGROUND INFORMATION

This includes (1) reviewing the pertinent literature and (2) becoming acquainted with the relevant characteristics of the organization or groups to be studied. The investigator uses the background information to locate the important factors operating in the situation and to formulate a theory and hypotheses.

Employees in this factory worked on an individual incentive system. Piece rates were set by time study and were expressed in units. One unit was equal to one minute of "standard" work, and 60 units per hour equaled the standard efficiency rating. It required a great deal of skill to reach 60 units per hour. The rating of every pieceworker was computed every day.

The investigators thought that learning a new job after transfer might be a factor in resistance to change. They made an analysis of the speed with which operators learned their jobs on first entering the factory. Then they compared these "learning curves" with the "relearning curves" of several hundred experienced operators who had been transferred to new jobs. They found that relearning after transfer to a *new* job was often slower than *initial* learning on first entering the factory. Only 38 per cent of the transferred operators recovered to the standard rating of 60 units per hour, and the other 62 per cent either became chronically substandard operators or quit during the relearning period.

What accounts for differences between initial learning and learning after transfer? Why should so many operators fail to recover their former unit ratings and even quit? Further investigation indicated that the interference of previous work habits in the learning of new skills did not play a crucial role. The investigators then interviewed a number of workers and made an analysis of production records and turnover. From their findings they developed the tentative theory that resistance to change was a result of the combination of two forces:

1. *The frustrations of transfer,* including the learning of the new job, the contrast of new status with former status, and the difficulties of reaching the standard piece rate.

2. *Negative attitudes induced in the individual from his work group.* The preliminary interviews suggested that groups with high "we-feeling" and positive co-operative attitudes about the change were the best relearners. On the other hand, groups with high "we-feeling" and negative attitudes toward management expressed strong resistance to change. Collections of individuals with little or no "we-feeling" displayed some resistance to change but not so much as the latter group.

The investigators attacked the problem of reducing resistance to change by (1) the reduction of the frustration of transfer and (2) the development of positive attitudes toward the change within the groups to be transferred. Would the group's participation in the plans for the change positively affect both of these factors? If group members were permitted to help plan the way their new jobs should be done and were consulted about the new standard piece rates, would the frustration of transfer (including the perceived difficulty of reaching a new arbitrarily set standard piece rate) be reduced? Through participation was it possible that the group, as a group, would agree that the change was necessary and develop positive attitudes toward the change? If the answers were "yes," the individual within his work group would be positively oriented toward the change.

STEP 3. STATING THE HYPOTHESIS

The third step in research is to state the hypothesis (or hypotheses) to be tested. The hypothesis guides the investigator in the collection of pertinent data, provides a standard to evaluate the findings, and allows other investigators to repeat the study. The hypothesis should be stated in such a way that it can be supported or refuted by the findings of the study.

The following hypothesis was suggested from the theory of resistance to change: *The greater the group participation in the plans for change, the less the resistance to the change and the faster the speed of relearning a new job.*

STEP 4. THE EXPERIMENTAL CONDITIONS

In an experimental *design, a number of groups are selected for study; the groups are matched on certain variables to give the experiment more precision.*

Four groups were roughly matched for (1) efficiency ratings (each group had reached a stable level slightly above the standard production of 60 units per hour); (2) degree of change that would be involved in the transfer; and (3) the amount of "we-feeling" observed in the group.

In an experimental design, a group (or groups) is subjected to experimental influences introduced by the investigator. This is the experimental *group. Another group (or groups) is not subjected to the experimental conditions, and it is the* control *group.*

After the experimental conditions have been imposed, the groups are observed to see what changes occur. The advantage of having a control group is readily seen. If the experimental group manifests change after the experimental conditions have been imposed and the control group does not, the investigator may state with some assurance that the change is related to the experimental conditions and not to some extraneous factors.

There are, of course, many variations of this basic "before and after" design.[38]

The four groups in the present study differed in their degrees of participation in the planning for the change-over.

Experimental group I had a meeting to discuss the need for the change. After discussion, the group agreed that the change could be made without affecting their

[38] Many problems in the use of this design cannot be discussed here. See, for example, Samuel A. Stouffer, "Some Observations on Study Design," *American Journal of Sociology,* **55** (1949–50), 355–61.

chances of earning high efficiency ratings. Management then presented a plan for changing over to the new job. The group approved the plan, which included choosing several operators to be specially trained and to set the new piece rate by time studies. The "special" operators met, and management asked for their suggestions about job procedures. The chosen operators worked out the details of the new job and consulted with the engineer in setting the piece rates. The new job and piece rates were presented at a second group meeting to all the operators, and the special operators trained the rest of the group on the new job.

Experimental groups II and III held meetings similar to those of experimental group I, but since these groups were smaller, all operators participated directly in the designing of the new jobs.

The control group (group IV) did not participate in the plans for change. The production department modified the job and set a new piece rate. A meeting was held and the group was told that the change was necessary because of competitive conditions in the market.

STEP 5. THE EXPERIMENTAL RESULTS

The experimental findings are stated as supporting or rejecting the hypothesis. Negative findings are quite as "good" and scientific as positive results.

The results of the present study support the original hypothesis. The rate of recovery to the standard efficiency rating was *directly* proportional to the amount of participation. Furthermore, turnover and aggression were *inversely* proportional to the amount of participation. The study is summarized in the Figure XVI:2.

The specific findings were as follows:

1. Experimental group I, at the end of 14 days, averaged 61 units per hour (the quota was 60 units per hour). No one quit in the first 40 days, and only one act of aggression against the supervisor was recorded. Obser-

vations indicated that the attitude of the group was co-operative.

2. Experimental groups II and III recovered faster than group I. After a slight drop on the first day of change, the efficiency ratings returned to a prechange level and showed sustained progress thereafter to a level about 14 per cent higher. They worked well with their supervisors, and no indications of aggression were observed. There were no quits in the first 40 days.

3. The control group did not reach its former production standard. There was no progress after transfer for a period of 32 days. Marked expressions of aggression against management occurred, and 3 of the 18 workers quit in the first 40 days. There was deliberate restriction of production.

To make sure that the results depended on group participation rather than on other factors, such as the personalities of members of the control group, the investigators brought the remaining members of the control group together again two and a half months after the original change. They were again transferred to a new job. This time they had the opportunity to participate in planning the new job procedures. The group then exceeded its previous level of efficiency, and there was no aggression or turnover for 19 days. This retesting of the control group strengthens the assumption that the important factor reducing resistance to change was the participation technique. However, at this point the group had lost three of its members, and they may have been dissident and obstructive ones.

STEP 6. INTERPRETATION OF THE FINDINGS

Interpretation consists of placing the findings in a broader conceptual framework. The discovery that participating groups exhibit less resistance to change than non-participating groups is a fact. But scientific knowledge does not consist solely of facts. Scientists must abstract from facts to generalizations.

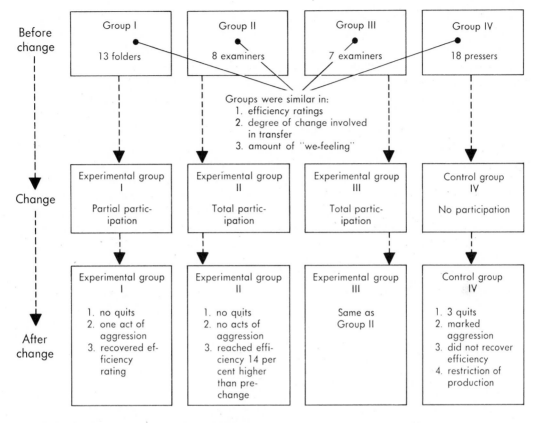

Fig. **XVI:2**   The Before-and-After Experiment

The findings of the present study suggest two generalizations: (1) pressures generated within a group for change are more compelling than pressures from outside, and (2) pressures for change will occur within the group if there is shared realization of the need for change. In the experimental groups, a new goal orientation took place, and inasmuch as it was shared by members of the group, it was socially reinforced, just as the former orientation of resistance to change was socially reinforced. If the goal or value of a group is either acceptance of or resistance to change, social controls are set up that tend to force the individual to conform. He depends on the group for the gratification of his social needs, and if he deviates from group values, he may be isolated from the group.

Section 4   **The labor force**

As societies become industrialized, the distribution of workers among various economic activities tends to change in a predictable way.

In the early stages the population is preponderantly engaged in agriculture and in the collection of raw materials for clothing and shelter. As the technology develops and industrialization proceeds, the productivity of agricultural workers increases, and at the same time workers are drawn into manufacturing and construction, where their efforts yield higher earnings. While the proportion in agricultural employment decreases and the proportion in manufacturing increases, a third trend appears. Growing numbers of workers enter service industries, such as the distribution of raw and finished products, the maintenance of communication, trade, and transport, and the training and care of the population.

INDUSTRIAL TRENDS

These broad trends, observable in many countries, are shown for the United States in Figure XVI:3. In the past 140 years the United States has changed from an agricultural nation with three-fourths of its workers in agricultural employment to a highly industrialized and urbanized country with less than 7 per cent of its workers in agriculture. About a third of the working force were employed in manufacturing and construction early in this century, and the percentage has remained about the same. Employment in the services paralleled the growth of industry until the beginning of the century, when it rapidly outstripped manufacturing employment. Service activities now employ substantially more than half of the working force.

The three major industrial divisions are sometimes treated under the headings of primary, secondary, and tertiary forms of pro-

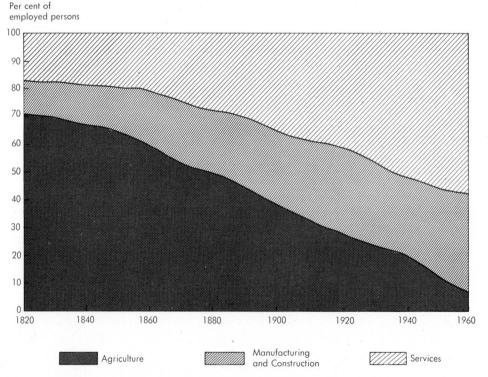

Per cent of employed persons

Agriculture   Manufacturing and Construction   Services

Fig. **XVI:3**   The Working Population of the United States: 1820–1960

After Eshref Shevky and Marilyn Williams, *The Social Areas of Los Angeles*
(Berkeley and Los Angeles: University of California Press, 1949), p. 4.
(Data for 1950 and 1960 added from *Census of Population*.)

1940: Average farmer fed himself and 9 others

1962: Average farmer fed himself and 25 others

Per cent of
employed persons

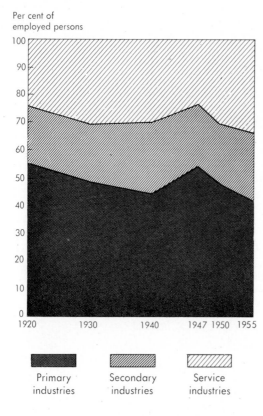

Primary industries   Secondary industries   Service industries

Fig. **XVI:4**   The Working Population of
Japan: 1920–1955

Source: Irene B. Taeuber, *The Population of Japan*
(Princeton: Princeton University Press, 1958),
p. 87. "Other and unknown" excluded from calculations.

duction.[39] Primary refers both to a stage of
industrial development and to the fact that
workers deal directly with raw materials. The
primary industries include agriculture, fishing, and forestry. *Secondary* industries, which
include manufacturing, construction, and
mining, are involved in the conversion of raw
materials into goods either for direct consumption or for further fabrication. *Tertiary*
industries include services, both professional
and personal, trade, transportation, and communication.

So broad a classification necessarily brings
very different things under one heading. For
example, in an early stage of industrialization service workers may be preponderantly
itinerant peddlers and personal servants. In
a highly industrialized economy, a large proportion of service workers are professionals,
semiprofessionals, managers, and skilled
white-collar workers. Although the trend
from primary to tertiary industry is nearly
world-wide, details vary from country to
country, and within a country change is uneven. For example, during an economic
depression the movement of workers out of
agriculture may be reversed temporarily;
during a war a heavy concentration in secondary industry will occur.

Differences among countries undergoing
industrialization are illustrated by comparison of Puerto Rico and Mexico. In both
places the proportion of workers in agriculture has declined and the proportion in services and manufacturing has increased. However, in Puerto Rico the size of the total
labor force has not increased, the excess
having been drained off by migration to continental United States. The number of Puerto
Ricans in service industries has expanded
only to the extent of the demand. In Mexico,
on the other hand, the labor force has grown
rapidly, emigration has not taken very many
workers, and the increase in service workers
has been greater than the requirements of the
country.[40] In industrializing countries with a
large labor surplus, such as Mexico, an increase in service workers will not mean the
same thing as a similar numerical increase in
a country where the labor supply is more
nearly in balance. In the former, service work
tends to be unskilled or semiskilled and
poorly rewarded. In a country with a small
labor surplus, the proportion of workers in
poorly rewarded activities declines as industrialization proceeds.

Figure XVI:4 shows the industrial distri-

[39] See Colin Clark, *The Conditions of Economic Progress*
(3rd ed.; London: Macmillan, 1957), esp. Chap. 9.

[40] A. J. Jaffe, *People, Jobs and Economic Development*
(Glencoe: The Free Press, 1959), p. 264.

bution for Japan. Although Japan is the most highly industrialized Asian country, the proportion of workers in agriculture and other primary activities remains high, and in 1955 was above 40 per cent. The proportion in manufacturing and construction, about 24 per cent in 1955, was substantially less than the 35 per cent for the United States at the same time. The figure also shows the industrial fluctuation connected with World War II, when manufacturing reached a high point. A similar "bulge" occurred in the United States and other countries. After the war there was a temporary decline in manufacturing and service industries in Japan, and a corresponding increase in agriculture, but the long-term trend toward a decline in primary industries soon reappeared.

THE UNITED STATES LABOR FORCE[41]

The United States labor force includes persons fourteen years old and over who are

Child labor in a Southern cotton mill, 1900.

Table **XVI:3** Employment Status of Persons Fourteen Years Old and Over, United States: 1960*

Employment Status	No. (in Thous.)	Per Cent
Labor force	69,877	55.3
(a) Armed forces	1,733	1.3
(b) Employed civilians	64,639	51.2
(c) Unemployed civilians	3,505	2.8
Not in labor force	56,399	44.7
(a) Students	10,326	8.2
(b) Inmates of institutions	1,760	1.3
(c) Over age sixty-four	12,443	9.9
(d) Keeping house and other	31,870	25.3
Total	126,276	100.0

*Data from *Census of Population, 1960,* Final Report PC-(1)-1C, Table 100.

[41] Donald J. Bogue, *The Population of the United States* (Glencoe: The Free Press, 1959), esp. Chaps. 16–19; A. J. Jaffe and Charles D. Stewart, *Manpower Resources and Utilization* (New York: Wiley, 1951); *Current Population Reports, Labor Force,* Series P–50 and P–57.

(a) members of the armed forces, (b) gainfully employed civilians, or (c) unemployed persons able to work and seeking work.[42] (See Table XVI:3.) The labor force is the part of the population that provides goods and services for some kind of economic reward, or is ready to do so if the opportunity presents itself. The rest of the population is not counted in the labor force: children, students, housewives not gainfully employed, adults in institutions, retired persons, unemployables, and other persons not seeking work.

The size of the labor force is affected by the age composition of the population, the amount of education demanded by the technology, and the efficiency of the system of production, which determines the ability of

[42] Unpaid family workers other than housewives who have no other job than keeping house are included in the labor force. Seasonal or other part-time workers are ignored unless they are working or seeking work at the time of enumeration.

the economy to support nonworkers. At present a large part of the population of the United States is in the productive years, and the labor force comprises 38.5 per cent, a correspondingly large percentage of the total population. (See POPULATION AND ECOLOGY, pp. 316–17.) In 1820 about 30 per cent of the population were gainful workers, and in 1900, 37 per cent. Women make up an increasing part of the labor force. In 1900 only 18 per cent of workers were female, in 1960 the figure was about 32 per cent, and there is every likelihood that it will continue to grow.

As the U.S. has become a mature industrial society with increasing education requirements, the age of entering the labor force has been postponed. In 1900 more than three out of five boys between fourteen and

nineteen years of age were in the working force; in 1960, less than half; and in 1975 it is estimated that only two out of five will be in the labor force.[43]

The labor force may be classified by industry or by occupation. Industrial distribution of workers is shown in Figure XVI:5 for 1910 and 1960. This is a more detailed breakdown than Figure XVI:3. The three major categories are given, but service industries are reported in additional detail because of the continuing development and diversification of services as well as the concentration of workers in these industries. Administrative and distributive services—transportation, trade, communications, etc.—have expanded with the growing complexity of the industrial

[43] *Current Population Reports*, Series P–50, No. 69. Also see Bogue, *op. cit.*, pp. 423–27.

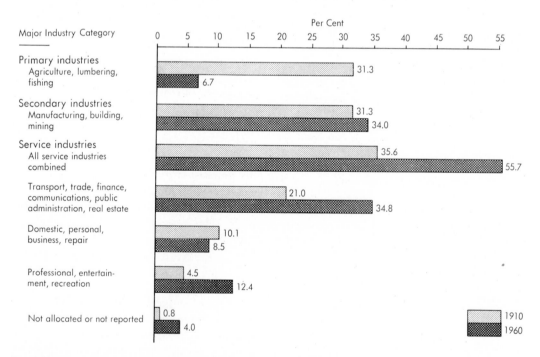

Fig. **XVI:5** Industrial Distribution of Workers: 1910 and 1960

Census data for 1910 from *Historical Statistics of the United States*, 1789–1945, p. 64; data for 1960 from *Census of Population: 1960*. Final Report PC(1)-1C, Table 91. Data should be interpreted with caution since 1910 and 1960 classifications are not strictly comparable. Data for 1910 are on gainful workers; for 1960 on employed persons.

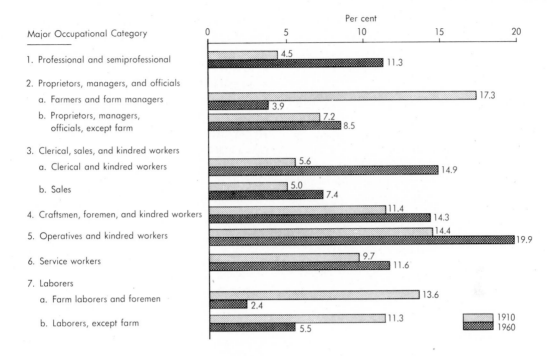

Fig. **XVI:6**   Occupational Distribution of Workers, United States: 1910 and 1960

Data for 1910 from Gladys L. Palmer and Ann Ratner, "Industrial and Occupational Trends in National Employment," Research Report No. 11, Wharton School of Finance and Commerce, September, 1949, p. 21. Data for 1960 from *Census of*

Population: 1960. Final Report PC(1)-1C, Tables 89 and 90. Data for 1910 are on gainful workers; for 1960 on experienced civilian labor force. "Occupations not reported" excluded from calculations.

order. The proportion of workers in professions, entertainment, and recreation is also greater. This trend is related to the higher values the society places upon education, medical care, welfare services, research, and recreation, and it is also a manifestation of a high productivity, which is able to support such specialized services. At the same time, industrial productivity is increased by the educational services, which impart needed skills, and by medical services, which maintain health and efficiency of the labor force and prolong the working life of experienced workers.

The largest proportion of the working force is employed by large industry. While the number of employees in the very largest industries declined somewhat after World

War II, about 0.1 per cent of all firms with 1,000 or more employees account for about 40 per cent of all paid workers.

Occupational Classification

An alternative breakdown of the labor force is the grouping of workers into occupational categories according to the kind of work they do, irrespective of their industrial classification. Figure XVI:6 shows this distribution for 1960 and 1910. Operatives (e.g., bus drivers, meatcutters) and kindred workers were the largest single group of employed persons in 1960, whereas half a century earlier farmers and farm managers were the largest category. The professional and clerical categories promise continued growth.

The classification of workers by occupation is an important tool of sociological analysis. For instance, the close relation of occupation and the class system in the United States is discussed in SOCIAL STRATIFICATION, pages 213–14, and in Russia, pages 180–81.

The industrial and occupational classifications of workers are important in determining policies and in making long-term plans for training and using manpower. Not only education, but welfare, retirement, and other programs must be based on an understanding of labor force trends. For example, there is often a large gap between the supply and demand for certain types of labor. The present shortage of engineers is one example, but workers are sometimes trained for jobs in little demand. This results in a surplus of manpower in some industries and occupations and a shortage of manpower in others. As the economy becomes more complex and as educational requirements are raised, full knowledge of the characteristics of the labor force is necessary to avoid serious waste and misallocation of manpower.

Chapter **XVII**

Political man*

Section 1 **Introduction**

One of the striking features of modern industrial and urban society is the ever-increasing
importance of politics and government. Urbanization and especially industrialization
are affected by public policy. Governments
are quick to see the implications for political
power and stability of industrial and commercial expansion. In the twentieth century
a large measure of government responsibility
for industrialization is taken almost for
granted, and the influence of politics is inex-
tricably mixed with the major social changes
discussed in the preceding two chapters.

Of equal sociological interest is the *effect*
of social change on the political order. Industrialization with its accompanying changes in
social relations has produced political crises
and upheavals, some of which have had the
gravest consequences for the security and
freedom of millions. Even when not accompanied by wars and revolutions, these master
trends have transformed the role of government. Compared to an earlier age, many

more people participate in political affairs;
many more are directly affected by the
government's decision to tax, conscript, or
educate. Modern man is political man no less
than he is urban and industrial man.

The Standpoint of Political Sociology

As in the study of industry, education, and
other special spheres of life, there is wide
recognition of the need to place political activities and institutions in a broader social
context, to see the influence of social groups
and forces upon the workings of the political
machinery. The sociologist contributes to this
fuller understanding in part by seeking out
the special political consequences of phenomena with which he is already familiar, such as
stratification, primary groups, collective behavior, and population movements.

Political sociology is especially interested
in the *underlying social conditions* that affect
government and politics. An understanding
of changes in the group structure of society,
such as the assimilation of ethnic minorities,
may throw light on the pattern behind the
shifting results of national elections. The outcome of elections, the stability of governments, the rise of new movements and parties

* This chapter draws on material included in earlier
editions in Chapter XIV, POLITICAL SOCIOLOGY, prepared by William A. Kornhauser in collaboration with
L.B. and P.S. We wish again to acknowledge our indebtedness to him.

—these and many other political events depend on what is happening in other areas of social life.

The social factors that influence the way men are governed and the way they make political decisions have been recurrent themes in the history of thought for many centuries. In *The Republic* Plato traced the connection between the integrity of statesmen and their social circumstances, holding that a degree of social isolation is necessary to protect the philosopher-guardians of an ideal state from the temptations and involvements of ordinary men. Aristotle studied the degeneration of forms of government and stressed the need for a middle class as a stabilizing force in the political order. Thomas Hobbes saw that government must rest on a social bond between rulers and ruled; otherwise, there would be unregulated use of physical force and life would be "solitary, poore, nasty, brutish, and short."[1] And James Madison, in the famous tenth Federalist paper called attention to the impact of group pressures on government and noted that "the most common and durable source of factions has been the various and unequal distribution of property."[2] Today many of these problems are still being explored, with somewhat less emphasis on speculative inquiry and more attention to the empirical testing of hypotheses.

Within political sociology, three broad areas may be distinguished:

1. Social foundations of *political order,* especially the way political arrangements depend upon social organization and cultural values. The main problem of political order is the regulation of the struggle for power, and political sociology considers basic constitutional questions. However, sociologists are less concerned with the formal aspects of government and law than with the underlying supports of these institutions.

2. The social bases of *political behavior.* Among contemporary social scientists "political behavior" refers mainly to the participation of individuals in politics—why and how they vote, hold political opinions, belong to political associations, and support political movements.

3. Social aspects of *political process,* including the types of organized groups in politics and their patterns of interaction. A major topic is the study of how interest groups, parties, and movements change or stabilize the political order.

In the course of analyzing some of the main political phenomena of the modern world, this chapter treats these topics. Section 2 deals with nationhood and political modernization. In Section 3 the nature of social revolutions is examined, followed in Section 4 by an outline of the chief characteristics of totalitarian society. Finally, Section 5 discusses the social foundations of freedom and democracy.

SOURCES AND READINGS

G. A. Almond and J. S. Coleman, *The Politics of the Developing Areas* (Princeton: Princeton University Press, 1960).

B. R. Berelson, P. F. Lazarsfeld, and W. N. McPhee, *Voting: A Study of Opinion Formation in a Presidential Campaign* (Chicago: University of Chicago Press, 1954).

Eugene Burdick and A. J. Brodbeck, *American Voting Behavior* (Glencoe: The Free Press, 1959).

Angus Campbell, P. E. Converse, W. E. Miller, and D. E. Stokes, *The American Voter* (New York: Wiley, 1960).

Heinz Eulau, S. J. Eldersveld, and Morris Janowitz (eds.), *Political Behavior* (Glencoe: The Free Press, 1956).

William Kornhauser, *The Politics of Mass Society* (Glencoe: The Free Press, 1959).

S. M. Lipset, *Political Man* (New York: Doubleday, 1960).

R. M. MacIver, *The Web of Government* (New York: Macmillan, 1947).

---

[1] Thomas Hobbes, *Leviathan* (Everyman's Library edition; London: J. M. Dent, 1914), p. 63. First published in 1651.

[2] Alexander Hamilton, John Jay, and James Madison, *The Federalist* (Everyman's Library edition; London: J. M. Dent, 1942), p. 43. First published in 1787/88.

Section 2   **The creation of nations**

Of all the dynamic social forces in the modern world, none is more important than nationalism. The nation is in many ways the decisive unit of social organization. It can summon profound loyalties; it can organize great economic and military efforts; it can give to millions of people a "consciousness of kind," a sense of common fate, a collective identity.

Nationhood has not always dominated the scene as it does today. For many centuries, in many lands, *kinship, social class,* and *local community* were the only abiding centers of loyalty. In Europe nationhood emerged only gradually as new institutions developed capable of (1) defining and defending national boundaries, (2) breaking down local barriers to trade and communication, (3) providing for political integration under an effective central government, and (4) creating a more or less uniform system of education transmitting an official language and a sense of common heritage.

Many conditions had to exist before these changes could be accomplished. Germany and Italy did not become fully organized nations until the nineteenth century, although centuries earlier the great Florentine writer Niccolo Machiavelli (1469–1527) had pleaded eloquently for the unification of Italy. In France and England vigorous monarchies contributed to the formation of nations. In doing so, the royal house had to change its own perspectives and self-image. The ruler had to "make up his mind whether he was the first of the nobles or the first of the magistrates and administrators." [3] As kings and queens came to think of themselves as chief administrators, they built up

a corps of tax collectors, judges, police, and other officials, distributed throughout the country and completely dependent on the central government. This helped lay the basis of the modern integrated nation-state.

The emergence of nations is a phenomenon of *widening loyalty and consciousness.* The nation is a broader, more inclusive unit than the local community. If a national identity is to be achieved, loyalty must go beyond the immediate bonds of locality and kinship. The individual transcends his primary group attachments. He embraces a more general and abstract idea—the concept of being French, Indian, Congolese, or Swiss. This widening of loyalty may not go very far. Only a small nation may emerge as a stable social unit. But extending or generalizing the individual's sense of his own civic identity is one of the most profound aspects of nation building.

Although national consciousness broadens loyalties, it also gives them focus and depth. New aspirations and demands are created, especially the demand for national autonomy. The nationalist patriot wants a government of his own to symbolize and protect the peculiar identity of his country. In this sense nationality also *limits* perspectives.

The combination of these broadening and limiting effects of nationalism produces a potent political energy. Nationalism creates power by making more men available for participation in its larger community. At the same time, this potential energy is given impetus and direction by the tendency of nationalism to seek ways of enhancing patriotic pride and fervor.

In today's world the nation-state plays a highly ambiguous role. Its capacity to mobilize a population and change old ways of life

[3] Albert Guerard, *France: A Modern History* (Ann Arbor: University of Michigan Press, 1959), p. xi.

makes the nation the major agency of modernization. In all parts of the world economic development and nationalism are closely associated. But nationalism is also a great threat to world stability.

This section is devoted to the social aspects of national development, primarily in the "new nations," and it will draw upon the considerable body of recent research on this topic.

COLONIALISM AS NATION BUILDING

Four hundred years of modern history (roughly 1500–1900) were marked by the penetration of European powers into the preindustrial areas of Asia, Africa, and the Americas. Spain, Portugal, Holland, France, Belgium, England, Italy, and Germany—all took part in the great commercial and political adventure called colonialism. They sought resources, markets, settlements, pride, power, and religious conversions. As they exploited, traded, settled, aggrandized, subjugated, and converted, they brought with them the culture of the Western world. This they transmitted, with uneven success, to at least the top layers of the societies with which they dealt.

For the most part the European powers entered lands that knew little of national identity. They were prenational as well as preindustrial. Some areas, such as North America, were relatively sparsely populated by tribal groups that lacked effective political organization. Elsewhere native communities, though densely populated and the seats of ancient cultures, were divided into small, scattered governmental units. Almost everywhere the conquerors were able to take advantage of existing conflicts within the indigenous population.

Where the land was largely unsettled, and the natives could be pushed aside, the newcomers acted as true *colonists*, exporting their own people and creating offshoots of the mother country in the new land. This is the familiar story of North America and South Africa. In other areas, such as India, *imperi-*

alism is a more apt term. There alien rule was established over a society otherwise left largely intact. In Latin America, the Spaniards did create true colonies, but these included large Indian populations held in subjection and tutelage by the new rulers.

Because the Europeans came to stay, and were not merely casual visitors or pirates, they faced the problem of establishing order. In solving this problem, they themselves laid the foundations for the emergence of new nations. They did this in three ways:

1. *By defining national boundaries.* In many areas the colonial governments simply drew lines on a map and gave a name to the new "country." Indonesia and the Philippines are good examples:

> The scattered lands inhabited by the peoples of Malay stock, including therein the Philippines, the entire Indonesian archipelago, and such parts of the Malay Peninsula as were primarily Malay were not laid out by nature or originally so settled by man as to make any one political partition of them more self-evident than another. The existing frontiers are, as far as both geography and ethnology are concerned, essentially arbitrary and reflect the limits of the colonial spheres carved out in the conflict of imperialisms.[4]

The new "national" boundaries were set partly for administrative reasons, so that the responsibilities of the colonial governor for a given territory could be fixed. In addition, boundaries were needed to establish claims and work out accommodations with rival European powers.

2. *By creating a more integrated social organization.* The colonial administrator typically proceeded with some vigor to establish centralized control over his domain. He had to pacify the territory, collect taxes, and protect his fellow-countrymen as they exploited and developed the resources of the colony. To achieve these ends, transportation

---

[4] Rupert Emerson, *From Empire to Nation* (Cambridge: Harvard University Press, 1960), p. 124.

Passing Styles: A monkey-skin-clad Kenyan tribesman and a city-dressed Englishman share a London sidewalk.

and communication were greatly improved, a national currency was established, and at least a rudimentary educational system was created. The result was readier and safer movement within the colonial boundaries, not only for government agents but for the natives as well. Men from hitherto isolated regions or tribes began to look upon one another not as potential enemies but as potential traders. Patterns of mutual dependency sprang up. It was easier to do business with people inside the colonial boundaries and this tended to establish new and enduring social bonds.

3. *By stimulating national consciousness.* The colonial government, it is sometimes said, created the conditions of its own destruction. By its very existence as a central administration for a defined region, the colonial government brought into being a new focus of loyalty and pride. Because it transmitted Western education and ideals, it created a group of people who would demand freedom in the name of those ideals, including the ideals of patriotism and national honor.

Perhaps most important, the colonial government itself became the target of opposition and rebellion. Anti-colonial sentiment stimulated national consciousness, even among settlers from the home country. Among non-Europeans, those who struggled for independence did not seek a return to the situation as it was before the Europeans came. Rather, they sought independence for precisely that nation which was the creature of the colonial power. For example, after the Indonesians gained their freedom following World War II they laid claim to the entire territory of the old Netherlands East Indies. This includes Irian (Western New Guinea, which was finally surrendered by the Dutch) although the people of the island are unlike the Indonesians both in race and culture.

Colonial nationalism has been strongest where the colonial government was most constructive. Where it invested in economic development of the country, educated the peo-

ple, brought them into government administration, and created or allowed free institutions, such as political parties and trade-unions, the growth of nationalism was rapid and strong. The British, especially, were relatively benign colonial rulers. By the same token, they were also the ones who did the most to make rebellion a practical possibility.

Direct and Indirect Rule

The policies and practices of the colonial powers followed no single pattern. They met many different problems and handled them in many different ways. However, there are two important types of colonial rule, each of which had a different effect on national development.

Under *direct rule* the colonial power set up its own administration and tried to regulate in considerable detail the economic and social life of the colony. For example, the British in Burma replaced the old monarchy with a governor-general,

whose staff gradually increased until the Secretariat came to house all types of departments and ministries expected of a modern government. Burma proper was divided into eight divisions, each consisting of three or four districts. In a ruthlessly logical fashion two or three subdivisions were created in each district, two to four townships in each subdivision. The townships were each divided into nearly fifty village tracts that became the prime units of local government.[5]

This is perhaps an extreme example of the effort to by-pass existing social organization and superimpose a centrally controlled administrative hierarchy upon the country.

In exercising direct rule, the colonialists used the ideas and methods they knew. They introduced Western concepts of law and administration, as in the creation of a Civil Serv-

[5] Lucian W. Pye, *Politics, Personality and Nation Building: Burma's Search for Identity* (New Haven: Yale University Press, 1962), p. 82.

ice and a Western-style judiciary by the British in large parts of India. The policy of direct rule limited and sometimes destroyed native institutions; but it did allow the recruitment of educated natives to serve in the government bureaus.

Under *indirect rule* the existing social organization was largely preserved. The colonial authority was exercised through the native leaders such as kings, tribal chiefs, village elders. This was the policy of the Dutch in Indonesia and of the British in various African territories. This system tended to minimize the Western impact. It supported local institutions and customary ways of life.

The choice of direct or indirect rule was usually pragmatic, depending on the traditions and strength of the colonial power. If it had only a weak outpost in the colony, occasionally reinforced by supplies sent thousands of miles from home, it was obviously prudent to come to some agreement with the native leaders who would, for a price, control their own populations. Indirect rule, requiring fewer paid officials, was also less costly.

Economic policy strongly influenced the choice of direct or indirect rule. Where the colonialists sought only a kind of tribute, extracting from the country cocoa or rubber or some other native product, this could be done rather easily through the use of local chieftains. On the other hand, if the native population was seen as a market for goods manufactured in the home country, or if local manufacturing was developed, direct rule was more appropriate. A more complex economy required a more efficient government, and this could be better supplied under direct rule.

What are the effects of direct and indirect rule on nation building? Paradoxically direct rule, though apparently more oppressive, lent itself more readily than indirect rule to the evolution of a united nation. Direct rule tends to create a cohesive political community *before* independence. When independence is achieved, the new rulers have some-

thing to work with. At least part of the job of centralization and training has already been done.

Indirect rule has often helped to make social change more acceptable to a tradition-bound people. Working through existing institutions has the effect of moderating the pace of change and associating it with a familiar and accepted authority, the local chiefs. On the whole, however, indirect rule kept the society weak, fragmented, and unprepared to enter the modern world. Because the central government was dependent on the co-operation of the tribal or village leaders, it remained weak, and indirect rule did not foster the development of an educated class.

The persistent strength of traditional authorities sustained by indirect rule is a source of difficulty after independence. When the colonial power is gone, they are reluctant to give up their power and they lack a strong commitment to the new state. Hence they represent a force for separatism along regional or ethnic lines.

TRIBALISM

The architects of the new nations of Asia and Africa must take account of pre-existing social organization. In their quest for modernization they must lead populations still very largely tradition-bound. Many millions of their people are untouched by the Western world. To them the immemorial ties of personal relatedness, ritual, and traditional authority are the true sources of security and satisfaction. For thousands of villages, isolation is still a paramount fact of life.

In the Congo, the village of Lupupa has its own way of describing the world:

The earth is conceptualized as a round, flat platter; if one approaches the edge (although the distance is too great to conceive of this as a real possibility) and is not careful, he will tumble off and into a limitless sea beyond which is only the unknown. In the exact center of this platter is Lupupa and, by extension, the Congo, while somewhere around the rim are placed

America, Belgium, and Portugal. These three countries, it is evident, figure in the world scene because they are the only ones known—America, because there had been American visitors there, Portugal because of the presence in Tshofa [a nearby village] of a Portugese trader, and Belgium for obvious reasons. . . .

The most sophisticated person in the village knew that this picture of the world was untrue, and told us so. He had learned the truth in school, he said, and the world, far from being a flat platter, was in reality a flat triangle, with Lupupa in the center, and Belgium, Portugal, and America at the various angles of the figure.[6]

Among these people, nationhood has little meaning. Moreover, for the villager the idea of a nation is very new, whereas local legends may trace the tribe back to the beginning of the world. It is reasonable to expect some reluctance to trade his old identity for a new one.

The tribe is a kinship-based, tradition-centered unit of social organization. It embraces people who share a sense of personal relatedness rooted very often in a real or imagined common descent. Tribal society of the African Gold Coast "was an amalgamation of family units into larger and larger kinship groupings in which totemic genealogy provided a major social guide."[7] Tribes may occupy and own a particular territory but this is less important for tribal organization than for the modern nation-state. It has been calculated that there are as many as six thousand tribes in Africa.[8]

Traditionally, the tribal bond has been an extension of family loyalties. One belonged to the tribe by way of his family membership. By the same token, the authority of the tribe over the individual was channeled through his kinship group. This was effective in rural areas where the family was an economic unit

and organized virtually the total life of the individual. As the tribesman moves to the city, however, family authority and identity weaken. The tribe comes to have a more direct influence on the person. In a subtle way, this may serve as a transition to a sense of national citizenship, because loyalty to a broader unit is encouraged. But the more immediate effects are less satisfactory, from the standpoint of national unity.

Tribes in the City

The persistence of strong tribal ties in the urban community is partly due to the capacity of the tribe to ease the transition from country to city. Fellow tribesmen can be looked to for practical help, and their presence is a source of psychological support. Moreover, the new urbanite maintains strong rural ties. He keeps up his interest in life at home and maintains continued and detailed contact with his tribal village. One reason is that the tribal home offers a possible refuge in old age.[9]

The effect of this continuing social bond is to make the tribe a significant political unit in the city. Participation by the tribesmen in political parties is often on a tribal basis. Because of tribal solidarity, tribal leaders can "deliver the vote" and thereby enhance the importance of the tribe in the new political setting.

African politicians have looked to the tribe for political support because

the tribe could provide them with a relatively secure political base, a fairly reliable personal following, and masses whose aspirations, belief systems, grievances, and tensions they knew intimately and therefore could most easily and legitimately appeal to or manipulate. Moreover, in many cases tribal unions have taken on the political functions of organized pressure or bargaining groups on behalf of tribes placed in a minority or disadvantageous position as a consequence of constitutional developments at the

[6] Alan P. Merriam, *Congo: Background of Conflict* (Evanston: Northwestern University Press, 1961), p. 176.

[7] David E. Apter, *The Gold Coast in Transition* (Princeton: Princeton University Press, 1955), p. 80.

[8] These are listed in George P. Murdock, *Africa* (New York: McGraw-Hill, 1959), pp. 425–56.

[9] Aldan Southall, "Kinship, Tribalism, and Family Authority," in Aidan Southall (ed.), *Social Change in Modern Africa* (London: Oxford University Press, 1961), p. 36.

territorial level. Finally, tribal unions were "organizations in being" which territorial politicians found highly useful . . . as an immediately available, developed organizational apparatus and a cadre of political activists.[10]

This is, of course, highly reminiscent of immigrant politics in the United States. For many years, and to a lesser extent today, ethnic and home-country ties formed the basis of effective big-city political machines.

In Nigeria, the three major tribal groupings —Ibo, Yoruba, and Hausa-Fulani—formed political parties. There were no less than 120 political parties in the Congo in 1960, almost all originating in a tribal grouping.[11] These new parties tend to perpetuate old tribal jealousies, fears, and separatist tendencies. After independence, tribes located in different parts of a country may seek separate political status in order to avoid possible domination by traditional tribal enemies.

In addition to this separatist effect of tribe-based parties, the continuity of tribal solidarity has other negative consequences for nationhood. For example, a stabilized national economy is difficult to achieve when men quit their jobs frequently to return home for the purpose of fulfilling tribal obligations. Capital invested in tribal lands rather than in industry may also be a hindrance to the national economy. Most important, however, men are encouraged to think of themselves as members of a particular tribe rather than as citizens of a nation.

NATIONHOOD AND MODERNIZATION

The emerging independent nations in Asia and Africa encounter many unique problems not previously faced by earlier new nations. Today's new nations enter a world scene charged with political and ideological conflict. The great industrialized protagonists feel the need to win co-operation and allegiance from the less developed countries. This has created unprecedented opportunities for international aid to promote development. At the same time, the new nations themselves eagerly seek industrialization with all that it means for full participation in the world community.

The Revolution of Rising Expectations

For many centuries the lives of millions of people in tradition-centered societies remained unchanged. A poor existence and short life were fatalistically accepted by many. These conditions were offset in part by the satisfactions of rich communal and family life. But one of the great sources of change in the modern world is the breakdown of these traditional perspectives, the rising demand for better health, more comfort, and all else that technology can provide. The change has been so drastic that a new phrase has been coined for it—"the revolution of rising expectations." [12]

These new expectations are in large part due to lessening isolation. As communication increases, especially the sort that brings the good news of high living standards to remote places, people become more aware of alternatives to their own way of life. It is easy to see that poverty is not man's inevitable fate. The newly awakening peoples do not see themselves as inferior, as in any fundamental way different from men who live in Western culture. They feel entitled to the benefits of advanced technology.

Raised aspirations are also encouraged by the dynamics of nationalism. The governments of the new nations must act fast to bind together their heterogeneous peoples when the colonial authority is removed. This they attempt to do by building up internal trade, improving transportation and communication, expanding educational facilities, establishing government-sponsored health clinics, damming rivers for electric power, and creating military establishments. Indirectly, all of

[10] James S. Coleman, "Current Political Movements in Africa," *The Annals*, No. 298 (March, 1955), p. 102.
[11] Merriam, *op. cit.*, p. 186.
[12] On the significance of changing perspectives, see COLLECTIVE BEHAVIOR, pp. 301 f.

these activities bring new values and perspectives into the traditional communities.

The struggle for independence from the colonial power brought with it new hopes for a better life. In the course of the struggle, nationalist propaganda offered visions of a rosy future once the foreigners were ejected. The very fact of a changed status helped produce the sense of an expanding world.

The revolution of rising expectations should be viewed in the light of one of the most important generalizations in political sociology: *It is not poverty or hardship as such that produces rebellion or other collective action; rather action is stimulated by a new awareness of alternative possibilities.* As a leader of the Russian Revolution of 1917 once said, "In reality the mere existence of privations is not enough to cause an insurrection; if it were, the masses would always be in revolt." [13]

The Charismatic Leader

The combination of continuing traditionalism, tribalism, and rising aspirations strongly affects the nature of political life in the new nations. Among the characteristic phenomena resulting from these circumstances is the "charismatic" leader.

Charisma means, in Greek, "endowed with grace." In ancient usage it had primarily a religious significance. Max Weber applied this idea in his analysis of authority and leadership. By charisma he meant "a certain quality of an individual personality by virtue of which he is set apart from ordinary men and treated as endowed with supernatural, superhuman, or at least exceptional powers or qualities." [14] The charismatic leader is perceived as a heroic, saintly, or otherwise peculiarly gifted man whose authority is based upon those personal qualities. It is not just that he occupies high office but that he himself is especially deserving of respect and even adoration.

Leadership based upon personal charisma tends to arise *when institutions are weak or subject to special stress.* Thus charismatic leaders become prominent in wartime and in periods of social upheaval. Winston Churchhill, Charles de Gaulle, and Adolf Hitler were charismatic leaders of the past generation— a combination which shows that charisma may attach to either good or evil leaders.

In the new countries, national institutions are weak. The charismatic leader serves as a unifying symbol; he can summon loyalty to the nation by way of devotion to his own person. Such a figure is Kwame Nkrumah, president and prime minister of Ghana, the former British colony known as the Gold Coast.

Before independence in 1957, Nkrumah's Convention People's Party recited nationalist prayers at mass meetings. A nationalist creed identified Nkrumah with Christ and the British Governor with Pontius Pilate. Nkrumah's imprisonment by the British in 1950 only added to his stature. "The word spread that the jail could not hold him and that he slipped out every night in the guise of a white cat." [15]

Nkrumah has done much to cultivate his charisma. The Constitution of Ghana names him Osagyefo—Redeemer and Leader. He is Life Leader of the Convention People's Party. His likeness is reproduced on stamps and coins and on the masthead of the party newspaper. In Accra, the capital, a large statue placed before the new Parliament building is inscribed, "Kwame Nkrumah, Founder of the Nation."

The charismatic leader combines qualities of the traditional village or tribal chieftain with those of the modern statesman-politician. As chief he is a personal and continuing

[13] A comment attributed to Leon Trotsky. See Crane Brinton, *The Anatomy of Revolution* (New York: Vintage, 1957), p. 34.

[14] See the picture and commentary, p. 630. For a discussion of charisma, see Max Weber, *The Theory of Social and Economic Organization* (New York: Oxford University Press, 1947), pp. 358–92, and Reinhard Bendix, *Max Weber: An Intellectual Portrait* (New York: Doubleday, 1960), Chap. X.

[15] John Gunther, *Inside Africa* (New York: Harper, 1955), p. 804.

The Nehru career: From English public school boy to revolutionary leader to head of state. Nehru as a young man; Nehru with his mentor, Gandhi.

Egypt's Populist Regime

Abridged from *The Arab World Today* by Morroe Berger (New York: Doubleday, 1962), pp. 419–23. Published in the British Empire by Weidenfeld & Nicolson, Ltd., London. Used by permission of the publishers.

The Egypt of King Farouk and the Egypt of Colonel Nasser are in a sense opposite models of the political evolution of countries that seek to change from a traditional agricultural to a modern industrial society. Though Farouk's regime was not liberal, it allowed a certain amount of freedom and political dissent. Partly, this was the result of a balance of forces among the palace, the British, and the various Egyptian groups who opposed both; the hesitation or fear of each one to assume all power enabled the others to survive and express themselves. But it stemmed also from the nature of the monarchy as a pre-populist regime. Such a regime and social system does not rest on public opinion. It retains considerable latitude by ignoring the masses, by not drawing them into political life, but leaving them undisturbed in their private misery and political apathy. It can therefore allow greater freedom at the top to the articulate groups—the press, political parties, professionals, students. By leaving the masses dormant, it affords some freedom for the elites.

Nasser's populist Egypt is something else. Having destroyed the organizations (especially the political parties and the economic bases of the groups that supported them) which enjoyed a modicum of freedom under its predecessor, the populist regime cannot allow these erstwhile elites or their remnants the same degree of freedom in politics. Instead, it seeks mass support by drawing new classes into the political process. These are the peasants and urban workers, who are wooed to add the strength of numbers to the regime's support in the army and the upper levels of the civilian bureaucracy. The political process no longer embraces competing parties and relatively free parliaments. Rather it includes (1) a single mass organization to arouse and channel political consciousness, (2) professional associations, peasant co-operatives, trade-unions, and religious groups harnessed to the regime's goals, and (3) plebiscites, and parliaments without parties.

Because the populist regime depends on the systematic cultivation of formerly isolated and ignored groups, it must rely on exhortation and propaganda to a greater extent than does the pre-populist regime. It communicates with the masses more directly and more often, creates opinions in them, arouses their passions, stimulates their desires and tries to make them work harder for the elite's goal of modernization. In such a society, where mass opinion is stirred, the expression of any opinion becomes all the more significant because it is no longer confined to the homogeneous and articulate thin layer at the top. The populist regime suppresses freedom at the top because freedom may now penetrate the lower levels and have serious consequences. And precisely because opinion and communication may now move the masses being brought into the political spectrum, the populist regime seeks to control expression everywhere. Increased communication does not itself constitute democracy though it enhances the role of classes formerly ignored.

1.   Social Processes

	PRE-POPULIST	POPULIST
COMMUNI-CATION	limited to elites and periphery	extended to whole society
VOLUNTARY ORGANIZA-TIONS	permits existence, makes some effort to control; few formal organizations, based either on religion or kinship	destroys or co-opts; creates mass organizations, substituting politics for kinship and religion; nationalizes loyalties
EDUCATION	emphasis on higher education and liberal professions; foreign schools permitted	greater emphasis on primary education and on science and technology; foreign schools nationalized
SOCIAL STRUCTURE AND STANDARDS	loose, many differences; individual closely bound to family and other groups and to locale	greater individual freedom from family and all non-political associations but deliberate effort to produce national uniformity

2.   Economic Processes and Policies

	PRE-POPULIST	POPULIST
ORGANIZA-TION	loose controls, private enterprise dominant	extensive controls, claims of socialism
INDUSTRY	small but growing	great emphasis on industrialization
AGRICUL-TURE	large holdings	land reform, state-controlled co-operatives
OWNERSHIP	private, with considerable foreign interests	nationalization in two senses: transfer of foreign property to native control, and state acquisition of private property
TAXATION	burden on middle and upper classes; chiefly indirect	extension of direct taxation to lower-income groups; appeals for "voluntary" contribution of labor and wages
PRICES	few controls	increasing control, mainly of food staples

3.   Political Processes and Programs

	PRE-POPULIST	POPULIST
NATIONAL-ISM OF DOM-INANT ELITE	strong but mixed with older loyalties	intensified, less influenced by other loyalties
PARTICIPA-TION	masses left largely quiescent	goads, exhorts, draws in masses
FREEDOM: MEANING	Western sense: individual liberty	synonymous with national independence
FREEDOM: INCIDENCE	some freedom resulting from competition for power among foreign interests, native elite in office, new native elite seeking power	no challenge to native ruling elite permitted
CLASS DIS-TINCTIONS	form basis of regime's policies	emphasis on social equality, economic democracy and appeal beyond classes
PARTIES	several	one, or a mass political organization not called a party
LEGISLA-TION	by parliament, with strong executive	rule by decree of leader or cabinet: parliament, if existing, based on plebiscite
PUBLIC AD-MINISTRA-TION	civil service a personal appendage to ruler; little effort at reform	efforts to introduce modern bureaucracy

source of power. This is important among nations unaccustomed to the periodic change-overs of leadership that accompany democratic elections.

Personal loyalty is familiar and meaningful to people not far removed from traditional ways of life. They can feel an attachment to the national hero which they cannot so readily feel for the abstract notion of nation-state. "In short, the hero helps to bridge the gap to a modern state." [16]

The Quest for Bureaucracy

In addition to political leadership, the modern state requires a dependable official-dom—a bureaucracy. This is especially important in the new nations because the role of government in stimulating and directing the economy is very large. This heavy responsibility creates the need for administrative and economic rationality in government. When a government does not have these responsibilities, it can maintain just enough law and order to keep itself in power; it can be lax in collecting revenues or dissipate them in supporting a nonproductive elite; it can tolerate much inefficiency and corruption within the government service. The new states, committed to rapid development, must take a different road.

Achieving rationality in government is no simple task. It requires a reconstruction of traditional approaches to the recruitment and supervision of government employees. This is the same basic process discussed in the preceding chapter in connection with the growth of rationality in economic behavior. The same fundamental change of orientation is required, from personal to more impersonal relations, from ascribed status to achieved status, from an emphasis on traditional loyalties and routines to a willingness to do what is needed to accomplish the task at hand.

In the developing areas, attitudes of impersonality and strict adherence to norms of

rationality are strange and may even be considered immoral. Thus Filipino administrators often feel that other loyalties are more important than loyalty to principles of efficient administration:

First, and most important, is loyalty to the family. Kinship ties more than any other factor determine political loyalties. Public office is often viewed more as an opportunity for fulfilling family responsibilities than as one for meeting responsibilities to the nation. For an appointing officer to fill a vacancy with a well-qualified stranger when a relative is looking for a job would subject him to a severe family criticism. [17]

Nepotism is only one of the obstacles to the development of a modern civil service. Political loyalties also play a large part. When government jobs are rewards for political support, it is difficult to maintain professional standards of administration. This is especially the case when patronage extends to the lower levels of the government administration. In the United States federal government and in many states, politics has much to do with the appointment of high officials but the lower levels tend to be recruited on the basis of the impersonal standards of the Civil Service. At an earlier period, however, the United States faced much the same problem, with respect to politics and administration, as now confronts the new nations.

From the standpoint of the modernizing country, however, impersonality and formality can be overdone. Development should be seen as *the creation of effective organizations.*[18] And organizational effectiveness depends on a blending of formal and informal relations. The breakdown of nepotism and other traditional ways is important, but the creation of new opportunities for personal satisfaction and group loyalty is also important. In the attempt to create a modern bureaucracy, there is sometimes an exagger-

---

[16] Immanuel Wallerstein, *Africa: The Politics of Independence* (New York: Vintage Books, 1961), p. 99.

[17] David Wurfel, "The Philippines," in George M. Kahin (ed.), *Governments and Politics of Southeast Asia* (Ithaca: Cornell University Press, 1959), p. 467.

[18] Pye, *op. cit.*, p. 38.

Upper: A Pakistani campaigning for office displays his party symbol.

Right: A First Voter in Colombia, with daughter, happily shows her registration form.

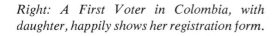

Candidates in Rampur, India hold ballot boxes with identifying symbols for voters unable to read.

ated emphasis on legalism and formality, with the result that the capacity of government to deal flexibly and rationally with complex problems may be impaired.

Democracy and the Modernizing Elite

In the new nations there is a continuing tension between democracy and authoritarianism. The dominant trend has been toward increased popular participation in political life—voting, membership in mass parties, attendance at political rallies and demonstrations. This new political awareness is part of the larger process by which national consciousness and loyalty are created. Voting for nation-centered parties and for national officers helps build a national civic identity. In addition the new leaders seek popular support to strengthen their own hands against the more traditionalist or separatist chiefs, or against other political opponents.

However, the modernizing leaders are not equally committed to mass participation. The table on page 681 summarizes the main differences between "pre-populist" and "populist" regimes. The distinction is useful, but it should be remembered that there are many "mixed" situations.

The emphasis on mass opinion by populist regimes does not necessarily mean that a great deal of political freedom is allowed. In Egypt under Nasser, for example, a mass organization, rather than competing political parties, is used "to arouse and channel political consciousness." Voting is a plebiscite rather than a real choice among alternative candidates. Other organizations, such as trade-unions and professional associations, are controlled by the government. See "Egypt's Populist Regime," pages 680–81.

The modernizing elite is mainly committed to economic development and increased national strength. It is less concerned about political forms. Often democracy is more nearly a slogan and a call to action than a specific way of making decisions. As a result new labels, such as "tutelary democracy" or "guided democracy," have come into use. These phrases describe regimes that encourage various forms of mass participation, but maintain effective control at the top.

In analyzing the weakness of democracy in the new nations, the following should be considered:

1. Modernization under unfavorable social conditions may indeed require considerable government initiative and control. And the political turmoil following independence may in some cases leave little alternative to a temporary authoritarian solution. It does not follow, however, that all cases in which freedom is abrogated can be justified on these grounds.

2. In some of the new or less industrialized nations, a relative lack of political freedom may be only a transitional phenomenon. We may expect the gradual strengthening of democratic institutions as economic and political development proceeds. However, where political freedom has been extinguished, or not allowed to emerge, such optimism is probably misplaced.

Section 3 **The age of social revolution**

In the modern world the common man becomes an actor on the stage of history. He learns to hold opinions and to make his aspirations known. His acceptance of things as they are is not taken for granted. He is wooed and placated, flattered and consulted. He is summoned to participate in great events. This "awakening of the masses" is perhaps the most fundamental social fact of our era.

Two key words of modern times are *democracy* and *equality*. The loosening of older social bonds has been accompanied by (1) a steady pressure to give more and more people a voice in political decision-making; and (2) a demand that traditional forms of inequality, especially those based upon inherited status, be modified. To a large extent, the expansion of democracy and equality has been a gradual process, the old order giving way in piecemeal fashion, step by step, to limited demands. On the other hand, the attack upon the old order sometimes has been accompanied by great social upheavals. When this occurs, a new set of forces comes into play. Revolution has its own effect on the pattern of social change.

THE MEANING OF SOCIAL REVOLUTION

There is a broad and a narrow sense in which the phrase "social revolution" is used. In the broad sense, a social revolution is any profound transformation of society, or of some aspect of society. Thus the term "industrial revolution" designates extensive changes in values and in social organization. Or it is said that a "managerial revolution" has taken place, affecting the social composition of the industrial and governmental elites in modern society. When used in this way, nothing specific is indicated as to the *method* of change. Reference is primarily to its scope and depth. It is assumed that many forces, acting in a variety of ways, have a profound and cumulative effect upon the social order.

The more restricted meaning of social revolution focuses upon a fairly definite set of events. In this sense social revolution is *a form of collective action* that has the following features:

1. It is directed at the overthrow of a government and the ousting of the social groups that support it from positions of power in the society.

2. Popular support is mobilized through methods of direct action such as mass demonstrations, rioting, refusal of soldiers to obey their commanders, and seizure of factories or of large agricultural holdings. These acts challenge existing authority and set passive elements of the population into motion.

3. Demands are general rather than limited, extending to basic changes in the political and social order.

There is a high probability that violence will be used in a revolution of this sort, either in the course of mass action or by soldiers recruited to the revolutionary cause. However, the use of force is not essential to a social revolution. In some cases, little or no violence may occur, particularly if the government is weak and chooses to flee or capitulate in the face of a well-organized and widely supported revolutionary group. Of course, the revolutionaries may use considerable force *after* they come into power, in suppressing opposition to the new regime, even though they used little force in actually taking over the government.

This discussion centers on the social revolution as a form of collective action. As such, it is distinguished from the simple *coup d'état,* in which a group outside the government takes over power by some form of intimidation, though with limited goals and without stirring a general social upheaval. Thus in 1962 the military leaders in Peru formed a "junta," and ousted the existing government in order to nullify the results of the presidential election. This *coup* had none of the features of a social revolution. On the other hand, a *coup d'état* can be *part* of a social revolution. A case in point is the Bolshevik *coup* in November,[19] 1917, which

[19] This is the New Style date, according to the Gregorian calendar. Before the Revolution, Russia used the Old Style (Julian) calendar. Under that system, the Czar was overthrown in February, 1917, and the Bolsheviks seized power in October. These dates become March and November under the New Style, which conforms to Western usage. The terms "February Revolution" and "October Revolution" are sometimes used in referring to the Russian events of 1917.

Vilfredo Pareto (1848–1923), an Italian economist, studied the non-rational bases of human conduct. No devotee of verbal economy, he produced a million-word treatise, The Mind and Society. His theory of elites considers decay within the governing class as a prelude to revolution. According to Pareto, divisions within the governing class and conflict among elites lead to social change. Social stability, on the other hand, presumes the "circulation of elites," that is, free access to the governing class by men of talent and determination and elimination of weaker members of the elite. While Pareto stressed the importance of elites, he did not defend aristocracy, which tends to interfere with the circulation of elites.

ousted the Provisional Government formed when the Czar was overthrown the preceding March. In this case the *coup* was a phase of the broader drama called the Russian Revolution.

Although they may involve mass action, social revolutions do not necessarily favor the extension of political democracy. The German Nazi regime of 1933–1945 was created by a social revolution. It was, however, contemptuous of democracy and quickly extinguished democratic institutions. Nor were the Bolsheviks (later called Communists) favorable to democracy. In each case, a self-appointed "vanguard" asserted the right to speak for the people and rule in their name, without, however, submitting itself to the test of free elections. The Nazi and Bolshevik revolutions are examples of a great historical paradox: the use of mass action, and the summoning of popular support, for dictatorial movements and governments.

Some of the social and psychological sources of antidemocratic mass action are discussed in Adaptation 44, pages 692 ff.

THE REVOLUTIONARY SITUATION

The conditions that make a society "ripe" for revolution are complex and variable and no simple formula may be stated. Nevertheless, several important conclusions may be drawn from a reading of modern history.

1. *Aspiration is as important as deprivation in stimulating revolution.* The significance of aspirations has already been indicated in the discussion above (p. 677) of "the revolution of rising expectations." Here it must be added that social revolutions are likely to be organized and led by groups that are fairly well off economically. It is not the lowest, most oppressed strata of the population that take the lead. For example, a study of the Jacobin clubs of the French Revolution, which were important centers of agitation and organization, casts light on the social position of the members. Table XVII: 1 shows the distinctly middle-class composition

Table XVII:1   Social Composition of the Jacobin Clubs
During the French Revolution

	Moderate Period 1789–1792 (Per Cent)	Violent Period 1793–1795 (Per Cent)
Middle class	66	57
Working class	26	32
Peasant	8	11
Total	100	100
Members	4,037 in 12 clubs	8,062 in 42 clubs

Source: Crane Brinton, *The Anatomy of Revolution* (New York: Vintage, 1960), p. 101.

of the clubs. The members "represent the abler, more ambitious, and successful of the inhabitants of a given town. It is as if our present-day Rotarians were revolutionists." [20]

The respectable and relatively well-situated revolutionists are led to revolt because they feel that the existing order does not give them the social status and the freedom of action to which they are entitled. For many, this represents a quest for full recognition and complete economic opportunity rather than a desperate effort to escape intolerable conditions. Deprivation may be important, however. The revolutionary situation is often marked by severe hardships brought on by food shortages, a sharp decline in the value of money, new and burdensome taxes, or a demand for unpopular military service. Desperation at the lower levels of society may produce sporadic outbreaks that highlight the weakness and incompetence of the government, encouraging the better-off elements to take action. At the same time, those most deprived become available for mass action in support of the revolutionary leaders. For all groups, it is *relative* deprivation that sharpens resentment and stirs revolt.

2. *Social revolutions occur when the ruling elite is weak and divided.* In the revolutionary situation a state of disorganization

spreads throughout the whole society. The revolution is a crisis of confidence, and this includes the *self*-confidence of the wealthy and the powerful. Members of the ruling elite are themselves affected by new ideas and by criticism of the existing order. Just before the French and Russian revolutions, many of the nobility were highly critical of the regimes and doubtful that the old way of life could continue for long. In such circumstances, beset by internal criticism and self-doubt, the government hesitates to take strong measures. Yet it is incapable of instituting the reforms that might stave off the revolution. Or such action may be too late.

Consequently, there is a breakdown of solidarity within the governing class. Some of its members openly espouse the revolutionary cause and even undertake to lead it. These upper-class rebels may be conservative in their backgrounds and social views, but they feel that the social crisis can be met only by overthrowing the government.

3. *The crisis calls into question the type of government represented by the existing regime.* Limited rebellions may demand only that particular men in power be turned out. Thus kings sometimes were forced to abdicate, to be replaced by another member of the royal family who might be thought more competent, less corrupt, or simply more willing to follow the policies proposed by the rebels.

[20] Brinton, *op. cit.*, p. 102.

In a social revolution, however, the attack goes beyond particular officeholders. A change in the form of government is demanded. This intensifies the crisis because the interests of those who derive their privileges from the existing form of government, and its institutions, are threatened.

Thus the revolutionary situation reveals weakness and incompetence at the top, widespread loss of confidence in the existing political order, and the availability of alternative groups in the society whose aspirations and self-confidence are high. These conclusions emphasize that revolutionary change is not a simple thrust from below. It is preceded by a corrosion that affects the entire social system.

THE NATURAL HISTORY OF REVOLUTIONS

The overthrow of the old regime is not an end but a beginning. What is most significant in social revolutions occurs *after* this initial event. How far social change will be pushed, and upon what principles the society will be organized, depends in large part on the character of the revolutionary leadership.

In the classic cases of France and Russia, power was at first transferred from the monarchy to a group of *moderates* who represented the official parliamentary bodies and who sought only a limited change in the nature of the government and society. But these men faced insuperable obstacles. They inherited an ineffective government organization and a host of political and social problems. Moreover, they were unprepared to assume the leadership of an aroused and excited public. They could not readily do so, because their moderate views inclined them toward compromise and gradual change rather than toward direct action and drastic measures. At the same time, they were committed to a new atmosphere of political freedom and this made them hesitate to curb the activities of those who held more radical views. The radicals believed that the political changes thus far wrought, in overthrowing the old govern-

ment, were not enough. The political revolution, they insisted, should become a social revolution.

Dual Power

The weakness of the moderates was acutely revealed in the existence of "dual power." In the early stages of the revolution, rival governments appeared. One was the official government, controlled by the moderates, the other was an unofficial government. Lenin, the leader of the Russian Bolsheviks, described the situation in this way:

The highly remarkable feature of our revolution is that it has established a *dual power.* . . . In what does this dual power consist? In the fact that side by side with the Provisional Government . . . there has developed *another government* . . . — the Soviets of Workers' and Soldiers' Deputies. . . . *This* power is of exactly *the same type* as the Paris Commune of 1871. The fundamental characteristics of this type are: (1) The source of power is not a law previously discussed and passed by parliament, but the direct initiative of the masses from below . . .; (2) the direct arming of the whole people in place of the police and the army, which are institutions separated from the people and opposed by the people; order in the state under such a power is maintained by the armed workers and peasants *themselves,* by the armed people *itself;* (3) officials and bureaucrats are either displaced by the direct rule of the people itself or at least placed under special control.[21]

Lenin wrote this statement in April, 1917, about a month after the overthrow of the Czar and six months before he himself was to assume power. When he speaks of "the people" he really means that certain organizations arise, based on groups not hitherto in power, that are capable of becoming powerful centers of loyalty. Dual power exists when these groups take over some of the functions of government, such as the maintenance of or-

[21] "A Dual Power," in V. I. Lenin and J. Stalin, *The Russian Revolution* (New York: International Publishers, 1938), pp. 20 f.

V. I. Lenin (1870–1924), organizer of the Bolshevik Revolution, addresses a crowd. To the right of the stand is Leon Trotsky, another intellectual who became a revolutionary.

der, while acting independently of the official government.

Russia of 1917 is the clearest case of dual power. On one side was the Provisional Government; on the other were the Soviets (Councils) within which the Bolsheviks and other radical groups were active. The same phenomenon, though not always so plainly evident, has occurred in other revolutions. In the English revolution of the 1640's, the radicals controlled the New Model Army, which represented a dual power rivaling the moderate-controlled Parliament. In the French Revolution of 1789–1795, a network of radi-

cal Jacobin societies provided the organizational basis of dual power.

The essential sociological feature of dual power is *the withdrawal of loyalty* by groups capable of establishing an alternative government. Such groups may take quite varied forms. Sometimes they have a geographical basis, as in the American South just prior to the Civil War; at other times, a sector of the official government—often the army—may become a "government within a government"; or new organizational forms may arise, usually based upon pre-existing political parties, churches, trade-unions, or other associations. In the 1930's a dual-power situation was created by the German Nazis, who built a network of organizations, including their own military units, that challenged the existing civil authority.

The phenomenon of dual power suggests two conclusions regarding the dynamics of social revolution:

1. The dramatic days of insurrection, when the old government is deposed, may only confirm and complete, with a minimum of violence, a transfer of power that has already occurred. If the unofficial rival government has established its own machinery, and won over the loyalty of units of the army or police, the revolution will already have taken place. In such cases, the final showdown will bring no surprises.

2. Social revolutionists do not so much "seize" power as destroy and re-create it.[22] The old institutions, already weakened, are helped to die. New ones, typically more vigorous and ruthless, are established. These new groups do not simply replace the old. They are more dynamic and bring additional resources into political life. Therefore, the total quantity of effective political power is increased in the course of the revolution.

Victory of the Extremists

The great social revolutions witnessed a deepening conflict between the moderates and the radicals. In part, these conflicts took place *within* the rival or shadow governments. The extremists pressed their views inside the Soviets, the Jacobin societies, military staffs, or other bases of dual power. When they became dominant there, they were ready for a final test of strength with the legal government of moderates who had replaced the old regime.

Characteristically, the extremists are only a small part of the total population. However, they come to power in two basic ways. First, by intimidating opponents, both physically and psychologically, they *neutralize* large

[22] See George S. Pettee, *The Process of Revolution* (New York: Harper, 1938), pp. 4–5.

parts of the population. As the crisis deepens, more and more people withdraw from political participation. Political life tends to be polarized, with high activity at the extremes but passivity among large numbers. Fear and confusion put many on the sidelines. The political arena is abandoned to those who are most ruthless and determined.

Second, because of their discipline and political passion, the extremist minorities are able to take advantage of popular manifestations of resentment or desperation. They place themselves at the head of the "masses," that is, of the most active and excited elements. This greatly increases their power, at least temporarily.

The radical leaders are often well aware of the fact that their chances of coming to power depend on a fragile combination of circumstances. They know that they must strike at the right time, when their potential opponents are neutralized and when there is enough excitement to provide a decisive measure of popular support. When the radicals do strike, it is in the form of a show of strength against the government, followed by the imprisonment, death, or exile of its leaders.

Once in power the radicals establish a "revolutionary dictatorship." Firmness and terror are the order of the day. Step by step, all opposition is suppressed. New and drastic measures are introduced. The social revolution is pressed from above. The government itself is now the main source of social change and the chief mobilizer of the people. Especially in the revolutionary dictatorships of communism and fascism, there is an emphasis on demonstrations of mass support, with huge parades and meetings addressed by the revolutionary leaders. Instead of holding elections, the leaders offer these "direct" activities as evidence of popular approval.

Thermidor

The leaders of the French Revolution underlined their break with the past by instituting a new calendar. For the warmest season of the year they chose the name Thermidor ("gift of heat"). On 9th Thermidor of the year II (July 27, 1794), the revolutionary leader Robespierre was deposed. He was executed the following day. There followed a period of reaction against the militancy of the revolution and the way was paved for Napoleon Bonaparte. This transition, to some extent duplicated in other social revolutions, has since been called the "Thermidorean Reaction."

As a phase in the natural history of revolution, Thermidor has the following significance:

1. The centralized power created by the revolution is taken over and stabilized by a "strong man"—Cromwell in England, Bonaparte in France, Stalin in Russia.

2. Revolutionary fervor is abated and accommodations are made with more moderate groups and older traditions. The revolutionary extremists are suppressed; peace is made with older institutions, such as the church; historic nationalist aspirations are reasserted.

3. The reaction is not complete. There is no return to the prerevolutionary situation. Rather, the period of Thermidor maintains and consolidates the chief social changes wrought by the revolution. But many of the ideals of the revolutionaries are shucked off. Thus under Stalin "socialism" became identified with state ownership of industry and state initiative in economic development, but the revolutionary ideals of "workers' control" and the "classless society" were abandoned.

Caution: The above discussion identifies patterns that are discernible in at least some rev-

olutions. Such an analysis helps us to look behind surface events and to ask meaningful questions. However, it is not possible to generalize for all revolutions. There is no single pattern of natural history, no inevitable set of stages.

THE OUTCOME

A great social revolution is not the work of a handful of conspirators or fanatics. Disciplined minorities can and do play a decisive role, but the upheavals occur because there are real problems that the old order seems incapable of solving. Some of these problems are immediate and relatively short-run, such as might be brought on by defeat in war or an economic crisis. These are not likely to lead to a social revolution unless important sectors of the society are ready to accept fundamental changes in the position of great institutions or social classes.

The Russian Revolution was begun by idealists that included in their number both moderates and extremists. "They dreamed of power with the object of abolishing power; of ruling over people to wean them from the habit of being ruled." [23] But the regime they created soon humiliated and destroyed the generation of militant idealists. Within a few years, a dictatorship had suppressed all opposition and set itself to build up its own and the country's power. Indeed, the chief accomplishment of the revolution was the modernization of Russia. [24]

[23] Arthur Koestler, *Darkness at Noon* (New York: Modern Library, 1946), p. 59.
[24] John Strachey, "The Strangled Cry," *Encounter* (London), November, 1960, pp. 7–8.

ADAPTATION 44

Escape From Freedom

Abridged and adapted from Erich Fromm, *Escape From Freedom*, Copyright, 1941, by Erich Fromm. Published by permission of Erich Fromm and Rinehart and Company, Inc. Responsibility for this summary should not be attributed to the author.

Many early sociological investigators regarded man as infinitely adaptable and entirely shaped by social forces. This view has been seriously challenged, notably by Freud and other psychoanalysts. In his analysis of the meaning of freedom for modern man, Erich Fromm holds that man is a creature of *limited* adaptability and suggests that when these limits are transgressed serious consequences for the social order ensue. While social forces mold man, man himself transforms society when it fails to meet his needs.

According to Fromm, man's psychological needs are as important as his physical ones, and when these psychological needs are not met he experiences anxiety. Because this is painful, it drives him to change the world in ways that will reduce his anxiety. Fromm believes that freedom in modern society has brought with it a burden of anxiety, and he attributes the growth of authoritarian social systems to an anxiety-laden search for psychological security. He believes that the anxiety growing out of contemporary forms of freedom is a persistent threat to modern democracy, and if democracy is to be a viable social order, it must develop in ways that will provide greater psychological security.

Escape From Freedom was an effort to diagnose the rise of Fascist totalitarianism. Since the book was published, the German and Italian Fascist states have been destroyed. Communist totalitarianism has spread rapidly, however, and the psychological basis of antidemocratic mass action remains an important problem.

The Acceptance of Totalitarianism

Modern European and American history is centered around man's effort to gain political, economic, and spiritual freedom. The conclusion of the First World War was regarded by many as the ultimate victory for freedom, but only a few years elapsed before new social systems emerged which denied the value of freedom. The essence of these new systems was the submission of all but a handful of men to an authority over which they had no control.

At first many people believed that the German and Italian people were the confused and unwilling victims of cunning, trickery, and terror. In the years that have followed, we have been compelled to recognize that millions surrendered their freedom willingly. This crisis of democracy is not a uniquely German or Italian experience. Rather it is a problem confronting every modern state. For many, freedom has become a burden too heavy to bear. Why is this so? What does it mean? What is "the burden of freedom"?

Freedom and Social Isolation

The burden of freedom is isolation, aloneness, and anxiety. Freedom runs the risk of being self-defeating because freedom *to* requires freedom *from*. As the child seeks freedom *to* develop and express his individual self unhampered by external controls, he must also seek freedom *from* those persons who gave him security and reassurance. Individuation is both a process of growing strength and integration of the personality and at the same time one in which the original identification with others is lost. This growing separation results in feelings of isolation and aloneness and creates anxiety and insecurity.

Since the Medieval period freedom has been a value in Western society. Unwilling to limit the process of his individuation, man has pursued it in ever-widening areas. He has demanded political, economic, religious, and intellectual freedom; he has sought status by his own achievements; he has struggled for the right to pursue his own ends and to act on the basis of his own convictions.

In seeking freedom to develop and express his independence and individuality, Western man has had to seek freedom from identification with traditional sources of psychological security. His ties to family, community, and church have been weakened. Although freed from the social control they exercise, he has isolated and alienated himself from his basic social institutions.

Capitalism and Protestantism testify to man's quest for freedom and his isolation from the community. In contrast to the feudal system of the Middle Ages under which everybody had a fixed place in an ordered social system, capitalist economy put the individual entirely on his own feet. What he did, how he did it, whether he succeeded or failed, was entirely his own affair. This increase in personal liberty is usually mentioned as an important item on the credit side of modern culture. But in furthering "freedom from," it helped to sever the ties between one individual and another and thereby isolated and separated the individual from his fellow men.

The teachings of the Protestant Reformation helped prepare for this development toward isolation. The relationship of the individual to God in the Catholic Church had been based on membership in the Church. The Church was the link between him and God, thus restricting his individuality but letting him face God as an integral part of a group. Protestantism had the individual face God alone. Psychologically, this spiritual individualism is similar to economic individualism. In both instances the individual faces the superior power of God or of impersonal economic forces alone.

Conditions Aggravating Anxiety

Over the centuries, society has developed in ways that have aggravated man's sense of aloneness. His early experience in freedom gave him a sense of power and significance, offsetting the negative aspects of his social isolation. He conquered and settled whole new continents, achieved a voice in government, and established public education for his children. Success came to few, but opportunity for advancement was real to many. The individual had the sense that his choices and decisions, his work and his achievements, counted for something.

Capitalism has built a vast industrial machine in which ordinary men play but a minute and negligible role. Technology has become increasingly important, while individual initiative, creativity, and opportunity have steadily diminished in importance. Man feels he is no longer the master of the machine but is instead its caretaker and servant; he feels insignificant and unimportant.

Economic crises, unemployment, war, and the remoteness of political decision add to this sense of powerlessness. Events occur in distant places—events which affect man's life profoundly but over which he has no control.

The Escape into Authoritarianism

The individual of our time is driven by his sense of isolation and powerlessness to seek new social arrangements. He feels, even if he does not understand, his need for integration into the community about him. He seeks understanding of his place in the order of things. Fascism offered the individual the semblance of the security he seeks in two ways:

1. *It offered the individual a pseudogroup to assuage his loneliness.* Fascist ideologists concentrated on developing the image of "the folk." They—"the folk," "the Nordic race" —claimed the allegiance of the lonely individual. In the place of clear-cut integration

into a functioning group, the individual was symbolically inducted into the community at large. A symbol of Fascism was the mass meeting in which unity was achieved through arranged hysteria. Even though their individuality was submerged and their responsibility denied, men escaped from their isolation.

2. *It allowed the individual to gain the semblance of significance through identification with a strong leader, and to achieve the sense of power by sanctioning aggression against the weak.* An essential element of authoritarianism is a strong leader. Identification with a strong leader offered an escape from the sense of insignificance.

The Need for Belonging

This analysis suggests that man has a psychological "need for belonging" rooted in his basic life situation. Relatedness to others is not a luxury with which man can dispense. Because the human infant is biologically helpless, relatedness to others is indispensable to human survival. It is also the necessary condition for the development of human personality and selfhood. We discover what and who we are only in our relations with others.

This relatedness to others is not identical with physical contact. An individual may be alone in a physical sense for many years and yet be related to ideals, values, or at least social patterns that give him a feeling of communion and "belonging." On the other hand, he may live among people and yet be overcome with an utter feeling of isolation which leads, in the extreme case, to the state of insanity called schizophrenia.

Does the analysis lead to the conclusion that there is an inevitable circle that leads from freedom into submission and a new bondage? There is a positive answer to the problem of freedom. Man can attain a freedom that does not isolate him from others. He need not be driven to deny his selfhood in compulsive subordination to the group.

Historically, freedom *to* has meant freedom to pursue goals, such as wealth, fame, success, power, and prestige. These goals were often not the expression of the genuine potentialities of the individual but were imposed upon him from without. They often required the suppression of whole areas of the personality. The meaning of life was found, not in the here and now, but in some future when wealth or power was finally attained. It was not so much the individual himself who was valued but the achievements he won.

Genuine freedom means freedom to be oneself; it consists in the spontaneous activity of the total, integrated personality. Spontaneous activity is to be contrasted with compulsive activity and that of the automaton. The automaton strives for goals imposed on him by others without regard for his individuality and uniqueness. Compulsive activity is activity driven by anxiety and by a need for security. Spontaneous activity is expressive of the self's genuine potentialities, values, and feelings.

The victory of freedom is possible only if democracy develops into a society in which the aim and purpose of culture is the growth and happiness of the individual, in which life does not need to be justified by success, and in which the individual is not subordinated to, or manipulated by, any power outside of himself, be it the state or the economic machine. Man will then be free to relate to the world and others through love and creative work.

Caution: Fromm's analysis is an example of the application of psychological theory to the interpretation of history. It assumes that large numbers of people can and do share similar life experiences and respond to these in similar ways. As in much analysis of human pathology, this theory appears to be most convincing when it stresses negative rather than positive aspects of personality. It is easier to identify an illness than to find a remedy. Fromm may be right in saying that man can find freedom and happiness in a spontaneous and creative relatedness to other people and to work. However, psychological theory has not yet precisely identified the behavioral meaning of the spontaneity and creativity to which Fromm refers.

Section 4 Totalitarian society

To many writers of the nineteenth century, for whom social change was social progress, the future of society seemed clear and hopeful. Industrialism and democracy would advance together. Traditional society based on status, privilege, and ignorance would be swept aside. A new and permanent era of rationality and enlightenment would gradually extend its sway. This optimistic view of a "progressive society" assumed that the darkest pages of human history, measured by brutality, tyranny, and political hatred, belonged to the past.

In the twentieth century, there is a more pessimistic note. Industrial society, and the technology on which it is based, have conferred many benefits. But they have also presented great problems and produced some unexpected and drastic responses. One of the most important of these responses is the emergence of twentieth-century totalitarianism.

Totalitarianism represents a fusion of state and society. It should be seen as an entire social system in which politics profoundly affects the whole range of human activities and associations.

The totalitarian social system differs markedly from older authoritarian dictatorships. In the latter, power is concentrated in the hands of a ruling few, but many spheres of life, such as religion and the family, are left untouched and more or less free from state control. Autocratic rulers of the past were often cruel, despotic, and ready to sacrifice others to their own power and glory. But they lived in a society that was poorly adapted to the exercise of centralized power. It is one thing to have the trappings and the doctrine of autocracy; it is another to have the means to put it into practice. Modern technology and social organization provide the most advanced tools of political dictatorship.

Total Power

The totalitarian regimes of communism and fascism have sought, and largely achieved, unlimited power. First, the government accepts no limitation on the *amount or kind* of coercion it may use to achieve its ends. It can execute people, exile them, place them in prison or in labor camps—all without effective restraint. Second, totalitarian power is unlimited in *scope*. It is all-embracing. The government asserts the right to control and regiment every phase of life.

Total power is not easily won or maintained. Every totalitarian regime supplements the more conventional powers of government by new devices and strategies for reaching the people and subjecting them to detailed surveillance and control. The most important controls are the following:

1. *The official political party.* Although there are no significant contests in the totalitarian state, much effort is devoted to maintaining a party organization. The regimes are sometimes called "party states" because of the important role played by the single political party in strengthening the hands of the top leaders. The totalitarian party consists of a relatively small percentage of the population,

but these include the most dedicated supporters of the system. The Communist Party of the Soviet Union includes about 4 per cent of the population of the country.[25]

The party is a training ground for future leaders and administrators; it is an army of volunteers who spend part of their time stimulating and reinforcing support for the government; its members greatly enhance the capacity of the government to observe the population and report subversive activities. Within the party, there are sometimes conflicts and debate among top leaders, but the membership itself does not participate in the determination of policy or the selection of leaders. The party is a dependable instrument of total power controlled from the top.

2. *Official ideology.* The totalitarian government is a propagandist and agitator. It seeks total conformity to an orthodox set of political beliefs. Ideology strengthens the regime in many ways. The government gains prestige as the spokesman for a new set of moral beliefs; the ideology provides material for the political indoctrination of the people, who thus learn whom to hate, what to cheer, and why they must sacrifice; loyalty is tested and "dangerous thoughts" detected and combated. Under totalitarianism the official ideology stands unchallenged. No competing doctrines may be openly promulgated. Furthermore, the official ideology is not restricted to one sphere, such as politics, religion, or economics. It is a total ideology, guiding all phases of conduct and belief. The common thread is subordination of the individual to the will of the state.

3. *Monopoly of public communication.* The government takes over the entire system of public communication: the newspapers, radio, television, cinema, and publication of books, magazines, and even academic journals. This monopoly has several uses for totalitarian rule. Most important, the prohibition of independent media of communication

stifles the organization of opposition groups, since such groups cannot maintain themselves without some means of communication. In addition, the government can filter out any news that might create unfavorable attitudes. Through its monopoly the government can undertake campaigns of "public education" to create a favorable climate of opinion.

4. *Control of organized group life.* When the totalitarian regime comes to power, it either breaks up or takes over most independent social groups. These include trade-unions, business associations, youth groups, churches, schools, political parties, and many other associations. It even seeks to place loyalty to the state above loyalty to family and friends, curtailing the autonomy of these primary groups. This is especially important in the early stages of totalitarian rule when the values transmitted by the family are not in full conformity with the demands of the state.

But totalitarianism is not the absence of social organization. On the contrary, associations of all kinds are created and supported by the totalitarian state. Government-controlled youth leagues, hiking clubs, trade-unions, and many other "people's" organizations have been important under both fascism and communism. Social groups under totalitarianism, however, are not autonomous, nor do they represent diverse interests. Instead, they are instituted and controlled from above to mobilize people for courses of action desired by the ruling elite and to prevent the development of independent groups and opinion.

5. *A managed economy.* The totalitarian state assumes control over the main sectors of the economy, especially the big corporations and banks. Under communism this means that all major enterprises are owned and run by the government. Under Hitler, private ownership remained, but the government established effective control over business management. Total power is not possible

[25] Herbert McClosky and John E. Turner, *The Soviet Dictatorship* (New York: McGraw-Hill, 1960), pp. 243–44.

when the government must defer to the independent decisions of businessmen or when the free play of the competitive market is allowed to decide who produces what and how much at what price.

6. *The police state.* Because the totalitarian regimes depend so heavily on the extensive use of arbitrary police power, they are often referred to as "police states." The police become weapons in the struggle for total power. Special police agencies, partly secret, are created to act as arms of the government in maintaining effective political surveillance of the population and in ferreting out potential opponents. Instead of being mainly concerned with suppressing conventional crime, the totalitarian police take on a decisive political function. Moreover, the police are not restrained by the legal requirements of speedy trial or fair treatment.

In its quest for total power, the totalitarian state combines the threat of violence with organization and mass persuasion. The ultimate achievement of total power would rest on complete and willing acceptance of the system and its existing leaders by the population. However, no totalitarian government is willing to test its hold on public opinion by removing the threat of imprisonment or worse and permitting the open debate of public issues.

Since the death of Stalin in 1953, there has been considerable relaxation of government by terror in the Soviet Union:

Purges of the elite within the Communist Party and political terror directed against the population at large were for a long time defined by many observers as distinctive and irremovable features of Soviet totalitarianism. Political controls of essentially nonpolitical activities and restrictions on freedom of movement and expression continue to characterize Soviet society. But the formerly ubiquitous forced labor camps have apparently largely been closed down, the purging of the ranks of the Party greatly reduced, and even the treatment of defeated "enemies" at the highest levels of the Party transformed from inevitable shooting to probable demotion and "internal exile." [26]

This relaxation is accompanied by an increased concern for consumer needs, some restraints on police power, and possibly a greater degree of professional and academic freedom. However, the government maintains the decisive instruments of total power. The government's continued stability and self-confidence may reduce the harshness with which these powers are used, and if this goes on for a long time the totalitarian character of the system may change. But there is insufficient evidence to conclude that such changes have occurred or even that they are likely.

In communist East Germany, the totalitarian state has a weak hold on public opinion, as evidenced by the mass efforts to escape to the West. The government rests on its own police and on the aid of Russian troops. The limits of total power in East Germany were tested in June, 1953, and those events are analyzed in Adaptation 45.

Totalitarianism and Industrial Society

From the standpoint of political systems and ideals, the totalitarian state is properly perceived as alien by the citizens of the free political communities. However, the *continuity* of the totalitarian industrial state and the democratic industrial society should not be overlooked.

1. The modern totalitarian state is a vehicle of rapid industrialization. Its power rests on advanced technology. Its values include a prizing of scientific and engineering progress. Indeed, in accordance with Marxist doctrine, the communists accept material progress as the main criterion of social worth. Insofar as advanced industrial organization defines the character of a society, totalitarian communism has points in common with other industrialized communities.

2. Totalitarian society, like the rest of the

[26] Alex Inkeles and Kent Geiger, *Soviet Society: A Book of Readings* (Boston: Houghton Mifflin, 1961), p. 249.

modern world, is a *participant* society. The totalitarian rulers ask more of their people than simple obedience. Through a large variety of government-controlled organizations and programs, the people are called upon to participate actively in public life—to volunteer for special duties, to show enthusiasm for their leaders, to read the government newspapers, to join in public criticism of lesser officials, to vote in great numbers for the official slate of candidates. The more totalitarian the society, the greater is the emphasis on *mobilization,* on driving the population toward greater effort to serve the state.

The emphasis on participation, plus the glorification of "the people" in totalitarian ideology, lends a pseudodemocratic cast to life in the totalitarian world. The very term "democracy" comes to take on a special meaning. It is identified with participation and popular consent, even if that does not involve the free choice of leaders, freedom of speech, or freedom of association. In the democratic age, the symbols of democracy, and some of its forms, come to be associated with even the harshest dictatorial regimes.

The Seventeenth of June

Based on news reports, especially those in the *New York Times,* June 17–19, 1953; Joseph Wechsberg, "A Reporter in Germany," *The New Yorker,* August 29, 1953; Norbert Muhlen, "The People Speak in a People's Democracy," *Reporter,* September 1, 1953; and "Der Aufstand im Juni: Ein dokumentarischer Bericht," *Der Monat* (Berlin), September and October, 1953.

There is much evidence that modern "monolithic" totalitarian states are extraordinarily capable of disciplining and controlling their populations. Supported by a mass political party and a system of state-sponsored organizations, such regimes have been able to reach down into the whole population and to forestall the development of independent groups and political action. The idea of a popular revolt, unsupported by outside force, has seemed remote. However, in the early summer of 1953 a surprised world was treated to a demonstration of mass action by the workers of East Germany.

At the end of World War II, East Germany, including a part of the old capital, Berlin, was placed under Soviet military occupation. In 1949 a nominally independent "German Democratic Republic" was organized as a one-party regime along police-state lines. It became the East German satellite of the Soviet Union. The ruling party was the S.E.D., *Sozialistische Einheitspartei Deutschlands* (Socialist Unity Party). This name was assumed by the Communist party after a forced coalition with a section of the former Socialist party. Under the S.E.D., the political and social life of East Germany was reorganized after the Russian model. Factories were nationalized; farms were collectivized; and trade-unions were placed under state control.

Although information was difficult to obtain, the East Germans did not appear to protest. However, refugees from East Germany entered West Germany from 1949 through 1952 at the rate of about one hundred and fifty thousand a year.

Between January and May, 1953, almost one hundred and eighty-five thousand refugees crossed the border. Emigration increased because of the economic deterioration of East

ADAPTATION 45

Germany and the increased severity of its government. Official East German and Soviet reports confirmed information that prices were rising and shortages increasing. Early in May, 1953, in an effort to deal with the economic problems of East Germany, the S.E.D. began an intensified drive for the complete transformation of Germany into a socialist state and called upon the workers to increase their production. The East German authorities announced a 10 per cent increase in work norms. Workers who did not increase their output by 10 per cent would have their wages correspondingly lowered. According to West German government sources, isolated and scattered strikes and demonstrations occurred in various industrial plants in East Germany. Some of these protests succeeded in re-establishing the old norms.

The Government Retreats

On June 12, 1953, a "new course" was announced by the S.E.D., admitting past errors and failures. Refugees were invited to return without reprisals; concessions were made to private business; collectivization would cease for the present; living standards of the workers would be raised. However, no change was made in work norms.

The evidence indicates that the new policy was dictated by the Soviet Union. Stalin died in March of 1953; Czech workers in Pilsen had struck on June 1; the situation in Russia and in her satellites was temporarily unsettled. The sharp reversal of policy left the impression of a weak and confused East German government, caught between the strategy of the Soviet Union and the evident misery of the East German people. According to some observers, the weakness of the East German government appeared not only in its public self-chastisement but also in its apparent reluctance to enforce strongly the new work norms. To many, the East German government seemed to have lost its morale, to be divided internally, and to be in no position to fight for its own survival.

The Strikes

On June 16, 1953, strikes, political demonstrations, and rioting broke out in East Berlin and spread rapidly to outlying districts and distant cities. At 7 A.M. on the morning of June 16, several hundred construction workers on a housing project in the Stalin Allee left their jobs and began to march toward Leipzigerstrasse where the Ministry of Labor and other government offices were located. Other workers joined the march. An estimated five to ten thousand people participated at the peak of the June 16 demonstration. In the Leipzigerstrasse the demand for a lowering of the work norms was soon replaced by political demands for free elections and the resignation of the East German government. The crowd called for Premier Otto Grotewohl and Walter Ulbricht, Secretary-General of the S.E.D. Neither appeared.

Several hours later the S.E.D. sent loud-speaker cars through the streets to announce that the new work norms would be reviewed and perhaps revoked. Nevertheless, demonstrations and street discussions among strikers and S.E.D. spokesmen continued all day. In the evening of June 16, strike leaders sent out loud-speaker trucks which they had seized during the day. They called upon the workers to continue their demonstrations the next day.

On June 17 from twenty to fifty thousand people, some from outlying districts, demonstrated in East Berlin. Workers from the Henningsdorf steel plant 25 miles away marched into Berlin. Soviet troops and armored cars moved into the city, and tanks appeared on the streets. Together with the *"Vopos"* (*Volkspolizei* or People's Police) the Soviet tanks kept the crowds from the approaches to the government ministries in the Leipzigerstrasse. Demonstrators moved toward the boundary between East and West Berlin. Rioting and violence occurred, directed against the symbols of Soviet and S.E.D. rule. The red flag atop the Brandenburg gate, flown since the beginning of the

Men Against Tanks in East Germany, 1953: Emotional contagion can do much to sustain courage against overwhelming odds. Mass strikes and demonstrations created a mood that dominated the streets.

Soviet occupation, was torn down, and the flag of the German Republic was substituted. Boundary markers between East and West were torn up. A border control shack and a propaganda booth were burned. Other official buildings were set afire, and government shops were smashed. In the afternoon martial law was declared by Major-General Dibrowa, Military Commandant of the Soviet Sector of Berlin, forbidding public assemblies of more than three persons. Soviet troops fired on demonstrators, and several people were run over by trucks and tanks. Soviet authorities seem to have withheld the tanks and troops until it became evident that the People's Police was unable to check the demonstrations and guarantee the survival of the East German regime. Faced by Soviet martial law and Soviet tanks, the revolt came to an end, although for several days large numbers of workers stayed away from their jobs.

Elsewhere in East Germany, June 17 was also a day of revolt and protest. Strikes and demonstrations occurred in 295 localities.

Workers struck and demonstrated in virtually every large state-owned industrial plant. Outside Berlin one of the first actions of striking workers was often to march to the nearest prison and release political prisoners. In Leuna, according to a participant, the prisoners were fellow workers. In most cities, as in Berlin, Soviet tanks and troops were called in to reinforce the "Vopos," who were often unwilling to use force and sometimes even joined the demonstrators. During June, 1953, 467 members of the *Volkspolizei* fled to West Berlin.

THE PATTERN OF POLITICAL REVOLT

Although unsuccessful, the East German uprising followed a familiar pattern of political revolt:

1. Demonstrations were inspired by economic hardship and began with economic demands.

2. Protests soon shifted from the economic to the political level. The demands for free speech, free elections, withdrawal of occupation troops, and abolition of the People's Police were designed to force the resignation of a government unable to meet the demands.

3. The demonstration appeared to take advantage of what was interpreted as weakness and division within the government. The success of a popular uprising depends in large measure upon the failure or unwillingness of the existing government to exercise the full measure of its authority. Division, dissension, loss of morale, unwillingness to assume responsibility for a policy and a program must usually occur at the top levels of government before popular revolt can be successful. It is sometimes said, therefore, that every revolution is a "palace revolution," and in a limited sense this is true.

4. Violence that marked the strikes and demonstrations was directed against the political symbols of authority, the "seats of power." Had the Ministries not been protected by an overwhelming armed force, the East Berlin crowds might have stormed the buildings and taken over the "seats of power."

5. Release of political prisoners has a symbolic significance beyond its meaning as a humane gesture. It is both a protest against the injustice with which a regime has been identified and a way of expressing solidarity with those who have overtly opposed it.

6. The rank and file of the police were uncertain of their loyalties, and some joined the demonstrators. The success of popular revolt often hinges on whether the government can rely upon its last resource—the police and the armed forces. The informal ties between a native police force and the populace can outweigh formal commitments in periods of crisis. Occupation troops are insulated from the loyalties which might prompt them to join a revolt or at least refuse to fire upon demonstrators. The fact that a puppet government is supported by an alien armed force may be an insurmountable obstacle to popular revolt.

SPONTANEOUS OR PLANNED?

Some interpreters of the June uprising have found it difficult to believe that the action was spontaneous. The rapid spread of the strikes and the similarity of slogans and actions seem to suggest preparation and prior organization. However, the testimony of participants interviewed in West Germany reveals no prior organization of the revolt, although its spread from Berlin to the rest of East Germany was aided by newspaper and radio reporting of the original actions. From these reports and from our knowledge of collective behavior, we can understand how leadership and a high degree of unity could develop even though the action was largely spontaneous.

The core of the revolt was a rather *homogeneous body* of industrial workers who shared a common economic plight and a common sense of frustration and deprivation. They worked side by side and were able to carry on a day-by-day communication by which their attitudes were sustained and supported and through which they could develop a measure of social organization. Mutual loyalties and understanding could readily develop. Informal leadership emerged, which in some cases quickly became a local "strike committee."

The decision to join the demonstration was rarely an individual one; strikers joined the march in a body, already protected by the anonymity and the emotionality of *crowd behavior*. According to reports, the original group of construction workers was gradually and spontaneously joined by other groups of workers as they marched through the streets.

Unifying symbols and slogans were devised to meet the needs of the immediate situation. One account by a participant who escaped to West Berlin shows how the strikers developed common slogans. On the spur of the moment he devised a rhyme: "Kollegen, reiht euch ein, Wir wollen freie Menschen sein!" (Fellow workers, join the ranks, we want to be free men!) He ran from group to group with it; it expressed the feelings of the participants; the rhyme caught on as a common slogan.

The response of the populace to the events of June 16 was a *shared sense of approval*. This tended to reinforce attitudes of protest and revolt and to inhibit feelings of fear and hesitancy. Schorn, a leader of the strike at the Leuna chemical works near Leipzig, reported that on June 17, as he rode to work on the streetcar, people cursed Walter Ulbricht, the Deputy Prime Minister and Secretary-General of the S.E.D., for whom the Leuna works had been named. Two "Vopos" standing on the rear platform ignored the talk. When Schorn arrived at the plant, no work was being done and workers were discussing the Berlin uprising. In the main workshop the men were talking of going on strike, and, finally, some of them ran into the courtyard. Their action stimulated others, and the strike was on.

Leaders emerged spontaneously as a result

of on-the-spot initiative or accident. According to Schorn, he was both pushed into leadership and willingly assumed it. The ranking German official (Dr. Eckard) in the Leuna plant urged the crowd to return to work, but the crowd became unruly, and the men gesticulated with their hammers.

I was standing not far below Dr. Eckard. The crowd had pushed me up there. One of the workers behind me, a fellow I knew, said, "Take over, Schorn, or something will go wrong." I stepped up toward Dr. Eckard, who was now talking about the necessity of fulfilling our norms, and said, "Pardon me, *Herr Doktor,* but I disagree with you." Then I stopped short. My voice had boomed all over the courtyard. In my excitement, I hadn't realized that I was now standing in front of the microphone. The crowd down below began to yell and applaud. A man just behind me shouted, "You tell them what we want, Schorn!" and then Dr. Eckard was somehow pushed away and I found myself standing in his place.[27]

Communication and organization developed quickly once leadership emerged. Schorn asked three volunteers from each workshop to step forward and form a strike committee. The committee decided to send a courier to the Buna plant at Halle where more than twenty thousand workers were employed producing synthetic rubber. Just as Schorn was announcing this over the loudspeaker, a man on a motorcycle drove into the courtyard. He was a courier from Buna, where a similar decision had already been made to ask the Leuna works to join the Berlin uprising.

In Berlin the demonstrators sent a delegation to RIAS, the American-sponsored radio station in the Western zone, and used its facilities to communicate information and resolutions to the East Germans. Loudspeaker trucks were commandeered. Elsewhere, an "initiative-committee" quickly thought of forcing a local newspaper to print

[27] Joseph Wechsberg, "A Reporter in Germany," *The New Yorker,* August 29, 1953, p. 40.

handbills for distribution to the people. A successful revolt could establish communications in a matter of hours.

Conclusions

1. Workers went on strike and demonstrated illegally despite the existence of a Russian satellite police state in East Germany.

2. Action occurred at a time of uncertainty behind the "iron curtain" due to the death of Stalin, and in response to increasing economic distress.

3. The East German regime had shown signs of weakness.

4. Action began with economic protest, but demands for political change quickly arose.

5. The uprising was largely spontaneous, but it depended upon the prior experience and social organization of workers and potential leaders.

6. The uprising was successful as a demonstration of anger and resentment, inflicting severe political damage on the regime at home and abroad.

7. Spontaneous action unsupported by sustained, effective organization has little chance of developing into a successful revolution. In this case, such a development was unlikely because of the presence of Soviet armed forces. The uprising burst forth as a dramatic instance of collective behavior, but within a few days it was under control.

[The events recounted in Adaptation 45 recurred in similar uprisings in Poland and Hungary in 1956.]

Section 5 **Social foundations of freedom and democracy**

The revolutionary changes discussed above—especially the rise of totalitarianism—direct renewed attention to the study of freedom and democracy:

1. The problem of *freedom,* that is, the restraint on the power of government and the protection of the individual from actual or potential oppression.

2. The problem of *democracy,* and the *quality of self-government,* that is, the degree to which civic participation is widespread, rational, and effective.

This section deals with these problems by considering (*a*) power and culture, (*b*) power and social organization, and (*c*) political socialization and participation.

POWER AND CULTURE

Constitutional law is a system of rules defining the rights and duties of those who govern and those who are governed. In a stable political order these rules are rooted in a people's traditions. If they are not so rooted, the political arrangements built upon them are weak and unstable. The democratic constitutional systems set up in some Latin American republics following their independence from Spain in the nineteenth century exhibited this weakness. Because there was no culturally rooted constitutional system, force was often used to decide who would rule, and the military held the balance in politics. On the other hand, the generally peaceful alternation of governments in England and the United States is attributable to the strongly held cultural values underlying their political systems. The shared belief in the democratic process, that is, in the *procedures* for seeking power, outweighs the desire to win. This morality is supported in practical ways when the people refuse to elect those who fail to follow the rules of the game. The orderly succession of governing groups is the crucial test of a political system, and in this the constitution is sustained by the beliefs and sentiments of the culture.

Only if there is some connection between power and culture can there be a stable and orderly group life. Unless people who seek power abide by socially approved rules, the outcome of political competition will not be popularly accepted. When this occurs, consent is withheld or given reluctantly, and the political system is insecure.

Power and Legitimacy

Political order is dependent on the *stability of authority*. Power-holders feel the need to justify their power, both in their own eyes and in the eyes of others. Without such justification, those who govern feel insecure, questioning their own right to rule; and those who are governed are less willing to obey, questioning the right of others to hold power. *Legitimacy* refers to the justification of power by reference to the community's cultural values. When power is made legitimate, it is called *authority*. Hence, the legitimacy of power depends on the group and its culture. By means of legitimation, consent to the exercise of power is gained, and governing is freed from primary reliance on naked force.

The *fact* of legitimacy is universal: all groups develop moral justifications for the unequal distribution of power. The *principles* of legitimacy vary: each culture justifies authority in accordance with its major values. Some of the different principles which have made power acceptable in specific groups are mentioned in the following quotation:

. . . ruling classes do not justify their power exclusively by *de facto* possession of it, but try to find a moral and legal basis for it, representing it as the logical and necessary consequence of doctrines and beliefs that are generally recognized and accepted. So if a society is deeply imbued with the Christian spirit the political

class will govern by the will of the sovereign, who, in turn, will reign because he is God's anointed. So too in Mohammedan societies political authority is exercised directly in the name of the caliph, or vicar, of the Prophet; or in the name of someone who has received investiture, tacit or explicit, from the caliph. The Chinese mandarins ruled the state because they were supposed to be interpreters of the will of the Son of Heaven, who had received from heaven the mandate to govern paternally, and in accordance with the rules of the Confucian ethic, "the people of the hundred families." . . . The powers of all lawmakers, magistrates and government officials in the United States emanate directly or indirectly from the vote of the voters, which is held to be the expression of the sovereign will of the whole American people.[28]

Some rule, and others obey, in part on the basis of shared beliefs in the acceptability and desirability of the arrangement. However, merely because legitimacy justifies a system of power, we should not conclude that principles of legitimacy are "mere quackeries designed to trick the masses into obedience."[29] Rather, such principles seem to answer real needs felt by rulers and ruled alike. Those who govern feel morally justified in controlling the lives of others; and those who are governed feel a more compelling reason for accepting discipline than the mere will of the stronger.

"Even the tyrant must sleep," observed Thomas Hobbes, and dictators strive for legitimacy, so that their rule may be stabilized and strengthened; they cannot rely solely on coercion. They must try to win consent and appear to conform to the basic sentiments and values of a major portion of the population. Adolph Hitler sought to legitimize his regime by claiming to represent the true German *Volk,* and Soviet rulers claim that their political order springs from the people and enjoys their support. These efforts have been

[28] Gaetano Mosca, *The Ruling Class* (New York: McGraw-Hill, 1939), p. 70. Used by permission of McGraw-Hill Book Company, Inc.
[29] *Ibid.,* p. 71.

only partially successful, and such regimes need elaborate systems of coercion. Indeed, if a dictatorship ever did become fully legitimate, it would no longer rest on force and would tend to accept restraints on its power. It would then be evolving toward some other political form.

Restrained Power

Legitimate power tends to be *restrained* power. Principles of legitimacy state what power-holders cannot do as well as what they are justified in doing. For example, if the principle of legitimacy is popular election, then the governing group cannot appoint its own successors but must hold elections to justify its continued power. In the case of monarchy, established principles of legitimacy governing accession to the throne, such as the right of birth or election by a council of barons, have checked continuous struggles for power on the part of feudal lords. The idea of a principle of legitimacy supports the broader notion of a restraining law that stands above the rulers, to which they are responsible and by grace of which they govern.

On the other hand, legitimacy makes it easier to take responsibility for the more or less arbitrary and often painful decisions that must be made, particularly at the highest levels of authority. President Truman's decision to send American armed forces into Korea in 1950 was taken on his own discretion. His action was accepted, in part because there was general agreement on the course pursued, but also because he was the legitimate chief of state and had the culturally prescribed obligation to safeguard the nation's security as he saw it. Furthermore, he placed great importance on legitimation by the international community, and when the action was endorsed by the United Nations, it was more widely accepted in the United States.

Too little legitimacy is a major source of political instability. Churchill so diagnosed the pre-Nazi German Republic, which he thought could have been adequately stabilized by a constitutional monarchy:

The victors imposed upon the Germans all the long-sought ideals of the liberal nations of the West. . . . A democratic constitution, in accordance with all the latest improvements, was established at Weimar. . . . Wise policy would have crowned and fortified the Weimar Republic with a constitutional sovereign in the person of an infant grandson of the Kaiser, under a council of regency. Instead, a gaping void was opened in the national life of the German people. All the strong elements, military and feudal, which might have rallied to a constitutional monarchy and for its sake respected and sustained the new democratic and parliamentary processes, were for the time being unhinged. The Weimar Republic, with all its liberal trappings and blessings was regarded as an imposition of the enemy. It could not hold the loyalties or imagination of the German people. For a spell they sought to cling in desperation to the aged Marshal Hindenburg. Thereafter mighty forces were adrift; the void was open, and into that void after a pause there strode . . . Corporal Hitler.[30]

Churchill's view of the situation after the first World War may well be disputed, but his statement underlines the practical importance of legitimate power for political order. He recognized that political order requires stable authority, which in turn must rest on the cultural heritage of the people. Of course, there may be many alternative ways of establishing this link between power and culture.

Legitimacy and Conquest

The close of the second World War also raised the problem of legitimacy in many countries. The capitulation of Japan was probably facilitated by the decision to retain the Emperor, who issued the Imperial Rescripts announcing the surrender. His accept-

[30] Winston S. Churchill, *The Gathering Storm* (Boston: Houghton Mifflin, 1948), pp. 10–11. Reprinted with permission of Houghton Mifflin Company.

ance of the military occupation undoubtedly aided the remarkably peaceful control of a country that had not been directly subdued by invasion. Thus the conquerors relied on the legitimate authority of the conquered.

The trial of enemy political and military leaders at Nuremberg in 1945/46 also posed the problem of legitimacy in an acute and still unresolved form. An International Military Tribunal was established by the victorious nations to try Nazis charged with "crimes against the peace," "war crimes," and "crimes against humanity." A strong effort was made to show that the Tribunal was legitimate, that is, a true court based upon established juridical principles. The judges maintained: "The Charter [of the International Military Tribunal] is not an arbitrary exercise of power on the part of the victorious nations, but in the view of the Tribunal. . . it is the expression of international law existing at the time of its creation." It was held that a succession of international treaties, and evolving custom, had outlawed wars of aggression. Therefore, the Nazis should be punished, not simply because they had lost but because they were criminals. This conclusion has been widely debated, but it indicates the strong pressure to make power legitimate.

POWER AND SOCIAL ORGANIZATION

Political freedom can be realized only in and through group membership. A single individual facing the power of government is too weak to resist encroachments on his freedom. But if he joins with others, he can find protection. The collective power of organized groups helps the individual to resist arbitrary interference with his liberty in other spheres of life as well as in his relations to government. A worker's freedom is enhanced because his union is able to prevent management from treating him arbitrarily, and this has been a chief reason for the widespread growth of trade-unions in modern times.

Many different social groups in addition to political organizations affect political freedom. Professional associations, trade-unions, business organizations, churches, fraternal orders, veterans groups, for instance, generate social power that can protect the individual, standing between him and hostile forces.

Three patterns of social organization and their effect on political freedom are:

1. *Highly concentrated power.* When one or a very few social groups become extremely powerful, the freedom of individuals and of other groups is endangered. There is such a preponderance of strength on one side that opposition can be quickly destroyed. It is easy to isolate the individual and break his power to resist. This situation is encountered where one group dominates a community or internationally when a single country dominates a continent.

When a single group or combination of groups achieves a virtual monopoly of power, it no longer has to take account of the interests of other groups. There are no effective checks on its power. Even though motivated by high ideals, any such group endangers the freedom of others.

2. *Fragmented power.* Freedom is also endangered when power is widely dispersed among many small competing groups and no group or combination is strong enough to organize the community and establish effective social control. Such a community is unstable and dominated by fear. Freedom of action is restricted to the narrow sphere within which safety can be won. A frontier society, in which each man is his own police force, is a case in point. Moreover, where power is fragmented, the community is vulnerable to any strong group that may arise. The conquest of England in 1066 by a small force from Normandy was made easier because of the fragmented character of social organization. Power was dispersed among many local lords, bishops, and sheriffs, and no adequate stabilizing force existed.

Within voluntary associations, fragmented

power makes it relatively easy for small con-spiratorial groups to become dominant. At a student convention or similar meeting, interest is often superficial and social organization is weak. That is, there are few ties among the delegates and no well developed leadership. The delegates may have little basis for voting beyond loyalty to a given school or locality. In such circumstances, even a small amount of concerted effort by a special-interest group can gain it a large amount of power, at least temporarily. However, most stable associations, such as a trade-union federation or political party, have a high degree of social organization, and the chances of capturing them are small.

3. *Balanced power.* Freedom is best protected when there are a large number of groups powerful enough to check each other and strong enough to maintain social order and organize the main activities of the society. Such a pattern of social organization is usually called "pluralism."

[The pluralist society is] characterized by the presence of large, well integrated groups representing significant divisions of interests and values. The various groups are limited in their power by the fact that the interests of other groups must be taken into account. The power of the state is limited by the power of organized public opinion and large special interest groups; the pressure exercised by business interests is counter-balanced by the forces of organized labor; both management and labor must take into account the interests of an integrated consumers' movement and other public agencies; no one religious group possesses a monopoly of spiritual values, and the various religious groups learn to accommodate themselves to one another; religious thought is denied absolute sovereignty over ideas by the presence of independent secular thought maintained by a free press, free universities, free literary movements, learned societies and organized scientific research. In the sphere of production, a pluralist society might allow for the operation of more than one form of economic organization: not only corporations and single entrepreneurships, but worker owned co-operatives and state organized collectives as well. Probably no community has ever achieved the optimum degree of pluralist organization, but the United States of America, Great Britain and Sweden may be considered as illustrative of societies tending to approximate the conditions of a pluralist society.[31]

Functions of Pluralism

Social pluralism limits the power of groups by providing a system of social checks and balances:[32]

1. Social pluralism encourages competition among groups and rivalry among leaders and therefore inhibits monopolies of power.

2. It limits leadership control by increasing the chances that members belong to several organizations. Each group tempers its attack on others to keep from losing the co-operation of those members who belong to the other organizations.

3. Social pluralism helps develop the skills of democratic politics. For example, participation in a pluralist society encourages the use of bargaining and negotiation.

4. Pluralism increases the availability of sources of information independent of government, church, or any single organization. This permits people to consider criticisms of and alternatives to existing policies and leaders.

If pluralism is to be a workable pattern of social organization, there must be a shared belief in its validity. This consensus helps to provide a "social constitution" to regulate the struggle for power. Diversity is valued, and certain kinds of competition and conflict are accepted as right and proper. For example, in labor-management relations, strikes and other legal forms of bargaining and controversy are recognized as necessary. The system works and accommodates the contending interests,

---

[31] Gerard De Gré, "Freedom and Social Structure," *American Sociological Review,* **11** (October, 1946), 535. See also Mosca, *op. cit.,* pp. 134 ff.

[32] See Robert A. Dahl and Charles E. Lindblom, *Politics, Economics, and Welfare* (New York: Harper, 1953), pp. 303–6.

Henry VIII (1491–1547) consolidated the power of the monarchy and split the English Church from Rome. Nevertheless, his power was limited by the social structure of his time. As king, Henry had no large standing army, no effective police, no extensive bureaucracy to carry out his will. He was greatly dependent on the landed gentry and the merchant classes, without whose co-operation he could not govern. His regime was autocratic and authoritarian, but not totalitarian.

because both trade-unions and employers have learned that they can realize most of their aims within the pluralist framework. There is now a common acceptance of collective bargaining among powerful representatives of business and labor, controlled to some extent by the intervention of government.

Agreement on fundamentals is more difficult to attain in pluralist than in communal social organization. A simple rural community is held together by strong ties of kinship, locality, and traditional belief. Pluralist social organization, however, has a greater diversity of values and interests, more impersonal relations, and, therefore, more conflicting loyalties. When few important life experiences are shared, consensus is difficult to achieve. But without agreement on fundamentals, pluralist social organization tends to break down into a society torn by conflict, and personal freedom is endangered. The significance of pluralism for political freedom is discussed further in Adaptation 46, pages 714–15.

POLITICAL SOCIALIZATION AND PARTICIPATION

Because political order is rooted in culture, the transmission of values is of major importance for political stability and change. If values are effectively transmitted, they become part of an individual's make-up—his personality, his understanding, his aspirations, his skills. Socialization prepares him for political participation. It gives him an understanding of the foundations of government and provides the motivations and skills he needs to govern or be governed.

The transmission of political values and skills, like the transmission of all cultural patterns, is not smooth and uniform. Political freedom, for example, is transmitted and maintained only with difficulty. Much depends on an appreciation of the spirit as well as the letter of the law, including respect for the views of others and a sense of fair play in political competition. Freedom also makes special demands on personality, and during times of stress many men abandon democracy for dictatorship.[33] Smoothness of transmission is also impeded because the members of society have different experiences which lead to distinctive approaches to politics, such as interest or indifference, optimism or pessimism. Wide variations in political experience and training affect the amount, quality, and direction of political participation.

[33] Erich Fromm, *Escape From Freedom* (New York: Rinehart, 1941). See Also H. D. Lasswell, *World Politics and Personal Insecurity* (New York: McGraw-Hill, 1935). (Cf. Adaptation 44, pp. 692 ff.)

Early Experiences and Political Outlook

Long before he reaches voting age, an individual begins to develop his political outlook in his family, peer group, and school. Political opinions are absorbed from parents and friends and "tend to persist into adulthood unless upset by a fundamentally different set of experiences and social relations." [34] In addition to the acquisition of specific attitudes and preferences, early experiences may also influence the *extent and quality* of political participation. They may determine, for example, whether a man seeks a political career or fails even to keep abreast of the political news, whether he feels that political activity is a duty or despises politicians. In other words, an individual's permanent orientations toward politics may be formed before he assumes his adult role as a citizen.

The evidence indicates that despite great social and political changes, most Americans vote as their fathers did. This tendency is not entirely due to socialization within the family. Most people resemble their parents in social class, religion, ethnicity, and in other ways that affect voting. However, family influence sometimes counteracts other social determinants. For example, although most workers are Democrats, workers with Republican fathers are as likely to vote Republican as Democratic. First voters are especially disposed to follow family political preferences.

Apathy and Political Competence

In a democratic society all adult citizens are expected to keep abreast of major political issues and vote in elections. Many, however, do not take the trouble to vote. National elections in the United States bring less than two-thirds of the adult population to the polls.[35] Still others are not really interested in politics even though they vote. Political apathy may be better understood if we examine differences in *skill* and in *feeling*, as these affect political participation.[36]

The complexities of modern politics make great demands on the understanding of the electorate. Candidates must be judged not only by the party they represent, but also by the particular wing within the party. A multitude of complex issues, from foreign policy to tax programs, need to be assessed for their long-run as well as short-run effects.

Voters vary widely in the level of their political skill. The educational and job experiences that produce skills are not uniform throughout the population. Social position has much to do with the ability to write letters, use the telephone easily, read the newspapers, and speak at meetings. Both poise and knowledge affect political competence. The conditions of lower-class life probably do not train people in techniques of co-operation and leadership that are taken for granted in many sections of the middle and upper classes.

Whether or not people have the skills, many do not *feel* competent to deal with political affairs. A sense of impotence keeps them out of politics because they wish to avoid areas of life that are frustrating. One study showed that the higher the income, the greater the feeling that individual political action does (or can) have an impact on politics. (See Table XVII:2.) Another found that "among the poorly educated, lower-income manual workers the sense of involvement in public, and particularly international affairs tends to be extremely limited and passive." [37]

---

[34] S. M. Lipset, P. F. Lazarsfeld, A. H. Barton, and J. Linz, "The Psychology of Voting: An Analysis of Political Behavior," in G. Lindzey (ed.), *Handbook of Social Psychology*, Vol. II (Cambridge: Addison-Wesley, 1954), p. 1144.

[35] Angus Campbell, P. E. Converse, W. E. Miller, and D. E. Stokes, *The American Voter* (New York: Wiley, 1960), p. 89.

[36] This discussion is based on: David Riesman and Nathan Glazer, "Criteria for Political Apathy," in Alvin W. Gouldner (ed.), *Studies in Leadership* (New York: Harper, 1950); David Riesman in collaboration with Reuel Denney and Nathan Glazer, *The Lonely Crowd* (New Haven: Yale University Press, 1950); and David Riesman in collaboration with Nathan Glazer, *Faces in the Crowd* (New Haven: Yale University Press, 1952).

[37] Gabriel Almond, *The American People and Foreign Policy* (New York: Harcourt, Brace, 1950), p. 130. See also Campbell *et al.*, *op. cit.*, especially pp. 103–5, 479–81, 490–91.

Table **XVII:2**   Income and the Sense of Political Efficacy

Income	Sense of Political Efficacy		
	High	Medium	Low
Under $2,000	11%	49%	38%
$2,000–2,999	19	54	25
$3,000–3,999	25	57	17
$4,000–4,999	33	51	16
$5,000 and over	43	46	10

Source: A. Campbell, G. Gurin, and W. E. Miller, *The Voter Decides* (Evanston: Row, Peterson, 1954), p. 191. A national sample of 1,582 persons replied to questions designed to gauge their "feeling that individual political action does have, or can have, an impact upon the political process, i.e., that it is worth while to perform one's civic duties. It is the feeling that political and social change is possible, and that the individual citizen can play a part in bringing about this change." The sample was asked to agree or disagree with such questions as: "Sometimes politics and government seem so complicated that a person like me can't really understand what's going on." [*Ibid.*, pp. 187–88.]

Among the lower classes the belief prevails that politics is not comprehensible or manageable. Even among higher-status groups, there are individuals who feel at the mercy of "forces" beyond their control.

Apathy and Political Affect

The great differences in feeling or emotion that people bring to politics are due in part to the wide variety of motives lying behind political interest. Traditionally, Americans have been exhorted to participate in politics in order to defend their private interests and to fulfill their duties as citizens. Self-interest is indeed a potent political incentive. The farmer, for example, must attend to politics in an era of government-supported prices, crop quotas, and subsidies. But for many citizens, private interests are only obscurely related to politics; the links to government action may seem remote or invisible, and even when clear, feelings of impotence may make political concern for private interests seem pointless. In mass democracy, self-interest is no sure motive for political involvement.

A sense of public duty is often a strong incentive. When social values are deeply implanted in the individual, he may feel the obligation to protect those values in politics, as in other spheres of life. Such a sense of duty has been historically most closely associated with upper-class tradition, for example in England and in New England. On the other hand, some people turn to politics for amusement, conformity, a sense of belonging, psychic escape, and other forms of gratification. They often turn away from politics for similar reasons. Group conformity probably has much to do with the level of political interest. When one's peers expect a person to be "up on politics," he is likely to follow the political news; but he has less incentive if his friends and associates view politics as dull or otherwise unvalued.

Combinations of Competence and Affect

Different proportions of emotional involvement and skill are associated with what Riesman has called "political styles." These ways of responding to politics cut across party affiliation or political ideology. They are rooted in socialization and character.

1. People of very low political competence and affect are *indifferent* to politics. They neither understand it nor feel personally involved in it. Politics to them is something alien, the province of others unlike themselves. Indifference was widespread at one time among women who viewed politics as the prerogative of men and among lower-class people who thought of politics as an upper-class responsibility. These "traditional indifferents" still form a large but indefinite proportion of the electorate in the United

States. In less politically mature countries, they remain the great majority.

2. People with more emotions than competence in politics often express themselves in an *indignant* manner. They respond to political disappointments with strong feelings of self-righteousness. Extreme "political indignants" are vulnerable to the appeal of ideologies and movements that promise to destroy all those groups not in agreement with their beliefs and to usher in a utopian order of "perfect morality."

3. People with a high level of political competence but little emotional involvement often express themselves in a *manipulative* manner. They see politics as an opportunity to manipulate people and things rather than as a way of supporting valued ideas and groups. They want to be "in the know," to "get the inside dope," because they believe "knowing your way around" and being an "operator" will insure approval from others. They avoid being on the wrong side. The manipulative person is careful not to become so emotionally involved in anything that he cannot quickly change his position. His lack of firm values does not provide a stable psychological base for democratic institutions.

4. An additional category is made up of people of high competence and high commitment. Such individuals are almost inevitably drawn to leadership roles. The most conspic-uous cases are from families that have a long history of public service and regard politics as a worthy and challenging career.

The Independent Voter

Among the more important conclusions of modern research on voting is a new assessment of the independent voter.

The ideal of the Independent citizen, attentive to politics, concerned with the course of government, who weighs the rival appeals of a campaign and reaches a judgment that is unswayed by partisan prejudice, has had such a vigorous history in the tradition of political reform—and has such a hold on civic education today—that one could easily suppose that the habitual partisan has the more limited interest and concern with politics. [However], far from being attentive, interested, and informed, Independents tend as a group to be somewhat less involved in politics. They have somewhat poorer knowledge of the issues, their image of the candidates is fainter, their interest in the campaign is less, their concern over the outcome is relatively slight, and their choice between competing candidates, although it is indeed made later in the campaign, seems much less to spring from discoverable evaluations of the elements of national politics.[38]

These conclusions, like many others in social science research, are based on the com-

[38] Campbell *et al.*, *The American Voter, op. cit.*, p. 143.

Table **XVII:3** Strength of Party Identification and Concern over Outcome, 1956

	Strong Party Identification	Weak Party Identification	Independents
Care very much or care pretty much	82%	62%	51%
Don't care very much or don't care at all	18	38	49
Total	100%	100%	100%
Number of cases	609	621	395

Source: Angus Campbell, P. E. Converse, W. E. Miller, and D. E. Stokes, *The American Voter* (New York: Wiley, 1960), p. 144.

ADAPTATION 46

parison of percentages. For example, Table XVII: 3 shows that in one study 82 per cent of people who strongly identified with a political party cared "very much or pretty much" about the outcome of an election. The corresponding percentage for independents was 51 per cent. Many independents are interested, although not so large a proportion as affiliated persons.

In a democracy, group membership is vital to the political process, partly to support a pluralist political order, as discussed above. In addition, the voting studies suggest that the affiliated citizen is more likely to be po-litically competent and involved than his "free-floating" compatriot.

A democratic order needs large numbers of people who are socialized in the skills of political participation and who believe that democratic values are worth having and protecting. However, it is not necessary that all members of the electorate must be politically involved all the time. A sizable group of less involved citizens is desirable to "cushion" the intense action of highly-motivated partisans. If everyone were highly and continuously interested in all issues, compromise and gradual solution might be reduced.

The Democratic Age

Abridged and adapted from *Democracy in America* by Alexis de Tocqueville. Translated by Henry Reeve and edited by Francis Bowen (Cambridge: Sever and Francis, 1862). For easy reference to other editions, general locations of quoted passages are shown.

Alexis de Tocqueville was born in Verneuil west of Paris in 1805 and died at Cannes in 1859. He studied law and, as a young man, began a career in the judiciary. In succeeding years, he developed a broad interest in the structure of French society, especially in the problems created by the interplay of a continuing aristocratic tradition and the rising tide of democracy.

In 1831, together with his lifelong friend, Gustave de Beaumont, Tocqueville obtained a commission from the French government to study the prison system and prison reform in the United States. This project was faithfully carried out, but the real interest of the two men lay in the entire political system of the new country. The result was a two-part study, *Democracy in America*. Part I appeared in 1835, Part II in 1840. This book has been called "perhaps the greatest work ever writ-ten on one country by the citizen of another."

Tocqueville saw the United States as a social laboratory. Here was a new country in which democratic institutions were being rapidly developed and given free rein. Here, if anywhere, the full significance of democracy might be studied. His aim was to draw some lessons from this experience for the guidance of his own countrymen. In pursuing this task, Tocqueville adopted a distinctly sociological perspective. He asked: What social conditions *sustain* the democratic political order? What are the consequences of democracy for manners and customs, for nonpolitical institutions, for the quality of life?

The following passages from Tocqueville show some of his major concerns.

It is not, then, merely to satisfy a legitimate curiosity that I have examined America; my wish has been to find there instruction by which we may ourselves profit. Whoever should imagine that I have intended to write a panegyric would be strangely mistaken, and on reading this book, he will perceive that such was not my design: nor has it been my object to advocate any form of government in particular, for I am of opinion that absolute excellence is rarely to be found in any system of laws. I have not even pretended to judge whether the social revolution, which I believe to be irresistible, is advantageous or prejudicial to mankind. I have acknowledged this revolution as a fact already accomplished, or on the eve of its accomplishment; and I have selected the nation, from amongst those which have undergone it, in which its development has been the most peaceful and the most complete, in order to discern its natural consequences, and to find out, if possible, the means of rendering it profitable to mankind. I confess that, in America, I saw more than America; I sought there the image of democracy itself, with its inclinations, its character, its prejudices, and its passions, in order to learn what we have to fear or to hope from its progress. (I. Introduction)

Despotism and Democracy

No sovereign ever lived in former ages so absolute or so powerful as to undertake to administer by his own agency, and without the assistance of intermediate powers, all the parts of a great empire: none ever attempted to subject all his subjects indiscriminately to strict uniformity of regulation, and personally to tutor and direct every member of the community.

When the Roman Emperors were at the height of their power, the different nations of the empire still preserved manners and customs of great diversity; although they were subject to the same monarch, most of the provinces were separately administered; they abounded in powerful and active municipalities; and although the whole government of the empire was centred in the hands of the Emperor alone, and he always remained, in case of need, the supreme arbiter in all matters, yet the details of social life and private

Alexis Charles Henri Maurice Clerel de Tocqueville

occupations lay for the most part beyond his control. The Emperors possessed, it is true, an immense and unchecked power, which allowed them to gratify all their whimsical tastes, and to employ for that purpose the whole strength of the state. They frequently abused that power arbitrarily to deprive their subjects of property or of life: their tyranny was extremely onerous to the few, but it did not reach the many; it was fixed to some few main objects, and neglected the rest; it was violent, but its range was limited. (II. Bk. 4, Chap. 6)

The notion of secondary powers, placed between the sovereign and his subjects, occurred naturally to the imagination of aristocratic nations, because those communities contained individuals or families raised above the common level, and apparently destined to command by their birth, their education, and their wealth. This same notion is naturally wanting in the minds of men in democratic ages, for converse reasons; it can only be introduced artificially, it can only be kept there with difficulty; whereas they conceive, as it were without thinking upon the subject, the notion of a single and central power, which governs the whole community by its direct influence. Moreover, in politics as well as in philosophy and in religion, the intellect of democratic nations is peculiarly open to simple and general notions. Complicated systems are repugnant to it, and its favorite conception is that of a great nation composed of citizens all formed upon one pattern, and all governed by a single power.   (II. Bk. 4, Chap. 2)

Every central power, which follows its natural tendencies, courts and encourages the principle of equality; for equality singularly facilitates, extends, and secures the influence of a central power.

I am of opinion that, in the democratic ages which are opening upon us, individual independence and local liberties will ever be the products of art; that centralization will be the natural government.   (II. Bk. 4, Chap. 3)

I believe that it is easier to establish an absolute and despotic government amongst a people in which the conditions of society are equal, than amongst any other; and I think that, if such a government were once established amongst such a people, it would not only oppress men, but would eventually strip each of them of several of the highest qualities of humanity. Despotism, therefore, appears to me peculiarly to be dreaded in democratic times.

On the other hand, I am persuaded that all who shall attempt, in the ages upon which we are entering, to base freedom upon aristocratic privilege, will fail; that all who shall attempt to draw and to retain authority within a single class, will fail. At the present day, no ruler is skilful or strong enough to found a despotism by re-establishing permanent distinctions of rank amongst his subjects: no legislator is wise or powerful enough to preserve free institutions, if he does not take equality for his first principle and his watchword. All of our contemporaries who would establish or secure the independence and the dignity of their fellow-men, must show themselves the friends of equality; and the only worthy means of showing themselves as such is to be so: upon this depends the success of their holy enterprise. Thus, the question is not how to reconstruct aristocratic society, but how to make liberty proceed out of that democratic state of society in which God has placed us. (II. Bk. 4, Chap. 7)

Freedom and Association

Aristocratic countries abound in wealthy and influential persons who are competent to provide for themselves, and who cannot be easily or secretly oppressed: such persons restrain a government within general habits of moderation and reserve. I am well aware that democratic countries contain no such persons naturally; but something analogous to them may be created by artificial means. I firmly believe that an aristocracy cannot again be founded in the world; but I think that private citizens, by combining together, may constitute bodies of great wealth, influence, and strength, corresponding to the persons of an aristocracy. By this means, many of the greatest political advantages of aristocracy would be obtained, without its injustice or its dangers. An association for political, commercial, or manufacturing purposes, or even for those of science and literature, is a powerful and enlightened member of the community, which cannot be disposed of at pleasure, or oppressed without remonstrance; and which, by defending its own rights against the encroachments of the government, saves the common liberties of the country.   (II. Bk. 4, Chap. 7)

There are no countries in which associations are more needed, to prevent the despotism of faction or the arbitrary power of a prince, than those which are democratically constituted. In aristocratic nations, the body of the nobles and the wealthy are in themselves natural associations, which check the abuses of power. In countries where such associations do not exist, if private individuals cannot create an artificial and temporary substitute for them, I can see no permanent protection against the most galling tyranny; and a great people may be oppressed with impunity by a small faction, or by a single individual.

The most natural privilege of man, next to the right of acting for himself, is that of combining his exertions with those of his fellow-creatures, and of acting in common with them. The right of association therefore appears to me almost as inalienable in its nature as the right of personal liberty. No legislator can attack it without impairing the foundations of society. Nevertheless, if the liberty of association is only a source of advantage and prosperity to some nations, it may be perverted or carried to excess by others, and from an element of life may be changed into a cause of destruction. A comparison of the different methods which associations pursue, in those countries in which liberty is well understood, and in those where liberty degenerates into license, may be useful both to governments and to parties.

Most Europeans look upon association as a weapon which is to be hastily fashioned, and immediately tried in the conflict. A society is formed for discussion, but the idea of impending action prevails in the minds of all those who constitute it. It is, in fact, an army; and the time given to speech serves to reckon up the strength and to animate the courage of the host, after which they march against the enemy.

Such, however, is not the manner in which the right of association is understood in the United States. In America, the citizens who form the minority associate, in order, first, to show their numerical strength, and so to diminish the moral power of the majority; and,

secondly, to stimulate competition, and thus to discover those arguments which are most fitted to act upon the majority: for they always entertain hopes of drawing over the majority to their own side, and then disposing of the supreme power in its name. Political associations in the United States are therefore peaceable in their intentions, and strictly legal in the means which they employ; and they assert with perfect truth, that they aim at success only by lawful expedients.

The difference which exists in this respect between Americans and Europeans depends on several causes. In Europe, there are parties which differ so much from the majority, that they can never hope to acquire its support, and yet they think they are strong enough in themselves to contend against it. When a party of this kind forms an association, its object is, not to convince, but to fight. In America, the individuals who hold opinions much opposed to those of the majority can do nothing against it; and all other parties hope to win it over to their own principles. The exercise of the right of association becomes dangerous, then, in proportion as great parties find themselves wholly unable to acquire the majority. In a country like the United States, in which the differences of opinion are mere differences of hue, the right of association may remain unrestrained without evil consequences.   (I. Chap. 12)

Amongst the laws which rule human societies, there is one which seems to be more precise and clear than all others. If men are to remain civilized, or to become so, the art of associating together must grow and improve in the same ratio in which the equality of conditions is increased.   (II. Bk. 2, Chap. 5)

TYRANNY OF THE MAJORITY

In my opinion, the main evil of the present democratic institutions of the United States does not arise, as is often asserted in Europe, from their weakness, but from their irresistible strength. I am not so much alarmed at the excessive liberty which reigns in that country, as at the inadequate securities which one finds there against tyranny.

I do not say that there is a frequent use of tyranny in America at the present day; but I maintain that there is no sure barrier against it, and that the causes which mitigate the government there are to be found in the circumstances and the manners of the country, more than in its laws.

It is in the examination of the exercise of thought in the United States, that we clearly perceive how far the power of the majority surpasses all the powers with which we are acquainted in Europe. The authority of a king is physical, and controls the actions of men without subduing their will. But the majority possesses a power which is physical and moral at the same time, which acts upon the will as much as upon the actions, and represses not only all contest, but all controversy. (I. Chap. 15)

When the ranks of society are unequal, and men unlike each other in condition, there are some individuals wielding the power of superior intelligence, learning, and enlightenment, whilst the multitude are sunk in ignorance and prejudice. Men living at these aristocratic-periods are therefore naturally induced to shape their opinions by the standard of a superior person, or superior class of persons, whilst they are averse to recognize the infallibility of the mass of the people.

The contrary takes place in ages of equality. The nearer the people are drawn to the common level of an equal and similar condition, the less prone does each man become to place implicit faith in a certain man or a certain class of men. But his readiness to believe the multitude increases, and opinion is more than ever mistress of the world. Not only is common opinion the only guide which private judgment retains amongst a democratic people, but amongst such a people it possesses a power infinitely beyond what it has elsewhere. At periods of equality, men have no faith in one another, by reason of their common resemblance; but this very resemblance gives them almost unbounded confidence in the judgment of the public; for it would not seem probable, as they are all endowed with equal means of judging, but that the greater truth should go with the greater number.

When the inhabitant of a democratic country compares himself individually with all those about him, he feels with pride that he is the equal of any one of them; but when he comes to survey the totality of his fellows, and to place himself in contrast with so huge a body, he is instantly overwhelmed by the sense of his own insignificance and weakness. The same equality which renders him independent of each of his fellow-citizens, taken severally, exposes him alone and unprotected to the influence of the greater number. The public has therefore, among a democratic people, a singular power, which aristocratic nations cannot conceive of; for it does not persuade to certain opinions, but it enforces them, and infuses them into the intellect by a sort of enormous pressure of the minds of all upon the reason of each.

The fact that the political laws of the Americans are such that the majority rules the community with sovereign sway, materially increases the power which that majority naturally exercises over the mind. For nothing is more customary in man than to recognize superior wisdom in the person of his oppressor. The intellectual dominion of the greater number would probably be less absolute amongst a democratic people governed by a king, than in the sphere of a pure democracy, but it will always be extremely absolute; and by whatever political laws men are governed in the ages of equality, it may be foreseen that faith in public opinion will become a species of religion there, and the majority its ministering prophet.

Thus intellectual authority will be different, but it will not be diminished; and far from thinking that it will disappear, I augur that it may readily acquire too much preponderance, and confine the action of private judgment within narrower limits than are suited either to the greatness or the happiness of the human race. In the principle of equality I very clearly discern two tendencies; the one leading the mind of every man to untried thoughts, the other which would prohibit him from thinking at all. And I perceive how, under the dominion of certain laws, democracy would extinguish that liberty of the mind to which a democratic social condition is favorable; so that, after having broken all the bondage once imposed on it by ranks or by men, the human mind would be closely fettered to the general will of the greatest number.

If the absolute power of a majority were to be substituted, by democratic nations, for all the different powers which checked or retarded overmuch the energy of individual minds, the evil would only have changed character. Men would not have found the means of independent life; they would simply have discovered (no easy task) a new physiognomy of servitude. There is,—and I cannot repeat it too often,—there is here matter for profound reflection to those who look on freedom of thought as a holy thing, and who hate not only the despot, but despotism. For myself, when I feel the hand of power lie heavy on my brow, I care but little to know who oppresses me; and I am not the more disposed to pass beneath the yoke because it is held out to me by the arms of a million of men.   (II. Bk. 1, Chap. 2)

DEMOCRACY AND ANOMIE

In certain remote corners of the Old World, you may still sometimes tumble upon a small district which seems to have been forgotten amidst the general tumult, and to have remained stationary whilst everything around it was in motion. The inhabitants are, for the most part, extremely ignorant and poor; they take no part in the business of the country, and are frequently oppressed by the government; yet their countenances are generally placid, and their spirits light.

In America, I saw the freest and most enlightened men placed in the happiest circumstances which the world affords: it seemed to me as if a cloud habitually hung upon their brow, and I thought them serious, and almost sad, even in their pleasures.

The chief reason of this contrast is, that the former do not think of the ills they endure, while the latter are forever brooding over advantages they do not possess. It is strange to see with what feverish ardor the Americans pursue their own welfare; and to watch the vague dread that constantly torments them, lest they should not have chosen the shortest path which may lead to it.

Their taste for physical gratifications must be regarded as the original source of that secret inquietude which the actions of the Americans betray, and of that inconstancy of which they daily afford fresh examples.

If, in addition to the taste for physical well-being, a social condition be super-added, in which neither laws nor customs retain any person in his place, there is a great additional stimulant to this restlessness of temper. Men will then be seen continually to change their track, for fear of missing the shortest cut to happiness.

Amongst democratic nations, men easily attain a certain equality of condition; but they can never attain as much as they desire. It perpetually retires from before them, yet without hiding itself from their sight, and in retiring draws them on. At every moment they think they are about to grasp it; it escapes at every moment from their hold. They are near enough to see its charms, but too far off to enjoy them; and before they have fully tasted its delights, they die.

In democratic times, enjoyments are more intense than in the ages of aristocracy, and the number of those who partake in them is vastly larger: but, on the other hand, it must be admitted that man's hopes and desires are oftener blasted, the soul is more stricken and perturbed, and care itself more keen.   (II. Bk. 2, Chap. 13)

When every one is constantly striving to change his position; when an immense field for competition is thrown open to all; when wealth is amassed or dissipated in the shortest possible space of time amidst the turmoil of democracy,—visions of sudden and easy fortunes, of great possession easily won and lost, of chance under all its forms, haunt the mind. The instability of society itself fosters the natural instability of man's desires. In the midst of these perpetual fluctuations of his lot, the present grows upon his mind, until it conceals futurity from his sight, and his looks go no further than the morrow. (II. Bk. 2, Chap. 17)

THE WORTH OF DEMOCRACY

In the present age, when the destinies of Christendom seem to be in suspense, some hasten to assail democracy as a hostile power, whilst it is yet growing; and others already adore this new deity which is springing forth from chaos. But both parties are imperfectly acquainted with the object of their hatred or their worship; they strike in the dark, and distribute their blows at random.

We must first understand what is wanted of society and its government. Do you wish to give a certain elevation to the human mind, and teach it to regard the things of this world with generous feelings, to inspire men with a scorn of mere temporal advantages, to form and nourish strong convictions, and keep alive the spirit of honorable devotedness? Is it your object to refine the habits, embellish the manners, and cultivate the arts, to promote the love of poetry, beauty, and glory? Would you constitute a people fitted to act powerfully upon all other nations, and prepared for those high enterprises which, whatever be their results, will leave a name forever famous in history? If you believe such to be the principal object of society, avoid the government of the democracy, for it would not lead you with certainty to the goal.

But if you hold it expedient to divert the moral and intellectual activity of man to the production of comfort, and the promotion of general well-being; if a clear understanding be more profitable to man than genius; if your object be not to stimulate the virtues of heroism, but the habits of peace; if you had rather witness vices than crimes, and are content to meet with fewer noble deeds, provided offences be diminished in the same proportion; if, instead of living in the midst of a brilliant society, you are contented to have prosperity around you; if, in short, you are of opinion that the principal object of a government is not to confer the greatest possible power and glory upon the body of the nation, but to insure the greatest enjoyment, and to avoid the most misery, to each of the individuals who compose it,—if such be your desire, then equalize the conditions of men, and establish democratic institutions.

But if the time be past at which such a choice was possible, and if some power superior to that of man already hurries us, without consulting our wishes, towards one or the other of these two governments, let us endeavor to make the best of that which is allotted to us, and, by finding out both its good and its evil tendencies, be able to foster the former and repress the latter to the utmost. (I. Chap. 14)

CONCLUSION

Tocqueville's argument may be summarized as follows:

1. In the democratic age, equality becomes a paramount value. This equalizing tendency breaks down the power and self-confidence of traditional elites. Whatever their defects, these elites did exercise some restraint on kings and other sovereigns. Democracy tends to create a strong centralized government before which all citizens are equal. Tocqueville thought this equality might become an equality of weakness. As a result, he saw a latent despotism in democratic society.

2. To make the citizens stronger, Tocque-

ville emphasized the importance of the autonomous association in the democratic community. He would have seconded the slogan of his contemporary, the French anarchist Proudhon, who said, "Multiply your associations and be free."

3. Tyranny can be cultural and psychological as well as political. Democracy, which gives all opinions equal worth, and honors the views of the majority, may usher in an age of conformity. This danger he referred to as the "tyranny of the majority."

4. Democracy and equality tend to stimulate ambition, loosen social bonds, and lessen respect for established forms of conduct. Thus democracy tends to be "anomic" (Tocqueville himself did not use that term) and runs the risk that dissatisfaction will produce irrational political responses.

Comment

Tocqueville's analysis should be understood as a diagnosis of some of the inherent weaknesses of democracy. In this sense, it is similar to the study by Michels (Adaptation 21, pp. 247 ff.). Tocqueville wrote mainly as a friend of democracy, although he drew on his aristocratic background and inclinations. At a number of points he expressed his faith in self-government.

CREDITS

Below are listed the pages on which illustrations appear by special permission, which we gratefully acknowledge. (Figures are suitably acknowledged at the place of their appearance.) We appreciate the right to reproduce the following illustrations:

4–Frontispiece from *The Positive Philosophy of Auguste Comte,* tr. and ed. by Harriet Martineau (New York: Blanchard, 1858).

27–Courtesy of The Macmillan Company.

28–Wide World Photos.

41–Photo by Lapie, Photothèque Française.

45–Frontispiece from *An Autobiography,* Vol I, by Herbert Spencer (London: Williams and Norgate, 1904).

54–Courtesy of Leonard Broom.

56–Courtesy of Standard Oil Co. (N.J.).

69–Courtesy of Maurice R. Davie.

72–The Bettmann Archive.

77–*The Toronto Telegram.*

84–Courtesy of Charles S. Rice, from *Meet the Amish* by Charles S. Rice and John B. Shenk (New Brunswick: Rutgers University Press, 1947).

87–John Launois, Black Star.

98–(Top) courtesy of Standard Oil Co. (N.J.); (bottom) photo from *Nigeria,* No. 37, 1951, p. 90.

101–(Top left) courtesy of Philip Selznick; (top right) courtesy of Leonard Broom; (bottom) courtesy of Douglas Davidson, Honolulu.

106–Frontispiece from *The Philosophy of the Act* by George Herbert Mead (University of Chicago Press, 1938).

116–Michel Descamps, Paris.

117–H. Roger-Viollet (collection Viollet), Paris.

120–Jerry Cooke, New York.

125–U.S. Coast Guard Photo.

131–Wide World Photos.

136–Courtesy of Standard Oil Co. (N.J.).

137–(Top) courtesy of Standard Oil Co. (N.J.); (bottom) John Zimmerman for *Sports Illustrated.*

144–Courtesy of Rentscheler Studios.

145–Courtesy of the U.S. Army.

162–Courtesy of the U.S. Army.

178–Courtesy of Yü Shan Han.

179–Courtesy of Yü Shan Han.

192–Culver Pictures.

195–*The New York Times.*

215–Courtesy of the Library of Congress.

253–Courtesy of Standard Oil Co. (N.J.).

259–Courtesy of LIFE Magazine. © Time Inc.

260–British Crown Copyright. Reproduced by permission of the Controller of Her Britannic Majesty's Stationery Office.

264–Courtesy of Brown Brothers.

273–Courtesy of the *Detroit Free Press.*

285–Reprinted from *Harper's Magazine.* © 1958.

303–UNATIONS (courtesy of Australian Government).

306–Frontispiece from *Essai sur le principie de population* (Paris: Guillaumin et Ce, 1852).

367–Courtesy of Standard Oil Co. (N.J.).

399–Richard Lannoy, Paris.

417–Don Normark, Los Angeles.

449–Courtesy of Professor Georges Balandier.

457–(Top) Lonnie Wilson, *Oakland Tribune;* (bottom) courtesy of Standard Oil Co. (N.J.).

506–Official U.S. Navy photographs.

521–(Top) courtesy of LIFE Magazine, H. Sochurek. © Time Inc., 1960; (bottom) Noel Clark, Black Star.

527–Courtesy of Brown Brothers.

558–Courtesy of LIFE Magazine. © Time Inc.

565–Courtesy of Jenaro Olivares G.

571–Wayne Miller, Magnum.

585–Courtesy of Qantas Empire Airways, Ltd.

590–Courtesy of Standard Oil Co. (N.J.).

598–Gerrymander cartoon from Roger Butterfield, *The American Past* (New York: Simon and Schuster, 1947), p. 51. Used by permission of Roger Butterfield and Simon and Schuster.

608–Courtesy of The Free Press.

628–Facsimile of engravings on wood, designed and engraved by J. Amman, sixteenth century. [From Paul Lacroix, *Manners, Customs, and Dress during the Middle Ages, and during the Renaissance Period* (London: Chapman and Hall, 1876). Reproduced by permission of the publishers.]

629–*Ibidem.*

630–From *Max Weber: ein Lebensbild* by Marianne Weber (Tübingen, 1926).

631–Frontispiece from *Histoire de la Vie . . . de Jean Calvin* by Hierosme Hermes Bolsec (Lyon: N. Scheuring, 1875). From a portrait in the Geneva Library.

637–Courtesy of The Singer Manufacturing Co.

652–Culver Pictures.

663–Courtesy of Shell Chemical Company.

665–Courtesy of the Lewis W. Hine Memorial Collection. From Roger Butterfield, *The American Past* (New York: Simon and Schuster, 1947), p. 312.

673–Keystone Press.

679–(Top) European Picture Service; (bottom) Wide World Photos.

683–(Top left) Pierre Streit, Black Star; (top right) Courtesy LIFE Magazine, F. Scherschel. © Time Inc., 1960; (bottom) Pierre Streit, Black Star.

686–Frontispiece from *The Mind and Society* by Arthur Livingston. Used by permission of The Pareto Fund.

700–Wide World Photos.

708–Frontispiece from *Henry VIII* by Edward Hall (London: T. C. & E. Jack, 1904).

713–The Bettmann Archive.

INDEXES

NAME INDEX

SUBJECT INDEX